W9-COZ-402

IMAGES IN THE DARK

IMAGES

IN THE DARK

An Encyclopedia of Gay and Lesbian Film and Video

Raymond Murray

TLA Publications

Philadelphia

Ref
PN
1995.9
.H55
M87
1994

Copyright © 1994 by TLA Publications, Inc. All rights reserved. No part of this book may be used or reproduced in any form or by any electronic or mechanical means, including information storage and retrieval systems without written permission of the publisher except in the case of brief quotations embodied in critical articles or reviews.

Printed in the United States of America

Published by TLA Publications®
1520 Locust Street
Suite 200
Philadelphia, PA 19102

TLA Publications® is a registered trademark of TLA Video Management, Inc.

Library of Congress Catalog Card Number: 94-060358

ISBN 1-880707-01-2

first printing: January 1995

Cover photo of *The Crying Game* courtesy of Miramax Films

SPECIAL THANKS AND ACKNOWLEDGMENTS

The completion of this book would not have been possible without the writing talents, valued input and editorial finesse of several people. Foremost in thanks is David Bleiler who, in addition to writing several biographies of stars and directors (especially those of Hollywood's Golden Era), has also served as Editor. His invaluable contributions and support are greatly appreciated.

Additional credit goes to Eric Moore, who organized and guided the book through the complete production process, including partial first edits and the final layout as well as the book cover design and editorial contributions.

I would also like to thank Kathleen Ziegler who created the book's design, and was the artist responsible for the initial layout; Ann Yarabinee for data entry; Rachel Tubman for film research and photo acquisition; and Claire Brown Kohler for production coordination.

While I've done the bulk of the writing, there have been several others who have contributed their insights by submitting various film blurbs. Adding a lesbian point-of-view have been Jenni Olson and Stacy Szymaszek. Other contributors include Byl Holte, Deni Kasrel, George Stewart, Irv Slifkin, Jay Medley and Ginger Osborne.

In acknowledging the assistance of others, I wish I could say that when I requested needed information, either from companies or people, that it was readily forthcoming. But frustratingly, that was not the case. Dozens of letters, information packages, faxes and phone calls went ignored or unanswered. Even companies that distribute gay/lesbian films were reluctant to supply me with information, photos, interviews or press kits, which only added to a frustrating and difficult process. And while this lack of help is not uncommon for any writer, I fear that the book's theme caused many an individual to bury my letter under a stack of papers. With that off my chest, I wish to thank the following individuals, festivals and companies for their help in making this book possible: The San Francisco International Lesbian & Gay Film Festival and its director Mark Finch; The Montreal World Film Festival; The London Gay & Lesbian Film Festival and its co-programmer Tim Highsted; The Los Angeles International Gay & Lesbian Film & Video Festival; The Academy Film Library; The German Consulate General; Barbara Grier of Naiad Press; Tom Able and Mark Harriot of Dangerous to Know; Lisa Birkin of First Run Features; Mike Stimler at Water Bearer Films; Steve Kramer of Mystic Fire Video; and the many other film and video companies who have made their films available for viewing and/or provided information.

EXPLANATION OF SYMBOLS:

▼ In Chapters 1-3, because so many of the films are not specifically gay/lesbian themed, this symbol indicates a title of particular interest for gay men and lesbians. The symbol is dropped in the subsequent chapters since all of those films have a queer interest.

⊛ If a film is or was at one time available for rental on home video in the United States, this symbol is placed at the end of its blurb.

PHOTO CREDITS:

Academy Entertainment, Award Films International, Basis-Film, Before Stonewall Inc., Bijou Home Video, Blush Entertainment Corporation/Fatale Video, Buena Vista Pictures, Cabin Fever Entertainment, CBS/Fox Video, Cinevista, Columbia Pictures, Connoisseur Video, First Run Features, Fox Lorber Home Video, Fox Television, Frameline, Grammercy Pictures, Greenwood/Cooper Home Video, Home Vision Cinema, House O' Chicks, Kino International, Kultur Video, Live Home Video, MCA Universal Home Video, MGM, Miramax Films, Mystic Fire Video, National Film Board of Canada, New Line Company, New World Pictures, New Yorker Films, Orion Pictures, Out on a Limb/Dangerous to Know Productions, Outsider Productions, Paramount Pictures, PolyGram Video, Republic Pictures, The Samuel Goldwyn Company, Sony Pictures Classics, Strand Releasing, Touchstone Pictures, Triboro Films, Troma Inc., 20th Century Fox Film Corporation, Universal Pictures, Warner Brothers, Water Bearer Films, Wolfe Video, Women Make Movies, World Artists, Zeitgeist Films

CONTENTS

IMAGES IN THE DARK

INTRODUCTION

When this project began two years ago, my goals were far more modest in scope than what eventually became this finished book. The original intent was to develop a video reference guide to gay and lesbian themed movies available on home video in the United States. In my capacity as an operator of a chain of video stores in Philadelphia, I had easy access to these titles and a professional desire to compile such a booklet. But as I started researching and sketching an outline, I discovered that a much more comprehensive publication was needed to incorporate the many lesbian and gay themed films that are both available on video and those not yet — perhaps never to be — on video. I also wanted to spotlight some of the thousands of lesbians and gays who have worked in the filmmaking process. Compiling such divergent information was not always a simple task.

While there are several books available on queer films and filmmakers, all focus on a particular theme or specific, limited subject. Where would I get information on a gay Spanish film I saw in a gay/lesbian film festival in 1981 and has since disappeared? Are there any gay themed films from Asia, and, if so, what are they? Information is available on most German and American gay/lesbian filmmakers but what about Mexican or Filipino directors? Many high-profile queer films (*Cruising, Desert Hearts, The Boys in the Band, The Killing of Sister George*) have been written about in books, but what about the less accessible, more specialized ones? There are/have been several prominent "out" filmmakers (Pedro Almodóvar, Gus Van Sant, Rainer Werner Fassbinder), but who are the others? What about lesbians behind and in front of the camera? These questions, and my frustration at the difficulty of finding answers, spurred me to expand the theme and goals of the book to the point that I aspired to make this the first comprehensive compilation on the contribution of queers to the art and commerce of filmmaking.

Upon organizing such material into a queer compendium, several options were available. I could take a historical approach, do a simple alphabetical listing, or combine similarly themed films and analyze them collectively. But the present structure, while admittedly breaking the alphabetical rules of a traditional "encyclopedia," is the one that came naturally and is one that I feel effectively breaks down the enormous wealth of information into easier reading, as well as providing a good reference point for others to delve deeper into their own analytical, political or historical interests.

While I use the all-encompassing term "encyclopedia" in the title, I actually make no pretense that this book is the *complete* cataloging of gay and lesbian participation and representation in filmmaking over the past 90 years. The goal was for it to be a comprehensive and at times admittedly subjective listing of: films and videos that have been written, scored, directed by, and starring gays and lesbians; and films that have gay/lesbian themes, or ones in which lesbian or gay characters are fleetingly presented. By concentrating on the idea of an encyclopedic approach to the topic, I've avoided essay-oriented discussion/analysis of certain film subjects or styles and have instead focused more on individual analysis of a much wider range of titles. And although pro-gay "cheerleading" is out of place in the critical descriptions of the films, I've tried to avoid unduly harsh attacks on a film or video's lack of Hollywood sheen, its not-quite-professional acting or plot deficiencies. My belief is that it would be an easy shot to lambast these technical faults. When a film's intentions are good (from my gay activist point-of-view), I've focused instead on its theme as it relates (effectively or not) to gay and lesbian issues.

In compiling the titles and artists for inclusion, I have used certain editorial restraints. The easiest qualifying criteria was a film or video's length. Generally, I included only works of at least 60 minutes in length. Exceptions have been either for historically important works (*Un Chant d'Amour, CBS Presents "The Homosexuals"*), shorts which have been grouped together for video release (*Boys on Film, Lesbian Lykra Shorts*) or when a particular filmmaker is highlighted and their important short films need to be discussed (Barbara Hammer, George Kuchar). With the recent proliferation of lesbian and gay film festivals around the world and the relatively inexpensive format of videotape, there has been a surge in the number of independently produced queer shorts, making their possible inclusion all too daunting. I've also ignored titles in which the film required excessive interpretation in order to arrive at a queer reading — an example is the works of John Woo, especially *The Killer*. When selecting a title, its queer elements had to be relatively evident.

The other, more troubling limitation has been the personalities, particularly actors and actresses who I wanted to include but did not because they are in the closet. Not wanting to out anyone, I have simply deleted them, hoping to include them in later editions. I could have included many without mentioning their sexuality, but their very inclusion would possibly have let the cat out of the bag. In numerous instances, I tried to confirm a person's sexual orientation through direct contact with them or their agent. Some asked not to be included (notwithstanding their sexual orientation) and, in the case of others, I was simply wrong in assuming they were gay. A case in point was director Allan Moyle who, despite making such gay/lesbian friendly movies such as *Times Square, Pump Up the Volume* and acting in *Outrageous!*, is in fact straight (but when contacted, he was amused to be thought of as gay and still wanted to be included). Some of the stars that made the final cut were included not because of first- (or second-) hand knowledge of their sexual orientation but through gossip (sorry, but true), "common knowledge" or references made on them in other books or magazines. Also present are still others who are of special interest to the reader because of the several gay/lesbian roles they have chosen to take. Hopefully, this book will generate letters and calls informing me of people and films who I missed. And maybe when the careers of those mentioned are not affected in any way, an avalanche of actors, directors and writers will contact me to complain of their absence and demand to be in the the next edition. I can dream, can't I?

The concept of "Images in the Dark" was not conceived in a literary vacuum. There have been several important books on the subject of lesbian/gay films that have preceded it. In the beginning there was Parker Tyler's wildly opinionated 1972 book of essays titled "Screening the Sexes: Homosexuality in the Movies"; a short but important book of essays and film listings published in 1977 was "Gays & Film" edited by Richard Dyer; and this was followed in 1981 with Vito Russo's definitive "The Celluloid Closet." After a decade-long lull, several more books have seen the light of publication, most notably Richard Dyer's "Now You See It — Studies on Lesbian and Gay Film" in 1991; and a veritable explosion of titles in 1993 that included Andrea Weiss' "Vampires and Violets — Lesbians in Cinema," Steve Stewart's "Gay Hollywood Film and Video Guide," "Gays and Lesbians in Mainstream Cinema" by James Robert Parrish, "The Lavender Screen" by Boze Hadleigh, and "Broadcasting It" by Keith Howes. While each of these books are important in contributing to the study (scholarly and entertainment-wise) of lesbians and gays in film, they have all focused on a specific limited number of film titles, be it lesbian, Hollywood, gay male, or just those on video.

In relation to these books, I've attempted a more inclusionary approach in recording the cinematic history of gays and lesbians in film. But while "Images in the Dark" is comprehensive, there are some obvious faults. I know my research and film viewing has been strong in regards to American and English films, good on German and French films, and much weaker when it comes to works from the other European countries. There are still many more films from these and other countries to be cataloged and commented on. An example of such is Australia, for although there has been an active queer rights movement there for years, my listing of films with lesbian/gay characters from that country is, I suspect, woefully underrepresentative. While there are few films pre-1991 from Asia, India and Africa, and, to a lesser extent, South America, I believe that I've missed only a few. In these countries, this lack of lesbian and gay images in the visual media can generally be ascribed to social and religious restraints, a weak gay/lesbian rights movement and a filmmaking environment controlled by governmental funding and its accompanying censorship.

With Chapter 1, I've compiled directors who are gay (interestingly those behind the camera [writers, directors and composers] have an easier time of coming out) while including some non-gay but gay-friendly personalities as well. In this chapter, I've separated "directors" from "independent filmmakers" — there seems to be a natural difference between the people who make Hollywood films and mass-market productions that are often not gay-themed, and independent films that almost always deal with issues concerning gays and lesbians. Chapter 2 highlights primarily American and British stars who are either gay/lesbian, have played several queer characters or who, though not gay, are of particular interest to readers of this type of book. As an editorial note, I feel that this chapter, while the largest, is also the weakest. One Academy Award nominated actor's agent, while not denying that the actor was gay, deemed it "inappropriate" for him to be included; the thought being that it could hurt him professionally/personally. Many stars rumored to be gay, lesbian or bisexual, including Barbara Stanwyck, Robert Taylor, Joan Crawford and several prominent stars of today were also not included. Chapter 3 focuses on writers, artists and composers, most of whom are/were gay or lesbian; again, the bulk of their work is not lesbian/gay themed. Chapters 4-9 make up the second and decidedly different part of the book. Here are the listing of films and videos broken down by genre or interest in a chapter, alphabetical format — Queer (of interest to both gays and lesbians), Lesbian, Gay, Transgender and Camp. The Camp section limits inclusions primarily to enjoyably cheesy films that feature gay/lesbian characters. The "gaydar" is set on high in the final chapter, Honorable and Dishonorable Mentions, a diverse selection of primarily non-queer mainstream movies that are analyzed for the way in which their gay and lesbian characters are featured, no matter how briefly. It is this final chapter - one that is filled with homophobic and inaccurate characterizations - that is the most troubling. For it is these films that the majority of filmgoers see and consequently form their inaccurate perception of lesbians and gays.

With the sheer number of titles in the book, one could have difficulty reaching conclusions on the history, politics or meaning of particular genres. For me, one of the most interesting aspects of the book is understanding the way lesbianism has been treated in film through the years. With lesbian involvement in mainstream cinema historically stultified, the images one sees (when there are images) have been formed for the most part by straight men, a vision fueled by both their sexual distrust of lesbians and filtered by their voyeuristic sexual intrigue. Hence, the lesbian is often seen as a slinky vampire, a sultry predator/seductress of the young and innocent, a frustrated man-wannabe, a threatening man-hater, a rich or decadent older woman on the prowl, a sadistic or lecherous prison warden/Nazi/spy and, if the filmmaker is in a particularly "sensitive" mood, simply as an unhappy (unfulfilled?, incomplete?) woman.

Happily these negative portraits are slowly fading away. Spurred by the queer activist movement, the "Lesbian Chic" media-frenzy of 1993 and the crossover box-office success of the invigorating and hopefully trendsetting *Go Fish* in 1994, the prospects for a new, fresh approach to lesbianism is in the offing. While there will always be lurid heterosexual cinematic fantasies of titillating lesbian sexuality (simply watch one of those "steamy" direct-to-video erotic thrillers), there are also the likes of Barbara Hammer, Su Friedrich, Pratibha Parmar and Greta Schiller and several other out filmmakers making movies and videos about lesbians and lesbian concerns. A new crop of independent lesbian filmmakers, unencumbered by the conservative morality of Hollywood, promise real and vibrant portrayals of lesbianism. Just two of the hotly anticipated lesbian features for 1995 are Marita Giovanni's romantic comedy *Bad Girls*, described by its producer as "...about love in the '90s. It's a 'Been out, done that, and I feel comfortable with myself' tale of lesbian love"; and Cheryl Dunye's feature-film debut with *Watermelon Woman*.

Another interesting trend that can be charted is the celebrated, much written about, but short-lived New Queer Cinema, a loosely assembled group of films and filmmakers (whose visible "mature" leaders include Gus Van Sant, Derek Jarman and Monica Treut). During a period of the late 1980s and early 1990s these directors and several other independent filmmakers produced refreshingly original and daringly defiant films. They shared a common theme, abandoning the "woe is me, the homosexual" line of thought to create works that reflected on the real-life situation of gays (and to a lesser extent, lesbians) in a world where the characters were young, out and outspoken. The stories went beyond examining the characters' sexual orientation and dealt instead with the many issues that affect them today: AIDS, social restlessness, sexual desire tempered with post-AIDS anxiety, the out queer as rebel, and the unification of gay men and lesbians. The result was a cacophonous chorus of "Yeah, we're queer, what the fuck you going to do about it!" Succinctly commenting on these in-your-face, unapologetically queer films (such as *The Living End, Via Appia, Swoon, No Skin Off My Ass, Poison, Nitrate Kisses, Mala Noche* and *Go Fish*), Paul Burston of London's *Time Out* said, "Some people describe them as 'negative,' 'dangerous,' 'politically incorrect.' Some lump them together and call them New Queer Cinema. I just call them fabulous."

What does the future hold for gays and lesbians in independent filmmaking, on the international cinema front and within the powerful but conservative behemoth that is Hollywood? Based on the recent outpouring of titles in the 1990s my conclusions are multi-layered. Queer American independent filmmaking is enjoying a mini-boom in production, accessibility and popularity while international cinema, in many cases, has continued to incorporate non-stereotypical lesbians and gays into their films as witnessed in the recent Cuban comedy *Strawberry and Chocolate* which features a startling and totally gay-positive character; Colombia's *La Estrategia del Carocol*, in which a transvestite is not only accepted by the community, but uses his/her homosexuality to help save the day; and the French *Pas Très Catholique* in which the lead character is a refreshingly original lesbian detective.

In the case of Hollywood, both a promising and troubling trend is emerging. Gay and lesbian characters are gradually being shown less in a predatory, sick or anti-social way (although these images still prevail) and are being more incorporated into mainstream films as non-threatening, intelligent, even hip (although most times minor) characters. This change is in of itself an advancement, but often this "liberal" approach produces images of queers as sexless, heteroized lead characters (*Philadelphia*) or in support as "friends" of the straight protagonists (*Naked in New York, Reality Bites*). The result is a laudable, but misdirected goal of making gay and lesbian characters palatable to the mass audience. An interpretation of this phenomenon is that these new queer characters are in effect replacing blacks as the token minority in a film's white, heterosexual story line. This trend, if taken in a conspiratorial vein, is more insidious than lesbian killer Catherine Trammell in *Basic Instinct* or the psychotic serial killer Jame Gubb in *The Silence of the Lambs*. For while these characters are insulting to the gay/lesbian community, they are also cartoonish in their stereotype, making them easily identifiable and criticized. Hollywood's attempt to market to mainstream audiences their sanitized interpretation of gay life and to make them "just like us" is more destructive, for, in a subtle way, it undermines the concerns, lifestyles and life stories of the lesbian/gay community. While we lament these false images, a self-satisfied Hollywood can claim a defense of, "Hey, we've thrown gay and lesbian characters into our films, and you're still not happy?" As the image of gays and lesbians undergoes this representational change, it becomes vitally important that we continue to insist on accurate, sensitive and relevant representation of queers in mainstream cinema and not to be co-opted into settling for a few cinematic crumbs.

The year 1995 holds the promise of being a watershed in Hollywood's handling of gays and lesbians, and especially transvestites. The film studios, always ready to jump on the profit-making bandwagon, must be quite happy with the surprise success of the Australian cross-dressing and transgender musical comedy *The Adventures of Priscilla, Queen of the Desert*. The film opened in late summer/early fall in 1994 and soon became a smash hit in the art/independent market. Its success came from a strong influx of non-queer audiences brought to the theatres with the guarantee of no homosexual sex, nary a kiss between the men and a promise of innocent, '70s-style musical fun. Continuing the trend and on the (high) heels of this is Beeban Kidron's *To Wong Foo, Thanks for Everything, Julie Newmar*, a Hollywood-backed film with a similar theme (a drag queen road movie) and featuring big name stars Patrick Swayze, Wesley Snipes and John Leguizamo. Other cross-dressing curiosities include an American remake of *La Cage aux Folles* with Robin Williams and Nathan Lane, and *Somebody to Love* starring Harvey Keitel, Rosie Perez and featuring a "sweet, energetic, red-headed, well-adjusted transvestite." With the success of *Philadelphia*, other AIDS-related productions include Francis Ford Coppola's *Cure*, a drama about the search for an AIDS vaccine written by Diana Johnson; Joel Schumacher's *Intimate Relations*; and the film version of Scott McPherson's off-Broadway play *Marvin's Room* with Robert De Niro producing.

At the risk of dating the book (this introduction being written in October 1994), the most eagerly awaited (but with the lowest expectations) queerish film of the 1994-95 season is certainly the film version of Ann Rice's *Interview with the Vampire*. The Neil Jordan-directed film features a creamy cast: Brad Pitt, Antonio Banderas and a blond Tom Cruise as the vampire Lestat. Other highlights are film versions of several gay plays: Paul Rudnick's *Jeffrey*, starring Steven Weber and Sigourney Weaver; the Disney-produced film version of William Finn's Tony Award-winning musical *Falsettos*; Larry Kramer's *The Normal Heart* produced and starring Barbra Streisand; and the most challenging and potentially most powerful of all of the gay/lesbian themed films slated for release, Robert Altman's adaptation of Tony Kushner's Tony Award-winning play *Angels in America*.

The most troubled production in Hollywood over the past few years has been the filming of Randy Shilts' *The Mayor of Castro Street*. Gus Van Sant was originally slated to direct the Oliver Stone-produced feature on the slain civil rights leader but that association ended. Rob Cohen was brought in but he left/was fired as well. Of the mainstream lesbian themed titles, the most exciting is the screen adaptation of lesbian mystery writer Katherine V. Forrest's *Murder at the Nightwood Bar* to be directed by Tim Hunter and starring Mary-Louise Parker as an L.A. police detective.

Not expecting Hollywood to readily change its stripes, a more propitious area for the redefinition of queer images is in independent filmmaking. In the past few years, there has been a proliferation of independently produced gay/lesbian themed films and videos. These works are finding audiences at the many gay/lesbian film festivals as well as in limited theatrical engagements (primarily in big city art-houses) and by marketing the works directly to home video. On this independent front, the most eagerly awaited film is *The Celluloid Closet*, based on Vito Russo's groundbreaking book on homosexuality in the movies and made by Rob Epstein, Jeffrey Friedman and Arnold Glassman. Other productions include the Todd Verow-directed, Marcus Hu-produced *Frisk*, adapted from Dennis Cooper's novel; Jill Godmillow's *Roy Cohn/Jack Smith*, with texts by Gary Indiana and Jack Smith; Todd Haynes' drama on a mysterious infectious disease, *Safe*; John Greyson's *Lilies*, based on a play by Montreal writer Michel-Marc Bouchard; and the film based on the life and work of artist/poet/activist David Wojnarowicz, *Postcards from America*. Amazingly, these films are just a sampling of the projected releases for the upcoming year, a year that hopefully offers lesbian/gay audiences a more sensitive and accurate look at queer life in the '90s.

Whether used simply as a handy queer video guide, a research source or a good, informational read, I hope "Images in the Dark" will be both useful, informative and entertaining. With dozens of productions in the planning/filming/editing stage, I feel that the book will need eventual updating, so I welcome all comments, corrections, additions, deletions and criticisms. You can contact me at TLA Video, 1520 Locust Street, Suite 200, Philadelphia, PA 19102.

Raymond Murray

1

FAVORITE DIRECTORS & INDEPENDENT FILMMAKERS

The featured filmmakers in this chapter, accompanied by a short biography and their filmography, are either gay/lesbian or, because of their work, are of special interest to the lesbian/gay viewer.

"It is difficult enough to be queer, but to be queer in the cinema is almost impossible. Heterosexuals have fucked up the screen so completely that there's hardly room for us to kiss there."

—Derek Jarman

"Just because a movie is gay or independent doesn't make it good. I'd rather go see fuckin' *Coneheads* than see most of them."

—Gregg Araki

CHANTAL AKERMAN

Innovative, demanding and provocative, Belgian-born Chantal Akerman has been called a filmmaker's filmmaker. Her works are primarily austere avant-garde or minimalist exercises which explore the emotional turmoil that lies underneath her characters' deceptively placid surfaces. In a style marked by the use of real time, long takes by an unswerving camera and a lack of many close-ups, Akerman's films, despite mostly being classified as "non-commercial," have attained legendary status in art cinemas in Europe as well as the United States.

Recurring themes in Akerman's films include loneliness and isolation; explorations into the communication between a mother and her adult daughter; and attempting to answer (or not to answer) the questions, "What is the meaning of life?" — and in her later works, "What is the nature of love?" Interestingly, Akerman has broken out of that mold on occasion with several engagingly buoyant and whimsical musical comedies.

Although a lesbian who focuses many of her films on female sexuality and feminism, she wishes to be associated with neither — it was reported that she once pulled *je tu il elle* from the New York Gay Film Festival telling festival director Peter Lowry, "I will never permit a film of mine to be shown in a gay film festival. I will not be ghettoized."

In addition to the films which follow, Akerman has made several documentaries including *Un jour Pina a demande'* (1983), *Letters Home* (1986) and *Histories D'Amerique* (1989).

"Comparable in force and originality to Godard or Fassbinder, Chantal Akerman is arguably the most important European director of her generation."
—J. Hoberman, *The Village Voice*

"Chantal Akerman is one of the most important European directors of our (post-'60s) generation. Not only are her films handily brilliant, but they're profoundly feminist as well."
—C. Ruby Rich, *The Village Voice*

"I won't say that I'm a feminist filmmaker...I'm not making women's films, I'm making Chantal Akerman films."
—Chantal Akerman

Chantal Akerman

Akermania Vol. 1 *(1968-84, 74 min, Belgium)*
A video compilation that features three shorts. *I'm Hungry, I'm Cold* (1984): Two young girls run away to Paris from their native Brussels and learn very direct, immediate approaches in getting their needs met. *Blow Up My Town* (1968): Living in a small flat, a young woman with too much unchanneled energy races through the mundane activities of daily life until she's caught in the vortex of their execution. This can be seen as a precursor to *Jeanne Dielman. Hotel Monterey* (1974): Without sound, the camera wanders through the lobby, into the elevator, hallways, various rooms and out to the roof of the hotel. This process eventually creates a portrait of impersonal space, and the people captured in it seem transient, impermanent, ephemeral. An eerie and disquieting experience. ⊛

▼ **je tu il elle** *(1974, 95 min, Belgium)*
This first feature film by Akerman is a charming yet demanding, innovative psychodrama that placed her in the same avant-garde company as Alain Robbes-Grillet and Margauritte Duras. The film, whose title means "I...You...He...She," opens with director/heroine Akerman lying alone and naked in bed eating from a bag of sugar. What follows is a deceptively simple story told in three segments, each containing an element of the traditional depiction of women. Initially, she is writing a sad letter to an (ex?)lover; another is a brief sexual encounter with a truck driver (basically a passive handjob as the trucker gives instructions); and, finally, a sexual relationship with another woman, depicted in a strangely unerotic fashion. While eschewing traditional narrative, Akerman thinks out such ideas as loss and separation, solitary introspection and voyeurism with startling clarity. In her book "Vampires and Violets," Andrea Weiss has described Akerman's

confused sexual messages in that, "Akerman dismantles both heterosexual romantic myths and the structures for male visual pleasure but she can not envisage any alternative film language for female desire." ☮

Jeanne Dielman, 23, Quai Du Commerce, 1080 Bruxelles
(1975, 201 min, Belgium/France)

Widely acclaimed as one of the most important films of the decade, Akerman's monumental saga of a frightfully ritualized existence covers three days in the stifling life of a bourgeois widow (Delphine Seyrig) who does household work, takes care of her teenage son and is a part-time prostitute; a tragic figure for whom the acts of cooking, cleaning and intercourse are performed with the same stoic efficiency. This epic explores the gradual unraveling of a frail human psyche. A bleak and original feminist tragedy and a highly rewarding realization of avant-garde filmmaking aspirations.

> "Beautiful...original and ambitious."
> —Vincent Canby, *The New York Times*

News from Home *(1976, 85 min, Belgium)*

In an avant-gardist mood, Akerman has produced in this static, repetitive exercise her own unique filmic symphony to New York City. Attempting to explore the differences between European myths of the city against its gritty reality, cinematographer Babette Mangolte captures the strangely stark beauty of an alienated, lifeless world while offscreen Akerman occasionally reads, in a monotone voice, letters from a Belgium mother to her daughter living in New York. A difficult, abstract work of art. ☮

▼ Les Rendez-vous D'Anna
(1978, 122 min, Belgium)

Filmed in a minimalist style, this quietly moving drama of alienation features a young Belgian director, Anna, who travels by train through Europe publicizing her newest film. Along the way, she meets a stream of characters: friends, lovers, relatives and strangers. During the course of her journey, she describes to her mother a sexual experience with another woman, explaining, "Our bodies happened to touch. Suddenly we were kissing. I don't know how it happened. I felt nauseous...I let myself go. It felt good." The pervading malaise enveloping Anna is brought out by Akerman's trademark style of static camera shots, understated images, monologues and silence. A grim portrait of one woman adrift as well as a vision of an insensate Europe. Starring Aurore Clement, Lea Massari, Helmut Griem and Jean-Pierre Cassel. ☮

Tout une Nuit *(1982, 90 min, Belgium/France)*

Abandoning standard narrative plot, Akerman's own minimalist, avant-garde story of the follies of sex and love is set on one torrid summer night in Brussels. Told in a series of amorous fragments, the film follows the various mating rites of several couples as they meet, fall in love, eat, drink and then break up. An ascetic yet strangely riveting experimental melodrama that is certainly not for all audiences. ☮

Les Annees 80 (The Eighties)
(1983, 82 min, Belgium/France)

The creative genesis of art and the filmmaking process is examined and deconstructed in this unusually fascinating and pleasurable film. Unlike Akerman's previous somber films, this is a giddy work: a musical set in a suburban shopping mall, and nothing like

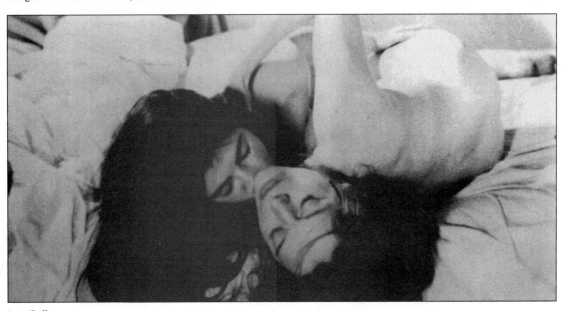

je tu il elle

the Hollywood musicals of the past. The first part of the film features a series of confusingly repetitive and jumbled scenes of a group of women singing, talking, discussing and arguing. Pushing the audience to the point of walking out (or turning off), the film changes direction completely in the second half to reveal the end result of all this confusion — a deliriously fun and lively musical extravaganza. A witty, tongue-in-cheek film that can be frustrating but proves to be well worth the wait. ⊛

Man with a Suitcase (L'homme a' la valise) *(1984, 63 min, France/Belgium)*

Akerman plays the lead in this almost stream-of-consciousness drama of power relationships, victimization and self-isolation. Upon returning to her Parisian apartment after a long trip, Akerman finds a friend-of-a-friend staying there. Unable to throw him out, she becomes obsessed with his presence. As her slight annoyance develops into outright hostility, the man increases his domination sending Akerman further into herself and a corner of the flat.

Window Shopping
(1986, 96 min, France/Belgium)

Set within the friendly, artificial confines of a Parisian shopping mall, Akerman proves that she is not limited to producing serious, experimental studies thanks to this delightful musical that pays homage to Jacques Demy and the old MGM musicals. Actually nothing more than a stylish soap opera, the story follows Lili, the manager of a hair salon, and her various suitors; which includes Delphine Seyrig's love-struck son. Plot twists abound, a chorus of shampoo girls breaks into song and love is always around the corner in this splashy, nonsensical lark that takes delight in its own frothiness while still retaining some insight into love in the modern age. ⊛

Night & Day
(1992, 90 min, France/Belgium)

A breezy, post-feminist comedy about a woman's loving relationship with two men, *Night and Day* is a deceptively simple blending of Eric Rohmer's obsession with talky young love and the filmic exuberance of early Jean-Luc Godard. Julie and Jack live and love in blissful isolation. He drives a taxi in the evening, and during the day they make love. This arrangement is altered but not upset after Julie meets Joseph, a fellow taxi-driving young man. They begin seeing each other while Jack works and eventually fall in love as well. Independent-minded Julie, however, is undeterred by thoughts of deceit, and is content to continue seeing both men, with no desire to choose between the two. Erotic, stylish and decidedly unconventional, the warm summer nights of Paris prove to be an inviting backdrop for this wryly blissful ménage à trois. ⊛

From the East
(1993, 107 min, France/Belgium/Portugal)

This impressionistic travelogue diary of the people of post-communist Moscow is a wordless, plotless experimental film. Shot from a slowly moving automobile, the film begins in the former East Germany in mid-summer and travels east through Poland before arriving in Moscow in blustery winter. Akerman's lens captures the almost expressionless, yet full-of-meaning faces of the population. The people are seen walking, waiting in long lines, selling household goods and simply standing on the street, possibly waiting for something to happen. Through the juxtapositions and editing and choice of images, Akerman manipulates the film, creating a quasi-fictional documentary. The almost endless stream of faces and places could strike some as the social antithesis of *Koyaanisqatsi* — a social/political film essay of a world without hustle, excitement, noise, music nor outward tension.

Jeanne Dielman, 23, Quai Du Commerce, 1080 Bruxelles

PEDRO ALMODÓVAR

Over the past several years, Pedro Almodóvar has rocketed to the top of Spanish cinema, so much so that he can claim to be not only Spain's leading "gay" filmmaker, but its leading filmmaker, period. Happily, he has achieved this stature without straying from his fundamentally iconoclastic and giddily pernicious point of view. His films, rollicking fantasies featuring characters ranging from glue-sniffing housewives to transvestite judges to lesbian punk rockers, are always infused with a gay sensibility, consistently poking fun at society's underbelly and always seeking to provoke. When asked at the Venice Film Festival what prize he would like to win for his 1988 watershed film, *Women on the Verge of a Nervous Breakdown*, he replied, "the prize for me would be to have the culture ministers ban it."

Coming as he did from the tiny town of Calzada de Calatrava in the La Mancha region of southwestern Spain, it's difficult to imagine where this cultural renegade got his outrageous style — rural Spain in the 1950s under Franco was not exactly what one would consider fertile soil for Almodóvar's brand of comic melodrama. So out of step was he with the pulse of his home town that in an interview with Vito Russo for *Film Comment* he declared that he felt like "an astronaut in King Arthur's court."

He left home at 17 and took a job as a telephone operator in Madrid where he became involved in the city's punked-out "hip" scene of the late '70s and early '80s — a bastion for gays, transvestites and drag queens. Upon Franco's death in 1975, he found himself in the center of the artistic community that would lead the country's cultural reawakening, a phenomenon known in Spain as "La Movida." He co-founded the cross-dressing punk rock band Almodóvar & McNamara as well as illustrated X-rated comic books. During this period, he began making home-styled, 8mm films with titles like *Fuck Me, Fuck Me, Fuck Me...Tim* (1978). Drawing cinematic inspiration from the works of Frank Tashlin (a one-time Warner Brothers cartoonist who made loopy '50s comedies), Douglas Sirk and Luis Buñuel, he went on to make his first 16mm film, *Pepi, Luci, Bom* (1980), which was an instant cult hit in Madrid.

His first commercial success came in 1986 with, of all things, his most personal and most outwardly gay-themed film, *Law of Desire*. *Law* set box-office records in Spain

Pedro and his minions

and gained the attention of international critics. Mass audiences didn't really get their first taste of Almodóvar's lunacy, however, until 1988 with *Women on the Verge...*, which established him as an international box-office draw and fueled interest in his earlier works.

Most of Almodóvar's films, though they feature many gay, transvestite or transsexual characters, have not been gay-themed per se. He sees nothing inconsistent in his approach, preferring to concentrate on human idiosyncrasies and passions over political agendas: "Even though I'm gay, I don't feel compelled to tell gay stories. I just tell a story that I'm interested in."

▼ **Pepi, Luci, Bom** *(1980, 80 min, Spain)*
A mock-pornographic farce, *Pepi, Luci, Bom*, Almodóvar's feature film debut, is rude, funny and *very* nasty. The inimitable Carmen Maura plays the heiress Pepi, who seeks revenge on the cop who deflowered her by becoming involved with his masochistic wife Luci and her lesbian rock-star friend Bom. Replete with drugs, kinky hetero and homo sex, erection-measuring parties, beatings and body fluids, this low-budget, raw and crude camp piece lacks the frenetic pace and lush panoramic color scheme of his later works; but as a curio, it is a must for Almodóvar fans. ☮

▼ **Labyrinth of Passion** *(1982, 100 min, Spain)*
Opening up with a dazed drag queen simultaneously guzzling booze, sniffing nail polish and cruising for action at a Madrid cafe, this hilarious low-budget comedy is intoxicatingly fun. The story centers around both Riza, the gay son of a deposed Middle Eastern

tyrant who likes to hang around with Madrid's sleazier denizens, and Sexi, an aspiring rock singer and unabashed nymphomaniac. The two fall for each other and decide to run away, but first they must deal with their respective rock groups, terrorists who are bent on kidnapping Riza, and a gay man (played by Antonio Banderas) with unusual sniffing abilities who is quite smitten with Riza and determined to make him his. A frantic, kaleidoscopic comedy bristling with loony humor. Don't miss the cameo of Almodóvar as a cross-dressing member of the rock band, Almodóvar & McNamara. ☻

Dark Habits *(1984, 116 min, Spain)*

While not Almodóvar's best work, *Dark Habits* nonetheless manages to carry the director's unparalleled sense of twisted, subversive and blacker-than-black humor. When Yolanda's boyfriend dies of an overdose of heroin, she decides it's better to run and hide than face the law. She winds up at the doorstep of the "Humble Redeemers," an order of heroin-addicted nuns who specialize in cases like hers — indeed they were all once cases like her! The cast includes some of the familiar Almodóvites: Julieta Serrano stars as the Mother Superior and Carmen Maura appears as the cloister's resident tiger keeper, Sister Sin. ☻

> "Deliriously warped! A good, sleazy wallow! This movie has exchanges so bizarre they make you giddy. It's pure subversion."
>
> —David Edelstein, *The Village Voice*

What Have I Done to Deserve This?

▼ What Have I Done to Deserve This?

(1985, 100 min, Spain)

This unbelievably funny, absurdist gem leapt out of the post-Franco liberalization with the velocity of a cannonball and was Almodóvar's first hit in the United States. Twisted and surreal, the film focuses on a modern Spanish clan. Mom is the head of the household, a frustrated No-Doze-addicted housewife who lives in

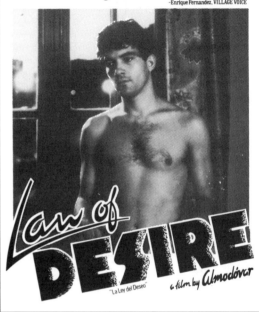

"Wickedly Funny!"
-David Lida, W.W.D.

"A lively cast, a turbulent plot... An entertaining jumble! Tina, the transsexual, is played vivaciously by Carmen Maura."
-Janet Maslin, THE NEW YORK TIMES

"Surreal humor...clearly an original talent!"
-Leo Seligsohn, N.Y. NEWSDAY

"Joyously sleazy...Almodóvar is the happiest, most entertaining hedonist in film today!"
-Enrique Fernandez, VILLAGE VOICE

Law of DESIRE

"La Ley del Deseo" a film by Almodóvar

Antonio Banderas takes it all off in *Law of Desire*

a tiny high-rise with her miserable cab-driving husband (who once forged Hitler's diaries) and two sons, one a 14-year-old drug dealer and the other a precocious 12-year-old who casually seduces his friends' fathers (and is finally sold to a gay dentist). Completing this thorny nest is their batty Grandma who longs to leave Madrid and, with her pet lizard and stick collection, find a place in the country. Underlying all of the madcap hilarity is a social critique on the breakdown of the family and the stifling conformity of urban living in Spain today. But don't let that interfere with the fun — this is a marvelously inspired black comedy. ☻

> "An absolutely wonderful black comedy. It is quite simply a small masterpiece."
>
> —*The New York Times*

> "A superb, absolutely mad film! This is like Buñuel doing John Waters, but seasoned with Woody Allen.
>
> —*L.A. Weekly*

Matador *(1986, 102 min, Spain)*

This wickedly twisted, satiric romp wallows in the world of desire as a series of bizarre sexual murders unfold. The police in Madrid are baffled until young Angel, believing himself to be guilty, turns himself in. Trouble is, he's innocent, but has been witnessing the killings clairvoyantly. His femme-fatale attorney knows of his innocence, as does his bullfighting instructor: for they are each responsible for the grizzly murders. In this dizzying ode to Hitchcock, Almodóvar has once again ripped away the facade of human behavior to reveal a hilarious, sometimes frightening subterranean view of a world ruled by passion and death. ☯

▼ Law of Desire *(1987, 100 min, Spain)*

Almodóvar's most prominent gay film is a wonderfully overheated sexual melodrama which basks in its farcical intentions. The story revolves around Pablo, a popular director of homoerotic films who, despite a hunky quasi-boyfriend, is yearning for a passionate love affair. Antonio Banderas is the darkly handsome but demented fan who attempts to win the director's heart by any means possible. Rounding out the wacky cast is Pablo's delightfully exuberant lesbian sister, Tina (Carmen Maura), who used to be his brother until he changed his sex in order to please his lover — their father! Their loves, passions and wild adventures are splashed on the screen with uninhibited eroticism, camp and outlandish wit. ☯

Women on the Verge of a Nervous Breakdown *(1988, 88 min, Spain)*

Almodóvar's comic masterpiece is largely responsible for familiarizing American audiences with his unique talents and is possibly his most inspired work. Based loosely on Cocteau's "The Human Voice," the story follows Pepa (brilliantly portrayed by Carmen Maura), an actress who comes home one day to find her lover has left. What follows is a hilarious escapade as she tries to piece her life back together. Julieta Serrano is fabulous as the insanely jealous wife and Maria Barranco is hysterical as a friend who is fleeing from Shiite terrorists. ☯

Women on the Verge of a Nervous Breakdown

Tie Me Up! Tie Me Down!
(1990, 101 min, Spain)

Lovers of Almodóvar's outrageous style will find this delirious comedy a pure delight. A recently released mental patient (Antonio Banderas) kidnaps a heroin-addicted porn star (Victoria Abril) and professes his love for her. Surprisingly sentimental for Almodóvar, this is an often hilarious tale of love and bondage which features a truly steamy sex scene and a water toy with a penchant for swimming into the nether regions of the female anatomy. ☯

▼ High Heels *(1991, 115 min, Spain)*

Almodóvar moves into new territory by looking a bit more closely at the human motives and desires he usually savages. The story revolves around a volatile estranged mother-daughter relationship. Upon reuniting, they come to realize that they have been sharing the same man. Quicker than you can say *Women on the Verge...*, the film fires headfirst into a series of alternately hilarious and tragic situations. Victoria Abril plays the successful but emotionally bankrupt daughter Becky. Marisa Paredes gives a virtuoso Joan Crawford-style performance as Becky's domineering and cold, but ultimately caring mother. Miguel Bosé turns in a head-turning performance as the transvestite nightclub singer Femme Lethal, and the musical lesbian prison number is a scream. Almodóvar's trademark visuals blend with tragic and comedic melodrama to wonderful effect. ☯

▼ Kika *(1993, 90 min, Spain)*

Almodóvar's newest and much-anticipated feature is this big-budget comedy-drama filled with outlandish costuming (by Jean-Paul Gaultier), neon-bright colors and wild characters, all filmed at the director's trademark frenetic pace. Once again, the women are the stars (Peter Coyote and Alex Casanovas play secondary roles) as the story alternates between farce and an examination of urban crises. Verónica Forqué is Kika, a sweet, sexy makeup artist who is forced to confront urban rape (committed by a recently released convict eager to "graduate" from queers to women), multiple murders, and intrusion of her privacy by the media's prying eyes. Her nemesis is Andrea Caracortada (Victoria Abril), a villainous femme disguised as the hostess of a "Cops"-like TV show, "Today's Worst." Andrea is seen clothed in black rubber, with a robotic camera helmet on her head and arc lights covering her breasts — if there's something happening in Madrid, she's going to capture it! Our heroine's rape, captured on video by a neighboring voyeur, falls into the clutches of Andrea who wants nothing more than to air it on national TV. This story of voyeurism and media manipulation also stars Bibi Andersen (not the Swedish actress), a statuesque transsexual who has been romantically linked to the director. The Picasso-faced Rossy Di Palma, an Almodóvar regular, is fine in support as Kika's lesbian maid who is madly in lust with her employer.

> "Willfully frivolous and superficial...Gloriously shot, beautifully dressed and skillfully acted, it is poorly plotted and characterized, its rogues' gallery of grotesque provoking little of the audience identification that Almodóvar was clearly hoping for."
> —Paul Julian Smith, *Sight and Sound*

LINDSAY ANDERSON

Lindsay Anderson (1923-1994) had been heralded as being one of the most gifted and influential directors of his generation. While a student at Oxford, he helped found, and was a leading critical voice in, *Sequence*, an independent film journal that attacked the staid and bourgeois British film industry. He moved from behind the pen to behind the camera with an industrial documentary, *Meet the Pioneers*, and with it began a long period in which he made innovative and award-winning documentaries.

During this period, he, along with Karel Reisz, was the prime inspiration behind the Free Cinema Movement, a collective of filmmakers committed to making films dealing with the working man and the importance of everyday life. Anderson won an Academy Award with his 1953 short, *Thursday's Children*, a Richard Burton-narrated film about the teaching of deaf students at the Royal School for the Deaf. Other important short films of this period include *Everyday Except Christmas* (1957), a grittily realistic, yet almost poetic night-in-the-life of the old Covent Garden Market, now gentrified into a shopping arcade; and the harrowing *O Dreamland* (1953). *This Sporting Life*, his first feature film, has been cited as a leading example of Britain's "kitchen sink" dramas — a genre similar to the Italian neorealism. With *If...* and *O Lucky Man!*, his anti-authoritarian philosophy was perfect for the turbulent 1960s and early '70s.

While his feature film output is not great (he was also a leading theatrical director) and his later films had been greeted to a critically lukewarm reception, his writings on film theory, his leadership in bringing about changes to British filmmaking, his many important social documentaries as well as his trendsetting, anti-authoritarian features assure Lindsay Anderson a place as one of Britain's most important filmmakers and critics.

This Sporting Life *(1963, 134 min, GB)*

Richard Harris gives a career performance as Frank Machin, a Yorkshire lad who tries to escape the restrictions of his working-class background and his personal limitations by becoming a star on the local rugby team. Gritty and stark, the film is peopled with great performances, among them Rachel

Lindsay Anderson

Roberts, as his landlady and doomed love interest, Colin Blakely and Arthur Lowe. Screenplay by David Storey, based on his book; produced by Karel Reisz. ⊛

▼ If... *(1968, 111 min, GB)*

Inspired by Jean Vigo's classic *Zero for Conduct*, this extraordinary allegorical film is set in a repressive public boarding school where Malcolm McDowell is one of three unruly seniors whose refusal to conform ultimately leads to a full-scale student rebellion against the authorities. McDowell made his film debut in this explosive, furiously funny attack on the British establishment that features a casual, almost matter-of-course depiction of homosexuality, adolescent sex and male companionship. Surreal and manic, the film has perplexed audiences with its alternating use of black-and-white and color photography. But rather than an artistic statement, Anderson had said that the reason for the switching was that he was not filming in sequence, and when he ran low on money, he was forced to shoot in black and white. ⊛

O Lucky Man! *(1973, 173 min, GB)*

Based on an idea by Malcolm McDowell, Anderson's mammoth and brilliant allegory stars McDowell as Mick Travis, a latter-day Candide buoyed by optimism in a sea of sham and corruption. Mick is an enterprising coffee salesman who pushes his way to the top only to fall and rise and fall yet again. A witty score is provided by Alan Price and there's sparkling support by Arthur Lowe, Ralph Richardson and Rachel Roberts. ⊛

In Celebration *(1974, 131 min, GB)*

Anderson's contribution to the American Film Theatre series is this rendition of David Storey's loosely autobiographical play about three grown-up sons who return home to their coal-mining home town to celebrate their parents' 40th anniversary. Alan Bates heads the original Royal Court Theatre cast. ☺

Look Back in Anger *(1980, 101 min, GB)*

Malcolm McDowell and Anderson team once again for this remake of John Osborne's explosive "angry young man" play. For theatre buffs, it's interesting to compare this rendering to the 1958 version starring Richard Burton and the 1990 version with Kenneth Branagh. ☺

Britannia Hospital *(1982, 115 min, GB)*

This scathingly funny and winningly absurd black comedy sums up the ailing state of the once mighty British Empire. Preparations for a visit by the Queen Mother to a floundering medical institution are set against the backdrop of violent demonstrations protesting the specialized care given to a ruthless African dictator. In the midst of the melee, every possible (and impossible) catastrophe arises until Graham Crowden (as the inimitably insane Dr. Millar) eloquently sums up the meaning of human existence. Malcolm McDowell stars, and Alan Bates and Joan Plowright appear in cameos. Ostensibly the concluding film of the Mick Travis trilogy (*If..., O Lucky Man!*), the film was savaged by the critics and greeted with indifference by the public. ☺

The Whales of August *(1987, 90 min, US)*

Lillian Gish and Bette Davis star in this eloquent rendition of David Berry's play about two aging sisters living out their final years together. Gish plays the tenderhearted and loving caretaker who patiently looks after sister Davis, who is blind, embittered and given to petulant outbursts. Both actresses play their parts exquisitely, each projecting a screen presence unscathed by the sands of time. Anderson leaves behind all the rampant political diatribe which are the hallmarks of his earlier works and concentrates on subtle human interaction; the result being a heartwarming look at the delicate process of growing old. Also starring screen veterans Vincent Price and Ann Sothern. ☺

Glory! Glory! *(1989, 152 min, US)*

Originally made as a two-part cable special, this hilarious satire of televangelism stars Richard Thomas as Bobby Joe Stuckey, an electronic preacher whose ministry is in disarray. His contributions are dwindling and cash flow is low. Things are so bad, in fact, that he hires a sexy rock 'n' roll singer (Ellen Greene) to help boost profits, and that's when the word of the Lord really starts to get turned upside-down. ☺

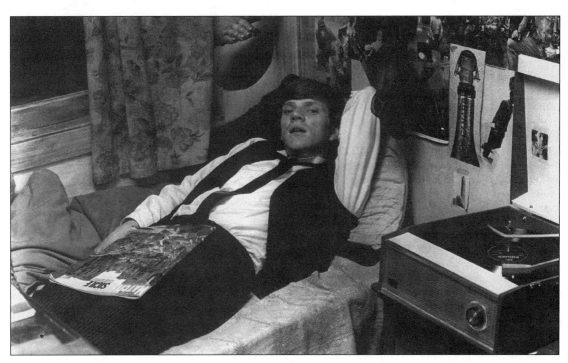

Malcolm MacDowell strikes an alluring pose in *If...*

EMILE ARDOLINO

A multi-talented and multi-award winning director (the recipient of an Oscar, a Peabody, an Obie, Emmys, and a Directors Guild of America Award), Emile Ardolino's fame was surprisingly limited in the public eye. Ardolino was a prominent figure in American dance and in the production of television specials on dance and their originators, and had a reputation as a creative film director with a knowledge of popular taste. However, his name at the time of his death from AIDS in November 1993 at the age of 50 was surprisingly less familiar than artists of much less success and talent. Ardolino's death cut short a career that was blossoming with both his *George Balanchine's The Nutcracker* and the Bette Midler-starring *Gypsy* premiering after his death. Born in New York City, Ardolino savored a lifetime interest in dance and theatre. He was involved early on, being an ardent theatregoer and starring in stage productions while attending New York's City College. His first professional job was in a touring version of "The Fantasticks."

His filmed segments for the risque Broadway show "Oh! Calcutta!" in 1969 won him an Obie. From there he formed his own production company, Compton-Ardolino Films, which specialized in dance documentaries. His duties in this company included producing, editing and directing. The company's best known work was making a series of 28 acclaimed dance documentaries for PBS. The series, called "Dance in America," featured films on The American Ballet Theatre, the Joffrey, the Pennsylvania Ballet, Pilobolus Dance Theatre and several other leaders in the field. In addition to being credited as producer to the above documentaries, Ardolino also directed several episodes of the TV series "Dirty Dancing" as well as television specials highlighting the works of Jerome Robbins, George Balanchine and Rudolf Nureyev and directed three shows produced by Joseph Papp: David Henry Hwang's "The Dance and the Railroad," Shakespeare's "A Midsummer Night's Dream" starring William Hurt, and "Alice at the Palace" with Meryl Streep.

Ardolino's golden touch continued as he won an Academy Award for his documentary *He Makes Me Feel Like Dancing*. His work in theatre included directing Leonard Bernstein's "Mass" and producing the multimedia effects for "Jesus Christ Superstar."

His Hollywood career was just as impressive. After some interesting "small" productions (*Rumplestilskin, The Rise and Rise of Daniel Rocket*), he stirred the interest of Hollywood with his surprise box-office success *Dirty Dancing*. He made two popular comedies, *Chances Are* and *Three Men and a Little Lady*, only to return to the rarefied mega-hit realm with his endearing comedy *Sister Act*, starring Whoopi Goldberg. His light, human-interest comedies were a direct result of his own attitudes toward life and film. He once said that "I am interested in scripts about character, whether it's a comedy, a romance or drama. I like audiences to feel something when they come out. I don't want them to come out numb. I really want them to feel and to think, mostly feel." He is survived by his domestic partner Luis M. Rodriguez-Villa.

Ardolino directs Danson, Selleck and Guttenberg in *Three Men...*

Rumplestilskin *(1982, 48 min, US)*
Made as part of Shelley Duvall's Faerie Tale Theatre series, Duvall stars as the gold-spinning queen whose promise to an evil troll (Herve Villechaize) spells trouble. ⊛

He Makes Me Feel Like Dancing
(1983, 90 min, US)
This stirring film, the winner of an Academy Award for Best Documentary, focuses on the life and charity work of former New York City Ballet dancer Jacques D'Amboise. The film was originally made for network television (NBC), and was also released in a limited theatrical engagement.

The Rise and Rise of Daniel Rocket
(1986, 84 min, US)
Originally made for PBS' American Playhouse series, this entertaining fantasy features an aviation buff (Tom Hulce) who becomes an international celebrity, but learns that even his illusion must remain fastened to the Earth. Timothy Dalton co-stars. ⊛

Dirty Dancing *(1987, 97 min, US)*

This sleeper hit of 1987 is a wonderfully nostalgic coming-of-age tale set in a Catskill Mountains resort in 1963. Patrick Swayze became a star thanks to his role as the handsome dance instructor who becomes involved with innocent teenager Jennifer Grey. Some good dancing and golden oldies highlight the film. ⊛

Chances Are *(1989, 108 min, US)*

This routine "switch" comedy is saved by Robert Downey, Jr.'s charming performance and Ardolino's skillful directorial hand. The spirit of Cybill Shepherd's deceased husband turns up in her daughter's boyfriend (Downey). With Mary Stuart Masterson and Ryan O'Neal as the confused partners of Downey and Shepherd. ⊛

Three Men and a Little Lady

(1990, 100 min, US)

While mildly entertaining, this sugar-coated sequel fails to live up to the original and is hampered by its predictability. Ted Danson, Steve Guttenberg and Tom Selleck all return from the original for this thin story about Selleck's snail-paced realization that he loves the little lady's mother, Sylvia (Nancy Travis). In one scene, the three fathers are on an interview and all of them vehemently deny being gay. The next scene, Danson tells the little lady it's okay to be different. ⊛

Sister Act *(1992, 101 min, US)*

A comic delight, Whoopi Goldberg stars as a Reno lounge singer who, upon witnessing a gangland murder, is sent to hide out at a San Francisco convent, run by the inestimable Maggie Smith. Captivating the order one by one, Whoopi does anything but lay low when she takes control of the church's choir and turns them into an overnight sensation. As would be expected, a lot of the humor stems from the nuns engaging in very un-nun-like behavior. But most of the comedy is sharper than that suggests. And though the premise is strictly formulaic, it's one Hollywood formula which works. As an elderly nun, it's good to see Mary Wickes again, and Kathy Najimy steals every scene she's in as an unbelievably perky sister. This surprise box-office hit was originally written by Paul Rudnick (*Addams Family Values*) for Bette Midler, but after she left the project, so did Rudnick. ⊛

George Balanchine's The Nutcracker

(1993, 96 min, US)

Box-office champ Macaulay Culkin suffered his first financial mini-bomb in his role as the Nutcracker Prince in this screen version of ballet's Christmas favorite. Staged at SUNY Purchase by Peter Martins, the film is unimaginative, even dull; its biggest problem being its straightforward shooting which stagnates the action and does not utilize the possibilities of opening up the play. This lack of directorial finesse might be attributed to Ardolino's ill health at the time. Possibly more interesting than the actual finished product was the gossipy infighting between the producers and Macaulay's father/manager Kit Culkin. Known for his tough bargaining positions on both money and artistic control, Kit is a feared force in Tinseltown, whose bigwigs have been forced to capitulate to his demands for the simple reason that everything little Macaulay touches turns to box-office gold. But Kit's insistence that the film not have narration and the producer's demand that he not interfere came to public blows resulting in juicy news items about the fighting. The Culkins publicly decried the film and refused to publicize it in any way, and the producer Arnon Milchen, saying enough-is-enough, told *The New York Times*, "I can take so much harassment, so much extortion, so much blackmail." ⊛

Bette Midler in *Gypsy*

Gypsy *(1993, 140 min, US)*

It is fitting that Ardolino's last production was his favorite musical, "Gypsy" (he saw it on stage 26 times). His love for the material is evident: This made-for-TV adaptation of the Broadway classic is a faithful and exhilarating remake. Taking over one of the most demanding and rewarding roles in musical theatre, that of the hard-driven stage mother Rose, is Bette Midler, who delivers a tour-de-force performance. It is to Midler's credit that with the ghosts of Ethel Merman, Rosalind Russell, Angela Lansbury and Tyne Daly circling overhead (all had previously played Rose), she is able to give a fresh interpretation of a time-honored role which more than one actress had stamped her name upon. Though this small-screen version may somewhat lack the energy and excitement of a live performance, there's little doubt that the story of Mama Rose and her daughter, actress/stripper Gypsy Rose Lee, is one of the greatest of all American musicals. ⊛

DOROTHY ARZNER

Arzner (at right) in her customary male attire

By far the most prominent woman director during Hollywood's "Golden Era" and, amazingly for the time, an overt lesbian, Dorothy Arzner's film career was rediscovered and reappraised by feminist film writers in the 1970s. Although her films were, for the most part, conventional studio comedies and melodramas, they were unusual in depicting women as independent, career-minded individuals.

Arzner began her career in the early 1920s working as a script girl, and soon became an editor and assistant director. Among others, she worked on Rudolph Valentino's *Blood and Sand* (1922) and James Cruze's epic western, *The Covered Wagon* (1923). Paramount finally gave her a chance to direct in 1927 with the frothy comedy *Fashions for Women*, and with the success of that film she went on to direct several other silent social comedies including *Ten Modern Commandments* (1927), *Get Your Man* (1927) and *Manhattan Cocktail* (1929). She worked steadily with several studios until her retirement from directing in 1943. Afterwards, she made Army training films for WACs, concentrated on her writing, and was a film teacher at UCLA in the 1960s.

Arzner's membership in Hollywood's all-male director's club was astonishing — supposedly her lesbianism and manner (she was well-known for her trademark mannish suits and short hair) made her acceptable to the boys. But her films stand for themselves in their positive portrayal of adventurous, attractive and free-spirited women.

▼ The Wild Party *(1929, 76 min, US)*

In the film that solidified Arzner's reputation as a top director, this early Paramount talkie is set in an all-girls' school and stars Clara Bow as a flighty student and Fredric March as the professor she loves. The melodrama is notable for the atmosphere of sensuality between the women, the depiction of the joy of all-female living in the dormitory and the projected dangers of the world beyond. Many critics see an undercurrent of covert lesbianism especially in the scene where Bow affectionately jumps on the lap of another student and embraces her.

On a technical note: Arzner has been credited by many as the originator of the boom, for in this film she supposedly instructed the technicians to attach a mike to a fishing pole, balance it on a ladder and have it follow Bow as she moved.

Sarah and Son *(1930, 76 min, US)*

Ruth Chatterton received a Best Actress nomination for her stirring performance as a woman who hires lawyer Fredric March to locate her long-lost son, taken from her years ago by her now-deceased husband.

Anybody's Woman *(1930, 80 min, US)*

A minor melodrama about a chorus girl's attempt to reform her drunken husband. Starring Ruth Chatterton and Clive Brook.

Honor Among Lovers *(1931, 76 min, US)*

A charming comedy about a young businessman who gets more than he bargained for when he marries his sassy secretary. Claudette Colbert, Fredric March and Ginger Rogers star.

Merrily We Go to Hell *(1932, 78 min, US)*

Sylvia Sidney plays an heiress who, on a whim, marries a self-pitying, alcoholic newspaperman (Fredric March) and lives to regret it. A deceptively satiric melodrama that co-stars Cary Grant.

Christopher Strong *(1933, 77 min, US)*

Arzner brings an enchanting perspective to this capable romantic drama with Katharine Hepburn in her element as a pioneering aviatrix who is forced to choose between romance and career. The film features the unforgettable scene of Hepburn dressed in a startling silver lamé body stocking and offers a sensational vision of an almost futuristic superwoman. ☮

Nana *(1934, 98 min, US)*

Arzner replaced the film's original director but could not save this lavish, but ill-conceived "star" vehicle based on Emile Zola's novel. Samuel Goldwyn's attempt to launch Russian actress Anna Sten as the new Garbo misfired in this story of a high-living woman and her tragic downfall. (GB title: *Lady of the Boulevards*)

Craig's Wife *(1936, 75 min, US)*

Rosalind Russell is outstanding as the selfish, materialistic wife whose maniacal, all-consuming obsession with her home and the social details that go with it ruins her marriage. Adapted from the Pulitzer Prize-winning play by George Kelly (the gay uncle of Grace). Remade in 1950 as *Harriet Craig* with Joan Crawford. ☮

The Bride Wore Red *(1937, 103 min, US)*

Arzner's nod to "Pygmalion" and "Cinderella." An eccentric count, trying to prove his theory about class distinction, sends nightclub singer Joan Crawford to a posh Austrian resort posing as royalty. She meets down-to-earth Franchot Tone and playboy Robert Young. Though not afforded the luxury of a classic screenplay, Arzner infuses a degree of high spirits into this entertaining social comedy. ☮

Dance, Girl, Dance *(1940, 90 min, US)*

In possibly her most explicitly feminist film, Arzner pairs Maureen O'Hara, as an idealistic young woman who dreams of becoming a ballerina, with Lucille Ball, the tough-as-leather show girl who doesn't take any shit from her leering, drunken audience. Ball convinces O'Hara to become partners in a burlesque troupe in this entertaining "the vamp and the virgin" comedy-drama. As "Bubbles," Ball is in great form. ☮

First Comes Courage *(1943, 88 min, US)*

Arzner's final feature film is a serious propaganda war drama starring Merle Oberon as a strong-willed Norwegian Resistance fighter who would rather fight the Nazis than flee with the man she loves.

Katharine Hepburn dazzles in silver lamé in *Christopher Strong*

ANTHONY ASQUITH

Famed British director Anthony Asquith's career can be summed up in the observation that his films reflected the best of England, both its citizens and its ideals. In a 40-year career, spanning from his directorial debut in 1928 until his death in 1968, Asquith at his best heralded intelligence and strength of character and he did so in an entertaining and sophisticated manner.

Asquith was the son of noted Liberal Prime Minister Herbert Henry Asquith (serving 1908-1916) and later Earl of Oxford. Anthony studied at Oxford, and in the mid-1920s, went on an extended visit to California. It was there, at the encouragement of Douglas Fairbanks and Mary Pickford, that Asquith took interest in a directing career. After an unusual introduction into the film business — he doubled (in a blonde wig) for actress Phyllis Neilson Terry in the silent *Boadicea* — he wrote and co-directed his first feature, *Shooting Stars*. During his long career, in which he created a handful of classics from the late 1930s thru the early 1950s, Asquith proved himself to be a director of sensitivity and integrity. It is his accomplished George Bernard Shaw adaptations and his eight-film association with writer Terence Rattigan in which the director is best remembered.

Asquith was openly gay, and was very much the model of a gentleman. An interesting sidenote about the character of the man is that in the 1950s, Asquith would leave the comfortable surroundings of his posh London home and work for an old Army buddy as a dishwasher at his friend's Yorkshire truck stop restaurant. Just try to imagine peering through the counter and seeing Steven Spielberg doing the same.

The Runaway Princess *(1928, 70 min, GB)*
Mady Christian plays a princess engaged to a prince she has never met. She runs away to London and falls in with the wrong crowd. Her prince ultimately comes to the rescue.

Underground *(1929, 60 min, GB)*
Asquith wrote and directed this drama centering on two lower-class youths (Brian Aherne and Cyril McLaglen), one a promising thug and the other a naive innocent, who are both in love with the same shopgirl (Elissa Landi).

Asquith (l.) with Dirk Bogarde

A Cottage on Dartmoor
(1930, 77 min, GB)
Melodrama about simmering jealousy when manicurist Nora Baring, who works for smitten barber Uno Henning, falls for customer Hans Schlettow. (US title: *Escaped from Dartmoor*)

Tell England *(1931, 70 min, GB)*
Asquith's first talkie has an anti-war theme to it in telling the story of the Battle of Gallipoli. Two friends (Carl Harbord and Tony Bruce) eagerly enlist but all-too-soon experience the horror of war firsthand. Asquith received good notices for this film, especially his handling of the battle sequences. (US title: *Battle of Gallipoli*)

Dance Pretty Lady *(1932, 64 min, GB)*
Romantic drama starring Ann Casson as a Cockney ballerina involved in an affair with aristocrat Carl Harbord. In a supporting role, Flora Robson made her film debut.

Marry Me *(1932, 75 min, GB)*
Another melodrama depicting romance between the classes. Renate Muller falls in love with Berlin aristocrat Harry Green. She becomes his housekeeper, and romance follows.

Lucky Number *(1933, 70 min, GB)*
Frantic comedy about a professional football player (Clifford Mollison) who leaves a lottery ticket as security at the local pub. He has his hands full trying to get it back when it turns out it's the winning number.

Unfinished Symphony
(1934, 90 min, GB/Austria)

This musical biography examines the life of composer Franz Schubert (played by Hans Jaray). The story concentrates on his romance with the daughter of his music professor, and the events which led to his writing the title piece and "Ave Maria."

Moscow Nights *(1935, 77 min, GB)*

Good period evocation enhances this war drama set in pre-WWI Russia. Laurence Olivier plays a Russian officer who falls in love with nurse Penelope Dudley-Ward. However, she is engaged, though not in love, with war profiteer Harry Bauer, a peasant-turned-merchant who is paying off her parents' mortgage in exchange for her hand in matrimony. (US title: *I Stand Condemned*)

Pygmalion *(1938, 96 min, GB, Anthony Asquith & Leslie Howard)*

George Bernard Shaw co-adapted the screenplay for this first real expert film translation of one of his plays. Wendy Hiller is captivating as Eliza Doolittle, the guttersnipe flower seller who is transformed into a proper socialite by the efforts of Professor Henry Higgins (Leslie Howard). Unfortunately lost in the shuffle since the international success of "My Fair Lady," this earlier, more modest version is exemplary of "classic" British cinema. ☮

French without Tears *(1939, 86 min, GB)*

Terence Rattigan adapted his own play to bring this acclaimed comedy to the screen. Set in the south of France, the story focuses on a group of British schoolboys who become distracted by the appearance of Ellen Drew, the sister of one of their fellow students. Ray Milland also stars. Edited by David Lean. A negative is not known to exist.

Freedom Radio *(1941, 95 min, GB)*

A gripping suspense melodrama giving voice to the brave anti-Nazi struggles of Germany's own citizens. Clive Brook plays a doctor who goes looking for a "better" Germany, only to find it in the secret radio broadcasts warning the world of Nazi oppression and aggression. Diana Wynyard plays Brook's wife. (US title: *A Voice in the Night*)

Quiet Wedding *(1941, 75 min, GB)*

Though made a decade before it, this is sort of a *Father of the Bride* as seen through the eyes of the bride. Co-written by Terence Rattigan, this charming comedy stars Margaret Lockwood in an effervescent performance as a bride-to-be who only wants a "quiet wedding." That's not what she gets after her family gets through with it. Derek Farr is her hapless fiancé. David Tomlinson and Peggy Ashcroft have supporting roles.

Cottage to Let *(1941, 90 min, GB)*

An excellent cast is featured in this spy thriller. Leslie Banks is a British inventor working on top-secret plane parts. John Mills is one of the Nazis who's after it. Alastair Sim plays a British agent on the Germans' trail. Michael Wilding is a young scientist in love with Banks' daughter Carla Lehman. Sim excels as the wily agent.

We Dive at Dawn *(1943, 93 min, GB)*

Recalling *In Which We Serve*, this effective war drama recounts life aboard a British submarine, which is assigned the task of sinking a German battleship. John Mills is the young lieutenant in charge, and Eric Portman is especially good as a crewman. ☮

The Demi-Paradise
(1943, 115 min, GB)

Asquith's capable hand brings to life this first-rate romantic comedy and satire on "foreigners" and British lifestyles. Laurence Olivier plays a Russian engineer who visits England just before the start of WWII. There he comes to terms with his preconceived prejudices as he experiences culture shock, and falls in love with Penelope Dudley-Ward. Also starring Margaret Rutherford. (US title: *Adventure for Two*) ☮

Fanny by Gaslight *(1943, 108 min, GB)*

Based on Michael Sadler's best-seller, this acclaimed romantic drama is set in late 19th-century England. Phyllis Calvert is Fanny, the adopted daughter of a burlesque couple. As she experiences heartbreak in her own romantic affair with upper-class Stewart Granger — whose family disapproves of their union — she also watches in distress her mother's affair with aristocrat James Mason, who was responsible for her father's death. (US title: *Man of Evil*) ☮

Uncensored *(1944, 83 min, GB)*

Wartime melodrama set in Occupied Belgium. A group of underground freedom fighters, including Eric Portman and Phyllis Calvert, distribute an anti-Nazi newspaper. They battle both the Germans, who are hot on their trail, and a jealous associate threatening to betray them.

The Way to the Stars
(1945, 87 min, GB)

Terence Rattigan wrote the screenplay for this stunning war film featuring exemplary direction by Asquith. The multi-layered story examines the lives of British pilots on the ground, in particular their personal relationships and the stress each soldier endures. Starring Michael Redgrave, John Mills, Trevor Howard and, in a small role, Jean Simmons. (US title: *Johnny in the Clouds*)

The Browning Version

While the Sun Shines *(1947, 75 min, GB)*

Terence Rattigan co-scripted this adaptation of his West End hit comedy. Set in wartime London, Barbara White plays an Air Force corporal who's engaged to aristocrat Ronald Howard (son of actor Leslie). But she has trouble getting to the church on time, especially when she meets up with handsome American G.I. Bonar Colleano, Jr.

The Winslow Boy *(1948, 117 min, GB)*

Asquith's outstanding direction and Terence Rattigan's intelligent adaptation of his stage hit combine to produce one of the best British films of the 1940s. Based on an actual incident, a 13-year-old naval cadet (Neil North) is expelled from school for an alleged theft. His father (Cedric Hardwicke), convinced of his son's innocence, tries to reopen the case. When the school refuses, the father hires a barrister (Robert Donat), who takes the case to court, and all the way to the House of Commons and to the Crown, itself. An exceptionally well-acted film with Donat in terrific form.

The Woman in Question *(1950, 88 min, GB)*

Intriguing whodunit about a murdered fortune teller (Jean Kent). As the police investigate her death, various friends, relatives and neighbors recall her in a series of flashbacks. This includes Dirk Bogarde as a music hall pianist who wanted her in his act, Susan Shaw as her sister, and, in a scene-stealing performance, Hermione Baddeley as a nosy neighbor.

The Browning Version *(1951, 93 min, GB)*

Michael Redgrave gives a stirring performance in this outstanding drama about a stodgy English boarding schoolteacher who finds himself being forced out of his teaching position and discovers his wife's infidelity. He finds redemption in an unexpected act of kindness when one of his young students gives him a copy of "The Browning Version" of Aeschylus' "Agememnon," a play which he has translated. Terence Rattigan scripted this adaptation of his own play, and his poignant screenplay, Redgrave's classic portrayal and a splendid supporting cast make this must viewing. ⊛

The Importance of Being Earnest
(1952, 95 min, GB)

Asquith was faulted by critics for this film's static, stage-bound setting, yet the film has endured as an impeccable rendition of Oscar Wilde's classic farce. Michael Redgrave, Dorothy Tutin, Edith Evans, Margaret Rutherford and Joan Greenwood star in this bitingly witty social comedy about the vagrancies of love set in the opulence of 1890s Victorian England. ⊛

The Net *(1953, 86 min, GB)*

Favorably compared to *Breaking the Sound Barrier* at the time of release, this drama centers on a group of research scientists working on an airplane designed to go three times the speed of sound. As they come together in their task, one of them is murdered and it is discovered secret information is being leaked. Phyllis Calvert, James Donald and Herbert Lom star. (US title: *Project M7*)

The Final Test *(1953, 91 min, GB)*

Terence Rattigan wrote the screenplay for this snappy comedy, which weighs Britain's fascination with cricket. A famed cricket player (Jack Warner) is playing his last game before retiring. All he wants is his poetry-loving son (Ray Jackson) to see him play, which is easier said than done. Robert Morley is priceless as a noted poet whom Jackson idolizes, but who'd rather watch old dad at the match.

The Young Lovers *(1954, 95 min, GB)*

David Knight plays a code room employee at the American Embassy in London. He begins a romance with Odile Versois, the daughter of a high-ranking Iron Curtain diplomat. Leaders from all sides break into a cold-war sweat. (US title: *Chance Meeting*)

Carrington V.C. *(1954, 105 min, GB)*

David Niven plays the title role in this film version of the London hit about the court-martial of a British Army officer. Niven stars as a former war hero who is charged with misappropriating funds — expense account money he helped himself to — and is brought up on charges by his adversarial commander. Margaret Leighton also stars as Niven's unsympathetic wife. (US title: *Court Martial*) ⊛

Orders to Kill *(1958, 111 min, GB)*

Personally Asquith's proudest achievement, this well-made espionage thriller stars Paul Massie as an American flyer who is assigned to murder a Parisian lawyer suspected of leaking information to the Nazis. However, when he befriends his intended victim, he's uncertain of the man's guilt; and suffers accordingly when he finally accomplishes his mission. Eddie Albert co-stars as an officer, Lillian Gish plays Massie's mother, and Irene Worth is a French agent.

The Doctor's Dilemma *(1958, 98 min, GB)*

Asquith's second film translation of a George Bernard Shaw play; and though not in the same class as *Pygmalion*, this is an enjoyable, if stage-bound adaptation. Roasting the medical profession, the film stars Dirk Bogarde as the amoral artist with the roving eye and Leslie Caron as his faithful wife who must convince a group of doctors his life is worth saving. Also with Robert Morley, Alastair Sim amd Alec McCowan.

Libel *(1959, 100 min, GB)*

Dirk Bogarde is Sir Mark Lodden, who returns from the war and picks up his life. An ex-POW (Paul Massie), however, accuses him of being an imposter, that he's really an actor taking over the role when the real Lodden was killed trying to escape. Olivia deHavilland is Lady Lodden, and Robert Morley is Bogarde's counsel when the case goes to court. Bogarde gets the opportunity to play three characters: the baronet, his imposter and a hideously deformed surprise witness. Made years before both *The Return of Martin Guerre* and *Sommersby*, the film is not as wholly successful as either of them.

The Importance of Being Earnest

The Millionairess
(1960, 90 min, GB)

Based on the George Bernard Shaw comedy, Sophia Loren and Peter Sellers rise above the static story of rich Loren in search of a suitable husband, setting her sights on doctor Sellers, who runs a clinic for the poor. She's shocked to learn he's not interested in either her or her money.

Guns of Darkness
(1962, 102 min, GB)

David Niven plays an Englishman living in a fictional Latin American land who helps overthrown president David Opatoshu escape the country. Leslie Caron is Niven's wife.

Two Living, One Dead
(1962, 92 min, GB)

A postal worker (Patrick McGoohan) is branded a coward and possible accomplice when he readily gives in to the demands of robbers. Bill Travers is one of his associates who is given a hero's reception when he is injured in the robbery. Virginia McKenna is McGoohan's wife who, like everyone else, begins to suspect her husband of duplicity.

The V.I.P.'s
(1963, 119 min, US)

In their follow-up to *Cleopatra*, Elizabeth Taylor and Richard Burton offer engaging performances in this slick, appealing *Grand Hotel*-like soaper set at the V.I.P. lounge of the London Airport. Though Liz and Dick are the stars of this episodic tale, it's the supporting players who elevate the film; especially Margaret Rutherford, who won an Oscar for her delightful performance as the Duchess of Brighton, and Maggie Smith as a devoted secretary. Asquith's steady hand keeps the drama moving at a brisk pace. ☻

The Yellow Rolls-Royce
(1964, 122 min, GB)

Asquith's final film is a slick but superficial drama, featuring the last collaboration between the director and writer Terence Rattigan. The episodic film is divided into three stories, and traces the lives of the various owners of the titular vehicle. They include politician Rex Harrison and his wife Jeanne Moreau; gangster George C. Scott and his moll Shirley MacLaine; and rich Ingrid Bergman and patriot Omar Sharif who help battle the Nazis.

PAUL BARTEL

With looks that suggest a deskbound accountant from New Rochelle, independent gay filmmaker Paul Bartel's real life and professional persona are quite the opposite. Possessing a devilish grin and mischievous eyes, Bartel's film career — as writer, actor and director — is one that has remained on the edge, with weird comedies featuring outrageous characters that suggest "a kinder, gentler" but no less off-the-wall John Waters. Although most of his films play in mainstream cinemas and malls, he stays committed to film topics that are decidedly non-mainstream. Bartel writes most of the scripts (although he prefers collaborating with a partner) and uses the same core of friends and crew members in his movies. From his entertaining foray into kinky sex with *Private Parts* to his cannibalism comedy *Eating Raoul* and his sexual shenanigans of the Hollywood elite in *Scenes from the Class Struggle in Beverly Hills*, Bartel takes delight in tweaking the cheek of the audience with his shockingly wacky satires, all filmed in a lighthearted, even playful approach. Even when dealing with S&M sex, murder and deceit, his films give the impression that there doesn't seem to be a mean bone in his body.

Brooklyn-born (in 1938) and New Jersey-raised, Bartel's initial start in film began when he was in the Army and worked as a script clerk and assistant director on training films and documentaries. He eventually went to UCLA film school, won awards for his animated shorts and even traveled to Rome on a Fullbright Scholarship, where he studied at the CinemaMontografia with fellow students Bernardo Bertolucci and Marco Bellocchio. He moved to New York in the early 1960s and became involved in the burgeoning underground filmmaking scene there. Bartel got a job in Roger Corman's independent company where he started as second unit director on *Big Bad Mama*, which led to the Corman-produced *Death Race 2000*, a cult favorite and surprise moneymaker.

In between making his own movies, Bartel has acted in many films, often times playing off his impish middle-class looks —from the teacher who supports the student rebellion in *Rock 'n' Roll High School* to appearances in such comedies as *Caddyshack II, Amazon Women on the Moon* and *Get Crazy*. Bartel has also had his share of serious roles, in films such as *Mr. Billion* and *Heart Like a Wheel*.

Paul Bartel

Gay references and characters do not abound in his eclectic comedies, although there are gay characters in *Private Parts* and in *Scenes...*. In the latter film, the lovemaking scene between Ray Sharkey and Robert Beltran was erotic and obviously a heartfelt offering (from this gay male point-of-view) of Paul Bartel's cinematic coming out.

The Secret Cinema/Naughty Nurse
(1966/1969, 29/8 min, US)
Bartel claims his first film "sprang from the darker reaches of my unconsciousness." It tells the tale of a paranoid actress living alone who is unable to decipher whether her life is real, or if she is simply the filmed subject of a diabolical director. In 1985, Bartel rewrote the story and directed and starred in it for Steven Spielberg's TV series, "Amazing Stories." Interestingly, that segment ran a few minutes shorter than his original, and cost one million dollars — over 200 times the original film's budget. The video also includes the Bartel short *Naughty Nurse*. ☻

▼ Private Parts *(1972, 86 min, US)*
A director's feature film debut won't come much more bizarre than this demented tale about the deviant denizens of a sleazy hotel. Turgid with sexual depravity, morbid obsessiveness and a general tone of anti-social behavior, the story centers on a runaway girl who discovers that auntie's San Francisco hotel offers a bit more than bed and breakfast. A delightful black comedy that takes perverse pleasure in wallowing in kinky sex, voyeurism and transvestism. ☻

Death Race 2000 *(1975, 80 min, US)*

As the survivor of a number of deadly crashes and outfitted with artificial limbs and devices, Frankenstein (played by David Carradine) takes on his challenger Machine Gun Viterbo (Sylvester Stallone) in this funny, somewhat campy but exciting action-satire. The film that made running over people for points famous; and remember, pregnant mothers qualify for bonus points! ⊛

Cannonball *(1976, 93 min, US)*

David Carradine once again stars in a Bartel-directed trans-American car race comedy. Many feel that this second version is funnier as the comic book-style comedy gets increasingly frantic. While not much of a plot line, the comic vignettes are quite entertaining. Featuring an amusing list of cameos including Bartel, Sylvester Stallone, and directors Roger Corman, Martin Scorsese, Jonathan Kaplan and Joe Dante. (GB title: *Carquake*) ⊛

Eating Raoul *(1982, 83 min, US)*

In his most consistently outrageous comedy, Bartel stars with Mary Woronov as Paul and Mary Bland, a mild-mannered couple who devise a diabolical scheme to raise funds for their entrepreneurial dream: Paul and Mary's Country Kitchen. Placing an ad in the local sex publication, they lure unsuspecting degenerates to their abode, club them with a frying pan and empty their wallets. Hunky Robert Beltran stars as the not-as-clever-as-he-thinks-he-is hustler Raoul. As close as a cannibalistic comedy can come to being family entertainment! ⊛

"A genuine treat for civilized cannibals." — *Time Out*

Not for Publication *(1984, 87 min, US)*

Bartel takes on the tabloids in this offbeat but oddly tame farce of muckraking journalism and political scandal. Nancy Allen is a moonlighting reporter who discovers her boss, the incumbent mayor of New York, at an orgy she is assigned to cover. David Naughton, Laurence Luckinbill and Alice Ghostley also star. ⊛

Lust in the Dust *(1985, 85 min, US)*

Gold lies somewhere in the squalid town of Chile Verde and the person who can line up the asses of Divine and Lainie Kazan will be able to follow the map tattooed thereon (half a map per cheek) to the treasure's whereabouts. Bartel has great fun with this wildly funny spoof of westerns that also stars Tab Hunter. ⊛

The Longshot *(1986, 89 min, US)*

A longshot that doesn't pay off, this not funny attempt at slapstick features Tim Conway, Harvey Korman, Jonathan Winters and Jack Weston as four losers who borrow $5,000 from their local mob moneyman to bet on a sure thing, only to bet on the wrong horse. A misfire that might be tolerable on TV late at night after a few beers...you better add some dope as well! ⊛

▼ Scenes from the Class Struggle in Beverly Hills
(1989, 102 min, US)

Bartel's most accomplished film to date. He stays true to his slap-dash style of comedy in this often hilarious, sometimes outlandish and always entertaining drawing room farce. Jacqueline Bisset stars as a Beverly Hills widow and ex-sitcom star who mourns the loss of her husband (Paul Mazursky) by plotting the sexual conquest of her Chicano male-servant (Robert Beltran) who has a bet with another servant (Ray Sharkey) on who can seduce the other's employer first. The stage is set for a no-holds-barred sex romp in which everyone is trying to get into bed with someone. The cast includes Ed Begley, Jr., Wallace Shawn, Bartel, and is rounded out by a terrific performance by Sharkey as a bisexual butler. Not to be missed is the unaccountably erotic gay lovemaking scene between Sharkey and Beltran. ⊛

Shelf Life *(1993, 90 min, US)*

Stricken with a fear of oncoming annihilation by "Commies and Martians," a mother and her three adult children escape to the confines of their basement/fallout shelter in preparation of the end. Mom quickly dies from contaminated canned salmon, leaving the "kids" to fend for themselves. Originally an L.A. stage production, the film features the original stage cast (Jim Turner, Andrea Stein and O-Lan Jones) and despite its transfer to film, retains the claustrophobic feeling of people trapped in an ever-tightening space. Of the film, Bartel commented, "(It's) unlike other films in that it does not have three distinct acts. Rather, it is comprised of a series of vignettes in which the three main characters act out some of their fantasies." Reportedly the Sundance Film Festival rejected the film, claiming that it "was not a Paul Bartel film." Bartel eventually presented its world premiere at the Palm Springs Film Festival.

Bartel and Mary Woronov in *Eating Raoul*

FAVORITE DIRECTORS

LIZZIE BORDEN

Lizzie Borden

Independent filmmaker Lizzie Borden's film career has to date been short — but controversial. Dealing with issues of feminism, lesbianism, political activism and sexual oppression, her films depict strong-willed women living on the fringe of society. Seeking to shed light on her idiosyncratic film career, Borden says, "What fascinates me is worlds that are closed to me and how they work." A filmmaker involved in all aspects of the business, Borden has set up her own production company, Alternative Current, and has, especially in her first two features, used women as her key crew members.

Born Linda Elizabeth Borden in Detroit in 1951 to an Ivy League family (her father was a stockbroker), Lizzie lived her early life a privileged child. The nickname "Lizzie" was adopted by her friends when young, in reference to the "40 whacks" nursery rhyme. Later in life she began to appreciate the infamous name of the suspected ax-swinging murderess and possible lesbian and enjoys the kinship with the notorious woman saying, "I like the idea of cutting and chopping. I think that it's ironic that my favorite part of film is editing."

Borden attended Wellesley (although she "hated it") and received two degrees: in painting and art history. She moved to New York after graduation and began work as an art critic. Having never attended film school, Borden taught herself all aspects of the film craft; including financing, editing, directing and scriptwriting. Her first effort, *Born in Flames*, a futuristic thriller of revolutionary women taking arms against the entrenched male oppressors, took her four years to complete on a budget of $40,000 and was financed in part from her job as a film editor. The film was quite controversial (alienating many feminists with the depiction of angry, gun-toting female revolutionaries), but was a critical and art-house box-office success.

Classifying herself as an "anarcho-feminist," Borden says of *Born in Flames*, "I made the film out of distress at the splits in the women's movement — the bars, the organizations are segregated white-black-Latina." While people began to understand her radical feminist politics as depicted in the film, she surprised and annoyed many others with her sympathetic portrayal of life in a brothel in her second feature, *Working Girls*. Filmed in her own Chinatown loft, the movie was, in many ways, diametri-

cally different from her first (although the casting of black lesbians remained).

On the heels of her independent success, Borden was enticed to Hollywood where she made *Love Crimes*, an erotic thriller that received only tepid response by critics and at the box office. Although, in keeping with her interest in her film's subject matter, she did research for the film by working for three weeks as a phone sex operator, taking home $7.00 an hour.

Although Borden is straight (involved in a five-year relationship with a man), she has had a relationship with a woman ("one of the leads in *Born in Flames*") of which she said, "The truth of the matter is during the time I did *Born in Flames* I was much more tied to women sexually and emotionally and everything in that sense. It was like a rebellious period." Of her sexuality, Borden commented: "I love women and I have loved women, so I think that once you know that capacity in yourself, if it's not the choice you take...I think that love is where you can find it." She says that "the heady atmosphere of feminism during the '70s" led to experimentation and personal growth. "For me, it came out of defining a sort of feminism for myself. Which is still kind of different from what I would call 'politically correct feminism' — which changes every few years."

Borden's current project is an omnibus film, *Erotique*, in which she, Monika Treut and Clara Law each contribute a 30-minute erotic film. Borden's segment is about an aspiring actress who works as a phone sex operator. It follows her sexual fantasies with a man who is a regular. Other projects she is working on are an adaptation of the book "The One True Story of the World" by Lynne McFall, about an abrasive, James Dean-type of heroine; and in pre-production is a film called *Rialto*, a drama about a woman operating a movie theatre during the era of McCarthyism.

Regrouping *(1976, 77 min, US)*

Much more experimental than Borden's other films, this non-linear experimental film focuses on a women's group — its formation, growth and its fractious closure. The multi-level narrative includes an exploration into the group's dynamics, its individual members' commitment to the cause, and shows as well the film-maker's difficulties in remaining objective to its close-at-home subject.

▼ Born in Flames *(1983, 90 min, US)*

Born in Flames is a science fiction tale of feminist activism and "women's empowerment from the underground" set in an imagined future, ten years after a socialist revolution that had left the patriarchal power structure intact. A band of female anarchists, led by a black lesbian and her adviser, do battle against an unresponsive government. This independent feature has a cinema verité quality which lends the story the raw power of documentary while conveying a hopeful fantasy of women of different races and sexual preferences working together against oppression. Borden said of the portrayal of the lesbian revolutionaries in the film: "I hoped to expose the dangers of being gay by showing a few women with their lovers and by revealing the FBI's fascination with their sexual, not just political, activities."

▼ Working Girls *(1986, 90 min, US)*

In cinematic terms, the prostitute is usually portrayed either as a statuesque, high-priced call girl with a heart of gold or as a drug-snorting, underaged, runaway streetwalker. *Working Girls*, on the other hand, is a wryly comical and nonjudgmental tale about another, less melodramatic side of the "sex-for-sale" business. Set at a Manhattan high-rise brothel, the film is a day in the life of the shrewish madam and her "girls" as seen through the eyes of Molly, an aspiring photographer who lives with her black lesbian lover and her lover's daughter. Borden, reflecting on Molly's lesbianism, said of her, "She didn't dislike men, but she didn't need them." The screenplay, co-written by Borden and Sandra Kay, reflects Borden's personal beliefs that there is a certain kind of strength in sexuality. Borden says, "If a woman decides she'd rather have sex with a man three times a week instead of working 40 hours a week in a Xerox store...I believe we should be allowed to make these choices." ⊛

Love Crimes *(1992, 85 min, US)*

Lizzie goes mainstream in this interesting, if slightly perplexing thriller. Sean Young stars as an unorthodox D.A. trying to build a case against a mysterious man who is impersonating a well-known photographer and is taking advantage of a number of unsuspecting and vulnerable women. Patrick Bergen plays yet another deranged and sadistic villain — not much of a stretch from Julia Roberts' abusive husband in *Sleeping with the Enemy*. Look for a solid portrayal of the Assistant D.A. from Arnetia Walker. Because of restrictions placed on her by the producers, Borden was forced into compromises with the story: "I wanted to go further in a woman's sexual exploration of that part of herself — the way that I felt *9½ Weeks* failed. I wanted to get into that territory — masochism." When Young discovers that the man can only hurt her, Borden wanted Young's character to "cut off his clothes, handcuff him and then rape him. Not an evil kind of rape, but a rape that would get him to finally have empathy...but because it implied anal penetration, they wouldn't let me do it." ⊛

Born in Flames

JAMES BRIDGES

An unusual inclusion in this listing of gay and lesbian directors, James Bridges' (1935-93) filmography does not offer much evidence of queerness. As a matter of fact, with the exception of employing several gay stars in his films and the character of Mike in *Mike's Murder* (who, despite the film's title, was only a peripheral figure), there are no gay themes or characters, major or minor, in his films. Twice nominated for an Academy Award, Bridges' commercial Hollywood career was a solid one. He embraced good storytelling with a film style that can be described as realistic and subtle, and cannily utilized the big "name" actors who appeared in his films. The results were generally good reviews and better-than-average box office. Bridges enjoyed critical success with the cultish *The Paper Chase* and big box office with *The China Syndrome* and *Urban Cowboy*.

Originally from a coal mining region of Arkansas, Bridges arrived in Hollywood at age 21 after the death of his idol, James Dean (much like the Richard Thomas character in *September 30, 1955*). He aspired to be an actor and had an interest and talent both for writing and eventually directing, which he did for both the stage and the screen. His first play as director was "The Candied Hour," written by Jack Larsen. He wrote a play, "Days of the Dancing," which directly led to his being hired as a writer on "Alfred Hitchcock Presents," as well as writing other scripts for TV. In 1973, Bridges was chosen by Tennessee Williams to direct the 25th anniversary staging of his "A Streetcar Named Desire." In addition to screenwriting or co-scripting all of his films, Bridges' other non-directorial screenwriting credits include *The Appaloosa* (co-writer), *Colossus: The Forbin Project*, *Limbo* and, most recently, *White Hunter, Black Heart*.

Interestingly, Bridges' gayness was not publicly known until the publication of his obituary. James Bridges died in June of 1993 at the age of 57 and in the notices, his 35-year relationship with writer and former actor Jack Larsen (who from 1951-57 played Jimmy Olsen on the TV series "The Adventures of Superman") was acknowledged.

Bridges directs Michael J. Fox in *Bright Lights, Big City*

The Baby Maker

(1970, 109 min, US)
Bridges' directorial debut, in which he also wrote the screenplay, proves that he got better with time. Barbara Hershey, in one of her first roles, plays a free-spirited woman who agrees to have a baby for a childless couple. ☮

The Paper Chase

(1973, 111 min, US)
Exceptional study of academia with Timothy Bottoms as a Harvard law student and John Houseman (in his brilliant Oscar-winning performance) as his professor and adversary. Also with Lindsay Wagner (as Bottoms' girlfriend and Houseman's daughter), Edward Herrmann and James Naughton. ☮

September 30, 1955

(1977, 101 min, US)
Richard Thomas heads a terrific youthful cast (which includes Lisa Blount, Tom Hulce, Dennis Quaid and Dennis Christopher) in this intriguing character study. The title refers to the day actor James Dean died, and the film traces the effect Dean's death has on an idolizing college student (Thomas) and his fellow classmates. The film alternates between the merry exploits of teenage hijinks and the drama of *East of Eden*-like soul searching. In one of his few starring movie roles, Thomas is excellent and successfully captures the essence of teenage alienation. ☮

The China Syndrome
(1979, 123 min, US)

Though this nuclear thriller greatly benefited from the timely publicity of the Three Mile Island accident, this outstanding drama would have succeeded without it. Jane Fonda is superb as a television reporter who inadvertently films an accident at a nuclear power plant, involving her in political intrigue. Jack Lemmon gives a superlative portrayal of a loyal plant supervisor whose search for the truth leads to tragedy. Michael Douglas is well-cast as Fonda's radical cameraman who helps in the investigation. A tension-filled examination of corporate cover-up which is both cautionary and unrelentingly suspenseful. ⊛

Urban Cowboy *(1980, 135 min, US)*

Cowboy John Travolta tries to lasso cowgirl Debra Winger at Gilley's Bar in Texas in this involving romantic drama. The film which created (for awhile) the mechanical bull stir. ⊛

▼ Mike's Murder *(1984, 97 min, US)*

An overly ambitious and quite unorthodox thriller written by Bridges that doesn't quite come together. Debra Winger is a mousy bank clerk who's involved in a casual sexual relationship with tennis bum Mike (Mark Keyloun). But Mike, after he and his slimeball friend Pete (Darrell Larson) get involved in small-time cocaine dealing, is killed. Winger begins her own sleuthing into his death and soon uncovers Mike's secret world of sex and drugs. During her investigation she meets record executive Phillip (Paul Winfield), the man who brought Mike to L.A., and who confesses that the two were a number and that he was in love with Mike. William Ostrander is Winfield's hunky houseboy/companion who aspires to be a Chippendale. ⊛

Perfect *(1985, 120 min, US)*

John Travolta plays a *Rolling Stone* reporter who is writing an exposé on Los Angeles health clubs and becomes infatuated with a club owner (Jamie Lee Curtis). Not one of Bridges' better efforts. ⊛

Bright Lights, Big City
(1988, 110 min, US)

Uptown boy Michael J. Fox doesn't realize that he should just say "No" in this adaptation of Jay McInerney's best-seller. Fox gives an earnest performance as a young magazine editor whose life becomes entrapped by an endless cycle of work, drugs and decadent nightlife. Kiefer Sutherland nicely plays Fox's sleazy bar pal, Tad. ⊛

John Travolta enjoys a ride in *Urban Cowboy*

L I N O
B R O C K A

Indisputably the Philippines' greatest filmmaker, Lino Brocka, who died tragically in an automobile accident outside Manila in 1991 at the age of 52, was not only a leading force in films of that country but also one of its leading political dissidents — an outspoken opponent of the country's martial law and censorship who clashed repeatedly with the repressive Marcos regime. In his films, as well as his politics, the openly gay Brocka championed the cause of the impoverished underclasses. A human rights activist as well as a gay rights advocate, Brocka was jailed by Marcos for sedition in 1985 after the release of his biting political drama *My Own Country* (*Bayan Ko*). He was released only after an international storm of protest forced Marcos to relent.

Born to a middle-class family in a small village, the young Brocka was raised a Catholic but soon became a Mormon and after graduation spent two years at a leper colony in Molokai, Hawaii. He also lived in San Francisco before returning to the Philippines in 1966 to work as an assistant on Monte Hellman's *Flight to Fury*. In addition to film directing, Brocka continued to work on TV and the stage — presenting Tagalog-language versions of Tennessee Williams' "Cat on a Hot Tin Roof" and "A Streetcar Named Desire."

His first directorial effort was in 1970 with *Wanted: Perfect Mother*, an adaptation of *The Sound of Music* that became an instant box-office hit. Bravely, he countered this popular success that same year with the film *Tubog Sa Ginto* (*Goldplated*), the first Filipino film with a gay theme. The drama, about the doomed love affair of an older man with a street hustler, featured a frank depiction of gay sex. It was condemned by the Catholic Church and did not do much at the box office.

His ensuing films, most set in the teeming slums of Manila (Brocka filmed there even after they were made off-limits by the government), ranged in themes from his country's social ills to entertaining mass market melodramas and impassioned political dramas. This insistence of focusing on hard-hitting realism and sympathy of the underclasses made him a thorn in the side of the Marcos regime, which was intent on depicting the country as a paragon of successful Asian capitalistic democracy. On more than one occasion he was taken in the middle of the night to Malacanang Palace to listen to First Lady Imelda rant about making entertaining films that "only reflect the good, the true, the beautiful."

When Marcos was overthrown in 1986, Brocka was one of 50 people appointed by President Corazon Aquino to the committee responsible for drawing up a new constitution for the country. At his insistence, a clause was inserted that reads "No law shall be passed abridging the freedom of speech and expression." But Brocka soon became frustrated on being a political insider, saying, "I have not done much in films since the revolution...I tried for three or four months to help, but I was going out of my head." He soon quit, resumed filmmaking and resumed as well his criticism of the ruling government.

Lino Brocka made over 70 films in a career that spanned only 21 years. He was president of the Directors Guild of the Philippines and was the first Filipino to sit on the Cannes Film Festival jury. In addition to the films which follow, his filmography includes *Tinimbang Ka Ngunit Kulang* (*You are Weighed in the Balance but Found Wanting*), a 1974 drama on the hypocrisies of small-town life; *Jaguar*, a 1979 release with a gay theme; and *Pacifica Falafay*, a popular sex comedy about an effeminate hairdresser and his coterie of cross-dressing friends who discover a baby on their doorstep and adopt it as their own. These and many other of Brocka's films have been limited to the Philippines.

▼ Manila: In the Claws of Neon (Maynila: Sa Mga Kuko Ng Liwanag)
(1975, 125 min, The Philippines)
Young fisherman Julio leaves his small village to travel to Manila to search for his young sweetheart who has disappeared. But deep inside the squalor of Manila's corrupting and dehumanizing slums, he is soon forced to support himself by reluctantly becoming a male prostitute. (Also known as: *Manila: In the Claws of Darkness*)

Insiang *(1976, 95 min, The Philippines)*
The film that established Brocka as a major international filmmaker, *Insiang* was the fist Filipino film to play at the Cannes Film Festival. The reception in 1980 was thunderous, not just because of the film but for his brave political opposition to Marcos. Set in the tough Tondo slums of Manila, this sordid melodrama centers on Insiang, a teenage girl who lives with her mother. When her mother's young lover rapes her, she is thrown out of the house; she is even abandoned by her fiancé. Insiang, played by Hilda Koronel (a veteran of over ten Brocka films), soon plots revenge on them all.

Bona *(1981, 83 min, The Philippines)*

The violative relationship between Bona, an 18-year-old girl, and Gardo, an abusive, philandering part-time movie actor, is the core of this drama that was Brocka's second film to play Cannes. After leaving her stable home for the obvious ingrate, Bona, faced with years of pain and sadness, must come to a quick decision on what to do with her life.

My Own Country (Bayan Ko)

(1984, 108 min, The Philippines/France)

The social and political turmoil affecting the country in the final years of Marcos is the topical theme of this forceful drama. Turing, a brawny young worker at a print shop, is caught in a no-win situation when he must decide whether to honor the picket lines of his friends and co-workers when they go on strike, or continue to work in order to pay for medicine for his sick wife. His dilemma leads him to being a scab, unemployed and a potential criminal. An interesting symbol of the social fractions of the country is exemplified in a scene where a company party is taking place. On the main floor, the managers and owners speak English, and the manual workers party down in the basement speaking the native tongue, Tagalog.

Manila: In the Claws of Neon

▼ Macho Dancer

(1988, 136 Min, The Philippines)

The eternal tale of the naive country boy who is seduced and corrupted by the evils of the big city is played out in this fascinating and erotic drama. Paole, a somnambulistic teenage beauty, is drawn to Manila after his American lover and supporter of his family returns to the U.S. The young man is soon enamored with the city's notorious gay bars and nightclubs and is seduced into a world of prostitution, sexually explicit dancing and "brown slavery." The film offers a voyeuristic glimpse into the tacky yet lascivious gay underground where sexual acts are performed onstage and then bought and sold offstage. While the film played in international gay and lesbian film festivals and is even available on home video in the United States and Great Britain, the film has never been shown uncut in the Philippines. Even after Marcos' martial law was lifted, Aquino's Board of Review, the powerful censorship committee, censored it, saying that it "endangers the morals of Filipino youth." ⊛

> "Romantic and sensual. This is a damned sexy movie. Your brain will react with arousal at the exposed flesh and sexual situations...one of the best movies ever to come out of the Philippines."
>
> —Steve Warren, *Bay Area Reporter*

Fight for Us

(1989, 92 min, The Philippines)

Filmed clandestinely, this stirring drama explores the political chaos and repression in the Philippines after the defeat of a dictator and the installation of an equally corrupt democracy. The story focuses on Jimmy, a former priest and political dissident recently released from prison, who confronts a group of vigilantes who commit mass murder all under the name of anti-Communism and democracy. His efforts to bring them to justice embroils him in a bloody fight that threatens an entire village as well as his wife, children and friends. ⊛

▼ Signed: Lino Brocka

(1987, 83 min, US, Christian Blackwood)

Signed is an involving documentary from director Christian Blackwood (*Roger Corman: Hollywood's Wild Angel*) which gives Brocka an arena to fully discuss his films and politics. Among various topics, Brocka explains why he continued to work in Manila's most notorious slums, and talks about his volatile political stands that caused him so much trouble with both the Marcos and Aquino governments. Brocka talks freely of his homosexuality and presents clips from *Goldplated*, his first gay-themed film, and allows Blackwood to record the rehearsals for his film-in-progress, *Macho Dancer*. Brocka's intellect, his passionate stand on politics and his willingness to be upfront about his gayness make this a very interesting film.

JEAN COCTEAU

Poet, novelist, dramatist, painter, ballet designer and screenwriter Jean Cocteau (1889-1963) directed only six films spread over the course of nearly thirty years; yet he occupies a unique position in the history of cinema. His films are personal and fantastic odysseys through the unreal reality of his poetic mind. From the magical world created in *Beauty and the Beast* to the vivid imagery of *Orpheus*, his works bear a style best described as lyrical surrealism. Cocteau once stated, "My dreams are detailed and terribly realistic," and this may explain his ability to form such absorbing fantasies devoted to capturing an elusive reality. As with his works in other mediums, Cocteau was inclined to experiment with a variety of styles and felt no desire to adhere to the confines of commercial filmmaking. Although his first film, *Blood of a Poet*, was successful, he waited over 15 years before making another, content to working in other arts as well as writing screenplays for others, which included *Les Dames de Bois de Boulogne* (1945, Robert Bresson) and *Le Baron Fantôme* (Serge de Poligny, 1943). Because of his uncompromising individualism and poetic vision, Cocteau was an enormous inspiration to the American avant-garde movement and the French New Wave.

Throughout his works, Cocteau's individualistic mythology is much in evidence. Recurring themes, symbols and images abound: the artist as magician, the poet as martyr to his art, the artist enamored with death, blood-speckled snow, and incestuous love. Death is a central theme: death of youth, death of love — although there is no sense of conflict or suffering. For Cocteau, life was a succession of passions, and as such, death had an altered meaning as the departed continued to return.

Since a childhood vow to make a mark on the world, Cocteau's personal life was just as colorful and exciting as his art. He was at the center of the artistic renaissance that enveloped Paris in the early part of the century and was friends with such luminaries as André Gide, Sergei Diaghilev, Sarah Bernhardt, Erik Satie, Pablo Picasso and Coco Chanel. He had, at least publicly, two great loves of his life. The first was novelist Raymond Radiquet ("The Devil in the Flesh"), whom he met in 1918 when Radiguet was only 15-years-old. Tragically, he died of typhoid fever at the age of 20 in 1923 and this had a profound influence

Jean Cocteau at work

on Cocteau. He wrote to his mother of his love: "I've lost something winged, noble and mysterious. I see Raymond's face the last night, his difficulty in speaking, his heavenly eyes. Tears and sorrow tear me apart." Years later he met and became lovers with actor Jean Marais, a relationship that evolved into an artistic collaboration as well until Cocteau's death in 1963.

Blood of a Poet (La Sang d'un Poète)
(1930, 58 min, France)
Considered one of the most influential avant-garde films of all-time, *Blood of a Poet* explores the plight of the artist and the forces of creative thought. Constructed as a collage of autobiographical revelations and enigmatic images, the film takes us on an odyssey into the poet's imagination. Although the film bears much in common stylistically with Buñuel's *L'Age d'Or* made the same year, Cocteau called his film "anti-surrealist" as well as "a realistic documentary of unreal events." Freud — possibly missing his mark as a film critic — said the film was "like looking through a keyhole at a man undressing." ☮

The Eternal Return (L'Eternal Retour)
(1943, 100 min, France, Jean Delannoy)
Although he did not direct it, Cocteau was present throughout the filming of this lavishly romantic and almost dreamlike modern retelling of the Tristan and Isolde legend. Jean Marais is Patrice, the nephew of a wealthy widower, who arranges a loveless mar-

riage between Nathalie, a beautiful young woman he meets, and his uncle. With the help of a love potion, Patrice and Nathalie are irrevocably attracted to each other, threatening the family with their "forbidden" love. Based on Cocteau's original screenplay, this poetic fable of tragic love is reminiscent of Cocteau's own *Beauty and the Beast*. ☮

Beauty and the Beast
(La Belle et la Bête)

(1946, 92 min, France)

This enchanting interpretation of the famous fairy tale is a sumptuous and beguiling adventure in surrealist cinema and enchantingly infused with Cocteau's own mythology and symbolism. Jean Marais gives a moving performance as the love-stricken Beast and Josette Day is the beautiful object of his amour. ☮

The Eagle Has Two Heads
(L'Aigle à Deux Têtes)

(1947, 99 min, France)

This extravagant and romantic melodrama was adapted from Cocteau's hugely successful play. Set in the 19th century, the film stars Jean Marais as a lederhosen-clad poet/anarchist (and double for the dead king) who sets out to assassinate the beautiful queen (Edwige Feuillére), but when the two lock eyes, it is love at first sight. In keeping with Cocteau's passion for linking love with death, the couple meets a tragic end. Probably the least successful of Cocteau's films.

Les Parents Terribles

(1948, 98 min, France)

An adaptation of Cocteau's play, considered by many to be his finest work, *Les Parents Terribles* is a riveting psychological tragi-comedy about the complicated tangle of sexuality, parental rivalry and jealousy within a troubled family. Cocteau creates a claustrophobic intimacy (only two sets, static camera, many close-ups, no exteriors) as this incestuously close family bares its soul. Yvonne deBray is wonderful as the domineering mother, Jean Marais plays the son, and Josette Day is the woman he (and his father) loves. (US title: *The Storm Within*)

The Human Voice

(1948, 35 min, Italy, Roberto Rossellini)

As part of his two-part film, *L'Amore* (*The Ways of Love*), Rossellini adapted Cocteau's play "The Human Voice" for the screen. Anna Magnani stars as a woman distraught by the breakup with her lover who, in a painfully personal monologue to her unseen and unheard lover on the telephone, attempts to persuade him not to leave.

Les Enfants Terribles

(1949, 107 min, Jean-Pierre Melville)

A landmark of French cinema and a strong influence on the New Wave filmmakers, this collaboration with Jean-Pierre Melville is a cinematic poem about the love and confused narcissism of a brother and sister, whose passion for each other is so intense that it flowers into perversity and eventual death. Interestingly, Melville, as much of the intense auteur as Cocteau, agreed to Cocteau being present during the shooting, but in order to lesson the writer's influence, he filmed much of the movie late at night while the 61-year-old Cocteau slept soundly nearby! While available on home video in the United States, the quality of the video is quite poor; hopefully it will be released with a restored print sometime in the near future. ☮

Jean Marais in *Beauty and the Beast*

Orpheus (Orphée) *(1950, 95 min, France)*

This haunting update of the Orpheus myth is a mesmerizing blend of the natural and the fantastic, poetry and science fiction, and is considered Cocteau's major achievement in cinema. Jean Marais stars as the successful poet who becomes enamored with the Princess Death — who travels between this world and the next via a chauffeur-driven Rolls Royce and is escorted by a convoy of satanic, leather-clad motorcyclists. ⊛

The Testament of Orpheus

(1959, 83 min, France)

"I shall present a striptease in which I shed my body to expose my soul." With this statement, Cocteau opens his final film, an ebullient farewell celebration to the screen and his art. Cocteau himself takes the lead in this private diary which exposes the relationship between the artist, his work and his dreams. He is "The Poet," who roams through a dream landscape replete with his friends as well as characters from his films and images from his art. A personal, some might call self-indulgent, summing up of his adventures in art that should be especially appreciated by those familiar with his work. As Cocteau says near the end after coming back to life after being speared, "A Poet can never die." ⊛

Thomas the Imposter

(1965, 93 min, France, Georges Franju)

Georges Franju (*Judex, Eyes without a Face*) was chosen by Cocteau to direct this film version of his novel. The result is a striking vision of fiction and fantasy merging with reality in images of unforgettable beauty and terror. Set duing World War I, the story follows the travails of Guillaume. A romantic, innocent adolescent, he impersonates the nephew of a general, Thomas, and goes to the front lines during the war where he meets a princess (Emmanuelle Riva) who is assisting the sick and injured. His fanciful dreams are shattered after being shot.

The Oberwald Mystery

(1980, 129 min, Italy/Germany, Michelangelo Antonioni)

Michelangelo Antonioni's remake of Cocteau's *The Eagle Has Two Heads* was poorly received when it was first released owing to the clash of the two artists' cinematic styles: Antonioni's formalism and interest in internalized alienation with Cocteau's more flamboyant even fantastic view of realism. Monica Vitti stars as a turn-of-the-century princess of a central European country who has been in hiding since the assassination of her husband ten years prior. When a handsome anarchist/poet arrives bearing a striking resemblance to her dead husband, she offers him refuge. They eventually become lovers but she soon comes to realize that the man is not her savior but rather her "Angel of Death."

Jean Cocteau: Autobiography of an Unknown

(1983, 56 min, US, Edgardo Cozarinsky)

In a career that spanned over 50 years and included successes with novels, plays, poetry, drawing and painting, in addition to making highly original movies, Jean Cocteau's life might seem an artist's dream. This documentary delves into the artist's creative process as well as allowing Cocteau himself to recount the extraordinary art scene in Paris in the early part of this century, where such luminaries as Picasso, Renoir, Nijinsky, Erik Satie and even Charles Chaplin befriended the young Cocteau. In the documentary, we are held captive by this catty and delightful man who, wanting to think of art as a game, never took it seriously but played the game quite well. ⊛

Jean Marais (l.), Marie Déa and François Périer in *Orpheus.*

GEORGE CUKOR

Of his many accomplishments on and off the screen, the one label which sticks in the mind about George Cukor is that he's the best "woman's director" ever to grace a director's chair. He made stars of and/or coaxed career performances from Katharine Hepburn, Greta Garbo, Rosalind Russell, Judy Holliday, Judy Garland, Joan Crawford and Ingrid Bergman, just to name a few. But as Cukor himself was always quick to point out, more men had won Oscars under his direction than women. But however he may be remembered, there's no doubt that George Cukor was above all a brilliant craftsman with a thorough knowledge of the filmmaking process. His 53-film career, which ended with his death in 1983, has produced, arguably more than any other director, the most beloved films ever to come out of Hollywood.

Kenneth Tynan once asked a noted screenwriter to name Hollywood's leading directors. After a list of six or seven without mention of Cukor, Tynan asked, "What about Cukor?" To which the writer replied, "Cukor doesn't make movies, Cukor just makes actors." Half of Cukor's film success was his ability to convey and instill a trust and confidence in his performers. Jack Lemmon, having only worked with him once, commented, "Cukor is the greatest actor's director I've ever worked with." Director William C. DeMille stated, "He's one of the few stage directors who really set out to study the motion picture as an art in itself." Therein lies the other half of his success.

Born in New York City in 1899, Cukor, the son of an assistant district attorney, started his professional theatrical career directing on the New York stage. Among his more acclaimed productions were "The Constant Wife," starring Ethel Barrymore, and Jeanne Eagles' last role, "Her Cardboard Lover." It was Cukor, incidentally, who was the very first director to "try-out" a production in stock. He came to Hollywood in 1930, and, like many stage-experienced directors, started as a dialogue coach. After all, most film directors had no experience with the spoken word. His first feature was as co-director on *Grumpy* that same year. After three co-directing chores, he finally helmed his first solo feature, *Tarnished Lady*. During the coming decade, Cukor had a string of financial and artistic successes which can only be described as phenomenal. He once commented, "Give me a good script and I'll be a hundred times better as a director."

Cukor directs Garbo in *Camille*.

Well, in 1938, a doozy had come his way: *Gone with the Wind*. Hired to direct it by producer David O. Selznick, Cukor spent one year on pre-production. Finally, it was time to film. Cukor got along with Vivien Leigh and Olivia deHavilland exceptionally well, but was having problems with both Selznick and star Clark Gable. Selznick was constantly looking over Cukor's shoulder, and the producer wasn't happy with the direction of the film. Gable was afraid of Cukor's "woman's director" tag and thought Leigh would upstage him. Finally, after three weeks of shooting, Cukor was fired. The famous "artistic reasons" was cited.

However, it was disclosed decades later that there was more to the parting. As detailed by Patrick McGilligan's biography "A Double Life," which Kenneth Anger also printed in "Hollywood Babylon," Gable had Cukor fired because of a drunken night a decade earlier, when Gable was seduced by actor William Haines, who was a friend of Cukor's. At a party during filming, someone commented "George is directing one of Billy's old tricks." The story got around Hollywood and infuriated Gable. Finally, in the middle of filming, Gable stormed off the set, saying "I can't go on with this picture. I won't be directed by a fairy.

I have to work with a real man." Gable protested to Selznick, who might have backed his director had not Cukor often stood up to Selznick's interfering. The next day, Cukor was fired, and Gable's pal, Victor Fleming, was hired to replace him. The homophobic attitude endured on the shoot. Selznick's assistant Marcella Raburn remembered, "(Gable and Fleming) always referred to Selznick as 'that Jewboy up there' and Cukor was 'that fag.'" Cukor returned to MGM to direct *The Women*. And during this time, both Leigh and deHavilland saw him for "moonlight direction," being coached for their roles of Scarlett and Melanie.

Cukor never hid the fact that he was gay ("I didn't put on any big act. [Guys] would go out with the girls and all that, and that's absolutely ridiculous. I didn't pretend"), and he continually battled homophobia at his home studio, MGM, as well. His contract had a "moral turpitude" clause which he fought to have removed at each renewal. Though the studio did come to his aid and covered up a potential scandal when Cukor was mugged by sailors when he was out cruising.

Cukor did his best to be discreet, or "gentlemanly" as he described it, though he was well-known for his Sunday afternoon pool parties, which would be all-male and very private. Cukor didn't tolerate a double standard in his personal life, and this carried over to his films, as well. He turned down *Cat on a Hot Tin Roof* because he said that it made no sense with the homosexuality element removed. It is that dedication to the written word, in addition to a glorious sophistication and wit which inhabit all his films, that makes George Cukor one of the all-time great directors.

His secret? In a typically self-effacing manner, Cukor shrugged and wondered, "The Cukor touch...I haven't a fucking idea what that is. Honest." But as François Truffaut once stated, "George Cukor is a director who out of five films will make one masterpiece, three that are good, and one that is interesting." With a filmography numbering over 50 films, Truffaut's mathematical equation suggests at least ten Cukor masterpieces. One only has to glance at the following titles to appreciate the accuracy of Truffaut's statement.

Grumpy *(1930, 74 min, US)*

Cukor's first film, which he co-directed with Cyril Gardner. Cyril Maude re-created her celebrated stage role (which she portrayed for 1,400 performances during the mid-teens) as a lovable, senile old "grump." Filmed once before in 1923.

The Virtuous Sin *(1930, 80 min, US)*

Cukor co-directed with Louis Gasnier. Set in war-torn Revolutionary Russia, the film stars Walter Huston as a dashing general who is seduced by Kay Francis in order to get her husband, medical officer Kenneth MacKenna, out of the war. She eventually falls in love with the military leader.

The Royal Family of Broadway

(1930, 68 min, US)

The first Cukor film to suggest the greatness to come. Co-directed with Cyril Gardner, this is a devastatingly on-target parody of theatre life and the great Barrymore clan, based on the George S. Kaufman-Edna Ferber stage hit. Fredric March rocketed to stardom with his uncanny portrayal of John B., and Ina Claire is Ethel. (GB title: *Theatre Royal*)

Tarnished Lady

(1931, 83 min, US)

Cukor's first solo directorial feature stars Tallulah Bankhead in her first sound film. The great Tallulah plays a New York socialite who marries wealthy Clive Brook for his money. She soon strays, only to realize she really loves him after all. Bankhead in her biography said of this soaper, "Was it any good? In a word...No!" It's not really as bad as that.

Katharine Hepburn (c.) dons drag to help her dad, Edmund Gwenn (l.), in *Sylvia Scarlett*

Girls About Town *(1931, 80 min, US)*

Gold-digger Kay Francis falls for rich and handsome Joel McCrea. They have a stormy courtship, but when he proposes, it turns out she's already married — or is she? Lilyan Tashman is the other half of the title.

One Hour with You *(1932, 80 min, US)*

This production started with Ernst Lubitsch as producer, and Cukor as director. Half-way through, Cukor quit due to interference, and Lubitsch finished. At any rate, it's a sumptuously sophisticated and funny musical/sexual satire which bears trademarks of both directors. In one of his best screen roles, Maurice Chevalier plays a doctor with a roving eye. Jeanette MacDonald is his jealous wife. When her friend Genevieve Tobin comes to call, she sets her sights on Chevalier. Charles Ruggles is Tobin's husband just waiting for the chance to divorce her. A remake of Lubitsch's 1924 silent *The Marriage Circle*.

What Price Hollywood? *(1932, 88 min, US)*

Adela Rogers St. John's story about an alcoholic director whose career spirals downward as the girl he makes a star eclipses him. Needless to say, this was the basis for the *A Star Is Born* films. Constance Bennett gives a strong performance as the Brown Derby waitress-cum-movie star in this surprisingly tough look at then-contemporary Hollywood. Lowell Sherman is the fading director. ☮

A Bill of Divorcement *(1932, 76 min, US)*

The film which introduced the ravishing Katharine Hepburn to the screen and began her illustrious 10-film association with Cukor. John Barrymore gives a fine performance as a veteran who returns home after a long stay at a mental hospital. He attempts to establish a relationship with estranged daughter Kate. Billie Burke superbly plays Barrymore's wife, whose plans of re-marriage significantly alter his hopes of a happy homecoming. The caliber of acting from these three performers make this a must see. ☮

Rockabye *(1932, 71 min, US)*

Cukor replaced director George Fitzmaurice after an initial poor reception of the film, but even he couldn't help. Constance Bennett plays a stage star who suffers through career, romance and motherhood, with Joel McCrea there to help pick up the pieces.

▼ Our Betters *(1933, 80 min, US)*

A lively if dated adaptation of W. Somerset Maugham's play with Constance Bennett shocking British society with her "scandalous ways" when she leaves her royal husband and embarks on a wild spree. Tyrell Davis plays a queeny dancing teacher in full stereotypical glory.

Rex O'Malley (c.) plays the gay Gaston in *Camille*

Dinner at Eight *(1933, 111 min, US)*

Cukor became part of Hollywood's directing elite thanks to this classic adaptation of the George S. Kaufman-Edna Ferber stage hit. Park Avenue shipping magnate Lionel Barrymore and his social-climbing wife Billie Burke throw a dinner party for a visiting British lord. On the guest list are fading screen idol John Barrymore; aging stage legend Marie Dressler; obnoxious financier Wallace Beery and his blousy wife Jean Harlow; and family physician Edmund Lowe. How their lives and problems intertwine is the stuff that great moviemaking is made of. Dressler and Harlow steal the show. ☮

Little Women *(1933, 115 min, US)*

Often asked what his favorite film was, Cukor mentioned this and *Camille* in the same breath, and it's easy to see why. This is a thoughtful, very faithful adaptation of Louisa May Alcott's book, featuring a wonderful performance by Katharine Hepburn as Jo, one of four sisters growing up in pre-Civil War New England. Joan Bennett, Paul Lukas, Frances Dee and Spring Byington also star. An impeccable production with flawless direction from Cukor, who received his first Oscar nomination as Best Director. The film was nominated for Best Picture. ☮

David Copperfield

(1935, 130 min, US)

Cukor's superbly crafted adaptation of Charles Dickens' novel was one of the box-office giants of the 1930s and with good reason. Freddie Bartholemew heads a stellar all-star cast as Dickens' young hero, who experiences the hardships and sorrows of orphaned life in 19th-century England. W.C. Fields is the perfect incarnation of Micawber, David's ne'er-do-well mentor; Edna May Oliver is splendid as his eccentric Aunt Betsy; and Lionel Barrymore, Maureen O'Sullivan and Roland Young are just a few of the outstanding supporting players. One of the finest filmic interpretations of classic literature. Oscar nomination for Best Film. ☮

FAVORITE DIRECTORS

Sylvia Scarlett
(1935, 94 min, US)
A rakish thief and his daughter (Edmund Gwenn and Katharine Hepburn) are on the run from the law, so Kate becomes a "he," and the pair hooks up with con artist Cary Grant. She keeps her disguise, but soon falls in love with him, forcing her to a decision. This is one of Cukor's fascinating misfires, which was crucified when released. Over the years, it has taken on classic status for its unusual premise and stylish tone. Grant's first real opportunity to play comedy, to which Hepburn observed, "George taught (Grant) how to be funny. He brought out the Archie Leach in Cary Grant." ⊗

Romeo and Juliet
(1936, 127 min, US)
Though leads Norma Shearer and Leslie Howard are much too old for the parts of star-crossed teenagers Romeo and Juliet, this is nevertheless an excellent screen version of Shakespeare's tragedy. Edna May Oliver (as Nurse), John Barrymore (as Mercutio) and Basil Rathbone (as Tybalt) offer excellent support. ⊗

▼ Camille *(1936, 110 min, US)*
Classic tearjerker with Greta Garbo, in arguably her greatest performance, as Alexander Dumas' doomed courtesan. One of the better examples of those opulent MGM productions in which the studio excelled. They could have found a better Armand than Robert Taylor, but Henry Daniell is sensational as the villainous Baron de Varville. First-rate direction from Cukor. Rex O'Malley appears as Gaston, the Oscar Wilde of Camille's Parisian party set. ⊗

Joan Crawford, Norma Shearer and Rosalind Russell are *The Women*

Holiday *(1938, 94 min, US)*
The second and more popular screen version of Philip Barry's Broadway hit. This delightful comedy stars Katharine Hepburn and Cary Grant as non-conformists up against an ever-restrictive world. Grant, at his most appealing, plays a free spirit engaged to socialite Doris Nolan, only to discover he has more in common with her sister Kate. Lew Ayres stands out as the alcoholic black sheep of the family, and Edward Everett Horton, repeating his role from the original 1930 film, is marvelous as Grant's mentor and friend. Another Cukor classic distinguished by sophisticated wit and bountiful charm. (GB titles: *Free to Live; Unconventional Linda*) ⊗

Zaza *(1939, 83 min, US)*
Claudette Colbert is a French cabaret singer who has an affair with married Herbert Marshall in this ordinary adaptation, the fourth film version of the Pierre Breton and Charles Smith play. In a supporting role, even Bert Lahr seems uninspired.

Gone with the Wind *(1939, 220 min, US)*

"Yes, Gone with the Wind is a painful topic. I shot the beginning, set the scenes, worked on the construction of the sets, researched the goddamned thing for a year."
—George Cukor

"I won't be directed by a fairy." —Clark Gable

"I would like people to know how grateful I am for the pains George took with me when I was trying to get myself into the character of Scarlett...He devoted himself for days at a time to teaching me mannerisms, coaching me in voice inflection, and trying to explain to me and implant in me something of the thinking and psychology that made Scarlett what she was...I shall be eternally grateful to George Cukor."
—Vivien Leigh

"Miss Leigh, you can stick this script up your royal British ass!"
—Victor Fleming to Vivien Leigh upon her request for his direction on a scene, to which Fleming said, "Ham it up," and Leigh countered with Cukor's advice, eliciting this response

The Women *(1939, 133 min, US)*
Based on Claire Boothe's Broadway hit, this uproarious comedy more than lives up to its title: The cast is entirely female. Norma Shearer heads an unbelievable all-star cast as Mary, a Manhattan socialite whose storybook existence is shattered when her husband leaves her for shopgirl Joan Crawford. This puts Mary "on the road to Reno," where she meets a group of other divorce-bound women: worldly Mary Boland; showgirl Paulette Goddard; and friends Joan Fontaine and Rosalind Russell (in a smashingly funny performance). It was Cukor who first tapped into Russell's as-yet-undiscovered comic potential. *The Women* is about as funny as they come. ⊗

Katharine Hepburn and James Stewart get all starry-eyed in
The Philadelphia Story

Susan and God *(1940, 117 min, US)*

Anita Loos (*Gentlemen Prefer Blondes*) adapted Rachel Crothers'
stage hit, a curious blend of sophisticated comedy and family drama.
Joan Crawford stars as a flighty socialite who finds religion, begins
preaching love and God, and interferes with her society friends'
lives. Fredric March is Crawford's alcoholic husband, who does not
benefit from his wife's new spiritual awakening. Crawford, under
Cukor's direction, gives an atypical, daffy performance, here resem-
bling a young Auntie Mame. (GB title: *The Gay Mrs. Trexel*) ⊛

The Philadelphia Story

(1940, 112 min,US)

Cukor's dedication to character, Philip Barry's delicious dialogue,
and three of the most enchanting lead performances ever to grace
the screen all combine to create the wittiest and most sophisticated
comedy of the 1940s. Katharine Hepburn repeats her stage role as
the Philadelphia socialite faced with a dilemma on her wedding
day: who to marry. James Stewart won an Oscar for his delightful
performance as a reporter covering Hepburn's wedding; and Cary
Grant is the essence of charm as Kate's ex-husband. Cukor's
second nomination as Best Director; the film received a Best
Picture nod. ⊛

A Woman's Face *(1941, 105 min, US)*

Joan Crawford has a juicy role as an embittered, facially scarred
woman whose personality changes when she undergoes plastic
surgery. An interesting melodrama enlivened by Crawford's dedicated performance and Cukor's competent direction. ⊛

Two-Faced Woman

(1941, 94 min, US)

Greta Garbo's last film. Much has been written of the fact that
Garbo was dissatisfied with the box-office results and the fact that
her mysterious image was diminishing. The film, also starring
Melvyn Douglas, isn't all that bad, and Garbo is quite good (she
was second runner-up in the Best Actress balloting of the New
York Film Critics awards). ⊛

Her Cardboard Lover *(1942, 93 min, US)*

With this second screen version of Jacques Deval's comedy,
Cukor returns to the source of one of his greatest New York the-
atrical triumphs, though with less successful results. Norma
Shearer, in her final role, plays a divorcée who hires playboy
Robert Taylor to pretend to be her lover to make ex-husband
George Sanders jealous.

Keeper of the Flame *(1942, 100 min, US)*

Solid performances from Spencer Tracy and Katharine Hepburn
distinguish this intriguing drama about reporter Tracy investigating the life of a deceased politician. He ultimately uncovers a dark
secret about the man. Kate is the widow. ⊛

FAVORITE DIRECTORS

Gaslight *(1944, 114 min, US)*

Charles Boyer is an effectively sinister counterpoint to Ingrid Bergman's fragile, luminous innocence in Cukor's classic treatment of manipulation and betrayed love. Boyer has a hidden purpose when he woos and weds orphan Bergman; to protect his secret, he begins a systematic attempt to drive her insane. Strong support from Joseph Cotten and, in her film debut, a very tarty Angela Lansbury. Bergman won an Oscar for her tortured portrayal. The film was nominated for an Oscar; Cukor was not. (GB title: *The Murder in Thornton Square*) ⊛

Winged Victory *(1944, 130 min, US)*

Cukor's underrated and usually forgotten stirring WWII tribute to the Army Air Force, based on Moss Hart's smash Broadway play. The story follows the experiences of Lon McCallister and fellow soldiers through flight training on their quest to become pilots. Judy Holliday has a small but memorable role.

Desire Me *(1947, 90 min, US)*

Cukor started this wartime melodrama, then left and Mervyn LeRoy took over the helm. The film was released without a director's credit, as neither wanted it. It's not quite as bad as that suggests. Greer Garson is the wife of G.I. Robert Mitchum. When he is believed killed in action, she falls in love with his buddy Richard Hart. Guess who returns.

A Double Life *(1947, 104 min, US)*

Ronald Colman won an Oscar for his triumphant performance as an acclaimed actor who can no longer separate his on- and off-stage lives — and now he's playing "Othello." Shelley Winters is terrific in support as his fateful girlfriend. A superior suspense drama directed with great flair by Cukor, who received his third nomination as Best Director. ⊛

▼ Adam's Rib *(1949, 101 min, US)*

Katharine Hepburn and Spencer Tracy are husband and wife lawyers handling opposite sides of a murder case. Impressive support by Judy Holliday as the defendant, a woman accused of trying to kill her philandering husband (Tom Ewell). David Wayne is the fey composer living next door, whom Tracy remarks that "he wouldn't have far to go" to be a woman. Garson Kanin and Ruth Gordon wrote the screenplay for this classic battle of the sexes, and Cukor's direction is on the money. ⊛

Edward, My Son *(1949, 112 min, US/GB)*

An unusual family drama based on Robert Morley's stage success. Spencer Tracy and Deborah Kerr suffer not-too-gracefully as parents of the spoiled Edward, who is not seen. Kerr's performance is the film's highlight as the wife who turns to drink at the pressures of familial crises.

A Life of Her Own *(1950, 108 min, US)*

Cukor coaxed an assured, textured performance from Lana Turner. Too bad Isobel Lennart's screenplay wasn't as inspired. Lana plays a Midwestern girl who moves to New York to start a modeling career. In no time, she's on all the magazine covers. She also becomes involved with married tycoon Ray Milland, with whom there can be no happy ending. The film is at its best peeking behind the scenes of the Big Apple's modeling circles; most of the drama, however, is a routine love story focusing on Turner as the other woman. ⊛

Born Yesterday *(1950, 103 min, US)*

Though Cukor's staging is more stage-bound than most of his adaptations, this is nonetheless a thoroughly delightful comedy which earned Judy Holliday an Oscar for her first starring role. Re-creating the part of Billie Dawn, which she played on stage, Judy gives one of the classic "dumb blonde" portrayals as a gangster's moll who comes under the tutelage of "cultured" writer William Holden. Broderick Crawford is her slobbish boyfriend. It was a remarkable win for Holliday, besting that year both Bette Davis (*All About Eve*) and Gloria Swanson (*Sunset Boulevard*). Garson Kanin adapted his own stage hit. A fourth Best Director nomination went to Cukor; the film was also nominated. ⊛

The Model and the Marriage Broker *(1951, 103 min, US)*

A high-spirited comedy offset by touching dramatics. Thelma Ritter runs a dating service, and helps model Jeanne Crain find a husband. Scott Brady is the perspective groom, an X-Ray technician. Zero Mostel co-stars. Cukor demonstrates a light touch, and gets pleasant performances from his cast. Screenplay by Charles Brackett.

The Marrying Kind *(1952, 92 min, US)*

Cukor, Judy Holliday and Ruth Gordon & Garson Kanin reunited after their rewarding associations in *Adam's Rib* and *Born Yesterday*. A sensitive comedy-drama, the story focuses on Holliday and husband Aldo Ray (in his film debut) as they relay their courtship and marriage to divorce court judge Madge Kennedy. ⊛

Pat and Mike *(1952, 95 min, US)*

This enjoyable sports comedy doesn't rate with the best of the Tracy-Hepburn comedies, but is nonetheless a pleasant comic diversion. Kate is a sports pro, and Spence is her gruff manager. Tracy gets to say of Kate, "Not much meat on her, but what there is is 'cherce.'" Kate gets to show off her athletic prowess. ⊛

The Actress *(1953, 89 min, US)*

Based on Ruth Gordon's semiautobiographical play, "Years Ago," this sensitive account of the actress/writer's young adulthood casts Jean Simmons as an aspiring actress. Spencer Tracy and Teresa Wright are her parents, who disapprove of her chosen career, but who ultimately stand behind her.

It Should Happen to You

(1954, 87 min, US)

Charming fluff about a New York City woman, Gladys Glover (Judy Holliday), who rents a Columbus Circle billboard — just to put her name on it; she becomes a media sensation. In his film debut, Jack Lemmon plays a budding filmmaker involved with the wacky Gladys. Holliday, of course, is nothing short of delightful. ⊛

A Star Is Born *(1954, 170 min, US)*

Cukor often referred to this as his "butchered masterpiece"; for just weeks after a critically acclaimed opening, the studio cut nearly 30 minutes from the film. After years of painstaking research and compilation, the film has been restored to its original length. The immortal Judy Garland gives her finest performance, both vocally and dramatically, as Vicki Lester, the young songstress who rockets to stardom while the career of the matinee idol who discovered her, Norman Maine (James Mason), begins to fade. Judy sings, among others, the unforgettable "The Man That Got Away." Mason's harrowing performance is not to be overlooked. ⊛

Bhowani Junction *(1956, 110 min, US/GB)*

Ava Gardner is a half-Indian, half-European who returns to her native India post-WWII. Though the British are withdrawing and anti-Anglo sentiments run high, Gardner falls in love with British major Stewart Granger against a backdrop of riots, train wrecks and political upheavel. Cukor impressively handles the huge spectacle scenes. ⊛

Les Girls *(1957, 114 min, US)*

Three showgirls take their former dancing partner to court; but during testimony, can't agree as to what really happened. A joyously entertaining musical with Gene Kelly in good form as the hoofer; and Mitzi Gaynor, Kay Kendall and Tiana Elg as his ex-mates. ⊛

Wild Is the Wind *(1957, 114 min, US)*

Anna Magnani and Anthony Quinn both offer tremendous performances in this otherwise average melodrama, with Magnani marrying her deceased sister's husband (Quinn).

Heller in Pink Tights *(1960, 100 min, US)*

A mixed-up comic western with Anthony Quinn and Sophia Loren as traveling entertainers making their way through the Old West. They arrive in rowdy Cheyenne and come afoul of sheriff Steve Forrest, Indians and bandits. A notorious flop which all disowned. ⊛

Song without End *(1960, 145 min, US)*

Cukor completed this film when original director and friend Charles Vidor died halfway through production. This could explain the lack of wholeness the film possesses. It's a musical biography of Franz Liszt, with Dirk Bogarde as the famed composer/pianist.

Let's Make Love *(1960, 118 min, US)*

A well-intentioned misfire, this sporadically amusing musical stars Yves Montand as a millionaire who learns he is to be parodied in an off-Broadway show. He becomes intent on closing the show until he spies leading lady Marilyn Monroe, and, well, you know the rest. This might have been better with someone other than Montand in the lead. ⊛

The Chapman Report *(1962, 125 min, US)*

Based on Irving Wallace's novel, this is a fictional account of the sexual dysfunction of the American housewife. Efrem Zimbalist, Jr. is the doc who interviews wives Jane Fonda, Shelley Winters, Claire Bloom and Glynis Johns.

My Fair Lady *(1964, 170 min, US)*

Although much will be lost in watching this enchanting musical extravaganza on the little screen, *My Fair Lady* still dazzles the viewer with spectacular sets and costumes, an inspired Lerner & Loewe score and wonderful performances by Rex Harrison and Audrey Hepburn. Winner of eight Academy Awards, including Best Film and Director, this musical version of George Bernard Shaw's "Pygmalion" tells the now familiar tale of Professor Henry Higgins, an arrogant linguist, who takes Cockney flowerwaif Eliza Doolittle under his wing on a bet he can transform her into a lady. It's hard to believe, in reviewing Cukor's filmography, that he never won an Oscar before this. He made other films after this, but *Lady* is his crowning achievement. ⊛

▼ Justine *(1969, 115 min, GB)*

Interesting character study of a lusty woman (Anouk Aimee) who seduces men while helping arm Palestinian Jews poised to revolt against English rule. Michael York, Dirk Bogarde and Robert Forster co-star. Cliff Gorman (*The Boys in the Band*) has a small role as a feyish murder victim. ⊛

Travels with My Aunt *(1972, 109 min, GB)*

Maggie Smith took over the role of Graham Greene's eccentric Britisher when Katharine Hepburn bowed out of the project, earning an Oscar nomination in the process. Smith's priceless performance highlights this outrageous and charming tale of stuffy banker Alec McCowen accompanying his aunt on a whirlwind trip around the world to rescue her kidnapped lover.

Love Among the Ruins

(1975, 100 min, US)

A captivating TV movie starring film legends Katharine Hepburn and Laurence Olivier at their regal best as former lovers reunited years later when barrister Olivier defends aging actress Hepburn in court. A sophisticated and totally grand romantic comedy, directed with panache by Cukor. Ⓐ

The Bluebird *(1976, 100 min, US)*

An all-star cast isn't able to elevate this third film version of the children's story. Two peasant children visit a fantasy land in search of the elusive Bluebird of Happiness. Along the way, they encounter Elizabeth Taylor, Jane Fonda, Ava Gardner, Cicely Tyson and Robert Morley. A young Patsy Kensit plays the young girl.

The Corn Is Green *(1979, 100 min, US)*

Cukor's elegant made-for-TV remake of the 1945 Bette Davis soaper, based on Emlyn Williams' popular play. Katharine Hepburn gives a gallant characterization of a devoted school-teacher in a small Welch mining town who tutors and encourages a promising student in hopes he will continue his educaton. Cukor and Hepburn's tenth and final film together. Ⓐ

Rich and Famous *(1981, 117 min, US)*

Cukor's last film is a likable, updated remake of *Old Acquaintance*, with Jacqueline Bisset and Candice Bergen taking over the Bette Davis-Miriam Hopkins roles as college friends and rivals. Both novelists, Bisset is the "serious" and single writer who careens from one sexual encounter to another. Bergen is the housewife who finds acclaim, but loses a husband, by writing lowbrow fiction. Director Robert Mulligan started filming, but hastily left, with Cukor quickly subbing. Writer Christopher Isherwood and his longtime lover Don Bachardy appear in a party sequence. Ⓐ

Though they're just friends, Jacqueline Bissett gazes rather longingly at Candice Bergen in *Rich and Famous*

TERENCE DAVIES

Terence Davies

More than most other directors, a biography of Terence Davies might very well be culled by simply viewing all of his films. For the films — three shorts compiled into one and his two features — are all, in fact, intensely autobiographical works. Unconventional and non-commercial, Davies' films are all similar in that they are leisurely paced, stylistically poetic works that contain scenes which, seemingly tranquil on the surface, are actually full of wrenchingly profound emotions of loneliness, fear and sadness. Collectively, his works seem to derive from his passionate feelings he had as a child growing up both gay and Catholic in post-war Liverpool. These formative years have provided creative inspiration although he is quoted as saying, "Believe me, I wouldn't live my teenage years over again if I were allowed to. It was a very painful period." Hence, one can feel in his films that almost palpable sense of melancholy; this pain of memory creates a unique filmic atmosphere as he bears his soul.

Born in 1945 to a working-class family of ten children, Davies' happiest childhood memories are of movies, when a dancing, Technicolored Gene Kelly and company provided a welcome escape from the austere life in Liverpool. He recalls that, "The movies had a very powerful effect on me. My love for the cinema is now connected to my memories of when I saw all of those fabulous Hollywood films for the first time. I still cry when I see *Singin' in the Rain*."

Davies' homosexuality is also a driving influence, seen especially in *Terence Davies Trilogy* and *The Long Day Closes*. Growing up, these intense feelings of being different caused him to withdraw into the delusory world of Hollywood films, as well as developing a close attachment to his mother especially after the death of his physically abusive father. Although he readily admits to being gay and his films reflect it, he is not on the forefront of the New Queer Cinema saying at one point, "I'm not glad to be gay and I would change it tomorrow if I could." Despite this bleak view of his sexuality, Davies insists that he is not bitter, announcing that his next film project will be his last autobiographical film and as evidence to that, he is currently working on a film titled *Vile Bodies*, which will be a thriller with a gay protagonist. In an interview in *Out*, Davies was quoted as saying, "If you're not

beautiful, nobody's interested. I speak from bitter personal experience. Nobody was ever interested. And I don't forget, I'll *never* forget."

Also in development is *The Neon Bible*, about a young boy growing up in a small Southern Bible Belt town in the 1940s. It will star Gena Rowlands and Denis Leary and is set for 1995 release.

▼ Terence Davies Trilogy
(1974-83, 101 min, GB)

Three short films, *Children*, *Madonna and Child* and *Death and Transfiguration*, were made over a ten-year period (including time spent as a student at the National Film School) and were all inspired from his own life. The films examine the harsh life — from boyhood to the grave — of Robert Tucker, a gay Liverpudian. While lacking in traditional narrative, this bleak yet stirring and powerful portrait follows one man's continual battle against the demons that drove him into loneliness and despair. Beginning in his bullied and tortured youth, Robert struggles with his conflicting homosexual desire and the tight restraints and ensuing guilt of his Catholicism. Through a complex use of flashforwards and flashbacks, he eventually comes out of the closet and sheds his childhood religion, but continues to be a haunted, mother-dominated adult — still tormented by his guilt-ridden sexuality and its emotional confusion. A richly evocative and unforgettable film.

"A real wrist-slasher that makes Ingmar Bergman look like Jerry Lewis."

—Steve Warren, *Bay Area Reporter*

"The trilogy is openly gay and a very bleak view of gay sexuality and how it destroys someone."

—Terence Davies

Distant Voices, Still Lives
(1988, 85 min, GB)

Winner of the International Critics Prize at Cannes, this unblinking, autobiographical account of a family's oppressive lifestyle in pre- and post-war England is like a timeworn photo album put on film. Davies wistfully recalls his adolescence and his strained family life as he, his mother and his older sisters struggle to mature despite their abusive father's tyranny. His aching memories features much joyful singing and family celebrations as well as several violent episodes that will have the viewer on the verge of tears — both in sympathy for the screen's characters and for evoking disturbing memories from one's own nearly-forgotten past. A passionate and haunting film on the pain of living between hope and hopelessness. ⊛

> "Ambitious, intelligent, profoundly moving, it thrills with a passion, integrity and imagination unseen in British cinema since Powell and Pressburger."
>
> —*Time Out*

▼ The Long Day Closes *(1992, 83 min, GB)*

Somber, melancholy and haunting, this restrained drama of a young boy's maturation is a very effective mood piece recalling director Davies' childhood. Filmed in a leisurely, almost floating style and obviously autobiographical, the story concerns Bud (Leigh McCormack), a pre-adolescent boy living with his close-knit family in a Catholic working-class neighborhood circa 1950s Liverpool. The film casts Bud as a thoughtful but shy boy, socially awkward with few friends, who immerses himself in escapist Hollywood musicals and develops an especially close relationship with his still quite pretty mother. In a sensitive and subtle fashion, Davies lets the viewer know of the boy's nascent homosexuality in the simplest way: The boy is seen gazing out the window and soon becomes entranced at the sight of a muscular, shirtless laborer, immediately evoking in him feelings of shame, fear and sexual excitement. Nothing more is needed. A visually stunning film, there is surprisingly little dialogue, and not much in the way of dramatic excitement or tension. Yet this poetic film is both entrancing and pensive. ⊛

> "Intelligent moviegoers — both gay and straight — have been longing for years for films half as good as *The Long Day Closes*."
>
> —David Ehrenstein

"Death and Transfiguration" from *Terence Davies Trilogy*

ELOY DE LA IGLESIA

Eloy de la Iglesia

Long before Almodóvar exploded on the scene with his outspoken gay consciousness, there was Eloy de la Iglesia. De la Iglesia, the first prominent Spanish intellectual to publicly declare his homosexuality, has enjoyed a prolific and popular career as a filmmaker despite censorship restraints from the old Franco dictatorship and repeated damnation from the homophobic Spanish press. Despite being an outspoken gay, staunch Socialist and Basque separatist, de la Iglesia, referred by many as Spain's Fassbinder, has made almost a film a year since 1966. But while he has enjoyed popularity at the Spanish box office and has won several international awards, de la Iglesia is still largely unknown in both the United States and Great Britain. This lack of recognition is baffling for a filmmaker who wants a large audience, saying in an interview that, "What good are films if they're not seen, and by the largest possible number?" When several of his gay-themed films finally made it to the United States in 1983, he was amused at his unfamiliarity, remarking, "When *The New York Times* reviewed my film, *El Diputado*, they talked about me as if I was this new discovery."

Born in 1945 in Zaruaz, in the Basque region of Spain, young Eloy studied art and philosophy in Spain and cinematography in Paris. Rejecting an early interest in the priesthood, he got his first job at the age of 19 as a television writer adapting classical novels, including Shakespeare, for TV. At 21, he directed his first film, *Fantasia Tres* (1966), which was based on three of his own children's stories. It was de la Iglesia's fourth film, *El Techo De Cristaz* (1970), that was his first commercial success. He has also made two English-language films including the 1973 thriller, *Una Gota de Sangre Para Seguir Amando* (*A Drop of Blood to Keep on Loving*), a take-off on *A Clockwork Orange*, starring Sue Lyon.

As he developed as a filmmaker, de la Iglesia's works began to share similar themes. Not interested in the foibles of the rich or presenting insipid comedies, his films for the most part are hard-hitting, gritty, naturalistic dramas focusing on the disenfranchised and marginalized members of society: the poor, the young and homosexuals. His themes deal with the economic and sexual exploitation of the privileged against those less so and include such contentious issues as gang warfare, pederasty, drug addition, prostitution, teenage pregnancy and suicide.

His first homosexual-themed film (many of his previous films had gay characters), *Los Placeres Ocultos* (1976), marked the beginning of a long collaboration with Gonzalo Goicoechea. Since that time, the two have worked closely together, co-writing several more films with Goicoechea's Opalo Films producing six of them. The five films which follow, all dealing explicitly or at least marginally with homosexuality, are again but a small sampling of his work as a whole. Other films by de la Iglesia include: 1967's *Algo Armago en la Boca* (*A Bitter Taste in the Mouth*); 1975's *Juego de Amor Prohibito* (*A Game of Forbidden Love*), which is loosely based on Sartre's "No Exit" and explores sadomasochism; and *El Pico* (which means "The Needle" to Spanish audiences, and to Latin American audiences it is slang for "The Cock"). *El Pico* was Spain's number one box-office draw that year and de la Iglesia followed it up with *El Pico II* the next year. In 1985, he and Goicoechea produced a controversial version of Henry James' "The Turn of the Screw," set in the Basque region. *La Mujer del Ministro* (*The Minister's Wife*), made in 1981, was his first film to feature a lesbian subplot yet claims that he is not the one to make them saying, "There should be a lesbian director to make movies about lesbians, but it is very hard for any woman in Spain to direct a movie, and would even be harder for a lesbian."

De la Iglesia finished his "gay trilogy" (the first two being *Los Placeres Ocultos* and *El Diputado*) with *Running Against the Wind*, a drama concerning a Spanish Civil Guard who begins a scandalous affair with the openly gay son of a Basque national hero. Featuring abundant nudity, the film caused an uproar with its story, not so much of the love between two men, but of two people from such bitter political extremes. De la Iglesia enjoyed the controversy and heated political discussions the film produced, remarking, "Everyone said that we were crazy, and that such a relationship could never exist, except in our imagination." It is that audacious imagination that has contributed to opening the barriers towards gays and human sexuality in Spanish cinema, paving the cinematic way for Almodóvar and others to follow.

> "I talk about the world of which the majority of filmmakers do not care to speak, the marginal world. I am a most unopportunistic filmmaker. I am the one who always wants to make the films that are not supposed to be made. I'm the one interested in the subjects that everyone else has agreed not to talk about."
>
> —Eloy de la Iglesia

▼ Los Placeres Ocultos (Hidden Pleasures)
(1976, 95 min, Spain)

This, Spain's first openly gay film, was de la Iglesia's 12th production and was made just as the Franco era was coming to a close. The story is an impassioned drama about a closeted bank director who prowls the streets of Madrid in search of male teenage prostitutes. His life is changed after he meets and falls in love with a poor 17-year-old straight student. The controlled, placid surface of their relationship is shattered by contradictory and sometimes violent interplay concerning differences of class, intellect and convention. The most positive gay scene in the film occurs when a young hustler asks the 42-year-old banker if what they do is unnatural. He replies, "Nature is as nature does." And when the boy asks that if there was a shot to cure homosexuality costing a million dollars, if he would he take it, the sexually troubled banker still says, "Not even it were for free." Possibly conscious of the difficulties the film was going to receive, de la Iglesia prominently included heterosexual coupling and extensive female nudity. On opening night in Madrid, the film was met with a massive street demonstration by gay liberationists, with de la Iglesia recalling that, "It was the first time a Spanish gay group came out in public, with its banners and presenting its demands." Ⓐ

> "Erotic, compelling, sensitive. Dares to embrace the forbidden and taboo."
>
> —*New York Native*

▼ The Cannibal Man *(1977, 90 min, Spain)*

A creepy, grisly and disturbing departure for de la Iglesia. Set in a Spain that is quickly becoming "modern" and depersonalized, the film stars Vincent Parra as Marcos, a seemingly normal young man who works in a slaughterhouse and enjoys a loving

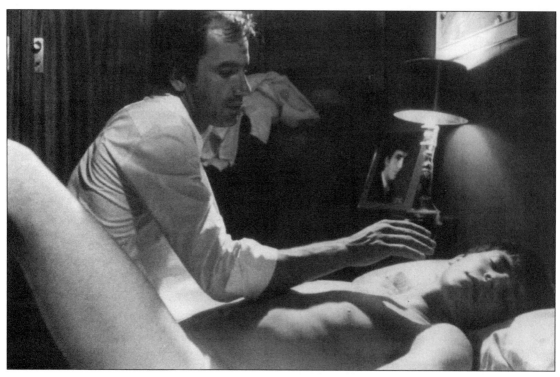

Hidden Pleasures

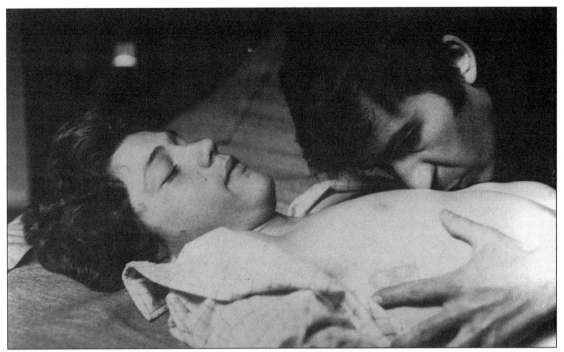

El Diputado

relationship with his fiancée. But after he accidentally kills a cab driver in self-defense, his mind snaps, sending him on a murderous rampage in which he kills his girlfriend, her father, his brother and several others. One of the people he does not kill is a middle-class gay man who befriends him.

▼ El Diputado (The Deputy)

(1978, 110 min, Spain)

Advertised on its initial United States release as "the most controversial film ever to come out of Spain," this highly praised and powerful thriller was de la Iglesia's first commercial release in the United States. A surprisingly huge success in Spanish-speaking countries, it played for over a year in Peru and two years in Mexico. The provocative story follows the political and sexual coming out of a young married politician in post-Franco Spain. The congressman's repressed homosexual desires are awakened while serving a brief prison term for a political matter. After a first encounter, he furtively seeks out sexual partners until he falls in love with a 16-year-old street hustler who in turn is hired bait in an undercover police blackmail plot. The film deals with the delicate balance between his life, his loving wife and his political goals. ⊛

> "May well be the most audacious film to play here all year...a satirical yet compassionate view of the interlocking of sex and politics."
> —Kevin Thomas, *Los Angeles Times*

▼ Navajeros (Knifers) *(1981, 100 min, Spain)*

Within the slums and bordellos of Madrid, an illiterate 16-year-old gang leader battles the police, prison authorities and rival gangs for love and acceptance. This hard-hitting, sexually charged film is based on a true story and features Mexican actress Isela Vega. De la Iglesia remarked about the star, who later denounced the film and its gay elements in the Mexican press, "She couldn't stand that I was gay and I was so open about it." ⊛

> "Gritty and uncompromising....as impassioned and lurid as the true events which inspired it. Devastating."
> —Kevin Thomas, *Los Angeles Times*

▼ Colegas (Pals) *(1982, 117 min, Spain)*

While not really gay-themed, this fine drama about the friendship between three teenagers in present-day Madrid does feature male prostitution and minor gay characters. Jose and Antonio have been friends for most of their lives, but their relationship is severely tested after it is discovered that Antonio's sister, Rosario, is pregnant by Jose. Their efforts to raise enough money to get an abortion in Catholic Spain lead them first to a Madrid gay bathhouse where their career as hustlers is short-lived. They eventually raise money by smuggling drugs into Spain for a homosexual Moroccan gangster. ⊛

> "A stunning celebration of homoeroticism and the gayest non-gay film ever made."
> —*Studflix Magazine*

FAVORITE DIRECTORS

SERGEI EISENSTEIN

One of the great pioneers of early filmmaking and one of its most important historical figures, Sergei M. Eisenstein (1898-1948) was a leading innovator of film techniques as well as a respected teacher and author on film theory.

The son of an architect, the young engineer-trained Eisenstein served in the Red Army and after his release began working in the theatre, first in production and costume design, then directing. He eventually turned to the new art form of film, in which he thought he found the medium to express his theories of proletariat drama — films that featured the masses, rather than individuals, as catalyst for dramatic action. In addition to his political and historical films which were popular successes, Eisenstein was influential in formulating several theories of film techniques, including montage: editing to enforce a film's plot and its overall meaning.

It was with his second film, *Battleship Potemkin*, that the intense genius gained international recognition. In 1929, buoyed by his celebrity, he embarked on what was to be a professionally disappointing European and American tour that included an invitation to Hollywood. His project for Paramount Pictures, a film version of Theodore Dreiser's "An American Tragedy," never went beyond the script stage and his projected film on Mexico, *Que Viva Mexico!*, was never finished after a falling out with financial backer Upton Sinclair. His return to the Soviet Union only continued his misfortunes. He was suspected of Western corruption and his "lost" film *Bezhin Meadow* (1935-37) was banned by authorities before its completion. He returned to teaching at the Moscow Film School and despite occasional attacks by authorities (who accused him of intellectualism), he became head of Mosfilm. He returned to directorial prominence with his sweeping, pre-Revolution historical epics, *Alexander Nevsky* and *Ivan the Terrible — Parts 1 & 2*. But his importance as an international figure in film by then had somewhat diminished.

Eisenstein's homosexuality was a closely guarded secret. Joseph Stalin, a great admirer of his, would no doubt have ended Eisenstein's career if his sexual orientation had become known. Although none of his films feature gay themes or characters, there can be found in several of them

Eisenstein in regal recline

a subtle yet quite distinct homoeroticism. This includes scenes juxtaposing muscular Russian men with elderly women in *The General Line*; the lingering of the camera on the primitive beauty of the abused, half-naked Mexican peasants in *Que Viva Mexico!*; and the shots of powerful, almost invincible soldiers in *Alexander Nevsky*. Eisenstein suffered a heart attack after completion of the first *Ivan the Terrible*. He had a second and fatal one after finishing the second part of his planned trilogy.

Strike *(1924, 82 min, Russia)*

In a remarkable directorial debut, Eisenstein introduced radical innovations in editing, montage and camera work in presenting this impassioned film about the struggles of pre-Revolution workers embroiled in a violent strike at a Moscow factory. Filmed at a relentless pace, he recounts the workers' hardships and exploitation as well as the devastating strike itself — the ensuing hunger, the presence of predatory infiltrators and ultimately the bloody massacre by the militia. ☻

Battleship Potemkin
(1925, 67 min, Russia)

This gripping account of the mutiny by the crew of the Potemkin and their part in the Revolution of 1905 is a landmark film for its groundbreaking use of editing and montage. The rebellion, the support for it by the people of Odessa, and the attack by Cossack troops still excite and overwhelm audiences today. ☻

October *(1928, 102 min, Russia)*

Commissioned to celebrate the 10th anniversary of the Revolution, this stirring portrait of an entire nation set on the edge of change was taken from American John Reed's writings. Eisenstein had endless resources to make the film and with the virtual absence of any footage of the real events of 1917, this powerful epic has been elevated into the realm of historical importance. (Also known as: *Ten Days That Shook the World*) ☮

The General Line
(1929, 90 min, Russia)

Eisenstein's last silent film, this dramatic satire focuses on one peasant woman's attempts to establish collective farming in her village. With his continued groundbreaking use of montage, a surprisingly vivid homoerotic poetic imagery, and extraordinary sadomasochistic undercurrents, the film was condemned by Soviet officials as "formalist" yet was a popular success. After the release of the film, Eisenstein began his world-wide travels. (Also known as: *The Old and the New*)

Que Viva Mexico!
(1930/1984, 84 min)

This famous aborted project has endured a long, rocky history. In 1930, Eisenstein traveled to Mexico in an effort to make a film on that country. The project was suspended after a dispute with his producer, the writer Upton Sinclair. With filming only partially completed, Eisenstein left for the Soviet Union expecting the rushes to be sent to him for completion; but they never arrived. The film stock was eventually edited several times, resulting in three different versions: *Time in the Sun, Thunder Over Mexico*; *Death Day*; and the current one. The project to edit the film more to Eisenstein's original intentions languished for over 40 years until Grigory Alexandrov, his former editor, obtained the rushes (from MoMA, of all places) and constructed a version Eisenstein might have done. The result is a glorious and compelling vision of a mystical Mexico. Told in five segments, Eisenstein explores different aspects of Indian life as well as their plight after Spanish conquest and Catholic indoctrination. Strikingly photographed, Eisenstein was taken by the beauty of the young peasant men of Mexico, resulting in poetic, homoerotic images of strong, determined and beautiful youths. ☮

Alexander Nevsky
(1938, 107 min, Russia)

After a period of ten years from his last film, Eisenstein's first sound film is a grand epic of Prince Nevsky's heroic defense of Russia against the invading Teutonic Knights in 1242. The final battle sequence on the ice of Lake Piepus is magnificent in its visual splendor and in the use of a stirring Prokofiev score instead of natural sound. ☮

Ivan The Terrible, Part 1
(1943, 99 min, Russia)
Ivan The Terrible, Part 2
(1946, 90 min, Russia)

This epic two-part biography of Ivan Grozny IV, proclaimed Russia's first Czar in the 16th century, was originally planned as a trilogy, but filming had only partially begun on part three before Eisenstein's death. A grand and uncharacteristically lavish spectacle, *Part 1* traces the emperor's coronation, his defeat and his eventual reinstatement. *Part 2* continues the tale as Ivan takes revenge on the friends who denounced him. The film features an original soundtrack by Prokofiev. The second part was interpreted by Soviet officials as possibly a critical allegory to Stalin's reign. It was shelved and finally released ten years after Eisenstein's death. ☮

The Secret Life of Sergei Eisenstein
(1985, 60 min, Italy, Giancarlo Bertelli)

Actually, this comprehensive documentary should have been titled *The Very Public Life of Sergei Eisenstein*. Based on his private memoirs (with some creative interpretation added), the documentary takes a first person, journalistic approach in detailing the life and works of one of the brilliant pioneers of film. Presented as a sensitive child who was raised by cold, indifferent parents, the film reviews his early personal life and then proceeds to analyze his works and present clips of newsreels of his travels to South America, Europe, Mexico and the United States. Also included are reminisces with friends D.W. Griffith, Brecht, Cocteau, Joyce, and Prokoviev. With a title that promises revelations into Eisenstein's homosexuality, this documentary sadly dismisses it, actually denying "my supposed latent homosexuality." The film, while successful as a comprehensive compendium of Eisenstein's film career, sadly fails in shedding any real light on the "secret life" of a man once described as "intense, joyous...and tormented." ☮

October

Rainer Werner Fassbinder

The boldest, most original and most important film talent to emerge from Europe in the 1970s, Rainer Werner Fassbinder (1946-1982), the irascible wunderkind of New German Cinema, died at the age of 36 from a combination of cocaine, sleeping pills and alcohol, leaving behind a wealth of 41 feature films in a career that spanned less than 13 years. His death shattered the film community as it was not burnout which concluded a sparkling career, but rather an abrupt demise for an artist in the midst of his creative life leaving a world that could hardly keep up with his prodigious talent.

The son of a doctor, young Fassbinder was obsessed with the American screen idols and melodramatic potboilers of Douglas Sirk and Samuel Fuller. He hated school, and when refused entry into the Berlin School of Film, he moved to Munich and started a theatre company; it was here he began writing scripts, staging the plays and acting in them, as well. His troupe included many of the actors (Hanna Schygulla, Ulli Lommel, Kurt Raab and Harry Baer) who would become regulars in his films. He soon began making films for German television and with the release of *Love Is Colder Than Death*, entered the theatrical film world.

As his filmmaking and writing career developed (he wrote most of the scripts for his films), so did his film style and themes. His early films were filmicly static, realism-tinged dramas featuring improvisational acting. With *The Bitter Tears of Petra von Kant*, however, highly stylized, over-the-top melodramas tinged with a camp sensibility began to emerge. Later, he proved he could film elegant, faithful adaptations with *Effi Briest*; and with his final films, Fassbinder sought to become sort of a Hollywood-on-the-Danube film factory with his bigger budget period pieces. Yet consistent with all of these styles was his choice of characters to focus on. They were not traditional heroes and great lovers, but losers and victims: battered people victimized by an oppressive economic system, alienated by the deceptive "economic miracle" of German post-war prosperity, tormented with personal despair, anguished by love affairs gone dead, and betrayed by the people around them.

Openly gay, Fassbinder also became a leading gay voice. While only a few of his features have a primary gay theme (*The Bitter Tears of Petra von Kant, Fox and His Friends, In a Year of Thirteen Moons, Querelle*), his films are imbued with an unabashed gay sensibility. Fassbinder once said, "Homosexuality is probably a factor in all of my films...not

The inimitable Mr. Fassbinder strikes a pose

all have a gay subject, but they all have the point-of-view of one gay man." In his private life, love and happiness were elusive. When asked by writer Boze Hadleigh on his work and thoughts on life, Fassbinder replied, "My work is not cynical, it is realistic. Pessimistic. Life is pessimistic in the end, because we die, and it is pessimistic in between..." Although he was known to be sexually active with both men and women, he had two great loves in his life: Algerian El Hedi Ben Salem (the Arab in *Ali: Fear Eats the Soul)* and German beauty Armin Maier. Each were contentious relationships, and both men ultimately committed suicide. The anniversary of Maier's death occurred during the production of Fassbinder's final film, *Querelle,* a tortured period for the director who died shortly thereafter.

The listing which follows, while exhaustive, is not complete; several more of his films have yet to become available in the U.S. or Great Britain including *Eight Hours Don't Make a Day* (1972, 87 min), *Rio Das Mortes* (1970, 84 min), *The Niklashausen Journey* (1970, 86 min), *Pioneers in Ingolstadt* (1971, 84 min) and *I Just Want You to Love Me* (1976).

"I don't like to be tortured. I can do that myself."
—R.W. Fassbinder

"There no longer can be any doubt about it: Rainer Werner Fassbinder is the most dazzling, talented, provocative, original, puzzling, prolific and exhilarating filmmaker of his generation."
—Vincent Canby, *The New York Times*

Love Is Colder Than Death

(1969, 88 min, Germany)

RWF's first feature film is a somber, stylized gangster film inspired by American B-movies and the works of Sam Fuller and early Godard. Ulli Lommel is a trench-coated mobster, Hanna Schygulla the femme fatale, and Fassbinder himself is a disheveled ex-con and pimp who gets in over his head. The no-budget, black-and-white film — uniquely Fassbinder — utilizes austere sets, and explores themes of loneliness, despair, love, death, manipulation and betrayal.

Katzelmacher *(1969, 88 min, Germany)*

Based on his own Anti-Teater (Fassbinder's repertory company) play, this chilling parable of latent bourgeois fascism is set in a grim provincial town outside Munich, where a Greek immigrant, played by Fassbinder, becomes victim to the country's violent xenophobia. The country's simmering dislike for "guest workers" turns to violence as he becomes entangled with a group of vicious working-class toughs and their promiscuous girlfriends.

Gods of the Plague

(1969, 91 min, Germany)

Deep in the backstreets of a sunless Munich, a den of sleazy gangsters and their molls stealthily plot their big heist only for it to end in betrayal and failure. A Fassbinder take on film noir starring Hanna Schygulla, Harry Baer and Margarethe von Trotta. ⊗

Why Does Herr R. Run Amok?

(1970, 88 min, Germany)

This devastating thriller on social conformity and the petit bourgeoisie stars Kurt Raab as Herr R., a successful professional who inexplicably (yet in Fassbinder's thinking, inevitably) goes berserk and takes his own life; but not before killing his wife, a neighbor and his little son. A doomed, taut polemic of failed expectations and the banality of existence. ⊗

Whity *(1970, 95 min, Germany)*

A strange western that starred his lover at the time, Gûnter Kaufman, as Whity, a half-black, overworked and exploited laborer who, spurred by a mouthy, sexually abused barmaid (Hanna Schygulla), kills his oppressive employers. Filmed in Spain, the tensions mounting on the set became the basis for Fassbinder's reflective film, *Beware a Holy Whore*, later that year. Co-starring RWF, Harry Baer and Ulli Lommel.

The American Soldier

(1970, 80 min, Germany)

RWF's mood-thick homage to American film noir and the milieu of Sam Fuller, Humphrey Bogart and Jean-Luc Godard's Lemmy Caution. It follows the fatalistic rounds of Ricky, a Vietnam veteran and professional killer hired by the German police to bump off a few problem crooks (and then some).

▼ Beware a Holy Whore

(1970, 103 min, Germany)

RWF's 8½, *Day for Night* and *Contempt*. An autobiographical meditation on the turbulent interactions and shifting power relationships which make up the filmmaking process. Based in part on Fassbinder's own experiences making *Whity*, the film follows a film crew and a group of actors who anxiously lounge around an opulent Spanish hotel arguing, drinking and becoming involved in destructive sex and power games as they endlessly wait for the film's star (Eddie Constantine), production money and especially the director (played by RWF) to bring them to life. Interestingly, this was RWF's last collaboration with the collective Anti-Teater. One of his first films to depict, in quite a casual way, homosexuality.

The Merchant of Four Seasons

(1971, 88 min, Germany)

RWF's first widely recognized film tells the life struggle of Hans: a born loser who is rejected by his bourgeois family, spurned by his "one true love," married to an unfaithful wife, cheated by his friends, and reduced to peddling fruit to sustain a meager existence. A superb mixture of black humor, melodrama and satire. Hans' suicide, by drinking himself to death at the dinner table in front of his stunned family, is bleakly unsettling. ⊗

▼ The Bitter Tears of Petra von Kant

(1972, 124 min, Germany)

This lurid and highly stylized account of the mangled web of domination, sadomasochistic passions and alternating jealousy among three lesbians is one of RWF's most controversial (and entertaining) works. Set in a single setting — fashion designer Petra's (Margit Carstensen) opulently appointed apartment — amid the music of Verdi and The Platters, the story focuses on the increasingly destructive power games between the mistress of the house and the object of her passion, the model Karin (Hanna Schygulla). Petra's maid also becomes involved in the mental mind games, which are played out to the hilt. For many lesbians, the film is quite misogynist, similar to the many straight men's films made on lesbians —*Les Biches, The Fox*, etc. The film was even picketed by lesbian groups when it played at the New York Film Festival in 1972. ⊗

> "It's a tragic love story disguised as a lesbian slumber party in high camp drag."
> —Molly Haskell, *The Village Voice*

Jail Bait (Wildwechsel) *(1972, 102 min, Germany)*

With the ballads of Paul Anka and the music of Beethoven in the background, Franz (Harry Baer), a 19-year-old worker falls for hefty 14-year-old Hanni (Eva Mattes). But Hanni's love turns into a power struggle of deception and betrayal in this melodramatic tale of teenage angst set in industrial northern Germany. Originally made for German television, its airing, spurred by the condemnation by original author Franz Kroetz and the luridness of its theme, caused quite an uproar. (GB title: *Wild Game*)

Martha *(1973, 95 min, Germany)*

In tribute to one of his greatest influences, Douglas Sirk, this hyperventilating melodrama of a woman's search for the man of her dreams is a campy tale of love gone awry and sadomasochism. Margit Carstensen plays the title character, a selfish and self-deluding woman of wealth who marries a virtual stranger only to discover his sadistic leanings, which are fully realized after she is paralyzed in an accident.

Nora Helmer *(1973, 101 min, Germany)*

Fassbinder tries his hand at Ibsen's "A Doll House" in this made-for-German TV videoplay. Stylistically exciting, this drama strips away the artifice and sentimental aspects of the play with RWF offering a cold look at the stifling world of the 19th-century bourgeoise.

Ali: Fear Eats the Soul

(1974, 94 min, Germany)

RWF's bittersweet love story between a lonely 60-year-old German cleaning lady and a reticent Moroccan auto mechanic half her age. The two find brief solace with each other in spite of family objections, social rejection and racial prejudice. One of Fassbinder's first films to play theatrically in the United States. ✆

Effi Briest *(1974, 140 min, Germany)*

This elegant adaptation of Theodor Fontane's 1895 novel has RWF exploring the subject of societal restraints in this beautifully photographed and impressively mounted production. Effi (Hanna Schygulla) is a vivacious young woman stifled in an oppressively loveless marriage to a much-older man. She becomes a helpless victim to his rage and unfounded jealousy when he discovers evidence of a long-dead affair of hers. Schygulla's performance is subtle, delicately layered and compelling. The film is often cited as among the director's best works. ✆

▼ Fox and His Friends *(1975, 123 min, Germany)*

RWF's first specifically male gay-themed film is a richly textured and powerful drama of the relationship between two gay men of vastly different social backgrounds. A lower-class carnival entertainer, Fox (played by Fassbinder), finds himself suddenly flush after winning 500,000DM. He soon becomes involved in an ill-fated romance with gold-digging Eugen, a rich, manipulative young man. The eternal class struggle and the continued exploitation of the poor and working class is tragically played out as the unwitting Fox is swindled out of his money and self-respect by his bourgeois lover and his family. Fassbinder's gay characters, Fox, his bar buddies and the morally bankrupt gays of "society" are quite complicated, non-stereotypical and unflinchingly honest. ✆

> "The first serious, explicit but non-sensational movie about homosexuality to be shown in this country."
> —*The New York Times*

> "One of the best films ever made about the life of homosexuals, their passions, their quarrels..."
> —*The Times* [London]

The Bitter Tears of Petra von Kant

Fear of Fear *(1975, 86 min, Germany)*

Made for television, this drama of despair and mental breakdown stars Margit Carstensen as a young housewife who, propelled by the pressures of a boorish husband, nagging in-laws and no prospects of improvement or meaning in her sorry life, is sent over-the-top with existential angst.

Chinese Roulette *(1976, 86 min, Germany)*

Anna Karina stars in this elegant gothic thriller. During a weekend retreat in a castle, a handicapped girl organizes a bizarre and fiendish truth game in order to psychologically attack her philandering parents and their respective lovers. With sweeping camera movement, and lush scenery and music, this cruelly humorous melodrama is pure Fassbinder. ⊗

Satan's Brew *(1976, 112 min, Germany)*

RWF's first comedy is a weird, vulgar and perverse story of the adventures of Walter Kranz (Kurt Raab), a "revolutionary" poet who imagines himself to be the 19th-century homosexual poet Stefan George. The film, shot in a black comedic slapstick style, boasts among its peculiar characters Kranz's butch wife (Ingrid Caven), a retarded brother, a wart-faced admirer and a troupe of prostitutes. Richard Roud, writing in *Film Comment,* suggests that "If you want (to know) where Fassbinder's head is at, this is the film to see."

Mother Kusters Goes to Heaven

(1976, 108 min, Germany)

Brigitte Mira is outstanding as Mother Kusters, an older woman whose gentle, ordinary life is thrown into turmoil when her husband goes mad at work, killing the paymaster and then committing suicide. She is soon exploited and assaulted by the yellow press as the media vultures descend, twisting the facts of her prosaic life to sell papers. Mother Kusters' outrage over the desecration of her husband's memory makes her a willing target for third-rate politicos promising the means of retribution. Mira's entirely believable performance and RWF's unerring cynical eye deliver a powerful treatise on the human propensity toward exploitation.

The Stationmaster's Wife (Bolwiesser)

(1977, 111 min, Germany)

Originally a two-part TV series running 200 minutes, this shorter theatrical version is set in 1920s and '30s Germany and concerns a sheepish, masochistic Bavarian stationmaster (Kurt Raab) and his nymphomaniac wife. A stylish drama of the lies and deceptions exchanged between two people.

Despair *(1978, 119 min, Germany)*

The first of Fassbinder's two English-language films (*Querelle* being the other), this critically maligned psychological drama,

based on a Tom Stoppard adaptation of a Vladimir Nabokov novel, is an interesting even riveting, but ultimately muddled puzzle. Dirk Bogarde stars as Russian emigré Hermann Hermann, a 1930s chocolate manufacturer who attempts to elude the Nazis by exchanging identities with a working-class double. The French title, *The Mistake*, might better describe Hermann's unbalanced schizoid state of mind when he concocts a plan of murdering his "double," collecting the insurance and then fleeing to Switzerland using the dead man's identity papers. ⊗

Fassbinder's take on gay-bashing from *In a Year of Thirteen Moons*

The Marriage of Maria Braun

(1978, 119 min, Germany)

Fassbinder's greatest international success and arguably his masterpiece is this sweeping drama that superbly mixes historical epic, offbeat comedy and social commentary. In a spellbinding performance, Hanna Schygulla stars as the prodigious heroine who rises from the ashes of post-war Germany to become a captain of industry. ⊗

▼ In a Year of Thirteen Moons

(1978, 129 min, Germany)

A passionate and pessimistic account of the final period in the doomed life of a transsexual named Elvira (ex-Erwin), who underwent a sex change operation on impulse to please a rich eccentric who no longer loves him/her. Now alone, Elvira seeks help from friends and her former wife, only to be repulsed and/or betrayed. This is one of RWF's most chilling and captivating efforts. As with his other films, he challenges and disorients the viewer with his sporadic sentimentality and harsh detachment. Volker Spengler excels as Elvira, an innocent sexual casualty in a desperate, and ultimately futile, search of aid.

> "...grotesque, arbitrary, sentimental and cold as ice. It's only redeeming feature is genius."
> —Vincent Canby, *The New York Times*

The 3rd Generation
(1979, 111 min, Germany)

"The world as will and idea." This is the cryptic code phrase for the "third generation" terrorists, bored and neurotic middle-class misfits who act blindly without any political passion or convictions. This band of determined but unintentionally absurdist guerrillas include Hanna Schygulla, Harry Baer and Volker Spengler. Beneath Fassbinder's typically mordant humor is the disturbing message that rebels without cause are the product of a society infected with violence. An explosive thriller, filled with sardonic humor and co-starring Eddie Constantine and Bulle Ogier.

Berlin Alexanderplatz
(1980, 930 min, Germany)

RWF's stunning 15½-hour epic is set in post-WWI Germany and continues through the birth and growth of Nazism. Simply told, a slow-witted Berlin transit worker, after accidentally killing his girlfriend and serving time, unwittingly becomes involved in the Berlin underworld. Originally produced for German TV, Fassbinder's monumental masterpiece is based on Alfred Doblin's novel and stars Gunter Lamprecht, Elisabeth Trissenaar, Hanna Schygulla, Brigitte Mira and Barbara Sukowa. ⊛

Lili Marleen *(1980, 120 min, Germany)*

Continuing his break from austere melodramas to elaborate big-budget, Hollywood-like bio-pics, *Lili Marleen* concerns a cabaret singer (Hanna Schygulla) and a Jewish musician (Giancarlo Giannini) caught up in a love affair amidst the hysteria of wartorn Germany. With the song "Lili Marleen," she records the unifying hymn to the glory of the "cause" while he plays an active role in the Resistance. Pretentious, overwrought and for many quite camp.

Lola *(1981, 114 min, Germany)*

Harkening back to his Sirkian melodramatic roots, this bitter satire deals with the mindless greed and corruption which spurred Germany's great economic "miracle" of the 1950s. A retelling and Fassbindering of *The Blue Angel*, the story centers on a reputable building inspector who falls helplessly in love with Lola, a sultry cabaret singer and moll to the town's unscrupulous kingpin.

Veronika Voss *(1981, 104 min, Germany)*

The stunning profile of a faded film star's descent into morphine addiction and emotional dependency is Fassbinder's eerie black-and-white tribute to Billy Wilder's *Sunset Boulevard*. A very un-Fassbinder-like cinematic tour-de-force, complete with ceaseless camera movement, this drama serves as the completion of his trilogy on the German condition during and immediately after WWII. ⊛

Fassbinder directs Rosel Zech as the morphine-addicted actress *Veronica Voss*

▼ Querelle *(1982, 120 min, Germany)*

Some say that RWF was past the point of dissipation as he worked on Jean Genet's 1953 existential homoerotic novel of lust and murder. There is no denying that the final result lacks the cohesion of the director's greatest works, but it reveals an artist perilously venturing into new frontiers. Brad Davis (who died of AIDS in 1992) is Querelle, a sexually brazen, amoral sailor who struts his sensuality for all to admire and swoon. A drug smuggler, Querelle kills a fellow sailor and takes refuge at a seedy seaside brothel, where he begins to discover his homosexual side. Franco Nero is his commanding officer who succumbs to Querelle's masculine swagger and Jeanne Moreau is the chanteuse who also lusts after him. A tale of violence, passion, degradation and intense sexual submission. The stylized, purposefully artificial sets of the port of Brest, complete with cock-shaped towers on the seawall and other exaggerated phallic symbols, is Fassbinder's final and, oddly enough, gayest film. ⊛

> "I saw *Querelle*. It made me hot for the whole day. I think the film will make lots of money. The kids will love it."
> —Andy Warhol to R.W. Fassbinder

Brad Davis in *Querelle*

Films about and starring Rainer Werner Fassbinder

Kamikaze `89
(1982, 106 min, Germany, Wolf Gremm)

This very strange and tense fantasy-thriller is based on Per Wahloo's best-selling novel, "Murder on the 31st Floor" and features Fassbinder's final screen appearance. He plays a detective who has four days to solve a mystery before a bomb explodes. ⊛

Wizard of Babylon
(1982, 83 min, Germany, Dietor Schidor)

A remarkable documentary on the filming of RWF's final and most explosive work — his film version of Jean Genet's masterpiece *Querelle*. Directed by the producer of the film, it is no mere promotional piece, but rather delves into the labyrinthine world of Fassbinder, his directorial style and his opinions on his past works. The film features fascinating footage of *Querelle* and candid, highly revealing interviews with cast members Jeanne Moreau, Franco Nero and a campy Brad Davis. Recorded, like the film, entirely on a single studio soundstage in a claustrophobic, unreal world where Genet's savage tale of homosexuality, violence, death and love comes to life. Included is a controversial 12-minute interview with a soft-spoken Fassbinder, donned in black leather and dark sunglasses, completed just hours before his death. A captivating portrait of a shy but zealous artist, consumed by his life's work.

A Man Like Eva
(1983, 89 min, Germany, Radu Gabrea)

Eva Mattes turns in a startling opposite-gender performance as a thinly disguised R.W. Fassbinder-like film director who loves, dominates and even terrorizes his cast and crew. This absorbing drama charts the inevitable self-destruction of an artist who longed for love but could not receive it. ⊛

I Don't Just Want You to Love Me
(1992, 96 Min, Germany, Hans Günther Pflaum)

Serious, analytical and as dry as the Sahara, this documentary on the life and work of Fassbinder provides interesting information on the prolific and fast-living director; although in a stifling style that limits the film to die-hard fans. Essentially a talking heads documentary, the interviewees include fellow German director Volker Schlöndorff, RWF regulars Ingrid Caven, Hanna Schygulla (looking uncharacteristically puffy and Mortitia-like), Harry Baer, Kurt Raab (interviewed shortly before his death from AIDS), his mother Lilo Eder and several other friends and colleagues. There are also, in a helter-skelter fashion, excerpts from many of his movies. A bit tedious, the film sidesteps RWF's homosexuality as well as his drugs and drinking problem. There is a fascinating film to be made on the enfant terrible of German cinema, but this isn't it.

Edmund Goulding

Born in London in 1892, Edmund Goulding was introduced to theatre life firsthand, acting at an early age. Coming from a theatrical background, Goulding soon became a leading man and Vaudeville headliner in London. After serving in WWI, he subsequently went to New York, where he earned a living as a playwright. It was in the early 1920s that Hollywood beckoned, and Goulding wrote several screenplays, including the silent hit *Tol'able David*, about a mama's boy who must prove his masculinity, and the Oscar-winning *Broadway Melody* (see Chapter 9) before directing his first film, *Sun-Up*, in 1925. Goulding quickly established himself as a capable storyteller, and like George Cukor, was anointed the tag "woman's director" thanks to his early, successful teamings with Greta Garbo, Gloria Swanson, Joan Crawford and Norma Shearer. One anecdote has it that during the filming of *Love*, Garbo was pulling a prima donna act and fussing over her hair, refusing to go on. Goulding grabbed a couple of bobby pins and fixed it himself.

An author, producer, director and composer, Goulding's filmography is peppered with a handful of classic melodramas, and during the 1930s and '40s, it was the three-hanky tearjerker in which he excelled. The director was oft-quoted: "The hardest thing about making a movie is landing the job to make it." Goulding married in 1927, but his wife died a short eight years later — he never remarried. Even during those years, however, the gay director was known for his extravagant lifestyle, wild parties and sexual affairs. He palled around with Errol Flynn and Tyrone Power (Goulding's home would often play host for liaisons between the two actors who were reportedly romantically involved), and was a visible gay presence in Hollywood's social scene. Goulding, who died at the age of 68 in 1959, was also a successful songwriter.

Sun-Up *(1925, 63 min, US)*
Goulding's first film stars Conrad Nagle as a hillbilly lad who marches off to war, returning home and becoming involved in a family feud.

Sally, Irene and Mary *(1925, 58 min, US)*
Constance Bennett, Joan Crawford and Sally O'Neill are the title characters in this silent tale of three chorus girls and their exploits on and offstage. William Haines plays O'Neill's boyfriend.

Paris *(1926, 67 min, US)*
Charles Ray plays an American youth vacationing in Paris who meets "underworld" moll Joan Crawford. He tries to elevate her socially and pursue her romantically — neither works out. Silent hokum all the way.

Love *(1927, 84 min, US)*
Greta Garbo and John Gilbert make a good romantic pair in this well-made silent version of "Anna Karenina." Garbo would play the role again in 1935.

The Trespasser *(1929, 91 min, US)*
Gloria Swanson was an Oscar nominee in this, her first talkie. Swanson's husband abandons her, leaving her on her own to raise their young child.

The Devil's Holiday *(1930, 80 min, US)*
Nancy Carroll received a Best Actress nod (up against Swanson in *The Trespasser*) for her winning portrait of a scheming working girl. Carroll marries and then leaves — complete with divorce settlement — millionaire's son Phillip Holmes. Can she find happiness without him, or will she return to him?

Reaching for the Moon *(1931, 90 min, US)*
Douglas Fairbanks is a successful businessman who gets drunk one night and chucks it all for a shipboard romance with Bebe Daniels. Goulding also wrote this fairly entertaining comedy-drama.

The Night Angel
(1931, 75 min, US)
Goulding wrote this unexceptional romantic drama set in Prague with Fredric March as a district attorney who falls in love with the daughter (Nancy Carroll) of a madam he incarcerated.

Grand Hotel *(1932, 113 min, US)*
Greta Garbo heads an all-star cast as the melancholic ballerina who "vants to be alone." John Barrymore is the debonair jewel thief who romances her. Also featured in this Oscar-winning Best Picture are Joan Crawford as a scheming secretary, Wallace Beery as a dishonest businessman, and Lionel Barrymore. Though Goulding's film did win Best Picture, he himself was not even nominated for Best Director. A startling oversight, to be sure. ☒

Blondie of the Follies
(1932, 97 min, US)
Marion Davies and Billy Dove were both veterans of the Follies, so their casting as two Follies beauties is doubly commendable. The story focuses on their on and offstage life, including as rivals in romance with Robert Montgomery. Jimmy Durante steals the show doing a very funny take-off on Goulding's own *Grand Hotel*.

Riptide *(1934, 90 min, US)*

Irving Thalberg's production stars his wife Norma Shearer as an American party girl who marries English lord Herbert Marshall after giving birth out of wedlock. He goes abroad, and she runs into former beau Robert Montgomery. A scandal ensues, and Marshall leaves her. When hubby has misgivings, he returns; Shearer must decide between him and Montgomery.

The Flame Within *(1935, 72 min, US)*

Ann Harding plays a psychiatrist who gets too involved in the lives of her patient Herbert Marshall and his girlfriend Maureen O'Sullivan. Goulding also wrote the plodding story.

That Certain Woman *(1937, 91 min, US)*

A remake of Goulding's *The Trespasser*. Bette Davis appears in the Swanson role as a secretary to attorney Ian Hunter. She falls in love with playboy Henry Fonda, they marry and split due to his parents' disapproval. She has a son, begins an affair with Hunter, and is torn between the two men when Fonda returns.

The Dawn Patrol *(1938, 103 min, US)*

Goulding proved himself quite adept with the action film after a string of romantic soapers. Errol Flynn had one of his best roles as a WWI flying ace assigned to keep the Germans behind enemy lines. Basil Rathbone is in good form as a tough officer who must send new recruits to an almost certain death. Also with David Niven. ℗

Dark Victory *(1939, 106 min, US)*

One of Goulding's best melodramas features Bette Davis in a quintessential performance. Davis plays a jet-setting socialite who discovers she has only a few months to live. As she slowly accepts her fate, she becomes more responsible, living her remaining months "beautifully and finely" as her doctor/lover (George Brent) suggests. Also starring Geraldine Fitzgerald, an oddly-cast Humphrey Bogart and Ronald Reagan as Davis' happily inebriated suitor. ℗

The Old Maid *(1939, 95 min, US)*

Bette Davis plays to the hilt the role of an unwed mother who, after her boyfriend is killed in the Civil War, gives up her child to be raised by her cousin (Miriam Hopkins). It's an acting tour-de-force as Davis and Hopkins battle it out with each other over daughter Jane Bryan. ℗

We Are Not Alone *(1939, 112 min, US)*

What could have been a melodramatic soaper is unexpectedly touching and full of life thanks to Goulding's sensitive direction, great performances, and original author James Hilton's nurturing screenplay. Set pre-WWI, Paul Muni stars as a country doctor married to Flora Robson, and she and Muni fall in love. However, things turn tragic when war breaks out and anti-Prussian sentiments run high (Bryan is of Austrian background) and both are suspected of murder in the accidental death of Robson.

Grand Hotel: Greta Garbo tells John Barrymore she "vants to be alone."

'Til We Meet Again *(1940, 99 min, US)*

Remake of 1932's *One Way Passage*, with Merle Oberon in the Kay Francis role of a fatally ill woman who becomes involved in a shipboard romance with con artist George Brent. Frank McHugh repeats his role from the original film.

The Great Lie *(1941, 107 min, US)*

Competent soaper with Bette Davis marrying George Brent, who used to be involved with Mary Astor. He disappears in a plane crash, Mary is pregnant, and Bette then raises the child as her own. Though Bette is her usual indomitable self, the acting honors go to Academy Award winner Astor. ⊛

Forever and a Day *(1943, 105 min, US)*

Goulding is one of seven directors in this impressive episodic drama chronicling the lives of several generations of a family and their London home. ⊛

The Constant Nymph *(1943, 106 min, US)*

Third screen version of the Margaret Kennedy play. Joan Fontaine gives an excellent performance as the daughter of a professor who secretly loves struggling musician Charles Boyer, who is living and studying at their home in the Austrian Alps. Complications arise when he marries Alexis Smith, only later to realize his true feelings for Fontaine.

Claudia *(1943, 91 min, US)*

Dorothy McGuire, repeating her acclaimed stage role, makes a splendid screen debut in this sweetly sentimental film version of the Rose Franklin play. McGuire plays the title role, a young bride married to Robert Young. The story follows their relationship together against the uncertainty of newly married life. Ina Claire is excellent as McGuire's mother.

Of Human Bondage *(1946, 105 min, US)*

Fair, at best, retelling of W. Somerset Maugham's novel, with Eleanor Parker essaying the role which made Bette Davis a full-fledged star. Paul Henreid plays the doctor done wrong by bad-girl Parker. Goulding ill-advisedly rewrote much of the dialogue. ⊛

The Razor's Edge *(1946, 146 min, US)*

After little success with W. Somerset Maugham's "Of Human Bondage," Goulding returned to another Maugham novel, but with far superior results. Tyrone Power goes through heaven and hell in search for spiritual truth. Anne Baxter won an Oscar for her heartbreaking alcoholic, and Clifton Webb should have won one as the cynical Elliott Templeton. ⊛

Nightmare Alley *(1947, 111 min, US)*

With the question "How do you get a guy to be a geek," this classic noir establishes itself as one of the most original, moody, bizarre and ultimately fascinating films of the 1940s. With a grotesque sideshow as its backdrop, the film follows carny Tyrone Power as he cheats his way to success as a nightclub spiritualist, only to incur a self-described fate worse than death. Joan Blondell is the mind reader he becomes involved with. Goulding's direction and sense of atmosphere is so overpowering its our loss he didn't continue in the genre.

Everybody Does It *(1949, 88 min, US)*

Paul Douglas is in good form as a gruff businessman who unwittingly becomes a singing sensation. He joins an opera company, and turns their peaceful lives topsy-turvy. Linda Darnell and Celeste Holm also star.

Mister 880 *(1950, 90 min, US)*

A captivating comedy with the wonderful Edmund Gwenn in the title role as a kindly counterfeiter (he calls his printing press "Cousin George"). Burt Lancaster is the Secret Service agent on his trail, which leads him to Gwenn's neighbor Dorothy McGuire and romance. Gwenn deservedly won an Oscar nomination for his spright performance, and he steals the film from one and all.

We're Not Married *(1952, 85 min, US)*

An engaging comedy about several married couples who learn they may not be legally married. Among them: Ginger Rogers, Paul Douglas, David Wayne, Marilyn Monroe, Eve Arden and Louis Calhern.

Down Among the Sheltering Palms
(1953, 86 min, US)

A South Seas musical with William Lundigan as an Army officer involved with missionary's daughter Jane Greer. Gloria De Haven is a journalist who falls for the G.I. Also starring Mitzi Gaynor as an island princess, and David Wayne as a soldier.

Teenage Rebel *(1956, 94 min, US)*

Ginger Rogers is reunited with her estranged teenage daughter, who returns to live with her and new stepdad (Michael Rennie) and stepbrother. Goulding wrote the film's theme song, "Mam'selle."

Mardi Gras *(1958, 107 min, US)*

Goulding's last film stars Pat Boone as a military cadet who finds romance with French actress Christine Carere during Mardi Gras. A modest ending to Goulding's notable film career.

JAIME HUMBERTO HERMOSILLO

It is quite surprising and encouraging that one of Mexico's most popular directors, Jaime Humberto Hermosillo, is also openly gay. Fiercely independent, Hermosillo discounts the problems of being gay in such a closeted and macho-obsessed environment, saying, "I have a serious career and people accept me." Speaking of his country's curious attitude towards homosexuality, he observes, "In Mexico, it's okay for a man to be a homosexual, but only in the active role." And possibly the active role of a director enables him to make films (most of them partially financed by the Mexican government) that feature gay characters without a public uproar, even enjoying popular support.

A graduate of the University of Mexico Film School, Hermosillo has made many of his films in his home town of Guadalajara. He has made over 20 features, most of them small independent films. Although his films play throughout Mexico, with the exception of *Doña Herlinda and Her Son* and possibly a few others, he is largely unknown to American and European filmgoers despite his films' humor, complexity and sophistication.

Best described as a more tranquil Almodóvar, he is similar to the Spanish director in that whether the film is gay-themed or not, they all embrace a gay esthetic. *Doña Herlinda and Her Son* was his first openly gay-themed film, although before that, and in almost every film since, a gay subplot or minor gay character appears. In many ways, this style of gay inclusion is more subversive than a gay film seen primarily by a gay audience, for his films play in front of the startled faces of all kinds of filmgoers throughout Mexico.

Hermosillo alternates his filmmaking career with the teaching of film at the University of Guadalajara and recently has been making films in association with his students. His two most recent productions, *La Tarea* and *La Tarea Prohibita*, were both conceived and developed in close collaboration with his students. Generally, Hermosillo leaves the conventional themes to others and is more interested in celebrating unusual characters. Whether in comedies or dramas, these roles range from sexually frustrated nannies itching to be bad, to a teenage son with the hots for his mother, to a mother who invites his gay son's lover to share his bed. Ironically, his characters are not from the type one usually associates with conservative Mexico.

In addition to the films which follow, he has made many more: including *The Dog's Birthday* (1974), a passionate marriage-on-the-rocks and murder-in-their-hearts marital melodrama; *El Corazon de la Noche* (*The Heart of the Night*) (1983), his first wholly government-subsidized feature; and *Bathroom Intimacy* (1989), a Warholian-like film in which a static camera, placed behind a two-way mirror, records the often times unusual bathroom habits of a bourgeois family and their maid.

A warm embrace in *Doña Herlinda and Her Son*

FAVORITE DIRECTORS

▼ Deceitful Appearances
(Las Apariencias Engañan)
(1978, 94 min, Mexico)

Banned in Mexico until 1982, when a new, more liberal government came into power, this strange soap opera of treachery, unrequited love and double identities stars popular Mexican actress Isela Vega. Made as an independent, non-union film, it was plagued by union protests and censorship problems. An out of work actor is hired to impersonate the long-lost son of a dying man in order to get him to sign over his fortune to a couple. Their plans go awry when the husband and, unbeknownst to him, the wife as well become "interested" in the young man. The twist is more than simple transvestism in this gender comedy as it soon becomes obvious that the husband is actually a hermaphrodite. Adding to the dying man's troubles is a particularly sadistic lesbian nurse.

Matinee *(1982, 90 min, Mexico)*

This entertaining fantasy-adventure is about a young boy whose life turns into a wild movie matinee when he runs away from his sister and mother and hitches up with a group of desperadoes. His new world, devoid of females, is soon filled with murder, passion, jealousy and revenge. While not a gay-themed film per se, the film features the bandits as having a natural love and attraction towards each other.

Mary My Dearest *(1983, 100 min, Mexico)*

This Mexican soap opera, adapted from a story by Gabriel Garcia Marquez, is a moderately interesting comedy of ill-fated love. After a mysterious eight-year absence, Maria, a beautiful young magician, returns to the home of small-time crook Hector. The couple falls in love a second time, but are soon separated when Maria, in a bizarre mix-up, is placed in an insane asylum and can't get out. ⊛

▼ Doña Herlinda and Her Son
(1985, 90 min, Mexico)

The film that put Hermosillo on the directorial map in the United States, this engaging and subversively heartwarming love story was one of the first films (if not the first) made in Latin America to deal positively with a gay theme. Set in an upper middle-class world of Guadalajara, Doña Herlinda is a shrewd yet always imperturbable mother who wishes for her son only that he live happily with mom, his wife...and another man if need be. Her son, Rodolfo, a sexually confused surgeon, is having a relationship with Ramon, a handsome music student. When mom realizes that their relationship is romantic and deep, she helps things out by inviting her son's lover to stay with them, reasoning that, "Rodolfo has such a large bed!" But a price comes with the compromise in this wickedly funny and uplifting comedy of sexual manners. Hermosillo has said that he wanted to avoid caricatures and create two gay men who are like everyone else except what they do in bed. ⊛

"A gay-lib Mother's Day card, a comedy that says you can have your mother's cake and your hot buns, too."
—David Edelstein, *The Village Voice*

▼ Clantestinos Destinos
(1987, 81 min, Mexico)

Reminiscent of a Roger Corman flick of old, and produced in conjunction with the University of Guadalajara, Hermosillo has obvious fun with this pseudo-political sci-fi camp serio-comedy that is filled with a wacky story line (written by Hermosillo), terrible acting and dark, dark comedy. The story is set in the near-future in northern Mexico, an area now controlled by the U.S., in a political climate where civil war seems imminent. With sex outlawed, a group of horny young people seeking to commingle with other flesh leave town and go camping. The cast of characters include handsome but suicidal Eduardo; Angel, a gay artist with the hots for Eduardo; Lila, a spoiled movie princess who goes by the name "Odinette Orozco"; a "Brad and Janet"-type couple; and Eduardo's neurotic dog, Ninón.

▼ The Summer of Miss Forbes
(1988, 87 min, Mexico)

Hanna Schygulla stars as a sexually repressed governess in this erotic, beautifully photographed but ultimately silly melodrama scripted by Gabriel Garcia Marquez. Set in a lush sea resort, a frenzied couple goes on a six-week cruise and hires Miss Forbes (Schygulla), a stern Prussian schoolteacher, to instill manners and discipline into their two chubby, calculating sons. Matronly dressed and militarily tough by day, Miss Forbes harbors another personality: for at night, she becomes a tequila-guzzling, cake-stuffing floozy, whose simmering sexual urges boil over. And while she is plotting the sexual conquest of the boys' beautiful diving instructor (unattainable because he is gay), they concoct a plan to rid themselves of her forever. While enjoyable, the film never completely works, with Ms. Schygulla miscast as the barely concealed basket case. ⊛

La Tarea (Homework) *(1990, 85 min, Mexico)*

Fascinating and inventive, *La Tarea* will remind many of a sexually charged version of Alfred Hitchcock's *Rope*. This slyly humorous, voyeuristic foray into Latino seduction and sexual game-playing begins when a woman invites a former lover to her apartment, ostensibly to rekindle their dormant affair. But she is actually videotaping the entire encounter for a school project. Filmed from the point-of-view of the hidden camera, the film was made to look like it was done in one take, with no editing. While there are no overt gay elements, there are references to AIDS, safe sex, the gay-themed film *Tea and Sympathy*, as well as Marcello Mastroianni's role as a gay man in *A Special Day*. Hermosillo prominently features the man (in full-frontal nudity) as the sex object rather than the feminine seducer.

La Tarea Prohibita
(Forbidden Homework) *(1992, 80 min, Mexico)*

More of a variation and expansion of a theme rather than a sequel, *La Tarea Prohibita* features Maria Roja, a veteran of more than ten films by Hermosillo, as an older woman lured to a rooftop studio for an acting job. The young filmmaker, a muscular pretty boy, is actually in love with the woman and hopes to seduce her during the course of the evening; all the time, secretly recording the entire proceedings. A witty and engrossing treatise on voyeurism and forbidden sexual yearning and, like *La Tarea*, the film has a great twist ending.

COLIN HIGGINS

Writer and director Colin Higgins, famous for his several enormously popular screen comedies, died of AIDS in 1988 at the age of 47. Although none of his films feature gay characters or subplots, Higgins' first success, *Harold and Maude*, was actually a disguised version of a gay love story. Higgins said of the film, "I'd have written a wonderful gay love story. But who would have filmed it? So I did the next best thing...I wrote something very quirky and interesting and which hopefully challenged convention."

Enjoying a varied and exotic life, Higgins was born on a French island in New Caledonia in the South Pacific to an American father and Australian mother. He grew up in Oakland, California, and spent the last two years of high school in a Franciscan monastery in Australia. After a stint in the Army and time spent at sea as a merchant seaman, Higgins became interested in film, both acting and writing, and enrolled in the UCLA Film School in 1967. While acting in several college productions, Higgins made a short film for $100 that was picked up by Filmways for inclusion in their "Genesis 1" program. With a Midas touch that continued professionally throughout his life, Higgins received his first big break while at school, which has become almost folklore on the UCLA campus: Working as a gardener for a Hollywood producer, Higgins gave his Master's thesis/screenplay, *Harold and Maude*, to the producer's wife. She loved it and in turn passed it on to her husband, resulting in it being picked up by Paramount and becoming one of the biggest cult films in movie history.

With this launch into Hollywood, Higgins' next project was the screenplay for *The Devil's Daughter*, a 1972 horror film and movie-of-the-week starring Shelley Winters. With *Silver Streak* in 1976, Higgins enjoyed a succession of hit comedies eventually directing several of them. Interesting projects that never came to fruition include a screenplay for *The Bluebird* he wrote for George Cukor when Katharine Hepburn was involved with the project; and a screen adaptation of *Hair* when Hal Ashby was set to direct. He wrote a Broadway play, "Retreat," that starred Janet Gaynor and had a brief run. While too busy to give any serious consideration to an acting career, he did appear briefly in the film *Into the Night*. Higgins' final project was as co-writer and co-producer of Shirley MacLaine's five-hour 1987 TV special,

The Best Little Whorehouse in Texas

Out on a Limb, based on MacLaine's book.

"My humor comes from a sense I have that life is a kind of cosmic joke. For me, laughter is very close to joy, joy is connected to bliss, and bliss is close to divinity."
—Colin Higgins

Harold and Maude
(1971, 90 min, US, Hal Ashby)
Hal Ashby directed Higgins' screenplay which became one of the most popular cult movies and repertory film-house favorites of the 1970s and '80s. Bud Cort is Harold, a pasty-faced 20-year-old obsessed with death. He finds meaning in life after meeting Maude (Ruth Gordon), an inimitable individual approaching 80 and full of joie de vivre. Vivian Pickles is a riot as Harold's daffy, domineering mom determined to find him a mate despite her son's penchant for suicide attempts on first dates. Gordon shines as the vivacious Maude who takes the grim Harold under her wing and teaches him to love and enjoy life. Black comedy at its darkest, this wonderful love story features the music of Cat Stevens. A favorite in France, Higgins adapted it for the Parisian stage where it ran for seven years. A 1980 Broadway engagement (produced without Higgins' involvement) closed quickly after its opening. ☿

FAVORITE DIRECTORS

Silver Streak

(1976, 113 min, US, Arthur Hiller)
Gene Wilder and Richard Pryor teamed for the first time in this engaging and often hilarious comedy written by Higgins (his second original screenplay) which tips its hat to Hitchcock and the mystery-aboard-a-train genre. Passenger Wilder gets himself mixed up with Jill Clayburgh, FBI agents, murder, con artist Pryor and spies as he travels from Los Angeles to Chicago. Pryor is a standout, and the cast includes Patrick McGoohan, Ned Beatty, Ray Walston and Scatman Crothers. ☯

Foul Play *(1978, 116 min, US)*

Based on the enormous popular success of *Silver Streak*, Paramount Pictures allowed Higgins to direct his first feature. Based on his own screenplay, Goldie Hawn stars in this funny comedy-thriller as a San Francisco librarian who becomes involved with detective Chevy Chase and a plot to assassinate the Pope. ☯

9 to 5 *(1980, 110 min, US)*

Higgins continued his streak of successful comedies with this topical battle-of-the-sexes comedy based on his own screenplay. Jane Fonda, Lily Tomlin and Dolly Parton proved to be a formidable team as three secretaries who team together to get even with their sexist, insensitive boss (Dabney Coleman). In doing so, they subsequently raise office efficiency and productivity to new highs in his absence. Tomlin's cartoon fantasy sequence is a hilarious highlight. ☯

The Best Little Whorehouse in Texas

(1982, 114 Min, US)
Director and co-screenwriter Higgins particularly enjoyed making this musical comedy: "I've always been a fan of film musicals, and that Universal gave me Burt Reynolds and Dolly Parton was better than any dream I've ever had." The two do bring a degree of charm to this glossy but uneven adaptation of the hit Broadway musical (which was directed by Tommy Tune) about a Texas bordello — called the Chicken Ranch — run by Parton and under attack by a local televangelist. Burt is the sheriff caught in the middle. Charles Durning received an Oscar nomination for his scene-stealing bit as the Governor. ☯

Ruth Gordon and Bud Cort are *Harold and Maude*

JDEREK JARMAN

One of Great Britain's most acclaimed directors and *the* leading gay filmmaker of our time, Derek Jarman had, in a career spanning over twenty years, created a body of work that is a highly focused, personal vision of life, infused with his strongly opinionated views on politics, sex and art. Despite his sickness from AIDS in the mid-1980s (from which he died in 1994 at the age of 52), he had continued to expand on these themes and with his later films began exploring gay sexuality and political radicalism with even greater fervor. Audaciously gay from his very first feature, Jarman has been both a beacon of queer artistry in film and a bold innovator in depicting positive images of male homosexuality. And because of his gay boldness and inventiveness, he has been credited as being the father to the New Queer Cinema movement.

Always the maverick, Jarman continuously worked the outer fringes of commercial cinema. Not primarily concerned with box office, big budgets, star egos and studio interference, he remained in England making films that interested him. The works, visually dazzling, are in varying degrees autobiographical, and do not always employ traditional narrative techniques. Many are dreamlike, avant-garde forays into his soul; others are imaginative interpretations of previously published works; all share his singular artistic integrity.

Born in 1942, Jarman studied fine art and enjoyed success not only as a filmmaker but also as a poet, writer and painter. He received his start in film working as the art director on Ken Russell's *The Devils* (1971) and *Savage Messiah* (1972). His first feature film, *Sebastiane*, shocked many not only for its use of Latin but also for its intense, poetic, homoerotic imagery. A surprise success, it was followed by the harsh fable on the possible future of England, *Jubilee*. Jarman has also reinterpretated the works of Shakespeare (*The Tempest* and *The Angelic Conversation*), and has carried on a career fascination with queer rebel heroes of the past (*Sebastiane, Edward II* and *Caravaggio*). In repeatedly steering away from the mainstream, his films are admittedly "specialized," but what he sacrificed with popular appeal, he made up with a singularly impressive body of intellectual and moving films.

Since his discovery in 1986 on being HIV-positive, Jarman's works took on a more urgent and militantly queer perspective. Despite repeated illnesses and hospital stays, he was remarkably productive, making a film a year, most of

Jarman

them exercises in ingenuity while belying their extremely low budgets. His most recent films, while provocative and intense, display an irreverent, comical sense of humor, as well. Despite his weakened condition, Jarman made the trip to New York and the New York Film Festival in October 1993 to screen his film *Blue*, where both he and his film were greeted with thunderous applause. Speaking before audiences and reporters, Jarman said of AIDS, "It has destroyed my sight, I couldn't make another film now because I can't see enough." Although the disease ended his career prematurely, he harbored no anger, no bitterness, saying in a *New York Times* interview, "You can sit there and feel sorry for yourself or get out and attempt to do something. I've tried to do the latter."

Jarman was also an author and painter. His paintings have been exhibited in galleries in London, and his books include "Dancing Ledge" and "The Last of England." He also wrote two memoirs: "Modern Nature" and "At Your Own Risk."

In the Shadow of the Sun
(1972-80, 51 min, GB)

Available on home video in Britain, this collection of several of Jarman's home movies and first Super-8 works are more experimental and non-linear than his feature films, suggesting Jarman's testing of the medium's waters. Images culled from footage filmed in the early 1970s are placed on top of other images of a 1980 car trip and are either slowed down or stopped, creating a dense, atmospheric, dreamlike vision. Musical soundtrack by Throbbing Gristle.

▼ Sebastiane *(1976, 82 min, GB)*

Sensual, lushly photographed and highly homoerotic, this vision of the legend of St. Sebastian is filled with beautiful images of male bodies and graphic scenes of sex and torture. The lives of few saints are as shrouded in mystery as that of the celebrated martyr Sebastian, whose arrow-pierced body has become one of the most familiar images in Christian iconography. In this film, he is shown as a Roman soldier who, because of his Christian beliefs, is sent to an isolated Sicilian encampment and into virtual exile by the Emperor Diocletian. His fellow soldiers and their captain, Severus, become involved in narcissistic and sado-masochistic intrigue which culminates with Sebastiane's death when he refuses the advances of the smitten captain. The film, co-directed by Paul Humfress, received a surprisingly strong commercial showing in Great Britain as well as in major cities in the United States. The music is by Brian Eno and it was filmed in colorfully lewd street Latin. ⊛

Sebastiane

Jubilee *(1978, 103 min, GB)*

Jarman's wildly inventive, highly personal punk fantasy of a post-apocalyptic future of a dying England takes off where *A Clockwork Orange* ended. The Queen is dead, Buckingham Palace is a recording studio and the police have it off with each other when they're not breaking the heads of young men. Queen Elizabeth I is transported by her astrologer to the close of the 20th century to witness the disintegration of order and the explosion of destruction and chaos. The cast of wasted, punked-out characters include a passively receptive and sexually mesmeric Adam Ant, Little Nell (of *Rocky Horror* fame), and a strong-willed Toyah Wilcox. Jordon's punk version of "Rule Britannia" is a musical highlight with additional music by Adam and the Ants, Siouxie and the Banshees, and Brian Eno. A fascinating culture shock look at a pre-Thatcherized England. ⊛

The Tempest *(1979, 95 min, GB)*

Jarman unleashes his prodigious talents on Shakespeare's "The Tempest" in this lighthearted and idiosyncratic screen version of the Bard's final play. Quite funny, outlandish and even camp, Jarman takes great liberties with the original text, condensing the tale and shifting it from an island retreat to a candle-lit Gothic mansion. Stylishly avant-garde, this absurdist adaptation features singing, dancing, and a montage of exotic and erotic visuals ending with a Elizabeth Welch rendition of "Stormy Weather." With Toyah Wilcox as Miranda, Heathcote Williams as Prospero, and Orlando as a grotesque Caliban.

> "The most truly spectacular British film in years...text and image are totally integrated to afford interpretation, not mere illustration. My enthusiasm for this rare film is unrepentant and unqualified."
> —David Robinson, *The Times* [London]

▼ The Angelic Conversation

(1985, 78 min, GB)

Eschewing narrative form, with the only dialogue being Judi Dench's offscreen reading of twelve Shakespeare sonnets, this cryptic assemblage of stop-action photography can be slow-going; but for those who persist, this allegorical mood piece can be a hypnotically beautiful film. Featuring several Bruce Weber beauties, Jarman, on a soul-searching mission, celebrates life and captures the sensual grace of male youth as well as his feelings on premature death caused by AIDS. With original music by Coil, the film is an affirmation of life, and an original and daring work. Jarman's favorite film, he said of it, "Extraordinary, with an almost archaic quality. The film is aces." ⊛

> "Jarman uses Shakespeare's sonnets as a way to make British culture leap out to join the imagery of Dante and Michelangelo, Cocteau and Kenneth Anger."
> —Harlan Kennedy, *Film Comment*

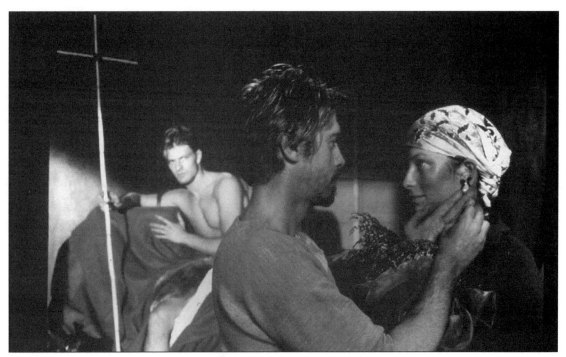

Sean Bean, Nigel Terry and Tilda Swinton in *Caravaggio*

▼ Caravaggio *(1986, 93 min, GB)*

Michelangelo Merisi Caravaggio (1573-1610) was the last, perhaps the greatest, and certainly the most controversial painter of the Italian Renaissance. This stylishly bold tribute to the violative artist features Nigel Terry as Caravaggio, a bad-boy of Italian aristocracy who scandalized the established order with his faintly erotic paintings of often naked saints modeled by prostitutes and street urchins. Jarman portrays Caravaggio as a man of intense passions — artistically, emotionally and physically — who was also a bisexual with a taste for "rough trade." Sean Bean is the bisexual Ranuccio, his rugged lover, and Tilda Swinton is Lena, his beautiful mistress who comes between them. A quirky yet elegant film blending anachronistic playfulness (a technique used again in *Edward II*) with a touching homoerotic love story, spectacular camera work and a complex, impressionist feel. Jarman spent seven years preparing for the film and when actual production began, he made it in only five weeks, all in an Isle of Dogs warehouse. ⊛

▼ The Last of England *(1988, 87 min, GB)*

Uncompromising in its vision, *The Last of England* is a beautifully photographed fragmented poem structured within a series of cross-cutting vignettes. Filled with homoerotic images, the film deals with the destruction of our physical and emotional world by the ravages of Thatcherism and the callousness of man. Accompanied by Nigel Terry's baleful narration, the visuals include shots of Jarman, male prostitutes and scenes of urban squalor and decay, as well as references to the Queen and the Falklands. ⊛

Highlights *(1989, 33 min, GB)*

Staged and directed by Jarman, this imaginative music video features eight songs from a Pet Shop Boys concert at Wembeley Arena in London. Seemingly light-years ahead of the audience, Jarman's hallucinatory sets and staging include mutated rubber creatures roaming the stage, an oh-so-pious, pitch-fork carrying Pope, a flamenco version of "Domino Dancing," and striking backdrop visuals. The music by the Pet Shop Boys, with songs that include "It's a Sin," "Shopping" and "Rent," is great but it is Jarman who really steals the show. ⊛

War Requiem *(1989, 90 min, GB)*

Jarman teamed with producer Don Boyd to create this elaborate symphony of sight and sound. Using the same non-dialogue format as Boyd's *Aria* (which featured a segment by Jarman), they have brought cinematic life to Benjamin Britten's immensely powerful "War Requiem." Written for the opening of the new Coventry Cathedral (the original was destroyed in WWI), Britten's oratorio is punctuated by the haunting poetry of Wilfred Owen — who was killed just prior to Armistice Day in 1918 at the age of 27. This exceptionally stirring piece captures Britten's theme of innocence ruined by the ravages of war. Not one of Jarman's favorites, he was quoted as saying, "It never goes through my mind that I ever made it." ⊛

FAVORITE DIRECTORS

▼ The Garden *(1990, 88 min, GB)*

While director Jarman fitfully sleeps in his garden, his cryptic dreams — culled from his subconsciouses and his fevered imagination — are played out in their fullest, queerest glory. The lyrical images of male love, tenderness and art are interspersed with images of natural beauty; but all collide against a backlash of homophobia, persecution and death. An allegory for AIDS, the film's main narrative thrust depicts two male lovers as they, in the manner of Jesus Christ, are taunted, arrested, tortured and are crucified for their beliefs. A stunningly filmed work of art, full of poetically realized images and fueled with an intense longing for understanding, peace and brotherhood. Supported by a haunting score by Simon Fisher Turner and featuring Tilda Swinton. ☉

▼ Edward II *(1991, 91 min, GB)*

Jarman reworked Christopher Marlowe's play into a homoerotic, sexually charged, radically relevant work for our times. Steven Waddington stars as the tragic King Edward, Andrew Teirnan plays his beloved Gaveston, Nigel Terry is the villainous Mortimer and Tilda Swinton also stars as the jealous and destructive Queen Isabella (for which she won the Best Actress Award at the Venice Film Festival). Graphically brutal, moving and surprisingly funny, the film blends Marlowe's prose with contemporary jargon and costumes, replete with positive portrayals of queer sex, profanity and ACT-UP activists. One of the film's most surprising sequences occurs when Annie Lennox appears crooning Cole Porter's classic "Ev'ry Time We Say Goodbye." Brilliant, daring and innovative, *Edward II* is contemporary filmmaking at its finest, and one of the best examples of modern queer cinema. ☉

▼ Wittgenstein *(1993, 75 min, GB)*

Displaying little of the queer militancy that has distinguished Jarman's recent films, and another in a series of biographies of gay historical figures (Sebastiane, Edward II, Caravaggio), this amusing, intellectual portrait of Austrian-born, British-educated philosopher Ludwig Wittgenstein is both a startling primer in low-budget filmmaking as well as a visually exuberant work. Considered one of the century's most influential philosophers, Wittgenstein's private and professional life is chronicled — from his prodigy childhood to his reluctant life as a professor at Cambridge. Jarman utilizes a pitch-black background, allowing the richly drawn, outrageously costumed characters and their witty, thought-provoking dialogue to take center stage. Karl Johnson plays the eccentric philosopher who tackled the weighty theories of logic and truth but was burdened with guilt about his homosexuality. Tilda Swinton is lavishly campy as Lady Ottoline and Clancey Chassey is delightful as the young but amazingly self-aware Wittgenstein. Shot in less than two weeks for under L300,000, this Channel 4-backed film proves to be an invigorating, uncompromising work.

▼ Blue *(1993, 76 min, GB)*

Jarman had been battling AIDS for six years prior to the making of this film. With deteriorating health and greatly impaired eyesight, Jarman — in what would be his final work — created a startling experimental film that is both a bold statement on AIDS as well as an important work of art. Inspired by the works of conceptual artist Yves Klein, Jarman invites the audience into his sight-deprived world, creating a womb-like meditative state by employing a completely blue screen throughout the film. This static, steadying vision is accompanied by several actors, including Tilda Swinton, Nigel Terry, John Quentin and Jarman, as they read from Jarman's journals. These often poetic diaries recount his medical complexities, his thoughts on the loss of many loved ones, and reflect on his life and art. Passages describing sickness, immobility and approaching death are amazingly devoid of anger and never succumb to polemical sermonizing nor maudlin self-pity. *Blue* is a fitting closure to his eventful career. Speaking from a London hospital where he was being treated for CMV retinitis, an eye infection, he said, "It's a hospital diary...we've packed it with reminisces and stories and things to do with the color blue. It makes a jolly good signing off film."

Glitterbug *(1970-86, 60 min, GB)*

Glitterbug is Jarman's collection of his video diaries set to music composed by Brian Eno. From mundane scenes at home, in his studio, through his travels in Europe, with his friends and on-location when making his feature films, Jarman's Super-8 snippets offer both a glimpse into his 1970s life as a British equivalent to Andy Warhol and his Factory as well as capturing something more personal — a joyful nostalgia filled with a sensuous innocence of his past. Featuring his friends and co-workers as well as William Burroughs, Jarman supervised the editing for this home video release and finished it before he died in February 1994.

The Angelic Conversation

BEEBAN KIDRON

A promising young film talent from England, London-based Beeban Kidron has, in just a few short years, rose from making political documentaries and small BBC-TV-financed features to directing a major Hollywood film with *Used People*.

Born in 1961, Kidron started her career in the arts as an assistant to photographer Eve Arnold. While attending the National Film School, Kidron worked on her first film, the documentary *Carry Greenham Home* (1986, 66 min), for which she shared directing credit with Amanda Richardson. The film followed the daily struggles, political activities and quiet heroism of a group of women encamped at the Greenham Nuclear Power Plant demonstrating for nuclear disarmament. The intensity of her commitment to the project was evidenced by the fact that she lived at the site for more than seven months, often times in harsh conditions while filming.

Her feature film career began in earnest after meeting lesbian novelist Jeanette Winterson at a party. They immediately hit it off, and worked together on the lesbian coming-of-age drama, *Oranges Are Not the Only Fruit*, which originally aired on BBC and eventually played to great acclaim in lesbian and gay film festivals around the world. Bouyed by the success, Kidron followed with her second feature, *Antonia and Jane*, a witty and insightful comedy-drama dealing with the strength and strains of two longtime friends. The film became a surprise art-house hit in the United States and, as usual in such cases, Hollywood sniffed a talent and began to court her. Instead of a "small" Hollywood-backed film, Kidron instead went head first with *Used People*, a big-budget comedy-drama with such tempestuous and renowned big-name stars as Shirley MacLaine, Marcello Mastroianni, Kathy Bates and Jessica Tandy. The film received mixed reviews and performed moderately at the box office; and while not the rousing success of Hollywood lore, it was by no means a failure and was quite a good "calling card" for future Hollywood film projects.

Kidron's film style, for the most part dictated by the constraints of television, is not that greatly developed. Her interest and talent lies more with her sensitive handling of her characters. As a general theme, she tends to focus on people struggling to discover their true selves. Presently, Kidron is working on several projects. She'll reunite with

Kidron (l.) directing *Vroom*

Winterson for a BBC production, *Bon Voyage*, to star Vanessa Redgrave, Dorothy Tutin, John Hurt and Jonathan Pryce, about a West Indian woman starting a new life in England; she's working on a drama about blacks and Jews in New York called *Payment in Full*; and in development is a film based on a play by Jim Cartwright. Kidron's latest production, however, is a road picture about three multiracial drag queens traveling cross-country who find themselves stranded in a Midwestern town, *To Wong Foo, Thanks for Everything, Julie Newmar*. The film stars Wesley Snipes, Patrick Swayze and John Leguizamo.

Vroom *(1988, GB, 89 min)*

Romantic and unpredictable, this engaging English road movie is set in the bleak northern city of Lancashire and centers around the lives of two free-spirited lads: Jack, a handsome devil loved by the ladies, and his mate Ringe, a charming, orange-and-spike-haired dweeb. Destiny plays a hand in changing their lives when a fetching woman arrives on the scene in a pink '57 Chevrolet, sending all on an escapist flight of fancy. This drama of youthful spirit in the face of disillusionment was wittily written by Jim Cartwright and originally aired on Channel 4.

FAVORITE DIRECTORS

▼ Oranges Are Not the Only Fruit

(1989, 90 min, GB)

Adapted for BBC-TV by Jeanette Winterson, from her novel of the same name, this three-part production chronicles the coming-of-age of a young British lesbian, Jess (Geraldine McEwanin). In her turbulent struggles with her domineering evangelist mother (Charlotte Coleman), Jess grows up to be a fiercely independent young woman. This poignant story features a marvelous ensemble cast and charming performances from its two lead actresses. The film received the Audience Award for Best Feature in the 1990 San Francisco International Lesbian and Gay Film Festival.

Antonia & Jane *(1991, 75 min, GB)*

This delightfully funny, low-budget gem, an Anglicized, feminist homage to Woody Allen, explores the loving but tempestuous relationship between two decidedly different women. Plain-looking, insecure but adventurous Antonia narrates the film's opening. She recounts her hilarious obsession with Jane, her pretty, married and seemingly well-balanced childhood friend she is about to meet for their annual lunch. Midway through the film, Jane takes over the narration duties and gives us her side of the story. Pleasantly amusing and deceptively simple. ☯

Used People *(1992, 116 min, US)*

The comparisons of *Used People* to *Moonstruck* and *Fried Green Tomatoes* are inevitable. All share a sentimental bent without being too cute about it; wacky characters find themselves in wackier situations; and members of near-dysfunctional families endear themselves not only to the viewer but, eventually, to each other. And if *Used People* does seem very familiar at times, it's the characters' familiarity which makes this slightly balmy, humorous and beguiling comedy-drama a welcome visitor. Heading a splendid cast, Shirley MacLaine plays a recently widowed Jewish wife and mother from Queens. On the day of her husband's funeral, she is asked on a date by determined Italian restauranteur Marcello Mastroianni. Against her better judgment, she agrees. What follows is a series of disasterous family get-togethers, culture clashes and romantic pursuits as Mastroianni tries to capture the no-non-sense heart of his intended. The film is immeasurably aided by the likes of Kathy Bates, Jessica Tandy, Sylvia Sidney and Marcia Gay Harden in supporting roles. ☯

Hookers, Pimps, Hustlers, and Their Johns *(1993, 85 min, GB)*

Made for Britain's Channel 4's unusual series on Christmas in New York City, Kidron ventured to the streets of the South Bronx and other areas of the Big Apple to examine the lives of those involved in the city's sex industry. Herself a former stripper (she ran away from home at the age of 17 and moved to San Francisco), Kidron treats both the sleazy enterpreneurs and the crack-addicted prostitutes with respect as the film delves, non-judgmentally and with vivid detail, the world of sex-for-sale. Highlights include Kidron donning the attire of a hooker and taking to the streets; and two pimps earnestly discussing the new wallpaper of their whorehouse. Kidron said that she "did not want it to be one of those films which is about how prostitutes are victims, pimps baddies and the police are the conquering heroes."

Antonia & Jane

LOTHAR LAMBERT

While generally unknown in the United States and Great Britain, Lothar Lambert (born 1943) has been successfully making enjoyably quirky and determinedly personal underground films in Berlin for over twenty years. He enjoys cult popularity at home and has been the subject of a retrospective in Toronto with several of his films also playing the gay/lesbian film festival circuit. What make Lambert's films so different, especially in contrast to other German gay and lesbian filmmakers (Rainer Werner Fassbinder, Rosa von Praunheim, Monica Truet, Werner Schroeder), is his idiosyncratic interests, unflinching honesty and a determination to keep his films in the ultra-low budget category. Lambert's films deal first and foremost with sexuality and sexual liberation. They can be raunchy in depicting the erotic revelries of the Berlin sex scene yet are disarmingly entertaining and satiric as he broadly spoofs all sexual and political persuasions.

Taking on the duties of director, producer, actor and writer, as well as being involved in the marketing and distribution end, Lambert's films are unquestionably his own and with the exception of *1 Berlin-Harlem*, all have been financed by Lambert himself, mostly from the money he earns as a journalist. While his films are breezy comedies, they also deal with such weighty issues as racism, individuals hopelessly lost in an oppressive system, sexual repression, and loneliness. What they are not about are concerns with women's issues (he has often been labeled misogynist) or with the Gay Movement. For although he often times plays a gay man or has his characters in gay situations, he is not interested in towing the line, and is quoted as saying, "I hate associations, parties — whatever you call them, because I feel that I have to give up some of my individuality, which I find hard to do."

Though he is the inspiration and leader of the German underground film movement and still a cult figure in that country, official recognition was not easily forthcoming. All of his earlier films were denied showings at the Berlin Film Festival because of what officials called "technical deficiencies." The outlaw status pleased Lambert at the time: "The official representatives of German cinema would hate that my dirty little films get to represent German culture. If my films have a message, it is just 'be yourself.'"

The following filmography is far from complete, but in addition to the films mentioned, he has also made *Faux Pas De Deux* (1976), a more explicit and less fanciful version of *Harold and Maude* which comicly tells of the love affair between an elderly actress and a young art student; *Sein Kamph*, an early film which was co-directed by Wolfram Zobus and is a sexual satire on the German Left; and *Now or Never*, a non-sync sound tale of a married man's discovery of his bisexuality while visiting New York City. In keeping with his unusual sexual politics, Lambert commented on the latter film's character: "I hope he stays with his girlfriend, and I hope she understands something about how, if he needs it, he may need different experiences than just her partnership."

1 Berlin-Harlem *(1974, 85 min, Germany)*

Tally Brown is a black G.I. misfit: he's disinterested in black activism and estranged from the white American establishment adrift in blond, blue-eyed Berlin. Made for $20,000 (a large sum compared to his other works, though this was his first movie to receive a state grant), the film deals with racial myths and racial tensions and co-stars Ingrid Caven and features a cameo by Rainer Werner Fassbinder as a trendy film director. Co-directed by Wolfram Zobus.

▼ Late Show *(1977, 95 min, Germany)*

An amusing and unusually sympathetic gay coming-out tale in which a man (played by Lambert) enjoys his gay sex life vicariously — through erotic gay fantasies seen in his head as a late-night movie. The fantasies become more frequent and more real until the two merge into one. Seen by one critic as "establishing a blasphemous dialectic between feminism and gay consciousness"; to others it was his most gay-positive and gay-centered film to date.

Fraülein Berlin

Nightmare Woman *(1980, 90 min, Germany)*

After her husband leaves her, a distraught, masochistic woman goes through some rough times, both psychologically and sexually, until she finds salvation as a punk rock singer. A German cult hit that ran for over eight months in Berlin.

▼ Fucking City *(1982, 95 min, Germany)*

A sex comedy and love-hate song to Berlin, *Fucking City* is about the obsessive sexual antics of four people: a sleazy porno filmmaker (Stefen Menche); his wife and frequent star of his increasingly exploitative flicks (Ulrike S.); a hefty and virginal country girl; and an effeminate gay butcher (played by Lambert). What they all have in common is a sexual interest in foreign "guest" workers, be they Lebanonese, Turkish or African. Played more for outrage than titillation, this comedy follows the foursome as they become involved in increasingly joyless and relentlessly exploitative sexual dalliances with the horny, ready-to-be-exploited collection of foreign men. Bitterly funny, the film has great fun in depicting all kinds of sexual variations including some simulated necrophilia — always a crowd pleaser!

> "*Fucking City* could be thematically located at the intersection of fellow Berlin Frank Ripploh's *Taxi Zum Klo* and Fassbinder's *Ali: Fear Eats the Soul*, but it's funnier, sadder and more compassionate than either of them."
> —*Variety*

▼ Paso Doble *(1983, 90 min, Germany)*

This wacky sexual comedy is about an uptight German couple whose vacation to Spain and a *paso doble* dancing lesson triggers their liberating breakup. Inhibitions are peeled under the hot Spanish sun as Mama quickly goes off with a Persian masseur and Pappa returns to Germany (and to his shocked children) with a hunky, mute gay waiter. The family's problem turns out to be their salvation in this hilarious look at married life and Germany's tight-lipped approach to sex.

Fraülein Berlin *(1983, 90 min, Germany)*

In an amusing self-parody, Ulrike S. plays an underground film star tired of the cheesy roles (her latest, *Monster Woman*) foisted on her by her domineering director. Frustrated, she travels to both Toronto and New York, where she meets an amusing number of real-life directors, critics and stars, including Norman Jewison, Jim Jarmusch and independent filmmaker Bette Gordon. Shot in English, the film is full of in-jokes and several outrageously amusing scenes.

> "A kind of a cameo-pegged *Greatest Story Ever Told* on the Underground circuit."
> —*Variety*

▼ Drama in Blood *(1984, 81 min, Germany)*

In what may be his funniest and most accessible film, Lambert stars as Gerharht, a boringly repressed bank clerk who begins to discover his true self after visiting a transvestite bar. Desperately wanting to don female clothing and sing his heart out, he finally cuts loose, and performs an entertaining Lili Marlene number; becoming in his own small way a nocturnal international chanteuse. This coming-out film uses drag rather than standard gay life as the liberating force in Gerharht's life.

Drama in Blood

▼ Forbidden to Forbid

(1987, 90 min, Germany)

Set amid Berlin's decadent sex district, this tale of raunchy sex and obsessive desire is structured as six different stories. Beginning with an opening prologue in front of a peep show, the stories focus on: two middle-aged women who peer at the activity of a group of gay men, prompting the women to speculate on how one contracts AIDS; an S&M tryst with a painter and his subject; a black biker; and a German bag lady who rails against the onslaught of foreigners and longs for a Hitler-like savior. Rainer Werner Fassbinder's ex-lovers, actress and cabaret singer Ingrid Caven and director Dietor Schidor, are featured.

MITCHELL LEISEN

Like George Cukor and Edmund Goulding, Mitchell Leisen was known as a "woman's director" — could it be this was a Hollywood code word for gay? The first to make the likes of Barbara Stanwyck and Joan Fontaine glamorous, Leisen was a perfectionist and very knowledgeable in his craft. In the 1930s and early '40s, he created a series of enduring sophisticated romantic comedies, many written by Preston Sturges or Billy Wilder. But his films were also known for a visual excellence, which can partly be attributed to a rewarding work relationship with Cecil B. DeMille.

Born in 1898 in a small Michigan town, Leisen spent his early twenties working for a Chicago architectual firm. He came to Hollywood to pursue an acting career, but after one experience decided he didn't like it. He found satisfaction, however, as a set decorator and costumer, and was considered an expert in the field. Performing these duties on such silent greats as *Robin Hood* and *Thief of Bagdad*, Leisen came to the attention of DeMille, quite by accident. DeMille's assistant recommended Leisen because she thought he had "interesting hands."

Leisen directed his first film in 1933, *Cradle Song*, and through the years became known for having a fine eye to detail and bestowing an extravagant look to his films. Leisen also personally supervised all aspects of his films, including costumes, sets, hair, makeup, etc. A tall, statuesque and impeccably dressed man (he once made the "best dressed" list), Leisen was a jack of all trades, and his interests included interior design, aviation, architecture, drafting, sculpture, clothing design and dance (he founded and directed a dance group called Hollywood Presents). In the mid- to late-1940s, Leisen's career began to wane. His films were out of style, and as Andrew Sarris wrote, with "the promotion of Sturges and Wilder from writers' cubicles to directors' chairs," screenwriters were now directing their own work, leaving Leisen in the "unenviable position of an expert diamond cutter working with lumpy coal."

Leisen was married once, in 1927, and the marriage lasted 15 years. The gossip columnists at the time often reported that for much of their marriage, they spent little time together. Leisen's Hollywood home proudly displayed a gigantic portrait of dance director and friend Billy Daniels, though no information could be found to indicate a relationship between the two other than good friends. Director Robert Aldrich, comparing the "outness" of certain directors, once commented that James Whale was blackballed for refusing to stay in the closet, while "Mitchell Leisen, and all of the others played it straight" and stayed out of trouble with the studio heads. Leisen experienced poor health in later life, including several heart attacks, and his right leg was amputated. He died at the age of 74 in 1972.

Cradle Song *(1933, 78 min, US)*

In her first American film, Dorothea Wieck (*Mädchen in Uniform*) stars as a nun who raises a foundling left at the door of her Spanish nunnery. In his directorial debut, Leisen's eye for production detail is well-served.

Death Takes a Holiday *(1934, 79 min, US)*

Maxwell Anderson's acclaimed Broadway drama makes for a fascinating and surreal film adaptation. Fredric March plays Death, who decides to take a three-day holiday. Disguising himself as royalty, he stays at a Spanish villa where he observes humans up close for the first time and to his surprise, falls in love.

Murder at the Vanities *(1934, 95 min, US)*

A pleasant if insubstantial musical murder-mystery comedy. Victor McLaglen is a police detective whose evening at the theatre is interrupted when attempts are made on the life of actress Kitty Carlisle and a chorine is found dead. The comic and musical segments surpass those of the murder-mystery subplot. ⊛

Behold My Wife *(1935, 79 min, US)*

Hokey melodrama with Gene Raymond as the spoiled son of a wealthy banking family. When his parents interfere in Raymond's engagement to a secretary, he travels West, meets Indian girl Sylvia Sydney, marries her and brings her home to embarrass his family.

Four Hours to Kill *(1935, 71 min, US)*

A *Grand Hotel*-like melodrama with the unusual setting of a Broadway theatre, where the lives of various audience members come together. They include escaped convict Richard Barthelmess, Reno-bound wife Gertrude Michael, and hat-check boy Joe Morrison.

Hands Across the Table
(1935, 80 min, US)

The hand of Ernst Lubitsch is apparent in this charmingly funny screwball comedy reportedly supervised by the famed director. Leisen's own hand is a capable one in telling the story of manicurist Carole Lombard and poor playboy Fred MacMurray. Each wants a rich mate, but their plans go haywire when they fall for each other. Ralph Bellamy is MacMurray's competition.

FAVORITE DIRECTORS

The Big Broadcast of 1937

(1936, 100 min, US)

In the third of Paramount's successful "Big Broadcast" series, Leisen built up the laughs in this funny variety musical-comedy. Jack Benny heads a good cast — which includes George Burns & Gracie Allen, Martha Raye and Bob Burns — as radio station manager Jack is driven crazy getting everyone on the air.

Thirteen Hours by Air *(1936, 70 min, US)*

Another *Grand Hotel*-type melodrama, this one set on a doomed airliner. Crashes, turmoil and even gangsters await pilot Fred MacMurray, society girl Joan Bennett, P.I. Brian Donlevy and several other passengers on a Newark-to-Frisco flight. Leisen unevenly mixes comedy and melodrama.

Swing High, Swing Low

(1937, 92 min, US)

A jazz updating of the play "Burlesque," with Fred MacMurray as a Panama Canal soldier who returns to the States to make sweet music with his trumpet. Carole Lombard watches his rise and fall. It's sappy all the way, but the earnest performances of MacMurray and Lombard make it of interest. ⊛

▼ Easy Living *(1938, 88 min, US)*

Preston Sturges wrote the screenplay for this consistently funny romp. Jean Arthur sparkles as a working girl whose life turns upside-down when tycoon Edward Arnold throws his wife's mink out the window, landing on Arthur. Ray Milland co-stars as Arnold's son who romances her. There's a great slapstick scene at an automat, and Franklin Pangborn, as a presumably gay and catty salesclerk, proves when it comes to dishing the dirt, he's second to none. ⊛

The Big Broadcast of 1938

(1938, 88 min, US)

The last of the "Big Broadcast" films, this go around is set aboard a transatlantic steamship. W.C. Fields heads the cast, which also includes Martha Raye, Dorothy Lamour, and Bob Hope singing (with Shirley Ross) his theme song, "Thanks for the Memory."

Artists and Models Abroad

(1938, 90 min, US)

Jack Benny rides again as Buck Boswell in this fun sequel to his popular 1937 comedy, *Artists and Models*. This time, Benny heads a troupe of American performers stranded in Paris, and has his hands full bailing everyone out of a succession of jams. Joan Bennett plays a millionaire's daughter, and there's a few musical numbers, too. (GB title: *Stranded in Paris*)

Midnight *(1939, 92 min, US)*

Leisen's most sophisticated comedy sports a delightful screenplay by Billy Wilder and Charles Brackett. Claudette Colbert plays a down-on-her-luck showgirl who is hired to impersonate a countess by baron John Barrymore (in a spirited comeback performance). It seems his wife Mary Astor is involved in a romantic indiscretion with playboy Francis Lederer, and it's up to Colbert to come between them. Which doesn't sit too well with cabbie Don Ameche, who's vying for Claudette's attention as well. A breezy lark.

Remember the Night *(1940, 93 min, US)*

Preston Sturges wrote the screenplay for this sparkling comedy. Barbara Stanwyck gets caught lifting a bracelet and lands in jail. Fred MacMurray is the assistant D.A. who's in charge of the case. It's Christmas, and MacMurray, in a moment of good will towards women, bails her. She then accompanies him back home to Indiana when he visits the family. Leisen keeps the comedy going at a brisk pace, and Stanwyck and MacMurray are in good form.

Arise, My Love *(1940, 113 min, US)*

Leisen mixes comedy, romance and suspense effortlessly as reporter Claudette Colbert and flyer Ray Milland cross paths (after she saves his life), fall in love, and each does their part in the war effort. A fabulous sophisticated comedy-drama in which Leisen extracts superior performances from his two leads. Billy Wilder and Charles Brackett wrote the screenplay; the film won an Oscar for Original Story.

I Wanted Wings *(1941, 131 min, US)*

Military salute to the Army Air Corps. Ray Milland, William Holden and Wayne Morris are the young cadets whose experiences are followed from training camp to the air. Constance Moore and Veronica Lake are the love interests, and Brian Donlevy steals the show as the future pilots' commander. Good aerial photography.

Hold Back the Dawn *(1941, 114 min, US)*

Olivia deHavilland's Oscar-nominated performance highlights this affecting wartime soaper written by Billy Wilder and Charles Brackett. Decades before *Green Card*, the story follows gigolo Charles Boyer as he courts maiden schoolteacher deHavilland in order to marry her and gain admittance into the United States. Paulette Goddard is Boyer's old flame. Fine direction by Leisen; his only film to be nominated for Best Picture.

The Lady Is Willing *(1942, 93 min, US)*

In a change of pace role, Marlene Dietrich plays a stage actress whose maternal instincts win out when she decides to adopt a baby. She lassos pediatrician Fred MacMurray into a marriage of convenience, and then daddy makes three. There's some laughs, though the story takes a needless dramatic turn at the end which almost sours what came before it. ⊛

Take a Letter, Darling

(1942, 88 min, US)
Rosalind Russell is a high-powered business executive who hires artist Fred MacMurray as her secretary/escort, prompting an inevitable clash and romance. More amusing than the predictable plot suggests. (GB title: *Green Eyed Woman*)

No Time for Love

(1943, 83 min, US)
Claudette Colbert plays a chic photographer for a *Life*-like magazine. On assignment, she meets construction worker Fred MacMurray, whose macho posturing entices her. A playful if familiar take on opposites attracting. Colbert is her usual sophisticated self. Colbert's fiancé, a sensitive composer played by Paul McGrath, is dubbed "dollface" by a taunting MacMurray.

The headline says it all!

Lady in the Dark *(1944, 100 min, US)*

Though much of the heart of the Kurt Weill-Ira Gershwin score has been removed, this lavish adaptation of the hit Broadway musical still manages to entertain in spite of itself. Taking over the Gertrude Lawrence role, Ginger Rogers plays successful but troubled magazine editor Liza Elliott, who reluctantly begins psychiatric counseling when career and romance push her to the edge. Ray Milland co-stars.

Frenchman's Creek *(1944, 113 min, US)*

Leisen's extravagant costumer certainly wears its high cost well, as this attractive romancer was Paramount's costliest production at the time. Joan Fontaine ably captures the tongue-in-cheek spirit Leisen strives for as an English lady who becomes involved with a notorious French pirate (Arturo de Cordova).

Practically Yours *(1945, 99 min, US)*

Fred MacMurray plays a Navy pilot who takes his plane on a suicide mission to sink a Japanese ship. Via radio transmission, he bids a last goodbye to his dog, Peggy. Back at home, all assume "Peggy" is ex-fellow worker Claudette Colbert. When MacMurray miraculously survives, the town arranges for them to reunite, with predictable results.

Kitty *(1945, 103 min, US)*

A sumptuous looking period drama based on Rosamond Marshall's novel. Set in 18th-century London, the film stars Paulette Goddard as the title character, a petty thief from the slums who crashes into polite society. Ray Milland is her lover. As would be expected, Leisen's film is a visual treasure.

Masquerade in Mexico *(1945, 96 min, US)*

Leisen misses the mark with this rehash of his wonderful *Midnight*. Dorothy Lamour is an American entertainer stranded in Mexico. She accepts the proposal of a millionaire (Patric Knowles) to divert the attention of a local bullfighter (Arturo de Cordova) who's paying too much attention to his wife.

To Each His Own *(1946, 122 min, US)*

Olivia deHavilland won the first of her two Oscars, giving a splendid portrayal of a small-town girl who bears a child out of wedlock, and is forced to give it up. She watches from afar as the boy grows from infancy to childhood to manhood. Leisen elevates this soap opera by offering sensitive direction which bypasses the usual melodramatic pitfalls; and deHavilland creates a three-dimensional character you can't help but care about.

Suddenly It's Spring *(1947, 87 min, US)*

Husband and wife Fred MacMurray and Paulette Goddard, who had decided before the start of WWII to divorce, return after the war from overseas. He's fallen for another woman, and eager to finalize the split. She's having second thoughts.

Golden Earrings *(1947, 95 min, US)*

An entire movie devoted as to why Ray Milland has pierced ears. Milland plays a British agent who must don the disguise of a Gypsy when the Gestapo is hot on his trail. He falls for beautiful Marlene Dietrich along the way. A modest WWII thriller.

Dream Girl *(1948, 83 min, US)*

Based on Elmer Rice's stage hit, Betty Hutton plays the flip-side of Walter Mitty as a day-dreaming socialite. The story loses some of its appeal by changing the character from middle-class bungler to high-society idler. Betty Field (whom Hutton sometimes recalls) played the part on Broadway.

Bride of Vengeance *(1949, 92 min, US)*

A lackluster retelling of the Lucretia Borgia tale. Paulette Goddard is the femme fatale, who marries the man (John Lund) she thinks killed her first husband. It seems she's in league with her brother who plans to take control of Lund's land. Then she discovers it was really brother MacDonald Carey who made her a widow, and it's Lucretia's revenge, once more.

Song of Surrender *(1949, 93 min, US)*

Claude Rains is the head of a museum in a small village. Wanda Hendrix is his bored wife, who begins an affair with visiting MacDonald Carey. A rather dull romantic potboiler.

Captain Carey, U.S.A. *(1950, 82 min, US)*

An appealing thriller with Alan Ladd as an ex-OSS officer who returns to the small Italian village where he was stationed during the war to find the traitor who betrayed him and members of the underground. Wanda Hendrix pops up as a former flame, long thought dead. Check out the Italian beefcake: five shirtless acrobats. (GB title: *After Midnight*)

No Man of Her Own *(1950, 98 min, US)*

Barbara Stanwyck's solid performance distinguishes this otherwise routine melodrama. Surviving a train wreck and on the lam, Stanwyck assumes the identity of a woman who is killed in the accident. Stanwyck's newfound happiness is short-lived, however, as a blackmailing ex-boyfriend enters the picture. Remade as the 1982 French film *I Married a Shadow*. ⊛

The Mating Season *(1951, 101 min, US)*

In this delightful comedy of mistaken identity, Thelma Ritter stands center stage, in possibly her best performance, as the working-class mother of newly married John Lund. When she visits her daughter-in-law Gene Tierney for the first time, she's mistaken for the new maid, so she decides to take the job and stick around for awhile. Though Tierney is thoroughly engaging, and Miriam Hopkins is smart in support as Tierney's interfering mother, it's Ritter's show all the way: She shoots those one-liners with the accuracy and timing of a Super Bowl quarterback.

Darling How Could You *(1951, 95 min, US)*

Based on James M. Barrie's play, "Alice-Sit-By-The-Fire," this old-fashioned comedy stars Joan Fontaine and John Lund as a married couple who return after a five-year absence to their London home and three children, one of whom thinks Fontaine is having an indiscretion with handsome doctor Peter Hanson.

Young Man with Ideas *(1952, 85 min, US)*

Lawyer Glenn Ford and wife Ruth Roman move from their Montana home to California to start life anew. He attracts the attention of law student Nina Foch, while she becomes involved with bookies. A slight comedy buoyed by agreeable performances and Leisen's whimsical direction.

Tonight We Sing *(1953, 109 min, US)*

A lightweight biography of Sol Hurok, a Russian immigrant who became a famous impresario to the likes of Pavlova, Feodor Chaliapin and Eugene Ysaye (played by Isaac Stern). Anne Bancroft appears as Hurok's neglected wife.

Bedevilled *(1955, 85 min, US)*

This must rate as Leisen's strangest film. Seminar student Steve Forrest becomes involved with on-the-run murderess/singer Anne Baxter in Paris. She's being pursued by both police and hoods, and Forrest attempts to help her escape from the country. Good location scenery gives background to some exciting chase scenes, but that story!

The Girl Most Likely
(1957, 98 min, US)

Leisen's last film is a harmless, fanciful musical remake of *Tom, Dick and Harry*. Jane Powell searches for Mr. Right; could it be Tom Noonan, Keith Andes, or handsome garage mechanic Cliff Robertson? Good support from Kaye Ballard as Powell's best friend. ⊛

Fred MacMurray (l.) checks out the merchandise as Claudette Colbert (r.) looks on in *No Time for Love*

JOSEPH LOSEY

Not the Englishman that many perceive him to be, Joseph Losey was born in 1909 in Lacrosse, Wisconsin. A self-exiled refugee brought about by the McCarthy hearings of the early 1950s, Losey moved to Europe, never to professionally return to the United States. He is considered one of Great Britain's best directors; *Cahiers du Cinéma* called him one of "the greatest of the great." It is generally assumed, however, that because he is not an auteur in the strictest sense of the word — he never produced his own films and relied on scripts written by others — he never received his proper due.

As a youth, Losey studied medicine at Dartmouth College before venturing into entertainment. His work included a stint as stage manager at Radio City Music Hall, a writer of film and theatre criticism, a producer and director of programs for radio and TV, and his first great love, stage directing. Losey supplemented his theatre work by directing documentary shorts, and after winning an Oscar nomination in 1945 with his short, *A Gun in His Hand*, he began, at the age of 39 and after 18 years in the theatre, to work in film. He began with smaller Hollywood films and had a promising career that was abruptly halted by his refusal to cooperate with the McCarthy witch hunts. He moved to England in 1952, working for many years under a pseudonym.

Despite a late start, Losey had a prolific movie career. His films share similar themes, most featuring characters who are ostracized by an intolerant society-at-large, or deal with innocent men threatened with blackmail and/or oppressive forces. With few exceptions, his works are serious, even downbeat dramas that deal more with character development than plot and action. Left wing in politics, Losey considered himself to be a "romantic...an emotional sucker." At his height in the 1960s, his association with playwright Harold Pinter brought popularity as well as critical praise. Losey's later films were not nearly as well received nor distributed.

Losey, who died in 1984, was married twice and had two children. He is included in this section of Favorite Directors primarily for three reasons: His personal history as an outsider has forced him (like many gays and lesbians) to view the world from a different point of view; He has worked with gay playwrights and has cast several gay actors; And finally, many of his films are thematically

Losey with Julie Christie filming *The Go-Between*

infused with a gay sensibility and feature either covertly or explicitly gay and lesbian characters. The following is an incomplete filmography, emphasizing his more important films and/or ones with gay themes or characters.

> "Even in the Midwest where I was born and brought up, I felt alien."
>
> —Joseph Losey

The Boy with Green Hair *(1948, 82 min, US)*

An involving WWII drama about a young war orphan who becomes a social outcast when overnight his hair turns green. A very young Dean Stockwell stars as the youth who is passed around from relative to relative and ultimately becomes a symbol of the futility of war and a cry against racism. ☻

M *(1951, 88 min, US)*

Taking on the difficult task of remaking Fritz Lang's expressionistic classic, Losey remained faithful to the story but changed its location (modern-day Los Angeles) and sympathies, with Losey saying at the time, "essentially Lang's villain was my hero." David Wayne is effectively creepy as the hunted child killer.

The Sleeping Tiger *(1954, 89 min, GB)*

Losey worked under the pseudonym of Victor Hanbury in this, his first British film made in self-exile. It's also the first collaboration between the director and Dirk Bogarde. Explaining in a later interview that he needed the work, Losey described the script as "a

FAVORITE DIRECTORS

lousy cheap story...a sort of bedtime story for senile stags." The plot, which deals with the darker forces of human nature and desire, features Bogarde as a seasoned criminal who after being paroled, is invited into the home of a psychiatrist in order for him to study and cure him of his criminal tendencies. What transpires, however, is that Bogarde soon hooks up with the doctor's lovely wife (Alexis Smith). A taut if improbable psychodrama.

> "We thought the script itself was frightful and it embarrassed us incredibly to do it."
>
> —Dirk Bogarde

▼ The Servant *(1963, 115 min, GB)*

Dirk Bogarde and James Fox star in one of Losey's most tantalizing, homoesque and complex films. Taken from Harold Pinter's first screenplay and based on a short story by gay novelist Robin Maugham, the story is about the developing role reversal and ensuing sadomasochistic relationship between Tony, a pampered, aristocratic weakling (Fox) and his manipulative and domineering manservant Hugo (Bogarde). Ostensibly dealing with the themes of the class struggle in England and sexual repression, this enticing tale never overtly deals with homosexuality, but Bogarde's seduction of Fox and their kinky relationship infuses the film with a gay consciousness. ⊛

> "It is one of the funniest pictures ever made. Nobody believes it. But I think it's really wicked."
>
> —Dirk Bogarde

▼ King and Country *(1964, 86 min, GB)*

An intense anti-war film set during World War I, this courtroom drama stars Dirk Bogarde as an officer assigned to defend a soldier who's been accused of desertion and faces the firing squad. The soldier (Tom Courtenay), the sole survivor of a bloody battle and seemingly shell-shocked, simply walked away from the battlefield. The deepening relationship between the accused and his defender suggests (although less so than in *The Servant*) a veiled homosexual subtext.

▼ Modesty Blaise *(1965, 119 min, GB)*

The great oddity of Losey's career, this comic-book adventure story of female super-secret agent Modesty Blaise (Monica Vitti) is a strange but entertaining satiric comedy that was poorly received in its initial release. With a stylishly outrageous set design, an effeminate, silver-wiged Dirk Bogarde as the super villain and a lesbian executioner whose leg muscles prove to be effective "jaws of death," this James Bond parody does not disappoint. Terence Stamp also stars in this delirious camp tale, which amazingly was scripted by Harold Pinter, based on a comic strip by Peter O'Donnell.

Accident *(1967, 105 min, GB)*

Harold Pinter wrote the script for this penetrating and thought-provoking examination of a love affair between a professor (Dirk Bogarde) and his student (Jacqueline Sassard). Bogarde and co-star Michael York both deliver sterling performances in this multi-leveled and complex psychological drama. ⊛

> "Unleashes the pent-up violence of sexual longing and onrushing age.
>
> —*Time*

> "Like a punch in the chest. Put together breath by breath, look by look, lust by lust, lie by lie. A compelling film."
>
> —*Newsweek*

▼ Boom! *(1968, 113 min, GB)*

Adapted by Tennessee Williams from his short play, "The Milk Train Doesn't Stop Here Anymore," this is an oddly comic drama about a dying millionairess (Elizabeth Taylor) who becomes enamored with wondering poet and "Angel of Death" Richard Burton. Filmed in the sunny island of Sardina, the film, considered pretentious and unintentionally funny, was one of the great box-office bombs of the 1960s. Noël Coward is featured as the bitchy Witch of Capri, a role originally written for a woman but played to the faggy hilt by Sir Noël.

> "It's a beautiful picture, the best ever made of one of my plays."
>
> —Tennessee Williams

▼ Secret Ceremony *(1968, 109 min, US)*

This campy psychological thriller stars Elizabeth Taylor as a middle-aged tart who becomes involved in a strange relationship with a mentally unbalanced rich orphan (Mia Farrow). Taylor's character, still in mourning over the loss of a young daughter, finds her emotional and financial needs fulfilled with "poor little doe" Mia. Liz is invited to live at Mia's mansion, where they play mommy and daughter, and soon become involved in mutually destructive emotional mind games. Their relationship is interrupted when Farrow's sexually abusive stepfather (Robert Mitchum) unexpectedly returns, prompting a dramatic escalation in the fevered characters. Interesting lesbian undertones are evident in the relationship of the two women: They take a bath together, Taylor enjoys a Farrow backrub, they kiss in bed, and the most erotically charged scene is when Farrow combs Taylor's long hair, spawning ecstatic looks on Liz's part. ⊛

The Go-Between *(1970, 116 min, GB)*

Julie Christie and Alan Bates star in this brilliant, richly detailed portrait of a forbidden romance and the lasting influence it has on the young boy who served as messenger for the illicit lovers. A visually sumptuous, fascinating study of deception and its lingering effects. Screenplay by Harold Pinter.

The Assassination of Trotsky
(1972, 103 min, GB/France)
Losey's uneven and historically derivative account of the last days of the exiled Trotsky is buoyed by an outstanding performance from Richard Burton as the Russian revolutionary. Alain Delon is effectively enigmatic as the Stalinist assassin sent to Mexico to hunt him down. ⊛

Galileo *(1973, 145 min, GB)*
Topol plays the 17th-century mathematician whose scientific theories on the universe is called heretical by the Catholic Church. Based on Bertolt Brecht's play (which Losey originally staged in its theatrical premiere in the United States in 1947), this was part of the American Film Theatre series. Also starring John Gielgud, Margaret Leighton, Tom Conti and Colin Blakely. ⊛

The Romantic Englishwoman
(1975, 115 min, France/GB)
A tired marriage between a frustrated novelist (Michael Caine) and his bored wife (Glenda Jackson) is stimulated when an attractive gigolo comes into the picture. Elizabeth (Jackson) travels on her own to Baden-Baden to get away from her stifling marriage and meets a poet (Helmut Berger), who's on the run from the mob. Elizabeth soon returns to her family in England and he follows, inveigling himself into the household. The husband, needing inspiration for his book and intrigued by the notion of jealousy, encourages their tryst, until things get out of hand. The sexual dynamics between the three make for intriguing melodrama in this elegantly witty film. Screenplay by Tom Stoppard and Thomas Wiseman. ⊛

Mr. Klein *(1976, 122 min, France)*
This disturbing mystery-drama deals with a self-centered, amoral art dealer (Alain Delon) in Nazi-occupied Paris. He takes advantage of the sweeping anti-Semitism until his world is suddenly shattered when he is mistaken for another — a Jewish Klein. ⊛

Roads to the South *(1978, 100 min, France)*
With cool directorial elegance and subtle perception, Losey creates a complex portrait of a man grappling with deep personal conflicts. Yves Montand stars as an exiled Spanish revolutionary who, after establishing himself as a successful screenwriter abroad, returns to his homeland to fight fascism. He instead battles a lifetime of personal deceptions, illusions and hypocrisies. ⊛

Don Giovanni *(1979, 185 min, France/Italy)*
Losey's brilliant screen adaptation of Mozart's operatic masterpiece features an all-star cast of singers including Jose Van Dam, Kiri Te Kanawa, Ruggero Raimondi and Teresa Berganza. Using a

The Servant

subtle blend of comedia dell'arte and morality play, Losey's loose interpretation of this Don Juan-based legend is a beautiful and bold marriage of opera and cinema. Sumptuously photographed on location in Venice and Vicenza, *Don Giovanni* is a visual treat. ⊛

▼ La Truite *(1982, 105 min, France)*
Isabelle Huppert is coyly sinister in this complex, funny and sensual melodrama about an innocent country girl who moves to Paris with her gay husband (Jacques Spiesser) and vows to succeed in the business world with the aid of her feminine wiles. Jean-Pierre Cassel is a wealthy financier lured by Huppert's coquettish manner, much to the chagrin of his neglected wife (Jeanne Moreau). (Also known as: *The Trout*) ⊛

Steaming *(1985, 95 min, GB)*
Losey's last film is an adaptation of the critically acclaimed play by Neal Dunn, and features the stellar female cast of Vanessa Redgrave, Sarah Miles, Pati Love and Diana Dors (in her final role). Set on "lady's day" at a London bathhouse, six women of wildly divergent backgrounds come together to discuss intimate secrets and commiserate about their place in the world. The production is perhaps a bit stagy, but it is carried by first-rate performances. ⊛

Merchant Ivory Productions
Ismail Merchant & James Ivory

Ivory (l.) & Merchant (r.) with Hopkins; from *Remains of the Day*

In surely what must be one of cinema's longest and most creative partnerships, director James Ivory and producer Ismail Merchant have worked together for over thirty years and have lived together for almost as long. The combination of the soft-spoken Ivory behind the camera with the more bombastic Merchant raising the money and controlling the production might offer the image, as evidenced in their films, of a smooth, trouble-free relationship; but the men are equally hard-willed, agree on the basics and entertain their regular crew members, actors and friends with their constant but benign bickering. Indian actor Shashi Kapoor said of the two men's relationship that it is "more than a marriage." And this unique team would not be complete without screenwriter Ruth Prawer Jhabvala as the third cog in the collaboration. Commenting on their unique relationship, Prawer said that "we're like one of those Hindu deities — with three heads and six arms and six heads. We're one person — a Jew, a Catholic and a Moslem — embodying good and evil." And actress Helena Bonham Carter noted, "Although Ruth is Polish and Jim is West Coast, they're all Indian." The three stay close even off the set with Ivory and Merchant having homes in London, New York's Upper East Side and a country house on the Hudson; and Jhabvala, when not with her husband in India, has an apartment one floor above them in New York.

The results of this union is an impressive collection of works. When *A Room with a View* opened to excited reviews, impressive box office and eventually received eight Academy Award nominations in 1985, it marked a popular and critical appreciation after laboring relatively unknown in the business for twenty-five years. With the exception of the misfire *Slaves of New York*, each succeeding film has been greeted with enthusiasm; their most recent films, *Howards End* and *The Remains of the Day*, represent the team's creative peak.

James Ivory was born in Berkeley, California, in 1928 into a wealthy lumbering family and raised in Oregon. He went to USC's film school where his thesis was *Venice: Theme and Variation*, a 1957 documentary made possible by a $15,000 gift from his father. Merchant was born in bustling Bombay in 1937, the only son of seven children.

His Muslim father operated stalls in the city's bazaar and after graduating college in India, Merchant traveled to the United States to make his mark in the business/entertainment world, although initially his jobs were as a United Nations messenger and, after briefly moving to California, a salesperson in a Los Angeles clothing store. It was there that Merchant also made a short, *The Creation of Women*, which was nominated for an Academy Award in 1961. Ivory's lifelong fascination with India brought the two men together. They met at the Indian Consulate in New York where Ivory was screening a short documentary on Indian miniature pictures. The two hit it off immediately and with $35,000 of Ivory's own money and a Ruth Prawer Jhabvala script in hand, they made *The Householder*. After their second film, *Shakespeare Wallah*, in 1965, Hollywood called and for the only time in their career, the two made a Hollywood-produced film, *The Guru*. But a troubled set, bad reviews and no box office effectively brought their Hollywood chapter to a close. The years following *The Guru* were prolific, creating several small-budget films with settings that alternated between India, London and the East Coast. Their loyal but limited "art" audience was greatly expanded with the release of *A Room with a View*.

It is easy to recognize a Merchant Ivory production: They usually begin with an adaptation by Jhabvala of a English novel and one that remains true to the spirit of the literary work. Writers have included Jean Rhys (*Quartet*), Henry James (*The Europeans, The Bostonians*), E.M. Forster (*A Room with a View, Maurice, Howards End*) and their latest, Kazuo Ishiguro (*The Remains of the Day*). Recurring themes in their films are intercultural conflict, a stranger in a new world, class differences, and repressed (sexually or otherwise) individuals who are offered a chance for freedom from the confines of restrictive conventions. The style of the films are urbane, leisurely paced and imbued with subtle emotional intensity from a cast of exceptionally fine actors. The locales and costuming (most of the films are period pieces) are meticulously detailed and lushly opulent, belying the production's relatively low cost. Their films are not without their detractors, however, who feel that the films are uncomfortably slow, passionless, laborious and pretentious Masterpiece Theatre knockoffs.

Although their E.M. Forster adaptation *Maurice* is considered by many to be a classic gay love story, gay/lesbian themes have been conspicuously absent in their other works. With the exception of Vanessa Redgrave's closeted lesbian character in *The Bostonians*, their films have been devoid of gay characters or issues. Although Merchant discounts this observation, "Homo-, hetero-, or bisexual...the story is what is attractive to me."

In 1993, Merchant Ivory signed a multi-picture deal with Jeffrey Katzenberg's Hollywood Pictures, a subsidiary of Disney Films. This surprising alliance is potentially explosive given the pair's history of independence and Disney's history of artistic interference. The best that can come out of the relationship is a new-found respect for filmmakers by Disney, and Merchant Ivory finally enjoying a dedicated source of funding and an established distribution system to get their works from the art houses and into the multi-screen suburban complexes of mid-America.

In development is *Jefferson in Paris*, to star Nick Nolte and Greta Scacchi. Ruth Prawer Jhabvala will pen the screenplay.

"If someone gave me $10 million to do a film, I wouldn't be very happy."
—Ismail Merchant on the joys of low-budget filmmaking

"A keen sense of the exquisite goes into making Merchant Ivory magic."
—Janet Maslin, *The New York Times*

Householder *(1962, 101 min, India)*
The first collaboration between director Ivory, producer Merchant and writer Ruth Prawer Jhabvala is this delightful and warmhearted but uneven comedy. Shashi Kapoor plays a young teacher who, pushed by his meddlesome mother, enters into an arranged marriage with a woman equally naive and inexperienced. Their troubles soon escalate as they find themselves unprepared for the difficulties of marriage and its financial responsibilities. While not one of the trio's best works, the film provides an interesting background for their future films. ⊗

Shakespeare Wallah *(1965, 120 min, India)*
The setting is India during the last days of the British Raj, when the struggling nation was trying to free themselves of British rule. Amidst all of this turmoil, an English Shakespearean acting troupe valiantly tours the countryside. The story concerns the budding love affair between the daughter of one of the actors and a young Indian. Their infatuation and innocence and persistence amidst the political upheaval help make this a charming and delightful tale. ⊗

The Guru *(1968, 112 min, US/India)*
East meets West in this drama featuring Michael York as a '60s rock star who travels to India ostensibly to learn the sitar from a worldy guru but soon discovers much more. Slowly paced, the film's emphasis is on the spiritual India. Rita Tushingham is featured as an Englishwoman on a spiritual quest.

Bombay Talkie *(1970, 108 min, India)*
Lucia (Jennifer Kendal), an American novelist, arrives in India in a desperate search for new sensations and experiences which will help her forget her approaching middle age. She soon meets and begins an affair with Vikram (Shashi Kapoor), a dazzling movie actor. Vikram eventually leaves his wife and family and destroys his life and career in a futile pursuit of an image that does not exist. ⊗

Savages *(1972, 106 min, US)*
By far the most offbeat result of the years of their collaboration, this is the story of a group of clay-covered savages who stumble across an abandoned mansion. Bit by bit, they assume the roles of the former, more civilized inhabitants until finally they have constructed their own little microcosm of the landed gentry. This strange and hypnotic film evokes images of *King of Hearts* and *The Emerald Forest*. ⊗

"A ridiculous premise for a film, as we all know, a joke but not quite a joke."
—James Ivory

The Wild Party *(1974, 107 min, US)*
Veteran character actor James Coco gives a poignant performance in a rare lead role as a fading silent comic in this evocative drama loosely based on the Fatty Arbuckle scandal. The wild Hollywood party that he and girlfriend Raquel Welch host, intended to harken his comeback, ends in murder and tragedy. ⊗

Autobiography of a Princess
(1975, 59 min, GB)
This delicate character study stars James Mason and Merchant Ivory favorite Madhur Jaffrey as an imperious princess, self-exiled in London and long-divorced. She invites her father's ex-tutor to a yearly tea to reminisce about a "happier" past, only to find that their memories of a Royal India differ. ⊗

Roseland *(1977, 103 min, US)*

Set in the famed, but at the time faded, New York dance hall, *Roseland* is a collection of three short character vignettes studying the tattered lives of the people who gravitate to the club. The three stories are all eloquent and quietly moving peeks into the lives of several lost and lonely characters. Exceptional performances come from Christopher Walken, Joan Copeland, Lou Jacobi, Lilia Skala, Geraldine Chaplin and Helen Gallagher. ⊛

Hullabaloo Over Georgie and Bonnie's Pictures *(1978, 82 min, GB/India)*

This film is a lighthearted romp through royal India — a world of princesses, palaces, tourists, precious art objects and the people who wheel and deal them. What's all the hullabaloo about? Georgie owns a priceless collection of ancient paintings which he loves, but his sister wants more practical objects and wants him to sell. Frantic art dealers are soon in hot pursuit as the royal couple are deluged with people who want to buy. A great double twist ending concludes this exotic film. ⊛

The Europeans *(1979, 92 min, US)*

Lee Remick stars in this lush adaptation of Henry James' novel about a 19th-century New England family whose lives are disrupted by the arrival of two European cousins — one a meddlesome, fortune-hunting countess. ⊛

Jane Austen in Manhattan *(1980, 108 min, GB)*

Two rival New York theatre companies vie for the rights to produce a recently unearthed Jane Austen manuscript written when she was 12-years-old. One wants to produce the piece as a period operetta, the other wants to make it an avant-garde performance piece. It's an interesting premise; however, the film is not one of the best to come out of the Merchant/Ivory/Jhabvala mill. ⊛

Quartet *(1981, 101 min, GB/France)*

This adaptation of Jean Rhys' novel stars Isabelle Adjani as a young woman who, upon being stranded in Paris, falls prey to a beguiling British couple played by Alan Bates and Maggie Smith. Excellent performances and Ivory's steady hand at the helm make this tale of hedonism and treachery a spine-tingling treat. ⊛

Heat and Dust *(1982, 130 min, GB)*

Lush and romantic, this tale, adapted by Ruth Prawer Jhabvala from her own novel, intercuts between 1920s India and the present in telling the story of two British women's parallel absorption into the mystical and carnal realm of the Far East. Julie Christie plays the independent contemporary woman who physically traces her roots through the life of her scandalous great-aunt, played by Greta Scacchi in a dazzling debut. ⊛

Vanessa Redgrave and Madeleine Potter in *The Bostonians*

Julian Sands and Denholm Elliott in *A Room with a View*

The Courtesans of Bombay
(1982, 74 min, India, Ismail Merchant)
In Ismail Merchant's first directorial effort, this intriguing and entertaining story follows the inhabitants of Pavanpul, the courtesan quarters, who by day carry on their daily domestic lives and by night, thrill and delight with exuberant singing, dancing and sex. Filmed in a pseudo-documentary fashion, the film is more of interest for its sociological stance rather than entertainment value. ⊛

▼ The Bostonians *(1984, 122 min, GB)*
An exceptionally strong performance by Vanessa Redgrave and a commendable portrayal from Christopher Reeve highlight this adaptation of Henry James' novel. Set in 19th-century New England, the story concerns a love triangle in which Redgrave, an early feminist heroine and repressed lesbian, and Reeve, a reactionary Southern lawyer, battle for the love (and political soul) of a young girl (Madeleine Potter). [Heterosexuality wins.] Ruth Prawer Jhabvala gleaned the emotional core out of James' work and her screenplay unearths the story's underlying passion. ⊛

A Room with a View *(1985, 115 min, GB)*
The first of three adaptations of the works of gay novelist E.M. Forster, this was a huge art-house success. Forster's classic novel of the sexual awakening of a young woman amidst the emotional repression of Victorian England is brilliantly captured in this comedy-of-manners. During a trip to Florence, Lucy's (Helena Bonham Carter) simmering sensuality is exposed when she meets and falls in love with a free-spirited and handsome young man. Chronicling the struggle between this love and the expectations of a "proper society," the film features uniformly outstanding performances by Maggie Smith as her insufferable aunt and Daniel Day-Lewis as her prissy English suitor. Also starring Denholm Elliott, Simon Callow, Julian Sands, Rupert Graves and Judi Dench. ⊛

▼ Maurice *(1987, 149 min, GB)*
Now considered a classic gay novel, "Maurice," E.M. Forster's self-suppressed 1914 love story, was not published until after his death in 1970. With the same reverence, sensitivity and regal authority that they brought to his *A Room with a View*, Merchant Ivory Productions has created an exquisite and sexually bold adaptation of the author's semiautobiographical novel. Set in pre-WWI England, the film examines the social and sexual repression of the era in this story of the emotional conflict facing a college student coming to terms with his homosexuality. James Wilby is perfectly cast in the title role, Hugh Grant gives a precise performance as his frustratingly platonic lover who transforms from free-spirit to social prig, and Rupert Graves is splendid as Alec, the handsome gamekeeper who awakens Maurice's dormant feelings. Their romantic first night together is filmed with a sexual longing that is both lyrical and erotic. Forster was reportedly determined to give

the book it's happy, if improbable ending and the result is an inspiring tale of a gay love that transcends class and social barriers. ⊗

Slaves of New York *(1989, 125 min, US)*

The transition from Edwardian England to the heady go-go days of 1980s New York failed in this disappointing and uninvolving screen version of Tama Janowitz's best-selling novel. Set against the trendy New York art scene, this episodic tale features Bernadette Peters as a struggling East Village hat designer involved in an impossible love affair with a self-centered artist. ⊗

Mr. & Mrs. Bridge *(1990, 105 min, US)*

A leisurely but fine character study highlighted by two bravura performances from Paul Newman and especially Joanne Woodward as an upper middle-class Kansas City husband and wife. Based on two Evan S. Connell novels, "Mr. Bridge" and "Mrs. Bridge," the film, set in the years between the two World Wars, examines with razor-sharp intensity and formidable wit the couple's everyday, and even mundane existence. A series of continuing and perfectly construct-

James Wilby and Rupert Graves as lovers in *Maurice*

ed stories, the film's most memorable scenes include Newman's "battle" with a tornado and Woodward's astonishing reaction at her son's Boy Scout meeting. ⊗

Howards End *(1992, 140 Min, GB)*

Merchant Ivory's third E.M. Forster adaptation is a sumptuous re-creation of the class struggle in the dying days of the Edwardian era. The story centers around the tragic confluence of three families from London's various social strata. Vanessa Redgrave and Anthony Hopkins personify the upper crust as the Wilcoxes. The Schlegel sisters (Emma Thompson and Helena Bonham Carter) represent the liberal middle class. And Leonard Bast (Sam West), an educated Cockney trying to make his way into the world of business, embodies the lower depths. Filmed with all of the pomp and circumstance one has come to expect of their films, and acted with loving attention to both the mannerisms and prose of the era, *Howards End* is a truly marvelous and engaging period piece. Thompson won a well-deserved Oscar for her portrayal of the elder Schlegel. ⊗

The Remains of the Day
(1993, 137 min, GB)

The unequivocal masterpiece of the Merchant/Ivory/Jhabvala collaboration. Spare in plot yet devastatingly powerful in its theme of repressed emotions and self-disillusionment, the deceptively simple story simmers with complex, unexpressed passions by its main characters. Adapted from Kazuo Ishiguro's 1989 subtly moving and quietly desolate novel, the story is set in a stately English manor with action being intercut from its 1930s heyday to its faded glory and near abandonment in the 1950s. In a magnificent performance, Anthony Hopkins stars as Stevens, the manor's long-time butler. With an unswerving and unquestioned devotion to his employer, Lord Darlington (James Fox), Stevens sacrifices any semblance of a personal life to serve what one discovers to be a well-meaning but incompetent Nazi sympathizer. As he looks back on his life and work, Stevens' greatest regret is the unconsummated relationship with the vivacious Miss Keaton (Emma Thompson), possibly the one person who could have given meaning to his life. Though this sounds somber and heavy-handed, the film is witty and entertaining, and is beautifully composed; even the slightest gesture by its characters creates almost unbearable tension and joy. ⊗

In Custody
(1994, 123 Min, GB, Ismail Merchant)

Ismail Merchant returns to behind the camera in this pleasant comedy-of-manners set in a small northern Indian town. A poor, under-appreciated schoolteacher and aspiring poet is assigned to interview Nur (Shashi Kapoor), a great Urdu poet. When he arrives and gets finally gets past Nur's two bickering wives, he sees the great writer now near the end of life — obese, sickly, cantankerous and confined primarily to his home. The film revolves around a series of aborted interviews (family, friends, food and sex seem to always interrupt them). One suspects that this simple story is actually a pretext for Merchant to offer lively discussions on the fading Urdu culture and language, and to have his actors read from the writings of the great Urdu poet Faiz Ahmad Faiz.

ROBERT MOORE

Although Robert Moore's professional life was primarily spent in the theatre both as an actor and director, he also worked in film, specializing in directing Neil Simon adaptations. His career was cut short when he died in 1984 at the age of 56. Moore was openly gay and once played a gay paraplegic in *Tell Me That You Love Me, Junie Moon*, but his films, with the exception of employing gays (Truman Capote, James Coco) were devoid of gay content.

Born in Detroit in 1927, Moore attended Catholic University and had a one-year stint in the military before seeking his fortunes on the Broadway stage. His acting debut came in the 1948 play "Jenny Kissed Me" and later successes included "The Owl and the Pussycat" and "Cactus Flower." During the 1950s, he also appeared on live TV. His Broadway directorial debut was with Mart Crowley's "The Boys in the Band" and what followed were a string of successes with Neil Simon: "Promises, Promises" (which he called "my butch musical"), "The Last of the Red Hot Lovers," "The Gingerbread Lady" and "They're Playing Our Song." Other non-Simon plays include "Woman of the Year" and "Deathtrap." Moore also directed the TV version of "Cat on a Hot Tin Roof" starring Laurence Olivier and Maureen Stapleton.

Tell Me That You Love Me, Junie Moon *(1969, 113 min, US, Otto Preminger)*

A deserved, overly sentimental flop about three emotionally and physically impaired outcasts who seek comfort and understanding by moving in together. The cast includes Liza Minnelli, who hyperventilates as a facially scarred young woman, and Ken Howard as a stuttering epileptic. Moore also stars as Warren, a gay paraplegic. It's hinted that his homosexuality is the result of being raised by a queeny stepfather (Leonard Frey); and later in the film, he is happily "cured" of one affliction (homosexuality) after a tryst with a black prostitute!

Thursday's Game *(1974, 100 min, US)*

Moore made an impressive comedic debut with this made-for-TV satire about two poker-playing buddies, and peppered with veteran comedians and TV sitcom personalities including Bob Newhart, Gene Wilder, Cloris Leachman, Rob Reiner, Nancy Walker and Valerie Harper. Scripted by James L. Brooks, the story revolves around the hectic work and home life of buddies Newhart and Wilder. ⊛

▼ Murder by Death *(1976, 94 min, US)*

Neil Simon wrote the screenplay for this delightfully zany spoof of movie detectives. An all-star cast does a number on Nick and Nora Charles (David Niven and Maggie Smith), Miss Marple (Elsa Lanchester), Charlie Chan (Peter Sellers), Hercule Poirot (James Coco) and Sam Spade (Peter Falk). The sleuths are summoned by millionaire Lionel Twain (a hilarious Truman Capote) to solve a particularly baffling murder. In one of the many red-herring revelations, it's disclosed that Sam Diamond (Falk) was picked up by Twain in a gay bar. Diamond explains, "I was working on a case." His girlfriend (Eileen Brennan) asks, "Every night for six months?" In the next scene, it's revealed that Diamond made up the scenario, though his girlfriend still wonders, "Why do you keep all those naked musclemen magazines in your office?" "Suspects!" ⊛

The Cheap Detective *(1978, 92 min, US)*

There are lots of laughs in Neil Simon's follow-up to *Murder by Death*. Peter Falk stars in this private eye parody (*The Maltese Falcon* in particular), ably assisted by Eileen Brennan ("If its something cheap you're looking for"), Ann-Margret, Dom DeLuise, Stockard Channing, James Coco, Madeline Kahn, Sid Caesar and Phil Silvers. Who cares if some of the jokes are forced, the film is in good humor and what a cast. ⊛

Moore (l.) with Ken Howard in *Tell Me That You Love Me, Junie Moon*

Chapter Two *(1979, 124 min, US)*

Neil Simon's autobiographical drama stars James Caan as a recently widowed novelist who meets recently divorced Marsha Mason. The two begin a romance but the scars of their personal loses soon affect the relationship. A bit somber for Simon although the film has moments of wit. Moore's final film. ⊛

F. W. MURNAU

Born Friedreich Wilhelm Plume in 1888 in Bielefeld, Germany, F.W. Murnau, the name which he used throughout his life, studied art and literature at the University of Heidelberg and later apprenticed under famed director Max Reinhardt. Well over six-feet-tall, his head ablaze in a tousle of red, Murnau's chances of making it as an actor were limited at best. This steered Murnau in another direction. Like Ernst Lubitsch, who was also studying under Reinhardt, Murnau watched the master director closely. After an intermission necessitated by World War I, Murnau found himself comfortably ensconced in Switzerland having landed there due to either a heavy fog or his poor abilities as a pilot. He passed most of the time directing amateur theatricals and working on propaganda films for their German embassy. By 1919 he was back in his homeland directing many films whose prints no longer exist.

As a director, Murnau can be ranked among the few greats of the silent era, one who greatly advanced the vocabulary of cinema. Under Murnau's cultured hand, mise-en-scene began to express for the first time psychological relationships.

In 1922, he began the film that would bring him international fame: an unauthorized version of Bram Stoker's gothic novel, "Dracula." In a half-hearted attempt to obfuscate the roots, Murnau called his film *Nosferatu*, and rechristened all the characters. Other than that, the film was more faithful to the novel than the 1931 Bela Lugosi film. Rather than employ some German expressionistic trick of stylized sets and dark shadows, Murnau chose to shoot on real locations, setting the nightmare firmly in the real world. Two years later, he created what many consider the greatest German silent ever, *The Last Laugh*.

By now Murnau had surrounded himself with a virtual repertory company of gay men who would work on all his projects on both sides of the camera. None was more talented than character actor Emil Jannings who, under Murnau's tutelage, would become such a big star that even the Nazis were willing to overlook his homosexuality and allow him to make propaganda films throughout the war. The international success of *The Last Laugh* led to entreats from Hollywood where Murnau created what *Cahiers du Cinéma* 25 years later would call the greatest film of all time: *Sunrise*. A story oddly lyrical, it's a dark tale of deceit and redemption when a country boy and girl go wrong in the big city.

F.W. Murnau giving direction

Two minor films followed and it was not until he formed a partnership with famed documentarian Robert Flaherty that he had a project worthy of his talents. Set in a magical, tropical paradise, *Tabu* (1931) is part documentary, part idyll. When the two strong-willed directors clashed, Murnau bought Flaherty out and it become totally his picture.

Murnau was stunned when a cavalier visit to an astrologer led to a prediction of tragedy if Murnau drove cross-country to attend the New York premiere of *Tabu*. Determined to be present at the event, he decided to travel by boat instead. Unfortunately for him, he allowed his 14-year-old Filipino valet Garcia Stevenson to drive him to the dock. They never made it. For years afterwards, the rumor favored by the rogues in Hollywood was that the poor lad's loss of control over the car was precipitated by his loss of control elsewhere — he came and went at the same time. Murnau was 42.

In addition to the films described below, Murnau's other films include several German films (now lost), including *Der Knabe in Blau* (*The Boy in Blue*) (1919), a film based on Gainsborough's painting; *The Grand Duke's Finances* (1924), a drama starring *Nosferatu's* Max Schreck; a silent film version of Moliere's *Tartuffe* (1926);

and *Faust* (1926), a lavish expressionist classic which starred Emil Jannings as the evil Mephistopheles. Murnau also made two American films, *Four Devils* (1929) and *City Girl* (1929), a film which was mutilated and transformed into a talkie by its producer after Murnau's death.

> "I am at home nowhere, in no house, and in no country."
> —Murnau in a letter to his mother

Nosferatu *(1922, 63 min, Germany)*
Murnau's "symphony of horror" is the first, and most macabre, of all the film versions of the legendary vampire, Count Dracula. Max Schreck's loathsome count, with his bald head, rodent face, long pointed ears, skeleton-like frame and talons, will chill the most callous viewer. ⊛

The Last Laugh *(1924, 73 min, Germany)*
One of the classics from Germany's "Golden Era," *The Last Laugh* features the great (and gay) Emil Jannings as the proud doorman of a luxury hotel who is demoted to washroom attendant. Once envied and respected by his neighbors, the baffled old man sees his world and status crumble; but in a surprise ending, he still gets the last laugh. That ironic ending was tacked on by Murnau after the studio decried its downbeat ending. German actress Lotte Eisner once said of the film, "This is a German tragedy that can only be understood in a country where uniform is king, not to say god." ⊛

Sunrise *(1927, 110 min, US)*
In his first U.S. film, Murnau curtailed the usual heaviness of German expressionism, evoking a deceptively American sort of souffle which foreshadowed the transparent narrative style of the talkies. Considered the apex of the art of the silents, it tells an unnervingly bleak tale about a married country boy whose life is ruined by a heartless vamp. Janet Gaynor won an Academy Award for her unforgettable performance as the wife. ⊛

Tabu

Tabu *(1931, 82 min, US/Tahiti)*
Filmed entirely on the seemingly idyllic island of Tahiti, and made through the unusual collaboration between directors Murnau and Robert Flaherty (*Nanook of the North*), *Tabu* is an early, rarely seen masterpiece. Set amidst the glistening sun and fine sand beaches of the island, the film tells the tragic tale of two young lovers, forced to separate after a tribal edict calls the girl "tabu" to all the men of the village. The video transfer is taken from a strikingly beautiful print that was restored by the UCLA film archives. ⊛

Nosferatu

SERGEI PARADJANOV

Always a nationalistic thorn in the Soviet Union's side with his controversial, regionally nationalistic films celebrating ancient myths and traditions, Sergei Paradjanov is considered one of the former Soviet Union's greatest directors who, upon his death in 1993, left behind an enigmatic collection of beautifully composed films dealing with Ukranian, Armenian and Georgian rural folk legends. Like Pier Paolo Pasolini, Paradjanov's singularly poetic visions were tinged with homosexual undercurrents, which caused the authorities to repeatedly persecute him. While Pasolini successfully battled in the courts for his artistic freedom, Paradjanov had the misfortune to work in the control-minded and homophobic Soviet Union, where the suppression of his films and eventual imprisonment succeeded in diminishing the man's artistic output.

Born Sarkis Paradjanian in Soviet Tbilsi, Georgia, of prosperous Armenian parents in 1924, Paradjanov played the violin, was educated at the Kiev Conservatory of Music and studied cinematography and film at the Moscow Film Institute. After working as an assistant director, his directorial debut was with the 1954 film, *Andriesh*. Though several films followed (all dismissed by Paradjanov as "failures"), it wasn't until the 1966 feature *Shadows of Forgotten Ancestors* in which Paradjanov received international acclaim. Soviet officials, however, viewing his works as imbued with offending "mysticism and subjective thinking," refused to allow him to travel abroad to film festivals and did not grant permission to make another film for several years.

In 1974, he was arrested under Article 121 of the Soviet Criminal Code (a "law" invoked many times by the KBG to imprison and effectively end the careers of many dissenters). He was absurdly charged with "incitement to suicide, speculation in foreign currency, spreading venereal disease, homosexuality and speculation in art objects." Despite the fact that homosexuality was not a criminal offense (homosexual acts are, however), the government succeeded in attaining a guilty charge and a sentence of five years of hard labor. Paying the price for what many of his colleagues believed to be his controversial films, Soviet officials, under pressure from Europeans and Americans, released him after serving a little more than four years. For over a decade after his release, he was refused permission to make another film, until 1985 when he returned to Georgia where he made *The Legend of Suram Fortress* and

Sergei Paradjanov

Ashik Kerib, despite constant government interference and continued charges of illegal currency dealings and bribery.

A burly, naturally gregarious and pointedly opinionated man, Paradjanov's career was cut short by a heart attack late in 1988 and his sudden death in 1993. His demise is especially sad given the impending collapse of the Soviet empire and resulting increase in Paradjanov's ability to expand on singular themes. Planned projects at the time of his death included a German production of "Faust" and a version of Longfellow's "Hiawatha" slated to be filmed in America.

A true cinematic original (who warned "that anyone who tries to imitate me is lost") as well as a painter, sketch artist and screenwriter, the film legacy that Sergei Paradjanov leaves behind is one of a dreamlike visual splendor which provides a document of an artist whose singular vision shone brightly during the darkest times of Soviet artistic repression. In his career, Paradjanov made three documentaries and six features (several of these confiscated by Soviet authorities). The following four films are the only films of Sergei Paradjanov to have been released in the States. He did other films, notably, *The First Lad* (1958), *Ukranian Rhapsody* (1959), and *A Little Flower on a Stone* (1962).

"I think the best filmmaking would be for the deaf and dumb. We talk too much, and there are too many words. Only in ballet do we see pure beauty, pure pantomime. That is what I am aspiring to."

—Sergei Paradjanov

Shadows of Forgotten Ancestors

(1964, 99 min, Ukraine)

The historical pageantry and epic legends of medieval times are enacted in this visually and musically vibrant love story. Set in 19th-century Ukraine, the drama centers around a young man who is trapped in a loveless marriage and haunted by his true, but dead, sweetheart. But make no mistake about its simple plot, for the film is a wonderful compendium of folk dances, religious zealousness and witchcraft. Mysteriously cryptic and erotic, it is filmed in a psychedelic rampage and has more spectacular effects, camera movements, wild experiments with color, and bizarre musical scenes than anyone could imagine in one film. ☮

> "I was put into prison for my films and for my sharp tongue. I shot *Shadows of Forgotten Ancestors* in Ukranian. Moscow wanted me to dub it into Russian and I refused."
>
> —Paradjanov

The Color of Pomegranates
(Red Pomegranates, Sayat Nova)

(1969, 75 min, Russia/Armenia)

Shelved after being termed "hermetic and obscure" by Soviet authorities, this poetic masterpiece was the last film Paradjanov made before his five-year imprisonment in 1974. *The Color of Pomegranates* focuses on the powerful works and spiritual odyssey of 17th-century Armenian poet Sayat Nova. Filled with oblique, symbolic imagery, this exotic mosaic of a film is divided into eight sections, each depicting, from childhood to death, a period of the poet's life. A tribute not only to Nova but to the spirituality of the Armenian people, Paradjanov's film is for specialized tastes and those devotees who have a knowledge of or interest in the poet and Armenia. ☮

▼ The Legend of Suram Fortress

(1985, 87 min, Georgia)

Based on ancient Georgian legend and dedicated to all Georgian warriors killed in defense of the Motherland, this unique, but for most viewers inscrutable tale has minimal dialogue and dazzling visuals. When a newly built Georgian fortress mysteriously collapses, the townspeople are at a loss and vulnerable to attack. An aging soothsayer claims that the only way to keep the walls standing is to have the son of the lover who jilted her buried alive inside the walls. Intoxicatingly abstract — part fairy tale, part Georgian folk legend, part Arabian Nights. ☮

> "An elliptical Arabian Nights fantasy...a challenging but rewarding experence."
>
> —*Los Angeles Times*

> "Extraordinary...delirious mixtures of gravity and humor...heterosexuality and homoeroticism."
>
> —*Time Out*

Ashik Kerib *(1988, 75 min, Georgia)*

Dedicated to the memory of Andrei Tarkovsky, Paradjanov's final film, co-directed with David Abashidzi, is an exotic and ebullient Georgian folk tale based on a story by Mikhail Lermontov. Although pregnant with symbolism and with oblique nationalist references of Georgia's ancient culture, the film remains accessible and even quite enjoyable; essentially because of its age old story of love conquering all. A handsome but poor minstrel whom "providence has given natural beauty and a good heart" must travel through the countryside to earn enough money to marry his young love, the beautiful daughter of a rich Turkish merchant. His fantastic adventures are spectacularly filmed in poetic and symbolic imagery — with scenes filled with strange creatures, flying carpets, spinning tigers and magic. Having little dialogue, this episodic story is infused with striking visuals and hypnotic traditional music and dances. If the film is interpreted as autobiographical, the minstrel can be seen as the director himself, an outcast artist and persecuted homosexual. It's often obscurely surreal but nevertheless riveting. Paradjanov was quoted as saying that, "The film ends like an American film. It has a happy ending." ☮

Ashik Kerib

PIER PAOLO PASOLINI

A gay Renaissance man for 20th-century arts, Pier Paolo Pasolini has achieved a legendary status as a provocative, scandalous and indisputably controversial figure. His personal, often contradictory beliefs permeated his work, for he was a fervent Marxist, an atheist (but with closeted quasi-Catholic tendencies), and an unapologetic and outspoken homosexual who was not only a filmmaker but a critically acclaimed poet, literary critic, essayist, linguist, screenwriter, teacher, painter and novelist. It was said that the three most important men in his life were Jesus Christ, Karl Marx and Sigmund Freud.

Despite his successes, he remained throughout his life an outsider, even an enemy of the powers-that-be. The ruling Right viewed him with unfettered distrust for his leftist beliefs; the Communists threw him out of the party because of a gay sex scandal; the Church thought of him as an immoral and blasphemous figure. His notoriety brought him into constant battle with the law, and his films and novels were often banned, with Pasolini being brought to trial almost a dozen times on charges of obscenity and blasphemy. Never one to shirk from the harsh spotlight, Pasolini took delight in vigorously defending his works, often writing long analytical essays on his films and novels.

Born in 1922 in the northern Italian city of Bologna, Pier Paolo's father was a fascist soldier of noble stock, but he identified throughout his life with his peasant-born mother. This identification, even obsession (both professionally and sexually), with the lower classes was conspicuous. His films usually focused on the plight of the sub-proletariat, and he used non-actors and people from the streets to act in his films. His sexual partners were usually these same street toughs. Filmmaking was not his first career, however. While growing up, poetry was his first love and today in Italy, he is considered one of their most important contemporary poets. When he finished college, young Pasolini moved to Rome where he began writing both poetry and novels. His first novels, "Una Vita Violenta" ("A Violent Life") and "Ragazzi de Vita" were popular, but viewed by the government as obscene. "Una Vita Violenta" led to his first trial, but Pasolini was acquitted. Before directing, Pasolini was a screenwriter on over 15 productions including Federico Fellini's *Nights of Cabiria* and Bernardo Bertolucci's *The Grim Reaper*.

With his first feature, the neorealist drama *Accattone*, Pasolini's contentious career began. While his film style and techniques evolved through the years, all of his films share

Pasolini

similar themes. These include religion (it's intrinsic power, corruption and folly), Marxism and the class struggle, mythology, sensuality, and sexuality. Pasolini's poetic treatment and an intellectual, revolutionary approach contribute to unify his body of work, which from 1954 to 1975 included 20 films and over 50 books.

Many saw his sensationalistic death in 1975 at the age of 53 as an appropriate epilogue to his dark vision of life as depicted in *Saló, or the 120 Days of Sodom*. But many others are not so convinced. The facts reported by the authorities are that a 17-year-old hustler, angered by Pasolini's sexual advances, lost control and brutally beat him up, smashed his skull and ran him over repeatedly in Pasolini's own Alfa Romero. Despite doubts on the accuracy of this scenario, and the likelihood that others were involved, the courts decided that the young man acted alone. That verdict on Pasolini's mysterious death has continued to fuel theories that enemies in either government, the police or the Church orchestrated his death. Today, the truth surrounding his death remains unknown.

"The world no longer wants me and doesn't know it."
—Pier Paolo Pasolini (1962)

"The more I live, the less faith I have in mankind."
—Pasolini

"Pasolini is one of the most original and perverse film poets of his generation. It's not always necessary to understand Pasolini to be riveted by what he does."
—Vincent Canby, *The New York Times*

Accattone *(1961, 120 min, Italy)*

Pasolini's first feature film is a harrowing, realistic and unsentimental look inside the slums of Rome, where its denizens — the prostitutes, hustlers and petty thieves — attempt to eke out an existence any way they can. Within this underworld of corruption is Accattone (Franco Citti), a young pimp who is torn between the easy pickings on the street and his efforts, motivated by love, to go straight. A brutal slice-of-life film which documents Pasolini's lifelong obsession with the outcasts of society. Pasolini was assisted on the film by a young Bernardo Bertolucci. ☻

Mamma Roma *(1962, 110 min, Italy)*

Set against the poverty- and crime-stricken slums of Rome, this anguished drama stars Anna Magnani as a prostitute whose efforts to bring about a better life for her teenage son are squashed by the hopelessness of her impoverished condition. Decidedly Marxist in philosophy.

▼ La Ricotta *(1962, 40 min, Italy)*

Made as part of the omnibus film, *RoGaPoG*, this short is a hilariously irreverent religious farce. At the Cinecittà film studio near Rome, a seemingly disinterested director (played by Orson Welles) begins shooting a film dealing with Christ's Crucifixion. Among the cast is a Jesus who has sex with boys in the bushes, and a peasant who plays one of the thieves crucified alongside Jesus — the actor literally dies on the cross, but not of inflicted wounds, but of indigestion caused by too much ice cream! The shocking comedy was seized by the government for insulting the religion of the state and Pasolini received a four-month suspended sentence for his "crime."

La Rabbia (The Anger) *(1963, 50 min, Italy)*

This was originally planned as half of a two-part documentary, but only Pasolini's segment was completed. This short is a passionate and poetic documentary that rails against history's continual succession of repressive governments and the resulting injustices and oppressions inflicted on the populace. Using extensive newsreel footage, the film presents a nearly unbearable montage of events including scenes of the Hungarian revolt, Castro's revolution, the Korean War, the Algerian War, and Arabs and Jews at Suez. Interspersed with the violence are shots of Ava Gardner's visit to Rome, Queen Elizabeth's coronation, Sophia Loren, and Marilyn Monroe's death. The crescendo is a collage of 30 atomic explosions.

> "It is a cry of anguish, a scream of rage. The profound moral fervor of this lonely genius burns through every frame of this subversive masterpiece."
> —Amos Vogal

> "As long as man exploits man, as long as humanity is divided into masters and slaves, there can be no normality, no peace."
> —Pier Paolo Pasolini

The Gospel According to Matthew
(1964, 135 min, Italy)

Dedicated to the memory of Pope John XXIII, Pasolini's remarkable film is a modern interpretation of Christ, told entirely through the writings of St. Matthew. Using non-professionals and filmed in a realistic, pseudo-documentary fashion in the arid regions of Calabria in southern Italy, the film depicts Jesus Christ as a man of the people and a revolutionary, fighting the social injustices of the time. Yet despite his faithful use of the scriptures, the film is imbued with a Marxist ideology, a situation which produced confused acclaim from Church leaders (the film was partly financed by the Church). Pasolini conspicuously did not include "St." in the film's title, although it was later added by the distributors. Look for Pasolini's mother in the role of Mary Magdalene. ☻

Love Meetings *(1964, 90 min, Italy)*

Love Meetings is a gritty cinema verité-style investigation of sex in Italy. The film includes appearances by author Alberto Moravia and noted psychologist Cesare Musatti. Pasolini interviews a wide range of individuals of varying ages and economic backgrounds to share their tales of love — including their thoughts on prostitution, homosexuality, jealousy, chastity, divorce and extramarital affairs. In reference to homosexuality, many replied that they felt pity while a businessman says, "In cases of that sort, I feel disgust, horror." ☻

Accattone

Hawks and Sparrows *(1966, 88 min, Italy)*

This post-neorealist parable is an unconventional story featuring Italy's beloved stone-faced clown Toto as an Everyman who, with his empty-headed son, travels the road of life accompanied by a Marxist talking crow, who waxes philosophically and amusingly on the passing scene. On their travels, they meet St. Francis who implores them to convert the crow to Christianity! Pasolini presents a tragic fable which shows two delightful innocents caught between the Church and Marxism. ☻

The Gospel According to Matthew

Oedipus Rex *(1967, 110 min, Italy)*

Filmed in and around an awesome, 15th-century adobe city in the Moroccan desert, Pasolini's version of the Oedipus legend retains the basic elements of Sophocles' classic tragedy. A young man, abandoned at birth by his parents, is foretold of his doomed fate by an oracle; nonetheless, he unknowingly murders his father and marries his mother. This tragic story of a man's intractable road to his destiny glistens with lavish costumes, bloody sword fights, sun-drenched locales and expressive performances by Franco Citti and Silvana Mangano. Pasolini once described this as being "the most autobiographical of my films." ⊛

▼ Teorema (Theorem) *(1968, 93 min, Italy)*

Pasolini's fusion of Marxism, sex and religion stars Terence Stamp as a divine stranger who enters the troubled household of a bourgeois family and profoundly effects their lives when he seduces the mother, father, son, daughter and maid. A surreal and sensual allegory with the Pasolini postulation that the ruling class can be undermined and destroyed by the one thing that it can not control — sex. Despite winning the Grand Prix at the Venice Film Festival in 1968, the film was publicly denounced by Pope Paul VI and banned as obscene in Italy. Pasolini was arrested but in a celebrated trial, was ultimately acquitted of all charges. ⊛

> "The most talked about foreign film of the year! Truly amazing in its decidedly homoerotic bias and extraordinary groin-oriented camera set-ups."
>
> —*Variety*

Porcile (Pigsty)

(1968, 99 min, Italy/France)

Two contrasting stories are interwoven in a single narrative in Pasolini's biting satire on society's darker nature and the entrenched powers-that-be who are compelled to squash it. One tale, set in a barren, mountainous land in medieval times, features Pierre Clementi as a wandering soldier who descends into cannibalism, eventually recruiting a cult of followers who feed the heads of its victims to the fiery volcano Mt. Etna. The contrasting story, set in modern times, stars Jean-Pierre Leaud as the bourgeois son of a former Nazi, now a successful industrialist, who is politically and sexually confused — so confused as to prefer the sexual companionship of his neighboring peasant's pigs to his attractive (and frustrated) fiancée (Anne Wiazemsky). While not as explicitly outrageous as *Saló, or the 120 Days of Sodom*, nor as whimsical as *The Decameron*, this brutal allegory of savage "innocents" and their threat to organized society is quite intense and involving. ⊛

Medea

(1970, 100 min, Italy/France/Germany)

With *Medea*, Pasolini presents a troubling vision of Euripides' classic tragedy. Soprano Maria Callas, in her only non-musical role (her voice, however, is dubbed), gives an intense and fascinating interpretation of a woman who kills her brother in support of her beloved Jason. But after Jason leaves her for Glauce, the daughter of King Creon, Medea enacts a terrible revenge with the help of magical powers. Pasolini has suggested a Marxist interpretation of the tragedy — with Medea representing the Third World's calamitous relationship with the materialistic nations of the developed world. ⊛

Notes for an African Orestes

(1970, 75 min, Italy)

This fascinating look at the artistic process of one of the world's most daring and creative filmmakers is, simply put, a cinematic notebook. The film follows Pasolini as he treks across East Africa scouring remote villages and crowded marketplaces for raw footage and discusses all of the possibilities for what he hoped would be a production of "The Orestia." Aeschylus' myth is truly one of the masterpieces of ancient Greek theatre and Pasolini's idea was to set the story in a rapidly modernizing Africa as a grand allegory for the painful and awkward period of development which swept through the Third World in the 1960s. For fans of Pasolini, this will prove to be a mesmerizing and poetic view of underdevelopment and the quest for modernization despite the social cost. ⊛

The Decameron *(1970, 111 min, Italy)*

Boccaccio's bawdy, earthy stories of sexual adventures during the 14th century is lustfully interpreted by Pasolini. Told in several humorous and lighthearted episodes, the stories illustrate the different facets of uninhibited human sexuality. The film takes special pleasure in depicting the Church's sexually repressed clerics frolicking lecherously among their flocks. The director's first in his "Trilogy of Life," this is perhaps Pasolini's funniest film and certainly one of his best. ⊛

The Canterbury Tales

(1971, 109 min, Italy)

Pasolini's second feature in his "Trilogy of Life" series is comprised of eight of the ribald stories contained in Chaucer's classic book. Set in England and featuring the director as Chaucer himself, the film explores the raciest, most exotic and controversial aspects of life in medieval times. Rumor has it that Pasolini, long known for working with non-professionals in his films, even used hitchhikers he picked up during his travels in England for major roles in the film. ☻

Arabian Nights *(1974, 130 min, Italy)*

This, the concluding film in Pasolini's "Trilogy of Life" series, is a bawdy and visually opulent fable of idyllic sexuality based on the classic Arabian tales. Told in dreamlike vignettes, the ten stories derive from three cultures — Persia, Egypt and India — and were shot on location in Iran, Eritrea, Yeman and Nepal using non-professionals and peasants. The stories range in setting from the 9th century to the Renaissance. A celebration of joyous sensuality rarely found in our present industrialized Western culture. ☻

▼ Saló, or the 120 Days of Sodom

(1975, 117 min, Italy)

Pasolini's last film is an unbelievably bleak and depressing vision of the human condition which shocked audiences with its brutally graphic scenes of sexual degradation and oppressive violence. The director transposes the Marquis de Sade's novel about the debauching of the four pillars of 18th-century French society to World War II Italy (Saló was the site of Mussolini's brief puppet government in northern Italy). There a group of four men, all fascist members of the power elite (a duke, a bishop, a banker and a judge) enact out their lust for power and control. They kidnap sixteen teenage boys and girls and systematically and sadistically force them to engage in a variety of perverse and repugnant acts including coprophilia, necrophilia, torture, sexual debasement and, eventually, murder. The startled viewer is the voyeur in Pasolini's descent into the evils of the human spirit. Condemned by Italian censors for its "aberrant and repugnant sexual perversion." ☻

Whoever Says the Truth Shall Die

(1985, 60 min, Holland/Italy, Philo Bregstein)

This provocative documentary probes into Pasolini's life and work in an effort to come to some understanding of the events which led to his death. From interviews with Bernardo Bertolucci and Alberto Moravia, and clips from his many films as well as biographical background, the film attempts to enter the private life of the director, who had a masochistic fascination with society's taboos and its unwanted denizens. Was he killed in a freakish isolated incident or was he assassinated? ☻

The Ashes of Pasolini

(1993, 90 min, Italy, Pasquali Misuraca)

Despite the 1993 copyright date, this personal insight into the political, social and intimate thoughts of Pasolini is actually a compilation of several interviews the director gave for Italian television's RAI during the mid-1970s. Far from the definitive film on the celebrated poet/artist/filmmaker, the video does offer extensive footage of Pasolini explaining his Marxist ideology, the reading of some of his poetry, reminiscences of his childhood and an explanation for his shift from the literary arts to filmmaking. Featured are several snippets from his films, but their titles are not noted and their inclusion seemingly made haphazardly. At times, the video provides a revealing and educational look into the mind of one of Italy's great artists of the 20th century, but it is also visually static and a meandering mess structurally. Except for his die-hard fans, this is a film most can live without. See his films and, if ambitious, read his poetry.

A little butt grabbing in *Saló, or the 120 Days of Sodom*

WOLFGANG PETERSEN

Unlike most of the talented crop of filmmakers that came out of the 1970s and '80s German New Wave, Wolfgang Petersen was not content to continue to make small-scale, human-interest dramas in his native country or in Europe, for he had long shown the talent of being a highly successful "entertainment" filmmaker. His work on TV had achieved a great popularity, and though he wasn't celebrated as a great auteur like Rainer Werner Fassbinder, Werner Herzog and Wim Wenders, his later theatrical films were thoughtful, inventive and in some instances controversial. He became famous overnight when, after a decade of directing for German TV and making small-budget films (he was known as a *tatort* or specialist in crime thrillers), he exploded onto the international scene with his big-budget *Das Boot*. He soon left Germany for the bright lights (and inherent dangers) of Hollywood and proceeded to experiment with a variety of genres, producing several offbeat films: a sophisticated children's fable with *The NeverEnding Story*; a thinking person's science-fiction fantasy in *Enemy Mine*; a psychological thriller with *Shattered*; and his latest film, the riveting political thriller *In the Line of Fire*, a box-office hit that squarely placed him on Hollywood's "A" list.

Born in 1941 in Emden, Germany, Petersen studied acting in Berlin and Hamburg before entering the Berlin Film & Television Academy in 1966, where he was quickly drawn to theatre direction. His first film, *Smog* (1972), caused a great deal of excitement, and resulted in continued employment. He eventually worked on over 20 TV productions, and at the same time made his second film, *Einer vons uns Beiden* (*One of Us Two*), a 1973 tale about an outsider trying to crash German society. This production marked the beginning of his long collaboration with actor Jurgen Prochnow, a partnership which included the gay-themed love story *The Consequence* and *Das Boot*.

Petersen, whose latest production is *Outbreak*, which follows the efforts to stop a deadly virus and stars Dustin Hoffman, Rene Russo and Morgan Freeman, now makes his home in Los Angeles.

For Your Love Only
(1976, 127 min, Germany)
This made-for-TV soap opera (released theatrically several years later) features 15-year-old Nastassia Kinski as a beautiful, sensi-

Wolfgang Petersen

tive student who finds herself trapped in a bizarre love triangle that escalates from forbidden passion to blackmail and murder. ℗

▼ The Consequence
(1977, 100 min, Germany)
A touching romance that focuses on the forbidden love between an actor jailed for an illicit sexual liaison and the young man he meets while in jail. Jurgen Prochnow stars as Martin, who is sent to prison for the "seduction of a minor." There, he meets and is immediately drawn to Thomas, the teenage son of one of the guards. After Martin's release, the boy runs away from home to live with him. And despite threats from the boy's father and the authorities, their love flourishes as the two are determined to live their life together — unprepared for the wrath triggered by their actions. Filmed in an almost documentary fashion from a script co-written by Petersen, the two men's relationship is depicted as sensual, tender and poignant. Petersen, while not discounting the homosexual theme, has said that the audience "should gradually forget that it is actually about the relationship between two men...(and) should feel empathy with two people who fall in love with each other but who happen to be men. Perhaps in this way, some of the people will be changed." Made for German TV, it was initially barred from airing but that ruling was even-tually overturned. Petersen's touching tale is a bittersweet plea for understanding and compassion.

Das Boot *(1981, 145 min, Germany)*

The film which put Petersen on the international map, *Das Boot* was, at the time, Germany's most expensive film ever made. The investment paid off as the film became an international smash, winning six Academy Award nominations and offering the world a rare glimpse of WWII German soldiers as non-sadistic, ordinary sailors fighting for their country. Few films convey the horror of war as powerfully as this claustrophobic account of a German U-boat's passage through hostile waters. Dispelling traditional film images of war heroism, *Das Boot* substitutes a truer vision of the waste and inhumanity inherent in battle. ⊛

The NeverEnding Story *(1984, 92 min, GB)*

Petersen's first English-language film is a near-classic fairy tale about a young boy who becomes so immersed in the book he's reading that he is magically drawn into the story and must help save the story's world from destruction. Wonderful children's fare, perhaps a bit scary for the wee-est of tykes, but filled with good special effects and an earnest young hero. Only a slight clumsiness and non-too-subtle allegorical message keep this from the highest pantheon of children's films. ⊛

Enemy Mine *(1985, 108 min, US)*

An intelligent, visually striking sci-fi adventure about two interplanetary enemies — a pilot from Earth and a warrior from the planet Drac — who become stranded together on a distant, deserted planet. Dennis Quaid and Lou Gossett, Jr. star in this space-age *Hell in the Pacific.* ⊛

In the Line of Fire

Shattered *(1991, 97 min, US)*

A post-modern whodunit whose psychological complexities, which obscure the action and violence, probably doomed this exciting and involving film at the American box office. Tom Berenger stars as a man left with amnesia after a near-fatal accident. In a series of ever-deepening twists he tries to get some idea of who he used to be, who he is now, and who he can trust to tell him the truth. This Hitchcock-inspired suspenser features Corbin Bernsen, Bob Hoskins, and Greta Scacchi as his supposedly loving wife. ⊛

In the Line of Fire *(1993, 123 min, US)*

A riveting suspense thriller and box-office hit which afforded Clint Eastwood a second opportunity to deliver a career performance. He plays a seasoned Secret Serviceman — who was present at JFK's murder in Dallas — who finds himself in another presidential assassination scenario as a routine investigation puts him and partner Dylan McDermott on the trail of a potential killer, played with great menace by John Malkovich. Much of the film's enjoyment lies in the cat-and-mouse relationship between would-be assassin Malkovich and Eastwood. Rarely has a screen duo's adversarial battle been as enthralling. ⊛

The Consequence

$R^{T \quad O \quad N \quad Y}_{ICHARDSON}$

An acclaimed director who alternated between stage and screen, and who created classics in both mediums, Tony Richardson was a driving force in the revitilization of British theatre in the 1950s and that country's cinematic rebirth of the 1960s. An Oscar-winning director, Richardson worked with the best the British theatrical and film communities had to offer, inspiring career performances and landmark productions.

Born in the north of England in 1928, Richardson, an only and sickly child whose father was a pharmacist-turned-politician, was introduced to theatre and film by both his grandmother and aunt. At eight years of age he saw a production of "A Midsummer Night's Dream" (his favorite play) and knew instantly what his life's work was to be. Richardson attended private schools as a youth, and was a loner who felt awful pangs of alienation. In his auto-biography "The Long-Distance Runner," he recalled, "My school was probably by no means the worst, but it is impossible to exaggerate the misery, the sordidness, the continual and recurring nastiness of a sentence to a gulag from which there was no escape." He directed and starred in school productions, but knew even at an early age that acting was not his forte. Richardson attended Oxford, where he directed college productions and formed a friendship with Lindsay Anderson, who would also become a noted director. Following graduation in the early 1950s, Richardson began an apprenticeship with the BBC, directing numerous television programs and shorts (one of which starred a young Denholm Elliott). On the strength of his BBC work, he was awarded a chance to direct on London's West End, and his first production there was "Mr. Kettle and Mrs. Moon."

After a brief tour of the United States in 1953, where he met Aldous Huxley, Christopher Isherwood (who would become a lifelong friend) and his idol Luis Buñuel, Richardson returned to London to write film criticism for *Sequence*, which would become *Sight and Sound*; and he would make his film directing debut with a 20-minute short (co-directed with Karel Reisz), *Momma Don't Allow*, a documentary on a North London jazz club. Also at this time, Richardson co-founded a London theatrical repertory company: the "unknown" cast members included Joan Plowright, Alan Bates, Mary Ure and Kenneth Haigh. Richardson's first production in association with his newly founded group was John Osborne's "Look Back in Anger" (Haigh appeared as Jimmy Porter and Bates and Ure also starred). The play was an immediate critical hit. Among his other London stage credits, Richardson directed "The Member of the Wedding," "The Entertainer" (with Laurence Olivier and Plowright), "Othello" (starring Paul Robeson), "Luther" and "The Seagull." His Broadway productions included Ionesco's "The Lesson," "A Taste of Honey" and a notorious flop, Tennessee Williams' "The Milk Train Doesn't Stop Here Anymore," with Tallulah Bankhead and Tab Hunter. Richardson made his feature film directorial debut in 1958 with the acclaimed adaptation of his stage hit, *Look Back in Anger*. Other film versions of his stage hits include *The Entertainer*, *A Taste of Honey* and the Nicol Williamson-starring *Hamlet*. In 1963, Richardson had his greatest screen success with the Oscar-winning Best Picture *Tom Jones*, a riotous, bawdy and fluid translation of Henry Fielding's novel.

Richardson was married once, to actress Vanessa Redgrave with whom he had two daughters, Natasha and Joely (both actresses). He also had another daughter, Katharine, with actress Grizelda Grimond. Though his bisexuality was known to close friends, Richardson would never acknowledge himself as such. He never makes mention of his gay affairs in "The Long-Distance Runner," and even goes to the extent of "closeting" gay associates. However, writer Gavin Lambert, in a *Sight and Sound* article on Richardson after the director's death to AIDS in 1991, recalled, "Even though (Richardson) introduced me to several of his male lovers, Tony's ground rule forbade us to discuss his sexual identity...Tony came of professional age in the stone age of the '50s, when open sexual non-conformity was a threat to almost anyone's career. Tony's lovers were always *Back Street* figures, and he could never allow himself to become deeply involved with them."

Posthumously released in 1994, Richardson's final film, *Blue Sky*, starring Jessica Lange, Tommy Lee Jones and Powers Boothe, concerns an engineer and his wife who discover a cover-up of a nuclear bomb test.

"The most prolific and the most prosperous of the *Sight and Sound* crop, and ultimately the least respected."
—Andrew Sarris

Look Back in Anger
(1958, 99 min, GB)
John Osborne's play made theatre history in England as a rebellious attack against the rigidity of the English establishment. Bristling with heated dialogue, the play represents the first signs of post-war dissatisfaction with the social immobility of life in a dying Empire — and the film expertly captures a nation's despair. Brilliantly performed by Richard Burton, Claire Bloom, Mary Ure and Donald Pleasence, this "angry young man" drama stars Burton as Jimmy Porter, a recent graduate who lashes out at society and those around him in a galvanizing attempt to survive. ⊛

The Entertainer
(1960, 97 min, GB)
Laurence Olivier gives an extraordinary performance in Richardson's depiction of a seedy vaudevillian on the skids who unwittingly destroys those around him. As the egotistical Archie Rice, Olivier captures the grotesque demeanor and futile yearnings of a defeated man. Also starring Joan Plowright, Alan Bates, Brenda de Banzie and Albert Finney. Based on John Osborne's play. ⊛

Sanctuary *(1961, 100 min, US)*
In his first American film, Richardson attacks William Faulkner's novel of Southern passions, but it unfortunately plays as second-rate Tennessee Williams. Set in the 1920s, the film stars Lee Remick as a married woman whose one-time affair with a troublesome Cajun sets the stage for intrigue and murder when he returns.

▼ A Taste of Honey *(1962, 100 min, GB)*
This lovely, heartbreaking film, adapted from a 1957 play by Shelagh Delany, is a minor masterpiece. An earthy, poetic tale about a group of social rejects in England's bleak industrial North, the film stars Rita Tushingham as Jo, a tough young woman who becomes pregnant after an affair with a black man who has since left her. Murray Melvin is Geoff, an effeminate homosexual and fellow outcast who befriends her. Transcending lower-class clichés, the story touchingly examines their lives; Jo and Geoff's relationship is one of tenderness and affection. ⊛

The Loneliness of the Long Distance Runner *(1962, 103 min, GB)*
Alan Silitoe's classic short story about a rebellious reform school boy whose athletic prowess earns him a shot at the Olympics is lovingly brought to life thanks to Richardson's sensitive touch. Tom Courtenay excels as the young runner and Michael Redgrave is superb as the school warden who takes him under his wing. A classic in the British "kitchen sink" style of filmmaking. ⊛

Tom Courtenay (c.) in *The Loneliness of the Long Distance Runner*

Tom Jones *(1963, 129 min, GB)*
An Academy Award winner for Best Picture, this sumptuous comedy richly evokes the tenor of its times — both in the setting of the novel and of the era in which it was filmed. Richardson uses every cinematic trick in the book — fast motion, jump cuts, rapid editing — to capture the joie de vivre of Henry Fielding's bawdy tale of a young rake's randy adventures in 18th-century England. Albert Finney is brilliant in the lead role, and his seduction of Joyce Redman in the classic eating scene will make a gourmand out of the most abstemious. Richardson won the Oscar as Best Director. ⊛

▼ The Loved One *(1965, 116 min, US)*
Evelyn Waugh's audacious satire on the Southern California way of life (and death) was adapted for the screen by Terry Southern and Christopher Isherwood. This classic black comedy, which was billed as "the film with something to offend everyone," features an all-star cast of characters: Robert Morse as the Candide-like nephew who travels to L.A. to visit his uncle; John Gielgud as his dearly departed relative, a gay art director; Rod Steiger as the Oedipal Mr. Joyboy; Liberace as a fastidious and gay casket salesperson; and Tab Hunter, Robert Morley, Roddy McDowall and Jonathan Winters. A refreshing slap in the face to both normality and eccentricity. ⊛

The Sailor from Gilbraltar
(1966, 91 min, GB)
Based on Marguerite Duras' novel, this existential dribble finds British tourist Ian Holm and French nymphomaniac Jeanne Moreau — on a world-wide search for her titular lover — finding solace with each other amid the boredom of an Italian coastal resort. Vanessa Redgrave plays Holm's museum-loving wife, and Orson Welles has a small cameo.

Mademoiselle *(1966, 103 min, GB)*

With a screenplay written in part by Jean Genet, Richardson is unable to fully realize this uneven drama about a French schoolteacher (Jeanne Moreau) whose love knows no bounds — even to the extent of criminal activity. ⊛

The Charge of the Light Brigade

(1968, 141 min, GB)

Entertaining if slightly muddled updating of the 1936 adventure film, as much an anti-war statement as a lavish spectacle. With Trevor Howard, Vanessa Redgrave, David Hemmings and John Gielgud. ⊛

Laughter in the Dark *(1969, 104 min, GB)*

Richardson's hand was heavy in bringing Nabokov's novel of passion and betrayal to the screen. Nicol Williamson gives an intense performance as an art critic who becomes obsessed with a youthful usherette (Anna Karina). When he moves in with her, they become engulfed in a series of vicious mind games which ultimately leads to tragedy.

Hamlet *(1969, 119 min, GB)*

Richardson brings his stage production to the screen with Nicol Williamson re-creating his acclaimed performance as the melon-choly Dane. Filmed at the now-closed Round House (London's equivalent of an off-Broadway theatre), the film is done in period dress and has a contemporary feel to it. All this is accented by dark, claustrophobic staging with little movement, which allows greater concentration on the intense faces of the characters. Williamson's portrait of a confused Hamlet, full of neurotic twitches and personal uncertainties, is riveting. Anthony Hopkins and Marianne Faithful also star. ⊛

Ned Kelly *(1970, 100 min, GB)*

Set in 19th-century Australia, this ambitious Outback western features the screen acting debut of Mick Jagger, who plays the title role, Australia's most notorious outlaw. Ned Kelly, accompanied by his band of fellow Irishmen, does battle against the repressive British authorities. Jagger, much better used in Nicolas Roeg's *Performance*, is out of place. A bit too scrawny for the role, he lacks any star quality. Lightning doesn't strike twice for Richardson in his attempt to mold the rude rocker in the fashion of "lovable rogue" as he did with Albert Finney in *Tom Jones*. Featuring music by Waylon Jennings. ⊛

A Delicate Balance *(1973, 134 min, US)*

A good cast in featured in Richardson's noble attempt to bring Edward Albee's Pulitzer Prize-winning play to the screen, another in the American Film Theatre series. Essentially a filmed play, the film revolves around a dysfunctional Connecticut family; and Katharine Hepburn, Paul Scofield, Joseph Cotten, Lee Remick and Kate Reid give strong characterizations.

Joseph Andrews *(1976, 104 min, GB)*

Even if this somewhat underrated comedy had been great, which it's not, Richardson would have been hard pressed to achieve the level of accomplishment of his earlier adaptation of a Henry Fielding novel, *Tom Jones*. Here, Peter Firth plays a lowly functionary who rejects the advances of the voluptuous Lady Booby (Ann-Margret) in favor of a peasant girl. ⊛

The Border *(1982, 107 min, US)*

Jack Nicholson stars as a U.S. Border Guard who gets caught up in the business of transporting illegal aliens to pay for the materialistic lifestyle his wife craves. His morals come to haunt him in the form of a young Mexican mother and her child, whom he comes to care for. An engrossing film with excellent performances from Nicholson, Valerie Perrine and Harvey Keitel. ⊛

▼ The Hotel New Hampshire

(1984, 110 min, US)

A felicitous actors' exercise which follows closely the John Irving novel. As with the author's "The World According to Garp," the serendipitous story examines the exploits of a highly unusual family and ranges in mood from the almost slapstick to the nearly tragic. While the direction tends to harbor self-indulgence, each actor's portrayal is inventive and endearing. Paul McCrane is the gay brother of Rob Lowe and Jodie Foster ("I am queer, ya know"). On a trip to Vienna, Foster expands her sexual horizons with Nastassia Kinski. As he was in *Fame*, McCrane is the only lead not romantically paired. ⊛

Penalty Phase *(1986, 100 min, US)*

Richardson made his U.S. TV debut with this absorbing drama examining the American judicial system. Due to a technicality, a judge must set a killer free, which he lives to regret. Starring Peter Strauss, Melissa Gilbert and Jonelle Allen.

Shadow on the Sun *(1988, 200 min, US)*

Made-for-TV drama about the life of 1930s aviatrix Beryl Markham, played by Stefanie Powers. Also with Claire Bloom, Trevor Eve, James Fox and John Rubinstein.

Phantom of the Opera

(1990, 200 min, US/GB)

Jumping on the "Phantom" craze created by Andrew Lloyd Weber's musical, Richardson directed this made-for-TV remake with an eye to physical detail. Charles Dance is an effectively romantic and sinister Phantom, and is supported by Burt Lancaster, Teri Polo and Jean-Pierre Cassel.

KEN RUSSELL

Ken Russell

He's been called genius, madman, historical revisionist, visionary, self-indulgent, and he has even had his works debated in both houses of Parliament. But say what you will of director Ken Russell — he never fails to excite the passions within a filmgoer: be they feelings of exaltation or exasperation. Probably no other director working in film today can lay claim to such fervent vocalization from his fans and detractors, alike. His signature style is one of excess and controversy. His films revel in visual fanaticism, tongue-in-cheek humor and extravagant abandonment of reason and serenity — all in what he calls "my subversive vision." Love him or hate him (and generally the critics love to hate him), there's no denying the man is an original.

Despite being "straight," Ken Russell has more gay sensibility evident in his movies than most gay filmmakers, even if the images are not always "politically correct." From exploring male-to-male sexual yearning in *Women in Love*, lesbianism in *The Rainbow*, the tortured homosexual artist in *The Music Lovers* or depicting a gayly decadent Oscar Wilde in *Salome's Last Dance*, his films are infused with gay characters and plots. Russell is also known for consistently working with gay writers, actors and set designers. With so much gayness running through his cinematic veins, it is no surprise that many think of him as being gay. He once said a very close friend called him a latent homosexual, to which Russell replied, "Fine, maybe I am, who knows. I don't think anyone knows themselves. We can all pretend, but I have no idea what I am. I'm me!"

Born in 1927 in Southhampton, Russell grew up obsessed with movies, often attending three films a day and many times accompanied by his mother. After enlisting in the Marines during World War II, Russell attempted several careers in the arts before settling on filmmaking. He made his initial mark on British television in the 1960s with a series of documentaries on famous artists including Wordsworth, Richard Strauss, Coleridge and Debussy. This fascination with classical music, artists and the creative process has remained with him throughout his career. On this oft-filmed theme, Russell has said that he "is merely the technician who's trying to unravel something about artists. The creative spirit is a mystery, and I never get tired of trying to find out what makes it what it is."

One of the strongest influences on Russell (other than his long marriage and collaboration with Shirley Russell whom he has since divorced and remarried) is his conversion to Catholicism. With his films immersed in sexual obsession, personal torment and death, this should come as no surprise. Russell says that "except for *The Boyfriend*, all of my films have been Catholic films, films about love, faith, sin, forgiveness, redemption."

He has rarely ventured into Hollywood, preferring to work in his native land; although, because of his individualist style, he belongs neither to the Free Cinema movement of the late 1950s-early '60s and its adherents (Lindsay Anderson, Karel Reisz), the mainstream British filmmakers of the past twenty years (John Boorman, Nicolas Roeg) nor the present wave of "new British cinema" (Stephen Frears, Julien Temple). The one director with whom he might share a similar esthetic vision might by Peter Greenaway. Russell decries much of his fellow countrymen's work complaining that "they are ashamed of England and like to show how terrible it is."

In the last few years, Russell has directed operas, worked for American television and has seen a greater difficulty in raising capital for several of his pet projects including *Evita* and film bios of Maria Callas and Cleopatra. In addition to the films mentioned, Russell also contributed short films to *Aria* (1988), starring a cross-dressing Theresa Russell in the lead, and *Women & Men — Stories of Seduction* (1990).

> "What Sen. Joe McCarthy did to people's reputations is nothing to what Ken Russell does...he is the chief defiler of celebrities of the past and present."
> —Pauline Kael, *The New Yorker*

> "I always start out thinking that I am going to make a pastoral film but the darker side eventually creeps in. All of my films are moral, or immoral, depending on your point of view."
> —Ken Russell

> "It's part of human nature, what's the big deal?"
> —Russell on his films' exploration of male friendship and homosexuality

> "I'm trying to reach a wider — and younger — audience...and make films that are visually stunning. They'll still be about love, faith, sin, guilt, forgiveness and redemption, which is what all my work is about. But I've never made a film I was totally happy with ...that's what keeps me going — the next one must be better."
> —Russell

French Dressing *(1963, 86 min, GB)*

Russell's first theatrical film is a limp satire of two schemers who attempt to bring some glamour to their plain British seaside resort, Gormleigh-on-Sea. Russell has said that he learned much from the making of the film, especially the fact that even during the filming he knew that the stars, TV comedians James Booth and Roy Kinnear, weren't funny.

Billion Dollar Brain *(1967, 111 min, GB)*

Michael Caine reprises his role of secret agent Harry Palmer in this final film of Len Deighton's spy thriller trilogy (the first two being *The Ipcress File* and *Funeral in Berlin*). In this story, Palmer is sent with a mysterious canister to Finland which soon involves him in an American megalomaniac's plot to rule the world.

Dante's Inferno *(1969, 90 min, GB)*

Russell's filmic fascination with artists tortured by personal weaknesses (*The Music Lovers, Mahler, Valentino*) is amply evident in this early, rarely seen film. Oliver Reed plays Dante Gabriel Rossetti, a morose, brilliant, drunken painter/poet who, as Russell sees it, was more interested in his flamboyant and excessive lifestyle than his artistic output. Rossetti drew into his pre-Raphael circle some of the most prominent figures of the late 19th century: his poetess sister Christina Rossetti, William Morris and his wife

Jane, the poet Swinburne, and the critic John Ruskin. Russell wonderfully re-creates the period in this engrossing tale of art, poetry, booze and sex. ✪

▼ Women in Love *(1969, 129 min, GB)*

Russell's powerful rendition of the D.H. Lawrence classic about two Midlands sisters and the tempestuous relationships they form. Resolute Gudren (Glenda Jackson) becomes involved with the strong but boarish Gerald (Oliver Reed) while her romantically inclined sister Ursula (Jennie Linden) falls in love with the handsome but aloof Rupert (Alan Bates), who is Lawrence's alter ego. Rupert craves for a relationship with both a man and a woman but finds this ideal illusive — although he comes close one evening when he engages in a nude wrestling match with Gerald. This scene is filmed in a seductive, erotic manner by Russell. Later in the film, Gudren soon becomes tired with Gerald and while they are on holiday in the Swiss Alps, she comes under the spell of gay "artiste" Crich (Alan Webb). Jealous of her attraction to what Gerald calls that "insect..rat," he wanders off into the snowy expanse to meet his fate. ✪

> "People come up to me and say, 'I loved your *Women in Love*.' Well, to me, it was one of the worst films I ever made. But it was a romantic film, and that's what people like."
> —Ken Russell

Focus on: *Larry Kramer*

Larry Kramer, who wrote the screenplay adaptation for this film, as well as writing the screenplay for Lost Horizon *(1973), is known today as an impassioned leading voice in the struggle for gay/lesbian rights and greater public and private commitment to ending the AIDS crisis. Kramer, the co-founder of the Gay Men's Health Crisis and ACT-UP, has also written several books including the novel "Faggots," and the AIDS-themed play "The Normal Heart," which is in film development with Barbra Streisand slated to direct and to star in the role of Dr. Linda Laubenstein.*

▼ The Music Lovers *(1970, 122 min, GB)*

This extravagant account on the life of Peter Ilyitch Tchaikovsky is wonderfully overacted and filled with wildly overstated imagery. Richard Chamberlain stars as the tortured, repressed homosexual composer, Christopher Gable his clinging blond boyfriend and Glenda Jackson plays his mad, nymphomaniac wife. Set in turn-of-the-century Russia, the film is impressively costumed and feverishly presented — with the hilarious, phallic and symbolism-laden "1812 Overture" dream sequence a personal favorite. ✪

The Devils *(1971, 109 min, GB)*

Any film that sacrilegiously features fenzied nuns sexually attacking a giant crucifix is pure enjoyment in my cinematic book. Oliver Reed stars as the martyred cleric and Vanessa Redgrave is the hunchbacked, sexually repressed nun in this gruesome and graphic account of witchcraft hysteria in 17th-century France. A memorable, lascivious adaptation of John Whiting's play and Aldous Huxley's book, "The Devils of Loudun." Astounding set design by Derek Jarman. ⊗

The Boyfriend *(1971, 140 min, GB)*

All-out musical numbers and spectacle abound in this lavishly entertaining musical — a glamorous tribute to Busby Berkeley — starring Twiggy, Tommy Tune and Christopher Gable. Glenda Jackson is featured as the star who, before opening night of "the big show," breaks her leg, forcing her mousy understudy (Twiggy) into the spotlight and onto the road to superstardom. The film was recently restored with additional footage. This version played at San Francisco's Castro Theatre with this promising marquee attention-grabber: "Ken Russell's Uncut Boyfriend!" ⊗

Savage Messiah *(1972, 103 min, GB)*

Turn-of-the-century sculptor Henri Gaudier-Brzeska (Scott Antony) and his four-year affair with the much older Sophie Brzeska (Dorothy Tutin) is told in this fierce, fragmented drama. Featuring Lindsay Kemp and Helen Mirren. ⊗

Mahler *(1974, 115 min, GB)*

Excesses were kept to a minimum in this sumptuously filmed and costumed biography of the famed Swedish composer Gustav Mahler. The film is a dazzling evocation of the loves, moods and music of the artist. Through flashbacks and beautiful dream imagery, it focuses on the tormented life and turbulent relationship he endured with his wife. Such Russellisms as a dream sequence with a Nazi Pope do sneak through. On the whole, however, this is Russell in a mellow mood. ⊗

▼ Tommy *(1975, 110 min, GB)*

The Who's rock opera stars Roger Daltrey as the "deaf, dumb and blind boy" who becomes a pinball wizard and New Messiah in this visually and aurally stimulating extravaganza. Ann-Margret is his mother who has an unforgettable encounter with a room full of beans, Elton John is the dethroned pinball champ, Eric Clapton is the preacher and Tina Turner is electrifying as the Acid Queen. The Who's drummer Keith Moon plays the boy's sleazy, degenerate Uncle Ernie. He baby-sits Tommy one evening and probably sexually molests him, gleefully singing, "Down with your bedclothes, up with your night shirt. Fiddle about. You won't shout as I fiddle about." Stepdad Oliver Reed comes home after the dirty deed is done with uncle sitting next to the sleeping boy reading *The Gay Times*. ⊗

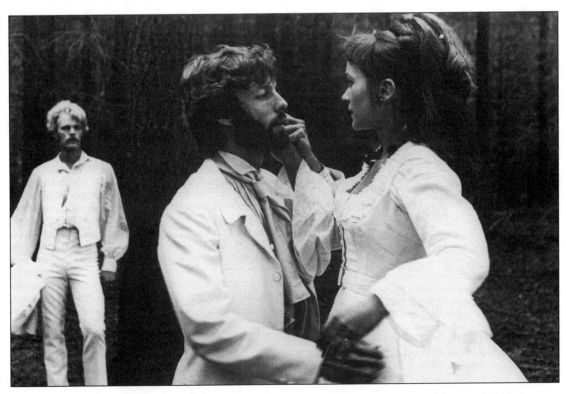

The Music Lovers: Playing Tchaikovsky, Richard Chamberlain (c.) romps in the woods as his lover (Christopher Gable) looks on

Lisztomania *(1975, 104 min, GB)*

The film that many feel took Russell over the top; resulting in an outlandish, phallic-symboled biographical assault on the life of Franz Liszt, classical composer and according to Russell, the world's first pop star. Roger Daltrey brings a certain East End Adonis-like quality to his role as Liszt. But it is Russell's garish, psychosexual images and frenzied storytelling in this rock opera that keeps an audience entranced, if they haven't already run out of the room or cinema. Ringo Starr makes an amusing appearance as the Pope. ☮

The Boyfriend

▼ Valentino *(1977, 127, min, US)*

This bizarre fantasy is a lurid exposé on the life of silent screen star Rudolph Valentino. Opening with the frenzied scene at his funeral, the film's flashbacks attempt to chart his rise to fame as well as uncover the man behind the image. Rudolf Nureyev stars as Valentino, and though he looks the part, he's woefully wooden and uninspiring. Though Russell downplays the homosexual aspects of the Latin Lover's life, he does offer some lesbian images including a funeral scene in which the "evil" Nazimova (Leslie Caron) accompanies Valentino's ex-wife/her lover Natasha Rambova (Michelle Phillips) to the funeral. ☮

Altered States *(1980, 102 min, US)*

In Russell's biggest box-office hit to date, William Hurt stars as an inquisitive scientist who experiments with powerful mind-altering drugs in a quest for his primal self. Gradually, he undergoes a series of mental and physical transformations and experiences some spine-chilling hallucinations. Though a sight and sound spectacular, screenwriter Paddy Chayefsky, who also wrote the novel, disowned this film version and had his name removed from the credits. The lovely Blair Brown co-stars as Hurt's long-suffering but compassionate wife. ☮

Crimes of Passion *(1984, 112 min, US)*

This sizzling tale of a sexually repressed street preacher and a mysterious prostitute carries a resounding wallop. Anthony Perkins stars as the deranged reverend who's hell-bent on saving the soul of China Blue (Kathleen Turner) — a well-respected fashion designer by day and slinky streetwalker by night. Openly gay screenwriter Barry Sandler (*Making Love*) infuses the film with camp humor and bizarre twists. Definitely one of Russell's most unique (a term which may be redundant when describing his work) and unforgettable ventures. A scene in which China Blue sodomizes a policeman with his own nightstick was cut from the theatrical prints but restored in some video versions. This prompted Russell to remark, "You can be as violent as you want in America but you talk about sex and everybody reaches for their chastity belts." ☮

Gothic *(1987, 90 min, GB)*

This unusual, dreamlike psychological thriller, set in the 1800s at Lord Byron's villa, depicts one hellish night spent by Byron and his guests, which include P.B. Shelley, his lover Mary, and author Dr. Polidori. The film suggests this fateful evening inspired Polidori to write "The Vampyre" and Mary (who would later marry her paramour) to pen "Frankenstein." Gabriel Byrne, Julian Sands and Natasha Richardson star. ☮

▼ Salome's Last Dance *(1988, 87 min, GB)*

Oscar Wilde (Nickolas Grace) and his lover, Lord Alfred "Bosie" Douglas (Douglas Hodge), visit a male brothel where they are entertained by an "illegal" performance of Wilde's play, "Salome," banned by the Lord Chamberlain in 1892 for its "licentious passion." The play itself represents Wilde's twisted vision of the fateful biblical encounter between Salome (daughter of King Herod) and John the Baptist. Here reenacted full of pulsating sexual innuendo, Russell eagerly sinks his teeth into Wilde's poetry and renders the play, in its entirety, at a frenetic pace. Imogen Millais-Scott is devilishly alluring as the coquettish, cockneyed Salome, and Glenda Jackson is nothing short of perfect as the steely, evil Queen Herodias. The film is infused with decadent gay images, both in the play and in the audience. In one scene, Wilde is watching the play while fondling a pageboy who is covered head-to-toe in gold body makeup. Russell, commenting on Wilde, said, "Wilde was a bit of a renegade who was upsetting the establishment...he led a double life: he was married with children, but also frequented the homosexual underworld of London...I wanted to give a flavor of what his life at the time was like, and at the same time give a hint of the homosexual relationship with Bosie that was really his downfall." ☮

The Lair of the White Worm
(1988, 94 min, GB)
Bram Stoker's final work receives a brilliant, tongue-in-cheek adaptation as Russell takes outrageous delight in offering a perverse tale of venomous vampirism and perverse paganism. Amanda Donohue offers up a truly kinky performance as a mysterious snake lady who slithers her way into modern England in search of virgins to feed to a giant worm god. Hugh Grant, Sammi Davis and Peter Capaldi make up the group of locals determined to stamp out this ancient evil. Russell's flair isn't lost as this slimy tale of rampant vampirism oozes with an abundance of camp humor, serpentine symbolism, phallic symbols and just about every daft snake joke in the book. ☮

▼ The Rainbow *(1988, 104 min, GB)*
Returning to D. H. Lawrence country, this "classic" adaptation of his novel is set in early 20th-century England and follows the sexual and spiritual liberation of young Ursula, the Jennie Linden character in *Women in Love*. Sammi Davis is great as the earnest and doe-eyed young woman whose sexuality and desires erupt all the while yearning for true love, self-respect and independence in a society which frowns on all three. The film reunites Glenda Jackson and Christopher Gable (from *The Music Lovers*) as the

parents of the restless, inquisitive Ursula. Stealing the show, however, is Amanda Donohue, who is delightfully decadent as Winifred (nicknamed "Fred" by her friends), Ursula's gym instructor, seductress and mentor. Donohue plays a willful, bohemian lesbian who when she first lays eyes on the fetching student becomes entranced. Their affair is depicted as romantic, loving, natural, affectionate. But like *Personal Best*, the young protagonist has more fish to fry as she uses her lesbian relationship as a stepping stone towards one with a man. ☮

Prisoner of Honor *(1991, 88 min, US)*
Russell is unusually restrained in this made-for-HBO retelling of the Dreyfus Affair, a scandalous incident of anti-Semitism in turn-of-the-century France. Richard Dreyfuss stars as an officer who refuses to allow his army to betray its honor by framing an innocent Jewish officer for treason. ☮

Whore *(1991, 92 min, GB/US)*
In a kind of follow-up to *Crimes of Passion*, Russell takes a less-successful walk down those streets of despair, leaving behind his bag of psychedelic tricks. Sadly, what is intended as a searing insight into the world of prostitution completely misses the mark under Russell's histrionic misdirection. Theresa Russell sleepwalks, er, streetwalks through this talky tale of a hooker on the run from her psychotic pimp. Also with Antonio Fargas. ☮

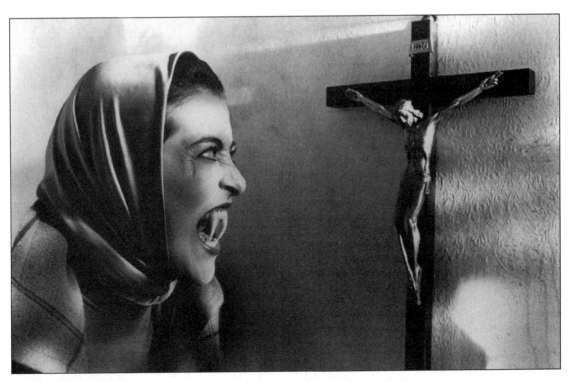

The Lair of the White Worm

JOHN SCHLESINGER

For nearly four decades, John Schlesinger has fashioned provocative films that deal with such issues as friendships, loneliness, social pressures, loyalty and both hetero- and homosexuality. Working in both his native England and in the United States, the openly gay film director has proven capable of handling mainstream Hollywood productions as well as daring, low-budget films.

Born in 1926, Schlesinger got his first chance at performing while in the armed services during World War II. After appearing in several plays while attending Oxford and, later in London during the 1950s, he honed his filmmaking skills on documentaries for the BBC. For one of these, *Terminus*, Schlesinger received great acclaim. A cinema verité study of London's Waterloo Train Station, the film won a major award at the Venice Film Festival. This led to directing *A Kind of Loving* in 1962. His first feature assignment, the complex, melancholy story details the lives of a lower middle-class man and his pregnant girlfriend who are forced into marriage. The film stands as one of the prime examples of England's gritty "kitchen sink" school of filmmaking.

Schlesinger followed *Loving* with *Billy Liar*, featuring Tom Courtenay as an Englishman whose drab existence leads him to retreat into a Walter Mitty-ish fantasy life. In 1965, Schlesinger filmed *Darling*, a stylish look at "swinging London" as experienced by model Julie Christie and the men in her life. Christie took home an Academy Award for Best Actress for her performance, while the film was nominated for Best Picture and Best Director. With these handful of films, Schlesinger was at the forefront of socially conscious cinema with his stirring and penetrating examinations of sexual themes and working-class characters.

It was with his American feature film debut, however, in which Schlesinger created one of the most important films of the decade: *Midnight Cowboy*. A powerhouse portrayal of the friendship between a Texas hustler (Jon Voight) and a handicapped New York con man (Dustin Hoffman), the film realistically depicts the squalor and glitziness of late-1960s New York, which mirrored the ensuing path of a nation. Though the film featured gay characters throughout, the essential relationship between Voight and Hoffman's characters was curiously less-developed — their loving relationship was treated in an "are-they-or-aren't-they"

fashion. The film received an "X" rating, and won Oscars for Picture and Director. Schlesinger continued with gay themes in: *Sunday, Bloody Sunday*, a landmark film in which, for the first time in a major production, two male characters kissed on the lips; and *An Englishman Abroad*, a BBC production with Alan Bates as British spy Guy Burgess. Though in his 1976 adaptation *Marathon Man*, a gay relationship featured in the book was completely ignored in the film version — that of government agents played by Roy Scheider and William Devane.

Schlesinger turned down writer Larry Kramer's request to direct the screen version of his acclaimed AIDS play, "The Normal Heart," in most probability due to his own interest to pursue his own AIDS drama, *The Midday Sun*. Schlesinger has spent over five years in trying to bring the story to the screen, written initially by novelist David Leavitt and, most recently, a re-write by Ramsey Fadiman. Of the project, Schlesinger said, "As a gay director, it matters to me desperately. If I'm going to tackle a subject as difficult as AIDS, I've got to do it awfully well. (The film) is one that deals with living with — not dying from — AIDS." Also in development are *Aspects of Love*, a film adaptation of one of Andrew Lloyd Weber's lesser stage musicals, and *Bad Desire*, an erotic thriller about a public official's secret life. His latest film, *The Innocent*, based on the novel by Ian McWean and starring Anthony Hopkins, Campbell Scott and Isabella Rossellini, is set for late 1994 release.

A tender embrace in *Midnight Cowboy*

Who's hustling who? Bob Balaban (l.) worms out of paying for sex with hustler Jon Voight in *Midnight Cowboy*

In addition to a Hitchcock-inspired cameo appearance in the thriller *Pacific Heights*, Schlesinger has appeared on the other side of the camera in *The Lost Language of Cranes*.

A Kind of Loving *(1962, 112 min, GB)*

Schlesinger's first feature film is a sensitive drama about a young couple living in the industrial North who marry because of pregnancy. While the film was unfortunately lost in the shuffle, having been released after its sensational "kitchen sink" counterparts *Room at the Top* and *Saturday Night, Sunday Morning*, it is nonetheless a witty, frank and poignant study of a lust gone awry. Featuring sterling performances by Alan Bates and June Ritchie as the young couple. ⊛

Billy Liar! *(1963, 96 min, GB)*

One of the benchmark films in the British "kitchen sink" school of filmmaking, this early Schlesinger effort is an outstanding examination of middle-class life. Tom Courtenay is splendid as a young undertaker clerk who is stuck in the mundacity of his boorish life.

In her film debut, Julie Christie is a wonderful young mod woman who offers Courtenay an escape into a world of fantasy. ⊛

▼ Darling *(1965, 122 min, GB)*

This highly influential classic brilliantly captures many of the manners, mores and morals of mod mid-'60s London. Julie Christie, who is nothing less than radiant, deservedly won an Oscar for her portrayal of a young London model who quickly climbs the social ladder by strategically jumping in and out of assorted beds. Dirk Bogarde stars as one of her conquests and Laurence Harvey is featured as one who escapes her enticing trap. Schlesinger received his first Oscar nomination as Best Director; the film was a Best Picture nominee. Ronald Curran plays Malcolm, a gay photographer who joins Christie on holiday in Italy. In one scene, he cruises a waiter, but *she* beds him. ⊛

Far from the Madding Crowd

(1967, 169 min, GB)

Julie Christie stars in this sumptuous adaptation of Thomas Hardy's novel as a ravashing femme fatale who manages to make emotional mince meat out of three men's lives (Alan Bates, Peter

Finch and Terence Stamp). Schlesinger's masterful touch combined with the brilliant cinematography of Nicolas Roeg make this an extraordinary viewing experience. ☹

▼ Midnight Cowboy *(1969, 113 min, US)*

No longer the shocking tale it was when first released, this classic slice of pop culture has evolved into a somewhat nostalgic reminder of the '60s mind-set, capturing the naiveté and upheaval of a society enduring growing pains. Jon Voight and Dustin Hoffman create a pair of legendary screen losers: Joe Buck, the aspiring Texan stud-for-hire; and Ratso Rizzo, his rodent-like mentor. Buck, a Texas "cowboy," travels to New York to make his fortune hustling rich older ladies. He encounters the tubercular Ratso, becoming his only friend as Ratso takes him under his wing and expands his services to the male population. Buck's gay encounters include high school student Bob Balaban in a dark movie theatre, and businessman Bernard Hughes whom, in a disturbing scene, Buck mercilessly beats up and robs. The homosexual attraction in the complex but tender relationship between Buck and Ratso is hinted at and seen as obvious by most, but it is never explicitly developed. Winner of three Academy Awards, including Film, Director and Screenplay. ☹

▼ Sunday, Bloody Sunday

(1971, 110 min, GB)
Glenda Jackson and Peter Finch give sparkling performances in this landmark work, a cause célèbre in the depiction of homosexuality and bisexuality in a mainstream film. Schlesinger has said that this small, personal film was a present from United Artists after his success with *Midnight Cowboy*. This quietly moving drama centers around the troubled participants of a bisexual triangle. Both Jackson and Finch are in a relationship with the younger, hippish Murray Head, a man who treats both aloofly and with almost bemused detachment. The passionate kiss between Finch and Head aroused an audible gasp from the audience of the day, a reaction that contributed to its box-office failure. Hollywood rewarded the film's groundbreaking intentions by nominating Finch, Jackson, Schlesinger and author Penelope Gilliatt for Oscars. ☹

The Day of the Locust *(1975, 144 min, US)*

A powerful, beautifully filmed screen version of Nathaniel West's novel of aspirations and forgotten dreams in 1930s Hollywood. Karen Black gives one of her best performances as an opportunistic, aspiring actress involved with both young studio set director William Atherton and lonely, slightly slow-witted Donald Sutherland (in a mesmerizing portrayal). Burgess Meredith received a well-deserved Oscar nomination as Black's boozing, sickly ex-vaudevillian father. An unforgettable though demanding film experience; the Hollywood premiere at the finale remains one of the most chilling sequences ever put to film. ☹

Marathon Man *(1976, 125 min, US)*

Nail-biting thriller with Dustin Hoffman as a Columbia University student who unwittingly becomes involved with the CIA, Nazi war criminals and the beautiful Marthe Keller. Laurence Olivier is splendid as one of the screen's most vicious villains, and Roy Scheider also stars as Hoffman's secret agent brother. Does for dentists what *Psycho* did for showers. Based on the William Goldman novel. There is no mention of the gay relationship between Scheider and William Devane's characters as featured in the book. ☹

Richard Gere in *Yanks*

Yanks *(1979, 139 min, US)*

An absorbing and literate WWII drama about American G.I.s stationed in England. Richard Gere and William Devane are but two of the "Yanks" who begin relationships with British women — Gere with young Lisa Eichhorn and Devane with married Vanessa Redgrave. In support, Rachel Roberts gives a smashing performance as Eichhorn's inflexible mother. Fine direction from Schlesinger, who has a keen eye for the detail and atmosphere of the era. ☹

Honky Tonk Freeway *(1981, 107 min, US)*

A major miscalculation on his part, this lame satire was a critical and box-office disaster, making it Schlesinger's *Heaven's Gate*. Trying to be wacky and frenetic, but coming off simply as a trying mess, the story revolves around a small American town that tries to become a tourist attraction despite no exit ramp from the new interstate. ☹

Separate Tables *(1983, 112 min, GB)*

Schlesinger's made-for-TV rendition of Terence Rattigan's pair of playlets is every bit as worthy as the 1958 film version with Burt Lancaster and David Niven. In "Table by the Window," Julie Christie plays an aging fashion model who travels to a seaside resort in the hopes of rekindling a relationship with her ex-husband (Alan Bates). In "Table Number Seven," Christie plays a woman who holds a secret love for an Army major (Bates) who is embroiled in a public scandal. Both Bates and Christie offer superb performances and excellent support comes from Claire Bloom and Irene Worth. ⊛

▼ An Englishman Abroad *(1985, 63 min, GB)*

Alan Bates gives a riveting performance in this brilliantly staged drama originally made for British TV. Based on a true incident, Bates plays Guy Burgess, the infamous British spy and traitor who defected to Russia. During a 1958 theatrical performance in Moscow featuring visiting actress Coral Browne (appearing as herself), a drunken Burgess, now years after his defection, promptly crashes backstage and sets up a friendship with Browne — desperate for Anglo companionship, cigarettes, drink and gossip from home. Browne, who is intrigued by this now paunchy, disheveled and quite eccentric outsider, comes to pity, despise and assist him after he invites her to his shabby flat. It is there that she meets his male lover (supplied by the State?) and comes to understand more about this almost broken man, called by one of her friends as "the notorious bugger." A touching and humorous film, with a witty, concise screenplay that, without artifice, includes Burgess' homosexuality within the story. ⊛

The Falcon and the Snowman

(1985, 131 min, US)

Acclaimed espionage thriller based on the true-life story of Christopher Boyce and Dalton Lee, who sold national secrets to the Soviets. Timothy Hutton and Sean Penn are outstanding as Boyce and Lee. ⊛

The Believers *(1987, 114 min, US)*

Suspenseful occult thriller starring Martin Sheen as a New York therapist whose counseling of a disturbed policeman leads him into a series of bizarre and gory ritual slayings. ⊛

▼ Madame Sousatzka *(1988, 122 min, GB)*

Shirley MacLaine gives a spirited performance as an eccentric and demanding piano teacher who dedicates herself to her new student — a gifted 15-year-old Indian boy. A lovely, lyrical film directed by Schlesinger with great sensitivity. Also with Peggy Ashcroft, Twiggy and Navin Chowdhry as the youth. Adapted for the screen by longtime Merchant Ivory collaborator Ruth Prawer Jhabvala. Lee Montague appears as an elderly gay neighbor. ⊛

Pacific Heights *(1990, 102 min, US)*

A "yupwardly mobile" couple (Matthew Modine and Melanie Griffith) pool their resources to purchase and renovate a large Victorian home (complete with two rental units) in an upscale San Francisco neighborhood. Enter Michael Keaton as sociopath Carter Hayes, a tenant from hell who seems to know that a lodger can do just about anything to his landlords and not be evicted — including non-payment of rent, destruction of property and cockroach breeding. ⊛

▼ A Question of Attribution

(1992, 72 min, GB)

A continuation of the homosexual Cambridge spy scandal (which included Guy Burgess, Anthony Blunt, Kim Philby and Donald MacLean) which shook Britain not once but twice — first when the ring was uncovered and secondly 30 years later when the "fourth man," previously protected by the government, was exposed. Like Schlesinger's previous *An Englishman Abroad*, this intensely witty drama was written by British playwright Alan Bennett. But the story instead focuses on that "fourth man" — Sir Anthony Blunt. James Fox is wonderful as the aristocratic Blunt, an intelligent, priggish and fey gentleman living in the rarified air of fine art but whose youthful "indiscretion" becomes his undoing. With a promise of immunity if he names names, Blunt engages in a taut cat-and-mouse game with a working-class government official as the film wonderfully uses discussions on paintings, art and artists as a symbol of Blunt's spying activities. The marvelously written exchange between a surprisingly intelligent, if cynical Queen Elizabeth and Sir Anthony is a high point of this absorbing and intelligent film. Like *Blunt: The Fourth Man*, which starred Ian Richardson, his homosexuality is taken as a given, with plenty of references but no overt name calling. A quality drama of the highest order. ⊛

Shirley MacLaine is *Madame Sousatzka*

MONIKA TREUT

Monika Treut, after only three feature films and several shorts, has become an exciting and visible leader in independent lesbian filmmaking — as one critic succinctly put it, "Her films were queer long before Queer Cinema was invented." Not content to make conventional, politically correct lesbian love stories, Treut's films are controversial in their celebration of non-mainstream issues such as lesbian sexuality (including S&M) and focusing on contemporary non-conformists and "bad girls" who speak out against traditional thought (Annie Sprinkle, Camille Paglia). Her works explore the liberating effects of diverse expressions of female and lesbian sexuality and they tend to shock the uninitiated, prod the timid and entertain the liberated. With subtle humor, a sensitive handling of the characters and a deft directorial touch, Treut avoids simple titillation or controversy-for-controversy sake in creating complex, challenging and sensitive films.

Born in Germany in a suburb of Dusseldorf in 1954, Treut studied literature and philosophy in college with her doctoral thesis being a study on the role of women in the works of Marquis de Sade's "Juliette" and Leopold von Sacher-Masoch's "Venus in Furs." In addition to being a filmmaker, Treut is also an avant-garde performance artist, author of several essays and books, and a lecturer in Europe. She currently resides in Hamburg and New York.

After working for several years in video, Treut entered the international film scene with a bang in 1985 with *Seduction: The Cruel Woman* (co-directed by Elfi Mikesch), which received its world premiere at the 1985 Berlin Film Festival. About that first showing, Treut stated, "That opening was like a riot. It's still a nightmare to me, which makes it hard to recall. It was packed, sold out three days beforehand...we didn't know what was going to happen...the audience got so mad. They attacked us. Only people who hated the film talked. That was only men. They just went crazy." Her next two films were based primarily in the United States. All three features played successful theatrical engagements in art houses in the U.S., no small feat for independent filmmakers.

Treut is currently working on *The Virility Factor*, a German-Canadian co-production based on the novel by Robert Merle ("The Day of the Dolphin") and set in Toronto. The film is to be a social satire about gender war. Set in the near future, the story charts a deadly disease that feeds on the testosterone of men of reproductive age. With such a theme at its core, Treut is destined to continue to bask in the contentious limelight.

"Being female is probably the source of my creativity.
—Monika Treut

▼ Seduction: The Cruel Woman
(1985, 84 min, Germany)

Co-directed by Treut and Elfi Mikesch (known for her experimental films like *I Often Think of Hawaii*), this highly stylized, dreamlike exploration of sadomasochism stars Mechtild Grossmann as Wanda. A glamorous, cooly detached dominatrix and proprietor of the local "gallery" of bondage, Wanda is an unusual business person who specializes in smashing sexual taboos with the staging of elaborate S&M fantasies. In her personal life, she moves from relationship to relationship, from a clinging female shoe fetishist to an American "trainee" (played by Sheila McLaughlin, the director of *She Must Be Seeing Things*). A slick, visual fantasy that plumbs the depths of the dark side of sexual desire. ⊗

"This is S&M by Avedon, outfits by Dior."
—Marcia Pally, *Film Comment*

"The most sophisticated lesbian film I've ever seen, carefully stylized in their color-coordinated mode of the late Fassbinder. Or like Helmut Newton photography come to life."

—C. Carr, *The Village Voice*

Seduction: The Cruel Woman

The Virgin Machine

▼ The Virgin Machine

(1988, 85 min, Germany)

This thought-provoking sexual odyssey tells the story of a young West German woman and her search for "romantic love." Frustrated by the emptiness and the emotional moraine of her native Hamburg, Dorothee decides to flee her home to search for her mother, who is living in San Francisco. Once she arrives, however, her trek turns into a process of sexual discovery as she encounters several characters of the sexual left and begins to understand the lesbian side of her persona. Filmed in a steamy black and white by Elfi Mikesch, the movie exudes a sensuality in which simple lust is transformed into glorious eroticism. A refreshing and funny feminist film about a woman's exploration of her own sexuality. ⊛

> "A lesbian 'Candide'...deliriously obscene."
> —*San Francisco Examiner*

▼ My Father Is Coming

(1991, 82 Min, US/Germany)

A comical story of sexual confusion, sexual awakening and self-discovery. Vicky, an aspiring actress and struggling waitress, finds her life in turmoil when she becomes involved with both a mysterious man and a female co-worker at the time her German father arrives for a visit. Having given the impression that she is a suc-cessful actress and happily married, Vicky vainly tries to impress her sour and demanding parent, even resorting to getting a Latino-loving gay friend to be her "husband." But papa doesn't get a chance to complain, for he is immediately swept up in a whirlwind of romance, TV commercial appearances and kinky sex — an odyssey which eventually leads to the bed of a lovely sex guru, played by Annie Sprinkle. The many characters in this charming comedy cover the spectrum of sexuality — from gay and straight to female-to-male transsexuals, with the results being an exuberant slice of life, New York style. ⊛

> "A cheerful cornucopia of kinkiness where genders and sexual preferences aren't simply bent, they are turned into corkscrews."
> —*The New York Times*

▼ Female Misbehavior

(1983-92, 80 min, Germany/US)

Amusing and provocative, this series of four shorts explores the expanded boundaries of female sexuality by focusing on four disparate, interesting individuals, all outlaws from conventional society as well as outsiders from mainstream feminism. ⊛

Bondage *(1983, 20 min)*
An unidentified woman explains the "pleasures" of bondage and tit torture and the "very warm, very safe, very secure" feeling that comes from it.

Annie *(1989, 10 min)*
Ex-porn star, now invigoratingly original performance artist, Annie Sprinkle offers an entertaining segment in which she allows the viewer to join her in examining (and admiring) her cervix with the aid of a flashlight and a speculum.

Dr. Paglia *(1992, 23 min)*
Dr. Camille Paglia, Professor of Humanities at Philadelphia's University of the Arts, came into prominence with the publication of her best-selling "Sexual Personae" in 1990. In this interview, the camera simply roles as the brilliant, highly opinionated, narcissist "anti-feminist feminist" and "academic rottweiler" discusses her theories as well as her disastrous sex life.

Max *(1992, 27 min)*
An interview with Native American Anita Valerio, who was formerly a stunning lesbian until she underwent an operation that transformed her into Max, a handsome heterosexual "almost" male.

> "*Female Misbehavior* is a totally accurate picture of my everyday life as a social and sexual alien."
> —Camille Paglia

FAVORITE DIRECTORS

GUS VAN SANT

Van Sant (c.) with Keanu Reeves and River Phoenix

One of the most daring, innovative and accomplished filmmakers working in cinema today, Gus Van Sant's career to date has been remarkably self-assured enjoying both critical and popular success. His "trilogy of the streets" all center on innocent down-and-outers scrounging for a living on the wet streets of the Pacific Northwest; and whether dealing with unrequited gay love in the gritty queer realism of *Mala Noche* and *My Own Private Idaho* or drug-addicted lovers/outlaws in *Drugstore Cowboy*, his characters retain a dignity and a self-awareness that would go unexplored by other filmmakers. On his use of these unusual subject matters and individuals, Van Sant remarked, "Most of my films fall into an area that's never been touched or mentioned except in news articles or documentaries." The success of the uncompromising Van Sant has undoubtedly inspired many aspiring young gay and lesbian filmmakers. Openly gay, Van Sant's films have a strong gay point-of-view, although he does not want to be pigeon-holed into being a "gay director," saying, "I don't want to propagandize being gay to the straight world."

Born in 1953 into a wealthy Connecticut family that eventually moved to Portland (where he still lives), Van Sant showed an early interest in filmmaking — using a Super-8 camera to make films beginning at the age of 12. He continued to make films as an art student at the Rhode Island School of Design. After graduating, he honed his skills with several three-minute shorts made for about $50 while working as a sound man in Hollywood as well as producing TV commercials in New York. The money from these jobs helped produce the $25,000 budget for his first film, *Mala Noche*, an out-of-nowhere independent feature that became a small hit in art cinemas and gay/lesbian films festivals around the country. Originally distributed by Van Sant himself, the film featured a matter-of-fact depiction of a gay man who was decidedly non-stereotypical. Its hero was a disheveled, handsome young man living on skid row who was all-too-aware of his own inevitable frustration in gaining the affections of his elusive sexual obsession: a straight teenage Mexican illegal immigrant.

This small film proved to be a gold-plated calling card to Hollywood as Van Sant's next film was the studio-backed (albeit small budget) drama, *Drugstore Cowboy*, which knowingly explored the drug culture and its denizens of the early 1970s. Defiantly flying against the rhetoric of Nancy Reagan's "Just Say No" anti-drug campaign, the film's critical response was quite strong: *Newsweek* called it "extraordinary"; the *L.A. Times* found it "electrifying"; and Vincent Canby dubbed Van Sant a leader in a new generation of filmmakers. His *My Own Private Idaho* was a critical and box-office hit, despite its "unsavory" theme and the casting of teenage heartthrob River Phoenix as a gay prostitute.

After getting off to a quick start, Van Sant's career in the past few years has been on hold. After devoting quite a bit of time to working on pre-production for the Oliver Stone-backed fiction film of Randy Shilts' best-selling book "The Mayor of Castro Street," about slain gay rights activist Harvey Milk, he left the project over conflicts with the producers over the original screenplay. While the producers claimed that he wanted to film "Harvey Milk meets *My Own Private Idaho*," Van Sant claims that he simply wanted to portray Milk less as a martyr and more on a human scale. His much publicized troubles with his adaptation of Tom Robbins' counter-culture comedy *Even Cowgirls Get the Blues* was a risky venture that proved difficult to pull off. After a less-than-enthusiastic response at the 1993 Toronto Film Festival, the film was pulled from its intended Fall opening and re-scheduled for a Spring 1994 release, reportedly so Van Sant could go back to the editing room. Despite the additional work, the film opened to generally unfavorable notices and tepid box office.

Currently, Van Sant is working on *To Die For* (not to be confused with Peter McKenzie Litten's gay ghost drama) from a screenplay by Buck Henry. Based on the 1992 novel by Joyce Maynard, the story centers on a woman's attempt to become a TV anchorperson by using her husband's death as an aid for advancement. Van Sant succinctly describes the film as "sort of a tragedy, but it's very funny, too."

Despite accolade from most gays and lesbians for his two gay-themed films, they have also disappointed and frustrated certain gays who want a clearer, more mainstream gay voice to rise in Hollywood, one in which gays are portrayed as positive, non-threatening and well-adjusted. Those proponents must wait for another, for Gus Van Sant is not the one. His vision is personal and troubling, which gives his films their power.

> "My films show a real severe world...if I tell things the way I see them, eventually it'll help."
> —Gus Van Sant

Shorts:

For several years, Van Sant made quickie three-minute shorts reportedly for around $50 each. They include: *My New Friend* (1984), a caustic autobiographical story in which Van Sant holds up a photo of a naked man and explains how he got a black eye; *Switzerland* (1986), which features a kid Van Sant meets on the street who claims he's from Switzerland; and *Ken Gets Out of Jail* (1987), about a street punk who's coming off a stint for robbing a store. In addition to these, he also made *The Discipline of DE*, a witty short about the William Burroughs-inspired attitude of "Do Easy." The latter can be found in the video compilation *Since Stonewall*.

▼ Mala Noche *(US, 1985, 78 min)*

Van Sant's first feature-length film, made on a shoe-string budget, proves to be a wry, perceptive meditation on obsessive love and thwarted lust. The film's gritty black-and-white photography intensifies Portland's colorful skid row where Walt (Tim Streeter), a cynical young man, spends his time selling Thunderbird to the panhandlers at the local *bodega*. Always with a weakness for Latinos, he becomes blindly infatuated with Johnny, an unresponsive 16-year-old illegal Mexican immigrant who is alternately abusive, taunting and appreciative. Frustrated by Johnny's stand of not giving it up, Walt becomes the compliant *puto* for Johnny's handsome immigrant friend Roberto. Refreshingly told from the amour-smitten hero's point-of-view, this early example of New Queer Cinema is a pleasure from beginning to end.

Drugstore Cowboy *(1989, 100 min, US)*

On the strength of his first low-budget film, *Mala Noche*, Van Sant received the backing of a major studio to make a non-gay themed drama and without abandoning his people-on-the-precipice interest, he adapted an unpublished novel by James Fogle who was at the time serving a 22-year prison term for drug-related crimes. This provocative exposé of four down-and-out drug addicts living in the Pacific Northwest in the early 1970s is one of the most highly original and profoundly honest films to come around in some time. Matt Dillon is perfectly cast as an icy-cool and unrepentant "drug fiend" who plays daddy to a rogue family of fellow junkies

— Kelly Lynch is his statuesque wife and James Le Gros and Heather Graham are his mindless junkie pals. Drawing its power from a surprisingly wry sense of humor and its wholly unapologetic even brazen tone, the film follows Dillon and crew as they wantonly romp from town to town and burgle the drugs they need from local apothecaries. William Burroughs is featured as wizened junkie Bob. ⊛

▼ My Own Private Idaho

(1991, 105 min, US)

Set on the mean streets of Portland and focusing on its burned-out denizens and the young male prostitutes on the edge of survival, this fascinating drama is a modern gay classic. River Phoenix is nothing short of brilliant in his portrayal of Mike Waters, a solitary, narcoleptic gay street hustler searching for his long-lost mother. Keanu Reeves co-stars as Scott, a slumming beauty and the unresponsive object of Mike's love. Van Sant deftly weaves in a subplot based on Shakespeare's "Henry IV, Pt II," even borrowing a smattering of the Bard's dialogue. Reeves gives strong support as Mike's Prince Hal-like friend and William Richert is superb as the Falstaff-derived Bob Pigeon. Dreamily photographed, with mood ranging from hilarious to tragic to highly erotic, the film is a tender, knowing look at life on the streets. River's quietly pleadful declaration (much of it improvised by the actor himself) of love to Keanu as they sit couched in front of an outdoor fire is a "perfect moment" in gay filmmaking. ⊛

▼ Even Cowgirls Get the Blues

(1994, 100 min, US)

A disappointingly vapid and lifeless misfire in the still short canon of work by Van Sant, this attempt to capture the hippie-dippy effervescence of Tom Robbins' 1976 novel completely fails to come to cinematic life. The comedy/adventure/drama/love story is filled with determinedly oddball cameos (including William Burroughs, whose one line is "Ominous"; Roseanne Arnold; Buck Henry; Crispin Glover; Angie Dickinson); and horribly stilted performances by the supporting actors (Keanu Reeves, Noriyuki "Pat" Morita, Lorraine Bracco); and a script that limps along, saddled by its attempts to be both post-modernist camp and politically and sexually relevant. Uma Thurman plays the pleasant if vacuous Sissy Hankshaw, a young beauty who is blessed/cursed with abnormally large thumbs and who lives the free life of the road. Encouraged by "The Countess" (a white-faced, over-the-top faggy John Hurt) to visit his dude ranch, The Rubber Rose, in Oregon, Sissy soon becomes embroiled in a cowgirl uprising headed by the "charismatic" Bonanza Jellybean (actually a catatonic Rain Phoenix). The lesbian affair is really the best-handled aspect of the film as the transfixed Sissy and gun-totin' Bonanza make for a believable and touching couple. While a failure on every level, the film is nonetheless easy to watch and does sport moments of fun; but its lasting effect is to remind one how films should not be made. k.d. lang provides a pleasant country soundtrack. ⊛

LUCHINO VISCONTI

An internationally renowned director who enjoyed success throughout his career, Luchino Visconti was a complex personality. He was born into one of Italy's most aristocratic families, though he eventually became a Marxist. His early films were moving, almost-documentary studies of life among the working poor, and his later films centered primarily around the rich, powerful and wealthy. He was a homosexual whose work contained few gay characters but were infused with a strong gay esthetic, and he was a successful filmmaker who spent much of his productive career working in theatre and opera.

Visconti, who died in 1976 at the age of 69, led a varied and interesting life. Reportedly a descendant of King Desiderius, the father-in-law of Charlemagne, Don Luchino Visconti di Morone began life as a privileged, pampered child who studied art, played the cello and who spent many an evening with his family listening to opera at La Scala. After a stint in the military, the young Visconti became a designer. He soon befriended Coco Chanel, and was introduced by her to the French filmmaker Jean Renoir. Visconti apprenticed under him for several films, then began his own directorial career with *Ossessione*. That film, made after being paroled from a fascist jail, launched the period of Neorealism, a type of film that focused on the daily lives of the working people and which often featured non-professionals in the roles. It was at this time Visconti, despite his noble lineage, developed a strong alliance with communism (although never becoming one). This dichotomy of values earned him the label, "The Red Count."

Visconti's film career can be easily divided into two periods: neorealist works which began with *Ossessione* and concluded with *Rocco and His Bothers*; and lavish melodramas produced on an operatic scale which began with *The Leopard* and were characterized by elaborate and meticulous set design, international financing and "star" actors. He was a master of both genres, although his detractors dismiss many of his later films as overly flamboyant and insubstantial. His political convictions did not generate as much controversy as did Pier Paolo Pasolini's similar beliefs. The emphasis in his films on social order and the role of the rich and of the aristocracy — far from leftist cinema — probably allayed the fears of many right-wingers.

Visconti with Charlotte Rampling

Openly gay, even a bit theatrical, Visconti always had an eye for male beauty, and his films were notable for featuring handsome young men in the leads and for their lack of strong female roles. Alain Delon received his real start in films in *Rocco and His Brothers*, Dirk Bogarde enjoyed international success with *The Damned* and *Death in Venice*, and Helmut Berger, his last love, starred in a couple of Visconti's final films, including *Conversation Piece* in which Berger played a captivating young man who entranced Burt Lancaster, the director's alter ego.

Not a prolific filmmaker, Visconti eventually made twelve features, as well as staging several plays (including works from Jean Cocteau and Tennessee Williams) in France and Italy and producing many operas both in Italy and at London's Covent Garden. Visconti died of a stroke soon after finishing *The Innocent*. In one of his last press conferences, Visconti wryly noted, "Here I am, ready to make another film, even if I do need a wheelchair. Next time it will be a stretcher, but I shall never give up."

Ossessione *(1942, 135 min, Italy)*

For his first feature film, Visconti adapted James M. Cain's powerful tale of ill-fated love, "The Postman Always Rings Twice," and transplanted it to wartime rural Italy. Gino, a virile young drifter, meets and falls in love with Giovanna, a beautiful yet desperately unhappy woman who is trapped in a loveless marriage with an older man. The two begin a doomed affair, conceived in passion and lust, but it ends in greed, murder and recrimination. This remarkable neorealist debut was banned by Mussolini during the war, and because it was an unauthorized version of the Cain novel, it was not permitted into the United States until 1975. Considered one of the first films (if not *the* first film) in the neorealist movement. ✆

La Terra Trema *(1948, 160 min, Italy)*

Visconti, who had initially intended to made a Communist Party-financed documentary short on the peasants of a poverty-stricken Sicily, abandoned this idea to work on an epic that focused on the harsh conditions of southern Italy's fishermen, factory workers and miners. He finished only this segment, "episodio del Mare," and the result is a neorealist masterpiece. Filmed on location with non-professional actors, the story tells of the struggles of an exploited fisherman's family and their unsuccessful revolt against insurmountable odds. With startlingly beautiful images, a simple narrative and a focus of social reality, this is one of his best films. ✆

Bellissima *(1951, 108 min, Italy)*

This neorealist tragicomedy follows the determined attempts of a pushy working-class mother who struggles to get her cute seven-year-old daughter into a film. Anna Magnani is wonderful as the mother willing to sacrifice everything to see her child a star. ✆

Senso *(1954, 120 min, Italy)*

A lavish and tragic tale of love and war, *Senso* is one of the landmarks of post-war Italian cinema. The story concerns the careless actions of an aristocratic woman (Alida Valli) who sacrifices her marriage and security for a handsome but cowardly soldier (Farley Granger). This lavishly romantic story is set in Venice in 1866 on the eve of the great conflict between Venice and Austria. Bankrolled by American money, the film's English-language dialogue is by Tennessee Williams and Paul Bowles. Visconti originally wanted Marlon Brando and Ingrid Bergman in the roles. (Also known as: *The Wanton Countess*) ✆

White Nights (Le Notti Bianche)

(1957, 107 min, Italy)

Based on a Dostoevsky short story and set within a misty, dreamlike seaside city, this sad love story was a great stylistic departure from Visconti's previous, neorealist features. Marcello Mastroianni stars as a young man, prowling the docks for a pick-up, who meets and fatefully falls in love with a mysterious, obsessive woman (Maria Schell). In a series of brief walks, chases and attempted escapes, she reveals to him that she is waiting for her lover who, before going to sea, promised to return to her. While talking only of her long-gone lover (Jean Marais), the two develop a relationship destined to end in tragedy. ✆

Rocco and His Brothers

(1960, 180 min, Italy)

Alain Delon and Claudia Cardinale star in this epic tale of five peasant brothers and their widowed mother who migrate to northern Italy only to find their dreams of happiness shattered when they confront the harsh economic realities of industrial Milan. The melodrama chronicles the family's struggle in this new world where family values and loyalty are lost to the new morality and individualism of contemporary society. The story centers on Rocco (Delon), the gentle and withdrawn brother, who tragically falls in love with Nadia (Annie Girardot), the girlfriend of his thuggish boxer brother. The escalating tensions between the two, fueled by the repressions and frustrations of an unfeeling land, build to a climax of rape and murder. A powerful operatic drama about opposing cultures, lust, greed and the will to survive. ✆

The Leopard *(1963, 185 min, Italy)*

A meticulous, atmospheric epic about 19th-century Italian nobility with Burt Lancaster in the title role as the Leopard, Prince Fabrizio de Salina, an aging aristocrat whose elegant world undergoes a dramatic upheaval during the social turbulence of the 1860s. Alain Delon is his opportunistic nephew who seizes the chance to become a prominent officer in the revolutionary regime. Claudia Cardinale co-stars as Delon's well-bred fiancée. A sumptuous portrait of a vanquished age featuring sparkling performances and a lavish Nino Rota score.

The Stranger *(1967, 104 min, Italy/France)*

A faithful, hypnotic adaptation of Albert Camus' existential treatise, this involving drama stars Marcello Mastroianni as Meursault, an individual seized by emptiness and isolated from society. Against the languid backdrop of Algiers, his detachment from existence abruptly ends when he commits a senseless murder and stands trial. However, this feeling stems not so much from the actual killing, but for his indifference to societal regulations. Imprisoned and stripped of his physical freedom, Meursault experiences a liberating resignation as he surrenders to the "benign indifference of the universe." A quietly powerful and unsettling work.

▼ The Damned *(1969, 155 min, Italy/Germany)*

A frantic international cast depicts Visconti's panorama of pre-war German decadence and Nazi narcissism. The action centers primarily among the vicious power struggles within a powerful Krupp-like family. Helmut Berger is memorable as Martin, the misfit son with a violent mother-fixation and a molester of little girls who does a mean imitation of Marlene Dietrich. Ingrid Thulin is his Lady Macbeth-like mother and Dirk Bogarde is the murderous man who wants in. The infamous slaughter of the homosexual-infiltrated SA Brown Shirts by rival SS troops, known as the "Night of the Long Knives," is shown with great detail for the sexual depravity although Visconti was forced to cut much more from the homosexually charged orgy preceeding the killings. ✆

▼ Death in Venice *(1971, 130 min, Italy)*

Visconti's adaptation of Thomas Mann's novella of an artist in search of purity and beauty but who ultimately becomes fatally obsessed with an exquisite young boy is a melancholy experience. Set in turn-of-the-century Venice, this languidly paced, darkly atmospheric film stars Dirk Bogarde as Aschenbach, an older man enamored with a flirtatious but unattainable blond youth (Björn Andresen), and who is gradually weakened by the cholera epidemic sweeping the city. Visconti changed the profession of Aschenbach from a writer to a composer, enabling him to fill a largely wordless film with the wondrous music of Gustav Mahler. ✥

> "The theme is not only homosexuality, but there is homosexuality. Although no sex at all. Still, Hollywood wanted me to change the boy to a girl. They do not even know of Thomas Mann!"
>
> —Luchino Visconti

> "Mann's 'Death in Venice' is, in fact, no more about homosexuality than Kafka's 'Metamorphosis' is about entomology...this film is worse than mediocre; it is corrupt and distorted...it is irredeemably, unforgivably gay."
>
> —*Time*

▼ Ludwig *(1972, 168 min, Italy/Germany/France)*

Rarely seen in the United States and then only in a truncated version (although an original uncut version finally opened in New York in 1987), this film was troubled during filming (Visconti suffered a stroke during the production) and was widely dismissed on its release as slow, incoherent and superficial. Helmut Berger stars as the young Ludwig, the reclusive mad king of Bavaria. As the ranting but attractive homosexual king is slowly driven mad, his paranoia increases as he hides in his Baroque castle and whose only pleasures are the music of Wagner (played by Trevor Howard) and in exquisite young men. Wonderful settings, and some fine acting (including John Moulder Brown, Helmut Griem and Romy Schneider) is featured, but the film is interminably long.

▼ Conversation Piece *(1974, 122 min, Italy)*

Burt Lancaster is memorable as a retired intellectual whose life of solitude amid his books, paintings and art is abruptly invaded by the arrival of a garish, "modern" family who moves in upstairs. His old-world comforts are shattered as he is both drawn to and forced to participate in their tawdry and hedonistic lifestyle. The invading family (which brings a breath of fresh air, life and love into the professor's life) includes the enchanting Countess (Silvana Mangano), her daughter (Claudia Marsani) and the Countess' student revolutionary boy-toy (Helmut Berger). The old professor is especially attracted to the sweet-talking young man, with the sexual tension between them almost palpable. ✥

The Innocent *(1976, 125 min, Italy)*

Visconti's final film is set in turn-of-the-century Italy and features a fine cast, sumptuous photography and stunning sets and costumes. Giancarlo Giannini is a chauvinistic aristocrat who ignores his beautiful and loving wife (Laura Antonelli) in order to pursue his adulterous affair with his mistress (Jennifer O'Neill). Revenge is sweet, however, as the lonely and frustrated wife takes a lover and turns the tables on her insensitive husband. Elegant and restrained, this tale of society's double standards for sexuality was made while Visconti was quite ill and was released after his death. ✥

A scene of Nazi debauchery from *The Damned*

VON PRAUNHEIM
ROSA

One of the world's leading gay directors and the enfant terrible of New German Cinema, Rosa von Praunheim has been a continual campaigner for gay rights in his films, although his controversial approach to the subject — which is highly opinioned, often bitterly critical and not always "politically correct" — has challenged and even offended many members of the gay movement. The tone of his gay-themed films is usually one of anger: towards bourgeois gay men content to associate gay rights purely in sexual terms; towards gays who work within the very system that oppresses them; towards gay leaders whose motivations may be suspect; and towards the political and social system bent on conformity and suppression. In his latest films, he targets the political and medical leaders who have not done enough to stem the AIDS epidemic. But not all of von Praunheim's films ring of impassioned urgency. Other subjects and people that interest him are the social outcasts of society, be they transsexuals and transvestites, or simple, eccentric older women bucking the system.

Born Holger Mischwitki in Riga, Latvia, in 1942, von Praunheim adopted a new name to go with his profession, taking delight in his sexually ambiguous first name. He studied painting in Berlin and soon worked as an assistant to gay filmmakers Gregory J. Markopoulos and Werner Schroeter. In addition to many Super-8 and 16mm shorts, he made several television-financed features such as *Die Bettwurst* (1970) and *Leidenschaften* (1972). Von Praunheim's *Sisters of the Revolution* (1969) was his first film to deal with a gay theme. In it, a three-part look at women's liberation, a group of homosexuals are shown fighting not for gay rights but for the feminist cause. *Homosexuelle in New York* (1970) recorded a gay rights march and advocates a new thinking for gays ostracized by a homophobic society.

A natural Brechtian, von Praunheim is less concerned with dramatic involvement in his work and more interested in provoking an unsuspecting audience and challenging their conventional thinking with his sharply political opinions. With the release of his latest film, the delightful *I Am My Own Woman* (1992), one finds a mellowed von Praunheim, who entertains the audience with a touchingly sweet tale of survival told from the point of view of a very unconventional person.

Von Praunheim recently finished his autobiography,

Rosa and his Burger Queens

"Fifty Years of Perversity," and is readying his latest project, *Nerviosa*, a seemingly morbid autobiographical video which he promises to be a comedic *Citizen Kane*, in which von Praunheim gets shot in the beginning and the rest of the film follows a sleazy reporter investigating his life.

▼ It Is Not the Homosexual Who Is Perverted, But the Situation in Which He Lives *(1970, 85 min, Germany)*

Credited as being a catalyst in the formation of gay liberation groups in several German cities, this politically charged drama, influenced by the radical filmmaking of Jean-Luc Godard, paints an unflattering portrait of gay life as it is structured around one man's gradual sexual coming out and political maturation. David, a closeted young man, begins the process of finding himself and in doing so uncovers the diversity (and sordidness) of Berlin's gay underground. He has his first affair with another man, becomes involved with the "wrong crowd," visits numerous gay bars and cruising areas and eventually settles down into an enlightened homo-hippie commune. Von Praunheim damns gay men's aping of bourgeois heterosexual society's values and in the process

FAVORITE DIRECTORS

paints a bleak picture of stereotypical gay men engulfed in a self-destructive lifestyle. Many viewed this harsh view of gay men as such an attack that it prompted the videotaping of a short, *Audience Response to "It Is Not the Homosexual..."*. It was shot during a screening and discussion/interview with von Praunheim in 1973 at New York's Museum of Modern Art, and currently preceeds many of the film's screenings.

▼ Army of Lovers or Revolt of the Perverts *(1979, 98 min, Germany)*

This controversial film documents various segments in the American gay liberation movement. Von Praunheim's camera records the celebrations of a San Francisco gay rights march, but he is much more interested in the people running the show, what he sees as an increasingly fractured leadership. Those interviewed include a gay Nazi; gay porno movie stars; spokespersons from the Gay Activists Alliance and its more conservative counterpart, the National Gay Task Force; leaders of the Mattachine Society; the founders of the Daughters of Bilitis; and novelist John Rechy, who defends gay male promiscuity against the director's contention that what is hurting the gay men's movement is the obsession with "discos, baths and orgy bars." Von Praunheim explores, among other themes, the initial unity formed after the Stonewall Riots, which was strengthened by the assault of the Anita Bryant-led, anti-gay initiatives, but which ultimately foundered into polarization and self-interest groups.

Red Love *(1982, 80 min, Germany)*

The subject of this bizarre, filmed biography is Helga Goetze, a 55-year-old former housewife and mother of seven who became a weird celebrity in Germany with her call, "All I want to do is fuck." Always willing to bare her far-from-perky breasts for the camera, the woman's sexual appetite would have any normal nymphomaniac gasping for breath. At one point, she elucidates on the advantages of sex with an older woman claiming that "Young cunt smells young. But old cunt...ah-ha-hah!...dat's like old wine und cheese...fully ripened." The story intercuts her tale with scenes from a novel by feminist writer Alexandra Kollontai.

▼ City of Lost Souls
(1983, 89 min, Germany)

Jayne (formerly Wayne) County (lead singer of the old punk band Jayne County and the Electric Chairs) stars in this hilarious low-budget musical satire about the lurid lives of a group of American expatriates living in Berlin and working in a sleazy diner, the Burger Queen. Director von Praunheim has fashioned a real curiosity which is reminiscent of the best of Andy Warhol/Paul Morrissey, John Waters and *The Rocky Horror Picture Show*. This outrageous musical comedy stars a bevy of happy misfits including transsexual Angie Stardust and transvestite Tara O'Hara. (Also known as: *Burger Queens of Berlin*)

▼ A Virus Knows No Morals
(1986, 82 min, Germany)

Never one to tread softly on a controversial subject, von Praunheim tackles the issue of AIDS in this archaic black comedy. With several stories intercut throughout the film, his cast of weird characters includes a sex club owner who refuses to change his policies, claiming that, "I won't let them take away our freedom"; hysterical members of the press who are bent on making a story; and workers at a hospital where the deluge of AIDS patients causes them to become so bored and jaded that the night nurses roll dice to see which patient will die next. Gallows humor abounds as the director seeks to provoke, embarrass and enrage the audience into understanding the effects of the crisis. ⊗

> "As suppressor cells multiply, the screen fills with songsters in drag, high-camp hospitals, and the general air of a Lana Turner melodrama choreographed by John Waters."
> —*Film Comment*

> "Courageous...subversive...von Praunheim's patron saint must be Joan Crawford."
> —*Boston Phoenix*

▼ Horror Vacui *(1984, 85 min, Germany)*

Filmed, as many of his films are, by Elfi Mikesch, this interesting neo-expressionistic drama/satire has been called a gay *Cabinet of Dr. Caligari*. Frankie and Hannes are students and lovers who are separated after Frankie attends a lecture and quickly becomes involved in a sinister cult operating as a self-help group called "Optimal Optimism," which is headed by an old Nazi professor, Madame C. (Lotti Huber), who is referred to as "the glittering sunshine monster." When the cult members discover that Frankie is gay, he is repeatedly raped by both the men and women of the group. Hannes must find a way to rescue him.

Anita: Dances of Vice
(1987, 85 min, Germany)

Lotti Huber stars as an old woman who thinks that she is the reincarnation of Anita Berber, the infamous nude dancer in Weimar Berlin who flaunted her bisexuality, acknowledged taking drugs and generally scandalized the nation with her notorious behavior. The film intercuts black-and-white footage of the ragged old woman spouting her outrageous claims with colorful re-creations of the old woman living the life of her alter ego. ⊗

> "*Anita* is a kind of lunatic, low-budget fandango, with a honky-tonk score and ravishing visuals that suggest a flea market amalgam of *The Cabinet of Dr. Caligari*, *Threepenny Opera, Reefer Madness* and the Ballet Russe... a combination of exuberantly tacky expressionism and pornographic insolence."
> —J. Hoberman, *The Village Voice*

Dolly, Lotte and Maria

(1988, 60 min, Germany)
Always interested in eccentric or outlandish performers, von Praunheim examines the hectic lives of three German stage and screen legends: dancer and clown Lotte Goslar, singer Dolly Haas and dancer Maria Piscator.

▼ Silence = Death *(1990, 60 min, US)*

Made in collaboration with Phil Zwickler, this documentary explores the reactions and response of New York's artistic community to the ravages of AIDS. Activists interviewed include representatives from the many arts organizations that have alerted the public to the crisis through performance art, music, theatre and literature — such as David Wojnorowicz, Paul Smith and Rafael Gamba. Particularly entertaining segments include Keith Haring admitting to nostalgic longing for the days of carefree sex and Allen Ginsberg's musing upon his shyer attitude about sexual experimentation. Even with the gentler voices, the film's undercurrent is an angry demand for action and recognition. ⊛

"A call to arms...raw, involving eloquence...seething with rage and disbelief."
—*The Village Voice*

▼ Positive *(1990, 80 min, US)*

Positive follows *Silence = Death* as the second part of von Praunheim and Phil Zwickler's trilogy about AIDS and activism (the third part, *Asses on Fire*, was never released). This film powerfully documents New York City's gay community's response to the AIDS crisis as they are forced to organize themselves after the government's failure to stem the epidemic. Activists who are interviewed include playwright Larry Kramer, People with AIDS Coalition co-founder Michael Callen (who died of AIDS in 1994), New York filmmaker and journalist Phil Zwickler, as well as representatives from ACT-UP, Queer Nation and the Gay Men's Health Crisis. ⊛

Affengeil *(1991, 87 min, Germany)*

The life of Lotti Huber, a German performance artist and star of *Anita: Dances of Vice*, is the focus of this homage/documentary to her determinedly scandalous life. Blending reality with what most certainly must be an active imagination, 79-year-old Huber vividly recounts the momentous events and successes of her life. She was a former prostitute and concentration camp survivor who managed to escape from the death camp; she traveled the world; later in life she became a cabaret performer, film "star" and restauranteur; and she enjoyed several marriages. Supposedly, it was Huber who persuaded close friend von Praunheim to make this film on her life. He also appears in the film, arguing with Lotti — but they always kiss and make up. (Also known as: *Life Is Like a Cucumber*)

▼ I Am My Own Woman

(1992, 90 min, Germany)
This wonderfully inspiring film of one person's determined efforts to be exactly what he wants is von Praunheim's best work to date and a must for all gay men and women facing the repression and wrath of a straight society. A documentary with re-created dramatic scenes intercut throughout, the film tells the courageous story of Charlotte von Mahsldorf, born Lother Berfelde in 1928, who, obsessed with wearing women's clothing, realizes his dream to live as a woman after receiving encouragement (and frocks) from his unusually understanding butch lesbian aunt. Informing people that he is not a transsexual but rather a transvestite, the story follows the dramatic events of her life, from her teenage years during WWII to her life near East Berlin, where she operated the country's only private museum — a mansion filled with period furniture from the turn-of-the-century. Despite the repression of the Communists, attacks by skinheads and public scorn, Miss Charlotte, living as a simple woman, retains an amazingly sunny approach as she freely and without restraint nor regrets, goes about her life as a woman. Two actors play the young Lother/Charlotte and Charlotte plays herself in the later years. One amusing scene has Charlotte — who was a constant source of encouragement to the actors — giving tips as to the proper position when bending over a barrel to receive lashes from a lover's whip. An unforgettable portrait of a courageous, unique individual, who ignored the conventions and repressions of the day to bravely live his life as she saw fit.

Charlotte von Mahsldorf (c.) flanked by the two actors who play her in *I Am My Own Woman*

ANDY WARHOL
PAUL MORRISSEY

Because their works are so intertwined in the public consciousness, the films of Andy Warhol and his protégé Paul Morrissey are included together in this section. Though their films are distinct, and Morrissey expanded on his mentor's original aesthetic in creating his own film style, their works remain closely connected. They're separate but the same — much like the Holy Trinity — a comparison that would no doubt be appreciated by the two Catholics. These two important filmmakers are divided into individual biographies.

ANDY WARHOL

Thought by many to be the most famous gay American filmmaker, Andy Warhol, who died suddenly during a gall bladder operation in 1987, reveled in creating and maintaining an enigmatic image both in his personal life as well as with his creative output. A prominent filmmaker, it's ironic that most people have never seen a Warhol film despite his prodigious production of over 80 films from 1963 to 1968. These films have rarely been revived in repertory cinemas and are currently unavailable on video (although there has been talk of releasing some in the near future). The movies the average filmgoer thinks of as a "Warhol Film" — *Trash, Flesh, Women in Revolt* and *Andy Warhol's Dracula* and *Andy Warhol's Frankenstein* — are, in fact, by Paul Morrissey and were films produced by Warhol or simply marketed with his name. While these popular titles might not be his own, it does not negate the importance of Warhol as a leading and especially influential figure, especially in the realm of underground, experimental and avant-garde filmmaking. His largely unseen canon of work from that period spearheaded changes in how film is structured and viewed, and were sexually groundbreaking.

The legacy of Andy Warhol began in McKeesport, Pennsylvania, where he was born Andrew Warhola in 1928, the son of Czechoslavakian immigrants (his father was a coal miner). He went to the Carnegie Institute of Technology in Pittsburgh and in 1949 moved to New York where he quickly became a successful commercial artist and illustrator for fashion magazines. His now famous

Andy Warhol

Campbell Soup can paintings in 1962 and other conceptual silk-screens propelled him in the artistic limelight, and it was with this image as a pop artist that he entered filmmaking in 1963 with his two-hour *Tarzan and Jane Regained...Sort Of*. His films soon became the rage in the arts and were hotly debated. *Sleep* (1963) was a hypnotic (or extremely boring) six-hour film of a naked man sleeping. Morrissey, commenting on the film, called it "cute, interesting. But I only stayed for about an hour." Warhol followed with the equally static and slightly longer *Empire* (1963), an eight-hour soundless recording of a night-in-the-life of the Empire State Building. His ensuing early endeavors were all silent, B&W films that eschewed traditional rules and narrative techniques: the camera was static, the "actors" non-professional and the plot totally improvisational. They were meandering, extemporaneous, and, at times, purposefully boring works. Warhol attempted, and succeeded, in being an anti-auteur. His films soon became "events" and he not only joined the American underground filmmaking community, he became its brightest star and its inarticulate spokesperson.

Making films at a breakneck pace from 1963 to 1968, his films, made primarily in an East 47th Street studio dubbed "the Factory," captured the antiestablishment, counterculture exuberance of the 1960s and the social upheaval and sexual revolution which followed (although Warhol himself was a devout Catholic who did not drink, do drugs and when it come to participatory sex, was asexual). Using the Factory as his version of a Hollywood studio, he developed a star system whose interesting personalities appeared in his films and would become "Superstars." This glamorous coterie included drag queens (Holly Woodlawn, Candy Darling, Mario Montez), hustlers (Paul America, Joe Dallesandro) and women (Edie Sedgwick, Viva, Nico, Bridget Polk).

As the years passed, and with the arrival of Paul Morrissey, Warhol's films developed complexity: the introduction of sound, use of color and the eventual use of editing and script. His development as a filmmaker was suddenly halted on June 5, 1968, when he nearly died after being shot by Valerie Solanis, a crazed Factory hanger-on and a member of SCUM (the Society for Cutting Up Men) and violent advocate of separatist feminism. Upon release from the hospital, Warhol became reclusive and abandoned directing; supplying the money and the name soon was his only link to the filmmaking process.

Due to poor cataloging and storage methods at the Factory, many of Warhol's early films are either lost, destroyed or incorporated into other films. A brief chronology of some of his films follows:

1963: *Kiss* (50 min); *Dance Movie* (45 min); *Eat* (39 min); *Haircut* (33 min); and *Blow Job*, a 30-minute reaction shot of a man enjoying what is in all probability a real blow job.

1964: *Batman Dracula* (120 min); *Harlot* (70 min); *13 Most Beautiful Women* (40 min); and *Taylor Mead's Ass* (70 min)

1965: *The 13 Most Beautiful Boys* (40 min); *Vinyl* (70 min), starring Gerald Malanga and Edie Sedgwick; *Beauty #2* (70 min), also with Sedgwick; *Bitch* (70 min); *Prison* (70 min); *Suicide* (70 min); *The Life of Juanita Castro* (70 min); and *Poor Little Rich Girl* (70 min)

1966: *Bufferin* (35 min), directed by Gerald Malanga & Andy Warhol and the first film to use split screen projection; and *The Velvet Underground and Nico* (70 min)

1967: *The Loves of Ondine* (86 min); and *I, a Man* (100 min)

> "When I got my first TV set, I stopped caring so much about having a close relationship."
> —Andy Warhol

Some of his most widely known works follow:

Couch *(1964, 40 min, US, Andy Warhol)*
The unblinking stationary camera (and Andy) gazes at a couch and the many people who sit, eat and have sex on it. Filmed in a series of eight single take five-minute episodes, the film features Factory regulars (Gerald Malanga, Ondine, Taylor Mead and Baby Jane Holzer) as well as others who happened upon the set (Jack Kerouac, Allen Ginsberg, Gregory Corso).

▼ Kitchen
(1965, 70 min, US, Andy Warhol & Ronald Tavel)
Comprised of two 35-minute takes, this camp comedy shows off silver-haired Edie Sedgwick in her best performance. The camera is set in a kitchen with Edie, her beau (Roger Trudeau) and another couple as they interact. There are arguments, sexual gossip, protestations of love and confessions of homosexual infidelities, all of which are met with indifference.

▼ My Hustler *(1965, 70 min, US, Chuck Wein)*
Warhol's style perceptively changed with the introduction of editing, "acting" and a rough treatment of a plot. Whether this is the result of Paul Morrissey (who worked as an assistant on his first Warhol film) or marked a new direction for Warhol is debatable. The setting is a Fire Island beachhouse where a group of friends and neighbors (including Ed Hood, Ed McDermott and Genevieve Charbon) lust after a blond hustler (Paul America). Hood, a witty, aging queen, tells his friends that he got the hunk from Dial-a-Hustler and is quite happy with the rental. All wanting to discover America, the guests make a bet on who will bed the youth first.

▼ Chelsea Girls *(1966, 210 min, US, Andy Warhol)*
Warhol's most famous film, this ambitious twin-screen, three-and-a-half-hour blockbuster was the first underground film to receive commercial distribution and marked Warhol's shift, begun in *My Hustler*, from static art films to a more commercial sensibility. Made for $3,000, the film was an art-house hit, playing in major cities throughout the country, but banned in Boston! Set in New York's Chelsea Hotel (years later it would be in the limelight again as the site where Sid Vicious bludgeoned Nancy Spungeon to death), the film presents stories from different hotel rooms which simultaneously occupy the screen, competing for the viewer's attention. The cast includes the entire coterie of Factory regulars including Nico, Eric Emerson, Ondine, Ingrid Superstar, Mario Montez, Mary Woronov, Bridget Polk, International Velvet, Gerald Malanga and Edie Sedgwick. Upon its opening, the ads named the segments by their corresponding hotel room numbers (such as "Room 723 — Pope Ondine," "Room 422 — The Gerald Malanga Story," "Room 116 — Hanoi Hanna," etc). But the Chelsea threatened a lawsuit, forcing Warhol to drop the room numbers and thereafter simply refer only to the names. The many strange, wonderful and exasperating characters (some presented as real, others acting a role) include gays, transvestites, drug addicts, lesbians, lovers — all in either conversation with themselves or directly at the transfixed camera creating an unforgettable confessional for its counter-culture denizens.

> "The lighting is bad, the camera work is bad, the sound is bad, but the people are beautiful."
> —Andy Warhol

FAVORITE DIRECTORS

★★★★ (Four Stars)

(1967, 1500 min, US, Andy Warhol)

Famous for being famous, this 25-hour film was shown only once: in New York City in 1967. In actuality, it was a loosely structured collection of several of the many films he made during the past year or so. The mega-film used two projectors with the images superimposed and included such provocative titles as *Gerald Has His Hair Removed with Nair* (30 min), *Imitation of Christ* (8 hours), *Katrina Dead* (30 min) and a full-length film, *The Loves Of Ondine* (86 min), which starred a teenage Joe Dallesandro, Viva, Ondine and Bridget Polk. It has been called a "repellent failure" by Warhol biographer Stephen Koch.

> "A morbid, flesh-bound, self-reviling vision...an obsessed pursuit of rancid pleasures."
> —Manny Farber, *Negative Images*

Nude Restaurant

(1967, 100 min, US, Andy Warhol)

No mystery here. The factory rented a restaurant and peopled it with young men (and Viva as the lone woman — a waitress). Clothes are shed, the camera is turned on and the talking begins. Stephen Koch, in his biography of Warhol, "Stargazer: Andy

Lonesome Cowboys

Warhol's World and His Films," derisively concludes that "I cannot think of a single inch of footage in *Nude Restaurant* that is worth looking at."

> "*Nude Restaurant* doesn't give a damn about the viewer's interests. It goes slowly about its natural, casual business, trusting its inspirational, occasional sparks...and through its seeming insignificance, it achieves — before you know it — a frightening seriousness of life."
> —Jonas Mekas

Bike Boy

(1967, 96 min, US, Andy Warhol & Paul Morrissey)

A Los Angeles stud, Joseph Spencer, who's a raw, tough-talking innocent, becomes the object of fascination and scrutiny for Warholites Viva, Ingrid Superstar and Bridget Polk. As they pepper him with questions (and occasional pleas to drop his pants), Joe becomes alternately befuddled, amused, cocky, and increasingly apathetic under the hilarious grilling of the women.

▼ Lonesome Cowboys

(1968, 110 min, US, Andy Warhol)

Dammed by some for its fractured editing, lack of drama and general incoherence, this ode to male beauty, sex and fraternity is actually quite a lot of fun. In a small Western town in Arizona, a whining Viva, the beauty of the West, and her stammering sidekick "nurse" Taylor Mead (sort of a '60s version of Gilbert Gottfried), find their tranquility invaded when a group of cowboys ride into town. And, even though the boys "rape" her at one point, they actually are more interested in comparing narcissistic beauty tips, wrestling each other, camping nude in the sagebrush and declaring love for one another. Mead, despite (or because of) his ramblings, is a scream. Joe Dallesandro and Eric Emerson have the best lines, and Julian Burrough's blond, youthfully muscular beauty stops Andy's leering camera in its tracks. At times hilarious, this entertaining film — the last project in which Warhol had total participation — provides a wonderful closure to the filmmaking career of Warhol.

Blue Movie *(1968, 133 min, US)*

Seized by the New York police at its opening on charges of obscenity, the credit for the making of this film is in dispute. Some say it should be attributed to Morrissey, who claims that the film was "entirely my idea" but supposedly he only set up the lighting and left, leaving Warhol and the film's stars, Viva and Louis Waldron, to continue. Others claim it was Warhol's final film in which he had a significant involvement. The film itself, despite its infamous reputation, is not really that explicit as it depicts the different sex games played out by its two leads and ends with the two cooking eggs as the sun rises. (Also known as: *Fuck*)

PAUL MORRISSEY

Though he's written and directed nine of his own features and has been prominently involved with several others, many of which vividly capture the thoughts and lifestyles of a generation, Paul Morrissey remains a relatively under-appreciated and under-publicized filmmaker. Despite over twenty years of independence, he has still not been able to fully escape from under the Warholian filmmaking umbrella. This can be directly tied to the fact that Morrissey evolved from an assistant in Warhol's films to gradually make his own films but retained the Warhol aesthetic and name in the titles.

It is interesting that while Warhol's films are known to the average filmgoer, few people have seen films actually directed by him. Most films associated with Warhol were, in fact, directed by Morrissey. His films, while conventional in structure, are far from so in subject matter, creating a strange hybrid of pop culture excesses and the restraints of commercial orientation. With his semi-scripted dialogue and casting of societal outcasts and often-time outrageous story lines, his films most closely resemble those of John Waters and Paul Bartel.

Born in 1938 in Manhattan to an upper middle-class family, Paul Morrissey was raised outside of the city in Yonkers. He received a Catholic education ("the best thing that ever happened to me") and attended Fordham University. After college, he moved to New York's Lower East Side where he stumbled upon the film industry when he began a short-lived business exhibiting 16mm films in a rundown storefront/apartment. As his interest in film was piqued, he began making several short films. In 1965, he ventured into Warhol's Factory around the time of *My Hustler*. Clearheaded and strongly opinionated, he quickly became essential to Warhol, initially working as production assistant, producer, writer, cinematographer and eventually becoming a full collaborator and driving force in the making of the films of the mid-'60s. Many Warhol-credited films, including *Chelsea Girls, Nude Restaurant* and *Lonesome Cowboys*, have been claimed by Morrissey as his own. In addition to filmmaking, Morrissey also managed Warhol's band, The Velvet Underground, worked on the magazine *Inter/View*, and took control of operations at the Factory. His increased presence and power stirred resentment at the often chaotic Factory, and he quickly forbad drugs and instituted other controlling measures which prompted Gerald Malanga to suggest that he was Warhol's "hatchet man."

Under Morrissey's guidance (or dismantling, as some Factory regulars have voiced), films from the Factory began to shift from static, often plotless avant-garde "event"-type films to more commercially oriented ones. These films emphasized more character development, featured some semblance of professional acting, and were structured with a loosely scripted plot. These changes were viewed as either needed evolution of the Warhol style or a much resented sell-out on the part of the more commercially minded Morrissey.

After the assassination attempt on Warhol in 1968, Morrissey began making his own films. Though produced by Warhol and featuring his marquee name, they were entirely works of Morrissey. He explored life among the druggies and fringe people in *Flesh, Trash, Women in Revolt* and *Heat*, and shifted gears with his European-financed cult films *Flesh for Frankenstein* and *Blood for Dracula*, eventually breaking free of the Warhol sphere, both in name and financing. After a fallow period, he returned to New York and to the seedier side of life with *Forty Deuce, Mixed Blood* and *Spike of Bensonhurst*.

Strangely, one of Morrissey's most disquieting attributes is his private political and morally conservative, even reactionary point of view. For a filmmaker who has featured, even championed, alternative lifestyles and people on the fringe of society, he has often been quoted as personally opposing much of this behavior. Once you get past the shock value, his films can be interpreted as advocating traditional values and a need for family — however unconventional.

Another recurring theme in most of his films is homosexuality, both male and female. Certainly one of his trademarks is the casting of hunky, handsome actors for major roles — despite their lack of professional training. These include Joe Dallesandro, long-haired beauty Dietmar Prinz (*Beethoven's Nephew*), Richard Ulacia (*Mixed Blood*) and the muscular Sacha Mitchell, who was physically idolized by the camera in *Spike of Bensonhurst*. In addition to the male casting, transvestites Holly Woodlawn, Candy Darling and Jackie Curtis had important roles in his films. Yet despite all of these seemingly gay/alternative lifestyle-friendly appearances, Morrissey's conservative thinking belies this. When his film *Forty Deuce* played the New York Gay/Lesbian Film Festival, festival director Peter Lowry said that "he didn't want his film in a festival 'that promotes homosexuality.'" A position as confusing and contradictory as the man is to himself.

> "Paul was nuts...he really believes all these wild theories he comes up with."
>
> —Andy Warhol

> "The politics in my movies is like the sex. It's always, always there to be funny."
>
> —Paul Morrissey

▼ Flesh *(1968, 105 min, US)*

A true artifact of the 1960s sexual revolution as well as a great example of the quirky New York independent filmmaking that came out of the Warhol film factory, this gritty comedy is a homage to the personality and body (with an emphasis on the latter) of Joe Dallesandro. The plot is simply a day-in-the-life of gay hustler Joe who utters immortal lines such as, "How am I going to make any money without clean underwear!" The story revolves around Joe, his wife (Geraldine Smith) and her live-in lesbian lover (Patti d'Arbanville). Joe is told by his wife to hit the streets to earn $200 for her girlfriend's planned abortion. Warhol Superstars Candy Darling and Jackie Curtis are featured in a funny eye-opening sequence where the two of them read magazines and talk while Joe is receiving a blow job from another. Seemingly drug-induced dialogue throughout includes the great philosophical thought, "The more you learn the more depressed you get." ⊛

▼ Trash *(1970, 103 min, US)*

Holly Woodlawn is truly memorable as the trash-collecting lover of impotent drug fiend Joe Dallesandro in this wonderfully realistic slice-of-life film about New York's druggies and counter-culture denizens. In this, her screen debut, Holly's character preserves her dignity and moral righteousness despite poverty, squalor and a forced-to-masturbate-with-a-beer-bottle-because-my-boyfriend-can't-get-it-up life. This is best exemplified in the exchange between her and a "with it" social worker who promises her welfare in exchange for a pair of silver platform shoes Holly found in the trash. She refuses, despite an obvious need for assistance. It is her character, and not the cute but almost catatonic Joe, which works against the film's not-so-subtle anti-drug message; an attitude which keeps with the director's moralistic and reactionary philosophy. Morrissey has commented that "the basic idea for the movie is that drug people are trash. There's no difference between a person using drugs and a piece of refuse." ⊛

> "Funny, provocative, affecting and somehow very fine. *Trash* is alive. Holly Woodlawn, especially, is something to behold, a comic book Mother Courage who fancies herself as Marlene Dietrich but sounds more often like Phil Silvers."
> —Vincent Canby, *The New York Times*

> "A masterpiece. A brilliant and funny film. Best movie of the year."
> —*Rolling Stone*

Focus on: *Holly Woodlawn*

Born in Puerto Rico in 1946 and subsequently raised in Miami, Harold Ajzenberg ran away at the age of 15 to the excitement of New York and was quickly transformed into Holly Woodlawn ("Holly" was for the Holly Golightly character in Breakfast at Tiffany's; *"Woodlawn" for the famous cemetery). Holly's rise to stardom began in 1969 when she was bouncing around the clubs of New York claiming to be one of Andy Warhol's Superstars. The sham did get her into a casting call for Morrissey's upcoming film* Trash, *and it was (professional) love at first sight for the two. Following her critical success in the film, she did indeed*

Holly Woodlawn (l.) in *Trash*

become a Warhol Superstar, eventually starring in Women in Revolt *and the 1974 underground cult classic* Broken Goddess *by Dallas. Hailed by Truman Capote as "having the face of the Seventies," Holly enjoyed a long period of fast living, including drug and alcohol dependency. She rebounded as a cabaret artist, stage actress (in Tom Eyen's "Neon Women" and Joe Orton's "What the Butler Saw") and as a writer with her 1991 autobiography "A Low Life in High Heels." In a 1970s appearance on Geraldo Rivera's talk show, Rivera goaded her by asking, "But what are you? Are you a man, a woman..." Holly stopped him in his tracks with the retort, "Honey, what difference does it make, just so long as you're fabulous!"*

▼ Women in Revolt *(1971, 97 min, US)*

Subversively outrageous and hilariously un-PC, this is the story of three women who fight against the yokel of male oppression and embrace the women's liberation movement (specifically, PIGS — Politically Involved Girls) only to eventually tire of the "idea" and revert to their old ways. Drag queen Superstars Holly Woodlawn, Candy Darling and Jackie Curtis make the unlikely threesome: Jackie is a frigid lesbian militarist, Candy is a rich deb and actress-wannabe and Holly is a fashion model and incorrigible bisexual nymphomaniac. But liberation takes a detour for the three as Jackie soon abandons her militant lesbian ways after paying to have sex with a former Mr. America and after her first orgasm ("I think I'm gonna go...I'm coming. Oh, now I know what we're against!"), gets pregnant, and becomes a happy single mother living in Jersey. Candy's acting aspirations lead her only on her back, and ditsy Holly ends up staggering through the Bowery as a boozy wino. The rise and fall of these three hapless heroines makes for a funny yet poignant gender-reversal satire. (Also known as: *Andy Warhol's Women*)

▼ Heat *(1972, 100 min, US)*

Kinky and funny, this many times vulgar takeoff of *Sunset Boulevard* stars Sylvia Miles as the shrillish Sally Todd, a fading movie star (actually a has-been chorus girl) who shares her dreary home with her lesbian daughter Jessie (Andrea Feldman) and Jessie's sadistic girlfriend. Their lives are briefly stimulated when

Joe Dallesandro, himself a former child actor in an old TV western, enters the scene. All have the hots for Little Joe, including mom and daughter (prompting the jealous mom to complain that "She can't even make a good dyke"), and even the boyfriend of Jessie's former husband. An insightful tale of unsatisfactory sex, elusive love and ever-present alienation masked as delightful camp. Featuring a John Cale soundtrack. When asked what his involvement with this film was, Warhol is said to have remarked, "Well, uh, I go to the parties." (Also known as: *Andy Warhol's Heat*) ⊛

L'Amour *(1972, 90 min, US)*
A big-budget ($100,000) first for producer Warhol and director Morrissey, this romantic comedy and satire on American vapidness centers around two hippie-esque American coeds, Jane (Jane Forth) and Donna (Donna Jordan), who travel to Paris to live and find love. Staying with fellow American Patti d'Arbanville, the two are soon transformed from mindless flower children to gold-digging pseudo-sophisticates, with Jane falling for deodorant king Michael (Michael Sklar) and Donna for Max (Max Delys), Michael's roommate.

Flesh for Frankenstein
(1973, 94 min, Italy/France)
B-movie dialogue, over-the-top performances and buckets of gore abound in this campy retelling of the classic horror story, served up with a weird sexual twist. Udo Kier is the mad baron who feverishly works on piecing together body parts from the recently dead to create a pair of perfect creatures — a beautiful female and

Joe Dallesandro, Sylvia Miles (l.) and Andrea Feldman in *Heat*

sex-crazed male. Joe Dallesandro plays the horny stud to the baron's wife/sister. Originally made in 3-D and rated a tantalizing "X," the film was a small box-office hit. (Also known as: *Andy Warhol's Frankenstein*) ⊛

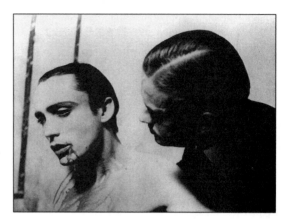

Udo Kier drips sensuality (and blood) in *Blood for Dracula*

Blood for Dracula
(1973, 93 min, Italy/France)
Spawned by the commercial success of *Flesh for Frankenstein*, this campy treatment of the well-worn Transylvanian tale features Udo Kier as Dracula, the creepy vampire in search of ripe, succulent throats and virginal blood. Leaving Hungary for the purer pastures offered in Catholic Italy, the count's toothy appetite for a fix of virgins proves elusive as the strapping Joe Dallesandro makes sure that the count's intended victims are no virgins, even if it means deflowering a 14-year-old. Featuring directors Vittorio De Sica and Roman Polanski. (Also known as: *Andy Warhol's Dracula*) ⊛

Hound of the Baskervilles
(1977, 85 min, GB)
Basil Rathbone can rest easy as this tepid Morrissey misfire, made as a comedic homage to Sir Arthur Conan Doyle's classic novel, falls laughlessly flat. Co-writers and stars Peter Cook and Dudley Moore should share blame, as well, as their antics are deadly unfunny. A good supporting cast (Kenneth Williams, Denholm Elliott, Spike Mulligan, Terry-Thomas and Prunella Scales) can't save this dud. An uncharacteristic film from Morrissey and certainly the nadir of his career. ⊛

▼ Madame Wang's *(1981, 95 min, US)*
This social comedy of a young Communist agent who tries to infiltrate America only to be infiltrated by America's insipid popular culture did not receive much in the way of commercial playdates and, consequently, is one of Morrissey's more obscure works. Patrick Schoene is Lutz, an East German KGB agent who goes undercover in Southern California in an effort to prepare for a Communist invasion. As he tries to enlist his likely allies (hip-

pies, Jane Fonda), he is instead propelled into and nearly seduced by a world inhabited by transvestite mothers (and fathers), pimps who sniff doorknobs, prostitutes, lesbian folksingers and the den of American youth's musical world — the Chinese Restaurant-punk club, Madame Wang's.

▼ Forty Deuce *(1982, 90 min, US)*

The first of Morrissey's trilogy on life on the tough streets of New York City (the others being *Mixed Blood* and *Spike of Bensonhurst*). This hard-hitting yet darkly humorous tale is an adaptation of an off-off-Broadway play by Alan Bowne. Its title refers to Manhattan's 42nd Street, a bleak, dead-end home to prostitutes, pimps, drug addicts and other social flotsam. Kevin Bacon is Ricky, a coked-up, greasy-haired male hustler who tries to pin the drug-induced death of a 12-year-old boy on Roper (Orson Bean), a rich "chicken hawk" john, and, in the process, blackmail him. The last half of the story is filmed in real time, and Morrissey doubles the action with split-screen projection.

Mixed Blood *(1985, 98 min, US)*

Morrissey's jet-black comedy is set in New York's notorious Alphabet City. A gang of drug-running Latin youths, under the guidance of a Fagan-like protector and her gorgeous (though monosyllabic) son, set out to control the neighborhood drug trade. Marilia Pera (*Pixote*) is unforgettable as the regal Rita La Punta, a June Cleaver-from-hell den mother who molds her blindly obedi-ent kids into a powerful weapon as she demands her piece of the rancid American pie. Richard Ulacia is a thuggish beauty as her son Thiago (but...the man can't act!), and Linda Kerridge is perfect as an icy Upper East Side blonde who goes slumming in the Alphabet and falls for his physical charms. An extremely violent and viciously funny social satire. ⊛

"*Mixed Blood* is often genuinely, knowingly funny and immediately afterward, so explicitly, nastily bloody that you might want to throw up."
—Vincent Canby, *The New York Times*

"A hip, tough black comedy for those who can take their social satire in savagery."
—Judith Crist

▼ Beethoven's Nephew
(1985, 103 min, France/Germany)

Morrissey sheds his well-deserved reputation as a sensationalistic chronicler of life on the fringe with this thoughtful, deadly serious and opulent story of the destructively possessive relationship between Ludwig Von Beethoven (Wolfgang Reichmann) and his handsome young nephew, Karl (Dietmar Prinz). Morrissey shows Beethoven in his later years as a furious and demanding "superstar" who, after winning a vicious court battle for the custody of his sis-ter's son, becomes consumed with an insanely jealous love for the boy. With surprising control in its examination of the composer's

Richard Ulacia and Marilia Pera in *Mixed Blood*

obsession, the film elicits a deep sympathy for his torment without compromising the severity of his tyrannical grip on the boy's life. ☯

"Weirdly engaging, offbeat and scrupulously accurate... full of homoerotic nuances."

—Vincent Canby, *The New York Times*

"It's inconceivable to think that Beethoven wanted sex with his nephew. That's a 'liberal,' Freudian idea...what he seemed to want was what Frankenstein and Dracula wanted, control and possession. That's a much more powerful and confusing emotion."

—Paul Morrissey on several critics' reading of a homosexual subtext

▼ Spike of Bensonhurst *(1988, 101 min, US)*

This witty mob satire stars Sasha Mitchell as Spike Fumo, an ambitiously arrogant two-bit boxer who on sheer chutzpa tries to climb his way to the top. Ernest Borgnine (in the best screen role he's had in decades) plays Baldo Cacetti, the befuddled neighborhood don who must contend with Spike after his pampered, groomed-to-be-a-WASP daughter Angel (Maria Patillo) falls under his seductively dangerous charms. After being "banished" from Bensonhurst, Spike sets up shop in Red Hook with a poor Puerto Rican family who include the hilarious Antonia Rey as his surrogate mom and the statuesque Talisa Soto as his new love interest. Geraldine Smith is unforgettable as Spike's lesbian mom with a protective and vocal lover ("How fuckin' dare you talk to your fuckin' mother like that") and Sylvia Miles steals a few scenes as a coke-sniffing congresswoman. Dark urban humor — including racial jokes — abound in this mean, lean comedy. And for leering gay men, the incredibly handsome and muscular 19-year-old Mitchell is a special treat. ☯

"Basically, it's another family comedy."

—Paul Morrissey

Additional films produced by or about Andy Warhol and Factory life

---

Ciao! Manhattan

(1965-71, 84 min, US, John Palmer & David Weisman)
This kaleidoscopic journey through the life of Warhol Superstar Edie Sedgwick is both a searing psychodrama of burnout syndrome and a dynamic potpourri of Sixties cultural paraphernalia. From Edie's rise to the throne of pop underground to her tragic plummet into drug abuse and mental illness, the quasi-documentary *Ciao!* manages to be comical, perplexing and poignant. Semi-fictitious, filming began in 1967, capturing the orgiastic frenzy of the Warhol Factory heyday. The fragile, silver-maned beauty enjoyed a rocket-like career in the limelight — becoming one of Warhol's first Superstars and starring in several of his productions including *Poor Little Rich Girl, Vinyl* and *Beauty II*. She was dubbed a "youthquaker" by *Vogue*. But her 15 minutes ended.

Filming was halted, only to resume after over 50 electric shock treatments and years of obscurity, booze and drug abuse, with a crumbling Edie living at the bottom of a swimming pool on the West Coast. Only months after completion of filming, Edie died of barbituate overdose. She was 28 years old. ☯

"This is *Sunset Boulevard* for real, an Acid Age *Snake Pit.*"

—*Time*

Andy Warhol's Bad

(1976, 100 min, US, Jed Johnson)
Directed by former Morrissey soundman and editor (*Trash, Women in Revolt, Heat, L'Amour*) Jed Johnson, Warhol lent his box-office producing name for this surprisingly slick, sick and subversive *Pink Flamingos*-like comedy of extremely bad taste. A slumming-for-dollars Carroll Baker stars as the tough, nefarious head of a female kill-for-hire organization based in Queens which specializes in especially difficult cases (i.e. eradicating a neighbor's pesky dog or a mother's screaming baby). All is going well for her and her immoral ingenues until a stranger (Perry King) enters the scene. Most prints and videos have edited out the infamous "baby splatter scene." Gross, highly offensive and disgustingly enjoyable. ☯

Warhol: Portrait of an Artist

(1988, 60 min, US)
The life of pop culture icon Andy Warhol, whose artistic output included painting, film, publishing, rock music and TV, is explored in this engaging documentary. Through interviews with friends, film clips and shots of his paintings and movies, we follow Warhol through his early days as a commercial artist into more heady times as a leading conceptual artist and patriarch of the avant-garde to his final days as a dazed celebrity maven. The filmmaker successfully argues that Warhol's talent and fame went far beyond simply painting Campbell Soup cans and that he should be considered one of the most important artists of the 20th century. ☯

Superstar: The Life and Times of Andy Warhol

(1990, 87 min, US, Chuck Workman)
Focusing on the exceptional life of Andy Warhol, this idolatrous, entertaining documentary probes not only his phenomenally exceptional career as a conceptual artist, filmmaker and publisher, but also takes a gossipy peek into the Club 54/Beautiful People club scenes that Warhol reveled in. From his childhood upbringing near Pittsburgh and his schooling at the Carnegie Institute of Technology, through his Factory days and finally to his unusual position as a pop icon, the film is well-researched and features interviews with such diverse characters as his farmer brother and aunts, to Dennis Hooper, Sally Kirkland, Liza Minnelli and Viva. A celebration of an enigmatic man and artist whose fascination with fame, beauty and soup cans earned him a remarkable place in 20th-century art. ☯

WJOHN WATERS

It's difficult to believe that the erudite fellow with the loquacious demeanor and pencil-thin mustache seen frequently on "Late Night with David Letterman" has given us some of the world's most disgusting movies. And while there's no denying that John Waters has lived down to his reputation as "The Prince of Puke," he's also an extremely funny and talented satirist who has tackled such topics as gender bending, sexual roles, capitol punishment, tabloid journalism, the dissatisfication of the middle class and other worldy topics.

Born in Lutherville, Maryland, in 1946 to an upper middle-class Catholic family (his father ran a profitable fire-fighting equipment company), Waters' childhood interests were different from the other kids — little John preferred to stage fake car accidents than play cowboys and Indians. A devotee of Rainer Werner Fassbinder, Andy Warhol's *The Chelsea Girls*, *The Wizard of Oz* (he rooted for the Wicked Witch), and the exploitation films of Herschell Gordon Lewis and Russ Meyer, Waters began making 8mm films in Baltimore — the titles included *Hag in Black Leather* and *Roman Candles* — when he was a teenager. Along with friends David Lochary, Mary Vivian Pearce, Mink Stole and Glenn Milstead, Waters started Dreamland Studios and graduated to 16mm with 1968's *Eat Your Makeup*, which showcased a tasteless reenactment of the Kennedy assassination. Milstead, soon to become the world's most famous transvestite, made his first appearance in drag as Divine in *Roman Candles*.

With $2,000, Waters filmed *Mondo Trasho* in 1970, which brought him attention outside of Baltimore thanks to midnight screenings in New England and New York, as well as favorable reviews from Pauline Kael and *Variety*. *The Diane Linkletter Story*, a ten-minute short depicting the LSD-induced death of Art Linkletter's daughter, followed; but *Multiple Maniacs*, an homage to *Freaks*, the Manson Family and Catholicism, helped bring Waters an even wider audience on the midnight circuit. With an elaborate budget of $10,000, Waters and Company next shot *Pink Flamingos* (1972), and the world has never quite been the same. This hilarious, disturbing and utterly disgusting "exercise in poor taste" was quickly tagged "the film with something to offend everyone" and eventually became one of the most successful films ever produced, making one hundred times more than its cost. With it, Waters and

John Waters

Divine became dysfunctional-household names.

Several other tasteless films followed, but it was in partnership with New Line Cinema in 1981 that Waters brought his delightfully deranged sensibilities overground with *Polyester*, a savaging of suburbia which featured "established" stars such as Tab Hunter. The film also boasted the wonders of Odorama, a scratch-and-sniff gimmick worthy of Waters' hero William Castle. Waters went even more mainstream (or was he just maturing?) with 1988's *Hairspray*, an affectionate, PG-rated salute to teen dance shows of the 1960s. After several aborted attempts to bring John Kennedy O'Toole's "A Confederacy of Dunces" to the screen, Universal and Imagine Pictures, a production company headed in part by Ron "Opie" Howard, backed *Cry-Baby*, Waters' 1990 musical salute to 1950s juvenile delinquent movies. In this uneven effort, Waters' struggle between directing a contemporary, studio-financed, PG-13 Saturday night date movie and being his unpredictable self is evident. Almost prophetically, Waters said in an 1983 interview, "To be perfectly honest, I don't think I would ever want to try to be that commercial. I don't have it deep down in my soul to reach all mankind. It's impossible to me. To attempt it would be suicide. I want as many people to see my films without pushing it."

His most recent effort is *Serial Mom* (1994), with Kathleen Turner as a murderess posing as a good-natured mommy. In addition to his directing efforts, Waters wrote "Shock Value — A Tasteful Book About Bad Taste," a fascinating autobiography that puts his obsessions in hilarious perspective.

> "If I see someone vomiting after seeing one of my films, I'd consider it a standing ovation."
> —John Waters

> "Waters cultivates sleaze like a rare orchid...he is to Baltimore what Ingmar Bergman was to Sweden."
> —*Baltimore Sun*

> "The patron saint and theoretical genius of Outlaw Cinema."
> —*Film Comment*

Mondo Trasho *(1970, 94 min, US)*

Ah...Just another day in the life of a 300-pound transvestite. Divine, in skin-tight, gold lamé Capri pants, runs over Mary Vivian Pearce in a 1959 Cadillac and commits other acts of mayhem. There's also sightings of the Virgin Mary, drug-addicted doctors, nasty 1950s rock tunes, nods to *The Wizard of Oz* and *Freaks*, and dismemberment of feet and hands that would make *Boxing Helena* gasp. Quiet! Waters at work. ☻

The Diane Linkletter Story

(1970, 15 min, US)

Extemporaneously filmed after hearing news reports of Art Linkletter's daughter's suicide, Waters and his cohorts have produced a quirky, semi-scandalous and hilarious "what might Diane's last minutes have been like?" scenario. Divine (in slight need of a shave) plays the young hippie Diane who just wants "to do my own thing!" with her new lover Bob. But parental interference by David Lochery and Mary Vivian Pearce and instructions to "go to your room" end in tragedy for all concerned. Let this be a lesson to all over-protective parents and fast-living teens.

Multiple Maniacs *(1971, 94 min, US)*

The film Waters claimed "flushed religion out of my system" is about a traveling carnival called "Lady Divine's Cavalcade of Perversions" which lands in Baltimore and disrupts the lives of the creeps living there. We're treated to a junkie shooting up on a church altar, bearded transvestites, the semi-classic scene of Divine being raped by a 15-foot lobster, Mary Vivian Pearce's rosary beads, cannibalism, Kate Smith's rendition of "God Bless America" and, perhaps most disturbing of all, shots of downtown Baltimore. ☻

Pink Flamingos *(1972, 92 min, US)*

Waters' name became one to fear after the release of this adventure in total sleaze, still one of the most disgusting and perversely funny films ever made. Zaftig matriarch Babs Johnson (Divine) and her family of egg-adoring Mom (Edith Massey) and chicken-loving son (Danny Mils) battle the repugnant Connie and Raymond Marble (Mink Stole and David Lochary) for the title of "filthiest person alive." The rest is history. ☻

Female Trouble *(1974, 95 min, US)*

Follow the trials and tribulations of Dawn Davenport (Divine): from cha-cha heel obsessed teen to rape victim to murderess to electric chair victim. Waters' ode to misguided teen traumas and prison melodramas includes satirical blasts at middle-class values, performance art ("Who wants to die for art's sake?") and really bad makeup. ☻

> "Where do these people come from? Where do they go when the sun goes down? Isn't there a law or something?"
> —Rex Reed, *New York Daily News*

Divine in *Pink Flamingos*

▼ Desperate Living *(1977, 90 min, US)*

A favorite for many JW fans, despite the absence of Divine, this high-volume, determinedly offensive camp comedy is also Waters' most blatantly queer film — featuring a transvestite cop, leather-clad biker boys and a bevy of tough-talking dykes accompanied by their buxomly kittenish girlfriends. Mink Stole stars as Peggy Gravel, a high-strung, borderline schizoid who, with the help of her 400-pound black maid, Grizelda (Baltimore schoolteacher Peggy Hill), kills her helpless hubby. Together, they go on the lam, eventually finding refuge in Mortville, a disgusting haven for perverts, murderers and worse, and ruled by porcine despot Queen Carlotta (Edith Massey). Lesbians with a sense of humor will take delight (humorless PC lesbians are cautioned to stick with another viewing of *Desert Hearts*) in the many lesbian characters including mole-faced butch Mo and her lingerie-queen girlfriend Muffy St. Jacques. Don't miss the lesbian glory hole scene where poor Peggy seeks a place of peace only to discover two bouncy breasts thrusted from the next cubicle. And in John Waters' warped sense of justice, his "happy ending" has evil overcoming evil as the outraged citizens of Mortville cannibalistically revolt. ⊛

Polyester *(1981, 86 min, US)*

Divine is a campy delight as Baltimore housewife Francine Fishpaw, who experiences her own private hell when hubby-with-a-bad-toupee has an affair, her daughter turns out to be a slut, and her revered son is cited as the notorious foot-stomper. Then, Golden Boy Tab Tomorrow (Tab Hunter) comes into her life. Waters tones down the crudeness to win new fans and succeeds — although number two on the scratch-and-sniff card is a doozy. We also like the drive-in that shows Marguerite Duras films. ⊛

Divine and Tab Hunter in *Polyester*

Hairspray *(1988, 94 min, US)*

Waters and Divine found new legions of fans when this nifty tribute to the TV dance shows of the 1960s opened in cineplexes around America. Ricki Lake is Tracy Turnblad, the chubby, beehived teen who competes against her arch-rival, the nasty Amber von Tussle, on "The Carny Collins Show." Divine plays Mom, and Sonny Bono, Pia Zadora, Rick Ocasek and Debbie Harry make appearances. Waters poignantly takes on issues of racism when Tracy's black friends are banned from the show; he proves up to the task of the racial issue, but wisely keeps the lid on all-out polemic and heavy-handedness by sticking with his strength — namely outrageous comedy. ⊛

Focus On: *Divine*

"The world's most famous transvestite" and "the most beautiful woman in the world" was born Harris Glenn Milstead in Baltimore in 1945. A childhood friend of director John Waters, Milstead was weaned on Elizabeth Taylor movies and recognized his penchant for cross-dressing at an early age. He made his screen debut in 1966 in Waters' 8mm opus Roman Candles, *then played in the director's* Eat Your Makeup *and* Mondo Trasho *before starring in* Multiple Maniacs *in 1970. With a loud and pushy demeanor, shaved forehead, an obvious fake wig, a large paunch, garish theatrical makeup and tacky, tight clothing, Divine drew attention in San Francisco in the early 1970s, performing in such revues as "Divine Saves the World" and "Vice Palace." Following the theatrical release of* Pink Flamingos *in 1972, Divine became a person that was both revered and reviled, performing perhaps the most revolting act ever committed on cellu-*

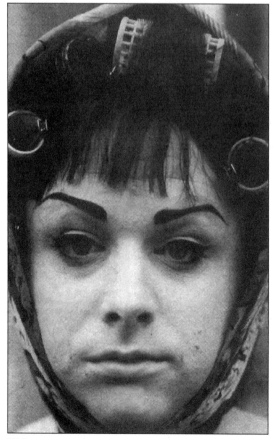

Divine

loid. Of course, he basked in the glow of the notoriety, moving to New York while appearing at the glitzy parties and the hip clubs of Hollywood. In "Shock Value," Waters' autobiography, the director recalled the press asking Divine if he was gay. The response: "Gay? Are you kidding? I've got a wife and two kids back in Omaha!"

Divine also made some recordings and starred in avant-garde plays like "The Neon Women" and "Women Behind Bars." Other films include Waters' Female Trouble *(1974)*, Polyester *(1981)* and Hairspray *(1988)*, as well as Paul Bartel's Lust in the Dust *(1985)* and, as a man, in Alan Rudolph's Trouble in Mind *(1985)* and Michael Shroeder's Out of the Dark *(1988)*. Sadly, Divine died of a heart attack in 1988, after the release of Hairspray and just as he was beginning to gain acceptance in mainstream film-making.

We love you Edie!

Cry-Baby *(1990, 85 min, US)*

Johnny Depp is "Cry-Baby" Walker, a hot-rodding, guitar-strumming Baltimore juvenile delinquent (and leader of the ultra-cool Drapes) whose swaggering style and tear-letting abilities help him land prissy rich gal Allison Vernon-Williams (Amy Locane), who has an itch to go "bad." Despite some dandy nods to Elvis and James Dean, a few exciting musical numbers and a Waters dream cast — including Traci Lords, David Nelson, Patty Hearst, Joe Dallesandro, Troy Donohue, Iggy Pop and Joey Heatherton — this one never really clicks into high-camp gear. ☽

Serial Mom *(1994, 95 min, US)*

Waters has created his most accessible film — a terrifically executed satire on suburbia, sex and violence, and our obsession with celebrity criminals. Even if this film had been made before the Menendez brothers and Lorena Bobbitt were enshrined in the public mindset, Waters' twisted and defiantly hilarious comedy would still hit a bull's-eye. Kathleen Turner is delicious as a June Cleaver-ish housewife. She cooks, cleans, listens to Barry Manilow, and even recycles. And she's a serial killer, too. Not indiscriminately, however; this Bloody Mama only kills to protect family and hearth. As husband and kids begin to realize the truth and the police close in, Waters lets loose a series of comic salvos which both tantalize and underscore his topical burlesque. You know you're in familiar Waters when Turner kills a victim with a leg of lamb and the score from *Annie* blares in the background. Longtime Waters co-hort Mink Stole is most memorable as a victimized neighbor. ☽

Johnny Depp is *Cry-Baby*

JAMES WHALE

Though director James Whale's filmography is comparatively a short one, his unique cinematic eye for atmosphere and mood and his stylized films firmly established him as one of the leading auteurs of the 1930s. Born in the English Midlands in 1889, he enjoyed his first artistic success with the acclaimed 1929 London staging of "Journey's End." The play proved to be so popular that he was immediately sent to New York to re-stage a Broadway version. Its subsequent success sent Whale packing to Hollywood, where he would stay until his death in 1957.

Howard Hughes, who in 1930 had just started his monumental epic *Hell's Angels*, hired Whale as dialogue director for that film. Afterwards, Whale made his directorial debut with the film version of *Journey's End*. It was named as one of the Ten Best Films of the Year by *The New York Times*, and Whale signed with Universal Pictures, for whom he'd make at least five more classics in as many years.

In addition to an uncommon mastery of the medium, what distinguished Whale's films was his own, self-described "perverse sense of humor." Elegant, witty and as unapologetic about his movies' non-mainstream edge as he was about his homosexuality — which he did nothing to conceal — Whale soon fell in disfavor with what he called "the New Universal": A new regime at the studio which continually challenged, censored and chastised him for "political" reasons (probably his openness about being gay). After the studio gave in to pressure from Nazi Germany in the cutting of *The Road Back*, the sequel to the studio's Oscar-winning *All Quiet on the Western Front*, Whale and Universal parted company and Whale became a freelancer. He would direct eight more films over the next 12 years, but Whale never captured the magic he had demonstrated earlier. After being fired in 1941 by Columbia while working on the film *They Dare Not Love*, Whale retired from the film business.

Having invested wisely, he lived comfortably, painting and occasionally directing at a small, local theatre company when the whim hit him. Whale lived for over twenty years with producer/studio executive David Lewis, splitting when in 1953 Whale "hired" a French youth as secretary/companion. In the mid-1950s, he was bothered by a series of strokes which greatly impaired him. At the age of 67, Whale wrote a suicide note and dived head-first

James Whale

into the shallow end of his swimming pool. However, the police ruled it as an accident as friends never revealed the existence of the note until many years later. Kenneth Anger's "Hollywood Babylon" reports a different scenerio in Whale's death, one involving murder and a young gay male, but this is contradicted by both Whale's friends and his biographer.

Journey's End *(1930, 75 min, US)*
Whale's first film is an acclaimed adaptation of his hit London and Broadway play, based on R.C. Sherriff's affecting anti-war story. It is presumed a negative no longer exists for this film.

Waterloo Bridge *(1931, 72 min, US)*
The first and less famous film version of Robert E. Sherwood's play, this melodrama set during WWI stars Mae Clarke as a prostitute who falls in love with a soldier (Kent Douglass), who is unaware of her true identity. A print was only recently discovered.

Frankenstein *(1931, 71 min, US)*
The granddaddy of 'em all. Whale creates a chillingly eerie atmosphere to tell Mary Shelley's ghastly story. Boris Karloff became a legend as the "Monster," Colin Clive is the demented doc, Mae Clarke is the requisite damsel in distress, and the film ushered in a whole new style of filmmaking. A masterpiece of suspense, mood and design, the film grossed an amazing five million dollars, and cemented Whale's reputation as Universal's reigning artistic champion. ⊛

The Impatient Maiden *(1932, 72 min, US)*

Romantic drama of a secretary (Mae Clarke) in love with a surgeon (Lew Ayres) who refuses to marry him until he makes a name for himself.

The Old Dark House *(1932, 75 min, US)*

Expecting another *Frankenstein*, Universal sold this strictly as a horror film, which only half tells the story. A devilishly sardonic and chilling masterwork, Whale's absurdist humor subverts nearly every frame as a group of travelers become stranded in a dark, mysterious and possibly haunted mansion. Charles Laughton, Boris Karloff, Gloria Stuart and Raymond Massey star. One of Whale's most accomplished films, and one of the best of its genre.

The Kiss Before the Mirror

(1933, 66 min, US)

Frank Morgan had one of his infrequent starring roles as a lawyer defending client Paul Lukas for murdering his unfaithful wife. Morgan soon discovers, however, that his own wife (Nancy Carroll) is having an affair. Remade five years later by Whale as *Wives Under Suspicion*.

The Invisible Man *(1933, 71 min, US)*

Claude Rains made his debut in Whale's bewitching comic horror tale based on the H.G. Wells novel. Playfully funny and featuring dandy special effects, the film casts Rains as a scientist who has discovered the secret to invisibility — at the cost of his own sanity. As the local snoop, Una O'Connor proves she can scream with the best of them. ☯

By Candlelight *(1933, 70 min, US)*

Whale is in Ernst Lubitsch territory with this beguiling romantic comedy. Paul Lukas plays butler to Nils Asther's European prince. When lovely princess Elissa Landi meets Lukas, complications arise when she thinks he's royalty.

One More River *(1934, 88 min, US)*

Whale and writer R.C. Sherriff (*Journey's End*) reteamed for this well-acted drama of divorce amongst the upper classes. Set in England, Diana Wynyard leaves cruel husband Colin Clive after he beats her, sending her into the arms of the waiting Frank Lawton. When he learns of their liaison, Clive brings Wynyard to divorce court — with Lawton as corespondent. The film features a splendid courtroom finale.

The Great Garrick

The Bride of Frankenstein
(1935, 75 min, US)
Dr. Frankenstein (Colin Clive) makes a bride for his creature (Boris Karloff), and all hell breaks loose. Arguably better than its predecessor, both emotionally and stylistically, Whale's moody sequel to his 1931 classic *Frankenstein* best illustrates the director's macabre sense of humor and filmmaking talent. Elsa Lanchester plays a dual role as "the bride" and as author Mary Shelley. Whale personally designed Lanchester's spiffy hair-do. ⊛

Elsa Lanchester as *The Bride Of Frankenstein*

Remember Last Night *(1935, 85 min, US)*
A society couple (Robert Young and Constance Cummings) join forces with a good-natured private detective (Edward Arnold) in solving a murder which occured the night before during a particularly drunken merry-making spree. Whale combines sophisticated comedy and murder mystery in this *Thin Man*-like yarn.

Show Boat *(1936, 113 min, US)*
This second of three film versions of the Kern-Hammerstein perennial is the best of the bunch thanks to Whale's sensitive yet firm direction and an immaculate evocation of 1880s America. A first-rate cast includes Irene Dunne, Allan Jones, Charles Winninger, and, in unforgettable voice, Helen Morgan singing "Bill" and Paul Robeson's staggering vocal of "Ol' Man River."

The Road Back *(1937, 103 min, US)*
Studio interference and a comedic bastardization of characters prevented Erich Maria Remarque's sequel to *All Quiet on the Western Front* from achieving the power of the first film. Handcuffed in his telling of the story of soldiers returning home after torturous years at war, Whale still managed somehow to create a number of effective scenes. More notable as the film in which Whale and home studio Universal parted company.

The Great Garrick *(1937, 91 min, US)*
Though critically well-received, Warner Brothers was not happy with the box-office results and let Whale go. A shame, for they lost a good director who gave them quite an enjoyable comedic souffle. Brian Aherne plays real-life 18th-century British actor David Garrick, who gets roasted by the Comedie Francaise when they think he has bad-mouthed them. Unfortunately this romp has been neglected over the years.

Sinners in Paradise *(1938, 65 min, US)*
Whale returned to Universal to direct this unusual melodrama about plane crash survivors stranded on a tropical island. John Boles is the recluse living there; Madge Evans, Bruce Cabot and Gene Lockhart are just some of the uninvited guests.

Wives Under Suspicion *(1938, 68 min, US)*
Whale remade his 1933 drama *The Kiss Before the Mirror*, this time around with Warren William as the cuckold husband, here a district attorney, who discovers similarities between a case he is prosecuting (a man convicted of killing his faithless wife) and his own life. Gail Patrick is William's philandering wife.

Port of Seven Seas *(1938, 81 min, US)*
Written by Preston Sturges, this updating of Pagnol's "Fanny" has its moments of interest. Wallace Beery is out of his element as the wayward sailor, though Maureen O'Sullivan is lovely as the woman who falls in love with him.

The Man in the Iron Mask
(1939, 119 min, US)
A dashing swashbuckler based on Alexander Dumas' tale of sibling rivalry between King Louis XIV and his twin brother, Philippe, who happened to be raised by the Three Musketeers. With Louis Hayward, Joan Bennett, Warren William and Alan Hale. ⊛

Green Hell *(1940, 87 min, US)*
Douglas Fairbanks, Jr. and Joan Bennett go searching for Incan treasures deep in the deadly jungles of the Amazon. Alan Hale, John Howard and George Sanders go along for the ride.

They Dare Not Love *(1941, 76 min, US)*
Austrian immigrants George Brent and Martha Scott become involved with Nazi agent Paul Lukas, refugees and the underground.

Hello Out There *(1949, 40 min, US)*
Whale came out of retirement to adapt William Saroyan's "Hello Out There," to be used in a compilation film. Reportedly well-received by preview audiences, the film was never released. Richard Roud reports in "Cinema: A Critical Dictionary": "As one of the lucky few who has actually seen (it), I can testify that it wasn't bad at all."

FRANCO ZEFFIRELLI

A true enigma both in his filmmaking career as well as his private life, Franco Zeffirelli has made some truly memorable, even acclaimed films (his Shakespeare adaptations and filmed operas, for instance), and has also been responsible for cinematic junk (such as *The Champ*, the embarrassing *Endless Love* and a 1988 disaster never released in the U.S., *Young Toscanini*, with C. Thomas Howell and Elizabeth Taylor). His schizophrenic abilities as a director seem to parallel his personal affairs. Although he came out in *The Advocate* several years ago and there was always talk of a possible relationship with mentor Luchino Visconti, his arch conservative politics and religious fundamentalism has repeatedly gotten him into trouble — the most controversial being his vocal opposition to Martin Scorsese's *The Last Temptation of Christ*, which Zeffirelli decried, blaming the Jews of Hollywood for its blasphemy.

Zeffirelli, who was born in 1923, entered filmmaking as an assistant to some of the greatest European directors of his time — Michelangelo Antonioni, Roberto Rossellini, Vittorio De Sica and the aforementioned Visconti. And although he's made over a dozen films in his career, in his native Italy he is regarded as a great stage director of operas. It is this background which might account for his film's trademark visual style and set design, typified by their lush photography, romantic settings and a keen eye for lyrical and poetic expression. When he is at the top of his form, as in *Romeo and Juliet* and *La Traviata*, the viewer can be lifted out of the doldrums of everyday reality and swept into an opulent world of beauty, love and tragedy. And when his films don't work, these same expressions can be seen as hokey, manipulative and mawkish.

In addition to the films which follow, Zeffirelli also directed a highly praised made-for-TV drama on the life and teachings of Jesus Christ, *Jesus of Nazareth* (1967, 371 min, Italy/GB/US). The drama was filmed with a largely American and British cast, headed by Robert Powell. In 1994, Zeffirelli was elected to the Italian parliament as a member of the right-wing Freedom Alliance party. He represents the Sicilian town of Catania.

"I hate to call certain human beings 'gay.' The moment you say 'gay,' I already see a movement or a category or a ghetto. I don't like that at all."

—Franco Zeffirelli

The Taming of the Shrew
(1966, 126 min, US/Italy)
This sumptuous screen version of Shakespeare's classic comedy was Zeffirelli's screen debut and he opens up the romp to great cinematic effect. Elizabeth Taylor and Richard Burton are perfect as the feuding couple; she's an unmarried "wildcat" and he's the only man in Padua willing to court her. Striking photography — soon to be a trademark in his films — and wonderful support from Michael York, Cyril Cusack and Michael Hordern help bring this battle of the sexes to spirited life. The story is the basis for the Cole Porter musical "Kiss Me Kate." ⊗

La Boheme *(1967, 104 min, Italy)*
In the first of several filmed operas available on home video in the United States, Herbert von Karajan leads the La Scala Chorus and Orchestra in this rousing Zeffirelli production of Puccini's classic. Soloists include Mirella Freni, Ruggeri Raimondi, Martino and Panerai. ⊗

Romeo and Juliet *(1968, 152 min, GB/Italy)*
With an eye for passionately romantic detail, Zeffirelli brings Shakespeare's immortal romantic tragedy to the screen with a flourish. His decision to cast teenagers Leonard Whiting and Olivia Hussey in the leads (and to sprinkle in some male and female nudity) helped make this film a perennial favorite for students in need of an accessible, lively and demystifying version of the dreaded Bard. Whiting and Hussey play the ill-fated lovers in 15th-century Verona in this lushly photographed and richly staged tragic love story. Also with Michael York as Tybalt. Music by Nino Rota. ⊗

Brother Sun, Sister Moon
(1973, 110 min, GB/Italy)
Sappy, meandering, hippie-esque (in the bad sense of the word) and plagued by a soundtrack by Donovan, Zeffirelli's romantic story of 13th-century St. Francis of Assisi is quite enjoyable nonetheless. A young man from a wealthy family has a burning quest for spiritual fulfillment which causes him to abandon all worldly possessions and pleasures and live a simple life among nature and the poor. An attractive and at one point nude Graham Faulkner plays the lead. ⊗

The Champ *(1979, 122 min, US)*
A maudlin update of the King Vidor 1931 tearjerker which starred Wallace Beery and Jackie Cooper, this version features Jon Voight as the punch-drunk, down-on-his-luck boxer and Ricky Schroeder as his young son. Trouble brews when ex-wife Faye Dunaway comes on the scene wanting custody of the boy. Forgettable. ⊗

FAVORITE DIRECTORS

Endless Love *(1981, 115 min, US)*

A plea of temporary insanity can be Zeffirelli's only logical defense for this infamously insipid movie on love gone mad (literally) featuring actress-wannabe Brooke Shields and Martin Hewitt. On nearly every critic's ten worst list that year, the film's interest today is that it features early screen appearances by James Spader and Jamie Gertz, and debuted Tom Cruise. A film which will always be remembered as the butt of Bette Midler's classic Oscar-night joke: "That endless bore — *Endless Love*." Ⓐ

> "As excruciating as the Diana Ross/Lionel Ritchie title tune."
>
> *—Time Out*

I Pagliacci *(1982, 70 min, Italy)*

Placido Domingo stars in this exciting Leoncavallo opera. Georges Pretre conducts the orchestra and chorus of La Scala, and Teresa Stratas and Juan Pons co-star. Ⓐ

La Traviata *(1982, 110 min, Italy)*

Zeffirelli's lavish, powerful rendition of Verdi's opera stars Placido Domingo and Teresa Stratas in emotionally charged performances as the doomed lovers. Not just for opera fans. Ⓐ

Tosca *(1985, 127 min, US)*

Zeffirelli staged this fiery, passionate production of Puccini's classic for the Metropolitan Opera. Hildegard Behrens and Placido Domingo are commanding under the direction of conductor Giuseppe Sinopoli. Ⓐ

Otello *(1986, 123 min, Italy)*

The dark treacheries and intense passions of Shakespeare's classic is vividly brought to the operatic screen by Zeffirelli. Set in an unreal Mediterranean locale, this soaring and lavish production stars Placido Domingo as the tragic, crazed king. Ⓐ

Hamlet *(1990, 135 min, GB)*

Taking an extreme career risk, Mel Gibson — Mad Max himself — took on Shakespeare's most challenging role, that of the mad Prince Hamlet. In a sumptuous retelling of the classic tragedy, Gibson gives a fiery, credible and even inspired interpretation of the melancholy Dane. And he is given remarkable support. Glenn Close is superlative as Hamlet's mother, Gertrude, who unknowingly marries her husband's murderer. Alan Bates makes an arresting Claudius, Helena Bonham-Carter is a fragile Ophelia and Ian Holm is a most amusing Polonius. Zeffirelli brings great energy to the work, and his stagings are carefully conceived and executed. Ⓐ

Romeo & Juliet

KENNETH ANGER

Throughout his career, Kenneth Anger has succeeded in creating his own myth to such an extent that little is known for certain about this allusive but brilliant filmmaker. He says he attended dancing school with Shirley Temple, and that he had a role in the 1935 film *A Midsummer Night's Dream*. Whatever the truth may be, it is his version of it that is significant, and like 1960s avant-garde compatriate Andy Warhol, Anger's cultivated image is as important as the films he makes.

Anger was born in 1929 in Santa Monica, California. He was surrounded by Hollywood lore and lure (his grandmother was a costume designer for silent films), and as a student at Hollywood High, he made 16mm films using fellow students (including John Derek) as actors. Perhaps his brush with the studio system is what gives his visionary cinema its professional sheen. Even the cruder titles of his youth, *Who's Been Rocking My Dreamboat?* (made in 1941 at the age of nine), *Tinsel Tree* (1942), *The Prisoner of Mars* (1942), *Puce Moments* (a six-and-one-half-minute film made in 1948 about an aging actress dressing to go out) and *Escape Episode* (1944-46), exhibit an interest in themes beyond his years.

Anger considers himself a magician: his camera is his conjuring tool, editing is his incantations. While many of his films were either started but not finished, held for ransom but not returned, or completed but not shown, Anger's reputation rests with his own curated retrospective referred to as "The Magick Lantern Cycle."

The earliest film in the series is his 1947 homoerotic masterpiece, *Fireworks*, made one weekend in the family home while his parents were away (he was 17 years old at the time). Titled so for the seminal image of a sailor's erection that ejaculates like a roman candle, it chronicles Anger's descent into the night as he scours the waterfront looking for rough sex — it's a visual pun worthy of Lubitsch. In the film, Anger says all that needs to be said about his sexuality, preferring to address other facets of his life and maintaining that homosexuality should be viewed as the Native Americans viewed it: a gift from the gods. Of historical note, *Fireworks* was one of the first homosexual-themed films to receive international acclaim and in 1960 was confiscated by the San Francisco police for being obscene. One particular admirer of the film was Jean Cocteau, and as Anger stated, "One fan letter from Cocteau and I hightailed it to Paris."

In 1950, he moved to France, where he assisted Cocteau on several projects — none of which came into fruition. While there, Anger reportedly tried to commit suicide, the details of which have gone unreported. How that affected his next films, *Rabbit's Moon* and *Eaux d'Artifice* (both 1950), is only conjecture, but both exhibit an odd, dreamlike state, like a somnambulist eager to return to bed. *Rabbit's Moon*, Anger's tribute to Méliès, is set in an iridescent forest where the sad clown prince Peirrot despondently dances in the cadence of a silent film, bathing in the cool blue lunar light. Where Occidentals see the face of a man on the moon, the Japanese — and Peirrot — see a rabbit. *Eaux d'Artifice* has been described by Anger, glibly one suspects, as an aging queen cruising for rough trade. That belies what is probably Anger's most beautifully constructed film, set in a magical garden of fountains and fauna, a visual fugue complementing Vivaldi's music, and is refreshing as the ever-flowing waters in the park.

Four years later, while back in Hollywood on a visit, Anger shot *Inauguration of the Pleasure Dome*, and recut it over a period of a dozen years after that to the form we see it in today. Based on one of Aleister Crowley's bacchanals and incorporating footage unused in *Puce Moments*, the short, which features Anais Nin in the role of Astarte, is his first overtly religious piece that concluded in 1980 with *Lucifer Rising*.

Somewhere during this time he wrote the French edition of "Hollywood Babylon," a compendium of nearly every sleazy story or rumor of debauchery by the stars of Tinseltown put in the worst light possible. So libelous was this notorious book that it wasn't until 1975 that an American edition appeared. *The New York Times* called it

Scorpio Rising

"a delicious box of poisoned bon-bons." In 1985, a second volume was published, every bit as morbid and fascinating. And a third volume is slated for release in 1995.

In 1962, Anger returned to America, moving to Brooklyn, which he described as "like visiting a foreign country. It was as strange to me as darkest Africa." The following year, he completed *Scorpio Rising*, a homoerotic ritual to that "masculine fascination with the Thing that Goes." The first film that reflected the sensibilities that would soon be responsible for Pop Art, *Scorpio Rising* found its Greek chorus in Top Forty radio, using the music of everyone from Bobby Vinton to the Rondells. Unfortunately, he used their music without asking, generating a legion of lawsuits that now keep the film out of video distribution, although it was released briefly in the mid-1980s. Upon the film's original release, it was confiscated by the LAPD, and Anger was sued by the American Nazi Party for "desecrating the swastika." With the song "Dream Lover" floating through the background of *Scorpio Rising*, some rough trade gently polishes his hot rod car. This was a harbinger of the camp sensibilities to come. 1965's *Kustom Kar Kommandoes* is the only fragment filmed of what was to be, according to Anger, "an oneiric vision of contemporary American (and specifically Californian) teenage experience."

After Anger's raw footage of his next project was stolen (by its star, Bobby Beausoleil, a member of the Manson family), Anger published his own obituary in *The Village Voice*. After a suitable period of mourning, Anger took what footage he had left and created part two of his Aleister Crowley trilogy, *Invocation of My Demon Brother*. As the Magus dances, Lucifer, the Bringer of Light, arrives reconciling opposites. Mick Jagger, dallying with demonology at the time, supplied a lackluster series of squeals and blips from his synthesizer for the soundtrack — which was eventually not used.

Anger's final chapter of his black trilogy was *Lucifer Rising*. The long-dead Egyptian gods Isis and Orsiris are summoned at sacred grounds around the world until they appear in their pink flying saucers over the ancient pyramids of the Valley of Kings. It's one of the most iridescent images ever put on film.

Since then, Anger seems to have done nothing new cinematically except to rework parts of his "Magick Lantern Cycle" for video release. He no longer lives in Los Angeles, where he had lived for many years, since a gang of ruffians capriciously shot his dogs in front of him while he was taking them for a walk near his home.

"The only devil I've ever worshipped is Mickey Mouse."
—Kenneth Anger

GREGG ARAKI

Determinedly un-PC in themes and social attitudes (especially when it comes to towing the "gay is good" viewpoint) and refreshingly belligerent when it comes to filmic style, Gregg Araki is certainly one of the most promising (but vocally reluctant) of the new generation of openly queer independent filmmakers. Filled with dark humor, societal at-large anger and raucous music, his films are raw but exceedingly witty examinations of disenfranchised Southern California youths (both gay, lesbian and straight) seeking to find a place in a straight, money-obsessed world. What Araki lacks in slick production values and its resulting professional sheen is more than made up with his involving, though not always likable characters and controversial story lines.

Araki credits the formation of his unorthodox personal approach to several European "art" and American independent directors. These filmmakers include Derek Jarman, John Waters and Andy Warhol, with his greatest influence being the works of Jean-Luc Godard. His jarring, in-your-face films have resulted in two independent hits — *The Living End*, his HIV-positive road movie and the critically praised gay teen angst drama, *Totally F***ed Up*.

Born in 1963, Araki (his 2 "g"'s in Gregg were given to him by his parents) was born in Santa Barbara, California, and worked at one point as a music critic for *L.A. Weekly* (where he once wrote of the anguished Leonard Cohen, "If he's so fucking depressed, why doesn't he just shoot himself?"). His public image, created by an often straight press, is one of being "arrogant and assaultive," while members of the gay press have been just as critical. In a *Genre* interview, Araki said, "The harshest criticism I've gotten is from gay journalists themselves, and it makes me wonder if they're the ones who are self-hating closet queens."

Araki is currently working on a new film, *The Doom Generation*, a "bizarre pop nightmare" that features in the kitschy cast Christopher Knight (Peter in "The Brady Bunch"), Lauren Tewes (Julie from "The Love Boat") and former porn stars Rex Chandler (real name: Paul Fow) and Zak Spears (Chris Rossianov). After *The Doom Generation*, Araki plans on making *Nowhere*, a film he promises to be a gay version of "Beverly Hills 90210."

"Being gay is definitely part of my personality and part of my sensibility."

—Gregg Araki

Gregg Araki

▼ Three Bewildered People

(1987, 92 min, US)
Made for only $5,000, Araki's first film is a witty drama about angst and despair in the modern world. The film follows three young Los Angelenos as they sort out their feelings and sexuality in a late night coffee shop.

"An exercise in twentysomething whining."
—*Film Threat*

▼ The Long Weekend (O'Despair)

(1989, 93 min, US)
This droll exploration of gay, lesbian and straight relations revolves around three college friends who get together with their bemused lovers for one long weekend, where angst is served for breakfast and sexual exploration for the evening snack.

▼ The Living End *(1992, 84 min, US)*

With its opening close-up shot of a bumper sticker that reads "Choose Death," one can rest assured that this self-described "irresponsible" black comedy, about two HIV-positive gay men who set out on a lawless road adventure, will not hesitate to cajole, provoke and otherwise incite strong reaction. Produced on a miniscule budget, the film presents an in-your-face reaction to society's disregard for the plight of HIV-positive people. Jon is a whiny, urban film writer and critic who happens into a relationship with fellow "positive" Luke, a free-spirited and rageful drifter who precipitates their angst-driven journey into anarchy. It's best to ignore the film's thinly written script, awkward scenes and less-than-professional acting and concentrate instead on its irresistible "Yeah, I'm HIV-positive and I blame society!" message; for despite its faults, it's a totally entertaining effort. ⊗

Note on Derek Jarman's reaction to *The Living End*:
In an open letter to Gregg Araki in London's daily The Guardian, *gay filmmaker Derek Jarman, weakened by AIDS, wrote, "You resolved your film in a sympathetic and gentle way with the boys sitting by the sea. Why didn't you allow them to blow their heads off in the love scene that proceeded this?"*

▼ Totally F***ed Up *(1994, 85 min, US)*

A "no-budget, labor of love" production, Araki's anti-stereotypical "homomovie" is an angry, entertaining and provocative drama that delves into the rarely seen subculture of queer teens. Set in a mostly nocturnal Los Angeles, the story follows the life, loves and fucked-up misadventures of six teenagers (4 gays and 2 lesbians) whose friendship and romantic relationships provide a decidedly '90s-style family unit. In almost Godardian fashion, Araki undercuts video "interviews" with a fractured "show how things really are" story of the bored, disenfranchised youths who desperately want "to cling to something besides TV." The teens, while quite different in personality, are all concerned — despite a tough exterior — with safe sex, the fear and guilt of promiscuity, love, relationships and romance. As the world turns on the teens, the flip side of love — sexual games, deceit, loneliness and regret — come into play. While each character has a story to be told, the narrative concentrates on one teen in particular: Andy (James Duval). A dark-haired River Phoenix look-alike, Andy is the most alienated and vulnerable of the group. Seemingly disinterested in everything except smoking and getting high, the young man finds himself pulled out of his shell when he meets another young man and gradually falls in love, only to have his heart broken. Funded by art grant monies (made for reportedly $25,000) and starring real teens in the roles (although interestingly, only one of the six actors is actually gay), the film was inspired by a true-life incident in which two teens committed double suicide rather than being separated by their parents. With an angry intelligence that promises a bright cinematic future, Araki has successfully combined such issues as homophobia, gay-bashing, AIDS and suicide into a witty, energetic, queerly subversive film.

"A rag-tag story of the fag-and-dyke teen underground...A kinda cross between avant-garde experimental cinema and a queer John Hughes flick."
—Gregg Araki

"Even when Mr. Araki's directorial affectations overshadow his film's lucidity, his daring, outrage and inventiveness are always clear."
—Janet Maslin, *The New York Times*

ARTHUR J. BRESSAN, JR.

Highly opinionated in his thoughts and uncompromising in his work and politics, Arthur J. Bressan, Jr., who died of AIDS in 1991 and who had only made three gay-themed features, should still be considered one of the more important gay filmmakers of the 1970s and '80s. From his sensitive handling of child abuse and the developing relationship between a thirtyish man and a 14-year-old boy in *Abuse*, to his exhilarating documentary *Gay USA* to his final film, the first fiction film to deal with the AIDS crisis, *Buddies*, Bressan showed courage and an unblinking focus on a variety of gay subjects at the time of Anita Bryant's ranting and the discovery of a new, deadly disease. He said that he made *Buddies* because film is the medium to reach people and he would be able to send the message that "AIDS is not a gay illness, that it hurts everybody, and that more money must be released for effective research and care."

Born in New York City in 1943, Bressan went from being a straight-acting teacher at a Catholic boys' school during his early twenties to living in a San Francisco commune where he came out and began his activist approach to gay politics and art. He received his start in film through the male porno industry — making distinctive sex films in Super-8 and 16mm that confused some of its viewers with their unusually romantic, sensitive handling of the characters. His first porn movie was *Passing Strangers* (1974) and he went on to make *Daddy Dearest*, *Juice* and *Pleasure Beach* (1984), which was voted one of the best 100 gay porn films ever by *Adult Video News*. These films paid the rent and helped in financing his three features. In addition, he also made several low-budget documentaries including *Thank You Mr. President — The Press Conferences of JFK* for PBS.

While a determined and concerned filmmaker, his strong personality also gave him a reputation as being belligerent and "difficult." On a personal note, I met Artie at a lunch in New York in 1985 to discuss his upcoming film, *Buddies*, which was to play at a cinema I operated in Philadelphia. After initial pleasantries, we were soon arguing and shouting with each other, one of the sticking points being his unwavering support of NAMBLA, the man/boy love group. It was a lively discussion that was a bit uncomfortable for the New Line Cinema representatives lunching with us. But my initial dislike soon changed to respect and

Arthur J. Bressan, Jr.

even affection when I met him again at the film's AIDS benefit at the Philadelphia premiere. He was eloquent, cajoling, persuasive and undeniably seductive. A man and film-maker sadly missed.

> "Arthur Bressan has always had trouble compromising his personal vision for the camera or for the audience; the result has been spare, no-nonsense films with an appeal somehow both gut-wrenching and elegant."
> —Vito Russo, *The Advocate*

▼ Gay USA *(1977, 78 min, US)*

The seminal 1977 documentary *Gay USA*, Bressan's acknowledged response to Anita Bryant's anti-gay political activities, is a fascinating feature-length slice of lesbian and gay Americana. Bressan commissioned filmmakers across the country to record all June 1977 Lesbian and Gay Pride marches. Intercutting this footage with on-the-street interviews, he documented this critical point in the history of the modern American lesbian and gay liberation movement.

> "It would be like my *Triumph of the Will*, only it would be called *Triumph of the Fag, Triumph of the Dyke*."
> —Arthur Bressan

▼ Abuse *(1983, 85 min, US)*

This daring and powerful yet sensitive account of a battered adolescent's coming to grips with his abusive parents and his awakening homosexuality caused quite a stir in the gay community with its positive approach to man/boy love. While filming a documentary on child abuse for his master's thesis, 35-year-old Larry (Richard Ryder) meets 14-year-old Thomas (Raphael Sbarge), the victim of abuse from his violent parents. The two become close, with Thomas beginning a healing process with the help of the older filmmmaker. Their nurturing relationship, spurred by the advances of Thomas, eventually turns to love, and faced with certain breakup and, for Thomas, more beatings, they flee together to San Francisco. This controversial film was rejected by just about every independent distributor until Cinevista, a New York-based company specializing in gay-themed films, picked it up.

▼ Buddies *(1985, 81 min, US)*

Buddies is the first dramatic feature film about the AIDS crisis. It tells the story of the friendship between Robert (Geoff Edholm), a 32-year-old man victimized by the disease, and David (David Schachter), a 25-year-old who volunteers to become his supportive "buddy." The two dissimilar men get off to a shaky start — David complains of Robert's unapologetically gay and political preachiness, saying, "Robert is not what I expected an AIDS patient to be like...he's not serious!" But as they get to know one another, a deep, tender relationship and love develops. Funny at times and extremely moving, the film was written by Bressan in five days and shot in nine, with the two actors being the primary cast. Bressan made the film to raise money for AIDS organizations and its opening features a computer sheet showing hundreds of names of people who had died of the disease with the date of their death and the word "AIDS" after it. However, due to legal ramifications, the names were all ficticious.

> "How many sick and dead friends does it take to make you want to do something? On the surface, *Buddies* is a simple story of two guys who meet in a crisis, strike up a relationship, and change each others' lives. On a deeper level, the film is a complex look at a unique love that transcends pain, fear, and even death."
>
> —Arthur Bressan

Buddies

JAMES BROUGHTON

"An odd bird in the aviary" is how England's *Guardian* newspaper succinctly described this effervescent poet/filmmaker. One of the early leaders of the American independent filmmaking community (others being Maya Deren and Kenneth Anger), and an original member of the "San Francisco School" of filmmakers which flourished in the late 1950s and early '60s, Broughton's shorts (he has never made a feature film) are lyrical, funny and uninhibited celebrations of life, love and sex. Although gay, his films do not always have gay images. Watching his films in chronological order, however, it is possible to see how his initial rejection of homosexuality (through celebrating the joys of heterosexuality) evolved into featuring gay love as one facet of the human experience while his later works has him coming out, exposing the joys of queerdom.

A playwright and teacher as well, Broughton made several films from 1946 through 1954. He did not make another film until 1968 — and these works were freer, hipper and wilder than before. Most of Broughton's shorts have been compiled into a six-part video series, "The Films of James Broughton." Immediately following are short descriptions of several of his films that are not in the collection and following that is the video series itself:

The Adventures of Jimmy
(1950, 11 min, US)

In what Broughton calls a "satiric version of the hero quest," this short features the director himself as a naive country boy on a journey of self-discovery and love. With a jazz score by Welden Kess.

Neptie *(1969, 14 min, US)*

The short celebrates a wedding of two older people; and features the ceremony, the banquet and a private beach ritual.

This Is It *(1971, 10 min, US)*

A two-year-old boy named Adam, a red balloon, an Eden-like garden and a miracle. Broughton said of the film, "This is It/This is really It/This is all there is/and It's perfect as It is."

High Kukus *(1973, 3 min, US)*

Broughton: "I have no meaning/said the Film/I just unreel myself...My most minimal film, my most profound nonsense."

▼ **Together** *(1976, US)*

Broughton's first completely gay film, *Together* was made in collaboration with his lover, Joel Singer. As poetry is read, the images of Broughton's two faces (the feminine and masculine) slowly merge into one.

▼ **Devotions** *(1983, US)*

Also made with Joel Singer, the film is a gay version of the sexual excitement celebrated in his mainly heterosexual 1968 film *The Bed*. Spiritual and lyrical, the film features leather men, male nuns on roller skates and other urban gay images, in addition to scenes with both Singer and Broughton.

The Films of James Broughton

Volume 1
Erotic Celebrations

The physical meets the philosophical in this celebration of love and eros. *The Bed* (1968, 20 min) is a delightfully lyrical homage to the bed and the various roles it plays in our lives. Broughton's inspiration for the film came when "I couldn't get out of my mind how all the great events in my life take place in bed." In *Erogeny* (1976, 6 min), sensual touch is compared to the exploration of landscapes. *Herme's Bird* (1979, 11 min) glorifies the male phallus; and *Song of the Goodbody* (1977, 10 min) is a sly attack on sexual taboos. ☮

Broughton playing sax in the nude

Volume 2
Rituals of Play

Three early avant-garde works. *Mother's Day* (1948, 22 min) is an ironic nostalgic collection of pranks, fetishes and rituals of a childhood dominated by a narcissistic mother obsessed with mirrors, big hats and proper behavior. *Sight and Sound* called it, "An unusually subtle, many-sided film, leisurely yet sharp, poetic and unsparing." *Four in the Afternoon* (1951, 15 min) tells of four people's search for love, based on Broughton's own poetry. Dylan Thomas described the film as "lovely and delicious; true cinematic poetry." The final short is *Loony Tom, the Happy Lover* (1951, 15 min), an homage to Mack Sennett. This slapstick comedy and Cannes Festival winner is about a woman-seducing tramp played by mime artist Kermit Sheets and is what Broughton calls "an impudent testimony to the liberating spirit of Pan." ☮

Volume 3
The Pleasure Garden

Made in Great Britain (1953, 38 min) and winner of a special prize for poetic fantasy at Cannes in 1954, this comic fairy tale, produced by Lindsay Anderson, was filmed at the ruined gardens of London's Crystal Palace. Allen Ginsberg calls it "on the side of the angels. It's a great testimony for love in the open." ☮

Volume 4
Autobiographical Mysteries

The world according to Broughton is told in *Testament* (1974, 20 min), a complex collage of personal imagery, songs and dreams. *Devotions* (1983, 22 min), co-directed with Joel Singer, is a personal vision of a world of brotherly love. *Scattered Remains* (1983, 22 min) is a filmed performance piece of Singer "doing" Broughton. ☮

Volume 5
Parables of Wonder

In this series of films, Broughton deals with metaphysical themes, especially Zen Buddhism and Lao-Tzu. Total running time is 56 minutes and it includes *The Golden Positions* (1970, 32 min), a lovely, erotic and humorous blending of anatomical tableaus and pantomime; *The Gardener of Eden*; and *The Water Circle*. ☮

Volume 6
Dreamwood

Dreamwood (1972, 45 min) is a spiritual odyssey into the landscape of a dream. Its poet hero, setting forth to rescue the bride of his soul, embarks on a voyage to a strange island where in a magical forest, he faces the most improbable experiences of his life. ☮

ROBERT EPSTEIN & JEFFREY FRIEDMAN

San Francisco-based filmmakers Rob Epstein and Jeffrey Friedman are award-winning documentarians who have concentrated their artistic efforts on addressing a variety of pressing gay and lesbian issues, including AIDS, lesbian/gay rights, coming out and gay leaders (Harvey Milk). The two men formed a TV and film production company called Telling Pictures in 1987.

Friedman's career has included stage acting and film and television editing, and he directed the PBS documentary *Faces of the Enemy* in 1987 before joining forces with Epstein with *Common Threads: Stories from the Quilt*. Rob Epstein, winner of a 1990 Frameline Award — presented annually by the San Francisco Lesbian and Gay International Film Festival to outstanding independent filmmakers working in lesbian and gay cinema/video — has also won two Academy Awards, a Guggenheim Fellowship, two Peabody Awards and three Emmys for his pioneering work. He began his career in film as one of the directors of the landmark 1978 film, *Word Is Out*, and, in addition to various Hollywood film work (*Never Cry Wolf, The Right Stuff*), he produced *Greetings from Washington, D.C.*, a 1980 documentary on the lesbian/gay civil rights march on Washington; and "The AIDS Show: Artists Involved with Death and Survival," made in 1986 for PBS and Bravo. Friedman and Epstein's latest project is the much-anticipated documentary of Vito Russo's landmark book on the history of gays and lesbians in Hollywood movies, *The Celluloid Closet*, which is scheduled for release sometime in 1995.

▼ The Times of Harvey Milk *(1984, 87 min, US, Robert Epstein & Richard Schmiechen)*

One of the most important gay films ever made, this extraordinary and compelling portrait of the slain San Francisco supervisor and gay political activist won a much-deserved Academy Award as the Best Documentary of 1984. Few films pack such a powerful wallop as it documents the true-life story of Harvey Milk, a Castro Street camera shop owner who became the country's first openly gay elected city official. His rise to power and success as a leader of minorities was abruptly ended on November 27, 1978, when he and Mayor George Moscone were assassinated by Dan White, an anti-gay former colleague of Milk's on the Board of Supervisors and a former police officer. The film reveals Milk's personal, political and activist life and provides a heartbreaking account of his tragic death. The film's coverage of killer Dan White's trial is a searing episode of injustice, triggering both rage and indignation especially after he used the infamous "Twinkie defense" and received a shockingly light sentence of eight years — a verdict that sent thousands of outraged gays and lesbians onto the streets of San Francisco. White was later released after five years and committed suicide soon after that. Eight of Milk's friends and associates were selected to be interviewed and their combined remembrances capture Milk's vibrancy, love and determination....and, indirectly, what it is to be gay. A stirring and important film. Narrated by Harvey Fierstein. ⊛

Robert Epstein, Harvey Fierstein & Richard Schmiechen

▼ Common Threads:
Stories from the Quilt

(1989, 79 min, US, Robert Epstein & Jeffrey Friedman)
In this Academy Award-winning documentary, Epstein and Friedman interview surviving relatives and friends of five people who died of AIDS and were memorialized through the AIDS Quilt. Narrated by Dustin Hoffman, the film presents an emotionally charged look into their lives, as told by those left behind through recollection, photographs and film. The storytellers infuse a spirit of being to the departed which obviously helps keep the memory of those loved ones alive. Not an eulogistic memorial, but rather personal and heartfelt reminiscences. ⊛

▼ Where Are We?

(US, 1992, 73 min, Rob Epstein & Jeffrey Friedman)
An 18-day vacation through the American South becomes an earnest sociological odyssey for filmmakers Epstein and Friedman. With camera in hand and a genuine interest of people and what makes them so different, the two travel to the diners, bars and street corners of heartland America. The kaleidoscope of people they meet reveal — with little prodding — many funny, sobering and poignant life stories all seemingly supported by an unwavering optimism despite lives filled with struggles, setbacks and broken dreams. Highlights of the film are the scenes at Camp Lejeune where they meet gay Marines and venture into a "forbidden" off-base gay bar; and when they encounter a couple who in homage to Elvis have constructed a mini-Graceland. One might be tempted to expect a degree of condescension in a story of two gay men traveling through the rural South, but that is far from the truth — the people interviewed are eloquent and the glimpses into their lives startling.

The Times of Harvey Milk

F̶RIEDRICH S U

New York-based Su Friedrich is a leading figure in independent experimental filmmaking with her series of short films that are "structuralist" in form yet personal in theme. Directing since 1978, her works have won numerous awards and have been screened and been the subject of retrospectives in both lesbian/gay film festivals as well as independent film festivals. Making her films almost single-handedly (she is the writer, director, cinematographer, sound recordist and editor), Friedrich's works can be both intriguingly avant-garde as well as accessible to the average (albeit adventurous) filmgoer.

Taking an artist's approach to the film medium, with a style that some have compared to fellow independents Stan Brakhage and Jonas Mekas, her early films have been described by one critic as being "scraped, scratched and scarred into being." This comment reflects Friedrich's technique of either scratching words and narrative directly on the film stock or otherwise altering the artifice of the film. She combines this with a personal approach to the themes and subjects of her films — many of which incorporate dreamlike memory, overlapping narratives, lesbian and feminist issues, and her family and lover — in a style that explores her private experiences in a public fashion.

Friedrich has said on her filmmaking initiative, "Whenever I set out to make a film, my primary motive is to create an emotionally charged, or resonant, experience — to work with stories from my own life that I feel the need to examine closely, and that I think are shared by many people." Commenting on how she approaches her topics, she said, "Many years ago I decided that I would do the work that I wanted to do without regard for external censorship (it's hard enough to overcome the external kind!). That meant speaking about my life as a lesbian whenever I felt like it, but always doing it in such a way that it took that identity for granted. I never explained, excused or compared it to being straight, unless that happens to be the point of the film (e.g. in *First Comes Love*, which is essentially an argument made on behalf of gay & lesbian marriage)."

Born in 1954, Friedrich graduated Phi Beta Kappa from Oberlin College and moved to New York City in 1976. In between her filmmaking, she teaches film production and writes on film. In addition to the following films, she has also made *Hot Water* (1978); *Cool Hands, Warm Heart* (1979, 16 min), a dreamlike film on a lesbian performance piece; *Scar Tissue* (1979, 6 min); *I Suggest Mine* (1980, 6 min); *Gently Down the Stream* (1981, 14 min); *But No One* (1982, 9 min); and her most recent film, *The Lesbian Avengers Eat Fire, Too* (1993, 55 min), made with Janet Baus about the lesbian activist group (The Lesbian Avengers) of which she was a member. Her latest project is a feature-length film titled *Bedtime Stories* which focuses, in Friedrich's words, "On the how, why, if and when we were born baby dykes." Not scheduled for completion until 1996, Friedrich is currently soliciting photos and life stories from lesbians from around the country for this independently produced project.

The Ties That Bind *(1984, 55 min, US)*

An unconventional portrait of her German-born mother, Friedrich's dreamlike memory film recalls her mother's haunting Nazi-era childhood. Friedrich creates an accompanying black-and-white visual narrative and includes her own self-reflections of her mother's tales. The visuals include a little girl building a toy house, shots of Germany taken during a recent trip, old family photos, and fragmented filming of her mother today. During her mother's often emotional reminisces, the director remains silent, posing her questions by scratching writing onto the surface of the film. Experimental and affecting.

▼ Damned If You Don't *(1987, 42 min, US)*

Friedrich's most acclaimed film, this experimental drama examines the conflict between religious repression and sexual identity and desire through a combination of four quasi-narratives: a nun's sexual awakening by a sultry neighbor; a young woman's narrative recalling her high school nuns and their effect on her nascent lesbian persona; a voice-over of the trial testimony of a 17th-century lesbian nun; and scenes from a deconstructed version of the 1946 Powell-Pressburger film of nuns in the Himalayas, *Black Narcissus*. The most conventional tale is the present-day story of a nun (Peggy Healey) whose latent lesbian desires are kindled by the presence of a beautiful stranger (Ela Troyano) who lives next to the convent. A lyrical meditation on repressed sexuality in relation to women living in a community of other women.

> "Sweetly passionate, genuinely innovative...a lyrical evocation of the mystery of memory and the development of sexual identity."
>
> —Amy Taubin, *The Village Voice*

Sink or Swim *(1990, 48 min, US)*

Heartbreaking and profound, this autobiographical film explores a teenage girl's memory of the relationship between her and her father. Structured as 26 stories, the young woman paints a startling picture of a rigid, career-obsessed father whom she loves and admires but also fears and eventually feels betrayed by. A complex and emotionally charged film.

> "Proudly personal and triumphantly artisanal, as accessible as it is uncompromising."
>
> —J. Hoberman, *Premiere*

Dammed If You Don't

First Comes Love *(1991, 22 min, US)*

The ritual of the marriage ceremony is the focus of this short that intercuts four different traditional, perfectly choreographed marriages all ironically set against the aural backdrop of popular love songs. As the cultural event concludes with the happy couples leaving the church, all that is left is an empty church and alterboys sweeping up the rice. Friedrich calls the film "essentially an argument made on behalf of gay and lesbian marriage."

▼ Rules of the Road *(1993, 31 min, US)*

A woman wistfully recounts the breakup of her love affair with another woman and focuses on not just the person she lost but a beloved object as well — their beige station wagon. A witty yet haunting study of the intangible things and moments which make up a relationship.

> "A study of the kind of separation anxiety that never makes it to the therapist. A funeral parade for a love that gets comically, and ironically, stuck in traffic."
>
> —Susan Gerhard, *Bay Guardian*

▼ The Lesbian Avengers Eat Fire, Too

(1993, 55 min, US)

Co-directed with Janet Baus and produced by the Lesbian Avengers, this impassioned and obviously biased documentary focuses on the people and issues behind this unique lesbian political action group. The film intercuts interviews with many of the jovial but determined women who have joined the Avengers along with a "you are there" reportage of several of their protest marches and education demonstrations. The dykes involved in the outspoken group strive for lesbian awareness and visibility and enjoy the empowerment that their consciousness-raising work has on an often ignorant or homophobic public as they demand equal rights and an end to discrimination and violence. Their actions include protests at a Queen's public school board meeting, impassioned marches down 5th Avenue, protests against the anti-lesbian/gay initiative passed in Colorado as well as a Valentine Day's commemorative at the Gertrude Stein statue located in New York's Bryant Park. ⊛

CONSTANTINE GIANNARIS

While not large in output so far, Constantine Giannaris' innovative film work to date offers great promise. The outspoken Englishman was the 1991 winner of London's *Gay Times* Jack Babuscio Award for Best Gay Filmmaker of the Year.

Jean Genet Is Dead *(1987, 35 min, GB)*

Dedicated to Mark Ashton, a gay political activist who died of AIDS, this poetic, highly personal collage features overlapping images set against the backdrop of a man reading from the works of Jean Genet. Accompanied by a mournful soundtrack, Genet's text explores love, friendship and loss.

▼ A Man and a Woman *(1988, 38 min, GB)*

Tongue-in-cheek humor highlights this melodramatic soap opera set in a South London flat where roommates Alan and Liz, both of whom shared the affections of a now-dead lover, find that their libidos are both piqued once again, this time for their new, attractive flatmate.

▼ Caught Looking *(1991, 35 min, GB)*

Winner of the Best Gay Short in the 1992 Berlin Film Festival, *Caught Looking* is a witty, sexy and highly inventive film which speculates on the future of personal relationships — particularly sexual ones — in the much-heralded era of the technological "information superhighway." An unforgettable homo/sci-fi successor to *Pink Narcissus*, the story follows the sexual exploits of a man who uses an interactive virtual reality machine to select his romantic fantasies. His options offer different sexual scenarios and characters, bringing to vivid life a world of idealized impersonal sex, muscular men cruising stylized tea rooms, and tattooed sailors. Stylish and subversive, the film was originally made for Britain's Channel 4's lesbian and gay television series, "Out," but its explicit sex scenes proved to be too much even for the normally adventurous network. ⊛

▼ North of Vortex *(1991, 58 min, GB)*

Quite different from his previous works, *North of Vortex* is a lyrical black-and-white road movie set in the vast expanse of the American West. A gay poet picks up a bisexual sailor and a waitress in his convertible. This leisurely paced film explores the shifting (and occasionally explosive) emotional and power relationships between the three. ⊛

MARLEEN GORRIS

There is probably no other filmmaker in this book more committed to a determined ideology than Dutch filmmaker Marleen Gorris. The three films she has made to date are all feminist militant cries against the injustices of the existing patriarchal society with stories filled with a visceral sense of rage. From the dogmatic attack against the brutal, oppressive nature of a male-dominated society in *Broken Mirrors* to the radical solution she proposes when she goes for the (male) jugular in *A Question of Silence* to her less stringent yet no less pointed illustration of man's tendency towards violence and his insipid follies in *The Last Island*, Gorris has maintained a steady, focused and radical vision of the bleak state of relations between the sexes.

Born in 1948, Gorris studied drama both in Holland and abroad. While attending a documentary film group in Holland, she read a news item about a woman arrested for shoplifting. She soon developed a screenplay from this and, since she had no experience in filmmaking, approached Chantal Akerman to direct. But Akerman encouraged Gorris to try filming herself, and with the aid of the Dutch government, which put up two-thirds of the production costs, her directorial career was launched with *A Question of Silence*. Her stylistic traits are not dazzling, although her use of crosscutting, flashbacks and tight editing — in addition to her screenplays — contribute to make her films intensely absorbing, undeniably powerful and always controversial.

Yet if her films were simple polemical militant feminist tracts, their effects on viewers would not be so great. But all three films are powerful, persuasive and impassioned and have been surprisingly successful commercially despite the inflammatory feminist themes. They grip the audience with tales of rape, revenge, oppression; offering a troubling glimpse into a rotting patriarchal system. Constructed as thrillers and action-adventure films, Gorris is especially effective in enticing the audience with her well-constructed stories and then walloping their collective heads with her admittedly rigorous politics.

Coupled with this vehement, beware-of-men feminist point-of-view is her much more subtle handling of lesbianism. While present, the inclusion of lesbianism as both a symbol of unity against men and as a legitimate alternative lifestyle is surprisingly muted although by no means wanting. Gorris prefers to depict the relationship between women as intensely emotional, physically close but non-sexual. The psychiatrist and the women prisoners in *A Question of Silence* attempt to reach out physically but are unable to do so. The prostitutes in *Broken Mirrors* appear to be physically intimate yet not sexually involved with each other, and in *The Last Island*, the female heroine could very well be a lesbian trapped on an island of sex-and-control starved men although her sexual orientation is left in question.

Gorris knows that her films are quite controversial, of which she says, "I make these films because I'm interested in the ways of the world, as far as the power struggle goes. And I think that women are often still seen as second-class citizens, and are treated that way as well. I suppose something should be done about it, although I don't see how I can. I'm merely showing what I see, in a fairly extreme form."

A Question of Silence

A Question of Silence
(1983, 92 min, The Netherlands)
Ostensibly a feminist thriller, this production is surely one of the most controversial and provocative films of the 1980s. The film chronicles the seemingly unmotivated murder of a male shopkeeper by three middle-aged women who had never met before and did not know their victim. A woman psychologist tries to piece together the puzzle of why they killed the man. Was it senseless murder or a political act — the rage of women against a male dominated society? Ⓐ

"An inflammatory, subversive (in the best sense of the word) black comedy."
—*Los Angeles Times*

Broken Mirrors (Gebrokene Spiegels)
(1984, 110 min, The Netherlands)
An impassioned attack on the economic, sexual and social injustices inherent in the patriarchal system, Gorris weaves together two parallel story lines: that of an intimate look into the degrading conditions of brothel life; and a sadistic killer's rampage through the countryside. The Amsterdam brothel called Club Happy House is depicted as a site of continual degradation, humiliation and violence against the women who, in the midst of it all, find solace and solidarity in their com-

mon hatred of men and their job. The serial killer scenes, in which a seemingly innocuous man kidnaps, tortures and then systematically kills several women, are almost to grisly to bear. The two plots merge in a shattering finale. Grim and fatalistic, this powerful feminist thriller equates women's suffering with men's pleasure and broadly indicts men as well as their destructive instinct to dominate and destroy.

"...*Broken Mirrors* has a lovely black humor...powerful, well-acted, full of rage."
—*New York Daily News*

▼ The Last Island
(1990, 101 min, The Netherlands)
Concluding her trilogy on radical feminism and anti-patriarchalism, this rousing polemic-filled adventure, sort of a *Swept Away...* meets *Lord of the Flies*, is a violent, graphic story of survival and social dysfunctionalism. When their plane crashes, seven survivors, including five men (a French scientist, a hot-headed American beach bum and Brad Pitt look-alike, two gays and a religious military man) and two women (a grandmother and a young Canadian lawyer), find themselves stranded with little hope of rescue. Their initial community organization of finding food, building shelter and constructing a bamboo raft is undermined by the men's increasingly aggressive nature for cruelty, domination and destruction. From attempted rape, mutilation and even murder, the men, spurred by the Rambo-esque religious fanatic and their own raging libidos, soon begin to run amok. Even the middle-aged gay man, initially viewed as reasoned and compassionate, allows his "natural instinct" to take over. The politics are simple: Man is the problem in organized society and a threatening force to life-affirming and nurturing Woman. As with her two previous films, this contentious theme works because the story is executed with the maximum amount of excitement and suspense.

BARBARA HAMMER

One of the brightest voices of the lesbian and independent filmmaking community over the past 20 years, Barbara Hammer is an award-winning filmmaker who has made over 70 experimental films and videos since 1968. Her 1974 film *Dyketactics* is the first lesbian lovemaking film to be made by a lesbian. Affectionately called "the grandmother of lesbian film" for her pioneering work, her films — all of which have been shorts until her most recent film *Nitrate Kisses* — are avant-garde in structure, often non-narrative in outlook and utilize dreamlike montages and abstract images to convey her personal thoughts. Topics culled from her poetic vision and approach to life include lesbian love, eroticism, women's spirituality, radical feminist politics, the goddess movement and the power of women. By remaining out of the feature and narrative form of filmmaking and concentrating on the theoretical and aesthetic elements of her work, her popularity has been limited with the general public but she has enjoyed continued strong support among a growing cadre of admirers.

Born in Hollywood in 1939, Hammer did not begin making films until she was 30. Before this, she worked as a counselor for emotionally disturbed teenagers, a teacher, a playground director and even as a bank employee — all what Hammer says were "social jobs." Her entry into the arts began with ceramic pottery and painting, but she eventually drifted into film after someone gave her a camera. She immediately made the 8mm short *Schizy* (1968), which deals with a person's dual feelings of masculinity and femininity. Her first 16mm film was *A Gay Day* (1973), a spoof of a lesbian marriage in which two women, both wearing bridal gowns, roll down a hill. This was followed by *Dyketactics* in 1974, a film that outlined her feelings of how her life has changed since she began making love to women. Claiming never to have been in the closet, Hammer did not "become a lesbian" until a year or so after making her first film, noting, "As soon as I heard about it, I did it." She personally financed all her films through 1984 (totaling approximately 35), and since then has been receiving grants for her work; most recently a $20,000 grant from the American Film Institute, money that Hammer says she applied for 20 years in a row.

Of her interest in experimental and avant-garde film-

Barbara Hammer

making, Hammer feels that the use of conventional film form to express a lesbian lifestyle is not possible for her. "I've always been at pushing for a change in political government and I'm pushing for a change in film form also." In her search for a lesbian iconography, she rejects conventional Hollywood movies as replicating the heterosexual lifestyle and of being patriarchal in form. Her films, especially her early ones, are concerned primarily with women's bodies (many times her own) and attempt through the film medium to explore the tactile sense.

Active in seeking out lesbian audiences for her films since the early 1970s, Hammer is an intelligent and impassioned speaker for both lesbian and independent film as well as an outspoken advocate for the arts. She has taught film production at several universities and has been a multi-award winner at film festivals, receiving retrospectives of her work at the Centre Georges Pompidou in Paris in 1985, the 1986 Berlin International Film Festival and at the Ann Arbor Film Festival in 1992.

Hammer's first feature-length film, *Nitrate Kisses*, a demanding documentary on the loss of queer history, enjoyed success in several festivals and is slated for limited theatrical engagements in 1994. Interested in reaching a larger audience with her films, Hammer wants her work to become more accessible while not losing their avant-garde edge. She is currently working on a documentary on breast cancer as well as a second feature-length film ("an alternative documentary"), *Tender Buttons*, which concerns the process of making autobiographies and how they are made in both Western and non-Western societies.

At the core of the film is Hammer's own autobiography filmed in montage and using her own archives in an effort "to construct a lesbian's life."

> "My films are often called visionary, but I am no visionary. I am living my lesbian life. I'm not waiting. My life is my vision. By documenting what others would call visionary, what I would call 'actionary,' I hope to spark the imagination of the audience."
>
> —Barbara Hammer

Many, but by no means all, of Barbara Hammer's films are available in the United States through four video volumes distributed by Facets Multimedia. The shorts available on home video are packaged as follows:

▼ Lesbian Sexuality ⊛

Dyketactics *(1974, 4 min, US)*
With 110 lesbian images in four minutes, Hammer has called this look at female sensuality and sexuality "an erotic lesbian commercial...a coming out film, celebrating what it was like to make love to a woman." Interestingly, Hammer attempted to restrict initial screenings of the film to women.

Double Strength *(1978, 20 min, US)*
Poetic and passionate, this study of a lesbian relationship, both performance (trapeze) artists, is taken from the romantic beginnings through an alienating breakup and eventually to a platonic friendship.

Women I Love *(1979, 27 min, US)*
Working from Hammer's comments that "the camera is a personal extension of my body, my personality," this erotic yet playful film features Hammer's four lovers — each wholly individualistic and exotic — captured over a five-year period.

▼ Lesbian Humor ⊛

Menses *(1973, 4 min, US)*
A comedy-drama about menstruation and the underlying patriarchal taboos accompanying it. The film revolves around several women who act out their own fantasies of the monthly event.

Superdyke *(1975, 22 min, US)*
Likened by Hammer as being similar to a Bugs Bunny cartoon, the story features a group of shield-wielding Amazons who descend on the city of San Francisco, taking its most important institutions (City Hall, Macys) before triumphantly returning to the wilderness.

Our Trip *(1980, 4 min, US)*
Hammer and her lover back pack to Peru in this "little ditty about lesbian travel."

Sync Touch *(1981, 12 min, US)*
Visual and tactile senses are explored in this ironic and humorous inquiry into the nature of the lesbian aesthetic.

Doll House *(1984, 5 min, US)*
A fast-paced montage with the central figure being a doll house.

No No Nooky, TV *(1987, 12 min, US)*
An exploration into the conflict between feminism and the electronic media and technology.

Nitrate Kisses

▼ Optical Nerves ⊛

This list of videos along with the ones in *Perceptual Landscapes* are more conceptual in outlook as they are concerned less with lesbianism, women's bodies and sexuality and delve into the nature of light, landscapes, pre-patriarchal monuments and life.

Optic Nerve *(1985, 16 min, US)*
An ambitious and personal film on family and aging revolving around the death of Hammer's grandmother.

Also featuring: **Place Mattes** *(1987, 8 min)* and **Endangered** *(1988, 18 min)*

▼ Perceptual Landscapes ⊛

Pools *(1981, 6 min, US)*
One of Hammer's underwater films, this short is an impressionistic swim by Hammer and co-director Barbara Klutinis as they swim through two pools designed by a woman architect at William Randolph Hearst's famed estate, San Simeon.

Bent Time *(1984, 20 min, US)*
An investigation into the premise that when one approaches the edge of the universe, time bends.

Also featuring two abstract looks at nature: **Pond and Waterfall** *(1982, 15 min)* and **Stone Circles** *(1983, 10 min)*

The following is a partial listing of Hammer's other films, none of which are currently available on home video.

▼ Sisters! *(1974, 8 min, US)*

A celebration of lesbianism, the film features footage of the Women's International Day march in San Francisco and the last night of the Lesbian Conference in 1972.

▼ Psychosynthesis *(1975, 9 min, US)*

The final film of a trilogy (*I Was/I Am* and *X* being the first two) is a feminist film dealing with the inner self and involves a witch, an infant, an athlete and a filmmaker. Using multiple and overlapping images, dissolves and superimposed images, the film explores internal conflict and evolving serenity.

▼ Multiple Orgasm *(1976, 6 min, US)*

The film begins with an extreme close-up of a vagina with a woman playing with her clitoris and evolves into her silently masturbating.

▼ Moon Goddess *(1976, 15 min, US)*

Co-directed by Gloria Churchman, the film is an exploration into "finding the mother within one's self" and a search for the feminine creative spirit. The story follows two lesbian lovers as they, guided by moon power and mutual respect, explore a "mythically suggestive" landscape.

Nitrate Kisses

▼ Sappho *(1978, 7 min, US)*

Made with seven of her students, this film brings to life the image of the ancient lesbian goddess, Sappho.

▼ Dream Age *(1979, 12 min, US)*

In a fractured, dreamlike structure, a 70-year-old lesbian feminist sends out her 40-year-old self in an effort for self-discovery.

Sanctus *(1990, 19 min, US)*

Jon Gartenberg, of the Museum of Modern Art Film Department, says of *Sanctus*: "Barbara eloquently and lyrically creates rich connections between her humanist self and perilous state of the world, as she evokes the co-fragility of human existence and the film emulsion, the artist's raw material onto which she creates images."

Vital Signs *(1991, 9 min, US)*

Hammer's latest video work explores Western conventions on death. It won the Grand Prize at the Black Mariah Film Festival.

▼ Nitrate Kisses *(1992, 63 min, US)*

Thematically returning to her seminal short film on lesbian sexuality, *Dyketactics*, Hammer's first feature film challenges the viewer with her thoughts on the loss of queer history as well as an unapologetic foray into both lesbian and gay sensuality and sexuality. The film begins with a short biography of writer Willa Cather, a presumed lesbian (Cather lived with a woman and preferred to dress in men's clothing) who, before her death, destroyed all personal records and correspondences, making it nearly impossible to learn more about her life. With this willful destruction of historical information, Hammer explores the life and sex of several older lesbians and juxtaposes through montage two gay men making love, scenes from the 1933 American avant-garde classic on male sensuality, *Lot in Sodom*, tattooed S&M dykes, German film footage from the 1930s and adds to this a multi-textured soundtrack including some amazingly queer blues songs. A demanding yet lyrical documentary film that is, among many things, a plea for gays and lesbians to record and rediscover and recover their own history.

TODD HAYNES

Having won the Sundance Film Festival's 1991 Grand Prize for *Poison*, Todd Haynes is one of New Queer Cinema's most visible filmmakers, both within the industry and to the movie going public alike. Haynes' films are unique in construction, and he has a keen ability to take an abstract thought and translate it into more accessible terms. Though he has an admitted allegiance to the manners and technique of a grand Hollywood style, Haynes has yet to make what one would presume to call a mainstream attraction, instead keeping his lens firmly focused in an avant-garde mode.

Haynes claims strong attachment to Jean Genet, whose inspiration is directly evidenced in *Poison*. He cites Alfred Hitchcock, Rainer Werner Fassbinder and Sam Fuller as his favorite filmmakers. Like these masters of the high art of cinema, Todd's films challenge viewers, provoking them into questioning their own objectivity via the creation of situations that are complex and which contain elements of the subversive. With *Superstar: The Karen Carpenter Story*, he constructed a completely unreal scenario by using Barbie dolls as main characters to tell a true story. In doing so, he humanized the title character — generally thought of as a dorky sugar popper and ultimate geek — so that viewers would gain sympathy and a strange identification with someone who's portrayed as being swallowed up by forces beyond their control. As is his custom, Haynes uses rather disturbed humor to break down our guards.

Haynes grew up in Encino, California, and he started making films while in secondary school. He attended Brown University, majoring in art and semiotics, the latter being the study of the philosophical theory of signs and symbols. He credits Brown's lack of a formal film department as the inspiration behind his inventiveness: "There were not a lot of facilities, not a lot of emphasis on technique, so people had to find creative solutions."

Notoriety gained from *Superstar* and *Poison* has resulted in Haynes' receipt of overtures to enjoy the financial rewards of mainstream movie production. He remains, however, an independent to insure autonomy and control over his projects. Haynes was also the co-founder of Apparatus Productions — a non-profit, grant-giving organization which funds emerging independent filmmakers.

His most recent film is *Safe*, set for a 1995 release. It's about a woman whose immune system breaks down. She leaves her L.A. home and moves to New Mexico in a quest for identity.

Todd Haynes

Superstar:
The Karen Carpenter Story *(1987, US)*

Made on the cheap, this student short has attained cult status and although not on video nor shown in cinemas, this wittily irreverent exposé of the famous anorexic singer only increases in noteriety. All of the characters are played out with Barbie-like dolls in an affectionately campy ode to the late bubblegum crooner. The reason for its unavailability is because of Haynes' admitted unauthorized use of Carpenter's songs.

FAVORITE INDEPENDENT DIRECTORS

▼ Assassins *(1987, 42 min, US)*

Haynes goes from the pop world to 19th-century France in this serious exploration on the tempestuous relationship between poet and adventurer Arthur Rimbaud and fellow French poet Paul Verlaine, who left his wife and home for the young man. Filmed in Providence, R.I., the film is less a documentary and more an arty meditative look at the two men. The film features a weirdly eclectic soundtrack including Iggy Pop, Offenbach, John Cage and Rossini.

▼ Poison *(1991, 85 min, US)*

Winner of the Grand Jury Prize at the Sundance Film Festival, this amazingly self-assured first feature by Haynes proved to be quite a controversial work when it was released in theatres. Interweaving three seemingly unconnected stories, each with its own individual filmmaking style, this low-budget independent effort will mesmerize many, perplex others and disgust more than a few. "Hero," the first tale, told in a semidocumentary form, recounts a young boy's killing of his abusive father and his miraculous flight away. "Horror," filmed in a '50s sci-fi/horror flick manner, follows the tragedy that strikes a scientist after he successfully isolates the human sex drive in liquid form. The final tale, adapted from the writings of Jean Genet, especially his first novel, "Miracle of the Rose," is "Homo," an intensely sensual and lyrical story of obsessive and unrequited love set in a prison. *Poison* is a wholly original, provocative, unsettling and intelligent film that is a "must-see" for adventurous videophiles. ⏁

> "(*Poison*) is a film that plays around with the act of telling stories while at the same time asking a few serious questions about the nature of deviance, cultural conditioning and disease."
>
> —Todd Haynes

Dottie Gets Spanked *(1993, 30 min, US)*

Filmed in a kitschy 1950s/early '60s "suburbia is the answer" style, this innovative short was originally made for PBS. Steven, a withdrawn six-year-old boy, becomes increasingly fixated on a Lucy-like television sitcom star, Dottie Frank (Julie Halston). Written by Haynes, the film examines the boy's obsession which is beginning to worry his parents. The story culminates with Steven going to the studio to watch a taping. That episode features the fictional Dottie getting spanked, which prompts Steven to confuse the scene with his own father's threats of punishment. The result is an impressive dream sequence where reality and imagination become comingled in the boy's mind.

Poison

MARC HUESTIS

San Francisco-based Marc Huestis is a veteran independent filmmaker who most recently enjoyed critical and popular success with his latest film, *Sex Is...*, a witty and perceptive documentary on gay men's sexuality in the AIDS era — the film has received several awards including the Audience Award for Best Gay Film at the 1993 Berlin International Film Festival. With the exception of *Men in Love*, Huestis writes and produces his films as well as directs. In addition to his filmmaking, Huestis formed Outsider Productions in 1977, a film production and distribution company "dedicated to films and videos which parallel the concerns of the lesbian and gay community." His first film was a 1977 short, *Unity*, a fervent response to the anti-gay actions of Anita Bryant and the Briggs Initiative, the latter a proposition placed on the California ballot that would have legislated discrimination against gays. That film also dealt with the persecution of gays and lesbians in Nazi Germany. In 1984, he made *Whatever Happened to Susan Jane?*, a raw, but quite funny film recalling the old Warhol/Morrissey films and one that has come to enjoy cult status.

A frequent guest lecturer at film events and at AIDS advocacy conferences, Huestis is also one of the founding members of the San Francisco International Lesbian & Gay Film Festival, the oldest and largest such festival in the country.

Huestis became a filmmaker after a rather abrupt departure from the theater. "I was in this group called The Angels of Light in San Francisco, which was a drag off-shoot of this group called The Cockettes — all of this is ancient gay history. Anyway, I played this alcoholic drag queen named Ellen Organ. One night when I was in this tantrum on stage, I accidentally threw this bottle that was in my hand into the audience and right into this guy's head, who had to get 20 stitches. At this point I knew that my career as a drag queen in San Francisco was over. So I thought, 'Well, I really like show business and since I can't be a drag queen anymore, maybe I can take some courses and learn how to be a filmmaker.'"

"I used to work in a video store and people would rent *All About Eve* and they would rent *All About Steve*, they would rent *Out of Africa* and they would rent *In and Out of Africa*. I knew that a lot of people were watching them (adult films) and that these images, for the gay market, would not be so shocking."
— Marc Huestis on his decision to include graphic sexual images into his documentary *Sex Is...*.

▼ Whatever Happened to Susan Jane?

(1984, 60 min, US)

Fed up with stifling domesticity in her suburban Virginia life, nerdy, bespectacled Marcy runs away, venturing to San Francisco where she looks up an old high school acquaintance, Susan Jane. Susan Jane, now Sujana, was a lonely outsider during her teen years. Having found acceptance in the big city, she wants no reminders of her past and nothing to do with the ogling Marcy. But she soon reconsiders and reluctantly takes her to her own favorite haunts filled with typical San Franciscans: bohemians, drag queens, exotic dancers, homosexuals and those "arty" types. An often hilarious comedy of self-discovery, fitting in and finding happiness. Co-edited by Rob Epstein. ⊛

"More colorful than *The Rocky Horror Picture Show*."
—*Bay Area Reporter*

▼ Chuck Solomon: Coming of Age

(1986, 57 min, US)

A celebratory, life-affirming documentary on San Francisco actor and theatre director Chuck Solomon who was suffering from AIDS, this film focuses on the man's defiant fight against the disease and his determined will to survive. Several people talk about the effect Solomon had on their lives, and his devoted mother — who was only recently told that he was gay and had AIDS — is also featured. Interspersed through the interviews are snapshots from his life, performances by Doris Fish, comedian Tom Ammiano, excerpts from "The AIDS Show" and scenes of Solomon's own struggle culminating in his joyous 40th birthday party attended by 350 friends. A winner of the Silver Hugo Award at the Chicago Film Festival, the film was part of the 14-film "Sex in America" package that was presented at the Moscow Film Festival and has also played on British, Spanish, German, Canadian and American television.

"What (*Coming of Age*) really does is present AIDS with tears and warmth and love."
—*San Francisco Examiner*

▼ Men in Love *(1989, 90 min, US)*

Terrible acting (by non-professionals), harsh direct-to-video cinematography and a painfully sentimental and bathetic story line involving love, AIDS and emotional/sexual rejuvenation offered through New Age spirituality contribute to make this film a disappointment in the Huestis canon of works. Pony-tailed Steven (with pale wide-eyed looks that reminds one of a silent film star) is mourning the loss of his lover, Victor, to AIDS. As promised to him before he died, he takes his lover's ashes to the paradise of Hawaii to throw them into the sea. There, he meets (and is immediately attracted to) Peter, and soon finds himself recovering from his grief through Peter and his friend's kindness and love. Not a film that he is proud of, Huestis says that he was simply hired to direct and did the best he could with the material. ⊛

"Bold, unique, stimulating...a sensual, life-affirming love story..."
—Deena Jones, *The San Francisco Bay Times*

FAVORITE INDEPENDENT DIRECTORS

Sex Is...

(1992, 80 min, US, Marc Huestis & Lawrence Helman)
Contemporary gay men's incessant preoccupation with sex and its side and after effects (love, relationships, AIDS) is entertainingly explored in this verbally and visually graphic documentary. Essentially a film of talking heads with some additional footage (mostly hard-core sex scenes), the film records the thoughts and opinions a several gay men, two cross-dressers, a porn star and a Protestant minister. They range from men of color to typical middle-class whites and their ages run from 20 to 70 years old. At times funny and surprisingly insightful, the men (including director Huestis who provides many memorable lines on tea room and S&M sex) recount their childhood sexual obsessions, fantasies, proclivities and dislikes while they all agree that sex is a mighty important aspect of their lives. Interestingly, as a group they have no qualms about distancing sexual desire and getting their rocks off with any connection to love or commitment. Raunchy, blunt and unapologetic, the film is an important testimony to gay men and their sexual lives before and during the age of AIDS. ☻

"...A boldface seismograph of gay male sex in America since the 1950s...boisterously entertaining and heartbreakingly sad. *Sex Is...* speaks out for sexual freedom with subtlety and force."
—Betty Sherman, *The Boston Globe*

"*Sex Is...* so welcome. It addresses male homosexual intimacy with a refreshing directness. At a moment when gay sexuality is often glibly equated with AIDS, it is firmly but responsibly pro-sex."
—Stephen Holden, *The New York Times*

Two interviewees from *Sex Is...*

GEORGE KUCHAR

Determinedly tacky, exhibiting a droll sense of camp humor and a savage self-depreciating approach to sexuality, George Kuchar's films (and there are hundreds) are just a cut above home movies, yet they exhibit a fresh openness and a pop-cum-trash mentality that result more often than not in pure kitschy delight. He has been making films for well over 30 years, primarily on his own, but has also worked with his twin brother, Mike, and fellow independent filmmaker Curt McDowell. His playfully overwrought melodramas lack McDowell's sexual explicitness and hard-edge approach to his subjects. Kuchar favors wacky humor laced with lilting romance and over-the-top tragedy — he admits his films are "turbulent from beginning to end." Kuchar's influence is obviously Hollywood of old, and in many ways that is what he gives to his ordinary characters: a touch of Hollywood glamour enlivening their often drab lives.

Born in the Bronx, Kuchar began his lifetime obsession with the camera at the age of twelve when his grandmother bought him and brother Mike an 8mm camera. Their family and friends became their earliest stars, although — as today — his cinematic efforts were not always appreciated by those in power. George, recalling his first run-in with a critic, recalls "I made a transvestite movie on the roof and was beaten by my mother for having disgraced her and for soiling her nightgown. She didn't realize how hard it was for a twelve-year-old director to get real girls for his movie."

In the early 1960s, the Kuchar brothers moved their base of operation to lower Manhattan and became part of the burgeoning underground filmmaking scene. While their distribution was limited to the Anthology Film Archives and similarly adventurous programmed venues, they were well-received, prompting Jonas Mekas in *The Village Voice* to call them "Pop Cinema at its best pop" and Jack Kroll of *Newsweek* to call them "the first holy innocents of the underground." Titles from their early avant-garde period include *Pussy on a Hot Tin Roof* (1961, 12 min); *Tootsies in Autumn* (1963, 15 min); and *A Town Called Tempest*. In 1965, George began to make films on his own and has never stopped — producing, directing, scripting (when one is used) and editing all his shorts. The films are by necessity very low budgeted, creating a constant need for efficiency and frugality. Kuchar once noted, "I work best under terrible pressure. Usually I

George Kuchar

write as the actors are getting ready for the scene."

Currently a professor at the San Francisco Art Institute, Kuchar has taught film since 1971. He has recently become less interested in 16mm short stories and become more involved with video diaries — videotaped recordings of the day to day experiences that interest him. His most often-filmed subject is weather, specifically tornadoes in Oklahoma. He has enjoyed several retrospectives including one titled "Gossamer Garbage: A George Kuchar Film and Video Retrospective" which was presented by New York's Museum of Modern Art and featured 64 of his films. While not the most well-known, nor the queerest, of the independent filmmakers highlighted in this book, his contribution to independent filmmaking has been great.

Because George Kuchar has been making short films seemingly continuously since his youth, a complete listing is difficult, but the following are some of his more celebrated film highlights.

Films made with Mike Kuchar include:

The Thief and the Stripper (1959, 20 min); *I Was a Teenage Rumpot* (1960, 10 min); and *Lust for Ecstasy* (1963, 45 min), described by Kuchar as his "subconscious, my own naked lusts that sweep across the screen in 8mm and color with full fidelity sound."

Solo efforts by Kuchar:

Mosholu Holiday (1966, 9 min) is a semi-documentary filmed during a particularly hot summer day in the Bronx and featuring Fran Leibowitz; *Eclipse of the Sun Virgin* (1967, 15 min) is a film poem that Kuchar says "must be seen by the victims of perversity, regardless of sex or age. Painstakingly filmed and edited, it will be painful to watch, too"; *Color Me Shameless* (1967, 30 min) was made while he and his cast were depressed — "the produc-

tion becomes a frozen, brittle enema bag that slowly thaws..."; *Unstrap Me* (1968, 78 min) is his longest film to date and was produced by Walter Gutman. Kuchar admits that he was drunk during much of the filming which was in Cape Cod, New Jersey and Florida; *The Mammal Palace* (1969, 31 min), of which Kuchar says: "The movie takes a rather negative look at things...this is a dramatic picture of exhausting conflicts and potential tragedy and should be on anyone's holiday list"; *Encyclopedia of the Blessed* (1970, 43 min) features artists Red Grooms and Mimi Gross and concludes with a theatrical production the three made at UCLA; *Pagan Rhapsody* (1970, 23 min) was "originally not scheduled to be a tragedy." But Kuchar remembers "things swiftly changed as the months made me more and more sour as I plummeted down that incinerator shaft I call my life"; *A Portrait of Ramona* (1971, 26 min) was filmed in Brooklyn with Kuchar singing the theme song, prompting him to compare his singing voice "to the final screams of a species doomed to extinction"; *Confessions* (1971, 10 min) features George confessing his "sins of the flesh" to his parents. Also, *KY Kapers* (1977, 16 min); *Prescription in Blue* (1979, 21 min); *Calling Dr. Petrov* (1987, 20 min); *The Rainy Season* (1987, 28 min); and *Motivation of the Carcasoids* (1988, 25 min).

Corruption of the Damned
(1965, 55 min, US)
Kuchar says of this film: "Overwhelming in plot, gargantuan in theme, trash-ridden in execution...this picture bursts from its girdle of traditional Hollywood pyrotechnics and falls all over the place in a paroxysm of flabby sensuality, senselessness and insanity."

Hold Me While I'm Naked
(1966, 15 min, US)
One of his more celebrated films, the story features a filmmaker who, after working all day filming a steamy love scene, returns home to his shabby Bronx apartment. Taking a shower, he breaks down, banging his hand against the wall in a gesture of loneliness and sexual frustration. Kuchar mockingly encapsulates: "A dazzling ruby in Kuchar's jewelry box of cinema gems and gossamer garbage. Financed with unemployment checks....(it) goes beyond the erotic into the world of hyper-neurotic, a world which exists behind the filmmaker's shower curtain."

The Devil's Cleavage *(1975, 107 min, US)*
A 16mm opus described by Kuchar as "an impressionistic series of romantic set pieces filmed in seedy interiors."

George Kuchar:
The Comedy of the Underground
(1983, 66 min, US, David Hallinger)
Kuchar stays in front of the camera in this documentary on his life and work.

Hold Me While I'm Naked

MC D OWELL
C U R T

Indiana-born Curt McDowell, once called the "bad boy of gay filmmaking" primarily for his raunchy, outrageous and often sweetly perverse subject matter, was a much-beloved cult director. His works, however, with the exception of his hilarious magnum opus, *Thundercrack!*, have rarely enjoyed commercial or even mainstream art-house exhibition. His films, largely consisting of shorts ten minutes or less, were sexually frank but never pornographic. He playfully explored the sexuality of his characters, and through them his own, admitting in one interview that "I'm trying to figure out my sexuality through my films."

McDowell, who died of AIDS in 1987, moved to San Francisco in 1965 at the age of twenty and attended the San Francisco Art Institute where he studied painting. He soon, however, became interested in film, thinking that "it seemed as if everything I've ever wanted to do in the arts — drama, painting, music — could be done on film." Working primarily in 8mm, he was nothing if not prolific, making a reported 50 shorts in 1969 alone. But it is his later films most of his fans are familiar with, as he dismisses most of his early shorts as "just test films really." Even after gaining select popularity with these longer films, he remained committed to short subjects, saying that they were simply sketches of people and ideas.

In the early 1970s, at a time when sexual explicitness was being explored in porno movies, McDowell's offbeat approach to the sticky subject was handled with disarming humor and was often self-consciously autobiographical, often making fun of his own gay sexual obsessions and desires (especially his penchant for rough trade heteros). He worked with a loyal group of people including fellow filmmaker George Kuchar and, since few of his films were picked up for distribution, raised the needed capital from various odd jobs and government grants.

In addition to the following films, McDowell made many more including *Truth for Ruth, Ainslie Trailer, Tastless Trilogy, Peed in the Wind, Nozy Tozy* (all in 1972 alone), *Lunch* (1973), *True Blue and Dreamy* (1974) and *Fly Me to the Moon* (1974).

Ascension of the Demonoids
(1986, 45 min, US)
Made with an NEA grant, the first one he ever received, this UFO epic was the culmination of his work in 16mm.

George Kuchar Goes to Work with Today's Youth *(1986-88, 45 min, US)*
One of the first of his many video projects, Kuchar drifts away from his lurid melodramas into semidocumentary work.

Weather Diary 1 *(1986, 81 min, US)*
This and several others videos (including *Weather Watch*) of similar theme are his observations of weather and clouds taken from a motel room where he annually stays in Oklahoma.

The Creeping Crimson *(1987, 15 min, US)*
Kuchar returns to the now-mean streets of his youth — the Bronx. He wanders the neighborhood holding the video camera at arm's length.

Video Album 5: The Thursday People
(1987, 60 min, US)
A haunting video recording made with his friend, filmmaker Curt McDowell, when he was dying of AIDS.

Big Ones Hurt *(1987, 25 min, US)*
And George should know it...a funny appreciation on the 1989 San Francisco earthquake.

Sherman Acres *(1991, 85 min, US)*
"Twin Peaks" is the object of satire in this six-episode takeoff on the celebrated television series.

Color Me Lurid *(1966-1978, 83 min, US)*
This video compilation includes "Hold Me Back While I'm Naked," "Mongreloid," "A Reason to Live," "Wild Night in Reno" and "I, an Actress." While not displaying any overt homosexuality in these particular shorts, they offer a queer audience a hilarious insight into the filmmaker and his fascination with tacky Hollywood melodramas.

> "My films are meant to be funny but I hate the idea of them being seen as comedies mainly because I hate jokes. I hate punchlines in films — like in Scorsese's films."
> —Curt McDowell

A Visit to Indiana *(1970, US)*

Feeding off his childhood memories of growing up there, this early film is a satire on the "Great Midwestern" lifestyle.

▼ Pornografollies *(1970, US)*

A surrealistic musical, or as one critic called it, "a bisexual scatological revue."

Weiners and Buns Musical *(1971, US)*

Called by the director "the destruction of the nuclear family by the tone deaf," this parody of sexual, domestic and movie conventions features two men and a woman who sing a song on the joys of life now that they've thrown their baby overboard.

Confessions *(1972, 16 min, US)*

Is the medium his way of purging childhood secrets (lying, stealing, even loving a girl) by revealing them to his parents through the camera or is he simply putting one over on the audience?

Siamese Twin Pinheads *(1972, 5 min, US)*

Best described by *The San Francisco Chronicle*, this is "an utterly revolting five-minute grotesquerie...its very loathsomeness automatically qualifies it as *tres punque*."

▼ Ronnie *(1972, 7 min, US)*

McDowell turns on the camera and allows his "star," a cocky male hustler, to ramble on about his prowess and straightness.

Boggy Depot *(1973, US)*

Co-directed by Mark Ellingeron, this "musical for the whole family" is a McDowellian musical spoof of *West Side Story*.

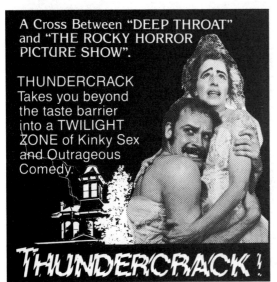

A Cross Between "DEEP THROAT" and "THE ROCKY HORROR PICTURE SHOW".

THUNDERCRACK Takes you beyond the taste barrier into a TWILIGHT ZONE of Kinky Sex and Outrageous Comedy.

THUNDERCRACK!

▼ Nudes: A Sketchbook *(1974, US)*

People's sexuality are voyeuristically explored and celebrated as McDowell sketches twelve of his friends: male-female, gay-straight, hunky and homely. At one point, with the camera right behind, he pulls the pants down on a particular reticent delivery boy.

Thundercrack! *(1975, 150 min, US)*

A very funny and outrageously sexy spoof of all those horror films in which a group of strangers is forced to spend a stormy night in an old dark house full of eerie sounds, bizarre happenings and, in this case, inhabited by a sexually active gorilla. Greeting the group of stranded motorists in her decayed mansion is a crazed hostess who initiates her unwitting guests in a series of increasingly bizarre sexual trysts. Fellow gay filmmaker and the film's screenwriter George Kuchar stars as one of the hapless and sexually ravaged guests. A sexually graphic camp classic that is a titillating scream. McDowell, commenting on the script said, "Basically the script is Mark Ellingeron's and mine; George added guilt and circus animals."

▼ Taboo *(1980, 55 min, US)*

Kevin Thomas of *The Los Angeles Times* says: "Begins amusingly but becomes an increasingly surreal equation of sex and death. It's virtually a nightmare, unfolding in ramshackle settings and involving intimations of incest and homosexuality. It's not nearly as erotic as *Thundercrack!* but is far more disturbing in its imagery as a projection of sexual fantasy and frustration."

▼ Loads *(1980, US)*

A raw and raunchy version of Gas Van Sant's *Mala Noche*, this sexually explicit comedy centers around the director luring tough straight young men into his apartment and convincing them to undress and masturbate. As the congenial host watches, the soundtrack has McDowell commenting on and rationalizing his obsessive desire for straight men.

▼ Taboo: The Single and the LP
(1980, US)

McDowell focuses his camera's gaze on an interesting Arab youth (and object of his desire) as he simply hangs out on the street and in McDowell's apartment.

Sparkle's Tavern *(1985, 90 min, US)*

Called by *The Village Voice* as the world's longest home movie, this lively fairy tale about sexual liberation features Marion Eaton as a sexually repressed mother who finally has an orgasm — much to the shock of her startled children. The film features George Kuchar as the magical Mr. Pupik. Commenting on the film, McDowell says, "It's 90 minutes, it's R-rated, it's funny. It's about enlightenment. It's about hiding things from your parents and them hiding things from you."

OᴜᴌᴚIᴋᴇ
OᴛᴛINGᴇR

Called by London's *Time Out* magazine as "Germany's foremost lesbian adventurist filmmaker," former painter Ulrike Ottinger, the co-winner of *The Gay Times'* 1994 Jack Babuscio Award, is part of the large, so-called New German Queer Cinema that has been in existence since the late 1960s. Ottinger, born in Germany in 1942, takes a more experimental and visually fanciful approach to her films (both documentary and fiction) than her more "realistic" compatriots, like fellow lesbian filmmakers Monica Treut, Alexandra von Grote and Elfi Mikesch and gay directors R.W. Fassbinder, Lother Lambert, Rosa von Praunheim, Frank Ripploh and Werner Schroeter. She writes, produces, photographs and directs all her films and has enjoyed a long collaboration with Tabea Blumenschein, who acts in her movies and is also the costume designer. Ottinger's work is infused with extraordinary art direction which produces striking visual images and settings. Many of her films center around empowered, rebellious, independent women engaged in adventure or travel. She adds to this a touch of surrealism and occasionally pokes fun at conventional narrative. Ottinger takes great pleasure in the use of depicting

women and lesbian sexuality and sensuality. Andrea Weiss, in her book "Vampires and Violets," says that it is Ottinger's goal to "(construct) visual pleasure for women."

After working as a painter in Paris in the 1960s, she made her first film in 1972, *Laokoon und Soehne.* Several other short films followed, including 1973's *Berlin Fever,* before she made her feature film debut with *Madame X — An Absolute Ruler* in 1977. In addition to the films which follow, Ottinger has made *A Ticket of No Return (Portrait of a Female Alcoholic),* a 1979 stylized, semidocumentary portrait of a lesbian drinking herself to death in Berlin; 1981's *Freak Orlando,* a free-form adaptation of Virginia Woolf's "Orlando" featuring Delphine Seyrig and Nina Hagen as a bearded Jesus Christ; and *China — The Arts, The People* and the 8½-hour *Taiga,* two documentaries she made while on location filming *Johanna d'Arc of Mongolia.* Her latest project is *Diamond Dance,* a drama concerning the lives of four Jewish families set in New York City's Brighton Beach environs.

▼ Madame X — An Absolute Ruler
(1977, 141 min, Germany)

Unlike any adventure yarn one has seen before, this feminist lesbian pirate movie's objective is to reinterpret the genre and parody its conventions. The results are a wildly uneven but unforgettable spectacle. Madame X, the self-proclaimed ruler of the China Sea, accompanied by her servant and sometime lover, Hoi-Sin, calls on the oppressed women of the world to leave behind their drudgery and travel with her on the ship Orlando and cruise the high seas.

Johanna d'Arc of Mongolia

The diverse group of women who answer her call include Betty Brillo, an American housewife; Blowup, a sexpot siren; a roller skating artist (played by filmmaker Yvonne Rainer); an Australian bush pilot who yearns to be an astronaut; a German athlete; and a skirt-wearing androgynous castaway picked up at sea. The one-armed, leather attired Madame X — described by the ship's psychologist Karla Freud Goldman as "a charismatic personality consumed by narcissism and whose lust for power grows" — leads this motley menagerie into both sexual and social exploration. At one point, all the women die only to reappear reinvented and revitalized. A lesbian cult classic.

Dorian Gray in the Mirror of the Popular Press *(1983, 150 min, Germany)*

This striking odyssey into surrealism stars Delphine Seyrig as a Dr. Mabuse-like head of an international press organization who concocts nefarious schemes to increase circulation. Women take over the roles traditionally awarded men including '60s model Veruschka von Lehndorff in the role of the narcissistic Dorian Gray.

▼ Johanna d'Arc of Mongolia

(1989, 165 min, Germany)

Dubbed "the lesbian *Lawrence of Arabia*" when it played at the San Francisco International Lesbian and Gay Film Festival in 1989, Ottinger's *Johanna d'Arc of Mongolia* is a very odd combination of elements. It's nothing you've ever seen before — unless you've seen an episode of Marlon Perkin's "Wild Kingdom" co-directed by Fassbinder and Cecil B. DeMille. An international cast, headed by Delphine Seyrig, portrays a delightful ensemble of characters traveling on the Trans-Mongolian railway. Their journey is interrupted by a band of nomadic Mongol horsewomen led by a Mongolian princess who kidnaps the train's female passengers. An astounding sense of composition characterizes the first half of the film as Ottinger incorporates mirrors and deep-focus cinematography to capture multiple planes of action onboard the Trans-Mongolian. In the second half of the film, we are abducted and carried into the geography of Mongolia. Plot takes a backseat to landscape as the film slides into a traditional ethnographic documentary mode.

"Wickedly delightful. Who would have believed that life in a yurt could hold this many temptations? Sophisticated, mysterious and deliriously beautiful."
—Sheila Benson, *Los Angeles Times*

▼ Countdown *(1991, 189 min, Germany)*

A fascinating chronicle of Germany's final days as a divided nation. Filmed in a period of ten days leading up to the June 1990 unification, Uttinger focuses not on the politicians and business people who engineered the change, but rather ordinary citizens, eliciting their thoughts on both the impending change and the possibility of traveling to sites that were instrumental in bringing about the division 45 years before. Uttinger visits the Reichstag as well as Jewish cemeteries; she films the first East German gay rights demonstration; and talks to West German bar patrons, Turkish "guest workers" and Rumanian immigrants.

J A N
OXENBERG

Although Jan Oxenberg's commercial output is low, she, along with Barbara Hammer, has been a pioneer in the field of independent lesbian filmmaking. Her groundbreaking 1970s short films played an important part in publicizing lesbian images and taking the idea of being lesbian from an underground lifestyle to one with greater social consciousness. The shorts played to often small but enthusiastic audiences — not always lesbian — and were a staple in early lesbian and gay film festivals as well as in many college and repertory cinema programs.

Unlike Hammer, her films use humor in driving across her sexual politics, a technique not always appreciated by critics at the time. Her parody of lesbian stereotypes in *A Comedy in Six Unnatural Acts* provoked cries of homophobia by certain activists but audience response to it was usually met with uproarious laughter and knowing appreciation. As with Hammer, her films are targeted towards a feminist-lesbian audience, with many early screenings restricted to women only. In an early interview, Oxenberg was quoted as saying, "It's really entertainment for the lesbian community. As far as I'm concerned, it's not being made for other people to see." Time and the political climate have changed, allowing a larger audience to take delight in her biting social and sexual commentaries.

Technically her filmmaking is not very complex as Oxenberg is seemingly more interested in ideas rather than cinematic manipulation of the medium. Notwithstanding their technical deficiencies, her films celebrate the lesbian experience and were invaluable in confronting a generation of socially and politically naive lesbians. Out of the filmmaking loop for many years, her comeback film was *Thank You and Good Night*, an entertainingly serious and insightful full-length documentary on death, her family and the living.

▼ Home Movie *(1972, 12 min, US)*

This landmark lesbian film is a reflective autobiographical work. Warm and funny, *Home Movie* is just that, featuring home movies from Oxenberg's childhood and adolescence (as a cheerleader in high school) intermixed with images relevant to her life as a lesbian adult (pride marches, a group of lesbians playing a friendly game of football). She provides the witty voice-over analysis of the accompanying images. The scenes of her as a child show how she played the game of physical and social conformity while her commentary reveals a totally different, queerer mentality. The fast-paced short knowingly expands on the disparity between exterior actions and interior thoughts and feelings. A more radical approach is offered by Andrea Weiss in "Violets and Vampires," suggesting that the film "takes up the radical feminist position that lesbianism is an antidote to male power. Rather than situate her film completely within a female community, Oxenberg juxtaposes images of patriarchal order with images of lesbian pleasure."

▼ I'm Not One of Them *(1974, 3 min, US)*

Lesbian denial is the theme to this tragi-comic sketch featuring a woman spectator at a roller derby event talking about her "unique experiences with lesbianism." Quite hilarious and provocative.

▼ A Comedy in Six Unnatural Acts
(1975, 26 min, US)

A cult favorite of many repertory cinemas and film festivals in the 1970s, this clever satire presents a series of skits each focusing on a particular stereotype of lesbianism. Six different clichéd lesbian characters are presented: "the wallflower," "role-playing," "seduction," "non-monogamy," "child molester" and "stompin' dykes." Oxenberg sets up each scene by giving just enough information on the character to lull the audience into jumping to a prejudiced conclusion, and then she offers cleverly twisted, table-turning endings to explode the myths. Behind the comedy is the serious issue of lesbian role playing and how it limits and deceives.

Oxenberg in *Thank You and Goodnight*

Thank You and Goodnight
(1991, 77 min, US)

"What is this thing called death? And what is eternity anyway?" Oxenberg breaks through the commercial film barrier with this humorous, irreverent, inventive and touching comedy-drama documenting her grandmother's death. Never maudlin nor morbid, she examines not only the life and personality of her 70-ish grandmother, a self-proclaimed kosher ham, but contemplates the mystery of death and the regret and sorrow of the living. The director intermixes interviews with her grandmother, a strong-willed, cranky Jewish New Yorker, with those of her friends and family, and intersperses these with imaginative use of life-size cutouts of herself and others in dramatic remembrances from her childhood. An emotionally powerful yet contemplative family autobiography that clutches at the heart and soul. The only complaint is the lack of any mention of the director's sexuality and how her family and grandmother have reacted to it. ⊛

PRATIBHA PARMAR

A feminist and activist, India-born Pratibha Parmar, winner of the 1993 Frameline Award and who now resides in London, has been making stirring documentaries on social and political issues since 1986. She has focused much of her attention on issues that greatly effect lesbians of color and the disabled and has dealt with such topics as AIDS, racism as well as highlighting several leading Indian and African-American women. Her latest film, *Warrior Marks*, made in collaboration with novelist Alice Walker, probes the repression and complex social context surrounding female circumcision, a cultural phenomenon (or mutilation) that occurs in many parts of South Asia and Africa. *Warrior Marks* has also enjoyed some specialized theatrical engagements and has played at festivals and universities. Parmar and Walker are currently finishing a book on the subject.

Emergence *(1986, 18 min, GB)*
Featuring four black and Third World women artists (including feminist poet Audre Lorde and Palestinian performance artist Mona Hatoum), this video work delves into their art and writing as well as focusing on the common problems facing them — including alienation from their community and loss of identity.

▼ A Plague on You *(1987, 58 min, GB)*
Produced by London's Lesbian and Gay Media Group, this "moving visual poem" is a sharp and impassioned rebuke of Britain's early AIDS awareness campaigns which preyed on fear and avoidance of the real issues. Originally airing on British television, Parmar focuses on England's advertising since the United States, under President Reagan, had yet to formulate a national awareness and prevention campaign.

Sari Red *(1988, 12 min, GB)*
Made in memory of Kalbinder Kaue Hayre, a young Indian woman killed in 1985 in a racist attack in England, this powerful documentary deals with racism and violence against South Asian women both in the community and in the home.

▼ Reframing AIDS *(1988, 36 min, GB)*
Expanding the debate platform from the typical gay white male perspective, Parmar gathers a multiracial group of gays and lesbians, all of who are affected by AIDS. In a series of interviews with them, she seeks to rebuke the myths of the disease as well as dealing with the social and political damage brought on the lesbian and gay community by AIDS.

▼ Memory Pictures *(1989, 24 min, GB)*
An exploration into racism, personal history and sexual identity, Parmar intercuts the life story of gay photographer Sunil Gupta, an

Indian who migrated to Canada, with footage of Parmar's own photography show, "Wall of Images."

▼ Flesh and Paper *(1990, 30 min, GB)*

Made for British television, this lyrical documentary focuses on the life, thoughts and writings of Indian lesbian poet and writer Suniti Namjoshi, a woman who was born into an Indian royal family, but who now lives and works in England. Author of "Feminist Fables" and "Conversations with a Cow," Namjoshi talks eloquently of her life as both an Indian and a lesbian.

A Place of Rage *(1991, 52 Min, GB)*

Parmar moves her social attention to the celebration of the achievements of African-American women. Featured in this documentary are interviews with activist Angela Davis, poet June Jordon and writer Alice Walker, and the subjects touched upon include Davis' commitment to radical politics with her involvement in the Black Panthers and the Communist Party, the Black Power movement, the struggles of the women's movement and the problems of overcoming homophobia and racism. Music soundtrack features Prince, Janet Jackson, the Neville Brothers and the Staple Sisters.

▼ Khush *(1991, 24 min, GB)*

The title is the Urdu word for "ecstatic pleasure" and is an ironic counterpoint to the difficult life experiences of several South Asian gays and lesbians living in Great Britain, North America and in India, where homosexuality remains illegal. The people recount both their feelings of isolation and displacement as well as their joys — their *Khush*. Intercut with the interviews are dream sequences, a dance segment and music.

▼ Double the Trouble, Twice the Fun
(1992, 25 min, GB)

Made for Channnel 4's "Out," this upbeat docudrama focuses on the lives of disabled lesbian and gay men. The film centers on Firdaus Kanga, an impishly witty and charming gay writer, and deals with the challenges faced and overcome by the women and men.

Warrior Marks *(1993, 54 min, GB)*

Parmar's latest film is a collaboration with Alice Walker, who acted as the film's executive producer. This thoughtful documentary deals with ritual female circumcision, or its more apt description, genital mutilation, a procedure involving the removal of the clitoris and one that is based on cultural and political traditions that effect a reported 100 million women worldwide. The act, often unsanitary and unprofessional, often leads to a life of health problems and, on occasion, death. Parmar traveled to Africa to film the ceremonies, and interviews women from Senegal, The Gambia, Burkina Faso, the United States and Great Britain who have both undergone the procedure and escaped it. Parmar's approach is not objective, seeing the practice as a form of subjugation of women as well as a form of child abuse and claiming that it is "torture, not culture." Called "dynamic, powerful and witty" by London's *Time Out*, this inspiring film also features readings by Alice Walker.

R MARLON RIGGS

Innovative American filmmaker Marlon Riggs, an Emmy Award winner and the 1992 recipient of the Frameline Award, is a leading documentarian whose films powerfully focus on the social and political issues that affect straight and, in particular, gay African-Americans. These short documenatries, often filled with anger and pain, are noted for their poetic eloquence and tender eroticism. In *Color Adjustment*, he takes an insightful historical approach in analyzing black stereotpyes in television, while *No Regrets* and *Tongues Untied* explore gay black Americans and the effects divergent concerns such as racism and AIDS play in their lives. Additional documentaries include *Ethnic Nations* and *Affirmation/Anthem*, a fascinating film on African-Americans and gay sexuality featuring four HIV-positive men, all of whom "refuse to be ashamed, refuse to be silent."

Riggs, who died at the age of 37 in April 1994, taught documentary filmmaking at UC Berkeley, and edited and contributed to the book "Brother to Brother: New Writings by Black Gay Men." Despite being sick, Riggs continued to work, filming but not completing *Black Is...Black Ain't* (1994), a look into black self-identity. Upon learning he was HIV positive, he said, "I felt that finally I knew what it was like...to really call forth all that is in you." Riggs is also the subject of two documentaries: the made-for-TV *The Creative Mind: Marlon Riggs*, and *I Shall Not Be Removed*, by Riggs' former student, Karen Everett, herself the director of *Framing Lesbian Fashion*.

Riggs, who received his Master's degree from Harvard University, is survived by his companion, Jack Vincent.

> "My work has been a way of not running from death or trying to undo death, which will come. It's living beyond death, to show people that there is a reason for living."
> —Marlon Riggs

> "Marlon's rejection of the so-called objective and professionally detached approach to documentary in favor of a more impassioned, emotionally engaged and heartfelt one, makes it possible for his films to touch and communicate to all people. His work rises above simplistic bounderies and connects with the universal aspects of the human condition."
>
> —Karl Knapper, President,
> Frameline Board of Directors

FAVORITE INDEPENDENT DIRECTORS

▼ Tongues Untied *(1989, 55 min, US)*

This highly acclaimed film combines poetry, personal testimony, rap and performance to describe the homophobia and racism that confronts gay African-Americans. Described by *The Village Voice* as "one of the rare works to deal with interracial homoeroticism from the black male point-of-view," the film garnered surprising controversy when some PBS stations, disturbed by its subject matter, refused to broadcast it. A personal and at times angry documentary that is an impassioned cry to speak out about the black gay experience. One of the characters in the film states, "Black men loving black men is *the* revolutionary act," and another asks, "If in America a black is the lowest of the low, what is a gay black?" ⊘

Color Adjustment *(1992, 88 min, US)*

This comprehensive and intriguing documentary charts and interprets 40 years of black images and black/white relations in television entertainment. Interspersed with many clips from such shows as "Amos 'n Andy," "Julia," "I Spy" and "The Cosby Show" are interviews with pioneering black actors, scholars and media professionals. Riggs also adds a biting political edge with extensive footage of the black civil rights movement happening at the time. The growing representation of blacks in TV is analyzed, providing not only an exposé of the not-so-subtle racism in such shows as "Amos 'n Andy" but also the troubling themes and ideas explored in the more positive, trendsetting shows that followed, such as "Good Times." An important interpretive piece on prejudice, perception and American race relations as seen through the popular art of television.

▼ No Regrets (Non, je ne regrette rien)
(1992, 38 min, US)

Edith Piaf's "Non, je ne regrette rien" provides the musical background and defiant attitude to this candid documentary as five black gay men, all infected with HIV, speak out about their illness and lives. The men recount their turbulent and contradictory emotions when confronted with the diagnosis, their panic and resignation, and also their emerging strength and resolve to fight the illness. Through music, poetry and stirring self-disclosure, the men talk of the need for a positive approach, supportive family and friends, and humor in dealing with the disease.

Tongues Untied

GRETA SCHILLER

Detroit-born and raised, Greta Schiller studied film and production at City College of New York and made her first film, *Greta's Girls*, before graduating. She was awarded a film arts fellowship from the New York Foundation of the Arts, received the first Fullbright Arts Fellowship and won an Emmy for *Before Stonewall*. In addition to her filmmaking, Schiller was the co-producer of the award-winning documentary *Greetings from Washington, D.C.*, and was the cinematographer on Charlie Ahern's hip-hop documentary *Wild Style* (1982) and Lizzie Borden's *Born in Flames* (1983). Additional television-backed documentaries include her 1979 documentary on aging, *Well, We're Alive!*, and her latest film is *Maxine Sullivan: Love to Be in Love*, a portrait of the legendary jazz singer.

Greta Schiller

▼ Greta's Girls *(1977, 60 min, US)*

Co-directed with Thomas Seid, Schiller's first film tells the simple story of a day-in-the-life of an interracial lesbian couple at the beginning of their relationship. In addition to the typical if mundane household activities, the two women's real affection for each other is prominently highlighted.

▼ Before Stonewall *(1985, 87 min, US)*

Co-directed with Robert Rosenberg, this extraordinary recollection/documentary traces the evolution of the gay/lesbian movement in the United States from the 1920s to the '60s and touches on the major milestones in the development of the queer consciousness. Narrated by Rita Mae Brown and aided by archival footage and memorable interviews, *Before Stonewall* vividly paints a picture of what it was like to be "in the life" during this period of repression. The pioneers of liberation recall their experiences — from the lesbian bars in 1920s Harlem to a gay soldier's experiences in WWII to what it was like for gay blacks and Native Americans. The unwritten history of the fight for gay rights comes alive in this entertaining tribute to the forces that shaped a fledgling community. ⊛

> "*Before Stonewall* should be required viewing for those unaware of the horror and oppression that were gay people's lot."
> —*Philadelphia Gay News*

> "A fascinating documentary...alternatively lively, funny, sad and intelligent."
> —*Chicago Tribune*

The International Sweethearts of Rhythm *(1986, 30 min, US)*

Produced and directed by Schiller and Andrea Weiss, this heartfelt tribute to a little-known jazz band from the 1940s is a fascinating rediscovery of feminist musical history. The 16-member band, led by singer Anne Mae Winburn, was a multiracial (although mostly black), all-women's band founded in the 1930s in Mississippi which enjoyed its greatest success during WWII, entertaining troops in Europe and America. Through archival footage and interviews with surviving members, the band's story unfolds as the women recall the difficulties — including the restrictive Jim Crow laws in the South that forced the band to travel and sleep together on a bus and forced one white member to use skin darkening makeup — and the triumphs — which included playing with the great jazz singers of the time. When the men returned from war and women were discouraged from working, bookings became scarce and the band soon disbanded, but not before musical history was made. ⊛

▼ Tiny and Ruby: Hell Divin' Women *(1988, 30 min, US)*

Co-directed with Andrea Weiss, this entertaining documentary centers on the life of jazz trumpeter and vocalist Ernestine "Tiny" Davis, a former star performer with the International Sweethearts of Rhythm, and her lover of over 40 years, jazz drummer Ruby Lucas (aka Renei Phelan). Tiny, who was once called "the female Louis Armstrong," makes for a commanding presence at the age of 76 as she and her partner recount their early touring days and their work after the band's demise in the 1950s. The film pays special attention to the two women's enduring relationship. Narration by poet Cheryl Clarke. ☮

▼ Waking Up: A Lesson in Love
(1988, 60 min, US)

Set in Austin, Texas, this lesbian soaper follows the real and imagined sexual odyssey of Susan (Hannah Moore), a free-spirited lesbian. The story line is thin and the acting is on the college theatrical level, but explicit sex scenes involving the erotic exploits of the promiscuous Susan keeps one's attention on the action. With a propensity for lingering baths and the inability to keep her few pieces of clothing on, Susan will remind some of a '90s lesbian Brigitte Bardot. She has sex on the brain as she tries to find real love amidst a series of unfulfilling one-night stands. A candid drama that features New Age lesbian dances, back-to-nature frolicking, a festive women-only square dance and exciting and varied sex scenes. The film is "dedicated to ending oppression of our sexuality as women and as lesbians." ☮

Before Stonewall

WERNER SCHROETER

Once called by the late Rainer Werner Fassbinder as his only equal in Germany, Werner "Mad Genius" Schroeter, born in 1945, is a relatively unknown figure in the international film circuit and especially with the American filmgoing public despite being an acknowledged influence to Wenders, Herzog, von Praunheim and Syberberg. His most recent film, *Malina*, was unlike most of his previous works in that it enjoyed a theatrical, albeit limited run at Joseph Papp's Public Theatre in New York. But despite generally puzzled but positive reviews, its engagement was confined to the one small cinema and has received very few additional bookings around the country.

Making films since 1968, his early works, which were primarily filmed in 8mm, were experimental and shared a common theme of opera and its accompanying excesses — to the point that they were often referred to as underground operas. Known for his avant-garde approach and his frequently flamboyant style of story telling, he gradually began making more quasi-commercial features, all low budget but made with a greater emphasis on a discernable (but never easy) plot. *Eika Katappa* (1969, 144 min) was one of his earliest films and featured a tragic gay love story in its overall frenzied, operatic tale. His harrowing documentary, *The Reign of Naples* (aka *The Kingdom of Naples*, 1978, Germany/Italy), is a vivid social history on the life of the poor and disenfranchised (including prostitutes and homosexuals) in Naples from 1944 to 1969. It was a surprising success for Schroeter with European audiences. In addition to his filmmaking, Schroeter continues to work as a director of live theatre and opera in his native Germany.

> "In my films, I want to live out the very few basic human moments of expressivity to the point of musical and gestural excess..."
>
> —Werner Schroeter

▼ The Death of Maria Malibran
(1971, 104 min, Germany)

This biopic of Maria Malibran, a renowned 19th-century German opera singer who died onstage at the age of 28 in 1836, is structured into a series of seemingly unconnected tableaux, each chronicling a part of her short but turbulent life. Filmed in a purposefully kitschy style and featuring a cast of mock lesbians and transvestites as well as Warhol Superstar Candy Darling and Schroeter's own superstar Magdalena Montezuma.

Werner Schroeter

"Each scene comes across with a decadent romanticism that lies somewhere between the pre-Rafelites and a quick fix through the pages of a 1940s *Vogue*...rich, strange and perverse."

—*Time Out*

Willow Springs *(1973, 78 min, Germany)*

Filmed in part in the United States, this exuberantly bizarre tale of feminism and female empowerment has been compared to Robert Altman's *3 Women* and Fassbinder's *The Bitter Tears of Petra von Kant*. Three women (including regular Magdalena Montezuma) set up a strange commune in the Mojave Desert where they lure men into their shack, force them to have sex, rob and eventually kill them. The eclectic range of accompanying music includes the Andrews Sisters, Bizet, Yugoslavian folk songs and the Blue Ridge Rangers.

Palermo or Wolfsburg

(1980, 175 min, Germany)

This epic, winner of the Golden Bear at the Berlin Film Festival and originally eight hours long, is a sweeping tale of social displacement, violence and redemption. A young Sicilian peasant, seeking a better life, emigrates to the German city of Wolfsburg to work as a "guest-worker" at the Volkswagen car plant. He soon falls in love with a pretty girl. But in true operatic fashion, tragedy strikes when his honor is impugned, resulting in the death of two Germans and his surreal trial and imprisonment.

Day of the Idiots *(1982, 110 min, Germany)*

A symbolism-filled, collage-like drama about an emotionally unstable young woman who, after she alienates her friends, family and lover, commits herself to a hellish insane asylum.

Laughing Star *(1983, 110 min, Germany)*

This thematic departure for Schroeter is set in the Philippines during the contentious Manila International Film Festival (Imelda Marcos was its benefactor and president). The film is a poignant but penetrating look at a fractured society as Schroeter takes his camera from the opulence of the festival down to the poverty-stricken streets nearby. A startling blend of satire and social realism.

De' L'Argentine

(1986, 92 min, France/Germany)

"First we kill all of the subversives, second their acolytes, third the sympathizers, and we'll finish with the weaklings." With this quote from a head of the Argentinian military government intent on squashing dissent, Schroeter plunges into this politically charged docudrama.

▼ The Rose King

(1987, 121 min, West Germany/Portugal)

Advertised as "a fever dream from the enfant terrible of German Cinema" and described as a "brilliant assemblege of Gothic rot and Catholic kitsch," this romantic homoerotic tale involves the obsessive love a young man (who is into growing the perfect rose) has for a handsome Italian gardener. With a half dozen different languages, a fractured narrative and music that alternates between Viennese waltzes and African chants, the film is set near the Mediterranean beach where a woman (Magdalena Montezuma) and her grown son, Albert, live. Albert, who is in lust with the young Fernando, witnesses him stealing from a church's poor box and in a series of unexplained incidents, kidnaps the young man. Imprisoning him, Albert begins to control his life, bathing him and feeding him the rose which he grew — a situation that leads to a form of sacrifice. Montezuma, who had worked with Schroeter since the beginning of his career, died of cancer two weeks after the completion of filming.

"(An) hallucinatory tale of Oedipal and homosexual passion, played out against an otherworldly Mediterranean landscape. Both entrancing and excessive."

—*Variety*

"Languidly elliptical and enveloped in a mystique of erotic suffering, it's pitched somewhere between the epicene of Richard Strauss's 'Der Rosenkavalier' and the tortured mysticism of Jean Genet's 'Miracle of the Rose.'"

—J. Hoberman, *The Village Voice*

Malina *(1991, 125 min, Germany)*

Adapted from a novel by feminist Ingeborg Bachman (who died in 1973), this French-language drama of *amour fou* was photographed by filmmaker/cinematographer Elfi Mikesch. Isabelle Huppert stars as a novelist suffering from a severe bout of depression and existential angst. She lives in Vienna with the much calmer Malina (Mathieu Carriére), a photographer. Fraught with Freudian symbolism, the often surreal and convoluted story centers on her new relationship with another man, made increasingly volatile by her troubled mental state.

2

FAVORITE STARS

The featured personalities, accompanied by a short biography and their filmogaphy, have been highlighted either because they are lesbian/gay, because their work has importance to gay/lesbian audiences or simply because they and their films have been embraced by the community.

"My being openly homosexual doesn't appear to have damaged my career in any way. That fact might offer encouragement to anyone who's still nervous of exiting the closet."
—Simon Callow

"I'm proud of who I am and I'm proud of my family. I live my life in the light. I'm not going to run into the shadows. The more we stand up and be counted, the harder it will be to discount our community. We need to put a face on gay America."
—Amanda Bearse

"Without homosexuals there would be no Hollywood, no theatre, no Arts."
—Elizabeth Taylor

Tallulah Bankhead

Though an accomplished stage actress for five decades, and to a much lesser degree a film star, it is the offscreen persona of Tallulah Bankhead which made her one of America's most popular celebrities.

Born in 1903 in Alabama, Bankhead came from a political and liberal family: her grandfather was a senator, and her father was Congressman William Bankhead, who served as Speaker of the House from 1936-1940. Her mother died giving birth to Tallulah, so she was raised by her paternal and progressive grandmother. Attending private schools most of her life, Tallulah was still a teenager when she won a beauty contest whose first prize was a role in a motion picture. After a second movie appearance, Tallulah went to New York to conquer Broadway. After several years of continued but anonymous employment, she moved to London, where she stayed for eight years, becoming a sensation (a British lord said, "There are only three people in England who are front-page news — The Prince of Wales, George Bernard Shaw and Tallulah Bankhead").

She returned to Hollywood a star, and made a succession of silents and talkies which helped cement her status at home, as well. The Hollywood love affair was short lived, however, and she went to New York in 1932 after reportedly saying she would never return (she later attributed this statement to a misunderstanding). Hollywood's loss was Broadway's gain. She went on to create, among others, the roles of Regina in "The Little Foxes" and Sabina in "The Skin of Our Teeth." She eventually did return to Hollywood, to star in Alfred Hitchcock's *Lifeboat*, for which she won the New York Film Critics' Best Actress award. She went on to appear in a handful of films over the next 20 years, but none were as rewarding as *Lifeboat* or her stage work.

Bankhead was also known for her strong political views, and she was one of the first to warn against the rising spread of Nazism (a famous drinker, she went on the wagon at the fall of Dunkirk and remained sober until VE-Day). In the 1950s, she lobbied Congress on behalf of the Unemployment Compensation Act.

But with all her achievements, no report on Bankhead would be complete without a mention of her infamous, scalpel-sharp wit. With her inimitable deep-voiced, exaggerated vocal delivery, Bankhead would aim her witty observations at herself ("I'm as pure as the driven slush"), as well as others. Alto-voiced reporter Earl Wilson once asked, "Have you ever been mistaken for a man on the phone?" "No, dahling," she replied, "have you?" She had accompanied friend Tennessee Williams to a screening of *The Fugitive Kind*, the film version of his play "Orpheus Descending." At the end, she turned to Williams, "Dahling, they've absolutely ruined your perfectly dreadful play." Of course, "Dahling" was part of the Bankhead mystique; Bankhead explained, "All my life I've been terrible at remembering people's names. I once introduced a friend of mine as Martini. Her name was actually Olive." The most famous and repeated Bankhead remark, seemingly handed down from generation to generation like gay folklore (and repeated by Tony Richardson in his autobiography "Long-Distance Runner"), occurred when she and Tab Hunter

Tallulah Bankhead in *Lifeboat*

were appearing in Baltimore in a pre-Broadway production of Tennessee Williams' "The Milk Train Doesn't Stop Here Anymore." Tallulah was asked, "Is Tab Hunter gay?" She turned, smiled and said, "I don't know, Dahling. He's never sucked my cock."

Meeting Joan Crawford for the first time, she said, "Dahling, I've had an affair with your husband. You'll be next." Though she may or may not have been joking, Bankhead never hid her bisexuality. Of herself, she once stated, "I've rejoiced in considerable dalliance, and have no regrets. I'm a single-standard gal. I found no surprises in the Kinsey Report." She also wittily remarked that she was "ambisextrous."

Tallulah was married once, for a very short time, to actor John Emery. She died of pneumonia in 1968 at the age of 65.

Her rarely seen silent films and early talkies include *When Men Betray* (1918), *Thirty a Week* (1918), *A Woman's Love* (1928), *His House in Order* (1928), *Tarnished Lady* (1931), *My Sin* (1931), *The Cheat* (1932), *Thunder Below* (1932), *The Devil and the Deep* (1932), and *Faithless* (1932). Of these films, she had her best role in *Tarnished Lady*, which was Bankhead's first talkie. Directed by George Cukor, Tallulah plays a socialite who marries for money. *Lady* is a somber, involving melodrama distinguished by Bankhead's dedicated performance.

Stage Door Canteen

(1943, 132 min, US, Frank Borzage)
Tallulah is one of the many celebrities to guest star and perform in this all-star tribute to the fighting men of WWII.

Lifeboat *(1944, 96 min, US, Alfred Hitchcock)*
As a pampered society woman, Bankhead gives a scathing, award-winning performance in this first-class Hitchcock suspenser about shipwreck survivors cast adrift in a lifeboat. Her best screen work. ☾

A Royal Scandal

(1945, 94 min, US, Otto Preminger)
Otto Preminger directed (with a little help from Ernst Lubitsch) Bankhead as Catherine the Great in this diverting comedy-of-manners. (GB title: *Czarina*)

Main Street to Broadway

(1953, 102 min, US, Tay Garnett)
Tallulah makes another cameo appearance in this backstage musical featuring a gallery of guest stars.

Fanatic *(1965, 97 min, GB, Silvio Narizzano)*
Tallulah's over-the-top performance — owing much to Bette Davis' *Baby Jane* — makes this thriller about a psychotic mommy a campy pleasure. (US title: *Die! Die! My Darling!*)

ALAN BATES

A British leading man for over thirty years, Alan Bates has become a memorable and enduring actor. He has enjoyed great versatility in the roles he's chosen and has on several occasions bypassed the money and publicity that roles in Hollywood films offer for more personally rewarding work on the British stage, in quirky small films and acclaimed television dramas. His shock of dense, unruly black hair, a seductive, modulated voice, a deceptively revealing grin, a stocky but attractive build and an often rumpled attire have combined to create a captivating if atypical international star.

Born in Derbyshire, England, in 1934 into a family of artists and musicians (although his father was an insurance salesman by trade), Bates decided by the age of eleven to become an actor. At seventeen, he was accepted into the Royal Academy of Dramatic Arts, where some of his fellow classmates were Albert Finney, Peter O'Toole and Tom Courtenay. After a two-year stint with the RAF, Bates made his acting debut at the innovative Royal Court Theatre in "The Mulberry Bush" in 1955. His third production there was as second lead as Cliff Lewis in John Osborne's trendsetting "Look Back in Anger," the first of the "angry young men" plays. His performance catapulted him to fame. He soon began to work extensively in West End plays, with his greatest success as the title character in "Butley," a role he originated in London and New York, winning a Tony Award for the Broadway run.

In interviews, Bates can be quite effusive when discussing his craft, but becomes cheerfully closemouthed when it comes to his private life. Typically, he will charmingly set the limits of an interview with such British aplomb as "Ask away, old chap, but let's not get personal." A bachelor until the age of 36, he married former actress Victoria Valerie Ward in 1970 and soon after had twin sons. Tragically, one of his sons, Tristan, died of an asthma attack at the age of 20 in 1990, and Bates' wife died two years later of a wasting disease. His other son, Benedick, is an aspiring actor on the British stage.

Bates' film acting has been in roles both varied and adventurous. He has played timid or inarticulate men (Frank in *The Entertainer*, Gabriel in *Far from the Madding Crowd*), the enchanting innocent (Jos in *Georgy Girl* and Private Plumpick in *King of Hearts*), a maniac/killer (Mick in *The Caretaker*, Charles in *The Shout* and Jimmy in *Nothing But the Best*) and even the

Alan Bates

debonair leading man (Saul in *An Unmarried Woman*, Rudge in *The Rose* and the roguish Captain Jerry in *The Wicked Lady*).

But there is possibly no other actor of Bates' renown who has played so many gay or bisexual men in films. Bates' venturous starring roles include *Women in Love*, in which he plays Rupert Birkin, a man who yearns for physical and emotional intimacy with both men and women (who could forget the nude wrestling scene with Oliver Reed); the self-destructive bisexual professor in *Butley*; the gay impresario Diaghilev in *Nijinsky*; the gay spy and traitor Guy Burgess in *An Englishman Abroad*; and Frank Meadows, the seemingly conventional civil servant in love with both Gary Oldman and his dog Evie in *We Think the World of You*. These wonderfully realized characters are never stereotypical or demeaning; nor are they saints. He imbues each with a sincerity, complexity and emotional fragility not often seen in male actors. Bates has also often worked with several gay directors including Lindsay Anderson, Franco Zeffirelli, Ismail Merchant/James Ivory, and John Schlesinger.

In addition to the titles whose reviews follow, Alan Bates has appeared in these films which can be found in their appropriate chapters:

> ***Brittania Hospital, In Celebration*** — directed by Lindsay Anderson
> ***Quartet*** — directed by James Ivory/Merchant Ivory Productions
> ***The Go-Between*** — directed by Joseph Losey
> ***The Rose*** — starring Bette Midler
> ***The Entertainer*** — directed by Tony Richardson
> ***Women in Love*** — directed by Ken Russell
> ***An Englishman Abroad, Far from the Madding Crowd, A Kind of Loving, Separate Tables*** — directed by John Schlesinger
> ***Hamlet*** — directed by Franco Zeffirelli

Whistle Down the Wind
(1962, 98 min, GB, Bryan Forbes)
This charming and extraordinary film is both a Christ parable and a poignant treatise on childhood innocence. In a remarkable directorial debut, Bryan Forbes brings a deft and heartwarming touch to this story of an escaped criminal (Bates) who is found by three young children in their barn and is thought by them to be Christ. ⊗

▼ The Caretaker
(1963, 105 min, GB, Clive Donner)
Bates is the sinister and sadistic brother of mentally ill Robert Shaw in this riveting performance of Harold Pinter's most popular play. Homosexual undertones rise to the surface, especially with the leather-attired Bates. Donald Pleasence is also featured as the derelict who invades their grubby South London flat. (US title: *The Guest*)

Zorba the Greek
(1964, 146 min, US, Michael Cacoyannis)
An exceptionally accomplished screen version of the acclaimed Kazantzakis novel, with Anthony Quinn giving the performance of a lifetime as the title character. Set in Crete, the fun-loving Zorba takes a reserved Britisher (Bates) under his wing, teaching him his philosophy of life. Lila Kedrova deservedly won an Oscar as Zorba's aging mistress. Featuring a terrific Mikis Theodorakis score. ⊗

Nothing But the Best
(1964, 98 min, GB, Clive Donner)
Frederic Raphael wrote the screenplay for this smashing black comedy, which could have served as inspiration to *A Shock to the System*. In a ferocious and funny performance, Bates stars as an ambitious working-class salesman who will go to any length to climb the ladder of success — but would he commit murder? Also starring Denholm Elliott and Millicent Martin. Photographed by Nicolas Roeg.

Georgy Girl

(1966, 100 min, GB, Silvio Narizzano)
Lynn Redgrave delivers a captivating performance in this uncommon British comedy about a frumpy young woman who's satisfied to live life vicariously through her swinging London roommate (Charlotte Rampling). A delightful adult comedy-drama of modern-day morals. James Mason stars as a wealthy man who desires the ugly-duckling Georgy as his mistress. Bates ably plays Rampling's lover who eventually falls for Georgy. ⊛

▼ King of Hearts

(1966, 102 min, France/GB, Philippe De Broca)
Bates became a cult hero thanks to this whimsical and disarmingly sappy comedy that celebrates the triumph of innocence. He stars as a Scottish soldier during WWI who is dispatched to a small French village where the only remaining inhabitants are the escaped inmates of the local asylum. Genevieve Bujold co-stars as Bates' waifish love interest. One of the local crazies is a gay barber. This was probably *the* most popular repertory film attraction of the 1970s. ⊛

The Fixer

(1968, 132 min, US, John Frankenheimer)
In a role that garnered him his only Academy Award nomination, Bates plays Yakov Bok, a Jewish handyman living in early 20th-century Czarist Russia who is arrested and wrongly accused of brutally killing a child. Based on the Pulitzer Prize-winning novel by Bernard Malamud, the drama's emotional power is captured early on with the realistic depiction of a Cossack pogrom in the Jewish quarters of the city, a harrowing scene that will remind some of the emptying out of the Jewish ghetto in Steven Spielberg's *Schindler's List*. Escaping the violence, Bok, uninterested in politics or religion, finds illegal employment in the Christian sector of the city but is eventually caught and jailed. It is there in prison that he is brought up on charges of murdering a Christian boy. Being guilty of only being a Jew in an anti-Semitic Kiev, he is nevertheless beaten and "encouraged" to confess to the

Bates and Oliver Reed wrestle in the nude in *Women in Love*

murder. An intense story of the endurance and triumph of the human spirit. The film also stars Dirk Bogarde as his haughty but strangely sympathetic lawyer, David Warner, Georgia Brown, Ian Holm and Hugh Griffith. ⊛

Three Sisters *(1970, 165 min, GB, Laurence Olivier & John Sichel)*

This is a brilliant version of the Chekhov play examining the lives of the three daughters of a recently deceased Russian military officer. Bates stars with a distinguished cast, including Joan Plowright, Laurence Olivier, Jeanne Watts and Louise Purnell.

A Day in the Death of Joe Egg

(1972, 106 min, GB, Peter Medak)
Bates and Janet Suzman give intense performances as a couple whose marriage is coming undone by the stress of caring for their spasmodic daughter. Peter Medak (*The Ruling Class, The Krays*) directed this black comedy of the darkest imaginable shade. ⊛

▼ Butley *(1974, 127 min, GB/US, Harold Pinter)*

Harold Pinter made his directorial debut with this American Film Theatre production of the play by Simon Gray. Bates is splendid as an acerbic, self-destructive professor who drives away both his long-suffering wife and his younger male lover with his bitter verbal assaults. Brimming with caustic wit, like "I'm a one-woman man, and I've had mine, thank God," the play provides a perfect vehicle for the energetic Bates who originated the role on both the London and New York stage. ⊛

The Royal Flash

(1975, 118 min, GB, Richard Lester)
A sword-wielding Bates plays hero to Malcolm McDowell's pesky nemesis in this free-wheeling swashbuckler. Adapted from one of the novels from George MacDonald Fraser's "Flashman" series, the film, shot in Lester's trademark action/slapstick style, is forgettable fun.

▼ The Collection

(1978, 64 min, GB, Michael Apted)
Bates, Laurence Olivier, Malcolm McDowell and Helen Mirren deliver outstanding performances in this gripping adaptation of Harold Pinter's critically acclaimed 1960 play. Harry (Olivier) and Bill (McDowell) are an embittered gay couple who come under attack from the menacing Bates when he accuses the much younger Bill of sleeping with his wife (Mirren). Veiled threats and jealousy give way to deception, disappointment and betrayal as all four characters become trapped in a series of recriminations. Olivier called the play one of the best of the British stage. ⊛

The Shout *(1978, 87 min, GB, Jerzy Skolimowski)*

Bates plays a mysterious and violently insane intruder who invades an English couple's household. Susannah York co-stars as the woman who succumbs to his emotional and sexual domination in this chilling tale of overwhelming menace and aggression. John Hurt also stars as the high-strung husband in this adaptation of Robert Graves' ("I, Claudius") short story. ⊛

An Unmarried Woman
(1978, 124 min, US, Paul Mazursky)
Jill Clayburgh's sensational performance is the heart of this penetrating drama about a dutiful wife (Clayburgh) who learns to be self-reliant after her husband leaves her for another woman. Bates is quietly seductive as Clayburgh's almost ethereal new lover. At the time of the film's release, his archetypical "sensitive New Man" had audiences swooning with unabashed sexual delight. Ⓐ

▼ Nijinsky *(1980, 125 min, GB, Herbert Ross)*
Herbert Ross, who scored a major triumph with *The Turning Point*, once again turns to the world of ballet with this expertly acted, rather melodramatic but intriguing biography about the legendary dancer Nijinsky (played by American Ballet Theatre star George de la Pena) and his professional and private relationship with his mentor/lover impresario Sergei Diaghilev (Bates in an impressive performance). Supporting cast includes Leslie Browne, Colin Blakely, Jeremy Irons, Janet Suzman, and Alan Badel in an outstanding turn as a wealthy patron of the arts. The film received an "R" rating in the United States, apparently because of an opening film scene in which Bates and de la Pena exchange a few peckish kisses through a handkerchief. The undeserved rating effectively restricted admittance to dance and ballet students although the distributor's marketing people used it to their advantage with an advertising tag line that read: "The first ten minutes of the film are the most shocking ten minutes in film history." Ⓐ

"The best gay weepie since *Death in Venice*."
—*Time Out*

Nijinsky

The Wicked Lady
(1983, 98 min, GB, Michael Winner)
Awkward remake of the 1945 programmer, this time with Faye Dunaway camping it up as the British noblewoman by day and highway bandit by night. Featuring a triumvirate of Britain's finest (Bates, John Gielgud and Denholm Elliott), the film nevertheless reflects the slipshod production usually associated with Cannon Films, and qualifies only as a guilty pleasure at best. Ⓐ

A Voyage Round My Father
(1983, 85 min, GB, Alvin Rakoff)
John Mortimer's superb television adaptation of his own hit play reunites Laurence Olivier and Bates. Semiautobiographical in nature, this often moving and sometimes funny reminiscence centers on the occasionally tumultuous relationship between an eccentric father (Olivier) and his son (Bates). Ⓐ

The Return of the Soldier
(1985, 101 min, GB, Alan Bridges)
The powerhouse cast of Bates, Glenda Jackson, Julie Christie and Ann-Margret (yes!) highlights this riveting psychological drama adapted from Rebecca West's first novel. During World War I, a soldier (Bates) experiences shell shock and amnesia and returns to his country estate without the memory of his past 20 years. His only recollections are of a bucolic childhood and a youthful love affair. Christie is wonderful as the pampered wife who is only familiar to her husband "like any other guest in the same hotel." A subtle, handsomely mounted and subtlely involving production. Ⓐ

Duet for One
(1986, 107 min, GB, Andrei Konchalovsky)
Julie Andrews gives a sensitive performance in this tragic tale of a world-renowned concert violinist whose career is brought to an abrupt end with the onset of multiple sclerosis. Bates appears as her unfaithful composer husband, Max von Sydow plays her psychiatrist and Rupert Everett is her embittered protégé. Ⓐ

A Prayer for the Dying
(1987, 107 min, GB, Mike Hodges)
Mickey Rourke delivers a subdued performance as a guilt-ridden IRA assassin in Mike Hodges' adaptation of Jack Higgins' novel. With their usual skill, Bob Hoskins, as a feisty priest, and Bates, as a cold-blooded racketeer, lend strong support. Though not as thrilling as its source, the film offers insight into the power of forgiveness and man's atonement for his sins. Ⓐ

▼ We Think the World of You
(1988, 92 min, GB, Colin Gregg)
This film version of J.R. Ackerley's best-selling semi-autobiographical 1960 novel about a love triangle between two men and a dog is not wholly successful and can be best described as an "interesting failure." Set in the rubble of post-WWII East End London, Bates

We Think the World of You

stars as the older, set-in-his-ways part-time lover of Gary Oldman, a roguish bisexual charmer who divides his affections between his wife Megan (Frances Barber) and his male lover. The situation is upset when Oldman is sent to prison for six months. The care and feeding of his beloved dog, Evie, a charmer in her own right, is left to his mother. But Bates, desperate for a replacement love, begins to care for her and becomes obsessed with the dog; able to see in her qualities that his gaoled lover could never possess. A decidedly offbeat and witty comedy of misplaced love. ⊛

Mr. Frost *(1989, 92 min, France/GB, Philip Setbon)*
Jeff Goldblum plays an icy serial killer (who believes he is Satan) who hasn't spoken in two years in this ineffective thriller. Alan Bates is the cop out to find his true identity and Kathy Baker (*Clean and Sober*) is the psychiatrist caught in the middle. ⊛

Club Extinction *(1989, 112 min, Germany/France/Italy, Claude Chabrol)*
This stylish futuristic thriller is about a still-divided Berlin plagued by pollution, crime and a series of violent, unexplained suicides. Bates is deliciously sinister as the megalomaniacal Dr. Marsfeldt (a super-criminal modeled after Fritz Lang's Dr. Mabuse), head of an all-powerful media organization and self-professed "travel agent" for whom death is the ultimate vacation. Jennifer Beales is oddly (but effectively) cast as Marsfeldt's unwitting ally and the ever-useless Andrew McCarthy has a brief cameo as an assassin. Fans of cerebral 1970s science fiction will find this a welcome treat. Inspired by Norbert Jacques' novel "Mabuse der Spieler." (GB title: *Dr. M*) ⊛

Secret Friends *(1991, 97 min, GB, Dennis Potter)*
Alternately impressive as well as tediously repetitive, this film by Dennis Potter, the writer of the acclaimed British series "The Singing Detective," stars Bates as a successful but high-strung artist in the throes of a nervous breakdown. Reality and his confused imagination result in increasingly violent fantasies, mainly involving the death of his sweet, much younger wife Helen (Gina Bellman). In a style reminiscent of a Nicolas Roeg collaboration with a subdued Ken Russell, the film features reenacted stories from his real and imagined past which are fueled by paranoia, tortured memories of childhood traumas and his increasingly lethal sexual obsessions. Bates is effective as the troubled man and the feverish dream sequences are impressive; however, the film goes no further than his breakdown, leaving one feeling restless and unsatisfied.

Silent Tongue *(1994, 98 min, US, Sam Shepard)*
The final theatrical release of River Phoenix, this involving though labored ghost story is slightly odd, but it achieves a poetic, mystical tone. Set in the Old West, the film casts Bates as a slimy sideshow owner who traded his Indian daughter to pioneer Richard Harris for his son (Phoenix) to marry. However, after the woman dies in childbirth, Harris returns to negotiate for Bates' remaining daughter to comfort his near-mad, grieving son — whose refusal to bury his wife causes her spirit to return to seek vengeance. *Silent Tongue* is an unusual, slowly paced but nevertheless gripping treatise on 19th-century Western culture, and features showy but sound performances from the entire cast. Shepard's direction is thoughtful and carefully realized. ⊛

AMANDA BEARSE

Best known to TV audiences as yuppie neighbor Marcy Rhodes Darcy on Fox-TV's long-running "Married...with Children," Amanda Bearse began her acting career in community theatre while studying acting in college. A member of the Neighborhood Playhouse in New York in the early 1980s, Bearse had a continuing role on the popular daytime soap opera, "All My Children," for two years. After that stint, she moved to Hollywood, where she appeared in several films before being cast on the hit Fox sitcom.

She caused many a lesbian heart to flutter when she officially came out in *The Advocate* in September 1993 — amazingly the first prime-time television regular to do so. "Roseanne"'s Sandra Bernhard had declared only her bisexuality — Bearse commented on Bernhard's half-step out of closet, "That ambiguity is part of her act." Bearse has said that she hasn't received any negative reaction: "The outing was quite a freeing experience. The industry's been very supportive. Plus, I've gotten many, many letters." Since her coming out, Bearse has become a leading and vocal spokesperson for lesbian/gay rights. Former lovers with Bernhard, Bearse is currently raising an adopted baby girl with her longtime lover, TV-commerical producer Amy Shomer.

Of her celebrity, Bearse said, "I'm in millions of people's homes daily because of "Married with Children," so people who don't know they knew what a lesbian looks like now know that they know what a lesbian looks like."

Amanda Bearse

Protocol *(1984, 96 min, US, Herbert Ross)*

Bearse has a small bit in her film debut playing a role of which she would know a great deal: a soap opera actress. ☻

Fraternity Vacation

(1985, 89 min, US, James Frawley)

Bearse has a supporting role in this harmless though moronic teenage comedy about a college nerd (Stephen Geoffreys) causing havoc during a Palm Springs weekend. ☻

▼ Fright Night

(1985, 105 min, US, Tom Holland)

In her only starring role to date, Bearse plays girlfriend to William Ragsdale, a teen who's certain next-door neighbor Chris Sarandon is a vampire. She helps in the investigation, and is reunited with *Fraternity Vacation* star Stephen Geoffreys. The plot calls for Sarandon's vampire and his gay servant, played by Jonathan Stark, to pose as lovers. In an *Advocate* interview, Bearse commented on director Holland's concern for her being gay. ☻

SANDRA BERNHARD

Sandra Bernhard

"I don't consider myself a gay woman in Hollywood. I consider myself a woman who makes choices without any pressure from society or family. I do what I want to do." And what Sandra Bernhard wanted to do as a child in Scottsdale, Arizona (where her parents had moved from Michigan), was to become famous.

"My mother's an artist. My father is a proctologist. I wasn't popular in high school, which was very white and racist. A good healthy dose of alienation was my feeling. I wasn't studious, either. I dreamed of traveling the world and pursuing show business. I was always moved by its excitement and glamour."

After high school, Bernhard followed the lead of her three brothers and went to live on a kibbutz in Israel. When she returned to the States, she studied cosmetology and while living in Los Angeles became a manicurist to the stars. After venturing into stand-up comedy ("I was 19 with a big mouth and a flair for being funny"), she was cast opposite Robert DeNiro in Martin Scorsese's *The King of Comedy*. The role brought her rave reviews and a National Society of Film Critics award for Best Supporting Actress.

Bernhard went back to stand-up and made appearances off-Broadway. Her style, like that of Bette Midler, was to find a cocky pride in the face of what others might call odd. A frequent theme in Bernhard's work is her own physical attributes. "I have a hard-to-believe face," she says in *Without You I'm Nothing*, "beautiful, sensual, sexy, dangerously beautiful." Others frequently describe her — with rangy body, boxer's nose and Medusa hair — as *jolie-laide*, or "the beautiful/ugly thing." To this Bernhard quips, "I'm not some blonde bimbo, but I'm fucking hot. A lot of people want to fuck me!" And she's right, a lot of people do find her alluring — designers have draped her in their fashions for couture shows and her naked image was spread across the pages of that pantheon of heterosexual lust, *Playboy*.

However, her first true mainstream acceptance came not in comedy clubs or film or theatre, but on TV as a frequent guest on "Late Night with David Letterman." Bernhard would appear on the show brandishing her forthright sexuality, wide Jagger-esque lips and direct come-ons like weapons that would make her button-

downed host squirm in his seat. On one appearance on the show, Bernhard surprised Letterman by bringing then-best friend Madonna on with her. The two sat, in matching outfits, making sly references to the fact that they were an item. Bernhard was once quoted as saying about the Material Girl, "She was the best lover I ever had."

It is Bernhard's sexual mystique as well as her own accomplishments — sold out one-woman shows, two books, a handful of choice movie roles and a recurring and acclaimed role on TV's top-rated "Roseanne," as the star's bisexual friend — which have cemented her pop-icon status; not to mention realizing a quest for fame.

The King of Comedy
(1983, 139 min, US, Martin Scorsese)
Robert DeNiro is Rupert Pupkin, an aspiring but psychotic comedian who schemes his way onto network TV and instant celebrity. Martin Scorsese directs a finely tuned cast, including Jerry Lewis as a cynical, Johnny Carson-like dean of the airwaves. Making a remarkable screen debut, Bernhard co-stars as Pupkin's crazed, rubber-faced accomplice. ☮

Sesame Street Presents: Follow That Bird *(1985, 88 min, US, Ken Kwapis)*

Bernhard makes a cameo appearance in this children's favorite. Big Bird travels to New York City after visiting the Dodo family; all his friends accompany him to ensure a safe trip. Other cameos include John Candy, Chevy Chase and Waylon Jennings. ⊛

An Evening at the Improv

(1986, 59 min, US)

Bernhard is one of the guest comedians appearing at the famous comedy club, and she gives a hilarious performance. Harry Anderson, Elayne Boosler, Billy Crystal and Michael Keaton are also featured.

Track 29 *(1988, 86 min, GB, Nicolas Roeg)*

Nicolas Roeg's playfully beguiling mystery stars Theresa Russell as a bored young woman trapped in a loveless and childless marriage with model train and S&M enthusiast Christopher Lloyd. The woman's life is changed when she is (possibly) visited by a young stranger (Gary Oldman), who claims that he is her abandoned-at-birth son. Is he a con man or prodigal son, a real person or only the figment of her rapidly deteriorating mind? Bernhard has a small but amusing role as the kinky dominatrix, Nurse Stein, who is involved with Lloyd. ⊛

Hudson Hawk

(1991, 95 min, US, Michael Lehmann)

One of the biggest flops of the '90s, this over-produced, half-hearted comic misadventure stars Bruce Willis as a cat burglar coerced into a series of robberies. Though the actors try to maintain a degree of lightheartedness, there's too much mugging and winking — the cast goes to extremes to show what a good time it's having. Even Bernhard, who is capable of rising above this kind of material, seems lost. She plays the self-indulgent wife of millionaire Richard H. Grant, who wants Willis to steal a Vatican artifact for him. ⊛

Without You I'm Nothing

(1990, 94 min, US, John Boskovich)

The film version of Bernhard's audacious off-Broadway hit brims with libidinous

Without You I'm Nothing

wit and inventive characterizations. With unabashed artistic daring, she plunges into a mélange of musical impersonations, poetry readings and monologues which put her on the cutting edge of stand-up comedy/performance art. Set in a sleepy nightclub, Bernhard's act is played to a thinning and impassive-looking audience and culminates in a desperate and very revealing go-go dance to the tune of Prince's "Little Red Corvette." Sprinkled with moments of inspired comedic brilliance, *Without You...* establishes Bernhard as a hip, thoroughly campy, urbane satirist. ⊛

▼ Madonna: Truth or Dare

(1991, 118 min, US, Alek Keshishian)

The biggest eye-opener of this fascinating behind-the-scenes look at Madonna's "Blonde Ambition" tour is not the dissing Kevin Costner gets from the Material Girl but the inadvertent outing of Bernhard by Madonna. Madonna and Sandra have a relaxed, friendly rapport which adds to the film's sometimes voyeuristic perspective. ⊛

▼ Confessions of a Pretty Lady

(US, 1993, 47 min, Kris Clarke & Sarah Mortimor)

Witty, irreverent and outspoken, Bernhard is beautifully captured in all of her outrageous glory in this entertaining documentary. Highlighted by several "see the real woman behind the fabulous image" interviews, as well as clips from her live performances, interviews with her mother, aunt and uncle and even featuring a critical analysis of the Bernhard persona by Camille Paglia (but interestingly no Madonna in sight or even in mention), the film attempts, in often hilarious fashion, to capture the "real" Sandra. From riding through L.A. escorted by Dykes on Bikes through her controversial centerfold modeling in *Playboy*, we see the self-acknowledged bisexual lesbian as a new force in feminism, a none-too-comforting thought to traditional minded feminists without a sense of humor!

▼ Inside Monkey Zetterland

(1993, 98 min, US, Jefrey Levy)

Bernhard plays the persistent but endearing romantic pursuer of neighbor and former child star Steven Antin in this quirky comedy which also features Patricia Arquette and Sofia Coppola as lovers. ⊛

DIRK BOGARDE

Bogarde in *Death in Venice*

Distinguished and respected, Dirk Bogarde has enjoyed decades of critical and popular success as an actor and in his later years as a writer as well. In a film career that has spanned over 45 years and over 65 films, Bogarde has played an impressively varied succession of characters. He has also played several gay roles and has worked with many of the most prominent gay directors of the time.

He began in England as a matinee idol, enjoying popular success in a series of now-dated comedies, romances, family pictures and thrillers. In 1961, his career dramatically altered after playing a gay barrister who stands up to a blackmailer in the groundbreaking film *Victim*. For years afterwards, he was a leading man in many British and international productions and worked under such directors as Joseph Losey, John Schlesinger and George Cukor. In the early 1970s, his career changed once again when he worked with Italian director Luchino Visconti in *The Damned*, and played the composer Aschenbach in Visconti's lush *Death in Venice*, based on the Thomas Mann novella. What followed was the most critically acclaimed era of his career in which he worked with such international name directors as Liliana Cavani in *The Night Porter* (1974), Alain Resnais in *Providence*, Richard Attenborough in *A Bridge Too Far*, R.W. Fassbinder in *Despair* and — in a return to the screen after a twelve-year absence — Bertrand Tavernier in *Daddy Nostalgia*.

Bogarde was born in Hampstead, London, in 1921 into an upper middle-class family. His father was the photo editor at *The Times* and his mother a retired actress. He attended college but soon became involved in live theatre. In 1939, he was the gofer at the Q Theatre at Kew Bridge. He worked his way up to stage manager and received his first acting job in the J.B. Priestly play "When We Are Married" when the lead actor became sick and he, as understudy, took over. His West End debut, in 1940, was in another Priestly play, "Cornelius." After several years in the Army during WWII, he resumed his acting career and was soon signed to a seven-year contract with the J. Arthur Rank Organization. His first film was the lead in *Esther Waters* in 1948, and his breakthrough film was two years later with *The Blue Lamp*, playing a cop killer. What followed was more than a decade of popular success and he even enjoyed the status of teen idol. In the Borstal melodrama *Boys in Brown*, he played a Welsh boy (although he like the rest of the cast were well into their twenties) who

corrupts the new boy, Richard Attenborough. His role as Dr. Sparrow in the 1954 hit *Doctor in the House* spurred three sequels and made him Rank's biggest star. But years of mediocre movies persuaded Bogarde to leave Rank and choose his own films and this is when he came into his own, tackling the "difficult" roles that have made him internationally famous.

Now semiretired, he lives in Provence in the south of France, his home since 1968. Bogarde works occasionally in television but spends most of his time writing and painting. Since 1980, he has written four volumes of autobiography and three best-selling novels.

In addition to the titles whose reviews follow, which is only a partial listing of the more important roles of his long career, Dirk Bogarde has appeared in these films which can be found in their appropriate chapters:

The Doctor's Dilemma, Libel, The Woman in Question — directed by Anthony Asquith
The Fixer — starring Alan Bates
Justine, Song without End — directed by George Cukor
Despair — directed by Rainer Werner Fassbinder
Providence — starring John Gielgud
Accident, King and Country, Modesty Blaise, The Servant, The Sleeping Tiger — directed by Joseph Losey
Darling — directed by John Schlesinger
Death in Venice — directed by Luchino Visconti

Quartet *(1948, 120 min, GB, Ken Annakin)*
First-rate episodic drama featuring four W. Somerset Maugham short stories, which are introduced by the author himself. The stories are: "The Facts of Life," "The Kite," "The Colonel's Lady" and "The Alien Corn," in which Bogarde plays a rich but talentless pianist. ④

Modesty Blaise

Doctor in the House

(1954, 92 min, GB, Ralph Thomas)

Bogarde stars in this hilarious farce about medical school students. The film was a box-office smash, and Bogarde reprised his role of the unassuming Dr. Sparrow in three sequels: *Doctor at Sea* (1955), *Doctor at Large* (1957) and *Doctor in Distress* (1963). ⊛

The Spanish Gardener

(1956, 95 min, Philip Leacock)

An involving but restrained drama with Bogarde as a not-too convincing Spaniard who takes a job at a British diplomat's (Michael Hordern) estate and strikes up a tender relationship with the man's neglected and lonely ten-year-old son (Jon Whiteley). Their friendship causes the embittered diplomat, jealous of the relationship, to accuse Bogarde of stealing. Adapted from a J. Cronin story, the book's original motivation of the man's jealousy— that he was sexually attracted to the gardener — was left out of the film.

A Tale of Two Cities

(1958, 117 min, GB, Ralph Thomas)

One of seven film versions of Charles Dickens' immortal classic about the French Revolution, this faithful adaptation of the romantic melodrama falls just short of the 1935 Ronald Colman version. A superior cast, including Bogarde, Dorothy Tutin, Cecil Parker, Donald Pleasence and Christopher Lee, makes this a worthwhile endeavor. ⊛

▼ Victim *(1961, 100 min, GB, Basil Dearden)*

A landmark film for its bold, complex and sophisticated treatment of homosexuality, this exceptional thriller was quite controversial in its day and was instrumental in changing the existing British law that made being a homosexual a criminal act. Bogarde stars as a married, homosexual barrister who risks his reputation by confronting a gang of blackmailers responsible for the death of his former lover (Peter McEnery). Sylvia Syms is also remarkable in the role of Bogarde's supportive wife. A thoughtful and compelling piece which Bogarde, whose matinee idol reputation was shaken by the portrayal, maintains that accepting the role was "the wisest decision I ever made in my cinematic life." ⊛

> "As a frank and deliberate exposition of the well-known presence and plight of the tacit homosexual in modern society it is certainly unprecedented and intellectually bold...presented honestly and unsensationally."
> — Bosley Crowther, *The New York Times*

Damn the Defiant!

(1962, 101 min, GB, Lewis Gilbert)

Alec Guinness is stellar as a British naval captain who must fend off a challenge for power by his first mate (Bogarde), a fierce, sadistic and merciless officer who is reviled by the crew. Set during the Napoleonic wars, the movie was filmed with an acute sense of historical detail. ⊛

The Night Porter
(1974, 115 min, Italy, Liliana Cavani)
As a sadistic partner in a bizarre S&M relationship, this was another controversial role undertaken by Bogarde. Few films equal the unrelenting intensity of this disturbing drama. After surviving physical imprisonment in a Nazi concentration camp and sexual subjugation under a SS storm-trooper (Bogarde), a Jewish woman (Charlotte Rampling) inadvertently encounters her former torturer/lover 15 years later working as a night porter at a Viennese hotel. Despite their reversed positions of power, they ultimately reenact their sadomasochistic roles in a gruesomely lecherous dance of death. ⊗

The Serpent
(1974, 121 min, Germany/Italy/France, Henri Verneuil)
A glossy Cold War espionage thriller about spies, double agents, defections and political intrigue. With Bogarde as the head of the British M16, Henry Fonda as head of the CIA and Yul Brynner as a high-ranking KGB defector. (US title: *Night Flight from Moscow*)

Permission to Kill
(1975, 96 min, GB, Cyril Frankel)
More international intrigue abounds in this complex spy thriller. Bogarde stars as the world-weary but ruthless head of a spy consortium who must prevent a political expatriate (Bekim Fehmiu) from returning to his fascist homeland where certain death awaits. Also with Ava Gardner, Timothy Dalton and Frederic Forrest. ⊗

> "It got me out of that awful rut after *Death in Venice* and *The Night Porter* when most of the scripts I was offered featured aging queers and perverts."
> —Bogarde on accepting the role in *Permission to Kill*

A Bridge Too Far
(1977, 175 min, GB, Richard Attenborough)
In the last of his international action/war/spy films, Bogarde is featured as the insensitive and ultimately incompetent General Sir Frederick "Boy" Browning, a real-life figure who was married to

Cliff Gorman (l.), Bogarde and Michael York (r.) in *Justine*

May We Borrow Your Husband?

author Daphne de Maurier. Attenborough's adaptation of Cornelius Ryan's book about a disastrous raid behind German lines in WWII Holland does offer a meticulous examination of the ill-fated mission. An all-star cast includes James Caan, Sean Connery, Robert Redford, Gene Hackman, Anthony Hopkins, Laurence Olivier and Liv Ullmann. ⊗

▼ May We Borrow Your Husband?
(1986, 107 min, GB, Bob Mahoney)
A gay comedy of sexual manners, Bogarde adapted Graham Greene's short story in this made-for-television feature. Set in sunny Cyprus, Bogarde stars as a writer who is befriended by Tony and Stephen (David Yelland and Francis Matthews), an absurd pair of gay interior decorators who have their collective eyes on Peter, the sexually confused newly wedded husband of the beautiful and innocent Poopsie Travis (Charlotte Attenborough). The calculating and catty Stephen soon plots a scheme to seduce and conquer the increasingly willing young husband as Bogarde slowly falls in love with the chagrined wife.

Daddy Nostalgia
(1990, 105 min, France/GB, Bertrand Tavernier)
Bogarde's latest film is this tender and wise story on the complex relationship between an aging and sick father, his wife and their daughter. In what may be his valedictorian performance, Bogarde is simply brilliant as the fastidious and at times insufferable father, an intelligent man cemented in his ways as well as being unable to express his feelings. Jane Birkin plays his gangly screenwriter daughter who travels to her parents' sun-splashed Côte d'Azur villa when her father takes ill. Completing the trio is Bogarde's wife (Odette Laure), a French woman who has become distant after enduring years with her grouchy, emotional diffident husband. Bertrand Tavernier insightfully delves into the characters' lives, thoughts and feelings as they attempt to understand each other and express their love. Emotionally devastating, yet never maudlin. (GB title: *These Foolish Things*) ⊗

BDAVID BOWIE

In a certain way, it is with reluctance that David Bowie is included as a Favorite Star, for he may well have been the first performer to "come out straight." But his influence on gay youth in the '70s, with his androgynous look, clothing and posturing, and theatrically flaunting his sexuality, cannot be underappreciated, and — like Tim Curry's Dr. Frank N. Furter — he gave a positive queer voice to gays everywhere. And though he once talked frankly about his gay affairs (he once said he met his first wife Angela when they "were both laying the same man"), Bowie has recently all but denied his sexual past.

Born David Jones in a rough-and-tumble section of London in 1947, the young musician changed his name in order not to be confused with The Monkees' band member. His father was "a drinker and a layabout for most of his life. I have a brother and a sister. We're all illegitimate." His father eventually became a publicist for a children's home, and his mother worked as a movie theatre usher. Leaving school at 16, Bowie went to work at an advertising agency. Unhappy there, he "looked for a profession that would let me be eccentric and express my idiocies." This led to several locally successful bands, as well as receiving training in mime from Lindsay Kemp (sort of a campy Marcel Marceau). Bowie said of Kemp, "Lindsay taught me more about what one can do with a stage than anyone." Utilizing this theatrical education, Bowie broke into the so-called mainstream in 1972 with the now-legendary tour of Ziggy Stardust and the Spiders from Mars. Based on his best-selling album, Bowie assumed the role of Ziggy, a sexually ambiguous rock 'n' roll star from outer space — and with it, he became one of the founding fathers of Glitter Rock. With female attire and makeup, Bowie was an androgynous icon for a generation.

After being cast in Nicolas Roeg's *The Man Who Fell to Earth* in 1976, Bowie embarked on a sporadic film career. In most of his earlier films, he played off his enigmatic sexual image (*Just A Gigolo* and *The Hunger*, for example), only to lose it for a mere hipness in his later films (*Absolute Beginners*, *The Linguini Incident*).

With his constantly changing image, from the frankly bisexual Ziggy in the 1970s to the Thin White Duke character that marked his stark German/cocaine-addicted days of the early '80s, Bowie has been labeled the chameleon of rock. However, in the mid-1980s, with even more financial success (albums, films, sold-out concerts), Bowie began to reject some of his more flamboyant past, including the idea that he was gay — "I was young. I was experimenting." In 1992, he married supermodel Iman, just around the time that a gag order was lifted from his first wife Angela's book (which was about their marriage). Containing more than one anecdote about her husband's sexual past, Angela (whom he divorced in 1980) recalled the now-famous tale of what happened when she opened a door one morning and found Bowie in bed with Mick Jagger: She made them breakfast.

> "I get offered so many bad movies. And they're all raging queens or transvestites or Martians."
>
> —David Bowie

▼ The Man Who Fell to Earth
(1976, 140 min, GB, Nicolas Roeg)
Bowie stars as the frail and mysterious visitor from another planet who unknowingly threatens American industry with his powers. An extremely original sci-fi drama presented with the surreal and mind-boggling sensitivities of Nicolas Roeg. Buck Henry is Oliver

Farnsworth, a gay lawyer who helps spaceman Bowie build his earthbound empire. Also with Candy Clark and Rip Torn. ☻

Just a Gigolo
(1980, 105 min, West Germany, David Hemmings)
Amid the glittery milieu of decadent post-WWI Germany, Bowie is a debonair escort to a host of society women. Kim Novak wants his body, David Hemmings wants his body and his soul while Marlene Dietrich (in her final film appearance) observes the goings-on while belting out the title tune. ☻

Christiane F.
(1981, 124 min, West Germany, Ulrich Edel)
A spine-tingling account of a young German girl lost in the dark abyss of drug dependency and prostitution. Based on a true story, the film has a striking authenticity acquired through the use of actual locales (Berlin's seamiest junkie havens) and a pallid complexioned cast. Bowie makes a guest appearance and provides the soundtrack music. ☻

Merry Christmas, Mr. Lawrence
(1983, 122 min, GB/Japan, Nagisa Oshima)
Nagisa Oshima's mesmerizing drama studies the conflicting cultures of East and West, which surface within the confines of a WWII POW camp. Bowie is a captured New Zealander whose stiff-lipped bravery and rebellious nature perplex his Japanese guards and intrigue the compound's commanding officer, who is gravely smitten by Bowie's allure. Possibly Bowie's best dramatic performance. ☻

▼ The Hunger *(1983, 99 min, US, Tony Scott)*
Style wins over coherence in this sensual vampire tale with Catherine Deneuve as the ageless beauty who takes on a different lover every two hundred years or so, bestowing on them temporary "eternal beauty." Bowie plays her current beau, John, who finds himself after centuries of bloodsucking, disco-going and clothes shopping suddenly aging rapidly. After looking every bit his 250 years, he finally succumbs, with his former lover soon baring her teeth and heart for sexy butch Susan Sarandon. ☻

Into the Night
(1985, 115 min, US, John Landis)
John Landis' off-center and very engaging comic thriller stars Jeff Goldblum as a likable Average Joe who gets tangled with beautiful Michelle Pfeiffer and Iranian terrorists. Bowie has a dandy extended cameo as a very lethal bad guy, and a good supporting cast includes Richard Farnsworth, Dan Aykroyd, Irene Papas and cameos by 12 noted film directors. ☻

▼ Absolute Beginners
(1986, 107 min, GB, Julien Temple)
This pulsating musical journey into the heart of the swinging teenage scene of London in the late 1950s also explores the brutal

racism which still afflicts that city today. Eddie O'Connell stars as a young photographer drawn into the music and fashion worlds; Patsy Kensit is the designer he's in love with. Bowie plays a slick associate of the nefarious James Fox, and sings the title tune. As many of the supporting characters prove, 1950s London was gay indeed: Eve Ferret is the vivacious Big Jill ("Chicks only for Big Jill, but a boy's best friend anyway"); Joe McKenna appears as the sprite Fabulous Hoplite ("Our own low-rent Oscar Wilde"); and Lionel Blair is chicken-hawk record producer Harry Charms ("Nobody's wild about Harry"). The music, orchestrated by jazz giant Gil Evans, is unbeatable and includes a truly seductive number by Sade. ☻

Labyrinth *(1986, 101 min, US, Jim Henson)*
George Lucas combined his talents with the magical puppet artistry of Jim Henson to create this imaginative fantasy. A young girl, searching for her kidnapped brother, is forced to weave her way through a treacherous maze where she encounters the deliciously maniacal elfin-like Bowie. As the King of the Goblins, Bowie gets to sing a couple songs. ☻

The Last Temptation of Christ
(1988, 164 min, US, Martin Scorsese)
Martin Scorsese's adaptation of the Nikos Kazantzakis novel is a controversial telling of the Christ story, and this epic exploration of the man behind the myth is a true article of faith for believer and non-believer alike. Willem Dafoe gives a stylistically brilliant performance as Jesus, who is locked in a battle with his own destiny. Scorsese's supporting cast is remarkable, including Harvey Keitel as a Lower East-Side Judas, Barbara Hershey as Mary Magdalene and Harry Dean Stanton as Paul. Bowie is a subtle Pontius Pilate. ☻

The Linguini Incident
(1992, 100 min, US, Richard Shepard)
Bowie is Monty, the new British bartender at the latest New York theme park restaurant, who needs to marry to get a green card. Or so it seems. Rosanna Arquette, Eszter Balint, Buck Henry, Andre Gregory, Viveca Lindfors and Marlee Matlin are some of the other characters in this giddy, convoluted and very entertaining foray into the world of Manhattan's super-rich, super-chic and wanna-be's. Escape artistry, Mrs. Houdini's wedding ring and some very serious wagers are a few of the backdrops to tell the tale of deception, survival and monetary gain in a place where robbery becomes performance art if you're wearing the right bra. A nifty score underlines the fun; and everybody looks good, too. ☻

Twin Peaks: Fire Walk with Me
(1992, 135 min, US, David Lynch)
Sort of a prequel to David Lynch's acclaimed but short-lived TV series, "Twin Peaks," this theatrical film takes place during the final week in the life of Laura Palmer. In a surreal, twenty-second appearance, Bowie plays an FBI agent. ☻

FAVORITE STARS

MARLON BRANDO

Generally acknowledged as the premiere American actor of his generation, Marlon Brando's rough-edged and naturalistic acting style has influenced dozens of actors from James Dean to Paul Newman. For over four decades, he has enjoyed a reputation as an actor without peer. Entering into his seventies, Brando is a true legend of the American silver screen — and his name still manages to excite when attached to a movie project.

Brando was born in Nebraska in 1924 to an upper-class family and lived in the Chicago suburbs as a youth. Nicknamed "Bud," Brando, who began to cultivate his "wild one" image early by being expelled from military school, moved to New York at age 19 to study acting — like his two older sisters before him. He had the good fortune to enroll in an acting school headed by Stella Adler, under whose tutelage Brando's talent and passion for acting flourished. He made his Broadway debut in 1944's "I Remember Mama," and appeared in numerous productions until he was cast in Tennessee Williams' landmark 1947 stage production of "A Streetcar Named Desire." Of course, this made him an immediate sensation, and led to his film debut in 1950's *The Men*.

In a few short years, Brando's brooding good looks, sensuous masculinity, rebellious nature and a remarkable acting ability propelled him to the forefront of American screen actors. (A torn tee-shirt baring nipple and a muscular chest certainly didn't hurt, either.) Over the years, Brando's classic screen portrayals, a highly-publicized private life which caused the actor to become almost reclusive, and a certain air of mystery have all combined to create a legendary persona.

Brando's sexual conquests — both male and female — have long been subjects of rumor and innuendo. And though he is predominantly straight, he has talked openly about his gay affairs: "Like many men, I too have had homosexual experiences and I'm not ashamed." In fact, rumor has long associated Brando with his lifelong friend and former 1940s New York roommate, actor Wally Cox, for whom Brando had always expressed affection.

During the last few years, Brando continues to work, accepting the infrequent film assignment if it is to his liking. His latest production is *Don Juan de Marco and the Centerfold* which will also star Johnny Depp and Faye Dunaway.

A Streetcar Named Desire

The Men *(1950, 85 min, US, Fred Zinnemann)*

Brando made his film debut with this sensitive and acclaimed story of injured WWII vets readjusting to civilian life. Solid acting all around, including Jack Webb and Richard Erdman as Brando's fellow patients, and Everett Sloane as the head doctor. ☻

A Streetcar Named Desire
(1951, US, 122 min, Elia Kazan)

Brando reprises his legendary stage role as the brutish Stanley Kowalski in this classic film adaptation of Tennessee Williams' immortal play of desire and deception. Academy Award winner Vivien Leigh is the fragile Blanche DuBois. Brando received his first Oscar nomination. Among the supporting cast, Karl Malden and Kim Hunter also won Oscars re-creating their stage roles. ☻

Viva Zapata *(1952, 113 min, US, Elia Kazan)*

Excellent biopic about the life and times of Mexican revolutionary Emiliano Zapata (Brando). Anthony Quinn won an Oscar as his brother. Another Oscar nomination for Brando. ☻

Julius Caesar
(1953, 120 min, US, Joseph L. Mankiewicz)

Brando is Marc Antony to James Mason's Brutus, John Gielgud's Cassius and Louis Calhern's Caesar. An outstanding adaptation of Shakespeare's classic drama. Brando's third Oscar nomination in as many years. ☻

The Wild One
(1953, 79 min, US, Laslo Benedek)
"Whatcha rebelling against, Johnny?" "Whatcha got?" Brando dons motorcycle jacket and tears up the countryside ridin' his hog. ⊛

On the Waterfront
(1954, 108 min, US, Elia Kazan)
Oscars for Picture, Actor (Brando), Director, Supporting Actress (Eva Marie Saint) and Screenplay (among three others) went to this searing drama of a crooked labor boss (Lee J. Cobb) and the man (Brando) who stands up against him. ⊛

Desiree *(1954, 110 min, US, Henry Koster)*
Brando is an animated Napoleon, Jean Simmons is a lovely Desiree and Merle Oberon is a stately Josephine in this otherwise muddled costume drama. ⊛

Guys and Dolls
(1955, 150 min, US, Joseph L. Mankiewicz)
Lively film version of the smash Broadway musical with Brando as gambler extraordinaire Sky Masterson and Frank Sinatra as "good old reliable" Nathan Detroit. Though Brando's voice can't compare with his famous co-star, Marlon acquits himself nicely. ⊛

The Teahouse of the August Moon
(1956, 124 min, US, Daniel Mann)
Hit film version of the John Patrick play with Brando as an Asian interpreter involved with American G.I.s in post-WWII Okinawa. As an Army captain, Glenn Ford steals the show. ⊛

Sayonara *(1957, 147 min, US, Joshua Logan)*
In one of the biggest hits of the 1950s, Brando finds himself back in post-war Japan; this time as an Air Force major in love with a Japanese woman. A hard-hitting examination of racial prejudice. Brando's fifth Oscar nomination. ⊛

The Young Lions
(1958, 167 min, US, Edward Dmytryk)
A rousing if somewhat overlong WWII drama with Brando as a Nazi officer, and Montgomery Clift and Dean Martin as American soldiers. ⊛

The Fugitive Kind
(1960, 135 min, US, Sidney Lumet)
This second Marlon Brando-Tennessee Williams collaboration is unfortunately a disappointment. Brando plays a drifter who visits a small Mississippi town and becomes involved with Anna Magnani and Joanne Woodward. ⊛

One-Eyed Jacks
(1961, 141 min, US, Marlon Brando)
Brando's only directorial effort is an intriguing western adventure of betrayal and vengeance. Bank robber Brando is out to settle the score with ex-partner Karl Malden, now a sheriff. ⊛

Mutiny on the Bounty
(1962, 179 min, US, Lewis Milestone)
Brando assumes the Clark Gable role of Fletcher Christian in this epic, toilsome but nevertheless entertaining remake. Trevor Howard co-stars as Captain Bligh, and it was reported that the two stars' off-camera relationship echoed their screen characters' enmity. ⊛

The Ugly American
(1963, 120 min, US, George Englund)
A complex cold war thriller with Brando as an American ambassador to a Southeast Asian country who becomes involved with an underground political group. ⊛

Bedtime Story
(1964, 99 min, US, Ralph Levy)
Brando and David Niven are con men out to swindle American heiress Shirley Jones. Remade as *Dirty Rotten Scoundrels*. ⊛

Morituri *(1965, 128 min, US, Bernhard Wicki)*
One of Brando's more fascinating failures casts him as an anti-Nazi German demolitions expert who helps the British disarm explosives on a German freighter carrying needed supplies. ⊛

The Chase *(1966, 135 min, US, Arthur Penn)*
Lillian Hellman adapted Horton Foote's novel of passion and revenge with Brando as a small-town Texas sheriff who prepares for the inevitable return of escaped convict Robert Redford; a possibility that transforms many of the "respected" townspeople into bloodthirsty vigilantes. There is a slight but palpable reading on "gaydar" in Redford's reaction to discovering that his wife, Jane Fonda, is shacking up with rich boy James Fox. For Redford, known as a dangerous and tough bully, simply accepts it, commenting that he doesn't care — "jail took things like that away from me." ⊛

Wild One

The Appaloosa

(1966, 99 min, Sidney J. Furie)

Lushly photographed western with Brando crossing the border to retrieve a prized stallion stolen by a Mexican bandit. ⊛

A Countess from Hong Kong

(1967, 108 min, GB, Charles Chaplin)

In Chaplin's last film, this uneven 1930s-style shipboard romantic comedy casts Sophia Loren as a Russian emigré who stows away in Brando's stateroom.

▼ Reflections in a Golden Eye

(1967, 108 min, US, John Huston)

Sexual repression abounds in this kinky version of Carson McCullers' novel. Brando is the latent homosexual Army officer and Elizabeth Taylor is his unsatisfied, contemptuous wife. Robert Forster is the hunky object of Brando's affection, and Zorro David is a fey houseboy. Not totally successful, the performances, however, make it slightly interesting. Unfortunately, the film suffers from being made at a time when there was a budding sexual freedom for all but gay characters; which made it impossible to fully explore Brando's character and sexual yearnings. The right director could make a helluva remake. ⊛

Candy

(1968, 115 min, US/Italy/France, Christian Marquand)

Brando is one of the guest stars who drools all over nubile Ewa Aulin in this hit-or-miss sex comedy, a substantial hit in its day. Richard Burton and John Astin are used to best effect.

The Night of the Following Day

(1968, 93 min, US, Hubert Cornfield)

Brando heads a team who kidnap Pamela Franklin in this rather stylish though flat suspense thriller. ⊛

Burn! *(1969, 112 min, France/Italy, Gillo Pontecorvo)*

Brando is terrific as a soldier-of-fortune who is sent by the British to investigate a slave uprising on a sugar-producing Caribbean island. He eventuallly becomes personally involved with the rebellion, in this complex, anti-colonial political drama. ⊛

The Nightcomers

(1971, 96 min, US, Michael Winner)

Weary prequel to "The Turn of the Screw" with Brando as a sadistic gardener who has a lasting influence on two small children. ⊛

The Godfather

(1972, 175 min, US, Francis Ford Coppola)

Brando won his second Oscar for his consummate performance as Mafia kingpin Don Corleone. Al Pacino, Robert Duvall, James Caan and Diane Keaton also star in this, one of the great epics of American cinema. ⊛

Last Tango in Paris

(1973, 129 min, France/Italy, Bernardo Bertolucci)

Brando won unanimous acclaim (and a seventh Oscar nomination) for his portrayal of an aging expatriate who begins a doomed sexual liaison with a young French woman (Maria Schneider). A landmark film which lays bare the primal nature of man. ⊛

The Missouri Breaks

(1976, 126 min, US, Arthur Penn)

Set in 1880s Montana, Brando plays a hired killer with a contract on horse thief Jack Nicholson. Brando even dons wig and female clothes to ferret out his prey. A financial and critical flop in its initial release, the film has acquired a cult following over the years. ⊛

Superman

(1978, 143 min, US, Richard Donner)

Brando was paid big bucks for his ten-minute contribution as Superman's father, Jor-El. It's Gene Hackman who steals the show, however, as Lex Luthor. ⊛

Apocalypse Now

(1979, 153 min, US, Francis Ford Coppola)

In a chilling performance, Brando plays an American officer-turned jungle diety who is the target of Intelligence assassin Martin Sheen. ⊛

The Formula

(1980, 117 min, US, John G. Avildsen)

In this muddled but hypnotic thriller, Brando plays a mysterious corporate magnate being investigated by policeman George C. Scott. The studio interfered with the final print, hence the reason for some of the film's static and confusion. ⊛

A Dry White Season

(1989, 97 min, US, Euzhan Palcy)

Brando received a Supporting Oscar nod for his brief but powerful turn as a South African human rights lawyer who brings a racist police official to trial for murder. An enthralling political and human drama. ⊛

The Freshman

(1990, 102 min, US, Andrew Bergman)

Brando has a lot of fun parodying his Don Corleone role in this entertaining and highly amusing comedy. Matthew Broderick also stars as a college student who is made an employment offer he "can't refuse." ⊛

Christopher Columbus

(1992, 121 min, US, John Glen)

Appearing as the Inquisitor Torquemada, Brando has a small role in this murky biography (the first of two in '92) of Columbus. He reportedly wanted his name removed from the credits. Can't blame him. ⊛

LOUISE BROOKS

Louise Brooks

With her haunting beauty, sexual mystique and trademark helmet of black bobbed hair, Louise Brooks was one of the greatest and enigmatic of the silent screen stars. Her career was a brief, meteoric one, for Ms. Brooks was an independent, intelligent woman who was filled with contempt for the "pestiferous disease" that was Hollywood. She rejected star status while at her height of popularity, made her best work in Europe and later in life became an outspoken writer as well as a leading film preservationist.

Born in Wichita, Kansas, in 1906, Brooks moved (with a spinsterly chaperone) to New York at the age of fifteen to study ballet. She found success early, first as a dancer with the Ziegfeld Follies and then signing a film contract with Paramount Pictures. Her first films were made in New York and included *The Street of Forgotten Men* in 1925, *The American Venus, A Social Celebrity, It's the Old Army Game* and *The Show Off* in 1926. When the Astoria Studios closed in New York, Brooks, now a rising star in Paramount's acting stable, moved to Los Angeles and was featured more prominently in such films as *Just Another Blonde* in 1926, *Evening Clothes* and *The City Gone Wild* in 1927. A year later, however, she appeared in Howard Hawks' *A Girl in Every Port* and became a star. But after only two additional pictures (*Beggars of Life* in 1928 and *The Canary Murder Case* in 1929), Brooks, an individualist who was not dazzled by the glamorous Hollywood life, shocked the powers-that-be by leaving the studio to make films in Germany with G.W. Pabst. Their collaboration — Brooks, the tempestuous femme fatale and Pabst, the dark realist — produced two unforgettable expressionistic melodramas: *Pandora's Box* and *Diary of a Lost Girl*. After starring in *Prix de Beauté* in France in 1930, she returned to America but was determined not to become trapped again. She rejected a contract at RKO, refused to remake a "talkie" version of *The Cat and the Canary* and turned down the female lead in *Public Enemy*, a role eventually given to Jean Harlow. A vindictive and unforgiving Hollywood, furious with Brooks' outspoken thoughts on the industry, soon spurned her. She wrote that Hollywood had "doused (me) with ugly publicity," keeping her from reclaiming her star status. She was offered only minor roles in such forgettable films as *Windy Reilly in*

Hollywood and *God's Gift to Women*. She retired in 1938, leaving Hollywood forever. Her final film was the John Wayne vehicle *Overland Stage Raiders*.

Rather than marrying a rich, starry-eyed suitor and becoming a Rodeo Drive-obsessed wife (she did marry once — to producer Edward Sutherland in 1926 but they divorced in 1928), she moved back East, working for a time as a salesgirl at Saks. Brooks eventually settled in Rochester, New York, writing film criticism and appreciation and working on film preservation. She also wrote her autobiography, "Lulu in Hollywood," in 1974.

The sexual allure and seductiveness of Louise Brooks has actually intensified over the years. She projects, in her best films, not the good girl image of her contemporaries such as Lillian Gish and Clara Bow, but instead a fiercely independent, sexually ambiguous, sensual woman resolute in going her way, no matter the consequences. Her screen image is also a reflection of her private life. Although not a lesbian, she has written about her strong lesbian friendships and has admitted to several lesbian affairs including a brief one with Greta Garbo. This combination of a captivating screen presence with an equally fascinating personal life has contributed to making her an icon to filmgoing lesbians for generations. This attraction was acknowledged by Brooks who recounts in letters written to her friend Kevin Brownlow in 1969 that even at the height of her fame she was thought of as a lesbian. She also wrote that by the time she arrived in Hollywood,

Pandora's Box

destructive path but not before she unwittingly destroys all who come close to her. For lesbian/gay audiences, the film is especially important in that it was the first film to present a well-developed lesbian character. Countess Geschwitz (Alice Roberts) is one of the people who falls in love with the temptress. Passionate, butch and long-suffering, the countess endures the teasing attentiveness of the hedonistic Lulu. Interestingly, the American censor originally demanded that the Countess' character be deleted from prints, although they were eventually restored. ☾

▼ Diary of a Lost Girl
(1929, 99 min, Germany, G.W. Pabst)
Pabst's final silent film stars the alluring Brooks in this parable of a woman's road to ruin. Brooks is a wronged innocent who is banished from respectability after being raped by her father's business partner and having a baby as a result of the assault. Forced to stay in a hellish but sexually charged "school for wayward girls"-cum-reform school, she escapes only to land in the false protective environment of a brothel. The startling drama also stars lesbian dancer and actress Valeska Gert. ☾

Prix de Beauté
(1931, 93 min, France, Augusto Genina)
Brooks' final starring vehicle, and her only film made in France, features her as a bored young office worker who, against the wishes of her jealous boyfriend, seeks fame and fortune by becoming an entrant in the Miss Europa beauty contest. A standard melodrama that is highlighted by another luminous performance by the enigmatic international star. Co-scripted by director Genina and Rene Clair, the film features the voice of Edith Piaf who sings "Je N'ai Qu'un Amour C'est Toi" for Ms. Brooks. ☾

Lulu in Berlin
(1985, 50 min, US, Richard Leacock & Susan Woll)
Louise Brooks' life and film work, which took her from Hollywood to pre-Hitler Germany and 1930s France, was exciting and controversial. Her remarkable career is recounted in this absorbing documentary that features the only filmed interview with Ms. Brooks as well as clips from several of her films. The filmmakers, renowned documentarians, capture the radiance of this articulate, seductive and beguiling woman. ☾

she was thought to be a lesbian and believed that this reputation influenced Pabst in choosing her for *Pandora's Box*. Additionally, she recounts in "Lulu in Hollywood" that while in Berlin, she frequented several gay and lesbian clubs.

A Girl in Every Port
(1928, 63 min, US, Howard Hawks)
Though not the star, Brooks' role as a femme fatale circus girl caught the attention of P.W. Pabst, which led her from the Hollywood she despised to Europe where she found her greatest fame. This hectic comedy follows the traveling antics of two carousing sailors who meet in a brawl but soon become inseparable buddies, only to have it threatened by the seductive Brooks. This was a huge box-office hit in its day.

Beggars of Life
(1928, 90 min, US, William A. Wellman)
Brooks plays the adopted daughter of a farmer whom she kills with a shotgun after he tries to rape her. On the lam from the authorities, she disguises herself as a boy, meets up with a tramp (Richard Arlen) and hits the road. Wallace Beery is featured as a bum, Oklahoma Red.

▼ Pandora's Box
(1928, 110 min, Germany, G.W. Pabst)
This expressionistic classic from G.W. Pabst features a luminous Brooks as the sexually insatiable Lulu, a prostitute who ensnares a series of men and one woman with her fetching beauty and beguiling indifference. Lulu's cavalier approach to love results in a self-

RAYMOND BURR

Raymond Burr made over 60 films throughout his career, appeared in numerous Broadway shows, and lived an unusual but fulfilling life — he even owned an island in Fiji. But it is for a wily TV lawyer named Perry Mason for which he'll be best remembered.

Born in British Columbia, Canada, in 1917, Burr lived in China for a few years as a young child, and in California during his adolescence. It was during his teens Burr was first introduced to acting when he worked one summer at a Toronto theatre — it was here Burr had decided his lifetime's work. Burr made his Broadway debut in 1941 in the play "Crazy with Heat," and before his tour of duty in the war, he appeared on the London stage. He also lived in Paris, working as a cafe singer. After his WWII service, Burr arrived in Hollywood to pursue a film career. He made his debut in the 1946 comedy *Without Reservations*.

Burr's large physique and intense mannerisms usually cast him as the villain, and he found steady employment on the screen through the late 1950s. It was in 1957, however, that the actor —who had remained mostly unheralded in his film work — found fame on the TV dramatic series "Perry Mason." The show aired for nine seasons, winning Burr two Emmy Awards in the process. The show was one of the most highly rated series of its time, and Burr had been catapulted into the upper echelon of TV actors during an era Lucy, Jackie Gleason and the Cartwright Family reigned over the airways. After "Perry Mason" went off the air, Burr returned in 1967 with a police drama, "Ironside," which ran for eight seasons. During the final years of his career, Burr reprised his Mason role for over 25 made-for-TV movies, most of which did surprisingly well in the ratings.

Burr refused to talk about his private life: "I've never yet seen a compelling reason to talk about (my life). I'm not sure it would really be any great shakes, anyway." In his studio biographies, Burr reported he had been married three times —

widowed twice and divorced once. However, his mother, sister, and closest friends reported never meeting any of his wives, and Burr steadfastly refused to discuss them. Burr died at the age of 76 of cancer in 1993. He is survived by his longtime companion and business associate, actor Robert Benevides.

In addition to the films which follow (which are Burr's most notable roles on screen), some of Burr's other, more well-known movies include: *Ruthless* (1948), *The Adventures of Don Juan* (1948), *Walk a Crooked Mile* (1948), *Station West* (1948), *Criss Cross* (1949), *Bride of Vengeance* (1949), *Key to the City* (1950), *Meet Danny Wilson* (1952), *Horizons West* (1952), *The Blue Gardenia* (1953), *Casanova's Big Night* (1954), *You're Never Too Young* (1955) and *Count Three and Pray* (1955).

Love Happy *(1949, 91 min, US, David Miller)*

A stone-faced Burr plays henchman to wicked jewel thief Ilona Massey in this mild Marx Brothers romp that also features Marilyn Monroe in a small role. ✪

A Place in the Sun
(1951, 118 min, US, George Stevens)

In a precursor to his Perry Mason role, Burr is especially good as the district attorney who prosecutes the case against Montgomery Clift, on trial for murdering Shelley Winters. And though he resorts to un-Mason-like theatrics, Burr's prosecutor is unrelenting and determined. ✪

Rear Window

Rear Window

(1954, 112 min, US, Alfred Hitchcock)

Burr is "whodunit" in this Alfred Hitchcock classic. James Stewart stars as a wheelchair-bound photographer stuck at home. Keeping a round-the-clock vigil on his neighbors, he becomes obsessed with the disappearance of a woman across the courtyard —Burr's wife. With the help of Grace Kelly and Thelma Ritter, Stewart proves the husband's guilt. As Lars Thorwald, this is probably Burr's best-known movie role. ⊛

Godzilla

(1954, 80 min, Japan, Inoshiro Honda & Terry Morse)

Burr plays American journalist Steve Martin (no kiddin') in this camp semi-classic Japanese horror flick. It seems a giant, fire-breathing monster is turning Japan into Baked Alaska, and reporter Burr is there covering the story. His scenes were added for the American release in 1956. (Japanese title: *Gojira*) ⊛

A Cry in the Night

(1956, 75 min, US, Frank Tuttle)

Burr gives one of his best screen performances in this creepy but effective thriller. He plays a Peeping Tom who kidnaps teen Natalie Wood after he gets caught spying on her and her boyfriend. Burr proves to be a totally menacing bad guy. Also with Edmund O'Brien and Brian Donlevy.

▼ P.J. *(1968, 109 min, US, John Guillermin)*

A violent but vapid detective actioner, *P.J.* stars George Peppard as a private eye who has seen better days and features Burr as William Orbinson, a shady business tycoon who hires P.J. to protect his moll/girlfriend. An interesting homophobic scene is when P.J., looking for a suspect, goes into the Gay Caballero Bar — a seedy dive populated by a throng of leather-and-earring-wearing homosexuals. A fight quickly ensues, with hetero P.J. besting them all!

Out of the Blue

(1980, 94 min, US, Dennis Hopper)

In a small but dramatic role, Burr plays the caring court-appointed psychiatrist for troubled teen Linda Manz, daughter of biker father Dennis Hopper (who also directed) and druggie mother Sharon Farrell. ⊛

▼ Airplane II: The Sequel

(1982, 85 min, US, Ken Finkleman)

Burr lets his hair down with a small but amusing cameo as the presiding judge at Robert Hays' incompetency trial. He doesn't get many jokes, but he keeps disorder in the court. Gay comic Stephen Stucker makes an appearance as the court stenographer. There's also an opening sequence sight gag of two businessmen saying goodbye at the airport; instead of shaking hands, they kiss, revealing they're lovers. ⊛

C S I M O N A L L O W

Simon Callow is probably best known on screen (to American audiences at least) as the slightly devilish Reverend Beebe, who with Julian Sands and Rupert Graves takes a naked romp in an icy pond in *A Room with a View*. But after nearly twenty years of celebrity status in his native England as an actor, director and writer, Callow remains relatively unknown in the U.S. — though his lively performance in *Four Weddings and a Funeral* may change that.

Born in London in 1949, Callow's father left his family just 18 months after his birth; consequently, Callow was raised entirely by women. In an *Advocate* interview, Callow recalled that when a man would come to visit, he would become "fantastically excited by the strangeness of them. Men were these terribly exotic creatures; they were glamorous and yet rather a frightening phenomenon to me, and I formed huge crushes on some of them."

Callow's entrance into the world of theatre had a certain distinction — he wrote a fan letter to Laurence Olivier. As he recalled in an article for *Vogue*, "I was under (Olivier's) spell more than most. (He was) what acting should be, and I wanted to do it." After attending performances at the National Theatre at the Old Vic, where Olivier was performing, Callow "sat down and wrote him a three-page letter. Olivier replied by return of post, 'Since you seem to like our theatre so much, why don't you come and work here?' My heart stopped. 'There is a vacancy at the box office.' I started breathing again."

After his stint at the box office, Callow attended the Queen's University in Belfast, Ireland, and the London Drama Centre. In the mid-1970s, Callow joined a traveling acting group, the Gay Sweatshop, and it was then he decided it was time to come out. His mother refused to talk about it, but the rest of his matriarchal family was — for the most part — supportive ("My grandmother was rather magnificent. She said 'Far be it from me to deny anyone the possibility of love.' Which was a very heroic remark").

In 1979, Callow had one of his biggest stage successes, creating the role of Mozart in the National Theatre production of "Amadeus" (he played a different role in the movie version). Callow also played Molina in a London stage adaptation of "Kiss of the Spider Woman," a role that he said enabled him "to draw upon my homosexuality as I never had." Callow also directed numerous stage productions in both London and New York, including "Shirley Valentine." In addition to his acting and directing, Callow is also a renowned author, and among his books are the definitive Charles Laughton biography, "Charles Laughton: A Difficult Actor," and "Being an Actor," an acclaimed book on acting and autobiography (which bares the first-page self-description "I was an infant transvestite"). In 1991, Callow made his directorial film debut with *The Ballad of the Sad Cafe.*

> "I am a gay actor rather than an actor who happens to be gay."
> —Simon Callow

Callow (far left) in *Four Weddings and a Funeral*

Amadeus
(1984, 158 min, US, Milos Forman)
Though he lost the part he originated on the London stage to Tom Hulce (who gives a thrilling interpretation of Mozart), Callow is splendid in a major supporting role as Mozart's actor friend, Schikaneder, who stars in a "common" staging of "Don Giovanni." ☮

A Room with a View
(1985, 115 min, GB, James Ivory)
Callow's Reverend Beebe brings an air of joviality to James Ivory's enchanting comedy-of-manners. His nude swimming scene is a particular highlight of the film. ☮

▼ Maurice *(1987, 135 min, GB, James Ivory)*
In the film's opening sequence, Callow plays a proper Victorian schoolmaster who takes his pupils on a seaside walk, including title character Maurice. Callow's reaction to a sexually graphic drawing in the sand provides a brief moment of levity. ☮

▼ The Good Father
(1987, 90 min, GB, Mike Newell)
Anthony Hopkins gives a multi-layered performance as a recently separated father exorcising his own demons through the custody battle of an acquaintance (well-played by Jim Broadbent). Callow is terrific as the slick, unscrupulous lawyer who represents Broadbent, using his wife's (Frances Viner) lesbianism as sole reason for her unfitness as a mother. An intelligent, considered exploration of the dissolution of marriage. ☮

▼ Postcards from the Edge
(1990, 101 min, US, Mike Nichols)
Carrie Fisher's first attempt at screenwriting is this breezy comedy based on her true-life battle with alcohol and drug-abuse. Meryl Streep and Shirley MacLaine are fabulously funny as the struggling Hollywood daughter and her aging diva mother. In a small but juicy role, Callow plays a catty film director who has a hilarious discussion with wardrobe mistress Dana Ivey as to what is really wrong with newly drug-free Streep. Playing a combination of Debbie Reynolds and Judy Garland, MacLaine's movie star is approached by two gays, one a drag queen — prompting her to exclaim, "You know how much the queens love me." ☮

Mr. & Mrs. Bridge
(1990, 124 min, US, James Ivory)
Callow plays — complete with accent — a joke-telling doctor and friend of conservative lawyer Mr. Bridge (Paul Newman) in this immaculate Merchant Ivory production. Joanne Woodward is superlative as Mrs. Bridge. ☮

The Crucifer of Blood
(1991, 131 min, GB, Fraser C. Heston)
Charlton Heston dons the cape, pipe and seven-per-cent solution of Sherlock Holmes in this entertaining adaptation of the Broadway mystery. Heston won't make anyone forget Basil Rathbone, Nicol Williamson or Christopher Plummer's interpretations, but he's suitable. Callow plays Inspector Lestrade, a South London detective investigating the murder of jewel thief James Fox and is continually outwitted (of course) by the famous sleuth. Richard Johnson makes a fine Watson. ☮

▼ Four Weddings and a Funeral
(1994, 100 min, GB, Mike Newell)
Taken at face value, this purely heterosexual romantic comedy's two gay characters could be seen as merely token in nature — yet another attempt at mainstream society to latch onto some perceived "gay-chic" hip factor. But fortunately that is not the case here. Simon Callow and John Hannah play a gay couple who feel right at home in an otherwise strictly-het retinue of semi-sophisticates who come together at a seemingly endless parade of weddings — sorry, no gay commitment ceremonies here, folks. Callow rollicks in his role of the bawdy bon vivant who is eager to lend his support to the hitchings of his straight friends. The film goes a long way in presenting a gay couple in a good light, not making an issue of their sexual orientation and treating their love as coincidentally as might be done with any other supporting characters. In fact, the film holds up their relationship as *the* paradigm to which their helplessly neurotic and romantically dysfunctional friends should aspire. The film is definitely a step forward for queer characters in the realm of non-gay cinema. ☮

RICHARD CHAMBERLAIN

Born in Beverly Hills in 1935, the exceptionally handsome Richard Chamberlain rose to fame thanks to his starring role in the 1960s TV series, "Dr. Kildaire." Chamberlain's first introduction to acting was as a theatre major in college. After a stint in the Army, he went to drama school, which led to numerous appearances on TV in the 1950s. Chamberlain made his film debut in 1960 in *The Secret of the Purple Reef*. After its release, he was signed to play the young Dr. Kildaire, a role he played for five seasons. Towards the end of that series' run, Chamberlain appeared in *Joy in the Morning*, featuring the actor in his first film lead. Paired with Yvette Mimieux, the film proved to be a surprise box-office hit. On the set of that film, however, there was not much joy as Mimieux made numerous comments about Chamberlain's masculinity, potential career-killing gossip which the actor basically ignored and survived.

After the run of "Dr. Kildare," Chamberlain concentrated on the New York theatre scene to improve his acting skills. London was next, and Chamberlain found success overseas; in fact, in 1969, he played Hamlet, the first American actor to play the role on the English stage since John Barrymore. During this time, Chamberlain also starred in a series of acclaimed British film productions. In 1980, Chamberlain starred in the TV miniseries "Shogun," which began his reign as "King of the Miniseries."

In 1992, Chamberlain gave an interview to the French magazine *Nous Deux*, in which he allegedly said in reference to his sexual orientation and hiding in the closet, "I've had enough pretending, and too bad for people who are upset by it." However, when word of this interview leaked to the more virulent American press, Chamberlain's manager denied the statement.

Chamberlain continues to alternate between TV miniseries, movies and plays, most recently touring the country and starring on Broadway as Professor Henry Higgins in an acclaimed revival of "My Fair Lady" and appearing in a 1994 made-for-TV adaptation of *The Night of the Hunter*.

The Secret of the Purple Reef
(1960, 80 min, US, William Witney)
Chamberlain's debut film is an average potboiler about two brothers investigating the death of their father.

A Thunder of Drums
(1961, 97 min, US, Joseph M. Newman)
Chamberlain gives a good performance in this standard cavalry western adventure about a fort's too-few soldiers battling warring Apaches.

Twilight of Honor
(1963, 115 min, US, Boris Sagal)
In his first substantial role, Chamberlain plays an idealistic lawyer who defends a murder suspect, with the help of elderly Claude Rains.

Joy in the Morning
(1965, 101 min, US, Alex Segal)
Yvette Mimieux and Chamberlain created a small sensation as struggling newlyweds in the 1920s Midwest. Though an uneven version of Betty Smith's novel, the film was nevertheless quite popular.

▼ Petulia *(1968, 103 min, GB, Richard Lester)*
This romantic drama is generally acknowledged as one of the best films of the 1960s, and its quirky camerawork, clever use of editing, strong performances, engaging use of San Francisco backdrops, and an intimate, compelling story line confirm its status. Chamberlain plays Julie Christie's neurotic husband, the spoiled son of Joseph Cotten. Though nothing is concrete in the script, there are many allusions to Chamberlain's sexuality. Whatever it may be, it's certainly not a flattering character: he's a wife-beater, weak-willed and possibly a pederast. ⊛

The Madwoman of Chaillot
(1969, 142 min, US, Bryan Forbes)
As a pacifist, Chamberlain is one of the many guest stars supporting Katharine Hepburn in this glossy but minor adaptation of Jean Giradoux' play. ⊛

Julius Caesar *(1970, 117 min, GB, Stuart Burge)*
Chamberlain plays Octavius in this satisfactory adaptation of Shakespeare's classic. However, the 1953 Marlon Brando version is far superior. ⊛

▼ The Music Lovers
(1971, 122 min, GB, Ken Russell)
Chamberlain arguably had his best moment on screen as Tchaikovsky in this deliriously bizarre and mesmerizing musical biography served up as only Ken Russell knows how. As the gay composer, Chamberlain creates a fascinating picture of the Russian legend, and Glenda Jackson matches him all the way with a helter-skelter portrait of his nymphomaniac wife. Though this is admittedly not for all tastes, and is overpowering in its energy and emotion, the film is ultimately rewarding for the adventurous. ⊛

Lady Caroline Lamb
(1972, 122 min, GB, Robert Bolt)
Like co-stars Sarah Miles and Jon Finch, Chamberlain doesn't fare too well in this romantic drama about the title character and her scandalous affair with Lord Byron. Nice costumes, though. ⊛

Chamberlain (l.) with Christopher Gable in *The Music Lovers*

The Three Musketeers

(1973, 105 min, GB, Richard Lester)
A gloriously entertaining, swashbuckling, slapstick adventure with Chamberlain as a splendid Aramis. The entire cast is delightful, though Raquel Welch steals the picture. ⊛

The Towering Inferno

(1974, 165 min, US, John Guillermin)
It's baked ham all around as Chamberlain holds his own with the likes of Newman, McQueen, Dunaway and Holden. Chamberlain plays the son-in-law from hell whose penny-pinching causes the titular disaster. ⊛

The Four Musketeers

(1975, 108 min, GB, Richard Lester)
It's almost as much fun as the original, which is saying a lot. Chamberlain returns as Aramis. (This was filmed simultaneously with *The Three Musketeers*.) ⊛

The Slipper and the Rose

(1976, 146 min, GB, Bryan Forbes)
With music by the Sherman Brothers (*Mary Poppins*), this charming musical version of "Cinderella" features Chamberlain as the handsome prince and Gemma Craven as Cinderella.

The Count of Monte Cristo

(1976, 103 min, GB, David Greene)
Chamberlain scores well as the imprisoned Edmond Dantes in this handsomely produced version of the Dumas classic. ⊛

The Man in the Iron Mask

(1977, 100 min, GB, Mike Newell)
Chamberlain has even more success with this second Dumas adaptation playing the dual roles of France's royal twin brothers Philippe and Louis XVI. ⊛

The Last Wave

(1978, 106 min, Australia, Peter Weir)
An acclaimed psychological thriller with Chamberlain as a Sydney lawyer who becomes involved in Aborigine ancient tribal magic, ritual and the spirit world. ⊛

The Swarm

(1978, 116 min, US, Irwin Allen)
Chamberlain barely survived the disaster of that big burning building; now there's some killer bees after him. The cast members aren't the only ones to get stung: there's the audience as well. ⊛

Shogun

(1981, 480 min, US, Jerry London)
Chamberlain became the "King of the TV Miniseries" with his portrait of a shipwrecked 17th-century Englishman who becomes Japan's first Western Samurai warrior chief, or Shogun. One of the highest rated series of all time. ⊛

Murder by Phone

(1982, 79 min, Canada, Michael Anderson)
As a college professor, Chamberlain investigates the murders of his students by an electronic gizmo which can kill over the phone. Don't call us...

The Thorn Birds *(1983, 486 min, US, Daryl Duke)*

This epic made-for-TV miniseries about a pioneer couple in Australia stars Chamberlain, Barbara Stanwyck, Rachel Ward, Bryan Brown, Piper Laurie and Richard Kiley, among many others. ⊛

King Solomon's Mines

(1985, 100 min, US, J. Lee Thompson)
This is more Indiana Jones than Allan Quartermain, and without the former film's chills and thrills. Though he may cut a dashing figure, Chamberlain can't elevate this above the average. ⊛

Allan Quartermain and the Lost City of Gold *(1986, 99 min, US, Gary Nelsen)*

Chamberlain is back as Allan Quartermain, and this sequel makes the original look like a classic. ⊛

The Bourne Identity

(1988, 200 min, US, Roger Young)
Exciting made-for-TV version of Robert Ludlum's novel with Chamberlain as an amnesiac spy caught in political intrigue. ⊛

Return of the Musketeers

(1989, 94 min, GB, Richard Lester)
Chamberlain and most of the original cast of *Three/Four Musketeers* return for this sequel which only occasionally captures the zaniness and high-spiritedness of the two 1970s classics. ⊛

FAVORITE STARS

C GRAHAM CHAPMAN

The son of a police inspector, Graham Chapman was born in Leicester, England, in 1941. He attended Cambridge University, where he studied medicine. However, he soon began writing, teaming with classmates John Cleese and Eric Idle, and the three would make the nucleus of what would become Monty Python.

At college, Chapman was a member of the Footlights, and subsequently appeared in the comedy revue "Cambridge Circus," which took him to London in the early 1960s. At that time, another college chum, David Frost, asked him to write for his TV show "That Was the Week That Was." Other scripts followed, including *The Rise and Rise of Michael Rimmer* and a TV special which starred Cleese, "At Last the 1948 Show." In 1969, the team of Chapman & Cleese met the team of Palin & Jones, and with Idle, formed their own TV show, "Monty Python's Flying Circus." Sporting goofy humor and silly sight gags, the show was a throwback to the comedy of The Goon Squad, a British comic staple of the 1950s which counted among its ranks Peter Sellers, Harry Secombe and Spike Milligan. "Monty Python" had revolutionized TV comedy.

"Monty Python" ran over a period of five years, airing four to six episodes a year. But the BBC was growing more conservative, and putting more restrictions on the group, and they decided to call it quits. It was about this time that the show aired on a PBS station for the first time in America. Within months, it became a cult favorite. It was during the show's second year that the newly formed Playboy Films, underwritten by Hugh Hefner, produced Monty Python's first film, *And Now for Something Completely Different.* The group reunited for their second film, *Monty Python and the Holy Grail.* The film's budget was so low, they couldn't afford to rent horses, so they galloped on foot to the sound of tapping coconut shells. The film was a surprise box-office hit, both in England and in the States. Though the group made many films afterwards, both individually and together, most of their works weren't as critically received or performed as well as *Holy Grail* (with the possible exception of John Cleese) .

Like most of the troupe, Chapman's best work was behind him. He continued to write— alone and with others — when the mood hit him, working on various film and TV projects, and dividing his time between London, New York and Los Angeles. In the late 1980s, Chapman was diagnosed with cancer. He died in 1989, one day shy of the 20th anniversary of the first broadcast of "Monty Python's Flying Circus." By his side were several members of the group.

Chapman was openly gay, and was an early supporter of gay rights. And though he was a parent, his preference was men: "I decided that I should do some clinical test on myself, so whenever I went in a taxicab, tube, train or bus, I would look at each passerby and tried to tell myself honestly which ones I would like to go to bed with. And the ratio of boys to girls was something like 7 to 3, which puts me clearly on the homosexual side of the scale." He even threw himself a "coming out"

Monty Python and the Holy Grail featuring Chapman (c.)

party. His longtime companion was Dick Sherlock. When a high-ranking member of the conservative National Viewers and Listeners Association heard that one of the members of the Monty Python troupe was gay, she sent them an angry letter. They promptly reassured her with their reply that "We have found out who it is and we've taken him out and killed him."

> "Graham Chapman was a loony. There was the quiet pipe-smoking doctor...the quiet pipe-smoking writer...the quiet pipe-smoking homosexual, who could calmly bring a party of Chinese boys down for breakfast in an extremely bourgeois German hotel, causing the manageress to request that he move to a more suitable establishment...the quiet pipe-smoking alcoholic who could reduce any drinking party to a shambles by consuming half a distillery and then crawl round the floor kissing all the men and groping all the women."

—Eric Idle

Monty Python's Flying Circus, Vols. 1-22
(60 min each, GB)
A 22-volume set featuring the best (and worst) skits from their five-year BBC comedy show. Just some of the classic skits include "Ministry of Silly Walks," "Taming Oscar Wilde," "Kamikaze Highlanders," "The Lumberjack Song," "The Dead Parrot Sketch," "Upper-Class Twit of the Year," "Nudge Nudge Wink Wink," "The Spanish Inquisition," "Killer Sheep," "Spam" and "The Cheese Shop." ☻

And Now for Something Completely Different *(1972, 80 min, GB, Ian McNaughton)*
Supreme silliness prevails in this, Monty Python's first movie. Essentially it's a collection of the best of their BBC television program and features dead parrots, transvestite lumberjacks, a killer joke, upper-class twits, and a lesson on how to defend yourself against a person who is armed with fresh fruit. A wink's as good as a nod to a blind bat, eh? Say no more... ☻

Monty Python and the Holy Grail
(1974, 90 min, GB, Terry Gilliam & Terry Jones)
The Python troupe takes on King Arthur in this insane farce set amongst the castles, lochs and moors of Scotland. Like the early works of Woody Allen, this is a scattershot affair with gags flying at every turn; miraculously, most hit their mark. The result is a hilarious and inspired excursion into knighthood, medieval pageantry, religious sentiment and transvestitism. ☻

Beyond the Fringe
(1976, 85 min, GB, Roger Graef)
Dudley Moore narrates this hysterical documentary of the Amnesty International 1976 April Fool's benefit show. Chapman, John Cleese, Michael Palin and Terry Gilliam lead the festivities with their typical barrage of inspired silliness. ☻

The Odd Job
(1978, 86 min, GB, Peter Medak)
Chapman developed the script for this comedy caper as a show-case for himself and his buddy Keith Moon — sadly, Moon's death intervened and Chapman was forced to complete the project alone. The result is a mildly funny tale about a downtrodden insurance salesman who, after he is dumped by his wife, hires a hit man to kill him. When he has a change of heart, however, he has a difficult time canceling the contract. ☻

Monty Python's Life of Brian
(1979, 93 min, GB, Terry Jones)
The Gospel According to Monty Python! This side-splitting spoof lampoons 2,000 years of religious thought and mankind's hysterical hankering for a good Messiah. Along with *Holy Grail*, Python's most accomplished feature. Just remember — always look on the bright side of life. Chapman takes center stage as Brian, the relectant savior. ☻

Monty Python Live at the Hollywood Bowl *(1982, 78 min, GB, Terry Hughes)*
Britain's premiere loonies invaded Los Angeles with this madcap series of sketches and routines. All of their favorite concerns, including God, death, and life in heaven, are hilariously explored. ☻

The Secret Policeman's Other Ball
(1982, 92 min, GB, Julien Temple)
Yet another benefit show for Amnesty International featuring the loonies of the Monty Python gang along with Peter Cook and other British wackos. An onslaught of hysterical skits is interspersed with the music of Pete Townshend of The Who. ☻

Monty Python's The Meaning of Life
(1983, 101 min, GB, Terry Jones)
This effort from the Python troupe is a wild collection of vignettes on the humorous aspects of existence — from conception through demise. Included are the educational song and dance production, "Every Sperm Is Sacred," and an unforgettable restaurant retching sketch. ☻

The Secret Policeman's Private Parts
(1984, 77 min, GB, Julien Temple & Robert Graef)
The zanies from the Monty Python gang are joined by Peter Cook, Connie Booth, Pete Townshend, Phil Collins and Pope Bob Geldof in this Amnesty International benefit show. A variety of sketches, filmed live, are guaranteed to evoke a state of sublime silliness. ☻

Yellowbeard
(1983, 101 min, GB, Mel Damski)
Chapman co-wrote (with co-star Peter Cook) and stars in this curiously flat takeoff on pirate films. A good cast is wasted, including Cheech & Chong, Marty Feldman, Eric Idle, Madeline Kahn and John Cleese. ☻

C MONTGOMERY LIFT

Montgomery Clift (1920-1966) began his professional career as a model at the age of thirteen. He was an extraordinary handsome youth, and his looks served him well as an adult when he began to pursue an acting career. But Clift proved to be more than a "pretty face," startling the New York theatrical community with his talent and range. He appeared in the original productions of "The Skin of Our Teeth" and "There Shall Be No Night," and numbered among his friends the Lunts, Lehman Engel and Thornton Wilder. He remained on the New York stage for 11 years, even turning down a lucrative contract with MGM in 1941. During this time, he was devoted to the theatre, and was one of the founding members of the famed Actors Studio.

Hollywood continued to beckon, however, and he finally succumbed in 1946, when he was signed to star with John Wayne in Howard Hawks' *Red River*. Though it took almost two years to hit the screen, Clift was an immediate hit. No actor before him had demonstrated such a combination of sensitivity and sensuality. In his subsequent film roles, Clift chose carefully, sometimes even turning down first-rate material (*Sunset Boulevard* among them). But all of Clift's roles were of a particular interest to him. In 1956, while making *Raintree County* with close friend Elizabeth Taylor, Clift was involved in a car accident in which he almost died. His face was disfigured, and it was months until he was able to finish filming. The accident, however, took a mental toll on Clift as well as a physical one, and he was never the same afterwards.

Clift's sexuality was rather well-known in Hollywood (on the set of *The Misfits*, Clark Gable referred to him as "that faggot"), though he did his best to keep his private life just that. He wasn't always successful: In 1949, he was arrested for trying to pick up a hustler on 42nd Street; the charges were subsequently dropped. Though a bisexual who took delight in sexual conquests of both men and women, Clift was not totally comfortable with his gayness (which was his preference), and he was often tormented by it. This anxiety, coupled with drug and alcohol abuse, caused the actor to burn-out before his time. John Huston, who directed Clift in *The Misfits*, said, "The combination of drugs, drink and being homosexual was a soup that was too much for him." Clift died of a heart attack at the age of 46.

Montgomery Clift

▼ **Red River** *(1948, 126 min, US, Howard Hawks)*
Clift's debut is this classic western with none other than John Wayne as a co-star. The story concerns a rugged, perilous cattle drive along Texas' Chisholm Trail. Wayne plays Clift's tyrannical guardian. Sexual repression runs rampant in this film, between both male and female characters. Most pronounced, however, is the unspoken love between Wayne and Clift's characters, and the flirtatious bond between Clift's Matthew Garth and John Ireland's cowpoke named "Cherry." Offscreen, Wayne and Clift did not get along. ✪

The Search
(1948, 104 min, US, Fred Zinnemann)
Clift received his first Oscar nomination as an American soldier stationed in post-war Germany who befriends a young Czech boy separated from his family and home. An endearing post-war classic. Clift rewrote many of his scenes to give the film a more realistic portrayal of G.I.s. ✪

The Heiress
(1949, 115 min, US, William Wyler)
Clift is just a gigolo in this sumptuous Victorian drama of an opportunist who romances a plain-looking heiress. Olivia de Havilland won an Oscar playing the title role. ✪

The Big Lift *(1950, 120 min, US, George Seaton)*

Clift returns to post-war Germany in this capable war drama as a pilot involved in the Berlin Airlift. ⊛

A Place in the Sun

(1951, 118 min, US, George Stevens)

Clift is the boy from the wrong side of town; Shelley Winters is his lower-class girlfriend; and Elizabeth Taylor is the society belle he pursues in this ambitious and poignant updating of Theodore Dreiser's "An American Tragedy." Oscar nominations went to Clift (his second) and Winters. ⊛

I Confess *(1953, 95 min, US, Alfred Hitchcock)*

Clift portrays a priest who hears a murderer's confession but refuses to divulge any information. He undergoes a crisis of conscience when he is badgered by all around him to break his vow.

From Here to Eternity

(1953, 118 min, US, Fred Zinnemann)

This is without question Clift's greatest performance. He plays a G.I., and gifted trumpet player, stationed in Pearl Harbor right before the bombing. The remarkable cast includes Burt Lancaster, Deborah Kerr and Frank Sinatra. Oscars for Best Picture, Director, Supporting Actor (Sinatra) and Supporting Actress (Donna Reed). Clift received a third nomination. ⊛

Indiscretion of an American Wife

(1954, 63 min, US/Italy, Vittorio De Sica)

Shot on location at Rome's Stazione Termini, Clift is the lover of Philadelphia wife Jennifer Jones, who's on holiday in Italy. The two come together to say a final farewell. (GB title: *Indiscretion*) ⊛

Raintree County

(1957, 187 min, US, Edward Dmytryk)

A fanciful Civil War epic with Clift involved with Southern belle Elizabeth Taylor. Though it wanted to be another *Gone with the Wind*, which it is not, it is nevertheless praiseworthy. ⊛

The Young Lions

(1958, 167 min, US, Edward Dmytryk)

Clift appears with Marlon Brando in this WWII drama. Monty's an American, Brando's a Nazi. ⊛

Shelley Winters and Clift in *A Place in the Sun*

Raintree County

Lonelyhearts

(1958, 101 min, US, Vincent J. Donehue)
Clift assumes the nom de plume of a female newspaper advice columnist and becomes too involved with his readers' lives. ⊛

▼ Suddenly, Last Summer

(1959, 112 min, US, Joseph L. Mankiewicz)
Clift and Elizabeth Taylor appeared together for a third and final time in this compelling Tennessee Williams' adaptation. Clift plays a psychiatrist who must determine why Liz flipped out while she was on summer vacation with her cousin. Katharine Hepburn is cousin Sebastian's mother. Though Clift is very competent, it's Taylor and Hepburn who mesmerize. ⊛

Wild River *(1960, 115 min, US, Elia Kazan)*

Beautifully realized drama with Clift as a Tennessee Valley Authority official who must relocate grandmother Jo Van Fleet, who refuses to give up her land.

The Misfits *(1961, 124 min, US, John Huston)*

Clift plays a disillusioned rodeo performer who crosses paths with cowboy Clark Gable and equally disenchanted divorcée Marilyn Monroe in this Arthur Miller drama. Gable and Monroe's final film. ⊛

Judgment at Nuremberg

(1961, 190 min, US, Stanley Kramer)
Clift's brief, stunning ten-minute scene as a Holocaust survivor who recounts his experiences at the Nuremberg trials earned him a Supporting Actor nomination. ⊛

Freud *(1963, 140 min, US, John Huston)*

Clift ably plays the Father of Psychiatry in this compelling drama which examines the five-year period Freud formulated his Oedipal theories.

The Defector

(1966, 108 min, Germany/France, Raoul Levy)
Clift's final film is not the most fitting epilogue to a striking film career. He plays a German spy on a dangerous mission involving a Russian defector.

C JAMES O C O

Born in 1930 the son of a Bronx shoemaker, James Coco spent his youth in the dark movie houses of his neighborhood — and it wasn't long before he knew what career to pursue. As a teenager in the late 1940s, Coco began a professional career that would span four decades.

Starting with local productions, Coco finally made his Broadway debut in 1957 in "Hotel Paradiso," and Coco worked steadily both on and off Broadway through the 1960s. But it wasn't until appearing in Terrence McNally's 1969 one-act play, "Next," that Coco made a name for himself. McNally had written the role specifically for his friend, and for it Coco won a Drama Desk Award. Neil Simon happened to attend one of the performances of "Next," and the author immediately knew he had found the actor for his next Broadway comedy, "The Last of the Red Hot Lovers." For that, Coco received a Tony nomination, and after over 20 years of various flops and anonymity, he had finally arrived.

Of Coco's twenty-plus films, his greatest moment — for which he received an Oscar nomination — came as overweight gay actor Jimmy Perino in *Only When I Laugh*. The actor's good cheer, marvelous comic timing and unpretentious demeanor have brightened both hits and duds alike. Coco died of a heart attack in 1987 at the age of 56.

It wasn't until the early 1970s that Coco found his niche in movie comedies. His earliest films include *Ensign Pulver* (1964), *Generation* (1969), *End of the Road* (1970), *The Strawberry Statement* (1970), *Tell Me That You Love Me, Junie Moon* (1970), *A New Leaf* (1971) and *Such Good Friends* (1971).

Man of La Mancha

(1972, 130 min, US, Arthur Hiller)
Coco is the only performer to acquit himself in this disaster. Based on the Tony Award-winning musical, Peter O'Toole and Sophia Loren are embarrassingly bad. As Sancho, O'Toole's servant and constant companion, Coco gives a spirited performance and manages to capture the flavor of the stage production. ⊛

The Wild Party

(1975, 100 min, US, James Ivory)
In his only starring role, Coco is very good in this Merchant Ivory production as a 1920s silent clown who, looking to make a come-

back, throws a party which leads to tragedy. Suggested by the Fatty Arbuckle scandal. Also with Raquel Welch and Perry King. ⊛

Murder by Death

(1976, 94 min, US, Robert Moore)
Doing a very funny takeoff on detective Hercule Poirot, Coco is one of the many all-stars (including Peter Sellers, David Niven and Maggie Smith) in Neil Simon's highly enjoyable comedy. The film marked the directorial screen debut of Robert Moore (see pg. 77 for more information on the film and the director). ⊛

Bye Bye Monkey

(1978, 114 min, France/Italy, Marco Ferreri)
Coco is one of the Manhattan denizens in this bizarre Gérard Depardieu black comedy.

The Cheap Detective

(1978, 92 min, US, Robert Moore)
More laughs with Neil Simon in this loving nod to 1940s detective movies, *The Maltese Falcon* in particular. Coco plays a Sydney Greenstreet-like cafe owner involved in political intrigue. ⊛

Charleston

(1978, 91 min, Italy, Marcello Fondato)
This Italian gangster comedy casts Coco as a mobster who gets swindled by con man Bud Spencer. He really hams it up here. ⊛

Scavenger Hunt

(1979, 117 min, US, Michael Schultz)
Coco is part of an all-star cast (including Ruth Gordon, Cleavon Little, Vincent Price and Arnold Schwarzenegger) which is wasted in this tired comedy about a group on inheritors forced to participate in a scavenger hunt. ⊛

Wholly Moses

(1980, 109 min, US, Gary Weis)
Another fine group of comedians (Coco, Dudley Moore, Dom DeLuise, Richard Pryor, Madeline Kahn) is wasted in this limp comedy which is supposed to have fun with religion. ⊛

The Wild Party

Only When I Laugh

▼ Only When I Laugh

(1981, 120 min, US, Glenn Jordan)
Coco's finest moment is splendid, indeed, as a struggling gay actor and confidant to recovering alcoholic Marsha Mason. As the supportive friend who wants to be "a big, big star," Coco is funny, touching, lovable, smart and big as life. He received a well-deserved Oscar nomination as Supporting Actor. ⊛

The Muppets Take Manhattan

(1984, 94 min, US, Frank Oz)
Coco is one of the guest stars who helps The Muppet gang get their show to Broadway. ⊛

▼ There Must Be a Pony

(1986, 100 min, US, Joseph Sargent)
In a part similar to his *Only When I Laugh* role, Coco plays the gay best friend to actress-on-a-comeback Elizabeth Taylor. Mama Liz worries that son Chad Lowe might be gay, but it's never really resolved. Based on James Kirkwood's novel, adapted by Mart Crowley.

The Chair

(1987, 90 min, US, Waldemar Korzenioswsky)
Coco plays a prison psychiatrist who locks horns with a sadistic warden in this killer-returns-from-beyond-the-grave thriller.

Hunk *(1987, 102 min, US, Lawrence Bassoff)*

Brainless shenanigans with Coco as the Devil who helps a California nerd become a California hunk. ⊛

That's Adequate

(1989, 83 min, US, Harry Hurwitz)
His last film is an episodic low-budget movie parody which, though silly, contains a couple of very funny skits. Coco plays the gangster studio mogul of Adequate Pictures (who gave us such hits as *Slut of the South* and *Singing in the Synagogue*). ⊛

D B R A D
A V I S

Becoming an "overnight" sensation for his outstanding work in 1978's *Midnight Express*, Brad Davis, like most other immediate success stories, worked hard and long to get there.

Born in Florida in 1949, Davis moved to Georgia after high school graduation to pursue an acting career. From there, it took two moves to New York to find work, but in the early 1970s, Davis began acting off-Broadway. It was during this time he studied at the Academy of Dramatic Arts. His stage work led to his movie debut, the TV hit "Sybil," and "Roots" followed. *Midnight Express* was next, which won him a Golden Globe for Best Acting Debut, and stardom. Though no film which followed equalled the success of *Express* (although his role as the sexy and violently gay sailor in Fassbinder's *Querelle* is possibly more memorable for gay fans), Davis was very daring in the roles he accepted. His friend, writer Larry Kramer, noted, "He was one of the first straight actors with the guts to play gay roles."

Davis contracted the AIDS virus in 1985, but in response to rampant anti-AIDS hysteria in Hollywood, he hid his status to continue working. In the last years of his life, Davis became a vocal and dedicated AIDS activist. Of Ronald Reagan, he said, "What an unbelievably ignorant, arrogant, bigoted person. How could he possibly think that his opinion on homosexuality had anything to do with a devastating disease that was ravaging people, reducing them to skeletons and killing them." Davis died at the age of 41 in 1991 but not before leaving a biting hand-written indictment of Hollywood's AIDS- and homophobia, which stated, "I make my living in an industry which professes to care very much about the fight against AIDS, that gives umpteen benefits and charity affairs. But in actual fact, if an actor is even rumored to be HIV-positive, he gets no support on an individual basis — he does not work." His widow, Susan Bluestein, continues his activist work.

Sybil *(1976, 198 min, US, Daniel Petrie)*
Davis gives an impressive performance in this classic drama as the street performer boyfriend of Sally Field's schizophrenic title character. ⓧ

The Campus Corpse
(1977, 92 min, US, Douglas Curtis)
Davis is a college student in this obscure turkey all about campus fraternity hazing.

▼ Midnight Express
(1978, 120 min, GB, Alan Parker)
Based on the autobiography of Billy Hayes, this intense film explores the hellish years Hayes spent in a Turkish prison for drug smuggling. Davis gives a remarkably complex performance as Hayes, and a good cast includes John Hurt and Randy Quaid. The film contains many good moments, but one frustrating scene involves a gay prisoner, Erich (Norbert Weisser), and Hayes. Seductively and tastefully filmed, Erich makes a pass at Billy in the shower. After a discreet kiss, Hayes politely brushes him off. Under most circumstances, that would be an admirable scene. But in real life, the two men were lovers during their prison stay. Hayes himself observed, "I wish that they'd let the steam in the shower come up and obscure the act itself instead of showing a rejection." Director Parker disagreed, however. It must be acceptable to have a hero smuggling drugs, or biting a person's tongue off, but evidently he can't remain a hero if he's lovers with another man. ⓧ

A Small Circle of Friends
(1980, 112 min, US, Rob Cohen)
There's much to recommend to this offbeat charmer with Davis, Karen Allen and Parker Stevenson as college friends in the late 1960s.

The Greatest Man in the World
(1980, 51 min, US)
Davis stars in this American Short Story Collection adaptation of a James Thurber tale as an airline passenger who gets more than he bargained for when he becomes the first person to fly non-stop around the globe.

A Rumor of War
(1980, 200 min, US, Richard T. Heffron)
Davis heads a terrific cast — which includes Keith Carradine, Michael O'Keefe and Brian Dennehy — in this outstanding made-for-TV Vietnam War drama. In a compelling and rich performance, Davis plays a newly arrived G.I. whose — like that of Tom Cruise in *Born on the Fourth of July* some nine years later — unblinking support of the war gives way to self-doubt and tragedy. ⓧ

Chariots of Fire
(1981, 123 min, GB, Hugh Hudson)
Davis has a small but choice role as an American athlete in this Oscar-winning look at Eric Liddell and Harold Abrahams, the two British runners who ran to victory in the 1924 Paris Olympics. Ian Charleson, who died of AIDS in 1990, plays Liddell. ⓧ

Midnight Express

Cold Steel

(1987, 90 min, US, Dorothy Ann Puzo)
This one Brad should have turned down. He plays a police officer who's out to get the psycho who murdered his father.

Heart *(1987, 90 min, US, James Lemmo)*
Derivative boxing story with Davis as a has-been fighter training for a last bout with glory. ⊛

When the Time Comes
(1987, 104 min, US, John Erman)
Bonnie Bedelia learns she has inoperable cancer, and decides to take her own life. Davis is her husband who can't have any part of it.

▼ Querelle *(1982, 106 min, W. Germany, Rainer Werner Fassbinder)*
Based on Jean Genet's homoerotic story of lust and murder, Davis plays the title character, the ruggedly handsome and lethal sailor who sets both men and women's hearts aflutter. Not one of Fassbinder's best, but its theme and Davis' narcissistic performance make it a fascinating oddity. ⊛

Chiefs *(1984, 200 min, US, Jerry London)*
Davis is a member of a mutli-generational law enforcement family in a small Southern town in this competent mystery starring Charlton Heston, Keith Carradine and Billy Dee Williams.

Robert Kennedy and His Times
(1984, 335 min, US, Marvin J.Chomsky)
As Bobby Kennedy, Davis turns in a charismatic performance in this engrossing biography based on the book by Arthur Schlesinger.

Vengeance *(1986, 100 min, US, Marc Daniels)*
Based on a true story, this made-for-TV drama casts Davis as Tony Cimo, who avenges his parents' murder by taking the law into his own hands.

Blood Ties *(1986, Italy, Giacomo Battiato)*
Davis is quite good in this brisk thriller as an American architect visiting Sicily who is blackmailed by the Mafia into killing his distant cousin (Tony Lo Bianco), a crusading, law-and-order judge. ⊛

The Caine Mutiny Court-Martial
(1988, 100 min, US, Robert Altman)
Re-creating the role that Humphrey Bogart had all but owned, Davis gives a fine, detailed performance as the infamous Captain Queeg. Where as Bogey's captain was all neuroses, Davis' portrayal is of a smug and officious commander. Stands up nicely to the classic 1954 version. ⊛

Rosalie Goes Shopping
(1990, 94 min, US, Percy Adlon)
Davis is delightful as Marianne Sagebrecht's endearing husband in this pleasant satire on American consumerism. Sagebrecht plays a housewife who goes overboard on her credit limit (she's juggling 37 credit cards) and devises ingenious ways to stay a few steps ahead of the creditors in her pursuit of the American Dream. ⊛

Child of Darkness, Child of Light
(1991,100 min, US, Marina Sargenti)
This occult chiller, made for cable, is pure hokum. The Church investigates mysterious, satanic goings-on. ⊛

Hangfire *(1991, 89 min, US, Peter Maris)*
Standard if lively actioner about a group of escaped convicts who make life a living hell for a small New Mexico town and the authorities who are after them. ⊛

JAMES DEAN

He starred in only three films, but few actors have had such an impact on American culture as legendary rebel James Dean. An authentic movie icon, Dean still represents — 40 years after his untimely death — the quintessential loner, the misunderstood youth, the picture of alienation.

Dean was born in 1931 in Indiana. His family moved to Los Angeles at age five, but after his mother's death, he returned to his home state, living on a family farm. After graduating high school, Dean fled to Los Angeles, where he studied acting at UCLA. He worked infrequently, appearing on TV commercials and cast in bit parts. In 1952, he moved to New York City, studying at the Actors Studio. He made his Broadway debut that same year in "See the Jaguar." It took two years and a series of odd jobs until Dean made his second Broadway appearance, in the 1954 production of André Gide's "The Immortalist," playing a homosexual Arab. The play also starred a rising young actress named Geraldine Page. For his work, Dean was voted one of the most promising stars of the year (others included Ben Gazzara, Eva Marie Saint, Harry Belafonte and Elizabeth Montgomery; Page and Paul Newman had been named the year before). Dean's performance led to a screen test at Warner Brothers, where he was subsequently signed to his first starring role in *East of Eden*. Upon that film's release, Dean was an immediate hit. However, Dean's time in the limelight was short-lived. He was killed in a car accident on September 30, 1955, before the release of his two other films, *Rebel without a Cause* and *Giant*. Dean received two posthumous Academy Award nominations for *Eden* and *Giant*. Ironically, right before his death, Dean had filmed a short on driving safety.

It wasn't until the mid-1970s that Dean's homosexuality began to be written about in various biographies. Dean had avoided the draft by "declaring" himself gay, and he was known to frequent backroom bars in Los Angeles. It was also known that Dean was heavily into S&M (gossip has it that he liked to be burned by cigarettes). It was reported that on the night before his accident, Dean had been in a fight with his lover over the actor's dating women for "publicity purposes." Dean was only 24 years of age at the time of his death.

Hollywood, always sensitive to the loss of one of their own, has two films currently in production to coincide with the 40th anniversary of Dean's death. *James Dean:*

James Dean

An American Legend is to be directed by first-timer Alan Houge. The film has been approved by the Dean estate. The second film is simply called *James Dean*, and is to be directed by Des McAnuff (Broadway's "The Who's Tommy") and released by Warner Brothers. The casting of the McAnuff film has not been finalized but leading contenders are Johnny Depp, Leonardo DiCaprio and Brad Pitt.

Dean had bit roles in the films *Has Anybody Seen My Gal* (which starred Rock Hudson), *Sailor Beware* and *Fixed Bayonets*.

Hill Number One
(1951, 57 min, US, Arthur Pierson)
Dean plays John the Apostle in this pietistic TV Easter sermon produced by St. Paul Films and sponsored by the Family Rosary Crusade. Set in Korea, the story centers on a group of soldiers who receives a lecture from the company pastor. Roddy McDowall and Michael Ansara also star. ⊗

Tales of Tomorrow *(1954, 60 min, US)*
Two episodes from the live science-fiction TV series. In one of the programs, Dean plays the assistant to scientist Rod Steiger. ⊗

East of Eden *(1955, 115 min, US, Elia Kazan)*

Dean's first film firmly established his outsider, misunderstood persona. Giving an affecting and sincere performance as a rebel with a cause, Dean searches for the truth about his mysteriously absent mother while at the same time seeking his father's affection. Based on the last chapters of John Steinbeck's novel, the film offers solid portrayals by Julie Harris, Raymond Massey and Oscar winner Jo Van Fleet. To establish an authentic screen bond, director Kazan had Dean and actor Richard Davalos, who played brothers, live together for a short period of time. Dean received his first Oscar nomination as Best Actor. ☮

▼ Rebel without a Cause
(1955, 111 min, US, Nicholas Ray)

A testament to adolescent angst with Dean as the prototypical angry young man at odds with his parents, himself and the future. A brooding film that cemented the Dean legend. In her first adult role, Natalie Wood offers an incandescent performance as a soul mate; and Sal Mineo is especially touching as Plato, a friendless youth who has yet to come to terms with his latent sexuality, and who is secretly in love with Dean's charismatic character Jim. ☮

Giant *(1956, 198 min, US, George Stevens)*

This sprawling saga of Texas oil aristocracy provided Dean with his final and most challenging role as the arrogant ranch hand, Jett Rink. A Best Director Oscar went to George Stevens while Rock Hudson earned a nomination for his finest screen work, and Elizabeth Taylor won acclaim for her sincere performance. Dean's second Oscar nomination. ☮

The James Dean Story
(1957, 80 min, US, Robert Altman)

Interviews with friends, associates and family are included in this rather one-dimensional documentary on Dean. Though there are some interesting moments, the film captures neither the mystery nor the power of the actor. ☮

James Dean
(1976, 100 min, US, Robert Butler)

Low-key and safe made-for-TV biography based on the novel by Dean's former roommate and friend, William Bast. Stephen McHattie gives a good performance as Dean, and Michael Brandon appears as Bast. (Also known as: *The Legend*) ☮

Rebel without a Cause

MARLENE DIETRICH

The quintessential femme fatale, Ernest Hemingway once said of Marlene Dietrich, "If she had nothing more than her voice, she could break your heart with it." That seductive voice may have been just as important as her sultry looks and considerable talent in the actress becoming an international star after the release of her first sound film.

Born in Berlin in 1901, Dietrich enrolled in acting school in the early 1920s. Throughout that decade she appeared in plays and numerous German silents, though Dietrich wasn't particularly well-known. But that would change after director Josef von Sternberg saw her in a play, and cast her in his new film, *The Blue Angel*. It was *Angel* which made her an international sensation, and brought her and director von Sternberg to Hollywood, where the actress would stay to become one of its most popular stars. Dietrich had a rewarding, seven-film association with her mentor von Sternberg, of whom she once said, "He breathed life into the nothingness."

With Dietrich's American popularity and the rise of Nazism, the actress hadn't set foot on her native soil since her arrival in Hollywood in 1930. By the late 1930s, this proved to be a sore point with Hitler, and the dictator courted Dietrich's return (it was reported that Hitler had wanted Marlene to be his mistress). Vehemently anti-Nazi, Dietrich not only stayed in America, vowing never to return as long as Hitler was in power, but after America's entrance into WWII, she became the symbol of a "free Germany" and tirelessly entertained troops and sold war bonds. In 1947, Dietrich was awarded the Medal of Freedom for her wartime services.

Continuing to appear in films in the 1950s, Dietrich branched out starring in a series of successful cabaret performances, which helped cement the actress' legendary stature. One of her appearances was in Berlin in 1960, marking Dietrich's first return to her native country in 30 years.

Dietrich was married once, though the relationship was a short-lived one, and the couple separated, though never divorcing. They had one daughter, Maria, who was one of the many authors in the early 1990s to write of her famous mother. (A film based on Maria's book, to be directed by Louis Malle and adapted by John Guare, is due in theatres in late 1995). Much was made of Dietrich's lesbianism by her biographers, including her daughter's book "Marlene Dietrich by Her Daughter." Kenneth Tynan once said of

Marlene Dietrich

Marlene, "She has sex but no positive gender. Her masculinity appeals to women and her sexuality to men."

As early as the mid-1950s, however, Dietrich's sexual orientation was subject to print: *Confidential Magazine* had done a front-page story on "the untold story" and mentioned Claire Waldorf, writer Mercedes de Acosta and socialite Jo Carstairs as among her lovers. In her biography, Maria talks of, among others, her mother's relationship with Colette.

Dietrich's films, especially *Morocco* and *Blonde Venus*, in which she dresses in male attire and kisses another woman, have cemented her as a lesbian icon. She offered a startlingly different approach to sexuality on the screen, enticing both men and women with her androgynous sex appeal and come-hither gaze.

In poor health, Dietrich spent the last years of her life a virtual recluse in her Paris apartment. She died at the age of 90 in 1992.

Though she appeared in over a dozen German films, Dietrich's movie success started with *The Blue Angel*. It is with this film in which her filmography begins.

The Blue Angel
(1930, 90 min, Germany, Josef von Sternberg)
Dietrich is the carnivorous cabaret chanteuse Lola-Lola whose lure marks the downfall of stiff-lipped professor Emil Jannings in this Gothic classic on social decay. She sings "Falling in Love Again." ⊛

▼ Morocco
(1930, 92 min, US, Josef von Sternberg)
The impossibly seductive Dietrich made her American debut as a cabaret singer in Morocco torn between Foreign Legionnaire Gary Cooper and wealthy Adolphe Menjou. Dietrich also dons top hat and tux, and kisses another woman on the lips. Marlene's only Oscar nomination. ⊛

Dishonored
(1931, 91 min, US, Josef von Sternberg)
Dietrich rises above the material in this espionage melodrama with Marlene as a spy during WWI; she eventually falls in love with Russian agent Victor McLaglen. ⊛

Shanghai Express
(1932, 80 min, US, Josef von Sternberg)
While en route through China aboard the Shanghai Express, prostitute Shanghai Lily (Dietrich) saves the life of her former lover (Clive Brook) by bestowing her favors on a revolutionary leader (Warner Oland). Dietrich makes this melodramatic train ride all the more enjoyable, and von Sternberg's direction is inspired. ⊛

Blonde Venus
(1932, 97 min, US, Josef von Sternberg)
The ever radiant Marlene is nothing less than stunning as a woman who leaves her husband when she becomes convinced that she is no good for him. Dietrich sings "Hot Voodoo" in a gorilla suit, and Cary Grant had his first starring role. ⊛

Song of Songs
(1933, 90 min, US, Rouben Mamoulian)
In her first film not directed by von Sternberg in many years, Dietrich gives a good performance in this otherwise standard romantic melodrama about a woman who falls in love with a poor artist, but marries his benefactor instead.

Dietrich (l.) in one of her gender-bending guises in *Morocco*

The Scarlet Empress
(1934, 104 min, US, Josef von Sternberg)
Dietrich and her Svengali, director von Sternberg, are at the top of their form in this exhilarating costumer with Marlene as Catherine the Great. ☮

The Devil Is a Woman
(1935, 76 min, US, Josef von Sternberg)
Dietrich casts a spell over the men of a 19th-century Spanish village in this appealing, beautifully photographed romantic drama.

Desire *(1936, 95 min, US, Frank Borzage)*
Ernst Lubitsch produced this handsome romantic comedy, and his "touch" is very much in evidence. Dietrich plays a jewel thief who is romanced by American car designer Gary Cooper. The two stars are just as well-matched in this, their second film together, as in *Morocco*.

The Garden of Allah
(1936, 80 min, US, Richard Boleslawski)
Marlene and Charles Boyer find true love, after 79 minutes of foreplay, in the Algerian desert. ☮

Knight without Armour
(1937, 108 min, GB, Jacques Feyder)
Dietrich plays a Russian aristocrat who is rescued from the Bolshevik Revolution by a British undercover agent (Robert Donat). Sumptuous production values, charismatic acting and lots of romance and atmosphere distinguish this James Hilton screen adaptation. ☮

Angel *(1937, 91 min, US, Ernst Lubitsch)*
Even the great Ernst Lubitsch is entitled to an off-day. Marlene plays a diplomat's wife who falls in love with debonaire Melvyn Douglas while on holiday.

Destry Rides Again
(1939, 90 min, US, George Marshall)
Dietrich sees "what the boys in the back room will have" in this classic western comedy. Marlene is a saloon singer who gets mixed up with sheriff James Stewart. ☮

Seven Sinners *(1940, 87 min, US, Tay Garnett)*
As a sultry singer, Dietrich tames Navy boy John Wayne and the high seas. ☮

The Flame of New Orleans
(1941, 78 min, US, René Clair)
Dietrich makes New Orleans burn just a little brighter when she's torn between wealthy suitor Roland Young and rugged Bruce Cabot.

Manpower *(1941, 100 min, US, Raoul Walsh)*
Clip-joint hostess Marlene comes between power line work-buddies Edward G. Robinson and George Raft in this action-packed tale.

The Lady Is Willing
(1942, 93 min, US, Mitchell Leisen)
Pleasant comedy-drama with Dietrich as a stage siren who marries baby doc Fred MacMurray just so she can adopt a tot.

Kismet

The Spoilers *(1942, 87 min, US, Ray Enright)*
Dietrich and John Wayne find romance and gold in the Yukon; Randolph Scott waits in the wings for Dietrich and the gold. ⊛

Pittsburgh *(1942, 90 min, US, Lewis Seiler)*
Dietrich, John Wayne and Randolph Scott had so much fun in the Yukon, now they're at it again in the coal mines of Pennsylvania. Not quite as good as *The Spoilers*, but it's the same mood.

Follow the Boys
(1944, 122 min, US, A. Edward Sutherland)
Universal Pictures' all-star tribute to our fighting boys features Dietrich in a cameo — getting sawed in half by Orson Welles.

Kismet *(1944, 100 min, US, William Dieterle)*
Not the musical. This Arabian Nights fable features Dietrich as a dancing girl (she's painted all-gold in one scene) and Ronald Colman as the "king of beggars" and sometimes prince.

Golden Earrings
(1947, 95 min, US, Mitchell Leisen)
Dietrich plays a gypsy who becomes involved with British agent Ray Milland during WWII. ⊛

A Foreign Affair
(1948, 113 min, US, Billy Wilder)
Billy Wilder's on-target farce of post-war morals, shot on location in Berlin, features Dietrich as an ex-Nazi singer who gives visiting congresswoman Jean Arthur some competition for the affection of G.I. John Lund.

Stage Fright
(1950, 110 min, GB, Alfred Hitchcock)
Clever, lighthearted Hitchcock thriller with Dietrich as the mistress of Richard Todd. She's wanted for murdering her husband. But who did it? ⊛

No Highway in the Sky
(1951, 98 min, GB, Henry Koster)
Top-notch suspenser with James Stewart as a professor who figures out the mystery to a series of plane crashes, but no one will believe him. Dietrich is a passenger onboard an ill-fated flight.

Rancho Notorious
(1952, 89 min, US, Fritz Lang)
Marlene is a saloon singer who runs the Chuck-a-Luck Ranch, western hideout for grungy cowboys and bandits. Into her life comes Mel Ferrer, searching for his fiancée's murderer. Extremely entertaining, and boasting good performances and colorful atmosphere. ⊛

The Monte Carlo Story
(1953, 99 min, Italy, Samuel Taylor)
Lovers Dietrich and Vittorio De Sica gamble away their love and money in Monte Carlo.

Around the World in 80 Days
(1956, 175 min, US, Michael Anderson)
Dietrich is one of the 43 star cameos in this big-budget, extraordinary entertainment. ⊛

Witness for the Prosecution
(1957, 114 min, US, Billy Wilder)
In her best latter-day career performance, Dietrich sizzles as the wife of accused murderer Tyrone Power. Charles Laughton stars as the wily defense attorney who takes on their case. There's trickery and twists at every turn in this Agatha Christie mystery, which features tour-de-force acting from all concerned. ⊛

▼ Touch of Evil
(1958, 108 min, US, Orson Welles)
Orson Welles directed and stars in this stylistic portrayal of corruption and decay in a town on the Mexican border. He plays Harry Quinlen, a cop with astute instincts and questionable morals. Charlton Heston and Janet Leigh star as the couple Welles is trying to frame. Dietrich appears in a stunning cameo as a fortune-telling, one-time flame of now-crooked cop Welles. An interesting scene has Leigh being roughed up by a gang of thugs in black leather jackets. Wait...one of them is a woman, a dyke, a butch with a snarl (Mercedes McCambridge), who simply "wants to watch." ⊛

Judgment at Nuremberg
(1961, 190 min, US, Stanley Kramer)
Dietrich has a small but showy role as the widow of a high-ranking Nazi officer in this impeccable drama of the Nuremberg trials. ⊛

Paris When It Sizzles
(1964, 110 min, US, Richard Quine)
Another cameo appearance. Even Marlene can't help this turkey about struggling screenwriter William Holden and his secretary Audrey Hepburn. ⊛

Just a Gigolo
(1978, 105 min, W. Germany, David Hemmings)
Dietrich was persuaded to come out of retirement to belt out the title tune and briefly appear as a madam. David Bowie is one of her charges. Marlene's final screen appearance. ⊛

Marlene
(1984, 96 min, W. Germany, Maximilian Schell)
Though she consented to be interviewed for the purposes of this hypnotic film biography, the legendary Marlene demanded not to be photographed. It's a small miracle, then, that Schell's film is as insightful and fascinating as it is as he interviews, confronts, compliments and does battle with the tough but vulnerable lady. An unconventional portrait of one of Hollywood's greatest stars. ⊛

RUPERT EVERETT

Rupert Everett has made a career playing alternately stuffy and languid upper-crust Brits, but with publication of his first novel, "Hello, Darling, Are You Working?," in 1992, he proved that he has a sense of humor as well as dramatic flair. Not only does the semiautobiographical work have a self-deprecating wit and a high camp sense of style, but on the jacket flap, amidst the rave reviews (i.e. "Everett has revealed an unexpected talent for bitchy, decadent comedy"), is a blurb from the *Times Literary Supplement*: "Deplorable."

Born in Norfolk, England, the son of a career army officer and a Scottish mother, Everett's formative years were spent in various army camps around the world until he finally settled at an English prep school. His stay at the school lasted only until Everett was 15, when he dropped out and spent some time in Paris where he attended a party. "There was some queen singing in a soprano voice and someone else playing a piano with candles on it. When I saw all this, I thought, 'I've finally arrived in my milieu.'" After Paris, Everett attended London's Central School for Speech and Drama, though he was summarily dismissed soon afterwards. Everett remembered, "When I came to London, I was catapulted into that whole Hooray junkie thing. Everyone I knew took heroin. I was certainly taking it. This was when I was into drama school and fortunately I was desperate to become an actor so I managed to get out of it."

Everett's professional acting career began at the Citizens Theatre, and shortly thereafter he starred in the West End production of "Another Country" as Guy Bennett. The play was an unexpected hit, and Everett's star had risen. The actor reprised the role in the film version three years later, and since then, Everett has successfully alternated between stage and screen. Interspersed in these years, Everett, a classically trained pianist, managed a not-entirely successful recording career of "housey acid dance music."

Like his alter-ego Rhys in "Hello, Darling," Everett, living a jet-set life in Paris and London, spent some time hustling. "I didn't set out to be a hustler. It was just on the street here. I don't know anyone who'd refuse it anyway." Though he points out, "The lead character is not me. However, I have taken things from my own character."

Called by *Time Out* as the "leader of the Brit Pack," Everett came out in 1992 in an interview in *Out*. He is probably the only openly bisexual (he acknowledges affairs with

Rupert Everett

both men and women) actor who still gets to play straight leading/romantic roles. About his decision to come out, Everett simply stated, "It's time for people to be honest about what they do."

In addition to the following titles, Everett has also appeared in *Bloody Chamber*, *The Man with the Gold-Rimmed Glasses*, *Intolerance*, and the short *Shocking Accident*; his latest release is the 1994 drama, *Remembrance of Things Fast*, appearing in a small role as a dying AIDS patient. Everett donated his time to the film, and it also stars Tilda Swinton.

Real Life *(1983, 93 min, GB, Francis Megahy)*
In his film debut, Everett plays a ne'er-do-well who takes a job with an antique store. Given to flights of fantasy about his personal life, he becomes involved in a relationship with an older woman (Cristina Raines). This is a tiresome romantic comedy/farce, though Everett quickly rebounded with his next film, *Another Country*.

▼ Another Country
(1984, 90 min, GB, Marek Kanievska)
A marvelously acted and elegantly photographed film version of Julien Mitchell's hit London play which speculates on the public school days of real-life traitor/defector Guy Burgess. Everett is the

languid "innocent," denied entry to the school's ruling elite because of an indiscreet homosexual affair. Cary Elwes is Everett's handsome lover. ⊕

Dance with a Stranger
(1985, 101 min, GB, Mike Newell)
This critically acclaimed tale of passion and mystery follows the path of the romantic self-destruction of Ruth Ellis, the last woman ever to be executed in Great Britain. This gripping examination of a murderous romance stars Miranda Richardson (in a sensational film debut) as a dance hall girl who murders her lover. As the selfish murdered boyfriend, David Blakeley, Everett gives a convincing and sensual performance of an emotionally shallow upper-class beauty (a role he'd go on to perfect) whose slumming leads to his demise. Ian Holm is outstanding in support. ⊕

Duet for One
(1986, 107 min, GB, Andrei Konchalovsky)
Taking a break from musical comedy, Julie Andrews gives a sensitive performance in this tragic tale of a renowned concert violinist whose career is brought to an abrupt end with the onset of multiple sclerosis. Everett plays Andrews' embittered protégé. ⊕

Hearts of Fire
(1987, 95 min, GB, Richard Marquand)
A notorious disaster — it was yanked from theatrical distribution and was sent straight to video — with Everett as a talentless musician who becomes involved with aging rock icon Bob Dylan and his protégé Fiona Flannagan. The soundtrack is complete with pretty bad '80s techno-pop sounds, which could have been enough to kill the musical genre. ⊕

Chronicle of a Death Foretold
(1987, 110 min, Italy/France, Francesco Rosi)
Based on Gabriel Garcia Marquez's novel, this absorbing tale of magical realism is set in early 20th-century South America where a mysterious stranger (Everett) is given a bride (Ornella Muti) — only to return her when he discovers she is not a virgin. The woman's brothers set out to find her former lover and enact their vengeance. Also with Irene Papas.

The Right Hand Man
(1987, 100 min, Australia, Di Drew)
Elegantly filmed but laboriously talky and pregnant with a meaning and plot the audience probably doesn't care about, this melodrama hints, but never develops, its idea of two men and a woman involved in a fully realized three-way relationship. Everett stars as Harry, the pouty, wealthy son of a domineering mother engaged in the carriage business in the 19th-century Australian frontier. His life changes after an injury caused by his increasingly dibilitating diabetes forces the amputation of his arm. He develops an intense friendship with Ned, a seasoned coachman (Hugo Weaving) and continues an affair with the beautiful Sarah (Catherine McClements). The three soon become intimately close and then he dies! ⊕

▼ The Comfort of Strangers
(1991, 102 min, US, Paul Schrader)
Paul Schrader (*Patty Hearst*) once again delves into the dark side of human nature with this visually exquisite production of Harold Pinter's screenplay about a young English couple (Everett, Natasha Richardson) who retreat to Venice to re-evaluate their relationship, and find themselves pawns in the twisted games of an Italian nobleman and his invalid wife (Christopher Walken, Helen Mirren). Marred only slightly by a seemingly unmotivated shock ending, this is a quirky entertainment of the highest order. The film touches on the sexual repression between Everett and Walken's character, but does not fully explore it. In the film, Walken owns a gay bar. ⊕

▼ Inside Monkey Zetterland
(1993, 98 min, US, Jefrey Levy)
Everett plays a gay activist who eventually falls in love with lesbian Patricia Arquette. In a comparatively small role, Everett abandons his usual upper-crust character to essay the part of a lower-class Australian doing time in L.A. ⊕

Everett (l.) and Colin Firth in *Another Country*

HARVEY FIERSTEIN

Probably the most visible gay actor of the 1980s, Harvey Fierstein was born in Brooklyn in 1954. At 13 years of age, he told his parents he was gay: "There was no crying or screaming in my presence. I was what I was and it wasn't a family decision." Fierstein began acting with a local Brooklyn theatre company in his teens, which led to his appearing in Andy Warhol's "Pork" at the famed La Mama. A few years later, he began writing, and one of his first works was "International Stud," which would serve as the first act of his play, "Torch Song Trilogy." For that Tony Award-winning production, Fierstein combined three of his one-act plays to tell the tale of Arnold Beckoff, a lovable drag queen from Brooklyn (Fierstein had worked briefly as a female impersonator), winning a Best Actor Tony for himself in the process. Fierstein would win a third Tony for his book of the musical "La Cage aux Folles."

Fierstein acknowledges the importance of gay characters in the theatre and on the screen: "Gays grow up listening to heterosexual songs and watching heterosexual movies. It's good for them to see one of their own struggling to be himself, rather than watching *Now, Voyager* and deciding whether they are Bette Davis or Paul Henreid."

Fierstein had bit parts in the films *Annie Hall* and *Dog Day Afternoon* before his success with "Torch Song Trilogy." He received an Emmy nomination for his appearance on "Cheers" as Rebecca's ex-boyfriend, and he created quite a storm providing the voice to the gay secretary who falls for Homer in "The Simpsons."

After the success of *Mrs. Doubtfire*, playing Robin Williams' gay brother, his most recent work is for the CBS sitcom "Daddy's Girls," playing the business associate of Dudley Moore, the star of the show. Fierstein noted that he is the first openly gay person to play a gay character on prime-time television. In development is *Plucked*, a comedy about a drag queen who cares for the children of his trailer-park resident sister. Harvey's newest film is *Dr. Jekyll & Ms. Hyde*, a contemporary telling of the Stevenson classic. It will star Sean Young and Tim Daly (TV's "Wings"). Release date is set for 1995.

> "I'd rather be a professional homosexual than have anyone assume that I'm heterosexual."
>
> —Harvey Fierstein

▼ Garbo Talks
(1984, 103 min, US, Sidney Lumet)
Ron Silver plays a dutiful son who searches for Greta Garbo — it's his mother's (Anne Bancroft) dying wish to meet her. On a ferryboat ride to Fire Island, he befriends Harvey, who plays a gay department store employee. His Bernie Whitlock is helpful and understanding to Silver's character, and Fierstein gives a sweet portrayal. ☮

Scott Capurro, Robin Williams and Fierstein attempt to create *Mrs. Doubtfire*

Torch Song Trilogy

▼ Torch Song Trilogy
(1988, 117 min, US, Paul Bogart)
Fierstein's breakthrough Tony Award-winning play (which ran almost four hours) about the life and loves of the most lovable drag queen in Brooklyn reaches the screen at half the running time but with most of the play's warm humor and acute insights intact. Fierstein, in a partly autobiographical role, is both touching and hilarious as Arnold Beckoff, whose life is presented in three, nonepisodic acts. The story examines his relationships with his bisexual boyfriend (charmingly played by Brian Kerwin), gay lover (Matthew Broderick) and mother (the always dependable Anne Bancroft). Though director Paul Bogart's TV sitcom roots sometimes are in evidence, the film is nevertheless noteworthy thanks to its star and author. ⊛

▼ Tidy Endings *(1989, 49 min, US, Gavin Millar)*
When Marian (Shockard Channing) and Arthur (Harvey Fierstein) lose the same man — her ex-husband and his lover — to AIDS, they are thrown into a battle by the loss. Both need to find a scapegoat for his death, but eventually they discover strength, love and friendship from each other. ⊛

> "Powerful and emotional. A fluid, moving work of considerable strength and depth."
>
> —*Daily Variety*

The Harvest
(1992, 97 min, US, David Marconi)
Miguel Ferrer stars as a Hollywood screenwriter who travels to a Mexican resort town to get away from it all and to rewrite his newest screenplay. Once there, he becomes involved in a convoluted series of events which lead to illegal organ transplants, murder and cover-ups. Harvey has a small but integral role as Ferrer's agent who convinces him to go in the first place. ⊛

▼ Mrs. Doubtfire
(1993, 105 min, US, Chris Columbus)
Robin Williams goes the *Tootsie* route and impersonates a woman to make himself a better man. Fierstein plays his gay brother, a movie makeup artist, who helps in the transformation. Their scenes of "creating" Mrs. Doubtfire are among the film's best. Comedian/performance artist Scott Capurro appears as Harvey's lover. Incidentally, this is the first film to gross in excess of $100 million to prominently feature a gay character. ⊛

> "I like the fact that my character had a visible lover. It's never an issue, him being gay. He's just Robin's gay brother. It's sort of the next step: gay characters who are just people."
>
> —Harvey Fierstein in a *Genre* interview

GRETA GARBO

With her husky, alluring voice, entrancing beauty, sexual seductiveness which attracted both men and women, and an enigmatic, elusive on- and offscreen personality, Greta Garbo was probably the most famous movie star of her time. And though it's been more than fifty years since her last film, the Garbo mystique endures.

Born Greta Lovisa Gustafsson in Stockholm, Sweden, in 1905, Garbo was born into a peasant family. Her father, an unskilled laborer, suffered from poor health late in life, and a teenaged Garbo had to work to support the family. Her father died when she was 14, and Garbo left school to work full time — she was employed at a barber shop and a department store. It was the latter job which led to her career in films. Thanks to her looks, she was cast in a short film sponsored by the store. This, in turn, was responsible for her starring role in her first theatrical film, *Peter the Tramp*. A four-hour film, it received mixed reviews in Sweden (a trimmed three-hour version was later well-received in Berlin). Garbo was awarded a two-year scholarship to Stockholm's Royal Dramatic Theatre Academy, where she was discovered by the leading Swedish director of the time, the gay Mauritz Stiller. He christened her Garbo, and directed her in her second film, *Saga of Gosta Berling*. After the release of the film, MGM studio chief Louis B. Mayer courted Stiller — he desperately wanted him to come to Hollywood and direct films for the studio. Stiller agreed, as long as Garbo was part of the package. Though Mayer thought that "American men don't like fat women" (Garbo was plump at the time), he agreed, and they arrived in 1925. Speaking little English, Garbo made her American film debut in *The Torrent*. She was an overnight sensation. In what could be the inspiration for *A Star Is Born*, Garbo's American career took off while Stiller's floundered — he returned to Sweden and died shortly thereafter. Reports at the stated he died clutching Garbo's picture.

Garbo's rise was meteroic, and she became one of the most popular stars of the silent screen. When sound was introduced, it took two years for Garbo to utter a word. But in 1930, amongst great hoopla, she made her sound debut in "Anna Christie." The ads read "Garbo Talks!" and the way the studio was pushing the film you'd think the actress had discovered speech all by herself. Through the decade, she appeared in a handful of classic titles, and most were hits at

Greta Garbo

the box office. At the end of the 1930s, her popularity began to wane, so they changed her image, and in 1939 she appeared in her first comedy, *Ninotchka*. It was a great hit. However, her next film, another comedy, *Two-Faced Woman*, was not so well-received at the box office. She temporarily retired from films, waiting for the end of the war. What was to be a few years became a lifetime. The closest she came to another film was in 1950 when she was to appear in a film directed by Max Ophuls, but the financing fell through at the last minute.

If there's a lasting image of Garbo, it's of a solitary woman requesting "I want to be alone." Though it's a line from *Grand Hotel*, Garbo is said to have echoed the sentiments on many an occasion, though later she clarified what she really said was "I want to be *let* alone." It is this reclusive eccentric — dodging photographers and fans alike — which stays in the mind.

A lesbian icon, Garbo — who never married — has been linked romantically to both men and women during her lifetime, including actress Louise Brooks, writer Mercedes de Acosta, co-star John Gilbert, director Rouben Mamoulian and conductor Leopold Stokowski.

Garbo died on Easter Sunday in 1990 at the age of 84. Smartly investing in Manhattan real estate, she left a sizable estate and lived extremely comfortably in her later life.

"In the gayest, maddest colony in the world, I became a hermit."

—Greta Garbo

Before her arrival in Hollywood, Garbo made *Peter the Tramp* (1922), *Saga of Gosta Berling* (1924) and *Joyless Street* (1925).

The Torrent *(1926, 68 min, US, Monta Bell)*

In her first Hollywood film, Garbo is captivating in this fairly routine silent melodrama as a Spanish peasant girl who is the unwilling object of nobleman Ricardo Cortez's affection.

The Temptress
(1926, 117 min, US, Fred Niblo)

Garbo is radiant as a woman driven to prostitution in this intriguing Parisian drama.

Flesh and the Devil
(1927, 112 min, US, Clarence Brown)

Garbo gives a seductive performance as a beautiful schemer who comes between lifelong friends John Gilbert and Lars Hanson. Garbo and Gilbert are an inspired romantic pair. ⊛

Love *(1927, 84 min, US, Edmund Goulding)*

Garbo's first (and silent) screen version of Tolstoy's "Anna Karenina" is not as polished as the 1935 remake, but it offers the actress a grand opportunity at classic tragedy.

The Mysterious Lady
(1928, 96 min, US, Fred Niblo)

Garbo rises above the material as a Russian spy living in WWI Berlin who becomes involved with Austrian officer Conrad Nagel.

A Woman of Affairs
(1928, 98 min, US, Clarence Brown)

A ravishing Garbo stars as a socialite whose free-spirited lifestyle takes its toll. Great acting distinguishes this melodrama also starring John Gilbert and Douglas Fairbanks, Jr. ⊛

Wild Orchids
(1929, 102 min, US, Sidney Franklin)

Garbo's sincere performance of a married woman involved in court intrigue in exotic Java is the only saving grace of this average melodrama.

The Single Standard
(1929, 73 min, US, John S. Robertson)

Garbo saves another routine drama with a ravishing performance as a socialite involved in a scandalous affair with a promising artist.

The Kiss *(1929, 89 min, US, Jacques Feyder)*

An innocent kiss leads to tragedy as young Lew Ayres misinterprets married Garbo's kindness. ⊛

Anna Christie
(1930, 89 min, US, Clarence Brown)

"Gimme a viskey, ginger ale on the side. And don't be stingy, baby." With these lines, the immortal Garbo evolved from silent star to legend. In this classic Eugene O'Neill adaptation, Garbo excels as a disillusioned prostitute who returns home after a 15-year absence. She received an Oscar nomination for her performance. ⊛

Romance *(1930, 76 min, US, Clarence Brown)*

Garbo's second talkie (for which she received her second Oscar nomination) is a stagey but compelling melodrama with the diva as an opera star involved in an affair with a young clergyman. ⊛

Inspiration
(1931, 74 min, US, Clarence Brown)

This minor romantic drama of love and sacrifice finds Garbo in her element as a Parisian artist's model whose past seems to get in the way of her new relationship with student Robert Montgomery.

Susan Lenox: Her Fall and Rise
(1931, 77 min, US, Robert Z. Leonard)

In her only pairing with Clark Gable, Garbo plays a poor farm girl forced to marry a brutish neighbor, though she's in love with engineer Gable. (GB title: *The Rise of Helga*) ⊛

Mata Hari
(1931, 100 min, US, George Fitzmaurice)

Garbo never looked lovelier than as the famed WWI spy whose exotic looks seduced every male she met. ⊛

Grand Hotel
(1932, 113 min, US, Edmund Goulding)

Garbo heads an all-star cast as the melancholic ballerina who "vants to be alone." This Academy Award-winning film boasts a gallery of first-rate performances, including those of John and Lionel Barrymore, Wallace Beery and Joan Crawford; but it's Garbo's show all the way. ⊛

Garbo and John Barrymore in *Grand Hotel*

As You Desire Me
(1932, 71 min, US, George Fitzmaurice)
An earnest performance by Garbo as an amnesiac who is reunited with husband Melvyn Douglas — only she doesn't remember him — highlights this fair adaptation of the Pirandello play. ⊛

▼ Queen Christina
(1933, 97 min, US, Rouben Mamoulian)
In one of her best performances, Garbo shines as the lonely but compassionate 17th-century Swedish monarch who renounced her throne rather than be forced into marriage to produce an heir. Exquisitely photographed, this classic drama features a severely beautiful Garbo as the reluctant queen who spends much of the film dressed as a male. Embraced by many as a crypto-lesbian love story, the film features an early scene in which a trouser-wearing Garbo hugs and plants a lips-on-lips kiss on her lady-in-waiting

Countess Ebba Sparre (Elizabeth Young). Their relationship is only hinted at, but a telling scene comes when Christina comes upon Ebba with a man and she's pledging her love for him and complaining that the queen "is so dominating." Christina is both jealous and hurt and impestuously runs away from the castle, eventually falling in love with the emissary of Spain's king (John Gilbert), and the drama quickly turns into a heterosexual love story. Another scene of interest to lesbians is the one in which Christina, dressed as a man, rents a room in an inn where she is attended to by a chambermaid — they flirt with each other, but sadly nothing comes of it. The final shot in which Garbo poses sphinx-like at the bow of a ship is unforgettable. ⊛

> "I shall die a bachelor."
> —Greta Garbo as Queen Christina

The Painted Veil
(1934, 83 min, US, Richard Boleslavski)
Not Garbo's best moment, but she is nonetheless appealing as a wife who travels to China with her husband (Herbert Marshall), only to fall for diplomat George Brent. ⊛

Anna Karenina
(1935, 95 min, US, Clarence Brown)
Tolstoy's tragic love story is immortalized by the outstanding performance of Garbo in the title role. This is the second time the actress appeared as the doomed heroine — the first being the 1927 silent, *Love*. ⊛

▼ Camille *(1936, 110 min, US, George Cukor)*
Arguably Garbo's greatest performance. As Dumas' doomed courtesan, Garbo suffers valiantly as she resists the advances of Robert Taylor for his own good. Rex O'Malley is Gaston, the Oscar Wilde of Garbo's Parisian party set. Garbo received her third Oscar nomination. ⊛

Conquest
(1937, 112 min, US, Clarence Brown)
Good romantic costume drama with Garbo as Napoleon's Polish mistress. Charles Boyer effectively plays the French ruler. ⊛

Ninotchka *(1939, 110 min, US, Ernst Lubitsch)*
Garbo's first comedy and she's captivating. The ads read "Garbo laughs," and so she does as a Russian envoy who risks honor and career when she falls for Paris and playboy Melvyn Douglas. A witty and enchanting classic co-written by Billy Wilder and Charles Brackett, and featuring impeccable direction from Ernst Lubitsch. A fourth Best Actress Oscar nomination went to Garbo. ⊛

Two-Faced Woman
(1941, 94 min, US, George Cukor)
Garbo's final film takes the shoulder of responsibility as to why she decided to retire from films. It's not all that bad, actually. In a turnabout of *The Guardsman*, Garbo plays a newlywed who decides to test husband Melvyn Douglas' felty by masquerading as her own twin sister. ⊛

Queen Christina

JOHN GIELGUD

Sir John Gielgud is considered — along with Laurence Olivier, Peggy Ashcroft and Ralph Richardson — one of the great British stage actors of the 20th century. In an illustrious career that almost spans the century, Gielgud's canon of work includes not only his acclaimed stage performances but directing West End productions, working on radio plays and television and, to a lesser but no less successful extent, acting in films.

Born in London in 1904 into a theatrical family, Gielgud decided at an early age that life in the theatre was for him. Success was swift and he soon became a fixture on the London stage, starring in over 100 different productions throughout the 1920s and '30s. One of his most celebrated performances was in the 1935 production of "Romeo and Juliet" in which he and Laurence Olivier switched between the lead and Mercutio. His work on the London stage reads like the highlights of 20th-century theatre with his greatest fame being a Shakesperean actor (he has appeared in over 32 different roles). He has also performed in the plays of Ibsen, O'Neill, Wilde, Shaw, Coward, Bennett and Pinter to name but a few.

Amazingly, his film career, which is still going strong at the age of 90, began in 1924 with the British silent film *Who Is the Man?* His debut, in which he played a dope fiend (in a role originated by Sarah Bernhardt), has been dismissed by Gielgud as being "the most ridiculous part I've ever played on screen." Unlike his flashier contemporary, Laurence Olivier, Gielgud did not like acting in the movies, finding the work alternately boring and difficult. What followed for the next several decades were occasional starring and supporting roles, most notably in roles which he created so successfully on stage —films based on the works of William Shakespeare. He appeared as Hamlet in *A Diary for Timothy* (1945, Humphrey Jennings); Cassius in the Joseph Mankiewicz 1953 version of *Julius Caesar*; Caesar himself in the Stuart Burge 1970 production; and had a short but memorable appearance as Clarence in Olivier's 1955 classic, *Richard III*.

Gielgud's indifference to film acting soon changed, however, after his work in Peter Glenville's *Becket* in 1964. For he found himself, at the age of 60 when many people are dreaming of Florida condos, beginning a new career as a memorable character actor in over 40 American

Gielgud in *Scandalous*

and British films. He received popular American attention at the tender age of 76 when he won an Academy Award for his portrayal of Hobson, the opinionated and hilariously officious valet in *Arthur*. More supporting roles followed as well as two memorable "leading man" roles in *Providence* in 1977 and *Prospero's Books* in 1991.

One of the few actors to have publicly come out, Sir John has been a longtime vocal supporter of gay rights. He was once denied an entry visa into the United States after it became known that he was once brought up on a morals charge — engaging in gay sex in a public rest room. He had just been knighted by the Queen and his arrest caused a loud but short-lived outcry from the more sanctimonious members of the media. At the age of 70, he moved from London to a grand country house in Buckinghamshire where he has lived for some time with his companion Martin Hesler.

His last appearance on stage was in 1988 in "The Best of Friends." Since that time he has concentrated on television, radio and film with his most recent feature being Disney's *Stick with Me, Kid*. At the end of 1993, he had also completed a broadcast of Kenneth Branagh's radio version of "King Lear." In his 1974 autobiography, "An Actor and His Time," Gielgud wrote that he "was not good at being idle" and in a *New York Times* interview in late 1993, Sir John impishly commented on his unceasingly active schedule, reasoning, "I've got a new agent, maybe he thinks it's important to make a little money out of me before I go."

A partial listing of films in which John Gielgud played supporting roles include:

Saint Joan (1957, Otto Preminger)
Chimes at Midnight (1966, Orson Welles)
The Charge of the Light Brigade (1968, Tony Richardson)
Oh! What a Lovely War (1969, Richard Attenborough)
11 Harrowhouse (1974, Aram Avakian)
Galileo (1974, Joseph Losey)
Murder on the Orient Express (1974, Sidney Lumet)
The Picture of Dorian Gray (1976, John Gorrie)
    [made for BBC Television]
The Elephant Man (1980, David Lynch)
Priest of Love (1981, Christopher Miles)
Chariots of Fire (1981, Hugh Hudson)
Inside the Third Reich (1982, Marvin J. Chomsky)
Scandalous (1982, Rob Cohen)
The Wicked Lady (1983, Michael Winner)
Wagner (1985, Tony Palmer)
Plenty (1985, Fred Schepisi)
Time After Time (1986, Bill Hayes)
    [made for BBC Television]
Quartermaine's Terms (1987, Bill Hayes)
    [made for BBC Television]
The Whistle Blower (1987, Simon Langston)

Secret Agent
(1936, 86 min, GB, Alfred Hitchcock)
Taken from an episode in W. Somerset Maugham's spy novel "Ashenden," this gripping story follows agent Ashenden (Gielgud) as he is dispatched to Switzerland to terminate a spy whose identity he doesn't know. Co-starring Madeleine Carroll, Peter Lorre and Robert Young. ☻

With Madeleine Carroll & Peter Lorre in *Secret Agent*

Julius Caesar
(1953, 120 min, US, Joseph L. Mankiewicz)
An interesting, if much debated translation of the Shakespeare play that features an astonishing cast including Marlon Brando as Marc Antony, James Mason as Brutus and Gielgud as Cassius — a performance which won him the Best Actor of the Year award from the British Film Academy. ☻

Richard III
(1955, 158 min, GB, Laurence Olivier)
Laurence Olivier leads an all-star cast as the physically grotesque and completely villainous Richard III, King of England. Sir Larry seems to revel in his part as the vile and fiendish hellhound who cavorts his way into conquest on the battlefield and in the boudoir. With a supporting cast of Claire Bloom, Ralph Richardson, and Gielgud as the sensitive Clarence. ☻

▼ **Becket** *(1964, 148 min, GB, Peter Glenville)*
Richard Burton and Peter O'Toole deliver magnificent and powerful performances in this gritty adaptation of the Jean Anouilh play. Burton is the stoic and indomitable Thomas Becket, Archbishop of Canterbury, whose long-standing friendship with King Henry II (O'Toole) becomes irrevocably frayed as they stray down opposite political paths. A gripping and powerful historical exploration of the inhuman burdens of power. Gielgud is elegantly charming as Louis VII, the King of France, a role which earned him an Academy Award nomination for Best Supporting Actor. Interest for gay viewers is the inordinately close relationship between O'Toole's Henry II and Burton's Becket, an intimacy that was not in the original stage production and one that prompted Andrew Sarris of *The Village Voice* to write, "O'Toole plays the king as a lovesick queen." ☻

▼ **The Loved One**
(1965, 116 min, US, Tony Richardson)
Evelyn Waugh's satire is brought to the screen in this calculatingly offensive black comedy. Among the wacky cast of characters is Gielgud as Sir Francis Hinsley, a veteran of the California bohemian life and victim to the cold-bloodedness of Hollywood. A longtime studio set decorator, he is fired from his job, causing the despondent man to hang himself. It falls in the hands of his befuddled nephew (Robert Morse) to bury him. ☻

Portrait of the Artist as a Young Man
(1977, 93 min, GB, Joseph Strick)
This beautifully filmed adaptation of James Joyce's autobiographical novel stars Bosco Hogan as Stephen Dedalus, a young man who is forced to question and confront his Irish Catholic upbringing before he sets out on life's journey. Age-old issues such as sexual guilt, familial repression and Church oppression are met with rebellion by the young man. Gielgud provides a highlight (and should wake up the nappers) with his spirited hellfire speech from the pulpit. ☻

Providence

(1977, 104 min, France,
Alain Resnais)

Gielgud creates a vivid character in the person of Clive Langham, a noted elderly author in this fascinating story on creativity and imagination by French director Alain Resnais. In what many consider to be his finest screen role, Gielgud plays the often drunk, foul-mouthed old man, who despite suffering from a fatal disease, spends a night hallucinating about members of his family while trying to plot out his next novel. Fact, fantasy and his unconscious thoughts and feelings as well as his growing senility are incorporated into the fabric of his tale. Filmed in English, this literate and involving film co-stars Dirk Bogarde, Ellen Burstyn and David Warner. ⊛

Caligula

(1979, 156 min, US, Tinto Brass)

Possibly needing some rent money, Gielgud joined the bombastic company of Malcolm McDowell and Peter O'Toole in this outrageously ridiculous, over-the-top production on the Roman Emperor Caligula and his frenzied reign of sexual excesses and madness. In a minor role, Gielgud plays Nerva, tutor to Tiberius who ultimately commits suicide (did he see the rushes?) by slitting his wrists in a bath. Gielgud has called the film "pure pornography." ⊛

▼ Brideshead Revisited *(1980, 581 min, GB,*
Charles Sturridge & Michael Lindsay-Hogg)

A brilliant and haunting adaptation of Evelyn Waugh's best-loved novel, this television miniseries chronicles a young man's enigmatic and obsessive relationship with a rich, aristocratic British family. Jeremy Irons heads an all-star cast, including Anthony Andrews, Claire Bloom, Diana Quick and Laurence Olivier. Spanning three decades from the early 1920s to the end of WWII, the story begins as a disenchanted British army captain, Charles Ryder (Irons), looks back on his earlier life in happier days. It was then he first encountered Sebastian Flyte — the dazzling ill-starred son of Lord and Lady Marchmain. Sebastian brings Charles to the family home of Brideshead, beginning Charles' compulsive love affair with this strange, doomed family. Gielgud steals some early scenes as Edward Ryder, the calculating and verbally assaultive father of Charles (Irons). Their acerbic dinner table repartee proves to be a witty highlight to the series. ⊛

The Conductor (Dyrygent)

(1979, 110 min, Poland, Andrzej Wajda)

Dubbed with a jarringly inappropriate Polish voice, Gielgud nevertheless is quite commanding as an elderly Polish émigré and internationally renowned maestro who returns to his homeland after a fifty-year absence. There, he rouses the provincial Gdansk orchestra with a stirring version of Beethoven's "Fifth

Richard Burton (l.) and Gielgud in *Becket*

Symphony." Gielgud, in one of his few starring roles, is believable as the baton-twirling conductor although the film never comes together. ⊛

Arthur *(1981, 97 min, US, Steve Gordon)*

Gielgud steals the show as Dudley Moore's acerbic valet and confidant in this inspired screwball comedy which stars Dudley Moore as the poor little rich man who risks his fortune to woo the charming (but penniless) Liza Minnelli. Gielgud won the Academy Award for Best Supporting Actor for his role as Hobson, the salty-tongued gentleman's gentleman. ⊛

Invitation to the Wedding

(1983, 89 min, GB, Joseph Brooks)

An American college student flies to England to attend a wedding and, during the dress rehearsal, is accidentally married to the bride by a bumbling country vicar (Ralph Richardson). The ensuing farce unfolds at a breakneck pace, but produces too few laughs. Gielgud makes a hilarious appearance as an Englishman turned Southern evangelist. ⊛

The Shooting Party

(1985, 108 min, GB, Alan Bridges)

Set on a great English estate in the autumn of 1913, this entertaining period drama casts a slightly jaded eye towards the landed gentry of an Edwardian England on the brink of World War I and the irrevocable changes that the war produced. It marvelously identifies the petty ceremonies and traditions of a declining ruling class and is filled with the crisp conversation of a cast of well-defined, idiosyncratic individuals. Starring James Mason, James Fox and Dorothy Tutin. Gielgud plays an eccentric animal rights campaigner who valiantly attempts to dissaude the group not to go on the hunt. ⊛

Appointment with Death

(1988, 108 min, US, Michael Winner)

Peter Ustinov returns as Agatha Christie's Belgian detective Hercule Poirot, here investigating the murder of greedy widow Lauren Bacall. It could have been Gielgud, Carrie Fisher, Piper Laurie or Hayley Mills, among others. This disappointing thriller will leave you caring little about "whodunit." ✆

Arthur 2: On the Rocks

(1988, 110 min, US, Bud Yorkin)

The presence of the original's writer-director, the late Steve Gordon, is sorely missed in this uninspired sequel. Dudley Moore manages to produce a few laughs despite the absence of a substantial script; but for the most part, this is tough, schmaltzy going. Liza Minnelli returns, as does Geraldine Fitzgerald and Gielgud, who, since he died in the first film, appears briefly as a ghost. ✆

Prospero's Books

(1991, 129 min, GB/The Netherlands, Peter Greenaway)

Peter Greenaway's kaleidoscopic, hallucinatory spin on Shakespeare's "The Tempest" is sure to leave the viewer with a visceral reaction — some will delight in his orgiastic vision, others will be turned off by the visual overload and others will simply be left dumbfounded. Whatever the reaction, there is no denying the sheer audacity of Greenaway's achievement as he splatters the screen with an endless procession of naked bodies and a level of bacchanalian spectacle never before seen in cinema. Gielgud not only stars as Prospero but also gives voice to every other character in the film. While the film sketchily follows the narrative, Greenaway pays more attention to the thematic content of the Bard's work and plays it up as an allegory for the conquering of the magical New World (read: the Americas). For adventurous viewers of cinema, this is a must, but be warned that a knowledge of "The Tempest" is extremely helpful in one's comprehension of the film. ✆

Gielgud (l.) plays uncle to Robert Morse in *The Loved One*

CARY GRANT

Whether searching for a leopard in a lush Connecticut estate, clinging perilously to Mt. Rushmore, or discovering to much dismay a body in the window seat, Cary Grant was the very essence of refinement and wit, the epitome of the urbane, elegant man-about-town. His sophistication and grace were a model (and still are) and are what all other actors are measured against.

Born Archibald Alexander Leach in 1904 in the English seaport town of Bristol, Grant spent his teens performing with an acrobatic troupe in Vaudeville. After a tour of America at age 17, Grant decided to stay in New York to pursue an acting career. Among his many jobs was playing straight man in a comedy act, no doubt where he learned his impeccable comic timing. His first big break came when he was 23 appearing as second male lead in the Oscar Hammerstein-Oscar Harbach operetta "Golden Dawn." This led to other stage roles, including a play called "Niki" — it was here young Leach played a character named Cary, the name co-star Fay Wray would later suggest as his new screen moniker. His break into films is classic — he played opposite an actress who was making a screen test for Paramount. They loved him, hated her. Grant's feature film debut was in a supporting role in the comedy *This Is the Night*. Grant's good looks and natural acting style attracted good notices, and in his next few films, he'd star opposite some of the leading ladies of the 1930s — Carole Lombard, Tallulah Bankhead, Sylvia Sidney and Marlene Dietrich among them. It was his eighth film, in 1933, which brought him national recognition: Mae West's *She Done Him Wrong*. In the years that followed, Grant solidified his leading man status, and his films were becoming bigger hits at the box office. But it was in 1937, in *The Awful Truth*, that Grant joined Hollywood's superstar elite. For the next thirty years, Grant was a top box-office attraction, and his film biography reads like a Golden Age favorites list: *The Philadelphia Story*, *His Girl Friday*, *Arsenic and Old Lace*, *Notorious*, *An Affair to Remember*, *North by Northwest* and *Charade*, just to name a few.

Although Grant's prestige is due, in most part, to his legendary performances in comedic roles, he was equally adept at dramatic ones as well. And though he was a comedian without peer, it is ironic that Grant received his only two Oscar nominations for dramas, *Penny Serenade* and *None But the Lonely Heart*. Grant stopped making films in 1965. His last film, released a year later, was *Walk, Don't Run*. In an eerie prophecy in the 1939 film *His Girl Friday*, Grant's character says he's good for 25 more years...evidently so was Grant.

Though he was married several times (one of his wives was Dyan Cannon with whom he had his only child), and none were for too long a period, there have been constant rumors about Grant's bisexuality since the 1930s. For a period of time, he lived with actor and co-star Randolph Scott, and the two were constant companions. Good friend Carole Lombard made a near-legendary comment on both their union and Cary's well-known frugality: "Their relationship is perfect: Randy pays the bills and Cary mails them." In 1980, Grant sued Chevy Chase, who on the "Tomorrow" show referred to him as "a homo. What a gal." After Chase apologized, Grant dropped the suit. Grant died — a genuine Hollywood icon — at the age of 82 in 1986.

Some of Cary Grant's earliest films include: *This Is the Night* (1932), *Sinners in the Sun* (1932), *Hot Saturday* (1932), *Merrily We Go to Hell* (1932), *The Devil and the Deep* (1932) and *Madame Butterfly* (1932). His career highlights follow.

Blonde Venus
(1932, 97 min, US, Josef von Sternberg)
In his first major role, Grant stars opposite the ever-radiant Marlene Dietrich as a former lover of chanteuse Marlene who rekindles the flame when they meet again in Paris. ⊗

She Done Him Wrong
(1933, 66 min, US, Lowell Sherman)
Mae West co-authored and stars in this classic comedy with Grant as the handsome next-door minister of the bawdy Diamond Lil, and he's intent on saving her soul — or is he? It's to Cary that West says the line: "Why don't you come up sometime and see me?" Sixty years have not dampened the snap and sizzle of West's retorts: She has the talk, and she has the walk. ⊗

Alice in Wonderland
(1933, 71 min, US, Norman Z. McLeod)
Grant plays the Mock Turtle in this all-star version of Lewis Carroll's classic children's story. The cast includes Gary Cooper, Edward Everett Horton and W.C. Fields as Humpty Dumpty.

The Eagle and the Hawk
(1933, 68 min, US, Stuart Walker)
Grant and Fredric March make a formidable team in this first-rate anti-war film set during WWI. Cary plays a hot-shot pilot who gets a lesson about heroism and friendship. Carole Lombard also stars as a society girl whom both Grant and March love.

I'm No Angel
(1933, 87 min, US, Wesley Ruggles)
"It's not the men in your life, but the life in your men" is just one of the many classic quips made by Mae West in this sparkling comedy. Mae plays a carnival performer who finds it as much a

breeze taming the men as she does the lions. When she crosses paths with businessman Grant, she promises "When I'm good, I'm very good. But when I'm bad, I'm even better." ☻

Thirty Day Princess

(1934, 75 min, US, Marion Gering)

Preston Sturges wrote the script for this very amusing comedy about an actress (Sylvia Sidney) who impersonates a princess who has taken ill while on tour in the United States. Cary is her romantic interest.

Wings in the Dark

(1935, 77 min, US, James Flood)

Earnest performances by Grant and Myrna Loy highlight this standard romantic drama with the two stars as pilots who fall in love. Their relationship is tested when Grant is blinded.

The Last Outpost

(1935, 70 min, US, Louis Gasnier)

Exciting action sequences punctuate this well-made adventure film set in the Sahara with Grant and fellow British troops standing tough against the Kurds.

Sylvia Scarlet *(1936, 94 min, US, George Cukor)*

Grant's first film with Katharine Hepburn is an offbeat charmer about the relationship between con artists Kate, her father Edmund Gwenn, and new partner Grant. Through most of the film, Hepburn dresses as a boy to elude the police, and is faced with revealing her identity when she falls for Cary. ☻

Suzy *(1936, 98 min, US, George Fitzmaurice)*

Jean Harlow is the title character, a chorus girl living in pre-WWI London looking for a rich husband. She settles for Irish inventor Franchot Tone, but after he presumedly is killed, she hooks up with French pilot Grant. Guess who didn't die. ☻

This Is the Night

The Awful Truth

(1937, 94 min, US, Leo McCarey)

Leo McCarey won a well-deserved Best Director Oscar for this hilarious screwball classic starring Grant and Irene Dunne at the peak of their comic abilities. They play a divorcing couple who keep interfering with each other's newfound romance. This is screwball comedy at its best. ☻

When You're in Love

(1937, 104 min, US, Robert Riskin)

Grace Moore plays a foreign opera star looking for a husband in name only. Grant is the obliging artist who marries her, then spends the rest of the film convincing her they're really in love. Moore performs a nice rendition of "Minnie the Moocher" in this '30s version of *Green Card.*

The Toast of New York

(1937, 109 min, US, Rowland V. Lee)

Good acting helps offset the awkward dramatics in this fictionalized biography of 19th-century tycoon Jim Fisk (well-played by Edward Arnold). Grant co-stars as Fisk's business partner, and Frances Farmer is Grant's lover (though in real life, her character was involved with Fisk). ☻

Topper *(1937, 97 min, US, Norman Z. McLeod)*

This delightful ghost comedy stars Grant and Constance Bennett as the Kirbys, who are killed in a car accident and return as spirits to haunt the ordered life of their banker, Cosmo Topper (Roland Young). Young's performance is priceless. ☻

Bringing Up Baby

(1938, 102 min, US, Howard Hawks)

The definitive screwball comedy, and one of the funniest films ever made. Grant gives one of his best comic performances as a hilariously befuddled anthropologist who becomes mixed up with daffy heiress Katharine Hepburn. A classic scene has Grant answering the door wearing a woman's robe, and is asked why he's wearing it. His response, after much exasperation: "Because I just went gay all of a sudden!" ☻

Holiday *(1938, 94 min, US, George Cukor)*

Grant and Katharine Hepburn are both marvelous as nonconformists up against an ever-restrictive world. The ever-charming Grant plays a free spirit who becomes engaged to socialite Doris Nolan, but soon discovers he has more in common with her sister Kate. Great support from Lew Ayres as Hepburn's alcoholic black-sheep brother (whose character could have been gay) and Edward Everett Horton reprising his role from the original 1930 film. ☻

Gunga Din

(1939, 117 min, US, George Stevens)

Grant is one of three rowdy, hard-fisted British soldiers in 19th-century India battling the Thugees and dropping wisecracks all the way. A classic adventure film. ☻

Only Angels Have Wings

(1939, 121 min, US, Howard Hawks)
Top-flight adventure with pilot Grant running a small air-line in the South American jungle. Also with Jean Arthur, Thomas Mitchell and a young Rita Hayworth. ⊗

In Name Only

(1939, 94 min, US, John Cromwell)
Tearjerker with Grant as a wealthy businessman who is trapped in a loveless marriage to social climber Kay Francis. Then he meets Carole Lombard. ⊗

My Favorite Wife

(1940, 88 min, US, Garson Kanin)
In this wonderfully funny comedy, Irene Dunne returns home after seven years lost at sea, only to discover husband Grant has just remarried. Also starring Grant's real-life roommate Randolph Scott as Dunne's hunky island mate. ⊗

Holiday

The Howards of Virginia

(1940, 117 min, US, Frank Lloyd)
Grant plays a Virginia backwoodsman in this average patriotic drama set in colonial times. Martha Scott is his high-bred wife whose gradual acceptance of America's independence mirrors the temper of an emerging nation. (GB title: *The Tree of Liberty*) ⊗

▼ His Girl Friday

(1940, 92 Min, US, Howard Hawks)
Grant and Rosalind Russell star in this fast-talking, wise-cracking, furiously funny sex-change version of "The Front Page." Cary is Walter Burns, a newspaper editor who resorts to every trick in the book to thwart the marriage plans of reporter and ex-wife Hildy Johnson (Russell). In one scene, Russell is describing the qualities of fiancé Ralph Bellamy. Grant replies: "He sounds like a man I oughta marry." One of the reporters, Bensinger, played by Cliff Edwards, is a poet-reading dandy who could be interpreted as homosexual. In Billy Wilder's 1974 remake, *The Front Page*, Bensinger is a swishy queen portrayed by David Wayne. ⊗

The Philadelphia Story

(1940, 112 min, US, George Cukor)
Grant and Katharine Hepburn's last film together is one of the wittiest and most sophisticated of all screen comedies. Kate is a socialite who's about to re-marry. Onto the scene comes ex-hubby Grant and photographer James Stewart. Oscar-winning performance by Stewart. ⊗

Penny Serenade

(1941, 95 min, US, George Stevens)
A sentimental, three-hanky tearjerker with Grant and Irene Dunne giving extremely compelling performances as a couple whose attempts to adopt after the death of their baby brings about tragedy. Grant's first Oscar nomination for Best Actor. ⊗

Suspicion *(1941, 99 min, US, Alfred Hitchcock)*

Joan Fontaine won an Oscar as a shy socialite who enters a hasty marriage with the charming Grant, who may or may not be a murderer. ⊗

The Talk of the Town

(1942, 118 min, US, George Stevens)
Grant stars as an escaped convict (framed, naturally) who hides out in the house of an old friend (Jean Arthur), who has just rented it to Supreme Court nominee Ronald Colman. There's romance ahead as Arthur and unsuspecting Colman try to prove Grant's innocence. A sparkling blend of romance and social comedy. ⊗

Once Upon a Honeymoon

(1942, 116 min, US, Leo McCarey)
Reporter Grant follows a Nazi spy who is on his shipboard honeymoon. Cary becomes involved with the agent's new wife, ex-burlesque queen Ginger Rogers. ⊗

Destination Tokyo

(1943, 135 min, US, Delmer Daves)
Grant heads a good cast in this taut WWII submarine tale about the crew whose invasion of mainland Japan laid the groundwork for the aerial strike of Tokyo. ⊗

Mr. Lucky *(1943, 99 min, US, H.C. Potter)*

Grant is the owner of a gambling ship who sets out to sting Laraine Day, but ends up falling in love with her instead. ⊗

Once Upon a Time

(1944, 89 min, US, Alexander Hall)
Grant plays a theatrical impresario who comes across a sure-fire act: a dancing caterpillar, owned by ten-year-old Ted Donaldson. Grant soon becomes involved with the youngster's mother, Janet Blair. James Gleason is particularly good as Grant's right-hand man. A whimsical and peculiar comedy. ⊗

FAVORITE STARS

None But the Lonely Heart
(1944, 113 min, US, Clifford Odets)
Grant received his second Oscar nomination in this moody Clifford Odets melodrama as a Cockney drifter who returns home to look after his dying mother (Oscar winner Ethel Barrymore). ☮

Arsenic and Old Lace
(1944, 118 min, US, Frank Capra)
Frank Capra's classic comedy features Grant in one of his best and most beloved roles. Cary is Mortimer Brewster, the only sane voice of the eccentric Brewster clan. His aunts are poison-happy, his uncle thinks he's Teddy Roosevelt, and his psychotic brother freaks out if you mention his resemblance to Boris Karloff. ☮

Night and Day
(1946, 128 min, US, Michael Curtiz)
It's Hollywood fiction all the way as Grant plays legendary songwriter Cole Porter. Of course, a film made in the 1940s would never have even hinted at Porter's homosexuality. Monty Woolley, Porter's best friend, appears as himself. ☮

Notorious *(1945, 96 min, US, Alfred Hitchcock)*
Grant and Ingrid Bergman make a ravishing duo as spies in postwar Brazil. Ingrid marries Nazi Claude Rains in order to keep tabs on underground fascist activities. ☮

The Bachelor and the Bobbysoxer
(1947, 95 min, US, Irving Reis)
Grant lets down his well-ordered hair by acting like a teenager. It seems "bobbysoxer" Shirley Temple is infatuated with artist Cary. When they are caught in a compromising position, judge Myrna Loy (and Shirley's sister) orders Grant to date Temple hoping she'll get over him. A delightful romp with Grant in good form. (GB title: *Bachelor Knight*) ☮

The Bishop's Wife
(1947, 109 min, US, Henry Koster)
An enchanting comedy with Grant as an angel who is sent to Earth to help bishop David Niven and his wife, Loretta Young. With Monty Woolley and Elsa Lanchester as a housekeeper. ☮

Every Girl Should Be Married
(1948, 84 min, US, Don Hartman)
Bachelor Grant has his hands full as he's pursued by shopgirl Betsy Drake who thinks the titular statement. ☮

Mr. Blandings Builds His Dream House
(1948, 94 min, US, H.C. Potter)
City couple Grant and Myrna Loy head to the country for the good life, but find it's not exactly what they expected. An enjoyable comedy of errors which was remade as *The Money Pit*. ☮

I Was a Male War Bride

I Was a Male War Bride
(1949, 105 min, US, Howard Hawks)
French Army officer Grant wants to be with WAC wife Ann Sheridan, who is returning to the States, so he dons wig and dress and poses as a nurse. An extremely funny farce. (GB title: *You Can't Sleep Here*) ⊛

People Will Talk
(1951, 109 min, US, Joseph L. Mankiewicz)
As he demonstrated in his two previous films, *All About Eve* and *A Letter to Three Wives*, writer-director Joseph L. Mankiewicz has a rare talent for combining comedy and drama. In this intriguing medical story, Grant plays a doctor under medical board review. Jeanne Crain plays one of his students who becomes his wife. ⊛

Monkey Business
(1952, 97 min, US, Howard Hawks)
Grant is the archetypal absent-minded professor, searching for a youth potion. He and wife Ginger Rogers give the elixir a test spin, spending much of the movie in regression. ⊛

Dream Wife
(1953, 99 min, US, Sidney Sheldon)
An engaging battle-of-the-sexes comedy. Grant breaks up with fiancée Deborah Kerr due to her feminist independence. He then gets engaged to a subservient foreign princess, but Kerr is back in the picture when she is hired as interpreter.

To Catch a Thief
(1955, 97 min, US, Alfred Hitchcock)
A fast-paced romantic thriller with Grant as a retired jewel thief who may be up to his old tricks when he meets wealthy and beautiful Grace Kelly on the French Riviera. ⊛

The Pride and the Passion
(1957, 132 min, US, Stanley Kramer)
Possibly Grant's worst moment. He plays a British officer overseeing a Spanish peasant revolt after Napoleon conquered that country. Also with Frank Sinatra and Sophia Loren. ⊛

An Affair to Remember
(1957, 115 min, US, Leo McCarey)
Grant and Deborah Kerr enjoy a shipboard romance in this touching remake of director Leo McCarey's 1939 classic, *Love Affair*. Despite what was said in *Sleepless in Seattle*, this can be enjoyed by everyone. A second remake was made in 1994 with Warren Beatty, Annette Bening and Katharine Hepburn, released under the original title, *Love Affair*. ⊛

Kiss Them for Me
(1957, 105 min, US, Stanley Donen)
Standard-issue Army comedy with Grant as one of three war heroes spending a little R&R in San Francsico. Ray Walston and Larry Blyden are his pals; Suzy Parker and Jayne Mansfield are the romantic interests.

Indiscreet *(1958, 100 min, US, Stanley Donen)*
Grant and Ingrid Bergman are well-matched in this beguiling romantic comedy with Ingrid as a European actress who is courted by American Grant. ⊛

Houseboat
(1958, 110 min, US, Melville Shavelson)
Grant plays a widower who hires Sophia Loren as a maid (though she's really a socialite) to take care of his three children and their houseboat. Of course, they fall in love. ⊛

North by Northwest
(1959, 136 min, US, Alfred Hitchcock)
A classic thriller — the best of the Hitchcock-Grant collaborations — with Cary as a Madison Avenue exec mistaken for a spy. He crosses paths with James Mason, Eva Marie Saint, a dusty cornfield and Mt. Rushmore. As Mason's right-hand man, Martin Landau uses his "feminine intuition" to deduce the real identity of agent Saint. ⊛

Operation: Petticoat
(1959, 120 min, US, Blake Edwards)
Grant is the captain of a crippled WWII submarine who has his hands full not only trying to make his ship seaworthy but looking after five nurses whom he rescued at sea. ⊛

The Grass Is Greener
(1960, 105 min, US, Stanley Donen)
Grant plays an English earl whose jealousy sparks a calamitous weekend affair when wife Deborah Kerr is given the royal treatment by visiting American millionaire Robert Mitchum. ⊛

That Touch of Mink
(1962, 99 min, US, Delbart Mann)
Pleasant '60s sex comedy with financier Grant chasing virginal working girl Doris Day. In a subplot, psychiatrist Gig Young thinks he's in love with Grant. ⊛

Charade *(1963, 114 min, US, Stanley Donen)*
The radiant Audrey Hepburn teams with Grant in this stylish thriller, a delightfully comic ode to Hitchcock. Newly widowed Hepburn finds herself terrorized by associates of her late husband, so she turns to government agent Grant...but is he who he appears to be? ⊛

Father Goose *(1964, 116 min, US, Ralph Nelson)*
Grant provides most of the laughs as a beachcomber reluctantly drawn into WWII by the Australian Navy. And now to make matters worse, six refugee children and their schoolmistress (Leslie Caron) have just been washed ashore. ⊛

Walk, Don't Run
(1966, 114 min, US, Charles Walters)
Grant's final film is an updating of *The More the Merrier*, set in Japan during the Olympics. Cary is an American businessman forced to share accomodations with Samantha Eggar and Jim Hutton. ⊛

WILLIAM HAINES

With the exception of die-hard movie buffs and cinema experts, there are probably very few born after the FDR adminstration who would recognize the name of William Haines. But during the 1920s and early '30s, Haines was an extremely popular film star who specialized as the innocent romantic.

Born in 1900 in Virginia, Haines was in the world of business before the business of show. After graduating from military school, he worked on Wall Street as an office boy and it was there that a Goldwyn talent scout offered the good-looking Haines a screen test. He was brought to Hollywood in 1922, and within a year he had become a leading man in silents. Haines' film debut was in the comedy *Three Wise Fools* (1923), and he would star in nearly 35 films in the next 12 years, surviving the sometimes career-ending transition from silent to sound films.

Like his friend the director George Cukor, Haines didn't hide his sexual orientation. And as long as his films were making money, his studio was happy to look the other way. However, by the mid-1930s, Haines could no longer get away

with playing the romantic matinee idol, and his popularity was in decline. In 1935, he was caught at a local YMCA with a soldier — and MGM studio chief Louis B. Mayer fired him almost on the spot. Fortunately, the story didn't end there, for Haines, probably realizing his days as an actor were numbered anyway, had already begun an interest in another field: interior design. And in the decades which followed, Haines was an internationally renowned decorator. His start came in the 1930s, and Joan Crawford was his first client (he once said of her, "Joan is a meticulous housekeeper"). After that, Claudette Colbert, Norma Shearer, Lucille Ball and Walter Annenberg were among his clients. He had even decorated the American Embassy in London. Haines lived well from his second career, and died fairly wealthy in 1974 at the age of 73.

Prints are no longer available for many of Haines' films, which precludes a complete, blurbed filmography. His best-known successes include: *Tower of Lies* (1924); *Sally, Irene and Mary* (1925), a light comedy also starring Joan Crawford; *Brown of Harvard* (1926), a big box-office hit at the time; *Tell It to the Marines* (1927); *Show People* (1928), a wonderful show business comedy co-starring Marion Davies which may be Haines' best film; *Navy Blues* (1929); *The Adventures of Get-Rich-Quick Wallingford* (1931); *Young and Beautiful* (1934), with Haines as a studio publicity chief; and *The Marines Are Coming* (1935), his final film.

For another story about William Haines, see George Cukor's biography in the Favorite Directors chapter.

Haines (l.) in *Remote Control*

ROCK HUDSON

Rock Hudson

He was one of the most popular box-office stars of the 1950s and early '60s, appearing in a series of successful melodramas and sophisticated sex comedies. He was voted more than once the world's most favorite actor. He was nominated for an Oscar. And he was the star of one of the most popular TV shows of the 1970s. But sadly it is not impressive acting credentials for which actor Rock Hudson is most remembered: for Hudson was the first well-known personality to die of AIDS, and to an entire nation he put "a face" to an "anonymous" disease.

Hudson was born Roy Scherer in 1925 in the Chicago suburbs where he grew up. Drafted in 1943, Hudson served in the Philippines as a Navy mechanic. He moved to Los Angeles after the war, and the handsome six-foot four-inch Hudson, after various odd jobs, received his first break, signing for a small role in the film *Fighter Squadron* in 1948. He appeared in many small parts, mostly in westerns, before receiving a substantial role in 1950's *Peggy*. But it was another four years of alternating between second leads and starring roles before Hudson became an "overnight" success with the hit film, *Magnificent Obsession*. Hudson proved to be so popular in the next two years that he was cast over William Holden, Clark Gable and Gary Cooper in arguably his greatest role, as Bick Benedict in *Giant*. Hudson's popularity continued through the mid-1960s, but towards the end of the decade changing tastes in film moved him towards TV, where he found great success, appearing for seven years in "McMillan and Wife."

Rumors of Hudson's sexual orientation had circulated throughout Hollywood since the 1950s. It was during this time a scandal sheet had threatened to reveal Hudson was gay, and his studio quickly arranged a marriage. It lasted for three years. It was not until 1984, when Hudson acknowledged that he had AIDS, that his sexuality became known. Writer Vito Russo had commented: "This is a watershed in shattering the myth of what gay people are. He really is gentle and macho and strong and soft-spoken...and gay. It shatters that old limp-wristed stereotype." And author Armistead Maupin said, "His visibility as a gay person would mean a lot toward cleaning up misconceptions the American public has about homosexuality."

Hudson died in 1985 at the age of 59. His last quote, read at an AIDS fundraiser, stated: "I am not happy I have AIDS, but if that is helping others, I can, at least, know that my own misfortune has had some positive worth." His words proved prophetic, as Hudson's death did bring national attention to the disease, and even got then-President Reagan, who for four years had not once publicly acknowledged the existence of the disease, to finally do so. Rock's director on *Giant*, George Stevens, once said of Hudson, "(His) image may be synthetic but the man is real. There is an inner core of warmth and decency there that can't be counterfeited — and it plays on the screen."

Hudson was the subject of Mark Rappaport's acclaimed documentary, *Rock Hudson's Home Movies*.

Hudson had bit/small roles in the following films: *Fighter Squadron* (1948), *Undertow* (1949), *I Was a Shoplifter* (1950), *One Way Street* (1950), *Winchester 73* (1950), *Shakedown* (1950), *The Desert Hawk* (1950), *Peggy* (1950), *Double Crossbones* (1951), *The Fat Man* (1951), *Bright Victory* (1951), *Air Cadet* (1951), *Tomahawk* (1951) and *Iron Man* (1951).

Bend of the River

(1952, 91 min, US, Anthony Mann)
Rock gets fourth billing as a gambler in the Old West who accompanies James Stewart on an Oregon-bound wagon train. (GB title: *Where the River Bends*)

Here Come the Nelsons

(1952, 75 min, US, Frederick de Cordova)
Ozzie and Harriet (before their TV series) play cupid for Rock and Barbara Lawrence. David and Ricky are on hand, too.

The Scarlet Angel

(1952, 81 min, US, Sidney Salkow)
Set in the 1860s, the film stars Yvonne De Carlo as a saloon gal from New Orleans who assumes the identity of a rich widow. Rock plays her former beau who comes back into her life. Shades of *No Man of Her Own*.

Has Anybody Seen My Gal?

(1952, 88 min, US, Douglas Sirk)
Rock gets second billing behind Piper Laurie in this dapper "flapper" musical. Charles Coburn is the real star, however, as a millionaire who plays both cupid and philanthropist. James Dean has a bit role.

Horizons West

(1952, 80 min, US, Budd Boetticher)
Hudson gives a sturdy performance as a cowboy who, after the Civil War, returns to his native Texas, where he and brother Robert Ryan come in conflict.

The Lawless Breed

(1953, 83 min, US, Raoul Walsh)
Hudson received top billing for the first time in this flavorful western tale. Rock plays infamous gunman John Wesley Hardin, who recounts his life and times.

Gun Fury *(1953, 83 min, US, Raoul Walsh)*

Familiar but competent western adventure with cowboy Rock on the trail of the bad guys who kidnapped his fiancée (Donna Reed).

Seminole *(1953, 87 min, US, Budd Boetticher)*

Rock plays an Army officer who tries to help save Florida's Seminole Indians from fort commander Richard Carlson and extinction.

Sea Devils *(1953, 91 min, GB, Raoul Walsh)*

Costumer set during the early 1800s with smuggler Rock becoming involved with spy Yvonne De Carlo.

Rock Hudson and his friend/leading lady Doris Day in *Pillow Talk*

The Golden Blade

(1953, 80 min, US, Nathan Juran)
Swashbuckling Rock saves princess Piper Laurie and defeats evil grand vizier George Macready with the help of the sword of Damascus.

Back to God's Country

(1953, 77 min, US, Joseph Pevney)
Injured captain Hudson and wife Marcia Henderson trudge through the Canadian wilderness with villainous Steve Cochran in pursuit.

Taza, Son of Cochise

(1954, 79 min, US, Douglas Sirk)
Entertaining sequel to *Battle of Apache Pass*, with Rock as the son of Indian chief Cochise, who tries to continue his father's quest for peace.

Magnificent Obsession

(1954, 107 min, US, Douglas Sirk)
Though Jane Wyman receives top billing and garnered the Oscar nomination, this is really Rock's film, and it propelled him to stardom. In one of the best soap operas of the 1950s, Hudson gives a strong portrayal of a reckless playboy whose wastrel ways lead to the blinding of a young woman (Wyman). Dedicating his life to a "magnificent obsession," Hudson becomes a surgeon determined to restore her sight. Agnes Moorehead is especially good as Wyman's nurse. Remake of the 1935 Irene Dunne-Robert Taylor tearjerker. ⊗

Bengal Brigade

(1954, 86 min, US, Laslo Benedek)
Standard adventure with Hudson as a British Army officer stationed in India. He comes in conflict with his commanding officer, falls in love with Arlene Dahl, and comes to the rescue of all in the nick of time.

Captain Lightfoot

(1955, 91 min, US, Douglas Sirk)
Hudson is cast as a 19th-century Irish rebel who takes on the British forces, almost single-handedly.

One Desire *(1955, 94 min, US, Jerry Hopper)*

Hudson and Anne Baxter star in this mushy romantic drama as gamblers who try to go straight. Julie Adams is the femme fatale who stands in their way.

All That Heaven Allows

(1956, 89 min, US, Douglas Sirk)
Hudson and Jane Wyman reuinted for this involving May-December melodrama with widow Wyman falling for gardener Rock.

Never Say Goodbye

(1956, 96 min, US, Jerry Hopper)
Based on a Pirandello play, Hudson plays a physician who is reunited years later with his wife, long thought dead.

Giant *(1956, 198 min, US, George Stevens)*

Hudson's greatest moment, and he earned an Oscar nomination for it. A sprawling epic of a Texas oil dynasty, Hudson shares the spotlight with Elizabeth Taylor and James Dean as rancher Rock, wife Liz and ranchhand Jimmy D. come in conflict as their fortunes rise. A classic production with three justifiably celebrated performances. ⊗

Battle Hymn *(1957, 108 min, US, Douglas Sirk)*

Hudson offers a sensitive performance in this heartwarming true story of a minister/Air Force pilot who helps evacuate orphans during the Korean War.

Written on the Wind

(1957, 99 min, US, Douglas Sirk)
Another successful Hudson-Sirk collaboration, this classic soaper follows the fall of an oil tycoon's family. Rock plays the lifelong buddy of scion Robert Stack, oil fortune heir. Dorothy Malone won an Oscar as Stack's nymphomaniac sister. Lauren Bacall rounds out the cast as Stack's wife. Highly entertaining and probably the prototype for TV's "Dallas" and "Dynasty." ⊗

Something of Value

(1957, 113 min, US, Richard Brooks)
Compelling screen version of Robert C. Ruark's best-selling novel about the Mau Mau uprising in Kenya and the effect it has on friends Hudson and Sidney Poitier.

A Farewell to Arms

(1957, 159 min, US, Charles Vidor)
Remake of the 1932 hit adaptation of Ernest Hemingway's novel of love and sacrifice during WWI. Hudson takes over the Gary Cooper role as a Red Cross ambulance driver who falls in love with an Army nurse (Jennifer Jones reprising the Helen Hayes role). ⊗

The Tarnished Angels

(1958, 87 min, US, Douglas Sirk)
Hudson, Robert Stack, Dorothy Malone and director Sirk reunited after their success in *Written on the Wind* for this fascinating adaptation of William Faulkner's "Pylon." Rock plays a newspaper reporter who gets caught up in the excitement of a traveling airshow, and becomes involved in the lives of stunt pilot Stack and his wife Malone.

Twilight for the Gods

(1958, 120 min, US, Joseph Pevney)
Captain Rock tries to lead a group of stranded passengers to safety after his ship, bound from the South Seas to Honolulu, springs a leak.

This Earth Is Mine

(1959, 123 min, US, Henry King)
To bootleg or not to bootleg is the question as three generations of Napa Valley vintners clash — including young upstart Rock and his dedicated grandpa Claude Rains.

Pillow Talk

(1959, 105 min, US, Michael Gordon)

The first film in a series of successful sex comedies for both Hudson and Doris Day. In this delightful romp, Hudson offers his funniest performance as a songwriter who shares a party line with designer Day. And though they detest each other without ever meeting, Rock has a change of heart when he catches sight of her; he then romances her by masquerading as a wealthy Texan. Terrific support by the always reliable Thelma Ritter and Tony Randall. ⊗

The Last Sunset

(1961, 112 min, US, Robert Aldrich)

Dalton Trumbo wrote the screenplay for this unusual and complex western adventure. Rock plays a sheriff who's after gunman Kirk Douglas. Dorothy Malone is the woman they both love, and Carol Lynley is Malone and Douglas' daughter — whom Douglas also falls for without knowing her real identity!

Come September

(1961, 112 min, US, Robert Mulligan)

Hudson again demonstrates a fine comic sensibility as a rich American who makes a surprise visit to his Italian villa, only to discover it's being used as a hotel during his absence. Gina Lollobrigida, Bobby Darin, Sandra Dee and Joel Grey also star.

Lover Come Back

(1962, 107 min, US, Delbert Mann)

Hudson and Doris Day reteamed, and the result is every bit as succesful as *Pillow Talk*. In this genuinely funny satire on Madison Avenue, Doris plays an ad exec determined to land the account of scientist Rock's new invention — only he's really a rival ad exec, and, of course, there is no new invention. Tony Randall encores in support. ⊗

The Spiral Road

(1962, 145 min, US, Robert Mulligan)

Possibly Hudson's worst moment as an unscrupulous doctor who undergoes a religious transformation in 1930s Java.

A Gathering of Eagles

(1963, 115 min, US, Delbert Mann)

Rock plays a Strategic Air Command officer whose dedication to his job jeopardizes his marriage and his personal well-being.

Man's Favorite Sport?

(1964, 120 min, US, Howard Hawks)

An amusing spoof on sports and manhood with Hudson as a renowned fishing expert who really can't stand the sport. When he is forced to make an appearance at a fishing tournament, public relations director Paula Prentiss has her hands full making Rock an outdoorsman. ⊗

Send Me No Flowers

(1964, 100 min, US, Norman Jewison)

Breezy marital mix-ups abound with Rock as a hypochondriac who mistakenly believes he is going to die. He sets out to find a suitable new husband for wife Doris Day. Hudson and Day's third and final film together. ⊗

Strange Bedfellows

(1965, 99 min, US, Melvin Frank)

More marital mix-ups, this time with Rock as an American oil exec stationed in London who tries to reconcile with wife Gina Lollobrigida to further his corporate career.

A Very Special Favor

(1965, 105 min, US, Michael Gordon)

Charles Boyer asks handsome playboy Rock to romance his daughter, psychiatrist Leslie Caron (he doesn't like her "girly" fiancé Dick Shawn). At one point, Rock pretends to be gay so he can be "cured" by her.

Blindfold *(1966, 102 min, US, Philip Dunne)*

Hudson plays a psychiatrist who unwittingly becomes involved in the kidnapping of scientist Alejandro Rey. Claudia Cardinale is Rey's sister.

Seconds

(1966, 108 min, US, John Frankenheimer)

With exception to *Giant*, Hudson offers his most accomplished screen portrayal in this riveting thriller. A distraught, middle-aged man undergoes cosmetic surgery, and is transformed into a young man — played by Hudson. But all is not as it appears to be. A bound and gagged Hudson being wheeled on a stretcher is as haunting and disturbing a scene as you're likely to see.

Tobruk *(1967, 107 min, US, Arthur Hiller)*

Routine WWII action with Rock and George Peppard out to destroy Rommel's fuel supply at the Mediterranean stronghold. ⊗

Ice Station Zebra

(1968, 152 min, US, John Sturges)

Large-scaled adventure film based on Alistair MacLean's novel. Rock plays an American submarine commander trying to retrieve vital satellite information in the Arctic before the Russians. Patrick McGoohan, Ernest Borgnine and Jim Brown lend a hand, too. ⊗

A Fine Pair

(1969, 88 min, Italy/US, Francesco Maselli)

A dud of a caper film. Claudia Cardinale tracks down family friend/policeman Rock and tricks him into helping her in a jewel heist.

The Undefeated

(1969, 119 min, US, Andrew V. McLaglen)

Low-key western with Hudson and John Wayne as former Civil War adversaries who join forces to take on Mexican bandits.

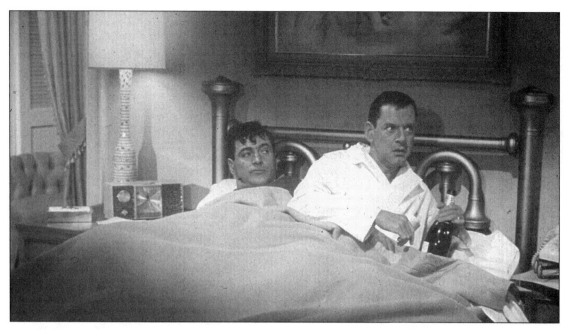

In bed with Tony Randall in *Send Me No Flowers*

Darling Lili *(1970, 139 min, US, Blake Edwards)*

A notorious flop (this is probably the inspiration for the film "Nightwing" in *S.O.B.*), this helped nail the coffin on big-budget musicals. But, with that said, *Lili* is actually quite an entertaining film full of surprising charms. Rock plays an American commander during WWI who becomes involved with German spy/entertainer Julie Andrews. ☮

Hornet's Nest *(1970, 110 min, US, Phil Karlson)*

Better-than-average war adventure, set in WWII Italy, with Hudson as an American soldier who with the help of a group of children sets out to destroy a strategic Nazi-occupied dam.

Pretty Maids All in a Row

(1971, 95 min, US, Roger Vadim)

Written and produced by Gene Roddenberry, director Vadim's first American film is a deft black comedy/thriller. Rock stars as a high school counselor who guides shy teen John David Carson towards his sexual awakening (with the help of Angie Dickinson) while he himself seduces and then kills half of the female student body.

Showdown *(1973, 99 min, US, George Seaton)*

Lifelong friends Hudson and Dean Martin are now on opposite sides of the law in this ordinary western tale. Susan Clark is the woman they both love.

Embryo *(1976, 108 min, US, Ralph Nelson)*

Interesting if muddled sci-fi yarn about scientist Hudson "growing" Barbara Carrera in his laboratory from a fetus. ☮

Avalanche *(1978, 91 min, US, Corey Allen)*

Tame disaster film featuring acceptable special effects. Rock opens a ski lodge where he was told not to. The mountain comes tumbling down, trapping the luckless guests, including his ex-wife Mia Farrow (in a pre-Woody role).

The Martian Chronicles, Vols. 1-3

(1979, 97 min ea, US, Michael Anderson)

Hudson stars in this capable made-for-TV sci-fi adventure, set at the turn of the second millennium. Rock plays an American colonel who spearheads the colonization of Mars. ☮

The Mirror Crack'd

(1981, 105 min, GB, Guy Hamilton)

An enjoyable, if slight Agatha Christie mystery, with Angela Lansbury as Miss Marple. Rock plays the husband of film star Elizabeth Taylor, who is the apparent target of an unknown assailant. ☮

The Ambassador

(1984, 90 min, US, J. Lee Thompson)

Rock's final theatrical film is an engrossing political thriller based on Elmore Leonard's "52 Pick-Up" (which was remade two years later under its original title) about an American ambassador (Robert Mitchum) caught in Israeli-Palestinian tensions.

DANNY KAYE

One of the screen's greatest and most beloved clowns, Danny Kaye was born in Brooklyn in 1913 to Ukrainian immigrants. He had originally intended to go to medical school, but his mother's death at the age of 14 changed Danny's direction. Kaye got his professional start in the early 1930s, playing the Catskills and New York clubs, ultimately becoming a headliner in the latter. He made his Broadway debut in 1939 in "Straw Hat Revue." Two years later, Kaye landed the role which brought him great acclaim (and the attention of Hollywood) as the fast-talking secretary in "Lady in the Dark." In that production, he managed the impossible and upstaged star Gertrude Lawrence by singing "Tchaikovsky," a patter song in which Kaye, in 39 seconds, rattled off the names of 50 Russian composers. Before making his movie debut with *Up in Arms* in 1944, Kaye also had great success on radio. When he finally went to Hollywood, he became one of the most popular box-office stars of the 1940s. His popularity waned in the 1960s, and he starred in an extremely successful Emmy Award-winning TV variety series.

The nimble, rubber-faced comedian was also known for his humanitarian efforts: For 35 years, he worked on behalf of the United Nations and was the Goodwill Ambassador of Unicef, traveling the world over. An avid baseball fan, Kaye was founder and one-time co-owner of the Seattle Mariners. In 1940, he married Sylvia Fine, with whom he had a terrific professional relationship, she penning many of Kaye's best songs and patter numbers in his movies. He had often said, "I'm a wife-made man."

In 1992, a biography of Laurence Olivier by Donald Spoto reported that the legendary actor and Kaye had had a ten-year affair.

Kaye once commented, "I wasn't born a fool. It took work to get this way. I'm just an entertainer. All I want to be is funny." And he certainly was.

Danny Kaye cavorts as *The Court Jester*

Up in Arms *(1944, 106 min, US, Elliott Nugent)*
In his feature film debut, Kaye wreaks havoc on an unsuspecting Army as a hypochondriac who gets drafted. He performs a few musical numbers, smuggles Constance Dowling on board his South Pacific-bound ship, and manages to capture a few enemy soldiers. Dinah Shore plays a nurse who's sweet on him, and Dana Andrews co-stars as Danny's bunkmate. There's an amusing scene in which Kaye and Andrews, seated next to each other on a bus, are telling Shore and Dowling, who are seated opposite of them, of their love. However, to the people around them, it looks as if Kaye and Andrews are talking to each other. Ditto for Shore and Dowling. ☻

Wonder Man
(1945, 98 min, US, Bruce Humberstone)
Kaye has a field day with this bright comic romp playing twins. When a twin brother, an outgoing and brash entertainer, is murdered, his ghost convinces his introverted sibling to impersonate him and find out who did the dastardly deed. Kaye has some wonderful bits, and is ably supported by Virginia Mayo, Vera-Ellen and S.Z. "Cuddles" Sakall. ☻

The Kid from Brooklyn
(1946, 113 min, US, Norman Z. McLeod)
Kaye is a dynamo as a timid milkman who unwittingly becomes a prize fighter. There's lots of laughs, and Kaye is a delight. Remake of the 1936 Harold Lloyd comedy *The Milky Way*. ☻

The Secret Life of Walter Mitty
(1947, 110 min, US, Norman Z. McLeod)
One of Kaye's most popular films, this funny adaptation of James Thurber's comedy has Danny as the timid, daydreaming hero whose ongoing fantasies get him involved in real-life adventures.

Kaye's constant co-star Virginia Mayo is lovely as ever, and Boris Karloff has an amusing supporting role as a psychiatrist. ☻

A Song Is Born

(1948, 113 min, US, Howard Hawks)
Director Howard Hawks remade his classic *Ball of Fire*, this time as a musical, with Danny taking over the Gary Cooper role. And though Danny and a fine jazz score are commendable, the film doesn't reach the original's inspired comic heights. What a treat, though, to see Benny Goodman, Louis Armstrong, Tommy Dorsey and Lionel Hampton all in one movie. ☻

The Inspector General

(1949, 102 min, US, Henry Koster)
Danny lets loose as an inept elixir salesman who is mistaken for the feared Inspector General by a small country village — whose citizens will do anything to please him. There's some good laughs and Kaye gets to perform a patter song or two. ☻

On the Riviera *(1951, 90 min, US, Walter Lang)*
Kaye won a Golden Globe Award as Best Actor for his delightful performance in this funny updating of *Folies Bergeres* and *That Night in Rio*. Danny plays dual roles: a cabaret entertainer and a famous financier. Gene Tierney is the wife of the latter who can't tell them apart.

Hans Christian Andersen

(1952, 120 min, US, Charles Vidor)
Kaye lends considerable charm to this classic children's tale about gay author and storyteller Hans Christian Andersen. Frank Loesser's score includes "Inch Worm" and "Ugly Duckling." ☻

Knock on Wood

(1954, 103 min, US, Norman Panama)
In one of his funniest films, Danny plays a ventriloquist/ nightclub entertainer who becomes mixed-up with spies and the lovely Mai Zetterling.

White Christmas

(1954, 120 min, US, Michael Curtiz)
Kaye and Bing Crosby make the most of a tuneful Irving Berlin score in this saccharinely sweet though very popular holiday-themed musical. Danny and Bing play entertainers who come to the rescue of their old Army commander. Mary Wickes appears as a housekeeper — don't you just love her? Kaye and Crosby do a drag number, which both perform very enthusiastically. ☻

The Court Jester

(1956, 101 min, US, Melvin Frank)
Danny's finest hour. To help restore the throne to its rightful heir, Kaye goes undercover, posing as a court jester; and in the process, of course, turns the palace upside-down. Basil Rathbone, Glynis Johns and Angela Lansbury offer great support. One of the funniest of all American comedies. And remember: "The pellet with the poison's in the vessel with the pestle." Or is that "the flagon with the dragon." ☻

Merry Andrews

(1958, 102 min, US, Michael Kidd)
Danny plays an English schoolteacher who sets out on an archeological dig but unearths a traveling circus instead. The merry exploits begin when he joins them.

Me and the Colonel

(1958, 109 min, US, Peter Glenville)
Kaye won a second Golden Globe award as Best Actor for his role in this adaptation of "Jacobowsky and the Colonel," a blend of satire and pathos. Danny plays the former, a Jewish refugee who is accompanied by an anti-Semitic Polish colonel (played by Curt Jurgens) while trying to outwit and elude the Nazis. Remade as the Broadway musical, "The Grand Tour."

The Five Pennies

(1959, 117 min, US, Melville Shavelson)
In his first semi-dramatic role, Kaye is quite good in this biography of jazz trumpeter Red Nichols. Barbara Bel Geddes plays his wife, and Louis Armstrong appears as himself. The film features a great score. ☻

On the Double

(1962, 97 min, US, Melville Shavelson)
With a nod to *I Was Monty's Double*, Kaye plays an American G.I. stationed in England. His expertise at impersonation involves him in a plot to double as a British general, who's a target of the Nazis, while the real military commander spearheads a secret invasion.

The Man from the Diner's Club

(1963, 95 min, US, Frank Tashlin)
Danny's last starring role is an okay comedy with the comic cast as a clerk for the Diner's Club who turns the city inside-out trying to retrieve a card he issued by mistake.

The Madwoman of Chaillot

(1969, 132 min, GB, Bryan Forbes)
As one of the many guest all-stars, Kaye, in his last theatrical film, plays the ragpicker who tries to help eccentric countess Katharine Hepburn outwit a group of greedy oil company bigwigs. The film is a disappointment, though Danny comes off best. ☻

The Best of Danny Kaye *(1993, 90 min, US)*
This video celebration/documentary on the life of Danny Kaye focuses primarily on his work in television. The infectiously funny and endearing entertainer is seen in songs and sketches from his award-winning television show with a special highlight being his "vessel with the pestle" tongue-twister made famous in his film *The Court Jester*.

CHARLES LAUGHTON

He was as unlikely a movie star the 1930s would see. He was portly, and though not ugly (however, he would continually call himself that: "I have the face like the behind of an elephant"), he had none of the desired matinee looks nearly all leading men had. But what he did have was an enormous amount of talent and commitment, a gift for getting into the core of a character and exposing its uniqueness. And in a ten-year period which saw the best from Fredric March, Spencer Tracy and Paul Muni, it is Charles Laughton who can be considered that decade's finest screen actor.

Laughton was born to a hotelier in the seaside town of Scarbrough, England, in 1899. He served on the front lines of WWI, where he was gassed shortly before the signing of the Armistice. At the age of 25, he entered the Royal Academy of Dramatic Arts in London, and had a handful of performances in the West End, where he was alternately celebrated and berated for his brilliantly mannered performances. Indeed, after a performance of "Pygmalion," George Bernard Shaw said to Laughton, "Young man, whatever your name is, you were horrible as my Higgins. But, nothing will stop you from getting to the top." All were impressed, however, when Laughton starred in "Payment Deferred," and he repeated the role in New York, which led to a Hollywood contract.

He made his American film debut in *The Devil and the Deep*, and followed this with a string of astonishingly remarkable performances, including his Oscar-winning *Private Life of Henry VIII*, *The Sign of the Cross*, *The Barretts of Wimpole Street*, *Mutiny on the Bounty*, *Ruggles of Red Gap*, *Les Miserables* and *The Hunchback of Notre Dame*, to name just a few. In the 1950s, Laughton returned to the stage with a series of successes as both actor and director. It was also in the 1950s Laughton directed his only film, the classic thriller *Night of the Hunter*. During the last years of his career, Laughton was often accused of over-acting, subjective to be sure, but there is no denying he was always enthralling.

In the late 1920s, Laughton married fellow bohemiam, actress Elsa Lanchester. Frequent co-stars, they were also kindred spirits, and their marriage, though at times rocky, lasted until his death in 1962. In a 1976 biography of Laughton, Lanchester for the first time in print revealed Laughton's homosexuality. It was two years into their mar-riage when he first told her, and only because he was facing a possible court case after picking up a youth in a park. When he told her about their tryst on the living room couch, she responded, with as much shock as understanding, "Fine. But let's get rid of the sofa." Asked why she wrote of her husband's orientation years after the fact, Lanchester responded, "Because times have changed, and such things can be discussed more openly than they were before." A definitive biography of Laughton is Simon Callow's "Charles Laughton: A Difficult Actor."

Laughton made a few British films before his move to Hollywood. These include *Wolves* (1927), *Bluebottles* (1928), *Daydreams* (1928), *Piccadilly* (1929), *Comets* (1930) and *Down River* (1930).

The Devil and the Deep
(1932, 78 min, US, Marion Garing)
Laughton steals the show from co-stars Tallulah Bankhead, Gary Cooper and Cary Grant. Laughton plays a submarine commander.

The Sign of the Cross

When he suspects young officer Grant is carrying on with wife Bankhead, he ships him out. Then Cooper enters the picture.

The Old Dark House
(1932, 71 min, US, James Whale)
Whale's classic chiller features Laughton as a stranded motorist who ill-advisedly seeks shelter from the storm at the old dark house.

Payment Deferred
(1932, 81 min, US, Lothar Mendes)
Laughton re-creates his acclaimed stage role, giving a stirring performance as a bank clerk whose financial difficulties lead him to murder. Maureen O'Sullivan and Ray Milland also star.

▼ The Sign of the Cross
(1932, 118 min, US, Cecil B. DeMille)
An intriguing religious drama with the typical DeMille flourishes. Laughton expertly plays an effeminate Nero, and is ably supported by Fredric March and Claudette Colbert, quite good as Poppaea. A scorching lesbian dance number and a scantily clad slave boy spurred protests from religious groups. The current version was cut in 1944 from its original 124-minute running time, with scenes involving sex and violence trimmed. ⊛

If I Had a Million
(1932, 83 min, US, various directors)
Ernst Lubitsch directed Laughton's sequence in this all-star episodic tale of millionaire Richard Bennett giving various people a million dollars. Laughton's is by far the best as an employee who works up a Bronx cheer for his boss.

Island of Lost Souls
(1933, 70 min, US, Erle C. Kenton)
Based on H.G. Wells' novel, Laughton gives a credible, if slightly hammy, portrayal of a mad doc whose experiments have created a race of half-humans, half-animals. "Are we not men?" is the credo of this exciting, extremely effective thriller. ⊛

The Private Life of Henry VIII
(1933, 97 min, GB, Alexander Korda)
Laughton won his only Oscar for his triumphant performance as England's 16th-century king in this superior costume drama. Laughton brings a depth of character never before seen in historical epics, and shades Henry with elements of egomania, gentleness, immaturity, rage and humor. Elsa Lanchester co-stars. ⊛

White Woman
(1933, 68 min, US, Stuart Walker)
Laughton plays one of his many scoundrels with relish. Set in Malay, Laughton sets himself up as "King of the River" over the local tribesmen. Carole Lombard is his wife, who opts to run away with Kent Taylor. Charles Bickford is good as Laughton's right-hand man.

The Barretts of Wimpole Street
(1934, 110 min, US, Sidney Franklin)
An exquisitely lovely romantic drama based on the life of 19th-century British poets Elizabeth Barrett and Robert Browning. Laughton gives a superlative performance as Barrett's possessive father (when told to avoid inferences of incest, he said, "They can't censor the gleam in my eye"). As Elizabeth, Norma Shearer had one of her best roles, and Fredric March is exemplary as Browning. ⊛

Ruggles of Red Gap
(1935, 92 min, US, Leo McCarey)
Laughton is priceless in this absolutely delightful comedy. He plays a proper English butler who heads to the American West to work for an unconventional family. Charlie Ruggles and Mary Boland offer terrific support as his new employers. Remade with Bob Hope and Lucille Ball as *Fancy Pants*. ⊛

Les Miserables
(1935, 108 min, US, Richard Boleslawski)
This excellent adaptation of Victor Hugo's novel features two outstanding performances from Laughton as the relentless police inspector Javert, and Fredric March as the hounded petty thief Valjean. ⊛

Mutiny on the Bounty
(1935, 132 min, US, Frank Lloyd)
Oscar-winning Best Picture and still the best of the three films depicting the infamous 18th-century mutiny. Laughton is at his best as the tyrannical Captain Bligh, and Clark Gable is a worthy Fletcher Christian. Amazingly, Laughton's only other Oscar nomination. ⊛

Rembrandt
(1936, 84 min, GB, Alexander Korda)
Laughton delivers an inspired and moving performance as the renowned Dutch painter. Laughton portrays Rembrandt as a complex and multi-faceted egotist whose deep religious faith drove him to ignore poverty and lack of sponsorship in pursuit of his art. An accomplished work. ⊛

I, Claudius *(1937)*
What could have been one of Laughton's greatest screen triumphs is no more than a cinematic footnote. After co-star Merle Oberon was injured in a car crash, production was halted after a third of the film was completed. The remaining footage is quite impressive. ⊛

Vessel of Wrath
(1938, 82 min, GB, Erich Pommer)
A brilliantly funny version of W. Somerset Maugham's novel featuring exceptional performances from both Laughton and Elsa Lanchester. Laughton plays a drunkard beachcomber happily content squandering away his monthly allowance. Lanchester is the hell-bent missionary out to rehabilitate him. (US title: *The Beachcomber*)

St. Martin's Lane

(1938, GB, 84 min, Tim Whelan)

Laughton excels as a London street entertainer who takes ambitious actress Vivien Leigh under his wing. Rex Harrison also stars. (US title: *Sidewalks of London*)

Jamaica Inn

(1939, 90 min, GB, Alfred Hitchcock)

A tense, suspenseful melodrama based on Daphne du Maurier's novel. Laughton plays an 18th-century country squire who is secretly the head of a band of pirates who wreck ships and ransom them. Hitchcock's last film made in England before his move to Hollywood. ⊗

The Hunchback of Notre Dame

(1939, 117 min, US, William Dieterle)

Laughton's tour-de-force performance highlights this outstanding adaptation of Victor Hugo's novel. Laughton brings heartbreaking pathos to the role of Quasimodo, the deformed bell ringer secretly in love with the gypsy Esmerelda (Maureen O'Hara). ⊗

They Knew What They Wanted

(1940, 96 min, US, Garson Kanin)

A semi-successful adaptation of Sidney Howard's Pulitzer Prize-winning play, greatly aided by strong performances from Laughton and Carole Lombard. Laughton plays an Italian grape farmer; Lombard is the waitress who becomes his correspondent fiancée. Remade as the Broadway musical, "The Most Happy Fella."

It Started with Eve

(1941, 90 min, US, Henry Koster)

Pleasant fluff with Laughton as a millionaire who plays cupid to his son Robert Cummings and hatcheck girl Deanna Durbin, whom Cummings hired to pose as his fiancée.

The Tuttles of Tahiti

(1942, 91 min, US, Charles Vidor)

Bright comedy about Laughton and family saying goodbye to the rat race and living the good life on a South Seas island. ⊗

Tales of Manhattan

(1942, 118 min, US, Julien Duvivier)

An all-star cast is featured in this episodic film which follows a tail coat from owner to owner. Laughton plays a conductor who runs into some bad luck after wife Elsa Lanchester picks it up in a pawn shop.

Stand by for Action

(1942, 109 min, US, Robert Z. Leonard)

An inferior war film with Laughton as a Rear Admiral. Top-billed Robert Taylor and Brian Donlevy battle it out with each other before taking on the Nazis.

Forever and a Day

(1943, 104 min, US, various directors)

An amazing all-star cast is featured in this excellent film chronicling the lives of various tenants of a London home. Laughton plays a butler during Victorian times. ⊗

This Land Is Mine

(1943, 103 min, US, Jean Renoir)

Laughton gives an extremely capable portrayal of a timid schoolteacher who becomes an unlikely hero when the Nazis invade his small French village. Maureen O'Hara nicely plays a neighbor on whom he has a crush. One of the better war films of the era.

The Man from Down Under

(1943, 103 min, US, Robert Z. Leonard)

Laughton can't add much lustre to this lifeless tale of an Australian soldier (Laughton) who returns home after WWI with two orphaned children.

The Canterville Ghost

(1944, 95 min, US, Jules Dassin)

Highly entertaining comedy based on the Oscar Wilde short story with Laughton gloriously chewing the scenery as a 300-year-old ghost. Laughton must find a relative to perform an act of bravery so his soul can rest. Robert Young is the chosen one, and young Margaret O'Brien also stars. ⊗

The Suspect

(1944, 85 min, US, Robert Siodmak)

Fine thriller with Laughton as a turn-of-the-century London shopkeeper who kills his nagging wife (Rosalind Ivan) after falling in love with a stenographer (Ella Raines). Stanley C. Ridges is the police inspector investigating the case.

Captain Kidd

(1945, 83 min, US, Rowland V. Lee)

Mediocre swashbuckler with Laughton as the notorious pirate. Laughton fares much better when Captain Kidd meets Abbott and Costello. ⊗

Because of Him

(1946, 88 min, US, Richard Wallace)

Laughton hams it up in this slight comedy as a successful stage actor. Deanna Durbin plays an aspiring actress who wants Laughton to be her Svengali.

The Paradine Case

(1948, 116 min, US, Alfred Hitchcock)

Laughton is in good form as a lascivious judge in this, his second film with Hitchcock. Gregory Peck stars as an attorney who risks his marriage and career when he falls in love with the enigmatic Mrs. Paradine (Alida Valli), on trial for murder. ⊗

Mutiny on the Bounty

The Big Clock
(1948, 95 min, US, John Farrow)
A competent thriller with Laughton as a crime magazine publisher who murders his wife, then sets reporter Ray Milland on the case, fixing the evidence to make it look like his ace journalist did it. Also with Maureen O'Sullivan, and Elsa Lanchester has a good supporting role.

Arch of Triumph
(1948, 120 min, US, Lewis Milestone)
Disappointing film version of Erich Maria Remarque's novel. Ingrid Bergman and Charles Boyer are the refugee lovers; Laughton plays a dreaded Nazi officer. ⊛

The Bribe
(1949, 98 min, US, Robert Z. Leonard)
Robert Taylor plays an American Secret Service agent investigating a Caribbean smuggling ring. Laughton is one of the gang; so are Ava Gardner and Vincent Price.

The Man on the Eiffel Tower
(1949, 85 min, US, Burgess Meredith)
A highly suspenseful psychological thriller set in Paris about a police inspector (Laughton) playing a mental cat-and-mouse game with a suspected murderer (Franchot Tone). ⊛

The Blue Veil
(1951, 113 min, US, Curtis Bernhardt)
Laughton appears briefly in this drama of dedicated nurse Jane Wyman and her various professional charges. Joan Blondell comes off best as the actress mother of ailing Natalie Wood.

The Strange Door
(1951, 81 min, US, Joseph Pevney)
A dreadful gothic horror tale based on a Robert Louis Stevenson short story with even Laughton in bad form, here playing a psycho French nobleman.

O. Henry's Full House
(1952, 117 min, US, various directors)
Henry Koster directed one of the five episodes all based on O. Henry short stories. In it, Laughton plays an amiable bum who tries to arrange a jail sentence.

Abbott and Costello Meet Captain Kidd *(1952, 70 min, US, Charles Lamont)*
Laughton reprises his role from the 1945 adventure film, and he manages to instill some comic life into a series which was beginning to lose steam. Laughton claimed he played Kidd again for this film because he wanted "to buy another painting."

Salome *(1953, 102 min, US, William Dieterle)*
Laughton chews the scenery as King Herod to Rita Hayworth's Salome. Also with Stewart Granger and Judith Anderson. ⊛

FAVORITE STARS

Young Bess

(1953, 111 min, US, George Sidney)
Laughton reprises his award-winning role of King Henry VIII in this appealing costumer about the early life of Queen Elizabeth I (played by Jean Simmons). ⊗

Hobson's Choice

(1954, 107 min, GB, David Lean)
Laughton offers a scintillating performance in this delicious working-class comedy about a tyrannical bootmaker who struggles to maintain his dominion over his three daughters. Brenda de Banzie shines as his strong-willed daughter who defies her father's authority by marrying the man of her choice. ⊗

Witness for the Prosecution

(1957, 106 min, US, Billy Wilder)
Based on the hit Agatha Christie play, this delightful adaptation proves to be an acting tour-de-force for all involved. Laughton is nothing short of terrific as an attorney who defends accused murderer Tyrone Power. Marlene Dietrich is Power's wife, who may or may not know more than she's letting on, and Elsa Lanchester upstages everyone as Laughton's watchdog of a nurse. ⊗

Under Ten Flags

(1960, 92 min, US/Italy, Signor Coletti)
This Dino De Laurentiis production, set during WWII, has Laughton as a British admiral who masterminds the sinking of a nefarious Nazi ship. Van Heflin plays the German captain.

▼ Spartacus

(1960, 196 min, US, Stanley Kubrick)
Kirk Douglas plays the title role, a rebel Roman slave. Laughton is commanding as Gracchus, a wily Roman senator. Kubrick's epic adventure is highlighted by remarkable action sequences and strongly developed characterizations, all set against the visual spectacle of the director's discerning eye for locale and cinematic tone. In a scene newly restored to the film, Roman master Laurence Olivier discusses oysters and preferences (dietary and otherwise) with lithe slave Tony Curtis, who only has eyes for Spartacus. ⊗

▼ Advise and Consent

(1962, 139 min, US, Otto Preminger)
Laughton offers an excellent performance in his final film role as a slick Southern senator. This fine adaptation of the Allen Drury novel examines the political machinations of a controversial Secretary of State nomination. As Senator Brigham Anderson, Don Murray is full of idealistic vigor as the chairman of a House sub-committee investigating the Secretary of State (Henry Fonda). However, when he refuses to endorse Fonda, he is blackmailed: He had an affair with another man while in the service. John Granger is Ray, Anderson's former lover, who now seems to be a hustler. Larry Tucker is Manuel, Ray's pimp; and Sid Gould is a very friendly bartender at the 602 Club. The first Hollywood film to go inside a gay bar. An interesting companion piece to *The Best Man*. ⊗

PAUL LYNDE

With a vocal delivery rivaled only by Tallulah Bankhead and a wit which bordered on the Wilde, Paul Lynde was one of the most familiar comedic character actors during the 1960s and '70s both on TV and in the movies. Though he had his own TV show (which was a ratings disappointment), he is probably best remembered for his TV appearances on "Bewitched" and "The Hollywood Squares."

Born in 1926 in Ohio, Lynde's early life was struck by tragedy when within three months of each other, his mother, father and brother died. Lynde studied acting at Northwestern University, and after graduating, he moved to New York to pursue an acting career. He toured in stock for a few years, and made his Broadway debut in "New Faces of 1952," which also featured other "New Faces" such as Alice Ghostley and Eartha Kitt. The entire cast repeated their roles in the movie version. After years of small parts and shows (including the 1956 TV comedy "Stanley"), Lynde hit it big in 1960 with his delightful performance as the excitable father in the Tony Award-winning musical "Bye Bye Birdie." After repeating the role in the hit movie adaptation, Lynde worked steadily until his death in 1981.

But for all his film work, it was TV which brought him fame. In 1964, he made a guest appearance on the hit TV comedy "Bewitched" as Elizabeth Montgomery's jokester relative, Uncle Arthur. He was such a sensation that his role was made into a recurring character, and that series' best episodes usually feature Lynde. He also appeared for one season on the comedy "The Pruitts of Southampton," which starred Phyllis Diller, and "Hey Landlord." In 1972, Lynde hosted his own short-lived series, "The Paul Lynde Show." During the early 1970s, Lynde began an association which would continue until his death with the TV game show "The Hollywood Squares." Always seated in the middle square of a giant tic-tac-toe game, Lynde's quick-witted retorts to a series of questions were legendary. "Do female frogs croak?" he was asked. "If you hold their little heads under water," he replied. One of the few visible gay voices on TV during the 1970s, Lynde's camp humor was always in evidence: "Why do motorcyclists traditionally wear leather?" His response: "Because chiffon wrinkles."

New Faces *(1954, 99 min, US, Harry Horner)*

The original cast of "New Faces of 1952" reprises their roles in this comedy/musical revue. Lynde is present in a few comedy sketches, as is Alice Ghostley (who would also co-star on TV's "Bewitched"), and Eartha Kitt is fetching in her couple of songs. The highlight of the show is the five-minute production number called "Lizzie Borden," which turns the infamous murder into a hoe-down musical! ⊛

Son of Flubber

(1963, 100 min, US, Robert Stevenson)

This sequel to the high-flying *The Absent-Minded Professor* is more earthbound and sillier than its predecessor. Fred MacMurray returns as a nutty professor, and Lynde has an amusing role as a know-it-all sportscaster. ⊛

Bye Bye Birdie

(1963, 112 min, US, George Sidney)

Lynde had his best screen role as the befuddled father to teenager Ann-Margret in this engaging version of the Broadway musical. A funny satire on rock 'n' roll, the story follows the calamitous day rocker Conrad Birdie arrives in small-town Ohio to kiss an average American teenaged girl. Dick Van Dyke re-created his stage role, and Janet Leigh took over for Chita Rivera. Lynde singing "Kids" is a great American musical moment. ⊛

Send Me No Flowers

(1964, 100 min, US, Norman Jewison)

Rock Hudson stars as a hypocondriac who thinks he's dying, so he tries to find wife Doris Day a new hubby. Lynde is extremely funny as a cemetery plot salesman who "really loves his work" (his motto: "When you're ready, we're ready"). ⊛

The Glass Bottom Boat

(1966, 110 min, US, Frank Tashlin)

Doris Day stars as a widow whose work relationship with scientist Rod Taylor leads to romance and espionage hijinks. As an overzealous security guard with a penchant for disguises, Lynde gives a splendidly funny performance. Lynde dressed in drag looks suspiciously like "Bewitched" co-star Agnes Moorehead, and there's a funny gag with him catching the eye of that "Man from U.N.C.L.E." Robert Vaughan. ⊛

Rabbit Test *(1978, 86 min, US, Joan Rivers)*

In Joan Rivers' hit-or-miss (mostly miss) comedy, Billy Crystal is the first pregnant man. Lynde plays Crystal's doctor who gives Billy his pregnancy test results ("Mr. Rabbitt has expired"), and then sees dollar signs and movie contracts in store for them. ⊛

The Villain *(1979, 89 min, US, Hal Needham)*

In essence a live-action Road Runner cartoon, this western spoof stars Kirk Douglas as the living incarnation of the coyote, a bandit trying to rob the elusive Arnold Schwarzenegger, who's escorting Ann-Margret and a tin of cash. Though the film provides a few laughs, it's overly broad and very silly. Lynde tries his best as an Indian chief named Nervous Elk. (GB title: *Cactus Jack*) ⊛

Lynde (l.) with Rock Hudson in *Send Me No Flowers*

IAN McKELLEN

One of England's greatest stage actors, Ian McKellen has been named in the same breath as fellow actors Anthony Hopkins and Derek Jacobi as the heir apparent to Laurence Olivier. Indeed, Olivier himself called McKellen "the greatest young actor in the English language." Openly gay, McKellen is almost as well-known for his gay activism as he is for his acting.

Born in 1935, McKellen started acting in school, and then majored in it at Cambridge. In 1961, he joined the Belgrade Theatre in Coventry and worked in various provincial rep companies before making his London debut in 1964 in "A Scent of Flowers." During the 1960s, McKellen had many successes on the West End, and worked with the National Theatre at the Old Vic (where he appeared in "Hamlet" and "Richard II" among others). He also enjoyed a remarkable four-year run with the Royal Shakespeare Company, starring in productions of "Dr. Faustus," "Twelfth Night" and "Pillars of the Community." A founding member of The Actors' Company, McKellen performed "Tis Pity She's a Whore" and "King Lear" with them. He created the role of Max in "Bent" at the Royal Court Theatre in 1979, and starred in its subsequent West End run. For it he won the Olivier Award, London's equivilent of the Tony. In total, the actor won four Olivier awards, and also won a Tony Award for the New York production of "Amadeus," playing Salieri.

For his contributions to the London theatrical community, McKellen was knighted in 1991, the first openly gay person to be so honored. A fervent gay and AIDS activist, Sir Ian came out during a BBC interview. It was in response to the anti-gay Clause 28. "Some friends argued there wasn't a single celebrated actor who'd come out. [Although Simon Callow had publicly come out five years earlier.] So I was ready to come out, and the ideal opportunity came with Clause 28 — it didn't seem I could make a public statement against it unless I was absolutely honest as to why I took it so personally." His knighthood proved to be quite controversial, as members of the gay community were split as to whether he should accept it or not. A group of well-known gay artists all came out in support of McKellen, including producer Cameron Macintosh, actor Alec McCowan, actor Stephen Fry, actor Simon Callow and director John Schlesinger. *The Guardian* called it "One of the most remarkable examples of gay solidarity since homosexuality was decriminalized (in Britain) in 1967."

Ian McKellen

Though a leading voice in the gay rights struggle, McKellen's openness has not really effected his career in films — instead of limiting his film choices, McKellen has appeared in a wide variety of movies, from art films to Hollywood mainstream productions.

> "Until (I came out), the only thing I felt expert in was theatre. Now I realize I have another expertise, and source of pride: my sexuality."
>
> —Ian McKellen

▼ A Touch of Love
(1969, 105 min, GB, Waris Hussein)
Sandy Dennis gives a compassionate performance in this insightful and affecting drama as a graduate student who has a baby out of wedlock. In a smart and sensitive portrayal, McKellen plays the bisexual BBC newscaster who is the father of her child. (US title: *Thank You All Very Much*)

Alfred the Great
(1969, 122 min, GB, Clive Donner)
David Hemmings plays the ninth-century King of England in this sluggish biography. The ambitious story chronicles Alfred's life, as soldier and ruler, but the awkward dramatics offset the well-staged battle sequences. McKellen co-stars with Michael York and Colin Blakely.

Priest of Love
(1981, 125 min, GB, Christopher Miles)
McKellen gives an excellent, shaded portrayal of author D.H. Lawrence in director Christopher Miles' elegantly photographed

and absorbing biography of the controversial writer's final days. The film details Lawrence's self-exile to New Mexico, his sojourn to Italy to write "Lady Chatterley's Lover," and the tempestuous relationship with his wife Frieda (played by Janet Suzman). Co-starring John Gielgud (in small role as a repressive English censor), Ava Gardner and Sarah Miles. ⊛

The Keep *(1983, 96 min, US, Michael Mann)*
From the director of *Manhunter* comes this stylish looking but empty-headed horror film set during WWII about Nazi soldiers holding up at an ancient site — where a demonic creature lays dormant. McKellen plays a professor who investigates the recent rash of killings. Also with Scott Glenn. ⊛

Windmills of the Gods
(1987, 95 min, US, Lee Philips)
Made-for-TV adaptation of a Sidney Sheldon novel. Jaclyn Smith plays the Ambassador to Romania who with aide and lover Robert Wagner becomes mixed up in political intrigue. McKellen has a small role as a dignitary in this trashy romantic adventure.

Scandal
(1989, 114 min, GB, Michael Caton-Jones)
First-time director Michael Caton-Jones' vivid enactment of the incredible sex scandal which brought a firmly entrenched, conservative British government to its knees in 1963. Joanne Whaley-Kilmer sparkles as Christine Keeler, a nightclub show-girl whose sexual liaisons with then-Minister of War John Profumo (stoically portrayed by McKellen) and a Soviet naval attache sparked what is still the biggest scandal in British political history. John Hurt also stars as the socialite and sexual provocateur whose manipulations brought about what came to be known as "The Profumo Affair." ⊛

McKellen as D.H. Lawrence in *Priest of Love*

Last Action Hero
(1993, 115 min, US, John McTiernan)
1993's most notorious bomb, this messy action-comedy stars Arnold Schwarzenegger as a fictional film hero who teams up with a 12-year-old boy who has magically entered the film he is starring in. There's lots of in-jokes (maybe too many), and a score of cameo appearances. The film's best bit features McKellen as Death in Ingmar Bergman's *The Seventh Seal* who literally walks off the movie screen and onto the streets of Manhattan. McKellen attacks his brief role with Shakespearean intensity, and in a moment of reckless surrealism, looks at the film's youthful hero and says "I don't do fiction" — it's a bizarre but wonderful moment. ⊛

▼ The Ballad of Little Jo
(1993, 120 min, US, Maggie Greenwald)
Part of 1993's parade of cross-dressing titles (including *Orlando*, *Farewell My Concubine* and *M. Butterfly*), this profound odyssey — based on a true story — examines feminine oppression in the tale of a young woman (Suzy Amis) who, after being attacked by a group of soldiers, masquerades as a man in a shabby mining town. McKellen gives great support as a miner who initially is seen as the only sympathetic man in the territory. But his personality soon radically changes, as he brutally injures a prostitute and villainously threatens Jo when he discovers her true sexuality. ⊛

> "(My character) has a difficulty dealing with women. He was probably gay without realizing it."
>
> —Ian McKellen

▼ And the Band Played On
(1993, 100 min, US, Roger Spottiswoode)
McKellen has a substantial role in this made-for-TV adaptation of the late Randy Shilts' controversial novel. He plays a San Francisco gay activist who campaigns for AIDS education at the cost of his lover, played by B.D. Wong. McKellen received an Emmy nomination for his performance. ⊛

▼ Six Degrees of Separation
(1993, 112 min, US, Fred Schepisi)
John Guare's acclaimed Broadway comedy exploring self-deception makes for an exhilarating screen work. McKellen plays a rich South African businessman and associate of Upper East Side art dealer Donald Sutherland who is equally charmed and duped by the charismatic gay hustler Will Smith. ⊛

The Shadow
(1994, 104 min, US, Russell Mulcahy)
Based on the popular 1930s radio program, a grim Alec Baldwin stars as the avenging hero/bad guy The Shadow in this lifeless cartoon "adventure" tale that borrows the set design ideas of *Batman* and *Dick Tracy* but not their excitement. One of the characters in the film includes McKellen as Reinhardt Lane, a befuddled scientist and loving father to The Shadow's love interest (Penelope Ann Miller). He performs the role in a mildly amusing, but perfunctory fashion. ⊛

SAL MINEO

An authentic rebel and a teenage hero to a generation, Sal Mineo's was a comparitively short-lived but varied career. An actor on Broadway, television and in films, he wrote, directed, painted and even had a brief fling with success as a singer. It is his haunting portrayal of Plato, the alienated gay teen in *Rebel without a Cause*, however, for which he'll be best remembered.

Born in 1939 in New York City, Mineo grew up on the tough streets of the Bronx. The son of a Sicilian-born coffin maker, Sal endured a hard childhood. A gang member as a youth, he was expelled from parochial school for troublemaking. To keep him off the streets, Mineo's mother signed him up in dance class. It was there that 11-year-old Sal was spotted by an agent, who immediately signed him to the Broadway run of Tennessee Williams' "The Rose Tattoo," opposite Maureen Stapleton. He stayed with the show for more than a year, and afterwards, he appeared in "The King and I" for a run of a year and a half. Mineo eventually made his way to Hollywood, and at the age of 16, made his film debut in the caper film *Six Bridges to Cross*. It was his next film, however, which brought him national attention and altered the young actor's career. Appearing with James Dean and Natalie Wood in *Rebel without a Cause*, Mineo and his co-stars acted with such conviction in conveying inner turmoil that they were heralded by their generation and Mineo and Wood both received Oscar nominations.

Mineo's subsequent roles in the 1950s cast him as the juvenile delinquent; embittered hoodlums fighting the system and who usually by the film's end went the straight and narrow. For these roles, Mineo became known as "The Switchblade Kid." He was such a hero to the youths of the street that once in 1959, Bob Hope jokingly told a TV audience that there would be no school in the Bronx the next day in honor of Mineo's birthday: Hundreds of Bronx high school students stayed home. Also that year, Mineo recorded a song, "Start Moving," which went gold.

During the mid-1960s and no longer a teen, Mineo found few good parts coming his way. He commented after being offered yet another psycho role, "Suddenly it dawned on me I was on the industry's weirdo list." In response, he left Hollywood in the mid-1960s for the seemingly more challenging roles being offered in Europe. He spent three years there, but the parts were not forthcoming. He returned to the States, where his film roles were few. He found greater success on the stage. He directed the Los Angeles premiere of "Fortune and Men's Eyes"; and appeared in the San

Dino

Francisco production of "P.S. Your Cat Is Dead" as a bisexual cat burglar.

A bisexual who made no attempt to hide his sexuality ("I like them all — men, I mean. And a few chicks now and then"), Mineo, unlike some of his comtemporaries (i.e. James Dean, Montgomery Clift), fought no demons over his gayness ("One time, when my Ma wondered how come I turned out gay, I asked her, 'Ma, how come my brothers *didn't*?'").

In 1976, Mineo was set to appear in the L.A. production of "P.S. Your Cat Is Dead." Coming home from rehearsals one evening, Mineo was stabbed to death outside his West Hollywood apartment in a botched robbery attempt. Contrary to rumors at the time, Mineo was neither killed by a hustler he had picked up nor by a crazed ex-lover. It is a sad irony that Mineo and his *Rebel* co-stars Dean and Wood all met untimely, violent deaths.

Six Bridges to Cross
(1955, 96 min, US, Joseph Pevney)
Mineo made his film debut in this enjoyable if slight caper comedy playing Tony Curtis as a youth — a juvenile delinquent who would as an adult mastermind the Brinks robbery. Also with Julie Adams and George Nader. *The New York Times* commented, "Mineo contributes an effective bit in the (film's) best scene."

▼ Rebel without a Cause
(1955, 111 min, US, Nicholas Ray)
In this testament to adolescent angst, Mineo plays Hollywood's first gay teenager, lonely rich kid Plato, who's not only in love with Alan Ladd (whose picture adorns his high school locker), but also with his only friend, Jim, played by James Dean. For his tender and haunting portrayal, Mineo received a Best Supporting Actor nod. ⊛

The Private War of Major Benson
(1955, 105 min, US, Jerry Hopper)
In this playful if predictable comedy, Mineo plays one of the mischievous cadets at a Catholic military boarding school who helps make new schoolmaster Charlton Heston's life hectic.

Crime in the Streets
(1956, 91 min, US, Don Siegel)
Based on Reginald Rose's acclaimed juvenile delinquent TV story, this tough youth drama adapted by the author himself casts John Cassavetes as a street punk planning to commit a murder. Mineo is good as one of Cassavetes' hoodlum co-horts (another is future director Mark Rydell). James Whitmore also stars as a do-good social worker. ⊛

Giant *(1956, 201 min, US, George Stevens)*
In his second film with James Dean (though they don't appear together), Mineo has a brief role as Angel, the Mexican son of Rock Hudson and Elizabeth Taylor's housekeepers. A soldier fighting in WWII, Hudson's Bick Benedict says of Mineo, "That boy's the best dang man on the place." ⊛

Somebody Up There Likes Me
(1956, 113 min, US, Robert Wise)
Paul Newman's fine performance as boxer Rocky Graziano highlights this sturdy biography, tracing the fighter's life from young hoodlum to boxing champion. Mineo ably plays Rocky's best pal and accomplice. Also with Pier Angeli, Robert Loggia and a young Steve McQueen. ⊛

Dino *(1957, 94 min, US, Thomas Carr)*
Re-creating his Emmy Award nominated performance, Mineo had his best "juvy" role in this film version of Reginald Rose's TV play, adapted by the author. Mineo plays the title character, a tormented juvenile delinquent who returns home after three years in reformatory school and experiences difficulty in readjusting. Brian Keith plays the caseworker who helps him along. Strong performances from Mineo and Keith elevate this involving drama.

The Young Don't Cry
(1957, 89 min, US, Alfred L. Werker)
Set in Georgia, this melodramatic youth drama casts Mineo as an orphan who desperately wants out of his work camp-like orphanage. When he does, he gets involved with hardened chain-gang prisoner James Whitmore (who's on the opposite side of the law from his *Crime in the Streets* role).

Tonka *(1958, 97 min, US, Lewis R. Foster)*
In this standard Disney adventure outing, Mineo gives a spirited performance as a Native American brave who rescues and trains a horse which survived Custer's Last Stand. Mineo looks pretty good in his skimpy Indian costume.

The Gene Krupa Story
(1959, 101 min, US, Dom Weis)
Mineo gives a good performance as the famous jazz drummer in this uneven musical biography examining Krupa's professional career and his personal life, including an almost career-ending drug addiction. Also with Susan Kohner, teen heartthrob James Darren, "Batgirl" Yvonne Craig and musicians Red Nichols and Buddy Lester. ⊛

A Private's Affair
(1959, 92 min, US, Raoul Walsh)
Getting to show off his singing talents, Mineo stars in this zany service comedy as one of three G.I.s (he's the beatnik of the group) who competes in a TV musical variety show. Barry Coe and Gary Crosby are his Army buddies; Barbara Eden, Christine Carere and Terry Moore are their romantic interests.

Exodus *(1960, 213 min, US, Otto Preminger)*
An epic version of Leon Uris' mammoth novel detailing the struggles of the new Israeli state. Paul Newman plays an Israeli resistance leader who becomes involved with American Army nurse Eva Marie Saint. Mineo received his second Oscar nomination for his intense performance as an embittered Auschwitz survivor who in a powerful scene reveals that he was raped by the Nazis ("...they used me as a woman"). Ralph Richardson is especially good as a British general. ⊛

Rebel without a Cause

FAVORITE STARS

Escape from Zahrain

(1961, 93 min, US, Ronald Neame)
Mineo is one of five escaped prisoners who flee their Middle Eastern jail and are chased through the desert. Yul Brynner and Jack Warden are two of the convicts, and James Mason has a cameo.

The Longest Day *(1962, 169 min, US, Ken Annakin, Andrew Marton & Bernhard Wicki)*

Classic WWII epic which accounts the Allied invasion of Normandy; the action here is carried at a brisk pace and with great attention to detail. The all-star cast delivers a plethora of strong performances from the likes of John Wayne, Henry Fonda, Richard Burton, Robert Mitchum, Sean Connery; the list goes on. Mineo is very good in his few scenes as an American Army paratrooper who gets fooled by a German rifle. ⊛

Cheyenne Autumn

(1964, 158 min, US, John Ford)
John Ford's last western is a sprawling account of the Cheyenne nation's grueling 1,500-mile journey from the arid Southwest to their northern homeland. Fine performances throughout, including Richard Widmark, Carroll Baker, Edward G. Robinson and Karl Malden. Not given much dialogue, Mineo's renegade Cheyenne brave is beefcake window dressing, but he's stalwart nonetheless. ⊛

The Greatest Story Ever Told

(1965, 141 min, US, George Stevens)
An all-star cast highlights this glossy though sluggish biblical epic about the life of Jesus (Max von Sydow). Cameos and supporting players include John Wayne as the Roman centurian overseeing Christ's crucifixion (hope we didn't give away the ending), Charlton Heston, Angela Lansbury, Sidney Poitier and Jose Ferrer. Amid the calculated reverence, Mineo manages to be touching as a "cripple" whom Jesus cures. ⊛

▼ Who Killed Teddy Bear?

(1965, 91 min, US, Joseph Cates)
This seamy thriller only occasionally delivers. Mineo plays a psychotic busboy at a swinging disco who stalks the club's beautiful hostess (Juliet Prowse). Elaine Stritch plays the bar's lesbian owner who in one scene puts the move on an uninterested Prowse.

Krakatoa, East of Java

(1969, 101 min, US, Bernard L. Kowalski)
A very unlively adventure film with Mineo as the latter half of a father and son balloonist team. They, Maximilian Schell, Diane Baker, Brian Keith and Rosanna Brazzi (as Mineo's dad) are in search of lost treasure.

Escape from the Planet of the Apes

(1971, 97 min, US, J. Lee Thompson)
In the third entry of the *Apes* series, futuristic simians Mineo, Roddy McDowall and Kim Hunter travel back in time to present-day Los Angeles. As Milo, Mineo isn't around too long. ⊛

ALLA NAZIMOVA

Emigrating from her native Russia in 1905, Alla Nazimova (1879-1945) became a beguiling and uniquely original actress of the New York stage. And although her talents were not best suited to the romantic melodramas and light comedies of the time, she also enjoyed a popular, if brief, film career. The sound of her exotic name combined with her raven-haired sultry persona stood in startling contrast to her contemporaries, like Mary Pickford, Mae Marsh and Lillian & Dorothy Gish — all of whom projected an innocent, Pollyana, all-American look. Nazimova was the first student of Stanislavsky to star in American film and theatre, and she was also the first to create — by promoting herself simply as "Nazimova" — an image of a film artiste. Her classical training resulted initially in an acting style noted for its realism. But as the years went by and Nazimova continued in the ingenue roles that she was much too old to play, her acting became overly affected resulting in an increasingly theatrical (even camp) performances (see *Salome*) that soon wore heavy with film audiences.

As her career flourished in the late 1910s and early '20s, she also became more bold in flaunting her bohemian lifestyle. Her famed mansion on Sunset Boulevard called "The Garden of Alla" became the site of many outlandish parties and the discreet meeting place for actors wanting to let their hair down. She also became the unofficial hostess of Hollywood's lesbian community and although married, her sexual interests varied, with her most notable relationship being with set and costume designer Natasha Rambova, with whom she collaborated on six films. As an ironic trivia note, she was also Nancy Reagan's godmother.

Nazimova married a Russian actor shortly before the two of them organized a repertory acting troupe and took it on a tour of the United States, where they performed to mostly Russian audiences. But while he stayed a few years and then returned to Russia, Nazimova remained. Determined to become an American star, Nazimova studied English and received her first screen credit in the 1916 film *War Brides* (GB title: *Motherhood*). She soon signed a contract with Metro, and with it, became known as an adept businesswoman as well as an ambitious actress, securing from the studio an extraordinary contract that called for a huge salary, her own production unit, and final approval on all stories, cast and directors. One of her most acclaimed roles was in the 1919 film *The Red Lantern*, a romantic drama set during the Boxer Rebellion in China, playing a dual role: an

Eurasian who becomes Queen of the Boxers and her English half-sister. After completing *Camille* in 1921 and the role of Nora in *A Doll's House* in 1922, Nazimova decided not to re-sign with Metro, choosing instead to produce her own movies with her own money. Her first (and last) production was the now famous *Salome*, her fanciful and quite homosexual interpretation of the Oscar Wilde play. Today, the film is considered a classic of avant-garde silent cinema; and though it was critically well-received, it cost Nazimova most of her fortune, a financial and emotional situation from which she never fully recovered.

She reentered the studio fold soon after, but — like Louise Brooks was to learn several years later — Hollywood can be a vindictive and unforgiving place. After being featured in three wholly unremarkable films — *Madonna of the Streets* (1924), *The Redeeming Sin* (1924) and *My Son* (1925) — she left Hollywood and resumed her stage career in New York and Europe, where she directed acclaimed versions of Ibsen classics and avant-garde works. She would return years later, at the urging of George Cukor, to work as a consultant on his film *Zaza* in 1939, and would enjoy several supporting roles until her death including playing mother to both Robert Taylor in *Escape* (1940) and Tyrone Power in the 1941 version of *Blood and Sand*.

Additional films starring Nazimova:
Revelation (1918), *Toys of Fate* (1918), *An Eye for an Eye* (1919), *Out of the Fog* (1919), *The Brat* (1919), *Stronger Than Death* (1920), *Heart of a Child* (1920), *Madame Peacock* (1920), *Billions* (1920), *The Bridge of San Luis Rey* (1944), *In Our Time* (1944) and *Since You Went Away* (1945)

▼ Salome *(1922, 35 min, US)*

Nazimova directed (under her husband Charles Bryant's name) this extravagant version of the Oscar Wilde play, with sets and costumes by Valentino's wife (and Nazimova's lover) Natasha Rambova (she based her work on the drawings of Aubrey Beardsley). Sensual and wildly stylized, the story of Herod's vixen stepdaughter who danced for the head of John the Baptist is even more outrageous here than in Ken Russell's entertainingly over-the-top *Salome's Last Dance*. Reportedly, the film was made with an all-gay/lesbian cast and crew. ☺

"The acting is excellent...an unusual, and at the same time, a visually satisfying spectacle...true dramatic intensity
—*The New York Times*

Salome

NRAMON OVARRO

"Ravishing Ramon," "Valentino's Greatest Rival" and "The Second Valentino" were only some of the publicity-inspired monikers ascribed to the strikingly handsome silent screen star of whom Pola Negri said at the time was "the greatest actor of the screen." His life read like a script: a young Mexican finds fortune and stardom as a leading man on the silver screen, as well as an acclaimed opera singer, film director and eventually a respected character actor in both movies and television. The storybook tale ended in tragedy, however, when a 69-year-old Novarro was found bludgeoned to death in his Laurel Canyon home, the victim of a botched robbery attempt by two hustler brothers picked up by the gay Novarro. His sadly violent end was fraught with rumors and innuendos, including the one in which the instrument of death was a black lead Art Deco dildo given to him by Rudolph Valentino. Known as a warm and generous man who was genuinely well-liked, his gayness, a well-known secret in the Hollywood community, became public after his murder.

Born Jose Ramon Samaniegos (from conquistadors and Aztec nobility as per his publicity material) in Durango, Mexico, in 1899, Ramon moved to the States as a teen and worked for a time both as a busboy and as a movie theatre usher in New York and Los Angeles. He also had a short stint in Vaudeville before beginning his career in the movies. He became an extra and acted in small roles in over 100 movies by the time he was "discovered" in 1922. His rise from obscurity to stardom was the result of Hollywood studios cashing in on the "Latin lover" craze that was spawned by the incredible success of Rudolph Valentino. Director Rex Ingram championed his cause after he played a part in his 1922 film *The Prisoner of Zenda*. His darkly seductive looks and surprisingly strong acting ability led to a contract at MGM where he played either a Latin or Italian in a series of romantic action films. He became very popular during the 1920s yet ironically racism still played a part in his career. One of his more interesting early films was the 1923 *Where the Pavement Ends*. In it, Novarro played a native boy in love with a female missionary. The film was a huge popular success but had a downbeat ending (he died). The immensely powerful exhibitors successfully petitioned MGM to provide a second ending, one in which Novarro, upon discovering that he has some white ancestry, lives and marries the woman.

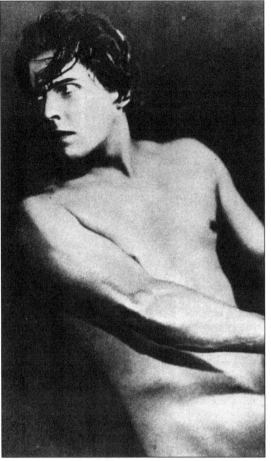

As a galley slave in *Ben Hur*

His greatest and lasting screen success was the lead in the big-budget spectacular *Ben Hur* in 1926, in which the sight of a near-naked Novarro as muscular galley slave Judah set many a woman and closet case's heart aflutter. Although the film was a box-office smash, Novarro's subsequent films, with the exception of *The Student Prince in Old Heidelberg*, were unexceptional.

With the advent of the talkies, Novarro continued to receive roles but with the public thirsting for new faces, he retired from films after his contract at MGM ran out. With his considerable savings as a safety net, he began a new career in music, becoming an opera singer and touring both the States and Europe. In the 1930s, he also directed Spanish versions of many of his American films including *La Sevillana* in 1930 and *Contra la Corriente* in 1936.

During the 1950s and '60s, he lived in his estate in Laurel Canyon near Studio City, appearing frequently as a character actor in films and television. His last film appearance was in George Cukor's *Heller in Pink Tights* in 1960, and on an episode of the television show "The Wild, Wild West" in 1968, playing a Mexican bandito.

In addition to the over 100 films Ramon Novarro appeared in before 1922, he also starred in the following:

The Goat (1922), *Scaramouche* (1923), *The Arab* (1924), *The Midshipmen* (1925), *Across to Singapore* (1928), *Forbidden Hours* (1928), *The Pagan* (1929), *Call of the Flesh* (1930), *Song of India* (1931), *The Son-Daughter* (1932), *The Barbarian* (1933), *Laughing Boy* (1934), *The Night Is Young* (1935), *The Sheik Steps Out* (1937), *We Were Strangers* (1948), *The Outriders* (1950) and *Crisis* (1950).

Ben Hur *(1926, 148 min, US, Fred Niblo)*

Novarro is unforgettable in this lavish Hollywood production, one of the greatest spectacles of all time, and a huge international hit when first released. The chariot race and the sea battle have never been equaled for sheer edge-of-your-seat excitement. Originally silent, the film was released with sound effects in 1931 and the video version features the original tinting and toning, plus a two-strip Technicolor sequence. The first half of the film offers Novarro in several semi-naked situations (reportedly an uncut version exists containing much nudity). ☻

The Student Prince in Old Heidelberg
(1927, 105 min, US, Ernst Lubitsch)

This silent film version doesn't really miss the music of Sigmund Romberg's operetta, for it displays a breezy charm which would become known as the "Lubitsch touch." Novarro is effervescent as the heir to the throne who gets to cut loose for the first time now that he's away for college. Everything would have been fine if he hadn't fallen in love with bar-frau Norma Shearer at the fraternity beer bash. ☻

Mata Hari *(1931, 90 min, US, George Fitzmaurice)*

This Greta Garbo star vehicle, in which she is a perilously beguiling WWI spy, also stars Novarro as one of the men entranced by her bewitching beauty. Also with Lionel Barrymore, the film features Novarro uttering the famous line, "What's the matter, Mata?" ☻

The Cat and the Fiddle
(1934, 90 min, US, William K. Howard)

A pleasant Jerome Kern-Oscar Hammerstein operetta starring Jeanette MacDonald as an aspiring actress who falls in love with Novarro, an equally struggling but temperamental composer.

The Big Steal *(1949, 71 min, US, Don Siegel)*

An exciting and slyly humorous cat-and-mouse adventure thriller starring Robert Mitchum, William Bendix, Patric Knowles and Novarro as four desperados on the lam and on the prowl in Mexico after a bank heist in the States. Highly entertaining with a fully satisfying labyrinthine plot. ☻

Francis X. Bushman (l.) lassos Novarro in the original *Ben Hur*

ᴾFRANKLIN PANGBORN

During the 1930s and '40s, Franklin Pangborn was Hollywood's best known "pansy." Appearing in supporting roles in over 100 films, usually as a flustered something-or-other, or a catty so-and-so, Pangborn was second-to-none in playing comedy and portraying effeminate characters who were clearly meant to be gay (the Hayes Code forbad homosexuals on-screen). He made such an impression in this string of comedies that it's difficult to imagine that Pangborn had a successful dramatic career in the theatre years before.

Pangborn (l.) consoles Eddie Bracken (c.) as William Demerest looks on in Preston Sturges' *Hail the Conquering Hero*

Born in 1893 in Newark, New Jersey, Pangborn served as an infrantryman in WWI. In fact, he was a hero at the battle of the Argonne, and was near-fatally gassed before the war's end. It was in the pre-war years that Pangborn began his professional career, appearing on the New York stage. After the war, he returned to New York, and in 1920, moved to Hollywood, continuing his theatre work there. Pangborn's resume included silent films, and a number of successful tours around the country, including one with Alla Nazimova. He also founded a local Los Angeles theatre company. In the early 1930s, he began appearing in sound films, and after a role in *International House*, turned to comedy. After that film, he became typecast as the sissy, a role he would always play with a straight face. And though he was playing what on paper were routine Hollywood stereotypes, Pangborn always demonstrated a splendid sense of comic timing which belied their stereotypical intent. Pangborn died in 1958 at the age of 65.

In addition to the following selected titles, some of the other films in which Franklin Pangborn appeared are: *Design for Living* (1933); *Young and Beautiful* (1934), starring William Haines; *Swing Hi, Swing Low* (1937); *A Star Is Born* (1937); *Rebecca of Sunnybrook Farm* (1938), starring Shirley Temple; *Vivacious Lady* (1938); *Carefree* (1938), with Fred Astaire and Ginger Rogers; *Topper Takes a Trip* (1938); Preston Sturges' *Christmas in July* (1940), *The Palm Beach Story* (1942) and *Sullivan's Travels* (1942); *Now, Voyager* (1942); *Holy Matrimony* (1943); and *The Horn Blows at Midnight* (1945).

International House
(1933, 70 min, US, A. Edward Sutherland)
Pangborn plays the harried manager of a hotel that crazy inventors W.C. Fields, George Burns, Gracie Allen and Bela Lugosi are calling home. ☮

My Man Godfrey
(1936, 95 min, US, Gregory LaCava)
In one of his best comic roles, Pangborn plays a flustered society organizer who tries to keep order while Carole Lombard and family, and other society types, engage in a frivolous scavenger hunt. A classic screwball comedy. ☮

Stage Door
(1937, 92 min, US, Gregory LaCava)
Pangborn makes the most of his few scenes as theatrical producer Adolphe Menjou's nearly acrobatic butler who also doubles as an escort (don't call him "stooge," he hates that word). ☮

Easy Living *(1937, 86 min, US, Mitchell Leisen)*
In a substantial supporting role, Pangborn ably plays a gossipy shop manager who helps ignite the false rumors of a love affair between working girl Jean Arthur and Wall Street magnate Edward Arnold ("Where there's smoke, there must be...somebody smoking"). ☮

Hail the Conquering Hero
(1944, 101 min, US, Preston Sturges)
Possibly Pangborn at his best. As a small town dignitary, Pangborn reaches inspired heights of comic madness as the organizer of mistaken hero Eddie Bracken's homecoming parade. All this takes place in the film's first 15 minutes. Thankfully, his role doesn't end there. A very funny performance. ☮

ANTHONY PERKINS

Though he made over 40 films, Anthony Perkins will always be remembered for one role: the crazed killer Norman Bates in Alfred Hitchcock's *Psycho*. It's an instance in which an actor became so identifiable with one role it was difficult or impossible to shed that particular character's image. It followed Perkins to the end of his acting career.

The son of Osgood Perkins, a noted actor of the early 20th century, Anthony was born in New York in 1932. He started acting as a teenager in summer stock, which led to his film debut in 1953's *The Actress*. Afterward, he appeared on TV, and on Broadway in "Tea and Sympathy," taking over for John Kerr. In 1955, he auditioned for *East of Eden*, obviously not getting the role. But a year later he did get the role of Gary Cooper's son in *Friendly Persuasion*, which brought him national attention, not to mention an Academy Award nomination.

Perkins was painfully shy, and not coincidentally many of his early roles shared this characteristic. It is in these parts in which Perkins excelled; his best performances (*Persuasion*, *Fear Strikes Out*, *The Matchmaker* among them) are founded in the sensitive young man mold. After the tremendous success in 1960 of *Psycho*, Perkins landed few good parts, due in large part to his identification as Norman Bates. In the 1970s, a more mature Perkins fared much better appearing in a series of character parts either in lead or secondary roles. He also co-wrote with Stephen Sondheim the thriller *The Last of Sheila*.

In the late 1980s, Perkins contracted AIDS, and like other actors, kept his status private in order to keep working (at this same time, the sensationalistic tabloid *National Enquirer* revealed that Perkins was HIV-positive). Before his death in 1992 at the age of 60, Perkins commented, "There are many who believe that this disease is God's vengeance, but I don't. I believe it was sent to teach people how to live and understand and have compassion for each other." In an 1983 interview with *People*, Perkins said he had numerous gay affairs, but termed them "unsatisfying." Perkins married late in life, and is survived by his widow and two children.

The Actress *(1953, 91 min, US, George Cukor)*
Based on Ruth Gordon's autobiographical play "Years Ago," Perkins made his film debut playing a shy suitor to Jean Simmons' aspiring actress.

Friendly Persuasion
(1956, 137 min, US, William Wyler)
Perkins received an Oscar nomination for his splendid work as the sensitive, headstrong son of Quakers Gary Cooper and Dorothy McGuire who are trying to maintain their religious beliefs in pre-Civil War Indiana. An absorbing adaptation of Jessamyn West's novel, expertly directed by William Wyler. ⊛

The Lonely Man
(1957, 87 min, US, Henry Levin)
It's almost funny to hear Perkins spout Norman Bates-like devotion to his dead mother in this pre-*Psycho* role. Jack Palance stars as Perkins' father, a notorious outlaw, who returns to rekindle a relationship with his unforgiving son. The scene in which Palance lassos and hog-ties Perkins has got to be seen to be believed. ⊛

Fear Strikes Out
(1957, 100 min, US, Robert Mulligan)
In his first starring role, Perkins offers a superlative performance as Red Sox outfielder Jimmy Piersall. Karl Malden also stands out in this unflinching biography as Piersall's father whose expectations on his son precipitate the youth's mental breakdown. ⊛

The Tin Star
(1957, 92 min, US, Anthony Mann)
Perkins plays the newly appointed sheriff to a small Western community. Henry Fonda is a former lawman who takes Perkins under his wing when trouble hits town.

Desire Under the Elms
(1958, 111 min, US, Delbert Mann)
A curiously uneven though seductive adaptation of Eugene O'Neill's drama. Set in mid-19th-century New England, the film stars Perkins as the son of farmer Burl Ives. He begins an affair with his stepmother (the miscast but alluring Sophia Loren). ⊛

This Angry Age
(1958, 111 min, US/Italy, Rene Clement)
Jo Van Fleet is the owner of an Indochinese rice field who struggles against the odds to farm the land. Perkins plays her son, and Silvana Mangano is his sister.

The Matchmaker
(1958, 100 min, US, Joseph Anthony)
Perkins' first stab at comedy is a rousing success in this enchanting film version of Thornton Wilder's hit play. Perkins plays Cornelius Hackl, grocery store head clerk, who finds love and happiness on a spree in New York City. Shirley Booth is a joy in the title role, the one and only Dolly Levi; and Shirley MacLaine and Robert Morse also star. The basis for the musical "Hello, Dolly." ⊛

Green Mansions
(1959, 104 min, US, Mel Ferrer)
Perkins is too restrained to fully bring to life his role of a fortune-hunting refugee who happens upon strange bird girl Audrey Hepburn in the Venezuelan jungle. An oddity at best. ☮

On the Beach
(1959, 134 min, US, Stanley Kramer)
One of the first cautionary tales of nuclear annihilation is also one of the best. In this first-rate adaptation of Nevil Shute's novel, Perkins plays a young Australian naval officer who finds love a little too late. Gregory Peck plays an American submarine commander, and Ava Gardner and Fred Astaire (in his dramatic debut) also star. ☮

Tall Story *(1960, 91 min, US, Joshua Logan)*
Jane Fonda made her film debut opposite Perkins in this light-weight but appealing comedy based on the Howard Lindsay-Russell Crouse play. Tony appears as a college basketball star who catches the eye of co-ed Jane. ☮

Psycho *(1960, 109 min, US, Alfred Hitchcock)*
What more can you say of Hitchcock's classic horror film about Kansas motel proprietor Norman Bates than it has forever altered the sanctity of the shower — not to mention tainting the reputations of taxidermists and loving sons everywhere. Perkins played Norman with such eerie perfection that it would shadow him the rest of his career. ☮

Goodbye Again
(1961, 120 min, US, Anatole Litvak)
Three-hanky soaper starring Ingrid Bergman as a middle-aged woman torn between law student Perkins and rich playboy Yves Montand. ☮

Phaedra
(1962, 116 min, US/Greece, Jules Dassin)
Perkins turns the head of another stepmother (as he did in *Desire Under the Elms*) in this updating of Euripides' "Hippolytus." Melina Mercouri plays the wife of shipping tycoon Raf Vallone; Tony is her stepson. They begin an affair. Good performances compensate for the sometimes heavy-handed material.

Five Miles to Midnight
(1962, 110 min, France/Italy, Anatole Litvak)
A visually stylish if muddled thriller starring Perkins and Sophia Loren. Tony is believed dead, so he devises a scam and forces terrified wife Sophia to collect his insurance money. But who do you think gets the last laugh?

The Trial
(1962, 115 min, France/Italy/Germany, Orson Welles)
Franz Kafka's nightmarish novel of a man arrested for a crime that is never explained to him is brilliantly adapted by Welles. Perkins is excellent in the starring role as Joseph K., a sensitive clerk pursued by a repressive bureaucracy, obsessed by an undefined guilt, and bewildered by the burden of living. Welles maintained complete artistic control over the project, and the result is a difficult but unforgettable expressionistic mood piece. ☮

The Fool Killer
(1965, 100 min, US, Servando Gonzalez)
Shortly after the Civil War, an abused child (Edward Albert) runs away from home and befriends an amnesiac war veteran (Perkins) — who may or may not be a mythical killer. A moody, provocative mystery drama. ☮

The Ravishing Idiot
(1965, 99 min, France, Edouard Molinaro)
Perkins stars in this slapstick caper comedy as a bungling bank clerk who, with walking disaster area Brigitte Bardot, unwittingly becomes involved with a Soviet spy ring. Edouard Molinaro also directed the first two *La Cage aux Folles* films. ☮

EXPLORING the BLACKNESS of the SUBCONSCIOUS MAN!

ALFRED HITCHCOCK'S MASTERFUL TALE OF TERROR and SUSPENSE...
A PARAMOUNT RELEASE

"PSYCHO"

starring
ANTHONY PERKINS · VERA MILES · JOHN GAVIN · and JANET LEIGH
MARTIN BALSAM · JOHN McINTIRE · as MARION CRANE

Is Paris Burning?

(1966, 185 min, US/France, René Clément)

Perkins is one of the many all-stars in this epic telling of the Nazi occupation of Paris and of its subsequent liberation. The cast includes Charles Boyer, Yves Montand, Orson Welles, Alain Delon, Jean-Paul Belmondo, Kirk Douglas and Glenn Ford. ⊛

The Champagne Murders

(1967, 107 min, France, Claude Chabrol)

This confusing murder mystery has a lot of style to it, thanks to director Claude Chabrol's deft touch. It has something to do with a corporation buying out a champagne company, and a mysterious series of murders. Perkins stars with Maurice Ronet and Stéphane Audran. (Also known as: *Le Scandale*)

Perkins with Tuesday Weld in *Play It as It Lays*

Pretty Poison

(1968, 89 min, US, Noel Black)

Perkins and Tuesday Weld offer a pair of splendid performances in this sly and ferociously entertaining black comedy/thriller. Perkins plays a disturbed parolee from an unnamed institution who teams with beautiful and innocent cheerleader Weld. She takes to the dark side quicker than you can say Darth Vader.

Catch-22 *(1970, 121 min, US, Mike Nichols)*

Perkins began a series of terrific character performances with a smashing portrayal of the ineffectual Chaplain Tappman in this powerful and subversively funny adaptation of Joseph Heller's anti-war novel. Alan Arkin stars as Yossarian, an American pilot stationed in the Mediterranean during WWII who is caught up in the absurdities of military life. Martin Balsam, Jon Voight, Richard Benjamin and Orson Welles are but a few of the all-star cast. ⊛

WUSA *(1970, 114 min, US, Stuart Rosenberg)*

In one of the best kept secrets of '70s cinema, Paul Newman stars in this exceptional political satire as a drifter who becomes a D.J. on a right-wing New Orleans radio station. Joanne Woodward also stars as his girlfriend. Both offer solid performances. However, it is Perkins' outstanding portrayal of a left-wing revolutionary which propels the film to dizzying heights. One of Perkins' best performances.

Ten Days Wonder

(1971, 101 min, France, Claude Chabrol)

Perkins stars in this Ellery Queen adaptation as a mentally and emotionally disturbed man who falls in love with his father's (Orson Welles) young bride (Marlene Jobert). A bewildering mystery of madness, adultery and blackmail, this distinctly original work should prove enjoyable to fans of the avant-garde and director Claude Chabrol. ⊛

Someone Behind the Door

(1971, 97 min, France/US, Nicolas Gessner)

Perkins plays a neurosurgeon who does a little tinkering on amnesiac Charles Bronson in a plot to murder his unfaithful wife (Jill Ireland). (Also known as: *Two Minds for Murder*) ⊛

The Life and Times of Judge Roy Bean

(1972, 120 min, US, John Huston)

Paul Newman plays the legendary outlaw in this not-quite-a-western. It's an interesting, unusually self-aware but uneven film with a star-studded cast including Jacqueline Bisset, Tab Hunter, Ned Beatty, Roddy McDowall, Stacy Keach, and Ava Gardner as Lily Langtry. Perkins is marvelously understated as a roving preacher whose demeanor suggests traveling performer rather than evangelist. ⊛

▼ Play It as It Lays

(1972, 94 min, US, Frank Perry)

Perkins and Tuesday Weld's riveting performances compliment each other in this aimless but nevertheless intense adaptation of Joan Didion's novel. Weld plays an actress undergoing a mental collapse and Perkins is her best friend, a suicidal gay producer; together they seek the meaning of life, but come up empty-handed. Though not a commendable character, Perkins brings an admirable conviction to his role.

Lovin' Molly *(1974, 98 min, US, Sidney Lumet)*

Atmospheric film version of Larry McMurtry's novel, sort of a western *Jules and Jim*. Perkins and buddy Beau Bridges are Texas farmboys who spend a lifetime lovin' Molly (exceptionally played by Blythe Danner). A charming, quirky film featuring a fine performance by Perkins.

Murder on the Orient Express
(1974, 127 min, GB, Sidney Lumet)
Agatha Christie's novel makes for a lavish mystery. Perkins is one of the many all-stars who try to figure who killed nasty industrialist Richard Widmark. Perkins plays Widmark's neurotic secretary. Albert Finney nicely plays detective Hercule Poirot. Lauren Bacall, Sean Connery, Vanessa Redgrave, John Gielgud and Ingrid Bergman are some of the other suspects. ⊛

▼ Mahogany *(1975, 109 min, US, Berry Gordy)*
An inferior, even ridiculous drama set in the fashion world with Diana Ross making it big as a model. Billy Dee Williams is her boyfriend, a community activist who disapproves of her profession. Looking like a fey Bernard Goetz, Perkins plays the photographer who discovers her and then goes all bitchy and neurotic when she rebukes his romantic overtures. Perkins' character is supposedly bisexual, as gossipy associates infer, and from the suggestion of a fight scene — which looks like a bad imitation of the wrestling match in *Women in Love* — between Perkins and Williams in which the latter inserts a phallic-shaped gun in the mouth of his almost willing adversary. Daniel Daniele plays Giuseppe, a hanky-waving fashion agency manager. ⊛

Remember My Name
(1978, 95 min, US, Alan Rudolph)
A moody, noir-ish drama with Geraldine Chaplin as a woman who is released from prison after 12 years. Having taken the blame for her husband's crime, she exacts a cool revenge against him. Perkins plays her ex. Both give sturdy portrayals in this stylish melodrama which suggests an updating of a 1940s Barbara Stanwyck movie. The film features a terrific score by blues great Alberta Hunter.

Les Miserables
(1978, 150 min, GB, Glenn Jordan)
First-rate made-for-TV production of Victor Hugo's classic novel. Perkins plays the relentless police inspector Javert to Richard Jordon's petty thief Valjean. ⊛

▼ Winter Kills
(1979, 97 min, US, William Richert)
A rare example of a film so wild, rambunctious and so bursting with energy it almost defies description. Jeff Bridges stars as Nick Keegan, a sole innocent searching for clues to the decade-old assassination of his half-brother, a Kennedy-esque president. Perkins has a small but pivotal role as the overseer of the Keegan family affairs. John Huston, as a Joseph Kennedy-type patriarch, says to son Bridges, "As a boy I was afraid you'd turn out to be a fag." Belinda Bauer plays Bridges' bisexual girlfriend. Eli Wallach plays a gay underworld figure who may have murdered the president (shades of *JFK*). Elizabeth Taylor has a small cameo as a famous actress who was once involved with the slain leader. ⊛

The Black Hole
(1979, 97 min, US, Gary Nelson)
Disney's answer to *Star Wars* is a slight but effective sci-fi adventure about a space expedition which comes in conflict with mad scientist Maximilian Schell. Perkins plays one of the crew (which includes Robert Forster, Ernest Borgnine and Joseph Bottoms). The film features a fine score by John Barry. ⊛

ffolkes
(1980, 99 min, US, Andrew V. McLaglen)
High-seas action with Perkins chewing the scenery as the leader of a group of terrorists who have taken over a supply ship. Roger Moore is the disheveled hero out to stop them. ⊛

Psycho II
(1983, 113 min, US, Richard Franklin)
Sporting an "if you can't beat them" attitude, Perkins gives in to the ghost of Norman Bates and reprises his famous role 23 years after the fact. Norman returns from the asylum, and tries to keep his hands (not to mention the shower) clean. Needless to say, it's not a very welcome home. ⊛

Crimes of Passion
(1984, 112 min, GB, Ken Russell)
Ken Russell's sizzling tale of sexual repression features Perkins in a showy turn as a deranged street preacher who travels to hell and back to save the soul of fashion designer-by-day/hooker-by-night Kathleen Turner. The film overflows with camp humor and bizarre twists. ⊛

▼ Twice a Woman
(1985, 90 min, The Netherlands, George Sluzier)
A divorced couple (Perkins and Bibi Andersson) begin separate affairs, unknowingly with the same woman (Sandra Dumas). ⊛

Psycho III *(1986, 96 min, US, Anthony Perkins)*
Perkins gets to direct for the first time as the Bates Motel is open for business, once more. It's all old hat by now, but Perkins' over-the-top performance makes it all quite entertaining. Norman becomes attracted to his new assistant (Diana Scarwid), who bears a striking resemblance to the ill-fated Marion Crane. The accent is on comedy and thrills ⊛

Edge of Sanity
(1988, 90 min, GB, Gerald Kikoine)
An inept Dr. Jekyll/Mr. Hyde horror spin-off with a bug-eyed Perkins as a doctor who accidentally concocts a mixture that turns him into a pasty-faced killer with a predilection for sleazy prostitutes. Set in Victorian London, this updating of the Stevenson classic offers few thrills and is not even enjoyable on a camp level. ⊛

Psycho IV *(1990, 96 min, US, Mick Garris)*
In Perkins' final film, he reprises the role of Norman Bates one last time. Norman gets hooked on talk radio, and soon recounts his childhood. Henry Thomas plays the young Norman living with his widowed, schizophrenic mother (Olivia Hussey). ⊛

P TYRONE OWER

Coming from a multi-generational theatrical family, Tyrone Power was born in Cincinnati in 1913. His father was a noted stage actor, his grandfather was a celebrated pianist, and his great-grandfather was a famous comedian in his native Ireland. There was ever little doubt as to what career young Tyrone would choose. After living in both Ohio and New York, his family moved to California when Power was seven because of the youth's ill health. After graduating high school, Power attended a Shakespearean drama school, and his first professional role was on the Chicago stage in a production of "The Merchant of Venice."

Power moved to New York in 1935, making his Broadway debut in 1936. It was his numerous stage appearances which led to a contract with 20th Century-Fox, and in 1936, Power moved to Hollywood to begin his film career (though he had appeared in one other film in 1932, *Tom Brown of Culver*, while visiting Los Angeles as a teenager). The exceptionally handsome Power became a star with his third Fox film, *Lloyds of London*, and for fifteen years afterward, was one of the studio's biggest box-office draws, except for the years (1942 thru 1945) he served as a Marine pilot in WWII. Though Power was very popular in the movies, he never turned his back on the theatre, and often returned to the Broadway stage and other theatrical venues for most of his life.

While living in New York in the years prior to his budding film career, Power was lovers with Robin Thomas, the stepson of John Barrymore. Their relationship lasted for several years, and was ended by Power when he moved to Hollywood. He soon married actress Annabella, which ended in divorce, and married twice thereafter. Rock Hudson was godfather to Power's son, Tyrone III. Hector Arce's "The Secret Life of Tyrone Power" more fully delves into Power's relationships with both men and women. Among the many reports on Power's personal life is that he had brief affairs with Errol Flynn and Lorenz Hart, among others; and was lovers with an unnamed actor and co-star who was Fox's biggest star of the 1940s. On the set of *Solomon and Sheba*, Power died of a heart attack at the age of 45.

Tyrone Power

Tom Brown of Culver
(1932, 82 min, US, William Wyler)
Still a teenager, Power made his film debut in a small part as a cadet. Tom Brown plays the similarly named title character, and the film also features, in another small role, Alan Ladd.

Girls' Dormitory
(1936, 66 min, US, Irving Cummings)
Power received ninth billing, but his small role in a nightclub sequence generated tons of mail, leading to a sizable role in his next film.

Ladies in Love
(1936, 97 min, US, Edward H. Griffith)
The first pairing of Power and frequent leading lady Loretta Young. Tyrone plays a wealthy nobleman whom working girl Loretta falls in love with. Also with Janet Gaynor and Don Ameche.

Lloyds of London
(1936, 115 min, US, Henry King)
Power's first lead role, and it made him a star. He plays the founder of the famous British insurance company.

Love Is News *(1937, 72 min, US, Tay Garnett)*
Power and Loretta Young reteamed for this screwball comedy with heiress Young announcing her ficticious engagement to reporter Power, who's been writing annoying articles about her.

FAVORITE STARS

Cafe Metropole
(1937, 83 min, US, Edward H. Griffith)
Gambler Power owes nightclub owner Adolphe Menjou big time, so he's forced to impersonate a Russian prince and woo heiress Loretta Young.

Thin Ice *(1937, 78 min, US, Sidney Lanfield)*
Ski instructor Sonja Henie falls in love with prince Power, unaware he's royalty.

Second Honeymoon
(1937, 84 min, US, Walter Lang)
With a nod to *Private Lives*, Power and Loretta Young are a divorced couple who reunite while on vacation and rekindle that old flame. Only problem: she remarried.

In Old Chicago
(1938, 115 min, US, Henry King)
One of Fox's biggest films of the 1930s is an impressive, if fictionalized account of the great Chicago Fire of 1871. Power plays Mrs. O'Leary's playboy son; Don Ameche plays her other son, the mayor. Alice Brady won an Oscar as Mrs. O'Leary. ⊛

Alexander's Ragtime Band
(1938, 105 min, US, Henry King)
Funtime Irving Berlin musical with Power as a bandleader who finds success with his music, but not much with singer Alice Faye. Don Ameche plays their pianist. ⊛

Marie Antoinette
(1938, 149 min, US, W.S. Van Dyke II)
Power plays lover to Norma Shearer's French queen in this lavish historical epic. Robert Morley is excellent as Louis XVI, and John Barrymore also stars. ⊛

Suez *(1938, 100 min, US, Allan Dwan)*
A historical drama which plays fast and loose with the facts. Power plays engineer Ferdinand De Lesseps, the engineer of the Suez Canal. He falls in love with Loretta Young, who would become Empress Eugenie. Co-stars Power's real-life wife, Annabella. ⊛

Rose of Washington Square
(1939, 86 min, US, Gregory Ratoff)
Thinly disguised biography of Fanny Brice, with Alice Faye as the singer and Power as "Nicky Arnstein." Al Jolson co-stars, basically playing himself. Some entertaining musical numbers.

Jesse James
(1939, 105 min, US, Henry King)
Exciting western adventure about the lives of bandit Jesse James (Power) and his brother Frank (Henry Fonda). Followed by a sequel, *Return of Frank James*, with Fonda reprising his role. ⊛

Second Fiddle
(1939, 85 min, US, Sidney Lanfield)
Movie publicist Power falls in love with the skating instructor (Sonja Henie) he's making a film star.

The Rains Came
(1939, 103 min, US, Clarence Brown)
The special effects department worked overtime for this story of an Indian doctor (Power), involved with socialite Myrna Loy, trying to aid his people after the earthquakes, flood and plague hit. ⊛

Daytime Wife
(1939, 71 min, US, Gregory Ratoff)
Uneven comedy with Power as an executive whose wife Linda Darnell, suspecting her husband of infidelity, takes a job as a secretary to playboy architect Warren William.

Johnny Apollo
(1940, 94 min, US, Henry Hathaway)
Straight-laced Power turns to a life of crime to help his dad, convicted embezzler/broker Edward Arnold. Dorothy Lamour is the gangster's moll whom Power falls for. ⊛

Brigham Young
(1940, 110 min, US, Henry Hathway)
Power plays a Mormon pioneer in this story of the religious leader (played by Dean Jagger) heading a trek across the country in the early 19th century to find a territory to settle, safe from religious persecution.

The Mark of Zorro
(1940, 93 min, US, Rouben Mamoulian)
Power's first attempt at swashbuckling, and he proves himself quite adept at it. He takes on an oppressive dictatorship, and tangles with the evil Basil Rathbone, always a worthy opponent with or without a sword. ⊛

A Yank in the RAF
(1941, 93 min, US, Henry King)
Power had one of his best roles as a cocky American flier who joins the British Air Force. Betty Grable co-stars as his girlfriend, a singer who's performing in London.

Blood and Sand
(1941, 124 min, US, Rouben Mamoulian)
A gorgeous looking and exciting remake of the Rudolph Valentino 1922 silent classic. Power plays a naive bullfighter who gets led astray by the sultry Rita Hayworth. Linda Darnell is the woman who loves him from afar. ⊛

This Above All
(1942, 110 min, US, Anatole Litvak)
Good WWII drama with Power as a British soldier who becomes disillusioned in the war effort. He deserts, and with the help of Joan Fontaine, regains his patriotism.

Son of Fury

(1942, 98 min, US, John Cromwell)
Flavorful adventure yarn with Power as the illegitimate son of a British nobleman who battles his greedy uncle, a tyrannical ship's captain and the South Seas to reclaim his inheritance. Gene Tierney is the island beauty he loves. ⊛

The Black Swan

(1942, 85 min, US, Henry King)
Power is at his swashbuckling best as a pirate captain who tries to go straight, all for the love of governor's daughter Maureen O'Hara. George Sanders co-stars as Redbeard, who stands in Power's way.

Crash Dive *(1943, 105 min, US, Archie Mayo)*

Power's last film before his WWII tour of duty. He plays a naval officer who serves on commander Dana Andrews' submarine. In between daring attacks on the Germans, he falls in love with Andrews' fiancée Anne Baxter. ⊛

The Razor's Edge

(1946, 146 min, US, Edmund Goulding)
Fine adaptation of W. Somerset Maugham's acclaimed novel with a much-matured Power going through heaven and hell in his search for spiritual faith. Gene Tierney co-stars as his shallow, society fiancée. The acting honors go to Clifton Webb as a snobbish society type and Anne Baxter as a heartbreaking alcoholic. ⊛

Captain from Castille

(1947, 140 min, US, Henry King)
Power plays a Spanish nobleman who finds himself up against the Inquisition, a greedy officer and a treacherous journey to the New World. Jean Peters co-stars as his wife, and Cesar Romero is Conquistadore hero Cortez.

Nightmare Alley

(1947, 111 min, US, Edmund Goulding)
Power asks the question, "How do you get a guy to be a geek?," then learns how in this classic noir. Power cheats his way to success as a nightclub spiritualist, only to incur a self-described fate worse than death. Joan Blondell is the mindreader he becomes involved with.

Basil Rathbone (l.) and Power appear to be more than just foes in *The Mark of Zorro*

FAVORITE STARS

The Luck of the Irish

(1948, 99 min, US, Henry Koster)

The puckish Cecil Kellaway steals the show as a lephrechaun in this whimsical comedy. Power plays an American reporter whose vacation to Ireland nets him Kellaway, who travels with him to the States. The magical elf helps Power in his romance with Anne Baxter, and steers his life in the right direction.

That Wonderful Urge

(1948, 81 min, US, Robert Sinclair)

Remake of Power's 1937 comedy *Love Is News*, with Gene Tierney taking over the Loretta Young role. Same plot: Tierney is a socialite who announces she's married to bothersome reporter Power. Slightly more amusing than the original.

Prince of Foxes

(1949, 111 min, US, Henry King)

Set during the Renaissance, the films stars Power as an Italian soldier working for the Borgias who ultimately rebels against the warlord (played by Orson Welles).

The Black Rose

(1950, 120 min, US, Henry Hathaway)

Thirteenth-century Saxon nobleman Power travels the world, meeting warlord Orson Welles while on his way to discover the secrets of China.

An American Guerilla in the Philippines *(1950, 105 min, US, Fritz Lang)*

Stranded naval officer Power helps the growing Filipino underground movement strike back against the Japanese.

Rawhide *(1951, 86 min, US, Henry Hathaway)*

Back in the saddle for the first time since *Jesse James*, Power plays a stagecoach station assistant who with passenger Susan Hayward must fend off the outlaws who've taken them prisoner. ⊛

I'll Never Forget You

(1951, 91 min, US/GB, Roy Baker)

Remake of the 1933 fantasy *Berkeley Square*, with Power reprising the Leslie Howard role. A scientist is transported back to 18th-century England, where he falls in love with a distant cousin (Ann Blyth).

Diplomatic Courier

(1952, 97 min, US, Henry Hathaway)

Intriguing spy thriller with Power as an American agent who is sent to Trieste to investigate the death of a fellow agent. There he meets and falls in love with Patricia Neal.

Pony Soldier

(1952, 81 min, US, Joseph M. Newman)

Power is a member of the Royal Canadian Mounted Police who's assigned liaison between an Indian tribe and the government. A convict held hostage by the Indians complicates matters.

Mississippi Gambler

(1953, 99 min, US, Rudolph Mate)

Set in antebellum New Orleans, the film casts Power as a roguish cardshark. He falls for Southern belle Piper Laurie in-between gambling and a few swordfights in this colorful costumer.

King of the Khyber Rifles

(1953, 99 min, US, Henry King)

Power is a half-caste officer in 1860s India, where he is assigned to quell an uprising led by a childhood friend. Terry Moore is the British commander's daughter he's in love with.

The Long Gray Line

(1955, 135 min, US, John Ford)

John Ford's patriotic biography of West Point athletic trainer Marty Maher makes for a satisfying, if overly sentimental drama. Power plays Maher, the Irishman who spent 50 years at the Point, and Maureen O'Hara co-stars as his wife.

Untamed *(1955, 111 min, US, Henry King)*

Lively adventure film with Power as a Boer commander who battles the Zulus and romances Susan Hayward.

The Eddy Duchin Story

(1956, 123 min, US, George Sidney)

Power ably plays noted pianist Eddy Duchin in this slick but familiar biography. Also with Kim Novak. ⊛

Seven Waves Away

(1956, 100 min, GB, Richard Sale)

An exciting adventure story reminiscent of both *Lifeboat* and *Souls at Sea*. After their luxury liner is sunk, a group of survivors struggle to stay afloat — and alive. Power is the officer in charge. (US title: *Abandon Ship!*)

The Sun Also Rises

(1957, 129 min, US, Henry King)

Uneven but nevertheless compelling version of Ernest Hemingway's novel of American expatriates living in post-WWII Paris. Power plays a reporter in love with society matron Ava Gardner. Errol Flynn made a sensational comeback, and best captures the spirit of Hemingway as a drunken rascal.

Witness for the Prosecution

(1957, 114 min, US, Billy Wilder)

Based on Agatha Christie's hit play, this delightful adaptation proves to be an acting tour-de-force for all involved. Power is on trial for murder, and attorney Charles Laughton is out to prove his innocence. Marlene Dietrich is Power's wife who holds the key to the mystery. Power's final film. ⊛

ELIZABETH TAYLOR

Cat on a Hot Tin Roof

As close to American royalty as is possible, Elizabeth Taylor has had the most remarkable of careers. An award-winning actress and headline maker throughout her life, she has lately devoted herself almost exclusively towards the fight against AIDS, and has even found a little time to be an entrepreneur. She may not have starred in a hit movie since LBJ was in the White House, but her boundless energy and commitment is timeless.

Born in England in 1932, Elizabeth was evacuated at age seven to Amercia at the start of WWII. Living in Los Angeles, she made her film debut when she was ten in *There's a Sucker Born Every Minute.* Appearing in bit roles, young Liz — who was an unusually attractive child — worked her way up the ladder at MGM Studios, and in 1944, 12-year-old Liz had her first great success with a leading role in the classic *National Velvet.* During the course of the 1940s, Liz went from child actress to adolescent star, though none of her films in those years equalled the success of *Velvet.* It was in 1951, however, when Elizabeth Taylor grew up — on-screen, anyway. As the society temptress who lures Montgomery Clift to an ill fate in *A Place in the Sun*, a teenaged Taylor demonstrated a sophistication well beyond her years and — most importantly — a genuine acting talent. The film was a big box-office hit, and it changed the direction Liz's career would go. During the 1950s, Liz proved to be one of its most popular box-office attractions, and as the decade matured, so did Liz. Her beauty was only rivaled by the considerable depth she demonstrated as an actress. In 1957, she received her first Oscar nomination for her performance in *Raintree County*, and received nominations in the next three successive years, capping it with a Best Actress Oscar in 1960.

The various points in Liz's career can be ascribed by decade, and if the 1940s was "Child Star" and the 1950s "Young Actress," the 1960s was "Liz and Dick." The story really began when Liz married Eddie Fisher, who had dumped Debbie Reynolds. Receiving most of the bad press, the media followed Liz's every move. Then in 1963, she met Richard Burton while filming *Cleopatra*, and when the two became romantically involved, the press went into a feeding frenzy. She eventually married Burton, and they became the decade's most famous, talked-about couple while appearing in a string of box-office successes.

However, as is Hollywood's anthem, success is fleeting, and the 1970s marked a down period in Liz's life. Her movies were mostly bombs, she split with Burton (twice), and she went through very public bouts with drug, alcohol and food abuse. But Liz's resilience cannot be undermined, and in the 1980s, movie career behind her, Liz began the most important fight of her life. In 1985, her good friend Rock Hudson had died of AIDS, and his death prompted a tireless battle against the disease for which she is probably most identified in the 1990s.

Those too young to remember Liz in her heyday may associate her only with her determined AIDS fight or her perfume, "Passion." But there is a wonderful acting career, there, too. And for both that and her stance against the disease, and her unyielding support of the gay community, we gladly acknowledge Elizabeth Taylor Hilton Wilding Todd Fisher Burton Burton Warner Fortensky as one of our Favorite Stars.

In addition to the titles whose reviews follow, Elizabeth Taylor has appeared in these films which can be found in their appropriate chapters:

> *The V.I.P.'s* — directed by Anthony Asquith
> *Reflections in a Golden Eye* — starring Marlon Brando
> *Boom!, Secret Ceremony* — directed by Joseph Losey
> *Winter Kills* — starring Anthony Perkins
> *The Taming of the Shrew* — directed by Franco Zeffirelli

Liz had small roles in *There's One Born Every Minute* (1942), *Lassie Come Home* (1943), *Jane Eyre* (1944) and *The White Cliffs of Dover* (1944).

National Velvet
(1944, 125 min, US, Clarence Brown)
Lovely family drama with farm girl Taylor (in her first starring role) and former jockey Mickey Rooney training a wild nag so they can enter it in the Grand National Steeplechase competition. Terrific entertainment. ⊛

Courage of Lassie
(1946, 92 min, US, Fred Wilcox)
Barnyard corn runs rampant as Liz trains Lassie to be nice again after serving in the war as an attack dog. ⊛

Cynthia
(1947, 98 min, US, Robert Z. Leonard)
Overly sentimental drama with Liz as a sickly, over-protected young girl who eventually learns to live her own life through her love of music. (GB title: *The Rich Full Life*)

Life with Father
(1947, 118 min, US, Michael Curtiz)
Liz has a pleasant supporting role in this near-classic comedy set in 1880s New York. William Powell gave one of his best performances as the gruff patriarch of a wealthy Madison Avenue family. Irene Dunne is his patient wife, and Liz plays a distant cousin who becomes romantically involved with Powell and Dunne's eldest son. ⊛

Julia Misbehaves
(1948, 99 min, US, Jack Conway)
Taylor plays second banana to Greer Garson and Walter Pidgeon in this whimsical marital comedy. Liz is a young bride-to-be; her wedding forces the reunion of her estranged parents, well-to-do daddy Pidgeon and actress mother Garson. The film is set at a snappy pace, and the three stars handle the comedy nicely. ⊛

Little Women
(1949, 122 min, US, Mervyn LeRoy)
An amiable second screen version of Louisa May Alcott's classic novel of pre-Civil War life in New England — though George Cukor's 1933 adaptation remains the definitive screen version. June Allyson reprises the Katharine Hepburn role as Jo, and Liz, Janet Leigh and Margaret O'Brien are her younger sisters. ⊛

Conspirator
(1949, 85 min, US, Victor Saville)
In her first adult starring role, Taylor brings a sophistication well beyond her 17 years of age. Visiting London, Liz marries British major Robert Taylor. However, unbeknownst to her, he's really a Communist spy who is dispatching secret information to the party. Mr. Taylor is too old to be playing a 31-year-old, and his stiff acting only further accentuates a weak romantic plot and a tired political thriller. ⊛

The Big Hangover
(1950, 82 min, US, Norman Krasna)
Liz and Van Johnson star in this featherweight comedy, which could be the inspiration for *Blind Date*. Johnson stars as a novice lawyer whose allergy to alcohol causes him to get intoxicated on one sip. Taylor is the boss' daughter who takes a liking to him. ⊛

Father of the Bride
(1950, 93 min, US, Vincente Minnelli)
In this delightful family comedy, Spencer Tracy may have proved the inspiration for every sitcom father who has ever had to deal with a teenager. But few have done it better. The story follows the comedic headaches facing father Tracy and mother Joan Bennett as they prepare for daughter Taylor's wedding. Remade with Steve Martin in 1991. ⊛

Father's Little Dividend
(1951, 82 min, US, Vincente Minnelli)
Cheerful sequel to the hit comedy *Father of the Bride*. Liz, Spencer Tracy, Joan Bennett and Billie Burke all repeat their roles as newlywed Taylor returns home — expecting. Steve Martin is set to appear in a 1995 remake of this sequel. ⊛

A Place in the Sun
(1951, 122 min, US, George Stevens)
An ambitious effort, and one of the few movies of its day to address the subject of class conflict in America. Montgomery Clift gives a great performance as a young man content to climb the social ladder by ordinary means. That is, until he meets rich soci-

ety girl Taylor. Although occasionally heavy and slow-moving, and the impending tragedy is perhaps all-too inevitable, this is still poignant material, and Clift and Taylor express genuine tenderness and passion. Shelley Winters is memorable as the girlfriend who Clift wishes would vanish. ⊛

Love Is Better Than Ever

(1951, 81 min, US, Stanley Donen)
Liz plays a small-town dance teacher who is taught some new moves by big city agent Larry Parks in this ordinary musical comedy. ⊛

Ivanhoe   *(1952, 106 min, US, Richard Thorpe)*

A young and absolutely ravishing Elizabeth stars in this rendition of Walter Scott's epic tale of Saxon honor and Norman villainy during England's Middle Ages. Robert Taylor stars as Ivanhoe, a knight torn between the honorable Rowena and the Jewess Rebecca, who is trying to bring the good King Richard back to England. Joan Fontaine and George Sanders co-star in this beautifully filmed historical drama. ⊛

The Girl Who Had Everything

(1953, 69 min, US, Richard Thorpe)
In this glossy though inferior remake of *A Free Soul*, Taylor plays the daughter of defense attorney William Powell, who numbers among his clients underworld figures. When one of them (Fernando Lamas) falls for Liz, daddy takes his revenge in court. ⊛

Rhapsody   *(1954, 115 min, US, Charles Vidor)*

A beautiful classical score highlights this otherwise routine romantic drama with the impossibly gorgeous Taylor torn between two lovers. Liz plays a spoiled heiress who travels to Zurich to be with Vittorio Gassman, a virtuoso violinist, and becomes involved with pianist John Ericson. Liz's breathless portrayal gives the film its moments of interest. ⊛

Elephant Walk

(1954, 103 min, US, William Dieterle)
A new wife travels to her husband's exotic plantation, where a battle ensues with nature. No, it's not *The Naked Jungle*, which had those neat killer ants, but the inferior *Elephant Walk*, which can only boast rampaging elephants. Taylor joins husband Peter Finch on his Ceylon tea plantation. There, she falls for foreman Dana Andrews, and contends with epidemic, drought, her husband's wrath and the aforementioned pachyderms. ⊛

Beau Brummell

(1954, 113 min, US, Curtis Bernhardt)
Liz looks great in her 19th-century costumes, but nothing else compares in this average costume drama. She plays mistress to British royal advisor George Brummell (Stewart Granger), who himself is at odds with the Prime Minister and Parliament. Peter Ustinov gives a showy turn as the prissy (though *not* gay) Prince of Wales. ⊛

Liz and Montgomery Clift in *A Place in the Sun*

The Last Time I Saw Paris

(1954, 116 min, US, Richard Brooks)
Romance blossoms between a young Army writer (Van Johnson) and a fun-loving socialite (Taylor) in post-war Paris. Donna Reed and Walter Pidgeon co-star. Based on the novel "Babylon Revisited" by F. Scott Fitzgerald. ⊛

Giant   *(1956, 210 min, US, George Stevens)*

Liz is nothing short of radiant as the compassionate wife of headstrong Texas cattleman Rock Hudson. As a neighboring oil tycoon, James Dean also stars in this, one of the biggest box-office hits of the 1950s. ⊛

Raintree County

(1957, 175 min, US, Edward Dmytryk)
Fanciful costume drama set during the Civil War with Taylor as a mentally troubled Southern belle who marries northerner Montgomery Clift. Good supporting cast includes Eva Marie Saint and Rod Taylor. ⊛

Cat on a Hot Tin Roof

(1958, 108 min, US, Richard Brooks)
Everyone has a skeleton in their closet in Tennessee Williams' Pulitzer Prize-winning drama. Taylor sinks her claws into the role of Maggie the Cat, the tormented, sexually frustrated wife of guilt-ridden ex-jock Brick (Paul Newman). The prototypic tale of family conflict and confrontation. The film does not make mention of Brick's homosexuality, which was explored in the play version. ⊛

▼ Suddenly, Last Summer

(1959, 114 min, US, Joseph L. Mankiewicz)
A blistering Tennessee Williams drama (co-scripted by Gore Vidal) about psychiatrist Montgomery Clift investigating what caused Taylor to crack while on summer vacation with Katharine Hepburn's son Sebastian. ⊛

Butterfield 8

(1960, 109 min, US, Daniel Mann)
Taylor won an Oscar (though many say it was because of her nearly dying of pneumonia) for her sultry portrayal of an expensive call girl who lives with her mom and doesn't think she's a prostitute. The film features great histrionics and a swell supporting cast, especially a charmingly slimy Laurence Harvey. A good, old-fashioned soaper with some fine, campy dialogue. ⊛

Cleopatra

(1963, 243 min, US, Joseph L. Mankiewicz)
Notorious epic about the Queen of the Nile. Whether it's more noted for the Taylor-Richard Burton angle (they met and fell in love) or the colossal sum spent on it or the dreary notices it received, the film, though spectacular looking, is a tough four-hour viewing. However, it does feature two award-calibre performances by Rex Harrison (as Ceasar) and Roddy McDowall. ⊛

The Sandpiper

(1965, 117 min, US, Vincente Minnelli)
Minister/schoolmaster Richard Burton is involved in a love triangle with wife Eva Marie Saint and free-spirited artist Taylor. Co-written by Dalton Trumbo. ⊛

Who's Afraid of Virginia Woolf?

(1966, 129 min, US, Mike Nichols)
Liz and Richard Burton deliver career performances as a tortured college professor and his vitriolic wife in Edward Albee's scorching domestic drama. As souls are bared and the lines betweeen truth and illusion are explored, George and Martha (Liz and Dick) are host to a late evening get-together of game playing and emotional revelations. George Segal and Sandy Dennis (at her mousiest) are Nick and Honey, the innocent young couple who are their guests. In this gut-wrenching adaptation full of caustic humor and searing drama, both Liz and Dennis won Oscars for their performances. There was talk in the early 1970s of producing an all-male version for Broadway, but the author vetoed this idea saying that the play wouldn't translate — this also gave Albee voice to contradict many people's assumptions that the play was based on gay characters. ⊛

Focus on: *Edward Albee*

A prolific writer for the stage, three-time Pulitzer Prize-winning author Edward Albee has curiously only had two of his works adapted for the screen: Who's Afraid of Virgina Woolf? *and* A Delicate Balance *(1973). Albee's writing success began in 1959 with the Berlin opening of "The Zoo Story." In 1962, at the age of 32, he enjoyed his first run on Broadway with his much-heralded "Virginia Woolf." Despite success and a critical output of over 27 stage plays, Albee has not reached the prominence that his early works promised. In 1994, his off-Broadway play, "Three Tall Women," won him his third Pulitzer, though it opened to mixed reviews. Although openly gay, Albee does not focus on gay characters (an exception being a separated gay couple in the 1982 play, "Finding the Sun"). He explained in an* Advocate *interview, "I don't like ghettoization of any kind of literature. I find that gay literature, gay theatre and gay playwriting is turning out to be a kind of limitation. Some of the characters are gay, and some are straight. And that's fine, because that's the way life is."*

Dr. Faustus

(1967, 93 min, GB, Richard Burton)
Colorful rendering of the Faustus legend with first-time director Richard Burton in the title role as a man who sells his soul to the devil for personal gain. While not the best telling of the tale, the film is notable for a cameo appearance by the director's wife, Taylor, in the role of "Helen of Troy." ⊛

The Comedians

(1967, 148 min, US, Peter Glenville)
Graham Greene adapted his own novel examining life in Haiti under the Duvalier regime, and the result is an ambitious, over-long, semi-successful film treatment. Richard Burton takes center stage as a cynical hotel owner who unwittingly becomes involved

Suddenly, Last Summer

in the rebel cause. In the film's least successful scenes, Liz plays a diplomat's wife having an affair with Burton. Great support from Alec Guinness, Peter Ustinov, Roscoe Lee Browne, Paul Ford and Lillian Gish. ☺

The Only Game in Town

(1970, 113 min, US, George Stevens)
Based on Frank Gilroy's play, this stagey but intriguing drama casts Liz as a chorus girl and Warren Beatty as a gambler who together find love against the loneliness of Las Vegas' casinos. Beatty gives a good performance; though the film is claustrophobic, no doubt due to being shot in Paris and therefore consisting of mostly indoor shots. ☺

▼ Zee and Company

(1971, 110 min, GB, Brian G. Hutton)
Imagine *Who's Afraid of Virginia Woolf?* with only three protagonists instead of four; this gives an indication of the mind games being played by all involved in this tacky romantic triangle. Guzzling alcohol, cursing and vomiting insults, a catty Liz plays the wife of philandering, well-to-do architect Michael Caine. Onto the scene comes designer Susannah York, who has an affair with Caine. As Liz and Michael do battle in a cheap George-and-Martha imitation, Taylor exacts a sexual revenge when she learns of York's bisexuality. Two minor gay characters include John Standing as Gordon, Liz's "poncy" confidant; and openly gay Michael Cashman (who played Colin, the gay yuppie, in "EastEnders") as Gavin, York's work assistant. (US title: *X, Y and Zee*) ☺

Under Milk Wood

(1972, 90 min, GB, Andrew Sinclair)
Set in lush and visually stunning Wales, this production of Dylan Thomas' classic play is performed with theatrical genius by Taylor, Richard Burton and Peter O'Toole. Thomas' glorious poetry sparkles in this tale of a day in the life of the mythical village of Llareggub. The film has been rightly accused of over-ambitiousness and, indeed, the sense of production does weigh some of the material down. But it still offers a sterling example of ensemble acting from three great thespians. ☺

Divorce His — Divorce Hers

(1972, 144 min, US, Waris Hussein)
The story of a failed marriage in which the couple (Richard Burton and Taylor) gets to tell their individual story of why their marriage failed. ☺

Ash Wednesday

(1973, 99 min, US, Larry Peerce)
Boringly trite melodrama with Taylor as the middle-aged wife of Henry Fonda who undergoes facial plastic surgery and comes out looking...well, like Liz. Helmut Berger is the youthful pick-up to ensure she got her money's worth. ☺

The Driver's Seat

(1973, 101 min, Italy, Giuseppe Patroni Griffi)
Taylor and Andy Warhol star in this complex melodrama. Liz plays a psychotic spinster involved in a series of adventures. (Also known as: *Psychotic*.) ☺

Night Watch

(1973, 105 min, GB, Brian G. Hutton)
As if Liz didn't have enough problems in the '70s, here she plays a widow (who's recovering from a nervous breakdown, no less) who witnesses a murder but can't get anyone to believe her. ☺

A Little Night Music

(1978, 124 min, US, Harold Prince)
A rather mediocre adaptation of the brilliant Tony Award-winning musical written by Stephen Sondheim (which was based on Ingmar Bergman's *Smiles of a Summer Night*). Taylor is miscast as Desiree, the actress who reenters the life of a newly married former beau (Len Cariou, repeating his stage role). Diana Rigg steals the show as the wife of a soldier (Lawrence Guittard) who is having an affair with Desiree. The film captures none of the magic which made the Bergman film and the stage play great hits; though "A Weekend in the Country" is admirably performed. ☺

The Mirror Crack'd

(1980, 105 min, GB, Guy Hamilton)
Before she went sleuthing in "Murder She Wrote," Angela Lansbury appeared as Agatha Christie's crack sleuth Miss Marple in this enjoyable, if slight mystery. Taylor and Kim Novak are well-cast as rival and catty movie queens, and Rock Hudson, Tony Curtis and Geraldine Chaplin round out the cast. Miss Marple becomes involved with show people when Taylor is almost murdered. ☺

The Flintstones

(1994, 105 min, US, Brian Levant)
Liz returned to the big screen after a 14-year absence to appear in the plum role of Fred Flintstone's mother-in-law in this appropriately cartoonish version of the popular TV animated series. John Goodman is Fred, Elizabeth Perkins is Wilma, Rick Moranis is Barney, and Rosie O'Donnell is Betty. This rates a big Yabadabadoo if for no other reason than marking Liz's return to pictures. ☺

T L I L Y O M L I N

An actress, writer and entrepreneur with a most decidedly feminist perspective, Lily Tomlin has had an enduring career in the fields of TV, stage and cinema for over 20 years. Best known for her work in comedy, she has sporadically taken jobs of strictly serious nature. "I make no distinctions between drama and comedy. To me, it's just performing...the difference is maybe stylistically, so you go a little further one way or another depending on the style of the piece, just how close you play it to reality."

Born Mary Jean Tomlin in Detroit in 1930, Lily was raised in a working-class environment. She attended Wayne State University originally as a pre-med student. However, she changed her major to theatre shortly thereafter. She credits her teacher, Peggy Feury, for instilling in her a passion for acting. Lily moved to New York in the mid-1960s, and briefly worked as a secretary to a casting director while performing comedy in Greenwich Village coffeehouses. She made her TV debut in 1966 on "The Gary Moore Show" (which gave series regular Carol Burnett her first chance in the spotlight), and also appeared on "The Merv Griffin Show." It was her performance on the latter — doing a comic bit about "the rubber freak" — which brought her to the attention of the producers of 'Laugh-In.' She once amusingly recalled, "I didn't want to go on "Laugh-In" because I thought it was too hip." For her audition, she used the persnickety telephone operator Ernestine and "The Tasteful Lady." Lily attracted widespread attention from her work on the TV variety series, also creating one of her most beloved characters, Edith Ann, during her second year on the show.

Staying with "Laugh-In" for three years, Tomlin left the series to pursue work in film and theatre, where she was able to fully explore her gift for characterization. Tomlin's first real acclaim came in 1975 with her debut film performance in *Nashville*, which garnered her an Oscar nomination. A year later, she made a spectacular Broadway debut in her one-woman show, "Appearing Nitely." In the years that followed, Tomlin alternated between both mediums. However, her theatrical engagements have brought her more success than her film career as she has appeared in acclaimed/box-office successes

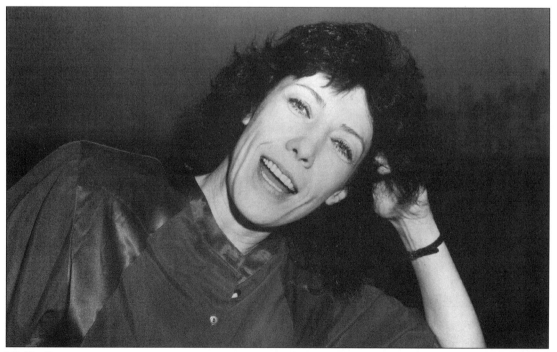

Lily Tomlin

(*The Late Show, All of Me, 9 to 5*) and duds (*Moment by Moment, The Incredible Shrinking Woman*) alike.

In 1992, Tomlin returned to the screen after a four-year absence to start an invigorating second chapter to her film career as a disciplined, accomplished character actress equally adept at both comedy and drama. Lily has shown a clear attraction to playing nurturing, sympathetic individuals, some who are in the throes of trying to come to terms with contradictory morals and beliefs, and she apparently enjoys ensemble acting, having distinguished herself in several movies of this format.

In her theatrical act, Tomlin transforms herself into different characters, both male and female. She's honed this trademark style of stage presentation in collaboration with Jane Wagner, her life partner, writer and producer on solo projects. The characters developed by the pair are generally disenfranchised persons east of a humane light. Their unique schtick is best illuminated in their film version of their Broadway hit, *The Search for Signs of Intelligent Life*, which also provides striking testament to Lily's pure acting ability.

Also in 1992, Lily set up her own company to distribute her performance videos (sometimes working from her own garage), and later set up a distribution deal with Wolfe Video, a small video company specializing in lesbian and feminist films.

Tomlin is currently involved in several projects, including pitching an animated version of Edith Ann as a TV series, and she is active in raising financial support for a cinematic adaptation of Vito Russo's "The Celluloid Closet." Her most recent films include *Blue in the Face*, directed by Wayne Wang and starring Harvey Keitel, Roseanne and Michael J. Fox, and *Getting Away with Murder*, a drama also to star Dan Aykroyd and Jack Lemmon which is set for mid-1995 release.

Saturday Night Live: Lily Tomlin

(1975, 67 min, US)
This early "SNL" episode, with guest host Tomlin, features the infamous Land Shark, an all-female construction crew cruising for beefcake, and John Belushi as Ludwig von Beethoven. ☻

Nashville   *(1975, 159 min, US, Robert Altman)*
Robert Altman's masterful, multi-layered mosaic of 1970s Americana. A wonderful ensemble of 24 characters interact at a Tennessee political rally resulting in comedic and often poignant vignettes. One of the greatest achievements of the decade, the film's stellar cast includes Ronee Blakely, Shelley Duvall, Henry Gibson, Keith Carradine, Barbara Harris, Barbara Baxley and Allen Garfield. Tomlin received an Oscar nomination for her stirring portrait of a gospel singer. Carradine won an Oscar for his song, "I'm Easy." ☻

The Late Show
(1977, 94 min, US, Robert Benton)
Two superior performances by Tomlin and Art Carney highlight this winning mystery comedy written and directed by Robert Benton (*Kramer vs. Kramer*). Carney plays an aging private eye who is thrown together with slightly daffy Tomlin as he investigates the death of his partner. Thoroughly enjoyable and a terrific homage to those great detective mysteries of the 1940s. ☻

Moment by Moment
(1978, 102 min, US, Jane Wagner)
This notorious bomb is probably one moment Tomlin would most like to forget. She plays a bored Malibu wife who begins an affair with beach bum John Travolta.

Lily Tomlin: Appearing Nitely
(1979, 70 min, US, Wendy Apple)
Tomlin's made-for-HBO special is a live recording of her acclaimed one-woman show, "Appearing Nitely." Alternately hilarious and poignant, Lily goes on an almost stream-of-conciousness tear as she mines remembrances from her childhood and youth to create a series of memorable characters and situations. She loses herself in the skits, becoming the shopping bag lady, the bratty adolescent and the geeky suburban girl ready to experiment in the wacked-out '60s. After the performance, the camera ventures backstage for a peek into her dressing room which is filled with famous well-wishers. And keep watching, for at the end there is a wonderful segment of Tomlin accepting an award at the Tony Awards and reliving her lifelong dream, not of stardom, but of becoming a waitress! ☻

9 to 5   *(1980, 110 min, US, Colin Higgins)*
A box-office bonanza, this amusing and topical comedy teams Lily, Jane Fonda and Dolly Parton as secretaries who turn the table on their sexist male boss (Dabney Coleman). As the office manager who trains the male newcomers only to have them get the promotions she's entitled to, Tomlin comes off best; and her cartoon fantasy sequence is a hilarious highlight. ☻

The Incredible Shrinking Woman
(1981, 88 min, US, Joel Schumacher)
In this humorous satire on consumerism and suburbia, Lily plays an average American housewife whose exposure to household products causes her to shrink. Charles Grodin is her hapless husband. Great production design and effects highlight the film. ☻

Lily: Sold Out   *(1981, 50 min, US, Bill Davis)*
Possibly the weakest of Tomlin's performance videos, despite the presence of several of her trademark characters and the cameo performances of Paul Anka, Dolly Parton, Liberace and Joan Rivers. With the lure of gobs of money, Lily agrees to do the "Strip" and venture into the tacky world of Vegas, but she soon finds out that her subtle "message-laden" character comedy is no match for the glitzy pizazz of Vegas superstar-lounge lizard Tommy Velour (Lily doing an on-target spoof of Wayne Newton) and his gaudy,

mega-charged ilk. But Lily decides to sell out and the result is a show that would make any polyester-wearing grandmother from Indiana flush with excitement. ☯

All of Me   *(1984, 93 min, US, Carl Reiner)*
Steve Martin's virtuoso comic performance highlights this very funny comedy about a dying invalid (Tomlin) whose soul is transported into the body of her lawyer (Martin). Tomlin is used to good effect (even if most of her performance is only seen in mirrors) in this bit of inspired silliness. ☯

Big Business
(1988, 97 min, US, Jim Abrahams)
Tomlin teams with Bette Midler in this tame identity switch comedy from the director of *Airplane!* Lily and Bette play two sets of twins switched at birth who are reunited 25 years later in New York. Though it features nice special effects and a few laughs, this is nevertheless a minor comedy for both its talented comediennes. ☯

Lily Tomlin
(1989, 90 min, US, Nick Broomfield & Joan Churchill)
A behind-the-scenes peek into both Lily herself, her longtime collaborator Jane Wagner and her employees. Ostensibly, the film charts the development of her hit Broadway show, "The Search for Signs of Intelligent Life in the Universe," as the show is initiated in tryout and ultimately is reworked to its finished form. Though she signed a contract giving her staff creative control and distribution rights, Tomlin sought — but failed — to win an injunction against the film's release. Lily's favorite characters are here, including Agnes Angst, Mrs. Beasley and Edith Ann, though the film is somewhat toned down due, in part, to the safeguarding Lily is given by her overly protective all-female staff.

The Search for Signs of Intelligent Life in the Universe
(1991, 120 min, US, Jane Wagner)
This delightful and engaging Tony Award-winning, two-hour, one-woman show can easily be considered Tomlin's magnus opus. The show centers around Trudy the Bag Lady as she escorts a group of visiting aliens from outer space and attempts to enlighten them on human idiosyncracies. Using this premise, Tomlin jumps from character to character portraying such scenes as Chrissie at her aerobics workout; the punked-out Agnes Angst and her visit to Grandma and Grandpa's; a male weightlifter at the gym; streetwalkers Tina and Brandi entertaining the press; and, as the centerpiece of all of this, the saga of Lynn, Marge and Edie (a middle-class white woman, a black radical and a drunken feminist) as they make their way through the '70s and the early days of the women's movement. The best humor in the piece comes from Trudy, however, as she pontificates on her own unique brand of cosmology and wisdoms. Amazingly, Tomlin makes her character transitions without the benefit of makeup or costume. This video occasionally cuts to staged re-creations of the vignettes. ☯

Lily for President
(1992, 50 min, US, Tom Trbovich)
While out promoting her upcoming movie, *The Seven Ages of Woman*, Lily finds herself caught up in a political whirlwind which eventually sweeps her into the White House! All of her stock characters, along with James Coco, Scott Baio, Pee-wee Herman and a host of other celebrities help her in her pursuit of the highest office. Imagine if you will: Lily as President, Ernestine as the White House switchboard operator, Judith Beasley as Lily's Consumer Advisor, Trudy the Bag Lady as the Chief of Stuff and, most importantly, five-year-old Edith Ann as the Secretary of the Future. It's enough to give Jesse Helms a heart attack. While not on par with her best work, and unfortunately shot directly on video, this briskly paced political satire is still a lot of fun and will provide plenty of amusement for Tomlin's fans. ☯

Shadows and Fog
(1992, 86 min, US, Woody Allen)
Lily, Jodie Foster and Kathy Bates steal the show in a hilarious scene as a trio of hookers who give Mia Farrow a lesson in life. Woody Allen's black-and-white comedy is a memorable homage to German expressionism. ☯

Short Cuts   *(1993, 183 min, US, Robert Altman)*
As one of 22 all-stars, Lily is reunited with *Nashville* director Robert Altman to bring this brilliantly observed adaptation of nine short stories by Raymond Carver to the screen. The film examines the comings and goings of a group of eclectic individuals residing in that microcosm of contemporary America: Los Angeles. Giving a particularly strong performance, Lily plays a waitress whose story of a hit-and-run accident provides the strongest segment of the film. Jack Lemmon, Tim Robbins, Andie MacDowell, Matthew Modine and Anne Archer are just some of the extraordinary cast. ☯

The Beverly Hillbillies
(1993, 93 min, US, Penelope Spheeris)
This sappy, big-screen version of the popular 1960s TV series is played so broadly it makes the TV show look subtle by comparison. In an A to B plot line, Arkansas hillbilly patriarch Jed Clampett (James Varney) strikes it rich and moves to Beverly (Hills, that is). The story has something to do with him becoming involved with swindlers. Of the film's cast, only Tomlin as Miss Hathaway and the underused Cloris Leachman as Granny will suffer the least ill-effect for their appearances. ☯

▼ And the Band Played On
(1993, 144 min, US, Roger Spottiswoode)
In this made-for-TV adaptation of the late Randy Shilts' controversial novel, Lily gives a determined performance as a caring, no-nonsense but overwhelmed San Francisco health department official doing her best to get the message out about AIDS. Tomlin received an Emmy nomination for her performance. ☯

RUDOLPH VALENTINO

Rudolph Valentino, the greatest screen lover of the silent era, was an Italian immigrant who quickly became a national obsession as well as one of the movies' greatest leading men. With his swarthy good looks and screen charisma he transcended simple matinee idol status to become a screen phenomena — and was idolized by millions of cinema-attending women. It is especially amazing that his time spent in the public spotlight lasted less than six years — from his first popular role in 1921 to his premature death in 1926. Valentino's foppish persona, romantic nature and come-hither stare appealed primarily to women, for finally there was a romantic leading man willing and able to fuel women's passions and sweep his conquests off their feet — and all this was accomplished in an undeniably sensual fashion. As much as he was idolized by women, he was equally derisively dismissed and ridiculed by many men. His greatest controversy was just months before his death when an editorial in the *Chicago Tribune* dismissed him as a "pink powder puff." This prompted Valentino to challenge the offending writer to a duel. His final recorded words, to a doctor at the hospital, were, "Do I behave like a pink powder puff?"

After a youth spent in a small town in Italy, Rodolfo Gugliemi emigrated to the United States in 1913 in hopes of becoming an agricultural engineer. But his first years were marked by poverty and simple jobs as a gardener. He found the money much easier as a dancer and earned sizable tips as a ballroom dancer and bedroom-eyed gigolo, sweeping enraptured dowagers off their feet. A friend soon encouraged him to try the movies and in 1917 he moved to Hollywood where he received his start as a walk-on in the 1918 film *Alimony*. Many more small roles, mostly as gangsters and thugs, came his way, but it was with *The Four Horsemen of the Apocalypse* in 1921 that the women of America took notice. His dark good looks coupled with a romantic, even effeminate persona was in stark contrast to the reigning all-American screen idols like Wallace Reid, Francis X. Bushman and Douglas Fairbanks.

As his film career rocketed, and his public persona was under constant scrutiny, Valentino's private life was bumpy at best. He was considered a very sweet man who felt overwhelmed by the attention. He was very private, and reportedly prone to depression although his home, Falcon Lair, was palatial and he seemed to enjoy the fast

The Sheik

life. Several (but not all) biographies conclude that Valentino was a bisexual. He wrote in his private journals of one sexual encounter with a man, and although he married twice, both of them were arranged by lesbian actress Alla Nazimova, including his second wife, lesbian set designer Natasha Rambova (formerly Winfred Shaunnessy).

On August 23, 1926, Valentino died suddenly at the age of 31 of a perforated ulcer. When news of his sudden death became public, a mass hysteria (some real, some manufactured) erupted. There were reports of actual suicides and 125,000 people lined up at his viewing. The funeral itself was quite theatrical with Rambova competing with other Hollywood stars as coffin drama queens. Mixed in with the real mourners were studio-paid wailers and fainters, there to add to the circus-like atmosphere and help drum up future business for Valentino's unreleased films. A sad but fitting end to one of the first victims to Hollywood's obsessive marketing.

"The symbol of everything wild and wonderful and illicit in nature."

—*Life Magazine*, 1950

FAVORITE STARS

There have been three film "biographies" on the life of Valentino: *Valentino* (1951, 102 min, US, Lewis Allen), with Antony Dexter as the star in a sanitized and romanticized Hollywood treatment; *The Legend of Valentino*, a TV movie starring Franco Nero; and *Valentino* (1977, 127 min, GB), Ken Russell's extravagant biopic that starred a decidedly uncharismatic Rudolf Nureyev as the seductive Latin Lover. Valentino appeared in many supporting roles before he catapulted to fame in *The Four Horsemen of the Apocalypse*. The highlights of his film career follow.

The Four Horsemen of the Apocalypse *(1921, 114 min, US, Rex Ingram)*
In his breakthrough film, Valentino plays Julio, a sensitive Argentinian youth, in this bleak anti-war film about two brothers who end up fighting on opposite sides during World War I. Valentino's tango scene entranced women worldwide in this drama that co-starred Alice Terry, Alan Hale and Wallace Beery. ☻

Camille *(1921, 77 min, US, Ray Smallwood)*
Valentino co-starred with Alla Nazimova in this, her first production after leaving the studio system to produce her own films. *Camille* is pure stylized art, with Nazimova playing her role as the tubercular Mlle. Gautier with the hyper-theatrics of a Norma Desmond. Valentino is engagingly effective as her playboy lover. Natasha Rambova, soon to be Valentino's wife, designed the art deco sets. ☻

The Sheik *(1921, 80 min, US, George Melford)*
Female fans flocked in droves to the cinemas to watch the impetuous, lovelorn Valentino entrance and ensnare Englishwoman Agnes Ayres into his luxurious tent in this unique (for its day) desert romantic adventure tale. Valentino was a sight — fabulously brilliantined hair, curvacious sideburns, penciled eyebrows and a hungry, sensual stare. The film begat the Valentino legend, catapulting him into superstardom. In a Hollywood tradition that flourishes today, the film and its star brought about a wave of similarly exotic Latino look-alikes and a series of romantic tales set in exotic lands. ☻

Blood and Sand
(1922, 80 min, US, Fred Niblo)
In one of his most famous roles, Matador Valentino can't decide between the good girl and the vamp, so he takes it out on the bull. While the acting style in this hyperbolic classic is humorously bug-eyed and stilted when viewed today, this proved to be one of Valentino's most popular films. ☻

The Eagle *(1925, 70 min, US, Clarence Brown)*
Full of romance, revenge, action and intrigue, this costume adventure yarn was adapted from an Alexander Pushkin story. Valentino plays a young Russian man who rejects the advances of the evil Czarina (Louise Dresser). As a result, he is banished. But he returns as The Eagle, a Tartar Robin Hood out to take vengeance against the Czarina as well as win the hand of the woman he loves (Vilma Banky). ☻

Son of the Sheik
(1926, 72 min, US, George Fitzmaurice)
Valentino's final film is this rousing sand and sword adventure yarn in which he successfully plays the dual roles of father and son. This sequel to his hugely popular *The Sheik* has Valentino as an Arab leader in love with dance girl Vilma Banky. ☻

Blood and Sand

CLIFTON WEBB

A popular Hollywood actor of the 1940s and '50s, Clifton Webb was as unlikely a box-office attraction and full-fledged movie star as there was. He wasn't traditionally handsome, though he was extremely sophisticated. He wasn't sensual, though in one of his most famous roles, he brilliantly played a scorned lover. And he projected an air of snobbishness which combined prissiness, acerbic wit and boredom. But for over a ten-year period, Webb was a leading player who was liked as much off the screen as he was on it.

Depending on which source you read, Webb was born in either 1896, 1893 or 1891, in Indiana (that's known for sure). As a teenager, he headed East with theatrical aspirations. At 17, he was singing with the Boston Opera Company, which marked the beginning of his musical career. He was an accomplished dancer, as well, and found great success in Broadway and London musicals. He was also a well-known ballroom dancer during the 1920s. Webb made his movie debut in 1920 in *Polly with a Past*. In the next six years, he'd appear in five films, but this proved to be a false start for the actor as these were of little consequence.

It was in the late 1920s that a turning point came for Webb: He was referred to as "just a hoofer" in a newspaper article. Infuriated, he gave up his musical career and turned to drama, instead. Thus began another chapter to his career, and during the 1930s and early '40s, he became an established stage star. Some of his hits included "As Thousands Cheer," "The Importance of Being Earnest," "The Man Who Came to Dinner" and "Blithe Spirit." Webb returned to Hollywood in 1944, appearing in Otto Preminger's classic mystery *Laura*. He and the film were an immediate smash (for it Webb received the first of his three Oscar nominations). Webb had completed his career cycle — from singer to dancer to stage actor to film star — and on the screen he not only achieved his greatest success, but was at his best.

Offscreen, Webb's sexuality was well-known among Hollywood circles. In fact, rumor suggested that more than one of the young, hunky actors of the 1940s got their start courtesy of Webb (including an Oscar-nominated actor whose career is still active in the 1990s). But it was more common to see Webb accompanied by his mother, Mabelle, than lovers or escorts. He was devoted to her to

Webb (r.) dispenses wit and wisdom in *Sitting Pretty*

such an extent that they were a legendary couple in Tinseltown — and more than once it was said they were the inspiration for Violet and Sebastian in Tennessee Williams' "Suddenly, Last Summer." When his mother died in 1960, Webb was left devastated. He was so overcome with grief and mourned for so long, it prompted Noël Coward to call him "the world's oldest living orphan." Webb died of a heart attack in 1966 at the age of 70, 73 or 75.

In the 1920s, Webb appeared in the following films: *Polly with a Past* (1920), *Let No Man Put Asunder* (1924), *New Toys* (1925), *The Heart of a Siren* (1925) and *The Still Alarm* (1926).

Laura *(1944, 85 min, US, Otto Preminger)*

With the question of "Who killed Laura?" (and *not* Palmer), Otto Preminger sets the stage for a complex, riveting and one-of-a-kind murder mystery. Dana Andrews plays a police detective investigating the murder of successful businesswoman Laura Hunt (the beautiful Gene Tierney). Through a series of flashbacks, cynical columnist Waldo Lydecker (Webb) recalls Laura's life up to the murder. Among the suspects are Webb, fiancé Vincent Price, and socialite Judith Anderson. Featuring extraordinary photography, a haunting score, unexpected twists, remarkable performances and scalpel-sharp wit, *Laura* is not to be missed. Webb — who received a Best Supporting Oscar nomination — gives a quintessential performance as the acerbic Lydecker ("I write with a goose quill dipped in venom"). Those only familiar with Price's horror movie career will be pleasantly surprised. ⊛

The Dark Corner
(1946, 99 min, US, Henry Hathaway)
Lucille Ball stars with Webb in this unfairly neglected film noir mystery. Lucy plays a secretary who sets out to prove the innocence of her private detective boss (Mark Stevens), who's been framed for murder. Second-billed, Webb plays a caustic, wealthy art dealer who's behind the frame-up. ✪

The Razor's Edge
(1946, 146 min, US, Edmund Goulding)
Webb received a second Oscar nomination (for Best Supporting Actor) in this sterling adaptation of W. Somerset Maugham's novel of spiritual awakening. Though Tyrone Power and Gene Tierney star, it's the performances of Webb and Anne Baxter which are most memorable. As the snobbish, cynical Elliott Templeton, Webb offers his best screen portrayal. His death-bed scene is terrific. ✪

Sitting Pretty *(1948, 84 min, US, Walter Lang)*
Webb received a third Oscar nomination (his only Best Actor nod) for his first stab at comedy, giving a hilariously finicky performance as babysitter/housekeeper extraordinaire, Lynn Belvedere. Maureen O'Hara and Robert Young are the young married couple he works for, and both manage to produce a smile or two, but it's Webb's film all the way. Followed by two more *Mr. Belvedere* films, this was the basis for the TV sitcom "Mr. Belvedere."

Mr. Belvedere Goes to College
(1949, 83 min, US, Elliott Nugent)
Mr. Belvedere leaves the serenity of suburbia in *Sitting Pretty* for the raucous dorms and hallowed halls of college life. Webb reprises the role with his customary aplomb, but the level of humor from the original is missing. Also with Shirley Temple and Alan Young.

Cheaper by the Dozen
(1950, 85 min, US, Walter Lang)
Webb is well-cast in this charmingly sweet comedy as an efficiency expert and father of twelve. The ever-classy Myrna Loy is his wife, and Jeanne Crain is one of the dozen. Followed by a sequel, *Belles on Their Toes*, with most of the cast returning except for Webb. ✪

For Heaven's Sake
(1950, 92 min, US, George Seaton)
This amiable comedy casts Webb and Edmund Gwenn as angels who look over married couple Joan Bennett and Robert Cummings, who are expecting a baby. Adapted from the play by Harry Segall, who had much more success with his other heaven-themed comedy, "Here Comes Mr. Jordan."

Mr. Belvedere Rings the Bell
(1951, 87 min, US, Henry Koster)
Webb fares much better in this final *Mr. Belvedere* film than he did in *Mr. B. Goes to College*. To prove his theory about the aging process, Mr. Belvedere has himself checked into a nursing home. Sentimental but amusing.

Elopement *(1951, 82 min, US, Henry Koster)*
Webb's funny performance elevates this otherwise average comedy. He plays Anne Francis' father, who objects to her boyfriend, college professor William Lundigan. When they elope, daddy is in hot pursuit.

Dreamboat *(1952, 83 min, US, Claude Binyon)*
Both Webb and Ginger Rogers are in good form in this inventive comedy which satirizes the then-new medium of television. Webb and Rogers play former silent screen stars whose films have renewed popularity on TV. Ginger promotes them, much to the chagrin of Webb, who is now a college professor and eager to forget his Hollywood past.

Stars and Stripes Forever
(1952, 89 min, US, Henry Koster)
A Hollywood-ized but nevertheless entertaining biography of turn-of-the-century bandleader/songwriter John Philip Sousa. Webb gives a cracking portrayal of the march king. (GB title: *Marching Along*)

Titanic *(1953, 98 min, US, Jean Negulesco)*
Barbara Stanwyck and Webb offer accomplished performances in this melodramatic retelling of the sinking of the famed, doomed luxury liner. The action is seen through the eyes of passengers/married couple Webb and Stanwyck, as opposed to the excellent British drama *A Night to Remember*, which uses the ship's personnel to tell its story. Also with Robert Wagner and Thelma Ritter.

Mister Scoutmaster
(1953, 87 min, US, Henry Levin)
Webb uses his persnickety Mr. Belvedere persona to good effect as a child-hating TV personality who takes command of a cub scout troop.

Three Coins in the Fountain
(1954, 102 min, US, Jean Negulesco)
A box-office smash, this Best Picture nominee follows the romantic adventures of three American women (Dorothy McGuire, Jean Peters and Maggie McNamara) living in Rome. A top-billed and debonair Webb plays McGuire's love interest. ✪

Woman's World
(1954, 94 min, US, Jean Negulesco)
An engaging cast is well-served in this sophisticated comedy-drama about big business. Webb plays a boss who calls his three top salesmen together to pick a new general manager. They include Van Heflin, Fred MacMurray and Cornel Wilde. Lauren Bacall, June Allyson and Arlene Dahl are their respective wives.

The Man Who Never Was
(1955, 102 min, GB, Ronald Neame)
A thoroughly absorbing WWII drama with Webb in an atypical performance as a British intelligence officer who devises an unusual plan to fool the Nazis — allowing the Germans to find a

With Gene Tierney in *Laura*

dead body which is carrying misinformation. The film divides its time between the evolution of the plan and its ultimate execution. Based on a true story. ☯

Boy on a Dolphin
(1957, 111 min, US, Jean Negulesco)
Webb plays a dastardly adversary to Alan Ladd's noble archeologist (shades of *Raiders of the Lost Ark*) in this weak sunken-treasure underwater adventure. Sophia Loren also stars in this tale set in Greece's Aegean Sea.

The Remarkable Mr. Pennypacker
(1959, 87 min, US, Henry Levin)
Remarkable is not the word which springs to mind to describe this comedy with Webb as a Pennsylvania businessman living with two different wives and families, both unknown to each other. Webb reteams with Dorothy McGuire.

Holiday for Lovers
(1959, 103 min, US, Henry Levin)
Lightweight comedy with Webb as a Boston psychiatrist who carts wife Jane Wyman and daughter Carol Lynley off on a South American vacation to keep his teenaged offspring away from the opposite sex.

Satan Never Sleeps
(1962, 126 min, US/GB, Leo McCarey)
Webb co-stars with William Holden as Catholic missionaries in post-WWII China who are in the path of the invading Communists. Webb and director Leo McCarey's last film, and not very fitting for either. (GB title: *The Devil Never Sleeps*)

FAVORITE STARS

KENNETH WILLIAMS

Epicene British comedian Kenneth Williams is probably best known to American audiences for his work in the *Carry On* series (including the taxonomically irregulars *Don't Lose Your Head* and *Follow That Camel*). An extremely popular star in his native England, Williams' trademark came naturally: a roll of the eye, or the flair of a nostril. "I like smutty old jokes," he once confessed. "Honest vulgarities the central tradition of English humor and uninhibitedness the essence of comedy."

Born in London in 1926, Williams began his career entertaining the troops during WWII, after a time spent as a lithographic draftsman. "Laughs are more important than tears," he once said. "There are plenty of people who can play serious roles but there are not many who can be funny." Only a few serious comedic roles ever came his way, the most noteworthy being The Inspector in Joe Orton's "Loot," which good friend Orton wrote specifically for him. (However, the role required a different physical type than Williams and the actor soon left the production after only several performances.)

Among his many film credits, Williams appeared in *The Beggar's Opera* (1952, GB), *The Seekers* (1954, GB), *Raising the Wind* (1961, GB) and *Twice Round the Daffodils* (1962, GB). His many *Carry On* films include: *Carry on Sergeant* (1958, GB), the first in the series; *Carry on Nurse* (1959, GB), which was a surprise hit in the States; *Raising the Wind* (1961, GB), which introduced Jim Dale to the series; *Carry on Cruising* (1962, GB); *Carry on Jack* (1963, GB), aka *Carry on Venus*; *Carry on Spying* (1964, GB); *Carry on Cleo* (1965, GB), one of the funnier outings; *Carry on Cowboy* (1967, GB); *Follow That Camel* (1967, GB), also starring Phil Silvers; *Carry on Doctor* (1968, GB), another highlight of the series; *Carry on Up the Khyber* (1968, GB); *Carry on Camping* (1970, GB); *Carry on Henry VIII* (1972, GB); *Carry on Loving* (1970, GB); *Carry on Behind* (1975, GB); and *Carry on Emmanuelle* (1978, GB).

Williams' death in 1978 was front page news in England as the actor had endeared himself with the British public through his film roles, TV work (including "The Kenneth Williams Show") and game show appearances. Speculation as to whether his death was a suicide was fueled by the last written words in his diary: "What's the bloody point?" Williams was never comfortable with his homosexuality — his four marriage proposals perhaps fooled no one but himself. And his self-loathing led to severe bouts of clinical depression. "I'm a suicidist — don't believe in existence at all."

Williams (far right) in *Carry on Nurse*

MONTY WOOLLEY

With his trademark bushy white beard, Monty Woolley delighted audiences on stage and on the screen during the 1930s and '40s in a series of comedies and musicals which usually cast him as an irascible curmedgeon. Like his off-screen persona, as well, his characters were quick-witted and to the point. It is this image of the raspy-voiced actor for which he is best remembered.

Born in New York City in 1889, Woolley grew up around celebrities as his father owned the famed Grand Union Hotel. Woolley studied at both Yale and Harvard, and it was while at the former that he met classmate Cole Porter. Together they put on student shows there, and they would remain close friends almost all their lives. After serving in France during WWI, Woolley taught at his alma mater, Yale, teaching English and Drama, and remained there for 12 years until he headed for the bright lights of Broadway. In 1927, he made his debut there as a director, and his very first show, "Fifty Million Frenchmen," with music by Porter, was a big hit. He also directed Porter's "Jubilee." In 1929, he appeared for the first time as an actor in "On Your Toes."

Hollywood soon beckoned, and after numerous stage successes in New York, Woolley headed West in 1937. His appearances, in such films as *Nothing Sacred* and *Three Comrades* were in small roles. However, that changed when he returned to New York to star in his greatest triumph, "The Man Who Came to Dinner." He played the role of the acerbic columnist Sheridan Whiteside for two years, and reprised it in the hit movie adaptation. His film roles after that were substantial, and he even played himself in *Night and Day*, the biography of his friend Porter. (Woolley was credited with coining the phrase "It's De-Lovely," which, of course, was one of Porter's biggest hits.) Woolley continued making movies into the 1950s, and died in 1963 at the age of 74.

Woolley never made a point of hiding his sexual orientation, though like his gay peers at the time he wasn't "out." The actor had a preference for black men, and this caused a falling out between him and Porter later in life. During his final years, Woolley fell in love with one of his employees, a black manservant, and the two lived together as lovers.

In addition to the following titles, Woolley also appeared in *Nothing Sacred* (1937), *Live, Love & Learn* (1937), *The Girl of the Golden West* (1938), *Three Comrades* (1938), *Lord Jeff* (1938), *Man About Town* (1939), *Never Say Die* (1939) and *Dancing Co-Ed* (1939).

The Man Who Came to Dinner
(1942, 112 min, US, William Keighley)
Though Bette Davis gets top billing, it's really Woolley who's the star of this hilarious adaptation of Kaufman and Hart's convulsive comedy. Re-creating his acclaimed stage role, Woolley gives one of the all-time great comic performances as Sheridan Whiteside, the cynical columnist who injures himself while visiting the small-town home of Billie Burke and family. Confined to a wheelchair, he becomes the epitome of the unwanted house guest, running everyone's life and sending the household into hysteria. As played by Woolley, Whiteside is non-sexual, but one can easily interpret the character, which was inspired by gay critic Alexander Woollcott, as homosexual. Bette plays Whiteside's secretary. ⊛

The Pied Piper
(1942, 84 min, US, Irving Pichel)
Rather than his classic interpretation of Sheridan Whiteside in *The Man Who Came to Dinner*, Woolley received a Best Actor nomination for his compelling performance in this heartwarming drama released the same year. He plays a crusty British father (whose son was lost in the war) who becomes an unlikely guardian when he escorts a group of children from Nazi-occupied France back to his native England.

Life Begins at 8:30
(1942, 84 min, US, Irving Pichel)
Based on the London stage hit, this sentimental comedy casts Woolley as a washed-up actor whose drinking ruined his career. His daughter (Ida Lupino), who has given up everything to look after him, begins a romance with a hot-shot composer (Cornel Wilde), who instruments a comeback for his future father-in-law. Excellent performances from Woolley (his drunken Santa Claus is priceless) and Lupino distinguish this otherwise maudlin tale. (GB title: *The Light of Heart*)

Holy Matrimony
(1943, 87 min, US, John M. Stahl)
Woolley is picture perfect as a famous English artist who masquerades as his dead butler when he buries his ex-employee under his own identity (at Westminster Abbey!). The marvelous Gracie Fields also stars as Woolley's new bride — whom his valet had arranged to marry through correspondance. They live the good, quiet life in the country until she sells one of his paintings. A brilliantly constructed comedy with both Woolley and Fields in rare form.

Since You Went Away
(1944, 172 min, US, John Cromwell)
Receiving his second Oscar nomination, Woolley gives a spirited characterization of his lovable curmudgeon. He plays a retired Army colonel who boards with Claudette Colbert — whose husband is fighting overseas — and her daughters Jennifer Jones and Shirley Temple. Despite his seemingly uncaring exterior, he becomes involved in their lives. A young Robert Walker plays his estranged grandson, who has joined the service to please his fami-

ly. Walker is referred to by Jones as "sensitive," "shy" and "timid"; these 1940s code words could raise the gay flag. "Gaydar" could also be used in the scene when Walker and Jones are out on a date and they meet the extraordinarily handsome Guy Madison, playing a sailor. The two men exchange words, scuffle, Madison knocks down Walker (establishing the master/servant roles?), and become immediate friends. Walker remarks of Madison, "He's good looking, isn't he?" Upon their meeting, Madison appears to be flirting with both Walker and Jones. ⊛

Molly and Me
(1945, 76 min, US, Lewis Seiler)
Woolley reteamed with Gracie Fields after their great success in *Holy Matrimony*. She plays a housekeeper who takes a position at the manor of curmudgeon Woolley. Shenanigans abound as she takes control of his life, eventually changing him for the better. Not as accomplished as their first pairing, but enjoyable nonetheless.

Night and Day
(1946, 128 min, US, Michael Curtiz)
Woolley plays himself in this ficticious biography of gay songwriter Cole Porter (though, of course, the film makes no mention of his homosexuality). Cary Grant portrays Porter, and Mary Martin makes a brief appearance singing "My Heart Belongs to Daddy." ⊛

The Bishop's Wife
(1947, 108 min, US, Henry Koster)
In this captivating comedy, Cary Grant plays an angel who is sent to Earth to help bishop David Niven and his wife Loretta Young. One of those who also benefits from his visitation is writer Woolley, who thanks to a little heavenly assistance resumes his stalled writing career. ⊛

Miss Tatlock's Millions
(1948, 101 min, US, Richard Haydn)
An unusual and rudely funny comedy with John Lund as a stuntman who impersonates a halfwit heir. He finds romance, comedy and wealth when he moves into the mansion of the cantankerous patriarch, played by Woolley.

As Young as You Feel
(1951, 77 min, US, Harmon Jones)
Woolley gives a spirited performance in this fetching comedy (based on a Paddy Chayefsky story) which takes a playful swipe at big business. Woolley plays an employee who is retired upon turning 65. In response, he impersonates the president of his firm's parent company to reverse the retirement policy. Things get out of hand when he is forced to continue the charade. Thelma Ritter co-stars as Woolley's daughter-in-law, and David Wayne and Marilyn Monroe also star. ⊛

Bette Davis and Woolley in *The Man Who Came to Dinner*

Gay Icons – 1930s

BETTE DAVIS

Bette Davis

If Clark Gable was the "King" of Hollywood in the 1930s and '40s, Bette Davis was certainly its "Queen." For a ten-year period beginning in 1937, Davis ruled the box office with an iron fist, appearing in an unprecedented string of commercial and financial successes which helped propel her to the status of most popular female star for a span of two decades.

From the start, Davis was an original, a mold-breaker. She didn't really look like a typical movie actress — when she arrived in Hollywood, she went unrecognized by a studio rep: "No one faintly like an actress got off the train." And she didn't really perform on the screen like most movie actresses. At the time Davis inaugurated her career, the accepted style of acting —both film and theatrical — had a tendency towards overplaying, melodramatic devices left over from the silent era. No wonder audiences took notice: Here was someone up on the screen who brought realism to her characters, reality to their situations, and humanized both strengths and weaknesses.

While at Warner Brothers Studios, audiences weren't the only ones on whom Davis left her mark. Unhappy with the films being selected for her, Davis took the studio to task, eventually winning a lengthy and costly battle for better roles: One only has to read her filmography to know the fight paid off. Leaving Warners in the late 1940s, Davis had a rough time finding roles which suited her talents. And in the 1950s and '60s, her films were comparatively few. During these years, Davis experienced more than one "come back" (*All About Eve* and *What Ever Happened to Baby Jane?* among them). But she more than once proved that with the right script, and no matter what late stage in her career, she never lost the magic.

Davis has long been a favorite with gay audiences, and may be the most imitated actress of the century. Who can resist at least once in their life pantomiming puffing a cigarette and with exaggerated glee, releasing it and proclaiming: "What a dump!" For her talent, energy, ambition, wisdom, conceit, independence, bitchiness, savvy, tempestuousness, versatility, and for leaving an indelible imprint on the face of American cinema, we include Bette Davis among our Favorite Stars.

Among Bette's earliest films are *Bad Sister* (1931), *Seed* (1931), *Waterloo Bridge* (1931), *Way Back Home* (1931), *The Menace* (1931), *The Man Who Played God* (1932), *So Big* (1932), *The Rich Are Always with Us* (1932) and *The Dark Horse* (1932). Davis credits George Arliss, the star of *The Man Who Played God*, for giving her her first big break as he gave a coveted role in that film to her against studio wishes. It's an excellent performance which paved the way to more important roles a year or two later. The following are highlights from Davis' career.

Cabin in the Cotton
(1932, 77 min, US, Michael Curtiz)
Bette immortalizes the line "Ah'd love to kiss ya but I just washed my hay-uh." In her first bad girl role, Davis plays a Southern vixen out to set a sharecropper's son on the road to ruin. The film's routine; Bette is not. ☻

20,000 Years in Sing Sing
(1933, 78 min, US, Michael Curtiz)
Bette plays Spencer Tracy's moll. He's a convict testing the prison's honor system; she's a one-woman, gun-totin' death squad.

Fashions
(1934, 78 min, US, William Dieterle)
Paris is the setting for this amiable comedy with Bette as a fashion designer who gets involved with con man William Powell. There's a musical production number directed by Busby Berkeley.⊛

Of Human Bondage
(1934, 83 min, US, John Cromwell)
This is the film which made Bette a full-flegded star. Davis is luminous and effectively trashy in W. Somerset Maugham's story as a waitress who spells disaster for artist Leslie Howard when he becomes obsessed with her. A small scandal occurred when Bette wasn't nominated for an Academy Award — prompting a huge but ineffective write-in campaign. ⊛

Bordertown *(1935, 90 min, US, Archie Mayo)*
Bette is teamed with Paul Muni, Warners' top actor at the time, in this involving melodrama. Playing the bored wife of businessman Eugene Pallette, Bette sets her sights on down-on-his-luck lawyer Muni.

The Girl from Tenth Avenue
(1935, 69 min, US, Alfred E. Green)
Bette gives a splendid performance as the working-class girlfriend of alcoholic lawyer Ian Hunter, whose wife has just kicked him out. His life falling apart, it's Bette to the rescue.

Front Page Woman
(1935, 80 min, US, Michael Curtiz)
It's a "battle of the sexes" between rival newspaper reporters Bette and George Brent as each tries to outdo each other's story in this snappy comedy. Bette's in good form.

Dangerous
(1935, 72 min, US, Alfred E. Green)
A consolation Oscar went to Bette for her *Of Human Bondage* snub the year before. Bette is actually quite good, but even she said the award should have gone to Katharine Hepburn for *Alice Adams*. The story is about an alcoholic actress in a career slump who gets some help from adoring architect Franchot Tone. ⊛

The Petrified Forest
(1936, 75 min, US, Archie Mayo)
Bette teams with Leslie Howard and Humphrey Bogart in this classic drama based on Robert E. Sherwood's play. Howard is a world-weary poet who stops by the small-town cafe where Davis works. Bogey is the gangster on the lam who holes up there. ⊛

Marked Woman
(1937, 97 min, US, Lloyd Bacon)
A taut gangster drama with Bette as a clip-joint hostess who is persuaded by D.A. Humphrey Bogart to testify against the racketeer boss responsible for her sister's disappearance. ⊛

Kid Galahad
(1937, 100 min, US, Michael Curtiz)
Sturdy boxing drama with Wayne Morris as the "Battling Bellhop"; Edward G. Robinson as his manager; Davis as girlfriend to both of them; and Humphrey Bogart as a rival manager. ⊛

It's Love I'm After
(1937, 90 min, US, Archie Mayo)
Bette shines in one of her flashiest comedic roles in this engaging screwball comedy with Davis and Leslie Howard as a theatrical couple on- and offstage. Olivia de Havilland is the woman who comes between them. Special mention goes to Eric Blore for his fabulous turn as Howard's dedicated valet ("I love you sir").

Jezebel *(1938, 103 min, US, William Wyler)*
Bette's battle with Warners paid off handsomely with the studio acquiring this specifically for her. Bette won a second, and much-deserved Oscar for her brilliant portrayal of a spoiled, Civil War-era Southern belle (any resemblance to Scarlet O'Hara is intentional). Henry Fonda is the object of her affection. ⊛

The Sisters *(1938, 95 min, US, Anatole Litvak)*
Bette is one of three turn-of-the-century sisters experiencing romance and marital woes. Errol Flynn is Bette's headache. ⊛

Dark Victory
(1939, 106 min, US, Edmund Goulding)
A classic Davis performance. Bette plays a jet-setting socialite who discovers she only has a few months to live. As she slowly accepts her fate, she becomes more responsible, living her remaining months "beautifully and finely." Oscar nominee Davis gives a superbly etched portrait of courage, fragility and temperament in this enthralling, first-rate soap opera. ⊛

Juarez *(1939, 132 min, US, William Dieterle)*
Bette, playing Napoleon III's wife Carlota, takes a back seat to Paul Muni's excellent portrayal of the Mexican revolutionary leader Benito Pablo Juarez in this expertly done biography. Claude Rains excels in support as the French leader. ⊛

The Old Maid
(1939, 95 min, US, Edmund Goulding)
Bette plays to the hilt the role of an unwed mother who must give up her child. It's an acting tour-de-force as Davis and adoptive mother Miriam Hopkins battle it out over the child. ⊛

The Private Lives of Elizabeth and Essex *(1939, 106 min, US, Michael Curtiz)*
A must see for Davis fans with Bette as Queen Elizabeth I and Errol Flynn as Earl of Essex. Davis chews up the exquisite scenery in this excellent period costume drama with great gusto. Bette appeared as Elizabeth once more in 1955's *The Virgin Queen*. ⊛

All This and Heaven, Too
(1940, 143 min, US, Anatole Litvak)
A handsomely produced tearjerker with Bette as a governess in 19th-century Paris who becomes involved with her aristocratic employer, Charles Boyer, which leads to tragedy. ⊛

The Letter *(1940, 95 min, US, William Wyler)*
A knockout (and second) screen version of W. Somerset Maugham's novel with Bette as the plotting wife of tycoon Herbert Marshall. Murder, deceit and sexual repression were never so much fun. Bette received her fourth Oscar nomination. ⊛

The Great Lie

(1941, 107 min, US, Edmund Goulding)
It's Mary Astor who walks away with the acting honors in this competent soaper with Bette on the flip side of *The Old Maid*, as she raises another woman's child; Astor is the birth mother. ✪

The Bride Came COD

(1941, 92 min, US, William Keighley)
Bette and James Cagney bring a lot of life to this zesty 1940s romp with flyer Cagney kidnapping bride-to-be Davis (at her father's request). Things get crazy when they crash land in the desert. ✪

The Little Foxes

(1941, 116 min, US, William Wyler)
This successful screen version of Lillian Hellman's play finds Bette at her bitchy best as the matriarch of a feuding Southern clan. Patricia Collinge and Teresa Wright stand out in support. A fifth Academy nomination went to Davis. ✪

The Man Who Came to Dinner

(1941, 112 min, US, William Keighley)
Though she's star-billed, Bette takes a backseat to star Monty Woolley in this hilarious adaptation of Kaufman and Hart's classic comedy. Davis plays a devoted secretary to Woolley's acerbic columnist Sheridan Whiteside. Bette is competent, but the lion's share of the laughs go to Woolley and a crazy cast of characters. ✪

In This Our Life

(1942, 97 min, US, John Huston)
Bette lets loose as a neurotic hussy whose tantrums and plottings ruin the lives of sister Olivia de Havilland, husband George Brent and, eventually, herself. ✪

Now, Voyager

(1942, 117 min, US, Irving Rapper)
In the '30s, it was *Jezebel*; in the '50s, it was *All About Eve*; in the 1940s, Bette's finest hour came as the lonely spinster who transforms from ugly duckling to high-flying swan. This classic tearjerker contains memorable dialogue and a great Max Steiner

Bette plays twin sisters in *A Stolen Life*

score, and Davis' transformation is stunning. Bette received her sixth Oscar nod. ✪

Watch on the Rhine

(1943, 114 min, US, Herman Shumlin)
Bette appears in her first Oscar-winning Best Picture. She plays the wife of Paul Lukas, a German refugee living in Washington D.C. and now wanted by the Nazis. Lillian Hellman wrote this powerful cautionary tale on the rise of Nazism. ✪

Old Acquaintance

(1943, 110 min, US, Vincent Sherman)
Bette and Miriam Hopkins pick up where they left off in *The Old Maid* in this extremely entertaining drama. They play lifelong friends and rivals, and both give expert performances. The basis for George Cukor's *Rich and Famous*. ✪

Mr. Skeffington

(1944, 146 min, US, Vincent Sherman)
Bette received her seventh Oscar nomination for her sensational performance as a youthful beauty who marries for money only to learn the true meaning of love. Claude Rains also stars in this grand soap opera as the title character, and matches Davis scene for scene. ✪

The Corn Is Green

(1945, 114 min, US, Irving Rapper)
Another sterling characterization from Bette, here as a teacher in a small Welch mining town who devotes herself to a promising student. In the 1970s, Davis appeared on stage in a musical version, "Miss Moffat," which closed in Philadelphia before its Broadway run. ✪

A Stolen Life

(1946, 107 min, US, Curtis Bernhardt)
Bette plays twin sisters in this okay melodrama, elevated by Davis' fanciful performance. When one sister dies, the other takes her place in marriage to the man they both loved. ✪

Deception *(1946, 112 min, US, Irving Rapper)*

A thoroughly captivating soap opera with Davis and Claude Rains once again matching wits, with Davis as a pianist torn between two lovers. ✪

June Bride

(1948, 97 min, US, Bretaigne Windust)
Bette sparkles in this lively battle-of-the-sexes comedy as a magazine editor who is accompanied by ex-lover Robert Montgomery to cover a small-town wedding. ✪

Beyond the Forest

(1949, 96 min, US, King Vidor)
Bette misses her mark as a murderous crack shot in this tepid melodrama about a country doctor's wife who wants out. She does, however, say the immortal "What a dump!" ✪

All About Eve

▼ All About Eve

(1950, 138 min, US, Joseph L. Mankiewicz)
Quintessential Davis. After forty years, this is still the definitive Hollywood film about theatre life. Bette, in arguably her greatest role, is Margo Channing, a first lady of the theatre whose life is changed forever when a seemingly starstruck woman, Eve Harrington (Anne Baxter), enters her life. A brilliantly scathing, enormously witty look behind the masks of the players who strut and fret their hour upon the stage. The character of Eve was originally written as a lesbian, but almost all context to her sexuality was deleted. There only remains two extremely subtle scenes — involving Eve's roommate and the film's finale — which even hint at her orientation. Bette's eighth Oscar nod. ☻

The Star *(1952, 89 min, US, Stuart Heisler)*

A ninth Oscar nomination went to Bette for her solid portrayal of a fading movie queen in this vitriolic Hollywood drama. Though Davis at the time was experiencing sort of a "comeback," there's no parallel — though the similarities are there to be interpreted— between Bette and her on-screen character. ☻

The Virgin Queen

(1955, 92 min, US, Henry Koster)
Bette reprises her acclaimed role from 1939's *The Private Lives of Elizabeth and Essex* as Elizabeth I. This outing, she comes in conflict with Sir Walter Raleigh (well-played by Richard Todd). ☻

The Catered Affair

(1956, 93 min, US, Richard Brooks)
Good performances distinguish this absorbing family drama with Bette as the wife of Bronx cabbie Ernest Borgnine and mother of bride-to-be Debbie Reynolds. (GB title: *Wedding Breakfast*) ☻

A Pocketful of Miracles

(1961, 136 min, US, Frank Capra)
Entertaining remake of Capra's own *Lady for a Day*, with Bette as the lady in question. Davis plays Apple Annie, an apple seller who — for the sake of her visiting daughter — masquerades as a society matron. ☻

What Ever Happened to Baby Jane?

(1962, 132 min, US, Robert Aldrich)
Director Robert Aldrich ushered in a new genre of Gothic horror and Bette made yet another remarkable "comeback" with this classic thriller. As an aging child star who slowly loses her sanity, Davis is simply remarkable, giving one of her most memorable (and popular) performances. Joan Crawford is the wheelchair-bound object of Bette's severe and deadly sibling rivalry. ⊛

Dead Ringer

(1964, 115 min, US, Paul Henried)
Bette's follow-up to *Baby Jane* may be a silly psychological thriller, but thanks to Davis' scenery chewing and grand histrionics, it's certainly a lot of fun. Bette plays (for a second time) twin sisters — one good, and one bad. (GB title: *Dead Image*) ⊛

Where Love Has Gone

(1964, 111 min, US, Edward Dmytryk)
Bette plays a society matriarch and grandmother in this slick adaptation of Harold Robbins' novel. The story, echoing the Lana Turner scandal of the late 1950s, concerns a teenage girl (Joey Heatherton) who kills the lover of her mother (Susan Hayward). ⊛

Hush...Hush, Sweet Charlotte

(1965, 133 min, US, Robert Aldrich)
More Gothic thrills, this time with Bette as a wealthy victimized hermit haunted by the memory of her dead lover. Olivia de Havilland (who took over for Joan Crawford) and Joseph Cotten also star, and Agnes Moorehead is terrific (and almost unrecognizable) as the family housekeeper. ⊛

The Nanny *(1965, 93 min, US, Seth Holt)*

Bette has a great time in this over-the-top and ripping thriller as the title character who ain't no Mary Poppins.

The Anniversary

(1968, 95 min, GB, Roy Ward Baker)
Bette is a bitter, possessive mother who gathers her three sons to help celebrate her and her late husband's wedding anniversary. This black comedy is heightened by Davis' campy performance (with eye-patch, no less).

▼ Connecting Rooms

(1969, 103 min, GB, Franklin Gollings)
Bette plays a street musician in this stagey melodrama examining the lonely lives of a group of tenants of a seedy British boardinghouse. Michael Redgrave plays an ex-schoolmaster who resigned after a scandal involving a young boy. The film was never released in the U.S.

Burnt Offerings

(1976, 115 min, US, Dan Curtis)
This creepy and scary horror film has Bette as a family's beloved aunt whose vitality is slowly sapped by the evil forces of their summer vacation home. Bette is splendid in this underrated chiller from the creator of "Dark Shadows." ⊛

Return from Witch Mountain

(1978, 95 min, US, John Hough)
Bette is a capable villainous out to learn the secret to an alien boy's powers in this Disney sequel to *Escape to Witch Mountain*. ⊛

Death on the Nile

(1978, 135 min, GB, John Guillermin)
As a pompous socialite, Bette is one of the many suspects in the murder of heiress Lois Chiles. This Agatha Christie mystery isn't quite as good as *Murder on the Orient Express*, but it's fun nevertheless. ⊛

The Whales of August

(1987, 90 min, US, Lindsay Anderson)
Two authentic screen legends come together in this eloquent, tender drama with Bette and Lillian Gish as sisters living out their final years together. Forget *Wicked Stepmother*, this is Bette's valedictory treasure. ⊛

Wicked Stepmother

(1989, 92 min, US, Larry Cohen)
An unfitting last film if ever there was one. Bette plays a witch who marries rich men, then shrinks them and absconds with their money. Bette withdrew from this film after a week, and a double was used in many scenes. ⊛

Towards the end of her career, Davis, as with many of her contemporaries, found it increasingly difficult to find quality roles in theatrical films — what with movies aimed at the under-25 age group almost dominating the market. In response, Davis turned to TV, where she found, for the most part, a number of high quality productions. These include: *The Judge and Jake Wyler* (1972), a charming detective mystery; *Scream, Pretty Peggy* (1973), a rather trite thriller; *The Disappearance of Aimee* (1976), a first-class courtroom drama exploring the mysterious disappearance of preacher Aimee Semple McPherson (played by Faye Dunaway); *The Dark Secret of Harvest House* (1978), a very potent thriller set in a small New England town; *Strangers* (1979), an excellent family drama of the renewed relationship between a mother and daughter (Gena Rowlands), which won Davis an Emmy Award; *White Mama* (1980), a touching drama about a poor widow and the black youth who befriends her; *Skyward* (1980), a sentimental tale with Bette as a former pilot who helps a paraplegic girl learn to fly; *Family Reunion* (1981), a beguiling drama of a retired schoolteacher who sets out on the road on an odyssey to rediscover her family; *Little Gloria...Happy at Last* (1982), an involving drama about the custody battle of young Gloria Vanderbilt; *A Piano for Mrs. Cimino* (1982), a sturdy character study of a widow forced to prove herself mentally competent; and *Right of Way*, a made-for-cable production which is noted more for the first-time pairing of Bette and James Stewart than for an artistic merit. Davis' TV filmography alone would have made any actress a star — a wry comment on both the modern usage of the word, and an homage to the perseverance and boundless talent of Miss Bette Davis.

Gay Icons – 1940s

JUDY GARLAND

Born Frances Gumm in Grand Rapids, Michigan, in 1922, Judy Garland was the leading female box-office attraction of the 1940s, had a film career which lasted nearly 30 years, was in show business for most of her 47 years, sold out concert halls throughout the world, was ravaged by drug abuse during most of her adult life, was married five times, and was an authentic legendary figure at the time of her death in 1969. Judy was also a longtime favorite with gay audiences, a love affair which still exists today, 25 years after she died — though her appeal is seemingly lost on the younger queer generation.

As one of her more famous lyrics suggests, Judy was almost "born in a trunk." Her parents were headliners in Vaudeville, known as Jack and Virginia Lee, and Judy made her first appearance on stage as a three-year-old — she was such a hit with the audience and so enjoyed performing that her father had to yank her off stage after three encores. In her later years, Judy would talk of her relationship with her father, who was gay. "I wasn't close to my father, but I wanted to be all my life. He was a gay Irish gentleman and very good-looking. And he wanted to be close to me, too, but we never had much time together."

Her family eventually moved to Hollywood, and at the age of fourteen, Judy made her first film appearance in a musical short, *Every Sunday*, which also featured a young Deanna Durbin. Judy was pushed into show business by her mother. She once commented, "I look at my three fine children and wonder whether I would want them to be entertainers, too. Applause alone doesn't sustain you at 3 A.M. when you can't sleep."

It was her appearance in *Every Sunday* which led to a contract at MGM Studios, and her feature film debut in *Pigskin Parade* in 1936. In a few short years, while still a teenager, Judy was one of the studio's most popular performers, and when she was teamed with Mickey Rooney, both their careers soared. In 1939, of course, things changed forever when she appeared in *The Wizard of Oz*. Shirley Temple was set to star in the film, but her studio, 20th Century-Fox, was asking too much. During the next decade, Judy was not only the biggest star — female or male — at the studio, but in the 1940s only Bing Crosby and Bob Hope sold more tickets. With her enormous success came heartbreak. During her years at MGM, Judy started taking drugs to help her stay awake during long shooting schedules. Given to mood swings and erratic behavior, it all became too much for her. She began to experience mental breakdowns, was taken off the film *Annie Get Your Gun* after only a few weeks of shooting; and in 1950, she attempted suicide. She lost her contract at the studio, and it took four years for her to make a comeback — which she did with *A Star Is Born*.

Though she would appear in several more films, Judy never captured the magic on screen that she possessed in the '30s and '40s. After a series of extremely successful live performances (one of the most famous being her brilliant "Live at Carnegie Hall" concert), Judy hosted her own TV variety series in 1963. It only lasted for one year. Judy did not find much happiness in her marriages, either; she was married five times — among them were conductor David Rose, director Vincente Minnelli (daughter Liza's father), and Sid Luft. While visiting London, Judy died of a drug overdose while with her fifth husband, Mickey Deans. They had been married for less than a year. In addition to her gifted musical ability, it is possibly Judy's tragic life which has made her so popular with gay audiences. In an era when there was no gay voice, Judy's songs of love, pain and sacrifice no doubt struck a nerve with the romantic aspirations of an invisible generation.

The following are highlights from Garland's film career.

Broadway Melody of 1938
(1937, 115 min, US, Roy Del Ruth)
In this all-star musical bonanza, Judy sings "You Made Me Love You" to a picture of Clark Gable. Pure magic. She also sings "Everybody Sings." From a large cast including Robert Taylor, Eleanor Powell and George Murphy, only Sophie Tucker is as memorable as Judy. ⊛

Love Finds Andy Hardy
(1938, 90 min, US, George B. Seitz)
Very entertaining entry in the *Andy Hardy* series with Judy as the new girl in town who turns the head of Mickey Rooney. A young Lana Turner also appears as another of Mickey's girlfriends. ⊛

The Wizard of Oz
(1939, 101 min, US, Victor Fleming)
As Dorothy Gale of Kansas, Judy endeared herself in the hearts of filmgoers for generations. Before availability on video, the film's showings on TV every year were "events" greatly anticipated by adoring fans — young and old, alike. Judy follows the Yellow Brick Road to meet the wonderful wizard of Oz in this all-time classic musical. In a scene-stealing performance, Bert Lahr excels as the Cowardly Lion: "Yeah, it's sad, believe me, missy/When you're born to be a sissy...I'm afraid there's no denying/I'm just a dandy lion." ⊛

Babes in Arms
(1939, 91 min, US, Busby Berkeley)
This trimmed-down but delightfully entertaining version of the Rodgers and Hart Broadway hit features Judy and Mickey Rooney as children of vaudevillians who put on a show to help their struggling parents. ⊛

Strike Up the Band
(1940, 120 min, US, Busby Berkeley)
There's a big-time high school band competition sponsored by orchestra leader Paul Whiteman, and Judy and Mickey are representing their alma mater. ⊛

Life Begins for Andy Hardy
(1941, 100 min, US, George B. Seitz)
In Judy's last outing in the *Andy Hardy* series, Mickey Rooney is off to the Big Apple to take a bite, but finds the big city can be tough on a small-town boy. ⊛

Babes on Broadway
(1941, 121 min, US, Busby Berkeley)
Judy and Mickey Rooney pull out all the stops in this highly enjoyable musical as future stars trying to make it big on Broadway. Looking back at these Garland-Rooney films, Judy's a wonderful sight, of course, but you really can't say enough about Rooney's energetic output. ⊛

The Wizard of Oz

For Me and My Gal
(1942, 104 min, US, Busby Berkeley)
Gene Kelly made his film debut opposite Judy in this first-rate backstage musical. They play a vaudeville couple during WWI hoping to make it big...which, of course, they do. Songs include "After You've Gone" and the title tune. Of his debut, Kelly once said, "I knew nothing about filming when we started and I was scared. It was Judy who pulled me through." ⊛

Girl Crazy *(1943, 100 min, US, Norman Taurog)*
A terrific George and Ira Gershwin score highlights this slam-bang musical with Mickey Rooney as a rich kid who's sent to an all-male school, where he meets neighbor Judy. Songs include "I Got Rhythm" and "But Not for Me." Choreographed by Busby Berkeley. ⊛

Meet Me in St. Louis
(1944, 114 min, US, Vincente Minnelli)
Garland had one of her biggest hits with this charmingly old-fashioned, sentimental musical — a loving reminiscence of turn-of-the-century family life. Judy sings "The Trolley Song" and "Have Yourself a Merry Litle Christmas." Little Margaret O'Brien steals the show as Judy's younger sister. ⊛

The Clock
(1945, 90 min, US, Vincente Minnelli)
A lovely romantic drama featuring Judy in a glowing dramatic performance. Garland plays an office worker who meets soldier Robert Walker while he's on a two-day pass. (GB title: *Under the Clock*) ☻

The Harvey Girls
(1946, 101 min, US, George Sidney)
Judy sings "Atchison, Topeka and the Santa Fe" as she and other well-bred young ladies head west to be waitresses at the new Fred Harvey railroad station restaurants. It's '40s sugar, but a talented cast plus smart musical numbers make it an enjoyable ride. ☻

The Pirate *(1948, 102 min, US, Vincente Minnelli)*
Gene Kelly's thrilling dance numbers highlight this charming musical about traveling acrobat Kelly being mistaken for a notorious pirate by love-struck Judy. ☻

Easter Parade
(1948, 104 min, US, Charles Walters)
A tuneful Irving Berlin musical with Judy and Fred Astaire as a song-and-dance team during the early 1900s. Songs include "Steppin' Out with My Baby" and "A Couple of Swells." ☻

In the Good Old Summertime
(1949, 102 min, US, Robert Z. Leonard)
Charming musical remake of Ernst Lubitsch's *The Shop Around the Corner*, with Judy and Van Johnson as bickering co-workers who unwittingly fall in love via the personals. ☻

Summer Stock
(1950, 109 min, US, Charles Walters)
Judy plays a farm girl and sings "Get Happy" in this entertaining musical about a theatrical troupe, headed by writer/dancer Gene Kelly, who plans to turn her family's barn into a theatre. (GB title: *If You Feel Like Singing*) ☻

A Star Is Born
(1954, 170 min, US, George Cukor)
Judy gives her finest performance, both vocally and dramatically, as Vicki Lester, the young songstress who rockets to stardom upon discovery by matinee idol James Mason. Garland sings the unforgettable "The Man That Got Away," and the film has been restored to its original running time. Judy received her first Academy Award nomination (as Best Actress), and should have won (Grace Kelly won that year for *The Country Girl*). ☻

Judgment at Nuremberg
(1961, 190 min, US, Stanley Kramer)
Though director Stanley Kramer lets Judy over-act, she still manages to be touching as a German war widow. Garland received a Supporting Actress nod. ☻

A Child Is Waiting
(1962, 102 min, US, John Cassavetes)
Judy gives a remarkably controlled performance in this poignant tale of a sympathetic woman's relationship with a mentally retarded youth. Also with Burt Lancaster and Gena Rowlands. ☻

I Could Go on Singing
(1963, 99 min, GB, Ronald Neame)
Judy's last movie reveals the legendary singer in commanding voice as a famous American entertainer who travels to England to retrieve her son, who is living with his father (Dirk Bogarde). ☻

Babes on Broadway

Gay Icons – 1950s

MARILYN MONROE

Marilyn Monroe

The reigning sex goddess of the 1950s, Marilyn Monroe started as a bit player contracted to 20th Century-Fox and within a few short years worked her way up to that studio's most popular actress. With a quintessential dumb blonde image on-screen, Monroe was anything but dumb off it as she herself nurtured that image and her subsequent meteoric rise in films. When she prematurely died in 1962, Marilyn had been a movie star for only ten years — and over thirty years later, she remains possibly the most famous sex symbol and the most famous actress of our times.

Born Norma Jean Mortenson in 1926 in Los Angeles, Marilyn's name was soon changed to Baker after her mother re-married. Raised in L.A., her youth reads like something out of a Dickens novel: Her maternal grandmother and mother were committed to mental hospitals; her father died in a car accident when Marilyn was only three; and young Norma Jean was passed from one foster home to another while her mother was institutionalized. Young Marilyn, who stammered as a child, had only one dream — to be a movie star. And in the late 1940s, she began her quest. After a brief modeling career (which included posing for nude photos) and a short-lived marriage to an L.A. policeman in 1942 (which ended in divorce in 1946), Marilyn signed with 20th Century-Fox, which cast her in bit parts as a sexy dumb blonde. Marilyn's screen presence was overwhelming; even with only two minor scenes in *The Asphalt Jungle*, everyone wanted to know who the blonde was. Fox gave her the build-up, and Marilyn smartly honed what could be called her breathy Lorelei Lee character.

As her career took off, however, she experienced heartbreak in her private life. She would marry two more times, both legends in their professions: baseball player Joe DiMaggio and author Arthur Miller; one lasting only nine months and the latter lasting four years. She had bouts of depression, was suicidal, and given to taking drugs. In trying to maintain her image, stay in the spotlight and "play the Hollywood game," she fell victim to the very same system which she had been trying to adhere to. In 1962, at 36

years of age, Marilyn was found in a hotel room dead of a barbituate overdose. She was naked and clutching a phone. Her death was ruled a suicide, though in the years which have followed, rumors of conspiracy are as rampant as those of JFK's death. It's also been rumored that at the time of her death, Marilyn was involved with the President. This is so commonly talked about that speculation has given way to common knowledge.

Marilyn's exuberance and sensual manner have made her a longtime favorite of gays. Evoking a fragile vulnerability, she had such an innocence pertaining to her own sexuality that she's ultimately non-threatening to a gay audience. In addition to her soft-spoken and inimitable personality, Marilyn's exaggerated sensual demeanor has made her one of the most popular acts of female impersonators.

The following are highlights from Marilyn's film career.

Ladies of the Chorus
(1949, 61 min, US, Phil Karlson)
Marilyn made this before she signed with Fox. In it, MM plays a Burlesque queen under the watchful eye of her dancer mother. She soon falls in love with a society type. Marilyn may appear in a few musical numbers, but this "B" drama is hokum all the way. The

video version of this film gives Marilyn star billing, but she was originally billed third under the title. ⊛

The Asphalt Jungle
(1950, 112 min, US, John Huston)

In only two scenes, Marilyn is most memorable as "some sweet kid," the mistress to shady businessman Louis Calhern. This taut John Huston heist drama is a brilliantly stylized crime story about a group of hoods plotting a major jewel robbery. ⊛

All About Eve
(1950, 138 min, US, Joseph L. Mankiewicz)

Marilyn has a short but sweet scene as one of Bette Davis' party guests, an actress "from the Copacabana school of dramatic art" who is escorted by the acerbic George Sanders. Speaking of a theatrical producer, MM asks the immortal question: "Why do they always look like unhappy rabbits?" ⊛

Clash by Night
(1952, 105 min, US, Fritz Lang)

Barbara Stanwyck gives a dynamic performance in this steamy psychodrama as the penned-up wife of a boring fishing boat captain (Paul Douglas) whose yearning for excitement leads her to her husband's best friend (Robert Ryan). Marilyn and Keith Andes give good support as a young couple. ⊛

Don't Bother to Knock
(1952, 76 min, US, Roy Baker)

Billed above the title for the first time, Marilyn plays an emotionally disturbed baby-sitter who is a danger to herself and the young girl she's watching. Richard Widmark lives across the courtyard and comes to the rescue. As a lounge singer involved with Widmark, Anne Bancroft made her debut. ⊛

Niagara   *(1953, 89 min, US, Henry Hathaway)*

The turning point in MM's career, this taut suspenser gave Marilyn her first big break towards stardom, and hinted at the legendary persona which would soon emerge. While vacationing at Niagara Falls, a faithless wife (Marilyn) plots to murder her husband (Joseph Cotten) and run off with her lover; but when the distraught husband gets wise, he has other ideas. The importance of this film in Monroe's career usually overshadows the fact that this is quite an accomplished thriller. ⊛

Gentlemen Prefer Blondes
(1953, 91 min, US, Howard Hawks)

Marilyn is the gold-digging Lorelei Lee, who's just a little girl from Little Rock. She and best pal/fellow performer Jane Russell head for Paris in search of well-heeled husbands. Howard Hawks directed this bright and brassy musical comedy loaded with unbeatable humor. Marilyn's first big hit as star and one of her most endearing performances; she sings the classic production number "Diamonds Are a Girl's Best Friend." ⊛

Marilyn (l.), Lauren Bacall (c.) and Betty Grable learn *How to Marry a Millionaire*

How to Marry a Millionaire

(1953, 95 min, US, Jean Negulesco)

Hollywood's first Cinemascope comedy is a witty and stylish souffle starring Marilyn, Betty Grable and Lauren Bacall as three Manhattan gold diggers out to trap (and marry) unsuspecting millionaire bachelors. David Wayne, William Powell and Cameron Mitchell are the catches. ⊛

River of No Return

(1954, 91 min, US, Otto Preminger)

A big, sprawling Cinemascope western with Robert Mitchum as a farmer who is double-crossed by gambler Rory Calhoun and sets out, with his young son and saloon singer Marilyn, to even the score. There's explosive chemistry between Monroe and Mitchum which propels the film well beyond the usual western adventure. ⊛

There's No Business Like Show Business

(1954, 117 min, US, Walter Lang)

This Irving Berlin songfest is a particularly sentimental but entertaining musical about the professional and personal ups and downs of a theatrical family. Ethel Merman and Dan Dailey are the parents; kids Donald O'Connor, Johnny Ray and Mitzi Gaynor soon join the act. Marilyn also stars as O'Connor's love interest, and she gets to sing "Heat Wave." ⊛

The Seven Year Itch *(1955, 105 min, US, Billy Wilder)*

Billy Wilder's witty and zany romp exposes the sexual fantasies of the middle-aged married man. Marilyn is the unintending temptress upstairs who becomes the object of Tom Ewell's Walter Mitty-ish, philandering escapades. ⊛

Bus Stop *(1956, 96 min, US, Joshua Logan)*

Marilyn displays her usual sex appeal as well as surprising pathos in this delightful adaptation of the William Inge comedy. MM stars as a torchy cafe singer who becomes the object of affection — and obsession — by young naive cowpoke Don Murray (who received

an Oscar nomination for his sensationally wild performance). Great support from Eileen Heckart as Marilyn's waitress confidant and Arthur O'Connell as Murray's seasoned manager. ⊛

The Prince and the Showgirl

(1957, 117 min, GB, Laurence Olivier)

By all reports, there was no love lost between Laurence Olivier and Marilyn on the set of this light romantic comedy. There was nothing lost on the screen, however; as a pair, they work extremely well together. Monroe plays a saucy American chorus girl who is courted by Olivier's Balkan prince at the coronation of King George V in London. Terence Rattigan provides a vivacious script based on his hit play "The Sleeping Prince." ⊛

Some Like It Hot

(1959, 122 min, US, Billy Wilder)

Director Billy Wilder's masterpiece rates as one of the funniest American comedies of all time, and it only gets better with age. Jack Lemmon and Tony Curtis, at their comic best, star as down-and-out musicians in 1920s Chicago who, upon witnessing the St. Valentine's Day Massacre, don wig and dress and join an all-female band to escape the murderous thugs looking for them. In one of the screen's best dumb blonde performances, Marilyn is Sugar Kane, the band's beautiful singer who the boys are enraptured by. Curtis (out of drag) romances MM, and Lemmon is courted by millionaire Joe E. Brown, who gets to deliver possibly the best closing line in movies. ⊛

Let's Make Love

(1960, 118 min, US, George Cukor)

Marilyn is one of the few bright spots in this curious musical misfire. She plays an actress who catches the attention of millionaire Yves Montand — the very person her off-Broadway production is spoofing. ⊛

The Misfits *(1961, 124 min, US, John Huston)*

A stark, poignant film with Clark Gable, Montgomery Clift and Eli Wallach as modern day cowboys, and Marilyn as a delicate divorcée entangled in their games of camaraderie and machismo. Scripted largely for MM by husband Arthur Miller, *The Misfits* marked her and Gable's final screen roles. ⊛

Gay Icons – 1960s

BARBRA STREISAND

Funny Girl

Born in 1942 on Pulaski Street in the colorful Williamsburg section of Brooklyn, Barbara Joan Streisand overcame a childhood of poverty and personal tragedy to become one of the most influential actresses/singers of her time. Upon her arrival on the entertainment scene in the 1960s, Streisand has been a particular favorite with gay audiences, and that loyal following, which helped propel the singer to mainstream popularity during that decade, has remained steadfast through a career which has triumphed in the fields of theatre, film and song.

The daughter of a teacher and a housewife, young Barbara (please note three "a'"s) was greatly affected by the death of her father, who died when she was only 15 months old. A shy and unusual looking child, Streisand felt her looks and personality set her apart from other children — and always thinking of herself as ugly, this childhood feeling of being different haunted her into her adult years, as well. Barbara would escape the realities of her life with rich fantasies casting her as a famous, beautiful actress. At the age of 14, she saw her first Broadway play, "The Diary of Anne Frank," and loved it. She convinced her mother, who was not supportive of her daughter's theatrical aspirations, to send her to summer acting school, which she attended for two years. While still a teenager, Barbra worked at varying jobs (usherette, switchboard operator) while trying to pursue an acting career. Making the exhausting rounds of auditions, Barbara found no luck — until she heard that a bar in the Village was having a singing contest, and the prize was money, food and a job — the hungry and cash-poor Streisand, although not really interested in a singing career, entered anyway.

As it turned out, it was a gay bar, The Lion, which was sponsoring the contest. Barbara, dressed bohemian and displaying a comic demeanor, stunned the bar patrons with her vocal ability. She won, and was awarded a brief stint singing there. This led to a very successful appearance at the upscale supper club Bon Soir, where Barbra (it was about this time that Streisand dropped the second "a") was wowing the trendy New Yorkers looking for the next future singing sensation. After making an appearance in the off-Broadway revue, "Another Evening with Harry Stoones," Streisand performed at the famous nightclub The Blue Angel. It was here writer Arthur Laurents saw her, requesting that she audition for his new Broadway musical, "I Can Get It for You Wholesale." Getting the part, Streisand made the most out of her small role as the lovelorn secretary Miss Marplestein, and received a Tony Award nomination. It was with this show that she met Elliott Gould, whom she married in 1963 (and would later divorce in 1971).

Streisand's career took off, and in 1963 alone, in addition to her Broadway triumph, she released her first record, "The Barbra Streisand Album," and was named *Cue*'s Entertainer of the Year. Successful nightclub engagements followed, but it was a year later that young Barbara's fantasies would come true — over such actresses as Anne Bancroft and Carol Burnett, Barbra was chosen for the lead of the musical "Funny Girl," playing entertainer Fanny Brice. Of course, it was the turning point in the career of Barbra Streisand. After the success of the stage show, and two highly-rated and acclaimed TV specials, Streisand made her film debut re-creating her "Funny Girl" role, winning an Oscar as Best Actress (in all, Streisand has won an Emmy, two Oscars, a Grammy and a special Tony). She went on to become the most popular female star of '70s.

A powerful player in Hollywood, Streisand is known for taking total control of whatever project with which she is associated; this has given her such wide-ranging descriptions as "bitch" and "perfectionist." In-between her many, and mostly financially successful films, Streisand has never turned her back on her singing, and has released nearly 20 albums since her debut in 1963. Privately, Barbra has lent her name to various political causes, and most recently, was an instrumental and visible supporter of Bill Clinton's run for the presidency. Also, she has been an early supporter of gay and lesbian rights (on the passage of Colorado's anti-gay legislation she was the first celebrity to call for a boycott) and has been involved in numerous AIDS charities.

Funny Girl
(1968, 155 min, US, William Wyler)
Streisand's Oscar-winning film debut, repeating her acclaimed stage role as the legendary performer Fanny Brice, made her a star. Though the film is somewhat melodramatic for a musical biography, Streisand's singing and clowning make it all worthwhile. There's good period design, and Barbra sings "My Man," "People" and "Don't Rain on My Parade." Also with Omar Sharif, Kaye Medford, Walter Pidgeon (as Ziegfeld) and Anne Francis. ✆

Hello, Dolly! *(1969, 146 min, US, Gene Kelly)*
Streisand shines in this elaborate and entertaining screen version of the hit Broadway musical comedy. Streisand plays turn-of-the-century matchmaker Dolly Levi, who sets her own sights on grocery store owner Walter Matthau. There are wonderful dance numbers, and a whimsical score by Jerry Herman. Though some of the production is rather overblown, it detracts nothing from the film's enjoyment. Also with Michael Crawford and Tommy Tune. Based on Thornton Wilder's comedy, "The Matchmaker." ✆

The Owl and the Pussycat
(1970, 95 min, US, Herbert Ross)
Streisand and George Segal are terrific together in this raucous and very funny screen version of Bill Manoff's Broadway play. Streisand, in sensational form, plays a hooker who is kicked out of her apartment after complaints made by neighboring writer Segal; so she moves in with him.

What's Up Doc
(1972, 94 min, US, Peter Bogdanovich)
In director Peter Bogdanovich's deliriously funny homage to screwball comedies, and *Bringing Up Baby* in particular, Streisand has never been funnier, and even the usually bland Ryan O'Neal is respectable. This lunatic story has to do with identical suitcases leading their owners on a merry chase throughout San Francisco. In her film debut as O'Neal's much-flustered fiancée, Madeline Kahn is priceless. ✆

The Way We Were
(1973, 118 min, US, Sydney Pollack)
Fine romantic drama with Robert Redford and Streisand meeting in college in the late 1930s and having an on-again, off-again affair over the next 15 years. Streisand plays a campus activist who is enamored by gorgeous WASP Redford, meeting years later when each has made a name for themselves. One of the first films to explore the Hollywood blacklist of the 1950s, though it is used merely as a subplot. ✆

▼ Funny Lady *(1975, 137 min, US, Herbert Ross)*
This adequate sequel to Streisand's smash musical *Funny Girl* finds her in excellent voice reprising her role as legendary performer Fanny Brice. With Nicky in prison, Fanny takes up with Billy Rose, who would become her second husband. Roddy McDowall appears as Bobby Moore, Fanny's gay confidant. James Cann, who plays Brice's husband Billy Rose, constantly refers to Bobby as "pansy," "pet poodle" and "dear." To his credit, McDowall brings more to his character than is written in the script. ✆

A Star Is Born
(1976, 140 min, US, Frank Pierson)
Though this third remake of the classic romance was dubbed by those-less-kind as "A Bore is Starred," it's not *quite* as bad as that suggests. Streisand takes over the Janet Gaynor/Judy Garland role as an aspiring singer whose romance with a faltering rock star leads to tragedy. Kris Kristofferson is the fading star. The least successful of the three screen versions. ✆

▼ Yentl *(1983, 134 min, US, Barbra Streisand)*
Streisand's musical set in turn-of-the-century Eastern Europe and based on a short story by Isaac Bashevis Singer teases the audience with homoerotic and transgender undercurrents. Streisand plays a woman who, determined to study the Talmud — an exclusive domain of men — disguises herself as a young man. At the Yeshiva, she stirs the confused sexual attractions of both fellow student Avigdor (Mandy Patinkin) and his fiancée Hadass (Amy Irving). She eventually is led into marriage with Hadass and must fend off her betrothed who desires an appointment in the marriage bed. Streisand and Irving kiss at one point and in subsequent publicity junkets made a big fuss about the "difficulty" of the peck. ✆

Streisand, pretending to be a man, marries Amy Irving in *Yentl*

▼ The Prince of Tides
(1991, 132 min, US, Barbra Streisand)
Streisand's acclaimed second directorial effort is a lush, exceptional looking film version of Pat Conroy's novel. Nick Nolte is outstanding as a married, Southern high school coach who travels to New York when his sister (Melinda Dillon) is hospitalized at a psychiatric hospital. There he meets her doctor (Streisand), and the two begin a brief affair. A touching romance and a rather harrowing childhood memory piece, *The Prince of Tides* will certainly satisfy the romantics in most of us; though those more cynical will probably be less impressed. George Carlin appears as Eddie, Dillon's gay neighbor. A fine stand-up comedian, Carlin is miscast here; his swishy interpretation lacks characterization or depth, and it's somewhat of an embarrassment. In the novel, Eddie is not at all fey. ✆

Gay Icons — 1970s

BETTE MIDLER

Charlie Chaplin was "The Little Tramp." Theda Bara was "The Vamp." Jimmy Durante had "The Schnoze." And wearing one of the most accurate monikers of 'em all, Bette Midler is "The Divine Miss M." With an almost legendary show business start, Midler has been a longtime favorite with gays since she first appeared at the Continental Baths in the early 1970s. It was that audience which helped define Midler's persona, and the brassy entertainer with the remarkable voice has for years been gay associated — it's only been since 1986 that she's gone mainstream thanks to a series of successful Disney adult-oriented comedies.

Born in Honolulu in 1946, Midler was a "young Jewish girl living in a poor Samoan neighborhood." One of four children, Bette studied drama in high school and college in her native Hawaii, where she never felt comfortable due to her looks and religion. After graduation, she moved to Los Angeles and then to New York to "make it as an actress." Though she appeared as an extra in the Julie Andrews drama *Hawaii*, Bette made her real professional debut in the chorus of "Fiddler of the Roof" on Broadway. She eventually went on to play the plum role of the eldest daughter Tzeitel. Immediately after her performances, she would leave the comfy confines of the theatre district to sing in coffeehouses in the Village. After she left "Fiddler," Bette helped support herself in jobs as varying as a go-go dancer in Jersey City and as a Manhattan department store clerk.

Still singing in clubs and making the rounds for auditions, she learned that the gay bathhouse, the Continental Baths, was providing live, weekend entertainment. With her pianist and musical director Barry Manilow at her side, Midler was an immediate hit. On the shy side, Midler's appearances at the Continental helped shape the personality which would also be known as "Trash with Flash." Her writer and friend Bill Hennessey said, "She started out very serious and dramatic, very Helen Morgan. Once she went to the baths, the 'Divine Miss M' came to the surface."

It was only a short time till Bette made her first album, the Grammy Award-winning, best-sellling "The Divine Miss M," released in 1973. From there, she appeared in numerous TV specials, and in several sold-out and acclaimed live performances on Broadway and on tour, the best being the "Clams on the Half-Shell" revue. Upon seeing her in person, Laurence Olivier commented that she was one of the greatest live performers he had ever seen.

Though she made a cheap, independent comedy called *The Thorn* in the mid-1970s, Midler made her feature starring debut in 1979 in the fictionalized account of singer Janis Joplin in *The Rose*. The film was a big box-office hit, and Bette received an Oscar nomination for her role. However, Midler's film career hit a snag as her next film, *Jinxed*, proved to be an accurate title. A demanding and emotionally draining experience, Midler almost had a nervous breakdown, and it took three years for her to make a "comeback" in films. This came via a Disney film —released through its adult distribution line, Touchstone — called *Down and Out in Beverly Hills*. It was a runaway hit, and began a successful association which is still in effect today.

With her boisterous image, it's difficult to think of Midler's offstage manner contrasting that of her onstage one. But as she once explained, "Offstage, I am basically a serious, sentimental, frequently maudlin person — the complete opposite of the wild, zany hedonist I play onstage." Married and living the life of a suburban housewife rather than the bawdy songstress for which she's most identified, Bette recently finished a successful concert tour, and has started her own production company, All Girl Productions.

The Bette Midler Show

(1976, 84 min, US, Tom Tirbouch)
The Divine Miss M offers comic skits and outlandish interpretations of "Boogie Woogie Bugle Boy," "Friends" and many others in this immensely entertaining "live from Cleveland" concert. This is live Bette at her best.

▼ The Rose *(1979, 134 min, US, Mark Rydell)*

Midler made an impressive starring debut as a hard-drinking, fast-living rock chanteuse struggling against the pressures of success. Alan Bates is her mean-spirited manager and Frederic Forrest is her on-again, off-again lover. Visiting a Greenwich Village drag club, Midler exclaims with delight, "That drag queen's doing me." She does a number with "Barbra Streisand," "Diana Ross" and "Mae West." Michael Greer is the club's Emcee. Later, Rose is reunited with an old girlfriend, Sarah (Sandra McCabe). The film, suggested by the life of Janis Joplin, doesn't really explore Rose/Joplin's bisexuality, with exception of a discreet encounter. ⊗

Divine Madness

(1980, 95 min, US, Michael Ritchie)
The Divine Miss Midler in concert. No joke is too cheap, no gag too crass as evidenced by the raunchy stage performance of Bette and her Harlettes. And she sings, too. ⊛

Jinxed

(1983, 103 min, US, Don Siegel)
This muddled black comedy about blackmail, blackjack and murder stars Midler as a Las Vegas singer and Ken Wahl as a gambler who hooks up with her. Rip Torn also stars as a dealer, he the

The Rose

"jinxed" of the title. This film is known more for the conflicts on the set than for what is presented on the screen. ⊛

Down and Out in Beverly Hills

(1986, 97 min, US, Paul Mazursky)
Paul Mazursky's boisterously funny social comedy stars Nick Nolte as a street person who is taken in by a nouveau riche Beverly Hills family when he tries to drown himself in their swimming pool. Richard Dreyfuss and Midler are in top form as the husband and wife whose lives are turned upside-down by their new boarder. Modern remake of the Jean Renoir 1932 classic *Boudu Saved from Drowning*. Much was written of a tasteless AIDS joke made by Midler, but it's the kind of comment her character would have probably said. ⊛

Ruthless People *(1986, 93 min, US, Jim Abrahams, David & Jerry Zucker)*

Larceny, infidelity and murder among California's nouveau riche form the core of this near-hysterical comedy. Danny De Vito plays an unfaithful husband who plots to kill his overbearing wife (played with hilarious gusto by Midler) who, fortunately for him, has been kidnapped by a not-so-ruthless couple whom De Vito swindled. Judge Reinhold and Helen Slater are the hapless couple. A hip, modern re-telling of O. Henry's celebrated short story, "The Ransom of Red Chief." ⊛

Outrageous Fortune

(1987, 92 min, US, Arthur Hiller)
One of the most hilarious films of the 1980s, *Outrageous Fortune* finds its success in the ingenious pairing of pretty, prim and proper bitch Shelley Long with flamboyant, aggressive, floozy Midler (and, as with Olivier's *Hamlet*, a role the Divine Miss M was born to play). The fireworks given off by these two is priceless. The truly outrageous plot finds the female odd couple searching for a "missing" boyfriend; they become involved with the CIA, Russian agents, biochemical warfare, and George Carlin. ⊛

▼ Big Business

(1988, 97 min, US, Jim Abrahams)
Lightning doesn't strike twice as *Ruthless People* star Midler and director Jim Abrahams reunite in this rather tame, though genial comedy. Midler and Lily Tomlin star as two sets of twins switched at birth who run across each other's paths in the Big Apple. A good premise, a nice turn from the Divine Miss M and some nifty special effects can't save this lightweight comedy; which, though it does manage a few laughs, is a disappointment considering the talent involved. As corporate execs and lovers, Edward Herrmann and Daniel Gerroll are Midler's officious lackeys, and they both fall victim to the rustic charm of country boy Fred Ward. ⊛

Beaches *(1988, 123 min, US, Garry Marshall)*

Midler and Barbara Hershey star in this effective tearjerker which follows the friendship — and its ups and downs — of two women through the years. Midler is dynamic, giving one of her patented larger-than-life performances as a singer/actress determined to make it in show business. Hershey, new lips and all, is slightly eclipsed in Midler's shadow, but nicely essays the role of an upper-class attorney beset by personal misfortunes. Get out the hankies for this one.

Stella *(1990, 109 min, US, John Erman)*

Even Midler can strike out on occasion, as proved by this turgid remake of the perennial classic. Bette plays the sacrificing and (supposedly) slovenly mother of teenager Trini Alvarado; but she's more schizophrenic as one moment she's wise and creative and the next crude with no fashion sense. It just doesn't work in the 1990s. John Goodman, Stephen Collins, Eileen Brennan and Marsha Mason co-star.

Scenes from a Mall

(1991, 87 min, US, Paul Mazursky)

The casting of Woody Allen and Midler as a married couple was inspired — on paper. And indeed, they work well together, but this slight farce, set against the glitz and streetfront glamour of the Beverly Mall, while providing the occasional laugh, is basically dull and flat. She's a high-powered psychologist and he's a major promoter. They wend their way through the seemingly endless mall and go through a series of petty fights, major revelations and other assorted marital spats. Director Paul Mazursky tries to squeeze some life out of the bone-dry script, but if it weren't for the talents of its two stars, this film would be only marginally less boring than going to the mall on a Saturday night.

For the Boys

(1991, 148 min, US, Mark Rydell)

Though she has long been associated with the music of the 1940s ("Boogie Woogie Bugle Boy," etc.), this is Midler's first on-screen foray into that decade. Unfortunately, it's not the perfect match one might have hoped for. Midler is paired with the miscast James Caan in this tale about the turbulent partnership of a song and dance duo — from their meeting during WWII to the present. When set in the '40s, the film has vitality and purpose, but it is overly ambitious and none-too-successful in tackling the Hollywood blacklist, and the Korean and Vietnam wars. As the bawdy Dixie Leonard, Midler is in excellent voice and her acting far outshines the rest of the cast, thereby propelling this otherwise mediocre film. A good soundtrack is amongst the film's few other outstanding attractions.

Hocus Pocus

(1993, 96 Min, US, Kenny Ortega)

The fact that Walt Disney Pictures released this not through Touchstone nor Hollywood Pictures, but their Buena Vista line, which is usually reserved for their children's films, tells a lot about this lightweight but amiable fantasy. Recalling the Fred MacMurray comedies of the 1960s, the film stars Midler, Kathy Najimy and Sarah Jessica Parker as three 17th-century witches who return to modern-day Salem and run "amok, amok, amok." With more hokum than hocus, the witches set out to steal the souls of all the town's children. Their only opposition are three spunky kids, one of whom released them from their 300-year sleep. Midler, who can perform this sort of comedy sleepwalking, sings "I Put a Spell on You," which is one of the film's only highlights.

Gay Icons – 1980s

MADONNA

Throughout her career, Madonna has been a vocal advocate of gay lifestyles and gay rights (she was one of the earliest entertainment industry supporters of AIDS charities); the images she uses in music videos and her picture book, "Sex," are often homoerotic; her documentary *Truth or Dare* has been praised as being gay-friendly; and she has received honors from the Gay and Lesbian Alliance Against Defamation. As she outlined in an interview in *The Advocate*, her identification with gays and lesbians started at 16 when her dance teacher, Christopher Flynn, took her to "my first gay club to go dancing. I'd only been to high school dances, and no guys would ever ask me to dance, because they thought I was insane. I felt like such as outsider. And suddenly when I went to the gay club, I didn't feel that way anymore. I had a whole new sense of myself."

One of six children, Madonna was born in 1958. Her mother died when she was only five, and the family was raised by her father. Madonna began her musical career when she left the University of Michigan after two years and moved to New York to pursue a career in dance. When this line of work did not produce the stardom she craved, she changed direction; playing drums and guitar, she recorded a demo, was a hit on the disco scene, and in 1983 recorded with Sire Records. Since then, her ambitious, outrageous musical career has made her the most famous woman of her generation, though her film career has been anything but meteoric.

She made a soft-core movie during her starving artist days in New York, but her real acting debut came in 1985 in the surprise hit, *Desperately Seeking Susan*. This low-budget "Alice in Wonderland" odyssey brought her national attention, and she was a hit with audiences and critics alike. Her ensuing films, however, have mostly been either critical or financial bombs — *Dick Tracy*, *A League of Their Own* and her documentary *Truth or Dare* are the obvious exceptions.

Madonna's personal life has garnered as much press as anything she has put on vinyl or film. Her rocky marriage and divorce to actor Sean Penn, affairs with Warren Beatty, baseball player Jose Conseco and various others have all been covered by the mainstream and tabloid press alike. However, it was her purported liaison with comedienne Sandra Bernhard that really got tongues wagging. And while Bernhard has said that Madonna was the best lover she ever had, the Material Girl is a little more ambiguous on the subject, content to playfully fuel the rumors of her bisexuality in print and on TV talk shows, alike. She says maybe she did and maybe she didn't, but "You know, I'd almost rather they (people in general) thought I did. Just so they could know that here was this girl that everyone was buying records of, and she was eating someone's pussy. So there."

> "Every straight guy should have a man's tongue in his mouth at least once."
>
> —Madonna

Desperately Seeking Susan
(1985, 104 min, US, Susan Seidleman)
Ignoring the soft-core film *A Certain Sacrifice* (which is easy to do), Madonna made her feature film debut in this hip comic adventure. Rosanna Arquette stars as a bored New Jersey housewife thrust into the heart of Greenwich Village bohemianism thanks to a konk on the head. Madonna is Susan, the free spirit whose life Arquette follows through the personals in *The Village Voice*. Also with Aidan Quinn. ☮

▼ Vision Quest
(1985, 107 min, US, Harold Becker)
Matthew Modine and the fiery Linda Fiorentino make an attractive twosome in this compelling drama about a high school wrestler going after the state championship. In a brief appearance, Madonna sings two songs. R.H. Thomson plays a gay sports equipment salesman who makes a pass at naive room service waiter Modine. ☮

Shanghai Surprise
(1986, 97 min, US, Jim Goddard)
One of the candidates for Worst Film of the Decade, this laughable adventure film teamed then-husband and wife Sean Penn and Madonna in the story of a missionary (Madonna) in 1930s China who enlists the aid of a down-and-out adventurer (Penn) to track a missing opium shipment. ☮

Who's That Girl?
(1987, 94 min, US, James Foley)
Madonna plays a spunky parolee out to clear her name who totally changes forever the mild existence of yuppie Griffin Dunne. An awkward attempt at screwball comedy. ☮

Bloodhounds of Broadway
(1989, 101 min, US, Howard Brookner)
An impressive, though rather restrained cast is the highlight of Howard Brookner's alternately charming and forced comic mystery

Madonna and her boys (oh, and yeah, one girl) in *Truth or Dare*

based on four Damon Runyon short stories. Set on New Year's Eve on Broadway in 1928, the story revolves around a group of gamblers, showgirls and aristocrats whose lives intersect after a local gangster is nearly slain. The colorful cast of characters include Matt Dillon as the worst gambler in NYC, Madonna and Jennifer Grey as showgirls, and Randy Quaid (who best captures the spirit of Runyon) as a dim-witted high roller in love with Madonna (that's a twosome!). ⊛

Dick Tracy *(1990, 104 min, Warren Beatty)*

Warren Beatty's colorful adaptation of the Chester Gould comic strip is a dazzling display of costumery and scenery. In the title role, Beatty is clearly having fun (for a change) with his role of the crime fighter; Glenne Headly is charming as his girlfriend Tess Trueheart; and Dustin Hoffman is hilarious as Tracy's informant, Mumbles. Madonna gets to sing a couple of breathy show tunes penned by the inimitable Stephen Sondheim, and all of her other attributes are used to perfection. It's Al Pacino, however, who steals the film with his showy, scene-stealing turn as Tracy's arch-rival, Big Boy Caprice. A highly entertaining romp — maybe now we can forget about *Ishtar*. ⊛

Madonna: Truth or Dare

(1991, 118 min, US, Alek Keshishian)

Though not technically a documentary, this fascinating behind-the-scenes look at pop icon Madonna's world-wide "Blonde Ambition" tour seeks to reveal the singer in on- and offstage actions and interactions. And though she is the Executive Producer, therefore with much at stake, Madonna is to be credited with "opening up" and revealing much about herself in front of the camera — calculated as that may be. That same camera also captures some fabulous live performances, with Madonna singing some of her greatest hits. Also on hand are Madonna's dancers, relatives and friends; not to mention a gallery of famous names, from beau Warren Beatty to Sandra Bernhard to Kevin Costner, whom Madonna "disses." Even those who aren't fans will come away with an appreciation of the talented and savvy entertainer. ⊛

A League of Their Own

(1992, 127 min, US, Penny Marshall)

A fabulously entertaining baseball comedy, *A League of Their Own* is inspired by the real-life antics of the all-girl baseball league founded in 1943, when most of the major league's players were away at war. Geena Davis and Lori Petty star as country-girl sisters who are discovered by the ever-acerbic Jon Lovitz. Whisked off to Chicago, they join Madonna and Rosie O'Donnell on the Rockford Peaches. As the team's over-the-hill, boozing manager, Tom Hanks gives a rich characterization; and his lecture about "crying in baseball" is one of the funniest moments of this or any other year. The entire cast, in fact, is excellent. Davis and Petty offer splendid performances. (And it doesn't hurt that they look good in uniform and can handle a ball and glove.) Madonna gleefully plays against her offscreen image, and gives a funny and rowdy performance. ⊛

Shadows and Fog

(1992, 86 min, US, Woody Allen)

As one of the many all-stars in Woody Allen's amusing tribute to German expressionism, Madonna has the small and unlikely role as the wife of the circus strongman. She also gets to fool around with the circus clown, played by John Malkovich. ⊛

▼ Body of Evidence

(1992, 99 min, US, Uli Edel)

Madonna and Willem Dafoe star in this lethargic psychosexual mystery that makes *Basic Instinct* look like the *Citizen Kane* of the whodunit-in-the-sack thrillers. The "body" in question is Madonna's over-exposed corpus; the evidence shows that said body was the lethel weapon in a classic case of come-and-gone lovemaking. Dafoe is Frank Delaney, the morally dubious lawyer who must prove that while S&M hellcat Rebecca Carlsen (guess who?) is a "killer" in bed (wielding handcuffs, candles and mega-developed inner thighs), she's not actually a murderer. But can he maintain professional distance and resist the pint-sized dynamo who "does it like animals do it?" Sure, Madonna's acting doesn't amount to much more than eyelash batting, hip-swiveling and lip-licking, but (and this is the sad part) she still out-acts Dafoe who gives the worst performance of his career. As the prosecuting attorney, Joe Mantegna can barely conceal his disdain for the entire affair. Frank Langella has a small role as Madonna's bisexual ex-husband. ⊛

Dangerous Game

(1993, 107 min, US, Abel Ferrara)

Director Abel Ferrara continues his examination of moral ambiguity with this verite *pas de trois* between a film director (Harvey Keitel) and his two leads (Madonna and James Russo). They're working on a nauseating little film in which Russo plays a husband who abuses his wife (Madonna) and subsequently she attempts to escape their life of drug abuse and debauchery. Using the device of a film within a film, Ferrara warps the distinction between illusion and reality as the three principals become ever more enmeshed in their on- and off-the-set shenanigans. Madonna, Keitel and Russo all perform well, and Ferrara shows a deft directorial hand, but that won't help most viewers overcome the film's repugnant core and unrelentingly nihilistic viewpoint.

3

THE ARTS

The writers, artists, dancers and composers in this chapter are all
either gay or lesbian, or have contributed greatly to a queer
presence in the arts.

"Most people do think of me as just another pinko faggot, a
bleeding heart, a do-gooder. But that's what I am."
                                        —Leonard Bernstein

P A U L
BOWLES

Paul Bowles in Morocco

(1970, 57 min, GB, Gary Conklin)

"If life is a question of being...then the best thing for him was to sit back and be, and whatever happened, he still was." Bowles, acclaimed writer ("Let It Come Down") and composer, is spotlighted in this intriguing documentary. Having left the United States in the 1940s to travel around the world, Bowles eventually settled in Morocco and it is there, in Tangier, his longtime home, that the filmmaker finds this urbane and fascinating man. Reading passages from his novels, recounting exotic stories from his past, visiting his favorite haunts and philosophizing about the Moroccan people and their lifestyle, Bowles rambles, but what captivating rambling it is! Interestingly, the film at times is less about the writer (and nothing at all is mentioned about his homosexuality) and more about the strange appeal of this mysterious Arab culture and land. ⊛

▼ The Sheltering Sky

(1990, 138 min, Italy/GB, Bernardo Bertolucci)

Against the vast backdrop of the sweltering heat and punishing sky of Northern Africa, Bernardo Bertolucci's intimate epic (adapted from Bowles' classic novel) follows the lives of three American travelers during the early 1950s. A husband and wife, Port (John Malkovich) and Kit (Debra Winger), and their traveling companion Tunner (Campbell Scott), embark from Tangier in search of the "real" Morocco. Slow moving, though featuring sumptuous photography, this sun-drenched existential journey should enthrall those with the patience. Malkovich is perfect as the arrogant and unfeeling husband who is overwhelmed by culture shock, and Winger's performance as a complacent woman who undergoes a life-altering transformation is mesmerizing. In support, Timothy Spall is quite effective as Eric, a sleazy, overweight homosexual, brow-beaten by his mother and sexually attracted to an unresponsive Port. ⊛

Paul Bowles in contemplative repose

W I L L I A M
BURROUGHS

Towers Open Fire

(1962-72, 35 min, US, Antony Balch)

Burroughs is featured in two shorts in this compilation of four art films from independent filmmaker Antony Balch. *Towers Open Fire* and *The Cut-Ups* attempt to make a cinematic equivalent to Burroughs' famous "cut and paste" style of writing — in which he would write sections of a book, physically cut the story into several pages and then randomly re-paste them together. As Burroughs narrates, we watch a visual collage of his writing containing many of the author's key themes. Although trying at times (watching five minutes of voice-over intoning repeatedly "yes-no" is a good test), the films are of great interest to both experimental film lovers and Burroughs fans. ⊛

Chappaqua

(1966, 82 min, US, Conrad Rooks)

Autobiographical account of Rooks' hallucinogenic (drug and alcohol-induced) impressions of a Parisian trip. Rooks stars in the surrealistic voyage that includes Burroughs, Allen Ginsberg and Ravi Shankar and Ornette Coleman.

Fried Shoes, Cooked Diamonds

(1979, 55 min, Italy/US, Constanzo Allione)

Narrated by Allen Ginsberg, this free-wheeling documentary focuses on the reunion of Beat poets (of the "Jack Kerouac School of Disembodied poets") at the Naropa Institute in Boulder, Colorado. Highlighted are relaxed poetry readings, music, and spirited discussions with such leading figures as Timothy Leary, Meredith Monk, Miguel Pinero, Gregory Corso, Amiri Baraka, Anne Waldman and Ginsberg and his longtime lover Peter Orlovsky. Burroughs, called by Ginsberg as "the invisible man," is also featured as he talks about, among other subjects, his philosophy of "do-easy" and Marxism. ⊛

Burroughs

(1983, 87 min, US, Howard Brookner)

The spiritual father of the Beat generation and author of several brutal and shocking novels ("Junkie," "Naked Lunch," "The Wild Boys"), Burroughs is vividly captured in this fascinating, funny and often touching documentary. Through Burroughs' cooperation, we visit his friends (Allen Ginsberg, Patti Smith), his home town of St. Louis and his then bunker-like residence in a former YMCA in the Lower East Side. Family scenes are the most revealing; the several encounters with his troubled son (who died during filming) and the particularly painful recounting of his wife's death in a William Tell-like experiment. With the many interviews, readings from his novels, a hilarious enactment of a scene from "Naked Lunch" and Burroughs' own honest and remorseless appraisal of his life, this is a splendid glimpse into the mind of a true literary genius. Director Brookner, who died of AIDS in 1988, made one other film: *Bloodhounds of Broadway*. ⊛

Burroughs (c.) with David Cronenberg (l.) and Peter Weller from *Naked Lunch*

(Burroughs, Allen Ginsberg, Gregory Corso) as well as its leading adherents of today (Marianne Faithful, Lydia Lunch, Richard Hell). With quotes like "'Howl' overcame censorship trials to become one of the most widely read works of this century," the documentary is prone to hyperbole and self-boasting, but nonetheless presents a vivid hour exploring the recollections and observations of today's performers and poets who together give us a teasing glimpse into creativity in the key of Beat. ⊛

Old Habits Die Hard
(1990, 60 Min, US)
Burroughs is featured in this John Giorno-produced video compilation that features additional performance pieces by such Beaters as Jim Jarmusch, Tom Waits, Love and Rockets, Coil, Star Sutherland, the Butthole Surfers, Giorno himself and others. ⊛

Poetry in Motion
(1985, 90 min, US, Ron Mann)
Burroughs, along with John Cage and Allen Ginsberg, are just three of the 25 artists (mostly straight) featured in this compilation documentary/performance film. In his trademark deadpan animated style, Burroughs reads from his writings which includes the line of advice, "Stay out of church and don't ever let a priest near you when you're dying. All they got is a key to the shithouse." Ginsberg offers a rousing rock poetry session and Cage passionately reads and discusses Henry David Thoreau. Other artists include Tom Waits, Charles Bukowski and Amiri Baraka. ⊛

Commissioner of the Sewers
(1986, 60 min, US, Klaus Maeck)
From the publication of his novel "Junkie" in 1963 through the present with the Hollywood-backed film version of his "Naked Lunch," William S. Burroughs has remained a controversial and fascinating figure. This documentary doesn't uncover anything new for seasoned Burroughs-philes, but for the uninitiated, it will prove to be enlightening as the author, with his dry wit and outlandish theories, pontificates on everything from his beliefs on death after life and art and artists to the meaning of his cut-up style of writing. He reads excerpts from his book "The Western Lands" and concludes with a reading of his now famous, and bitterly sarcastic, "Thanksgiving Prayer." ⊛

Gang of Souls
(1988, 60 min, US, Maria Beatty)
This tribute to the Beat Generation is comprised of various interviews with members of the first generation of the '50s movement

Naked Lunch
(1991, 115 min, US, David Cronenberg)
Based on Burroughs' 1950s free-form, underground classic, *Naked Lunch* — a book whose non-linear narration and fantastical and shocking imagery have been long thought of as "unfilmable" (indeed, as have all of his other works) — has been successfully brought to the screen in this witty and imaginative interpretation by "straight" horror-meister David Cronenberg. Far from being a literal translation of the celebrated novel, this hallucinatory, horror/sci-fi/comedy/drama freely borrows scenes from the novel and mixes in classic Burroughs leitmotivs (such as Burroughs' shooting of his wife while playing a game of William Tell). Also thrown in are some Beat Generation characters and philosophies, along with Cronenberg's usual assortment of grotesque and phallic-shaped creatures. Sadly missing, however (no doubt for commercial considerations), is any reference to Burroughs' penchant for violent and graphic gay sex, including his obsession with autoerotic strangulation. Peter Weller stars as Burroughs' monosyallabic alter-ego, Bill Lee, an exterminator who, along with his sharp-tongued wife (the amazing Judy Davis), gets hooked on his own bug powder. Lee, swimming in a narcotics-induced paranoia, sees his Remington typewriter come alive in the form of a slimy, bug-shaped creature who informs him that he is really an underground agent on a mission to fight a worldwide "Interzone" conspiracy. This leads him to "travel" to Morocco, where he meets other agents Ian Holm, Julian Sands and, in an additional role, Davis. An audacious and demanding foray into the psyche of a drug-addicted artist that will prove for some to be disgusting and incomprehensible — a response that should delight Burroughs. ⊛

C T RUMAN APOTE

Beat the Devil

(1954, 92 min, US, John Huston)

This offbeat black comedy left audiences in a daze when first released. Reportedly, the filming began without a finished script, forcing John Huston and a young Capote to collaborate daily before shooting and allowing the actors to ad-lib many scenes. The result is a zany spoof of spy thrillers dealing with a gang of international crooks concocting a uranium swindle. The peculiar cast includes Humphrey Bogart, Gina Lollobrigida, Jennifer Jones (blonde-wigged and brilliant as a compulsive liar), Peter Lorre and Robert Morley. ⊛

Breakfast at Tiffany's

(1961, 114 min, US, Blake Edwards)

Based on a Capote story, this winning romantic comedy stars Audrey Hepburn as small-town Texas girl Holly Golightly, who leaves home to conquer the Manhattan party scene. The film features zesty direction by Blake Edwards, and a fanciful Henry Mancini score including the Oscar-winning "Moon River." Reportedly, Capote did not like the film version. ⊛

In Cold Blood

(1967, 134 min, US, Richard Brooks)

A truly remarkable screen adaptation of Capote's novel. A straightforward presentation in moody black and white avoids sensationalizing the already potent story of random slaughter by two aimless, rootless lost boys (Robert Blake and Scott Wilson). Director Richard Brooks, aided by a masterful script, conveys complex information and muted emotional states with assured skill and humane empathy. Unsettling, discomforting, rewarding. ⊛

Truman Capote's A Christmas Memory

(1966, 51 min, US, Frank Perry)

Beginning with his cousin's observation, "Oh my, it's fruitcake weather," this Emmy Award-winning short film is a sweetly nostalgic recollection of Capote's youth in the rural South during the Depression. In an award-winning performance, Geraldine Page stars as his homespun "cousin" who takes care of the young Capote, with the story centering on their warm home life, their touching relationship and her Christmas tradition of making over 30 fruitcakes as presents. A simple, quiet drama of love narrated by the author himself. ⊛

Truman Capote

▼ The Glass House

(1972, 73 min, US, Tom Gries)

Capote co-wrote the screenplay (with Wyatt Cooper) for this harrowingly realistic depiction of prison life that was a landmark made-for-television drama. Shot in an actual Utah state prison and using real inmates as extras, the film depicts the often savage, predatory conditions in the brutal "glass house" where control lies in the thuggish hands of Hugo Slocum (Vic Morrow) and his gang of goons. One memorable scene involves the gang rape of teenage newcomer Allen (Kristoffer Tabori) by the henchmen of a spurned Hugo, a vicious act that leads to the boy's suicide. Also starring Alan Alda and Billy Dee Williams.

Murder by Death

(1976, 95 min, US, Robert Moore)

Capote makes a rare (and quite campy) acting appearance as Lionel Twain, a wispy lispy-voiced millionaire who invites a group of famous sleuths to his Gothic mansion to solve a mysterious murder. An enjoyable whodunit spoof scripted by Neil Simon. ⊛

COLETTE

L'Ingénue Libertine
(1950, 88 min, France, Jacqueline Audry)
Jacqueline Audry, director of the lesbian-themed *Olivia*, enjoyed a directorial career that began in the 1940s and lasted until the '70s. Her films dealt primarily with independent women, a particularly rare theme in the male-obsessed motion picture community. She worked on several screen adaptations of Colette novels including *Gigi* (a 1948 French version), *Mitsou* and this sexually adventurous melodrama. Daniéle Delorme stars as a young wife who becomes sexually distant with her older husband who offers her no respect. They are brought back together only after she has two liberating affairs with other men. The theme of a happily philandering wife caused an uproar in Britain where the film received the country's first "X" certificate. (US title: *Minne*)

The Ripening Seed
(1954, 105 min, 1953, France, Claude Autant-Lara)
Condemned by the Catholic Church as "immoral and obscene," this now tame (but at the time scandalous) love triangle involves a youth (Pierre-Michel Beck) who is torn between his childhood love (Nicole Berger) and a seductively alluring older woman (Edwige Feulleré). Adapted from Colette's novel. (US title: *The Game of Love*)

Mitsou *(1956, 95 min, France, Jacqueline Audry)*
Audry's final adaptation of a Colette story is this lavishly produced costume drama set in Paris during World War I. The story revolves around a pretty chorus girl (Daniéle Delorme) who is spurned by her more class-conscious soldier-boyfriend. In "Pygmalian"-style, she asks the assistance of an older admirer to teach her refinement and elegance.

Gigi *(1958, 116 min, US, Vincente Minnelli)*
The second adaptation of Colette's novel is this enchanting Oscar-winning musical about a French girl (Leslie Caron), being groomed to be a courtesan, and her romance with a handsome playboy (Louis Jordan). Maurice Chevalier also stars and is most memorable as young Gigi's guardian. Winner of nine Academy Awards, including Best Picture. Terrific Lerner & Lowe score includes "Thank Heaven for Little Girls" and "I Remember It Well." Cecil Beaton was the costume and production designer. ☮

▼ Becoming Colette
(1992, 97 min, US/France, Danny Huston)
While never quite overcoming its pedestrian handling of a potentially illuminating subject, this steamy drama, sort of a poor man's *Henry and June*, is filmed in the tradition of European "art" films, replete with female frontal nudity and "shocking" lesbian love scenes, all filmed in a lush, bombastic and romantic style. The story concerns the early years of the life of Sidone-Gabrielle Colette, one of France's most popular 20th-century writers. As an enchanting teenager in rural France, young Gabrielle is introduced to Willy (Klaus Maria Brandauer), a sweet-talking bon vivant 22 years her senior. She quickly sweeps him off his feet and they move to Paris to begin a carefree life of society living. But when Gabrielle shows him some of her writing, he publishes the work as his own and becomes the talk of the town. Frustrated at being merely cash-producing chattel for her now philandering husband, the young woman begins a lesbian relationship with a friend, and with her assistance and support, the increasingly sophisticated Colette is born. The love scenes between the women are tender, sensuous and eventually life-affirming while her husband is portrayed as an abusive, deceptive leech. Despite director Huston's heavy-handedness, the film is nevertheless entertaining in telling the story of one woman's growth, maturation and success, all accomplished on her own terms. ☮

NOËL COWARD

Easy Virtue *(1927, 79 min, GB, Alfred Hitchcock)*
Hitchcock meets Noël Coward. It's tempting to simply leave it at that. Based on a story by Coward, this early silent comes up a little short dramatically, but it does have flashes of the director's later style. The story has to do with melodramatic sufferings an alcoholic's wife (Isabel Jeans) endures. ☮

Private Lives
(1931, 84 min, US, Sidney Franklin)
One of Coward's most delightful stage comedies is given sparkling treatment in this very funny screen adaptation. Norma Shearer and Robert Montgomery are a divorced couple who meet each other on their respective second-marriage honeymoons. In a flash, they leave their spouses and run off to rekindle their relationship — and their bickering. The film is ripe with those scintillating Coward witticisms, and if Shearer and Montgomery weren't the perfect choices to recite them (the Lunts made *The Guardsman* that same year), they nevertheless handle this sophisticated hilarity with great charm. ☮

Cavalcade *(1933, 110 min, US, Frank Lloyd)*
Coward's 1930s stage hit is given superior treatment in this Oscar-winning adaptation. Clive Brook and Diana Wynyard head an upper-class British family at the turn-of-the-century. The film follows their lives thru World War I and into the 1930s. Though she was nominated for a Best Actress Oscar, Wynyard's performance seems exaggerated and dated, but the film does not. First-rate production values and an engrossing story make this one of the classics from its era. ☮

FAVORITE WRITERS

Design for Living

(1933, 90 min, US, Ernst Lubitsch)

The talents of director Ernst Lubitsch and writer Coward are well put to use in this smart and very funny (if watered down) film version of Coward's play. Substantially rewritten for the screen by Ben Hecht, the film stars Miriam Hopkins, Fredric March and Gary Cooper as three struggling bohemians in 1930s Paris. Cooper is an artist, March is a writer, and Hopkins (in an enchanting performance) is the woman they both love. Even though much of Coward's original sexual innuendo has been removed, the film is still enjoyable in part to the three leads' spirited portrayals and the director's deft "touch." Edward Everett Horton stands out in support as Hopkins' fussy, cliché-quoting husband.

The Scoundrel

(1935, 74 min, US, Ben Hecht & Charles MacArthur)

Coward appeared in his first (adult) starring role in this unusual and scintillating supernatural comedy-drama written and directed by the writing team of Hecht and MacArthur ("The Front Page," "20th Century"). Coward plays an egotistical, cynical publisher who dies and returns to earth in a last search for love. Ahead of its time and extremely witty (*Variety* said it's "good Hotel Algonquin literati stuff, but not for the Automat trade"), the film's sophisticated story line, masterful (and Oscar-winning) screenplay and strong performances make this a one-of-a-kind film experience. Gay critic Alexander Woollcott — the inspiration for Sheridan Whiteside in "The Man Who Came to Dinner" — has a sizable role.

In Which We Serve

(1942, 115 min, GB, Noël Coward & David Lean)

One of the masterpieces of British cinema, *In Which We Serve* provided director/writer/actor/composer Coward with his finest screen hour. Based on the real-life experiences of the British war-ship HMS Kelly, the film recounts — mostly in flashback — the story of the men of a torpedoed destroyer awaiting rescue. Coward brings all the right qualities of leadership and resolve to his role of the ship's captain, and excellent in support are John Mills, Michael Wilding, Richard Attenborough and Celia Johnson (both in their film debuts), and Kay Walsh. Daniel Massey, who would play Coward in *Star!*, also made his debut playing a youngster. The film marked the directorial debut of David Lean, and Coward won a special Oscar for his "Outstanding Production Achievement." ⊛

This Happy Breed

(1944, 114 min, GB, David Lean)

Coward's keen adaptation of his own hit play about the affairs of a lower middle-class family was immensely popular in its day. Set between the two World Wars, the film delves into the petty bickerings and small triumphs of the Gibbons clan as they grapple with the difficulties of a world ravaged by social strife and war. Director David Lean makes excellent use of Ronald Neame's penetrating camerawork. ⊛

Blithe Spirit *(1945, 96 min, GB, David Lean)*

Coward's enchanting classic stage production makes for an equally captivating film comedy, adapted for the screen by Coward himself. Taking over Coward's stage role, Rex Harrison stars as a cynical author whose life turns upside-down when the ghost of his deceased first wife materializes during a seance. Kay Hammond is a delight as the returning spectre, and Constance Cummings is splendid as Harrison's second wife. But it's the hilarious and spirited performance of Margaret Rutherford as the medium Madame Arcati which is most memorable. ⊛

Brief Encounter

(1946, 86 min, GB, David Lean)

A masterpiece from Britain's post-war cinema, this extraordinary romantic drama stars Trevor Howard and Celia Johnson, both giving impeccable performances, as two ordinary, middle-aged people involved in a short but passionate extramarital affair. Subtle, masterful direction from David Lean. Based on Coward's one-act play, "Still Life." ⊛

▼ Star!

(1968, 194 min, US, Robert Wise)

Though a colossal failure upon its release, this handsome, song-filled musical biography of actress/singer Gertrude Lawrence is glorious entertainment hampered by only its extravagances and excesses. Julie Andrews gives a sturdy performance as Lawrence, who rises from poverty to become the toast of two continents. Daniel Massey received an Oscar nomination for his well-studied, tempered portrayal of the gay Noël Coward, Lawrence's best friend and co-star. The film's musical numbers, especially "Jenny," are first-rate, and while Coward's gayness is played down, any mention of Lawrence's reported bisexuality is nonexistent. ⊛

Kay Hammond, Rex Harrison and Constance Cummings in *Blithe Spirit*

DU MAURIER

DAPHNE

Jamaica Inn
(1939, 90 min, GB, Alfred Hitchcock)
This tense, suspenseful melodrama by Alfred Hitchcock, starring Charles Laughton and Maureen O'Hara, is based on the best-selling novel by Du Maurier. The story is set in the 18th century and is about a country squire (Laughton) who is secretly the head of a band of pirates who wreck ships and ransom them. This was Hitchcock's last film in England before he began his "Hollywood period." ⊗

▼ Rebecca
(1940, 115 min, US, Alfred Hitchcock)
Alfred Hitchcock's first Hollywood movie is a Gothic masterpiece based on the book by Du Maurier. Joan Fontaine plays a passive and awkward paid companion ("friend of the bosom") for the snotty dowager Mrs. Van Hopper. While on vacation at Monte Carlo, she falls in love with the ominous and rich Maxim de Winter (Laurence Olivier) who whisks her off to his mansion. However, his mysterious attachment to his deceased first wife wreaks havoc upon their marriage. The most durable performance comes from Judith Anderson as the creepy Mrs. Danvers, the fanatical devoted housekeeper (paramour?) of the first Mrs. de Winter, whose eventual death/suicide echoes that of the "mad woman in the attic" in "Jane Eyre." A chilling script and superb acting and direction won *Rebecca* an Oscar for Best Picture. ⊗

The Birds
(1963, 120 min, US, Alfred Hitchcock)
Long before the heyday of disaster films, Hitchcock helmed this frightening tale of nature gone awry, as swarms of ferocious fowl attack a tranquil California town. Evan Hunter adapted Du Maurier's menacing short story, and Rod Taylor, Tippi Hedren, Suzanne Pleshette and Jessica Tandy star. Pleshette's character, that of the schoolteacher, could be interpreted as lesbian. ⊗

Don't Look Now
(1973, 110 min, GB, Nicolas Roeg)
This stylish, visually beautiful mystery established Nicolas Roeg as a master of his craft. In addition to creating one of the most famous sex scenes in the history of the cinema, Roeg brilliantly taps into one of the most primal fears of many adults — the death of a child. Based on a novel by Du Maurier, the film stars Julie Christie and Donald Sutherland as bereaved parents who attempt to contact their child

through a medium. Roeg's haunting imagery of winter in Venice is breathtaking. ⊗

Focus on: *Daphne Du Maurier*
Although writer Daphne Du Maurier lived a quiet suburban life with her husband and three children, her bisexuality has been long open to speculation. She had acknowledged having a schoolgirl affair with a female teacher in her French boarding school, but it was with the publication of Margaret Foster's biography, "Daphne Du Maurier: The Secret Life of the Renowned Storyteller," that details of her other life surfaced. Foster claims that Du Maurier thought of herself "not a lesbian, but a half-breed, someone internally male and externally female." The great but unrequited love of her life was Ellen Doubleday, wife the publisher Nelson Doubleday. After this ended, Du Maurier soon became involved with actress Gertrude Lawrence when she was starring in her play "September Tide." Strongly individualistic, Du Maurier once remarked about lesbianism, "Nobody could be more bored with the 'L' people as I am."

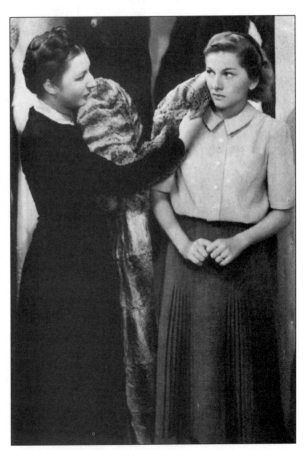

Rebecca

E.M. FORSTER

A Passage to India

(1984, 163 min, GB, David Lean

Master filmmaker David Lean proved himself capable of pulling yet another beautifully crafted "big" picture out of his hat with this meticulous adaptation of the Forster novel about the clash between British and Indian cultures and classes in the colonial India of the 1920s. A superlative cast (Judy Davis, Victor Banerjee, Peggy Ashcroft, James Fox and Alec Guinness) is featured and Lean's evocation is rich in flavor and nuance. ⊛

A Room with a View

(1985, 115 min, GB, James Ivory)

This enchanting period comedy-of-manners is the first of three film adaptations of Forster's works by Merchant Ivory Productions. During a trip to Florence, Lucy's (Helena Bonham Carter) simmering sensuality is kindled when she meets and falls in love with a free-spirited and handsome young man. The struggle between this love and the expectations of a "proper society" features uniformly outstanding performances by Maggie Smith as her insufferable aunt and Daniel Day-Lewis as her prissy English suitor. Also starring Denholm Elliott, Simon Callow, Julian Sands, Rupert Graves and Judi Dench. ⊛

▼ Maurice *(1987, 149 min, GB, James Ivory)*

Called a trite maliciously the "closet queen of the century" by biographer Andrew Hodges, Forster's life and work should be of great interest to gays and lesbians. Born in 1879, Forster became a celebrated novelist of elegant (heterosexual) drawing room dramas and a professor of English at Cambridge. He was never "out" although he did have a lover, Bob Buckingham, and once wrote of his love, "From 1951 to '53, I have been happy, and would like to remind others that their turn can come too. It is the only message worth giving." His coming out was done posthumously with the publication in 1971 of his tenderly romantic gay love story "Maurice," written in 1914. The characters and story in the novel were based on an actual incident while he was a student at Cambridge. Max Garnett and fellow student Ernest Mertz (Clive in the book) were close friends, but when Ernest found out that his love was soon to be married, he committed suicide. Reportedly Forster met Mertz on the night he died, in 1909, and he was the last person to see him alive. Translating the incident to paper, Forster wanted to offer a happy ending to their relationship. The possibility that working-class Scudder and college boy Maurice could sustain a gay relationship in 1914 England (especially since both would have been drafted to fight in World War I) stretches believability, but romance and love is eternal and fiction has no restraints. On this romantic conclusion to the tale, Forster wrote, "A happy ending was imperative.

Maurice

I shouldn't have bothered to write otherwise. I was determined that in fiction, anyway, two men should fall in love and remain in it forever and ever that fiction allows." Describing the main character he wrote, "In Maurice, I tried to create a character who was completely unlike myself...someone handsome, healthy, bodily attractive, mentally torpid, not a bad businessman and rather a snob. Into this mixture I dropped an ingredient that puzzles him, wakes him up, torments him and finally saves him." ⊛

Where Angels Fear to Tread

(1991, 113 min, GB, Charles Sturridge)

This overlooked adaptation of Forster's novel is impressively produced, superbly acted and an extremely worthwhile effort. Helen Mirren stars as Lilia Harriton, a wealthy widow who enrages her stodgy in-laws when she runs off to Italy and marries a swarthy young peasant, thereby threatening the family fortune. Scandalized, their matriarch (Barbara Jefford) dispatches Mirren's brother and sister (Rupert Graves and Judy Davis) off to Italy to try to talk some sense into the merry widow. Helena Bonham Carter tops off the cast as Mirren's devoted traveling companion. All of the performances are first-rate, but Davis steals the show with her truly over-the-top portrayal of the histrionic Harriet Harriton. The film sports a darker sense of humor and more tragic twists than the standard Forster fare produced by Merchant Ivory. ⊛

Howards End

(1992, 140 min, GB, James Ivory)

The third time is certainly a charm as Merchant Ivory Productions have outdone even themselves with this sumptuous re-creation of Forster's tale of class struggle in the dying days of the Edwardian era. In this truly marvelous and engaging period piece, Emma Thompson won a well-deserved Oscar for her portrayal of a middle-class woman who marries into the upper crust, and Anthony Hopkins matches her handsomely as her newly married husband. One of Merchant Ivory's biggest box-office successes. ⊛

JEAN GENET

▼ Un Chant d'Amour

(France, 1950, 20 min, Jean Genet)

Although only 20 minutes long, *Un Chant d'Amour*, the only film made by Genet, is one of most important works of gay cinema. Set in a French prison, the film records the erotic dance of death and passion enacted out by three inmates and their masochistic guard. The hardened men strive for love and affection in the cold, isolated world of their cells, furtively succeeding at times: in one scene, two men share a cigarette through a small hole by one blowing the smoke into the mouth of the other; and in another a bunch of flowers are blindly given through barred windows. There are explicit scenes of masturbation and the threat of violence and retribution hangs heavy (a voyeuristic guard enters the cell of one of the prisoners and places a gun in his mouth). Poetic and lyrical, the film is a startling work on the flowering of homosexuality despite repression by the powers-that-be. Genet's lover at the time, Lucien Sénémaud, is one of the actors in the drama. The film, which has been rarely seen, suffered decades of censorship including a case in Los Angeles in which the courts banned the film on grounds of obscenity.

▼ The Balcony

(1963, 83 min, US/GB, Joseph Strick)

Genet's allegorical play set in a brothel comes to life in this vivid and boisterous low-budget film. Shelley Winters is the beleaguered lesbian madam of the bustling brothel. This "house of illusion," where people play out their dreams, is left undisturbed, despite a ravaging rebellion outside its doors. An interesting, and at times, surreal find which also stars Peter Falk, Ruby Dee, Lee Grant (who plays Winter's lover) and Leonard Nimoy. ☯

> "A shocking film, but one worth being shocked by"
> —*The New Yorker*

▼ Deathwatch

(1965, 88 min, US, Vic Morrow)

Actor Vic Morrow, whose career included several roles as a juvenile delinquent or thug (*Blackboard Jungle*, *The Glass House*), directed his only film in this adaptation of Genet's first play, "Haute Surveillance." Set in a bleak French prison, it follows the struggles of one man (Leonard Nimoy) to gain acceptance in the criminal society as well as to wrest sexual control of a muscular convict (Michael Forrest) from the clutches of a murderer (Paul Mazursky). Originally presented on stage, this production is bound to the prison cell of the three inmates creating a tense, claustrophobic atmosphere. It was said by critic Stuart Byron that the film was the first in its print advertising campaign to be directly marketed to a gay audience. Previously unavailable in the United States since its initial release, the film enjoyed a revival at the 1990 San Francisco Lesbian & Gay International Film Festival.

Mademoiselle

(1966, 99 min, France/GB, Tony Richardson)

Genet is credited with the scenario in this atmospheric drama although reportedly several others were involved (including Richardson) at some point in the writing. The story unfolds in a French farming village which has seen its tranquility upset by a series of floods, fires and poisoning of animals. No one suspects the real culprit — the classy spinster schoolteacher (Jeanne Moreau) who, under a mask of respectability, is a sexually repressed, emotionally disturbed and malicious creature. The townspeople come, instead, to suspect a virile, pleasant Italian woodcutter (Ettore Manni) who is also the object to Moreau's sexual scheming and bridled lust. A quietly brooding tale of evil and the suffering of the innocent. ☯

▼ The Maids

(1975, 95 min, GB, Christopher Miles)

Genet's feverish play about the sadomasochistic games brought on by sexual and emotional frustrations between two servants is brought to the screen in this faithful, if overheated theatrical adaptation. Glenda Jackson and Susannah York give stellar performances as the docile maids to a bossy woman (Vivian Merchant)

The Balcony

who, when her back is turned, elaborately stage a series of sexual fantasies involving domination and submission.

▼ Maidsplay (1983, 80 min, US, Nicole Dreiske)

Genet's classic play *The Maids* was inspired by a real-life incident where two incestuous sisters employed as maids murdered their mistress and her daughter. This filmed play is inspired both by the actual transcripts of the original murder trial and Genet's play. The result is an experimental play featuring stylized acting and rapid-fire dialogue in which the two sisters, fueled by frenzied jealousy and bizarre role-playing, conspire to commit a heinous crime. The video transfer is below average and the play seen on TV loses some of its power and is a difficult watch. ⊛

▼ Querelle

(1982, 108 min, Germany, Rainer Werner Fassbinder)

Although slow-moving and teetering on the self-parody, R.W. Fassbinder's adaptation of Genet's 1947 homoerotic tale of lust, obsession, domination and murder is still quite impressive. The teaming of Fassbinder and Genet makes for an interesting marriage — with RWF's interest in working-class (sometimes gay) losers being a fine compliment to Genet's tortured, sexually charged story. Brad Davis is enticing as the dangerously attractive and narcissistic Querelle whose raw sexuality captures heart and crotch of both Captain Seblon (Franco Nero) and a dockside chanteuse (Jeanne Moreau). Much of the film's success is in the atmospheric, phallic-intensive set design which transform's the docks of Brest into a dark, wet, determinedly artificial prison of the soul. ⊛

▼ Jean Genet

(1983, 95 min, France, Antoine Boun Seillem)

This documentary about the controversial French writer is composed, for the majority, of Genet explaining his views on everything from his support of the Black Panthers and the Palestinians to freely talking about his relationships with his several lovers. In his first appearance on film, Genet is an assured speaker. While on the surface he may seem to be an old and respected writer he is in actuality a literary and social renegade who has spent a life refusing to succumb to expected behavior. Born in 1910, Genet's early years were spent in and out of reform school and as a teenager he became a hardened criminal and prostitute. His time spent in prison soon unleashed his artistic talents and it was in the dank, dark cell where he wrote several brilliant, if disturbing novels, including "Our Lady of Flowers." His work sparked an interest with the French intelligentsia and with the aid of Jean Cocteau and Jean-Paul Sartre he was released from prison and given a pardon in 1949. The film, which is little more than a filmed interview, features Genet pontificating on a variety of subjects including memories of his past, all which reveal his intelligence and creativity. Breaking up the monologue are readings from several of his works which deal explicitly with raw homosexuality, violence, domination and submission. Genet died of throat cancer in 1986. ⊛

Saint Genet

(1986, 60 min, Nigel Williams & Charles Chabot)

This fascinating BBC interview with a feisty Genet was completed just days before the French writer's death. One learns more of his combativeness and encouragingly defiant nature than actual biographical information or personal insights. The film's crew and interviewer (who barely speaks French) seem genuinely startled by the antagonism of the mocking and generally uncooperative Genet.

▼ L'Equilibriste (Walking a Tightrope)

(1991, 128 min, France, Nico Papatakis)

Reportedly based on an episode in Genet's life, this overwrought drama stars Michel Piccoli as a Genet-like writer who becomes enamored by the masculine beauty of a German/Algerian floor sweeper at a visiting circus. Determined to save (destroy?) him from his nondescript life, the author assists the young man in gaining his dream of becoming a star trapeze artist. But his benefactor soon loses interest in him when he becomes obsessed with the potent charms of an aspiring racing car driver. A disturbing drama which depicts older gay men as lecherous exploiters who prey on the innocence and vulnerability of young men.

▼ Poison

(1990, 85 min, US, Todd Haynes)

Gay independent filmmaker Todd Haynes makes his feature film debut with this ambitious, disquieting drama made up of three separate stories, all focusing on troubled outsiders. Inspired, in part, by the writings of Genet, the interwoven tales include "Hero," about a boy who kills his abusive father and then mysteriously flies away; "Horror," in which a scientist's laboratory experiments on sexuality turn him onto a horribly disfigured outcast; and "Homo," a Genet-like tale of tortured love, humiliation and violent sexuality set in a boy's borstal and a prison. In "Homo," John (Scott Renderer), a homosexual thief, finds solace in incarceration and in his adopted family of criminals. He soon becomes obsessed with Jack (James Lyons), a fellow prisoner and former acquaintance at a teenage reformatory. When John's sexual advances are rejected, the two engage in a violent and sexy dance of domination and, eventually, submission. Haynes, who received partial government funding for *Poison*, upset several conservative politicians who railed against the film for the unabashed depiction of one facet of homosexual love and, particularly, a disturbing scene of degradation of Jack as a teenager. The film throughout quotes from Genet's "Miracle of the Rose," "A Thief's Journal" and "Our Lady of Flowers" and concludes with the Genet quote: "A man must dream for a long time in order to act with grandeur, and dreaming is nursed in darkness." ⊛

WILLIAM INGE

Come Back, Little Sheba

(1952, 99 min, US, Daniel Mann)
Long before she played "Hazel" on TV, Shirley Booth set the stage and screen afire with her remarkable performance as a downtrodden wife in Inge's blistering drama. In an Oscar-winning portrayal, Booth stars as the spouse of an alcoholic (nicely played by Burt Lancaster). When they rent a room to a pretty boarder (Terry Moore), the stage is set for jealousy and recriminations. This excellent adaptation is punctuated by Inge's efficient and penetrating dialogue and outstanding performances from a talented cast. ⊗

Picnic *(1955, 115 min, US, Joshua Logan)*

Riveting film version of Inge's play about the sexual frustrations and longings in a small town in Kansas (where the gay author was born and raised). William Holden is the beefy drifter who sets hearts aflutter; Cliff Robertson is his old college friend; Kim Novak is Robertson's girlfriend who prefers Holden; and Rosalind Russell gives an electrifying performance as a spinster involved with Arthur O'Connell. O'Connell received a well-deserved Oscar nomination; however, Russell would have probably won the Supporting Actress statue but she refused to be in that category. ⊗

Bus Stop *(1956, 96 min, US, Joshua Logan)*

Marilyn Monroe displays her usual sex appeal as well as surprising pathos in this delightful adaptation of Inge's comedy. MM stars as a torchy cafe singer who becomes the object of affection — and obsession — by young naive cowpoke Don Murray (who received an Oscar nomination for his sensationally wild performance). Great support from Eileen Heckart as Marilyn's waitress confidant and Arthur O'Connell as Murray's seasoned manager. ⊗

The Dark at the Top of the Stairs

(1960, 123 min, US, Delbert Mann)
An expertly acted film version of Inge's Pulitzer Prize-winning play. Robert Preston heads an exceptional cast as the patriarch of an Oklahoma family in the 1920s. As seen through the eyes of a young boy coming-of-age, the story focuses on a family's fortunes and misfortune, misunderstandings and prejudice. Dorothy McGuire, Angela Lansbury, Eve Arden and Shirley Knight also star.

Splendor in the Grass

(1961, 124 min, US, Elia Kazan)
Beginning with screendom's first French kiss, this tale of two teenagers' coming-of-age is somewhat sentimental; but even after thirty years, it still has heartbreaking and timeless appeal. Bud and Deannie find themselves hopelessly trapped: by overbearing parents and social class lines, and by the boundaries of young love. Earnest performances by Warren Beatty (in his film debut) and

Natalie Wood, keen direction by Elia Kazan and an Oscar-winning screenplay by Inge are sure to cause a tear or two as they poignantly bring all the memories of bittersweet young love to mind. ⊗

All Fall Down

(1962, 110 min, US, John Frankenheimer)
Adapted for the screen by Inge, *All Fall Down* centers on a dysfunctional Cleveland family headed by alcoholic Karl Malden and domineering Angela Lansbury. A young Warren Beatty is the eldest son Berry-Berry, a louse of a drifter who returns home at the insistence of his idolizing brother Brandon de Wilde. Eva Marie Saint rounds out a first-rate cast as a family friend who, unfortunately, becomes involved with Beatty. Inge and director John Frankenheimer concentrate on the dark side of the American family, exploring a bruised familial psyche with numerous open wounds. And thanks to its perceptive direction and script, the film cuts deeper than the usual Gothic drama. It's Lansbury who walks away with the acting honors, though Barbara Baxley is fine in a small but potent role as one of Beatty's pick-ups. Based on James Leo Herlihy's novel. ⊗

The Stripper

(1963, 95 min, US, Franklin Schaffner)
Joanne Woodward's competent performance saves this Inge melodrama about an aging stripper and her affair with a young man. Richard Beymer, Claire Trevor and Gypsy Rose Lee co-star. ⊗

▼ Bus Riley's Back in Town

(1965, 93 min, US, Harvey Hart)
Using the pseudonym of Walter Gage because of the many rewrites on the part of the director, Inge wrote the original screenplay for this interesting but muddled drama. The charismatic Michael Parks stars as Bus Riley, a serviceman who returns to his small Midwestern hometown after his tour of duty. Ann-Margret also stars as his ex-girlfriend, a married woman determined to renew their relationship. As Bus searches for fulfillment, he considers taking a job with a gay friend, Spencer (Crahan Denton), a mortician. But when Spencer suggests living together and "comes on to" him, Bus is out of there like a greyhound.

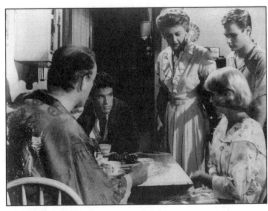

All Fall Down

CHRISTOPHER ISHERWOOD

Cabaret

I Am a Camera

(1955, 98 min, GB, Henry Cornelius)

I Am a Camera is a screen version of a 1951 John Van Druten play which was based on characters and stories in Christopher Isherwood's "Berlin Stories." With intelligence and wit, this excellently acted drama (not a musical) features Julie Harris as Sally Bowles (a character later made truly famous by Liza Minnelli in Bob Fosse's *Cabaret*) and Laurence Harvey as Christopher. Isherwood, who was working on the screenplay for *Diane*, was unable to do the adaptation, a task that John Collier assumed. Supposedly they concluded that audiences would not believe (or be able to handle the implications) that two young, attractive single people (Sally and Christopher) would remain platonic friends so in this version, the two marry. The film opened to generally mixed to negative reviews and Isherwood wrote to a friend that he and John Van Druten thought the film to be "disgusting...near pornographic trash." ☻

▼ Cabaret *(1972, 124 min, US, Bob Fosse)*

Bob Fosse's splashy musical adaptation of Christopher Isherwood's stories of 1930s Berlin stars an effervescent Liza Minnelli as nightclub singer and carefree bohemian Sally Bowles and Michael York as Isherwood's alter-ego Brian Roberts. The short-lived decadent world of pre-Hitler Berlin as well as the rising nationalistic tide of Fascism are effectively captured in this trend-setting musical. Unlike *I Am a Camera*, Brian's bisexuality is touched upon although in retrospect, too evasively. Helmut Griem also stars as the wealthy and debonair Maximilian van Heune, who sweeps both Brian and Sally off their feet (and in a sense, literally). The musical numbers at the Kit Kat Klub (filled with outlandish characters — check out the transvestites and "gay types") are just some of the film's rousing highlights, a collection of great songs performed by both Minnelli and Academy Award winner Joel Grey as the devilishly cynical MC. ☻

▼ Christopher Isherwood: Over There on a Visit *(1977)*

This intimate portrait of the brilliant openly gay writer is set in Isherwood's Santa Monica home, with whom he shares with his lover, painter Don Bachardy. Born in 1904, Isherwood came from a wealthy English family, but after an education in the best public schools and time spent in Oxford, he began, with the help of W.H. Auden, his literary career. He lived for a time in Germany and emigrated to the United States in 1939, settling in Los Angeles where he wrote several novels ("Prater Violet," "Down There on a Visit," "A Single Man"), his autobiography ("Christopher and His Kind"), philosophy ("An Approach to Vedanta") and screenplays (includ-

ing *Rage in Heaven, Forever and a Day, Diane, The Loved One, Sailor from Gibraltar* and *Frankenstein: The True Story*). The series of interviews in this film touch in these works as well as his relationships, his enduring friendship with Auden, his homosexuality, and his deep feelings for the principles of Hinduism.

Memories of Berlin: The Twilight of the Weimar Culture *(1979)*

Isherwood is one of the featured interviewees in this documentary on the intellectual, sexual and artistic freedoms that flourished in Berlin between the wars. In addition to the reminisces of Isherwood, other celebrities include Louise Brooks, Elizabeth Bergner and Arthur Koestler. ☻

HANIF KUREISHI

▼ My Beautiful Laundrette

(1986, 94 min, GB, Stephen Frears)

An unpredictable and charming social comedy that was director Stephen Frears (*Prick Up Your Ears, Dangerous Liaisons, The Grifters*) first commercial hit. The story follows the unlikely success of a young English-born Pakistani (and budding capitalist) and his punk friend/lover (Daniel Day-Lewis). Together they brave the ugly spectre of racism as well as transform a dingy East Side laundrette into a glitzy and profitable emporium. An early and definitive example of New Queer Cinema, for the two gay characters' gayness is open and matter-of-fact, loving and sexual and, most importantly, not troubling to themselves. Kureishi won numerous awards for his refreshingly smart and penetrating screenplay. ☻

▼ Sammy and Rosie Get Laid

(1987, 100 min, GB, Stephen Frears)

Director Frears and Kureishi reunited after their triumphant *My Beautiful Laundrette* to fashion another brilliantly scathing portrait of present-day London. Sammy (Ayub Khan Din), the son of a right-wing Pakistani politician, is involved with a sexually liberated English woman (Frances Barber). When his father, fleeing political enemies, comes to live with them, their informal relationship begins to mirror the mounting social unrest in the streets outside their window. ☯

▼ London Kills Me

(1992, 107 Min, GB, Hanif Kureishi)

Where Kureishi's *My Beautiful Laundrette* dealt with working-class aspirations, sexuality and morality in a racist, Thatcherized London, *London Kills Me*, Kureishi's directorial debut, goes a few rungs down the economic ladder in a humorous exploration of life on the fringe underbelly of a post-punk, beyond-hope society. The story centers on Clint, a pale, emaciated, sexually abused-as-a-child 20-year-old who, despite being mired in a seemingly hopeless world of drugs, homelessness, petty thievery and prostitution, retains a cheery, optimistic approach to his prospects of survival and success. Hope springs eternal after an exasperated owner of an upscale Portabello Road restaurant promises the bedraggled Clint a job if he returns the following week with a new pair of shoes. With this promise of respectability, Clint begins a frantic odyssey to acquire this elusive pair of shoes. A fascinating, yet flawed comedy-drama that, despite a tagged-on happy ending that borders on the bizarre, is fun nonetheless and vividly captures this part of London. Like *Sammy and Rosie Get Laid* and the television adaptation of his novel *The Buddha of Suburbia*, this story is essentially a straight tale of survival, yet there are several gay and lesbian characters in the background of all three films. ☯

▼ The Buddha of Suburbia

(1993, 240 min, GB, Roger Michell)

Kureishi's serio-comic novel of life among the bohemians and bohemian-wannabes in 1970s London has been adapted for the screen in this four-hour miniseries by BBC Television. The story focuses on handsome Karim (Naveen Andrews), a bisexual teenager of an conventional English mother and an surprisingly eccentric Indian father who longs to escape the confines of suburban Bromley and experience "life." Karim desperately loves his neighbor Charlie Hero (Steven MacKintosh), an aspiring rocker in the David Bowie-Billy Idol vein but when that goes no further than a hand-job, he goes on to newer (and straighter) relationships. The story gains speed when he moves into a frenetic, punk-filled London with his father and his father's girlfriend. Sort of an English version of *Tales of the City*, this sprawling slice-of-life story created some controversy when it first aired in Britain, prompting a front page scream in London's *Sun* which decried the film's sex orgies, nudity and homosexuality. It also comes as no surprise that there is no date set for an American television airing. Original music by David Bowie.

C ARSON M CC ULLERS

The Member of the Wedding

(1953, 91 min, US, Fred Zinneman)

McCuller's Broadway hit is successfully transposed to the screen in this mournful but electrifying drama. Julie Harris, in a role she originated on stage, plays Frankie, a lonely 12-year-old tomboy awkwardly teetering between childhood and adolescence but belonging to neither. Ethel Waters is her understanding nanny and Brandon de Wilde his her six-year old cousin. French director Claude Miller made an uncredited adaptation of this play with his 1985 film, *An Imprudent Girl*. ☯

▼ Reflections in a Golden Eye

(1967, 108 min, US, John Huston)

McCullers' 1944 novel is bombastically brought to the screen by John Huston. In this teapot of repressed sexuality, mental illness and hyperventilating desire is Marlon Brando as Major Penderton, the impotent, closet-cased husband of Leonora (Elizabeth Taylor). Brando seethes with lust for one particularly attractive man, Private Williams (Robert Forster), who is assigned to take care of Leonora's horses and who himself has a kinky penchant for nightly bare-assed horseback riding and sneaking into Taylor's bedroom to watch her sleep. Brando is memorable as the sadomasochistic Major who reverts to violence when he is "betrayed" by the man who he can not have. Critic John Simon once wrote that the world of Carson McCullers is one where "aberration is the norm and perversion is worn as a badge." ☯

The Heart Is a Lonely Hunter

(1968, 125 min, US, Robert Ellis Miller)

Based on McCuller's lyrical first novel, this poignant drama stars Alan Arkin (in an Academy-nominated performance) as a sensitive deaf-mute who befriends, supports and, then in some quiet fashion, is betrayed by a small group of fellow social outcasts. Set in the South, this tender tale features Sondra Locke (another Oscar nominee) and Stacy Keach (both in their screen debuts). ☯

▼ The Ballad of the Sad Cafe

(1991, 108 min, US, Simon Callow)

The Deep South has played host to many a curious tale, but none more strange or bewildering than this wildly uneven but nevertheless hypnotic adaptation of the Edward Albee play, itself based on McCullers' novella. Never a stranger to risk-taking, Vanessa Redgrave gives a bold, mesmerizing performance as Miss Amelia, the butch town tycoon whose crew-cut and gangly walk sends fear into the local residents. All except Lymon (Cork Hubbard), a hunchback dwarf who arrives one day claiming to be Miss Amelia's cousin. A ne'er-do-well, Lymon convinces her to open a cafe, which becomes the pulse of the tiny town. However, rela-

FAVORITE WRITERS

tionship and allegiances change drastically when Miss Amelia's estranged husband, Marvin (Keith Carradine), returns from prison. As Lymon turns his affections towards Marvin, the stage is set for a battle-of-the-sexes showdown which culminates in an unbelievable fist-fight finale. Although there is no overt homosexuality, queer emotions bubble to the surface as the combined talents of gay actor/director Simon Callow, the gay Edward Albee and the bisexual McCullers make for a fascinating, if strange drama. ✪

JOE ORTON

▼ Entertaining Mr. Sloane
(1969, 94 min, GB, Douglas Hickox)
Two years after his violent murder by his jealous longtime lover Kenneth Halliwell, playwright Joe Orton's scathing 1963 black comedy about a young stud's entry into the lives of a middle-aged brother and sister was adapted, more or less successfully, to the screen. Beryl Reid (*The Killing of Sister George*) is a riot as the sex-starved, self-delusional sister, Harry Andrews is her latently homosexual leather-fetished brother and Peter McEnery is the handsomely menacing hustler. After the tartish Reid picks up the young man at the public library and brings him home, a farcical and eminently scandalous power struggle ensues between the sib-

lings as they vie for the affections and appendages of the aforementioned young stud. While some of the "opening up" of the play by director Douglas Hickox drags a bit, the scintillating Orton dialogue remains intact, resulting in a superbly acted and boldly original rendition of one of Britain's most daring playwrights. ✪

▼ Loot   *(1972, 101 min, GB, Silvio Narizzano)*
Orton's frantically paced, door slamming black comedy — one of the most original and uproarious plays ever to grace the British stage — receives a less than successful screen adaptation. But for those unfamiliar with the play, this truncated film version will still prove to be a genuinely bizarre and at times uproariously funny farce. The story concerns a pair of misguided youths (Roy Holder and Hywell Bennett) and sometimes lovers who, having knocked over a bank, hide their dough in the coffin of one of the young men's recently deceased mom. All hell breaks loose as the distraught duo tries to retrieve their booty before the police catch on and the casket is buried. The failure of this version, other than the editing out of some of the original text, was with the actors ignoring Orton's stage instructions that the acting should be done seriously, allowing the dialogue and the increasingly frenetic action to generate the comedy. The result is broad performances from such seasoned veterans as Lee Remick, Richard Attenborough and Milo O'Shea. Yet despite the faults, Orton's mordant satire comes through. ✪

▼ Prick Up Your Ears
(1987, 108 min, GB, Stephen Frears)
Adapted from John Lahr's 1978 biography of Orton, this chilling and graphic portrayal of the life and death of the enfant terrible of British theatre is a masterful tribute to a man who fearlessly attacked English restrictive morals and customs. Gary Oldman is eerily transformed into Orton, a hugely talented, defiantly gay writer who seduced all with his easy going charm and mischievous grin and who gained fame almost overnight with his outrageous and viciously funny social comedies. Alfred Molina co-stars as Kenneth Halliwell, Orton's tormented lover, sometime collaborator and eventual murderer. The film, much to its fault, focuses primarily on the stormy relationship between the two dissimilar men and almost ignores Orton's prodigious talent as a playwright and his rise to fame with such brilliantly written plays as "What the Butler Saw," "The Ruffian on the Stair," "Loot" and "Entertaining Mr. Sloane." What the film does not flinch from is depicting Orton's acknowledged partiality to public restroom sex, at a time when homosexual acts were outlawed. On a trivia note, Lahr plays off Orton's mischievousness with the book's title, with the word "ears" in *Prick Up Your Ears* being an anagram for "arse"! ✪

Peter McEnery gets the once over from Harry Andrews in *Entertaining Mr. Sloane*

GORE VIDAL

The Catered Affair
(1956, 93 min, US, Richard Brooks)
Gore Vidal began his career in the arts as a novelist, writing his first book, "Williwaw," in 1946 at the age of nineteen and his controversial gay novel, "The City and the Pillar," the first American novel to deal openly and sympathetically with homosexuality, in 1948. In the 1950s, Vidal continued writing books but also began scripting for television for such programs as "Omnibus," "Studio One" and "The Philco-Goodyear Playhouse." His first screenwriting credit was with this MGM drama based on a Paddy Chayevsky teleplay. Bette Davis trades in her Hollywood glamour for a Bronx kitchen in this tale about a working-class taxi driver (Ernest Borgnine) and his wife (Davis) who plan an extravagant wedding for their daughter (Debbie Reynolds). Vidal's dialogue nicely captures the aspirations, frustrations and cadence of life in the Bronx. ⊛

I Accuse! *(1958, 99 min, GB, Jose Ferrer)*
From a Vidal script, this sincere courtroom drama deals with the turn-of-the-century conviction of Capt. Alfred Dreyfus for treason, a decision that caused intense controversy at the time and whose impact still reverberates in France today. Jose Ferrer plays Dreyfus who is defended by writer/activist Emile Zola (Emlyn Williams).

▼ The Left-Handed Gun
(1958, 102 min, US, Arthur Penn)
Vidal's television play, "The Death of Billy the Kid," is transposed to the big screen in this provocative western that in the very subtlest of ways, offers the possibility that Billy was a repressed homosexual. The depiction of Billy by the intensely handsome Paul Newman is that of a pensive, misunderstood but hot-headed loner — a tormented youth in the fashion of James Dean and Hamlet. After his boss, with whom the illiterate, insecure Billy forms a tender father-son relationship, is innocently gunned down, Billy and his two best friends/followers, Tom (James Best) and Charlie (James Congdon), become obsessed with gunning down the man's killers, only to be killed themselves by another father-figure in the guise of Pat Garrett (John Dehner). Vidal, who has described the film as "the first sort of strange western ever made," was unhappy with the results, blaming the autuer-obsessed Penn with tampering with his original ideas. ⊛

▼ Suddenly, Last Summer
(1959, 114 min, US, Joseph L. Mankiewicz)
Tennessee Williams' one-act play was scripted for the screen by the gay writing team of Williams and Vidal. Although the film is often credited as being the first Hollywood film to deal with homosexuality, the actual face of homosexuality, that of Sebastian Venable, is never actually shown in the film. The Catholic Church and Hollywood's own censorship rules forced Vidal to make several changes in the original script. Thinking back, Vidal has been quoted as saying that he thought Williams "hated" his adaptation for *Suddenly* but egalitarianly concluded that he himself has been "badly served by the movies" and that Williams' feelings were "...dreadful justice. What I have done to others, others have done to me." ⊛

▼ Ben-Hur *(1959, 212 min, US, William Wyler)*
Vidal was an uncredited script collaborator on this biblical epic filmed on a scale even the Caesars could appreciate. The tale concerns two boyhood friends, Judah Ben-Hur (Charlton Heston) and Messala (Stephen Boyd), who become enemies at the time of Jesus. Despite deletions of any direct homosexual references, the intense relationship between the two virile men says otherwise. In an interview, Vidal said that he proposed to director William Wyler "that the two had been adolescent lovers and now Messala has returned to Rome wanting to revive the love affair but Ben-Hur does not." After Wyler agreed to this covert motivational ploy, Vidal informed Stephen Boyd (and pointedly not Heston), resulting in Boyd successfully playing off the role of a spurned lover, especially when he cries, "Is there anything so sad as unrequited love?" Wyler once said, "The biggest mistake we made was the love story. If we had cut out that girl (Haya Harareet) altogether and concentrated on the two guys, everything would have gone better." ⊛

> "*Ben-Hur* is the ultimate Technicolor meditation on homoerotic, S&M and master-slave relationships...looking at it now (1990), the film's homoerotic subtext is the film's most obvious draw."
>
> —*L.A. Weekly*

▼ The Best Man
(1964, 102 min, US, Franklin J. Schaffner)
Outstanding adaptation of Gore Vidal's vitriolic play centering on two politicians campaigning for the presidential nomination, each trying to woo support of the party and the ailing ex-president. Cliff Robertson is Joe Cantwell, a ruthless conservative presidential nominee running against the idealistic William Russell (Henry Fonda). It is alleged that Cantwell had a gay affair; "dirty" politics Russell doesn't want any part of ("Even if it's true, so what?"). ⊛

▼ Myra Breckenridge
(1970, 94 min, US, Michael Sarne)
What was in some 20th Century-Fox's collective head when they green-lighted this outrageous project — an X-rated version of Vidal's "scandalously" satiric transsexual novel (with Vidal co-writing the screenplay) that would feature Rex Reed and Raquel Welsh as the male and female embodiment of the same person, feature some acting oddities (Mae West, John Huston, Farrah Fawcett and a mustache-less Tom Selleck); have a talentless Michael Sarne direct and imbue it with a slap-dash Sixties mentality. The result was, predictably, an epic disaster, sending critics running to their thesauruses looking for words stronger than "repugnant" and "atrocious" and audiences (however small) running to the exits. But was it so bad? YES! But yes in a campy, smirky, hipper-than-fag sort of way. Just watching Raquel, on a male ego-deflating rampage, rape a strapping stud of a cowboy (Roger Herren) with objects that

should remain in utility closets is enough to nominate this deliciouly vulgar comedy, along with Russ Meyer's *Beyond the Valley of the Dolls*, as one of the best films of 1970! ⊛

"About as funny as a child molester." —*Time*

Caligula *(1979, 156 min, Italy/US, Tinto Brass)*

Intriguing for what it is not and decadently enjoyably for what it is, this controversial X-rated tale on the carnal, digestive and power excesses of Caligula is if anything, a butchered, orphaned mess. Originally titled *Gore Vidal's Caligula*, the $15 million production was plagued with constant infighting between the producer, *Penthouse Magazine's* Bob Guccione, Vidal and director Tinto Brass. Brass was eventually replaced, Guccione's hacks reedited the film and in restructuring it, deleted the many gay sequences, angering Vidal who successfully sued to have has name and credit removed from the finished piece. As a guilty pleasure, the film is actually not all bad, with Malcolm McDowell dancing about as the crazed Caligula, the fourth of the twelve Ceasars, who was finally assassinated after four tumultuous years of unrivaled debauchery and defilement (my kind of guy!). ⊛

"A fellatio rise and fall of the Roman Empire. Something for every appetite in pants or panties."

—*Variety*

Gore Vidal: Portrait of a Writer

(1979, 57 min, West Germany, Hans Jörg Weyhmüller)
An impish Vidal holds court to an entranced filmmaker in this entertaining and informative film that follows Vidal around Roman ruins, the coast of Italy and in Rome as he pontificates on a wide range of subjects. Vidal reveals his thoughts on the origins of religion, Western civilization, his political aspirations, the Mafia, the Kennedys, his work in film, Federico Fellini and, in some cattier moments, his opinions on Truman Capote ("a pathological liar") and Norman Mailer ("a fat little old lady, not unlike Colette"). ⊛

▼ Dress Gray *(1987, 91 min, US, Glenn Jordan)*

This riveting gay murder mystery set in a military academy during the Vietnam War is based on the novel by Lucian K. Truscott IV and adapted for television by Vidal. Alec Baldwin stars as a cadet who becomes embroiled in a cover-up over the mysterious death of another cadet. An athletic, macho young "pleb" is found dead by a river near the school. After an autopsy, it is discovered that he had been raped immediately before his death. Fearing a scandal involving homosexuality and murder, the embarrassed commandant (Hal Halbrook) and his staff decide to cover up the death as a simple accidental drowning. But as the truth slowly begins to unravel, Baldwin, the secret object of the dead cadet's affections and the ex-boyfriend of his sister, becomes embroiled in the increasingly complex web of lies and deceit, all invoked in the name of the military's code of duty, honor and valor. Like a high stakes Hardy Boys mystery, the cadet attempts to clear his name and uncover the real killer with the mystery unraveling in a genuinely tense and exciting fashion. Both a well-told story, a forray into the secretive military establishment and a well-developed analogy to America's involvement in Vietnam and Watergate. Also starring Eddie Albert, Lloyd Bridges and Lane Smith. Vidal's best work for television. ⊛

Raquel Welch as Rex Reed's alter ego in *Myra Breckenridge*

Gore Vidal's Lincoln

(1988, 191 min, US, Lamont Johnson)
Adapted by Ernest Kinoy from Vidal's best-selling novel, this sprawling, made-for-TV historical epic attempts to humanize (trivialize?) the turbulent presidency of Abraham Lincoln. Sam Waterston, arguably too young and too good looking to play the part, is Lincoln, while Mary Tyler Moore is superb as his mentally troubled wife, Mary Todd Lincoln. The action begins with his inaugural and progresses into the calamitous war between the States, but focuses primarily on his home life and the intensifying mental breakdown of his wife. Good but far from great. ⊛

Gore Vidal's Billy the Kid

(1989, 100 min, US, William Graham)
Made for cable television, this, Vidal's second film of the life and death of Billy the Kid, is enjoyable enough but does not come close to the complexity and nuances that were much in evidence in *The Left-Handed Gun*. Val Kilmer plays Billy, but a Billy that is less tormented, more heterosexual and a bit more goofy than Newman's interpretation. There is much less character development as the story treads the same territory as the first, focusing primarily on the friendship between Billy and the man who finally guns him down, Pat Garrett. With toothy good looks, Kilmer makes for an attractive renegade but his role in ultimately undermined by the traditional, strictly-by-the-numbers approach to the legend. This story might have been less tampered with than his *Left-Handed Gun*, but it is also less interesting, more pedestrian. ⊛

OSCAR WILDE

In addition to the titles which follow, films based on the works of Oscar Wilde can be found in their appropriate chapters:

The Canterville Ghost — starring Charles Laughton
Salome — starring Nazimova
Salome's Last Dance — directed by Ken Russell

Lady Windermere's Fan

(1925, 80 min, US, Ernst Lubitsch)
Wilde's witty 1892 drawing room comedy is updated to the 1920s in this splendid silent film. The story centers around a mysterious society lady, Mrs. Erlynne, whose past almost brings scandal to her circle. A charming romantic comedy that stars Ronald Colman, May McAvoy and Irene Rich.

The Picture of Dorian Gray

(1945, 110 min, US, Albert Lewin)
Wilde's classic study of greed, narcissism and decadence stars Hurd Hatfield as the extraordinarily handsome Dorian Gray who sells his soul to George Sanders, the elegantly corrupt devil, for eternal beauty and that picture in the attic. An earlier version of Wilde's ominous tale, one reportedly with a homosexual subplot, was the German film *Das Bildnis des Dorian Gray* (1917). ⊛

The Importance of Being Earnest

(1952, 95 min, GB, Anthony Asquith)
Michael Redgrave, Dorothy Tutin, Edith Evans, Margaret Rutherford and Joan Greenwood star in this impeccable rendition of Wilde's classic farce. Wilde's play is certainly one of the hallmarks of British theatre and it represents the height of his genius.

Oscar Wilde

He joyously pokes and jabs at the hypocrisy of British society while using the most widely accepted conventions of the stage to present his most radical ideas and social criticisms. Sterling performances from the entire cast make this one of the most outstanding comedies to grace any screen, large or small. ⊛

▼ Oscar Wilde

(1959, 96 min, GB, Gregory Ratoff)
Robert Morley, in a reprisal of his stage role, gustily exudes the wit and decay of the famed playwright during his notorious 1890s trial for libel, during which he was accused of sodomy and sexual perversion. A superb Ralph Richardson co-stars as the Queen's council in this sophisticated drama on the turbulent later years in the life of the playwright.

▼ The Trials of Oscar Wilde

(1960, 123 min, GB, Ken Hughes)
From the director of the horrendous guilty pleasure *Sextette* as well as *Chitty, Chitty Bang Bang* and *Casino Royale* comes this drama that was filmed almost simultaneously with the above mentioned *Oscar Wilde* and covers basically the same period in the author's life. Peter Finch, who projects greater sexual appeal than Robert Morley, is the vainglorious Wilde who sued his lover's father, the Marquis of Queensbury, for libel after the man impugned his reputation (i.e. called him a fag). After he lost the ill-conceived suit, he in turn was charged with sodomy and found guilty. The film amazingly tones down considerably the gay implications and offers instead an elaborate and intriguing courtroom drama. Also starring Nigel Patrick and James Mason. (US title: *The Man with the Green Carnation*)

THE STORY OF A MAN WHO TRADED HIS SOUL FOR ETERNAL YOUTH!

The PICTURE of DORIAN GRAY
with
George SANDERS
HURD HATFIELD
DONNA REED
Angela LANSBURY
Peter LAWFORD
Richard FRASER

FAVORITE WRITERS

293

▼ Dorian Gray

(1970, 93 min, GB/Italy, Massimo Dallamano)
Swingin' London of the '60s is the setting for this modernized retelling of Wilde's allegorical play. Blond, blue-eyed beauty Helmut Berger stars as Dorian, an innocent and naive young man who becomes fatally obsessed with a portrait of himself and sells his soul in exchange for eternal youth while his portrait grows increasingly old and hideous. There are several allusions to Gray's homosexuality and to a gay international jet-set. Although the film drags in parts and, at times it borders on the cinematically tacky, this cautionary tale of corruption is, if anything, a wonderful compendium of outlandish 1960s mod clothes and the slightly right-of-hip denizens who assist Dorian in his descent to Hell. (Also known as: *The Secret of Dorian Gray*) ⊛

The Canterville Ghost

(1986, 96 min, US, Paul Bogard)
John Gielgud plays a spooky but ineffectual apparition who tries to frighten an American family in this updated version of Wilde's supernatural tale. Made for television, the story is only saved by Gielgud's high-spirited role as the earthbound spectre. Also featuring Ted Wass, Andrea Marcovicci and Alyssa Milano. ⊛

▼ Forbidden Passion

(1980, 120 min, GB, Henry Herbert)
The tragic life of Wilde, who was imprisoned for homosexuality, is the subject of this engrossing and disturbing BBC drama. Michael Gambon plays the flamboyant Wilde, a man who, although married, continued to enjoy the pleasures of rent boys and the excesses of gay life until he fell in love with the insolent charms of Lord Alfred Douglas. The fateful affair between the love-struck Wilde and Douglas caused Douglas' father, the Lord of Queensbury, to begin a one-man campaign of revenge. The film chronicles the author's early successes, his trials and imprisonments as well as his final years in France, depicting Wilde as a stubborn man who, by refusing to live a lie, unwittingly fell victim to the hysteria of the times. ⊛

The Sins of Dorian Gray

(1983, 98 min, US, Tony Maylam)
This made-for-television drama attempts to wring any possible life out of this often filmed tale by changing the sex of Dorian and updating the action to the present electronic era. Belinda Bauer is a beautiful actress who sells her soul to the devil and instead of a portrait, it is her video image that ages horribly. An insipid take on the macabre classic that also stars Anthony Perkins and Joseph Bottoms.

W T H O R N T O N W I L D E R

Our Town *(1940, 90 min, US, Sam Wood)*

Wilder's stage masterpiece makes for exceptional film drama in the telling of small-town life in pre-WWI America. Set in the New England hamlet of Grover's Corners, the focus lies on George and Emily (keenly played by William Holden and Martha Scott), youthful next-door neighbors who wed and experience the cycle of life in their short time together. The play's celebrated ending has been slightly altered, but the film retains the power of the original work. ⊛

The Bridge of San Luis Rey

(1944, 89 min, US, Rowland V. Lee)
Adapted from Wilder's acclaimed novel, this static drama, while ambitious, is mostly unsuccessful in bringing life to the story's characters and events. Five people are killed when a bridge in Peru collapses. The story recalls their lives and what brought them to that moment. Starring Lynn Bari, Frances Lederer, Nazimova, Louis Calhern and Akim Tamiroff. ⊛

Shadow of a Doubt

(1943, 108 min, US, Alfred Hitchcock)
Cited by Hitchcock as one of his personal favorites, this cat-and-mouse, spellbinding psychological thriller stars Joseph Cotten as an apparently ordinary fellow who visits his small-town kin. However, his diabolical past gradually becomes evident, and threatening, to his suspicious young niece (Teresa Wright). Wilder wrote the screenplay. ⊛

The Matchmaker

(1958, 101 min, US, Joseph Anthony)
Enjoyable screen version of Wilder's play, with Shirley Booth giving a wonderful performance as turn-of-the-century matchmaker Dolly Levi. As Horace Vandergelder, one of her clients and romantic interest, Paul Ford is in good form. Also with Anthony Perkins and Shirley MacLaine as youthful lovers, and Robert Morse as Perkins' sidekick. The basis for the musical "Hello, Dolly." ⊛

Mr. North *(1988, 92 min, US, Danny Huston)*

John Huston's son Danny took over the reigns of this quirky comedy when his legendary father died just before the start of the production. Anthony Edwards plays the ingratiating title character, who warms himself to the flaky citizens of Newport's upper class. Also with Robert Mitchum, Lauren Bacall, Anjelica Huston, Mary Stuart Masterson and Harry Dean Stanton. A real charmer based on Wilder's "Theophilus North." ⊛

TENNESSEE WILLIAMS

Tennessee Williams

A Streetcar Named Desire
(1951, 122 min, US, Elia Kazan)
Marlon Brando is the brutish Stanley Kowalski, who psychologically strips his fragile sister-in-law Blanche (Vivien Leigh) until her breakdown is complete. Williams' masterpiece is layered with sexual symbolism and haunting imagery. Excellent supporting work comes from Karl Malden as a well-intentioned suitor and Kim Hunter as Stanley's beleaguered wife. Leigh, Malden and Hunter all won Oscars. The film does not explore the play's homosexual subplot in which Blanche recalls her marriage to a gay man who ultimately committed suicide. ⊗

The Rose Tattoo
(1955, 117 min, US, Daniel Mann)
Anna Magnani gives an extraordinary performance in this riveting adaptation of Williams' play as a widow, still obsessed with the memory of her late husband, who begins an affair with trucker Burt Lancaster. Magnani won the Oscar for her portrayal, and is matched all the way by Lancaster. ⊗

Baby Doll *(1956, 114 min, US, Elia Kazan)*
This steamy Williams scripted drama set in rural Mississippi created quite a controversy when initially released in 1956 (it was condemned by the Legion of Decency), though it appears rather tame by today's standards. Carroll Baker stars as the child bride of lascivious Karl Malden, and Eli Wallach is the sleazy businessman out to use both of them. ⊗

Cat on a Hot Tin Roof
(1958, 108 min, US, Richard Brooks)
Everyone has a skeleton in their closet in Williams' Pulitzer Prize-winning drama. Elizabeth Taylor sinks her claws into the role of Maggie the Cat, the tormented, sexually frustrated wife of guilt-ridden ex-jock Brick (Paul Newman). The prototypical tale of family conflict and confrontation. In keeping with the censorship of its time, MGM eliminated any direct references to Brick's gayness and blurred the otherwise sensual relationship between him and his best friend Skipper, thereby confusing the reason of why Skipper committed suicide. ⊗

▼ Suddenly, Last Summer
(1959, 114 min, US, Joseph L. Mankiewicz)
A blistering Williams drama (co-scripted by Gore Vidal) about psychiatrist Montgomery Clift investigating what caused Elizabeth Taylor to crack (and whether she needs a lobotomy) while on summer vacation with over-bearing Katharine Hepburn's son Sebastian. The kicker is that Sebastian (whose face is never seen) is gay (which is never mentioned) and that he was viciously killed (and "eaten") by a gang of Spanish youths. Based on a Williams one-act off-Broadway play, BBC recently produced a version of it, shorter than this film and more faithful to the original play with Maggie Smith playing the villainous Mrs. Violet Venable who wants doctor Rob Lowe to lobotomize her distraught neice Natasha Richardson. ⊗

The Fugitive Kind
(1959, 135 min, US, Sidney Lumet)
Disappointing though gritty version of Williams' play, "Orpheus Descending." Marlon Brando stars as a Mississippi drifter who becomes involved with two women (Anna Magnani and Joanne Woodward) while staying in a small Southern town. ⊗

The Roman Spring of Mrs. Stone
(1961, 104 min, US, Jose Quintero)
Vivien Leigh is Karen Stone, a middle-aged widowed actress who retires and settles in Rome to live in peace and solitude. Through a vulgar procuress (Lotte Lenya in a campy performance), Mrs. Stone meets a swarthy young stud, Paolo (Warren Beatty). Before long, Mrs. Stone succumbs to the suave gigolo's chicanery, and she soon finds herself losing both her money and her self-respect. Beatty's accent may cause a chuckle or two, but the film, based on a Williams novella, does come off, thanks to Leigh's tender portrayal. ⊗

Summer and Smoke
(1961, 118 min, US, Peter Glenville)
Geraldine Page repeats her acclaimed stage role in Williams' searing drama, and she should have won an Oscar for it. In a tour-de-force performance, Page plays a sexually repressed minister's daughter who falls in love with dashing playboy Laurence Harvey.

FAVORITE WRITERS

Set in a small Mississippi town in 1916, the story is a sensitive treatise on unrequited love and ignored passion. Also with Una Merkel, Pamela Tiffin, Earl Holliman and Rita Moreno. ✪

Period of Adjustment

(1962, 112 min, US, George Roy Hill)
As far as screenplay adaptations go, this Williams piece didn't fair as well as *Baby Doll* or *A Streetcar Named Desire* when Hollywood stepped in. Two strained marriages form the central action in this early '60s melodrama based on a classic Williams theme of illusion versus reality. The first couple, Jane Fonda (a sweet Southern belle) and Jim Hutton (an emotionally scarred Korean War veteran with lots of bravado to make up for his insecurities) are newlyweds who, on their honeymoon night, are wondering just what they've gotten themselves into. They flee to the house of the husband's war buddy (Tony Franciosa) in Florida for comfort only to find he himself is experiencing marital difficulties with wife Lois Nettleton. What follows is a comic and tender exploration of love and marriage, as well as male bravado and sexual compatibility. In this early role, Fonda portrays the confused bride with vigor, but the rest of the acting seems a bit stagey. ✪

Sweet Bird of Youth

(1962, 120 min, US, Richard Brooks)
An expert adaptation of Williams' critically acclaimed play stars Geraldine Page as a former movie queen whose career has given way to achohol and compromise. Searching for seclusion, she arrives in a small Southern town accompanied by ne'er-do-well hometown boy Paul Newman. Ed Begley won an Oscar for his powerful portrayal of the town's corrupt boss who has it in for Newman. Elizabeth Taylor and Mark Harmon starred in an unremarkable 1989 made-for-TV production. ✪

▼ Night of the Iguana

(1964, 118 min, US, John Huston)
In this expertly acted film version of Williams' steamy Broadway play, Richard Burton, Ava Gardner and Deborah Kerr give stellar

Suddenly, Last Summer

performances as participants in a love triangle in a small Mexican resort town. Burton plays a defrocked priest turned bus tour guide who becomes involved with young nymphette Sue Lyons, sexually repressed Kerr and fiery hotel proprietor Gardner (who is stunning in possibly her best screen portrayal). Grayson Hall (TV's "Dark Shadows") received an Oscar nomination for her stirring portrait of Lyons' lesbian guardian who engages Burton in a psychological battle for her soul. Interestingly, Hall's chaparone is the only gay character to be featured in one of Williams' works, to which he commented, "I have never found the subject of homosexuality a satisfying theme for a full-length play." ✪

This Property Is Condemned

(1966, 110 min, US, Sydney Pollack)
Francis Ford Coppola was one of three writers who adapted Williams' one-act play for the screen. Natalie Wood is touching as a tubercular Southern belle living at her mother's Mississippi boarding house. Loathing her small-town life, she becomes involved with transient Robert Redford whom she sees as her ticket out of town. ✪

Cat on a Hot Tin Roof

(1984, 122 min, US, Jack Hofsiss)
A superlative made-for-TV adaptation of Williams' play, with particularly exceptional performances from Jessica Lange as Maggie the Cat; Rip Torn as Big Daddy; and Tommy Lee Jones as Brick, Big Daddy's favorite son, an alcoholic ex-jock with a burden from his past that he cannot resolve. Strong support from Kim Stanley, David Dukes and Penny Fuller as other members of the conflicted Southern family. ✪

The Glass Menagerie

(1987, 134 min, US, Paul Newman)
The sterling performances of Joanne Woodward, John Malkovich, Karen Allen and James Naughton elevate this handsome production based on Williams' classic play. Allen brings a heart-wrenching vulnerability to Laura, the lonely and lame daughter of faded Southern belle Woodward. Malkovich is well-cast as Woodward's troubled son Tom, and Naughton rounds out the cast as the Gentleman Caller. Two other film versions were made: in 1950 with Gertrude Lawrence and Kirk Douglas; and a 1973 made-for-TV production starring Katharine Hepburn and Sam Waterston. ✪

Orpheus Descending

(1990, 117 min, US, Peter Hall)
Peter Hall directed this searing made-for-TV adaptation of Williams' drama about a forbidden love in a sleepy Southern town. Reprising her acclaimed West End and Broadway role from the hit revival, Vanessa Redgrave stars as Lady Torrence, an unhappily married woman whose repressed sexual passions erupt when she encounters a mysterious young drifter (Kevin Anderson). As the two revel in their tryst, her tyrannical, bedridden husband plots his revenge. ✪

FRANCIS BACON

Francis Bacon

Francis Bacon
(1985, 55 min, GB, David Hinton)

Francis Bacon, who died at the age of 82 in 1992, was one of Britain's greatest painters of this century. His life and work are entertainingly uncovered in this free-wheeling documentary. With Melvin Bragg prodding him with questions, the two roam galleries, his studio, a restaurant and a lively bar as Bacon explains his work and reveals a little of his private life. Born in 1909 in Ireland to wealthy English parents, Bacon moved as a child to England only to leave at 15 for the excitement of Berlin and Paris. He returned home and began work as an interior designer, and in the early 1930s he began painting under the mentorship of Roy de Maistre (who was also his lover). He would soon become a highly praised and innovative artist despite (or as he would think because) having never attended art school. An opinionated man, Bacon describes his painting style as "deforming and reforming reality" as both he and Bragg review and analyze his paintings and his contemporaries. When Bacon gets sufficiently plastered on wine, he acknowledges that "I like men." And with the ice broken, some personal information comes forth, although much more is still left unsaid. Not your standard bio-documentary, the film effortlessly enters Bacon's world, one that on the surface seems calm and self-assured but on canvas takes on a new meaning with his trademark shocking images. ⊛

PAUL CADMUS

Paul Cadmus: Enfant Terrible at 80
(1984, 64 min, US, David Sutherland)

In his Connecticut studio drawing a nude, Paul Cadmus reminices about his background, his artistic inspirations and the techniques

of his work in a career which saw his brash, satirical and sexually provocative paintings create scandal and controversy as far back as the 1930s. This award-winning documentary lets Cadmus do all the talking as the erudite artist takes us through his stormy career and explains his paintings and drawings as well as the people who inspired him. ⊛

Paul Cadmus: Enfant Terrible at 80

CARAVAGGIO

Caravaggio *(1991, 28 min, US)*

Not to be confused with Derek Jarman's film, this made-for-TV documentary, while only 28 minutes, is an amazingly informative look at the revolutionary painter whose realism and humanistic style of painting (as well as his disturbing homoerotism) challenged tradition and infuriated authority. Much of the video is taken up with an academic analysis of many of Caravaggio's better known works while also providing biographical information on the painter's short but tumultuous life. An invaluable primer for a viewer who wants to know more about art appreciation and Caravaggio's role in the advancement of painting. ⊛

LEONARDO DA VINCI

The Life of Leonardo Da Vinci
(1972, 270 min, Italy, Renato Castellani)
Poorly dubbed and strangely constructed, this nonetheless compelling film biography of Leonardo Da Vinci, one of the great geniuses of the Renaissance, is a curious and exhaustive made-for-Italian television production that "historically" dramatizes the life of the renowned painter ("Mona Lisa," "The Last Supper"), scientist, astronomer and engineer. An often intrusive "fact-giving" goateed man in modern dress narrates the film which begins with Da Vinci's bastard birth in 1475 and proceeds to his death in 1564. While the film strives to be historically accurate, a subject of debate is its handling of the arrests of Da Vinci when he was a youth. The documented fact is that Da Vinci was arrested twice but was released on one of these charges for insufficient evidence. The film keeps the accusations vague, suggesting heresy as being the charges against him. In other publications, it has been said that the actual charge was the sodomy of a 17-year old boy by a 24-year-old Da Vinci. While ignoring this "evidence" of his homosexuality, the film does show his lifelong disinterest in women and many close relationships with men. Also stressed is his prodigious artistic output in painting and architecture and his many inventions. Hokey at times, and speculative other times, the film should be of great appeal for anyone interested in the life and artisitc output of this fascinating man. ☮

KEITH HARING

Drawing the Line: Keith Haring
(1990, 30 min, US)
When gay artist Keith Haring died in February 1990 of complications due to AIDS, he left behind an astounding artistic legacy. In his 31 years, Haring had gone from being an anonymous

Keith Haring at work on a mural

graffitist who drew chalk figures on New York City subway posters to become a popular and outspoken artist, with his work hailed as the successor to Andy Warhol and Roy Lichtenstein. Haring's hieroglyphic-like drawings, which have become an ubiquitous sight around New York, incorporated social issues such as the fight against Apartheid, crack and AIDS. This revealing profile contains interviews with gallery owners, fellow artists and actor Dennis Hopper as well as a close-up look into Haring's passionate art. ☮

DAVID HOCKNEY

▼ A Bigger Splash
(1974, 90 min, GB, David Hockney)
Controversial British painter David Hockney stars as himself in this penetrating, semi-ficticious portrait of his personal and artistic life. Centered around the actual breakup of Hockney and his lover/model, Peter Schlessinger, this witty and revealing work meditates on the relationship of art to life. Vignettes of Hockney with friends, lovers and ex-lovers create an impressionistic study of the swirling influences in one artist's world. ☮

David Hockney: Portrait of an Artist
(1985, 52 min, GB)
David Hockney is the most popular British painter of his generation, but in recent years, his painting has taken a back seat to photography. We are invited into the London studio of the artist where we witness his applications of still photography innovations to moving pictures. The result, on camera, is Hockney's first experiment in making "fine art" out of cinematography. ☮

▼ Hockney at the Tate
(1988, 55 min, Alan Benson)
With a quizzical Melvyn Bragg in tow, Hockney walks through the Tate Gallery's exhibition of his paintings as he analyzes them — from his first oil portrait in 1955 (casually described by Hockney as "a dull art school painting") through to his L.A. swimming pool paintings including "A Bigger Splash." Hockney is not reticent about discussing his homosexuality as it refers to his work. The film is a fascinating opportunity for art and Hockney fans alike to watch an artist "read," interpret and criticize at length his own work. ☮

A Day on the Grand Canal with the Emperor of China
(1990, 60 min, US, David Hockney & Philip Hass)
One of the most accessible documentaries on art available, this unusual film is a vivid journey down a 72-foot long 17th-century Chinese scroll. Narrated by artist David Hockney as he unrolls the elaborately painted and richly detailed scroll, the life of Emperor Kangxi and the bustling life of his kingdom comes alive. Hockney

David Hockney

also spins an interesting discourse on Eastern and Western perspectives and their relationship to his own artistic vision. ⊗

"The film easily and subtly reveals as much about Mr. Hockney's own work as it does the scrolls...splendid."
—Janet Maslin, *The New York Times*

FRIDA KAHLO

Frida *(1984, 108 min, Mexico, Paul Leduc)*
The life of painter, revolutionary and woman-of-the-world Frida Kahlo is brilliantly brought to the screen in this insightful and poetic biography. Told from her deathbed in surreal flashbacks reminiscent of her own canvases, the film recalls Frida's stormy relationship with muralist Diego Rivera, her dealings with Leon Trotsky, her involvement with the cultural renaissance in Mexico in the 1930s, as well as capturing the spirit and determination of one of the dominant painters of the 20th century of who Rivera once described as "hard as steel, delicate and fine like a butterfly's wings." ⊗

Frida Kahlo — A Ribbon Around a Bomb
(1990, 75 min, US, Ken Mandel)
The fascinating but painful life of painter Frida Kahlo comes alive in this ambitious documentary that blends archival footage, examinations of her paintings, interviews with many of her contemporaries and friends, and a stage production in an attempt to piece together the mysterious puzzle that was Kahlo. We learn that Kahlo was physically debilitated throughout her life because

of a bus accident as a youth but which became the impetus for her art — one that was self-revelatory and imbued with images of death, blood, internal organs and suffering. Her partnership and tempestuous marriage to Diego Rivera is also explored, a relationship that was strained not only because of the great differences in age but Rivera's many affairs, including one with Kahlo's sister Christina. Many of the women of whom she was intimate speak out on this very special woman who has gone on to become an artistic legend today.

MICHELANGELO

The Agony and the Ecstasy
(1965, 140 min, US, Carol Reed)
Not considered one of the better films from the director of such classics as *Odd Man Out* and *The Third Man*, Carol Reed's historical account follows Michelangelo di Lodovico Buonarroti Simoni's aesthetic battles with Pope Julius II as he toiled on the Sistine Chapel. Charlton Heston and Rex Harrison provide worthy performances, but the film's slightly overblown production values and its considerable length overshadow their efforts. It will also come as no surprise that there is no mention of the artist's homosexuality. ⊗

Return to Glory:
Michelangelo Revealed *(1986, 52 min, Japan)*
Obscured by centuries of soot, pollution and bad restoration attempts, only now is the true vibrancy of the Sistine Chapel revealing itself. When this latest restoration began in 1980, no one expected that Michelangelo, far from being a solemn and shadowy painter, was in actuality a bold colorist who painted with astonishing subtlety and skill. Narrated by Edwin Newman. ⊗

▼ Michelangelo Self-Portrait — The Life and Death in His Own Words
(1989, 90 min, US, Robert Snyder)
The master of the Renaissance, Michelangelo, is explored in this "you are there" documentary. Oscar-winning director Robert Snyder narrates as the film travels in a flashback style to where he lived and created. Michelangelo's works stand today as some of the most impressive of all time. A painter, architect, sculptor, engineer and poet whose work includes "David," "The Pieta," "Moses" as well as the murals on the ceiling of the Sistine Chapel, Michelangelo's life is detailed from his youth to his old age and death at the age of 89. The film paints a portrait of a gifted and tormented soul who struggled all his life to find a balance between humanity and ego, flesh and spirit. Included are Michelangelo's love sonnets written for the much younger nobleman Tommasso Cavalieri.

FAVORITE ARTISTS

TOM OF FINLAND

▼ Boots, Biceps & Bulges — The Life & Works of Tom of Finland
(1988, 30 min, US, James Williams)
Not to be confused with the similarly themed *Daddy and the Muscle Academy*, this fascinating film documents the life and the unique erotic art of Tom of Finland. Tom, who died in 1991 at age 72, developed over the years a strong underground following for his fanciful and sexually graphic depictions of gay men from around the world. Exaggerating their features and equipment, his homoerotic drawings of super-masculine, ruggedly handsome men, usually in uniforms or leather, have become gay icons. The film intersperses an interview with Tom in 1988 with shots of hundreds of his drawings. A mesmerizing look into the thoughts and works of a genuine gay folk artist. ⊕

▼ Daddy and the Muscle Academy
(1992, 60 min, Finland, Ilppo Pohjola)

This involving documentary on the life and art of Tom of Finland has enjoyed acclaim both in lesbian and gay film festivals as well as from straight critics through its several theatrical engagements in the United States. The film explores the evolution of Tom's art from his crude but sexy drawing of German soldiers during Finland's occupation by Nazi forces during WWII, to his work as one of the most popular illustrators of gay erotic images — reaching a point in his craft that he has become an icon in the realm of gay male erotica. Tom himself is interviewed, shortly before his death. He reminisces about his unusual childhood obsessions, the influences on his work and his interest in erotic-romantic images that are filled with musclebound, well-endowed men in various stages of dress and undress wearing uniforms, leather and chains. Hundreds of his drawings are shown in this almost adulatory film on this celebrated artist. ⊕

▼ Tom's Men *(1992, 28 min, US)*
Unlike the two documentaries available on home video on Tom of Finland, *Tom's Men* is an all-too-short foray solely into the artist's entertainingly erotic art. Basically a videoized dirty comic book, the stories vividly detail erotic adventures of the men Tom dreams of — unbelievably endowed, mustached macho men in uniform jumping on each other's bones! A real eye and zipper opener! ⊕

MEREDITH MONK

Meredith Monk
(1983, 60 min, GB, Peter Greenaway)
The exotic artistry of avant-garde composer, singer, dancer, film-maker, choreographer and performance artist Meredith Monk is captured in this Peter Greenaway documentary originally aired on Britain's Channel 4. Her unusual approach to music is the most startling aspect of the film — for Monk eschews, for the most part, recognizable words and presents instead sounds, many of them bird-like chants. This new hybrid offers for her a greater range of communication, the result being musical pieces that feel both ancient and futuristic. Greenaway intermixes a Monk performance with interviews with the spirited artist and offers clips from several of her experimental films. ⊕

RUDOLF NUREYEV

An Evening with the Royal Ballet
(1963, 85 min)
Featuring a young Nureyev, who had two years earlier defected to the West, this video features a compilation of some of The Royal Ballet's greatest works, including "Le Corsaire," "Sleeping Beauty" and "Les Sylphides." Margot Fonteyn co-stars. ⊕

Romeo and Juliet *(1966, 124 min)*
Considered by many in ballet as the greatest dance partnership, Nureyev and Margot Fonteyn are captured at the height of their careers in this rousing production. Featuring The Royal Ballet, and with music by Prokofiev and choreography by Sir Kenneth MacMillan. ⊕

Don Quixote
(1973, 109 min, Rudolf Nureyev & Robert Helpmann)
This film version of Marius Petipas' colorful ballet was co-directed by Nureyev (who also plays Basilio) and Robert Helpmann (who appears in the title role). The film also stars Ray Powell, Lucette Aldous, Francis Croese, and the dancers of the Australian Ballet. The score is by Ludwig Minkus, and the film is lavishly photographed by noted cinematographer Geoffrey Unsworth. ⊕

"An exciting, intelligently conceived spectacle."
—*The New York Times*

Rudolf Nureyev (r.) palling around with Divine

"The finest full-length dance film ever."
—Dance Magazine

I Am a Dancer
(1973, 93 min, GB, Pierre Jourdan & Bryan Forbes)
An absorbing documentary portrait of one of this century's greatest dancer. The film follows Nureyev through his training to his arrival on the international scene. He dances with Cynthia Gregory and Dame Margot Fonteyn. ⊛

Giselle *(1979, 78 min)*
Nureyev stars as Albrecht in this popular ballet that features the Canadian ballerina Lynn Seymour and the Royal Ballet's Monica Mason.

Fonteyn and Nureyev:
The Perfect Partnership *(1985, 90 min)*
Focusing on the lasting and inspiring dance partnership of Dame Margot Fonteyn and Nureyev, this video offers highlights from several of their ballets including "Romeo & Juliet," "Swan Lake" and "Le Corsaire." ⊛

Rudolf Nureyev
(1991, 90 min, GB/Germany, Patricia Foy)
A fascinating video biography for anyone interested in the life of Nureyev. Through interviews with a reflective and wistful Nureyev (just a year before his death to AIDS), the film chronicles his life, from his poor Tartar Muslim peasant childhood and his education and dancing at the Kirov Ballet, to his news-making defection to the West in 1961 and his international success as a pop ballet icon and international celebrity. Stating that "from early years I knew how to be on stage and how to command it, how to shine," Nureyev recounts his run-ins with Kirov teachers, Soviet Communist authorities, his contemporaries and his battles with the board of the Paris Opera Ballet when he headed it. In addition to many excerpts from his ballets, the documentary also interviews his childhood dancing teacher, his first dancing partner and delves

into his legendary professional relationship with his greatest partner, Dame Margot Fonteyn. Projecting him as a fiery, independent artist who is not shy about voicing his opinions, the film sidestep's Nureyev's homosexuality and personal life, preferring to ignore this aspect of his life by simply labeling him a deep-thinking loner. Yet despite the absence of any personal information or any reference to his illness (painfully obvious in the interviews), the film presents a temperamental, independent man at peace with both his life and his work. ⊛

HOWARD ASHMAN

Little Shop of Horrors
(1986, 88 min, US, Frank Oz)
Science fiction, comedy and musical do-wop blend wonderfully in this glorious screen version of Howard Ashman and Alan Menken's hit off-Broadway musical based on Roger Corman's 1960 exploitation flick. Audry II, the alien Venus Flytrap with an appetite for human blood, befriends a nerdish Rick Moranis in its fiendish plot to take over. The many show-stopping scenes include a maniacal Steve Martin as a sadistic denist who meets his match in Bill Murray's hilariously masochistic patient. Ashman, openly gay lyricist who collaborated with composer Menken to create a handful of classic modern musicals, died of AIDS in 1992. His ability to create witty, intelligent and sophisticated lyrics — deceptively complex rhymes which perfectly complimented his partner's melodic scores — easily put him in a musical class with contemporaries such as Sondheim or Andrew Lloyd Weber; and his talents were more than once compared to those of Cole Porter. ⊛

The Little Mermaid
(1989, 82 min, US, John Musker & Ron Clemens)
Ashman and Menken's joyous score, combined with outstanding animation, a thoroughly enjoyable story and a bewitching cast of characters, all contributed in making *The Little Mermaid* Disney's most accomplished film since *Mary Poppins* and initiated an artistic renaissance for the studio which is still in effect today. This delightful tale tells the story of Ariel, a young mermaid, who falls in love with a handsome human prince, much to the chagrin of her father, ruler of the underwater kingdom. An Oscar winner for Best Score and Best Song (the enchanting "Under the Sea"). ⊛

Beauty and the Beast
(1991, 85 min, US, Gary Trousdale & Kirk Wise)
On the heels of *The Little Mermaid*, one of Disney's finest animated features, comes an even more impressive achievement, the first animated film to be nominated for an Academy Award as Best Picture. Based on the classic fairy tale, Disney animators have created a masterpiece of color and scope, complete with refreshingly good humor and a captivating text. But what makes *Beauty* soar is the outstanding musical score by Menken and Ashman. Including the Oscar-winning title ballad and the exuberant "Be Our Guest,"

the score has the style and brilliance of a classsic Broadway musical rather than — what most musicals are today — a promo for a best-selling soundtrack. Menken and Ashman's music would be equally remarkable for a live-action film. A total delight for all ages, *Beauty* is not to be missed. ⊛

Aladdin
(1992, 87 min, US, John Musker & Ron Clements)
Based on the classic "Arabian Nights" tales, *Aladdin* is a consistently entertaining and incredibly funny achievement. The film features a charming musical score by Ashman, Alan Menken and Tim Rice, delightful animation and wonderful laugh-out-loud jokes. This alone makes the film first-class. But *Aladdin* also has Robin Williams. As the voice of the genie whose iconoclastic references will split any side, Williams catapults the film to inspired comic heights — and the Disney artists have matched his vocal escapades with sensational drawings. A marriage made in cartoon heaven, this is Williams and Disney at their best. Not to be overlooked is Gilbert Gottfried's wonderful turn as a side-kicking parrot. A film adults will love even more than children. *Aladdin* was Ashman's final project, and the terrible loss of his artistry is especially apparent in Disney's latest animated feature, *The Lion King*. Though a box-office smash, *Lion*'s score (by Tim Rice and Elton John) is unmemorable, which only further accentuates the film's less-than-remarkable story line. ⊛

LEONARD BERNSTEIN

On the Town
(1949, 98 min, US, Gene Kelly & Stanley Donen)
A grand, energetic and immensely enjoyable adaptation of the popular Broadway musical with a score by Bernstein and a book by Betty Comden and Adolphe Green. Directors Gene Kelly and Stanley Donen have opened up, with location shooting, the exuberant tale about three sailors on a 24-hour pass, and of their romantic adventures in New York City. Kelly, Frank Sinatra and Jules Munchin are the men in uniform; and Vera-Ellen, Betty Garrett and Ann Miller are the women with whom they meet and fall in love. Includes "New York, New York" and "Come Up to My Place." ⊛

On the Waterfront
(1954, 108 min, US, Elia Kazan)
Bernstein composed the music for this gritty drama starring Marlon Brando as a former fighter and dock worker who gets into trouble with the union mob after he sings to the law about dockside corruption. ⊛

West Side Story
(1961, 152 min, US, Robert Wise & Jerome Robbins)
Whether referring to the stage or film version, this Bernstein-Stephen Sondheim musical is one of the all-time greats. Natalie

Leonard Bernstein

Wood and Richard Beymer are the star-crossed lovers in this updated "Romeo and Juliet" set against the backdrop of gang warfare in New York's Upper West Side. Russ Tamblyn and George Chakiris (Oscar winner) are the gang leaders, and Rita Moreno (also an Oscar winner) is Chakiris' girlfriend. Expertly directed by Robert Wise and Jerome Robbins (who also choreographed the classic dance numbers). Winner of 11 Academy Awards, including Best Picture. Bernstein's score is at once pulsating, hypnotic, melodious, haunting and alive with the verve of a tumultuous day in New York City. ⊛

Leonard Bernstein —
Verdi: Requiem *(1970, 97 min, GB)*
Bernstein conducts the London Symphony Orchestra within the imposing grandeur of St. Paul's Cathedral. Featuring Placido Domingo and Ruggero Raimondi. ⊛

Leonard Bernstein — Beethoven:
The Ninth Symphony *(1970, 78 min)*
Performed at the Konzerthaus, Vienna, Bernstein conducts the Vienna Philharmonic Orchestra and Vienna State Opera Chorus. Features Gwyneth Jones, Shirley Verrett, Placido Domingo, Marti Talvera. ⊛

Bernstein in Vienna:
Beethoven Piano Concerto No. 1
(1970, 45 min, US, Humphrey Burton)
Prepared for the 200th anniversary of Beethoven's birthday, Bernstein conducts the Vienna Philharmonic in this performance of Beethoven's Piano Concerto No. 1 in C Major. He also performs (keyboard) and narrates the tale. Soloists include Gwyneth Jones, Placido Domingo, Shirley Verrett. ⊛

Leonard Bernstein's
Young Peoples Concerts
From 1958 thru 1972, Leonard Bernstein presented a series of hour-long educational concerts and shows on CBS. In commemo-

ration of his 75th birthday in 1993, Sony Pictures and the Smithsonian in Washington came together and released all 53 of the old television programs on 25 different videos. ⊛

Trouble in Tahiti *(1973, 48 min)*
Inspired by jazz and American musical theatre, Bernstein conducts his own score in this satire on the emptiness of materialism and the false promise of suburban comforts. Featuring a live-action cast and an animated set. ⊛

The Unanswered Question *(1973, US)*
In 1973, Bernstein, as the Charles Eliot Norton Professor of Poetry at Harvard University, gave a series of lectures on music history and diversity. This compilation of six videos follows Bernstein as he delves into explanations and demonstrations of all types of music and searches for a innate musical grammar. The programs include performances by Bernstein, the Boston Symphony Orchestra and the Vienna Philharmonic. ⊛

Volume 1: Musical Phonology *(104 min)*
Bernstein explores the origins and development of music and language with a performance of Mozart's Symphony No. 40 in G Minor. ⊛

Volume 2: Musical Syntax *(95 min)*
Using the same piece of Mozart music, Bernstein explains the structure of music and speech. ⊛

Volume 3: Musical Semantics *(142 min)*
Bernstein conducts the Boston Symphony in Beethoven Symphony No. 6 in F Minor, Op. 68. ⊛

Volume 4: The Delights and Dangers of Ambiguity *(142 min)*
Composers Berlioz, Wagner and Debussy are musical examples as Bernstein explains the movement for new tonal field by composers of the Romantic Era. ⊛

Volume 5: The Twentieth Century Crisis *(133 min)*
The theme of Bernstein's lecture is the atonality movement by Arnold Achoenberg. Musical selections include works by Mahler, Ives and Ravel. ⊛

Volume 6: The Poetry of Earth *(177 min)*
Bernstein concludes the series with an examination on how Igor Stravinsky keep tonality viable while experimenting freely with dissonance. Features a complete complete performance of Stravinsky's "Oedipus Rex" with the Harvard Glee Club. ⊛

Leonard Bernstein — Tchaikovsky *(1974, 48 min)*
With the New York Philharmonic performing in the recently opened Sydney Opera House, Bernstein conducts Tchaikovsky's Symphony No. 6 in B Minor Pathetique. ⊛

Leonard Bernstein — The Ravel Concerts *(1975, 87 min)*
The program opens with "Alborada del graciosa" followed by Bernstein performing Ravel's Piano Concerto No. 1 (the maestro conducts from the keyboard). Concludes with Ravel's masterpiece "Bolero." ⊛

Leonard Bernstein — Berlioz: Requiem *(1975, 88 min)*
Set in the Chapel of St. Louis des Invalides in Paris, Bernstein conducts Berlioz's monumental work. ⊛

Leonard Bernstein — Chichester Psalms *(1977, 80 min)*
With the Israel Philharmonic Orchestra at the Philhamonie in Berlin, Bernstein conducts three of his own compositions: "Chichester Psalms," "Jeremiah" and "The Age of Anxiety." (Also known as: *Bernstein Conducts Bernstein*) ⊛

Leonard Bernstein — Schumann: Symphony No. 1/Shostakovich: Symphony No. 5 *(1979, 93 min)*
Bernstein conducts the New York Philharmonic at the Bunka Kaikan in Tokyo. ⊛

Leonard Bernstein Conducts West Side Story *(1985, 89 min, US)*
Bernstein conducts Kiri te Kanawa, Jose Carreras, Tatiana Troyanos and Kurt Ollmann in the making of the newly recorded version of "West Side Story." ⊛

West Side Story

Ode to Freedom —
The Berlin Celebration Concert
(1990, Germany/US, 92 min, Humphrey Burton)
In celebration of the unification of Berlin and Germany, this fes-
tive outdoor concert features Bernstein conducting the Barvarian
Radio Symphony Orchestra in Beethoven's Symphony No. 9 in D
Minor, Op. 125. ⊗

Candide *(1991, 147 min, US/GB, Humphrey Burton)*
Performed in 1989 at London's Barbican Centre, Bernstein's
own composition of Voltaire's satiric book comes alive with a
youthfully animated Bernstein conducting the London
Symphony Orchestra. Lyrics are by the combined talents of
Bernstein, Lillian Hellman, Dorothy Parker and Stephen
Sondheim. With Jerry Hadley-Land as Candide and June
Anderson as Cunegonde. Songs include "Glitter and Be Gay"
and "The Best of All Possible Worlds." ⊗

BENJAMIN BRITTEN

The British Documentary Movement
— Benjamin Britten
In addition to his operas, Britten also wrote music for films including the four short documentaries in this video compilation. *Coal
Face* (1935, 12 min) goes deep into the coal mining pits of Whales.
Night Mail (1936, 24 min) follows the labyrinthine and massive
postal service in a social documentary fashion. *Instruments of the
Orchestra* (1947, 20 min) and *Steps of the Ballet* (1948, 24 min)
examine not the industrial system of the previous two shorts, but
rather the various components in the creative process. The images
are not in the finest of shape, but Britten's lyrical, often soaring
musical accompaniment is heard quite well. ⊗

▼ A Profile of Benjamin Britten —
A Time There Was...
(1980, 102 min, GB, Tony Palmer)
Possibly the quintessential biography on an artisan, this documentary on composer Benjamin Britten — a fascinating divulgence
into Britain's greatest 20th-century composer — seeks to know
and gently understand this man who spent his life not as a tortured,
temperamental genius spurred into trailblazing creativity by simple inspiration but rather a hard-working professional "from the
middle classes." Leonard Bernstein once said of Britten, "(He
was) a man at odds with the world...and he didn't show it." The
film, aided by fascinating archival footage of performances from
his operas, scenes of him conducting and composing, and photos
and films from his childhood and youth, follows this Suffolk boy
from his birth in 1913 through his professional and personal life, which
ended with his death in 1976. The film is certainly not a
"talking head" documentary but does include interviews with both
his contemporaries (Rudolph Bing, Julian Bream) and friends and

employees. His lifelong relationship with tenor Peter Pears is also
explored, a union described by Pears as "passionate, devoted and
close" (their house cleaner/cook describes the couple as "very
clean people"). While Britten and Pear's relationship is taken as a
given, gay references are kept to a minimum, with the only overt
moments being Pear's discussion of his unease with the word
"gay" and its "lifestyle." For fans and novices alike, this award-
winning film is especially effective in revealing Britten's work
ethics and the recurring themes found in his operas, symphonies
and concertos including his interest in the beauty and danger of
relationships, his pacifist believes and his rebellious male heroes,
many of them homosexual. ⊗

A Midsummer Night's Dream
(1982, 156 min, GB, Peter Hall)
Set in an enchanted forest, lit only by the rising moon and a late-
day sun, this magical Glyndebourne production features Ileana
Cotrubas as the majestic Tytania.

> "This *Dream* looks absolutely ravishing, gliding from one
> sumptuous and glittering tableau to another."
> —*London Evening Standard*

Gloriana *(1984, 146 min, GB, Derek Bailey)*
Sarah Walker plays the indomitable Queen Elizabeth I in this
English National Opera production of Britten's passionate tale.
Considered a modern masterpiece, this opulent but poignant opera
also stars Anthony Rolfe Johnson as the Earl of Essex. Mark Elder
conducts.

Albert Herring
(1984, 147 min, GB, Peter Hall)
Britten's comic opera, adapted from a story by Guy de
Maupassant, features John Graham-Hall in the title role as the
gullible, naive and good-hearted greengrocer. Much to his
embarrassment, Albert has been made the Village May King
when it is discovered that there are no local girls with the necessary virtuous qualities to be Queen (no, the village's boys do not
get a chance at the title!). A Glyndebourne production conducted
by Bernard Haitink.

Peter Grimes *(1985, 155 min, GB)*
Britten's masterpiece "Peter Grimes" is considered one of the
great works of 20th-century opera. Originally composed in 1945,
this version by the Royal Opera Company with Colin Davis conducting stars Jon Vickers in the title role. Set in a small fishing
community, the story focuses on the proud and misunderstood outsider Peter Grimes, who must battle opposition from fellow fishermen and a vindictive community. ⊗

War Requiem
(1988, 92 min, GB, Derek Jarman)
Produced by Don Boyd (*Aria*), director Derek Jarman provides
visually imaginative images to accompany Britten's music with
the result being a jarring, exhilarating metaphor on the folly of

war. Originally written to commemorate the reopening of the Coventry Cathedral, destroyed during the war, Britten's story draws its inspiration from the poetry of WWI footsoldier Wilfred Owen. Laurence Olivier is the old soldier whose remembrances form the narration, with Tilda Swinton featured as Nurse, Nathaniel Parker as Poet and Owen Teal as Unknown Soldier. ⊛

Billy Budd
(1988, 157 min, GB, Tim Albery)
Adapted from the Herman Melville story, this gripping opera of persecution and injustice aboard an 18th-century British ship features a text by E. M. Forster and Eric Crozier with music by Britten. Filmed originally for BBC television, this English National Opera production centers on the innocent youth Billy Budd (Thomas Allen) who, after being unjustly accused of mutiny, strikes and kills his tormentor, the master-of-arms, John Claggart (Richard Van Allen), which in turn prompts Captain Vere (Philip Langridge) to order Budd's execution for murder. ⊛

▼ Benjamin Britten's Death in Venice
(1990, 13 min, GB, Stephen Lawless & Martha Clarke)
Britten's final opera, which is based on Thomas Mann's novella, is presented here by the Glyndebourne Touring Opera Company with music conducted by Graeme Jenkins. Tenor Robert Tear is Aschenbach, the elderly composer who becomes tortured by the complex beauty and innocence of a youth he sees while in Venice. The homosexual elements are much stronger than in the novella and in Visconti's film version as Aschenbach becomes transfixed by a image that is both elusive and destructive. Michael Change plays the blond boy and Alan Opie appears in a multitude of roles. ⊛

JOHN CAGE MERCE CUNNINGHAM

Merce Cunningham
(1979, 60 Min, GB, Geoff Dunlap)
Made for London Weekend Television, this documentary focuses on the meritorious contributions Merce Cunningham has made to the art of dance. Cunningham, one of the most important choreographers of his generation, is seen rehearsing as well as working on music (with longtime friend John Cage), painting, theatre and filmmaking. Cunningham's unique, instinctive approach to choreography is presented through interviews with dancers Karole Armitage, Carolyn Brown and Chris Komar, and Cunningham himself. Exuberant performance excerpts are featured from "Exchange," "Squaregame," and "Travelogue."

John Cage
(1983, 60 min, GB, Peter Greenaway)
As part of Peter Greenaway's four-part series on American composers (others include Robert Ashley, Meredith Monk and Philip Glass) made for Britain's Channel 4, this startling film provides an overview, or sampler of the works of the modernist "percussion composer" John Cage. Set in the deconsecrated shell of St. James Church in Islington, London, a series of performances are staged to commemorate Cage's 70th birthday. Intercut between Cage's readings and interviews are performances from his works of the 1940s through to the late 1970s. The environmental sounds that many people think of as simply noise become the key to Cage's kaleidoscopic approach to music — an approach that challenges traditional musical thought. Greenaway's camera sweeps through the church as if part of the musical performance. ⊛

Points in Space   *(1986, 55 min, US)*
The longtime collaboration of composer John Cage and Merce Cunningham (former lovers who evolved into a creative partnership in music and dance) is explored in this BBC-produced production. The first part is an interview with the two eclectic artists and the second is a filmed performance of "Points in Space," as performed by the Merce Cunningham Company.

John Cage:
I Have Nothing to Say and I'm Saying It
(1990, 57 min, US, Allan Miller)
While possibly a bit too analytically dense for neophytes of the musical avant-garde, this film on the work of controversial composer John Cage is both informative and, for fans of his approach to music and art, fascinating. Experimental and innovative, Cage's aversion to harmony did not deter him from becoming a conceptual composer, pioneer in electronic music, visual artist and lecturer on the appreciation of alternative music. With excerpts from many of his compositions, including his famous (or for some, infamous) "4' 33"," a musical piece featuring a piano and pianist and complete silence, we learn more of both the man and the artist. Interviewed are Cage himself, his longtime collaborator Merce Cunningham and many others in the adventurous left field of art. ⊛

Cage/Cunningham
(1991, 85 min, US, Elliot Caplan)
Through archival footage that dates back to the beginning of their friendship and present-day interviews, this film chronicles the extraordinary 45-year collaboration between avant-garde composer John Cage (who died in 1991) and choreographer Merce Cunningham. Dealing primarily with their professional relationship, the documentary explores their artistic output together which includes work in art, dance and music.

"Beautifully filmed, it erases the ordinary boundaries between life and art. It suggests in some indefinable way that Cage and Cunningham have made work that transcends time."

— Stephen Holden, *The New York Times*

FAVORITE COMPOSERS

COLE PORTER

The following is a selected list of some of the films containing Cole Porter music.

Broadway Melody of 1940

(1940, 102 min, US, Norman Taurog)
A sparkling backstage musical starring Fred Astaire, George Murphy and the great Eleanor Powell. Excellent dance numbers, and a lovely Porter score includes "Begin the Beguine" and "I've Got My Eyes on You." ⊛

DuBarry Was a Lady

(1943, 100 min, US, Roy Del Ruth)
Based on Porter's Broadway hit, those two crowned heads of comic tomfoolery, Red Skelton and Lucille Ball, take over the Bert Lahr and Ethel Merman roles. And though Red and Lucy are just fine, Hollywood once again outsmarted itself in the translation of a stage musical, here keeping only three of Porter's songs ("Friendship," "Do I Love You" and "Katie Went to Haiti"). Red's in love with nightclub entertainer Lucy. He sips a mickey and dreams he's Louis XV of France to Lucy's Madame DuBarry. Also with Gene Kelly and Zero Mostel. ⊛

Night and Day

(1946, 128 min, US, Michael Curtiz)
As Hollywood fiction, this is fairly entertaining stuff; but as the true biography of legendary songwriter Porter, it's laughably inaccurate. And though no one ever complained about seeing Cary Grant in a film, he's not exactly the perfect choice to play the composer. Also starring Alexis Smith as Mrs. Porter (his wife, not mom), and Monty Woolley plays himself as Cole's best friend. Mary Martin has a small scene singing "My Heart Belongs to Daddy." Of course, a film made in 1946 would never have even hinted at Porter's well-known homosexuality. ⊛

The Pirate

(1948, 102 min, US, Vincente Minnelli)
Gene Kelly's thrilling dance numbers highlight this charming musical about traveling acrobat Kelly being mistaken to be a notorious pirate by love-struck Judy Garland. Porter's score includes "Be a Clown" and the Nicholas Brothers are sensational in support. ⊛

Kiss Me Kate

(1953, 119 min, US, George Sidney)
One of Porter's best scores highlights this vibrant adaptation of the Broadway musical about a divorced theatrical couple who are reunited for a performance of Shakespeare's "The Taming of the Shrew." Howard Keel and Kathryn Grayson are wonderful as the estranged husband and wife; and the dance sequences featuring Ann Miller, Bob Fosse, Tommy Rall and Bobby Van are terrific. Originally shown in 3-D. Songs include "Too Darn Hot" and "Why Can't You Behave." (The also featured "From This

DuBarry Was a Lady

Moment On" is not from the original stage show, but a cut song from Porter's "Out of This World.") ⊛

High Society

(1956, 107 min, US, Charles Walters)
Musical remake of *The Philadelphia Story* with songs by Porter. Grace Kelly, Bing Crosby and Frank Sinatra take over the Katharine Hepburn, Cary Grant and James Stewart roles. It's a pleasing rehash, but nowhere near the original. Porter's songs include "True Love" and "Well, Did You Evah!" ⊛

Silk Stockings

(1957, 117 min, US, Rouben Mamoulian)
Porter's score elevates this charming musical remake of Ernst Lubitch's *Ninotchka*, with Fred Astaire in the Melvyn Douglas role as a movie producer, and the lovely Cyd Charisse in the Garbo role as the Russian envoy. ⊛

Can-Can *(1960, 131 min, US, Walter Lang)*

The powerhouse cast of Frank Sinatra, Shirley MacLaine, Louis Jordan and Maurice Chevalier isn't enough to offset the many lethargic moments in this only occasionally entertaining Porter musical. Shirley wants to dance the "shameful" title dance; the police say no, lawyer Frank says she can-can. Songs include "I Love Paris" and a few not in the original stage production. ⊛

STEPHEN SONDHEIM

A Funny Thing Happened on the Way to the Forum *(1966, 99 min, US, Richard Lester)*

A rip-roaring, bawdy and hilarious adaptation of Sondheim's hit Broadway musical for which he wrote both music and lyrics. Zero Mostel had one of his best roles onstage, and here on-screen, as a conniving Roman slave who sets out to obtain his freedom. Sexual innuendo, slapstick and feverish chases are the order of the day as Mostel uses every trick in the book in his glorious quest. Jack Gilford also repeats his stage role as a fellow slave, and Michael Crawford is their young, love-struck master. Also with the zany Phil Silvers and Buster Keaton. Sondheim's score includes "Everybody Oughta Have a Maid" and "Comedy Tonight." ⊛

Company: Original Cast Album

(1970, 53 min, US, D.A. Pennebaker)

Behind-the-scenes look at the recording sessions of Sondheim's Broadway musical "Company." The original Broadway cast, including Dean Jones, Elaine Stritch, Barbara Barrie and Charles Kimbrough (TV's "Murphy Brown") shine and grind it out in this truly revealing documentary of the creative process at work. ⊛

▼ The Last of Sheila

(1973, 120 min, US, Herbert Ross)

Entertainingly puzzling to the very end, this star-studded murder mystery features James Coburn as a game-obsessed film producer who invites six of his Hollywood jet-set "friends" on a cruise in the Mediterranean where a mean-spirited game, begun by him and designed to expose a dark secret of each member, backfires. Twists and turns abound in this plexus story written by real-life puzzle freaks Anthony Perkins and Sondheim. The "innocent" guests include James Mason, Dyan Cannon, Joan Hackett, Richard Benjamin and Raquel Welch. ⊛

A Little Night Music

(1978, 124 min, US, Harold Prince)

A rather mediocre adaptation of Sondheim's brilliant Tony Award-winning musical (which was based on Ingmar Bergman's *Smiles of a Summer Night*). Elizabeth Taylor is miscast as Desiree, the actress who reenters the life of newly married Len Cariou (repeating his stage role). Diana Rigg steals the show as the wife of soldier Lawrence Guittard, who is having an affair with Taylor. The film captures none of the magic which made the Bergman film and the stage play great hits. Though "A Weekend in the Country" is performed quite admirably. ⊛

Sunday in the Park with George

(1984, 140 min, US, James Lapine)

A thrilling adaptation of Sondheim's Pulitzer Prize-winning Broadway musical, filmed directly from the stage, about the life of 19th-century French artist Georges Seurat and his painting of the masterpiece "Sunday Afternoon on the Island of La Grand Jette." The original Broadway cast is featured in this superb production, including Mandy Patinkin, Bernadette Peters, Charles Kimbrough and Dana Ivey. ⊛

Sweeney Todd *(1984, 140 min, US)*

A live performance of Sondheim's Tony Award-winning musical. Magnificently re-created for video, Angela Lansbury (also a Tony Award winner) and George Hearn repeat their stage roles as, respectively, the evil Mrs. Lovett and the demonic barber Sweeney, who together conspired to murder his customers and serve them up in her meat pies. An unusual topic for a musical, to be sure, but the genius of Sondheim's music and lyrics and Harold Prince's original staging combine to create a musical masterpiece. Hearn, who stepped into the role after Len Cariou, gives one of the greatest performances to be seen in the theatre in recent memory. An unforgettable theatre piece, and not to be missed. ⊛

Dick Tracy *(1990, 104 min, US, Warren Beatty)*

Warren Beatty's colorful adaptation of the Chester Gould comic strip is a dazzling display of costumery and scenery. In the title role, Beatty delivers what might be his only good performance in years; Glenne Headly is charming as his girlfriend Tess Trueheart; Dustin Hoffman is hilarious as Tracy's informant, Mumbles; and Madonna gets to sing a couple of breathy show tunes penned by Sondheim, who won an Oscar for the song "Sooner or Later." ⊛

Follies in Concert *(1990, 90 min, US)*

An all-star cast is featured in this one-time performance of Sondheim's classic Tony Award-winning musical "Follies." Without sets or costumes, the likes of Carol Burnett, Mandy Patinkin, Barbara Cook and many others perform the entire score in a concert-like setting. Though everyone is in fine voice, it's Patinkin who steals the show with his energetic rendition of "Buddy's Blues." ⊛

Sondheim: A Celebration at Carnegie Hall *(1992, 90 min, US, Scott Ellis)*

In 1992, an all-star musical tribute in honor of Sondheim was held at Carnegie Hall. Among the performers were Liza Minnelli, Patti LuPone, Glenn Close and Bernadette Peters. Songs include "Send in the Clowns," "Being Alive," "Old Friends," "Children Will Listen" and many others. ⊛

A Funny Thing Happened on the Way to the Forum

4

OF QUEER INTEREST

The alphabetical listing of titles for this chapter have been selected because of their relevancy to both gay men and lesbians.

"Lesbians are so great, they get so much done in a day."
—A rhapsodizing Bruce McCulloch of the
comedy troupe Kids in the Hall to his group
of vagina-envious poker playing pals

"I'm proud of my lifestyle...you can't make me ashamed."
—A middle-aged lesbian in *Why Am I Gay?*
Stories of Coming Out in America

Acting on Impulse
(1993, 93 min, US, Sam Irvin)

Made for cable's Showtime, this comic thriller has its tongue planted firmly in cheek, as with director Sam Irvin's previous outing *Guilty as Charged*. The ravishing Linda Fiorentino plays a "scream queen" goddess of B-horror films. After a fatal argument in which her producer is found dead, Fiorentino sets out for a little R & R, where she is stalked by "adoring" fans; and then the body count starts piling up. Featuring a little lesbian teasing between a playful Fiorentino and Nancy Allen, and a steamy Fiorentino-C. Thomas Howell sex scene, the film is leisurely paced, offers a few well-placed jabs at the horror film industry, and has an eclectic supporting line-up, including the late gay actor Dick Sargent (the 2nd Darrin of "Bewitched" fame), Paul Bartel, Adam Ant, Isaac Hayes, Zelda Rubinstein and Mary Woronov. Openly gay director Irvin is currently working on a futuristic western, *Oblivion;* as well as *CopCat*, a serial killer film that Irvin says will have a major gay subplot. Irvin's other dream projects include a gay James Bond movie and a film version of Grant Michael's gay mystery novel "A Body to Die For." ⊛

Agora
(1992, 73 min, US, Robert Kinney & Donald Kinney)

Directed by twin gay brothers Robert and Donald Kinney, this low-budget melodrama's theme looks at gays and lesbians' "outlaw" status in America — one in which society rejects them for what they are and, in turn, their refusal to conform. Set primarily in a seedy Midwestern motel, the film focuses on five social misfits. Crab is a young closeted gay who's awkward, shy and works at the hotel's reception desk; Swallow is an agressively scrappy convict on the lam who is holed up in the hotel with his lover, Jack; and two lesbians, Katch, who was recently thrown out of the Army, and her flighty lover Joy, are also staying there. While the story meanders, it is still interesting to a queer audience for its matter-of-fact way of depicting its gay and lesbians characters — unapologetically and without stereotypes.

All Out Comedy
(1993, 78 min, US, Bohdan Zachery)

Queer stand-up comedians finally get their stage spotlight in this intermittently funny tape which features two gay male and two lesbian comedians. Filmed live at San Francisco's Josie's Cabaret and Juice Joint, each comedian is interviewed briefly before going on stage. Featured are Karen Ripley, a sad-sack looking lesbian ("Is it OK to hate men but dress just like them?"); Scott Capurro ("I'm only funny when I'm queer"), whose nelly queen act is not-so-funny as an eerily quiet audience sits yearning for better material; Marilyn Pittman follows, and overcomes thin material with her humorous bellowing delivery and sexually tinged jokes; concluding the segment is veteran Tom Ammiano, the so-called "Mother of Gay Comedy." ⊛

And the Band Played On
(1993, 144 min, US, Roger Spottiswoode)

Mini-history of the making of the film: The much hyped and eagerly anticipated film version of the late Randy Shilts' controversial best-selling novel on the early years of the AIDS epidemic was embroiled in its own controversy even before its September 1993 airing on HBO. The difficulty of getting the film made was legendary (reportedly taking over six years, and then only after considerable support by many actors including Richard Gere and Lily Tomlin). After all principle photography was completed, HBO — under pressure from Shilts and gay organizations who previewed the film — fired director Roger Spottiswoode, banned him from the editing room, and refused to let him screen it at the Cannes Film Festival. Bill Couturie (co-director of *Common Threads*) replaced him to re-edit and add more documentary footage. Shilts thought that the film was unbalanced and needed more positive gay role models, saying at the time, "My only concern is with the portrayal of gays. I've gone through hell with the gay community over my book and it's made me more sensitive." Spottiswoode, director of *Under Fire* and *Shoot to Kill*, kept his name on the film, but believes that the new version "trashed" his original and has said, "They sanitized the movie. It was supposed to be a tough film, but equally tough on everyone."

The review: By structuring the film as an investigative medical thriller, this star-studded and emotional drama fights an almost insurmountable problem in that the villain is a virus, its discovery brings no joy and there cannot be a happy ending. Nevertheless, *And the Band Played On* is historically and scientifically comprehensive, as well as fast moving, at times humorous and exceedingly focused in unraveling the mysterious illness that baffled science and medical experts for years. Shilts' contention in the book was that in the initial discovery, various organizations and individuals, motivated by greed, ignorance and pride, stymied research and allowed the AIDS virus to spread to epidemic proportions. For the sake of dramatic focus, the story follows one government virologist, Don Francis (Matthew Modine), as he, almost single-handedly, works on solving the mystery that resulted in unexplained illness and death among male homosexuals, Haitians, hemophiliacs and Africans. With the exception of a few passing references, the focus is on male American homosexuals. The high-caliber cast includes Lily Tomlin as a persuasive, dedicated San Francisco health official; Richard Gere in a seemingly much-edited, disguised role as choreographer Michael Bennett; Phil Collins as a profit-obsessed bad-boy owner of a gay bathhouse; Ian McKellen as a San Francisco gay leader and B.D. Wong as his lover. Alan Alda savors his role as the vain, fame-seeking Dr. Robert Gallo. The story slowly unravels in a chronological and almost educational fashion as the knowledge of what is causing the deaths becomes clear. The film indicts nearly everyone involved: the Reagan-led U.S. government; uncooperative gays who felt that their sexual freedoms were being threatened; hospital and blood bank officials who felt their profits were being threatened; and publicity-seeking scientists bent less on research and more on glory. Admittedly powerful and engrossing, the film does suffer in its depiction of gays (the first on-screen gay is an effeminate transvestite with AIDS and an attitude) and the general perception that it took the intense work of a group of straight men and women to come to the rescue of the helpless gay community. ⊛

Armistead Maupin's Tales of the City

(1993, 360 min, US/GB, Alastair Reid)

Taken from Armistead Maupin's endearing and popular 1978 novel, which in turn was derived from his weekly columns in the *San Francisco Chronicle*, this boldly original and faithful adaptation follows the interconnected lives of a group of San Francisco eccentrics (both gay and straight) during the halcyon 1970s. Adapted by openly gay scriptwriter Richard Kramer ("thirtysomething"), this six-part miniseries, which covers the first six volumes of the book, centers around exotic earthmother Anna Madrigal (Olympia Dukakis), landlady of 28 Barbary Lane. The colorful extended family of the residence includes innocent Mary Ann (Laura Linney), a recent arrival from Cincinnati; bisexual/fag hag Mona (Chloe Webb); and Michael (Marcus D'Amico), a hopeless romantic eternally searching for Mr. Right. Soon the lives of these people and others come together in an amazingly complex series of eye-opening episodes which involve marital infidelity, ribald sexuality, racial denial, recreational drug use and scenes of the emerging gay lifestyle. Frank and racy dialogue and lingering but playful scenes of gay men kissing and caressing help in bringing a glimpse of the queer world to the general public. A completely engrossing six hours called "high class, soft camp soap opera" by London's *Gay Times*, *Tales...* is funny, provocative and totally unpredictable. Also starring Donald Moffat, Paul Gross and Barbara Garrick with support and cameos by Edie Adams, Lance Loud, Paul Bartel, Rod Steiger, Karen Black, Mary Kay Place, Ian McKellen and McLean Stevenson. ⊛

Marcus D'Amico, Laura Linney and Chloe Webb in *Armistead Maupin's Tales of the City*

Notes on the production: This, Armistead Maupin's first novel, is set in San Francisco but was produced primarily by Britain's Channel 4 with additional financing provided by San Francisco's local PBS station KQED and PBS' "American Playhouse." Getting the book adapted for the screen was no easy task for Maupin, due in large part by its open depiction of homosexuality — the book suffered through years of "development hell." Warner Brothers first showed interest in 1979 but nothing came of it. HBO followed in 1982, planning a 13-part series, but that too was scrapped. After almost 15 years of options bought and fruitlessly expired, it was finally made by an enterprising British production company at a total cost of $8 million. Even after the film was completed and shown in England, controversy erupted in the States when the film's fleeting nudity and depiction of casual drug use (let alone the sight of kissing and affectionate queers) prompted many stations to express concern. One station in the South refused outright to air it while others ran a different version which had the nudity pixilated out. Maupin, reacting to the editing, remarked that he wanted as many people as possible to see his film and was "delighted that PBS has taken the stance that America can watch what British grandmothers have already seen."

Basic Instinct

(1992, 127 min, US, Paul Verhoeven)

What *Cruising* was to infuriated gay men in 1980, this ultra-chic, sexually explicit thriller was to equally incensed lesbians in 1992. Surrounded by controversy and picketed in several cities, the film raised a red flag for lesbians, gays and feminists with its shocking "retro" stereotypes of man-hating lesbians with a "basic instinct" for murder. Essentially an adolescent sex fantasy disguised as a murder mystery, the film follows burned-out San Francisco detective Michael Douglas as he absurdly falls in "lust" with the prime suspect in a series of brutal ice pick murders. Sharon Stone, in an admittedly star-making performance, plays Catherine Trammell, a beautiful bisexual author of best-selling murder mysteries who, under her elegantly cool veneer of white trash class, might very well be (OK, she *is*) a duplicitous killer. Captured within her dangerous web along with Douglas are her butch lesbian lover Roxy (Leilani Sarelle) and old college flame Beth (Jeanne Tripplehorn). Joe Eszterhas' misogynistic screenplay takes special delight in making all three women dangerously alluring, attractively attired and eminently psychotic. ⊛

The Best of "Out" and "Out on Tuesday" *(1989-1991, 75 min, GB)*

Unlike anything found in the States, Great Britain's upstart commercial network, Channel 4, has been in the foreground of both supporting (through production monies) and showing gay and lesbian themed works. From *My Beautiful Laundrette* to *Oranges Are Not the Only Fruit* to even *The Crying Game*, to name just a few, the network has been truly a savior in getting queer images out to the general public. This videotape, currently available only in the U.K., offers highlights from "Out" and "Out on Tuesday" — two programs made by gays and lesbians and aired on Channel 4. Issues explored include a short on hair and its relevance to gays and lesbians, a segment on the 1991 London Gay/Lesbian Pride March as well as short documentaries on the joys of lesbianism, Asian and Indian struggles dealing with being queer, why straight women go to gay bars and the strange attraction we have towards drag shows.

The Best of "The Kids in the Hall"
(1989-91, 120 min, Canada)

The Kids in the Hall (the five member all-male Toronto-based comedy troupe which includes Scott Thompson, Dave Foley, Bruce McCulloch, Kevin McDonald and Mark McKinney) is a wildly funny group which enjoys fervent cult status both in Canada and in the United States, primarily from their hip and deadly on-target television series on HBO and, most recently, with a series on CBS. While only one of the members, Scott Thompson, is openly gay, the group is amazingly queer-friendly (to the point where many viewers might assume they are all gay) and have a special penchant for cross-dressing. Their female characters go beyond simple men-in-drag stereotypes to become actual characters in their own right. The boys transform into tittering secretaries and proper wives and mothers and even softball-playing dykes. Even when not in drag, their skits remain queerish; one example in this compilation finds the five playing poker, and in a lull, each begins to reveal his secret desire to become a woman — either to enjoy breast-feeding, have a period or to become a dyke. As one says, "Lesbians are great, they get so much done in a day." Included in this video is Thompson's most famous character, Buddy Cole, a swishy and dishy, wise-cracking bar queen who, when not wittily dissecting racial and sexual stereotypes, becomes the martini-drinking guest manager of a lesbian softball team named the Sappho Sluggers (all, of course, played by the troupe). ✪

Bright Eyes
(1984, 85 min, GB, Stuart Marshall)

Gay historian/documentarian Stuart Marshall created with *Bright Eyes* one of the earliest British films to deal with the impending AIDS crisis. Made for Channel 4, this three-part investigative work takes a historical approach while dealing with the human element to the disease. Included with the collage of images are thoughts on the meaning of homosexuality and an overview of how the print media, propelled by its homophobia, either ignored or mishandled the initial reportage of the impending epidemic. Marshall also includes a look at the history and suppression of Magnus Hirschfield and his groundbreaking homosexual rights work with the Institute of Sexual Sciences and its eventual destruction by Fascist forces in 1930s Germany.

> "Stated concisely, the point I wanted to make was that the historical construction of homosexual identity as an inherently pathological subjectivity formed the powerful subtext of contemporary journalistic representations of AIDS as "the gay plague."
>
> — Stuart Marshall

Changing Our Minds: The Story of Dr. Evelyn Hooker
(1992, 77 min, US, Richard Schmiechen)

Nominated for an Academy Award for Best Feature Documentary of 1992, this inspiring film recounts the life and work of pioneering psychiatrist Dr. Evelyn Hooker, whose studies on homosexuality in the 1950s paved the way for its greater understanding and acceptance, especially in the professional fields. The film recounts, with the aid of archival footage and interviews, the McCarthy-fueled hysteria in post-WWII America when the general public's fear of homosexuality resulted in police actions in which bars and even parties were raided and gay men and women arrested and prosecuted. And it is in this atmosphere of hatred and misunderstanding that Dr. Hooker began her work. The main reason for her fame is underdeveloped, but what we do learn is that she spearheaded a groundbreaking scientific study with the result showing no discernable difference between her gay and straight subjects — a result that disputed the general notion of homosexuality as a mental disorder. For before that time, psychiatry was in the "Dark Ages" as it historically advocated the "treatment" of the "mental illness" with lobotomies, castration and electro-shock therapy. Dr. Hooker's paper, presented to the American Psychiatric Association (APA) in Chicago proved to be the beginning of greater understanding of homosexuality although it was not until 1974 that the APA finally removed from its platform the belief that homosexuality is a form of mental illness. While not a rousing documentary, the film is memorable mainly through the interviews with the articulate and courageous Dr. Hooker who emotionally recalls her life and historic work. An important film on the history of gays and lesbians.

Coming Out Under Fire
(1994, 71 min, US, Arthur Dong)

Adding yet another significant chapter in transposing oral lesbian/gay history onto film/video, this entertaining and eye-opening documentary centers on nine lesbians and gay men and their experiences as "undesirables" in the armed forces during World War II. Based on Allen Berube's "Coming Out Under Fire: The History of Gay Men and Women in World War II," the film provides both a historical overview of the American government's shifting attitudes towards gays in the military as well as allowing the interviewees to describe vivid personal experiences of the discriminatory practices of their own government. Especially timely given President Clinton's compromised "Don't Ask, Don't Tell" policy, the film comes alive when the often eloquent vets recount both their good times (camaraderie with other gays/lesbians, wartime romances) and bad (being arrested and discharged) living as closeted homosexuals in an organization that viewed them as unfit for military service and saw their sexual orientation as either a mental illness, morally suspect or potentially hazardous to unity and moral. The award-winning film also provides historical and factual information, including the statistic that at least 9,000 gay men and women were dishonorably discharged during World War II.

Coming of Age
(1982, 60 min, US, Josh Hanig)

The divergent attitudes of teenagers living in the Reagan era are explored in this film set in a week-long encounter seminar involving 200 teens. Dealing with such issues as sexuality, racial relations, religion and family, the inner-city students — white, black and Asian as well as gay and lesbian — discuss their thoughts and reveal their emotional needs with surprising candor in this simple but passionate documentary.

Comrades in Arms
(1990, 50 min, GB, Stuart Marshall)
From documentary filmmaker Stuart Marshall (*Desire, Over Our Dead Bodies*) comes this very funny look at homosexuality in Britain's armed forces. Originally aired on Channel 4's gay program "Out on Tuesday," the film features interviews with six gay and lesbian veterans of World War II who recount, in alternately poignant and entertaining fashion, their amorous adventures while defending Queen and country. The people deal less with the persecution of homosexuality and more with the positive aspects of their experiences, including furtive sexual fulfillment, the joys of serving in the armed forces and the many lifelong friendships (sexual and platonic) they have formed.

The Conformist
(1971, 115 min, Italy, Bernardo Bertolucci)
This fascinating exploration of the emotional roots of Fascism in pre-war Italy ranks as one of the best Italian films of the 1970s. Jean-Louis Trintignant stars as Marcello, a repressed homosexual traumatized by a childhood incident in which he shot the family chauffeur after a seduction attempt. Now as an adult, Marcello longs for conformity and appears to find it when he joins the Italian Fascist Secret Service and tries to hide his homosexuality by marry-

ing a vapid, petite bourgeois woman whom he barely tolerates. Sent to assassinate his former professor who is now a leading dissident, he meets and is "attracted" to Dominique Sanda — who appears as a lesbian and anti-fascist and who eventually develops into the moral adversary to Trintignant's perverted beliefs. While the initial scenes have Sanda playing the role a bit too mannishly (director Bernardo Bertolucci probably didn't want anyone to miss the signs), her free-spirited, naive nature and pureness of conviction makes her character a strong counterweight to Trintignant's Marcello. ⊛

Cut Sleeve: Lesbians & Gays of Asian/Pacific Ancestry
(1993, 24 min, US, N.A. Diaman)
Despite a running time of only 24 minutes, this mini-documentary is included because of its interesting handling of the sexual and racial prejudices encountered by gays and lesbians of Asian and Pacific ancestry. This little publicized minority within a minority has had to face the double difficulties of their patriarchal and traditionally homophobic culture as well as being accepted within the "white" queer community. Filmed on a bare-bones budget and shot in a simple style, the film interviews eight "typical" men and women as they recount their struggles with sexual and ethnic self-identity. Director N.A. Diaman is author of five novels (including "Ed Dean Is Queer," "The Fourth Wall" and "Castro Street Memories") and is working on a new documentary video, *The Stonewall Generation*.

Damned in the USA
(1991, 68 min, GB, Paul Yule)
Tackling the question of whether art has the power to corrupt, this hard-hitting documentary examines the growing cry for censorship in film, music and the fine arts. The film gained notoriety when its distribution was temporarily halted by a lawsuit by Fundamentalist minister Donald Wildman over "unauthorized" interview footage of him. Insightful and often satirical, the film's interest for gay/lesbian audiences is when it focuses on the censorship of photographer Robert Mapplethorpe's blatantly homosexual work.

Desire (1989, 88 min, GB, Stuart Marshall)
Utilizing incredible archival footage as well as interviews, this intense talk-fest documentary chronicles the birth, growth and eventual suppression of Germany's gay/lesbian movement, from 1910 through Hitler's crackdown. Marshall takes an intellectual approach in his exploration of the emerging gay culture and birth of the "erotic idealism" inherent in the movement that flourished in the 1920s and '30s before ending when it was outlawed by the Nazis, resulting in the systematic oppression and eventual imprisonment of its members in concentration camps. Also explored is turn-of-the-century Germany's scientific "discovery" of homosexuality and how people reacted to this "breakthrough." Through interviews with expert sociologists, sexologists, historians and actual lesbian and gay survivors of the camps, the film offers a fascinating glimpse into a relatively unknown subject and proves to be a vital document in queer history. ⊛

> "A well-made and engrossing documentary...*Desire* is the equivalent of *Before Stonewall*...its ultimate effect is to show us how sometimes hideous things are perpetrated in seemingly benign settings."
>
> — *The Advocate*

Desire

A Different Story
(1978, 107 min, US, Paul Aaron)

Actually nothing more than a TV situation comedy, this is the same old story: Two unlikely people initially dislike each other, but eventually fall in love — with the twist being that he's gay and she's a lesbian. Albert (Perry King) arrives in L.A. accompanied by famous classical conductor Douglas (Peter Donat), who from the start is depicted as an obnoxious, vindictive and philandering homo. Albert's life as his boy-toy is short-lived and he's soon thrown out. He quickly meets Stella (Meg Foster), a lesbian who offers him a night on her couch; but a night turns out to be quite a bit longer as the two are slowly drawn together. They get married (ostensibly to keep Albert, who's Belgian, from being deported), make love, become heterosexual, have a kid, he gets a successful job, she quits hers and to prove that they are now straight, begin to have marital problems. The film uses the gay subtext simply as a gimmick, dwelling little on their original sexual orientation and more on their male-female love. The pre-fucked King is obviously a homosexual — he's a neatness freak, a great cook and knows more about women's clothing than women. Stella's lesbian life is less conspicuous, limited basically to her relationship with her lover Phyliss (Valerie Curtin), who is seen as a neurotic, emotional mental case (in obvious need of a man) and no real threat to Albert and the advancement of heterosexuality. The gay stereotypes aside, and the notion that queers can be cured with a good hetero fuck, the film is forgettable. ⊗

"The movie's use of their homosexuality is indeed exploitive, insensitive and offensive in a variety of ways."
— *The New York Times*

Enchanted
(1992, 89 min, Germany, Dorothee von Diepenbroick)

Gays and lesbians living in Germany during the Nazi era are the subject of this compelling documentary. The Nazis' rise to power brought an end to Germany's status as the center of gay/lesbian culture in Europe during the 1920s and early '30s. Article 175, making homosexuality illegal in Germany, marked the beginning of years of persecution — a situation that was not rectified at the end of the war; for, shockingly, West Germany's new constitution of 1949 retained Article 175. Life in Nazi Germany for gays and lesbians is vividly brought to life as 13 men and women from Hamburg recall their lives during this period of deadly oppression. Now in their seventies and eighties, they freely talk about the secrecy required by the danger of being gay in a society that had one woman arrested for simply having a picture of another woman in a swimsuit in her apartment.

Family Values
(1988, 56 min, US, David Stuart)

Less an objective documentary and more a heartfelt tribute, this video gives thanks to the many lesbians who have been deeply involved in helping ease the suffering inflicted on gay men by the AIDS epidemic. Despite being in the lowest risk group for contracting the disease, San Francisco's lesbian community has been mobilized into action, involved in activities such as nursing sick patients, organizing food banks, publishing newsletters, taking

Not just another boy meets girl story.

A Different Story

care of the pets of sick and hospitalized patients and fund raising. Interviewed are the many women who have devoted much of their time and energies. They talk of what spurred them into community service and what it all means in their lives. Also interviewed are several gay men, mostly AIDS patients, who have been the beneficiaries of these resolute and untiring women.

Feed Them to the Cannibals!
(1992, 65 min, GB, Fiona Cunningham Reid)

With the title referring to the suggestion by a New South Wales governor 200 years ago that "them," meaning homosexuals, and the cannibals, being New Zealanders, meet for a meal, this irreverent and wildly exuberant film chronicles the bacchanalian extravaganza that is Sidney's Mardi Gras. The event, the largest gay/lesbian happening in the Southern Hemisphere, has its history traced to a simple march in 1978 which turned violent (after police disruption) to defiantly become today a month-long gay and lesbian celebration. From a spectacularly staged and wildly costumed "Sleaze Ball" to sporting and social events and even a queer dog show, the month's activities culminate in a plasmorganic parade — rivaling Greenwich Village's Halloween Parade — in which 400,000 spectators gather to join the fun of celebrating gay and lesbian pride. After viewing the film, many will want to cancel their tickets to New Orleans and head Down Under to join the festivities.

> "In my opinion it's not only offensive, but obscene and blasphemous...In the beginning God created Adam and Eve not Adam and Steve."
> — Rev. Fred Niles, Australian Christian Fundamentalist

A Florida Enchantment
(1914, 63 min, US, Sidney Drew)
Considered one of the earliest films to feature ambiguous sexual attraction, this cross-dressing comedy, based on an 1896 Broadway play, is set at an elegant Florida resort. A young woman (Edith Storey), frustrated at her fiancé's philandering, ingests magic seeds from the African Tree of Sexual Change which quickly transforms women into men and vice versa. While she remains feminine looking (though she does sprout a cute mustache), she immediately assumes the behavior of a man: swaggering belligerently, smoking furiously and making repeated advances on other women. She kisses several women on the lips with surprisingly little protest and essentially becomes a philandering straight man in a woman's body, eventually proposing to a woman. The seeds ultimately fall into the hands of her former fiancé, who becomes an effeminate female in a male body. While not really gay or lesbian themed, the film is years ahead of its time in humorously exploring men and women's sexual roles. ⊕

Framed Youth
(1983, 45 min, GB, Lesbian & Gay Video Project)
Winner of the Grierson Award for Best Documentary in 1984, this short documentary, aired on Britain's Channel 4 in 1986, deals with what it is like for young people to be gay and lesbian in Britain today. Utilizing music (including Jimmy Somerville), interviews, film clips and cartoons, the film's subjects talk about coming out, first love and their families' responses. Those involved in the making of this enlightening tape include filmmakers Constantine Giannaris (*Caught Looking, North of Vortex*), Isaac Julien (*Young Soul Rebels, Looking for Langston*), Nicola Field and musicians Somerville and Richard Coles.

Gay for a Day
(1976-78, 45 min, US, Tom Palazzolo)
This video time capsule features two short films which celebrate the heady days of the 1970s, a pre-AIDS time period when being gay or lesbian simply meant freedom of personal expression and sexual liberation. The first, *Gay for a Day*, documents the 1976 Gay Pride Day Parade in San Francisco, where sequins, balloons and half-naked men abound and squeals of, "I love those shoes!"

were heard throughout the land. The second, *Costumes in Review*, takes a humorous look at a festive, and at times raunchy, gay costume party. Rambling and poorly photographed, this is by no means great cinema, but a document of an important (and in retrospect innocent) period of gay/lesbian history. ⊕

Gay Games III *(1990, 192 min, US)*
More of a simple recording of an important gay/lesbian event than a traditional documentary, *Gay Games III* videotapes the opening and closing ceremonies of the 1990 Gay Games which were held in Vancouver, Canada, in the summer of 1990. Since its inception in 1982, which drew 1300 male and female participants, this third Gay Games (the use of the word "Olympics" had been barred by a court order) grew to include 7000 athletes from all around the world. Two 96-minute volumes record the "rah-rah" enthusiasm of the crowd as well as 20 marching bands, several live musical performances and the introduction of the athletes to a curiously half-empty B.C. Place Stadium. Lesbian activist and comic Robin Tyler sparks the crowd with her funny comments as a succession of politicians and organizers offer rousing speeches. The second tape, much less interesting, passively views the closing ceremony as the viewer asks what happened to *any* outtakes from the actual sporting events! A nice video to own if you were there. ⊕

Gay Youth

Green on Thursdays

Gay! Gay! Hollywood

(1994, 85 min, US, Nick Bougas)
Upon first look, *Gay! Gay! Hollywood* promises to be the video equivalent of this very book; sadly it fails to deliver. The incessant, often stumbling voice-over sounds like a poorly written college term paper on the subject ("homosexuality is one of the oldest traditions in theatrical life") and the images, often unconnected to the narrative, rely too much on public domain footage and film trailers. Name-dropping is the key as the usual cast of characters are introduced with their stories filled with the maximum amount of gossip and innuendo and the minimum amount of fact. Focusing primarily on men (although Joan Crawford, Janet Gaynor, Garbo and Dietrich are mentioned), the film delves into the professional and personal lives of such stars as Cary Grant (maybe he wasn't gay), James Dean ("a human ashtray"), Rock Hudson (notorious homo), Montgomery Clift (traumatized by his small dick) and many more. It teases about some (Cesar Romero), discounts others (Errol Flynn, Ray Sharkey) and luridly depicts the alleged sexual predilictions of several more (Dan Dailey was a cross-dresser, Tyrone Power was reportedly a coprophiliac). There is some good material in the video and one will be lured to it for what sexual secrets it may reveal, but overall it's a disappointment — read the book! ✆

Gay Games IV from A to Q

(1994, 60 min, US)
Through the combined efforts of the queer electronic media, including Dyke TV, The Gay Cable Network, Gay Entertainment Television, "In the Life," and Network Q, this documentary provides the visual highlights of the 1994 Gay Games IV held in New York City in June 1994. Its short running time forces the videomakers to race through the opening ceremonies, on to rapid highlights of the competition and conclude with segments from the closing ceremonies held at Yankee Stadium. ✆

The Gay Rock 'n' Roll Years

(1991, 50 min, GB, Shauna Beaven & Clare Beaven)
Originally broadcast on British television and subsequently screened at various lesbian and gay film festivals, this fast-paced, high-energy documentary follows rock 'n' roll from its birth in the 1950s through the 1990s. With musical clips, commentary and interviews, the video features the groups and individuals, as well as the memorable events and important musical performances, that have helped shape gay and lesbian life in Great Britain.

Gay Youth *(1992, 40 min, US, Pam Walton)*

Produced as an educational video and designed for viewing by high school students (the tape includes a study guide when purchased), this stirring documentary addresses the need for tolerance and understanding for young gays and lesbians and calls for an end to homophobia, especially among teenagers. The story follows the lives of two widely divergent gays: Bobby Griffith, a troubled gay youth who committed suicide at the age of 20; and Gina Gutierrez, a 17-year-old lesbian who has accepted her lesbianism and, in turn, has received support and encouragement from family and friends.

Green on Thursdays

(1993, 78 min, US, Dean Bushala & Deidre Heaslip)
This disturbing documentary on violent homophobia in Chicago provides a complex look at a tense situation. In interviews, several victims of gay-bashing (men and women, black and white) recount the attacks on them, their injuries and their confused feelings of rage and frustration afterwards. The film points out that with the wide openness of gays and lesbians in many big cities, there has been a steady rise in hate crimes directed at them. After several horrifying stories, the viewer, along with the victims, feels a sense of resignation at the overwhelming hatred of homophobes which is compounded by police bias and indifference, an ineffectual legal system and politicians' avoidance of the issue. But we are offered a glimmer of hope with the rise of several gay and lesbian activist organizations dedicated to confronting and stopping the violence. The Pink Angels, a group of citizens that patrol troubled sections of Chicago's gay/lesbian area, becomes an effective tool which, coupled with the formation of the Chicago Anti-Violence Project and the rise of political activism in the form of raucous demonstrations and marches, offers witness to the determined militant spirit of the community. The film reveals progress in confronting the prejudice, but can offer little in the way of a solution to this sobering, all-too-true predicament.

Greetings from Out Here
(1992, 60 min, US, Ellen Spiro)

Ellen Spiro, a "Southern expatriate who escpaced to New York," packed a few bags, her camcorder and dog into a van and headed off in search of the "new gay South." The result is a delightfully educational and illuminating whirlwind tour that ventures down the back roads and into the small towns of the Deep South. Along the way, she visits a lesbian music fest, a gay Texas rodeo, a gay Mardi Gras ball and a meeting of the Radical Faeries in the hills of Tennessee. Her travels also involve interviews with an African-American lesbian living in a broken-down bus in Arkansas, a gay preacher in Alabama, and Michael Monks and Allan Gurganus, who collaborate to write *Monk Magazine* (Gurganus is author of "The Oldest Living American Confederate Widow Tells All"). Twenty-seven-year-old Spiro, originally from Richmond, Virginia, has said that, "Going back, I found a rich and diverse gay culture. I was also interested in showing the human South that breaks away from the New York stereotype of Southerners as cross-burning racists."

Grief *(1993, 92 min, US, Richard Glatzer)*

With the same quirky, endearing qualities which distinguished producer Yoram Mandel's previous gay film *Parting Glances*, independent writer-director Richard Glatzer has taken his personal experience as a writer for TV's "Divorce Court" and fashioned an engaging and funny comedy-drama about friendship, love, bereavement and trash TV. Craig Chester (*Swoon*) stars as Mark, a gay writer for a daytime courtroom drama who is nearing the one-year anniversary of his lover's death to AIDS. Set during an eventful workweek, the film follows Mark's relationships with his co-workers and superiors, as he comes to grips with office politics, an office crush, homophobia, and his loss. Jacki Beat (in a "Divine" bit of casting) co-stars as Jo, the overweight producer who mother-hens and browbeats her crew at the same turn, and who serves as narrator and resident wit. Alexis Arquette plays Bill, a bisexual fellow employee who is involved in a secret office affair with the no-nonsense Jeremy (Carlton Wilborn), and the object of Mark's affection. Highlighting the film are campy renditions of the show the characters write, which includes everything from lesbian circus performers to schizophrenic divas. These bits include cameos from Paul Bartel, John Fleck and Mary Woronov. ⊛

He and She and Him
(1978, 90 min, France, Max Pecás)

Slightly a cut above (or below?) porn, this sex drama revolves around a predatory lesbian and her gay accomplice. Greta, an innocent blonde Swedish student, is down on her luck and wandering the streets of Paris. She is "rescued" by Claude, a dark-haired, wealthy lesbian who takes her home, dons black leather shorts, boots and a whip, drugs little Greta into a pleasant stupor and has her Sapphic way with her. The film goes on to "justify" Claude's lesbianism as resulting from being raped by three boys while she was in school! ⊛

Alexis Arquette (l.) and Carlton Wilborn as lovers in *Grief*

Hearing Voices

(1990, 89 min, US, Sharon Greytak)

Numbed into quiet boredom by the shallow, manipulative world of fashion modeling and physically scarred after reconstructive surgery, Erika floats aimlessly through her successful but empty life. She is saved emotionally after meeting Lee (sort of a Pauly Shore on Prozac), the gay lover of her doctor. Their relationship, infused with tender caresses and revealing intimacies, is an unusual love, which, while not altogether fulfilling and ultimately doomed, does help in their respective healing processes. This story, a "romantic" relationship between a gay man and a straight woman, provides a great premise; but the film, hampered by languid pacing and stilted acting, becomes a ponderous exercise in Bergman-esque "message cinema," reducing it to an earnest but lifeless viewing experience. ✆

Heavy Petting *(1989, 85 min, US, Obie Benz)*

This amusing and entertaining satire on America's repression of and obsession with sex chronicles those "innocent" days (when "good girls didn't") with clips from '50s "B" movies and funny, insightful, and occasionally stupid anecdotes from the likes of David Byrne, Sandra Bernhard, Ann Magnuson, Laurie Anderson, Spalding Gray, Allen Ginsberg and William Burroughs. Despite its more-than-fair queer representation, the film takes a mainly straight-and-narrow approach to the subject. ✆

The Historic March on Washington

(1987, 58 min, US)

The highlights of the Octobet 1987 Lesbian and Gay March on Washington, the largest gay rights demonstration up to that date, are documented. The rally and march are seen along with the unveiling of the Quilt and the mass queer wedding ceremony. ✆

Improper Conduct (Mauvaise Conduite)

(1984, 110 min, France, Nestor Almendros & Orlando Jimienez Leal)

This provocative documentary investigates the oppression and abuse faced by Cuba's gay and intellectual populace under the hyper-machismo reign of Castro. Twenty-eight Cuban exiles — homosexuals, poets, artists and former government officials — are interviewed, each detailing their conflicts with a system that suppresses civil rights and considers homosexuality a crime. ✆

In the Life: The Funny Tape

(1992-93, 60 min, US)

"In the Life" is the first American television series focusing exclusively on issues of lesbian and gay interest. Similar to Britain's "Out" and "Out on Tuesday" on Channel 4, "In the Life" is syndicated on PBS, although its availability has been limited by the refusal of many local PBS stations to carry the show. This home videotape features stand-up comedy highlights from its first season, including such comedians as Kate Clinton, Karen Williams and Garret Glaser. Also featured are the musical/comedy group The Flirtations, drag artist extraordinaire Charles Busch (as 1940s screen idol Mary Dale), Randy Allen as a nearly mummified Bette Davis and some interesting footage of author Vito Russo ("The Celluloid Closet") with Lily Tomlin. ✆

Inside Monkey Zetterland

(1993, 93 min, US, Jefrey Levy)

An all-star queer and queer-friendly cast, coupled with good intentions, cannot save this emotionally empty, occasionally funny but generally uninvolving "wacky family comedy" which fails to match the anarchic humor of the film it steals from the most, Tony Richardson's *Hotel New Hampshire*. The story revolves around the life of "painfully average" Steven Antin, a former teen actor living with his soap opera diva mother (Katherine Helmond), his lesbian sister Grace (Patricia Arquette) and his bulimic tenant (Martha Plimpton) who is shacking up with a wasted (in both senses of the word) Rupert Everett (who inexplicably speaks with an Australian accent). The plot revolves around L.A. yuppie terrorism, but the film is most interested in introducing its touchy-feely Left Coast too-much-time-on-their-hands eccentrics. The queer angle is the estranged relationship between Grace and her now-pregnant lover Cindy (Sofia Coppola). The family fully accepts her although still following the Vito Russo "rules of treating homosexuals" that was prevalent throughout the 1950s-1980s — one of the lesbians is inexcusably killed off. The film also features Ricki Lake as a lonely star stalker and *Out*'s Lance Loud. ✆

Heavy Petting

Liquid Sky

Lick Bush in '92

(1993, 89 min, US, Gabriel Gomez & Elspeth Kydd)
Using as one of her campaign slogans, "If a bad actor can be elected president, why not a good drag queen," the presidential ambitions of Chicago's black transvestite diva Joan Jett Blakk are wittily chronicled in this entertaining yet underlyingly serious documentary. What began as a joke, Blakk's campaign steamrolled through the Second City and culminated with her appearance at the Democratic National Convention in New York. Throughout, Blakk proves to be both a droll and intelligent voice of reason — her pledge to do away with the military and replace it with Dykes on Bikes just might work! Ultimately too long (a 60-minute feature would have been better), the film is most effective when, through the sheer balls of the "Boss in Lip Gloss," she creates publicity on such issues as homelessness, AIDS and queer rights.

Liquid Sky

(1983, 112 min, US, Slava Tsukerman)
Flying saucers, fatal orgasms, rampant androgyny and relentless nihilism make *Liquid Sky* one of the most original and hallucinatory films in memory. Co-author Anne Carlisle stars in dual roles as Jimmy, a snarling junkie, and Margaret, his female nemesis, a languid model with an unusual kiss of death. Perched atop Margaret's

penthouse terrace are mite-sized aliens who crave the sensation of a heroin rush which, it seems, is duplicated organically during human orgasm. A stunning cultural collage that offers an alien's-eye view of Manhattan's lurid clubs, majestic skyline and jaded populace. ☮

Living Proof: HIV and the Pursuit of Happiness *(1993, 70 min, US, Kermit Cole)*
Refusing to pessimistically portray people with AIDS simply as victims of a deadly disease, this documentary focuses on some of the many HIV-positive men, women and children who are living life to the fullest. Buoyantly upbeat, *Living Proof* centers around one man, George DeSipio, who, after being diagnosed with AIDS in 1990, found that there was very little in the way of positive role models for PWAs. He soon teamed with photographer Carolyn Jones to work on a photographic essay that would celebrate these very courageous people. The project eventually included over 40 people from all walks of life, all of whom share a common commitment not to give up, but to fight the disease and lead productive, even joyous lives. The interviewees, ablaze with an almost religious fanaticism, talk about how the knowledge of being HIV-positive is far from being a death sentence. The film follows the photography sessions which eventually opened in a gallery in New York in 1993 and culminated with a

book of the photographs which was given to President Clinton at the White House in early 1994.

> "I think what the film does is highlight the enormous personal courage PWAs had to muster and provides them with a context to express what's been good as well as bad in an air of community and celebration."
> — director Kermit Cole

> "Exhilarating...amazing! There's lots of humor, and an attitude explosion that's contagious. If you don't believe there's such a thing as transcendent energy, go see this film."
> — Jay Carr, *The Boston Globe*

March On! *(1993, 56 min, US)*

Far from being a dry account of a protest march, *March On!*, one of several videos made on the 1993 Lesbian & Gay March on Washington, is an entertaining yet informative look at social and political activism in the queer community. With its goal to celebrate the civil rights march, an event that many feel was a beginning of an organized, united stand by gays and lesbians to voice their demand for full civil rights, the video goes beyond simple talking head documentary and takes a meandering role in recounting the many events which were scheduled during the march. Along with scenes of the march itself, the video includes interviews with many surprisingly eloquent participants including gay scouts, a mother of two gay sons, a lesbian biker, straight Miami police officers who attended the march in support, and includes some touching moments at a mass queer marriage ceremony. ⊗

March in April

(1994, 60 min, US, Stephen Kinsella)

Unlike the many "you are there" documentaries that were made on the April 1993 Lesbian and Gay March on Washington, this "personal video" focuses on a group of gay men who convene on the weekend of the march in a Washington home for a friendship reunion. Super low-budget and mildly interesting, the video chronicles the host's frantic preparations as well as his relationships with his lover and visitors. The discussions between these "guppies" touch on such issues as coming out, gays in the military and gay/lesbian rights, but they are marred by a simplistic, "Can't we all just get along" mentality. ⊗

Marching for Freedom!

(1993, 78 min, US)

Upbeat, slick and fast-paced, this video document of "The Gay Woodstock" (the April 1993 march on Washington) has some of its profits earmarked to benefit the National Gay & Lesbian Task Force Policy Institute. Set against a backdrop of high-energy music, the video, one of several such documents of the event, offers clips from speeches by Rep. Patricia Schroeder, Rep. Gerry Studds, New York Mayor David Dinkins, actress Cybill Shepherd, activist/tennis star Martina Navratilova, NOW President Patricia Ireland and an especially stirring Dorothy Hajdys, whose son, Alan Schindler, was the victim of a deadly gay-bashing while in the Navy. Celebrating unity, pride and empowerment, there are snippets from interviews with marchers, a brief look at the Quilt,

talks with former military veterans discharged because of their homosexuality, and a montage of smiling faces from the mass queer wedding ceremony. ⊗

Network Q — Television for Gay America

With its catchy media slogan, "All Queer, All The Time," Network Q, a monthly alternative news and entertainment video-mag, has, in a little over two years, become a vital communications link for gays and lesbians. Its founder, and in later programs its narrator, David Surber, has as his goal to promote and highlight the diverse queer lifestyles that mainstream media neglects and even censors. Each monthly episode, beginning with September 1992, is two hours long and features travel, art and political information, documentaries, AIDS updates, independent short films, comedy skits and other stories that highlight issues and events of interest to the gay and lesbian community. Entertaining and educational, these tapes effectively fill the information void left open by the straight media. ⊗

No Alternative *(1993, 67 min, US)*

Made in conjunction with MTV, this benefit for AIDS Education and Relief is an intoxicating mix of music, poetry and short films from various artists from the U.S. and U.K. that also features interviews and information regarding AIDS aimed especially at teens and young adults. Musical performances include Matthew Sweet, the all-male Goo Goo Girls, Buffalo Tom, Smashing Pumpkins, Patti Smith and Suede. Poetry readings are provided by Maggie Esstep and Lou Reed and shorts by Hal Hartley, Matt Mahurin, Jennie Livingston (on lesbian activism) and Derek Jarman, who provides the backdrop visuals to Suede's song as well as a final short. Unusually well made, watchable and hopefully instructional for young viewers. ⊗

Not All Parents Are Straight

(1986, 58 min, US, Kevin White & Annamarie Faro)

Despite Dan Quayle's (remember him?) idyllic vision of the American Family — a husband and wife and their children all living together under one roof — the reality of the situation could not be further from the truth. Through divorce, death, abandonment and other social factors, more and more children are raised in single parent or non-typical households. This compelling documentary examines gay and lesbian parents — there are an estimated 4-5 million in the United States parenting 8-10 million children. Through interviews with several children and parents of such households, the film looks at the challenges and prejudices they face, both in school and with neighbors. The film also examines their fear of custody battles, a less-than-supportive legal system, and the emotional conflicts within the families themselves. The overall impression one gets is that those interviewed are generally happy, well-adjusted family units, possibly strengthened by the pressures of the outside world.

On Being Gay *(1986, 80 min, US)*

Boston-based author Brian McNaught ("On Being Gay," "Gay Issues in the Workplace") expounds on the problems facing young gays and lesbians as he attempts to "replace the myths about homosexuality with the facts of being gay." Presented in the form of a homespun lecture, the tape is of interest primarily to teens and young adults, especially those facing the difficult decision of coming out to their family and friends. McNaught delivers his message of self-acceptance and the need to overcome childhood misconceptions of homosexuality in a folksy, non-threatening manner that makes him John Bradshaw's equivalent for queers. He underscores his talks of gay/lesbian self-hatred, problems of coming out in the workplace and family support with anecdotes of his personal experiences. The earnest first three-quarters of the video offer the viewer no warning for the final section, in which he brandishes the Bible and attempts to dispel the widely held misconception that it condemns homosexuality. Suddenly the entire tone changes from levelheadedness to wholly inappropriate and needlessly sectarian, and ultimately borders on Moonie-esque fanaticism. ☉

On Common Ground

(1992, 70 min, US, Hugh Harrison)

Using the format of a low-budget soap opera, this charming, funny yet politically savvy film chronicles the changing nature and maturity of a divergent group of denizens of the gay bar The Purple Parrot. We follow them from the pre-Stonewall time of naiveté and repression through the sex-filled disco days of the '70s and ending in the

Out: Stories of Lesbian and Gay Youth

'80s where AIDS casts a shadow on them all. The acting sometimes falls short of being professional and the video production values are bare bones, but they prove to be of little importance as the earnestness of the cast and director shines through as they tackle a violent police crackdown, premature death, racism within the community, gay/lesbian rage and eventual political activism. The film is followed by a short documentary, *On Common Ground — The Real Story*. The 30-minute film is a series of interviews with older lesbian and gay activists who reminisce about "the life," the underground bar scene and police harassment in the 1940s thru the '60s. ☉

One Nation Under God *(1993, 84 min, US, Teodoro Maniaci & Francine Rzeznick)*

Providing another invaluable piece of queer history, this low-budget documentary explores the organizations and people who proselytize that gays and lesbians should change their homosexual orientation. The film offers screen time to both sides of the debate including interviews with the directors of "recovery programs," professionals opposed to their work, ex-gays who claim they are now straight and the former ex-gays who claim that it is all a farce. Fearing that homosexuality has reached "epidemiological proportions," Christian groups such as Exodus International and Love in Action seek to "cure the disease of homosexuality" through "motivation and guidance," behavior modification, orgasmic therapy and hocus pocus psychological sessions that are reminiscent of Alex's "rehabilitation" in *A Clockwork Orange*. The film's most eloquent and perceptive speakers are Michael and Gary, founding members of Exodus and now former ex-gays who voice the strongest condemnation of these organizations that espouse radical "curative" treatment. Entertaining, humorous and informative. ☉

Out for Laughs *(1992, 30 min, US)*

Queer comedy comes into its own with this very funny and witty collection of comedy skits modeled after "Saturday Night Live" and "Kids in the Hall." The troupe of five female and five male performers spoof stereotypical images of gays and lesbians with such topics as "Myths about How You Become a Homosexual," which includes a hilarious look at boot camp; and "Camp Camp," where men and women "learn" to become fags and dykes. There is a gay news program, a mini-movie about two fashion-conscious drag queens from outer space and much more. Best watched with a crowd of fellow queers, this tape hopefully is only the first of many from the San Francisco-based comedians. ☉

Out: Stories of Lesbian and Gay Youth *(1993, 79 min, Canada, David Adkin)*

Made for the National Film Board of Canada, *Out* delves into the lives of several well-spoken and out gay and lesbian youths. Primarily from small towns in Canada, these young people, including whites, blacks and natives, describe their own difficulty in accepting being "different," their coming out to their parents, the isolation and homophobia of their fellow students, and their determination to be open about their sexuality. The film obviously sides with them as it presents a positive view of young lesbians and gays while making an effective plea for tolerance and acceptance. The most touching scenes are with the parents — or rather, the mothers, for the fathers are a rare sight. They embrace their gay/lesbian children by not only accepting them as they are but by also attending support groups and walking as proud parents of lesbians and gays in marches. Keeping in mind that being different and coming out in rural and small-town Canada is quite daunting, the young people demonstrate a resilient strength despite moments of isolation, ignorance and the threat of violence. A film that could make a difference for many if shown throughout the United States and Canada's high schools — but that is unlikely.

Over Our Dead Bodies
(1991, 84 min, GB, Stuart Marshall)
Stuart Marshall, who died of AIDS related complications at the age of 43 in May 1993, was a pioneering force in the emergence of gay/lesbian and AIDS activism. He made influential documentaries that have played on British television and in lesbian/gay film festivals worldwide. *Over Our Dead Bodies* delves into gay/lesbian groups' reaction to the enveloping AIDS crisis and the rapid rise of several more politically charged organizations such as ACT-UP, Queer Nation and OutRage. Statistics are provided, opinions offered, and charges leveled against the response to the epidemic by governments, health organizations and religious groups. Taking a tough approach to a contentious subject, Marshall keeps the documentary more on an intellectual level by dealing less with individual stories and more on the overall political picture. Marshall's final project at the time of his death was a video portrait of his father titled *Robert Marshall*.

The Passion of Remembrance
(1986, 82 min, GB, Maureen Blackwood & Isaac Julien)
Produced by Sankofa, a British collective of black feminist and gay filmmakers, their first feature is a stunning political film that examines the diversity, complexities and disputes within the black experience in Britain from the 1950s to the present. Individual black men and women, gay and straight, speak on a number of politicized issues. One man complains that "every time a black face appears on the screen...it has to represent the whole race." Intercutting documentary footage with acted scenes, the film features a confrontation between a radical black woman and a younger gay black man; discussion by older blacks on the civil rights movement; and contrasting thoughts by younger activists on today's struggle for feminist and gay rights.

Out for Laughs

Portrait of Jason
(1967, 100 min, US, Shirley Clarke)
This striking documentary is a look into the life, loves and philosophy of an articulate black gay street hustler. Director Shirley Clarke simply places a camera in front of Jason Holiday (nee Aaron Payne), prods him with a few offscreen questions and lets him take over. Drinking throughout the film, Jason, a natural and animated storyteller, brings us into his world — a gritty, troublesome place where fantasy blends seamlessly into reality. His tragicomedic story is peppered with witty comments and observations, but the minimalist approach taken by Clarke might prove to be troublesome to those who are not taken in by the antics of the roguish Jason. ⊛

> "The most extraordinary film I've seen in my life...for two hours a black homosexual tells us on the screen about his life as a prostitute. It is absolutely fascinating."
> — Ingmar Bergman

Positive Image   *(1992, 37 min, US)*
Despite its short running time, this tape is included because of its intended audience: the parents of gays and lesbians. Sponsored by the non-profit PFLAG (Parents and Friends of Lesbians & Gays), the film is an upbeat documentary on how parents should deal with the admittedly traumatic experience of having a child come out to them. Interviewed are several parents who recount their reactions and preconceived opinions of gays. One mother says, "I was very homophobic. I knew nothing." Others discuss their feelings of ignorance, denial and anger, emotions which — through the help of this support group — turned into acceptance, understanding and a strong love for their child. Interviewed also are the gay and lesbian children (all white and in their twenties) who relate how they felt about coming out. Enlightening and queer-positive, but the film's disco-driven, *Superman*-like theme music has gotta go! ⊛

Pout — queervideomag
With queer video magazines the current rage, *Pout* stands out from the others (*Network Q* and *Man for Man*) in that it does not produce but instead solicits work from the gay/lesbian community. For those who long ago tired of "Breeder TV," the resulting series of experimental shorts, which range from camp to irreverent, can be quite entertaining and humorous. Ranging greatly in quality, professionalism and approach to queer issues, these mini-features offer a much needed media outlet for queers who want their voices and opinions heard. The vidmag includes, as of this writing, three issues (volumes one thru three show increasing professionalism) and additional videos are scheduled to be released on a quarterly basis. Issue One includes "homohoroscopes," a discussion on what is sexy for gay men and women and lots of drag. The second issue is narrated by Angel Perv and the third and most accomplished tape, titled "Safer Sex TV Dinner," tackles topics concerning sex through a diverse selection of "Camcorder Classics" including an amusing, balletic dance through a supermarket with some hunky queers and a psychedelic spoof of Dr. Who titled, "Dr. Poof." An interesting side note: Issue #3 comes with an assortment of safe sex helpers including a condom, rubber gloves, KY jelly and an emery board?! (Available in Great Britain only.)

Prelude to Victory   *(1993, 60 min, US)*
From the award-winning producers who brought you *Part of the U.S.A.!* (a video on the 1987 march on Washington), comes this equally compelling account of the April 1993 march. While there were other videos made that recorded the historic civil rights gathering, *Prelude to Victory*, by its very title, takes a more aggressive stance in documenting the event and its political significance. The video captures segments from many of the scheduled speakers at the march including Ralph White, an aid to Senator Nunn who was fired simply because of his sexual orientation, gay and lesbian veterans, Sir Ian McKellen, Martina Navratilova, Patricia Ireland and Dorothy Hajdys, mother of slain sailor, and queer-bashing victim, Alan Schindler. An impassioned documentary that possibly overstates the importance and success of the march (as witnessed by the inability to lift the ban on gays in the military); but regardless of the film's occasional hyperbole, it is an invigorating and pride-inducing documentary. ⊛

Pridetime Travels —
Lesbian and Gay Travel Videos
Pridetime Travels, a Boston-based video company, has produced an informative series of travel videos on various vacation cities that are of interest to the gay and lesbian community. Similar to programs on the Travel Channel, the tapes highlight (in a determinedly upbeat manner) the best hotels, bars, beaches and restaurants in each city while at the same time providing a history of its gay and lesbian community. The quality, depth of prevalent information and running times vary with each tape, but coupled with one of the queer travel books available, for anal-retentive gays and lesbians who must *know*, these tapes should help in filling the information void. Tapes include the following cities: *Provincetown* (Part 1, 25 min) & (Part 2, 25 min), *San Francisco* (45 min), *New York City* (29 min), *Key West* (26 min), *Montreal* (21 min), *Fort Lauderdale* (26 min), *Palm Springs* (20 min), *Washington D.C./Rehobeth Beach* (40 min), *Amsterdam* (45 min), *London/Brighton* (60 min). Upcoming productions will include New Orleans and Chicago. ⊛

Sacred Lies, Civil Truths
(1993, 58 min, US, Catherine Saalfield & Cyrille Phipps)
Expressly made to educate, motivate and organize lesbians and gays into an activist stand, this urgent "call to arms" video could find no better villain/threat than homophobic Christians operating under the umbrella of the "Religious" Right. The first part deals with hate-filled Christians' unstated goal of creating a theocracy in the United States and focuses on its leaders (Jerry Falwell, Pat Robertson, etc.) and their actions mainly in organizing anti-gay/lesbian initiatives in the ballot boxes of Colorado and Oregon. Part two turns away from the enemy and deals primarily with the people who make up the lesbian/gay community, and touches on such topics as gay youth, queer-bashing and political organizations. A serious, political and effectively impassioned documentary.

Score *(1973, 89 min, US, Radley Metzger)*

A good-natured sex romp from soft-core eroticism king Radley Metzger, *Score* follows the sexually insatiable romps of Elvira (Claire Wilbur) and Jack (Gerarld Grant), a bisexual swingin' married couple who wager bets on who can seduce who in a set amount of time. Following a plot not dissimilar to *Dangerous Liaisons*, the calculating pair sets their eyes and loins on the naive couple next door, Betsy (Lynn Lowry, looking like Susan Dey in her "Partridge Family" era) and blond closet case Eddie (Cal Culver, aka porn star Casey Donovan). The entire movie revolves around getting the young things into their lair and seducing them. The emphasis is on boy-boy and girl-girl couplings (and it is all quite explicit for its time) as Elvira gradually beds the demure, but waiting-to-be-corrupted Betsy and Jack, a self-acknowleged sex fiend who would fuck a porcupine if he fancied it, schemes his way into Eddie's tight-fitting Levis. Of course, their mission is accomplished and *viola*, two more queer converts! ⊛

Seize the Day! — A Guide to Living with HIV *(1993, 92 min, US)*

With volumes of HIV/AIDS information available at clinics, hospitals and libraries, a person recently diagnosed as HIV-positive might easily be overwhelmed by the material. This vitally important video (the first volume in a projected series) can easily provide simple, direct, knowledgeable and practical information on the disease and how one should handle being HIV-positive. Taking an upbeat but not a foolish approach to the illness, HIV-positive actor Michael Kearns hosts a panel discussion with seasoned experts in the field of caring for people with AIDS. Stressing that a positive diagnosis is not necessarily a death sentence, the team offers a variety of advice on many subjects that help maintain and prolong one's health and assist in keeping an optimistic mental approach. The panel members include Dr. Neal Rzepkowski (a gay, HIV+ physician), Dr. Carol Ireton-Jones (a nutritionist and dietary expert) and Dr. Paul Froman (a psychologist who is also HIV+). Kearns asks the questions many AIDS patients have on their minds and the panel provides answers on a variety of subjects such as accepting one's condition, exercise, proper nutrition, medical information, support from family and friends, and strong advice on keeping healthy by avoiding unsafe sex, drugs, excessive alcohol and smoking. Never succumbing to quackery or unrealistic advice, the experts provide fascinating advice told in layperson's terms on the above topics as well as on such matters as acupuncture, herbs, experimental drugs, AZT/DDI/DDC and holistic medicine; and all four advocate that HIV+ people take an active role in both medication and a healthier, life-prolonging lifestyle. Breaking up the discussion are segments on food preparation and food buying by Michael Ivie (with startling advice such as avoiding certain cheeses and sushi, washing all fresh fruits and vegetables and avoiding wooden utensils), HIV humor with comedian Joseph Leonardi, and the tape concludes with singer/songwriter Darien Martus. The advice and opinions presented in this video will certainly help HIV/AIDS patients in many ways, especially in ending thoughts of simply being a victim to becoming a positive-thinking activist, successfully managing a strong fight against the disease. A must see for all those who are infected by HIV. ⊛

Sex and the Sandinistas
(1991, 30 min, GB, Lucinda Broadbent)

Although only 30 minutes, this compling documentary sheds much light on the underground gay and lesbian culture in Managua, Nicaragua. From the repression of pre-revolution life through the liberating period of the Sandinista Revolution and into the murky future of the democratically elected (but right wing) government in 1990, this video interviews many Latino queers and reveals a nascent but thriving culture that is once again threatened. Former Sandinista President Daniel Ortega is interviewed along with many gays and lesbians including a 14-year-old lesbian military guerilla. Also shown are gay/lesbian dances and drag bars, and innovative AIDS education programs, all of which explore and celebrate gay life despite Latin America's traditionally homophobic beliefs.

Silent Pioneers
(1984, 40 min, US, Lucy Winer)

The lives of older gay men and lesbians are explored in this short documentary. Nine elderly gay people — men, women, white, black, Catholic, Jewish — are interviewed, offering insight into their own particular problems of growing old, including self-doubts on the lifestyle they had led, loneliness and fear as well as positive moments of pride in their "different" orientation.

A Simple Matter of Justice
(1993, 56 min, US)

Produced by the Committee for the 1993 March on Washington Inc., this highly professional and, at times, moving documentary is the "official videotape" of the much-filmed march. The camera delves both behind the scenes with lesbian and gay leaders and organizers as well as into the march itself, capturing the festive and expectant mood of the gathering. While containing much of the same footage as other videos of the event (*March On!, Prelude to Victory*), *A Simple Matter...* is more slick and fast-paced, offering glimpses of the mass queer wedding, the Holocaust memorial ceremony and the Dyke March as well as interviews, snippets of speeches (from Eartha Kitt and RuPaul to Alan Schindler's mother) and musical performances (The Flirtations, Holly Near, Melissa Etheridge). ⊛

Since Stonewall *(1971-1991, 80 min, US)*

Independent gay and lesbian filmmakers are the focus in this entertaining ten-short compilation that deals, both seriously as well as humorously, with such topics as AIDS, female impersonation and coming out. Highlights include Gus Van Sant's *Discipline of DE* — (DE, or Do Easy, refers to an at-peace approach to life and inanimate objects inspired by William Burroughs); *Bust*, in which Holly Brown becomes a multiple-personalitied Bette Davis-type mother-in-law from hell; and *Queerdom*, an animated tale of a muscle man who wakes up one morning suddenly "feeling a little queer." Other shorts include *Final Solution* by Jerry Tartaglia, *Anton* by Robert Dunlap and *976-* by David Weissman. ⊛

Stonewall 25: Global Voices of Pride and Protest *(1994, 90 min, US)*

Originally broadcast on PBS from information culled from both the In the Life Media Network and New York's WNYC, this celebratory documentary provides highlights of the different events surrounding the Gay Games IV and the Stonewall 25 march, both held in June 1994 in New York. In addition to some historical background, the film presents footage of the marches and interviews with several of their participants, and also shows highlights from the Gay Games' sporting events and includes snippets from the speeches of such queer and queer-friendly luminaries as Ian McKellen, Kate Bornstein, Chita Rivera, Joan Rivers, Charles Busch, Lee Grant and the always scintillating Quentin Crisp. ⊗

Stop the Church
(1990, 30 min, US, Robert Hilferty)

Gaining notoriety after PBS refused to air the program, this political film, with its sympathies clearly on the protesters' side, documents ACT-UP's discussions, planning and execution of a march and "die-in" at St. Patrick's Cathedral in 1989. With its stated goal of "offending" the church and its anti-gay New York diocese leader, Cardinal O'Connor, the action was organized to protest the Catholic Church's insensitive position on gay rights as well as AIDS awareness and treatment. With a shaky handheld camera focused on the action, director Robert Hilferty's best moments are at an ACT-UP meeting, where the morality and righteousness of a protest within the church building itself is heatedly discussed. Whether one approves of the ensuing protest (not to be confused with another demonstration in which protesters received and then spit out the Host), the film is a fascinating exposé of radical political thought and contentious action. ⊗

Sun Chi *(1992, 60 min, US, Thomas Mitchell)*

Narrated by Neil Tucker, this instructional video on "the techniques of relaxation and positive imagery" is specifically aimed at PWA, HIV-positive people and others who seek ways to relax from the day's daily stress. Tucker's melodic voice resonates as he explains his Oriental principles and demonstrates the simple exercises in front of a small audience. Seeking inner calm, some techniques include massage therapy for the hands ("where fear is stored"), full body massage, the healing sounds of the Kototama, dialogue with your non-dominant hand and simple meditation. While an earnest, helpful self-care workshop, its most appreciative audience will be already-converted adherents to New Age remedies. ⊗

Ten Cents a Dance (Parallax)
(1986, 30 min, Canada, Midi Onodera)

Using a split-screen representation of three intimate, interpersonal scenarios, *Ten Cents a Dance* portrays an erotically charged lesbian dinner-date; an anonymous sexual encounter between two men in a bathroom; and hetero phone sex. A dry commentary on the relational differences between lesbian, gay and straight sexuality.

A Time of AIDS
(1993, 200 min, GB/US, Joseph Beven, Jenny Barraclough & Katherine Carpend)

Produced by the Discovery Channel and Channel 4, this fascinating, factual and comprehensive documentary reviews the first 12 years of the AIDS epidemic. While treading similar ground as was covered in Randy Shilts' book *And the Band Played On* (and the film version), this documentary is in many ways much better, eschewing the restraints of a fictional film. *A Time of AIDS* delves into the myriad of issues, locales and personalities connected to the disease and comes to the same conclusion as Shilts; that is, through "intrigue, jealousy, genius and stupidity," the government, blood banks, pharmaceutical companies and the medical profession all contributed in allowing the disease to reach — what are today — epidemic proportions. Beginning in 1979, the film charts the gay sexual liberation, during which the community was first struck by the virus, which was rapidly spread through what one gay man calls the "sexual smorgasbord" of the period. Another gay man, intoning a certain "blame the victim" mentality, says "A sexually transmitted disease

Urinal

that is fatal...now there'll be hell to pay." Also explored is the "patient zero" theory that one man, a French-Canadian airline steward, was mainly responsible for the initial rapid spread of the virus. Switching to the medical profession where much of the film focuses, doctors involved in treating the mysterious illness are baffled as they begin the long, frustrating odyssey of uncovering the cause and seeking a cure. The unethical professional misdeeds of Dr. Robert Gallo are explored with several interviews of Dr. Gallo explaining, defending and damage-controlling. There is also a behind-the-scenes look into the work of Professor Luc Montagnier, the man credited with discovering the HIV virus which is thought to be the cause of AIDS. The film wisely increases its focus to include other early victims (IV-drug users, Haitian immigrants, hemophiliacs, Africans) and hints at the general in-roads to the heterosexual public. The search for a cure, the availability (and price-gouging) of AZT, the growth of the gay political voice as evidenced with demonstrations, fund-raising and ACT-UP are also explored along with the American public's hysteria, homophobia and its quick "solution" which blames the victims. Narrated by actor Alec Baldwin, the video is a vitally important, compassionate, informative, surprisingly objective and enlightening overview of this horrifying disease.

To Forget Venice
(1979, 110 min, Italy, Franco Brusati)
Franco Brusati (*Bread and Chocolate*) has fashioned this sensitive and refined story of a group of people (two gay men and two lesbians) who together visit an old country estate. The film explores the important events of their past, their first sexual encounters and their worried looks to the future. A very good film, but one in which many will debate the accuracy of the film's sexual politics (i.e. that there was one moment in each of their lives that made them gay). ⊛

To Support and Defend
(1993, 30 min, US, Julian Siminski & Rob Wilson)
Essentially a counterpoint video made as an angry response to the anti-gay diatribe *The Gay Agenda*, which was distributed to U.S. political and military leaders early in 1993, *To Support and Defend* was not made for general distribution (although it has been popular in many lesbian and gay film festivals). The film features interviews with various individuals who share the common belief that the current military ban against gays and lesbians should be ended. Introduced by Cybill Shepherd, the video, a simple but stirring "talking heads documentary," includes accounts by 20 people including Marine Sergeant Justin Elzie who was proclaimed Marine of the Year in 1992, Green Beret Eugene Gannuzio and other former soldiers and sailors whose careers have been destroyed by their coming out. An unlikely defender of ending the ban is Dr. Lawrence Korb, former assistant Secretary of Defense who was responsible for administering the anti-gay policy under President Reagan. Co-director Julian Siminski states at one point, "Gays and lesbians in the military have supported and defended our Constitution bravely and with honor. Many have died for it. It's time the Constitution defended them."

Too Much Sun
(1990, 100 min, US, Robert Downey)
It's best to leave your political correctness aside when viewing this amusingly tasteless comedy, which can be quite stupid and, if seen immediately after attending an ACT-UP meeting, might seem insultingly homophobic. From the film's opening shot of a swishy gay couple sending their poodles (one wearing a pink bonnet) off to day camp, you know that no gay stereotype will be spared. Eric Idle and Andrea Martin play Sonny and Bitsy, the middle-aged gay and lesbian children of millionaire Howard Duff. Dad finds out his kids are queer from a scheming priest, Father Kelly, who blackmails him with photos of his daughter making love with another woman. When dad has a heart attack, brought on when Idle comes out, Father Kelly, a Cardinal Richelieu-wannabe, cons him into signing a will stipulating that in order to receive the inheritance (Catholics are on the receiving end as much as gays), one of the two children must bear a child "in the conventional way." What follows is an admittedly stupid and predictable, but at times hilarious effort on the part of Sonny to have sex with a succession of women while Bitsy tries to locate the son she gave up for adoption when she was 16. Too complicated to dismiss as homophobic, the film portrays Martin and her foreign lover Susan (Laura Ernst) as loving and affectionate. Idle and his bearded lover, George (Leo Rossi), are shown dancing together, kissing (on the cheek), making references to their bedroom activities and arguing over the sanity of the totally gay Idle's attempts to produce an heir. An amusing line comes at the deathbed of his father when Idle says, "I apologize for every homosexual experience I ever had...and ever will have" (very gay and very Catholic!). Rounding out the cast is a swishier-than-swish Robert Downey, Jr. as a conniving real estate agent, and the surprisingly funny Ralph Macchio also stars as his partner. Despite being made by a straight man (Robert Downey, famed director of *Putney Swope* and *Greaser's Palace*), the film exudes a playful gay/lesbian sensibility and, despite the self-depreciating jokes, a queer sensitivity. ⊛

Urinal *(1991, 100 min, Canada, John Greyson)*
Less provocative and explicit than the title suggests, this low-budget Canadian production is a documentary-style talk fest centering on homosexual repression through the ages and, more specifically, the well-publicized entrapment cases and crackdowns in Ontario's public rest rooms by a homophobic police force. The film's premise is that several prominently rumored homosexuals and lesbians from the past (Yukio Mishima, Sergei Eisenstein, Frida Kahlo, Frances Loring, Langston Hughes and Florence Whyle) are mysteriously brought together in a Toronto apartment where they hold a series of discussions on the sociology of homosexuality and how to counter gay repression. Despite its static and awkward dramatic pretensions, the film is an interesting and literate examination of gay and lesbian history as well as a call for action against discrimination. ⊛

Voices from the Front *(1990, 90 min, US, Robyn Hutt, Sandra Elgear & David Meieran)*
This impassioned documentary focuses on the AIDS crisis, but rather than offer a "balanced" look at its "victims," the ongoing search for a cure or a summary history of the epidemic, the filmmakers instead focus on the several political action groups that have mobilized against a passive press, unresponsive and/or ineffectual government programs and agencies (including the DDA and the National Institute of Health) and the multinational pharmaceutical companies and medical establishment who are profiting from and exploiting the situation. Made by the New York group Testing

the Limits, the film centers on the actions of so-called "fringe" groups like ACT-UP and People with AIDS Coalition and other "empowerment movements" who collectively wage an information campaign, stage demonstrations and employ confrontational tactics engineered to draw attention to the dire need for action. ⊗

"Impatient, energetic and terrifically articulate."
— Vincent Canby, *The New York Times*

"A testimony to the most riveting political movement in gay and lesbian politics since Stonewall."
— *City Limits* [London]

Why Am I Gay? Stories of Coming Out in America

(1993, 60 min, US, Kenneth Paul Rosenberg)
The director of this compelling HBO documentary, which examines the lives of several gay men and women, is also a psychiatrist, which might explain the somewhat clinical, but still pro-gay approach. The film consists of several in-depth character studies of gays who have openly confronted their homosexuality and interviews with medical professionals who all confirm, each using a different approach, that homosexuality is "in all probability" a born-with trait. The three main voices are Edgar Rodriquez, a Bronx-born, Puerto Rican policeman in New York; Michael Callen, a singer in the openly gay a cappella/comedy group The Flirtations, who died of AIDS in 1994; and Ira, a bible-toting Christian gay committed to "overcoming" his homosexuality through group support. Also featured, but less prominently, are gay/lesbian teens and their families and a middle-aged lesbian couple, one of whom eloquently says, "I'm very proud of my lifestyle...and you can't make me ashamed." Definitely gay supportive, the subjects all recount their feeling of being different and alone in a straight world and their efforts to overcome these feelings, accept their homosexuality and deal with family and friends.

Witches and Faggots — Dykes and Poofters *(1979, 45 min, Australia)*

Independently produced, this stirring social and political documentary on gay/lesbian oppression powerfully recounts the police attack on the gay/lesbian revelers of Sydney's 1978 Mardi Gras celebration and relates its social conditions with similar incidents from history. The filmmakers contend that this was no isolated incident, but rather followed the usual reactive course in history when gays and lesbians made their presence too loud. A powerful documentation of the historical roots of gay/lesbian rights. Another film on the subject of homophobia confronting the gay and lesbian organizers and participants of Sydney's Mardi Gras is *Feed Them to the Cannibals!*

Word Is Out — Stories from Some of Our Lives *(1978, 130 min, US)*

Originally conceived as a documentary titled *Who Are We?*, this fascinating exploration of gay culture and history from the Mariposa Group is made up of interviews with 26 lesbians and gay men. Ranging in age from 18 to 77, and representing many divergent types — from a beehived housewife to a sultry drag queen — the film captures their vivid experiences of growing up gay in America and at the same time, helps destroy decades of accumulated stereotypes. A moving and important gay document. ⊗

"An electric piece of living history."
— Vito Russo

"The most intelligent, telling cinematic look to date at the homosexual experience in America."
— *The San Francisco Chronicle*

Zero Patience

(1993, 95 min, Canada, John Greyson)
From the director of the very serious *Urinal* comes this unexpectedly outrageous and satiric musical-comedy about life in the age of AIDS. The story centers around "Patient Zero" — Gaetan Dugas, a French-Canadian airline steward who was reported by health officials to be the man who brought AIDS to North America and helped rapidly spread it with his promiscuous sexual activity. Gaetan returns from the dead to restore his name and solicits the help of 19th-century explorer, now 20th-century AIDS researcher, Sir Richard Burton. But Burton has his own agenda: to gather all the damaging information he can on Gaetan and others for an exhibition on contagious disease in a museum's "Hall of Contamination." Burton's development from a self-centered heterosexual homophobe, open to distorting the truth for personal advancement, to an ACT-UP-styled queer in the front lines of activism is the centerpiece of this amazing story. And if this strange plot is not enough to keep your attention, the film features several bizarre musical routines, inventively choreographed and sporting wittily queer lyrics. These numbers include a duet by a pair of singing assholes and one inside a PWA's bloodstream featuring The Flirtations' Michael Callen as a falsetto-voiced Miss HIV. Audaciously political, filmicly inventive, AIDS/HIV-informative and queerly radical.

Focus on: *John Greyson*

Toronto-based videomaker John Greyson's two feature productions, Urinal *and* Zero Patience, *have put him in the forefront of politically committed and adventurous gay film and video makers in North America. In addition to these two features, he has made over 15 videos and shorts including* The AIDS Epidemic, *about the new disease "Acquired Dread of Sex";* Moscow Does Not Believe in Queers, *on gays in Russia;* You Taste American, *in which gay luminaries Michael Foucault, Tennessee Williams and Montgomery Clift come together for a chat; and* A Moffie Called Simon, *a short on the gay black South African activist. He has also made several shorts on AIDS.*

Zero Patience

O F Q UEER I NTEREST

5

OF LESBIAN INTEREST

In alphabetical format, the following films have either been made by lesbians, have a lesbian theme or feature a lesbian actor or lesbian characters.

"You've never had a man. I think that's your problem. Isn't that what you need?"
—Keir Dullea to Sandy Dennis in *The Fox*

"We live completely dyke lives. Our life is so regular to us and foreign to everyone else."
—Guinevere Turner, star
and co-producer of *Go Fish*

"I think that post-menstrual women should run the world."
—A post-menstrual lesbian
interviewee in *Forbidden Love —
The Unashamed Stories of Lesbian Lives*

Les Abysses

(1963, 90 min, France, Nico Papatakis)
A scandalously violent film for its time, this drama was based on the actual 1933 French case that inspired Jean Genet to write "The Maids." As a family decides to move from their country mansion to a smaller house, the two maidservants (played by real-life sisters Francine and Colette Berge) become increasingly worked up at the prospect of losing their jobs. The desperate sisters, unpaid for three years, and involved in a troubling incestuous affair, begin to destroy parts of the house and terrorize the family. Eventually, they brutally murder the wife and daughter (killed despite her lesbian fixation on the younger sister) while the husband helplessly watches. The film created an uproar when first shown at the Cannes Film Festival.

"The cinema has given us its foremost tragedy."
— Jean Paul Sartre

Afternoon Breezes (Kazetachi No Gogo) *(1980, 105 min, Japan, Hitoshi Yazaki)*

This beautifully bleak account of a Tokyo day care worker's obsession with her roommate captures the bittersweet pain of unrequited love. Natsuko's co-worker Etsuko asks her how she feels about men. "Not for me," she says, "I won't degrade myself." Based on an actual newspaper story, *Afternoon Breezes* presents Natsuko's repressed lesbianism as a crush which evolves into an obsession. With lots of real-time sequences and a complex use of sound, the film has surprisingly little dialogue, conveying meaning through a wonderfully simple use of action and objects.

Aileen Wournos — The Selling of a Serial Killer *(1993, 87 min, GB, Nick Broomfield)*

A chilling crime and justice documentary that would make the events in *The Thin Blue Line* seem like a paragon of legal competence, this mesmerizing and tenacious investigative film by Nick Broomfield (*Soldier Girls, Lily Tomlin*) attempts to gather the facts in the case against convicted serial killer Aileen Wournos. Wournos, a lesbian and prostitute, was convicted of brutally killing seven men on the Florida highways between 1989 and 1990. Broomfield outlines the seemingly open-and-shut case against her including her own confession and guilty pleas for four of the murders. But what becomes clear as he digs is an elaborate web of deception and profiteering both on the part of law enforcement officers (who already had signed a TV deal on the murder even before Wournos' arrest), her "friends" and, most painful of all, the betrayal of her lover, Tyria. Exploitatively proclaimed the "Angel of Death," "the nation's first female serial killer" and the "lesbian serial killer," Wournos instead is seen as a thoughtful and rather intelligent woman who, while probably guilty, did not receive an ounce of justice as she was railroaded to several convictions and a date with death in the electric chair. The cast of characters interviewed border on the deliriously psychotic and, in scenes that would make John Waters proud, are seen as greedy, manipulative, even monstrous opportunists. Included in this group are Arleen Pralle, a nervously smiling born-again Christian who adopted Aileen as her daughter while she was in prison, and Steve Glazer, her comically deranged lawyer. The two are seen as money and publicity whores whose interest in Aileen is minimal if not nonexistent. The lasting effect of the film is not only a document of the gross miscarriage by the judicial system, but a look at a personal tragedy as well — of a seemingly normal woman propelled for many reasons into violent acts and the personal tragedy of being betrayed by all those around her. ⊗

Älskande Par

(1964, 118 min, Sweden, Mai Zetterling)
Swedish actress-turned-director Mai Zetterling's (*Scrubbers*) debut effort is an adaptation of several works by Agnes von Krusenstjerna, a Swedish writer famous for her treatment of lesbianism. Very Bergman-esque in style and somberness, the drama is set at the beginning of this century. In a series of interlocking flashbacks, it tells of the lives and loves of three pregnant women all in a hospital ready to give birth. Adele is an unhappy woman stuck in a loveless marriage whose baby is stillborn. Agda is a carefree spirit who gives birth to a healthy child, but in the flashbacks it is revealed that the father of the child arranged a marriage between Agda and a gay friend of his. Instead of being upset (especially when the man comes into church holding hands with his male lover), she instead is exhilarated and "free." The third woman is Angela, a lesbian living with her lover Petra. She is by far the happiest of the three as she and her lover show affection towards each other and talk gushingly of "our child." The lesbian couple also gets the best lines, with such heterosexual digs as "marriage is like falling asleep for the rest of your life." (Also known as: *Loving Couples*)

Alternative Conceptions

(1985, 35 min, US, Christina Sunley)
The issue of lesbian biological parenting is explored in this balanced and thoughtful documentary. Through interviews with several lesbian parents in the New York area, one begins to understand the many difficult questions facing the women. The initial decisions to be made include whether to have artificial (alternative) insemination or actual sex with a man (all those interviewed

Anne Trister

chose the former); having the male donor be anonymous (semen from a sperm bank); or receiving it from a (gay) friend, or even a relative of one's lover. The medical procedures involved in the birthing is also important. Also elicited from the women are the very real problems encountered after birth, including legal ones involving the rights and prospective custody battles by the male donor, as well as the child's perceptions of growing up in an environment of same sex parents as well as their eventual desire to find out more about their fathers. By raising so many points on the topic, this video is quite illuminating, especially in light of the many legal challenges facing the rights of lesbian parents.

Amor Maldito
(1986, 90 min, Brazil, Adelia Sampaio)
Scheduled to play the 1986 San Francisco International Film Festival, *Amor Maldito*, the first Brazilian film to deal with lesbianism, never got its showing — the Brazilian government (the producer) at the last minute refused to subtitle the print. The simple story follows Sueli and Fernada's friendship which evolves into an intimate affair. But following the Vito Russo theory that the homo should die for his/her sexual orientation, what follows for the women is a suicide, a false murder charge and a sensationalistic trial where lesbianism is derisively heralded as the unnatural passion that fueled the alleged murder.

Amorosa *(1986, 117 min, Sweden, Mai Zetterling)*
Based on the often scandalous life of Swedish author Agnes von Krusenstjerna (*Älskande Par*), this understated, moody but affecting drama focuses on the writer's final years as mental illness destroyed both her professional and personal life. In Venice during Carnival in 1935, the writer (played by Stina Ekblad), who was known for her startling erotic novels, suffers a nervous breakdown. Her husband sends her to a Catholic insane asylum to recuperate. It is here, through the story of her latest manuscript, that her emotionally tumultuous past is explored. As an idealistic 19-year-old, Agnes falls in love with Gerald, but he rejects her sexual advances — and may well be involved with Agnes' brother. Frustrated, she finally succumbs to her best friend Ava's advances, only to be again rebuffed. She also discovers that her future mother-in-law is involved in a lesbian affair with one of the young servants. Agnes finally escapes this web of repression, homosexuality and madness by marrying David (Erland Josephson), a much older man. But salvation continues to be illusive as he begins to control her life, gets her addicted to morphine and introduces her into greater sexual experimentation, including a three-way with their sexy female maid. While the description of lesbianism and homosexuality is not presented in the best light, it works well in this sobering story.

Anne Trister *(1985, 115 min, Canada, Lea Pool)*
This melancholy Canadian feature from Lea Pool tells the story of Anne, a young Jewish painter who, distraught over the recent death of her father, leaves her boyfriend and goes to Montreal to stay with her friend Alix. Deciding to stay in Montreal, Anne finds a studio space and begins to work on an immense floor-to-ceiling abstract mural. As the mural develops, the relationship between the women intensifies. The film is not a completely satisfying lesbian love story, but they do both leave their boyfriends in the end.

Another Way

Another Way
(1982, 102 min, Hungary, Karoly Makk)
This courageous and intelligent lesbian love story, Eastern Europe's first film dealing with a gay or lesbian issue, is set in Hungary immediately after the 1956 uprising and concerns the mutual attraction and budding relationship between two female journalists. Livia, married to an army officer, shyly begins accepting the advances of Eva, an outspoken reporter with whom she shares an office. Director Karoly Makk (*Love*) juxtaposes this tender but doomed love affair with the high hopes and bitter suppression of the Budapest Spring. An impassioned plea for tolerance in a land long bereft of it. ⊛

Another Woman's Lipstick: The Red Shoe Diaries 3 *(1993, 90 min, US, Zalman King)*
Zalman King's "classy" soft-core hetero erotica series continues to enjoy great success on home video. Structured as three stories revolving around different women's erotic fantasies, the segment of interest to a lesbian audience is the second, "Another Woman's Lipstick." Zoe and Robert's upwardly mobile L.A. marriage is shaken after Zoe discovers lipstick on her husband's collar (literally, we are not talking originality here!). But instead of throwing an ashtray at him and yelling, "You shit!," she follows her husband to a restaurant where he meets a beautiful young woman and then, through a window, she watches the two make love. She soon becomes obsessed with the beguiling woman, forgetting her unfaithful husband and musing, "Every day, day and night, all I could think about was her. I had to touch her." Then in a cinematic leap of faith, she dresses in men's clothing (complete with a wiry mustache) and goes to a club, meets up with the "Other Woman," dances with her and they both go off to an empty office for "privacy." In a surprisingly sensitive and sensuous fashion, the two explore each other's bodies, with the woman knowing all along that the man is a woman, which only excites her more. Zoe, dazed by her lesbian desire, quietly

protests, "I've never done anything like this before" only to gently succumb to the situation and her awakened passion. All is destroyed when she returns home and forgives her husband...after all, this is a straight man's filmic fantasy. ⊛

Bathroom Sluts (Amateur Lesbian Video #1) *(1991, 45 min, US)*

The opening shaving scene is the hottest thing in this tape (with black-and-white photo stills by Tracy Mostovoy intercut with the video action). Five women in various combinations do a bit of fucking, voyeurism, bondage and light whipping in the ladies' room. Fast forward through the (too) long, standing fuck in the shower and get to the bathroom stall scene. A little, white boy-femme and a buxom, Latina femme watch a butch with a strap-on fuck another girl on the tile floor. Variations and combinations between them are at least interesting, if not always very hot. A finale fist fuck scene is fucked up by Blush's decision to self-censor (using a pink circle instead of a black bar). The pink dot obscures her pink spot and actually makes it look like they're faking it. Self-censored pornography? Please! Wrap-up interviews with the participants after the shoot are the most interesting aspect of the tape. The women discuss their feelings about having sex with each other in front of the camera and the butch with the strap-on reveals that it was her first one. Well-produced for an amateur tape. From Blush Productions/Fatale Video. ⊛

Because the Dawn

(1988, 40 min, US, Amy Goldstein)

A lesbian Gothic vampire thriller which, through its outrageous art direction, hilarious dialogue (such as "Vampires have always had the worst publicity" or "Joan of Arc? I got her into a lot of trouble"), and reversed story line (a woman longs for the elusive female vampire), has the makings of a camp favorite. Marie is a sultry, self-absorbed vampire who meets fashion photographer Ariel (Sandy Gray). Marie knows that she does bad, but desperately wants to be admired by the modern world. Ariel, on the other hand, is immediately fascinated with her seductive image, eventually becoming obsessed and begins hunting her down on the streets of Manhattan.

The Béguines (Le Rempart des Béguines)

(1972, 90 min, France/Italy, Guy Casaril)

Schoolgirl Helene (Anicée Alvina), the solitary only daughter of a widowed politician, begins to learn more than her ABC's when her father's sexy mistress takes an amorous interest in the young lady. The mistress Tamara (Nicole Courcel) is seen slinking around, smoking black cigars and looking exotic in flowing kimono robes as she and the girl soon find themselves involved in a passionate affair; one that is highlighted by demands of submission and outbursts of violence by the fiery Tamara — and Helene thought nuns were strict! The older woman eventually marries Helene's father, if only for the money and a reason to be close to the girl. This French soft-core sex flick is elegant (in an *Emmanuelle* sort of way) as lesbian sexuality and emotions threaten to engulf the entire house!

Les Biches

Belle

(1992, 99 min, The Netherlands, Irma Achten)

This lesbian *Citizen Kane* tells an interesting but trying tale of one woman's corruption and the loss of her great love (to a woman), all caused by her greedy quest for power and money. Belle, a pretty blonde rich girl, finds love in the arms of Marthe, a slightly older working-class woman. Her schoolgirl's affection is romantically portrayed — a lyrical poem to Sapphic love — but the affair doesn't last as she develops into a ruthless businesswoman who drops her lover for a more conventional relationship with a man. As money and heterosexuality play a number on her, she finds herself in a stifling, loveless marriage causing her to become indifferent to the passions that surround her and longing for her abandoned Marthe. A revealing moment comes when she, unbeknownst to her husband, writes the name "Marthe" in butter on his bare back. The highly stylized melodrama is quite a debut for lesbian filmmaker Irma Achten, but its vacillation between damnation, sympathy and pity for Belle's plight is frustrating. For, although the lesbian love scenes are touching and passionate, and desire is portrayed as feminine, a long term love between two women is ruled out, leaving the viewer forced to sympathize with a regret-obsessed woman who squandered the love of her life all in the pursuit of "normalcy."

The Berlin Affair

(1985, 121 min, Italy/Germany, Liliana Cavani)

From the director of *The Night Porter* comes this erotic and provocative tale of sexual obsession and domination set in pre-war, 1938 Berlin. The lovely Gudrun Landgrebe (*A Woman in Flames*) plays Louise von Hollendorf, the headstrong but bored wife of a Nazi diplomat who in her art class is immediately entranced by the elegant beauty of Mitsuko (Mio Takaki), the daughter of the Japanese ambassador. Impervious to the wagging tongues of her fellow students, Louise and Mitsuko begin a love affair that is shown as sensuous, loving and terribly romantic. But when her jealous husband, Heinz, suspects that the two are more than just friends, the situation changes and Mitsuko becomes sexually involved with him as well. The seemingly submissive Mitsuko soon reveals her domineering, manipulative side as she makes the love-struck couple sexual slaves using as weapons her sexual wiles, bouts of jealousy, drugs and blackmail. This elegant psychodrama, poorly received on its initial release, emphasizes with great tenderness the lesbian relationship. Also featured in the film is a gay general who is purged by the increasingly violent and moralistic Third Reich. ⊛

Betty Dodson — Self-Loving
(1991, 60 min, US)
Betty Dodson, artist, author and unusual sex instructor, has been a leading public advocate for women's sexual liberation for over twenty years. With a mantra-like philosophy that "Masturbation is the ongoing love affair with ourselves," Dodson leads a two-day workshop involving ten women with the goal to get to know and love one's body, increase one's sexual self-awareness and enhance sexual pleasure. The women in the seminar are primarily heterosexual (with only one woman openly lesbian and another bisexual) and range in age from 28 to 60. Beginning with simple breathing exercises, the women go on to explore and marvel at each other's genitals, experiment with the use of vaginal bar bells to strengthen the pelvic area, perform clitoral stimulation with a vibrator and eventually rise to a group crescendo of ecstasy as each woman achieves a prolonged, vocal and obviously satisfying orgasm. The video concludes with group massages and special bonding between the women. Boldly graphic yet never exploitative, this fascinating hour of sexual exploration is a type of seminar that seems impossible for similarly heterosexual men to participate in. ⊛

Les Biches
(1968, 104 min, France/Italy, Claude Chabrol)
Stéphane Audran has never looked more elegantly decadent than in this twisted bisexual drama of sexual domination, obsession, despair and revenge, filmed in Claude Chabrol's trademark cool, detached style. Audran is Frederique, a glamorous woman of lesbian leaning who, on a trip to Paris, meets then seduces a poor, enigmatic young woman named Why. She soon whisks her new love off to her home in St. Tropez to continue their affair, but the balance is changed when a man (Jean-Louis Trintignant) enters the picture and, after a brief attraction to Why, takes up permanently with Frederique. The centerpiece of this explosive love triangle is Audran's wanton sexual appeal, a power that eventually leads to bitter consequences. ⊛

Bilitis *(1982, 93 min, GB, David Hamilton)*
Well-known as a photographer of young female erotic art, David Hamilton makes his first venture into the world of film with this account of a 16-year-old girl's sexual awakening. The softly focused photography works well with the plot, making for a very moving and sensual experience. ⊛

Bittersweet *(1993, 28 min, US, Alice B. Brave)*
A professional dominatrix's work is never done! When a beautiful red-headed woman returns home, still attired in her work clothes — an elaborately designed leather outfit — she begins a busman's holiday with her submissive, bondage-playing roommate. Passionate, violent and steamy yet oddly loving S&M lesbian sex ensues with a piercing incident that will never allow you to look at a needle and thread the same way again! ⊛

Black Widow
(1987, 102 min, US, Bob Rafelson)
Theresa Russell and Debra Winger square off in this spine-tingling suspense story. Russell is a jet-setting sophisticate whose husbands have a habit of dying shortly after their wedding day. Winger is the Justice Department agent who catches on to Russell's shenanigans and sets out to uncover her deadly scheme.

NEW REALM DISTRIBUTORS presents

That exquisite moment of a girl's sexual awakening

Bilitis

X

IS A YOUNG GIRL.
A FILM BY DAVID HAMILTON
ORIGINAL MUSIC by FRANCIS LAI
starring PATTI D'ARBANVILLE
MONA KRISTENSEN, BERNARD GIRAUDEAU
GILLES KOHLER and MATHIEU CARRIERE
Original Soundtrack Available on UNITED ARTISTS RECORDS & TAPES

Instead, the two become locked in a heated tête-à-tête (or more appropriately coeur à coeur) which sizzles with underlying sexual tension. Their relationship — Winger, the loveless butch tracking down her prey, and Russell, the bewitching femme who wants her pursuer so much — is nicely handled, but in a vague, slightly frustrating and dissappointing fashion. ⊗

Blood and Roses

(1960, 74 min, Italy, Roger Vadim)
Annette Vadim stars as the sexy Carmilla in this lush and provocative Italian-made feature. Seduced by her lesbian vampire ancestor who takes over her body, the lusty Carmilla first jumps a young maid and then her beautiful cousin. Although the cousin is engaged to be married, the women make eyes at each other throughout the film (in that Euro-soft-porn sort of way), and director Roger Vadim plays up every lesbionic inch of it. Not as lurid as the Hammer Studios lesbian vampire movies (*The Vampire Lovers, Twins of Evil* and *Lust for a Vampire*), but much more lively and very well-produced. ⊗

The Blood Splattered Bride (La Novia Ensangrentada)

(1972, 84 min, Spain, Vicente Aranda)
Sexy lesbian vampires are on the prowl once again in this erotic, bloody and creepy Spanish production. A pretty young bride marries a wealthy and handsome man, but when disturbing visions keep her out of their honeymoon hotel, the couple are forced to go to the young man's palatial Gothic estate. Heterosexual sex is the problem here as Susan, horrified by the violence and domination of her husband's sexual advances, retreats into her own world haunted by visions of knife-wielding beauties and castrated husbands. Her life is "saved" when Carmilla, a mysterious and elegant stranger, arrives. Carmilla, a centuries-old vampiress, and the innocent bride are immediately attracted towards each other and seal their relationship with a memorable kiss filled with blood and sexual ecstasy. Now united, the two lovers plot the death of her hated husband who "Pierced my flesh to humiliate me. Spat inside me to enslave me." A shocking and violently bloody finale will keep the viewer engrossed as this kinky horror film brings new meaning (and warning) to the problems of marital life. Take that Mr. Man! ⊗

Blood and Roses

BurLEZk Live!

Bound and Gagged: A Love Story

(1993, 96 min, US, Daniel Appleby)
Everything *Three of Hearts* should have been but wasn't, this frantic "My girlfriend's left me, but I'm gonna get her back" lesbian comedy is an amazingly self-assured independent feature by Daniel Appleby. Cliff is a hetero slacker who gets by playing Santa Claus at the local mall and is thrown into a suicidal funk by his wife's gleeful, vindictive departure with another man. His best friend is Elizabeth (Elizabeth Saltarrelli), a fun-loving but irrational bisexual who sleeps with men but is hopelessly in love with Leslie (former porn queen Ginger Lynn Allen), a young woman stuck in a marriage with an abusive husband. When Leslie's Neanderthal hubby demands that the two stop seeing each other, Elizabeth, with a befuddled Cliff in tow, abducts her and goes on the road, roaming the Midwest in a queer *Thelma and Louise* fashion. A snappily bizarre romp filled with weird, zany, and not always likable characters which mischievously explores the mysteries of obsessive, but elusive love. ⊗

Breaking the Silence

(1985, 62 min, GB, Melanie Chait)
The social and court-sanctioned prejudice faced by lesbian mothers in Great Britain is the focus of this impassioned documentary. Director Melanie Chait probes the long-standing difficulties of a political system intent on preserving its narrow vision of the conventional family unit and follows lesbian mothers who speak out

against a legal system intent on denying them their rights. Also explored are the personal struggles of a lesbian-headed household and the many ongoing custody battles they often face. An effective, clearly subjective film which successfully handles this contentious subject.

BurLEZk Live!

(1987, 90 min, US, Nan Kinney & Debi Sundahl)
Adding new meaning to "girls' night out," this sexually tantalizing peek at a women's-only striptease club was taped live at a San Francisco nightclub, where women strip and dance for the enjoyment of other women. The types of the dances run the gamut of styles. The event, which is comprised of safe but sleazy lesbian fun, has been running for over three years and has reportedly attracted over 15,000 women to the nightclub. Now it's your turn! ☉

BurLEZk II Live!

(1988, 60 min, US, Nan Kinney & Debi Sundahl)
The steamy eroticism heated up by the gyrations and teasing dances of female stripping in front of a lesbian audience continues in this entertaining Fatale Video-produced tape. Artistic pretensions meet raunchy sensuality as the campy Stella sings a love song to her dildo, Fanny Fatale performs a dance to safe sex and other women dance up a sexy storm. It may not be politically correct, but it's all harmless fun. ☉

Cancer in Two Voices

By Design

(1981, 88 min, Canada, Claude Jutra)
The sexual revolution travels north in this quirky comedy directed by Quebecois Claude Jutra. Patty Duke (Helen) and Sara Botsford (Angel) star as two fashion designers, business partners and lovers who decide they want to have a baby. Rejected by the adoption agency and finding artificial insemination "gross," the frustrated pair decide that a stud is needed. After slapstick encounters cruising the straight discos, bars and construction sites of Vancouver, Helen and Angel choose Terry, an oafish photographer who eagerly accepts the mission. The deft handling of the relationship between the trio makes this an offbeat and touching comedy. ☉

Cancer in Two Voices

(1993, 43 min, Lucy Massie Phenix)
Emotionally muted and highly analytical, this intimate video chronicles the challenges faced by a loving lesbian couple when one of them develops breast cancer. Barbara and Sandy's eight-year relationship is put to the test when Barbara's prognosis of advanced breast cancer brings illness and imminent death into their young lives. Similar to the challenges faced by gay male couples confronting AIDS, the video records — over a three-year period — the two women's struggle as Barbara undergoes chemotherapy (resulting in the loss of her hair), radiation and surgery. A moving testament to love, acceptance and letting go.

Carmilla *(1989, 60 min, US, Gabrielle Beaumont)*
Carmilla, the sultry vampiress with a fondness for beautiful young women, returns to the screen in this campy, but surprisingly pro-lesbian cable TV movie. Set in a mansion in the American South in the late 19th century, the story follows the lonely Marie who finds a friend (and much more) when Carmilla (Meg Tilly) arrives after surviving a deadly carriage accident. Tempestuous and impetuous, Carmilla soon wins over Marie's father, enabling her to chomp to her fang's content on the supple neck and soft breasts of the innocent belle. But, before she can complete her seduction, a vampireologist (an animated, it's-only-for-the-rent-folks Roddy McDowall) arrives on the scene, determined to stop Carmilla's nocturnal nibbling. The relationship between Carmilla and her pretty victim starts with hand-holding, advances to quick, tender kisses and culminates in some steamy trysts in the forest. Instead of opting for a simple seduction of the unwilling, Marie reciprocates in the lesbian relationship, quickly falling in love with Carmilla and pleading with her father not to "take away the only joy I have in my life." Sexy, creepy fun that doesn't obscure the story's lesbian undercurrents. ☉

Cass *(1981, 90 min, Australia, Chris Noonan)*
Made by a man, this wrenching drama deals with a young female filmmaker whose life is thrown into crisis after making a film about a primitive, tribal society. Fascinated by their matriarchal rituals, the woman returns to "civilized society" and her husband. She soon realizes, however, that she is a changed person with new values and eventually becomes isolated from her husband, ridiculed by her boss and finds herself falling in love with another woman. The film focuses on her attempts to resolve her newly discovered inner conflicts. ☉

The Cats

The Cats

(1964, 93 min, Denmark, Henning Carlsen)

This powerful drama about the oppression of women in Sweden is based on the successful play by Valentin Chorelle. Set at a laundry plant, the story centers on the women who labor there. Trouble brews for the quiet manager Marta (Eva Dahlbeck) after Riki (Gio Petre), one of the workers who's a hot-tempered borderline nymphomaniac, accuses her of making sexual advances. The other women, all sexually starved or frustrated in their own way, begin to humiliate the woman until Riki is forced to admit she lied. The interesting angle of the film is that Marta eventually admits to the younger woman that she is indeed attracted to her, leading Riki surprisingly to offer herself to her.

Celine and Julie Go Boating

(1974, 192 min, France,
Jacques Rivette)

"Alice in Wonderland" meets Cocteau in this entertaining, dreamlike drama. Celine (Juliet Berto) is a magician who becomes fast friends with librarian Julie (Dominique Labourier) after they meet at the foot of Montmartre. They soon become involved in a series of strange, fantastic adventures when they take magical candies which transport them to a mysterious house where they become involved in its dramas. While this surreal escapade has an element of lesboeroticism to it, with the two lead characters displaying physical affection for one another and basically being the primary focus of each other's lives, the lesbian subtext is very subtle. A playful, exhilaratingly strange and engrossing feature that offers up a lot of fun for lesbian audiences.

The Children's Hour

(1961, 107 min, US, William Wyler)

William Wyler's second screen adaptation of Lillian Hellman's play (1936's *These Three* was his first) tells of the devastating effects of gossip and scandalous rumors about two women. Wyler, attempting to right the wrong of his original film version which was stripped of any lesbian inferences, this time addresses the lesbian theme — so important in Hellman's play — if only flimsily. Interestingly, although this was the first major Hollywood film dealing with lesbianism, the word itself is never spoken and the two women never consummate their relationship. Audrey Hepburn is Karen, the sensitive heterosexual and Shirley MacLaine is Marthe, the possessive lesbian-in-hiding. Together they operate a girls' boarding school which is ruined when a horrible little girl, Mary (a potential lesbian), accuses the two of having an affair. Miriam Hopkins is the vindictive Aunt Martha who views their relationship as "unnatural." The unsubstantiated allegation ignites a self-righteous community (shades of the McCarthy witch-hunts) which eventually destroys the careers and lives of the two women. (GB title: *The Loudest Whisper*) ⊗

Choosing Children

(1984, 45 min, US, Debra Chasnoff & Kim Klauser)

From the director of the Academy Award-winning documentary *Deadly Deception* comes this engaging documentary on lesbians who decide to become parents after they have come out. Six families are profiled ranging from domestic lesbian lovers to two non-lover lesbians living together to a lesbian and gay man who do not live together, but share custody of a child. Their experiences, both painful and joyous, are revealed in this touching film.

Focus on: *Debra Chasnoff*

Lesbian documentarian Debra Chasnoff caused quite a stir after she won an Academy Award for Best Documentary Short in 1991

Shirley MacLaine (l.) and Audrey Hepburn in *The Children's Hour*

Claire of the Moon

for Deadly Deception. *The film is a 29-minute exposé on General Electric's pervasive pattern of misinformation in disclosing their involvement in dumping nuclear wastes, radiation leakage and their work in nuclear weapons development. In accepting the award, Chasnoff damned the multinational corporation and thanked her lover for her help and support in completing the film.*

Claire of the Moon
(1992, 106 min, US, Nicole Conn)

While not the breakthrough lesbian film that many had hoped for, *Claire of the Moon* is an earnest, if amateurish drama of simmering female sexual desire and equally strong denial. At an oceanside women writers' retreat in Oregon, Dr. Noel Benedict (Karen Trumbo), a brooding psychologist and lesbian author of "serious" books (reminding one of a constipated Carol Burnett), finds herself rooming with her opposite — Claire (Trisha Wood), a willowy, yet cynical straight blonde woman who is determinedly messy and fun-loving. Their budding relationship becomes a tense and inadvertently amusing cat-and-mouse game of "I want you...I don't want you" as they alternately try to overcome their insecurities, accept their true feelings and pounce on each other! A refreshingly intimate lesbian romance that works as a love story despite being a talky and didactic soap full of typical lesbian stereotypes and featuring a wooden script, stilted acting, and an overload of lingering glances. ☻

> "They should have called it, 'Lesbianism for Beginners, with Added Psychobabble'...But it's fabulous anyway — packed with tension and angst, labored breathing and hovering lips, torment by tantalization."
> — Megan Radclyffe, *Time Out*

Clips
(1988, 30 min, US, Nan Kinney & Debi Sundahl)

Three creative, if uneven vignettes from Blush Productions which push back the boundaries of lesbian sexuality. The first, a surreal piece which incorporates slow-motion and the distorted images of a masked woman, celebrates self-love and penetration. In the second, a woman takes a silk scarf and then her lover's fingers into her body. Safe sex is reflected as she returns the pleasure by stimulating her lover orally using a dental dam. Role-playing and sex toys are the keys to the third segment as a bored "housewife" seeks to spark the interest of her inattentive "husband." ☻

Club des Femmes
(The Women's Club)
(1936, 90 min, France, Jacques Deval)

This gorgeous comedy-drama had a brief run in New York City in 1937 after censors removed dialogue between the lesbian character (Josette Day) and her unrequited love interest (Elize Argal): "You're so pretty...if I were a man, I'd really love you." Set in an all-women's hotel in Paris, *Club des Femmes* features a positive portrayal of a lesbian character, a man who dresses in drag to get into the hotel to visit his girlfriend, and a lot of great dialogue that the censors didn't clip. The film was considered too racy for the general public and never received national release. ☻

Coming Out Is a Many Splendored Thing *(1992, 35 min, US, Debbie Daliege)*

Proving that Lesbian Humor is far from an oxymoron, Debbie Daliege almost single-handedly presents this comic short film on lesbian self-realization, coming out and getting that first date! Beginning with a "trailer" of a forthcoming film titled *Super Execudyke*, Daliege goes on to recount her childhood ("crushes with other girls and a spiritual bond with Lily Tomlin") and the moment when she figured out that she was a dyke. With that settled, she goes on to a series of vignettes recounting her first day as a real lesbian, coming out to her "mother" ("Oh no, your grandmother was one, too!") and entering into the crazy world of dyke fashion, lesbian bars and dating. Genuinely funnier than many of the queer videos out on the market, *Coming Out*, despite below average production values and a poor video transfer, is both witty and insightful. ☻

Committed
(1984, 77 min, US, Sheila McLaughlin & Lynne Tillman)

Committed tells the striking story of film star/leftist iconoclast Frances Farmer (*Come and Get It, The Toast of New York*). While dealing with the same subject as the 1982 Hollywood feature *Frances*, which starred Jessica Lange, this independent production

Clips

avoids some of its mainstream counterpart's theatrics and offers a solid feminist interpretation of her life. In 1935, Farmer was an overnight Hollywood sensation, but within ten years she was in a state mental institution. From stardom to a locked ward to her lobotomy, the film presents a compelling and multi-layered reconstruction of the life and repression of this culturally defiant woman. While there is no lesbian subplot or theme in the film, it was co-directed by New York independent filmmaker Sheila McLaughlin, the director of the lesbian love story *She Must Be Seeing Things*. ☮

Complaints of a Dutiful Daughter
(1994, 42 min, US, Deborah Hoffman)
This loving video self-portrait centers on the involving relationship of the director with her elderly mother who is suffering from Alzheimer's. Doris, director Deborah Hoffman's mother, is seen as a wonderful, educated woman whose increasing illness results in disorientation, loss of memory and increasing dependence on her lesbian daughter. Far from being somber or dwelling on medical problems, the video humorously captures the spirit of this effervescent 84-year-old woman as well as documenting the love

and struggles of the daughter as she faces her mother's illness. Emotional, involving and wonderfully tender.

O Corpo (The Body)
(1991, 84 min, Brazil, Jose Antonio Garcia)
Two dissimilar women are both happily involved with the same man, but when they discover he is cheating on them with a prostitute, they are drawn even closer together, emotionally and sexually. As amorous moonlighting threatens the stability of the women, they grow to despise him and plot his death.

Crocodiles in Amsterdam
(1989, 88 min, The Netherlands, Annette Apon)
This zany women's buddy film from lesbian director Annette Apon has a "magical realist" quality similar to Jacques Rivette's *Celine and Julie Go Boating*. Anything can happen — plot, motivation, sense and structure can be abandoned at any moment. Though the relationship between Gino and Nina is not identified as lesbian, their affection for one another is intensely portrayed. And as Nina explains, if you don't see any crocodiles in Amsterdam, "lack of a sighting doesn't mean they don't exist."

Crush
(1992, 97 min, New Zealand, Alison MacLean)
This unnerving psychological thriller is infused with a brooding sense of doom and complex but subtle lesbian tensions. Set against the bubbling geysers of rural New Zealand, themes of passion, betrayal, desire, jealousy and revenge surface when two women, Lane (Marcia Gay Harden) and Christina, become involved in a car accident, leaving Christina severly injured and Lane (whose carelessness was the cause of the accident) unscathed. Lane inexplicably abandons her comatose friend and leaves the scene, eventually arriving at the home of a novelist, Colin. There, with an easy sensuality, she immediately befriends (and eventually seduces?) Angela, the boyish 15-year-old daughter of Colin. In black widow-like fashion, Lane soon drops the girl for her father, thereby threatening the father-daughter relationship. The now-spurned Angela visits the

Crocodiles in Amsterdam

Crush

hospital and, in turn, befriends the slowly recovering, but brain-damaged Christina. The story takes a shocking turn when Christina, still severely handicapped and suffering from amnesia, meets up again with Lane. The film works best when delving into the three women's constantly shifting and troubling relationships and sexual games. While there is no overt lesbianism, there are unanswered questions including: Were Lane and Christina lovers or ex-lovers? (Lane says that Christina "didn't get along with men"); and did Angela fall in love with the teasing and duplicitous Lane? A twisted, stylish, tension-filled feature film debut for Alison MacLean. Ⓐ

Daughters of Darkness
(1971, 96 min, Belgium, Harry Krümel)

One from the vaults! Delphine Seyrig stars as a Hungarian countess and present-day vampiress who, in order to continue her daily blood baths (a youth and beauty preservative), must continually prowl for nubile virgins. Her blood-gathering soirees take her to Belgium where she, along with her lesbian secretary, seductively stalks the hotel for a quick fix. Campy, funny and erotic, this elegantly decadent fairy tale for adults explores the darker side of sexuality with shocking frankness. Ⓐ

> "Seyrig slinks around like a satanic Auntie Mame, all cheekbones, patent leather and feather boas. It's a bit like seeing the devil in drag."
> — *Variety*

> "I cannot quite think of anyone trash-oriented enough to tolerate, yet alone revel in, *Daughters of Darkness*...be warned to bring barf bags."
> — John Simon, *New York*

Depart to Arrive
(1982, 89 min, Germany, Alexandra von Grote)

A story of self-discovery from Alexandra von Grote, director of *Novembermoon*, this, her debut feature, deals with a woman breaking up from a lesbian affair and her ensuing search for meaning. Anna (Gabriele Osburg) and Regina (Ute Cremer) have been in a relationship for a year when Regina, whose previous relationships had been with men, begins to drift away. Anna, who had demanded total intimacy and commitment, soon discovers that Regina is also romantically involved with Gaby, a mutual friend. In an

impulsive moment, Anna leaves her job, borrows a car and runs away from Berlin to the south of France to meditate. Intensely somber and sexually candid, the film features several hallucinatory sequences that spice it up as it sensitively reveals the nuances of lesbian love and a woman's obsession with another.

Desert Hearts *(1985, 93 min, US, Donna Deitch)*

Desert Hearts, considered by many to be the best "mainstream" fiction film about lesbians, was also one of the first Hollywood films to deal with, in a sensitive manner, a lesbian relationship. Cay (Helen Shaver), an uptight English professor from New York, heads out to a dude ranch in Reno, Nevada, in order to process her divorce. There, she meets, is immediately attracted to, and eventually falls in love with Vivian (Patricia Charbonneau), an openly lesbian (and openly sexual) free-spirited sculptress/casino worker. Cay's attraction to this dark-haired iconoclast mystifies her, but however hard she tries to thwart Vivian's advances and hold on to the conventional order of her life, her heart and desires ultimately overtake her reason and repression and she finally lets herself be seduced. The romantic story, set in 1959, was written by Jane Rule (based on her novel, "Desert of the Heart") and features strong characterizations and great acting by Shaver and Charbonneau. Truly a landmark film in its positive and very realistic depiction of a love affair between two attractive and intelligent women, *Desert Hearts* offers the viewer a human-scale, tender treatment of two women in love. Deitch has jokingly referred to it as her remake of John Huston's *The Misfits*. Ⓐ

Desert Hearts

Focus on: *Donna Deitch*

Desert Hearts is considered by many to be the best independent lesbian film ever made. But getting Jane Rule's novel to the screen was no easy task for Donna Deitch, who wrote the screenplay as well as acted as the film's producer and director. The film's $850,000 budget was arduously raised by Deitch through the sale of $1,000 units of the film to small investors and friends. The investment was easily paid back when the film became a critical success and a large art-house hit, an unprecedented situation for a lesbian-themed production. Deitch, born in 1945 and originally a *painter, received her film education at UCLA where she made several documentaries and experimental shorts including* Woman to Woman *(1975), a documentary about housewives and prostitutes, and* The Great Wall of Los Angeles *(1978), about the longest mural in the world. She worked on many short and feature film productions as a still photographer, cameraperson and editor before making her feature film debut with* Desert Hearts. *While not having equaled the popular success of that film, Deitch has continued to work in the film industry. Her latest production was the four-hour, Oprah Winfrey-produced television drama* The Women of Brewster Place *in 1989.*

Diabolique
(Les Diaboliques [The Fiends])
(1955, 106 min, France, Henri-Georges Clouzot)
This white-knuckle thriller, set in a shabby boys' school, stars Simone Signoret as Nicole, the battered mistress of the school's headmaster (Paul Meurisse). Tired of his sadistic bullying, she conspires with Christina, his sickly wife (Vera Clouzot), to kill him. In grisly fashion, they drug the husband, drown him in a tub and dump the corpse in a pool. But mysteriously, the body disappears and evidence of their crime begins to haunt them. The heart-stopping climax and twist ending will have you on the edge of your seat. Based on Boileau and Narcejac's "La Femme qui E'tait," this powerful film adaptation omitted the book's premise that the two women were lesbian lovers — a much more plausible explanation of their murderous actions. Despite the deletion of the lesbian subplot, one can still enjoy the notion that the two women were motivated by their mutual attraction for each other and the need to get rid of the unwanted male member of their ménage à trois. ⊗

The Dozens
(1980, 80 min, US, Christine Dall & Randall Conrad)
The Grand Prize winner for Best Dramatic Feature at the U.S. Festival, this low-budget drama is a moving story about a woman and her relationship with her incarcerated lover. Sally, a scrappy 21-year-old recently released from prison armed with a wry sense of humor, determinedly attempts to bring about a normal life for her and her young daughter, but finds that her strongest emotional support comes from her lover who remains behind bars.

> "As a portrait, *The Dozens* is powerful...an interesting heroine against a vivid social background."
> — Janet Maslin, *The New York Times*

Dracula's Daughter
(1936, 70 min, US, Lambert Hillyer)
Along with boarding school settings, another popular milieu for lesbian-themed films is the world of the supernatural — many mainstream horror films (*The Vampire Lovers*, *The Hunger*) have employed the stereotype of the predatory lesbian (primarily as vampires and witches). One of the earliest Hollywood appearances of the lesbian as vampire is seen in *Dracula's Daughter*. Gloria Holden stars as the titular vampire, whose attempts to escape her bloodthirsty inclinations (through the help of a sympathetic doc-

Dream Girls

tor) are dashed when she develops an affinity for a young woman whom she seduces and vampirizes. ⊗

Dream Girls
(1993, 50 Min, GB, Kim Longinotto & Jano Williams)
Japanese fascination with cross-dressing, young girls' attitudes towards men and their obsession with cleaning are just a few of the subjects touched on in this provocative documentary. The film goes behind the scenes of a strange theatre school, set up over 90 years ago to train girls for a type of theatre/cabaret circuit that employs only women for both the female and male roles. The film shows the young women's rehearsals, interviews with their intensely adoring female fans and a focus on the troupe's star, Takarazuka, a young woman who specializes in the sexy, often romantic male roles. While there is no attention given to lesbianism, the idea of it permeates the film, as the women form strong bonds with one another and reject (at least temporarily) relationships with boys. Included are several snippets from the troupe's elaborately staged cross-dressing romance musicals. A rare insight to a uniquely Japanese tradition.

Dreamers of the Day *(1990, 94 min, Canada, Patricia Spencer & Philip Wood)*
From the *Claire of the Moon* school of lesbian love and sexual coming out is this enjoyable, if a bit amateurish video drama. Set in Toronto, the story revolves around the friendship between openly lesbian Andra (Lorna Harding), an aspiring filmmaker dedicated to making lesbian-themed films, and Claire (Julie Lemieux), a

married, professionally successful film producer. Written, produced and co-directed by Patricia Spencer, the film follows their budding friendship which is undermined by Andra's attraction to the "straight" Claire, who is unable to deal with the increasingly sexually tinged relationship. She resorts to evasion and lying, all in a vain attempt to deny her queer feelings. Despite their repeated assertions of being "just friends," these two attractive career women strike up a relationship that leads them inexorably to a smoldering bed. A tender and believable love story (that has played in several lesbian and gay film festivals), *Dreamers of the Day* suffers a bit from a standard story line, often stilted acting, and a static camera. ☻

Dress Up for Daddy (Amateur Lesbian Video #2)

This lesbian Daddy/Girl tape gets an "A" for ambition. Unfortunately, this second amateur venture from Blush Productions doesn't live up to its potential. A basic white, butch/femme scenario with a Daddy twist (military daddy, specifically), the tape opens with real-life lovers Cecilia and Jay dressing up and talking about their relationship (butch/femme, light S&M, role-playing, dressing up). Daddy gets a dildo blow job and fucks his girl. The butch flips to get fucked (the femme gets out the rubber gloves — the only visible latex in this tape). After a major Daddy orgasm, the femme gets a spanking and a finish-up fuck. Definitely amateurish on all counts — self-conscious performances, shaky camera, poor sound and lighting, random editing and, of course, cheesy music on the soundtrack. ☻

Dry Kisses Only

(1989, 75 min, US, Jane Cottis & Kaucyila)
Through film clips, lively interpretation, gossip and hilarious commentary, *Dry Kisses Only* explores the lesbian subtext that lies beneath the heterosexual facade of many classic Hollywood films. From *All About Eve* to *Johnny Guitar*, the film offers up dyke interpretations of the revered icons of femininity and hidden lesbianism. Films are imaginatively re-edited to reveal their "true" meanings; Dykella and Dykenna chat about lesbian vampire stereotypes; and Lady Manilla Lively provides the lighthearted gossip on hidden lesbians in today's Hollywood.

Dracula's Daughter

Each Other

(1979, 90 min, Israel/France, Michal Bat-Adam)
After playing the lead in *I Love You, Rosa*, Israeli-born Michal Bat-Adam turned to directing in this erotic lesbian love story which she wrote as well as stars in. Bat-Adams plays Yola, an Israeli writer who meets Anne (Brigitte Catillon), a vacationing French photographer, on a Tel Aviv-Jerusalem train. They become friends and eventually lovers, a situation that endangers her marriage with Avi (Assaf Dayan). The film is structured in a series of flashbacks, as their relationship, filtered through their memories, develops.

> "Tender and moving...the screen explodes with unusually graphic (but never pornographic) sex scenes."
>
> — *After Dark*

The East Is Red *(1992, 95 min, Hong Kong, Ching Siu-Tung & Raymond Lee)*

Move over Supergirl. Your days are numbered Wonder Woman. Asia the Invincible, the first transsexual lesbian superhero is now the reigning queen! This spectacular kung fu fantasy is 95 minutes of non-stop action featuring awesome special effects and enough flailing bodies and exhilarating fight sequences to keep any fan of the genre enthralled. With magical powers (including flying across the screen and flinging killer needles at her foes), Asia (Brigitte Lin-Ching Hsia) is a fiery villain/hero who goes on a rampage fighting neighboring armies, Spanish conquistadors and even a bevy of fake Asias all in a Herculean effort to regain the affections of the ravishing Snow. A particular highlight is an opium-induced

The Elegant Spanking

lesbian lovemaking scene. With action that makes John Woo's *The Killer* seem like a Bergman opus, this dazzling live-action cartoon film is startling in its matter-of-fact depiction of a woman who would do anything to recapture the girl of her dreams!

The Elegant Spanking

(1994, 30 min, US, Maria Beatty & Rosemary Delain)
Not for the sexually squeamish, this black-and-white porn (for lack of a better word) film — sort of a lesbian version of a Jean Genet scenario — features performance artist Rosemary Delain as "The Mistress" who sexually dominates, humiliates and satiates her submissive maid Kitty (independent filmmaker and "sex worker" Maria Beatty). A silent film accompanied by music composed by John Zorn, the sensual tale includes gentle spanking, graphic lovemaking and a memorable scene involving water sports (bedroom cocktails?). Not for straight men nor the faint of heart. ✪

Emilienne & Nicole

(1970, 95 min, France, Guy Casaril)
Is this tenderly erotic story a tale of two women who love one another, or is it simply the work of an exploitive man who enjoys his leering voyeuristic peek at women "making it" with each other? Guy Casaril, director of several films that feature lesbian relationships and sexuality (1986's *L'Astragale* and 1972's *The Béguines* [*Le Rempart des Béguines*]), directs this ménage à trois love story between two women and a man. Claude and Emilienne, affluent and seemingly happily married, find their stability shaken after Claude begins an affair with a young student, Nicole. But Nicole becomes attracted to Emilienne, as well, and the two begin an affair. Emilienne, smitten with love, throws out Nicole when

she discovers she has been sharing her with her husband. But remorse (and an unsuccessful night at a lesbian bar) soften her cold resolve and she soon pleads with her husband to get Nicole to return. Nicole does but shacks up with Claude and becomes pregnant. Emilienne, the third cog in the affair, moves out and into a flat with a lesbian friend. But love can be fickle in this sexy tale as Nicole soon grows tired of Claude and begins to seek out her former lesbain lover.

Emmanuelle

(1974, 94 min, France, Just Jaeckin)
The reigning queen of the art-tinged soft-core sex films of the 1970s, *Emmanuelle* was a huge box-office hit which spawned a veritable cottage industry of "Emmanuelle clones." Masking its pornographic intentions with soft-focus photography, exotic locales and only teasing glimpses of exposed flesh, the story follows the sexual adventures of Sylvia Kristel, the naive and sexually innocent bride to a worldly diplomat. Our fawn-like heroine moves to Bangkok and there, amidst the bored housewives of foreign dignitaries, she begins her sexual education. What made this film so different was its emphasis on lesbian love. Her first encounter with a woman is when an older, lecherous blonde beauty pounces on her while sunbathing in the nude ("Oh, you frightened me!" prompting the remark, "I always frighten people"). Emmanuelle's pent-up desires are released as our inquisitive neophyte begins a series of encounters with women, including a mutual masturbation scene with a boyish vixen and first Sapphic love with a self-assured

Entre Nous

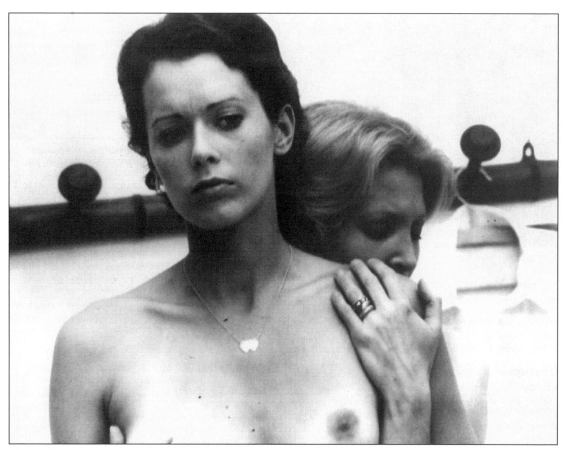

Emmanuelle

woman archaeologist who eventually breaks her heart. There are encounters with men, but the film holds its gaze and attention towards Emmanuelle's tender lesbian trysts. ⊛

Note: On the heels of the overwhelming success of the film, there was for years an outpouring of *Emmanuelle* sequels (including many with Sylvia Kristel, the latest being *Emmanuelle Goes on Social Security*) and rip-offs, most of them containing the requisite but often leering depiction of soft-core lesbian sex and relationships.

The Enchantment
(1989, 109 min, Japan, Shunichi Nagasaki)
This polished sexual psychodrama belies its low budget as it tells the complicated tale of a Tokyo psychiatrist who becomes enchanted with a mysterious female patient. Miyako cryptically reveals to him that her bruises were given to her by her jealous girlfriend Kimmie who thinks she is seeing a man. Called a "seductively cunning suspense movie...with lots of twists" by *Time Out*, the stylish melodrama involves a death, an obsessional

cab driver and the doctor's secretary/mistress who also begins an affair with another woman.

Entre Nous *(1983, 110 min, France, Diane Kurys)*
Based on the lifelong relationship of Diane Kurys' mother and her friend, this beautiful rendering of the strength and complexity of love does not contain any overt lesbianism. Yet, despite even Kurys' public denial of any sexual relationship or attraction between the two women, the film's sexual ambiguity and its characters' intensity and commitment towards each other suggests otherwise. Isabelle Huppert portrays Lena, a reticent housewife resigned to the numbing security of her husband and family. Through a chance encounter, she meets Madeleine (Miou-Miou), a vibrantly bohemian sculptress whose love and companionship opens the door to Lena's self-discovery. The film radiates with the delicate nuances of a woman's sensibility and sensuality. ⊛

Erotic in Nature
(1985, 40 min, US, Cristen Lee Rothermund)
Soft-core porn for New Age Dykes! Cris Cassidy, replete with long blonde hair, ample breasts and a nipple ring, lounges around

Erotique

the great outdoors playing with herself and friends while accompanied by the sounds of chirping birds and melodic elevator music. Unintentionally funny, this bucolic love-in-the-sun film features Cris as she makes love to a cherry red dildo, a surging water hose and has a scene where she inserts an ice cube into another woman. Ahhh...the cube that refreshes! ✪

Erotique   *(1994, 90 min, Lizzie Borden, Monika Treut & Clara Law)*

Erotique is an omnibus film that features three 30-minute shorts by women directors all of which share the theme of sexual fantasies as seen through feminist eyes/imagination. Lizzie Borden's *Let's Talk About Sex*, written by Borden and Susie Bright, follows a feisty Latina woman who, while working as a sex telephone operator, becomes obsessed with one of her male customers. With the assistance of her lesbian L.A. policewoman friend (a relationship that is left tantalizingly oblique), she acts in a very masculine fashion when she hunts down the body belonging to the voice. *Taboo Parlor*, by Monika Treut, is a wonderfully decadent and sensuous tale of female exploitation by a pair of lipstick lesbians. The two lovers, an older but glamorous fashion executive, the other a bisexual femme beauty, decide to add spice to their already active sex life by picking up a posturing male and having their way with him. Sensual and surprisingly funny. The final film, Clara Law's *Wonton Soup*, is a strictly heterosexual affair about a young couple living in today's Hong Kong.

Et L'Amore
(1993, 23 min, US, Mary Kumiss & Ellen Seidler)

This short film is about a purely sensuous, erotic encounter between two women who meet and spend the rest of the film exploring each other's bodies in a realistic and passionate way. Featuring no dialogue, the action is filmed with a surreal quality, blurring the lines between fantasy and reality, lover and stranger. It is sexy, soft, billowy and, at times, boring. In the end, we see one woman walking down the street while the other is still in bed

ruminating, presenting an important challenge to the stereotype that women aren't interested in one-night stands, if that's what this erotic encounter was. ✪

Extramuros (Beyond the Walls)

(1985, 120 min, Spain, Miguel Picazo)
Carmen Maura, long a favorite of Pedro Almodóvar, stars in this fascinating and strange story of lesbian love and lusty ambition behind a convent's walls. While the Plague ravages all around, a poverty-stricken convent becomes the center of attention after Sister Angela injures her hands and fakes the miracle of Stigmata. The nun, with her lover Sister Ana (Maura), staves off the despotic Mother Superior to eventually become the prioress herself, until the members of the Inquisition pay a not-so-friendly visit to the "saint." Throughout the bizarre ordeal, the two nuns' love for each other remains sensual, true and strong. A strange melodrama that borders on the deliriously unreal — a curious mix of the combined excesses of Ken Russell's *The Devils* and the Watergate conspiracy! ✪

Fantasy Dancer
(1990, 33 min, US Linda Vista)
A film of contrasts: A woman, Alex, is taken to a strip club by her fiancé and is surprised to find herself as excited as he is by the strikingly beautiful black stripper, Nicole. As Nicole dances, she draws Alex into a dreamworld of erotic excitement. One thing leads to another and eventually clothes and inhibitions are stripped away. ✪

The Farewell
(1980, 90 min, Sweden, Tuija-Maija Niskanen)
The familiar Swedish family drama of repressed passions and simmering family tensions is given a lesbian angle in this slow-moving but engrossing drama. The story, set almost entirely in an opulent home from the 1930s thru '50s, focuses on Valerie, a young woman who, along with her sister and cowering mother, grows up in a household ruled by her tyrannous and puritanical father. Feeling from the start her father's disappointment that she was not a son, Valerie has a lonely childhood with no one to turn to. Sensitive and moody, she grows up fearful of her domineering father, yet eager to try to win his affection. Her mother is also distant and this complex relationship with her parents creates a longing for escape, but she is unable to break the familial bonds. After an attempted suicide, she finds affection, self-respect and love in the arms of Marie, a fellow acting student. Their brief affair, which Valerie surprisingly does not keep from her family, predictably angers the blustering father who, through sheer force, ends the affair. But he can not crush the young woman's lesbian leanings nor her struggle for independence. An absorbing portrait of an intense family's love/hate relationship written by director Tuija-Maija Niskanen and filmed with the production crew often used by Ingmar Bergman.

Flaming Ears *(1992, 84 Min, Australia, Ursula Pürrer, Angela Hans Scheirl & Dietmar Schipe)*

Originally shot on Super-8 and then blown up to 16mm, this provocative lesbian sci-fi thriller, told in an almost comic book style, is a guilty-pleasure sleeper. The year is 2700 where, in a bombed-out and dangerous town, a bizarre group of nearly wild lesbians attempt to eke out an existence. The story revolves around the often times violent interplay, fueled by jealousy, lust and revenge, of three lesbians: the romantic Spy, Volley (a pyromaniac sex fiend) and Nun. The film's absurdly low budget actually enhances this almost surreal, post-apocalyptic tale.

Forbidden Love — The Unashamed Stories of Lesbian Lives *(1992, 85 min, Canada, Aerlyn Weissman & Lynne Fernie)*

If at all posible, see this very funny and insightful documentary with an audience of queers because its perceptive approach to a serious and under-documented subject (Canadian lesbian history) will certainly charge and unite the crowd. The filmmakers weave archival footage, amusing interviews with older lesbians, Sapphic artifacts and a reenactment of one particularly lurid tale of love in

The Fox

fleshing out what life was like for lesbians in the repressed Canada of the 1950s and '60s. The nine women interviewed include a butch ranger who could have just come from a Marlboro shoot, a kittenish femme housewife and a Native American woman, all of whom vividly recount the days when lesbianism was only whispered and love affairs and even same-sex parties were quite illicit. Interspersed throughout are shots of hilariously cheesy covers from lesbian paperback potboilers of days gone by. An unforgettable and compelling film with many colorful lines such as this one spoken by an older lesbian, "I think that post-menstrual women should run the world!" ⊛

The Fox
(1967, 110 min, US, Mark Rydell)

With the basic postulation that all a lesbian really needs is a man, this somber drama, adapted from a D.H. Lawrence novella, is one of the more deceptively homophobic pictures to come out of Hollywood in the 1960s. Jill (Sandy Dennis) and Ellen (Anne Heywood) are two lesbians living on a farm in a desolate area of Canada. Jill is the skittish, man-fearing femme whose attraction to other women is "explained" through a childhood incident that she overblows into a trauma. Ellen is the pants-wearing butch. Together they contentedly work their farm until the arrival of a drifter, Paul (Keir Dullea), who quickly brings about "nature's order" by seducing Ellen, much to the torment of her helpless lover. Filmed in an overly arty and symbolic manner (Dullea is the "Fox" who creeps into the henhouse, Dennis is ultimately killed by a phallically suggestive tree), the film views lesbianism as an unsatisfyingly aberrant behavior that can be readily fixed. Dullea, with his eyes on Heywood, confronts her lover at one point, challenging her with lines like, "You've never had a man. I think that's your problem. Isn't it what you need?" It is a narrow-minded definition of lesbianism that helps to foster the notion that lesbians (and gay males) have something wrong with them; that they are not fully realized and mature individuals. Their inclusion in '60s and '70s American films was limited to the roles of heavies, perverts or persons to be pitied and who, in many cases, were cinematically killed off.

Framing Lesbian Fashion
(1992, 58 min, US, Karen Everett)

Beginning with a montage of various outfits and "uniforms" worn by lesbians over the last four decades, this entertaining documentary traces the herstory of how apparel has helped shape and define the lesbian mystique — its attitudes, politics, sociology and personal role-playing. By tracing the fashion trends of lesbians, the films touches on such themes as the traditional butch and femme look, lesbian clones of the '70s and the Birkenstock-and-flannel radfems to today's world of greater freedom and individuality where fashion definition has been blurred and where lipstick lesbians and dykes with long hair, makeup and dresses are as much a part of the lesbian culture as women into body piercing, leather and even corporate drag. Intercutting archival photos with clips from movies (Katharine Hepburn and Marlene Dietrich in drag) and interviews, director Karen Everett takes us through a fascinating journalistic tour of the evolving lesbian community, its culture and its shifting self-identity. A vital addition to the recent collection of films (*Last Call at Maud's*, *Forbidden Love* and *Thank God I'm a Lesbian*) which aim to create greater awareness by uncovering lesbian history. Originally made as Everett's master thesis at UC Berkeley. ⊛

Framing Lesbian Fashion

Fresh Kill
(1994, 80 min, US, Shu Lea Cheang)

An excitingly dense sci-fi political comedy that might prove to be a landmark in independent lesbian cinema, *Fresh Kill* is an audacious directorial debut for New York video artist Shu Lea Cheang. Written by Jessica Hagedorn, this futuristic tale is set in a seriously contaminated and eerily glowing New York City, a world where racial and sexual orientation barriers seem to have disappeared only to be replaced by greedy yuppies who rape everything and everybody while whining and dining in the finest traditions (where fish lips are the latest rage). Sarita Choudhury (*Mississippi Masala*) and Erin McMurty are featured as lesbian parents who get caught up in a Byzantine plot involving industrial waste spread through radioactive sushi. The two women are seen as just another nuclear family trying to keep their daughter from glowing in the dark. When their daughter disappears, they and others organize against the multinational corporations responsible for the mess. Cameos include Ron Vawter, Karen Finley, Laurie Carlos and Robbie McCauley.

Fried Green Tomatoes
(1991, 130 min, US, Jon Avnet)

Adapted from Fannie Flagg's novel "Fried Green Tomatoes at the Whistle Stop Cafe," this endearing adaptation centers on the relationship between two pairs of women in separate time frames: Idgie (Mary Stuart Masterson) and Ruth (Mary-Louise Parker), friends and business partners in the 1930s; and Evelyn (Kathy Bates) and Ninny (Jessica Tandy), who meet in the present. The elderly Ninny relates to Evelyn the story of Idgie and Ruth, childhood friends from her youth in a small Alabama town. Though at the core of the film is the friendship between Idgie and Ruth, the film only slightly hints at the romantic relationship between them — which was more significant in the novel — with several scenes awash with sexual tension. Of this, director Jon Avnet said, "You can take it how you want to. I had no interest in going into the bedroom." The acting from the entire cast is excellent, though Masterson is superb as the "dyke heroine" Idgie, who spends her time gambling at the River Club, charming bees (an act which swoons Ruth) and ultimately rescuing and protecting her fair amour. ⊛

Fun with a Sausage/L'Ingenue
(1985, 30 min, US, Ingrid Wilhite)

Outrageous and offensive, this pair of short subjects offers a dated look at lesbian tomfoolery. In the first piece, a young filmmaker from Idaho finds her sexual initiation in San Francisco at the command of a leatherwoman. The second film is a silent piece about the adventures of a young woman who decides to dress up as a man — all the way down to the sausage she stuffs in her jeans to obtain that proper "bulging" silhouette. ⊛

Fuses *(1967, 23 min, US, Carolee Schneemann)*

1960s avant-garde filmmaking has never been more erotic than in this short collage of images depicting the physical and emotional intensity of lovemaking filmed from a woman's point-of-view. With a backdrop of ocean waves and the sounds of seagulls, Carolee Schneemann takes her images and over-exposes them, dips them in acid, burns them and generally obscures the graphic, but never pornographic visuals of human bodies at play as she explores their mystery and sensual beauty.

The Gemini Affair
(1974, 98 min, US, Matt Cimber)
A very interesting and gratuitous nudity-filled independent production about how a great friendship between two women develops into physical love. Not featuring the greatest production values or acting talents, the film is, however, quite lesbian-friendly, especially for Hollywood circa 1974. Jessica, a New York actress, flies to L.A. to stay with her best friend from high school as she tries to break into the modeling/acting biz. Her friend Julie, sort of a Joey Heatherton-wannabe, welcomes her to her opulent Beverly Hills digs, made possible by her high-class prostitution. The two have a wonderful time becoming close again, and despite a house of mammoth proportions, they sleep in the same bed. When a lecherous lesbian talent agent makes the moves on her, a naive Jessica imperiously rebuffs the "recruiting" effort. Later, Julie refers to the agent as "a snotty, bitchy cunt," to which Jessica replies, "I knew a woman like her in New York. She smoked cigars and had hands like a teamster." While the two spew homophobic remarks, unsaid Sapphic emotions begin to percolate — Jessica says at one point, "I'm hungry but I don't know what I want." Finally the two make love, shown as tender and loving, but afterwards Jessica is repulsed and runs away with the unapologetic Julie in pursuit. They eventually discuss the situation (while never uttering the "L" word) and despite acknowledgements of love and physical attraction, realize tough times lie ahead. It's difficult to say who the intended audience was for this curiosity: It certainly was not marketed at lesbians and while the sex and nudity were probably a turn-on for straight men, the film's theme would undoubtedly leave them cold. ⊛

Gertrude Stein: When You See This Remember Me
(1970, 82 min, US, Peter Miller Adato)
The amazing life of lesbian author, famous personality and art collector Gertrude Stein comes alive in this tribute/documentary. The world and thoughts of Stein are revealed through her own words, those of her many famous friends (Virgil Thompson, Jacques Lipshitz, Bennett Cerf), and home movies with her lover Alice B. Toklas. The film pays special attention to the halcyon days of Paris in the 1920s where Stein and Toklas played hostesses to a venerable "who's who" in the arts including Picasso, Thornton Wilder, T.S. Eliot, James Joyce, Edith Sitwell, Ernest Hemingway and Jean Cocteau. Also featured is a recording of the only radio broadcast she ever made. Other films dealing with Gertrude Stein and Alice B. Toklas include the 1986 PBS film *Waiting for the Moon* with Linda Hunt and Marian Seldes, and *Gertrude Stein and a Companion*, a 60-minute BBC production made in 1985, based on the stage play by Sonia Fraser and starring Miriam Margolyes as Gertrude and Natasha Morgan as Alice B.

Fresh Kill

Getting Ready
(1976, 55 min, US, Janet Meyers)
This sensitive, unusually perceptive drama, though lacking professional actors, is a sharply realized tale of two young women entering their awkward adolescent years. With its frame of reference set firmly in the tacky '70s, the story revolves around the evolving friendship (and possible love) of two New York City teens (one played by a young Annabella Sciorra). Though more about their tender friendship, the film definitely contains lesbian undercurrents and a suggestion of what might come to pass. Chosen by lesbian filmmaker Jan Oxenberg as a selection at the 1994 London Lesbian & Gay Film Festival.

Girlfriends *(1978, 86 min, US, Claudia Weill)*
A flawless performance from Melanie Mayron as a photographer who makes it "on her own" after her best friend and roommate gets married makes this independently made feature well worth watching despite its less than fair treatment of a lesbian character. Susan (Mayron) finds success as an artist while Ann (Anita Skinner) struggles to balance being a wife and mother with being a writer. The real focus is not on the conflict and jealousy between the women, but rather on Mayron's character and her daily life. One scene of note: Susan picks up a young female hitchhiker (Amy Wright) who ends up staying with her even though Susan knows she is a lesbian. The girl eventually makes a non-threatening pass at her, is rejected (the "eternal triumph" of heterosexuality) and is soon dispatched from the apartment and Susan's life. ⊛

Girlfriends
(1993, 80 min, US, Mark Bosko & Wayne Harold)
This kinky tale of a pair of likable lesbian serial killers is an inventive, low-budget combination of *Henry: Portrait of a Serial Killer* and *Pink Flamingos*. Pearl (Lori Scarlet) and her butch lover Wanda (Nina Angeloff) make a modest living picking up a variety of men, blowing their heads off and making off with their

Director Rose Troche (l.), V.S. Brodie (c.) and Guinevere Turner of *Go Fish*

wallets. In the midst of the casual carnage, Pearl decides she wants to have a baby — pity the poor father-to-be. *Girlfriends*, not to be confused with the Claudia Weill film, is an ironic thriller loaded with shockingly graphic splatter effects, sly humor and a surprise ending. ⊛

Glitter Goddess of Sunset Strip

(1993, 115 min, US, Dick Campbell)

An innovative, autobiographical psychodrama about the life and times of ex-glam rock groupie and sexual maverick Llana Lloyd. Beginning with her birth in 1952 into the strange, domineering world of a man-loathing lesbian mother and a schizophrenic father, Lloyd turned her psyche-tested, tormented existence into a positive learning experience and made it her claim to fame. With the story being told through a series of John Waters-influenced dramatic "reenactments" and talk-show footage (some featuring an Afro-endowed Oprah Winfrey), we get a unique fly-on-the-wall perspective into a strange, complex world of gender role-playing and ahead-of-its-time sexual politics, with Lloyd and real-life daughter Alana playing the mother/daughter roles. ⊛

Go Fish

(1994, 85 min, US, Rose Troche)

An unlikely candidate to join the ranks of epochal lesbian-themed films, this delightful yet knowing independent romantic comedy by first-time Chicago filmmakers Rose Troche (co-writer/director/co-producer) and Guinevere Turner (co-writer and co-producer) is more than simply the *Desert Hearts* of the 1990s. *Go Fish* feels no need to deal with the difficulties of coming out, of self-acceptance, of discovering one's self — themes that many films including *Claire of the Moon* obsess over. Here, the women are dykes, plain and simple, living and breathing dyke values, lifestyles and loves. Made on an extremely low budget, filmed in black and white and featuring primarily non-professionals in the major roles, its very grittiness helps in making its characters more real, honest and accessible. What the film lacks in professional pizzazz and slick acting is more than made up with its witty screenplay (peppered with several Spike Lee touches), its vividly drawn characters and its deceptively simple plot. Seriously cute and boyishly hip Max (Turner), after a drought of ten months, is looking for love and possibly finds it (through the prodding of her friends and roommates) with Ely (V.S. Brodie), a semi-dorky, slightly older woman. How the two women meet, become attracted to each other and possibly get together is the crux of the film. Will Max get past the looks and into the person. Will Ely shed her hippie-ish look and loosen up a bit? Will their friends just back off and let nature take its course? These and other queries are wonderfully handled in a light, effervescent fashion that combines to paint a finely detailed and on-target depiction of young lesbian life. Other memorable members of the circle include Max's levelheaded roommate and college professor Kia (T. Wendy McMillan), Kia's Latina lover Evy (Migdalia Melendez), and their horny, always-on-the-prowl friend Daria (Anastasia Sharp).

"It's 'girl meets girl, girl gets girl, girl has sex with girl on screen' kind of thing...We live completely dyke lives. Our life is so regular to us and so foreign to everyone else."
—Guinevere Turner

The Handmaid's Tale

(1990, 108 min, US, Volker Schlöndorff)

Volker Schlöndorff's adaptation of Margaret Atwood's novel has a few minor structural problems in trying to cover so much ground. Overall, the film is very powerful and compelling as it combines the most insidious and subtly horrific aspects of early American Puritanism with the military-industrial terror of a supposedly futuristic, but quite contemporary looking police state. Marketed as a sexy movie (the film's newspaper ads used

Playboy's reviewer Bruce Williamson's quote, "A psychosexual movie shocker...cool eroticism, intelligence and intensity" to sell it), *The Handmaid's Tale* is actually a film with a very timely political point to make about the implications of state control over women's bodies. So, don't expect some kind of mindless Hollywood fluff that you can watch for two hours and forget about. Also, Elizabeth McGovern is great as Moira, the token lesbian. When Natasha Richardson asks her why she's been taken by the authorities, she explains, "Gender treachery. I like girls." ☻

Hayfever

(1990, 105 min, US, Cristen Lee Rothermund)
This lesbian comedy tells the tale of two women who must collect their inheritance from a great-aunt at a roundup. On the way, there is plenty of adventure, sexual and otherwise, including a run-in with a mysterious villain who would foil their plans. Full of different types of women, music, dancing and sex. If not taken too seriously, this film is great fun. ☻

Henry & June

(1990, 140 min. US, Philip Kaufman)
The first film to earn the MPAA's NC-17 rating, director Philip Kaufman's steamy adaptation of Anais Nin's novel about the passionate love triangle between herself, writer Henry Miller and his wife June is a glorious sexual and literary odyssey through the streets of 1930s Paris. Exquisitely photographed, *Henry & June* sumptuously evokes a frenzied carnival atmosphere and makes for an extraordinary sensual cinematic experience. Newcomer Maria de Medeiros is dazzling as the doe-eyed Anais, a prolific diarist who vigorously committed herself to the pursuit of complete sexual abandon. As Miller, Fred Ward is excellent, exuding a sleazy sexuality and the tenderness of a love-struck poet. Uma Thurman gives a lusty portrayal of the voluptuous bombshell June. ☻

Her Summer Vacation

(1972, 90 min, Brazil/France, Victor DiMello)
Passions erupt, clothes shed and sexual taboos are thrown on the bedroom floor after Giselle, a young Maria Schneider look-alike, spends the summer learning all about sex at her father's Brazilian ranch. Our Latin American nymphette, imbued with an insatiable and "anything goes" sexual appetite, soon develops torrid relationships with her lovely stepmother, the ranch's handyman, her bisexual cousin and even an all-too-willing former baby-sitter. All kinds of sexual proclivities are gleefully displayed in this soft "X" sexual smorgasbord including bisexuality, lesbianism, incest, voyeurism, rape, and pedophilia, with a hint of beastiality thrown in as well. Art? Hell no! But it is enjoyable fun for those who associate "art" films with yearning naked bodies set against exotic locales. ☻

Home-Made Melodrama

(1982, 51 min, GB, Jacqui Duckworth)
Stark, low-budget and admittedly autobiographical, *Home-Made Melodrama*, filmed over a two-year period because of budgetary problems, is a lesbian-feminist take on a ménage à trois involving three women. The love triangle is seen as difficult, even painful at times, while positive aspects of the relationships, including sexual exploration, are seen as well. Features Lyndley Stanley, Cass Bream and Joy Chamberlain (director of *Nocturne*).

How to Female Ejaculate

(1992, 60 min, US, Nan Kinney)
On Our Backs publisher and "pro-sex feminist" Fanny Fatale, the "Jane Fonda of genital aerobics," is the knowledgeable and enthusiastic narrator of this instructional video on female ejaculation: What it is, what it is not, and how to achieve it. Beginning with a lecture that focuses on medical particulars and physical descriptions using charts and diagrams, Fatale ultimately uses her own vagina for a close-up look at feminine ejaculation. She explains that it is more than simple orgasm, that particular vaginal exercises help bring it about and that there are two kinds of female ejaculation: clitoral and uterine (G-spot). The second half of the video finds Fatale joined by three women in a discussion that concludes with a group masturbation exercise that brings about several sexually graphic female eruptions. Not all women can readily achieve ejaculation and some con-

Maria de Medeiros (l.) holds hands with Uma Thurman as Fred Ward looks on in *Henry & June*

Fanny Fatale in *How to Female Ejaculate*

fuse the watery discharge as urine, but as one of the participants explains, the ejaculation fluid tastes like "a cross between a sea salty, kind of briny taste and buttered popcorn." Explicit but never gratuitous, the women, through discussions and demonstrations, compare sexual notes and offer suggestions and exercises for women to achieve their own ability to ejaculate. ⊗

How to Find Your G-spot

(1993, 36 min, US)
The San Francisco-based lesbian video company House O'Chicks continues to present tapes that humorously educate and celebrate the enjoyment potential of female sexuality. Entertaining and super low-budget (simply an apartment, a camcorder and a smooth-talking demonstrator), the video features Dorrie Lane — "sex worker, sex educator, prostitute, mom and lesbian" — as the enthusiastic guide who takes the audience on an exploration of women's G-spots (or better yet, Goddess spots) through the use of the Wondrous Vulva Puppet, drawings, a road map and, finally, a personal, up-close demonstration. After just one viewing, no woman should ever get lost finding her own (and another's) pleasure zones. Come the Queer Revolution, high schools all over America will be screening this video during sex education classes! ⊗

How to Have a Safe Sex Party

(1992, 30 min, US)
Produced by House O'Chicks, this no-budget sex instructional tape features a room full of eager-to-begin women who engage in a series of sexually explicit safe sex techniques. Actually not much different in style than many run-of-the-mill porno shorts, this video is of interest because it was made by, with and for lesbians and does not feature the usual wham-bam sex scenes. Instead, it

depicts the women engaged in hot sex, tender kissing and lingering caressing, all videotaped in a playful spirit. ⊗

The Hunger   *(1983, 99 min, GB, Tony Scott)*

Dripping with cinematic style and chic sexual intrigue, *The Hunger* is less vampire horror film and more a sensuous drama of lesbian attraction and desire. Catherine Deneuve is Miriam, an icy, elegant vampiress, hundreds of years old, who goes on the prowl for a new mate after her 200-year lover (David Bowie) quickly ages. Her affections find their way to Sara (Susan Sarandon), a doctor who has written on the subject of accelerated aging. From the moment the two lock eyes — Sara in her butch t-shirt and trousers, Miriam in suggestive designer dress — one knows that Sapphic love is in the offing. The two romp, fall into each others arms and make love — and, of course, share blood. Although a body double was used in place of Deneuve in the more explicit sex scenes, the two stars create unprecedented sensual sizzle. After their tryst, Miriam declares "You belong to me. We belong to each other" and promises Sara "eternal youth" and an everlasting relationship — but read the small print on Bowie's coffin, Sara! ⊗

Hungry Hearts

(1989, 30 min, US, Nan Kinney & Debi Sundahl)
Produced by Fatale Video, the leaders of lesbian erotica, this short tale is set at an ocean resort where two real-life strippers, Pepper and Reva, engage in sensual and passionate lovemaking. Made by women for women, this bawdy tale of sex includes a striptease, a much-used dildo, a harness and a most unusual bath. Lingerie lovers will love this one. ⊗

I've Heard the Mermaids Singing

(1987, 81 min min, Canada, Patricia Rozema)
Sheila McCarthy, star of this enchanting comedy, is nothing short of a revelation. The film itself is cute and whimsical but it is McCarthy as Polly, the day-dreaming romantic Gal Friday, who steals the show as well as our hearts. An avid photographer who dwells in her own fantasy world, Polly secures a job as a temp at an art gallery where she becomes infatuated with the female curator. Her innocence and joie de vivre prove to be a bracing tonic in a world dulled by pretension and greed. A film and a performance which should lift your spirits. ⊗

I, the Worst of All (Yo, La Peor de Todas)

(1990, 100 min, Argentina/Fr, Maria Luisa Bemberg)
From the director of *Camila* and *Miss Mary* comes this unconventional story of 17th-century Mexican poet and nun Sor Juana Inez de la Cruz. Confined to a prison-like cloister, Sister Juana's passionate, philosophical poems become the "rage" amongst both the rich and poor, causing problems for the virtually sealed-off convent and prompting an intimate relationship (though mostly through bars) with a beautiful vicereine (Dominique Sanda). The film is elegant and intelligent, though the women's relationship never goes beyond lingering glances, which leaves the viewer more *wishing* for an affair than actually getting one.

Hungry Hearts

The Ice Palace

(1987, 78 min, Norway, Per Blom)
This crypto-lesbian, Nordic *Picnic at Hanging Rock* is a moody, often silent drama filled with a haunting sexual mysticism. Unn (Hilde Martinsen) and Siss (Line Storesund) are two 11-year-old friends who, while playing in Unn's attic bedroom, take off their clothes for each other, but don't touch. Their nascent sexuality is awakened, but both are disturbed by the incident. The next day, a troubled Unn ventures down a frozen waterfall and eventually dies within a maze of underground ice tunnels. Pregnant with meaning, this mood piece is quite effective in its theme of sexual repression and isolation.

Images *(1986, 54 min, US, Janet Liss)*

Images is a dramatic love story about a happy lesbian couple whose relationship is tested by "the other woman." This first-rate film portrays positive characters and combines a tender love story with gentle eroticism. ⊛

Immacolata e Concetta

(1981, 110 min, Italy, Salvadore Piscicelli)
A passionate and defiant love between two Neapolitan women is at the center if this intense and ultimately violent love story. Immacolata and Concetta, both attractive, if severe women, meet and fall in love while in prison. Upon their release, Immacolata moves in with Concetta, scandalizing her family and neighbors and effectively pushing aside Concetta's agitated husband. Their relationship is depicted as loving and the sex scenes are equally erotic. Their flaunting of village conventions eventually leads to tragic, almost inevitable repercussions.

In the Best Interests of the Children

(1977, 53 min, GB, Elizabeth Stevens,
Cathy Zheutlin & Frances Reid)
"A woman has the right to be a lesbian, but lesbians don't have the right to raise children." This stinging, homophobic opinion by a judge in a New York custody case offers a vivid example of the tough legal roadblocks suffered by lesbian mothers. The lives of eight lesbian mothers and their children are profiled in this provocative and intelligent documentary on the subject of lesbian parenting.

Le Jupon Rouge

(1987, 90 min, France, Geneviève Lefèbvre)
Three women of greatly differing ages and backgrounds engage in a complicated and, at times, contradictory ménage à trois. Manuela (Marie-Christine Barrault) has a nominal relationship with her boyfriend, but it does not stop her from other close relationships or her political work. She meets an older woman, Bacha (Alida Valli), a Holocaust survivor and activist, and the two strike up a closely physical but platonic friendship. Their relationship becomes strained when Manuela begins a passionate love affair with the lovely and much younger Claude (Guillemette Grobon). Feeling lonely, betrayed and jealous, the distraught Bacha admits to Manuela that "you with that girl brings out the worst in me." Manuela, who doesn't want to lose her friend but is equally determined to explore this love with another woman, is faced with a difficult decision. A tender, well-acted drama touching on themes of desire, sensuality and possessiveness in relationships as well as a subtle reminder of the tenuousness of life and love. (Also known as: *Manuela's Loves*)

I, the Worst of All

Julia *(1977, 118 min, US, Fred Zinnemann)*

In a 1976 article in *The New York Times*, Jane Fonda said of *Julia*, "It's about a relationship between two women. It's not neurotic or sexually aberrant." Asked by interviewer Judy Klemesrud in an October 1977 *New York Times* issue whether there were overtones of lesbianism in the film, Vanessa Redgrave responded, "No, I don't think so, not at all. There is no hint of it in the way Lillian Hellman writes of their friendship. In fact, in the book where Lillian views Julia's body in the funeral parlor she says something like, 'It wouldn't matter if I never even kissed her, so I just touched her face.'" When a male character in the film suggests that, "Everyone knows about you and Julia," Jane Fonda slugs him. Redgrave is absolutely stunning as Julia. And Jane Fonda as Lillian is totally crushed out on her. Similar to Diane Kurys' *Entre Nous*, the friendship between Fonda and Redgrave contains strong overtones of lesbianism. Could Hellman's real-life relationship with Julia have been the inspiration for her play, "The Children's Hour"? ☻

Just Because of Who We Are

(1986, 28 min, US)

Though short, this powerful film eloquently deals with violence against lesbians — a troubling situation that is especially prevalent with lesbians of color. Interviewed are a series of women who discuss and recall the horrors of violence against them: taunts and unprovoked physical abuse from strangers (male) on the street; arrests in lesbian bars by police; parents who abhor the knowledge that their daughter is a lesbian; medical authorities; and even, in one case, a particularly violent former lesbian lover. The physical and psychological scars inflicted on the women by this homophobia (the film focuses primarily on violence in New York City and Northampton, MA) leads to organized protests and support groups. While a change of thinking, re-education and re-socialization is needed for the offenders to change, the film concludes with a naively happy ending at New York City Council, where equal right for lesbians and gays legislation finally, after six attempts, passes in 1986.

Just the Two of Us

(1970, 82 min, US, Barbara Peters)

Quite possibly the most unheralded lesbian-themed film ever made in the United States, *Just the Two of Us* tenderly tells the love story between two married women and features (surprising not only for 1970 but for the 1990s as well) a happily Sapphic ending. Much like *Go Fish*, the film is ladened with low production values and sub-par acting, but both films rise above these flaws with an engaging pro-lesbian script. Pretty and sensible Denise (Alicia Courtney) and the sweetly ditsy blonde Adria (Elizabeth Plumb) are lonely housewives living in suburban L.A. who become close friends. While lunching at a restaurant one day, they spot two women at another table holding hands and later kissing. Both are transfixed — Denise excited and envious, Adria perplexed but intrigued. An idyllic romance (complete with torrid lovemaking) soon ensues between the two, but troubles brew when the bisexual Adria thinks of their relationship more as a fling, soon becoming bored and eager to meet men, much to Denise's frustration and jealousy. An aspiring actor/stud-wannabe soon enters the picture,

with whom Adria falls in love, summarily dumping Denise. If the film followed the familiar pattern of these types of films, the mainly straight woman drops her lesbian desires for the pleasures of a man and the "other woman" is soon killed off or suffers some calamitous fate. But this is not the case here. Denise, heartbroken and carrying the torch for her love, is encouraged by some of her lesbian friends to attend a party. There, she is led to the bedroom of the sultry hostess; but before anything can happen, Denise flees the scene, still pining for her true love. Meanwhile across town, Adria and her stud boyfriend are paid a surprise visit by her musclebound and furious husband. Do the two women reunite? Will Adria find happiness with either man? Will Denise get over her hurt and begin dating women? Will true love win out? The outcome to these questions will bring a collective smile on the faces of lesbian audiences. An undiscovered gem that should receive revival exposure in lesbian/gay film festivals. ☻

Kamikaze Hearts

Kamikaze Hearts

(1986, 80 min, US, Juliet Bashore)

Reality and fiction are intriguingly merged in this fascinating film-within-a-film-within-a-film which is centered around two women working in the porno business: Sharon (Mitch) Mitchell and her lover Tigr Mennett. Porn star Mitch (who, if she lived in 1960s New York, would have likely been a Warhol Superstar) is an unusually sexy young woman who goes to San Francisco to star in a porn film somewhat based on the Bizet opera "Carmen." At the same time, a film crew is following her shooting a documentary (*Truth or Fiction*) on her life. Her lover Tigr, a film producer, is a pretty blonde with "hurt little boy" looks who is wildly in love with the hero-worshipped Mitch ("I didn't fall in love with her because she's beautiful, but because she's powerful"). The majority of the film takes place on the set of the upcoming porn extravaganza and, as filming proceeds, strains between the two women become evident, with Tigr especially jealous of Mitch's lesbian sex scenes. Mitch, a veteran of over 119 films ("Some of them unfortunately are not smut; you gotta pay taxes on something"), is the center of attention as the sassy statuesque "star." A complex, sexually explicit and ambitious film which works both as a revealing exposé of the porn biz, and as a story of two women who meet in it, fall in love and are eventually distanced by its pressures. ☻

The Killing of Sister George

(1968, 138 min, GB, Robert Aldrich)

One of the great and infamous lesbian "breakthrough" films of the '60s, this story of an aging lesbian who loses her job and her young lover is a shrill, even grotesque exposé on lesbian lifestyles. Beryl Reid is magnetic in her portrayal of George, the loud and aggressive, cigar-chomping dyke whose girl-chasing ways (she even accosts a cab full of nuns!) and domineering personality drive away all who care for her. The triangle of lesbian stereotypes include: butch George; the predatory, sophisticated middle-aged dyke (Coral Brown); and Childie, the kittenish but neurotic femme (Susannah York). An entertainingly dated tale of love

Last Call at Maud's

and loneliness that treads a strange line between comedy and sensationalist, perverted drama. In possibly a first for mainstream films, some scenes were shot in an actual London lesbian bar, the Getaway Club. Despite the stereotypes and heavy-handedness, this lesbian soap opera is a "must see" for all cinematic queers. ⊛

Labor More Than Once

(1983, 52 min, US, Liz Mersky)

This touching personal documentary follows a young mother's valiant struggle against a homophobic judicial system to regain custody of her son. Not having seen her son for almost two years, the woman faces a legal system that is bent on denying her custodial rights solely on her sexual preference and is on the verge of

The Killing of Sister George

granting a petition of adoption to her ex-husband's wife. Her refusal to back down and abandon the fight led to a landmark court trial in 1981.

Last Call at Maud's

(1993, 75 min, US, Paris Poirier)

The 1989 closing of Maud's Study, a lesbian bar and institution in San Francisco since 1966, propelled filmmaker Paris Poirier to explore the 23-year life of the bar and its patrons as well as offer a fascinating mini-history of recent (post-WWII) lesbian life and the role that lesbian bars played in it. Many longtime patrons of Maud's are interviewed, providing vivid case histories as they nostalgically recall their first experiences in a lesbian bar, their early relationships and the significance of Maud's closing. Their recollections offer a lively and informative account of lesbian life from the 1940s to present, with stories of the many raids and police harassment of "queer" bars which surprisingly lasted until the early '70s, even in San Francisco. Topics also touched on are the nascent gay/lesbian movement of the '70s, the changing Sapphic perspective on the role of bars and the not always smooth relationship between lesbians and gay men. An engaging and informative documentary which celebrates lesbian life and provides an essential chapter in the social and political history of lesbians. ⊛

Laurie Anderson: Home of the Brave

(1986, 90 min, US, Laurie Anderson)

Laurie Anderson continues her ascension from cult performance artist to pop performance star in this visually sensational musical art film that is an eye-popping combination of video, wild choreography and a compelling fusion of conventional rock instruments and loopy electronic sonics. She leads her band through 18 compositions including "Language Is a Virus" and an atmospheric

OF LESBIAN INTEREST

"Gravity's Rainbow." Always inventive, Anderson brings a wealth of talent to this effort. Aside from her witty, intriguing lyrics and talents as a dancer and comedienne, she has a genius for an array of expressive gimmicks and unexpected sleights of hand. Sporting an infectious grin and spiked haircut, Anderson is riveting as she turns her entire body into a percussion instrument, dances a tango with William S. Burroughs and all this with her tongue planted firmly in her cheek. ☮

Learn to Country Western Dance with Donna E

(1993, 60 min, US, Irene Young & Melanie Mocium)
D.J. and dance instructor Donna E is credited for having popularized country dance amongst the gay and lesbian set with her classes at Women's Music Festivals and gay/lesbian clubs throughout the United States. This video features Donna, in step-by-step fashion, demonstrating such classics as "The Texas Two-Step," "The Waltz," and the line dances "The Tush Push" and "The Tahoe Kick." Featuring music from Wynnona Judd, Teresa Trull and Laurie Lewis. ☮

Lesbian Lykra Shorts

(1984-1991, 114 min)
Hyped by its distribution company as the first video in the U.K. to be produced for a lesbian audience, this entertaining and challenging compilation features four disparate shorts:

Domestic Bliss *(1984, GB, Joy Chamberlain)*
Made for British TV, this breakthrough dyke soap opera is a humorous farce of a lesbian couple who just can't seem to find any time alone, with intimacy constantly interrupted by an inquisitive daughter and a parade of neighbors and ex-husbands. Dianna, a successful doctor and anal-retentive housekeeper, finds her life in emotional and neatness turmoil after her new lover, Emma, moves

Lianna

in. Emma not only brings along a daughter, but also her pet rat and a penchant for disorganization.

Can't You Take a Joke? *(1989, Australia, Vicki Dunn)*
An enjoyably strange Down Under short. Jenni looks for help after her sense of humor is stolen. With police unable to help, she seeks out Laura Hunt, the sleuthing private eye of comic book lore. But while Jenni discovers that Laura was buried a few weeks back, Amanda, the artist who drew Laura, agrees to take on the case.

She Don't Fade *(1991, US, Cheryl Dunye)*
African-American independent filmmaker Cheryl Dunye, based in Philadelphia, contributes with this 23-minute sexual comedy in which Dunye, in a self-reflective mood, looks at her past loves and relationships and sets out to find "new ways to meet women."

Reservaat *(1988, The Netherlands, Clara van Gool)*
A seven-minute experimental short that features two women dancing silently through a secluded forest as the leaves slowly fall. (Available only in Great Britain)

Lesbian Tongues

(1989, 90 min, US)
By capturing the opinions and feelings of several "out" lesbians, this documentary plays an important part in heightening awareness of lesbian history. Much more educational than entertaining, the film's greatest fault is in its lack of editing, for while the women interviewed are interesting, their sessions seem to ramble on forever, deadening the interest of all but the most enamored viewer. The interviewees include comedians/performance artists Peggy Shaw and Lois Weaver; a couple who operate a goat dairy farm in the South; Donna J. McBride and Barbara Greir, co-owners of Naiad Press; and several other eloquent women. At its best, the film captures revealing glimpses of the women's thoughts on living and working together as openly lesbian women, as well as the importance of love and relationships. ☮

Lesbian Lykra Shorts: Reservaat

Lesbionage *(1988, 90 min, US, Joyce Compton)*

This low-budget lesbian thriller from Pop Video centers around two bickering lovers whose relationship and private detective partnership are revitalized when they are employed by a blackmailed lesbian congresswoman. The cast of suspects in this humorous and sexy sleuther includes her three jealous lovers and the case soon involves the KBG, a kidnapping and government corruption. ✪

Lianna *(1982, 110 min min, US, John Sayles)*

Director-writer John Sayles' exceptional and humorous exploration of the coming out of the "good wife." Lianna confronts her husband's infidelity, falls in love with her graduate instructor and sets out on her own. A lesbian film directed by a straight man you say? Well, the film might have some flaws, but it more than compensates with many vulnerable and tender moments of budding lesbian self-realization. ✪

The Lickerish Quartet
(1970, 90 min, It/Germany/US, Radley Metzger)

Taking a more lurid approach to a theme that was similarly explored in *Something for Everyone* and Pasolini's *Teorema*, director Radley Metzger's (*Thérèse and Isabelle*) tale involves a stranger (a woman this time) who comes into a household and seduces all in sight. A bored bourgeois family — a husband, wife and teenage son — live in an opulent Italian castle and idle away their time watching porno movies — the son watches in disgust while the parents comment and enjoy both the hetero and lesbian sex scenes. Afterwards, while visiting a traveling circus, they meet a beautiful female motorcycle daredevil who bears a striking resemblance to one of the women in the "smoker." She is invited back to the castle and after all four milk the situation with endless sidelong glances and hungry, yearning stares, the games begin. She is "seduced" by the husband, has a tender outdoor tryst with the brooding son and finally goes back and pounces on mom, still an attractive and youthful woman. This humorously ridiculous soft-core European "art" film effectively intercuts the scenes described with the black-and-white adult movie as well as yet another murder/suspense plot line. The lesbian seduction scene, long in coming, is pretty explicit, but although both characters are into it, it is essentially a one-sided affair. (GB title: *The Erotic Quartet*) ✪

Lifetime Commitment
(1987, 30 min, US, Kiki Zeldes)

Despite its static, almost amateurish direction, this moving story of Karen Thompson's struggle for legal access to her hospitalized lover proves to be a compelling tale. Sharon Kowalski was critically injured in an auto accident in 1983, leaving her in need of constant medical attention. Despite the fact that Karen and Sharon had lived together for four years, exchanged rings and made a lifetime commitment to each other, Sharon's parents denied that their daughter was a lesbian. Backed by the courts, they blocked Karen from many rights traditionally accorded a family member. Karen recounts her frustration in trying to care for her lover and discusses her personal growth, going from a closeted woman — afraid to frequent a lesbian bar — to a national advocate for lesbian and gay partnership rights. Since the film was made, Karen won her case; the December 1991 Minnesota court ruling stated that a "family of affinity...ought to be accorded respect." ✪

Lilith *(1964, 114 min, US, Robert Rossen)*

Jean Seberg (star of Jean-Luc Godard's *Breathless* and Otto Preminger's *Joan of Arc*) gives a strong performance as a schizophrenic woman in a resort-like institution. Warren Beatty plays Vincent, an ex-Army officer training to be an occupational therapist. While trying to help Lilith come to terms with her mother's mental breakdown, he falls in love with her, and as her name's biblical reference suggests, is "persuaded to sin with her." But enter lesbian subplot. Blonde Lilith and her brunette girlfriend (Anne Meacham) walk through the woods holding hands, very aware that jealous Vincent (Beatty) is stalking them. He bursts into the barn just as they are putting on their pants and calls Lilith "a dirty bitch." She retorts with one of her many memorable lines, "If your god loved others as much as he loved you, would you hate him

The Lickerish Quartet

OF LESBIAN INTEREST

for it?" The enraged Vincent, in an effort to "straighten" Lilith out, proceeds to make semi-forcible love to her. Later, as she caresses her own breasts, she tells him she wants to leave the mark of her desire on every living creature. The movie is a bit long and tries to deal with too many complex issues, but is nonetheless poignant as it questions why some people are labeled insane and others are not. ⊛

Long Awaited Pleasure
(1989, 90 min, US, Giovanna Manana)
Lois Weaver and Peggy Shaw, co-founders of the inventive lesbian comedy/musical troupe Split Breaches, are the saving graces in this low-budget production that follows two women who meet and fall in love. Rory, a gangly thirtyish New York dentist, moves to a small Southern city after breaking up with her longtime lover. It is there she meets Sue, a willowy blonde undertaker anxious for a partner. The simple story deals primarily with their initial, tentative talks and dates, which lead up to the dramatic moment of their first kiss and the beginning stages of a love affair. A fine, honest depiction of the awkward moments and exhilarating highs of a budding lesbian relationship. ⊛

Long Time Comin'
(1994, 52 min, Canada, Dionne Brand)
Two African-Canadian women, painter Grace Channer and singer Faith Nolan, both lesbian artists committed to feminist causes and social change, are finely drawn in this revealing and involving documentary. Believing that higher education and the arts have been too long dominated by the entrenched white patriarchy, the two friends work together to create a voice for their community. Through Nolan's politically charged folk songs and Channer's lesbian Afro-centric canvases, the two celebrate their social concerns: feminism, lesbianism and being black. A fine portrait of two memorable women.

Love Game
(1990, 90 min, US, Joyce Compton)
This lesbian romance comedy from Pop Video tells the story of lesbian tennis star Dana Johnson (Georgia West) and her amorous off-the-court melodramas. Dana is an in-demand celebrity, and her partner (Nikki Lake) subsequently tires of never seeing her and running all of her errands. Out of jealousy and anger she starts sleeping with Dana's manager (played by poet Jewel Gomez). Meanwhile, Dana puts the moves on a woman who almost ran her over in the street. The movie's strong points are not its plot or acting, but that it is very funny and that it was made from a lesbian point of view; that alone makes it refreshing. The video includes outtakes, some of which are funnier than the final cut. ⊛

Mädchen in Uniform
(1931, 89 min, Germany, Leontine Sagan)
This 1931 German production is the first in a long line of lesbian-themed films set in boarding schools. Based on the play "Yesterday and Today" by lesbian poet Christa Winsloe, *Mädchen in Uniform* tells the story of a young girl's love for her teacher. Manuela (Hertha Thiele) is sent to a boarding school attended by the daughters of Prussian military officers. There, she develops a deep attach-

ment to her teacher, Fraulein von Bernbourg (Dorothea Wieck). While the headmistress declares Manuela's affections to be scandalous, her classmates convey their support and understanding. When released in America in 1932, the American distributor allowed the censors to make cuts in an attempt to remove what was seen as offensive lesbian content. While the censors' cuts tempered the strength of Manuela's passion, diluting it to appear a simple "schoolgirl crush" to the average straight audience, those who were listening for it could still hear quite clearly the strains of "the love that dare not speak its name." The film went on to be selected by the National Board of Review as one of the Ten Best Foreign Pictures of 1932. The film has enjoyed two, albeit lesser received, remakes over the years: *Muchachas en Uniforme* (Mexico, 1950) and *Mädchen in Uniform* (Germany, 1958). On the political front, the film, seen by many as a plea for humanism during the period of rising fascism, was eventually banned by Goebels and at one point a pro-Nazi ending was tacked on. Soon after the making of the film, director Sagan and many of the cast left Germany. ⊛

Mädchen in Uniform
(1958, 91 min, Germany, Geza Radvanyi)
This lackluster remake of Leontine Sagan's classic 1931 drama stars an effective Romy Schneider as a sensitive student attracted to a teacher (Lilli Palmer) at a repressive girls' boarding school. More lesbian-explicit than the original, the Technicolor film suffered censorship problems in the United States and did not debut there theatrically until 1965.

The Magic of Female Ejaculation
(1991, 14 min, US)
There's magic, but it's on the short side (due to the running time) to this atypical how-to video. The documentary opens with a woman's testimonial on her experiences ejaculating and proceeds to demonstrate, through diagrams and breathing and exercise techniques, how natural and easy it is to ejaculate. ⊛

Mano Destra
(1985-86, 53 min, Germany, Cleo Ubelemann)
Fast becoming a European lesbian cult classic primarily for its insightful handling of its theme of lesbian S&M. The film explores bondage, domination and sensory manipulation among women of all types. Director Cleo Ubelemann's physiological approach to the contentious subject has had some more militant adherents dismiss the film as a mushy romanticization of an intense experience.

The Minders
(1985, 50 min, New Zealand, Judy Rymer)
A strangely ethereal sci-fi, feminist-lesbian film which features a "heaven" populated and ruled by benevolent women and a few equally mellow men. When Stella, an abused housewife, is killed by her husband, she joins the Minders, who in turn observe the earth and telepathically offer encouragement and advice to the needy in pseudo-Guardian Angel fashion (although they never help Stella with her thuggish husband). Bending the rules, Stella is allowed a second chance and is transported back, eventually becoming the roommate to her former husband's current girl-

friend. While there is no overt lesbianism, the relationships between Stella and her roommate and among the female Minders are affectionate, caring and supportive.

Mirror Images II
(1993, 92 min, US, Gregory Hippolyte)

Gregory Hippolyte, director of such lesbian-tinged exploitation flicks as *The Other Woman, Sexual Intent, Secret Games* and the first film of this series, has become the unquestioned king of lesbian titillation for the R-rated heterosexual male video viewer. In this sex-filled thriller, two identical sisters lock heads with each other. Carrie is a sexually uptight woman traumatized by a childhood murder, while Terri is her evil, thought-to-be-dead bisexual twin sister (both are played by Shannon Whirry). Terri, when not working as a prostitute, enjoys fucking Carrie's boyfriends, employees and eventually her husband; taking devilish delight in the rouse. Messed up by all of this, Carrie visits a female psychiatrist, who listens patiently and when Carrie tells her that she is beginning to have sexual feelings for her, the Doc (while placing her hand strategically on her thigh) says, "It's called transference. It's a good thing, don't worry about it." This said, the two quickly undress and make passionate, tongue-lashing, lip-smacking softcore love. Sibling rivalry turns deadly in this tale and although the lesbianism is shown for purely gratuitous reasons, Hippolyte erotically films it with a sensitive, nonjudgmental approach ⊛

Moments — The Making of *Claire of the Moon* *(1992, 70 min, US)*

Fans of the independent lesbian feature *Claire of the Moon*, and those simply interested in the filmmaking process, will enjoy this behind-the-scenes documentary. Essentially a video scrapbook, it takes the viewer into the initial casting sessions, through the frantic, on-location shooting and concludes with the film's enthusiastically received theatrical premiere. Outtakes from the film, five years in the making, and interviews with the beleaguered but determined director Nicole Conn are also included. Some cynics might see this film as simply a vanity production (for the film was made by the same company as *Claire of the Moon*), but it is nevertheless — on its own merit — an interesting peek into how an independent film is made. ⊛

Monsieur Hawarden
(1968, 106 min, Belgium, Harry Kümel)

The film debut of Harry Kümel, the director of the elegant lesbian feature *Daughters of Darkness*, this stylish and inveigling crossdressing lesbian murder mystery is based on a true story set at the

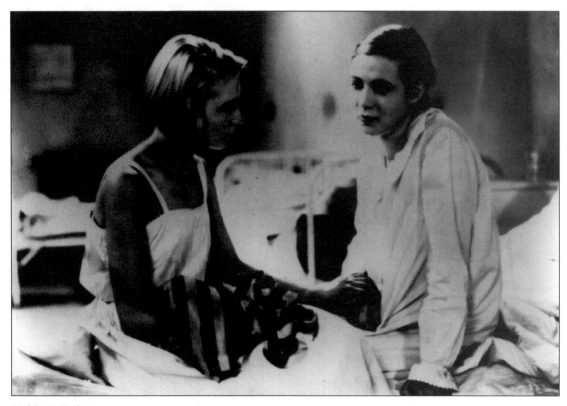

Mädchen in Uniform

turn-of-the-century. The melodrama follows Monsieur Hawarden as he travels to a remote farmhouse with his lovely maid, Victorine. The subject of gossip by the simple residents, Victorine is soon found dead, and her likely killer gone. Being that the film is rarely seen, the mystery can be revealed — for the monsieur is actually Meriora Gillibrand, an aristocratic woman with murder on her hands. Filmed in stark black-and-white photography and dedicated to Joseph von Sternberg, Kümel develops this story of sexual identity, lesbian passion and female drag in an impressively seductive manner.

My Two Loves

(1986, 100 min, US, Noel Black)

Co-written by Rita Mae Brown ("Rubyfruit Jungle") and made for ABC-TV, this tepid drama is still a bit of a classier outing than Brown's previous script, that for the slasher pic *Slumber Party Massacre*. The story revolves around a recently widowed woman (Mariette Hartley) with a teenage daughter who is romantically torn between her new boyfriend (her husband's ex-partner) and a woman executive (Lynn Redgrave). Previously 100% heterosexual, her lesbian side is kindled by the persistent and aggressive Marjorie (Redgrave).

Nea — The Young Emmanuelle

(1978, 140 min, France, Nelly Kaplan)

At 16, Sybille (Ann Zacharias) is already an accomplished book thief and writer of erotic literature ("better than de Sade"). Although she doesn't sleep with women in the movie, she anticipates the opportunity and is more than happy when she spies her mother and her father's sister making love. She later tells her mother that she saw them and asks her what it is like to know the body of another woman. Sybille soon grows tired of being a voyeur and wants to gain experience. She convinces the man who published it that they should sleep together in order to give her material for her next effort. Their relationship sours when she falls in love with him and he starts taking credit for the book. They end up rowing off in a boat together, a traditionally romantic ending for an otherwise unconventional script. Her mother, with Sybille's blessings, leaves her stuffy husband for her female lover. Ⓐ

Night Rhythms

(1992, 99 min, US, Alexander Gregory Hippolyte)

In a role that would make *Basic Instinct*'s Catherine Trammel seem like a lesbian role model, Delia Sheppard plays Bridget, a woman who, when not obsessing about her female lovers or venting rage against men, is plotting revenge-filled murder schemes. Nick West (Martin Hewitt) is an obnoxious late night D.J. whose specialty is whispering sweet little nothings into the pleading ears of his sexually starved female listeners. But he soon finds himself framed for the murder of Honey (Tracy Tweed), a sexy siren he finds dead after the two make love. We give away the "surprise" ending to this sexy (read: semi-porno) thriller (à la the placards carried by feminists and lesbians proclaiming "Catherine Did It!"): After all are said and fucked, we find that Bridget, Nick's radio assistant, was also Honey's former lover and in a rage over Honey's leaving her (and furious that Nick was getting all the girls), she kills Honey. The final

shot of her is as a deranged psycho being carted away by the police. The most amusing scene is a Hollywood fantasy-filled depiction of a sleek lesbian bar, filled with luscious, big-haired women dancing the tango, kissing each other and generally looking decadent. Ⓐ

Nocturne *(1990, 58 min, GB, Joy Chamberlain)*

Made for British TV, *Nocturne* is a perverse acting out of repressed lesbian desire and has been heralded as one of the best lesbian films in years. Marguerite (Lisa Eichhorn), a 45-year-old upper-class woman, returns to her family mansion to attend her mother's funeral. Two young lesbian runaways break into the house, and, in a night of revelry, revelations and flashbacks, Marguerite confronts the buried truth about herself, her mother and her childhood governess. The film is quite disturbing in the style of Hitchcock. Subtle psychological and emotional dynamics between the three characters are developed and are exposed gradually throughout the film. Director Joy Chamberlain carefully constructs the frigid atmosphere of an upper-class British home, offsetting the building tensions of the present with the remembered tensions of Marguerite's past.

Novembermoon

Northern Exposure: "Cicely"

(1992, 52 min, US, Rob Thompson)

Along with routinely making references to Jung, Nietzsche, Kafka and other intellectual icons during their first several seasons, the producers of the television series "Northern Exposure" have routinely introduced gay characters into their mix. The show revolves around the quirky inhabitants of Cicely, a small town on Alaska's Kenai Peninsula. While the operators of the town's bed and breakfast are an openly gay couple, the show's real contribution towards normalizing gay and lesbian characters on primetime TV (see "Roseanne" for the other) came with its "Cicely" episode. This nearly hour-long segment tells the tale of the town's founders, a pair of Sarah Lawrence-educated lesbains (Rosilyn and Cicely) who arrive in Alaska at the turn-of-the-century determined to turn a little backwater mining town into a cultural Mecca. Not only does the episode unflinchingly portray the two women as lovers, but more importantly, it shows them to be the moral superiors of the town's surly denizens. Of course, in the end they must do battle with the town's nefarious villain, resulting in the inevitable tragedy for which the town's name was dedicated. A note of interest: the actress portraying Rosilyn now makes occasional appearances on the show as a schoolteacher. ☯

Nothing to Lose *(1989, 30 min, US)*

"Fat is beautiful" is the message of this low-budget production which features 15 defiantly proud and vocal overweight women. Not a documentary per se, the women alone or together simply read poetry, sing or stage short scenes — all with the theme that they are fed up with the diet-crazed, fat-hating world they live in. With humor and anger, they lay claim to the pride of accepting and loving themselves as they are. ☯

Novembermoon

(1984, 107 min, Germany, Alexandra von Grote)

This ambitious WWII drama by Alexandra von Grote stars Gabriela Osburg as November, a plucky Jewish lesbian whose flight from the Nazis leads her to Paris and freedom. But when Occupation forces enter the city, she is again threatened. Her Parisian lover, Ferial, at grave risk, poses as a collaborator in an attempt to save the life of the woman she loves. A moving film experience that reaches beyond the horrors of WWII as it speaks out against violence, war and the persecution of all minorities.

Obscenity *(1992, 29 min, UK, Joan Bereridge)*

Although only 29 minutes long, this short deserves special mention for its subject matter — that of the 1928 public obscenity trials in the United States and Great Britain on Radclyffe Hall's groundbreaking lesbian novel, "The Well of Loneliness." The film stylistically intercuts re-created courtroom scenes with interviews with various lesbians on their thoughts on the book's relevance to lesbians of today.

Odd Triangle *(1969, 76 min, US, Joe Sarno)*

This cheapie, pre-hard-core porn exploiter is a terribly acted drama which has some appeal for its handling of a housewife's initiation into the boundless possibilities of extramarital lesbian sex. Poor little rich girl Allison, bored and sexually uptight (but who never considers a job), asks her sexually active friend, a toothy bleached blonde named Janet, to help her out. They rent a houseboat with the intent of extra-sexual activities, and to Allison's surprise, Janet brings another woman to the boat. The two make love and eventually entice Allison into the action. Afterwards, guilty but aroused, she is torn between her oafish husband and the possibilities of this forbidden fruit. Sexually explicit for the time, the film's clearly lesbian theme is well developed, although the intent of the film was to excite male audiences with the woman-to-woman lovemaking. ☯

Olivia *(1951, 88 min, France, Jacqueline Audry)*

A young student falls in love with her teacher in this sensitive, moving tale of desire and intrigue set in a turn-of-the-century boarding school. Written, directed and acted by women, the film was based on the 1928 English novel by Dorothy Bussy. Simone Simon (*Cat People*) and Edwige Feuillére star as two sisters who run a school for girls. When a new student, Olivia (Claire Olivia),

arrives, she is enchanted by the place and with the headmistresses, each of whom has her own coterie of girls. A tender relationship between the one sister, Julie (Feuillére), and Olivia soon develops. The film portrays the girls not as victims, but as willing participants and their affair is affectionate and even sensual. Prints were heavily edited on its initial release in Great Britain and the United States, where it was retitled *The Pit of Loneliness* (an obvious reference to Radclyffe Hall's unfilmed lesbian novel, "The Well of Loneliness") and was first advertised with the tag line, "The daring drama of an unnatural love!" Director Audry made 18 features in her long career including a 1955 adaptation of Jean-Paul Sartre's *No Exit* and also worked closely with novelist Colette to bring three of her novels to the screen — *Gigi* (1948), *L'Ingénue Libertine* (1950, US title: *Minne*) and *Mitsou* (1957). ☯

> "Superior to the famous picture with a similar theme, *Mädchen in Uniform...Olivia* falls nothing short of magic!"
>
> *— Time*

> "A frank treatment of abnormal emotionalism in a girls' school."
>
> *— New York Daily News*

> "Beautifully realized...Jacqueline Audry has handled the subject with sensitivity and a wistful, fragile grace...tremendously tender and moving."
>
> — Bosley Crowther, *The New York Times*

On Guard

(1983, 51 min, Australia, Susan Lambert)

A political and social commentary disguised as a thriller, this Australian suspenser begins innocently enough with the depiction of the seemingly ordinary life of a lesbian couple and their children; but underneath the tranquil homelife, an unsettled disquiet is felt. For the women, along with two others, are preparing for an industrial sabotage scheme against a company engaged in genetic reproductive engineering. The execution of their midnight raid on the heavily guarded plant is shown, but the film's real intent is to show these women taking decisive action in a fight for their right to self-determination and against the existing oppressive political (male) structure.

Only the Brave

(1994, 59 min, Australia, Ana Kokkinos)

A lesbian Down Under take on *River's Edge*, this brooding yet touching drama examines the restlessness and alienation of youths (in this case teenage girls) living in the working-class suburbs of Melbourne. The story centers around the intense friendship and eventual breaking up of two daughters of Greek immigrant families: Alex (Ellen Mandalis) and Vicki (Dora Kaskanis). Alex is a budding lesbian attached to her heterosexual friend Vicki. Complicating her life is a developing crush on one of her female high school teachers. Depicting a grim, often times violent dead-end world, very unlike one's typical vision of sunny, carefree Australia, the film follows the two girls' close and sometimes sensual friendship, which undergoes drastic changes as Alex begins to seek her own identity. Unlike most American teen angst dramas,

Only the Brave does not cop out by presenting a light at the end of the tunnel, instead retaining its unrelentingly grim view of love and life. An unflinching drama that promises much from lesbian director Ana Kokkinos.

Other Mothers *(1993, 54 min, US, Lee Shallat)*

American television's history of handling gay and lesbian themes has been earnest, if a bit stilted and far too few. This CBS Schoolbreak Special is a drama about a teenage boy who faces prejudice in his school when people find out that he has two mothers. Definitely a cut above the "heartbreak of being queer" dramas that are so prevalent, the special is quite effective in handling many aspects of lesbian/gay parents' battles to gain acceptance in a homophobic world. Will, a budding sports jock who makes the varsity basketball team in his freshman year, is an affable, "normal" kid who seems to have had no problems being raised by his mother and her lover since he was two. His parents — his birth mother Linda (Joanna Cassidy) and her lover Paula (Meredith Baxter) — are both loving to Will. They are presented as successful executives living in typical heterosexual upper middle-class suburbia. Problems arise when the two women want to join the team's booster club, fueling animosity and gossip that results in Will's teammates, classmates and even his coach giving him the cold shoulder. He loves his parents but doesn't want to be different and has a difficult time bearing the cross of having queer parents, eventually becoming ashamed of them for the first time. How he (and the two

women) handle the tough situation is presented with sensitivity and realism. The depiction of the two lesbians is surprisingly complex: they are attractive, non-stereotypical and successful, although Paula is a little too headstrong (and militant) in expecting even narrow-minded people to accept them. With the issue of lesbian and gay parents increasingly in the news (according to the Gay and Lesbian Parent Coalition, between six and eight million children are being raised in gay or lesbian households), this drama hopes to calm the fires of fear and prejudice. The teledrama was written by Amy Dunkleberger and the executive producer was Joseph Stern, who spent four years pushing the project past reluctant TV executives.

P4W — Prison for Women
(75 min, Canada, Janis Cole & Holly Drake)

Canadian documentarians Janis Cole and Holly Drake (*Hookers on Davie; Minimum Charge, No Cover*) enter into Canada's only federal prison for women and the result is a personal, touching and harrowing look at five of its inmates. Reportedly taking four years to make, the film reveals the reasons why the women are there (their convictions range from drug dealing to murder), their prison relationships and daily routines, as well as their ensuing loneliness, bitterness, pain and survival instincts. While not really a lesbian film, there is a sensitive depiction of a behind-bars lesbian relationship. A simple, humanistic look at prison life, the film's haunting power comes mainly through the voices of its subjects.

Persona *(1966, 81 min, Sweden, Ingmar Bergman)*

A fascinating, complex story about Elisabeth, a well-known actress (Liv Ullmann), who suddenly decides to stop speaking, and Alma, her nurse (Bibi Andersson), who takes her to an island to convalesce. Alma is planning a conventional life whereas Elisabeth is shunning her husband and son, apparently struggling with her identity as artist and as mother. Ullmann gives a haunting performance without uttering a word. Her physical warmth puts Alma at ease and allows her to use the silence as a void to project the personality of a perfect friend. In this atmosphere of forced intimacy, she tells Elisabeth her secrets and soon falls in love with her. After Alma reads a letter from Elisabeth to her doctor which discloses Alma's secrets, Alma starts to take her silence personally. Do they want to *be* each other or *beat* each other? A vicious struggle for identity ends with Elisabeth scratching Alma's arm and sucking her blood. The movie is an erotically charged and remarkably intuitive (not to mention beautifully shot in black and white) look at the dark side of the two women's relationship. ☮

Personal Best
(1982, 124 min, US, Robert Towne)

Award-winning screenwriter Robert Towne directed this tale of two women who become friends and lovers during tryouts for the Olympics. Of course, heterosexuality triumphs as the outcome implies that autonomy and lesbianism don't mix. Mariel Hemingway plays the fast but feckless Chris who gets a chance to make the team through her involvement with Tori (Patrice Donnelly). Feeling that Chris is in denial about the nature of their relationship, Tori says, "We may be friends, but every once in awhile we fuck each other." Their jealous, bitter coach (Scott Glenn) adds to their relationship's demise by pitting them against

Other Mothers

each other personally and professionally. Chris ends up dating a man while Tori remains firmly and proudly lesbian, a sexy one at that. They both make the Olympics. Tori congratulates Chris on the medal and her boyfriend, saying he's cute, "for a man." The movie runs a bit long and the cinematography is unimpressive with too many lingering group shower scenes and crotch close-ups. ⊛

Poison Ivy *(1992, 89 min, US, Katt Shea Ruben)*

Drew Barrymore fans should not miss her as the sleazy teen (Ivy) who befriends Sylvie (Sara Gilbert), a self-proclaimed "politically correct feminist type" who thinks she might be a lesbian. A familiar battle for identity ensues as the two outcasts venture to see if a slut and an intellectual can maintain a friendship. Ivy soon manipulates her way into Sylvie's wealthy family and sets her sights on seducing dad (Tom Skerritt), whose wife (Cheryl Ladd) is dying of emphysema. The two teens eventually graduate from stick-on tattoos to real ones, but the focus soon turns away from their seemingly tender friendship and towards Ivy's quest to usurp mom's place in daddy's bed. She starts wearing Sylvie's mother's clothes and eventually pushes her out of the bedroom window, leading everyone to believe it was suicide. The infamous kiss between Barrymore and Gilbert comes just before the former plummets to the same fate as Ladd. This movie may be melodramatic, predictable and based on many unfortunate stereotypes, but it sure makes for amusing trash. ⊛

Personal Best

Portrait of a Marriage

(1990, 220 min, GB/US/NZ, Stephen Whittaker)

Made in conjunction with the BBC, Boston's PBS affiliate WGBH and New Zealand television, this opulent melodrama tells of the passionate but tempestuous love affair between writers Vita Sackville-West (Janet McTeer) and Violet Trefusis (Cathryn Harrison). Disregarding the protestations of Sackville-West's husband, politician Harold Nicolson (played by David Haig), Trefusis' fiancé and social decorum, the two women openly loved each other, creating one of the great scandals of their time. Their romance, played against the backdrop of post-WWI Europe, is eventually undermined by the two women's increasing obsessiveness with each other, spawning destructive feelings of possessiveness and jealousy. Written by Penelope Mortimer, the film's strength is in its good acting, elegant art direction and impressive cinematography, but it suffers from a slow moving, uninvolving screenplay. *Portrait of a Marriage* aired without problems in Great Britain and New Zealand, but for American PBS stations, 34 minutes were censored, primarily the lesbian love scenes.

Prisonnieres

(1988, 100 min, France, Charlotte Silvera)

The opening scene in this hard-hitting women-in-prison drama is set at the Montparnesse station in Paris where seven chained women are led to a train that will take them to the notorious Rennes women's prison in Brittany. There, behind the stone walls, episodic tales unfold of prison life: of the petty repression and harsh cruelty of the guards and matrons, as well as the violence, resignation, rebellion and bonding (sexual and otherwise) of the prisoners. Unlike the many lurid films of the genre, *Prisonnieres* attempts to be evenhanded, non-sensationalistic and even sympathetic to the prisoners' plight. Marie-Christine Barrault, Annie Girardot, Agnes Soral and Bernadette Lafont star in this film which features a diversity of lesbian life behind bars.

Private Pleasures

(1985, 60 min, US, O. Wow)

This safe sex, erotic video from Fatale Video offers an exploration into two real-life lesbian lovers' fantasies and sexuality. While Asian beauty Mariko peeks voyeuristically, attractive brunette Teri and blonde bombshell Caerage, at home in a ritzy penthouse apartment, engage in a variety of sexual games, including butch/femme seduction, play dressing and simple down-on-the-floor fucking. ⊛

Privilege *(1990, 103 min, US, Yvonne Rainer)*

Veteran New York-based independent filmmaker Yvonne Rainer, known for her experimental, avant-garde films (*Lives of Performers*, *Film About a Woman Who...*) on feminist issues and the performing arts, directed this semidocumentary about menopause. Rainer structures the film through the eyes of a black filmmaker named Yvonne (Rainer is white) who interviews several witty and eloquent middle-aged women. Interspersed throughout are scenes from old "educational" films, a snippet of a Lenny Bruce monologue and a collection of computer-driven facts and figures. Not lesbian themed, the film is an important document for all women and features as one of its characters Brenda (Blaire Baron), a lesbian who reads from Joan Nestle's erotic novel "A Restricted Country" to an unlikely group of lawyers, men and professionals.

Queen of the Night (La Reina de la Noche) *(1994, 117 min, Mexico, Arturo Ripstein)*

Deadly somber, darkly lit and with a story that unfolds at a snail's pace, this lurid, fictionalized account of Lucha Reyes, famed Mexican torch singer of the 1930s and '40s, would be a forgettable film if it were not for director Arturo Ripstein's startling exposé on the troubled woman's lesbianism. The story begins at the start of Lucha's (Patricia Rayes Spindola) long, torturous downfall, precipitated by her intensely jealous love for a philandering man she impestuously marries. This singular heterosexual facet of her life is counterbalanced by her more dominant unapologetic lesbian side — one that includes a lifetime love for Jaira (Blanca Guerra). Included are scenes of her fondling unsuspecting women in nightclubs, her possible incestuous intentions on her teenage stepdaughter and (in a possible cinematic first) an encounter in which she takes home a young female prostitute who reminds her of her now-gone Jaira. Amidst the booze, drugs and sexual excesses lies a supremely independent woman who (for reasons never satisfactorily explained) descends into a pit of self-despair. Despite its failures, however, the film presents a singularly vivid portrait of a sensuous woman who is fearless in expressing her lesbian desires.

Quest for Love

(1988, 94 min, South Africa, Helena Nogueira)
Based on Gertrude Stein's short novel, "Q.E.D.," this intriguing lesbian love story and political thriller was South Africa's first woman-directed commercial feature. A tenderly told lesbian love triangle between three attractive women unfolds surrounded by the taut drama of Southern Africa's political instability and governmental repression. Alexandra is a bisexual writer and activist who, in the aftermath of black independence in the fictional nation of Mozania, embarks on a leisurely cruise on a yacht with Dorothy, a woman who desperately loves her, and Mabel, a flighty young woman who in turn has fallen in love with Dorothy. While the shifting alliances of the women continue, Alexandra's boyfriend Mike, who is involved in some shady political maneuvering, comes on board, rocking the fragile situation. Unusually affectionate and unstereo-typical in its depiction of the lesbian love interests and the women's sensuality, the film is also daring in depicting South Africa's political heavy-handedness, torture and government-sanctioned murder. Stop reading if you have not seen the film and want to be surprised...but another exciting twist in the film is that Alexandra, heterosexually torn not only by Mike but by a black artist as well, chooses to go with her lesbian side and Dorothy in the end. ⊗

A Question of Love

(1978, 104 min, US, Jerry Thorpe)
Based on a true story, this made-for-TV drama is about a nurse in Ohio who moves in with her female lover accompanied by her two sons. When the older child wants to go back to his father, a tem-

Private Pleasures

pestuous and hard-fought court battle ensues. Great performances are delivered by both Gena Rowlands and Jane Alexander. ⊗

Red Heat

(1985, 104 min, US/West Germany, Robert Collector)
Linda Blair and Sylvia Kristel team up in this pedestrian Cold War women-in-prison flick set in a nameless communist country. Blair, an American innocent, is captured by Communists after inadvertently witnessing the abduction of a political dissident. She is sent to a hellhole women's prison where the lesbian warden is sexually kept in check by one of her prisoners, Sophia (Kristel). Kristel camps it up as Sophia, a red-haired, power-hungry vixen who reigns over her bevy of tatooed beauties with a mixture of cruelty and sexual control. Containing the requisite hair-pulling-in-their-underwear fight scenes and snippets of gratuitous nudity, the film's darker, anti-gay side makes this action drama of real social interest for its equating of lesbianism with communism and repression — only the "bad girls" are lesbian. Scenes of orgies, outright rape and sexual violence are all part of a futile system intent on controlling the masses. Kristel's Sophia, a slinky, sadistic, lesbian seductress, borders on the deplorable; but if one ignores the politics, she's simply an over-the-top camp caricature. ⊗

Reflections: A Moment in Time

(1987, 37 min, US, Janet Liss)
Megan and Xavier reminisce over breakfast on the beginning of their three-year relationship. Warm and tender, the film also deals with issues of racism and homophobia. ⊗

Richard's Things

(1980, 104 min, GB, Anthony Harvey)

Originally made for British TV, but released theatrically in the U.S., this drama wallows in somber pretentiousness and is unusually stagnant for its subject matter. Liv Ullmann stars as a widow who is seduced by her late husband's girlfriend. The two get together initially out of curiosity, a desire for companionship and to share their feelings about the man they loved. But what soon develops is a deeper relationship, and the two women begin a lesbian affair and fall in love. Good premise, but sexual seduction never looked so dreary as Ullmann goes through the film as if stuck in the frozen existential wasteland of Bergmania. ⊛

Rome — Open City

(1945, 101 min, Italy, Roberto Rossellini)

A harrowing account of ordinary citizens caught up in the horrors of war, this early neorealist classic was made just before the end of the war and was filmed on the streets of the ravaged city, utilizing mainly non-professional actors. Set in 1944 during the final bloody months of German occupation, the story concerns three people: an Italian Resistance fighter, a pregnant woman who is killed assisting him, and her sister who takes up the cause only to be betrayed by an informer. That informer, Marina (Maria Michi), is depicted as a fun-loving opportunist: a drug addict who plays informant and sexual play thing to a particularly evil lesbian Gestapo agent. From the first sight of the agent — in dark clothing, sporting thin, arched eyebrows and a lecherous grin — one knows she's trouble. She is shown fawning over the complying young woman, offering gifts, caressing her — even at a Gestapo party where the male officers remain unfazed by the two. She demands "affection," uses her and casts her aside when done. A startling depiction, and possibly one of the first films to luridly associate lesbianism with debauchery and domination. ⊛

The Room of Words

(1990, 115 min, US/Italy, Franco Mol)

Before Philip Kaufman's *Henry & June*, there was this more pedestrian yet racy screen version of the steamy relationship between artist Anais Nin, writer Henry Miller and June, the woman they both loved. Filmed entirely in New Orleans, the film features elegantly dressed people in equally elegant surroundings spending their time expounding on love, desire and lust in the most elegant and tasteful manner, of course! Showing off plenty of gratuitous naked women's flesh, the story revolves around the ever shifting power relationships between the seductive Nin, the manipulative and insecure Miller and the pretty blonde bombshell femme June. A little awkward at times, especially in the acting department, this titillating look at the dangerous sexual games of the threesome could have resulted in just a straight man's lurid peek at lesbian love. But instead it's sensitively filmed and with a surprisingly strong amount of true longing and love between the two women.

Safe Is Desire

(1993, 60 min, US, Debi Sundahl)

Lesbian erotica gets no hotter or safer than in this sizzler locally produced in San Francisco by Blush Entertainment. Dianne and Allie are an interracial couple whose mutual sexual attraction gets a cold slap in the face when the two can not agree on the need for safe sex. In an effort to win Dianne over to the joys and protections of safer sex, Allie takes her to a lesbian sex club where a group of highly charged performers, the Safer Sex Sluts, demonstrate the pleasures of dental dams, saran wrap, latex, role-playing and protected sex toys, culminating in a frenzied orgy. Far from simple dyke porn, the film's graphic sex scenes are never (OK, rarely) gratuitous, as it attempts to be both funny and informative in its depiction of lesbian romance coupled with sexual responsibility. ⊛

Salmonberries

(1991, 94 min, Germany, Percy Adlon)

Written and directed by Percy Adlon (*Celeste, Sugarbaby*), *Salmonberries* has much in common with his earlier *Bagdad Cafe* (surreal cinematic flights of fancy, a haunting soundtrack and lots of landscape). Set in the desolate, no-man's land of Alaska, the quirky drama portrays the developing emotional bonds between two women of very different backgrounds. Singer k.d. lang plays an orphaned Eskimo who hides her/his gender beneath baggy layers of clothing and who develops an attraction to Roswitha, the local librarian of the town of Kotzebue. Roswitha (Rosel Zech) resists her affections; however, lang's determined courting climaxes in a tremendous tease of a love scene...or not a love scene, as it were. Although ultimately frustrating as a lesbian film because of this lack of consummation, *Salmonberries* is satisfying for other reasons, the most notable being the presence of k.d. lang and her haunting soundtrack featuring the theme song, "Barefoot." ⊛

Scrubbers *(1982, 90 min, GB, Mai Zetterling)*

Far from being another lurid, exploitative women-in-prison film, this intense drama about a tough crop of women inmates at a dingy British Borstal is told with daunting realism and sensitivity. Observing a diverse cross-section of inmates, from the black lesbian lovers (one who returns to prison just to rejoin her faithless lover) to the mute anorexic, the leather-jacketed tough girl and the baby-faced heroine, the film documents their small joys,

Scrubbers

oppressive duties and interpersonal sparring and painful yearnings. Bawdy, crude and harrowing, this serious yet, at times, funny film features performers who are feisty and unforgettably human. ☮

"A comic and tragic tale about tough women in a hellhole girls' prison. There's plenty of violence, humor, lesbianism...real and gripping."
— Dori De Galle, *The New York Native*

The Seashell and the Clergyman
(1928, 44 min, France, Germaine Dulac)
Written by surrealist Antonin Artaud, this pioneering work, one of the most celebrated avant-garde films ever made, caused an uproar upon its initial release. French audiences groused that director Germaine Dulac "feminized" the original script, while in England it was banned by the British censors for being "so cryptic as to be almost meaningless." The censors went on to write, "If this film has a meaning, it is doubtless objectionable." The story centers on the frenzied fantasies of a sexually repressed but celibate clergyman whose dreams take on lusty and bizarre twists. A fascinating avant-garde classic.

Focus on: *Germaine Dulac*
Lesbian filmmaker Germaine Dulac (1882-1942), who was born in France as Germaine Saisset-Schneider, was a pioneer in avant-garde and feminist filmmaking during the prodigious arts explo-

Germaine Dulac

sion that was centered in Paris in the 1920s. Her The Smiling Madame Beaudet *(1923) deals with the liberation of a repressed bourgeois housewife and is considered one of the first, if not the first, feminist films ever made. Dulac began working as a theatre critic and playwright before venturing into conventional filmmaking in 1916 with* Les Soeurs Enemies. *She soon embraced the tenets of the avant-garde movement, also known as French Impressionism, and alternated between her abstract, experimental style and films of a more conventional nature. She eventually moved into documentary filmmaking and worked until her death, making newsreels for Pathé-Journal and Gaumont.*

The Second Awakening of Christa Klages
(1977, 93 min, Germany, Margarethe von Trotta)
Director Margarethe von Trotta's first solo effort is an intense political drama that embraces the theme of closeness between women. Christa (Tina Engel) is a young mother who, distraught over the prospect that her children's day care center is running out of money, executes a bank robbery with the assistance of her lover Werner and another friend. Werner is killed during the attempt and when it becomes clear that the police are after her, Christa flees to the Portuguese country house of her friend Ingrid. A lesbian relationship is suggested between the two women, a situation that threatens both women's safety.

Focus on: *Margarethe von Trotta*
Recurring themes in the films of Margarethe von Trotta include feminism, the sisterhood of women and radical politics as an answer to political repression. The women in her films are intelligent, committed and contradictory yet mutually dependent on one another. Although lesbianism is only a marginal sub-theme in a few of her films, her feminist approach often includes two distinctly different women (one the pragmatist, the other a romantic) involved in an intense, conflict-filled relationship. She has gained an international reputation with such films as Sisters on the Balance of Happiness *(1979),* Marianne and Julianne *(1981) (featuring a lesbian protagonist),* Sheer Madness *(1982) and her nonfiction film on the German revolutionary* Rosa Luxemburg *(1987). Born in Berlin in 1942, von Trotta, who is married to fellow director Volker Schlöndorff, began as a stage and film actress in both Berlin and Paris, but soon began to work as a screenwriter and eventually became a director. Early in her career, she worked with Claude Chabrol and Rainer Werner Fassbinder, acting in several of their films including* Gods of the Plague *(1969) and* Beware of a Holy Whore *(1970). It was at that time she began the longtime professional collaboration with her husband, scripting, acting in and co-directing seven films with him including* A Free Woman *(1972),* The Lost Honor of Katharina Blum *(1975) and* Coup de Grace *(1976). In 1981, she wrote the screenplay for his riveting drama* Circle of Deceit.

Seven Women *(1966, 87 min, US, John Ford)*
Anne Bancroft stars as the chain-smoking, cowboy cross-dressing Dr. Cartwright. She's tough, bold, intelligent and doesn't take shit from anyone (until the end, when she is forced — albeit heroically — into a submissive role). The film also features Margaret Leighton as Agatha Andrews, the repressed lesbian spinster with

She Must Be Seeing Things

the hots for Sue Lyon. Set in 1935 China in an all-women's mission, *Seven Women* is remarkable for offering an intense psychological study of its female characters. Unfortunately, the portrayal of the film's Mongolian robbers is not so enlightened, falling into the usual Hollywood racist stereotypes in the last half of the picture. Director John Ford's last film.

Shades of Black
(1993, 115 min, US, Mary Haverstick)
Alternately refreshing and frustrating, this independent lesbian drama of first love was filmed not in a big city where lesbian activism flourishes, but in the Pennsylvania Dutch city of Lancaster. A first feature for Mary Haverstick, the story centers on the evolving relationship between the pretty but insecure Kate (a bicyclist and photographer) and the slightly older, and much more fucked-up, Lilly. Hired to photograph an avant-garde dance piece, Kate is immediately attracted to the sensuous Lilly who, though aggressive, is sensitive to Kate's undefined lesbian identity. Their love affair never materializes, however, as prospects of a normal relationship are constantly blunted by Lilly's neuroticism (comically reminding one of a lesbian Glenn Close in *Fatal Attraction*) which violently and repeatedly flares up. While this earnest effort is a step in the right direction for American independent lesbian features, the film suffers from being overly long and much too leisurely paced to keep a general audience interested. *Shades of Black* does provide an interesting example

of just how differently lesbians and gay men approach filmmaking: In a typical low-budget male gay film, sex comes fast and furious and the sorting out of the personal aspects of the relationship comes later; here, the sexual interest between the two women is kept at a high level with no pay-off in the end (see *Claire of the Moon* for a similar, although consummated, story line). The emotional and sexual attraction between the women is the entire basis of the story, making the sexual aspects of the relationship secondary in importance.

Shadows (1985, 30 min, US, Caerage & Teri)
Leather and the lesbian couple! Fatale Video's series on lesbian erotica received its start with this steamy sexual drama starring real-life lovers Caerage and Teri. After a romp on a motorcycle, the couple playfully descend into a basement where, with the aid of whips and other sexual paraphernalia, they engage in sucking, fucking, whipping and riding (not actually in that order). The couple's knowledge of each other's bodies is evident in this quality production. ✪

She Must Be Seeing Things
(1988, 85 min, US, Sheila McLaughlin)
Independent New York filmmaker Sheila McLaughlin's lesbian love story explores the complex sexual and emotional commitment of two women professionals. The story follows the rocky relationship of Agatha, a lawyer, and Jo, a filmmaker. While Jo is out of

town, Agatha comes upon her diary and photos which suggest that she is developing an interest in men and may be unfaithful to her. Agatha's growing jealousy and her frantic attempts to keep her wavering lover interested result in her donning men's clothing and spying on her unsuspecting partner. While not entirely successful there are moments of great insight and fine acting by Sheila Dabney and Lois Weaver. ⊛

"A wryly sophisticated comedy...plays like a lesbian homage to *Unfaithfully Yours*."
— *Boston Globe*

The Silence

(1963, 95 min, Sweden, Ingmar Bergman)

This, the final installment of Bergman's trilogy on faith which includes *Through a Glass Darkly* and *Winter Light*, is a characteristically intense and disturbing family and sexual drama. Anna (Gunnel Lindblom), a free-spirited mother of a ten-year-old boy, and her repressed lesbian sister, Ester (Ingrid Thulin), unexpectedly stop in an unnamed Eastern European city when Ester becomes ill. Holed up in a luxury hotel, the sisters' long simmering tensions with each other begin to come to the surface. Despite a lifetime of being emotionally and physically close, Anna strives to break away from her domineering sibling. With her hair severly pulled back, Ester is depicted as a lonely, tormented woman who, despite her respiratory sickness, resorts to smoking, drinking and masturbation to stave off her increasing feelings of emptiness. She feels contentment only when in the presence of her sister, but Anna, in a determined effort to break free, flaunts her affections by having sex with a stranger, which only fuels Ester's jealousy. Far from being a sympathetic portrayal of lesbianism, Bergman uses Ester's sexuality as a symbol of her neuroses contrasted with the life-affirming activities of the heterosexual Anna. ⊛

The Silent Thrush

(1992, 100 min, Taiwan, Shengfu Cheng)

This bombastic melodrama, set among the very unhappy members of a traveling popular opera cast and crew in present-day Taiwan would receive little notice if it were not for its interesting lesbian subplot. While everyone is shouting and generally heaving themselves about, Chia-feng, the show's butch dyke star, quietly falls in love with Yuh, a pretty young crew member. Their backstage romance, which the cast and crew suprisingly accept nonchalantly, provides just about the only sweet moments in this otherwise hyperventilating soap opera. A second, even tougher lesbian, the troupe's business manager, is also depicted with humor and sympathy.

Silkwood *(1983, 128 min, US, Mike Nichols)*

Meryl Streep gives one of her many remarkable performances in the role of Karen Silkwood, a nuclear plant worker who died under mysterious circumstances after uncovering damaging information on the plant's hazardous working conditions. Written by Nora Ephron and Alice Arlen, the drama is tense, harrowing and compelling. Kurt Russell co-stars as her boyfriend Drew and Cher plays Silkwood's lesbian roommate, Dolly Pelliker. Cher's portrayal of the personable but lonely Dolly is quite refreshing, complex and

affecting. She is seen in a tender but short-lived relationship with a lover, Diana Scarwid, who is quite funny as her lover Angela, an outrageous mortuary beautician. The relationship between Karen and Dolly, who regard each other in very different ways, is indicative of the unrequited love familiar to so many gays and lesbians who develop affections for their straight friends. Before taking the role, director Nichols said to Cher of Dolly, "It's a wonderful part. She's a lesbian, but she's a wonderful lesbian." Cher has said that "I didn't want to play Dolly with a pack of Marlboros rolled up in my T-shirt sleeve...the result is refreshingly unconventional." ⊛

Simone *(1986, 90 min, France, Christine Ehm)*

Written and directed by 19-year-old French filmmaker Christine Ehm, this first feature played at the New York Gay Film Festival, International Gay and Lesbian Film Festival (Amsterdam) and Women's International Film Festival (Paris). Simone, a mysterious stranger, enters the life of a suicidal young woman, Francoise. A bond between them gradually develops and although the evidence of a lesbian relationship between them is minimal (one kiss and many exchanged glances), an erotic tension develops between the two as they spend time together in Francoise's apartment. The director's striking use of a mutating color palette is a fascinating visual element of this film.

Singapore Sling *(1992, 90 min, US)*

Film noir meets kinky sexuality in this bizarre tale of a mother-daughter's incestuous love and the (male) stranger who tears them apart. A young man's search for his lost girlfriend leads him to a dark mansion where a French- and English-speaking woman and her American daughter live. First seen burying alive a beaten and stabbed man, the two women live out their lives dressed in slinky lingerie and playing various sexually charged S&M games with each other. While obviously deranged, the two women prove to be a dangerous pair as they capture the man, chain him up, and sexually abuse him (and much more). Part splatter film, part sex film and part David Lynch nightmare, the film's cavalier attitude toward lesbianism is possibly its most sane angle. Not for the squeamish. ⊛

Sister Emmanuelle

(1981, 90 min, Italy/US, Joseph Warren)

A fevered, mostly lesbian, romp, this cheesy exploitation film "in the tradition of *Emmanuelle*" offers exotic locales (Venice and a castle-like convent), a nymphomaniac beauty (Laura Genser as Monika) and a bevy of sexually starved women and nuns. This entertainingly lurid and sexually explicit tale follows the amorous adventures of blonde sexpot Monika who, after bedding her beautiful stepmother, is sent to a convent school to cool down her libido. However, she soon sends several of the students into a frenzy of sexual corruption. Monika seduces her studious roommate Anna, quickly turning her into a quivering mass of Sapphic desire and jealousy. She then sets her ravenous eyes on Sister Emmanuelle, a statuesque and sexually repressed black nun. Truly ridiculous, the film was made by and for men, but the lesbian lovemaking scenes are surprisingly erotic and effectively handled. True, a lesbian bombshell who pounces on all is not exactly positive role-playing, but in purely sexual terms, it's a stimulating watch. ⊛

Silkwood

Sluts and Goddesses Video Workshop
(1993, 52 min, US, Maria Beatty & Annie Sprinkle)
Few will be prepared for this wildly entertaining, sexually frank and humorously tongue-in-cheek all-female video workshop which attempts to dispel and explore the myths of female sexuality. Former porno film star, now celebrated performance artist and nascent filmmaker, Annie Sprinkle is a delight as a demented sex education teacher/guru who takes us on an exploration into women's many pleasurable and exciting sexual personas. Sprinkle, along with her ten "Transformation Facilitators," offers helpful tips like, "When it comes to makeup, too much is never enough" and "You haven't lived fully until you've had your body painted." This enjoyable search for your "inner slut" also includes suggestions on how to have fun with body hair, body piercing, choosing a new name as well as essential sexercises — from group masturbation and female ejaculation demonstrations (featuring a five-minute orgasm!) to learning about your private parts ("Can you find your cervix?"). A must for feminists and lesbians with a sense of humor. ⊛

Sonia Speaks — Going Farther Out of Our Minds *(1988, 100 min, US)*
In an exhilarating speech, videotaped at UC Santa Cruz, Sonia Johnson lectures on the theme of patriarchy and how women are enslaved and colonized by 5,000 years of "violence and political terrorism" caused by the existing system. Rejecting the "practical" feminist approach of gaining power and eliciting change (i.e. working within the system), Sonia, as the vocal outsider, is compelled to seek a vision of women leaving the "senile patriarchal" society behind and beginning to live in a new world right now. Sonia's ideas (which in this tape do not deal with any aspects of lesbianism) are fascinating, insightful and do not become bogged in intellectual or metaphysical details. See it with some men in attendance and watch the fireworks! ⊛

Sotto Sotto
(1984, 104 min min, Italy, Lina Wertmuller)
The prototypical machismo-obsessed Italian male must come to grips with the sexual freedoms and diversity of the late 20th century in this wild sexual comedy that is both illuminating and troubling in its depiction of two women in love with each other. Set in Naples, the story revolves around Ester and Adele, two friends who witness two women kissing in a Roman ruins garden. Transfixed by the sight, the two unhappily married women look forlorn, seemingly wishing for a special, hitherto unfelt kind of love. The next day Ester recounts a dream in which she saw herself as Ingrid Bergman in the film *Notorious* while Adele, in the Cary Grant role, plants on her a "real kiss, a slow kiss." With this revelation, the two fall in romantic, but unconsummated love. They return home to their husbands, but both lose interest in them as they pine away for each other. Adele's husband is sent away while Oscar, Ester's husband becomes upset with the notion that his wife is in love with another. He soon works himself into a jealous rage, determined to find the man who has taken away his wife's love. During this time, he discovers that the world is not so clear-cut in its sexual relations; he meets bisexuals (one who claims that in 20 years 80% of people will be bisexual), gays, transvestites and transsexuals. He becomes especially violent when he discovers that his rival is a woman. The final outcome will disappoint, but the love between the women (though limited to a quick kiss) is terrifically romantic and tender. ⊛

The Spy Who Came
(1969, 71 min, US, Ron Wertheim)
This independent, pre-porn murder mystery is notable for its images of a beautiful but particularly sadistic lesbian. A young detective goes to the 9th Circle Bar in Greenwich Village (interestingly, this was a longtime gay bar which has since closed) and picks up an almost skeletal woman. This encounter soon gets him involved with a group of hippie, queer and Arab blackmailers who run a white slavery ring. The women in charge of prepping the girls is a slinky blonde lesbian who likes to sample the wares when she's not torturing the unwilling. What really upsets her is when her boss forces her to have sex with the detective. When she is accused of being sick, she retorts venomously, "Is it I who is sick, or is it you, Mr. Man!" Her girls get her in the end.

Suburban Dykes
(1990, 30 min, US, Debi Sundahl)
From Fatale Video comes this featurette, another in their series of lesbian safer sex erotica. Pepper and Nina Hartley are a couple who, on a whim, decide to use a phone sex service. Their call soon turns into a steamy sexual encounter. Emboldened by their initial try, the two women hire Sharon, a butch female escort who takes their fantasies and makes them hot realities in an orgasmic three-way encounter. ⊛

Terrorist Bridesmaids
(1991, 45 min, US, Deana Bomhof)
Fans of lesbian comedians and performance comedy acts should be interested in this video featuring four comedians — Helene Lantry, Betsy Salkind, Dorothy Dwyer and Susan McGinnis. The video transfer is a bit below average and the sound is not as clear as it should be, but the comedians more than make up for the production shortfalls. ⊛

Thank God I'm a Lesbian *(1992, 55 min, Canada, Laurie Colbert & Dominique Cardona)*
One of the more celebrated of the lesbian documentaries that played the lesbian/gay film festival circuit in 1993, *Thank God I'm a Lesbian* is both entertainingly animated and enlightening in its

attempts to define (and at the same time expand the definition of) what it means to be a lesbian today. Juxtaposed with footage from the Toronto Gay Pride Parade are interviews with articulate women of all ages and ethnic origins including writers Sarah Schulman, Dionne Brand, Nicole Broussard and musician Lee Pui Ming. They, and others, offer a wide range of opinions on such topics as coming out, racism, bisexuality, S&M, outing, fidelity, AIDS and the evolution of the feminist and lesbian movement.

Thelma and Louise

(1991, 120 min, US, Ridley Scott)
A wildly entertaining and remakably accomplished road movie that stars Geena Davis and Susan Sarandon as the title characters, two friends who leave their male counterparts and embark on a leisurely weekend outing. En route, however, their vacation turns deadly when Davis is assaulted and Sarandon guns down the would-be rapist. Stylish and witty, the film follows their series of escalating crim-inal escapades as the two women break away from

Thelma and Louise

the confines of a male-dominated world (periodically venting their rage) and search for their own identity. Sarandon and Davis are both tremendous, each creating enormously appealing and sub-stantial characters. The microcosm of male society is represented by Harvey Keitel, Michael Madsen and Brad Pitt. Though thor-oughly mainstream in its outlook, the film struck a nerve among women and before long "Thelma and Louise Live" bumper stick-ers were cropping up everywhere. ⊗

These Three

(1936, 93 min, US, William Wyler)
In 1936, Samuel Goldwyn Company bought the rights to Lillian Hellman's controversial play, "The Children's Hour," knowing full well that the work's lesbian theme would not pass the restrictive Hayes Code (they even forbade the use of the play's original title including its mention in advertising or promotion). Hellman was hired to adapt her story, and she changed the play's "scandalous" relationship from a lesbian one to a heterosexual triangle. Karen (Merle Oberon) and Martha (Miriam Hopkins) are compassionate teachers who open a girls' school. Karen is engaged to Joe (Joel McCrea), whom Martha is also in love with. Trouble begins when a student falsely accuses Martha and Joe of engaging in "strange acts." A scandal ensues, their school closes, and their lives fall apart. Hellman's text is strong commentary on the destructive power of gossip and the so-called innocence of youth. Director William Wyler remade the story in 1962, using the play's original name and theme; Shirley MacLaine and Audrey Hepburn starred in that version. In *The Children's Hour*, Martha hangs herself. In *These Three*, Martha ends up friendless and penniless. ⊗

Three of Hearts

(1993, 101 min, US, Yurek Bogayevicz)
While this much-publicized romantic sex comedy does not hold up to the promise of being a breakthrough Hollywood lesbian film (it cops out early on, of course), the film is still remarkably charming

and far from a complete failure in terms of how it deals with the issue of lesbianism. The fine acting on the part of Kelly Lynch (as the jilted, but true-blue lesbian), Sherilyn Fenn (as the bisexual fence sitter) and William Baldwin (as the prostitute with a heart of gold) keeps the film interesting and believable. Stung by her sud-den breakup with Ellen (Fenn), the lovelorn Connie (Lynch) con-cocts a wild plan of reconciliation by hiring a male hustler (Baldwin) to entice her into falling in love with him and be dropped by him, thereby breaking her heart and, hopefully, send-ing her running back to Connie's loving embrace. But the plan goes haywire when Joey, the male escort and now a roommate and friend of Connie, inadvertently falls in love with the charming uni-versity teacher. Yes, the best moments in this lighthearted and humorous film are the tender, romantic (heterosexual) scenes with Joey and Ellen. And yes, the only scene with the two lesbians together is when they are breaking up. But the film is saved (and avoids being lumped in with such dreck as *A Different Story*) by a script that depicts an attractive, intelligent and funny lesbian and a bisexual woman who, although she breaks up with a woman, defends their love and the affectionate friendship between a gay woman and a straight man. The result may veer into the comfort-ing embraces of heterosexuality, but the film throughout projects lesbians in a warm, complex and positive fashion. An interesting side note to the American marketing of the film: Before the film was released on home video, store owners around the country were given the unprecedented chance to change the film's ending. The two endings, in which Baldwin gets the girl and the other where he does not, amazingly left out the option of Lynch getting the girl! The original theatrical (and much better, but not best) ending was eventually chosen. ⊗

Thérèse and Isabelle

(1968, 102 min, France, Radley Metzger)
Set in an all-girls Catholic boarding school, this milestone film is a tender glimpse at the erotic affair of two young women. Unlike

many other works of the period, this provocative drama offers a non-exploitative picture of budding female sexuality, some very hot love scenes and lots of schoolgirl emotional tension. With voice-over narration taken directly from Violette Leduc's autobiographical novel, the film is genuinely sweet in spite of a lingering Euro soft-porn atmosphere. ⊛

Times Square *(1980, 111 min, US, Allan Moyle)*
Infused with a lesbian love angle, this big-budget rock 'n' roll rebellion film is rousing fun. Timid but intelligent Pamela (Trini Alvarado) meets the butch, tough-talking Nicky (Robin Johnson) while they are both undergoing psychiatric tests at a New York hospital. Becoming quick friends, with Nicky playing Pammy's protector, they escape and run off to the city. Setting up a makeshift home amidst the trash of an abandoned warehouse, the two spurn authority and Pammy's well-connected parents as they fall in love (with each other), freely run around the seedy sections of an oddly nurturing New York, become heroic inspiration to frustrated teenage girls and begin putting together a renegade rock band. Tim Curry embarrassingly overacts as a "hip" radio D.J. who assists their fantasy-filled odyssey. The love interest between the two girls is muted; reportedly the more blatant aspects of their relationship were edited out before the film's theatrical release. But even without the missing scenes (remaining in the final cut is Pammy's love poem to Nicky), one can easily see the love and affection between the two. The soundtrack features the best of '80s alternative rock, with Patti Smith Group, Lou Reed, Suzi Quatro, David Johansen, The Ramones, The Pretenders, XTC, The Cure, Talking Heads and Roxy Music. ⊛

Focus on: *Allan Moyle*
Although Canadian-born Allan Moyle has made only four feature films in 13 years, his sensitivity towards the treatment of gays and lesbians cannot be overstated. His first film, Rubber Gun *(1977), had a gay theme and was a gay film festival favorite. Its success, and the prodding of producer Robert Stigwood (*Saturday Night Fever, Grease*), lured Moyle to Hollywood to make a musical drama on teenage runaways. That film,* Times Square, *was a box-office bomb, possibly in part due to the studio-directed last minute editing of the film. Moyle calls the film "a horrible movie, a mis-*

Touch Me

management of my own script." His run-in with the Hollywood moguls and the ensuing tensions contributed to his sudden and total loss of hair caused ostensibly by a skin condition. After a several-year hiatus in which he made a living writing screenplays (including the script for Lizzie Borden's Love Crimes*), he triumphantly returned with the cult hit* Pump Up the Volume, *a teen rebellion movie which starred Christian Slater and called "A Talk Radio for teenagers" by Moyle. The film featured the sympathetic handling of a despondent gay teenager. Recently married for the second time, Moyle's most recent film is the comedy* The Gun in Betty Lou's Handbag *(1992).*

To My Women Friends
(1993, 64 min, Russia/Germany, Natasha Sharandak)
To say that lesbian/gay life in post-Communist Russia is a fascinating and worthy subject cannot be denied, but this film sadly fails to do more than cursorily glance at it. More of a simple document of lesbians in Russia than a documentary, the film relies on nothing more than static, unedited talking head interviews with six ex-Soviet lesbians. Though the women (included are a bus driver, a folk singer, a former prisoner and a butch Afghanistan veteran) are at times animated and opinionated, the film's format results in a simplistic, unelucidating, frustrating and ultimately boring picture.

Touch Me *(1993, 30 min, Australia, Paul Cox)*
This Paul Cox-directed lesbian drama is a short which is included in the feature titled *Erotic Tales*. Set in Melbourne, the story revolves around the developing tender relationship between two women. *Erotic Tales* is a series of twelve shorts exploring eroticism produced by Regina Ziegler. Other directors who have completed their films include Bob Rafelson (*Wet*), Susan Seidelman (*The Dutch Master*) and Ken Russell (*The Insatiable Mrs. Kirsch*). Other filmmakers scheduled to submit films include Emir Kusturica, Melvin van Peebles, Andrzej Wajda and Jiri Menzel.

Twice a Woman
(1985, 90 min, The Netherlands, George Sluizer)
This pleasantly tender and romantic lesbian love story stars Bibi Andersson (*Wild Strawberries, Persona, Cries and Whispers*) and features Anthony Perkins as her ex-husband. Set in Amsterdam, the tale begins immediately with a pick-up. Laura (Andersson) is a successful 41-year-old restorer. She meets Sylvia, a charming young girl (Sandra Dumas) barely half her age, on the street and takes her back home. Laura, who admits that this is her first time, is calmed by the more experienced Sylvia and they eagerly make love. Sylvia soon moves in and they begin a relationship which faces special difficulties due to differences in age, education and income. Perkins plays Laura's sleazy ex-husband who, after registering his disapproval at his ex "becoming a lesbian," himself becomes romantically interested in Sylvia. A tangled web of passions soon develops as the women's love affair abruptly ends when Sylvia runs off to Paris with Perkins. Although the film approaches a happy, lesbian-positive ending, death to one of the women is "necessary" in preaching the same old warning that two

women cannot live happily and romantically together without men. Despite the predictable ending, the film is wonderfully satisfying in its complex portrayal of a lesbian relationship, the difficulties of telling one's parents, and the problem of societal disapproval. An especially interesting scene finds the two women on a holiday in Nice where they cooly come out to people in a bar, a restaurant, and in the hotel indifferent to the homophobia that surrounds them. From the director of both the Dutch and American versions of the chilling thriller, *The Vanishing*. ✪

Twin Bracelets *(1990, 100 min,*
Taiwan/HongKong, Huang Yushan)
Written and directed by women, this simply told but engrossing saga follows one woman's struggle for independence against a restrictive patriarchy and her determined efforts to capture the heart of the woman she loves. Hui-hua is a pretty, rebellious teenager living with her hard-working family in a small fishing village, which is ensconced in ancient traditions and social rules that keep women firmly in subservient, chattle-like positions. From an early age, pouty Hui-hua has had a crush (nurtured by romantic interludes and close physical contact) on schoolmate Hsui which eventually turns to love. Hui shamelessly flirts with her girlfriend in front of her family and is quick to show jealousy when she does not get the attention she craves. While she makes no attempt to hide her feelings, her family sees it all, but understands nothing of her true emotions. As dictated by tradition, Hsui is married off, but despite this, the two teenagers vow to live their lives as "sister, man and wife; to live together and to die together." Hui's own family attempts to marry their daughter off in an arranged marriage, but fails, as she tries to stay true to her love despite insurmountable odds.

Nothing satisfies like a bite on the breast: *Twins of Evil*

Alice Walker in *Visions of the Spirit*

Twins of Evil *(1972, 85 min, GB, John Hough)*
Lukewarm but somewhat engaging follow-up to the far superior *Vampire Lovers*, featuring real-life twins and *Playboy* playmates Madeleine and Mary Collinson. There's black magic ceremonies, mild lesbianism (of the petting and pecking variety), witch burnings and Peter Cushing, who shows up to decapitate the vampire twins. The lesbian vampires not only seduce their female victims, but feed by biting them on the neck and on the breast. ✪

Two in Twenty *(1988, 160 min, US, Laurel*
Chiten, Cheryl Qamar & Rachel McCollum)
Originally slated to air on a public access station in Boston, *Two in Twenty* is an entertaining, amusing and ambitious lesbian soap opera. The show's five episodes (on three tapes, with outtakes on the third) are structured as an actual TV soap "aired" on WCLT, complete with humorous spoofs on commercials. The stories revolve around two lesbian households, and deal with such topics as bisexuality, promiscuity among lesbians, racial problems, lesbian child rearing and various other joys and problems that befall the many lesbian characters. The tape's finale focuses on a dramatic courtroom battle for custody of a 15-year-old girl living with her lesbian mother and lover. While not slick in production values, nor acting prowess, the show's strength is in its ability to depict — honestly, directly and from a lesbian perspective — a slice of several lesbian lifestyles. ✪

Vampire Lovers
(1970, 88 min, GB, Roy Ward Baker)
The voluptuous Ingrid Pitt stars as a lesbian vampire in this sexy but faithful redo of J. Sheridan Le Fanu's "Carmilla." The sensual seductress' best scene comes when she entices the innocent Emma (Madeleine Smith) from the arms of her male lover and into her cloying embrace. Produced by Hammer Studios, the film

was a groundbreaking and daring attempt to breathe new life into the horror genre by adding lesbian bloodsuckers and sexy seductions for what was, and still is, an essentially heterosexual male audience. After the success of the film, Hammer Studios released a torrent of sexy lesbian vampire movies from 1970 to 1974 with the most successful being *Twins of Evil* (1971) and *Lust for a Vampire* (1971). ⊗

Vampyres *(1974, 86 min, GB, Joseph Larraz)*
Two sexy lesbian vampires lure unsuspecting men to their isolated English mansion for nights of passion and bloodletting. Featuring a surprising amount of nudity (although many video versions have been cut), the film is effectively creepy and erotic as the mysterious women, Miriam (Anulka) and Fran (Marianne Morris), when not feasting on the blood of their lecherous (and soon to be drained) houseguests, are in each other's passionate embrace. ⊗

Visions of the Spirit: A Portrait of Alice Walker
(1989, 58 min, US, Elena Featherston)
The life and work of poet, mother, activist, feminist and Pulitzer Prize-winning author Alice Walker is explored in this intimate documentary whose only problem is its pedestrian, "educational TV" approach. Interviewed are friends, family, critics and, in a small segment, the cast and makers of *The Color Purple*. In the second part, Walker herself takes center stage, recounting her personal struggles and recalling incidents from her childhood, time spent at Sarah Lawrence and Africa, and her civil rights activities in Mississippi where she lived while married to a white man. The interviews with her and Alice's mother in their rural Georgia home are most evocative. Early on, the film refers to the omission of the lesbian relationship between Celia and the blues singer Shug in Steven Spielberg's film version of Walker's *The Color Purple*, but as quickly as it is mentioned, it is dropped — unresolved.

Waiting for the Moon
(1987, 87 min min, US, Jill Godmillow)
The story of the tumultuous relationship between author Gertrude Stein and her lover/companion Alice B. Toklas. The film is minimalistic with long periods of dialogue between the women, in a style reminiscent of *My Dinner with Andre*. Upon its release, most critics disapproved of the film's downplaying the women's lesbianism, which opts instead for a more "matter of fact" attitude. Linda Hunt and Linda Bassett star. ⊗

Walk on the Wild Side
(1962, 114 min, US, Edward Dmytryk)
The stage is set for the battle over the soul of call girl Capucine in this enjoyably trashy '60s psychodrama. Laurence Harvey plays Dove, a drifter who, with fellow roadie Kitty (Jane Fonda), arrives at The Doll's House, a posh bordello in New Orleans. He's there to rekindle a relationship with former girlfriend Hallie (Capucine), who's now working for lesbian madam Jo (Barbara Stanwyck). Hallie is one of Jo's favorites, and they're "special friends." Once he finds her, the film takes on a moralistic tone, and glorifies hetero-

sexuality and the power of love. Eventually, tragic fates await all; except for Dove, who flies away. Fonda comes off best as Kitty, who eventually becomes another inhabitant of The Doll's House. ⊗

The War Widow *(1976, 83 min, US, Paul Bogart)*
Pamela Bellwood stars as Amy, the lonely wife of a World War I soldier. Amy meets Jenny (Frances Lee McCain) in a New York tea room and they develop a friendship which gradually becomes "passionate." On a vacation together at the beach they realize the depth of their relationship. As Amy's husband is about to return from overseas, she is forced to make the ultimate choice between her family and her lover. This charming television drama has been a lesbian favorite for years.

Well Sexy Women *(1993, 55 min, GB)*
Although lesbians are thought to be a low risk group when it comes to contracting HIV, there is still a small possibility of transmission. This interesting, frank and informative video was made in response to this situation, as well as out of concern for lesbians who might contract other sexually transmitted diseases. Written, produced and directed by The Unconscious Collective — comprised of Sophie Moorcock, Michele Hickson, Lulu Believeau and Liz North — the video features six opinionated lesbians captured during a group discussion that involves suggestions on how lesbians can reduce their risk to STDs and generally lead safer sex lives. Gloves, sex toys, latex and dams are discussed, as well as anonymous sex and even helpful fist-fucking tips ("That's why

Well Sexy Women

when I'm fisting, I use gloves"). Interspersed in the discussion are several graphic safer sex scenes, proving that the women practice what they preach. ⊛

> "The most important, honest presentation of safer sex techniques...personal, moving and erotic vision of safe sex for our age."
>
> — *Gay Times* [London]

West Coast Crones

(1991, 28 min, US, Madeline Muir)

The particular problems, challenges and experiences of elderly lesbians are explored in this all-too-short documentary. Proudly proclaiming themselves "Old Lesbians," an articulate group of nine white, mostly middle-class women meet to discuss issues as diverse as their initial sexual experiences, coming out, their decision to have or not have children, their self-perception, friendships and relationships with other women as well as the expectancy and mental preparation for an approaching infirmary and death. A revealing glimpse into some very interesting women. The film makes an interesting companion film with *An Empty Bed*, a film that focuses on the situation of elderly gay men. ⊛

What You Take for Granted

(1983, 75 min, US, Michele Citron)

An unusual blend of documentary and fiction, this film delves into the lives of several women employed in non-traditional jobs that have been usually held by men. Culled from more than 40 interviews, the film intercuts those stories with fictionalized ones including a tale that explores the growing, if a bit tentative, friendship between a feisty lesbian truck driver and a straight, upper middle-class female doctor. A "psycho-documentary" that explores stereotypes in employment, race, class and sexual orientation.

Where There's Smoke

(1986, 33 min, US, Lynx Canon)

While little more than lesbian porn, this video is saved by the fact that it was made by and for lesbians and that the lovemaking between Cris Cassidy and Lee Rothermund is videotaped in a vastly different fashion than one sees in the straight, male pornography that seems always to feature at least one "girl-girl" scene. The sex is explicit, tender, exploratory and varied. ⊛

Wild Flowers *(1989, 66 min, GB, Robert Smith)*

Filmed in a warmhearted and seductively subtle fashion, this made-for-TV drama follows the deepening friendship and understanding between two dissimilar women. Sadie, a young woman from Glasgow, visits her boyfriend's working-class family in a small seaside town in Scotland, and there meets his vibrant and attractive mother. She becomes increasingly interested in the fascinating woman, and their relationship takes on a new wrinkle when Sadie discovers that the older woman is bisexual. The sexual openness of the older woman helps in releasing the sexual repressions in the younger one.

Windows *(1980, 96 min, US, Gordon Willis)*

In the annals of film homophobia, this ridiculous thriller is viewed by many to be the lesbian equivalent to *Cruising* and a precursor to *Basic Instinct* in its depiction of a rich, attractive lesbian who commits murderous deeds. In his defense, cinematographer-turned-director Gordon Willis has said of the lesbophobic picture, "*Windows* is not about homosexuality — it's about insanity." Elizabeth Ashley is Andrea, a psychotic lesbian who develops a fatal passion for the mild-mannered heterosexual Emily (Talia Shire). Tensions arise when the predatory Andrea, desperate for her *object d'amour*, becomes increasingly jealous and concocts a plan to have Emily raped, thereby sending her into her clutching arms. Adding to the luridness is that Andrea becomes sexually aroused by repeatedly listening to a tape recording of the assault. Heterosexuality wins out in this poorly acted and terribly written film that was greeted with protests from the lesbian and gay community, received poor reviews and performed abysmally at the box office.

A Woman Like Eve

(1979, 100 min, The Netherlands, Noichka van Brakel)

The life of a bored Dutch housewife is turned around when she rejects her bourgeois marriage, discovers feminism and then becomes romantically involved with another woman. This sensitive drama stars Monique Van De Ven (*Turkish Delight*, *Keetje Tippel*) as the married Eve, whose secure but unhappy marriage ends in divorce when she finds fulfillment in the arms of Liliane, a free-spirited lesbian folk singer played by Maria Schneider. An early European effort at depicting a positive portrayal of lesbians which was made by a production crew of primarily women.

Focus on: *Maria Schneider*

A "self-acknowledged bisexual" who in 1975 declared publicly "the right to be insane" and committed herself to a Rome mental institution to be with her hospitalized girlfriend Jane Townsend, Maria Schneider has led both a tumultuous private and professional life. Born in Paris in 1952, she quit high school at age 15 to make her Paris stage debut in "Superposition." That led to bit parts in films, but her first starring role came in Bernardo Bertolucci's controversial classic Last Tango in Paris *with Marlon Brando in 1973. Another international success was her passionate performance opposite Jack Nicholson in Michelangelo Antonioni's* The Passenger *in 1975. Soon after, she began working with some of Europe's most important directors including Roger Vadim, René Clement and Jacques Rivette. But a reputation for being tempestuous resulted in her walking off or being fired from* Caligula, 1900, That Obscure Object of Desire *and* I Never Promised You a Rose Garden. *Over the past few years, Schneider, who is an avid painter as well, has continued working in Europe and most recently starred in Dani Levy's 1991 German-American co-production* I Was on Mars.

Women Like Us *(1989, 55 min, GB)*

Originally aired on Channel 4's gay magazine series, "Out on Tuesday," this queer historical documentary features 16 older lesbians — ranging in age from 50- to 60-years-old, and from diverse political, economic and racial backgrounds — who were culled from all different parts of the country. The interviews deal with what it is like for these women to be lesbian today as compared with years past. The women recall their lesbian youth, love and romance, feminism and politics, role-playing, and coming out to their family and friends. Interestingly, most shared a common and difficult search for positive role models and cultural images that could help them develop and strengthen their lesbian identity.

The Women of Brewster Place
(1989, 200 min, US, Donna Deitch)
Director Donna Deitch's first work since her lesbian love story *Desert Hearts*, this made-for-TV production was produced by Oprah Winfrey and focuses on the intertwined lives of seven black women all living in the same tenement. Based on Gloria Naylor's award-winning novel, the cast of characters range from welfare mothers to a sophisticated lesbian couple who all attempt to overcome their poverty and create strong family ties. The cast includes Winfrey, Moses Gunn, Robin Givens, Paul Winfield, Jackee and Paula Kelly. ⊗

The Women Who Made the Movies
(1990, 56 min, US, Gwendolyn Foster-Dixon & Wheeler Dixon)
A promising title that actually limits its focus to the women pioneers of the silent film era in Hollywood and gives little attention to the women who followed. Made for Nebraska Educational Television, the film highlights, using a dry, educational approach, the many now-unknown women who successfully made films when the industry was in its infancy. Women like Kate Corbally (*80 Million Women Want?*, 1913), actress and director Lois Webber (*Japanese Idyll*, 1912) and Dorothy Davenport (Mrs. Wallace Reid) receive the bulk of the attention while Dorothy

Arzner, Leni Riefenstahl, Germaine Dulac while the many women who followed receive only passing reference. ⊗

Women on the Roof
(1989, 90 min, Sweden, Carl-Gustaf Nykvist)
This bisexual tale of attraction and betrayal is set in 1914 Sweden. New to Stockholm, Linnea (Amanda Ooms), a timid and naive young woman, is soon befriended and used by the suave and alluring photographer Anna (Helena Bergstrom). Both women, coming off abusive relationships (Linnea with her father, Anna from a male lover), quickly become romantically involved. The arrival of Anna's former boyfriend breaks the idyllic spell between the entranced women and brings about retribution and bitterness. Directed by the son of famed cinematographer Sven Nykvist, the film is beautiful to look at, but suffers from poorly developed characters and a painfully slow story line.

Yes (To Ingrid My Love Lisa)
(1968, 90 min, Sweden, Joseph W. Sarno)
American "nudie" director Joseph W. Sarno, taking advantage of greater tolerance, moved his base of operations to Sweden for several years in the late 1960s, and, among others, produced this deliciously overwrought tale of lesbian longing. Successful but sexually repressed Lisa is a thirtyish fashion designer who drowns her loneliness with booze and futile attempts at sluttish excess. But it's love/lust at first sight when she meets her neighbor's teenage daughter. Blonde Ingrid, a naive country girl, is soon swept off her feet by Lisa, who hires her as a model, plies her with food and drink and even has her move into her flat — but no amount of inticement on the part of the Sister George-like older woman can get the waif into her bed. After a few trysts with some lecherous men, however, Ingrid thinks, "What the hell, it is the '60s, after all," and finally jumps into bed with the appreciative Lisa. The almost intolerable tease of "will they or won't they" will remind some of the 1993 classic of the genre, *Claire of the Moon*. An enjoyably campy, over-the-top tale of a lesbian's sexual obsession and intense frustration which also features Nils, a flamboyant young gay man who is Lisa's only friend, assistant and confidant. ⊗

Your Heart Is All Mine
(1992, 50 min, Germany, Elke Götz)
Funny, sexy and affecting, this quirky lesbian love story centers around two women who not only have to contend with who is the butchest but a clinging semi-incestuous mother as well. Hilde is a plain-looking workaholic secretary who blossoms when she finds first love in the arms of the seriously cute Gisela (Gigi), a motorcycle-loving butcher. Bordering at times on the bizarre, their fairy tale love is complicated when Hilde's mother won't let go of her daughter/playmate/lover. A delightfully endearing film, spiced with many campy scenes, that tries to find out literally who gets to wear the pants in the family.

Your Heart Is All Mine

6

OF GAY MALE INTEREST

In alphabetical format, the following films have either been made by gay men, have a gay theme or feature a gay actor or gay characters.

"Your dick knows what it likes."
—Explanation of male sexual orientation
by Peter (Adam Nathan) to Nick
(Steve Buscemi) in *Parting Glances*

"It's fine if straight actors want to play gay roles because I'm a gay actor who also wants to play straight roles."
—Alexis Arquette

AMG — The Fantasy Factory/Revisited/A Third Visit

(60 min ea, US)

Pre-dating modern male pornography, the Los Angeles-based Athletic Model Guild, guided by Bob Mizer from the years 1956 thru 1969, produced thousands of nudie flicks that were for the most part the only sexually suggestive images available for gay men of that period. The films were not the feature length hardcore fuck 'n' suck videos of today, but almost-chaste displays of male beauty (mainly the "boy next door" type) based around scenes of models posing, wrestling, and enactments of playful fantasies and male iconography (cops, Roman gladiators, prisoners, friendly roommates, bikers, bodybuilders). Featuring men either scantily clad in posing straps or, in later films, flaccidly naked, these videos, narrated by Steve Malis, are compilations of many of these short (running two to nine minutes) black-and-white films that take the viewer nostalgically back to a more discreet time in male erotica. ☮

Absolutely Positive

(1991, 85 min, US, Peter Adair)

From the producer of *Word Is Out* comes this touching documentary about people living with HIV and AIDS. In addition to talking with several outspoken gays, including black filmmaker Marlon Riggs, the film also features interviews with several "typical Americans" on how they feel about the disease. The film aired on Britain's Channel 4.

Aclá *(1992, 86 min, Italy, Aurelio Grimaldi)*

The inordinately harsh life of Sicilian peasant miners, and one blond, 11-year-old boy in particular, in 1930s Italy is the subject of this unrelentingly grim drama. Young Alcá, a handsome youth with a streak of independence, comes of age to accompany his father and his two older brothers to the underground sulfur mines where they work six days a week for little pay and food. He is sold off as an indentured worker, a virtual slave, for 500 Lira and must endure horrible conditions made worse by the casual brutality inflicted on him. Using poetic (pederastic?) license, the director displays all of the workers (many gorgeous) in the excessively hot mines laboring only in loincloths, revealing for the audience, and the increasingly horny miners, endless panning shots of chalky but inviting backsides — the scenes suggest paintings by Caravaggio. When the work is over, the men huddle in a single room to sleep; their lust drives them to either fuck men their own age or, better yet, buy some of the boys with a few olives and then have their way with them. As one of the miners observes, "We fuck boys during the week and our wives on Sundays." Aclá never allows anyone to touch him, however, despite pleas from the normally heterosexual men. He dreams of the sea and escape while struggling against the inhumanity, determined not to have his spirit broken. Although sex is always in the dusty air, it is filmed discreetly, as the director is content with flesh rather than action. The only tender relationship in the entire film is one between Aclá's older brother and another miner — at one point the two, obviously in love, are seen with their eyes locked onto one another, dancing to the entranced stares of their fellow miners. ☮

Aclá

Adieu Bonaparte

(1984, 114 min, France/Egypt, Youssef Chahine)
From Egypt's greatest director comes this period-piece family drama which contains homoerotic elements. Set during the French dictator Bonaparte's assault through Egypt, the drama focuses on one family as they struggle to survive. The family and their three sons flee Alexandria and stay with relatives in Cairo. Bakr is the oldest son, a married Moslem; Yehia, at 16, is the youngest and Aly is a poet. When the army begins to occupy the city, Aly's intriguing nature leads him to an uneasy friendship with a French general, Cafferelli (Michel Piccoli) — a one-legged advisor to Bonaparte as well as a scientist and inventor. The general's sexual attraction to the two young brothers is obvious, being interested in Aly for his mind and Yehia for his body. His outgoing personality emotionally seduces the two boys, but the war destroys their friendship.

Adios, Roberto

(1985, 90 min, Argentina, Enrique Dawi)
Winner of the Audience Prize as the Best Film in the 1987 New York Gay Film Festival, this good-natured comedy on the "conflicting" forces of machismo and homosexuality was made only after Argentina's return to democracy and the subsequent relaxation of artistic censorship. The story follows Roberto, a macho young man who moves in with a friend's relative after separating from his wife. Marcelo, the roommate, is gay and though for a while it seems as if Roberto will never catch on, they eventually become close friends. One night in a drunken stupor, Roberto has sex with Marcelo, and when he sobers, he faces his own conflicting feelings as well as ridicule and damnation from his wife, family and even his confessional priest. Despite the opposition, however, their relationship deepens into love in this witty, well-observed story that is full of surprises.

The Affairs of Love (Las Cosas del Querer)

(1990, 100 min, Spain, Jaime Chavarri)
From the director of *To an Unknown God* comes this delightfully lighthearted musical drama about three members of a vaudeville troupe set in 1940s Madrid. The performers include the handsome heterosexual Juan, his fiery girlfriend Pepita, and Mario, a dropdead-gorgeous gay piano player who is Pepita's dancing partner. Mario, who is in love with the macho Juan, finds his advances rebuffed, but instead of brooding, he accepts the rejection and goes about seducing a bevy of handsome men, from backstage workers to appreciative audience members. But when Mario breaks up with a pampered nobleman, the spurned lover's mother gets into the act, determined to exact revenge. Depicted as a pleasant, sweetly tempered and charming individual, Mario is a dream gay man: handsome, strong, talented and completely at ease and unapologetic about his homosexuality.

Alexander: The Other Side of Dawn

(1977, 100 min, US, John Erman)
It is surprising, taking into account American television's prurient nature, that a telemovie on the highly contentious subject of a boy's descent into male hustling and homosexuality could ever be given a green light. Yet this telefilm was made and aired on NBC. The drama follows Alexander (Leigh McCloskey), an attractive youth from the sticks who, when he can't find a job in the big city, begins life as a male prostitute, working for both male and female clients on the streets of Hollywood. Alex soon begins a series of run-ins with police and at one point he is counseled by Ray (Earl Holliman), a worker at the Gay Community Center. But Alex, confused about his sexuality, refuses help, claiming that he is not gay. As he continues tricking with men, Alex eventually meets a gay football player (Alan Feinstein), moving into his Malibu beach house. But, of course, this is television and the boy finds the error of his ways, and with his fellow ex-prostitute girlfriend (Eve Plumb) in tow, he leaves the evil city for a new, straight life elsewhere. ♨

Alexandria — Why?

(1978, 132 min, Egypt, Youssef Chahine)
Winner of the Special Jury Prize at the 1979 Berlin Film Festival, this autobiographical WWII drama of illicit love is set in the teeming port city of Alexandria in 1942, where life in the besieged city remains strangely undisturbed despite the fact that advancing Rommel is only 60 miles away. The story explores the taboo love affairs between a Muslim man and a Jewish woman, and between a handsome Egyptian teenager (and aspiring actor) and a young British soldier. While not explicitly gay, this entertaining drama is an important film as an Arabic treatment of the tender relationship between two men. Interestingly, although Chahine has made over 30 films since 1950, none have ever played theatrically in the United States.

Amazing Grace (Hessed Mufla)

(1992, 95 min, Israel, Amos Gutman)
Set in Tel Aviv, this intense, melancholy drama focuses on Jonathan, a gangly and romantic teenager who faces an early-life crisis when he finds himself alone after his lover moves out of their apartment. Frustrated by his self-absorbed mother and disenchanted by the horde of drug-taking friends and relatives who invade his apartment, the youth's passions are rekindled after he befriends Thomas, the handsome, HIV-positive older son of his upstairs neighbor, who is visiting from New York. Their budding yet tentative relationship provides the backdrop for this ambitious social and sexual drama which touches on such issues as AIDS, death, drug abuse, the gay milieu of Tel Aviv and family dysfunctionalism. Although the film attempts too much, it remains a serious, thought-provoking gay drama.

Focus On: *Amos Gutman*

Hungarian born director Amos Gutman, who died of AIDS in February 1993 at the age of 38, made several feature films in his adopted homeland of Israel, including the acclaimed Drifting *(the first Israeli film to deal with homosexuality),* Bar 51 *(1986),* King of Jerusalem *(1987) and two gay-themed shorts:* A Safe Place, *a drama of a teenage boy's coming out and sexual initiation at a cinema, and* Afflicted, *the story of a closeted man's enlightening visit to a drag bar.* Amazing Grace, *his final film, won Best Feature at the 1992 Jerusalem Film Festival.*

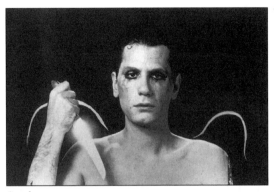

Angel

American Fabulous

(1992, 105 min, US, Reno Dakota)

A gay, white-trash Spaulding Gray, bitchy motor-mouth Jeffrey Strouth dominates the screen in this amusingly campy one-man performance piece. Shot primarily in the back seat of a '57 Cadillac as it cruises across country, Jeffrey — like a mincing Tallulah Bankhead — extemporaneously pontificates on any subject that enters his mind, elaborately weaving tales culled from his past, and his wild imagination; stories that are at once unbelievable, hilarious and semi-tragic. With razor-sharp wit, the thirtyish Southerner recounts significant moments from his childhood and free-living adulthood while the filmmaker, obviously fascinated by the Wildean character, simply lets the camera roll, offering free reign to the catty and amusingly vicious storyteller. There are a few problems with the film — visually it is numbingly static and a bit too long — and while enjoyable, a better night might be had with some of your animated and tackier gay friends! ⊛

"A tour of the wild, low-life gay existence...captivating, hilarious, yet touching. Strouth displays a wit that might conceivably amuse Oscar Wilde."
— Kevin Thomas, *Los Angeles Times*

Anders Als Die Anderen (Different from the Others)

(1919, Germany, Richard Oswald)

This, the first film to positively portray homosexuality and plead for the tolerance of "The Third Sex," was produced by Magnus Hirschfeld, founder of the Institute of Sexology in Berlin and staunch opponent to Germany's anti-homosexuality law, known as "Paragraph 175." The film, about a prominent gay man who is blackmailed, opened in 1919 to generally good reviews and healthy box office. But by 1920, it was banned in many cities (including Vienna, Munich and Stutgart) and was allowed to be viewed only by professionals in the educational, scientific and medical fields. All known prints were probably lost after the Nazis raided the offices of Dr. Hirschfeld in 1933 and destroyed his work. Today, the only existing print, found in 1976 in Ukraine, has a running time of only 30 minutes, much shorter than the original film. Gay actor Conrad Veidt stars as Paul Körner, a famous pianist who falls in love with one of his students, Kurt. Kurt moves in with his teacher, but soon Paul becomes the victim of blackmail by one of their acquaintances. Rather than paying off the man, Paul confronts him in court, but with homosexuality against the law, both receive jail sentences. Upon his return from prison, Paul, a broken man, commits suicide and at his casket, his former lover vows to change the laws against homosexuality. Hirschfeld is featured in the film as a sex researcher who assures Paul that there is nothing to be done about his homosexuality and that he can lead a good life. The film was either remade or reedited in 1927 by Hirschfeld and Oswald under the title, *The Laws of Love* (*Gesetze der Liebe*), although no prints are known to survive. An important first in the history of the depiction of gays in film.

Angel *(1982, 126 min, Greece, Yorgos Katakouzinos)*

When this film made the circuit of Gay/Lesbian Film Festivals several years ago, it caused quite stir with its negative images of homosexuality. Yet, despite (or because of?) this downbeat approach, the film (the first Greek feature to deal with homosexuality) was a commercial smash in Greece, swept the awards at the Salonika Film Festival and was even well received at Cannes. The film is a harrowing, tragic account of a shy young man from a dysfunctional family (dad's an alcoholic, mom's a former whore) who thinks that he's found love after meeting a macho sailor. Their relationship soon becomes abusive, with the young man forced to become a transvestite prostitute on the mean street of Athens. His helplessness and humiliation soon end in inevitable violence. From the "'Tis a pity he's a homosexual" school of filmmaking.

Anguished Love

(1988, 105 min, Thailand, Pisan Akkaraseni)

A sequel to Pisan Akkaraseni's previous gay-themed film *The Last Song*, this pseudo-documentary is a gritty exposé about life, lust, death and revenge on the mean streets of Bangkok.

Apartment Zero

(1989, 114 min, GB, Martin Donovan)

A multi-layered, stylish thriller which never fails to elicit a strong emotional response, *Apartment Zero* creates an atmosphere of wicked sexual tension through the subtle use of suggestion and innuendo. Set in an English-speaking community in Buenos Aires, the film stars Colin Firth as Adrian LeDuc, a sexually repressed cinephile with a penchant for the classics who takes in a swaggering, handsome American boarder (Hart Bochner) with many skeletons in his "closet." Suspicions abound as gruesome political murders haunt the Argentine city upon the arrival of Adrian's new roommate. Firth and Bochner shine in their roles, as do a talented supporting cast. Director Martin Donovan uses stylish camerawork and extreme close-ups to seduce the viewer into his world of intrigue. Co-written by David Koepp, whose screenplay for *Bad Influence* also explored sexual repression by way of an underlying homoerotic relationship between a seducer and his prey. ⊛

Arch Brown's Top Story

(1993, 118 min, US, Arch Brown)

A gay soaper for the '90s, this video production centers around the daily traumas and bumpy love lives of a group of Southern California gay men (lesbians are featured, but only in support).

The interlocking stories are fast-paced, and though the story line is not uninteresting, the video suffers from awkward and uneven acting. The many mini-stories center around a group of men living in a large Spanish-style house. They quickly form relationships with special attention given to Tim (Jerry Ferracio), a cute closet case who finally drops his girlfriend and succumbs to the charms of Will (John Finch). Trouble brews for all of them after Tim's overbearing, homophobic mother decides to run for elected office on a staunch "family values" platform. Her sexual McCarthyism forces Tim to confront her and publicly declare his homosexuality. There is incidental nudity, lots of cuddling and romantic coupling by the leads. While not of queer film festival quality, *Top Story* is an earnest and at times accurate depiction of gay life. Called "the man who invented porn" by the late porn director Christopher Rage, Arch Brown is a veteran of over 16 male adult films made during the 1970s and early '80s including *Dynamite, Musclebound* and *The Night Before.* ⊛

Armistead Maupin: Is a Man I Dreamt Up

(1992, 60 min, GB, Kate Meynell & Kristiene Clarke)
Armistead Maupin, one of America's most famous and accessible writers, is the entertaining subject of this interesting portrait. Captured through interviews are his reminiscences about his Southern childhood, his days when "Tales of the City" was a weekly column in the *San Francisco Examiner*, and even his bizarre meeting with Richard Nixon. He also gives testimony to the fact that Armistead Maupin is his real name and not an anagram for "is a man I dreamt up." He freely discusses his writing and personal life as well as reading from some of his stories. Friends and colleagues also provide witty testimony to this important gay novelist and storyteller.

The Art of Touch

(1992, 45 min, US, Craig Cooper)
Not confining itself solely to massage, this video demonstrates the therapeutic and pleasurable effects simple, but "time tested," touching techniques can offer a couple. Six attractive male models engage in various forms of touch, caress and massage exercises as a narrator describes every move, and New Age music intones in the background. The demonstrations should be of help to many couples interested in increasing intimacy and physical exploration, although its sappy approach ("Get lost in the embrace," "If you

Apartment Zero

Asa Branca

come in contact with the genitals, slowly graze them and move on") distracts from its real intent. ⊛

The Art of Touch II — A Taoist Erotic Massage *(1993, 50 min, GB, Mike Esser)*

Notwithstanding its gimmicky, but undeniably fun 3-D effects (one receives two pair of glasses with the tape), this instructional massage video demonstrates the tender, relaxing and erotic possibilities offered in the Oriental massage technique called Taoist Erotic Massage. With six seriously cute instructors (nude and occasionally enjoying the massage a little *too* much), the video is ideal for gay couples who want to go beyond simple sexual intimacy and travel into an area where the effective use of the hands can "channel the sexual energy of the massage into a spiritual experience." But what can be spiritual for some will be tantalizing and titillating for others as the beautifully sculpted men pull, stroke, caress and touch each other. A warning to those susceptible to motion sickness — in their effort to heighten the 3-D look, the camera is constantly revolving around the massage bed, creating a potentially dizzying effect, so keep handy both your body oils and Dramamine! ⊛

As Is *(1986, 86 min, US, Michael Lindsay-Hogg)*

Based on the acclaimed Broadway production, this powerful, opened-up play stars Robert Carradine and Jonathan Hadary as ex-lovers who are brought together when the former is stricken with AIDS. Often humorous and never morose, author William Hoffman doesn't pull his punches with either his portrayal of a gay lifestyle or of the emotional toll the disease takes. ⊛

Asa Branca — A Brazilian Dream

(1982, 95 min, Brazil, Djalma Limongl Basista)
This coming-out drama of sexual repression and homosexual desire is set amidst the machismo sport of soccer. An attractive young athlete, Asa Branca, whose gay sexual longings have been

Being at Home with Claude

long suppressed, begins to express his desire for another man. A sensual and lyrical tale that provoked fury in its native country with its premise that there is a homoerotic aspect to the relationship between the sport's male fans and their scantily clad heroes.

The Attendant/Caught Looking

The Attendant (1992, 8 min, GB, Isaac Julien): Though only "eight queer minutes," Julien's witty and stylish short remains quite memorable. A middle-aged black museum guard allows his wildly gay fantasies to take over after the galleries are closed. His S&M desires are let loose as several 19th-century paintings come to vivid life. *Caught Looking* (1991 35 min, GB, Constantine Giannaris): This unforgettable homo/sci-fi successor to *Pink Narcissus* follows a man who uses an interactive virtual reality machine to select his sexual fantasies. His four options offer different sexual scenarios and characters in different worlds featuring idealized, impersonal sex, hunky men cruising stylized tea rooms, and tatooed sailors. For more information, see page 138. (These two shorts are available together on home video in Great Britain only. In America, *Caught Looking* is double-billed with *North of Vortex*.)

Basileus Quartet

(1982, 118 min, Italy, Fabio Capri)
This Italian art-house melodrama provides a classic example of the serious straight cinema equating homosexuality with immaturity, lecherousness and madness. When one of the elderly members of a staid classical quartet dies, he is replaced by Eduardo, a handsome young man. Eduardo's effervescent approach to life and music proves to be both a tonic and a curse for the others in the group, but one of the most affected is Guglielmo, the closeted gay member. We learn of his homosexuality early on when he cruises for trade in a movie theatre. He buys an ice cream cone for a young man who appreciatively puts his hands on the older man's thigh and Guglielmo flees in horror. Now established that Guglielmo has real sexual problems, it comes as no surprise that his relationship with Eduardo is tumultuous. Under the guise of protective "fatherly" love, Guglielmo fawns over the curly-haired youth and soon becomes overly obsessional and increasingly jealous. His creepy smothering leads to an awkward kiss, a quick rejection and more self-destructive behavior; eventually he has masochistic sex with a hustler (chained to a chair and whipped) which, naturally, leads him to be committed to an insane asylum! ☻

Beautiful Dreamers

(1990, 108 min, Canada, John Harrison)
Rip Torn stars as Walt Whitman in this touching drama in which he befriends the superintendent of a Canadian insane asylum. Their friendship results in the young doctor challenging the beliefs and practices of his profession as he tries to put a more human face on the psychiatry of the late 1800s. The film portrays the conflict between the Christian-based hierarchy of the day and the nascent humanism represented by Whitman — it's a struggle which, it could be argued, is still with us. Torn puts in a strong performance as the free-thinking poet whose homosexuality is never mentioned, although it is alluded to when someone wonders why he never married. ☻

> "While there is one rawly naturalistic scene of female frontal nudity, Whitman's homosexuality is so shyly suggested that anyone who did not know that Whitman was gay would miss the point."
> —*The Village Voice*

Behind Glass

(1981, 70 min, The Netherlands, Ab van Leperen)
The life cycle of a gay relationship is charted in this interesting but overly serious soap opera. A middle-class radio reporter and a working-class window washer become lovers despite their obvious differences in class, education, outside interests and money. Beginning as a seemingly happy couple, life soon becomes a battlefield of mini-wars and injurious power games for the pair as they shed their domestic niceties for the raw emotions of jealousy and resentment. Sort of a gay version of *The War of the Roses*, the film proves that even gay men are not immune to domestic turmoil.

Being at Home with Claude

(1991, 90 min, Canada, Jean Beaudin)
Queer criminality meets romantic love in this riveting and unconventional murder mystery. Set in Montreal, this adaptation of Rene-Daniel Dubois' taut, claustrophobic play opens up the action and heightens its original dramatic force. Relying less on the "whodunit" angle and more on "why-did-he-do-it," the film opens

with an erotic, hyperkinetic sequence focusing on a steamy sex scene which ends with a brutal murder. Three days later, Yves, a sexy male prostitute, summons the police to a judge's chamber and admits to the apparently senseless crime. Unapologetically gay and not the killer type, Yves, the lover of the deceased Claude, soon becomes embroiled in a harrowing interrogation which lays bare his tortured soul to the tough, but strangely sympathetic cop. A fine drama that works both as a suspense thriller and an absorbing tale of gay passions and desperate love. ☻

Best of Howard and Dave
(1991, 85 min, US)
Of interest primarily to Southern Californians who know of their show, or fans of these "wacky" TV hosts, this low-budget video features the best segments from Howard and Dave's gay-oriented cable TV program, which has gained notoriety over the past few years. ☻

The Best Way
(1976, 85 min, France, Claude Miller)
A summer camp for boys is the setting for this absorbing study of the tensions and sexual attraction of two male counselors. Marc, the overly masculine sports director, discovers Philippe, the music teacher, dressed in women's clothing. His inability to deal with his repressed feeling causes him to humiliate and persecute Philippe to the point were he must deal with the truth of his actions. A fine drama on sexual identity and male friendships. ☻

The Best of "Soap" — Vols. 1-2
(1978, 74 min, US, J.D. Lobue & Jay Sandrich)
Billy Crystal shot to fame thanks to his role as Jody, the crossdressing gay son of the eccentric Campell family in this popular 1970s TV comedy — a sometimes very funny and often unpredictably sentimental takeoff of TV soap operas. In this show's beginning, Jody is trying on his mother's dresses, much to her dismay. His stepfather (Richard Mulligan) drops homophobic remarks, which bother Jody's brother Danny (Ted Wass) more than they do Jody. As the series progressed and found a sizable audience, Jody dropped his transvestite antics (and his desire for a sex change) and started dating a handsome football player. At the same time, as if to follow in the footsteps of shows such as "Dynasty" where gay men started dating women, Jody soon fathered a child and was involved in a court custody battle with the mother. At the end of the series' run, Jody became asexual, and when his baby is kidnapped, he loses his mind, and begins to think he's a 70-year-old man. That was the last show of the series and Jody's sexuality was never resolved. Though a lot of the humor directed towards Jody's char-

acter was obvious, Crystal always managed to present Jody in a positive light, and his humor, intelligence and warmth made him one of the series' most popular characters. ☻

Beyond Therapy
(1987, 93 min, US, Robert Altman)
Christopher Durang co-adapted his own hit off-Broadway play for the screen in this Robert Altman-directed comedy about the frantic goings-on of a group of sex-obsessed neurotics and their equally unbalanced psychologists. Jeff Goldblum is the bisexual Bruce who lives with semi-swishy Bob (Christopher Guest), but tastes a little of the straight side with a hopelessly frazzled Prudence (Julie Hagerty). Telling a quivering Prudence on their first personal ad-arranged date of his gay inclinations and relationship with Bob, Prudence tries to run out of the restaurant after bleating, "I hate gays." Group therapy-addicted Bob, told by his "theatrical" mother of the secret rendezvous, is hysterical, but unable to do anything about his lover's roving libido. Tom Conti and Glenda Jackson play two equally crazy psychiatrists whose advice only makes everyone more crazy. Roundly panned on its initial release, the film, while wildly uneven, is quite charming and at times hilarious, with a gay sensibility that reigns supreme. Cris Campion is featured in support as a gay waiter and Jackson's son. ☻

Bezness
(1992, 100 min, France/Tunisia, Nouri Bouzid)
From the director of *Man of Ashes*, a shrill drama of a tortured homosexual youth, comes this tale of cultural invasion and moral corruption in Tunisia. "Bezness" are young prostitutes who work the tourist trade, providing their bodies to all comers. A French photographer is sent to do a story on them and is quickly befriended and protected by Roufa, a handsome bezness who dreams of earning enough money to move to Europe. The photographer sees firsthand the dichotomy of his lifestyle — he willingly has sex with men or

Beyond Therapy

Billy Budd

Blind Trust (Pouvoir Intime)

(1987, 86 min, Canada, Yves Simoneau)
This riveting suspense thriller chronicles the planning, execution and bloody aftermath of a failed armed robbery attempt in Montreal. Successfully balancing its sympathy for both the criminals as well as a guard held captive in the armored truck, this taut crime caper should keep the viewer enthralled throughout. Of note is that the guard who decides to fight back is gay. ⊛

Blonde Cobra

(1959-63, 25 min, US, Ken Jacobs & Bob Fleischner)
One of the earliest examples of the New York avant-garde filmmaking movement which flourished from the late 1950s thru the early '70s, *Blonde Cobra* is a no-budget, improvisational shambles which deliriously explores homosexuality, transvestism and transsexuals in a style that was meant to startle and excite the gay and underground audience and put off the mainstream folk. It was photographed by Bob Fleischner, edited by Ken Jacobs and acted and narrated by fellow filmmaker Jack Smith (*Flaming Creatures*).

> "A masterpiece of the Baudelairean cinema, and it is a work hardly surpassable in perversity, in richness, in beauty, in sadness, in tragedy...a great work of personal cinema."
> —Jonas Mekas, *Film Culture*

The Blue Hour

(1992, 88 min, Germany, Marcel Gisler)
The vulnerability and loneliness of a pretty "rent boy" and a flighty salesgirl is the theme of this absorbing drama by Swiss-born director Marcel Gisler. Theo is a Berlin hustler, a handsome young man who, despite selling his body, retains an amazingly sweet and trusting, if a bit secretive, nature. Despite living the "good life," Theo begins feeling a little old, tired and alienated. His sadness is relieved a bit when he strikes up an uneasy friendship with his next door neighbor, Marie. Marie, a punkishly outlandish French woman, no longer in the spring of her years and whose good-for-nothing boyfriend just moved out, is also looking for something better. This tentative friendship — between two disparate people brought together by a common need for intimacy and understanding — is not the stuff of high drama, but rather a simple, surprisingly touching and sensitive tale of an unlikely love between two social outsiders. The film is the third in a kind of "Berlin Trilogy" by director Gisler, with the other films being *Hanging Around* (*Tagediebe*) in 1985 and *Sleepless Nights* (*Schlaflose Nachte*) in 1988. ⊛

women while at the same time engaged to a traditional Arab woman and acts puritanical with his family. What the photographer discovers is that the permissive West, in the form of seemingly harmless tourism, invades Muslim lands and corrupts their young.

Billy Budd *(1962, 123 min, US, Peter Ustinov)*

Taken from Herman Melville's last work, a novelette that was not published until 1924, this rousing allegorical sea yarn set in the late 18th century is a fascinating study of good and evil, innocence and treachery, the ineffectiveness of civilized justice, and subtle homosexual obsession. A beautiful young merchant marine, Billy Budd (a luminous Terence Stamp), is pressed into military service on the H.M.S. Avenger and comes under the sadistic command of First Mate Claggard (an intensely sinister Robert Ryan). Against his own wishes, Claggard finds himself attracted to the young man, an attraction that he fatally fights off. Peter Ustinov also stars as the gentler Captain Vere, equally troubled by this personification of virtue and comeliness. A stirring yet troubling drama. ⊛

Focus on: *Herman Melville*

Nineteenth-century American novelist Herman Melville (1819-1891) was a popular writer of action-adventure sea tales who ultimately fell out of favor with the public and finished his life working in anonymity for 19 years at a U.S. Customs House in New York. It was not until many years later that his works began to gain immense popularity. His stories were about strong, adventurous men on the high seas who many times were bound by duty, love and affection for each other. Although he was married with three children, his unrequited love for fellow author Nathaniel Hawthorne is considered a revelatory relationship in his life. Additional film versions of Melville's novels include John Huston's 1956 production of his immortal sea classic Moby Dick *with Gregory Peck in the role of Captain Ahab; and a 1970 independent production of his short novel of alienation,* Bartleby, *directed by Anthony Friedman and starring Paul Scofield.*

Blue Jeans

(1981, 101 min, France, Hughes Burin des Roziers)
First love and the fickleness of adolescence is the theme of this charming, if slight drama. The story follows a pretty blond French youth who is sent with his classmates to an English seaside resort for the summer to study English. It is there that he first meets and "falls in love" with a girl, but when the girl spurns him for an older teenager, his attentions and affections are soon shifted to him. His unresponsiveness is frustrating but not lethal for the boy (see *To Play or to Die* for a more somber approach to this subject) in this touching and sensitive tale. ⊛

Blunt: The Fourth Man

(1992, 86 min, GB, John McGlasham)

Anthony Hopkins is a delight as Guy Burgess, the British government official who fled England before the discovery that he and several other high government employees were spies for the Soviets and traitors to their country. Knowledge of this story will prove helpful to would-be viewers, for the film goes about its business with the assumption that the audience is well aware of this much-publicized scandal. At the center of the tale is Burgess' fellow spy, Anthony Blunt (wonderfully played by Ian Richardson), who recruited Burgess, Kim Philby and Donald McLean while they all attended Cambridge in the 1930s. Set in the early 1960s, the film shows Blunt as a well-respected art historian and "keeper of the Queen's paintings." When his well-ordered life is threatened with exposure, Blunt begins an elaborate cover-up and damage control campaign to safeguard his network of fellow spies and himself. His biggest challenge is in protecting Guy Burgess, his former lover and close friend. The handling of the characters' homosexuality is both sensitive and explicit, for although the film is about men who betray their own country, it is also a quietly tender love story between the two older men. While Richardson plays Blunt as a fastidious semi-queen, Hopkins has great fun as the foppish Burgess, an openly gay carouser who never waivers from his freewheeling, boozing and sexually active persona while plotting his clandestine defection. ◈

A Boy Like Many Others
(Un Ragazzo Come Tanti)

(1983, 96 min, Italy, Gianni Minello)

Evoking a neorealist mood, this touching low-budget drama tells the harrowing and familiar tale of a fresh-faced teenager who comes to the big city filled with dreams only to encounter poverty, exploitation and indifference. Stefano Mioni plays Pino, the country boy, a handsome youth who, despite his initial aversion and shame, takes the advice of his new city friends and becomes a prostitute. What follows is Pino's increasingly depressing and degrading encounters with seedy johns and urban low-lifes as he eventually becomes involved in petty crime and drug dealing. In an unlikely ending, the boy finds possible happiness and understanding in the arms of a gay artist. Taking a *Pixote*-styled social realism approach, this fascinating and engrossing film, which features mostly non-professionals, depicts the young people involved in homosexuality, drug taking and prostitution in a non-judgmental, even sincere fashion.

The Boys in the Band

(1970, 118 min, US, William Friedkin)

Historically and politically significant despite (or because of) the pervading self-loathing and wallowing self-pity of its gay characters, *The Boys in the Band* continues to ignite contentious debate a quarter of a century after its release. Mart Crowley produced and adapted his own award-winning 1968 play which featured the original off-Broadway cast and was directed by William Friedkin (who would go on to helm *The French Connection* and the infamous *Cruising*). The stage-bound, hyperventilating comedy-drama features eight friends who get together one rainy New York evening for a simple birthday party. What ensues during the course of the night is enough emotion, acid-laced barbs and self-analysis to last a normal queer's lifetime. Michael (Kenneth Nelson), the host of the party, is an over-consuming, "can't deal with being a faggot" Catholic with a drinking problem; Harold, wonderfully played by Leonard Frey, is the birthday boy, a pot-smoking, pock-marked Jew. Other characters include a bickering couple (Keith Prentice and Laurence Luckinbill as a pipe-smoking bisexual family man); a seemingly well-adjusted black man who is devastated when confronted with his past; Cowboy, a brainless but beautiful hustler (Robert La Tourneaux); and Emory (immortally played by a limp-wristed, lisping Cliff Gorman). As the evening wears on, the playful bickering turns into vengeful attacks and the men come to realize the almost overpowering sadness and loneliness of being a homosexual. A pre-liberation classic which features many memorable lines (some funny, others not) such as Emory's plea, "Who do you have to fuck to get a drink around here?" and Michael's "Show me a happy homosexual and I'll show you a gay corpse." Dated but hilarious and often times suprisingly offensive to '90s gay sensibilites, the film is nonetheless an important step in the depiction of gays in film. On a side note, the film's 1970 theatrical premieres across the country were true events, despite most critics' denunciation of the film; the controversy even made its way into the advertising campaign. The original film poster was a split screen image of Leonard Frey on the left with a line saying, "Today is Harold's birthday"; on the right was a photo of a grinning Robert La Tourneaux, and underneath written, "This is his present." Most newspapers, including the *Los Angeles Times* and *The New York Times*, rejected it. On a sad note: Leonard Frey (who would receive an Oscar nomination with his next film, *Fiddler on the Roof*), Kenneth Nelson, Frederick Combs (who played Michael's friend Donald) and Robert La Tourneaux all have died from AIDS. ◈

The Blue Hour

Boys of Cell Block Q

(1992, 90 min, US, Alan Daniels)

Teetering between being an enjoyably cheesy C&A "boys in prison" spoof and actual drama, this poor man's *Fortune and Men's Eyes* works best for those seeking humor and skin (but alas, no sex!). The setting is Sunnyvale Labor Farm for wayward boys — a veritable hotbed of homosexuality, pumped up pecs, sadistic guards, lecherous priests, and a coterie of pretty boys who seem to be in various stages of undress. The story focuses on one cell of boys: Tim, the innocent "virgin" with a murderous past; Beef, the hunky chieftain and self-proclaimed "Top Cock"; and Lana, the acid-tongued queen. Adapted from a John C. Wall play and filled with campy lines such as, "He thought that it would be bad to be a homosexual in love with a minor who kills people" and "Put that in your crockpot and simmer it," the film won't be confused with Shakespeare, but then again, what was the last Shakespeare play with studs entangled in a steamy, naked brawl in the showers? ☻

"It's *Prisoner: Cell Block H* but with cute guys and loads of dick...a camp horny comedy."

—*Boyz* [London]

Boys of Cell Block Q

The Boys of St. Vincent

(1992, 186 min, Canada, John N. Smith)

This compelling drama of physical and sexual abuse at a Canadian boys' orphanage unravels like a wrenching sexual horror film, making for riveting, if uncomfortable viewing. The time is 1975 and the setting is St. Vincent, a Catholic orphanage in Newfoundland run by an order of brothers. Instead of being a place of compassion and understanding by the group of "celibate" guardians, it is a pervasive atmosphere of sexual tyranny and gross abuse of authority. The center of the story is Kevin (Johnny Morina), a withdrawn 10-year-old boy who is the sexual pet of Brother Lavin (Henry Czerny), the dictatorial and devil-like principal. There are scenes in which the boys, trapped inside the walls of the orphanage with no one to turn to, are physically and sexually abused — it is almost too painful to watch. A sympathetic janitor alerts the police, but Church complicity and police reluctance to interfere conspire to cover up the problem and solidify the veil of secrecy. The second part of this shocking psychological thriller is set 15 years later, as the boys, now young, emotionally scarred men, successfully prod the authorities to bring criminal charges against the brothers involved. Especially effective in this part is 25-year-old Kevin (Sebastian Spence), who is forced to relive his traumatic past. The story, based on true events, is quite disturbing, but it is noteworthy that despite portraying men abusing boys, the film does not consider it a "gay" issue; in fact, all involved are nominally straight, even the evil Brother Lavin, who is seen as married with two children. This controversial two-part video was banned on TV in Ontario and Quebec and its home video release in Canada was delayed for a year. ☻

Boys on Film, Vols 1-3

An introduction about the shorts: Spurred by the relative affordability of video and a greater willingness to focus on queer themes, hundreds of lesbian and gay shorts are being made every year. But despite many of these works being programmed together at the various lesbian and gay film festivals around the world, greater distribution after the festival circuit has been difficult, if not insurmountable. A case in point is the film and videos in this very book — I've ignored, for the most part, any film that is less than 50 minutes, thereby eliminating an entire video and filmmaking movement that is currently in full bloom. British distributor Dangerous to Know and Frameline, the producer of the San Francisco Lesbian & Gay International Film Festival, have begun to address this distribution and availability problem with the packaging of several shorts into feature-length programs that are being promoted both theatrically (*Boys Shorts*) and directly to home video in the case of the *Boys on Film* series. Lesbian compilations include *Lesbian Leather Shorts*, *Lesbian Lykra Shorts* and *She Is Safe*. Hopefully, the success of these initial offerings will pave the way for many additional programs.

Boys on Film: 1

Dangerous to Know, the British video distributing company specializing in queer-themed films and videos, is releasing video compilations of the many gay and lesbian shorts that make the festival circuit. The company's goal is to present an "invigorating selection of contemporary gay short films from across the world."

The following video, the first of a projected series, is available only in Great Britain, although *The Dead Boys' Club* can be seen in the U.S. in the *Boys' Shorts* compilation released through Frameline.

The Dead Boys' Club
(1992, 25 min, US, Mark Christopher)
A stylish and funny AIDS-era short that celebrates the vitality of the 1970s gay generation. While sorting through the belongings of his recently deceased lover, a fortyish man offers a pair of his lover's disco shoes ("his slut shoes") to his young, shy and closeted cousin. Strange, wonderful things happen to the young man when he puts on the shoes — magically transporting him to the carefree, boisterous days of disco, exuberant sexual energy, bathhouses, bell-bottoms and the music of Sylvester and Donna Summer.

The Dead Boys' Club

Pool Days
(1993, 45 min, US, Brian Sloan)
Wryly humorous, sexy and sensitive, this coming-out story is set in a gym where handsome 17-year-old Justin gets a summer job as a lifeguard/attendant. Still confused about his sexuality, the gay world comes to him as steam room sex, naked male bodies and one particularly enticing swimmer cloud his head with sex, sex and more sex. After a furtive stab at seducing a female member, Justin eventually lets his gay side come out, with happy results.

Boys on Film: 2

To Play or to Die
(1990, 50 min, The Netherlands, Frank Krom)
Filmed with unusual flair for a small independent film, his hyper-ventilating psychosexual drama tells the story of a nerdish teenager's intense crush on a bullying but attractive classmate. With his parents away, 15-year-old Kees, fueled by a masochistic puppy love for the unresponsive and cruel Charel, has his plans for seduction and revenge unravel after he invites the other boy to his home. A simple premise, and while not at all homophobic, its theme of equating homosexual desire with madness and death is a

sad, frustrating one, especially problematic coming from a promising gay filmmaker. ✪

Tell Me No Lies
(1992, 30 min, GB, Neil Hunter)
Set among college students in London, this droll coming-out comedy revolves around three best friends, all of whom are gay but are unable to come out to others. Interesting, if a bit too dry.

Relax
(1991, 25 min, GB, Christopher Newby)
This humorous take on one man's decision to take an AIDS test is both visually atmospheric and refreshingly original. Steve (Philip Rosch), after much internal debate, decides to take the dreaded AIDS test and in the ensuing ten days of waiting for the results, goes through the gamut of emotions — from thoughts of paranoia to fatalism to suicide. He rejects his friends and fears the worst from his past unprotected sex. A promising, imaginative short. Christopher Newby recently directed his feature film debut with *Anchoress*.

Boys on Film: 3

Bad News Bachelors
(1990, 25 min, Australia, Franco di Chiera)
The eternal search for Mr. Right is the theme to this pleasant comedy. Set in a gay Sydney, the film follows thirtyish Stuart as he roams the city's cafes, bars and cruising areas looking for a man to love but finding only sex (which is more than most find) with a series of likable men, none of whom offer the likelihood of a relationship.

Resonance
(1991, 11 min, Australia, Stephen Cummins)
Visually impressive, with a memorable soundtrack and several classical dance numbers, this artily abstract story starts with a brutal queer-bashing and proceeds to juxtapose the subsequent strengthening of the victim's relationship with his lover and the crumbling life of the attacker and his girlfriend.

To Play or to Die

Beyond Gravity

(1988, 44 min, New Zealand, Garth Maxwell)
Gay love blooms in Aukland in this romantic tale about the unlikely love between a nerdish, astronomy-obsessed young man and a free-wheeling Italian con man. Richard's unassuming routine working as a mild-mannered scientist and living in the closet is thrown into disarray after he meets Johnny, a slyly attractive and mysterious stranger who invades and quickly throws his well-ordered life into delirious turmoil. Throwing caution to the wind, Richard becomes involved with the unpredictable Johnny, and together they set off for adventure. One of the few gay-themed films from New Zealand.

Boys' Shorts

(1990-92, 119 min, US/GB/Australia)
This collection of videos was screened theatrically in the United States in 1993. ⊛

R.S.V.P. *(1991, 23 min, Canada, Laurie Lynd)*
As they listen to a classical station belatedly play his request for Jessye Norman's recording of Berlioz's "La Spectre de la Rose," a group of students remember their teacher who has died of AIDS.

Anthem *(1990, 9 min, US, Marlon Riggs)*
From the director of *Tongues Untied* comes this poetic rap exploration of love and desire as it relates to gay African-Americans.

Relax *(1991, 25 min, GB, Christopher Newby)*
For description, see *Boys on Film: 2*

Resonance *(1991, 11 min, Australia, Stephen Collins)*
For description, see *Boys on Film: 3*

Billy Turner's Secret

(1990, 26 min, US, Michael Mayson)
Professional and very entertaining, this humorous film focuses on two lifelong friends who share a Brooklyn apartment. Tensions rise when Billy, an African-American, decides that he has to tell his none-too-enlightened friend that he is living with a queer.

Boys' Shorts: R.S.V.P.

The Dead Boys' Club

(1992, 25 min, US, Mark Christopher)
For description, see *Boys on Film: 1*

The Broadcast Tapes of Dr. Peter

(1990-92, 60 min, Canada, David Paperny)
Dr. Peter Jepson-Young, a physician and educator living in Vancouver, British Columbia, was diagnosed with AIDS in the late 1980s. Instead of simply sitting back and acting the victim, he decided to videotape his diary entries and his life. Structured in a series of 111 half-hour episodes over a two-year time frame, the videos were originally broadcast on a local Canadian news program and eventually compiled and edited down to one hour for broadcast on BBC. The film journal begins with the handsome, 33-year-old, fun-loving doctor already partially blind. But in sharp contrast to *Silverlake Life*, Dr. Peter puts his best face forward, keeping his private life largely secret, as well as his emotions and intimate thoughts. But one does get to see a man determined not to be brought down by the disease, and he is seen skiing, playing the piano and engaging in several other activities. Having no self-pity, this invigorating portrait charts his inevitable deterioration as the disease begins to ravage his body — he eventually died in November 1992. A poignant PWA tale that is alternately upbeat and quite sad.

Broken Noses

(1987, 75 min, US, Bruce Weber)
No photographer has captured and defined the male erotic image as Bruce Weber. Now the prolific Weber has entered the area of documentary filmmaking with his lush and subtle *Broken Noses*. A small boxing club in Portland, Oregon, a second home to boys in age from 10 to 16, provides the perfect opportunity to highlight youthful beauty as the young men talk of their dreams and aspirations. At center stage is 19-year-old Andy, a young boxer with a promising future. Weber's camera caresses Andy's smoldering physique while exploring his narcissism and machismo. Filmed primarily in black and white, the film has a rich '50s feel which is enhanced by a West Coast hip jazz soundtrack. ⊛

Burning Secret

(1988, 106 min, US/GB/Germany, Andrew Birkin)
Taking what might be considered a minority — some would say sick — interpretation of this elegant drama, one can view *Burning Secret* as a reversed *Death in Venice*, with a 12-year-old boy falling in love with an older man — a man who teases but remains elusive, resulting in the death of the boy's innocence. Set in 1919 at a luxury hotel in a wintry Marienbad, the film stars David Eberts as Edmund Tuckman, a lonely asthmatic boy who is desperate for affection and is recuperating with his lovely and equally lonely mother Sonja (Faye Dunaway), while his much older father stays in Vienna. He clings to mom until one day he becomes transfixed by a sports car owned by a mysterious and alluring Baron (Klaus Maria Brandauer). The Baron sees the boy and his first comment is, "Would you like more than just a look...go for a ride." And with this pick-up line, they become

Broken Noses

uncomfortably close friends. Sexual tensions are heightened as the two become inseparable. Mom gets nervous about the relationship, but is relieved when it becomes apparent that the Baron was only using the boy to get to her. When the boy realizes this, he becomes jealous, moody and determined to win the man back; an effort that ends in failure. In one of the most bizarre episodes in the film, Sonja and the Baron begin making love in the Baron's room down the hall. The boy's sleep becomes increasingly troubled and his moaning (as in a sexual frenzy) succeeds in coitus interruptus. The lies and deceptions the adults inflict upon the sensitive and trusting boy only toughen him as he grows up in a hurry and begins to recover from his first love. And then again, the film could simply be a simple love story between two adults... ⊛

Busting *(1973, 89 min, US, Peter Hyams)*

Patently offensive to gays and lesbians as well as blacks and other members of the disenfranchised, this standard police comedy-drama doesn't pit cops against robbers, but rather cops against the socially and sexually deviant. Despicable and at times painful in its violent homophobia, the film stars Elliott Gould (remember when he "starred" in movies?) and Robert Blake as two out-of-control vice cops, rampaging through the underworld of prostitution and gay bars undeterred by the Bill of Rights and basic justice. The gay sequence, in which the two cops "disguise" themselves as fags and raid a "fruit bar" turns violent after the queers (depicted as limp-wristed queens), sick of another police incursion, aka Stonewall, and led by professional homosexual Antonio Fargas (*Next Stop, Greenwich Village; Car Wash*), refuse to go quietly and begin a riot, fighting off the two until overcome by additional police. Anti-gay slurs abound, but there are fun moments including Gould and Blake awkwardly dancing arm-in-arm at the gay bar. ⊛

CBS Presents "The Homosexuals"
(1967, 52 min, US)

This pre-liberation TV special is hosted by Mike Wallace and purports to "enlighten" the American public about the lifestyles of the "average homosexual." While possibly unfair to criticize its end result, ignorant good intentions certainly abounded. Wallace interviews five male homosexuals and in an effort to be unbiased, presents two of them (all five of their faces were obscured) as happy with their lifestyle, two as quite troubled and one as unsure. Psychiatrists are also called in to present the "medical experts'" opinion on this deviant behavior. Despite painting a bleak view, several critics found it too homosexual-friendly and before it was aired, it was edited to make the two "happy" homos less so. After one showing, one of the interviewees who had their views distorted sued CBS, effectively preventing any future airings of the controversial program.

> "The average homosexual, if there is such, is promiscuous. He is not interested in, nor capable of, a long lasting relationship like that of a heterosexual marriage."
> —Mike Wallace

The Cage *(1988, 90 min, US, Rick Cluchey)*

Filmed in front of a live audience at L.A.'s Odyssey Theatre by the San Quentin Drama Workshop, this drama on the inhumanity of man suffers from both a poor video transfer and a script that is perhaps too earnest. The result is an awkward, stylized, preachy and altogether unbelievable "exposé" of prison life. A naive, and possibly innocent, young man is thrown into a cell with three other inmates. When he is not being brutalized by the sadistic guards, he becomes the object of his cellmates' power and fantasy games, who taunt and abuse him, sexually and physically. His fellow prisoners include a crazy older man (writer and director and former con Rick Cluchey), a self-proclaimed agent of God; a handicapped weirdo and sex fiend (William Hayes, author of *Midnight Express*); and a Marine-like boxer bent on deflowering the new cell mate. Attempting to be impassioned and haunting, the tale develops instead into a stage-bound drama with a story seen many times before. The original stage production might have made for a more effective experience as evidenced by the many great reviews for the play including this quote from *The National Observer*: "Mr. Cluchey's play is surreal, fantasy-oriented and moves beyond rampant homosexuality to consider the ways in which men behind bars handle their guilt." ⊛

La Cage aux Folles
(1978, 91 min, France/Italy, Edouard Molinaro)

This frolicsome farce that finally made drag respectable stars Ugo Tognazzi and Michel Serrault as gay lovers who must, amid mounting complications, pose as mom and dad for the sake of a prospective daughter-in-law and her straight-laced parents. The film was a big art-house hit upon its theatrical release, and spawned two sequels and an American musical remake for the Broadway stage. ⊛

La Cage aux Folles II
(1980, 101 min, France, Edouard Molinaro)

This sequel to the popular comedy reunited the original stars (Tognazzi & Serrault) who, as gay lovers Alban and Renato, become involved with spies and are forced to flee the country.

Alban's valiant attempts to masquerade as a Sicilian peasant woman is one of the hilarious highlights to this otherwise fair sequel. ☺

La Cage aux Folles III: The Wedding
(1986, 88 min, France, Georges Lautner)
Who saw this tepid sequel when it came out theatrically? Judging from the box-office receipts, not many. Gay cabaret star Alban learns he is to inherit a fortune — but only on the condition that he marry and provide an heir in 18 months. ☺

Cap Tourmente
(1993, 115 min, Canada, Michel Langlois)
Square-jawed Roy Dupuis (the hustler who killed for homo love in *Being at Home with Claude*) stars in this entertaining and ridiculously somber tale of simmering incestuous passions set in the remote regions of Quebec. Bringing new meaning to family dysfunctionalism, Dupuis, looking like a dreamy sailor who fell off the pages of "Querelle," is Alex, an aggressively troubled young man returning (home from the "sea") to his world-weary mother (Andree Lachapelle) and his unhappy sister Alfa (Elise Guilbault). Joining them is leather-jacketed family friend Jean-Louis (Gilbert Sciotte). Outward appearances deceive as it is quickly revealed that all have in the past been sexually involved with the others (a mathematically impressive number!). The sexual shenanigans remain frustratingly on the lingering glances, quick kiss level as the foursome attempt to work out an acceptable partnering relationship. Alex, although a mental case, is the only one who would be happy to bed all three (all at the same time if the bed was big enough). His bisexuality is taken completely matter-of-factly, although in comparison to lusting after one's mother and sister, homosexuality looks conventional by comparison!

Casta Diva
(1982, 107 min, The Netherlands, Eric de Kuyper)
Belgian director Eric de Kuyper, whose background is in structuralism and semiotics, has worked previously as a theoretician in film production with Chantal Akerman. *Casta Diva*, his feature-film debut, is a hallucinatory and haunting experimental film. Shot in black and white and using non-sync sound, the film consists of ten scenes of approximately ten minutes each. Filmed with a steady, almost static camera, he records singular, seemingly innocuous daily activities of solitary men (i.e. a man leisurely bathing, someone trying on a pair of trousers, another working on a car). The result is a muted celebration of the male form and a personal analysis of solitary man interacting with his physical self.

Céleste *(1981, 107 min, Germany, Percy Adlon)*
Set in 1913, this moving drama is based on the memoirs of the real Céleste Albaret. With no plot to speak of, it is a subtle yet involving and ultimately inspiring love story that chronicles the daily routine of an uneducated peasant girl (the wonderful Eva Mattes) who is hired as the housekeeper for the ailing author, Marcel Proust. The film's power lies in the evolving relationship between the intellectual Proust and the simple, caring woman who, in the course of nine years, not only tends to his house but becomes his companion, secretary, friend and surrogate mother, as well. ☺

Focus on: *Marcel Proust*
French writer Marcel Proust (1871-1922) was a much celebrated novelist who overcame a lifelong series of illnesses (he was an invalid much of his life), homosexuality and being a Jew to become the toast of Parisian society with his love stories centering around high society. With his classic "Remembrance of Things Past" and several other novels and writings, he became a respected and admired man of letters who was influential with writers such as André Gide and Jean Cocteau. While he was widely known as a homosexual (for a time the word "Proustian" became a polite form of saying homosexual), it was only in the 1921 journals of Gide that his homosexuality was revealed publicly. Gide writes that Proust "Transposed all of his attractive and charming homosexual recollects to fill out the heterosexual portions of his mammoth work." His later years were spent as a recluse, where he hired many gay men as servants and reportedly enjoyed a long relationship with his chauffeur, Alfred Agostinelli, who moved into his home and became his secretary. The only major film version of his works is

La Cage aux Folles II

Swann in Love *(1984, 155 min, France, Volker Schlöndorff)*, a beautifully rendered adaptation of the author's illustrious "Swann's Way." Jeremy Irons stars as the dashing, cultivated Charles Swann who loses his heart and esteem in a passionate tryst with a pouting courtesan *(Ornella Muti)*. Alan Bates played Proust in the made-for-British television film 102 Boulevard Haussmann *in 1991.*

Chain of Desire

(1992, 105 min, US, Temistocles Lopez)

From the director of the intriguing *Exquisite Corpses* comes this stylistically inventive and wittily droll observation on sexual yearning and unrequited love in the age of AIDS. Linda Fiorentino is Alma, a singer in a slick New York nightclub who sleeps with Jesus, a married, Hispanic worker. This successful coupling begins a humorous but sexually frustrating daisy chain of purely sexual encounters with a succession of New York characters. Malcolm McDowell is featured as a cheesy closeted journalist with a taste for street urchins and Seymour Cassel plays a philandering artist who catches his previously chaste wife humping a startled canvas stretcher. A titillating highlight (and the most sexually satisfying for the film's characters) is a three-way, voyeuristically-charged masturbation scene (both gay and straight) between three people in three different curtain-less high-rise apartments. While never actually mentioning the word "AIDS," the disease hovers over all in this erotic updating of *La Ronde* which explores sexual desire (but oddly omits lesbianism) and has been described by the director as a "story about desire, not lesbianism." ✪

> "My film is about desire, with moments of love...I wanted to say that no matter what your sexuality, there's no wrongs or rights; sex is to be seen as a force — relentless — which has no boundaries of any kind. It is true that the gay material was longer than any other part of the script, but that is what I wanted as a gay director."
>
> —Temistocles Lopez

Focus on: *Temistocles Lopez*

Although Temistocles ("call me Temmie") Lopez has made only two feature films, Chain of Desire *and his 1989 debut* Exquisite Corpses *(and neither is per se a "gay film"), he still is a shining star in gay independent American filmmaking for the '90s. Openly gay (or as he is quoted, "preferably gay"), Temmie's first act of coming out was to his super macho father who, when Lopez told of his homosexuality at age 18, responded, "There's only one thing for you to do: shoot yourself." Lopez said, "I was devastated, although I had never felt badly about being gay. I never felt it was wrong to be gay. Never." Lopez's two provocative films include in their wacky casts of characters gay men and, to a lesser extent, lesbians. Responding to complaints that* Chain *was soft in its depiction of lesbians, Lopez explained that "I had originally written the scene between the chanteuse (Linda Fiorentino) and her masseuse (Suzanne Douglas) to be flat-out lesbian, but Fiorentino refused to do it." Born in Caracas, Venezuela, Lopez was educated in Europe and attended the London Film School. He honed his filmmaking skills by making shorts, Spanish features, Italian TV programs and directing stage productions in South America*

before moving to New York and successfully raising the $100,000 needed for Exquisite Corpses. *He is currently working on a new project called* The Touch, *which again contains several gay characters.*

Changing Face

(1993, 103 min, US, Robert Tate & Robert Roznowski)

A direct-to-video release, this earnest independent production is an interesting (albeit frustrating) example of the current state of queer film/video production — now almost explosive in the United States. While far from being theatrically viable or even being gay film festival material, *Changing Face* takes the politics and "deviance" out of being gay by presenting, in a conventional soap opera structure, the inconsequential life of a stable gay couple. Filmmakers Robert Tate and Robert Roznowski star as Tom and Dan, two ordinary men as bland as their names. The two — twentysomething yuppies involved in a long, monogamous relationship (very '90s!) — find themselves, despite their young age, suffering from midlife identity crisis. Around their vapid lives, filled with petty squabbling and matronly pecks on the cheeks, are their familiar collection of wacky New York friends. These types (lonely men and women looking for the right person, a gay couple on the rocks) provide some semblance of life when compared to the orderly domesticity of Tom and Dan. The film's greatest problem is lack of a plot, a failing that forced the directors into the mistaken path of using the couple's heightened bickering as the film's only evidence of dramatic tension. While the film is a disappointment, its importance lies in its very conventionality. Now that some gays and lesbians are successfully integrated into society at large (a situation that only exists in the big cities) and have surrounded themselves with the conveniences and superficiality of American consumerism, will queer filmmaking begin to reflect this? Will filmmakers who are currently working on documentaries and more heated dramatic features become placated by capitalistic comforts? ✪

Cheers: "Boys in the Bar"

(1983, 25 min, US, James Burrows)

Episodes of the long-running television sitcom "Cheers" have recently been released on video and one of the two-episode tapes includes a gay-themed opus entitled "Boys in the Bar." In it, Sam (Ted Danson) invites his old pal and fellow ex-professional baseball player, Tom (Alan Aurty), to his bar to celebrate the publication of Tom's autobiography, which, unbeknownst to Sam, centers around Tom's coming out. Insipid stereotypical images (fern lovers, lite beer drinkers, etc.) are the main butt of the homophobic humor as Sam remarks "guys should be guys" and his homophobic pals fear that their beloved bar will soon be overrun by fags. As barmaid Diane, Shelley Long provides the only calming and reasoned voice in this show's limp attempt to be current and "liberal." The ending scene is, and I admit this begrudgingly, funny. Though the first, this is not the last gay-themed episode on "Cheers." Harvey Fierstein played a gay friend of Rebecca's (Kirstie Alley), and the show demonstrated a greater gay sensibility and sensitivity. ✪

Chippendales: Tahitian Adventure — Stranded

(1992, 65 min, US)

Having long flourished under the protective veil of heterosexual men showing off their classically chiseled, gyrating bodies to the innocent ogling of women, the Chippendales can now come directly to your home via this sun-splashed, flesh-baring video. Meet your favorite beauties as they frolic in the sun, with nary a stitch of fabric to clothe their bronzed, muscle-bulging physiques. This silly tease just might be the tonic for those who find hard-core porn leaves nothing to the imagination. ☹

Chippendales: A Musical with Muscle

(1993, 71 min, US)

With bulging biceps, skimpy, skin-tight G-strings, shaved chests and pretty faces, one almost expects that the Chippendales will eventually star in a TV series — an updated "Charlie's Angels" just might be the ticket. But before any development deals are realized, fans will have to contend with this, the Chippendales' video version of their stage musical "A Musical with Muscle." Filmed live at London's Strand Theatre, these skimpily-clad, cross-dressing Rockettes put on a lively, fleshy performance with a high energy musical score and lavish "Let's put on a show" dance numbers. Almost anachronistic in its sexual outlook, the video will prove to be harmless, almost-tantalizing fun, but 71 minutes of sexual teasing and accompanying pulsating, chiseled male bods will drive many a male to their lockers in search of something harder. ☹

The Choirboys

(1977, 120 min, US, Robert Aldrich)

This awful adaptation of Joseph Wambaugh's novel (he disassociated himself from the film), directed by Robert Aldrich (*The Killing of Sister George*), is unbelievably vicious in its homophobia. For starters, there's Jack DeLeon (some may remember him as the swishy lover on "Barney Miller") as a faggot with a capitol "F" — he comes complete with pink poodle and purse, and delights at finding a naked man handcuffed to a tree. Then there's vice cop Vince Tayback's fag routine in a men's room, pretending to come on to a bigoted cop. How about young gay Michael Willis, caught cruising a men's room and brought to vice cop Burt Young, who can say only, "How long have you had this problem?" Patrolman James Woods jokes at one point, "How about shooting at fags?" And then, to top off this incredulous gay-bashing, Willis returns, this time to the park where it seems only gay men and police officers congregate, and (after opening a locked police van!) gets blown away by a crazed officer, to which his fellow cops confer, "It's only a fag." If one or two of the police officers possessed these anti-gay feelings, it could be presumed that the film is a tough-minded, brutal exploration of homophobia (as in *The Boys Next Door*). But all the characters act and feel this way: it's an accepted behavior. This is a dispicable film with reprehensible ideas — only more disturbing is the fact that it got made in the first place. ☹

Chris Hayward plays a gay doctor in *The Clinic*

Citizen Cohn

(1992, 112 min, US, Frank Pierson)

Based on the novel by Nicholas von Hoffman, this engrossing biographical and political drama on the life of Roy Cohn — Communist headhunter, ruthless lawyer and closeted homosexual who died of AIDS in 1986 — is great explosive fun. Using his trademark hyper-energy coupled with his on-edge, often grating on-screen personality to unforgettable use, a seemingly possessed James Woods stars as the charismatic, but at times demonic Cohn. Made for HBO, the film is structured in a series of flashbacks, as the now disbarred Cohn lies semiconscious in a hospital bed, dying of AIDS and hallucinating on many of the contentious incidents from his life — a past full of grievances, perceived slights and a relentless, blood-thirsty quest for glory. Pulling no punches, the story chronicles Cohn's early triumphs as the prosecutor at the Rosenbergs' trial, his work as henchman/conciliator to Joe McCarthy during the Communist witch-hunts as well as his later years as an arrogant lawyer and power broker. Adding spice to his many professional confrontations are scenes that touch on his secretive personal life, that of a free-wheeling homosexual who, as the film "reveals," was close chums with fellow homos J. Edgar Hoover and Cardinal Spellman. ☹

Clay Farmers *(1988, 60 min, US, A.P. Gonzalez)*

This odd tale of man-boy friendship and homophobia is set in a small farming community in northern California where Mike (Nicholas Rempel) and Dan (Todd Fraser), two strapping, often shirtless young men tend a farm. The other farmers, many of them impoverished, form an uneasy acceptance of the two. But when they befriend and comfort a young boy who was physically abused by his father, the father has no trouble stirring up homophobic hatred against them. The film, while not altogether satisfying, does create an effective atmosphere of impending doom, and includes some touching scenes between the two hard-working men and leaves open the question of their sexuality by cryptically remarking "Homophobia runs deep, it ruins friendships. I have had relationships where the friendship could not be close because the men were afraid it would have to be homosexual." ☹

On the same video is *My First Suit* (1985, 29 min, New Zealand, Stewart Main), written by Peter Wells and directed by Stewart Main, the production team responsible for the 1993 cult extravaganza *Desperate Remedies*. *My First Suit* is a funny and evocative short about Steve (Conrad Crawte), a shy, bespectacled teen whose divorced parents both want to buy him a new suit for a school dance. But the wistful Steve is more interested with his fantasies involving masculine, muscular men and the confused beginnings of his gay sexuality.

"A knowing glance through gay adolescence."
—*Bay Area Reporter*

The Clinic
(1984, 93 min, Australia, David Stevens)
A comedy about social disease? It may sound strange, possibly in bad taste and potentially off-putting, but *The Clinic* is a surprisingly fresh and funny frolic about one day in the life of a Sydney V.D. clinic. Chock full of bawdy doctor/patient vignettes, the film is never derisive and maintains a gentle understanding for the afflicted denizens of this madcap milieu. Gay men are featured throughout this pro-sex, pro-gay and pro-woman comedy with the star of the film (the clinic's head doctor) being a well-adjusted gay man (Chris Hayward) who not only tends to be affected, but also handles some subtle homophobia by a young intern (Simon Burke). ⊛

Closing Numbers
(1993, 95 min, GB, Stephen Walker)
Similar in theme to the 1991 French drama *The Lie*, this made-for-British TV potboiler concerns itself with deceptive bisexuality and AIDS in the typical family. Anna (Jane Asher) is the happily married, middle-class wife of Keith (Tim Woodward). Her life is drastically altered when she discovers that he is having an affair, not with a woman, but with another man. She eventually meets the lover, Steve (Patrick Pearson), and surprisingly befriends him. Through their friendship, her life is opened up to the world of AIDS and its accompanying prejudices and pain as she befriends Steve's acquaintance Jim (Nigel Chernock), who is hospitalized with the disease. The harsh realities of AIDS ultimately hit home when Keith, who refused to be tested, begins showing signs that he has the disease.

Cock & Bull Story
(1992, 80 min, US, Billy Hayes)
Directed by Billy Hayes, the writer of *Midnight Express*, this potent two-man drama was performed by the San Quentin Drama Workshop and videotaped before a live audience. The story is set in a small English town in a gym locker room where Jocko (Mark Sheppard), a boxer with hopes of making it big in London, trains for an upcoming fight. His best mate, the fast-talking Travis (Trevor Goddard), hangs around and they engage in a series of tension-filled, sexually charged admissions and revelations about their personal feelings. Amidst the taunts and the macho posturing by the working-class youths comes the reality that the two can only express themselves through violence, despite their deep feel-

ings to the contrary. Flat sound quality due to the live recording mars this otherwise gripping story. ⊛

"The play is violent, bawdy, funny and ultimately heartbreaking as rampant homophobia compromises and then destroys friendship."
—*L.A. Village View*

A Cold Coming
(1992, 70 min, US, David Gadberry)
Earnest intention from playwright Howard Casner and director-star David Gadberry cannot breathe life into this stage-bound gay drama. Lovers for more than three years, Dave and John find themselves stranded one day at a train station during a blizzard. It is there that they begin to confront the reality that, despite emotional ties, their relationship is crumbling. Through flashbacks of their happier courtship days, the couple discuss, kvetch and argue on what has gone wrong while attempting a reconciliation. A low-budget production that is marred by being short on dramatic punch. Note: The sound clarity and volume fluctuate during the second half of the video. ⊛

Colonel Redl
(1984, 144 min, Germany/Hungary/Austria, Istvan Szabo)
Klaus Maria Brandauer (*Mephisto*) gives a bravura performance as a man driven by his lust for power. The son of a poor Jewish railway worker, Redl rises in rank to become head of military intelligence and commander in the Austro-Hungarian Army just before the start of WWI. A sweeping historical epic of intrigue, love and treason set in Austria during the turbulent years leading to the breakup of the Hapsburg Empire, the film concentrates chiefly on Redl's military career, only superficially examining his homosexuality. Laszlo Galffy is the handsome agent hired to seduce Redl to obtain military secrets. Based on John Osborn's play, "A Patriot for Me," and winner of the Special Jury Prize at Cannes. Although Szabo's film only hints at it, Alfred Redl's fall from power was due directly to his homosexuality. As head of Austrian Intelligence, Redl's career was yet to peak when the Russians used evidence of his homosexuality and transvestism (reportedly pictures of him naked with different men and love letters) to compel him into being a double agent for Tsarist Russia. When his treason was discovered by Austrian officials, he was given the honorable way out, suicide by revolver. Redl's case has been long used by military and government officials as an example of how homosexuals are susceptible to blackmail and thus are a security risk in highly sensitive jobs. An earlier film on Redl is the 1931 German feature, *Der Fall des Generalstabs-Oberst Redl*. ⊛

Coming Out
(1989, 109 min, Germany, Heiner Carow)
Premiered on the night the Berlin Wall came crumbling down, this, East Germany's first and only gay-themed film, is a gripping study of a man searching for his true sexual identity. Philip, a schoolteacher in East Berlin, becomes involved in a close, but passionless relationship with a woman. When he meets an old school

chum with whom he had a gay affair, his heterosexuality is thrown into doubt. Soon his emotions are torn between staying on the straight and narrow and accepting his new gay self and continuing the relationship with a handsome teen he met at a rock concert. Reminiscent of independent, quasi-autobiographical films (and all involving schoolteachers) like *Taxi Zum Klo* and *Nighthawks*, the film was shot in the many underground gay bars of East Berlin. A sentimental but frank tale which offers a rare glimpse into the "perils" of homosexuality behind the now crumbled Iron Curtain.

Compulsion
(1959, 103 min, US, Richard Fleischer)

The 1924 Leopold and Loeb murder case, in which two young men (both homosexuals) killed a boy basically for the thrill of it, has been adapted for the screen two other times. In Alfred Hitchcock's 1948 *Rope*, homoeroticism is playfully hinted and Tom Kalin's 1992 *Swoon* delivers a more blatantly queer interpretation. This intense drama, based on Meyer Levin's best-selling novel, stars Dean Stockwell and Bradford Dillman as the two privileged college students involved in a relationship that culminates in the murder of a 14-year-old boy. The cold and calculating Artie (Dillman) dominates the more sensitive Judd (Stockwell) while their "perfect crime" quickly unravels, leading them to prison and the possibility of a death sentence. Orson Welles, in the Clarence Darrow role, is featured as the impassioned lawyer who defends them. The homosexuality is inferred, enough so that critics at the time characterized the two "dirty little degenerates" as homosexual lovers.

Consenting Adult
(1985, 100 min, US, Gilbert Cates)

Praised when first aired on ABC in 1985, this earnest, made-for-TV movie is little more than a near two hours of uninterrupted preaching about the torment and pain of homosexuality. Interestingly, despite ultimately embracing themes of healing and "understanding," there is more homophobic ranting and hokey pounding-of-the-breast ravings in this liberal film than one would expect from a typical Jesse Helms speech. Marlo Thomas and Martin Sheen play a loving, upper middle-class Seattle couple whose lives are torn apart when their son announces, "Mom, I am a homosexual." The son, Jeff, played by Barry Tubbs, is a loving, blond jock studying pre-med at college (in other words, the perfect young man every family wants) who tells his mom that he hasn't done anything yet (this is Hollywood) and would like help with the "affliction." Mom smiles and says, "Thanks for telling me," and then, out of view of her son, cries and hysterically wonders what she did wrong. Determined to find a way to make him normal, the quietly domineering mom (Thomas is quite good in the role) tries to cure him of his "illness" by taking him to a quack psychiatrist who claims a 25-percent conversion rate; Dad, who has his own sexual hang-ups just about disowns him. Curiously, despite living in the big city, Jeff never seems to come in contact with other gays, but he begins to accept his true self nonetheless. In his best scene, he explodes about his doctor while describing his feelings to his mother, screaming, "He can't cure me! I'm not sick!" and soon after proclaims for all to hear, "I'm a queer, a fag, a fairy, a homosexual." Eventually, with the ache of failure still in

their hearts, his parents stop the tears, hysteria, regret and denial and accept their son as he is. Actually quite involving despite its many problems, the film, which is based on a 1975 novel by Laura Z. Hobson, went much further than other TV films of its time. Still, it was these very films and their "sanitized" image a homosexuality which led to the emergence of the New Queer Cinema. Ⓐ

Corrupt *(1983, 99 min, Italy, Roberto Faenza)*

Kinky S&M sexual tensions simmer to the boiling point in this weird police thriller. Harvey Keitel plays a bad good cop (that is, he's a hard-working cop on the take) who lives in a Brooklyn walk-up, but clandestinely shares an expensive, Upper East Side condo with another officer. The relationship between the two cops (the other is married) is never explained, although thoughts of a homosexual nature cannot be far away. The story begins when a pasty-faced creep (Johnny Lydon — aka Johnny Rotten of the Sex Pistols and Public Image Ltd.), looking for "someone special," begins stalking Keitel. Lydon, an heir to a fortune but saddled with a passion for punishment, insinuates himself in a sadomasochistic relationship with the frazzled policeman, who participates, initially out of fear, but eventually out of sick pleasure. Although there is no overt sex and Keitel dismisses his captive as simply a "faggot" (and denies being gay himself), the situation is steeped in homosexuality. Hints to the gay undercurrents are provided when Keitel, secretly searching his tormentor-victim's room, sees a copy of *The Advocate* and male bondage magazines. This teasing of the gay theme works to the film's advantage, producing a gratifyingly demented and taut psychological drama. Ⓐ

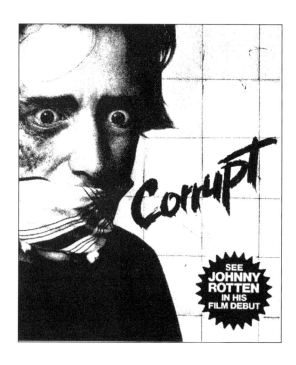

SEE JOHNNY ROTTEN IN HIS FILM DEBUT

Coup de Grace

*(1976, 95 min,
France/Germany,
Volker Schlöndorff)*

Set in a ravaged country house some-where in the Baltics during the 1918-19 civil war between German sympa-thizers and Communist insurgents, this heavy-handed psychological drama stars Margarethe von Trotta as Sophie, a middle-aged woman whose home becomes the headquarters for German soldiers. What develops over the bleak winter months is an agoniz-ing, never consummated love triangle between Sophie, who falls in love with Erich, a German soldier secretly in love with Sophie's brother. Yearning for his touch and complete-ly ignorant of his true feelings, Sophie is slowly driven to desperate measures in trying to capture his interest. He, in turn, is quite unhappy and incapable of expressing his true

Cruising: Al Pacino goes undercover in Greenwich Village

homosexual feelings. Finally, in an act of defiance and rebellion, she becomes a Communist sympathizer and political enemy to Erich. From the artsy school of emotional constipation and sexual angst, this drama never comes together and its gay sub-plot is always there but never dealt with. ⊛

The Creation of Adam

(1993, 93 min, Russia, Yuri Pavlov)

Heralded by its director as the first gay-themed film from Russia, this mystical drama will disappoint many by its oblique handling of the gay angle. Set in the industrialized port area of St. Petersburg, the story fol-lows handsome designer Andrei (Alexander Strizhenov) who is stuck in an unfulfilling relationship with his equally unhappy wife, Rita. After saving an effeminate teen from a group of queer-bashers, he is quickly accused — by both the thugs and his wife — of being a homo-sexual. Mired in a melancholy mood, his life is soon transformed when he meets Philip, a mysterious, self-assured young man. The younger blond man, who's made a fortune in the new capitalism of post-Communist Russia, sets his dark Tonya Harding-like eyes on Andrei's lost soul. Their ensuing relationship, handled in a weird, dreamlike manner, is one of both seduction and brother-like guidance, with the overall effect being that Philip is his guardian angel sent from above to teach him to love. The two kiss and share a bed at one point, but whether either is gay is unexplored; a situation that, while still a breakthrough for Russian filmmaking, will frustrate Western audiences wanting a more unambiguous depiction of a gay relationship.

Cruising *(1980, 106 min, US, William Friedkin)*

The most notorious film from the late-1970s, early-'80s assault of Hollywood-inflamed homophobia (*The Choirboys, Windows, Partners*), this hyperventilating police thriller united the gay commu-nity at the time of its release, and resulted in pickets and a boycott of

the movie. The film is set in the leather bars, cruising areas and sweat-ing, pulsating discos of Greenwich Village where a psychotic is killing gay men. Al Pacino is Steve Burns, a seemingly well-adjusted heterosexual cop who is assigned to go undercover and flush out the killer. With nothing more than some skin-tight shirts, a revealing leather ensemble and an apartment in the "heart of darkness" (read: a gay neighborhood), he begins his investigation. But muscular men and the prospects of satisfyingly violent sex cause him to question his own sexuality. The lurid and inarticulate depiction of gay life, as well as the notion that contact with gays could lure a man into their web, infuriated gays at the time. Today, long after the fury has died down, the film proves to be an entertaining and (for those born too late to enjoy the sexual excesses of pre-AIDS gay life) fascinating if ridicu-lous glimpse into gay life — albeit Hollywood's version of gay life. The sight of a wide-eyed Pacino "working" the S&M gay bars is as absurdly unreal as the den of lustful lesbians in the bar scene in *The Killing of Sister George.* Having lost its power to offend, the film is now part of queer film history and a testament to how a frightened Hollywood treated a disenfranchised minority. ⊛

> "This isn't a film about gay life. It's a murder mystery with an aspect of the gay world as background."
> —William Friedkin

Da Vinci Body Series — Vol. 1

(1993, 60 min, US, Robby Dix)

More than simply a gimmick exercise tape featuring naked men (although the five beautifully sculpted models are not bad), this primer exercise video, the first in a projected series, focuses on exercises that strengthen and tone the upper body — abdominals, chest, shoulders and triceps. Offering helpful tips and suggested exercise routines for both the novice and the serious bodybuilder,

OF GAY MALE INTEREST

the tape illustrates warm-up stretching, over 20 different exercises and concludes with a needed cooldown. Informative and semi-titillating. ☻

Da Vinci Body Series, Vol. 2 — Lower Body Workout

(1993, 50 min, US, Kevin Glover)
While bulging crotches were the main obsession of the 1970s, today's young gay men are just as obsessed with bulging muscles. This series of exercise and health and fitness tapes earmarked exclusively towards gays takes advantage of that interest. This volume, the second of the series, was "designed by its makers to give the viewer an exercise program that is visually erotic and beautiful." It takes off where the first left off, concentrating on exercises that build and strengthen the lower body including biceps (lower body?), back, abdominals, buttocks and legs. The hook, as in many of the tapes, is that the five finely chiseled youths demonstrating the exercises are nude. So there are plenty of lingering close-ups of flaccid cocks to accompany the workout. A narrator explains each exercise and the models do their thing. A better-than-average tape for those who have outgrown Jane Fonda! Also released is *Vol. 3 — Aerobic*, featuring five hard-bodied men demonstrating low-impact aerobic exercises (all in the nude, naturally). ☻

Dafydd *(1993, 90 min, Wales, Ceri Sherlock)*

Dafydd is the first Welsh-language gay film. Its distribution has been limited to Welsh television and several film festivals. It has been described by Berwyn Rolands, director of the Welsh International Film Festival as "Wales' late contribution to queer cinema." Director Ceri Sherlock's script focuses on a young Welsh boy who acknowledges his homosexuality after becoming a male prostitute in Amsterdam. The film's sexual content was cut down considerably when it was broadcast on BBC Wales.

A Darker Side of Black

(1993, 55 min, GB, Isaac Julien)
Gay British filmmaker Isaac Julien (*Looking for Langston, Young Soul Rebels*) takes a socio-political view in this thoughtful documentary as he explores the homophobia and advocacy of violence present in the lyrics in today's hip-hop, gansta' rap and reggae music. Far from being a simple indictment of the reactionary extremism of much of the music, the documentary seeks "a nihilistic response to a nihilistic situation" and puts things in perspective by exploring the cultures that have spawned these attitudes. Interviewees include rapper Shabba Ranks, cultural theorists as well as fans. While the gay aspect of the discussions is important, Julien effectively broadens the scope to deal with racism, slavery, the escalating gun culture and other factors.

The David Burrill Nude Aerobic Workout *(1993, 35 min, US, Sum Hung Man)*

Joining a burgeoning field of gay-oriented exercise tapes on the market is this amusingly ridiculous vanity production. Disregarding any of the artistic pretension or cosmic naturalness of exercising naked, this homemade video cheesily celebrates the sexual titillation offered in watching an attractive young man play with barbells all the while sporting a respectable semi-hard-on. The exercises are basic with generic gay disco music accompanying the action as the camera glides up and down David's body, resting for a breather several times

The making of a "six pack" in *Da Vinci Body Series Vol. 2*

in the groin area! And to show that this is no ordinary exercise tape, David heads off to the shower for a graphic masturbation exercise to complete the workout. Stupid and fun, but for the exercise-minded individual, it's a waste of time. ⊛

The Days of Greek Gods

(1947-68, 79 min, US, Richard Fontaine)

Along with Tom of Finland, Richard Fontaine is considered one of the leading early creators of modern gay erotica. Through his company, Zenith Films, he used his Athletic Model Guild studio in Los Angeles as a base to make a series of provocative shorts. Though tame by today's standards, they were quite adventurous for the time. His early short, *The Days of Greek Gods*, made in 1947, is thought to be the first gay erotic film to play theatrical engagements. This documentary is a campy, cult favorite for fans of bodybuilding magazines of the 1950s and of the almost innocent gay male erotica that flourished before the onslaught of hard-core pornography. The film traces Fontaine's progression as filmmaker through the use of muscleman magazines, photos and snippets from his early posing-strap shorts and sexually teasing "historical" films of the 1950s and early '60s.

Dafydd

Dear Boys

(1980, 90 min, The Netherlands, Paul de Lussanet)

This funny and candid Dutch oddity about an aging gay Don Juan and his entourage is a lusty and humorous story of sexual obsession. Wolf, a novelist plagued by writer's block and an aging sexual adventurer and self-proclaimed "servant of beauty," finds his creative juices flowing once again after he meets and becomes helplessly smitten by Muscrat, an attractive but indifferent young man. In his attempt at seduction, Wolf lures him (along with his ancient Sugar Daddy) to his country house, where he lives with his handsome "ex," Tiger. And there in his den, the persistent Wolf stalks his prey. When straightforward seduction fails, our horny hero resorts to telling imaginative homoerotic fantasies to Muscrat hoping to stimulate, arouse and dispel the diffidence of his newfound love. A funny and candid look at one gay man's frantic attempts at keeping his sexual mystique and grasping an unattainable love. ⊛

Death in Venice, CA

(1994, 30 min, US, David Ebersole)

Though only 30 minutes, this wry sexual drama is a surprisingly professional and pleasurable tale on the perils of romantic love. Using Thomas Mann's classic novella "Death in Venice" as its inspiration, the film follows the relationship between an older English writer and a youth he meets while staying with distant relatives at the California beach town. An uptight writer, Mason Carver (reminding one of Sam Shepard), finds his sexuality both piqued and confounded when he meets Sebastian Dickens, a gay youth of 18 whose bedroom eyes, finely muscled body and West Hollywood good looks proves to be a passionate tonic for the repressed Mason.

Death on the Beach

(1988, 101 min, Mexico, Enrique Gomez)

Repressed homosexuality, vicious murders and lovely bronzed bodies dominate this silly melodramatic thriller set under the Acapulcan sun. The story revolves around a handsome but misunderstood teenager who returns home (a mansion overlooking the Pacific) to find his domineeringly buxom mother shacking up with a fiercely heterosexual lover. The boy, sexually and emotionally confused, becomes agitated when they begin to introduce a succession of young girls to him. Instead of saying, "No thanks, mom," the boy's pent-up and unspent passions erupt in a violent and unpredictable way. A film not for card-carrying members of ACT-UP, as the filmmaker equates homosexuality with deranged, psychopathic behavior. Take the politics out, however, and you have a generally silly but fun sexual thriller. ⊛

Deathtrap *(1982, 116 min, US, Sidney Lumet)*

Ira Levin's smash Broadway murder mystery is brought to the screen in this satisfactory adaptation. Michael Caine plays a down-on-his-luck playwright who sees a chance at reclaiming success when a former student (Christopher Reeve) shows up with a sure hit script. Caine plots to murder him and take the play as his own. The twist (yes, revealed now that the film is well over a decade old) is that the two men are actually gay lovers who concocted the elaborate hoax in order to startle Caine's troublesome, weak-hearted wife (Dyan Cannon) into a quick and fatal coronary. The two men thankfully do not camp up their gayness or resort to any stereotypical mannerisms, and their full-mouthed passionate kiss shocked audiences in its day — not so much that the kiss revealed the twist in the mystery, but demonstrating how strong an audience's aversion was to the two male stars kissing each other. ☹

Desperate

(1991, 91 min, US, Rico Martinez)

Rico Martinez's first film (his latest is the transsexual documentary *Glamazon: A Different Kind of Girl*) is an inventive, low-budget black comedy that, in a style reminiscent of John Waters' early films, follows two losers who desperately seek quick, easy success. They try their luck at a litany of fashion and cultural fads of the late 1970s and early '80s including liposuction, punk rock and pyramid schemes. Born in 1964 in San Diego of Chinese-Filipino/Mexican-American parentage, Martinez's first two films indicate we have much to look forward to from this talented queer filmmaker. His newest film project is *Micro Mini* — a science-fiction feature about Asian and Hispanic transvestites/transsexuals who live on a planet that exists on a micro chip.

> "I want to make films that are somewhere between *Valley of the Dolls*, *Saturday Night Fever* and Kenneth Anger's *Scorpio Rising*."
>
> —Rico Martinez

The Detective

(1968, 114 min, US, Gordon Douglas)

Frank Sinatra stars as a jaded but "tolerant" New York City detective in this gritty actioner set for the most part in the city's nefarious homosexual haunts. He is assigned to find the killer of a wealthy gay man (James Inman), found brutally murdered and castrated. In an effort to quickly conclude the investigation, he and his violently homophobic co-worker comb the gay bars and cruis-

ing areas of the city hoping to ferret out the suspected killer. Tony Musante plays the dead man's former roommate and lover who is coerced into confessing to the crime and is eventually sent to the electric chair. But rather than an open and closed case, things get complicated when it seems that Musante was innocent. Sinatra soon uncovers police corruption leading to the murder and the discovery that closet case William Windom, who has since committed suicide, had killed the man, leaving a note "explaining" that, "I was more ashamed of being a homosexual than a murderer." Robert Duvall is featured as a queer-bashing cop. ☹

Devil in the Flesh

(1947, 110 min, France, Claude Autant-Lara)
(1986, 110 min, Italy/France, Marco Bellocchio)

The original version of this adaptation of Raymond Radiquet's novel was quite controversial upon its initial release in 1947. Set during WWI, the film is a beautifully acted and exquisitely filmed tale of the passionate love and tragic involvement between a young male student and a mature married woman. Years later, Italian director Marco Bellocchio made a notorious updating of the story under the same title. Bellocchio's version tells the story of a sizzling love triangle between an imprisoned terrorist, his sultry girlfriend, and a teenage boy she lured from the schoolyard. The themes of political intrigue, betrayal and madness take a backseat to the erotic couplings and explicit oral sex scenes between the sensuous young woman, Maruschka Detmers, and her enamored young victim, the handsome Federico Pitzali. ☹

Focus on: *Raymond Radiquet*

The above two versions of Raymond Radiquet's semiautobiographical novel are both purely heterosexual tales of amour fou, but they are included because they are the only screen versions of works by Radiquet, an immensely popular and praised literary prodigy who died tragically in 1923 of typhoid fever at the age of 20. Radiquet, already well-known at the age of 15, was introduced by French poet Max Jacob to Jean Cocteau, a man 15 years his senior. They became lovers until the time of his death, a loss that greatly affected Cocteau and had a lasting influence on his art. Reflecting on Radiquet's death in a letter to his mother, a devastated Cocteau wrote, "I've lost something winged, noble, mysterious. I see Raymond's face the last night, his difficulty in speaking, his heavenly eyes. Tears and sorrow tear me apart."

The Devil's Playground

(1976, 105 min, Australia, Fred Schepesi)

This compelling drama, set in a boys' seminary, probes the torment of young students and their instructors as they grapple with sexual yearning and the harsh codes of religious discipline. The story concerns one particular boy's struggle to deal with both his divine calling and his pent-up sexual needs. A sometimes funny, always hard-hitting indictment of repression. ☹

Deathtrap

The Devil's Playground

Diary of a Hit Man

(1991, 90 min, US, Roy London)

Forest Whitaker, though miscast, makes a strong showing as a hit man who meticulously saves the earnings gained from his murderous profession for a down payment on a co-op. Normally unperturbed by his work, he faces a mental crisis when he is paid to knock off an annoying (to her coke- and commodities-addicted husband) wife and her infant. Sherilyn Fenn co-stars as Whitaker's intended final victim in this strangely personal thriller. Although director Roy London was gay, there are no gay undercurrents in this, his first and only film. ⊛

Focus on: *Roy London*

Roy London, who died at the age of 50 in August 1993 of lymphoma, marked his directorial debut with Diary of a Hit Man. *Openly gay, he enjoyed a varied career as an actor, acting coach, stage director, playwright and screenwriter (*Tiger Warsaw, *a 1988 drama starring Piper Laurie and Patrick Swayze). In addition to more than 150 stage appearances, he also directed several episodes of "It's Gary Shandling's Show" for Showtime and "The Larry Sanders Show" for HBO. He was also a private coach for many well-known actors including Geena Davis, Sharon Stone, Jeff Goldblum and Michelle Pfeiffer.*

A Different Kind of Love

(1981, 60 min, GB, Brian Mills)

After a slow start, this British teleplay about a man coming out to his mother picks up some emotional steam. Joyce Redman is appropriately overbearing as the domineering mother of Peter ('Pumpkin' to her), a recently divorced father of a young boy. She vainly attempts to set him up with available women, blind to the possibility that her 30-year-old son, now living with another man, might not be interested. Pinter-esque in dialogue, the film succeeds in capturing the inarticulate tensions between mother, son and lover. The gay men, who look so alike it is difficult to tell them apart, are not as finely detailed as the regal, ball-busting mom — which might be the point, as the mother refuses to allow her son his own identity. Made for television, the film is a quietly revealing drama of the stereotypical relationship between a gay man and his mother. ⊛

The Disco Years

(1991, 30 min, US, Robert Lee King)

Set in sunny California during the *Saturday Night Fever*-influenced, bell-bottom wearing 1970s, this humorous and optimistic coming-of-age story will touch many with its universal tale of sexual self-discovery. Tom Peters, an attractive and "straight-acting" high school student, finds his sexuality awakened after sleeping with and falling in love with another boy. Gwen Welles is especially good as Tom's hippie-ish mother who has a tough time accepting her son's sexuality. A refreshingly on-target story of one person's gradual acceptance of himself.

Dog Day Afternoon

(1975, 130 min, US, Sidney Lumet)

Before Al Pacino embarrassed himself *Cruising* the leather bars, he gave a first-rate performance as a gay thief whose attempt to rob a bank (to pay for his lover's sex change) brings the city of New York to a standstill. An often delightful comedy, the film is flavored with warm characters and deft humor. In supporting roles, Charles Durning as a police liaison and Oscar-nominee Chris Sarandon as Pacino's lover are standouts. Based on a true incident. ⊛

Doing Time on Maple Drive

(1992, 100 min, US, Ken Olin)

An unusually affecting, sensitively handled and gay-positive made-for-TV drama which marked the directorial debut for actor Ken Olin ("thirtysomething"). Teenager Matt (William McNamara), a star athlete and honor student courageously comes to grips with his sexuality and comes out to his parents (James B. Sikking and Bibi Besch). The revelation strips away the veneer of the "typical" suburban American family and exposes their repressed dysfunctionalities, including alcoholism, abortion, school difficulties and, finally, Matt's homosexuality. Matt's confrontation with his parents occurs after he attempts suicide in the family car. When he returns home, he explains, "It's better to be dead than to tell you that I'm gay."

OF GAY MALE INTEREST

The Dreaded Experimental Comedies
(1991-92, US, John Toppling)

Seen in part on Network Q and in several gay and lesbian film festivals, this collection of humorous shorts, little more than home movies, will remind many of a queer version of *Moron Movies*. The writer, director and star is John Toppling, and while the work is wildly uneven (on short simply shows fingers drumming a tune on a naked butt), there are some funny bits, including "My New Lover" — an imaginative story of a lonely man who "creates" the man of his dreams. ⊛

Dream Man
(1991, 75 min, US, David Edwards)

Gay theatre at its most provocative, this, the premiere release in "The Pride Playhouse Collection" of landmark gay-themed plays on video, is a savagely funny and intensely moving piece written by James Carroll Pickett. Michael Kearns stars as an over-the-hill hustler, an acid-tongued purveyor of phone-sex fantasies, who confronts his customers' most perverse requests. Performed on more stages and in more countries than any other gay play, the *L.A. Times* has called it, "Brooding and on the edge...sad and funny!"; while the *L.A. Weekly* says it is filled with "Bitchy humor, sexual hysteria and old-fashioned romance." ⊛

The Dresser *(1983, 118 min, GB, Peter Yates)*

Albert Finney and Tom Courtenay are both outstanding as, respectively, a grandiloquent, aging actor and his devoted dresser. Finney is the head of a second-rate touring company besieged by financial and wartime woes; Courtenay is his gay confidant/secretary/valet who watches over him with the eye of a hawk and the perseverance of a den mother. A brilliant, moving and often funny peek behind the curtain of theatre life. ⊛

The Dresser

Daniel Auteuil as an unrepentant killer in *The Elegant Criminal*

Drifting (Nagua)
(1983, 80 min, Israel, Amos Gutman)

Director Amos Gutman's acclaimed first feature is also the first gay film made in Israel. The story follows Robi, a 24-year-old would-be filmmaker who isolates himself completely in the gay world and grows increasingly troubled; not by the political turmoil in his country, but by his increasingly aimless and frustrated life. His ennui causes him to reject his friends and lover and withdraw into self-destruction, at one point even offering refuge to a pair of murderous Arabs who then sexually humiliate him. This sensitive and moving drama takes a serious look at one man who is forced to question his role in the straight world. When the film was programmed at the Montreal Film Festival in 1984, the Israeli government protested and attempted to suppress its screening, claiming that the film, because of its gay theme, was not representative of Israeli culture. A sensitive and moving drama. ⊛

An Early Frost
(1985, 100 min, US, John Erman)

The first TV movie to deal with AIDS, *An Early Frost* is an outstanding, thoughtful and undeniably powerful drama about Michael (Aidan Quinn), a young, successful gay lawyer who learns he is HIV-positive and decides to confront his family with both his sexuality and illness. The effect of his announcement on him and his family is at the core of the drama. Quinn gives a sensitive, commanding performance in the lead role, and Gena Rowlands, Ben Gazzara and especially Sylvia Sydney offer strong support as, respectively, Quinn's mother, father and grandmother. John Glover is remarkable as Victor, a dying AIDS patient. The film also offers a surprisingly realistic portrayal of the relationship between Michael and his lover, Peter (D.W. Moffett). ⊛

The Elegant Criminal
(1991, 120 min,
France, Francis Girod)

Long dependent on Hollywood for its cinematic diet of lurid depictions of evil (Dr. Hannibal Lecter in

Silence of the Lambs, Max Cady in Scorsese's *Cape Fear* and Henry in *Henry, Portrait of a Serial Killer*, to name just a recent few), the French now have an evil genius to call their own. In this fascinating portrait, based on the true story of the notorious 19th-century murderer Pierre-Francois Lacenaire, director Francis Girod (*The Infernal Trio, L'etat Sauvage*) has avoided the cheap, gory route and instead has fashioned an intimate, witty and complex look into the dark abyss of unrepentant evil. Daniel Auteuil (*Jean de Florette, Manon of the Spring*) is riveting as Lacenaire — a failed playwright, refined gentleman, persuasive conversationalist, as well as thief, con man and knife-wielding mass murderer, who despite (or because of) it all, received the respect of his jailers and became a national celebrity. Why this film is of interest is its off-handed approach to Lacenaire's

An Empty Bed

homosexuality. He and his lover/accomplice have such an open relationship that the authorities allow the two men to share in one final meal (actually a feast) before his execution. While it is refreshing to see such a matter-of-fact portrayal of homosexuality, it's a shame that the killer, though respected and intelligent, is still a mass murderer who is executed for his crimes. ✆

Empire State *(1987, 104 min, GB, Ron Peck)*

Independent gay filmmaker Ron Peck (*Nighthawks, Strip Jack Naked*) goes mainstream with this underworld crime thriller set amidst the 1980s boom of the rapidly gentrifying docklands of London's East End. Seemingly countless characters and subplots are weaved through this violent tale of drugs, scheming real estate speculation, greedy yuppies, bruising boxers, male prostitutes and elegant moles. The central story follows the attempt of a young turk and former male prostitute to try to take over a glitzy gay/straight nightclub owned by Frank (Ray McAnally). The interest for gay viewers is how the gay characters (and there are many) infiltrate the tale, with the two most prominent being Martin Landau as a bisexual American businessman who likes "the rough stuff" and is willing to pay for it; and Lee Drysdale as a charming and enterprising rent boy who works overtime to raise money to go to the States. The other gay characters are generously interspersed throughout this frenetic gangster flick. Not a great film; it opens promisingly, but concludes in a mess of unanswered questions. The use of gay characters in an essentially straight thriller, however, is rare and provocative and hopefully a harbinger for future films. ✆

An Empty Bed *(1986, 60 min, US, Mark Gasper)*

This rarity among gay-themed films, focusing on the concerns of elderly gay men, features John Wylie as a gay man in his sixties. The story follows his reflections on his younger days, the choices he has made, and the prospect of an empty bed; for he lives alone, having been unable to commit himself to a relationship. He looks back, not with regret or bitterness, but with a feeling that things could have turned out differently. ✆

"A lovely, moving, familiar experience for viewers of any age"

—*The Advocate*

Ernesto *(1983, 95 min, Italy, Salvatore Samperi)*

This lush period drama revolves around the emotional and sexual maturation of an impetuous Italian teenager who quickly discovers the power of youth, beauty and money. Set in the town of Trieste in 1911, the story follows Ernesto, the son of a wealthy merchant who, wielding his emerging sexuality with wanton abandon, becomes involved with a hunky stevedore only to cruelly discard him. The lad immediately enters into an unlikely love triangle with a younger boy and his twin sister. Throughout his amorous romps, Ernesto, not a particularly likable lad, remains a figure of vacillating loyalties and reckless sexuality. The handsome Michele Placido is perfectly cast as the helplessly infatuated workman. ✆

"*Ernesto* is the most complex rendition of homosexuality yet to reach the screen. The film reconciles the legacies of Pasolini and Fassbinder with that of Jean Renoir, a happy accomplishment and a useful one for Americans."

—Richard Goldstein, *The Village Voice*

OF GAY MALE INTEREST

Fantasy Men

Erotikus: History of the Gay Movie

(1975, 70 min, US, L. Brooks)

The birth, maturation and eventual proliferation of gay erotic cinema is chronicled in this dated but interesting documentary narrated by superstar porno director Fred Halsted. The film explores the beginnings of gay erotica with physique magazines of the '50s and '60s and its evolution onto the big screen with the "innocent" bodybuilding films from the Apollo and Guild Studios. The film's historical approach to the evolution of gay filmmaking goes from the suggestive to the explicit when the film segues into a sexual montage of highlights from several hard-core films of the 1970s. Halsted's humorous recounting of this "art form" keeps it compelling but unfortunately can't explore the explosion of male adult films in the '80s brought about by the video revolution. ⊛

An Evening with Quentin Crisp

(1980, 91 min, US, James Cady & Arthur Mele)

Floridly disclaiming to be simply "a straight talk from a bent speaker," Quentin Crisp's performance piece/lecture filmed in front of an appreciative audience is full of the celebrity's Wildean witticisms and droll reflections on living as a gay man today.

Patently outrageous and always entertaining, the British-born author ("The Naked Civil Servant" and "How to Watch Movies"), promising "a consultation with a psychiatrist who is madder than you are," holds court as he offers helpful hints, droll opinions and practical advice on such subjects as the avoidance of dreary housework, how to be oneself, how to dress and look smart, and how, generally, to live with style regardless of one's economic situation. Introduced by John Hurt, who memorably played him in the film version of his book, *The Naked Civil Servant.* ⊛

The Everlasting Secret Family

(1987, 93 min, Australia, Michael Thornhill)

With an outrageous premise — a highly organized secret society of pederasts stalk area schools for young male victims whom they then ravage and reprogram to their way of life — this as an enjoyably ludicrous drama that despite its sinister idea, still makes for strangely riveting, erotically charged entertainment. Mark Lee, costar of *Gallipoli*, plays a gorgeous young boy who is spirited away by a wealthy, middle-aged senator. He soon tolerates the sex and begins to enjoy the power and prestige he attains as the "boy-toy" of the politician. But as is wont for a finicky pederast, the senator soon drops him for younger flesh. Now fully indoctrinated into the society, and aging rapidly, Mark must go off himself in search of an innocent victim; and the boy he chooses is the senator's young son! Enjoyable camp once you ignore its sinister and incendiary harangues. ⊛

Every Night in Thailand

(1991, 65 min, US/Thailand)

The go-go boys of Bangkok, the 1990s gay sex capital of the world, are featured in this amateurish but stimulating travelogue/exposé. The camera wanders into the multitude of gay bars in the city and becomes transfixed on the young, handsome Asian men as they dance and strip to disco music, as well as engage in masturbation and simulated sex. ⊛

Exquisite Corpses

(1989, 95 min, US, Temistocles Lopez)

Refreshing, inventive and unapologetically gay, this is *Midnight Cowboy*-meets-a-queer-*My Fair Lady*; it's a pansexual comedy/thriller which follows the success of a naive country boy who rises from hick to chic. Stripped of everything on his first day in the big city, young Buck is rescued from poverty by a handsome gay casting agent who transforms the cowboy from a rough-and-tumble Chet Atkins to a sexy Chet Baker. But the young man loses his soul in the process and becomes a shallow, sexually ambiguous user — the perfect New Yorker! While tasting his gay side with his pony-tailed Henry Higgins, the young man becomes a decidedly no-talent, all-looks cabaret performer, soon finding that his road to fame is littered with dead bodies. An engagingly witty and offbeat gem that is part murder mystery, part exposé on the rotting underbelly of New York posturing and a warts-and-all look at gay relationships, love triangles and bisexuality. Writer-director Temistocles Lopez develops his sexual themes even more in his provocative *Chain of Desire.* ⊛

Faerie Tales

(1992, 20 min, US/France,
Philipe Rogues)

This amusing mini-documentary travels into the forests of Oregon in its perceptive peek into the lifestyle and thoughts of "Radical Faeries" and "Crusty Queers," two back-to-nature New Age gay groups comprised of free-spirited men of all ages who leave the coldness and hardness of the cities to live out a playful life of peace, openness and love. An interesting look at a decidedly fringe group within a fringe group that is proud to be different.

Fantasy Men — Vols. 1 & 2

(1994, 100 min, US)

Essentially high-class soft- (I mean flaccid) core porn for those who are more interested in the sensuality of the male body than its sexuality, this voyeuristic tease features 12 handsome, athletic and mainly naked young men in mini-scenes set in bathhouses, bedrooms, the woods, a deserted beach and other such locations where one usually finds men enjoying themselves. With an actively horny narration as the aural backdrop to the pictures of finely sculpted bodies, the video is intended to get one going without actually delivering (Catholic schoolgirls being the straight man's equivalent?). (GB title: *Euroboy*) ⊛

Farewell My Concubine

(1993, 154 min, China, Chen Kaige)

An exotic Chinese gay love story told on an epic scale, this big-budget spectacle recounts the tempestuous relationship between two Peking Opera stars as they live through five decades of turbulent Chinese history. It begins in the 1920s when a prostitute signs over her androgynous little boy Dieyi to an opera company training school steeped in conformity, hard work and mindless cruelty. Pretty but tough, Dieyi (Leslie Cheung), soon befriends the older Xiaolou (Zhang Fengyi) wherein begins their lifelong involvement with each other. The two young men soon become Peking Opera stars, famous for their rendition of "Farewell My Concubine," in which a concubine (Dieyi) loves her king so much that when military defeat is apparent, she kills herself with his sword. But in the tragedy of his real life, the gay Dieyi, celebrated for his female roles, finds his love slipping away when the affectionate, but heterosexual Xiaolou meets and marries a fiery former prostitute (Gong Li). Carrying a dramatic torch for his elusive love, the two men find themselves intractably

Zhang Fengyi (l.) and Leslie Cheung in *Farewell My Concubine*

intertwined, each needing the other, despite Xiaolou's clinging wife and the tribulations of Japanese occupation, post-war upheaval, Communist control and the horrors of the Cultural Revolution. Featuring exotic locales, sweeping photography, colorful costumes and an emotionally draining love story told with compassion and sympathy, the film is a riveting experience. ⊛

On the politics surrounding *Farewell My Concubine*: Despite sharing the top prize at the 1933 Cannes Film Festival (with *The Piano*) and being one of the most acclaimed Chinese films ever, *Farewell My Concubine* has endured a tough time with Communist officials. Because of either the homosexuality or, more likely, the film's harsh criticism of Communist rule, the film was originally banned in China. An edited version was initially made available, but eventually, bowing to pressure, the film was released in China in its original version.

> "We pretend not to see the reality of homosexuality in China, but sooner or later we must face the fact."
>
> —director Chen Kaige

Fast Trip, Long Drop

(1993, 54 min, US, Gregg Bordowitz)

Breaking with the traditional handling of AIDS documentaries, Gregg Bordowitz has produced an ambitious, involving and thoughtful autobiographical video on HIV/AIDS-infection and how it is handled by its sufferers, the media and the gay community's self-appointed leaders. The work is memorable because of its deft blending of biting satire (fake television programs "dealing" with AIDS infection, hilarious stock footage of death-defying daredevils and a loud-mouthed speaker called Larry Blamer) with interviews with his parents and scenes of political activism. Diagnosed as HIV-positive in 1988, 23-year-old Alter Allesman (Bordowitz's alter ego) changed his lifestyle, came out to his parents, sought to rediscover his Eastern European Jewish heritage, and became committed to political action, especially in respect to the media's "containment" and codification of the epidemic. For instead of simply accepting his condition, he develops a direct confrontational style ("I'm no longer a person with AIDS, I am AIDS," "I'm sick and I don't want a cure," "I want to be the protagonist of my own story") and his revelatory thoughts on his anger, mortality and in-your-face approach both entertains and awakens the viewer with his personal pain and urgency to action against the disease.

Fellini Satyricon
(1970, 129 min, Italy, Federico Fellini)
Set in Nero's decadent Rome, this wild and purposefully shocking phantasmagoria is a free-form adaptation of the Petronius book. Two handsomely athletic youths, the blond Encolpius and the grinning, raven-haired Ascyltus, are first seen fighting over the affections of Giton, a strangely pretty boy. The two meet up repeatedly in this dreamlike tale which takes them through wild adventures in a world peopled with hermaphrodites, dwarfs, a Minotaur, prostitutes, nymphomaniacs and homosexuals. Boldly bizarre and visually exciting, the film is imbued with homoeroticism, despite its mainly heterosexual story. Because of this, gay historian Tyler Parker once wrote that the film was "the most profoundly homosexual film of all time." ⊗

The Fifth of July *(1984, 100 min, US)*
Made for PBS' "American Playhouse" series, this extremely well-acted, first-rate adaptation of Lanford Wilson's acclaimed Broadway comedy-drama (with most of the original cast reprising their roles) is slightly opened-up yet still retains its intimate theatricality. In a splendid performance, Richard Thomas plays a gay disabled Vietnam veteran and schoolteacher who faces an emotional crisis upon returning to the classroom. Jeff Daniels is his supportive lover whose even temper and good will are put to the test when Thomas' college friend Swoosie Kurtz (who won a Tony Award for her portrayal), a free-spirited and now successful singer, arrives with her entourage for a short stay. As the characters recall the past and face the future, secret passions, betrayals and insecurities are brought to the surface. Wilson's poetic dialogue is funny, tender, intelligent and remarkably assured, and though two of the three lead characters are gay, refreshingly their homosexuality is matter-of-fact and not a source for individual neuroses or misgivings.

Film (Fill 'Em)
(1991, 45 min, Canada, Sky Gilbert)
Filmed in a fake cinema verité style and in homage to early Warhol films such as *Bike Boy* and *Chelsea Girls*, this amusing short film is simply the straight ahead recording of an obnoxious narcissistic gay hustler and his ditsy, stripper-cum-fag hag roommate. With the characters moving in and out of the gaze of the static camera, the film records the two's everyday conversations which includes the boy's claim of being the biggest dicked hustler in Toronto and the girl's oddly innocent desire for breast implants. A humorous and promising first film.

Film for Two
(1985, 31 min, US, Victor Mignatti)
Set in New York's West Village, this atmospheric, and at times provocative tale follows two young men as they embark on their first love affair. Explored are the singular problems facing gay relationships as well as the universal interpersonal gulfs that endanger everyone. The two men attempt to overcome their communication barriers, their fears of intimacy and the destructive power games which keep them isolated.

Fire on the Mountain — An Intimate Guide to Male Genital Massage
(1992, 40 min, US, Joseph Kramer)
Weaving the "erotic with the sacred," sex instructor Joseph Kramer has made a name for himself and his EroSpirit Institute with his courses and lectures on the mystical techniques of Taoist Erotic Massage. Or in layman's talk, instruction on the finer points of caressing a cock. Obviously sexually explicit, the video is not meant to be titillating. With Kramer's voice in the background describing the moves, two models demonstrate the various techniques of the massage of the body and the penis, including breathing exercises and 25 different genital massage strokes. Cumming is not the point in the exercises as Kramer believes that the erotic massages increase orgasmic energy, which, in turn, "connects the genitals to the heart, producing an ecstasy that opens onto spirituality." And keep your mouth shut, for it's the hands that play the role in pleasure giving! Probably not of interest to "Wham, bam, thank you sir" devotees, it might prove invaluable to those interested in New Age teachings and/or those open to ideas that might increase sexual pleasures. Promised upcoming titles by Joseph Kramer Productions include *An Intimate Guide to Female Genital Massage, Advanced Anal Massage* and *Phallic Reflexology*. ⊗

> "The difference between a 'hand job' and Taoist Erotic Massage is the difference between banging on a piano or playing Mozart."
>
> —Joseph Kramer

The First Annual Gay Erotic Video Awards *(1993, 90 min, US)*
Jumping on the bandwagon of self-congratulatory awards shows, the gay adult video industry's first awards ceremony is presented in this video that is, in all likelihood, of interest only to the die-hard fans of the genre. With poor sound quality, the show, hosted by an outrageously multi-costumed Chi Chi LaRue, features many of the adult video stars (Joey Stefano, vet Jack Wrangler, Ryan Idol) and directors giving out the Oscar-esque statuette to such winners as Best Solo, Best Safe Sex, Best Cum Shot and the more pedestrian Best Picture, Best Director, etc. The most frustrating aspect of the show is the utter lack of titillation (read: no film clips of the winning performances). ⊗

Flaming Creatures
(1962, 43 min, US, Jack Smith)
Reportedly made for $300, this now-quite-tame avant-garde extravaganza became a cause célèbre when it was seized by New York City

police at its premiere showing and eventually banned when New York's Criminal Court labeled it obscene. Filmed in murky black and white, this underground classic, thought of by many as a masterpiece of camp, is a loosely edited, semi-homage to Hollywood "B" actress Maria Montez which features an array of vampy transvestites, hermaphrodites, drag shows, a sexually ambiguous vampire, a drugged-out orgy and a beefy cunnilingual rapist.

> "A most luxurious outpouring of imagination, of imagery, of poetry, of movie artistry — comparable only to the works of the greatest, like von Sternberg."
>
> — Jonah Mekas

Focus on: *Jack Smith*

A leader of the American avant-garde underground filmmaking movement of the late 1950s and 1960s, Jack Smith (who died in 1989) was often artistically linked with such contemporaries as Kenneth Anger, Andy Warhol and Gregory Markopoulos. In addition to making movies, Smith also was a performance artist and actor, appearing (many times in drag) in such classics of the underground movement as Star Spangled to Death *(1959) and* Blonde Cobra *(1960), both by Ken Jacobs,* Queen of Sheba Meets the Atom Man *(1963, Ron Rice),* Camp *(1965, Andy Warhol) and* The Illiac Passion *(1964-66, Gregory Markopoulos). His work in film, while not technically proficient, was groundbreaking, defiantly queer and outrageous for its time. His films were infused with a "hysterical intensity" as they celebrated sexual and sensual freedom by featuring casts that included tranvestites, transsexuals and explicit scenes of homosexuality. While* Flaming Creatures *was actually his only completed film, he made many others throughout the years (although many do not exist today), often freely interchanging footage and dialogue as seemed appropriate. His first film was* Buzzards Over Bagdad *(1951-56); others include* In the Grip of the Lobster Claw *(1966),* No President *(1969) and* Landlordism of Lobster Lagoon *(1981). The follow-up to* Flaming Creatures *was his more commercial, all-color extravaganza, Busby Berkeley tribute titled* Normal Love *(aka:* Normal Fantasy*) (1963, 55 min) which was also never completed. It featured a fascinating blend of East Village beatniks, gays and gender-benders — some in drag, some dressed as mermaids, werewolves and monsters from old Hollywood films. It was a silent film which was accompanied by music, and featured nudity, dancing and scenes involving a huge Claus Oldenberg-designed cake.*

The Flavor of Corn

(1991, 93 min, Italy, Gianni da Campo)
Best likened in theme to the much more explicit Dutch drama *For a Lost Soldier*, this tender drama of friendship and enveloping love between a young teacher and a 12-year-old boy is hampered by amateurish acting and an overly serious tone. University student Lorenzo (Lorenzo Lena) travels to a rural region of northern Italy for his first teaching assignment. The handsome young man discovers that Duilio (Marco Mestriner), one of his pupils, is in "puppy love" with him. Equally attracted

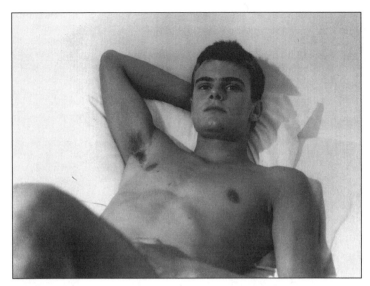

The Flavor of Corn

(although initially platonically), Lorenzo becomes friends with the precocious boy; only after his self-destructive relationship with a woman ends does he consider the sexual attraction to the boy. Although the two never have sex — their affection is limited to holding hands, looking longingly into each other's eyes and a brief peck on the lips — their attraction for each other becomes increasingly intense. Their impossible relationship becomes strained after Duilio's peasant family suspects something is up and asks the teacher to cool his visits. A surprisingly tasteful, restrained and bittersweet tale of first love and the internal conflict of accepting one's sexual feelings. ⊗

The Flower Thief

(1960, 70 min, US, Ron Rice)
This landmark example of New American Cinema harkens back to silent film days when Hollywood productions often employed a "wild man" — a person who, when the directors were exhausted, would stir things up with his antics. Poet, funnyman and future Warholite Taylor Mead fulfills that role in this celebration of freedom and the Beat Generation. The camera follows the adventures of this innocent "homo-man-child" as he wanders the city streets, enjoying life and impetuously living for the moment. One particularly wild scene shows Meade cruising a bum and follows the two as they have a tryst on the beach.

> "Rice, by deliberately flouting established moviemaking traditions, reveals himself primarily as a professional rebel rather than the leader of a new movement. But...he has produced a major work."
>
> —*The New York Times*

Focus on: *Ron Rice*

Before he tragically died in 1963 in Mexico where he ostensibly went to film and to escape constant police harassment in New York, Ron Rice showed great promise as a leading gay voice in the emerging American avant-garde and independent filmmaking movement. His fellow filmmakers included Ken Jacobs, Jack Smith, Gregory Markopoulos and Stan Brakhage. Other films of Rice include: Senseless *(1962, 28 min), a series of images surrounding several people's frenzied fantasies of their upcoming trip to Mexico; and* Chumlum *(1964, 26 min), filmed in a poetically dreamlike fashion and showcasing several exuberant drag queens as they make themselves up, childishly frolic (and cruise) at a park, and simply lounge around on hammocks — all this accompanied by melodic Eastern meditation music. Rice also left an unfinished work called* The Queen of Sheba Meets the Atom Man *(1963, 70 min), a humorous, sexually explicit (for its time) phantasmagoria featuring, among others, Taylor Mead and fellow independent filmmaker, and drag aficionado, Jack Smith. On presentation of a rough cut to an audience before he died, Rice wrote, "This is only 70 minutes of a protracted three-hour epic by the director of* The Flower Thief. *This is your opportunity to challenge the Hollywood stranglehold on morals, expression, and art and what have you. Dig us."*

For a Lost Soldier

(1993, 92 min, The Netherlands, Roeland Kerbosch)
The potentially explosive subject of man-boy love is delicately handled in this touchingly romantic drama of a boy's coming-of-age in The Netherlands during WWII. Jeroen (Maarten Smit), a handsome, rosy-cheeked boy of 13, is sent by his mother to the countryside to stay with a farming family in order to avoid the war and food shortages. It is there that his adolescent sexual yearnings for those of his own sex begin to take hold. Initially interested in his girl-crazy best friend, Jeroen finds his true love with the older Walt (Andrew Kelley), a handsome Canadian soldier stationed in the area as part of the Liberation forces. It is love-at-first-sight for the two who, undeterred by their language barrier, develop a friendship that begins first as buddies and develops later into a full-blown love affair. Their one lovemaking scene, in which Walt calls the boy his little prince, is achingly romantic with an intense, sexually charged atmosphere. And while not sexually graphic, it is certain to shock, especially with its cavalier, naturalistic view of their tender love. A gay version of *Summer of '42*, this wonderful love story never feels the need to even mention homosexuality nor offer the typical warnings or tragic aftereffects of such an affair — a stance which makes the film that much more powerful for a gay audience. Jeroen Krabbe is featured as the now-adult Jeroen who frames the story at the beginning and end as a nostalgic reminiscence for his first and greatest love. ✪

Forever Mary

(1990, 100 min, Italy, Marco Risi)
A tougher look into modern urban Italian life than one usually sees. This hard-hitting prison drama, set in a Palermo juvenile detention center, takes an unflinching look at the "rehabilitation" of a group of teenagers. Essentially a spaghetti-*To Sir with Love*, the story follows Marco (*Ernesto*'s Michele Placido), a taciturn, yet dedicated teacher who volunteers to spend some time trying to educate a clamorous group of teenagers. Their initial scorn soon turns to respect and much to the director's credit, the story avoids sentimental pitfalls and retains its hard edge. The title refers to Mario, a transvestite prostitute who falls in (puppy) love with the teacher. ✪

For a Lost Soldier

Fortune and Men's Eyes

(1971, 102 min, Canada/US, Harvey Hart)

John Hubert's play about homosexual brutality in prison comes to the screen in this taut, claustrophobic and sensationalistic drama. Behind bars for the first time, young Smitty (Wendell Burton) finds himself the prized sexual catch to a thuggish Rocky (Zooey Hall). Sexual humiliation, domination and abuse fill the halls of the seemingly guardless prison as the inmates enact a frenzied dance for power and gratification. Michael Greer (the swishy queen in *The Gay Deceivers*) is alternately hilarious and terrorizing as Queeny, the affectionate, limp-wristed fairy cell mate to Rocky and Smitty who, when threatened, turns into a dangerously violent psychopath. ⊗

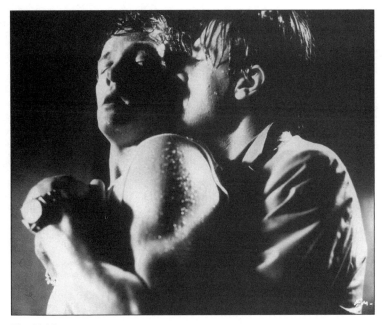

The 4th Man

The 4th Man

(1984, 110 min, The Netherlands, Paul Verhoeven)

A wonderful hallucinatory thriller that bristles with dark, forboding humor and sexual paranoia. The story concerns a brooding bisexual novelist entwined in the web of a mysterious beautician and her handsomely sculpted lover. Starring Jeroen Krabbe and the hauntingly beautiful but oh-so dangerous Renee Soutendijk. ⊗

Frankie and Johnny

(1991, 118 min, US, Garry Marshall)

Adapted for the screen by Terrence McNally from his hit off-Broadway play "Frankie and Johnny at the Claire de Lune," this romantic comedy, though a tale of straight love, does feature a positive portrayal of a well-adjusted and supportive gay man. Al Pacino is an ex-con who takes a job as a short order cook in a greasy-spoon diner and falls for the waitress, played by Michelle Pfeiffer. Nathan Lane is Tim, Pfeiffer's confidant and neighbor. The "gay best friend with a killer wit" is nothing new; Lane, however, gives it a refreshing take. Sean O'Bryan is his lover Bobby. Nice to see the gay confidant romantically involved for once. ⊗

Focus on: *Terrence McNally*

*Texas-born playwright ("Bad Habits," "Lisbon Traviata" and "Lips Together, Teeth Apart") and screenwriter (*The Ritz*), Terrence McNally is an openly gay author who wants to be known for his artistic output rather than his sexuality. He has said, "I am a gay man who earns his living writing plays; I am not a playwright who writes gay plays. I know, if you don't identify yourself as a gay playwright some people think you're not being out there. It's almost who can be gayer than the next. I'm a gay man who writes plays."*

Friends Forever

(1986, 95 min, Denmark, Stefan Christian Henszelman)

A teenage boy's sexual and emotional development is the theme in this pleasant Danish drama by gay filmmaker Stefan Christian Henszelman, who died of AIDS in October 1991. Kristian is a shy and innocent 16-year-old who becomes friends with two very different boys — Henrick, a slightly effeminate and determinedly non-conformist student and Patrick, a blond thug. When Patrick tells him that he is gay and introduces him to his older lover, Kristian is thrown into emotional turmoil. Similar to Denmark's other adolescent gay drama *You Are Not Alone*, this simple, yet unpredictable story presents a positive outlook on a young man's sexual coming out and its effect on his friends. ⊗

Fun Down There

(1989, 89 min, US, Roger Stigliano)

This independently produced drama is notable only for its gay coming-of-age theme and should be of interest solely to an audience that accepts the film's earnest intentions and ignores its less-than-professional acting, plot and production values. A gangly young man, feeling frustrated and alone in his upstate New York town, moves to New York City determined to explore his gay tendencies. Although not really attractive and possessing the personality of a piece of driftwood, the neophyte lover finds sexual success and excess in the Village. ⊗

> "A film about one man's coming to terms with his homosexuality without Sturm und Drang or apologies to anyone...*Fun Down There* is not only about understanding, it demonstrates it with élan."
> —Vincent Canby, *The New York Times*

Fun Down There

Funeral Parade of Roses

(1968, 105 min, Japan, Toshio Matsumoto)

This obscure, avant-garde film, a modern gay version of the Oedipus legend, is the first Japanese film to deal with homosexuality and has been called by many a masterpiece of gay filmmaking. Eddie is a young gay teenager who, as fate decrees, kills his mother and sleeps with his father! This melodramatic spoof on the ancient myth features male prostitutes, a gay bar called Genet, impressive cross-dressers (including Peter, a famous Tokyo female impersonator) and the film crew and actors themselves, discussing the production and their own sexuality.

The Gay Deceivers

(1969, 99 min, US, Bruce Kessler)

What has time done to this low-budget '60s comedy about two "perfectly normal" guys who try to evade the draft by posing as homosexual lovers? Is it offensively homophobic drivel or simply a frequently hilarious, naively camp curiosity? Filmed in a "Laugh-In," sitcom style, the film's funniest scenes come when our hapless heroes, under investigation by a suspicious Army recruiter, must move into a gay bungalow complex, populated by the most outrageous gay stereotypes this side of Fairyland. Michael Greer adds both a campy humor and surprising gay dignity as he steals the show as Malcolm, the boy's "queer as a three dollar bill" landlord. If you mind swishy, lisping, prancing, mincing "fags" and the jokes that come with them, avoid this at all costs. For others, this anachronistic sex comedy will provide some laughs and an appreciation of how much things have changed in 25 years. ⊛

Gay Erotica from the Past, Volume 1

(1990, 60 min, US)

Beginning with a scholarly introduction by a serious, bearded man, this compilation video offers a sampling of the many silent, black-and-white "smokers" that were made before the advent of video and the porno explosion in the early 1970s. Collectively, the shorts are long on posing, tight underwear and muscles and short on any real full-frontal nudity or hard-core sex, but as a historical document of gay sexuality, they are quite fascinating. The first vignette features an over-accomodating man who invites all who come to his doorstep. The film has innocence, humor and lots of shower scenes as well as a friendly free-for-all wrestling scene. The second short is set in a late-'50s/early-'60s gay bar, where hunky sailors, cowboys and clones all have a hard time keeping their clothes on. "Cellmates," the third short, is the best at sexual teasing. An innocent boy is thrown in jail and is befriended by a muscular "daddy." In "Ben-Hurry," Roman gladiators find better things to do with their lances than simply killing Christians! The tape ends with "Fanny's Hill," an amusing, hippie-inspired homage to nudity, free-love and pie-throwing. ⊛

Gay Erotica from the Past, Volume 2

(1991, 60 min, US)

The cock tease continues in this second volume of gay "smokers" from the 1950s and '60s. Buns, flaccid penises and over-enthusiastic wrestling are the recurring themes in these often-funny shorts. The opening short proves that sometimes "water sports" is simply a frolic in the shower. Others include a sculptor whose Adonis-like marble statue comes to life, but he doesn't know what to do with it! There's a short from Apollo Photography Studio with a greasy posing session. The final few shorts all feature California boys frolicking naked poolside and channeling their sexual frustrations into relentless wrestling sessions. The final short, "Three's a Crowd," is an entertaining tale of two campers who meet up with a voyeuristic reptilian alien. Let 'em cruise on their own planet! ⊛

The Gay Man's Guide to Safer Sex

(1993, 50 min, GB, David Lewis)

Made with the support of The Terrence Higgens Trust, the U.K.'s leading HIV/AIDS charity, this serious and discreetly explicit documentary candidly explains the erotic possibilities of safe sex as well as cautions on unsafe practices. The young but informative narrators clarify what is and what is not unsafe sex while six attractive models put into vivid demonstration variations on the safe sex theme. Emphasizing the "play safe" mantra, the film offers ideas on the use of condoms ("Keep them everywhere!"), sex toys, and role-playing along with practical tips for the sexually active ("Wash your fingers between asses"). An important primer for those interested in knowing more about avoiding contacting the HIV virus while still enjoying a full sex life. ⊛

Gay Voices, Gay Legends *(1988, 58 min)*

Some of America's most famous gay men (oddly no lesbians are to be found) are featured in this compilation video. More conversational than standard interview in style, and more entertaining and funny than informative, the film features such people as porn star Al Parker, female impersonator and entertainer Charles Pierce, Leonard Matlovich (an early opponent of the military's ban against homosexuals), Michael Hardwick, Michael Murray and Norris Knight. ⊛

Gay Voices, Gay Legends 2

(1989, 60 min)

Insightful and amusing interviews with famous American gay men continues in this video follow-up which features writer Paul Monette, Mattachine co-founder Harry Hay, Rev. Troy Perry (founder of the non-denominational church for gay people, the Metropolitan Community Church) and actor Michael Kearns. ⊛

The Genesis Children

(1972, 84 min, US/Italy, Anthony Aikmen)

Tough call on this one: Is *The Genesis Children* a celebration of the beauty and innocence of youth and a bold expression of naturism or is this crudely made independent feature merely a thinly veiled excuse to leer at the naked bodies of the many boys shown in the film? With poor production values, chintzy tourist footage and terrible acting from the leads, this semi-home movie follows the frolicking antics of a group of mostly naked boys aged 10 to 15. What keeps the movie from being soft-core kiddie porn is the absence of any overt or even implied sexuality. ⊛

Getting It Right:
Safer Sex for Young Gay Men

(1993, 55 min, GB, Mike Esser & Chris Hughes)

After the success of their instructional video *Gay Man's Guide to Safer Sex*, Pride Video has released this similarly themed tape which is aimed specifically at gay men under the age of 25. With AIDS being a top concern for this high-risk group, the video offers, through explicit sexual demonstrations with several handsome young models, various safer sex activities. Also included are interviews with young men on coming out and health information. ⊛

Giarres

(1983, 90 min, Germany, Rienhard von der Marwitz)

With startling black-and-white photography and a dreamlike, almost poetic story line, this gay love story and murder mystery is quite interesting. The story begins on a train where two men meet. The one tells the other a story of two men's intense love for each other. Near the Sicilian town of Giarres, two men are found shot. A local boy confesses to the double murder despite appearances that the deceased men might have been involved in a lovers' suicide pact. Did they hire the boy to kill them or are there other circumstances that could solve the mystery?

Goat Boy and the Potatoe Chip Ritual

(1992, 30 min, US, Tim McCarthy)

Chubby, hippie-dippy cross-dressing gay naturalists of Wolf Creek Radical Faerie Sanctuary reenact playful rituals and myths in this low-budget short originally made for the Gay Cable Network. Preceeding the film is Brian Gamon's "Come Out Voting" — the first gay and lesbian "get out the vote" commercial seen on network TV. ⊛

The Great Unpleasantness

(1993, 80 min, US, Dorne Penies)

This comedy-drama by North Carolina independent filmmaker Dorne Penies, while a bit awkward in plot and acting, makes up for its rag-tag looks in its interesting, if not exactly positive inclusion of a gay couple in the story's plot. A hip but penniless straight couple are about to be evicted from their seedy Charlotte home. Also affected are their upstairs neighbors, an often feuding, often imbecilic gay couple who argue over paint color (their apartment is a lavender-walled, plastic male figure-art faggot dive), call each other names ("You're a K-Mart queer!") and even take to shooting at one another. While seemingly in the throngs of violently breaking up, the two are reunited by the headstrong girlfriend from the apartment below. Their negative depiction (but is it simply negative or actually realistic and inclusionary?) abruptly changes when they make up just in time to become allies in the fight against the greedy developer. The final part of the film shows the two Southern gays to be tender and affectionate towards each other. ⊛

Gymnastikos: Power & Grace

(1993, 42 min, US, Layne Derrick)

Hypnotic and unusual, this balletic appreciation of the male form in motion features five world-class gymnasts who are filmed while warming up and performing incredible gymnastic exercises. Self-described by the makers as "the video equivalent of a 'high-end' coffee table book," the hook for this visually stunning video is that the young men, all from Eastern Europe, are seen both with and without their clothing. The nudity, gratuitous to some, enjoyable to others, helps in revealing the amazing physical strength and fluidity of the athletes. Producer and director Layne Derrick was determined to create a gymnastic art film with men in the nude remarking, "We thought our biggest challenge would be finding top, internationally ranked gymnasts willing to perform without clothes. We learned that nudity was not an important issue to Europeans." ⊛

Hamlet *(1976, 67 min, GB, Celestino Coronado)*

Feverish, dreamlike and campy to a '70s fault, this outlandish interpretation of William Shakespeare's "Hamlet" is a low-budget, druggy, flesh-filled drama staged by the Lindsay Kemp Company. Twin brothers (Anthony and David Meyer) play the often-naked, much-tortured lead, Helen Mirren is both Gertrude and Ophelia and a much-made-up Quentin Crisp is Polonius. This Fellini-esque

Giarres

adaptation, condensed and altered a bit, takes place in front of a gauze background, and is mostly suited to fans of the avant-garde. All caution is thrown to the wind as gay director Celestino Coronado (who also helmed Kemp's rendition of "A Midsummer Night's Dream") fills the screen with erotic dances, futuristic costuming, transvestites and two Hamlets running around clothed only in jockstraps.

Happy Birthday, Gemini
(1980, 107 min, US, Richard Benner)

Ridiculous stereotypes, terrible acting and a tired script make this film version of Albert Innaurato's 1977 Broadway comedy-drama "Gemini" a messy failure. Set in the row houses of Italian South Philadelphia, the story revolves around a closet case, Francis (Alan Rosenberg), who, while in the midst of a sexual identity crisis, must contend with his wacky neighbors, overbearing father and the unexpected arrival of two of his WASPy Harvard friends. Problems arise when schoolmate Judith (Sarah Molcomb) wants to resume their tentative college affair, but Francis is actually attracted to her blond brother Randy (David Marshall Grant). His tormented indecision finally comes to a head as he begins to accept his homosexuality (although he does not show any affection towards another man, has never had sex with a man and never once says he's gay). Included in the constantly screaming and bickering menagerie of grotesques are Rita Moreno and Madeline Kahn. From the gay director of *Outrageous!* and *Too Outrageous!* ⊛

Haunted Summer
(1988, 106 min, US, Ivan Passer)

Languid (read: boring), beautifully filmed (read: the countryside is more interesting than the characters), evocative period piece (read: pretentious costume drama drivel) and shocking (read: a failed attempt at titillation), this drama retreads the often-traveled grounds of the fateful summer that Percy Shelley, his lover and future wife Mary Goodwin, her half-sister Claire Claimont and the roguish poet Lord Byron spent together on the shores of Lake Geneva in 1816. Were these "beautiful people" highly talented, sexually adventurous bohemians whose great works of art were fueled by each other's company, or were they simply rich, spoiled, indolent dilettantes with whom history has been extremely kind? It would be prudent to withhold judgment on this foursome if one's only source is this ridiculously "serious" story of their times. Shelley is played by flower-sniffing, sonnet-espousing Eric Stoltz, the abused Claire is played by Laura Dern and the role of Mick Jagger, oops, Lord Byron is played by Philip Anglim, who is seen alternately as seductive and obnoxious, a mixture that entices Mary (Alice Krige) and ensnares the homosexual Dr. Polidori (Alex Winter). The gay scenes are limited to Byron's sexual domination of the wimpy Doctor who suffers a painful love for the philandering Byron. ⊛

For those interested in the life, work and sexual adventures of Lord Byron (nee George Noel Gordon — 1788-1824), this film is certainly not the best. The famed Romanticist poet whose bisexuality was an open secret is best known for his epic satire "Don Juan," his Faustian tragedy "Manfred" and "The Prisoner of Chillon." He began his sexual adventures as a youth in boarding schools and continued imbibing in forbidden fruit (boys, lords, married women and even his half-sister

Gymnastikos: Power & Grace

Augusta) until his death. The most notable of the biopics of this colorful character was Robert Bolt's 1972 drama *Lady Caroline Lamb* which stars Sarah Miles, Jon Finch and Laurence Olivier with Richard Chamberlain as Byron. British actor Hugh Grant also starred as the poet in the 1988 Spanish feature *Rowing in the Wind*, directed by Gonzalo Suarez. A heterosexualized version of his life can be found in the 1948 British film *The Bad Lord Byron* with Dennis Price in the title role. For those who want their biographies devoid of most fact and infused with a most camp sensibility, Ken Russell's dreamlike psychological thriller, *Gothic*, filmed in 1987, is a must.

Hin Yin for Men: Ancient Secrets of Relaxation and Self-Eroticism

The onslaught of soft-core exercise and relaxation tapes for the gay audience continues with this classy demonstration video. Called "very erotic, sensual and even educational" by the *Gay Video Guide*, the film aims to increase men's awareness of their body and its erotic, pleasure-giving potential by revealing "ancient Chinese secrets" of relaxation, personal hygiene and anal and penile massage. Avoiding its potential for being cheesy and exploitative, the tape is actually quite tasteful (but not in that way) as three male models demonstrate the exercises and engage in self-eroticism. ⊛

> "A refreshing look at sexuality! A Jane Fonda exercise tapes for New Age queers."
>
> —*Hunt Magazine*

Holy Bunch
(1981, 89 min, Germany, Heinz Emigholz)

From gay underground director Heinz Emigholz (*Die Basis des Make-up*), comes this witty, thought-provoking drama about death and the feelings of those left behind. Set in New York, a group of artists (a writer, an architect, a photographer, a comic illustrator and a translator) are forced to examine their lives after one of their friends dies. Featuring New York performers Kyle de Camp and

John Erdman as well as Wolfgang Muelter and the late Bernd Broaderup (*Taxi Zum Klo*).

Homosexual Desire in Minnesota

(1981-85, 59 min, US, Jim Hubbard)

Filmed in Super-8, this twelve-part compilation film provides an interesting historical and political view of gay life in the American Heartland from the late 1970s to early '80s. New York independent filmmaker Jim Hubbard is known primarily for his varied political shorts (*Stop the Movie* [*Cruising*], *Elegy in the Streets*, *Two Marches*) which have become staples in lesbian and gay film festivals. Included in the film are scenes of the 1980 and 1981 Gay Pride celebrations, a raucous but affecting look at a group of drag queens as they primp and prepare for a show, scenes of the filmmaker's former lover and casual affairs, as well as intimate portraits of several other individual gays and lesbians.

The Hours and the Times

(1991, 60 min, US,
Christopher Münch)

Taking the historical, if seemingly unimportant fact that The Beatles' manager, and early guiding force, Brian Epstein took John Lennon on a four-day vacation to Barcelona, Spain, just months before the meteoric rise of the Fab Four, director Christopher Münch has fashioned a fictional "what-might-have-happened" queer drama. Epstein — Jewish, upper-class and gay — and Lennon — a Liverpudlian working-class musician with unlimited but raw promise — seem an unlikely pair although their mentor-student relationship is quite intense, especially at this crucial juncture in their lives. Their vastly different lifestyles and attitudes both attract and distance the two and is especially evident in Epstein's sexual attraction for the appreciative but hopelessly straight Lennon. This sexual tension provides the dramatic centerpiece in this understated and low-budget picture which is both an engrossing exploration of the shifting nature and intensity of friendship and a touching example of unrequited love. David Angus portrays Epstein, and Ian Hart is Lennon, a role he'd repeat in the 1994 film *Backbeat*. ☮

The Hugh Holland Collection

(1989, 75 min, US)

This unusual and erotic video is a filmed analog of more than 150 stills from the works of photographer Hugh Holland. His models, athletically beautiful young men, are photographed amidst the lush locales of Mexico and California. ☮

I Am a Man

(1988, 89 min, Thailand, M.L. Bhandevanop Devakul)

Mart Crowley's "The Boys in the Band" is transported to Asia in this low-budget but faithful interpretation of the comedy-drama which features a macho dancer in the role of the hustler cowboy. Described by the San Francisco International Lesbian and Gay Film Festival as a "cross between a 1968 episode of 'Hawaii Five-O' and a Herschel Gordon Lewis epic."

I Don't Kiss (J'embrasse pas)

(1991, 116 min, France, André Téchine)

The age-old story of an innocent country youth becoming corrupted by the big city is given a gay angle in this initially involving but ultimately trying sexual drama. Pierre (Manuel Blanc) leaves the safe bosom of his mother to live in the unforgiving "mean streets" of Paris. His initial jobs as a low-paid dishwasher don't pan out, so a friend introduces this straight young man to the world of male prostitution. Before he takes the plunge, however, Pierre instead becomes the boy-toy of a wealthy middle-aged matron. But the

The Hours and the Times

lure of the street, with its easy money (and nighttime work), beckons, eventually turning him into a seasoned hustler who warns his clients, "I don't kiss, suck off or take it up the ass." This reluctance offers him an excuse to claim that he is not gay. Also featured is Philippe Noiret (the film's producer) as a wealthy television personality with an obsession for street trade. His interest in Pierre, though never fully explored, is centered less on his body and more on his soul. But this unorthodox gay coming out tale eventually turns into a heterosexual love story as the hardened Pierre falls in love with an equally world-weary female prostitute (Emmanuelle Béart). This interesting, but disappointing story made watchable by Blanc's inexpressive performance is a glimpse into the nocturnal world of gay hustling.

I Love You No More
(1975, 88 min, France, Serge Gainsbourg)
Years — even deacdes — ahead of its time, this bizarrely brutal love triangle about two gay lovers and the woman who comes between them is played out in a vaguely Gallic Southwestern American landscape. Joe Dallesandro and Hughes Questar play two junk men, Krassky and Padovan, who roam the sun-drenched countryside eventually coming upon the boyish Johnny (Jane Birkin), a bored but sexy "small-titted, big-assed" waitress in a backwater cafe. Krassky takes a liking to the boney waif, but being mostly gay, can not get it up unless Johnny pretends that she is male and lets Krassky fuck her up the ass. The only problem is that Johnny's cries of pain when entered causes them to be thrown out of every cheap motel in the area. Compounding the problem is the increasing jealousy of Padovan (a masochistic drama queen if ever there was one), whose pent-up rage against Johnny eventually erupts in violence. The tense triangular relationship is "resolved" in an off-the-wall surprise ending. Enjoyable for both the relaxed depiction of the gay relationship in an environment not known for nurturing such and for the attractive (and often naked) bodies of the three lovers. An artily atmospheric and exceedingly involving tale that will remind some of a queer *Last Tango in Paris*. Also starring a young Gérard Depardieu, who won't fuck Padovan because he would "tear him apart" with his big dick, and Michel Blanc, as a mousy thug who likes to watch. Why this film is not considered a classic of '70s filmmaking is beyond me.

I Love You, I'll Kill You
(1971, 94 min, Germany, Uwe Brandner)
Rural Germany, the romantic sight of countless domestic "yodeling" films of the 1950s and ealry '60s, is portrayed as a destructive and violent hell in this disturbing film. The story takes place in a seemingly idyllic town where the initial scenes of daily life seem picture-perfect. Closer scrutiny reveals, however, that the villagers have been doped into complacency, and when drugs don't do the trick, a repressive police presence functions to "keep the peace" and prevent anyone from entering the adjoining forest, the site of mysterious activity. Counterbalanced against this tense scene is a sensitive relationship between two men. The blond, slightly effeminate school-teacher (Rolf Becker), a recent arrival, meets his butch opposite in a dark and gruff forester (Hannes Fuchs) and the two find themselves drawn together in an increasingly tender love affair. Their relationship ends in betrayal and death, however, as the teacher ventures into the forbidden forest to poach only to be turned in by his love. He is summarily shot, provoking his lover to rebel himself. An adventurous and dense story which *Time Out* calls the *"L'Age d'Or* for the valium generation" and "a rural version of *Performance.*"

I'll Love You Forever...Tonight
(1992, 76 min, US, Edgar Michael Bravo)
Made for under $100,000 by 31-year-old Edgar Michael Bravo as his thesis film at UCLA, this searing yet quite funny film focuses on life for a group of young friends. What begins as a quiet weekend retreat in Palm Springs soon develops into much more for a petulant photographer and his lover. Their peace and solitude are shattered when the two are joined by a raucous gathering of friends, lovers, former lovers and possible future ones. The proceedings soon turn bitchy, as an around-the-clock party of heavy drinking and emotionally cruel sexual games reveal the young men's loneliness, self-deceptions and their simple longing for love and understanding. Alternately described as "Pinter-on-Fire Island" and "a queer *Big Chill*," this gritty tale of life for the post-AIDS twentysomething crowd is alternately compassionate and devastating, but always perceptive.

> "Suggests Mart Crowley's 'The Boys in the Band' as it might be adapted and updated for 1993 in the spirit of Bret Easton Ellis' novel, 'Less Than Zero.'"
> —Stephen Holden, *The New York Times*

I'm Still Alive
(1986, 58 min, Germany, Michael Aue)
Originally broadcast on German television, this documentary is an intimate, somber story of Peter S., a gay German with AIDS who moves back to his native land after eight years in San Francisco. The film chronicles his parents' distrustful reactions as well as Peter's strong but admittedly fearful battle with the disease, including his determined efforts to explore his own emotions and to keep outside tensions and strains to a minimum. Emotional and heartfelt.

Imposters
(1979, 110 min, US/Germany, Mark Rappaport)
Independent New York filmmaker Mark Rappaport (*Rock Hudson's Home Movies*) has fashioned, with the help of Charles Ludlam (the late founder of New York's Ridiculous Theatre Company), an absurdist, convoluted and extremely strange comic soap opera about two incestuous twin brothers (who are not twins and one of whom is gay) whose interests include magic, love triangles, assassinations and stolen Egyptian treasures. Produced on a miniscule budget and told episodically in a hysteria-driven labyrinthine plot (Rappaport has said that there's "enough plot to choke a horse"), this very "'70s" picture might seem rudderless and even senseless to many, but others will find it quite entertaining, intellectually puzzling and original.

> "A succulent and tasty mango, an insolent high-camp comedy about magic, obsession, role-playing and love."
> —David Denby, *New York Magazine*

In a Glass Cage

(1986, 98 min, Spain, Agustin Villaronga)
Although definitely not for the squeamish, this sexually bizarre and violent thriller is a real find for those aficionados of no-holds-barred horror. Set a few years after WWII, the story concerns a former Nazi doctor and child molester who, because of an accident, is confined to an iron lung. The tormentor becomes the tormented after a mysterious young man, employed to be the paralyzed man's nurse, is instead bent on revenge. Mixing the style of *Diva* with the graphic sadomasochism of Pasolini's *Salo*, the film treads on ideas rarely ventured in commercial films. An uncompromising psychosexual drama that is both erotic, painful and terrifying. ✪

Inside Men: Video Agenda *(1991, 60 min)*

Porn star and lube-promoter Rex Chandler and Steve Schulte co-host this gay male video magazine that started in late 1991. The featurettes include an interview with baseball's gay umpire Dave Pallone, a sneak behind the making of an adult movie, and a short story on the struggles of openly gay cops. Also, a video personals is tagged on at the end of the newsmagazine. ✪

Jeffrey Dahmer — The Secret Life

(1993, 95 min, US, David R. Bowen)
Gross, obscene and revolting, this low-budget bio-pic on serial killer Jeffrey Dahmer is a horribly sick film experience that sympathetically portrays the killer; it is saved only by the possibility that it might actually be an inadvertently black, black comedy. Screenwriter Carl Crew stars as Dahmer, a misunderstood man who, mistreated by his unloving parents and ignored by an insensitive government, takes his childhood fascination with cutting up dead animals, combines it with his kinky homosexual desires and proceeds to kill, mutilate and dismember at least 17 young men. Incredibly, Dahmer is the narrator, recounting his "troubles" and explaining his actions with, "I was trying for the normal life; to be good." He dismisses his sickness and violence as "crimes of love" and justifies his first murder with, "I just didn't want him to leave, I didn't want to be alone again. I never wanted to kill." The acting is terrible and the plodding story line only adds to the difficulty of watching Dahmer prowl gay bars, pick up men with the promise of money, drug them and then excrutiatingly kill his weakened victims. This confessional form of depicting the grisly story lacks the power or effectiveness of *Henry: Portrait of a Serial Killer*, and its depiction of Dahmer as a sensitive youth with a problem is just unthinkable. The film is "dedicated" to Dahmer's victims. ✪

Jerker *(1991, 90 min, US, Hugh Harrison)*

Robert Chesley's controversial homoerotic play about two men who, through a series of sexually charged telephone calls, begin to become friends and learn something about themselves is alternately intriguing, sexy and emotionally hard-hitting. The story begins when a young man is woken up by a stranger who wants telephone sex. He obliges, and through a series of these calls, their talks shift slowly from mere sexual games and into monologues and conversations about personal ambitions and frustra-tions. The alternate title is "Helping Hand — A Pornographic Elegy in Twenty Telephone Calls, Many of Them Dirty." The *Philadelphia Gay News* called it, "Raw, honest and unapologetic in its portrayal of gay sexuality." This video features, at the conclusion, an in-depth interview with Chesley on the writing and production of his play. ✪

The Jim Bailey Experience

(1990, 54 min, US, Compiled by Stephen Campbell & Rick Flynn)
Culled primarily from old TV clips (including an appearance on "The Lucille Ball Show"), this fluffy promotional documentary focuses on "actor-illusionist" Jim Bailey, arguably the most "accepted" of the female impersonators/impressionists today. Included are segments from his acts, whose subjects include Barbra Streisand, Phyllis Diller, Peggy Lee, Judy Garland and, in an effort to stay current, Madonna. ✪

Joey Breaker *(1992, 92 min, US, Steven Starr)*

Essentially a heterosexual story of a selfish man's social enlightenment, the film features several gay characters who "assist" in his conversion. Joey (Richard Edson) is a high-powered, nothing-will-get-in-my-way New York entertainment agent who, despite living in New York in the 1990s, remains sexist and homophobic. His education comes in several forms — befriending a person with AIDS, representing a black gay comedian and falling in love with a Jamaican woman. Obsessed only with deal making, Joey is asked to accompany a co-worker as she visits a friend, a 46-year-old man stricken with AIDS. His initial meeting with the sweet, former librarian is tense, with Joey afraid of casually catching the disease. But he continues visiting the man, until the point where they form a bond. While beginning to understand about gay men and AIDS, he also confronts gay militancy when it dawns on him that a hot black comedian whom Joey desperately wants to sign up is also gay. Hip Hop Hank (Erik King), recently released from prison, brings along his male lover to their first meeting, revealing an openly gay relationship. Joey suggests that it would be better for Hank's career to keep his gayness a secret but the comedian angrily informs Joey that his private life is his own. Joey's acceptance of their relationship coupled with his love of a remarkable black woman, opens him up to the multiple possibilities in life. Sort of a gay, black version of *A Christmas Carol*, this American independent film has its faults, but not when it comes to depicting interesting and intelligent gay characters. ✪

Johnny Minotaur

(1971, 60 min, US, Charles Henri Ford)
Writer-poet Charles Henri Ford's semiautobiographical underground film is a dreamlike film-within-a-film in which a middle-aged American artist visiting Crete becomes erotically obsessed with several young men on the island, site of the ancient legend of the minotaur. Handsome young men and boys are seen making love and showing homoerotic affection for each other as the artist, fueled with a lust for one particular straight Greek painter, composes his own personal fantasy-myth.

Judgment *(1990, 89 min, US, Tom Topor)*

The sexual abuse of minors by priests is the delicate issue handled quite effectively in this serious and focused HBO-produced drama. Keith Carradine and Blythe Danner star as devout Catholics whose faith in both the law and the Church are shattered when their son reveals that he has been sexually abused by a priest. When their son, Robbie, is picked by the kindly parish priest, Father Aubert (David Strathairn), to train to be an alter boy, they couldn't be more proud. And they are especially glad at the special religious attention Robbie is receiving when Aubert proposes overnight stays at the rectory and weekend camping trips. But when Robbie becomes distraught, agitated, admits to rectal bleeding and displays a fear of the priest, they are shattered. Along with other parents in the parish, they begin a persistent but painful campaign to remove Aubert and have him prosecuted as a sex offender. The challenges they face include a reluctant legal system and a secretive Church hierarchy bent on denial and self-preservation. They reject neighbors' pressure and a compromise Church settlement offer in their drive to protect their child and exact justice. An all-too-true and sad story which is given expert handling here, with all of the personalities treated fairly — even the perpetrator is seen as a victim. ⊛

The Kiss (o Beijo No Asfalto)
(1985, 80 min, Brazil, Bruno Barreto)

From the director of such heterosexual celebrations as *Doña Flor and Her Two Husbands* and *Gabriela* comes this interesting thriller about homophobia in Brazil. Based on a play by Nelson Rodrigues, the film hinges on a scene in which a man sees a dying man on the street and instinctively kisses him on the lips. That one act precipitates an avalanche of hatred. Persecuted by a cynical, corrupt press intent on milking the incident, his life soon becomes a nightmare, where even his boss calls him a "faggot."

Kiss of the Spider Woman
(1985, 120 min, Brazil, Hector Babenco)

Hector Babenco's spellbinding meditation on political idealism and self-delusion stars Academy Award winner William Hurt and Raul Julia who portray two dramatically opposite inmates thrown together in a dungeon-like cell somewhere in South America. Julia, a cold political realist and activist, is forced to endure the fantasies of Hurt, a hopelessly romantic and politically naive homosexual. An exotic Sonia Braga plays both Julia's one-time lover and Hurt's imagined heroine. ⊛

Focus on: *Manuél Puig*

Expatriate Argentinian writer Manuél Puig, a flamboyantly gay personality who was called by fellow South American writer Mario Vargas Llosa "one of the masters of contemporary Latin American fiction," lived alternately in Rio de Janeiro, Colombia and New York City, where he taught at Columbia University. He died in 1990 officially from a heart attack brought on by a gall bladder operation — many of his friends suspected, however, that it was an AIDS-related death. He was celebrated for his

Kiss of the Spider Woman

enjoyable novels, which were crammed with nostalgic movie references, outrageous camp, tender romance, surprisingly strong political issues and were peppered with many homosexual themes. Three of his books were adapted for the screen: "Kiss of the Spider Woman," "Pubis Angelical" and "Heartbreak Tango," which he also scripted. The Argentinian film Naked Tango *was "inspired" by an idea of his. Other novels include "Eternal Curse on the Reader of These Pages" (written after a love affair ended), "Betrayed by Rita Hayworth" and "The Buenos Aires Affair." Always outspoken and witty, Puig gained international attention with the success of the screen version of* Kiss of the Spider Woman, *and in response to William Hurt's performance as the wistful homosexual he said, "La Hurt is so bad she will probably win an Oscar." In an interview with the Colombian newspaper El Tiempo, he cited his three greatest influences: Greta Garbo, Ernst Lubitsch and Sigmund Freud.*

L'Homme Blesse

(1984, 105 min, France, Patrice Chereau)
Adrift in the French underworld of hustlers and pick-ups, the innocent Henri (Jean-Hughes Anglade) experiences a brutal awakening to his gay sexuality. He witnesses a trick being beaten in the train station toilet, surrenders to the culprit's fierce embrace and finds himself hopelessly lost in ardor for this mysterious thug. Suddenly drawn to the rough trade, Henri undergoes a number of hardships before finding liberation in a shocking final act of conquest. ⊗

"Absolutely amazing in its erotic power. A whirlwind of frustrated adolescent passion."
—Joel Weinberg, *New York Native*

Last Exit to Brooklyn

(1989, 103 min, Germany, Uli Edel)
This fevered production of Hubert Selby, Jr.'s 1957 underground classic is a hard-hitting, no-holds-barred look at life in hell on the docks of Brooklyn in the early 1950s. This isn't simply Ozzie and Harriet in reverse; it's an all-out indictment of the American experience as seen through the eyes of Brooklyn's lower depths. Gripping and undeniably overwhelming, one of the film's main characters is Harry (Stephen Lang), a handsome but inarticulate union worker who, despite being married with a child, harbors repressed homosexual desires. He finds momentary happiness and a chance to explore his gay sexuality when, at a bizarre dock workers/drag queen party thrown by the neighborhood's resident queer, George/Georgette (Alexis Arquette), he meets Regina (Zette), an attractive but self-serving young man. The bewildered Harry's brief respite from the pain of living ends abruptly when, all at once, he loses his job, his lover and his reputation. Alexis' George, a drug-addicted, semi-transvestite gay man, and Jennifer Jason Leigh, as teenage hooker Tralala, are just two of the film's beautiful losers. ⊗

Alexis Arquette (r.) in *Last Exit to Brooklyn*

The Last Song

(1986, 90 min, Thailand, Pisan Akkaraseni)
The first part of director Pisan Akkaraseni's fascinating glimpse at the gay lifestyle in Bangkok (the other being *Anguished Love*) is a grand-style melodrama featuring drag queens, macho dancers and other denizens of the cabaret district.

The Last Supper

(1994, 96 min, Canada, Cynthia Roberts)
A filmed reenactment/creation of the last 90 minutes of a man's life, *The Last Supper* makes for an unlikely and not altogether successful film. Filmed in a cinema verité style, in real time and in an actual AIDS hospice in Toronto, the story centers on Chris (Ken McDougall), a former dancer, now an emaciated, bedridden AIDS patient who has decided to end his life rather than continue. At his bedside is his lover/partner Val (Jack Nicholsen). The two talk, eat a meal, drink wine and, accompanied by cherished music and memories, prepare for his upcoming death, to be administered via an injection by a sympathetic doctor. The film attempts to tackle many subjects including PWAs' struggle for dignity, the deep love between

The Leather Boys

Let's Get Lost
(1987, 119 min, US, Bruce Weber)

The life and music of the late jazz great Chet Baker is the subject of this poignant, fascinating documentary by noted photographer Bruce Weber. In fact, Weber's roots show to tremendous effect as this examination of a tortured artist's genius and self-destruction looks every bit as handsome as its subject in his early years. Weber splendidly intercuts rare recording sessions, interviews with family and friends, and even includes clips from Baker's short-lived movie career in the 1950s. The scenes of Baker's later years are heartbreakingly sad as the ravages of drug addiction had clearly taken its toll on this legendary trumpeter. ☯

the two men and euthanasia. Taken from a play, the dimly lit film is rough going; if the filmmakers were attempting to make a gut-wrenching tearjerker, they failed. Unlike such documentaries as *Silverlake Life: The View from Here* and *Cancer in Two Voices*, two films that deal in real-life death among lovers, the film's theatrical artifice distances the viewer and mutes the power of the real tragedy it presents. This criticism aside, the film will bring back painful memories for anyone who has been at bedside with a terminally ill person. McDougall, who performs a touching "dance" during the film, himself died of AIDS soon after the film was completed.

The Leather Boys
(1963, 107 min, GB, Sidney J. Furie)

An implied homoerotic tension between Pete (Dudley Sutton) and Reggie (Colin Campbell) is the primary theme of this British drama. Gradually this tension becomes identified as the probable reason for Reggie's lack of sexual interest in his new wife, Dot (Rita Tushingham). Director Sidney J. Furie presents a very subdued treatment of the issue until the last half hour of the film when Dot accuses Pete and Reggie of being "queer." Denying her charge, they agree that they are just good friends. After a few melodramatic twists, Pete and Reggie decide to sail off to America together and are about to get on a ship when, stopping at a waterfront bar, Reggie realizes that Pete really *is* gay. Reggie abandons Pete and walks off alone. In contrast to the drugs, girls and rock 'n' roll ambience that American biker pics are associated with, *The Leather Boys* is rather staid in its drama. The "sensational" biker backdrop is distinctly British, and really the film is a serious drama focusing on the lives of its young working-class protagonists (who just happen to be very interested in motorcycles). ☯

Libera *(1993, 83 min, Italy, Pappi Corsicato)*

With over-the-top melodramatic excesses, color-splashed sets and a manic comic gay approach that would make Almodóvar proud, Naples-based Pappi Corsicato holds much promise in this, his first feature film. The film is structured as three separate stories all dealing with women and their "tragic" tales of elusive love and broken dreams. *Aurora* is a dippy, over-consuming woman who loses not only her monied, lecherous husband, but when true, though penniless love comes her way, she flubs that as well. Wittily told, the story features a gay priest-cum-chantuese and many inventive comic touches. The second episode, *Carmela*, is the gayest of the three. Sebastiano, a gorgeous gay youth, has just returned to his single mother Carmela after spending time in reform school. It is obvious to everyone but mom and the horny upstairs neighbor that he is gay (he goes goo-goo eyed over a masculine street merchant), but before he has a chance to tell mom his secret, she, in a hilarious turn, tops him with her own secret about his long-gone father. In the final story, *Libera*, a woman who discovers that her husband is cheating on her comes up with a particularly satisfying form of revenge. Setting the stories (all of which star Ciro Piscopo) in a rapidly changing Naples, Corsicato imbues them with a gay sensibility and a mischievous streak that suggests a queer Buñuel. (Also known as: *The Neopolitans*)

> "Naples now has its own Pedro Almodóvar...Corsicato's tales all have an extraordinary liveliness and an exceedingly wired sense of humor."
>
> —*Variety*

Liberace *(1988, 96 min, US, Billy Hale)*

Possibly the most famous closet case in the entertainment business, Liberace parlayed a talent for the piano with a natural enthusiasm for flashy showmanship to become one of the icons — albeit tacky — of television and Las Vegas. With outrageous, sequined and colorful costumes clinging to his scented body dripping with baubles, Liberace's feyness was amazingly ignored by his thousands of adoring (mostly blue-haired) fans. Despite a successful palimony suit by reported longtime lover Scott Thorson, and even up to his death in February 1987 of AIDS (his doctor initially falsified his death certificate), Liberace steadfastly refused to acknowledge his homosexuality. In the aftermath of his death, two television movies were commissioned. This drama, the first to air, featured a lackluster, Liberace estate-approved script and starred Andrew Robinson as the flamboyant entertainer. The "G" word is never heard and AIDS is only fleetingly mentioned.

Liberace: Behind the Music
(1988, 96 min, US, David Greene)

Promising to reveal the man behind the legend, this biopic takes a slightly more lurid approach to the public and private life of the bejeweled and ermine-cloaked showman. Victor Garber in the lead does not bear any physical resemblance to Liberace, but the story line is more believable and upfront. His affair with Scott Thorson is dealt with as is his life-ending battle with AIDS. Co-starring Maureen Stapleton as Liberace's domineering mom.

Ginsberg (l.), a seated William Burroughs and director Jerry Aronson: *The Life and Times of Allen Ginsberg*

The Lie (Mensonge)
(1993, 89 min, France, François Margolin)

The sympathies of many narrow-minded people for those suffering with HIV infection of full-blown AIDS has been limited to hemophiliacs, children born with the disease or those people (often women) who have unknowingly contracted the disease from an unfaithful partner. It is that third category that is the focus of this harrowing melodrama. Emma (Nathalie Baye) is happily married to reporter Charles (Didier Sandre) and the two live quite the normal family life in Paris. Tragedy strikes when Emma discovers, after a routine pregnancy test, that she is both pregnant with a second child and HIV-positive. Stunned and on the verge of a nervous breakdown, she has no one to turn to — her husband is on assignment in America, her friends are away and her family is strangely unsupportive. With her emotional stability unraveling, she begins a determined investigation to uncover the source of her infection, with all signs pointing to her husband and his heterosexual infidelities. After a frantic and fruitless search for girlfriends, she soon finds out that her husband has led a secret and promiscuous gay life. After her initial shock, Emma must confront the deadly disease and deal with a relationship that has been built on deceit and lies. The drama, while sobering and occasionally affecting, suffers from a ponderous self-pity on the part of Baye's character, leaving the better part of the film to simply wait until she gets over the shock.

Life and Death (1980, 90 min, Norway, Svend Wam & Petter Vennerod)

This deceptively breezy, romantic comedy of sexual liberation is one of Norway's few contributions to gay cinema. A young married doctor finds homosexual hormones stimulated when he meets, and eventually falls in love with, a gay medical student. Against a musical background of ABBA, the doctor brings his love home to his accepting-of-the-situation wife and what begins as a determined attempt by the three to develop a loving, non-traditional threesome ends in tragedy thanks to society's heavy, homophobic hand.

The Life and Times of Allen Ginsberg
(1993, 83 min, US, Jerry Aronson)

Emotional, enlightening and highly entertaining, this intimate portrait of visionary Beat Poet and self-proclaimed "faggot individualist" Allen Ginsberg seeks to venture beyond his fame and controversy to explore the man who has dedicated his work and life "to ease the pain of living." Told in chronological order and recounted through photos, interviews with relatives and with Ginsberg himself, the film begins with his influential North Jersey childhood where he lived with his poet father, his brother and his mentally ill mother. It follows him to his Greenwich Village days and initial success as a poet as well as his friendships with the Beat "leaders" — Jack Kerouac (whom he loved) and William Burroughs (thought by Ginsberg's family to be a decadent millionaire and bad influence). Evolving from beatnik to hippie, Ginsberg became involved with anti-Vietnam demonstrations culminating with his calming influence at the 1968 Chicago Democratic Convention and his effect on '60s leaders such as Abbie Hoffman, Timothy Leary and Joan Baez. His "mellower" period follows when he explored yoga, meditation, chanting and teaching. But while the historical accounts are fascinating, it is his own readings of his poems that will stir and move. His anguished poem, "Howl," is recited in parts from both a 1955 recording and from a 1992 reading. His tender, heartbreaking ode to his mother, "Kaddish," is also read. Ginsberg's homosexuality seems always present, although his personal life, with the exception of his love for longtime companion Peter Orlovsky, is kept to a minimum. Richly detailed, this exploration into the life of the elder statesman of American poetry is nothing less than inspiring. ⊛

Longtime Companion
(1990, 99 min, US, Norman René)
One of the most stirring American fiction films to deal with the AIDS crisis, *Longtime Companion* is an exceptional look into the lives of a group of gay friends and how the disease affects them, both collectively and singularly. Beginning in 1981 at Fire Island and ending in 1989, the film charts the change in the characters, from carefree innocents enjoying their sexual freedoms to men numbed by suffering, forced to cope with the death of friends and lovers, amd mobilized into action. Director Norman René and writer Craig Lucas (who teamed up again in the making of *Prelude to a Kiss*) succeed in creating full dimensional characters, and the film is rich in sharp observations and keen wit. There is a terrific ensemble cast, including Campbell Scott and Dermot Mulroney, but Bruce Davison must be given a special mention for his superlative portrayal of the lover who slowly watches his longtime companion succumb. Simplistic, maudlin and too rich, white and male for some, the film's message of love, support and hope overshadow these faults. ⊛

Looking Back — 1987/1988: A Gay Review
(1987/1988, 58/60 min, US)
Among the first of the queer video magazines, these two tapes attempt to be a "comprehensive look back at the major developments that shaped gay life in 1987 and 1988." The 1987 video features farewell mini-portraits of the recently deceased Michael

Looking for Langston

Bennett, Liberace, Charles Ludlam and Andy Warhol. The tape also covers Gay Pride Celebrations, the 1987 March on Washington, the National Gay Rodeo and a visit to Inferno, the year's "hottest leather party." The 1988 tape visits that notable pride parade, parties, the Quilt, and highlights gays in the news.

Looking for Langston
(1989, 45 min, GB, Isaac Julien)
This pensive, yet celebratory meditation on black poet Langston Hughes is an original work of cinematic art. Stylish and sexy, the film incorporates the lyrical poetry of Essex Hemphill and Bruce Nugent with archival footage of the Harlem Renaissance of the 1920s. Reenacted Cotton Club scenes, romantic shots of two intertwined lovers, Robert Mapplethorpe's photographs of beautiful black men and the pounding disco beat of "Can You Feel It" are also used in telling the story of black consciousness in a culturally evolving America. ⊛

> "One of the most visually satisfying and intellectually stimulating gay films made to date."
> —*Outweek*

The Lost Language of Cranes
(1992, 90 min, GB, Nigel Finch)
Changing locales from a Jewish Upper West Side Manhattan family to a WASPy suburban London one surprisingly does not tarnish David Leavitt's critically acclaimed novel. For this BBC feature film production successfully retains the book's powerfully emotional central story of a troubled family's crisis with homosexuality. Phillip, a young, handsome gay man, falls in love and begins to feel the need to tell his parents about his true sexual self. The twist is that the young man's father, Owen, a successful middle-aged professor, is also gay/bisexual but keeps his yearning closeted from his wife and family — finding release in weekend cottaging in dark movie theatres and anonymous bars. The parallel stories of these two men and the emotionally distraught wife and mother caught in-between results in an undeniably painful melodrama that is exceptionally sensitive to the issues of homosexuality, bisexuality, coming out and familial miscommunication. The director John Schlesinger and Rene Auberjonois are featured in small but humorously touching roles as the unconventional "parents" of Phillip's lover. ⊛

Lot in Sodom
(1930, 28 min, US, James Watson & Melville Webber)
This European-influenced, avant-garde interpretation of the Old Testament tale of the trials of Lot features homoerotic imagery, sensual dances and distorted multiple images in telling its tale of a good man and his family living amidst a sexually charged band of homosexual Sodomites. The handsome angel, sent down by God to find 50 good men in the city, finds only writhing, half-naked bodies and thus destroys the city. ⊛

A Love Like No Other
(Wie geht ein Mann?) *(1983, 104 min, Germany, Hans Stempel & Martin Ripkins)*
This queer drama takes a serious look at the problems facing a gay couple in Berlin. Two longtime lovers, one a bookseller and the

Longtime Companion

other a teacher, find their long-term relationship on the rocks and both are exasperated by their upwardly mobile but superficial lifestyle. Along with facing problems similar to straight couples, the two men must come to grips with their barely concealed anger and disappointment with each other.

Luc, or His Share of Things
(Luc ou part des choses) *(1982, 80 min, Canada)*

Described by one Canadian reviewer as "a working-class *Making Love*," this tender and engaging low-budget drama of sexual self-discovery was co-produced by the Quebec Ministry of Education for the training of psychologists and social workers. The story, set during a steamy summer in a seemingly idyllic small Quebec town, revolves around the intense friendship between two 20-year-old men. One of them is a closeted gay who is "lured" into his first homosexual act with a stranger by a lake. When word of the tryst becomes known, he is made a victim of derision and scandal, although his friend remains true. After a failed suicide attempt, he gathers his emotional strength, bids farewell to his straight past, and buddy, and heads to (gay) Montreal.

El Lugar sin Limites
(The Place without Limits)
(1977, 101 min, Mexico, Arturo Ripstein)

Veteran Mexican director Arturo Ripstein's (*Queen of the Night*) curious drama is set in a brothel owned by a drag queen, "Manuela," and his daughter, "The Japanese Girl." Father/daughter rivalry takes an unusual twist as both find themselves attracted to the same man: Pancho, the brutally macho lover of the girl. After one particularly violent episode when the drunken Pancho is especially abusive to his daughter, Manuela, though harboring a real fear of the man, nonetheless confronts him in his own way; offering himself in place of his daughter in front of a room full of startled onlookers and in the process exposing the conflicting fury and cowardice underlying the machismo facade.

Making Love
(1982, 113 min, US, Arthur Hiller)

Although slick and superficial, and at times a groaner for queer audiences, *Making Love* is nonetheless an important breakthrough film — for it marked the first time Hollywood produced and marketed a gay-themed film to a general audience. This romantic drama features Michael Ontkean as a successful doctor who leaves his wife (Kate Jackson) for a handsome writer (Harry Hamlin). One of the first mainstream films made in the U.S. to feature well-adjusted characters in non-supporting roles, and to show two men kissing. With all its "good intentions," the story is at times soap opera-ish, but involving nonetheless. Good performances from its three lead players. ⊛

The Male Couple
(1985, 90 min, US)

Based on the best-selling book, this instructive video is the result of a five-year study of male couples by Drs. David McWhirter and Andrew Mattison. It explores the myths surrounding gay relationships (most obviously, that they don't last), the difficulties facing gay couples and innovative ways for developing and maintaining these relationships. Included in the video are ways for dealing with sex (both inside and outside the relationship), how to cope with jealousy, income and age differences. The tape also details useful techniques to assist couples in working out the problems which are often responsible for ending relationships. ⊛

The Male Escorts of San Francisco
(1992, 42 min, US, Matthew Link)

This talking heads documentary focuses on the world of male models/escorts/masseurs (never hustler or prostitute) in the sex-obsessed queer capital on the bay. Five men are interviewed and they offer all kinds of thoughts on what led them to this kind of work, what is involved with a typical appointmemt with a "client," why they are different from your average whore-on-the-street, and what has driven a few of them away from the profession. The men, encompassing all different kinds of looks (daddy bear, Latino lover, boy-next-door), are not really eloquent (actually the problem of the filmmaker and editor), but what they do talk about makes for an intriguing film — that is, in a seedy, guilty-pleasure sort of way.

Mambo Mouth
(1992, 60 min, US, Thomas Schlamme)

With razor-sharp satire and hilariously inspired portrayals of the diverse personas of the American Latino, John Leguizamo proves that he is a talent to be reckoned with in this hugely entertaining video adapted from his off-Broadway show. A skilled critic, Leguizamo creates six different aspects of the Latino — from the sexual bravura of a misogynist macho male, to a goofy 14-year-old homeboy's first sexual experience with a prostitute, as well as an acid-tongued, hip-swiveling prostitute. A wonderfully revealing commentary on the self-image and perceptions of the Latino in America. ⊛

Man for Man

(1992, 59 min, GB, Gordon Urquhart)
The first quarterly video magazine for British gay men is the U.K.'s answer to the States' Network Q, presenting a diverse range of subjects for its viewers including gay travel news, fashion tips, episodes from Great Britain's first gay soap opera and erotic stories. Because of the country's restrictive anti-pornography laws, the "steamy" erotic tales are tame in comparison to the hard-core product that is readily available in America, but with its romantic safe sex depiction of gay love, set in unusual settings, the stories are quite appealing. (Available in Great Britain only)

Man for Man 2   *(1993, 60 min, GB)*

The second edition of Great Britain's gay video magazine contains several shorts and a travelogue through gay Amsterdam. Included are *Deep South*, an artsy, black-and-white soft-core romp between a horny college student and a tatooed truck driver; the second installment of the gay soap opera "Buckingham Palace"; *Angelo*, a witty noir-ish thriller/serial called by the *London Sun*, "Sherlock Homo!"; and *Chains of Love*, proving the Spanish Inquisition was a great place to meet half-naked men! (Available in Great Britain only)

Man of Ashes

(1986, 109 min, Tunisia, Nouri Bouzid)
The first Arab film to deal openly with homosexuality, *Man of Ashes* caused quite a controversy when it played in film festivals for its less-than-sympathetic treatment of the subject. The story follows Hachemi, a young woodcarver in the town of Sfax, whose engagement is threatened by his constant tormented memories of being sodomized as a child by his overseer. Also raped in the incident was his friend Farfat, who has since turned openly gay and is now the laughing stock of the town. Hachemi's suffering and doubts about his masculinity has his family in a frenzy, with dad whipping him (to rid him of the demons) and the rest of the family hoping for a change. He is "cured" after a quick visit to a knowing, gentle prostitute. Farfat responds to his rapist in a different fashion: Ten years after the incident, he approaches his abuser, knives him in the groin and quickly leaves the village. While strikingly photographed, the film's overly simplistic approach borders on the hysterical.

Mardi Gras Celebrations

Penises on parade! Yes, more than you could ever shake a stick at in this voyeuristic peek at the many men who shed their pants and underwear at the drunken, bacchanalian orgy that is Mardi Gras, New Orleans-style. Except for the truly hard-core fans, the two-hour running time will prove exhausting (but no, not in that way), so keep your finger on the fast-forward and savor the many different shapes, sizes and colors of man's best friend. The filming of the New Orleans revelers dropping their drawers for beads, appreciation, applause and more has become an annual video event. The stars themselves come in two varieties: hard and soft. The following videotapes are available (their flaccidity levels are in parentheses): 1990 (hard); 1991 (soft & hard); 1992 (hard); 1993 (hard); and 1994 (hard). ⊛

Il Mare (The Sea)

(1962, 104 min, Italy, Giuseppe Patroni Griffi)
With its sweeping camera capturing the desolate beauty of off-season Capri, *Il Mare* is a beguiling and enveloping drama that depicts the constantly shifting relationships between two men and a woman. Umberto Orsini stars as "The Man," a handsome actor of around thirty who comes to the resort to temporarily escape. There, he meets "The Boy" (Dino Mole), an attractive but troubled teenager in the midst of a self-destructive drinking binge. The two soon engage in a strange and violent dance of attraction, with the boy obviously interested in the older man. Before anything can develop, however, "The Woman" (Françoise Prevost) arrives on the scene, luring the man with her flip sensuality and devil-may-care attitude. With the island as their playground, the three become dangerously involved with one another, but the boy finds himself slowly being pushed out of the triangle. Claimed by director Derek Jarman as a major influence, this sexual and psychological melodrama is filmed in the school of Michelangelo Antonioni and Jean Cocteau and evokes the atmosphere and deep sexual longing of Visconti's *Death in Venice* (filmed several years later). With a minimum of dialogue and the absence of any direct homosexual references, the film succeeds in developing, especially between the boy and the man, a romantic, drunken, sensual and often violent tale of sexual tension and unrequited love.

Marquis

(1990, 80 min, France, Henru Xhonneux)
Sort of an X-rated "Ren & Stimpy"-visit-the-French Revolution, and arguably one of the strangest films released in the last few years, this bizarre tale tells of the Marquis de Sade's imprisonment in the Bastille during the upheaval of 1789 — with the twist being that all of the cast play out their roles in grotesque animal costumes. Devilishly witty and shockingly vulgar, this bestial satire's cast includes, in a leading role, Colin, de Sade's frisky and dialectically opinionated penis; the Marquis himself (a horny, but pensive hound-faced intellectual); a lusty prison guard in love with the Marquis who is intent on being buggered by him; and a whip-wielding, horse-faced dominatrix who flails at the flanks of the decadent rulers. Despite being bogged down by the intricate 18th-century French politics, any film that delights in wallowing in excessive perversity and politics (is there a connection here?) will certainly shock some, and entertain, amuse and titillate others. From the producers of the equally inventive *Delicatessen*. ⊛

Massillon   *(1991, 90 min, US, William Jones)*

This debut gay, experimental, autobiographical feature challenges some of the most firmly entrenched conventions of filmmaking. *Massillon* has no human actors and consists almost entirely of long, static, landscape shots. The film's gentle editing is complemented by the reassuring intonation of director William Jones' voice-over (describing his childhood, his researching of state sodomy laws, and the etymology of the language of sexuality). His prose literary, his images painterly, his timing ponderous and his humor dry, Jones crafts a film exceptional for its coherent utilization of the unique capabilities of the medium. Divided into three parts ("Ohio," "The Law" and "California"), the deeply hypnotic

Massillon ranges through the personal to the political and back again as it delves into one man's isolation and the despair of his sexual coming-of-age.

Ménage
(1986, 84 min, France, Bertrand Blier)
Family values are turned inside-out in this outrageously wacky sexual farce that takes demonic delight in its vulgarity, misogyny and demented sexual mores. Life changes abruptly for the feuding, poverty-stricken couple Antoine (Michel Blanc) and his wife Monique (Miou-Miou) after they meet the bombastic and dangerously exciting Bob (Gérard Depardieu), who showers them with money and promises of the good life — made possible by inviting them to his nightly burglary raids of rich homes. But the rewards of the bourgeois life has its price, especially after the burly Bob falls passionately in love with...no, not the sexy Monique, but the bald, mousy and frantically tight-lipped Antoine! Watching Depardieu wax poetic and become all girlish in front of the bewildered Antoine is a hilariously priceless moment in French cinema. (Also known as: *Tenue De Soirée; Evening Dress*) ⊛

> "Original, unsettling, crazily funny...a farce of breathtaking energy and disorienting reason."
> —*The New York Times*

Michael's Death (La Muerte de Mikel)
(1984, 88 min, Spain, Imanol Uribe)
A somber, yet involving drama, this film, paralleling political and sexual repression in Spain, is structured in a series of flashbacks beginning with the funeral of a handsome young man, Michael. Dark-haired and fiery, Michael (Spanish star Imanol Arias) is a

leading Basque separatist stuck in an unhappy marriage. His sexual frustration reaches such a point that, while having sex with his wife, he bites her genitals with so much force, that he sends her to the hospital. Inexplicably, he finds himself attracted to a drag queen and even more surprisingly, does not hide that affection in public — an action that might have led to his death.

Michaël   *(1924, 74 min, Germany, Carl Dreyer)*
The second film adaptation of "Mikaël," gay novelist Herman Bang's "decadent" tale of homosexual love between a teacher and his student, is less gay-positive than Mauritz Stiller's *The Wings*, but is still quite candid. Made by Danish director Carl Dreyer (*The Passion of Joan of Arc, Ordet, Vampyr*), this impressionistic study of unrequited love and loneliness stars the Danish director Benjamin Christensen as elderly painter Zoret who adores and "loves more than a son" his model Michael. But Michael is lured to the arms of the mysteriously seductive Princess Zamifoff, breaking Zoret's heart. On his deathbed, the painter proclaims his love for his young student, "Now I may die content, for I have known great love."

A Midsummer Night's Dream
(1984, 77 min, GB, Celestino Coronado)
The very gay Lindsay Kemp and his equally outrageous and inventive troupe, The Lindsay Kemp Company, interpret Shakespeare's whimsical romance. The result is this charming and magical, if unorthodox theatrical film infused with balletic and operatic touches. Managing to remain true to the spirit, if not the writing of the Bard's play, some liberties are naturally taken including not only that the feuding couple switches partners, but sexual tendencies as well. Kemp himself stars as a maniacal Puck and The Incredible Orlando (Jack Birkett) is Titania. A filmed theatrical spectacle that downplays the dialogue while emphasizing visuals and a lush score in capturing both the optimism and dark mystery of love.

Miller's Crossing
(1990, 115 min, US, Joel Coen)
A very interesting and unusual film for gay audiences. While its gay subplot went over many people's heads, this Coen Brothers send-up of gangster flicks features three gay characters in a love triangle and its convoluted plot involves gay love, deceit and murder. But while these are not the positive images one usually wishes to see on the screen pertaining to gays, they are imaginatively integrated into the story as a whole. By changing the central character of the triangle from woman to man, the standard *femme fatale* is replaced by a *homme fatale*. Bernie Bernbaum (John Turturro) is a weaselly, double-crossing bookie who gets in trouble with a gang boss. That boss' right-hand man is Eddie "The Dane," a hard-as-nails thug with a soft spot for Mink (Steve Buscemi), a mob underling. Granted, this is only the subplot, but you can read a straight book for the main plot! Bernie, unbeknownst to The Dane, is getting a little on the side with Mink and when the heat is on for his own neck, knocks Mink off, only infuriating the smitten, now boyfriend-less bad guy. The leads refer to all this bed hopping in couched '30s gangster lingo, spouting lines like "Cozy as lice and it ain't just business" and "jungled up together" when referring to the intimacy of the three. And when Bernie tells the hero that his

OF GAY MALE INTEREST

girlfriend, Bernie's sister, once had sex with him, he states that she was simply trying "to save me from my friends." A great film which non-judgmentally depicts the characters' gay sexuality and, unlike countless other "gay-themed" films, never dwells nor leers when revealing that side of their character. ⊛

Mishima: A Life in Four Chapters
(1985, 121 min, US/Japan, Paul Schrader)
Yukio Mishima, Japan's most celebrated novelist, stunned his country in 1970 when, after a bizarre attempt at a political over-throw, he committed *seppuku* (ritual suicide). With this puzzling event at its center, Paul Schrader has created a daring film that tries to understand the man through his writings. With the final day of Mishima's life as the background, the film features three stylish episodes from his novels, which are intercut with flash-backs from his childhood. A fascinating look at an obsessed artist. Because of restrictions imposed by his widow, any references to Mishima's homosexuality or his homoerotic writing were barred in the making of the film, a condition that sadly dilutes the impact of this otherwise absorbing film. ⊛

Focus on: *Yukio Mishima*
The outstanding Japanese writer of his generation, Yukio Mishima's life was anything but simple. He was a gay man with a taste for rough trade despite the fact that he was married with two children; he was an advocate of traditional Japanese values yet lived an opulent Western lifestyle; and most of all, he was a cele-brated artist who became fatally obsessed with bodybuilding and militarism. The young Mishima shocked the post-WWII Japanese literary world with his passionate, often violent novels and plays, several of which focused on homosexuality and featured, propheti-cally, a fascination with eroticism, death and self-sacrifice. One of his earliest novels, now considered a Japanese classic, is "Confessions of a Mask," an autobiographical story of a tortured adolescent who is forced to come to grips with the fact that he is gay. His gay love story "Forbidden Colors," a more sinister homosexual tale of obsession and corruption, cemented his repu-tation with gay readers. With his many other novels and plays he soon became a vastly popular writer for Japan's general audience and the most widely read Japanese writer in Europe and America. Born in 1925, Kimitake Hiraoka, better known by his pen name, Yukio Mishima, wrote hundreds of novels, plays, stories and essays before his spectacular and bizarre death in 1970. It was after he had completed writing "The Decay of the Angel," the final installment of his four-volume opus, "The Sea of Fertility," that Mishima, a fervent right-wing activist, donned military cloth-ing and led a devoted group of virulent followers on a ridiculous attempt to overthrow the government, restore the emperor and return to ancient virtues. When he was defeated, Mishima and fol-lower/lover Masakatsu Morita committed ceremonial seppuku, a public self-disembowelment. Although many of his writings would translate well to the screen, only the novel "The Sailor Who Fell from Grace with the Sea," a striking and erotic story about a group of young schoolboys who commit a ritual murder upon a visiting sailor, has been adapted. Mishima can be seen as a living statue in the hilariously campy crime caper spectacle, Black Lizard (see page 454).

Montreal Main
(1974, 90 min, Canada, Frank Vitale)
Using a cinema verité approach with a non-professional cast and improvised dialogue, Frank Vitale directed and stars in this earnest, low-budget drama about the relationship between a man and a 13-year-old boy. Frank (Vitale) is an inarticulate artist/photographer who befriends Johnny, a teenage suburban boy. The two become close during a moment of mutual need, but social differences and the boy's parents soon pull them apart. Humorous, sensitive and touching, the story, set in a squalid area of Montreal, suffers from awkward filming, sub-par acting and the lack of any discernable plot. The decision to cloak Frank's sexual orientation (he has sex with a male friend but neither considers themselves gay) adds a dimension of confusion to the intense relationship of man and boy.

More Love
(1984, 65 min, Japan, Koshi Shimada)
One of the first Japanese films to focus exclusively on homosexuali-ty, this improbable and melodramatic potboiler was a breakthrough with its intensely erotic depiction of gay sex and a gay lifestyle. The story revolves around a young rock star who becomes immersed in Tokyo's gay milieu, and is obsessed with the notion that he has AIDS. Adding to his problems are his fanatically Catholic mother and a devilish priest. The young man's efforts to find happiness with his homosexuality are doomed as a homophobic tabloid press cou-pled with religious hypocrisy, familial hysteria and his own inability to accept himself lead him to commit ritual suicide.

Movie Buff: The Video *(60 min, US)*
If you think only women do cinematic nude scenes, then think again. This compilation of male nude scenes spans from rare 1910 buff shots all the way to the present day. Clips feature the bods of Don Johnson, Gregory Harrison, Bruce Boxleitner, Johnny Depp, Alain Delon and Jan-Michael Vincent. And just to prove he's no prude, host Steve Malis also includes one of his own cinematic *au naturals*. ⊛

Movie Buff: The Sequel *(60 min, US)*
More male nudity in the movies with your host Steve Malis. This time, clips feature the "king of male nude scenes" Malcolm McDowell, along with assorted buff shots of Michael Douglas, bad-boy Rob Lowe, Jeff Bridges, Ken Howard, Julian Sands, Brad Davis and many others. ⊛

Movie Buff: The Threequel *(60 min, US)*
Continuing to uncover and expose the actors who decide to bare all, this amusing foray into cinematic voyeurism travels around the world seeking exposed skin. Excerpts include scenes from *A Room with a View; Brother Sun, Sister Moon*, and the films of Pier Paolo Pasolini. Featured actors include Peter Firth and Patrick Dempsey, as well as Patrick Swayze and his firm backside. ⊛

Movie Buff: The Four Play *(60 min)*
Will this beefcake never stop? Apparently not, by the looks of this, the fourth *Movie Buff* installment. Bared stars include Don Johnson, William Katt, Andrew Stevens, Charlton Heston and Harry Belafonte. Harry Belafonte? ⊛

Mr. Nude Universe
(1993, 60 min, US, Paul Borghese)
Playgirl Magazine, that literary bastion of revealing, if limp beefcake marketed exclusively towards "women" is responsible for this cheesy beauty-cum-"strip and bare the family jewels" contest. Featuring six unbelievably long-haired, pumped-up, body-shaved, butt-swaying contestants who go on stage in front of a horde of appreciative women and perform an elaborate strip tease, each ends their act in a finale unveiling their frisky best friend. Not content to just let the viewer ogle at the goods, the film goes behind the scenes and guess what?... they talk as well! A fun rental for a cold and wet Tuesday hanging out with the girls. ⊛

Muscle *(1993, 60 min, Japan, Hisayasu Sato)*
Provocative, sexually explicit, extremely controversial and almost unwatchable during its graphic scenes involving violent S&M lovemaking (looking at an exacto knife will never be the same!), this kinky drama of gay sexual obsession makes for brutal, almost painful but absorbing viewing. A seemingly mild-mannered editor of a muscle magazine finds his sexual desires ignited when he becomes involved in a sadomasochistic relationship with a muscular bodybuilder. Not able to take the intensity of pleasure/pain, he cuts off his lover's arm in the midst of sexual excitement. After his release from prison several years later, the young man combs the sordid streets of Tokyo desperately looking for his now one-armed love. The film makes several references to the films of Pier Paolo Pasolini (especially *Saló, or the 120 Days of Sodom*), but goes several steps further in depicting a world of violent, self-destructive love.

The Naked Civil Servant
(1980, 80 min. GB, Jack Gold)
Based on the autobiography of Quentin Crisp, this is a witty examination of the process of growing up gay in the repressive England of the 1930s and '40s. John Hurt's portrayal of Crisp is nothing less than superb as he fights back against society's intolerance, ostracism and violence with pointed, razor-sharp humor. ⊛

"A LANDMARK FILM IN ITS REALISTIC PRESENTATION OF A HOMOSEXUAL LIFE!"
Los Angeles Times —KEVIN THOMAS

NIGHTHAWKS
A COMPLEX PORTRAIT OF A GAY LONDON SCHOOLTEACHER

Naughty Boys
(1983, 105 min, The Netherlands, Eric de Kuyper)
Set in an elegant country mansion, this plotless, avant-garde film from the director of *A Strange Love Affair* and *Casta Diva* deals with gay sensibilities in film and theatre. The film features musical numbers, fag hags and a bevy of handsome (gay?) men, who wander about in a manner described by one reviewer as "waiting for a Noël Coward play to begin."

Night Out
(1989, 50 min, Australia, Lawrence Johnston)
A short feature about homophobia, gay-bashing and the effect it has on two gay men. Tony, whose lover Steve is away on business, cruises a nearby beach where he is brutalized by a group of toughs. The attack forces the two men to examine their tenuous relationship.

Night Zoo
(1987, 117 min, Canada, Jean-Claude Lauzon)
A schizophrenic film if there ever was one — is it a darkly violent crime thriller or a heartwarming human drama of the rapprochement of a man with his father? The film focuses on both themes and suffers for it. After being released from prison, Marcel, an angry punk of questionable sexuality, tries to readjust to life on the outside but his efforts are thwarted by two sleazy gay cops. While Marcel is getting into hot water with thugs and lowlifes, he also tries to reach out to old dad; you know, the one with the wizened ticker. Set in a dark and dangerous Montreal, the film's action sequences are exciting, but generally the film bogs down when it deals with the sappy familial angle. ⊛

Nighthawks
(1979, 113 min, GB, Ron Peck & Paul Hallam)
London's gay scene, and one man's search for belonging in it, are explored in this sensitive and intelligent drama which was Britain's first independent gay-themed film. Ken Robertson plays a quiet teacher who divides his time between the classroom and the closet and evenings spent aimlessly cruising the city's gay bars and discos. Using mostly unprofessional actors, this gritty, heartfelt drama has surprising depth despite the lack of any discernable plot, as it sympathetically portrays one man's homosexual lifestyle without resorting to theatrics, hysterics and stereotyping. Made over 15 years ago, the film has a "period" feel, offering strong evidence to the rapid change of gays both in how they accept their homosexuality as well as the social possibilities offered.

> "A landmark film in its realistic matter-of-fact presentation of homosexual life."
> —*Los Angeles Times*

> "A breakthrough film...Perhaps the most uncompromisingly honest and probably the best gay film ever made."
> —*Soho News*

On the British video release of *Nighthawks*, this early Ron Peck short is included:

What Can I Do with a Male Nude?

(1985, 25 min, GB, Ron Peck)

Among Margaret Thatcher's conservative policies was the crackdown on sexually explicit works, which caused many censorship problems for London's bookstores. They were forced to battle Customs and Excise in order to import works from the United States and Europe by such artists as Allen Ginsberg and Jean Genet. With this political situation in mind, this short comedy features a photographer preoccupied with the difficulties and legal taboos of dealing with people in the nude. As he has his model dress in various outfits and uniforms, the photographer wittily ruminates on "what might be permissible in respect of a male nude."

No Skin Off My Ass

(1990, 85 min, Canada, Bruce La Bruce)

The onslaught of New Queer Cinema (*Swoon, Poison, The Living End, The Hours and the Times, Edward II*) continues with this wry, low-budget and sexually explicit comedy about a punkish hairdresser who, in an homage to Robert Altman's *That Cold Day in the Park*, becomes obsessed with a tough-looking, but shy skinhead. Filmed in grainy black and white and blown up from Super-8, the story opens when the coiffeur (who also narrates) invites the seemingly lost, baby-faced skinhead home. Sort of a fag version of the beautiful and near-catatonic Joe Dallesandro in *Trash*, the skinhead passively and diffidently accepts his offers of a bubble-bath and a place to live. Rounding out the cast of characters is the skinhead's lesbian sister who gets cheap thrills by undressing her brother in front of her friends. While the gay sex scenes are hard-core at times, they are also romantic. And while the film takes a gay male perspective, it is the skinhead's lesbian sister who gets the two together by telling her brother, "Queer is smart...everyone's a fag, even skinheads. Haven't you got that yet?" Note: Due to censorship constraints, the British video release of the film is edited. Censorship problems also arose in Canada, where the film was seized by the Morality Squad of Toronto and was charged with three violations: bondage, nudity with violence and the sucking of toes. But director LaBruce retrieved the print without deleting any footage. ⊗

> "Sweeter than Warhol, subtler than Kuchar, sexually more explicit than Van Sant, and second only to Ken Jacobs and Bob Fleischner's *Blonde Cobra* in the aesthetic-of-poverty sweepstakes."
> —Amy Taubin, *The Village Voice*

Focus On: *Bruce La Bruce*

Although he has only made two independent features, filmmaker/actor Bruce La Bruce (or BLaB) is on the lips of many a film lover. A self-labeled "fag," the "post-queer," Toronto-based La Bruce (born on the same day as Judy Garland's death!?) made his local name with several 8mm shorts including Boy/Girl (1987, 15 min), I

Know What It's Like to be Dead (1988, 15 min), Slam (1989, 10 min) and Home Movies (1989, 12 min). With the film festival success, and international cult status, of No Skin Off My Ass, a quirky love story featuring counter-culture queers, skinheads, lesbians and surprisingly hard-core gay sex scenes, La Bruce has become something of a celebrity and cause célèbre. Because of its unorthodox view, the film has been both applauded and damned by members of the gay/lesbian community, prompting a shrug of the shoulders by BLaB, who said, "Personally, I'm just not interested in being mundane and boring as everybody else but I happen to be gay." His latest film is Super 8½ (1994, 99 min), his queer turn on the Fellini classic, 8½, with a promised ad tag-line that will read "If you thought 8½ was big, wait til you see Super 8½. La Bruce describes the film as "a faux-documentary...composed largely of interviews and movies-within-the-movie tracing the rise and fall of our unfortunate hero, Bruce." BLaB is also currently working on the script for his next feature, Homicidal, a film on a gay serial killer.

Nocturne

(1993, 100 min, US, Mark Townsend Harris)

Not to be confused with Joy Chamberlain's lesbian film of the same name, this involving drama of one man dealing with his turbulent sexuality won the Best Film award at the Gay Film Festival in Turin, Italy. Set in New York City, the story follows Martin (J. Ryder Smith), a sexually repressed young musician (bearing an unsettling resemblence to Erik Menendez) who has recently moved to the city. Although anxious at the thought of picking up one of the many handsome men who come his way, he finally meets and beds Gino (Gabriel Amor), a sweetly charming and cute

No Skin Off My Ass

NYU acting student. The tryst, a casual one-night stand for Gino, becomes an emotionally shattering experience for Martin when he comes to believe that their romp was the beginning of a relationship. He quickly becomes obsessed with the "failed" love affair and determined to confront, violently if necessary, his now-gone "lover." Harris films this tale of *amour fou* in high-contrast black and white with a restful camera, which keeps its unblinking gaze on the characters long after they speak their lines. The film is especially insightful in depicting the tenuous moments of a rendezvous/relationship, but its weakness is its Bergman-esque heaviness, tinged with wispy poetry, and too many long solitary gazes onto water (à la *Claire of the Moon*). A low-budget movie that approaches greatness. ⊛

"An insightful look at casual sex that will make audiences either squirm in frustration or nod in recognition."
—*Outweek*

Noir et Blanc
(1986, 80 min, France, Claire Devers)
This understated yet bizarre drama, adapted from Tennessee Williams' "Desire and the Black Masseur," deals with an increasingly intense sadomasochistic realtionship between two men. Infused with oblique "meaning" and sexual ambiguity, and strangely compelling, the black-and-white tale begins when a mousy but not unattractive accountant begins working at a health club. Seemingly heterosexual (he has a girlfriend), the shy man begins taking advantage of the gym's perks, especially the free massages with a silent, muscular black masseur. Their sessions begin to take on increasingly violent elements, resulting in damaged skin and broken bones; but the two participants, unable to break away from the intoxicating relationship, continue their fatal dance of violence. A dark story of a curious, intense relationship with an ending designed to shock its audience.

Norman, Is That You?
(1976, 92 min, US, George Schlatter)
This gay sex farce tries to have it both ways — making fun of faggots while espousing a what-will-be-will-be sexual philosophy — and the result is a surprisingly inoffensive and politically incorrect comedy. The story revolves around Norman, a handsome black man of 23 who lives with Garson, his cute, swishy lover in West Hollywood. Trouble brews when his father and eventually his mother (Redd Foxx and Pearl Bailey), neither of whom know that he is gay, land at his doorstep for an extended visit. The film's dialogue is at times hilarious despite some lame jokes, stupid stereotypes (Norman is a window dresser, he has lavender curtains and loves Judy Garland) and a regular lexicon of innocuous gay namecalling that includes: queer, sissy faeries, homosexuals, closet queens, tinkerbell, three-dollar bill, cream puff, fruit, funny, and even Juliet. Dennis Dugan as Garson steals the show doing a "FABulous" fag routine, but no, the two men never kiss or even show affection towards each other. Wayland Flowers and his sassy puppet Madam add to the campy humor. ⊛

Norman, Is That You?

Northern Exposure — The Gay Wedding *(1994, 52 min, US)*
This famously quirky television series, known for being gay/lesbian friendly (the Alaskan town where it takes place was founded by lesbians, and gays are featured occasionally), attempted in this episode to be trendsetting and deceptively non-controversial by having a gay couple marry on screen. Longtime lovers, and bed & breakfast operators, Ron (Doug Ballard) and Eric (Don R. McManus), who are the only queers in town, decide to enact the traditional heterosexual bonding ceremony only to develop second thoughts. Joyce Van Patten plays Eric's mother, a loving woman who wants only the best for her son and loves them both, but still suffers because it was "not the marriage I envisioned..." The marriage eventually goes off without a hitch, but a sour taste develops for politically aggresive queers. Several elements of the show contribute to undermine its groundbreaking intentions: The couple are not seen as happy, not even compatible; they argue throughout (their problems are never resolved); and their "kiss" at the conclusion of the ceremony is shown as barely more than a heterosexual hug. Frustrating because the makers of the show decided to be daring yet backed away from any truly sensitive and accurate handling of it. As is always the case in "family values"-obsessed Middle America, several CBS affiliates refused to air the program.

Not Angels But Angels
(1994, 80 min, Czech Republic/France, Wiktor Grodecki)
The world of male prostitutes in the recently democratized Czech Republic is the lurid subject of this talking heads documentary (that throws in shots of hard-core pornography involving the teens as well). With either rap or somber classical music playing in the background, the director interviews more than ten boys, ranging in age from 14 to 19 years old, who work the train station, discos and streets of Prague. They answer questions about their family background (most come from broken homes), how they got their start selling themselves, what they do to a john and for how much, what kind of men employ their services (mainly German tourists), whether they consider themselves gay or not (50/50), their fear of contracting AIDS and what their aspirations are. The boys'

responses offer a fascinating glimpse into a seldom seen world — although one gets the uncomfortable feeling (aided by the fact that the boys were paid by the filmmakers to lay bare their lives and the use of the pornographic footage) that both the viewer and the filmmaker are involved as well in the exploitation of these vulnerable young men.

Nude Dudes *(1992, 60 min, US, Joe Tiffenbach)*

While the appropriateness of including a video that is simply a collection of soft-core shots of naked men in this book is indeed questionable, this entertaining nudist romp, a "celebration of the male body," is innocuous fun. Hosted by Dan Steele, the tape shows models of all types going about in naturalist abandon: skinny-dipping, exercising and riding a bike. Sensual but not really erotic, the film is actually a compilation from Tiffenbach's other videos, *Just Naked Men, More Naked Men* and *Stark Naked Men.* ⊛

Okoge *(1992, 120 min, Japan, Takehiro Murata)*

Japan's teeming if still underground gay life is explored and celebrated in this pleasant story of the relationship between two gay lovers and the effervescent woman who befriends them. Beginning at a rock and cement covered urban beach populated with the full spectrum of gay male "types," the story centers around Goh, a young, self-employed man, and Tochi, an older married "corporate" worker. Their inability to rent a hotel room or find a suitable spot for their lovemaking is solved when Sayoko, a naive young woman who inexplicably finds herself drawn to gay men, befriends them and offers her small bed as a convenient love pad. The simple plot line follows their relationship and their friends — mainly drag queens from the local gay bar. Funny, but deceptively lighthearted for beneath the tacky drag shows and extravagant characters lies the serious theme of the homophobia that pervades Japan — from a family's refusal to accept a gay family member to the tight-assed work place where coming out would be tantamount to losing one's job. A note on the title: "*okama*" is the Japanese word for a rice pot as well as a slang insult word for gays; "*okoge*" is the rice that sticks to the bottom of the pot and also is the slang for women who hang around gay men. ⊛

Oliver
(1983, 85 min, The Philippines, Rosa de Maynila)

This independent film examines the transvestite and male prostitute's life in poverty-stricken Manila. The main character is Oliver, a young man who makes a living for both himself and his family as a gay hustler and as a performer at a local club. His bizarre act includes his "spiderman" routine, in which he puts spools of thread in his anus and dances across the floor creating designs!

Olivier, Olivier
(1991, 109 min, France, Agnieszka Holland)

Essentially a reworking of the *Return of Martin Guerre* theme — that of a person returning to his home after many years away but whose identity is challenged (and supported) by those close to him. Olivier, a precocious nine-year-old coddled by his doting mother at the expense of his older sister, one day mysteriously disappears without a trace. His family is torn apart by the loss but are reunited six years later when a 15-year-old homosexual prostitute working the Parisian public toilets claims to be their long-lost son. The family, especially the emotionally charged mother, desperately wants to believe that this savvy teen is indeed the innocent of years past, although nagging doubts linger as to why he ran away. This engrossing drama unfolds on two fronts: that of the boy learning about love and trust; and the unraveling of the mystery of his disappearance. The interest for gay viewers is twofold: first, that director Agnieszka Holland (*Europa, Europa*) presents the teenaged Olivier as a cocky but caring scavenger and unrepentant gay hustler; the second and more troubling point is the presence of a dim-witted pederast, child rapist and killer. That villainous role will remind many of the transvestite killer in *The Silence of the Lambs.* ⊛

One Adventure
(1973, 90 min, US, Pat Rocco)

This historically significant travelogue documentary centers on a group of eight gay men as they travel throughout Europe looking at the sights and meeting other gays and "homophile organizations." The generally older (50s

Okoge

and 60s) men — most of whom sport seriously intense sideburns and fashionably loud clothing — include The Rev. Troy Perry, founder of the Metropolitan Community Church, and other early gay activists. Director Pat Rocco, who also becomes part of the entourage, films in a leisurely fashion both familiar tourist footage as well as the group's encounters with several nascent gay rights organizations — gatherings which include discussions, lectures and screenings of Rocco's earlier films. Adding spice to the proceedings are innocently romantic mini-dramas of gay love, with a different story for each country they visit. While the quality of the footage is only a cut or two above home movies, the film is a distinct piece of gay history, capturing gay men (no lesbians) doing battle on the early gay rights front. ⊗

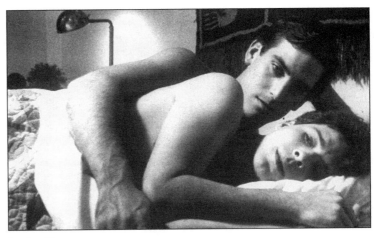

Parting Glances

One Foot on the Banana Peel, the Other Foot in the Grave

(1993, 83 min, US, Juan Botas & Lucas Platt)
Intrigued by the diverse personalities and thoughts of his fellow AIDS patients, artist Juan Botas conceived this cinema verité document in which he simply videotaped the interactions of several men as they received AIDS treatments in a New York City doctor's office. Finished by filmmaker Lucas Platt after Botas' death in 1992, the film vividly captures the opinions, life stories, wit, camaraderie, intimacy and expressions of love between the many men who arrive in the waiting room, christened "The Dolly Madison Room." Inspiring and emotional, the film soars above its bargain-basement production quality in presenting a lively group who have much to say — not only about their lives and loves, but about their indomitable will to fight, as well.

100 Days Before the Command

(1990, 70 min, Russia, Hussein Erkenov)
While not overtly gay, this melancholy, dreamlike meditation on passive resistance and the disintegration of the rigidity of the old Soviet Union is included because of its prevailing homoerotic imagery. In an army basic training facility, a group of young men —when not undergoing grueling military exercises — engage in Jean Genet-like camaraderie and languid bathing rituals, with one gently washing the naked torso of another. The camera eyes these scenes of naked young flesh (played by real-life Russian soldiers) with a tenderness that is lacking in all other areas of their lives. When not dwelling on male beauty, the almost silent film becomes a mystical, symbolic tale of the restlessness of a young Russian generation who, living more like prisoners than soldiers, long to break free of their Communist restraints.

Our Sons *(1991, 100 min, US, John Erman)*
From the director of *An Early Frost* comes this intelligent and moving AIDS drama. Julie Andrews and Ann-Margret star as the mothers of gay lovers Hugh Grant and Zeljko Ivanek. Andrews is a wealthy businesswoman who remained close to her son after he came out while Ann-Margret, a barmaid from Arkansas, refuses to accept her son's sexuality and rejects him. When the latter's son becomes sick with AIDS, Andrews is persuaded by her son to meet his lover's mother and try to get the two to reunite. A serious, straightforward story which, while suffering a bit from a talking heads-style of filmmaking, remains quite compelling and compassionate.

Outcasts *(1986, 102 min, Taiwan, Yu Kan Ping)*
After being caught having sex with another student, young Ah-Ching is both expelled from school and beaten out of his home by his father. Befriended by a middle-aged photographer as well as by other young gays, Ah-Ching rebuilds his life with the help of his new surrogate family and begins to explore his own sexuality. The first film from Taiwan with a gay theme, *Outcasts* is, at times, unintentionally funny in its heavy-handed melodramatic excesses, but is nonetheless a powerful and sensual look at a youth finding a place in an uncaring and insensitive world. ⊗

Paris, France

(1993, 111 min, Canada, Gerard Ciccoritti)
Deliriously paced and entertainingly saturated with numerous and inventively diverse sexual couplings, this tale of mid-life crisis, regret, longing and sexual repression is anything but your standard melodrama. Set in Toronto, the story involves the three owners of a small publishing company: a married couple, Lucy (Leslie Hope) and Michael (Victor Ertmanis), and their business partner William (Dan Left). The stability of their lives is thrown into an emotional maelstrom with the arrival of Sloan (Peter Outerbrige), a former boxer turned writer whose first book (on a serial killer) is about to be published. The hunky and frequently naked Sloan immediately gets in over his head with the sexually ravenous and intellectually frustrated Lucy, who longs to re-create her S&M-filled days in Paris years gone by. But he soon goes from her sweat-soaked bed

to the bed of the openly gay William. Sloan's complex sexual needs soon lead to confusion: Is he a gay top man or a straight bottom boy (with Lucy administering the half-nelsons and whip-snapping)? All the while, the befuddled Michael is slowly going crazy until a sexually surprising ending sets him on a new course. Beyond the steamy sex scenes and the characters' ranting about poetry, commitment and "Paris" is the uninhibited notion of exploring all of one's many sexual needs. Interestingly, while the three straight/bi characters are bed-jumping, the one monogamous and sexually sane character is the gay William.

Parting Glances
(1986, 90 min, US, Bill Sherwood)

This wonderfully rich and seductively appealing independent production is considered by many to be one of the best gay films of the 1980s. The action takes place within a 24-hour period and centers around Michael (Richard Ganoung) and Robert (John Bolger), a gay New York couple who are about to temporarily separate as Robert is transferred overseas. Their attempts to keep the relationship strong (made tense when Michael's former lover develops AIDS) and to understand each other is the core of this simple but wise comedy-drama. The supporting cast of mainly gay friends who throw a farewell party for Robert are all finely drawn, creating familiar types for gays; not gay stereotypes. But despite the solid cast, it is Steve Buscemi who steals the show by giving a bravado performance as Nick, a young rock singer dying of AIDS. While not suspenseful or complicated in plot, the film's strengths lie in its simple and honest moments — a loving embrace or a telling confession. Writer-director Bill Sherwood, who sadly died of AIDS in 1990, has fashioned a joyful, knowing gay love story. ⊛

Partners *(1982, 98 min, US, James Burrows)*

An odious cop comedy with a "fag" angle. Vito Russo in *The Celluloid Closet* considered this homophobic drek one of the worst gay-themed films ever made. But rather than quickly dismissing the film, a closer look is called for as this was a Hollywood film of the '80s made by people who were thinking that it was both funny and possibly even gay sensitive! Ryan O'Neal plays Benson, a pretty-boy straight (read: normal) detective who is reluctantly teamed up with an effeminate, frigid, in-the-closet desk cop named Kerwin (John Hurt) to go undercover as gay lovers to investigate a gay serial killer. Told to "live in their neighborhood, eat in their restaurants and shop in their stores," the film begins to indulge itself with every conceivable homophobic stereotype. Hurt, whose wardrobe seems to consist entirely of pink and lilac, is a scared, helpless femme who, in the course of the job, takes on the "wife's role," becoming a cleaning, ironing, souffle-making queen who eventually falls in love with the couldn't-care-less O'Neal. The many homosexuals depicted are seen as promiscuous, lisping, limp-wristed queens who should basically be laughed at and pitied. With lines like, "Those two faggots look exactly alike, just like all faggots," the film is almost painful to watch although it does feature police harassment of gays (but only mildly condemning it). Surprisingly, as is the case in so many of these kinds of films, the fag doesn't die at the end, although he is shot in the stomach! Watch it and wince! ⊛

> "Hollywood's latest crime against humanity in general and homosexuals in particular is a dumb creepshow...stupid, tasteless and homophobic..."
>
> —Rex Reed

Pauline's Birthday or the Beast of Notre Dame
(1977-79, 80 min, Germany, Fritz Matthies)

Set in a Hamburg gay bar, this somber pseudo-documentary belongs to the "it's a terribly sad and empty life for the homosexual" school of filmmaking. The film starts off with several patrons deciding to begin an underground theatre. What follows are interviews with the men behind the formation of the venue, rehearsals of the play and finally its premiere performance, which turns out to be a tragic-comic morality play on gay life. The "stars" include the gay men and neighborhood boys who call the bar home and the force behind them all, the bar's owner and resident power queen, Harry Pauly (aka: Mutter Courage — Pauline).

Performance
(1970, 105 min, GB, Nicolas Roeg & Donald Cammell)

A disturbingly intoxicating blend of violence, hallucinatory drugs, rock music and blurred sex roles, Nicolas Roeg's directorial debut features a very handsome James Fox as a Cockney "enforcer" for a London gang who finds himself on the other end of the fist when he has a falling out with the crime organization. Hiding out in the Notting Hill flat of a reclusive rock icon (a pouting, androgynous Mick Jagger), his well-ordered gangster world is turned inside out when an intriguing game of sex and power unfolds. Jagger's two female lovers, one a boyish young

Partners

woman, the other the bewitching Anita Pallenberg, are involved with both Mick and each other as well as having an interest in Fox, who will "try anything once." The sexual games include a definite attraction of Jagger to the thuggish and often shirtless Fox. Another man interested in Fox is Harry, the corpulent and bespectacled head gangster who is obviously gay — his bedroom/office is littered with male porn magazines and while his gangster underlings don't bat an eye, a handsome number flits about the room. Ⓐ

> "You don't have to be a drug addict, pederast, sadomasochist or nitwit to enjoy it, but being one or more of these things would help."
>
> —John Simon

Antonio Banderas (l.) and Tom Hanks in *Philadelphia*

Philadelphia
(1993, 119 min, US, Jonathan Demme)

Hotly debated in the queer community mostly for what it is not, *Philadelphia*, Hollywood's first attempt at a big-budget, big-star treatment on the AIDS crisis, while riveting and emotionally powerful, and determinedly "politically correct," fails on many levels when it comes to successfully dealing with both AIDS and homosexuality. Nonetheless, it remains a tightly focused family and courtroom drama about one man's politicization in the face of homophobia and AIDS discrimination. Tom Hanks took home the Oscar for his solid performance as Andrew Beckett, a hot-shot corporate lawyer for a prestigious (read: powerful) Philadelphia law firm. After he is fired (ostensibly for poor performance, but in actuality because he is a gay man with AIDS), he boldly decides to fight the firm, eventually hiring a homophobic, ambulance-chasing lawyer (Denzel Washington) to defend him. The outcome of the trial is a given, so for queer analysis, the film's handling of gay issues and AIDS and its effect on the general public and queer audiences become more important. The film doesn't really tread any new ground in the realm of AIDS and its sufferers, although Hanks' gradual physical deterioration is sure to elicit strong emotions. The film preaches about how one gets it (although only in a clinical fashion) and the prejudice ensured by those who have it.

More troubling perhaps than its handling of AIDS is the film's depiction of gay men (except for the mention of a woman who is gay, lesbians are conspicuously absent). Despite a screenplay by the gay Ron Nyswaner and direction from a normally sensitive heterosexual Jonathan Demme, the film relegates gays to minor supporting roles. This film is for heteros to go see other heteros wrongly discriminate against handsome, successful, WASPish,

straight-acting gay men with AIDS rather than throw into the collective face of America more "disturbing" images of gays/lesbians and their lifestyles. The role of Hanks' longtime lover, Miguel, effectively played by Spanish actor Antonio Banderas, has been obviously cut. Affection between the two men is kept to a minimum, with the only real kiss between them occurring on Hanks' death bed, and even then Banderas only kisses Hanks' fingers. In addition to this very important gay character being downplayed, the couple's gay friends are almost nonexistent. Shockingly, the only time that the two men are not seen as post-college hetero roommates comes when they throw a gay Halloween party, which features outrageously costumed gays (including professional fag Quentin Crisp and The Flirtations). While the party scene is far from offensive, it is the only scene where gays are seen in a social setting; the couple is not seen at gay restaurants or bars, or simply enjoying other gays' company — gays only come out of the dark to party and camp it up. This is quite possibly the most damaging aspect of the film.

Gay-point-of-view complaints about the film could continue, but might undermine the good, even courageous (again only by Hollywood standards) position of the film. As a primer for straights (its intended audience) who know of AIDS only through media reports and think of gays in a less-than-positive way, this drama might prove to them to be enlightening. Director Demme is quoted as saying, "It would be fair to say it's big, old-fashioned entertainment. *Terms of Endearment* is a good reference for me." For the more politically oriented gays and lesbians not impressed with the film's weak posturing in terms of its handling of homosexuality and AIDS, *Philadelphia* will seem trite, evasive and troublingly misleading. It's a filmic equivalent to the Woody Allen joke about a restaurant, "The food is terrible, and such small portions!" Ⓐ

Pink Narcissus

(1971, 78 min, US, Anonymous)
A longtime favorite of gay audiences, this legendary erotic creation was rediscovered in New York in 1972. Made by Anonymous, the film was reportedly shot over a seven-year period and is reminiscent of the films of the 1960s New York Underground and Kenneth Anger. Straddling the line between underground art and gay porn, the film is a classic of gay male erotica. The hero, teenage beauty Bobby Kendall, drifts into slumber and his dreams, fueled by a lively imagination and sexual fantasy, take on a surreal and amatory air. Poetic, tender yet sexually potent, we are taken through his erotic revelries: from scenes of tea room sex, to Bobby becoming a toreador, a Roman slave, and eventually involved in Arabian Nights debauchery. ⊛

A note on the British video release of *Pink Narcissus*: Remarkably, despite strict censorship rules, *Pink Narcissus* was passed by the British Board of Film Classification without any cuts. The video release is in much better condition than the one available in the United States. The film's distributor, Dangerous to Know, electronically restored the film, enhancing the visuals and removing much of the blurriness of the original 16mm print, which itself was blown up from 8mm.

Pink Ulysses

(1989, 98 min, The Netherlands, Eric de Kuyper)
Using Ulysses' return from 20 years of exile in Troy as its nucleus, this sex-drenched oddity from the director of *Naughty Boys* and *Casta Diva* goes where no Steve Reeves vehicle dared to venture. Featuring the obligatory loin-clothed beefcakes, the film also depicts Ulysses' wife Penelope as having the incestuous hots for her attractive son. Stirring the kinetic mix is a cheap esthetic which permeates this visual melange. If the film had any distribution other than the gay film festival circuit, it's a bet it would have been a cult favorite. ⊛

Pixote *(1981, 127 min, Brazil, Hector Babenco)*
A brilliant, disturbing film about a band of youths who escape a brutal youth detention center, where rape and violence is commonplace, to resume their desperate lives of petty crime in the slums of

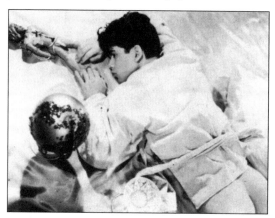

Bobby Kendall dreams of love in *Pink Narcissus*

São Paulo. Two of the three boys, Dito, an older super-macho teen and Lilica, an effeminate boy, become lovers while the youngest one, 10-year-old Pixote (Fernando da Silva), remains an aloof outcast. They get involved in a drug smuggling scheme and soon befriend an aging alcoholic prostitute, Cristal (Marilia Pera), who offers them a brief respite of tenderness as a mother figure and a lover. The gun-toting Pixote, a desperate boy in a hopeless situation, acts out his tragic existence with wide-eyed innocence and trailblazing violence. From the director of *Kiss of the Spider Woman* and from a novel by Jose Louzeiro. ⊛

Prelude to a Kiss

(1992, 110 min, US, Norman René)
Craig Lucas and Norman René, the writing and directing team that produced the heart-wrenching AIDS drama *Longtime Companion*, reteamed to bring this captivating romantic fantasy, based on their Tony Award-winning play, to the screen. Alec Baldwin (reprising his Broadway role) and Meg Ryan star as a couple who meet, fall in love and marry. However, on their wedding day, the souls of Ryan and an uninvited guest, a 70-year-old man (played with high spirits by Sydney Walker) are transposed. As this AIDS allegory continues, Baldwin suddenly finds his mate, once young and healthy, now sickly and old virtually overnight. He must find a way to reverse the process before the change becomes permanent. A tale with great humor that gives thoughtful testament to the responsibility, resilience and consummate power of love. ⊛

Pretty Boy

(1993, 86 min, The Netherlands, Carsten Sonder)
This dark, kinky and violent tale of one youth's rough coming-of-age takes place amidst the lurid world of teenage male prostitution. Nick (Christian Tafdrup) is a handsome and innocent 13-year-old runaway who quickly falls in with the wrong crowd when he arrives in Amsterdam. Befriended by a hardened, violence-prone gang of teen prostitutes (oddly headed by a tomboyish girl), Nick, called by one of his johns "the sweetest young chicken," soon is immersed in a world where middle-aged pederasts prowl the train stations and parks for boys, sex is performed only for money and where love rarely comes into play. The boy, who really wants nothing more than a caring family life, soon falls prey to the self-destructive lure of the streets. ⊛

Prime Suspect 3

(1994, 230 min, GB)
Unflinchingly tackling themes of pedophilia, AIDS infection, teenage male prostitution, gay policemen, cross-dressing and child pornography, it is a surprise that this television crime drama was ever produced, let alone played on British and American television. Continuing in her role from the first two miniseries, Helen Mirren is Jane Tennison, now promoted to Detective Chief Inspector, but transferred from the criminal division to the vice squad at the Charing Cross police station. There, she is confronted with the mysterious death/murder of 15-year-old Colin Jenkins (Greg Saunders), a homeless rent boy who perished in a fire. Fighting sexual discrimination, interference in her own department and her own personal crisis, D.C.I. Tennison continues the

investigation; one that hints at police and political complicity. Initially, her main suspect is Jimmy Jackson (David Thewlis), a villainous opportunist who haunts the city's train stations recruiting wayward boys into a life of petty crime and prostitution. She soon finds herself drawn into the nefarious underworld of the sex-for-sale industry, kiddie porn and sexual lowlifes who prey on vulnerable youth. A riveting, groundbreaking and compulsively watchable drama that, although it does not paint a positive picture of gay lifestyles, is certainly not homophobic or exploitative — a rare achievement for such a contentious subject. Written by Lynda La Plante, the program also features a memorable Peter Capaldi as transvestite Vernon/Vera, the owner of the flat where the boy was burned to death.

Pixote

Prince in Hell (Prinz in Hölleland) *(1992, 96 min, Germany, Michael Stock)*

Germany's answer to New Queer Cinema, this bizarre modern-day fairy tale begins where *Christiane F.* ended as it follows the lives of several junkies, queers, lowlifes and anarchists all living in glorious squalor in a trash-strewn, post-unification Berlin. With pulsating music, raunchy S&M sex and a "fuck life" attitude, the story's main characters are Jockel and Stefan, two gay lovers. The two are in the throes of breaking up, slowly being separated by promiscuity, heroin addiction and booze. Gay life is presented as matter-of-fact, but on the extreme fringe in this hard-hitting story where alternative lifestyles and political alienation clash with neo-Nazi violence and economic hardship. Queer romantic nihilism for a ravaged, turmoil-filled Germany.

The Prince of Pennsylvania

(1988, 93 min, US, Ron Nyswaner)

An offbeat dude (Keanu Reeves) wants to avoid following in his blue-collar father's footsteps, so he kidnaps his pop and holds him for ransom. The problem? No one wants him back. Fred Ward, Bonnie Bedelia and Amy Madigan co-star. Gay writer-director Ron Nyswaner wrote the screenplays to *Philadelphia* and *Smithereens*. ⊛

The Prodigal Son

(1992, 97 min, Finland, Veikko Aaltonen)

This fascinating Finnish drama explores the sadomasochistic relationship between a straight man and a gay man. Esa is a handsome young thug just released from prison after several years. Unable to find a conventional job, he is hired as an enforcer, a man who beats up people for a price. This "career" turns a bit kinky when Linstrum, a wealthy, corpulent, older psychiatrist, becomes his client — with the unusual arrangement, however, that Esa does not beat up others, but Linstrum himself. Their S&M sessions become increasingly violent and

sexual, to the point that Linstrum begins masturbating while being beaten to a pulp. Other activities between the two include whipping and, in an implied fashion, the use of a large black dildo. Esa, after initial reluctance, comes to accept these meetings nonchalantly, until his attraction to a young woman causes his increasingly jealous client to take drastic measures to insure the continuation of their "relationship." The homosexual Linstrum is depicted as a sick, vindictive, violent and evil individual, unable to have normal sex or a normal affair. But although he is the villain in this riveting tale of violence and redemption, homophobia can probably be ruled out; his character is well-drawn and his evil seems to come more from his wealth and success than from his homosexuality.

Pubis Angelical

(1982, 117 min, Argentina, Raul de la Torre)

Gay novelist and playwright Manuél Puig ("Betrayed by Rita Hayworth," "Heartbreak Tango" and "Kiss of the Spider Woman") adapted, in collaboration with director Raul de la Torre, his novel for the screen. A young Argentine woman, in a Mexican hospital for cancer, slips in and out of sleep, troubled by vivid dreams that are infused with nightmarish visions of the manipulation, disappointments and deceit she has suffered at the hands of the men in her life. The fantasies, in which she is alternately an actress, prostitute and spy, come to symbolize her real-life existence, especially after a former lover, now a right-wing Peronist insurgent, comes to her bed seeking help in kidnapping another former lover, an important figure in the Argentine government. A complicated tale of one woman torn between her illusions of a happy life and the realities of her disappointments. Although the novel was a best-seller in Spain and the film contains only fleeting moments of interest, Puig might have been only slightly hyperbolistic in calling it "a true horror." ⊛

Quand L'Amour est Gai

(1994, 56 min, Canada, Laurent Gagliardi)
Similar in style to *Sex Is...*, this video essay might more appropriately be called *Homosexuality Is...*. Interviewed are men of all ages who discuss their homosexuality, the importance of their gayness in their lives, the level of acceptance of their sexuality (ranging from complete to closet cases) and the relationship/camaraderie that exists among gay men. It does not try to ram the idea of homosexuality into the face of a less-than-receptive society, but rather simply attempts to show the faces of gay men and, in one scene, the tender love between two men. Hopefully the result will be a neutralization of pervading ignorance and prejudices regarding homosexuality.

Race D'Ep

(95 min, France, Lionel Soukas
& Guy Hocquengem)
This four-part film documentary postulates that gay liberation did not begin in the 1960s-'70s, but rather had its roots in the turn-of-the-century. Taking its title from Paris street slang for homosexual, the film traces gay history through four historical and fictional "reveries." Part 1 is titled "The Pose Period" and focuses on the art and life of Baron von Gloeden, a photographer noted for his pictures of nude Sicilian boys. Part 2, "The Third Sex," is about Dr. Magnus Hirschfeld and his famous work on homosexuality with his Institute of Sexual Research in Berlin. The institute was eventually closed down by the Nazis in 1933. Part 3, "Sweet Sixteen in the Sixties," changes pace by being a jazzy recollection of a man's sexual liberation through the reading of a gay love letter. The film concludes with "Royal Opera," a gay *Rashomon* in which an American businessman and a French "Follies" queen meet. Low-budget, with non-sync sound and the use of non-professional actors, the film imaginatively offers several independent thoughts on homosexual history.

Rainbow Serpent

(1983, 90 min, France, Philippe Vallois)
From Philippe Vallois, director of the lyrical *We Were One Man*, comes this entertaining satire of musicals and detective films. In keeping with his recurring theme of homosexuality among heterosexuals, the director focuses on the budding sadomasochistic relationship between a beefy bodybuilder and the rookie cop sent to investigate him. Flashy musical numbers are interspersed throughout this strangely unreal, comic thriller.

Rebels of the Neon God

(1993, 85 min, Hong Kong, Tsai Ming-Liang)
While not an explicitly gay-themed feature, *Rebels of the Neon God* is a fascinating drama of one boy's obsession and confused sexual feeling for another boy. Set in an unbelievably congested Tokyo, the film primarily follows teenager and college student Ah Tze and his lonely personal life. Unable to form any meaningful relationships or friendships, he soon becomes interested in a self-assured, slightly older petty criminal. Ah Tze stalks his "love" through the city and in a moment generated by either his latent homosexual feelings, mixed-up hero wor-

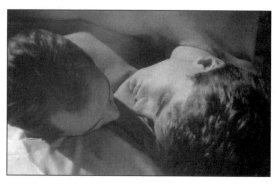

Quand L'Amour est Gai

ship or simply run-of-the-mill jealousy, destroys the boy's motorbike and scrawls "AIDS" all over it.

> "...a crisply made first feature that evidences much tender regard for boys in jockey shorts."
> —Tony Raynes, *Sight and Sound*

Remembrance of Things Fast

(1993, 61 min, GB, John Maybury)
This dreamlike, multi-image experimental work from gay video-maker John Maybury unfolds as if we are watching the director lying in bed at night channel surfing through the memories of his and his friends' past. Featured in the video are Tilda Swinton, Rupert Everett, porn star Aiden Brady and several bitingly witty drag queens. In this almost hallucinatory landscape, culled from reality, near reality and complete fiction, several mini-tales unfold, with the most enlightening being about a transvestite who recounts a sexual pick-up that ends in violence. Confrontational, political and viewer-demanding, *Remembrance*, made for only $40,000, is also entertaining, provocative and is a vivid example of the current state of young queer videomaking.

Resident Alien

(1990, 85 min, GB, Jonathan Nossiter)
Gay celebrity and writer Quentin Crisp ("The Naked Civil Servant") is the central attraction of this British quasi-documentary television production. Following Crisp's move to New York, the action is filmed in his apartment and features many of his friends including Sting, John Hurt, Holly Woodlawn and even Sally Jesse Raphael.

Rich Boy, Poor Boy

(1992, 94 min, The Philippines, Piedro de San Paulo)
Sort of a Filipino-style *Maurice*, this romantic and erotic gay love story, banned in the Philippines, is also a melancholy drama of the class problems afflicting the Third World. Mark, a rich, Americanized young man returns from the States to visit his mother at her country estate where he meets and falls in love with Pilo, a sexy, yet sincere servant. Their love blossoms despite Mark's mother's attempts to push young women in his direction and her eventual discovery of the affair. But it is the political turmoil in the countryside that proves to be an even larger obstacle to the naive

lovers. Note: A short film, *A Boy Named Cocoy*, also by the director, precedes the feature. This entertaining and erotic tale, which plays like a Filipino J.O. fantasy, follows Cocoy, a 20-year-old country boy who arrives in the Big City only to lose all of his clothing and money to thieves. He is saved from a life in the streets by a friendly young man named Tony. And when Cocoy discovers that he is gay, he repays him the only way he knows how! ✛

Riot *(1968, 97 min, US, Buzz Kulik)*

This typical prison breakout flick features several incidents with gay prisoners — some good, most quite negative. While the straight ringleaders (Gene Hackman and Jim Brown) plot strategies, the men in "Queen's Row" (the homosexual wing) set up, in the absence of guards, a makeshift gay bar, surrealistically filled with men kissing, cruising and camping it up. There's even a striptease drag act performed in front of many entranced fellow prisoners. The film contains two really interesting scenes: one in which a fellow prisoner, Mary (a name by choice) attempts to seduce the almost baited Jim Brown (quite explicit for 1968); and, sadly, the first death occurs when a fellow prisoner stabs a gay man with a pair of scissors when he tries to break out with the others. There are also many anti-gay epithets ("faggot psychologist"). Filmed in an actual state prison in New Mexico, the supporting characters (including most of the Queen's Row habitués) were actual prisoners. ✛

Robby *(1968, 60 min, US, Ralph C. Bluemke)*

"Robinson Crusoe" meets "Sesame Street" in this mildly diverting kiddie version of survival and friendship on a desert island. Robby, a nine-year-old white-haired castaway, finds life not so bad on the idyllic island after he befriends a native boy whom he soon calls Friday. The adventure story, made on a shoestring budget, features beautiful South Pacific beaches, naked boys frolicking in the crystalline waters and a simple, universal story. ✛

Robert Having His Nipple Pierced
(1970, 33 min, US, Sandy Daley)

The year is 1970. Robert Mapplethorpe is having his nipple pierced. You are there. Robert's boyfriend comforts him while Robert's roommate, Patti Smith, gives a drugged-up voice-over

Rainbow Serpent

babelogue about her bizarre childhood, her tits, her transvestite brother, shaving her pubic hair, Bob Dylan and whatever else crosses her amused little mind.

Rock Hudson's Home Movies
(1992, 63 min, US, Mark Rappaport)

Often hilarious, highly original and utterly convincing, this revisionist interpretation of Rock Hudson's film career and life seeks to discover the "real" Hudson through his "reel" persona. Was Hollywood hunk, and celebrated closet case, Rock Hudson — star of innumerable heterosexual sex comedies — completely out of touch with his secreted sexuality or did he, throughout his career, offer his audience subtle — and not so subtle — hints of his true sexuality? Exploring this idea, Rappaport's insightful and unconventional biography cleverly dissects, through freeze frames, slo-mo, and replays, many of Hudson's films, seeking clues and overtly gay signals. What was really happening in all of those coy sex comedies, when Hudson had to play "gay" to get the girl (Doris Day, Paula Prentiss, Elizabeth Taylor, Dorothy Malone) only to be interrupted before anything really happens. What was the true relationship between him and his fey co-star Tony Randall? Structured around a Rock Hudson look-alike (Eric Farr) who narrates, Rappaport's premise is that Rock freely chose to star in these types of films and that his gayness was an open secret all along, the viewer only had to read between the straight lines. ✛

Focus on: *Mark Rappaport*

While Rock Hudson's Home Movies *has just recently thrusted Mark Rappaport into the queer limelight, he is far from a neophite. A filmmaker since the mid-1960s, his works have played film festivals around the world with several of them enjoying limited theatrical engagements in both Britain and the United States. Winner of the British Film Institute Award, Rappaport's films can be characterized as a zany mix of camp, melodrama, comedy and surrealism, all fashioned through an avant-gardist's cinematic eye.* L.A. Reader *has written that "Rappaport's sexual comedy of manners has a teasing intellectual wit that easily puts to shame Woody Allen's better-appointed tales of urban sophisticates-in-crisis." His earliest film was* Strike, *a short made with Richard E. Brooks about the 1966 New York subway strike. In the intervening years he made his feature film debut with* Casual Relations *(1973, 80 min), a no-budget New York comedy about lonely, neurotic characters. Other notable films include* Imposters *(1979, 110 min) (see page 411) and* Mozart in Love *(1975, 83 min), a theatrical, aria-filled comedy about Wolfgang's relations with the three Webster sisters.* Local Color *(1977, 116 min), an offbeat modernist melodrama examines the lives of eight couples, one of whom is gay. Vincent Canby of* The New York Times *called it "...a failed attempt to make camp melodrama in the style of the Kuchar brothers," and Roger Ebert of* Chicago Sun Times *dubbed it "...a strange and wonderful movie; absolutely original, haunting and starkly beautiful." His 1978 film,* The Scenic Route *(76 min), is a wryly humorous jealousy- and revenge-filled soaper about an incestuous triangle formed by two sisters and the man caught between them. Roger Ebert called it "A movie of great, grave, tightly controlled visual daring...you've never seen anything like it before."*

James Stewart (l.) confronts John Dall (c.) and Farley Granger in *Rope*

The Room of Chains

(1972, 68 min, France, Gerard Trembasiewicz)
With the combustible mixture of sex, violence and religion, this trashy exploitation picture links homosexuality with fiendish depravity. George (Jack Bernard) is a respectable antique dealer who works with both his wife and the much younger Mark (Oliver Neal). Unbeknownst to the wife, the two men are lovers who engage in a murderous hobby in which they kidnap beautiful women, chain them in a dungeon in their estate and slowly kill them. The police are confused when they investigate, puzzled by the fact that the women weren't sexually violated in their ordeals. Add *Room of Chains* to the list of films which feature murderously psychotic gays and lesbians.

Roommates

(1994, 100 min, US, Alan Metzger)
A made-for-TV movie/disease-of-the-week tearjerker, *Roommates* takes an earnest but ultimately simpleton approach to dealing with people suffering from AIDS. Eric Stoltz glides through his role as Bill, an educated gay man from a privileged background who improbably leaves his loving parents to live out his last days in a Seattle hospice for PWAs. His assigned roommate is Jimmy (Randy Quaid), a hulking, obnoxious, heterosexual and homophobic ex-con who contracted the disease from a blood transfusion and who loudly pontificates on the disease being "God's way of cleaning house." From the moment the two clash over who will have the larger bedroom, you know that in short time, they will begin to soften, and become the best of friends despite their opposite natures. Watch as the gruff Quaid (doing a weird John Wayne imitation) finally comes around to acceptance, changing from a beer-guzzling bully to a sensitive Melville-reading companion. The other members of the hospice (gays and a prostitute) are seen as only minor background characters. Essentially "The Odd Couple Contracts AIDS," the film is

nevertheless not without its merit. Stoltz's gay characterization is well balanced, without stereotype, with him as the intellectual and emotional pillar of the film.

Rope

(1948, 80 min, US, Alfred Hitchcock)
The Master of Suspense's audacious experimentation with real time and ten-minute takes gives this murder-thriller both a kinetic and claustrophobic atmosphere. Suggested by the Leopold-Loeb case, the story concerns two homosexuals (played by Farley Granger and John Dall) who murder an old school mate for the thrill of it, stuff his corpse in an old chest, and then proceed to hold a party around the makeshift casket with attendees including the victim's father and fiancée. The film's screenplay was written by gay writer Arthur Laurents (*West Side Story, The Way We Were*). ⊗

Sacred Passion

(1989, 60 min, US,
Emerald D.H. Starr)
An orgy for the soul! Infused with lofty, mystical (and pretentious) narration by poet Gavin Geofrey Dillard and featuring loads of naked men lounging about in lush Hawaii, this sensual guide to tantric sex will prove to be more of interest to ex-hippies than to today's ACT UP-oriented gays. There's lots of kissing, nudity and even non-sexual grinding — all in all, a plotless look into the possibilities of love freed from compulsion. ⊗

Safer Sex for Gay Men, and Men Who Have Sex with Men

(1993, 50 min, South Africa, Jeff Van Reenen)
Joining the burgeoning list of safer sex demonstration tapes is this well-meaning, if unexceptional video from South Africa. It begins with a serious and informative introduction on the do's and don'ts regarding unsafe sexual practices, including such catchy phrases as "blood means danger" and "don't brush your teeth before oral sex." Also included is a series of demonstrative sexual encounters by several well-toned male models seen groping themselves and each other through underwear, and eventually without their Calvins in a series of safer sexual acts. Despite the video's box art which warns of "sexually explicit scenes," they are in fact quite tepid, as the makers of the tapes obsessively avoid showing the stated willies in action! Also, the tape says that oral sex is generally safe if the person does not cum in their partner's mouth. This stance is contradicted by many people as being overly dismissive of the risks involved by unprotected oral sex. The video's reception in South Africa has been far from open-armed. The gay theme and the use of interracial couples caused the video to be labeled by the South African Directorate of Publications as being "devoid of a moral message" and bordering on pornography. ⊗

Salon Kitty

(1976, 110 min, Germany/Italy/France, Tinto Brass)
Salon Kitty is a sleazy, sexually graphic shocker joining the ranks of "Nazis-and-their-sexual-degeneracy"-themed movies like *The Night Porter*, *The Damned*, *Salo: 120 Days of Sodom* and even *Ilsa: The She-Wolf of the SS*. A crazed (but exceptionally handsome) Helmut Berger stars as a powerful SS officer who will do anything to get dirt on his fellow officers and their wives. In the cheap thrills category, Berger's long-awaited death in the film occurs with him naked — in full frontal nudity, save a Swastika armband. Self-proclaimed anarchist and director of *Caligula*, Tinto Brass explains his fascination with sexual zealots and mass murderers by saying, "I am always on the side of the losers." An erotic and, at times, disturbing probe into the sickness of man. ⊛

Salut Victor!

(1988, 83 min, Canada, Anne Claire Poirier)
Made for television, this French-Canadian gay love story, though a bit predictable, is a simply told and poignant tale about love in life's later stages. Set in a retirement home, the film follows Philippe, a wealthy gentleman who begins to feel the pain and loneliness of losing his health and sense of freedom. He is reluctantly pulled out of his doldrums by his friendship with Victor, a talkative, exuberant man who recently lost his lover in a plane crash. These disparate men soon strike up an affecting, tender relationship as this delicate tearjerker adds new meaning to the term "old-fashioned," and breaks new ground through its portrait of older gay men, ultimately charming one and all with its sentimental style. ⊛

Sand and Blood

(1987, 101 min, France, Jeanne LaBrune)
Coming on the heels of Pedro Almodóvar's exploration of sex and violence in the bullring with *Matador* comes this much more thoughtful yet equally provocative, erotically charged drama. An upcoming matador from "the wrong side of the tracks" meets and befriends a wealthy doctor who is morally opposed to the violence of the bullfight. Their unlikely relationship affects both their lives and their families as together they confront their hidden secrets

Sacred Passion

and fears. Be forewarned: the bullfighting and slaughterhouse scenes in the film contain bloody and graphic images of violence against animals. ⊛

Saturday Night at the Baths

(1974, 85 min, US, David Buckley)
The transformation of a homophobic straight man into "one of the boys" is the theme of this independently made comedy-drama. Michael, who lives with his girlfriend Tracy, finds his already unstable sexuality challenged after he gets a job as a pianist at the gay Continental Baths. At first denying any male attraction, his defenses melt, especially after the baths' manager, Scotti, finally beds him, releasing a torrent of pent-up memories and sexual desire. It is an exploration of one man's sexuality which, while featuring amateurish acting and a stilted screenplay, is nonetheless quite entertaining.

> *"Saturday Night at the Baths* is the first motion picture to take a sympathetic, gutsy look at the defenses we erect against complete sexual expression."
> —Original ad copy in print campaign

Savage Nights (Les Nuite Fauves)

(1992, 126 min, France, Cyril Collard)
Possibly the most personal and controversial of all the films dealing with HIV-infection and AIDS, *Savage Nights* is a startlingly knowing semiautobiographical melodrama from former rock star and writer Cyril Collard (the director who died from AIDS at the age of 36 in 1993 just four days before the film nearly swept the Cesar Awards, winning Best Director, Best Picture, Best Debut Film, Best Actress and Best Editing). Adapted from Collard's 1989 novel and filmed in a style reminiscent of the early French New Wave, the film stars Collard as Jean, a high-living bisexual photographer who discovers after a trip to Morocco that he is HIV-positive. Despite this, he is determined to live life to the fullest, eventually becoming involved with love-sick 17-year-old Laura (Romana Bohringer) and S&M-obsessed, neo-Nazi rugby player Samy (Carlos Lopez), as well as immersing himself in increasingly degrading anonymous rough-trade sexual encounters. The story revolves around these two tumultuous relationships as the outwardly calm Jean, with his ever-present smirky smile and handsome easy-going charms, tries to forget about his illness through physical and sexual comforts. He explains to Laura that "Sometimes I'll do anything just to forget I'm wasting away. Can you imagine coping with that threat every day?" But his self-absorption and inability to give of himself to others prove to be his undoing as the people that love him are forced either to leave or eventually are replaced with others. The portrait is raw and unflinching as Jean (Collard) offers a "fuck-you" approach to AIDS, the most controversial aspect of which is his continued unprotected sexual antics, despite the probabilty of spreading the disease. With its jagged, almost documentary feel and homemade quality, the film effectively and unapologetically delves into the feeling and life of a non-hero and his personal response to coping with AIDS. The film was dedicated to gay Filipino filmmaker Lino Brocka. ⊛

Sand and Blood

companion, Clyde Tolson. Were the two simply lifelong, "monastic" bachelors and best friends, or were they "sex deviants"; was Hoover being "terrorized by his urges?" Interviewing former FBI agents and eyewitnesses, the documentary lays claim that the two were not simply lovers committed to each other for almost half a century, but rather, outlandish homosexuals who "held each other's hands" and engaged in sex parties (without women!) — one woman even claimed to have seen Hoover as a cross-dressing dowager named Mary who wore "a black chiffon dress with black lace, ruffles, black high heels, a black wig and black eye lashes." [Sounds both practical and fashionable to me!] Mafia informers lay claim that the mob had blackmailed him with pictures of the normally staid Hoover giving head to Tolson! While Hoover might well have been a corrupt, even despicable man, I could not help feel a little sorry for him as this subtly anti-gay documentary tears his career and personal life apart. ☻

The 2nd Annual Gay Erotic Video Awards *(1994, 120 min, US, Michael Bruno)*

Organized by *Gay Video Guide* and hosted by the elegantly attired Chi Chi LaRue, this curious awards show is a much snazzier production than the previous year's. Videotaped at L.A.'s Tomkat Theatre, this talky, low-rent version of the Academy Awards draws the biggest names in the male adult video industry. In addition to the presentation of the awards (for such categories as Best Supporting Actor, Best Solo Performance, etc.), the show features music and comedy from such performers as drag diva Gender, Harriot Leider and Paul Jacek, as well as behind-the-scenes interviews with the stars. Those expecting to see some raised appendages will be disappointed as the performers only go so far as some playful G-stringed simulated sex. Even segments from the nominated films are sadly absent. Porn favorites Jeff Stryker, Ryan Idol, Jon Vincent and Rex Chandler are just a few of the presenters in this video that will be of interest primarily to die-hard fans of male adult videos. ☻

The Secret File on J. Edgar Hoover

(1993, 60 min, US, William Cran)

Originally broadcast on PBS, this hard-hitting exposé seeks to reveal, "for the first time," the "depth of Hoover's personal corruption." The investigation hits on his gambling problems, the misappropriation of public funds for personal use, his unexplained laxity in battling the growth of the Mafia and his hidden homosexuality. As FBI director for 48 years, Hoover had enjoyed amazing popularity as a hero in his lifetime; but now, after his death, floods of reports have revealed his tyrannical control and abuse of power. The most lurid of the revelations concern his homosexuality and his relationship with his assistant and constant

Secret Passions *(1989, 85 min, US)*

From its humble, yet noble inception as part of California's public access cable system, "Secret Passions" was welcomed as the soap opera geared to address the medium's very present, but largely ignored gay audience. Unfortunately, all this campfest proves is that even the best of intentions can go astray. This laughably bad introduction to the people and problems of a small (seemingly all-gay) Orange County community tries to cram so much information to its audience, that one is left with the feeling of having walked in on a "Dynasty" spoof as performed by its unappreciated crew members! While this production should at least be lauded for its long-overdue attention to such taboo subjects as male homosexuality and lesbianism, the slipshod story line seems to be just an excuse for a catty barrage of one-liners. ☻

A Separate Peace

(1972, 104 min, US, Larry Peerce)

Despite calf-cake galore, John Knowles' best-selling novel makes a not-all-together successful transition to film in this sun-splashed teenage drama of friendship, initiation and betrayal. Reminiscent of *Summer of '42* and the first part of *Brideshead Revisited*, the action, set at a prep school at the beginning of WWII, focuses on two roommates' developing friendship and unspoken love. Parker Stevenson is the freshly-scrubbed narrator Gene who falls under the charismatic spell of the athletic and domineering Finny. Their ensuing friendship is tested after a freak accident, possibly caused by Gene, injures Finny. Gene's betrayal, while never explicitly explained can be interpreted as a result of his jealousy as well as a confused, repressed sexual yearning for his blond, blue-eyed friend. While their is no overt homosexuality, the film gazes lustfully on the many half-naked teenage boys that grace the screen, giving some visual excitement after the action slows to an aimless crawl. ☯

> "By giving us yards of exposed flesh, Peerce attempts to convey the unrealized homosexuality that lurks beneath the Levis and sweatshirts of his protangonists."
>
> —*Newsweek*

The Sergeant *(1968, 107 min, US, John Flynn)*

On the heels of the similarly themed *Reflections in a Golden Eye* came this hyperventilating drama of a repressed homosexual military man whose "unnatural" passions become his violent undoing. Rod Steiger is Master Sergeant Callen, who is tortured by his seething but closeted homosexuality for which he overcompensates by being a macho, bullying "man's man" and immerses himself in the military life. But his homosexual passions are inflamed after he sees and falls in lust with handsome blond Private Swanson (John Phillip Law). Unable to articulate how he feels to anyone, including the obviously straight private, Sergeant Callen just about emotionally explodes and in one brief moment of release, grabs the private and plants a furious, intense kiss on the lips of the startled man. Overcome with shame and self-loathing, the sergeant takes his pistol, heads to the woods and blows his brains out! If it were really so easy! The original advertising campaign featured the tag line, "Just one weakness. Just one."

Sergeant Matlovich vs. the U.S. Air Force *(1978, 100 min, US, Paul Leaf)*

The intriguing but dramatically uninspiring real-life story of Sergeant Leonard P. Matlovich's battle with the United States military does not fare well on-screen in this tepid made-for-TV drama. Brad Dourif plays Sgt. Matlovich, a Vietnam veteran, Purple Heart and Bronze Star-awarded soldier in the U.S. Air Force who declared to his commanders that he was gay, prompting a drive to dishonorably discharge him. Instead of accepting the actions of the Air Force, Matlovich fought back in the courts charging discrimination by the military's blanket ban of gay men and lesbians. Since the issue is even more contentious today, one would expect that his efforts did not meet with full success, for he was eventually discharged, but honorably.

Serious Charge

(1959, 99 min, GB, Terence Young)

A few years before the groundbreaking blackmailed homosexual drama, *Victim*, came this rarely seen story of the nature of prejudice (and to a lesser extent, homophobia) directed by Terence Young (*Dr. No, Thunderball, Wait Until Dark*). A small-town juvenile delinquent (Andrew Ray) vengefully accuses the town's gentle vicar (Anthony Quayle) of sexually molesting him after the minister implicates the boy in the death of his girlfriend. The film is notable also in that it marks rock idol Cliff Richards' screen debut as Ray's younger brother. Based on a play by Philip King, a dramatist ("How Are You Johnny?," "The Lonesome Road") who included several gay characters in his works.

The Shadow Box

(1980, 100 min, US, Paul Newman)

A well-made and sensitive version of Michael Cristofer's Tony and Pulitzer Prize-winning play, this Paul Newman-directed drama explores the lives of three terminally ill patients as they and their families spend a day at an experimental retreat in the California mountains. The main story focuses on Brian (Christopher Plummer), a middle-aged gay man suffering from cancer who is living with Mark (Ben Masters), a much younger man. Tensions arise when Brian's former wife Beverly (Joanne Woodward) visits the two men. Brian is glad to see his former wife but Mark, a former gay prostitute in San Francisco, is threatened by their easy friendship. Mark's anxiety is needless, however, as Brian confides to Beverly that Mark has revitalized his life and that he deeply loves him. The free-spirited Beverly, who remarks that Mark "doesn't look like a faggot," readily accepts their relationship and works on a rapprochement with both men. Although the two men show no physical closeness, the film depicts a gay relationship in a positive, upbeat fashion. ☯

Sharing the Secret

(1981, 84 min, Canada, John Kastner)

Originally banned in Australia and very controversial when it aired on Canadian television, this powerful and dated (thankfully) documentary attempts to correct the misconceptions of homosexuality by delving into the personal lives of five gay men. The film reveals that despite ten years of advocacy, these men continue to be torn between pride and pain as a result of their attempts to be both individuals as well as to "blend" into the majority. The selection process, reportedly involving 50 men during a nine-month period, had as its goal to find "typical" gay men — the silent, non-stereotypical members of society at large. The five men include Andre, a 22-year-old stockbroker; Peter, a young man struggling with his religious background; Lee, who works on getting his ultra-conservative family to accept him; and Alex, a 44-year-old just recently out of the closet.

Short Eyes *(1977, 104 min, US, Robert M. Young)*

Miguel Piñero's powerhouse play, scripted during his stint in Sing-Sing, is a gritty, nerve-rattling glimpse of life behind bars. The prison is peopled by Muslim zealots, angry blacks, knife-wielding Latinos and a smaller group of tough, but cautious whites, all of whom hate one another. The depiction of the prisoners' casual brutality includes male rape and a constant barrage of sexual taunts (threats like "blood on my knife and shit on my dick"). A young Latino prisoner called Cupcake (Tito Goya) is the object of more than one prisoner's violent lust. But racial tensions dissolve as the prisoners become more united in their hatred of Clark Davis (Bruce Davison), a white, first-time offender who, after they discover that he is a child abuser ("short eyes"), becomes the target of an onslaught of threats and bloody violence. ☯

Sidney Shorr: A Girl's Best Friend

(1981, 100 min, US, Russ Mayberry)

Tony Randall stars as a lonely gay New Yorker who finds friendship and platonic love with a woman in this feature-length televi-

Silverlake Life: The View from Here

impending death. He becomes reinvigorated and sexually intrigued after seeing Siegfried, a curly-haired blond youth who performs a juggling act in a traveling circus. The boy is quickly lured from his circus life into the older man's world of art, liquor and fine clothes. Drawicz tries to seduce Siegfried while he is posing naked, but his advances are violently refused. In the film's humorously O. Henry-type of twist ending, the old man does not die (like Aschenbach) but succeeds in "capturing" the boy's youth and beauty. ☻

Silverlake Life: The View from Here

(1992, 99 min, US, Tom Joslin & Peter Friedman)
Possibly the most harrowing vision of death and dying ever recorded, this emotionally devastating video diary of two lovers both diagnosed with AIDS and slowly succumbing to the disease is far from a morbid recording of one's own death. Rather, it's an emotional celebration of life and of the enduring love the two men have for each other. Tom Joslin, film teacher and filmmaker, and his lover for over 22 years, Mark Massi, decided after the beginning signs of the onslaught of AIDS-related illnesses to record their lives — including the virus' debilitating effects, Tom's family's reactions and especially their relationship, strained and yet strengthened during the ordeal. The camera follows them as they go to the doctor, buy medicine and herbal "cures," and visit the park, but stays primarily in their apartment located in the Silverlake section of Los Angeles. Refusing to live under a death sentence, the two men attempt to continue leading productive lives despite the frustration of their physical incapacities and their increasing inability to perform the simplest household tasks. Although Mark was the first diagnosed with the disease, it is Tom who first begins to become ill. And it is these scenes of Tom battling the body's deterioration with unflagging spirits that would even wrench the heart of a Reaganite. At one point, as they sit on their balcony pretending to be narrating a sea cruise, Tom wishes to keep the viewer "informed of our continuing journey — it's shorter than I thought it would be...but that's life." Peter Friedman, a former student of Tom's, and friend to both, completed the film after Tom's death. One's immediate feelings after the sadness of their story is an acknowledgement of their overriding commitment to one another, making this personal diary an astonishing love story, told with humor, great insight and an enduring life-affirming belief. Winner of the Grand Jury Prize, 1993 Sundance Film Festival and Best Documentary, Teddy Bear Awards, 1993 Berlin Film Festival. ☻

sion drama that served as the pilot for his short-lived situation comedy "Love, Sydney" (1981-83). Exhibiting the same fastidious mannerisms that he perfected in his heterosexual role as Felix in "The Odd Couple," Sidney is a middle-aged man who, recovering from the death of his younger lover, befriends an aspiring actress (Lorna Patterson) who soon moves in with him. The homosexuality of the lead character is severely downplayed and was essentially eliminated in the television show.

Siege

(1982, 81 min, Canada, Paul Donovan & Maura O'Connell)
A film that should inflame the argumentative passions of and militarize any self-respecting gay person, this blatantly homophobic diatribe is couched as a simple reaction film, but beware! When the police go on strike in Halifax, Nova Scotia, a crowded gay bar is invaded by gun-wielding thugs of the New Order. Scores of helpless "homos" are killed in the ensuing carnage but one young man escapes and runs to a nearby farmhouse to hide (running literally into a closet!). It takes the enterprising and strapping heteros (both men and women) to defend themselves and the poor waif after the house comes under assault from the killers. A violent, nefarious independent production that makes *Cruising* seem innocuous.

Siegfried

(1986, 91 min, Poland, Andrzej Domalik)
This unusual drama is an interesting variation on the theme of old age transfixed by youthful beauty — a subject best explored in Visconti's *Death in Venice*. Stefan Drawicz (Gustax Holoubek) is a wealthy art connoisseur who feels the weight of old age and

Sincerely Yours

(1955, 115 min, US, Gordon Douglas)

Liberace, the outrageously flamboyant entertainer whose sequined, fur-draped costumes and jewel-dripped appendages delighted blue-hairs and camp-lovers alike, stars in this entertainingly awful tearjerking melodrama. With a screenplay by Irving Wallace, this inexcusable remake of *The Man Who Played God* co-stars Dorothy Malone and features Liberace as a celebrated concert pianist whose life abruptly changes when he loses his sight. Not surprisingly, this travesty ended any prospects for a real film career and he did not appear in a film again until ten years later in the hilarious part of a casket salesman in *The Loved One*. His concert stage and Las Vegas shows became his speciality with many television specials (several available on video including the classic, *Liberace Shows His Home*). Despite his celebrated fey persona and underground reputation, Liberace lived his whole life in the closet even after losing a palimony suit by a young man. He unequivocally denied being a homosexual, up to the point of his death in 1987 to AIDS. ⊛

> "Given sufficient intoxication, you could find this movie amusing."
>
> —*Saturday Review*

Sis: The Perry Watkins Story

(1994, 60 min, US, Chiqui Cartegena)

This inspiring documentary tells the story of Perry Watkins, the U.S. Army sergeant who became the first person to successfully challenge the military's ban on gays and lesbians. After serving 15 years, Watkins was discharged in 1982 on the grounds of homosexuality. Because he acknowledged his gayness on his draft papers in 1967 and he had an exemplary record, his nine-year court battle ended with victory when the Supreme Court declined to rule on a lower court's decision to reinstate him. Watkins, a charismatic speaker with an infectious smile, proves to be a seductive subject — an African-American who was openly gay and, on occasion, performed in drag (as "Simone") to throngs of appreciative soldiers. His unique case turned him from a simple military clerk into a leading public speaker on civil rights. Those interviewed include some of the soldiers who had worked with him; his commanding officers; and legal experts on the ban on gays. A rare film on the subject of gays in the military — rare because it has a happy ending.

Six Degrees of Separation

(1993, 112 min, US, Fred Schepisi)

The charismatic and slyly cute Will Smith (aka Fresh Prince) stars in this complex and involving screen version of John Guare's witty Broadway play about self-deception. Loosely based on a real incident, the story revolves around a strange but uncommonly charming young man who ingratiates himself into the households of several rich New Yorkers by claiming to be a friend of their children as well as the son of Sidney Poitier. One of the scammed couples is Upper East Side art dealer Flan (Donald Sutherland) and Ouisa Kittredge (Stockard Channing, a marvel in the role that she originated on stage). An interesting dimension to the story (which justifies its inclusion in this book) is the fact that the con man, Paul, is an unapologetic gay man. He has a ton of emotional and mental problems, but his sexual orientation is not one of them. Despite the controversy of Smith's discomfort playing the gay scenes, there are several that stand out, including his sexual romp in bed with a blond pickup; his seduction and semi-stripping scene with a gay student (Anthony Michael Hall) and his wining and dining of an innocent Utah boy whom he eventually deflowers in a horse-drawn carriage in Central Park. Most reviews of the lauded film either neglected to mention that he is gay or simply referred to it in passing, a major step in integrating gay characters in films that are not necessarily gay in theme. This positive portrayal is accomplished despite Smith's oft-repeated protestations against kissing another man on-screen. He publicly stated during the filming that despite being "totally committed" to the project, he would not do an on-screen kiss with another man (though he had no problem picking one up and stripping him and telling another that he wanted to "fuck" him). He said that "I have kissed girls on-screen. I could work that out. The difference is how people perceive it. If I kissed a guy then went home, they'd be like, 'Yo man, why'd you do that?...You kissed a dude. Something's wrong with you, man.' I just didn't want to hear it." He has softened his homophobic position since the release of the movie. Ian McKellen is featured as a rich South African businessman who also becomes enchanted with the young man. ⊛

The Slight Fever of a 20-Year-Old

(1993, 114 min, Japan, Ryosuke Hashiguchi)

The curiously empty lives and unrequited loves of two young male prostitutes in Tokyo are the focus of this earnest and reasoned but slow moving film. Tatsuro is a sullen youth who helps himself

The Slight Fever of a 20-Year-Old

through college by nonchalantly turning tricks at the Pinocchio Bar. Not much more than a child, he remains an aloof, dour (I believe he does not smile throughout the entire film) professional, never one to refuse a trick or blanch at their kinky suggestions. His other-worldliness is shaken when Shin, a fellow rent boy, declares his love for him, forcing Tatsuro to confront real emotions. Rounding out the cast are the two boys' platonic girlfriends who provide an escape into normalcy and who are in the dark about the boys' high-paying night jobs. With a subject that offers the promise of scandal and a chance to explore the rarely seen world of male prostitution in Japan, the young director lacks the technical skills to bring about any warmth or feeling for the alienated characters who robotically go about life, wallowing in hopelessness and displaying little youthful exuberance or joy. Utilizing a static camera with few close-ups, the film's visual style, using long extemporaneous scenes in single takes, eventually takes its toll on the viewer. The film's only humorous scene is when Tatsuro's girlfriend brings him home to her parent's apartment only for him to encounter her father, a former customer.

Smoke (1993, 90 min, US, Mark D'Auria)

An initially intriguing but ultimately trying independent film, *Smoke* borrows heavily from Martin Scorsese's seminal drama *Mean Streets*. Michael, a puffy, almost handsome 30-ish man is a bathroom attendant with a penchant for overweight, older men. With a laborious style and pretentious pacing, the film explores the clash between Michael's kinky obsessions and sexual desires and his Catholic guilt. Although the film is 100% queer, and the idea of a man's attraction to the antithesis of gay men's ideal (young, handsome, built and thin) is interesting, the film is slow going and is of interest mainly to patrons of the gay/lesbian film circuits. ⊛

> "Mark D'Auria has created a mini-masterpiece on very little pocket money...*Smoke* strings together as many eye-popping images as a Jane Campion film...an arresting, audacious debut."
>
> —*Out*

Some of My Best Friends Are...

(1971, 110 min, US, Mervyn Nelson)

Although made by a gay man, this independent melodrama's painfully clichéd depiction of gay stereotypes places the film squarely in the pre-liberation, "it's a lonely, pitiful life for a faggot" period. Originally titled *The Bar*, the film is set on one action-filled Christmas Eve at the Blue Jay, a Manhattan gay bar. Its habitués include vulnerable but acid-tongued drag queens, spiteful fag hags, sympathetic straights and confused closet cases. Dismissed on its limited release as a lurid *Boys in the Band* rip-off, the film is full of self-loathing with gays the seemingly helpless victims to an oppressive heterosexual majority. An important film in the evolution of gay filmmaking which, when seen today, simply borders on the ludicrously camp. An interesting cast includes Candy Darling, Fannie Flagg, jazz singer Sylvia Sims, David Drew and Carleton Carpenter.

> "It is almost as if the guests at Crowley's party (in *The Boys in the Band*) were so miserable because their alternative was the Blue Jay."
>
> —Vito Russo, *The Celluloid Closet*

Der Sprinter

Something for Everyone

(1970, 112 min, US/GB, Harold Prince)

Broadway director Harold Prince's directorial film debut is this witty black comedy that stars a seductive Michael York as a cunning, amoral opportunist who insinuates himself into the household of the flamboyant Countess von Ornstein of Bavaria (Angela Lansbury). Once inside, he proceeds to infiltrate the bedrooms of both her and her son. Lansbury camps it up wonderfully, acting as though she were a drag queen on stage at a New York fashion show, unveiling her fabulous frocks to an enraptured audience. Anthony Corlan plays Helmut, the countess' gay teenage son, whose dark and sullen good looks prove to be a nice contrast to York's fair complexion. When the two of them are in a canoe on a lake, Helmut accuses York of being able to sleep with anyone; York replies, "But I have my preferences" and the boy melts into his duplicitous arms. Jane Carr plays Lansbury's corpulent daughter who has the last laugh. Sly fun and sophistication abound in this charming gem. (GB title: *Black Flowers for the Bride*) ⊛

Song of the Loon (1970, 90 min, US)

Long considered a classic of independent gay filmmaking, *Song of the Loon* is an earnest tale of love and brotherhood among men as well as a naturalist's delight. Set in northern California in the 1870s, the story follows the odyssey of Ephraim McKeever, a young man in search of love and happiness. By using non-professional actors, not showing hard-core sex scenes and featuring such silly lines as "Dammit, you're beautiful," the film is at times awkward and dated, but it is also a welcome change from the normal X-rated fare that abounds. ⊛

A Special Day (1977, 124 min, Italy, Ettore Scola)

The day Hitler arrived in Rome to meet Mussolini in 1938 is the setting for this touching drama. Antonette (Sophia Loren), an oppressed housewife and mother of six, sees her children and husband off for the festivities, leaving her alone for the day. She meets and befriends Gabriel (Marcello Mastroianni), a tenent in the building. He soon reveals to her that he is a homosexual who has lost his job as a radio announcer because his secret was discovered. Having already lost his lover, who is in exile, Gabriel faces a troubled future in the homophobic Fascist state. These two opposite people are drawn together out of mutual fear, sadness and curiosity. They eventually make love, but to the film's credit, while Gabriel enjoys the closeness, he remains gay. Mastroianni received a nomination for an Oscar for this quietly revealing drama of sex and politics. ⊗

Spetters
(1981, 109 min, The Netherlands, Paul Verhoeven)
Three Dutch youths find themselves at the crossroads of adulthood in this arresting drama by Paul Verhoeven (*The 4th Man*). Seeking to escape their working-class destinies, they dream of fame and fortune racing motorcycles, but are sidetracked by the fateful intervention of a scheming hash-slinger (the sultry Renee Soutendijk). One of the youths (Toon Agterberg) is a closet case whose repressed sexual feelings are awakened when he is gang raped. He finds that he likes it rough and soon becomes lovers with Soutendijk's beefy brother. Emboldened by his new openness, he comes out to his father — who severely beats him. Bloodied but undaunted, he embraces his new lifestyle. ⊗

Der Sprinter
(1985, 90 min, Germany, Christoph Boll)
A witty social satire about a young closeted gay man who, in order to please his mother, decides to be "normal." Wieland Samolak portrays our confused hero, a pale, wide-eyed young man with expressionistic silent film star looks and a charming comedic touch. He chooses sports, specifically running, as his entrance into the straight world. His attempts at sports produce little until he meets and falls in love with a buxom butch female shot putter. Oh, the price to pay for conformity! ⊗

Squeeze
(1980, 89 min, New Zealand, Richard Turner)
A warm, engrossing drama that follows the dilemma of a businessman who falls for an effeminate teenage boy on the eve of his marriage. The first gay film from New Zealand, this serious, but often humorous soap opera takes an interesting look at bisexuality and the vagaries of love.

> "Superbly cast...a well observed study of a bisexual."
> —Stuart Byron, *The Village Voice*

Staircase *(1969, 96 min, GB, Stanley Donen)*
Considered by many to be one of the most insulting and homophobic pictures of all time, this disaster (which is "sadly" not available on home video in the United States) is an embarrassment for all involved. Based on Charles Dyer's play, this "comedy" features Rex Harrison (considered a card-carrying homophobe in his time) and Richard Burton as two aging, pathetic homosexuals (and hairdressers, natch) who after 20 years of living together in their dingy London flat, can't stand one another. Burton, as Harry, is the queen to Harrison's slightly more composed Charlie. Amidst their bickering (and total lack of affection), little incidents keep the wailing at a pitched level. Charlie brings home a number which puts Harry in a tailspin, and an attempted suicide. Charlie is arrested for doing drag at a gay bar and for solicitation when it is raided by the police; Harry, the poor little poof, has to gather his strength and stand by his man.

Viewing this in front of a well-intoxicated gay crowd would certainly prove to be a camp delight, but the underlying assumptions with which it was made are certainly disturbing, although one would think that with films like *Cruising, Partners* and *The Choirboys*, we would have toughened our collective skins and psyches. A contemporary audience looking beyond the dense layer of homo-hatred that envelopes the film can feel an intense sympathy for these characters who are trapped in a pre-Stonewall Cinemascope rendering of an intensely homophobic stage play.

> "Perhaps most actors are latent homosexuals and we cover it with drink. I was once a homo, but it didn't work."
> —Richard Burton in a *People* interview

Straight for the Heart
(1988, 92 min, Canada, Léa Pool)
Returning from a harrowing trip to Nicaragua, where he has witnessed and photographed the horrors of war, prize-winning photojournalist Pierre arrives home in Montreal only to find that Sarah and David, his lovers in a ten-year ménage à trois, have both left him. This absorbing drama, unusual for its matter-of-fact approach to bisexuality, explores the man's devastated life — from his futile attempts to reunite the threesome, to his pain and loneliness at being abandoned, to his recovery through the love of a handsome deaf-mute and his wanderings through the city photographing urban decay. An intriguing, melancholy love story and a quiet study of one man's emotional void; reminiscent in part to Alain Tanner's *In the White City*.

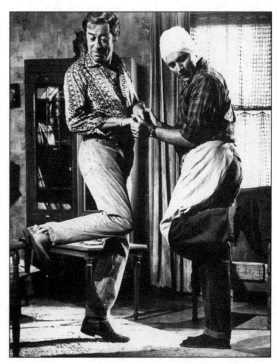

Staircase

A Strange Love Affair

(1985, 92 min, The Netherlands, Eric de Kuyper)
From the director of *Casta Diva* and the wicked sex comedy *Dear Boys* comes this unusual meditation on gay love. Beautifully shot in black and white and filmed in quasi-Hollywood "weepie" style (and throwing in many film references), the drama focuses on Michael, an English university film professor who falls in love with Chris, a rugby playing, classical guitar strumming student who he meets while teaching a class on Nicholas Ray's *Johnny Guitar*. While the two lovers are on a trip to Belgium, Michael meets Chris' father, who coincidentally was his lover many years before. The ensuing romances, both new and rekindled, are played out in an imaginative and melodramatic fashion.

The Strange One

(1957, 97 min, US, Jack Garfein)
Calder Willingham's sensational screenplay, based on his own controversial Broadway play "End as a Man," is a bit toned down, but retains enough innuendo for the *Daily Herald* to remark at the time, "This is the first English-language film ever to portray a homosexual. It does so in an adult, non-sniggering way." The story, set in a Southern military college, is about Jocko de Paris, a sadistic cadet (a creepily dangerous Ben Gazzara in his screen debut) who rules over the others. It takes one brave cadet (the gay!) to lead a group of freshmen against the bullying menace. A weird and compelling drama that was surprisingly frank for its time. Also starring George Peppard, Pat Hingle and Julie Wilson.

Strawberry and Chocolate *(1993, 110*

min, Cuba, Tomás Guitiérrez & Juan Carlos Tabío)
Both a delightful comedy of friendship and love as well as a surprisingly critical political drama, *Strawberry and Chocolate* also has what is surely one of the best drawn gay characters in film. The tale, set in modern-day Havana, centers on the unlikely friendship between David (Jorge Perugorría), a shy, straight and lost soul who blindly believes in the righteousness of the Revolution, and Diego (Vladimir Cruz), a swishy but intelligent, witty and opinionated gay man (and opera queen). Diego, who initially lusts after the innocently attractive college student, soon seduces him, not through gay sex, but by his free-thinking appreciation of art (Communist as well as the illicit Western), the "enemy's drug" (Johnny Walker Red) and his effervescent personality. With Diego's gentle teaching, David learns to take his political blinders off and in the process opens himself up to the differences in people — both politically and sexually. Also prominent in David's re-education is Nancy (Marta Ibarra), Diego's fag-hag neighbor who amusingly initiates the virgin David in the ways of love. In the person of the flamboyant, defiantly gay Diego, we see a man who stands tall and remains outspokenly combative despite a lifetime of criticism, censorship and eventual abandonment by the people and country he loves.

Streamers *(1983, 118 min, US, Robert Altman)*

Director Robert Altman utilizes the intensity of the theatrical experience with the opportunities offered through film in this adaptation of David Rabe's award-winning play. *Streamers* is an ensemble piece, set in a claustrophobic Army barracks, featuring four ill-assorted young soldiers waiting for assignments to Vietnam. The men must grapple with their hidden fears and prejudices which, in turn, generate sexual intolerance, racial distrust and a misunderstanding that leads to violence. This carefully crafted work stars David Alan Grier as Roger, a quiet, moderate black; Matthew Modine as Bill, an intellectual farm boy haunted by insecurities; Mitchell Lichtenstein as Richie, a gay Ivy-Leaguer who taunts his bunkmates with truths and half-truths; and Michael Wright as Carlyle, a street-wise black, tense and confused, and the catalyst for the film's unforgettable climax. The entire cast won the Golden Lion Award for Best Acting at the Venice Film Festival. ⊛

Street Kid

(1990, 89 min,
Germany, Peter Kern)
With a lion's mane of pompadoured hair, skin-tight jeans, flashy cowboy boots and a cocky attitude, 14-year-old Axel prowls the mean streets of Dusseldorf selling his body to pederasts — all of whom are out to taste forbidden fruit. Similar to *Christiane F.* in depicting the gritty and harsh life of teenagers on the streets, the film's sardonic humor keeps it from being somber as it follows the bisexual Axel, who, despite abusive parents (his own father rapes him at one point), possesses a fun-loving and tender attitude. Life takes an unexpected change for the boy after he meets an unhappily married man who falls in love with him. ⊛

Streamers

Strip Jack Naked — Nighthawks II

(1991, 60 min, GB, Ron Peck)
Intercutting outtakes from his groundbreaking 1978 gay film *Nighthawks* (reportedly the first independent gay film made in Great Britain) with new footage, director Ron Peck narrates this personal journey of sexual and political self-discovery and growth and links it with the nascent 1970s gay liberation movement as well. In this mesmeric documentary, the director recounts his childhood growing up a closeted gay, his first forays into the secretive gay world of the London bar and pick-up scenes, and his determination to make a film about that lifestyle. The best sequences are the ones describing the 1970s world of gay men's sexual abandonment, where liberation meant having sex with as many men as you could. It is the change of thinking from the sexual to the social and political that changed both the life of the director as well as the direction of the gay movement. A fascinating subject in gay history, made with great insight and feeling.

The Sum of Us *(1994, 100 min, Australia, Kevin Dowling & Geoff Burton)*

From the 1991 off-Broadway play comes this endearing family comedy-drama about the unusual relationship between a father and his son. Set in a working-class area of Sydney, the story centers around the widowed but fun-loving Harry (Jack Thompson) and his football-playing son Jeff (Russell Crowe). What makes their story so different is that dad not only knows that his twentysomething son is gay, but is quite enthusiastic and accepting of it, hoping that he eventually will find Mr. Right. The reasons for this attitude is both his strong love for Jeff and the fact that his own mother, after her husband died, became involved in a 40-year love affair with another woman. With wit and charm, the two men's wacky home life is explored. Jeff falls hard for a handsome gardener and dad finds temporary happiness with a widow. Funny, tender and just a bit maudlin, the film breaks many sexual stereotypes, barriers and taboos. In many respects a groundbreaking film in dealing openly and evenhandedly with homosexuality.

Super 8½

(1994, 85 min, Canada, Bruce La Bruce)
A mild disappointment after his audacious debut with *No Skin Off My Ass*, Bruce LaBruce's (BLaB) much anticipated second film is a surprisingly hard-core (much graphic sex — yes, cum shots and all), film-within-a-film autobiographical drama that, while containing fascinating scenes, is a structural mess. BLaB himself stars as a washed-up porn star/filmmaker whose life of "It's not who you know it's who you blow" loses some of its bite when his talents are not wanted. Living off his hustler boyfriend, Pierce (Klaus Von Brücker), his life is changed when lesbian underground filmmaker Googie (Liza LaMonica) begins making an experimental movie on his life (she's also working on her own opus, *Submit to My Finger*). LaBruce, who reminds one of a more romantic but sexually aggressive Gregg Araki, shows off his cocksucking abilities to good effect; but while all of the sex is appreciated, it bogs down the movement of a potentially interesting tale. Also featured is "Kids in the Hall" star Scott Thompson, as former porn star Buddy Cole, and fellow independent filmmaker R. Kern.

Swann in Love

(1984, 115 min, France, Volker Schlöndorff)
Volker Schlöndorff beautifully renders the emotional intricacies and period flavor of gay author Marcel Proust's illustrious "Swann's Way." Jeremy Irons is the dashing, cultivated Charles Swann who loses his heart and esteem in a passionate tryst with a pouting courtesan (Ornella Muti). A sparkling ensemble of supporting players includes Alain Delon, Fanny Ardant and Marie-Christine Barrault. ⊛

Swoon *(1992, 95 min, US, Tom Kalin)*

The scandalous 1924 murder trial of Nathan Leopold and Richard Loeb for the inexplicable murder of a young boy is given a slightly tilted, definitely New Queer Cinema treatment in this intriguing independent feature that will certainly fascinate some and probably frustrate and upset others. Filmed in grainy black and white, homosexual lovers Leopold and Loeb, both intelligent college students from wealthy Jewish families, get their visceral and sexual kicks in petty crimes. Their intense but perverted love culminates in a bungled scheme to kidnap a boy, resulting in the boy's cold-blooded killing. The two are eventually tracked down by the police, arrested, tried and sentenced to life in prison. But director Tom Kalin's real interest lies less in the horrendous act of the unlikely criminals and more with the lovers' secretive, intense and self-destructive relationship. A controversial, compelling story, guaranteed to stir debate even within the gay community. Other films adapted from the notorious murder are Alfred Hitchcock's *Rope* and Richard Fleischer's *Compulsion*. ⊛

Le Symphonie Pastorale

(1946, 105 min, France, Jean Delannoy)
The only film version of an André Gide novel, this romantic drama won the Best Film award at Cannes in 1946 and tells the story of a blind orphan girl (Michele Morgan) who is taken into a Swiss family where both the father (Pierre Blanchar) and his son (Jean Desailly) fall in love with her, only to meet with tragic consequences. Cooly directed by Jean Delannoy (also the director of Jean Cocteau's *The Eternal Return*).

Focus on: *André Gide*

Although La Symphonie Pastorale is the only film adaptation of André Gide's work, this Nobel Prize-winning novelist deserves mention here for his outspoken defense of homosexuality. In 1924, Gide wrote two works, "Si le grain ne Meurt (If It Die)," in which he discussed his homosexual experiences while traveling in North Africa, and his startling "Croydon," a book that eloquently defended homosexuality. Born in Paris in 1869, Gide's most famous novel is "L'Immoraliste (The Immoralist)," a story about a repressed homosexual written in 1902, the English translation of which was not permitted to be published until 1930. He also wrote "The Counterfeiters" and "Lafcadio's Adventures" as well as several plays, essays and travel books. He was a friend of Oscar Wilde, reportedly with a fascination with Arab boys, and had a relationship with French producer/director Marc Allegret. Interestingly, two years after his death, a New York stage production of "The Immoralist" starred the young James Dean.

Tao Yinn: The Chinese Art of Self-Massage *(1987, 90 min, US, Alan Carrol)*

It's a wonder that with all of these secret "ancient Chinese techniques" for self-relaxation and self-massage that there are so many Chinese! Tao Yinn, the "ancient Chinese" method that delves into the stress relief and self-relaxation benefits resulting from the manipulation of one's own energy centers, is demonstrated step by step by master Neil Tucker. ☯

Tarch Trip
(1993, 64 min, Japan/Germany, Hiriyuki Oki)

This low-budget experimental film, in all probability the work of a young gay Japanese film student, explores boredom, sexual longing and desire. Primarily a silent film (street noise makes up much of the soundtrack), this *nouveau vague* exercise is composed of lingering static shots of urban life as witnessed by a forlorn teen and his friends from the balcony of his second floor flat. The result of all this posturing is an effectively thoughtful and minimalistic treatise on the numbing effect of everyday life and the elusiveness of love. One very short hard-core depiction of the youth masturbating provides a jarring counterpoint to the rest of the meditative scenes.

Taxi Zum Klo
(1980, 94 min, West Germany, Frank Ripploh)

The consciousness and perception of gay men was revealed to a surprisingly large heterosexual audience when this witty and charming, but controversial social comedy opened theatrically in the United States in 1981. Unflinchingly honest and unpretentious, this first film by director-screenwriter-star Frank Ripploh is a "warts and all" portrait of one gay man's lifestyle. The film unabashedly presents scenes of promiscuous pre-AIDS sex, including tea room sex romps and thirst-quenching water sports, that could not be shown in today's more conservative climate. Frank stars as a secondary schoolteacher alternating between his "straight" work life and his nocturnal homosexual leisure activities. His sexual cavortings are temporarily halted when he falls in love with a movie theatre manager who believes in home life and monogamy. One of the many humorous sex scenes features Frank in a public rest room where he, seated on a toilet, begins grading exams while fondling genitals thrust at him through a glory hole and pondering whether or not to attend the faculty's weekly bowling match. Made on a budget of $50,000 (and no government subsidies), this engaging autobiographical travelogue is a brash, invigorating work which considers the dilemmas of gay fidelity and intimacy without succumbing to maudlin sentimentality or cynicism. ☯

> "A breezy, funny, aggressively candid autobiography."
> —Vincent Canby, *The New York Times*

> "The best and brightest film made in Germany in the last few years!"
> —Elliott Stein, *Film Comment*

> "The first masterpiece about the mainstream of male gay life!"
> —Stuart Byron, *The Village Voice*

Taxi Nach Kairo
(1989, 90 min, Germany, Frank Ripploh)

Frank Ripploh's follow-up to his gay classic *Taxi Zum Klo* is a disappointing let down. Retaining his autobiographical roots, this comedy concerns Frank's mom and her persistent attempts to have Frank end his S&M ways, find a nice girl, get married and claim the family's inheritance (a similarly themed but altogether funnier version of this tale is *Too Much Sun*). Frank, who would rather fight than switch, finds an airline stewardess who agrees, for a price, to pose as his betrothed, but with an Almodóvar-inspired outrageousness, his well-laid plans fall apart in a farcical finale which includes a free-for-all between mom, Frank, his "wife," his neighbor (and his former lover) and a muscle-bound cop. Overall frustratingly tame, with none of the sexual explicitness or fresh originality of his debut effort.

Tea and Sympathy
(1956, 123 min, US, Vincente Minnelli)

Adapted (and watered-down) by Robert Anderson from his own Broadway play, this tale of a sensitive teen (John Kerr) at a New England boarding school who is falsely accused of being a homosexual is frustratingly tame and queerly unsatisfying. Kerr plays a 17-year-old boy from a broken home who is accused by his bullying schoolmates of being a "sister boy" after being seen sewing buttons on his shirt and refusing to play football. Deborah Kerr is the headmaster's wife who, frustrated by the lack of attention from her husband (Leif Erikson), befriends the boy and eventually exorcises any of his latent homosexual leanings by sleeping with him. Due to restrictions imposed by the Hayes Code and religious organizations, the film ignores any homosexual longing by either the youth or the repressed headmaster. A misdirected plea for tolerance, not for gays, but for boys who are different; less macho, but still straight. ☮

Tenderness of the Wolves
(1973, 90 min, Germany, Ulli Lommel)

With queer vampirism usually taking a lesbian angle, this creepy low-budget shocker offers the viewer a gay blood sucker, albeit a sick, murderous one. Adapted from the same story that inspired Fritz Lang's *M*, Rainer Werner Fassbinder regular (and Peter Lorre look-alike) Kurt Raab stars as the sleazy predator who lures pretty young boys to his attic lair and there, strips them of their clothing and has his way sexually before sucking their blood. Topping off his treachery, he sells off their body parts as meat to unsuspecting buyers. Filming the scenes with a tantalizing mix of titillation, gore and black comedy, this low-budget gem is both disturbing and oddly entertaining. Featuring Fassbinder (who also produced the film), Ingrid Caven and Jürgen Prochnow.

Thailand: Through a Traveler's Eyes
(1990, 60 min, US)

Similar to *Every Night in Thailand*, this film chronicles the sexual antics of Thailand's notorious gay bars, but with additional tourist-oriented coverage of Bangkok, Pattaya and Chang Mai. ☯

That Certain Summer
(1972, 73 min, US, Lamont Johnson)

This landmark television movie, which for the first time brought the issue of homosexuality into the homes of millions of

Taxi Zum Klo

Americans, is a solid, sensitive drama. Hal Holbrook gives a great performance as a divorced man who, after his visiting 14-year-old son learns he is gay, must open up and discuss it with him. Martin Sheen is Holbrook's lover and while these two stars play gay, there is no passion nor kissing between the two. The film is earnest in its intent to be positive about the subject, but it is not entirely successful — for in what might be an appeasement of right-wing homophobes, Holbrook confesses that, "A lot of people — most people, I guess — think it's wrong. They say it's a sickness, that it is something that has to be cured. I don't know. I do know that it isn't easy. If I had a choice, it's not something I'd pick for myself."

The Third Sex
(1958, 77 min, Germany, Frank Winterstein)
Intriguingly contemporary, especially for its time and place (West Germany in the mid-1950s), this historically important potboiler melodrama features a gay relationship torn apart by a mother and father determined to make their son "normal." Klaus, a sleek, handsome teenager, is in a relationship with fellow classmate Manfred, an effete, pouting blond. By making no effort to conceal their closeness, the two soon become the talk of the school. Klaus' domineering father, aghast at his son's "sickness," goes about trying to break the two apart. And while dad's off making trouble for his son's gay friends, his alternately sympathetic and calculating mom plots to get the pretty maid into her wayward son's bed. Family troubles really mount, however, when mom is sent to jail

for "procuring prostitution." But it's a small price to pay after Klaus drops the lovelorn Manfred and aggressively (a little too much perhaps?) embraces heterosexuality. Notwithstanding the ridiculous ending, the film is quite extraordinary in its depiction of gays, society's extremist reaction to them and the clash between the old Germany and the new. There's plenty of lingering handshakes and romantic touches between the two lovers and several of the film's characters offer spirited defenses of homosexuality (the word is never actually spoken) and there is even a trip to a lively drag bar. The most interesting character in the film, however, is not the self-sacrificing pimp mom, but Boris Winkler, a 50-year-old sweet talking devil who attracts young men to his home and "corrupts" them with electronic music and the appreciation of modern art, poetry and literature, with some Greek wrestling thrown in. Corruption was never so intoxicating. Also on the video with *The Third Sex* is *Vapors* (1965, 25 min, US, Gerald Jackson). Set in the notorious St. Mark's Bathhouse, this fascinating, stagey short film deals with anonymous sexual encounters and the craving for love and intimacy. A nervous young man visits the bathhouse for the first time and, despite taunts from the bevy of nelly queens who roam the hallways, meets an older, sexually confused married man. But instead of just the standard quickie, the two engage in thoughtful conversation dealing with desire, intimacy and soul searching. Like *The Boys in the Band*, made five years later, the film is both tender and understanding towards the "anguish" of homosexuality. ⊛

This Special Friendship

(1964, 99 min, France, Jean Delannoy)
Set in a Catholic boarding school in France, this love story smolders with the youthful homoerotic bonds between several boys in the school. Their love and friendship is touching and beautifully handled by director Jean Delannoy. ⊛

> "A masterpiece...shocking in the best sense of the word!"
> —*Los Angeles Times*

Focus On: *Roger Peyrefitte*

"Special Friendship," from which this film was adapted, was the first novel of openly gay writer Roger Peyrefitte. Written in 1944, Peyrefitte said of the two boys' releationship, "The two boys enter into their relationship of their own volition... it is a subtle way of showing that homosexual feelings are perfectly natural and not automatically the result of an 'incitement to immoral behavior.'" He explained that his writing was an act of defiance against the Diplomatic Service where he was employed at the time. A prolific writer of novels and essays and an outspoken voice for gay rights in his native France, Peyrefitte's other novels include "Diplomatic Conversations," "The Exile of Capri," "The Jews" and his latest, "Voltaire e Frederic II."

Threesome

(1994, 93 min, US, Andrew Fleming)
Another mini-leap forward for Hollywood in its willingness to include gay, lesbian and bisexual characters in its films. This often perceptive and funny story revolves around the friendship and evolving sexual relations between three college students sharing the same dorm suite. Stephen Baldwin is Stuart, a droopy-eyed, sex-obsessed jock, Eddy (Josh Charles) is the "sexually ambivalent" (Hollywood code word for gay) narrator and roommate and Alex (Lara Flynn Boyle) is the sexually aggressive woman mistakenly assigned to their room. Complications arise when love and lust rears its ugly head — Alex has the hots for Eddy who has his eyes on the well-formed butt of Stuart who wants to jump the bones of the disinterested Alex. Sure it's "high concept," but what saves the film from being tiresome and predictable (although there are really no surprises) is the witty script which is crammed with hilariously accurate thoughts and comments on gays, straights and today's college life. When one examines the film's gay/bisexual politics, however, the film falls apart. Eddy is seen as a sexually confused young man who is probably gay with slightly straight leanings. But what the film's narration describes, and how the plot develops, are two entirely different matters. To make the character palpable for American audiences, Eddy is made a gay virgin who during the course of the film has spirited sex with a woman on several occasions, violently rejects the advances of a gay student, develops a hazy, almost platonic crush on roommate Stuart and when the climactic threesome sex scene happens, the only gay action is Eddy gingerly placing his hand on the naked backside of straight man Stuart. No kisses, no groping, no sex, no threat America!

Its gay outlook makes *Philadelphia* seem like gay porn by comparison. With the release of this film, *Reality Bites*, *Three of Hearts*, *Naked in New York* and the aforementioned *Philadelphia*, Hollywood is beginning to feel comfortable including gay charac-

This Special Friendship

ters in the story line. And although this seems like a radical step in the queer direction, so far these films are all mildly disappointing and certainly frustrating in developing realistic, sexually active, non-sexually confused queer characters who show outward interest and affection for members of their own sex. Actor Josh Charles has exacerbated things in interviews in which he complains how hard it was to play a gay! The one other gay character in the film is completely out Alexis Arquette who plays an alternately aggressive and coquettish student/desk clerk who is interested in Eddy, but well before hands or lips meet, Eddy flees in horror as if he was doing a Stephen Rea imitation from *The Crying Game*. ⊛

> "I play a quintessential fag role...When I say 'fag,' I don't mean homosexual, I mean *fag*. I'm not really proud of that role. For gays, it's not a good thing."
> —Alexis Arquette

> "I thought it would be nice to have a film where the lead is no Mr. Victim or Mr. Swish or Mr. Psychopath... (although) it wasn't my intention to further any kind of gay agenda. I wanted to present a normal gay character who folks would identify with...non-gays included."
> —Openly gay director Andrew Fleming

Time Off *(1990, 45 min, Israel, Eytan Fox)*

Though only 45 minutes long, this daring drama is of great interest because it is the first Israeli movie to deal with homosexuality in the military. Set at the outbreak of the 1982 invasion of Lebanon, a young gay soldier, before he is sent off to basic training, breaks off from his colleagues and wanders through the streets of Jerusalem.

While cruising a park, he meets, to his amazement, his burly, macho lieutenant. A passionately intense and absorbing tale.

To Catch a Killer

(1991, 95 min, Canada, Eric Till)
The police investigation and arrest of serial killer John Wayne Gacy is the subject of this crime drama that has been significantly edited down from its original miniseries length. Rather than being cheap sensationalistic exploitation, the film is actually quite suspenseful and sensitive to the fears of gays that he would be unfairly associated with them. In fact, the film never mentions the words "gay" or "homosexual," yet never flinches from dealing with Gacy's sexual attraction to teenage boys. Brian Dennehy is believable as the demented Gacy, a stocky construction contractor who was eventually sent to death row for kidnapping, sexually torturing and killing at least 33 teenage boys and then burying their bodies in the dirt basement of his Illinois home. Without the mystery of whodunit, the film instead focuses on the police's frantic efforts to track down the mass murderer. A determined young detective (Michael Riley) takes charge of the case, and when evidence is only circumstantial, he engages a cocky Gacy in a cat-and-mouse game as they slowly piece together the evidence needed for an arrest. Margot Kidder is featured as a psychic who aids the police (actually the silliest part of the film). Sad, creepy and riveting. ⊛

To an Unknown God
(A Un Dios Desconocido)

(1978, 95 min, Spain, Jaime Chavarri)
This evocative and richly detailed, if somewhat confusing and enigmatic contemporary memoir is a meditation on growing old, homosexuality, Franco's dictatorship and, especially, the poetry of Federico Jose Lorca. Jose, a gay magician who lives with a somewhat younger and affectionate lover, is suffering a middle-age crisis which leads him on a journey of self-discovery through his past. This obsession directs him to his childhood town of Granada and to the home of gay poet and political activist Federico Jose Lorca, triggering a traumatic memory from 30 years before when he, while making love to Lorca's brother in the garden, witnesses the assassination of the poet. A complex film which openly depicts the characters' homosexuality in a frank, non-sensational fashion.

"...handsome, densely packed...lovely to look at, highly cultivated and poised and very, very difficult to get to know."
—Vincent Canby, *The New York Times*

Together Alone

(1991, 87 min, US, P.J. Castellaneta)
Winner of the "Teddy Bear" for Best Gay Feature at the 1992 Berlin Film Festival, this sensual, funny and perceptive two-character drama is set entirely in a single bedroom and bed. Two men, who met anonymously at a gay bar, have just had (unsafe) sex, but instead of the usual kiss on the cheek and "I've got to go...," the two begin to talk well into the night. Bryan, who lives in the apartment, is an out and outspoken gay while Brian is a married bisexual with a complicated past. Filmed in black and white, the two men discuss and argue about a wide range of issues:

AIDS, sexual responsibility, dreams, betrayal, the cause of homosexuality, honesty, loneliness, abortion and relationships. Their attempts to understand one another and reveal something of themselves is both believable and forceful. With a reported budget of $7,000, P.J. Castellaneta, the director, writer, producer and (as listed in the credits) caterer, has made an intellectually invigorating queer drama, and the actors Todd Stites (Bryan) and Terry Curry (Brian) are perfectly cast as the two "strangers in the night" who stop just long enough to feel, learn and understand. ⊛

"...sensitive, funny, daring and timely...Castellaneta is probably a born filmmaker and *Together Alone* is almost good enough to give one-night stands a good name."
—Jay Scott, *Toronto Globe & Mail*

Tosca's Kiss

(1984, 87 min, Switzerland, Daniel Schmid)
Casa Verdi, the home for retired opera singers established by Guiseppi Verdi in 1902 in Milan, provides the setting for this affectionate and often funny tribute to the elderly denizens of the once elegant palace. The stars of this documentary are the aging, but still vibrant opera singers who shamelessly perform, argue and preen before the camera. The film is enlightening, surprisingly humorous and quite moving. ⊛

Focus on: *Daniel Schmid*

Swiss director Daniel Schmid, quite popular in his native country for both filmmaking and the direction of operas, was one of Rainer Werner Fassbinder's first lovers. Reportedly, just days before his overdose death in 1982, Fassbinder talked with Schmid and promised him that he had flushed all of his drugs down the toilet, a less than truthful confession. Other films directed by Schmid include Hecate, *starring Lauren Hutton, and* Notre Dame de la Croisette, *featuring Bulle Ogier.*

Track Two *(1982, 90 min, Canada,*
Harry Sutherland, Jack Lemmon & Gordon Keith)
In 1981, the normally placid city of Toronto erupted, becoming a prejudice-fueled battleground between Christian fundamentalists and police on one side and gays and lesbians fighting for their rights on the other. This conflagration was ignited when the police orchestrated a series of raids on several gay bathhouses. "Track 2," police slang for the gay/lesbian area of the city ("Track 1" is for the red light district), soon became a maelstrom of controversy as the city was torn apart, and tensions escalated to the point of violence. Indiscriminately labeled "criminals" by the police, the gays and lesbians soon organized and eventually formed a community and became a powerful political force. The film re-creates the police raids and mass arrests, records the midnight marches for justice, and interviews many of the people involved and, in turn, creates a raw but stirring account of nascent gay solidarity.

"*Track Two* is easily the best documentary yet made about what it means to be gay in North America. Honest, intelligent and full of wit and courage, *Track Two* must also be seen by the straight audience."
—*The Hollywood Reporter*

Tracks in the Snow

(1984, 95 min,
Norway, Orlow Seunke)

This remarkable film maps the psychological and sometimes physical combat that ensues between two wildly different brothers who embark on an arduous journey through the bitter Scandinavian winter to attend to their dying father. The brothers, Simon, a down-at-the-heels gay cabaret performer who has been disowned by his father, and Hein, an imperious and wealthy stockbroker, are thrown together for the first time in twenty years. Reminiscent of the films of Ingmar Bergman and Fassbinder, the tale is structured as a thriller, complete with slowly discovered twists and revelations and a dazzling finale. Simon's homosexuality, an obvious cause for the estrangement between him and his father and brother, is interestingly handled — it is Simon who is loving, understanding and forgiving with his straight brother, who harbors hate and despair.

The Two of Us

Le Triche (The Cheat)

(1984, 101 min, France, Yannick Bellon)

The prototypical French police thriller is given an interesting gay angle in this surprisingly big box-office winner in France. The film follows a bisexual Bordeaux police inspector (Victor Lanoux of *Cousin, Cousine*) whose professional and family life is laid open to possible ruin when he becomes involved with Bernard, a handsome young musician who is also the prime suspect in a murder. The decision to arrest, protect or believe in the innocence of his new lover, as well as his co-workers' increased suspicions about his sexuality, combine to create a riveting, satisfying actioner.

La Triche

Turnabout: The Story of the Yale Puppeteers

(1993, 58 min, US, Dan Bessie)

Another hitherto unknown chapter of gay history is unearthed in this amusing and fascinating account of the lives of Harry Burnett, Forman Brown and Roddy Brandon, founders of the Turnabout Theater — a traveling comedy and musical puppet troupe which captivated thousands of children and adults with their witty skits and satirical songs from the 1930s through the '60s. Playwright-novelist Brown and producer Brandon, lovers for over 50 years, and Brown's cousin Burnett, who lived with them, were the guiding force behind the successful troupe, which included such regulars as Odetta and Elsa Lanchester. Using archival footage, home movies and interviews with Burnett and Brown, now both in their 90s, the film not only captures an innocent entertainment era, but also documents an enduring and productive relationship between three gay men.

Twinkle *(1992, 103 min, Japan, George Matsuoka)*

With the almost simultaneous release of *Okoge, The Slight Fever of a 20-Year-Old, The Wedding Banquet* and this hugely entertaining comedy-drama, 1992 seems to be a watershed year for gay filmmaking in Japan. A closeted gay doctor and an alcoholic young woman are forced by their "concerned" parents into an arranged marriage. The man, Mutsuki, drops his college student lover for the sake of conformity while Shoko, an effervescent dynamo who wonderfully suggests a young Audrey Hepburn with balls, takes the marriage in stride, working on her job as a translator, not expecting sex and hitting the bottle with wreckless abandon. But when the free-thinking Shoko encourages her husband to resume his affair with his lover, he, the lover and both sets of parents are thrown into a tailspin. This comedic melodrama, fueled by a memorable performance by Hiroko Yakushimaru as Shoko, is great fun, offering both a rarely glimpsed view of the "new Japanese woman" as well as depicting a fair, balanced view of a gay relationship.

The Two of Us *(1987, 75 min, GB, Roger Tonge)*

This touching story of two teenage boys in love has had a tumultuous history since it was made in 1987 for the BBC Schools TV series "Scene." Repelled by the film's pro-gay stance, and propelled by the repressive Clause 28 — a government directive that called for sex education classes to stop teaching that homosexuality is an acceptable form of human behavior — the BBC initially withdrew the film and finally broadcast it only after several cuts and a new "choose straight" ending. But now on video, with the cuts and original ending restored, it can be seen; although currently only in the U.K. The story, written by Leslie Stewart, concerns the deepening friendship between Matthew, a handsome youth and recent high school graduate, and his best mate Phil, an outgoing senior. He begins to realize that he has sexual feelings for his friend but vacillates between him and his girlfriend. Tired of the taunts of "nancy boys" from Phil's classmates and harassment from their friends, family and authorities, the two go off to a seaside resort defiantly telling people that they are on their "honeymoon." But Phil's indecision about commitment and his bisexual leanings put a strain on their budding relationship. A sensitive, sweetly romantic and ultimately uplifting story of love and being true to one's self. ⊛

Under Heat

(1992, 102 min, US, Peter Reed)

Peter Reed, a dancer and filmmaker of short films, died of AIDS in May 1994 in his home in Manhattan at the age of 40, just a month before this, his feature film debut, premiered at the San Francisco Lesbian and Gay International Film Festival. Filmed in an "American Playhouse"-style fashion, the family drama centers on the summer visit of Dean (Eric Swanson) to his rural New York

Turnabout: The Story of the Yale Puppeteers

A Very Natural Thing

family of brother Milo (Robert Kneeper) and his mother (Lee Grant). Ostensibly, his return is to tell his family that he is HIV-positive, but troubles with his drug-addicted brother and his mother's cancer scare contribute in keeping his revelation a secret. Swanson's Dean character, a somewhat queeny New Yorker, is the film's weakest part (although Swanson's acting ability is suspect). It is hard to believe that he, at the age of 36 and almost clonish in demeanor, is not out to his bohemian mother and easy-going brother. The other characters, especially Grant (who has by far the best lines) as a flighty mom, are well developed and the occasional humor helps relieve the tensions generated by the intensely raw emotions that pour out of each family member. The film's sappy approach and predictability undermine an otherwise worthy effort.

Vaudeville

(1990, 55 min, US, Ira Sachs)

Filmed in stark black and white, this drama about the childish infighting among the seven members of a dreadfully awful vaudeville troupe is notable primarily for the group's mostly gay and lesbian makeup. While playing to near-empty houses in backwater towns of the rural South, a group of young performers, strained by their own lack of talent and a genuine dislike for each other, succumb to vicious mind games, attempted seductions and family-like arguing. The film's matter-of-fact approach to the members' sexuality is refreshing, although their quarrelsome and bitchy nature will make many glad that the film is only 55 minutes long.

A Very Natural Thing

(1973, 85 min, US, Christopher Larkin)

An important film in the history of American gay filmmaking, *A Very Natural Thing* is considered the first feature film on the gay experience made by an out-of-the-closet gay to receive commercial distribution. The simple but insightful story involves a 26-year-old gay man who leaves the priesthood and moves to New York City in the hopes of finding a meaningful gay relationship. Now a school-teacher, he soon falls in love with a handsome young advertising executive. While detractors find the film a bit too sappy and soap opera-ish, others see it as sensitively told and refreshingly romantic.

> "The idea of a film about gay relationships and gay liberation themes come out of my own personal reaction to the mindless, sex-obsessed image of the homosexual prevalent in gay porno films."
>
> —director Christopher Larkin.

> "A breakthrough in the portrayal of homosexuals on the screen."
>
> —*Los Angeles Times*

Via Appia *(1991, 90 min, Germany, Jochen Hick)*

When Frank, a young German flight attendant, wakes up after a one-night stand with a street hustler in Rio, he finds scrawled on the bathroom mirror, "Welcome to the AIDS club." Back in Germany with the disease beginning to take hold of him, he decides to return to Brazil (with an accompanying film crew) to find the prostitute, having only his name, Mario, as a lead. The grim search, all set in a film-within-a-film style, involves combing the sleazy bathhouses, back streets and even a beach known as the "AIDS Farm," inquiring as to Mario's whereabouts. He interviews various male prostitutes and lowlifes in what soon becomes, for Frank and his film crew, a meandering, existential odyssey. With time running out, the young man's longing to find the "cause" of his impending death is both gut-wrenching and disturbing. A powerful and suspenseful story filled with sexy images of an unapologetically hedonistic netherworld which continues unabated despite the looming spectre of AIDS. ☻

Villain *(1971, 98 min, GB, Michael Tuchner)*

Coming off his pitiful role of the despondent fag Harry in *Staircase*, Richard Burton butches it over-the-top in this sordid and extremely violent crime drama set in London's East End. Possibly inspired by the gay crime boss in *Performance*, Burton plays Vic Dakin, a brutal yet craven homosexual thug who commands a band of gangsters. Vic is a nasty piece of celluloid evil — a leering killer with an obsessive devotion to mom (Cathleen Nesbitt) and an equally obsessive sadistic streak towards his enemies. ☻

The Virgin Soldiers

(1969, 96 min, GB, John Dexter)

Beautiful cinematography enhances this little-known gem about the end of innocence (both sexually and otherwise) for a group of young British recruits going to battle in 1950s Singapore. A dewy-fresh Lynn Redgrave stars as the girl who escorts one of the boys (Hywell Bennett) into manhood. ☻

Focus on: *John Dexter*

John Dexter, who died in 1990 during heart surgery, directed three films, The Virgin Soldiers, I Want What I Want *(1971) and* Sidelong Glances of a Pigeon-Kicker *(1970), but his true fame was being one of England's greatest theatre and opera directors. His long career included stints at the National Theatre (with productions such as "Othello" with Laurence Olivier and "The Royal Hunt of the Sun"), West End productions ("Equus" being one of his most successful) and a turn in America as the head of New*

We Were One Man

York's Metropolitan Opera, albeit a problem-plagued stewardship. He successfully worked with playwrights Peter Shaffer and Peter Hall and directed such luminaries as Diana Rigg, Alec McCowen, Joan Plowright, Rudolf Nureyev and Maria Callas. Some of his most recent productions include "M. Butterfly" and "Threepenny Opera" which starred Sting. Despite an illustrious career, Dexter had an unenviable reputation as a catty, difficult, temperamental, even vicious director who was known for his run-ins with actors. In his autobiography, "The Honorable Beast: A Posthumous Autobiography," he writes of his friend, Academy Award-winning actor Anthony Hopkins, "A shifty, spineless Welsh cunt. Has AA helped him? I don't think so, once a cunt always a Welshman." He is survived by his longtime companion, actor Riggs O'Hara.*

Vito and the Others

(1992, 90 min, Italy, Antonio Capuano)

Pubescent, angel-faced boys rove the streets of a decaying Naples terrorizing all with their petty crimes, drug dealing and prostitution in this lurid *Pixote*-influenced "exposé" on urban hopelessness. Twelve-year-old Vito, living with abusive relatives after his father wipes out his family in a murderous rampage, joins up with a band of future juvenile delinquents who cut school and spend their time robbing homes, knocking over old ladies and setting homeless men on fire. Sent to a prison after a busted drug deal, he slips further away after he is repeatedly raped by a 16-year-old. He returns to the streets a hardened hooligan, indifferent to emotion or love. Violent and chilling, the film's over-the-top vision of a society submerged in poverty and numbed by senseless crime features a cast made up largely of non-professionals infusing the film with moments of realism; but unlike *Pixote*, we never get to know much about young Vito, nor do we care much about his vicious anti-social behavior. While the film is essentially straight, the camera often lingers over the many boys in various stages of undress and keeps with its theme of total corruption by presenting the only gay person as a sleazy pederast who takes pleasure in seducing cute young boys for a few lira. ☻

"Voluptuous innocence slowly drifts into poverty and decay, as these children are inexorably dragged into a world of crime and violence."

—*Variety*

We Are There *(1976, 25 min, US, Pat Rocco)*

Structured in a style similar to newsreels of old, this historically important documentary captures the events that were staged for Gay Pride Week in both San Francisco and Los Angeles in 1976. Captured are the celebratory exuberance and the now-lost innocence of men and women proclaiming their free-spirited sexuality and their newly realized political rights. The group organizing the events, Christopher Street West, is seen working behind the scenes while on the streets the marches, parades, carnivals and even a circus keep the crowd entertained. On the critical side, Pat Rocco films the proceedings without critical commentary, providing a promotional rah-rah-rah narration while the visuals scream out for more insightful analysis. This lack of political awareness plays as a fascinating counterpoint to the more politically charged demonstrations of the AIDS era. Director Rocco provides a five-minute introduction (filmed in 1994) to the documentary.

We Were One Man
(1981, 90 min, France, Philippe Vallois)

This unusual love story chronicles the budding relationship between a wounded German soldier and the young French peasant who nurses him back to health. Excitable but dim-witted Guy's lonely existence is brightened when he comes upon Rolf in the forrest. The two develop a close affection for each other, with Rolf deciding to clandestinely stay with him even after he is well. The two constantly play around, but each is reluctant to make the first sexual move. Eventually, Rolf can't take any more teasing from the bisexual Guy and jumps him. Torrid sex ensues ("Kiss me as if I were a woman!") but their happiness is fleeting as the war reenters their lives and tries to separate them. ☻

The Wedding Banquet
(1993, 111 min, Taiwan/China/US, Ang Lee)

La Cage aux Folles Asian-American style! This wholesome gay comedy crossed over to mainstream audiences, not only in America, but to notoriously homophobic Asian audiences as well. Witty and perceptive, this Taiwanese-financed comedy follows the family drama of Wai Tung (Winston Chao). A transplanted Taiwanese gay man, now New York real estate entrepreneur, Wai lives in "guppie" bliss with his American boyfriend Simon (Mitchell Lichtenstein) in the West Village. Exasperated at his traditional parents' persistent inquiries into his marital prospects, he announces a mariage-of-convenience with a wacky artist from Shanghai who's desperate for a green card. His ruse to please and deceive them backfires, however, when they announce that they are coming to New York to meet the bride! Frantically, the two lovers remove all vestiges of their relationship from the apartment, posing as landlord-tenant and bringing in the *faux fiancée*. The plan seems to be working fine until the parents spearhead an elaborate wedding banquet that involves a night of gaudy excesses and some unwanted surprises. The delightful characters are the real attraction in this sexual and cultural comedy that might easily have turned into another *A Different Story* or *Three of Hearts* (gay or lesbian discovers the joys of heterosexuality and "switches"). Director Ang Lee, a 38-year-old Taiwanese-American NYU film school graduate who, strangely enough, is not gay, won the Golden Bear Award at the Berlin International Film Festival for his crowd-pleasing independent feature. ☻

The Wedding Banquet

Westler: East of the Wall
(1985, 94 min, Germany, Weiland Speck)

Winner of the 1986 Max Ophuls Prize, *Westler...* is the first feature of Weiland Speck, a veteran of many intriguing and queer short films. A romantic and involving gay love story set before the fall of the East German Communist government and the crumbling of the Berlin Wall, the film follows the seemingly doomed love affair between Felix, a West Berliner, and Thomas, an unemployed East Berlin waiter. Having met during a visit to Alexanderplatz, the two young men soon fall in love, but discover that forces beyond their control conspire to keep them apart. The relationship flourishes despite a curfew that forces Felix to return to the West every evening and border guards who become increasingly suspicious. Shot clandestinely on Super-8, which gives the film a semidocumentary feel, this strongly pro-gay love story will enthrall and delight queer audiences. ⊛

"...a confident, touching, intelligent and promising work."
—*The Times* [London]

Who Killed Cock Robin?
(1989, 80 min, US, David Stuart)

Tongue is planted firmly in cheek in this ordinary though eager-to-please gay murder comedy. Sort of a homosexual *Dirty Harry*, a gay cop investigates the murder of a porn star, uncovering a variety of types in and out of the industry. Most of the jokes are forced, and the humor is all camp. But it is hard to really dislike any production which has a film-quoting dowager doing his best to single-handedly bring back Gloria Swanson. Though the adult film

Wonderland

world is the backdrop, there is neither nudity nor sex (with the exception of a simulated sex scene done strictly for laughs). ⊛

Wild Blade *(1991, 53 min, US, David Geffner)*

This punky independent film is high on style but a bit slow going. Clark, a greasy comedian, dies while choking on a piece of meat (symbolism?). At the funeral, his wife, who's been getting a little on the side from her sexy girlfriend, is told that her husband was keeping a young male hustler on the "payroll." The rent boy, with looks that will remind one of the illegitimate son of Marsha Mason and Kevin Bacon, is an attractive, deaf teen, who, when not brooding intensely, becomes the fought-over object of desire between his abusive horse-faced pimp and the now hustler-obsessed woman. No one gets what they desire in this "interesting" effort that features a good jazz soundtrack, but is hampered by collegiate-level theatrical acting. ⊛

Wild Life *(1985, 40 min, US, John Gross)*

Two 15-year-old Chicanos living in Los Angeles are the subjects of this no-budget video that blends documentary footage and fiction to explore the young men's sexual and social coming-of-age. Caesar and Carlos, best friends and "sisters," are two high school students who are questioned in front of the camera, asked to act out conversations and are videotaped wandering about West Hollywood. They are a bit inarticulate and what they say is by no means earth-shattering (when they realized they were gay, how they feel about women, how they feel about clothing), but *Wild Life*'s interest lies in that gay Mexican-born/American-raised teenagers are given a forum to air their thoughts. ⊛

The Wings (Vingarne)
(1916, 80 min, Sweden, Mauritz Stiller)

Adapted from the 1906 Danish novel, "Mikaël," by gay novelist Herman Bang, this early melodrama about the homoerotic relationship between a teacher and his young pupil might also be the earliest film to depict a gay relationship and lifestyle. Stiller, a popular and influential gay Swedish director of breezy comedies and, later in his career, dramas based on literary classics, is actually best known (outside of Sweden) as the man who "discovered" Greta Garbo. Look for gay iconography in the background, especially a bewinged male nude sculpture, and works by gay sculptor Carl Milles and painter Magnus Enckell. Thought to be long lost, a print has been recently uncovered and is being restored.

Wonderland
(1989, 103 min, GB, Philip Saville)

This intriguing British thriller delves into an often overlooked subculture: gay youth. *Wonderland* is the story of the friendship between two gay teenagers from Liverpool, Eddie and Michael, who are forced to flee the city when they witness a gangland slaying at a local gay bar. Taking refuge at the home of a manipulative wealthy couple in Brighton, the boys' idyllic existence of freedom and safety is shattered when they meet the killers in a deadly confrontation. Both Emile Charles as the dolphin-loving, soft-hearted Eddie and Tony Forsyth as the streetwise, caring hustler Michael are excellent as the youths. (Also known as: *The Fruit Machine*) ⊛

The Worst Boy in Town

(1989, 60 min, Mexico,
Enrique Gomez Vadillo)

If this film received the exploitation treatment, the advertising angle might be something like, "Pepe: marauding macho thug by day...coquettish transvestite whore by night!" Set in the slums of Mexico City, the film features Mexican TV star Raul Buefil as the roguish Pepe, the leader of a gang of strapping thugs who spend their days playing pool, intimidating the neighbors and harassing young girls. But there is more to Pepe than his beefy body, tight pants and macho exterior. After the sun sets, he dons makeup, a wig and a sexy dress and visits the local transvestite bar, and in "her" new kittenish persona, looks for a good strong man who can give him a good....! Not to be confused with great art, this entertaining melodrama is nonetheless cheesy fun. ⊛

You Are Not Alone

Wrecked for Life —
The Trip and Magic of
Trocadero *(1993, 60 min, US, John C. Gross)*

This video is a simple remembrance of San Francisco's famous gay disco, The Trocadero Transfer, which operated from 1978 to 1983, a period one could consider the best part of the gay underworld's innocently decadent heyday. Interviewed are several former employees and members of the cavernous club who collectively evoke a carefree era of Donna Summer, mirror balls, drugs and, to a lesser extent, alcohol and free-wheeling sexual experimentation. Although potentially interesting, the static visuals (all talking heads) and uninspired structure (5-10 minutes would have been fine) make for an eventually trying time for all but the most die-hard of disco fans. ⊛

You Are Not Alone *(1981, 94 min, Denmark,*
Lasse Nielsen & Ernst Johansen)

Filmed in a gentle, lyrical style reminiscent of François Truffaut, this tender (and just a bit soft-core) tale of gay first love is notable for its upfront, matter-of-fact depiction of the sexual attraction and love between two young boys in a private boarding school in Copenhagen. The headmaster catches on to their relationship and tries to put an end to the sexual shenanigans, but love conquers all in this joyful, lighthearted film. ⊛

> "A freshly scrubbed soft-core slice of life from Denmark, about the precocious kids in a boarding school and the rather astonishing variety of their various initiations into sexuality."
>
> —Roger Ebert, *Chicago Sun Times*

Young Hearts, Broken Dreams

(1990, 37 min, US, Jerry Neal)

The first in what is projected to be a series, this low-budget gay soap opera has good intentions but the stilted acting and horrible script undermine the effort. The story, about the budding relationship between a young movie star hooked on drugs and an innocent delivery boy with an urge to be corrupted, doesn't go anywhere. With plenty of blond California beefcake, this gay porno flick without the sex simply teases and never delivers the goods. ⊛

Young Soul Rebels

(1991, 103 min, GB, Isaac Julien)

Winner of the Critic's Award at Cannes, *Young Soul Rebels* is a 1977 period piece that tells the story of two black disc jockeys (one gay, one straight). Late '70s British culture (notably punk and funk) comes through as the primary strength of the film, with lots of good music and fun clothes. The murder of a closeted gay man in a park known as a gay cruising place provides the dramatic tension and the ongoing hubbub of Queen Elizabeth's Silver Jubilee celebration makes for an almost surreal backdrop to the story. Well-produced and beautifully shot (by Nina Kellgren), director Isaac Julien's feature film debut oddly received very limited playtime in cinemas in the United States.

Zero for Conduct

(1933, 44 min, France, Jean Vigo)

Jean Vigo's first fiction film was banned for anti-French sentiment and was reissued in 1945 after the liberation. It is, in part, an autobiographical account of the director's boyhood in boarding school as well as a rendering of childhood fantasy. Realistic, anarchic, poetic and subversive, it tells of four boys' rebellion against the petty repressiveness of adults and abusive school authorities, who are imaginatively represented in the buffoonish dwarf principal. One of the boys, Tabard, is a pretty, long-haired youth who is assumed to be a homosexual and who strikes up a closeness with another classmate. An inspiration to Cocteau, Truffaut and especially Lindsay Anderson who made the similarly themed *If....* ⊛

7

OF TRANSGENGER INTEREST

The films in this chapter feature, or are of special interest to,
transgendered people — transsexuals, transvestites and drag
queens...and their fans.

"If a bad actor can be president, why can't a good drag
queen?"

—The rallying cry of presidential aspirant
Joan Jett Blakk in *Lick Bush in '92*

"Get me transvestites! I need transvestites!"

—Ed Wood (Johnny Depp) to Bunny (Bill
Murray) concerning the casting for his
upcoming opus *Glen or Glenda* in *Ed Wood*

An Actor's Revenge

(1963, 113 min, Japan, Kon Ichikawa)
With magnificently stylized sets, vibrant color and a spectacular performance by Kabuki actor Hasegawa, this elaborate tale of revenge and murder ranks as one of Japan's greatest films. Set in the early part of the 19th century, Hasegawa plays an *onnagata* (female impersonator) of the Kabuki theatre, who discovers the identity of the three nobles who forced the suicide of his parents many years before. In an elaborate scheme of revenge, our hero/heroine exacts a plot that does not have him simply kill them, but rather have the men turn against themselves or die at their own hands. A complex period melodrama that concerns itself with opposites: love/hate, illusion/reality, masculinity/femininity. ☮

The Adventures of Priscilla, Queen of the Desert

(1994, 102 min, Australia, Stephan Elliott)
1960s international sex symbol Terence Stamp (*Billy Budd, Teorema, The Collector*) is a transgenderized marvel as the mature, demure but tough transsexual Bernadette who teams up with two transvestites on a cross-country trip through Australia's Outback in this rousingly fun cross-dressing musical comedy. Muscular Felicia (Guy Pearce), the sad-sack Mitzi (Hugo Weaving) and the wisecracking Bernadette (nee Ralph) leave the safe but under-appreciative confines of Sydney to travel in a ramshackle tour bus (named Priscilla) across country to a four week casino engagement in Alice Springs. Along the way the fabulously attired threesome encounter more than their fair share of problems but through it all keep their spirits high, their feathers and sequins unruffled and their gravity-defying wigs straight (so to speak). There are moments of seriousness when homophobia, potentially violent culture clashes and regret at roads not taken (in life as well as on Priscilla) confront them, but they readily conquer all in this buoyant and infectously good-natured tale.

The Ballad of Little Jo

(1993, 120 min, US, Maggie Greenwald)
While this fascinating feminist western does not contain any gay or lesbian references, it is notable for its curious theme: that of a solitary woman, facing innumerable dangers, who decides to live her life as a man. Josephine Monaghan (Suzy Amis), thrown out of her Eastern home for having an illegitimate baby, travels west. But after surviving a kidnap/rape attempt, she decides the untamed land is no place for a woman and she changes her identity and sexuality by cutting her hair, exchanging petticoats for pants and scarring her face. The story revolves around her life in a small mining town, where she is accepted as Little Jo, a frail young man. Far from being an idyllic portrayal of frontier life, the film depicts the harsh conditions of the West as well as showing the men as piggish brutes. Ian McKellen turns in a fine performance as Percy, portrayed initially as a decent man but who eventually shows his true misogynist colors. ☮

Black Lizard

(1968, 86 min, Japan, Kinji Fukasako)
Mix elements of *What's Up, Tiger Lily?* with *Beyond the Valley of the Dolls*, throw in lurid color schemes and weird camera angles by a seemingly drug-imbued cinematographer and you'll have some idea of the makeup of this wildly campy detective yarn. Japan's most famous female impersonator, Akihiri Maruyama, stars as the villainous jewel thief, The Black Lizard, a fatally seductive temptress who'll stop at nothing to get her dainty hands on the fabulous Star of Egypt diamond. Yukio Mishima, who adapted the original novel for the stage, is featured in this entertaining curiosity as a naked human statue in the glamorous chanteuse's demented private museum. She's so evil! ☮

Blank Point: What Is Transsexualism?

(1991, 58 min, US, Xiao-Yen)
An award-winning documentary (Blue Ribbon, American Film & Video Festival; First Prize, Athens International Film Festival; Silver Medal, Houston International Film Festival) which offers balanced insight into transsexualism. Through interviews with two male-to-female and one female-to-male transsexuals, the film seeks to answer what motivates a person to change their gender. They talk candidly about their decision, the operation itself, their new lives and the difficult psychological and social challenges that confront them.

The Adventures of Priscilla, Queen of the Desert

Boy! What a Girl
(1945, 70 min, US, Arthur Leonard)
Tim Moore (who played "The Kingfish" on the popular 1950s "Amos 'n Andy" television series) stars as a butch drag queen pursued by three men with marriage on their minds in this all-black cast musical. The black comedy team of Patterson and Jackson co-star, along with a line-up of musical talent that includes the Slam Stewart Trio, Sid Catlett Orchestra (with a cameo performance by Gene Krupa), Deek Watson and his Brown Dots, composer/pianist Mary Lou Williams, Ann Cornell and the International Jitterbugs. The plot revolves around a pair of small-time producers, Jim and Harry (Elwood Smith and Duke Williams), trying to stage a show while wooing the daughters of the show's wealthy backer. The acting is less than natural, at times, and the plot less than subtle, but these were defining characteristics of most of the big-studio, white musicals of the '40s as well.

Bugs Bunny in one of his many drag stints in *What's Opera, Doc?*

Boys from Brazil
(1993, 68 min, GB, John Paul Davidson)
Made originally for the BBC, this documentary, filmed over a two-year period, ventures to Brazil and explores the life of the city's many *travesti*: gay, transsexual and transvestite prostitutes. The main focus is on the dangerous, often short lives of the *travesties* (chicks with dicks), males who live their lives as women, taking hormones and injecting silicone in their breasts, buttocks and hips. The "mother-daughter" relationship of Samira and the attractive Luciana provides some of the drama as the film also takes a peek into the city's drag bars, watches the girls work the streets, and explores their camaraderie and bitchy in-fighting. There are several telling moments, particularly when one *travesti* says, "We're not happy, we pretend to be happy so as to survive." An eye-popping, titillating but ultimately sad look at this doomed fringe sexual group.

Bugs Bunny
Born in 1937, the legendary, wise-cracking rabbit with a penchant for asking "What's up, Doc?" first appeared in the Warner Brothers cartoon *Porky's Hare Hunt*. Called "dispicable" and "rascally" by his more envious peers, Bugs always got the upper-hand with his adversaries, who more often than not was the hapless Elmer Fudd ("Sh-hh! I'm hunting wabbit"). Bugs was a smart-aleck, witty, resourceful, and his humor was often very gay (he refused to comment on his sexual orientation, only stating that his body of work speaks for itself). In *Water, Water Every Hare*, Bugs finds himself prisoner in a spooky castle and hunted by a monster. In a quick moment of improvisation, Bugs dons the persona of a dishy hairdresser, commenting in a heavy lisp to his startled foe, "My, you monsters lead such *interesting* lives." In the 1938 short *Slick Hare*, Bugs received on-screen a fake and very fey Oscar, his first brush with the Academy. Twenty years later he would win one for real with *Knighty Knight Bugs*. The most common theme

in his work is man's inhumanity to hare, and with great cunning Bugs would escape near-death situations by slinging a snappy retort and, if need be, dressing in drag and/or dancing, kissing or even marrying his male opponent. In the precursor to *The Crying Game*, Chuck Jones' *What's Opera, Doc?*, Bugs dons wig and gown to play the role of the blonde, buxomed Brunhilda to Elmer's anxious lover. In *Rabbit of Seville*, Bugs marries Elmer at the story's end. Towards the end of his career, there were rumors running rampant in Hollywood that Bugs — a lifelong bachelor — was lovers with the late Mel Blanc, though it could not be confirmed. Probably the most popular cartoon character of all time, Bugs' cross-dressing antics and gay sensibility have made him a gay icon and a rabbit for all seasons. ☮

Calamity Jane
(1953, 101 min, US, David Butler)
Doris Day stars as every tomboy's hero! She's the fast-shootin', tough-talkin', cross-dressin' (real-life lesbain cowgirl) Calamity Jane! Of course, we know enough about the real Calamity to ignore the film's heterosexualized narrative and read it the other way around — which is easy enough when Calamity brings sexy Katie Brown to Deadwood and they move in together and paint "Calam & Katie" on their front door. This also happens to be a great old-fashioned musical with a bunch of fun songs and dance numbers, including "Whip Crack Away," "Secret Love" and Dick Wesson's fantastic drag performance of "I've Got a Hive Full of Honey" — and all in brilliant Technicolor. The film is, unfortunately, less than enlightened on the subject of Native Americans as it features every stereotype in the book. Admiring the natural beauty of South Dakota, Day unwittingly notes the injustice of the conquest of Native American land as she quips, "No wonder injuns fight so fierce to hang onto this country." ☮

The Christine Jorgensen Story
(1970, 89 min, US, Irving Rapper)
Based on her autobiography, this transsexual drama of a man "trapped in the wrong body" made its first mistake in casting the masculine looking John Hansen in a role that required someone of a more androgynous appearance. The real 1952 story of the first man to undergo a sex change operation fascinated the nation; but the film, made almost 20 years after the event, fails to effectively handle the sensitive subject. Taking a sympathetic but almost clinical approach to the story, the film follows the unhappy (and ridiculously) asexual George as he finally decides to have the operation that turns him into Christine. In describing just how ludicrous Hansen was as Christine, Parker Taylor in *Screening the Sexes* writes that Hansen "behaves like a remarkable Amazonian maiden who has been rejected as a beauty contestant because she is 40 pounds overweight, has husky shoulders, a very masculine neck, and a bosom that seems to be two oversized wens on either side of a dimple."

The Crying Game
(1992, 112 min, GB, Neil Jordan)
In a brilliant marketing coup, the folks at Miramax Films released this film strongly advising people not to give away its "secret." Word of this "secret" quickly swept the nation and everybody was dying to see what would have otherwise been another *Defence of the Realm* or *Hidden Agenda*. Thankfully, director Neil Jordan's tautly realized political thriller is worthy of all the praise and press it generated. Stephen Rea received an Oscar nomination for his role as an IRA terrorist with a troubled conscience who promises a captured British soldier (Forest Whitaker) that he'll look after his girlfriend in London. Sometime later, Rea has opted out of the terror game and is trying to lead a quiet life of obscurity in London, where he decides to look her up. Newcomer Jaye Davidson's portrayal of the slender and exotic hairdresser is a knockout and also garnered an Oscar nomination. Trouble comes in spades when one of Rea's old Republican comrades, Miranda Richardson (who, as an actress, redefines the word versatile), shows up to test his loyalties. An exciting and highly entertaining story which is sprinkled with drama, comedy and plenty of intrigue. ⊗

Focus on: *Jaye Davidson*
Winning an Academy Award nomination in the Best Supporting Actor category for his first feature film, Jaye Davidson's future film career has been eagerly anticipated. After over a year off, he is scheduled to play an intergalactic ruler named King Ra in the sci-fi fanatsy Star Gate, *which stars Kurt Russell and James Spader. The French-financed film was released in Fall 1994.*

Dirty Daughters
(1981, 80 min, Germany, Dagmar Beirsdorf)
Director Dagmar Beirsdorf stars as Rita, a warmhearted transvestite prostitute (in films, is there any other kind?) who takes in a cute Lebanese exile who passes himself off as Puerto Rican. Fellow underground director Lother Lambert, who also wrote the screenplay, plays Betty, a gutsy, overly-dramatic transvestite and

Eat the Rich

best friend of Rita. A wacky, exuberantly camp film despite its downbeat ending. The German title for the film is *Die Hure und Der Hurensohn*, which translates into English as *The Whore and the S.O.B.* Made for a reported $10,000 (entirely financed by Beirsdorf and Lambert), the film is a classic example of the fun-loving productions that came out of the Berlin Underground filmmaking group during the 1980s. Featuring Ingrid Caven and Ulrike S. and a host of nonprofessionals.

Dr. Jekyll and Sister Hyde
(1971, 97 min, GB, Roy Ward Baker)
Transsexual serial killer? Yes, that and much more in this Hammer Studios-produced variation on the Robert Louis Stevenson story. Set in a perpetually foggy London in the 1890s, hard-working researcher Dr. Jekyll, sporting a weird, pseudo Prince Valiant hair-do, works on an elixir to prolong life. But when his experiments require recently killed female hormones from young women, he soon develops into a deranged necromaniac and mass murderer, justifying it all with, "gotta do bad to do good." And if this wasn't bad enough, when he tries his experiment on himself, he finds himself transformed into a foxy, big-breasted woman! His shock turns to delight as his feminine alter-ego takes over, wetted with an insatiable sexual appetite for both young and older men as well as accomodating prostitutes. Was his sex-starved "sister" simply acting on his own deep-rooted desires? Forget any serious analysis and enjoy this witty chiller, but remember what one observer says of the situation, "It's a queer business, very queer." ⊗

Dream Boys Revue
(1985, 74 min, US, Howard Schwartz & John Moriarty)
For those interested in female impersonation but can't or won't go to a drag bar, this cheesy cross-dressing beauty pageant, hosted by superstars Ruth Buzzi and Lyle Wagoner, should satisfy. Over 30 contestants gathered in Houston for the Female Impersonator of the Year show — and Howard Stern, who should have been the host, is nowhere in sight. The event is a carbon copy replica of a typical beauty pageant, replete with judges voting on each lady's beauty, poise and talent as well as behind-the-scenes cavorting,

interviews with the excited contestants and a finale spotlighting the crowning of a tearful but happy new queen. The proceedings are sanitized for the home viewer, with all references to sexuality and homosexuality removed and Buzzi explaining that "female impersonation is respectable, popular and downright fashionable." Displaying both glitz and tackiness, the show's funniest moment occurs when the camera ventures backstage as the contestants prepare and glamorize, all accompanied by the music of Tom Jones' "She's a Lady." The talent segment of the show is also fun, with the gorgeous, big-haired lovelies belting out impersonations of the standards: Bette Davis, Barbra, Marilyn and Liza. ⊗

Eat the Rich
(1987, 100 min, GB, Peter Richardson)

Director Peter Richardson's *Eat the Rich* is a scathing attack on the British class system parlayed, in the tradition of Lindsay Anderson's *Britannia Hospital*, through thoroughly outrageous, and at times grotesque, humor. Alex (played by transsexual Lanah Pellay) is fired from his job as a waiter at a ritzy-glitzy restaurant called Bastards for failing to show the proper respect for the upper-class twits who frequent the place. In response, he teams up with an ex-bouncer and the discarded mistress of the British Home Secretary to start the revolution. They begin by taking over Bastards and renaming it "Eat the Rich" which is exactly what the unsuspecting patrons do. Hilarious evidence that the spirit of revolt survives even in Thatcher's revisionist England. ⊗

Glamazon: A Different Kind of Girl

A Fairy for Dessert
(1991, 84 min, Germany, Dagmar Beirsdorf)

In the wacky, low-budget style of Lother Lambert's underground films, Lambert regular, actress Dagmar Beirsdorf, directed this offbeat yet gentle melodrama of a decidedly different nuclear family. Lambert stars as Julchen, a meddling drag queen-cum-hausfrau who befriends Nina, the half-Moroccan daughter of his housemate. Concerned that she and her daddy are estranged from their mother, the tenacious transvestite is determined to patch things up and create one big happy family. Hilarious and often times bordering on the surreal, this endearing story celebrates both the freedom to be who you are and the strength of adopted family units.

First a Girl *(1935, 94 min, GB, Victor Seville)*

This entertaining cross-dressing musical is an English version of the 1933 German film *Viktor und Viktoria*. A third film, Blake Edwards' *Victor/Victoria*, successfully reprised the plot with Julie Andrews in the lead in 1982. Jessie Matthews stars as a shopgirl who finds confused fame when, at the urging of a drag artist (Sonnie Hale), she becomes a wildly convincing gay man impersonating a woman in a cabaret act. Although the film veers from any direct gay/lesbian sexual overtones, a queer presence is much in evidence with Matthews' wonderful portrayal of the sexually ambiguous performer.

The Girls of 42nd Street
(1971, 84 min, US, Andy Milligan)

A nudie exploitation flick definitely a cut above the typical dreck, this entertaining tale is about an enterprising girl looking for happiness on her back. Dusty (Diana Lewis), a pretty 42nd Street prostitute, seasoned at the age of 20, meets up with older friend, drag queen and fellow prostitute Cherry Lane (Lynn Flanagan). Dusty moves in with the often hilarious, wise-cracking, seen-it-all and done-'em-all Cherry and they join forces in turning tricks. But when Dusty falls for a nice guy from Staten Island, her hopes of love, respectability and domestic bliss are falsely raised. Cherry, "whose office stretches from upper Broadway to the end of Christopher Street," is one of the screen's priceless transvestite characters. She likes a little of the rough stuff and dons colorful mod frocks when working the West End docks. In her most revealing moment, she describes her early life, her disappointments and loneliness, lamenting, "I'd love someone to love or someone to love me. It ain't easy being a freak." And although she is portrayed as a bit pitiful, and turns out to be a rotten friend, she is still a sharp, sympathetic character who can handle most of what life throws at her. (Also known as: *Fleshpot on 42nd Street*)

Glamazon: A Different Kind of Girl *(1993, 83 min, US, Rico Martinez)*

This offbeat documentary delves into the life of Barbara LeMay aka Glamazon, an outrageous 61-year-old transsexual go-go dancer. The film follows Barbara as she returns after many years to her poor West Virginia backwater home town to visit relatives and old friends. She takes center stage as she recounts her entertainment life, from running away from home to work at a circus freak show to her success as a legendary exotic dancer in the world of strip shows and burlesque. Something of a motormouth, Barbara, who died shortly after the completion of the film, fervently believes in her talent, her beauty and her show business success. Her homecoming borders on the surreal, as all accept her as she is and listen in rapture as she tells stories from her fabulous life. In addition to showing a few of her hoochie-coochie routines, the film also reenacts several of her stories, including one in which a man, in order to escape prison, had to resort to home surgery to make himself a hermaphrodite. At times rambling and repetitive, the film is nevertheless an oddly inspiring tale of survival against almost insurmountable odds.

Glen or Glenda?

(1953, 67 min, US, Ed Wood)
From grade-Z cult director Ed Wood, himself a heterosexual aficionado of cross-dressing (he reportedly landed on the beaches of Normandy wearing panties and a bra under his uniform), comes this hilarious but completely sincere plea for greater tolerance for transvestites. Cast in the mold of a scientific exploitation flick, a bulging-eyed Bela Lugosi warns us, "Beevare the beeg green dragin!" as he introduces us to the hopelessly confused Glen (director Wood), a young man possessed with a passion for angora and an uncontrollable urge to don female garb. An unredeemable schlockumentary and one of the most ill-conceived and funniest works of all time. "Vat are little boys made ov? Is it puppy dog tails? Big fat snails? Or maybe *brassieres! high heels! garters!...*" (Also known as: *I Changed My Sex; I Led Two Lives; Transvestite*) ⊛

Hookers on Davie

(1984, 85 min, Canada, Janice Cole & Holly Dale)
Set in Vancouver, the "Prostitution Capital of Canada," *Hookers on Davie* is a "you are there" style documentary that features the many prostitutes — male, female, transsexual and transvestite — who work along side each other on a pimp-less street in an otherwise typical middle-class neighborhood. Capturing both the danger as well as the boredom of the "chosen" profession, the camera eavesdrops on conversations and exchanges between the working "women" and their johns, with such price negotiations as, "$50 for head, $75 for tail and $90 for half and half." Some of the hookers interviewed include: Joey, a laid back Olive Oyl-like woman of 22; Michelle, a tough-talking 24-year-old transsexual with gravity defying tits; Bev, a surprisingly aware veteran of the streets; and Tiffany, a 20-year-old transvestite waif. Their collective tales of broken homes, sexual violence and tough-luck living are all told without pity — these survivors accept their lot in life and live it to the fullest. An unusual, insightful approach to an often told subject. ⊛

I Wanna Be a Beauty Queen

(1979, 81 min, US, Richard Gayor)
For "three seconds of fabulousness," contestants (women and drag queens alike) vie for the "coveted" Alternative Miss World title and this tongue-in-cheek documentary captures it all. Set in a big tent in London's Clapham Common, the festivities were organized by Andrew Logan and hosted by America's then-reigning drag queen Divine. The film details the entire event — from the show's preparations and the erection of the tent to the arrival of the audience and the elaborately costumed stage show that ends with the crowning of the new queen. Unfortunately, it's not as fun as it might sound, as the film suffers from sloppy editing and a decided absence of wit and humor; both from a seemingly bored and confused Divine and the contestants who, while looking quite outrageous, have nothing to say when the mike is thrust in their face. The fun is innocent and the costumes border on the surreal. Look for a young John Maybury (director of *Remembrances of Things Fast*) as a slimy post-nuclear Creature from the Black Lagoon. (Also known as: *The Alternative Miss World*) ⊛

I Want What I Want

(1971, 97 min, GB, John Dexter)
Surprisingly sensitive and non-exploitative, this somber drama follows a young man's life as he explores his desires to initially dress as a woman and eventually have the operation to become one. Anne Heywood stars as Roy, a timid and sullen real estate agent and secret cross-dresser who is forced to move out of his super-macho father's house after being caught in women's clothing. On his own, he bravely decides to dress full-time as a woman and adopts the name Wendy. As a woman, (s)he moves into a bedsit and tentatively explores her new life. Strong-willed and determined, (s)he responds to her sister after being asked if (s)he can be cured, by saying, "I am cured." After an awkward attempt with a man, Wendy decides to go all the way and undergo the operation. Heywood is good in the lead role, not so much in the beginning playing the effeminate Roy, but in the part of a woman playing a man playing a woman. The sexual frustration and loneliness suffered by Wendy when (s)he falls in love with a brutish man is the most effective part of the film. ⊛

Just Like a Woman

(1994, 90 min, GB, Christopher Monger)
Adrian Pasdar stars in this gentle, gender-bending comedy about an American banker living in London whose penchant for lingerie gets him in trouble with his wife, who thinks he's seeing another woman. She kicks him out, and he winds up lodging with Julie Walters, who's just ended a 22-year marriage. After they strike up a relationship, he divulges his secret to Walters and rather than react with revulsion she helps him fulfill his fantasies. The film follows Pasdar, whose heterosexuality is never called into question, on a trip to a transvestite club and depicts his humiliating arrest by the police. While basically a straight love story, the film nonetheless is an entertaining examination of gender roles in relationships. Based on Monica Jay's book "Geraldine."

Just One of the Girls

(1993, 94 min, US, Michael Keusch)
The standard teen sex comedy is given a '90s transgender twist in this likable and occasionally funny cross-dressing tease. Corey Haim (the cute Corey) stars as Chris, a music-minded high school

student who resorts to disguising himself as a girl in order to avoid trouble with Kurt, the school's bully (an even cuter Cameron Bancroft). This being Hollywood escapist fantasy, the now buxom Chris (pretty in the old East German athlete sort of way) soon gets into his newfound persona — he shaves his legs, joins the girls cheerleading team and risks detention by flirting with a lovelorn Kurt. The most homoerotic scene is when Kurt tries feeling up the demure Chrissy and succeeds in planting a kiss, broken off abruptly when Chris says she's allergic to tongues. The charade gets out of hand, however, as Chris is suspected by both his gym teacher and girlfriend as being a lesbian while his dad thinks he's gay or at least

a drag queen. Heterosexuality reigns supreme in the finale, although the gender roles are pleasantly parodied. ⊛

Lady Boys (1992, 50 min, GB, Jeremy Marre)

The thriving underworld of Thailand's drag queens and transsexuals is explored in this documentary originally made for Britain's Channel 4. The film follows several of the female impersonators and "surgically created" women, most of them young, as they stage beauty pageants, work in drag bars like the "Go Orgy Go" and earn their living as prostitutes. A mesmeric and oddly glamorous world that ultimately, however, proves rather sad.

Let Me Die a Woman
(1978, 77 min, US, Doris Wishman)

Despite its 1978 copyright, this hilariously awful "sensitive exposé" on transsexuals has its ideas planted too much in the "1950s Glen or Glenda school of filmmaking" to be an enlightened documentary. Shrill and lurid, the film is narrated by a Dr. Leo Wollman ("M.D., PhD, surgeon, psychologist, minister and medical writer") who "understands this phenomena" — that is, a person's loss of sexual identity when the psyche of a man or woman is trapped in the body of a woman or man. There is a lot of time spent lecturing (heavy on the medical terminology), as well as interviews with several man-to-woman transsexuals, and some woman-to-man conversions (who supposedly make up 20% of all operations). The goodly doc takes his pointer several times to the naked bodies of his patients, explaining to the viewer the "unique characteristics" of these people. There are frank discussions about and filming of sex acts between transsexuals and their partners; there is also one particularly grisly operation removing the penis and testicles of a patient. The film exhibits moments of insight, but is hampered by its sleazy intentions and remarks like, "If the glands do not develop properly, the result is homosexuality, lesbianism, transvestism or transsexualism." ⊛

Linda, Les and Annie (1991, 40 min, US)

A uniquely funny and at times disturbingly entertaining docu-drama about transsexual Les Nichols and his transformation from female to male. Beginning with his roots as a lesbian, we follow Les on the journey to manhood: from hormone treatments, to surgery — including graphic medical photos — and finally the night when he and ex-porn star and sex educator Annie Sprinkle try out his newly constructed penis. Shockingly frank and not for all tastes, Linda, Les and Annie is a must see for the sexually curious. ⊛

Lip Gloss (1993, 70 min, Canada, Lois Siegel)

Montreal's surprisingly bustling world of drag shows, tranvestites, female impersonators and drag queens takes center stage in this low-budget documentary. Interviewed are the stars (many older and heavyweight), including Armand Monroe, Guilda, Bobette, and Derek of the comedy drag ballet troupe, Les Ballets Trockadero de Monte Carlo. As a document of a fringe gay lifestyle, the film is interesting, if somewhat downbeat. On a critical front, however, the interveiws "drag" on a bit (in the bad sense of the word) and the film depicts a disturbing misogynistic streak among many of the interviewees. This "Montreal Is Burning" took almost eight years to make and captures the spirit of

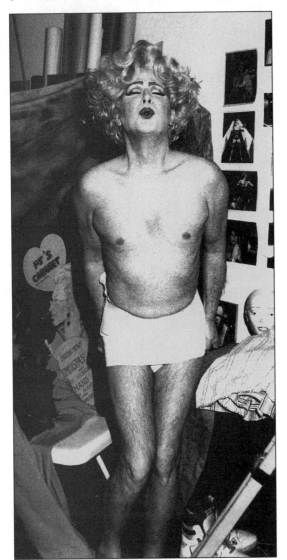

Lip Gloss

Montreal's gay and transgender population, a mostly overlooked and unrecorded segment of the queer community. Since filming began in 1984, several of the performers have died and many of the featured clubs (PJs and Bellevue Tavern) have closed.

A Little Bit of Lippy

(1992, 75 min, GB, Chris Bernard)
Although determinedly heterosexual, this made-for-British TV film is of interest primarily for its theme of transvestism. Set in a working-class neighborhood somewhere in the industrial north of England, the story is about Rick (Danny Cunningham), a hunky pretty boy who is married to his high school sweetheart, Marian (Alison Swann). Trouble explodes when Marian catches her motorcycle-driving hubby all dressed up in drag. She immediately runs into the narrow-thinking arms of her parents, but her love for Rick forces her to try to understand his penchant for dresses, slinky underwear and lace stockings. Helped by a wise, campy drag queen, and her husband's contention that he is purely heterosexual, they try to sort things out. A delightful comedy that doesn't allow its strong plea for cross-dressing acceptance to get in the way of the fun. The only problem with this otherwise terrific film is its almost obsessive presentation of a non-gay world — for with the possible exception of the drag queen, all of the cross-dressers and the entire audience at a drag show are straight, which might cause some naive TV viewers to believe that transvestism is an exclusively heterosexual obsession.

Luminous Procuress

(1971, 87 min, US, Steven Arnold)
Return to the innocent, pre-AIDS days of queerdom with this outrageous drag celebration that was called a "West Coast *Satyricon*" on its opening. Determinedly silly and featuring loads of nudity, the film stars San Francisco's Cockettes, Divine and Sylvester and has in its cast: whores, musclemen, kewpie dolls, fairy godmothers, monkeys, vegetable people, Sufi holymen, transvestite mimes, visionaries and male nuns (bearded, of course!). In addition to this feature-length extravaganza, The Cockettes made such celluloid classics as *Tricia's Wedding*, *Elevator Girls in Bondage*, *Tinsel Tarts in a Hot Coma*, *Journey to the Center of Uranus* and *Palace*, a backstage look at a Cockettes stage show.

M. Butterfly

(1993, 100 min, US, David Cronenberg)
The much-anticipated screen version of David Henry Hwang's hit play is somewhat of a letdown. Inspired by a true story, the tragic tale tells of a man's self-delusional love for and betrayal by an alluring Chinese woman who is actually a man. Set in 1964, the film stars Jeremy Irons as Rene Gallimard, a fidgety, deer-in-the-headlights-like accountant at the French Embassy who becomes entranced with singer Song Liling (John Lone) during a recital of music from the opera "Madame Butterfly." Lone, beautifully dressed and in heavy makeup, plays a convincingly demure woman with a melodic voice, although for many scenes, (s)he is cast in shadows or from afar (trying to hide that 5 o'clock mustache shadow). The two unlikely lovers begin an affair, "the most forbidden of loves," that fills Irons' character with an awkward self-importance which leads to his promotion to vice-council, his

Miss Mona

eventual dismissal and then his ridicule by his peer and betrayal of his country. This sexual variation on the Puccini opera deals with self-deception, self-importance, corruption and intense love, all in the elaborately lush and exotic setting of Beijing, Paris and Budapest. The action unfolds quite slowly along with the emotional level, which never seems to rise beyond the simmering point; it's a grand tragedy reminiscent of a Bertolucci spectacle. The relationship between the Irons and Lone characters is romantic, tender and touching, although "the ancient Oriental ways of love" that Liling talks about are in actuality simple blow jobs and anal sex with clothes pulled up. A thoughtful, at times disturbing story of wayward love that is involving despite the film's many faults. ☮

Mascara

(1987, 98 min, Belgium/Fr/US, Patrick Conrad)
Strange does not begin to describe this stylishly shot psychosexual thriller that combines incestuous elements of Cocteau's *Les Enfants Terribles* with the violence and sexual confusion of *Cruising*. Michael Sarrazin stars as a sexually repressed police inspector on the brink of murderous insanity triggered by a particularly pretty dress he fancies. Charlotte Rampling is featured as his sister and object of his incestuous desires. Filled with themes of lust, love and violence, the action takes place in a kinky gay after-hours club called Mister Butterfly peopled by S&M aficionados and hermaphrodites and awash in transvestism and transsexuality. Enjoyably weird with one scene that pre-dates *The Crying Game*'s shocking appendage revelation! ☮

Minimum Charge, No Cover

(1976, 83 min, Canada, Janice Cole & Holly Dale)
Social documentarians Cole and Dale, who share the functions of director, producer and editor, delve into the nocturnal underworld of Toronto's "sleazier" side in this engaging film. While showing an empathy for its denizens, the film focuses on the area's prostitutes, transsexuals, transvestites and drag queens, as well as the petty criminals who hover around it all.

Mirror, Mirror

(1978, 107 min, Denmark, Edward Fleming)
An unusual film which sensitively mixes comedy with melancholy in depicting an astounding group of Copenhagen drag queens.

Featuring many well-known Danish actors including Frits Helmuth as Bent, the film shows the mostly middle-class transvestites and their friends (including a mom who regrets that her son was not a girl so they could have been a dancing team) as resilient individuals who use illusion and reality bending to get them through life.

Miss Mona
(1987, 95 min, France, Mehdi Charef)
Veteran French screen actor Jean Carmet (*Black and White in Color, Buffet Froid*) stars as Miss Mona, an aging transvestite/prostitute who wants to die a "real" woman. Her long illusive goal of going under the knife becomes possible after meeting a young illegal Arab immigrant. The vulnerable boy, also down on his luck, teams with Miss Mona, who tells him, "I'll bring you a lot of old queers, we'll make a lot of money and you'll be able to buy fake ID papers and rent a room." The youngster agrees, not knowing that he is actually working towards Miss Mona's operation.

The Mystery of Alexina
(1985, 84 min, France, René Féret)
This somber, literate and beautifully photographed film tells the tale of Alexina, a convent-bred maid who goes to teach at a girl's elementary school. There she falls in love with another girl, at which time it is discovered that she is actually a man. The erotic sequences between Alexina and her lover are beautifully rendered and the film makes this extraordinary story seem both mythic and tragic. The remarkable Alexina is played by French artist Vullemin, whose androgynous characteristics are perfectly suited to the role. Based on a mid-19th-century memoir by a hermaphrodite, Herculine Barbin, the evocative screenplay was written by director René Féret and Jean Gruault (*Jules and Jim, The Wild Child, Two English Girls* and *Mon Oncle D'Amerique*). This is an

intriguing if understated piece of filmmaking which poses questions of identity and character in a romantic, stylish setting. ✪

Orlando
(1993, 93 min, GB/Russia/Fr/It, Sally Potter)
Adapted from Virginia Woolf's 1928 modernist novel, this wholly original, sumptuously filmed comedy of sexual mores, attitudes and gender-switching stars as our hero/heroine the luminous Tilda Swinton (star of many Derek Jarman films) as Orlando. The tale begins in 1600 when the bewitchingly androgynous Orlando captures the eye of the aging Queen Elizabeth I (regally played to the hilt by Quentin Crisp) who promises the nobleman the deed to his family's estate on the condition that he retain his beauty and does not age. As the decades and centuries go by, the immortal Orlando strolls through the elaborate pageant that is English history — from its Colonialist period to the Parlor Room days of the mid-1700s to the Victorian era and eventually to the present — and during her adventures for love and self-discovery, he changes sexes, yet all the while, retaining his/her independence, kind heart and a droll sense of humor to her adventure-filled fate. Spectacularly staged and costumed, reminding one of Peter Greenaway's *The Draughtsman's Contract*, and featuring a hypnotic soundtrack (which even has the falsetto-voiced Jimmy Somerville as a singing and flying angel), this witty, enchanting story is infused with wry jokes and emotional truths and is a thrilling adventure that should not be missed. ✪

Focus on: *Virginia Woolf*
It will come as no surprise to readers of Virginia Woolf that other than Orlando *and* To the Lighthouse *there have been no other screen adaptations of her many novels. Her work is original, experimental and demanding, and much of her storytelling focuses on the interior thoughts of her characters rather than relying on simple, familiar narrative. An acclaimed critic, fervent feminist, prodigious writer, and clebrated member of the Bloomsbury Group, Virginia Stephen was born into a literary family in 1892. She was a sensitive child who was greatly affected at the age of three by her mother's death and suffered a nervous breakdown as a teenager after the death of her beloved father. She married Leonard Woolf, but theirs was to be a sexless marriage, with Woolf's greatest love being socialite Vita Sackville-West, reportedly the inspiration for "Orlando." Emotional problems and insanity plagued her throughout her life until she ended it, committing suicide by drowning in 1941.*

Outrageous!
(1977, 10 min, Canada, Richard Benner)
A wildly funny and affecting Canadian film about a female impersonator and his touching friendship with a schizophrenic girl. Craig Russell's impressions of Streisand, Garland, Midler, West and others are flawless, and Hollis McLaren is captivating as the young woman. Followed by a sequel, *Too Outrageous!* ✪

Quentin Crisp (l.) as Queen Elizabeth and Tilda Swinton in *Orlando*

Paradise Is Not for Sale
*(1985, 60 min, Denmark,
Teit Ritzau)*

A sensitive and personal look into the lives of four transsexuals: an opera singer and veteran of several films by Federico Fellini; Christine Jorgensen (still the world's most famous transsexual); a taxi driver; and a female-to-male transsexual. The documentary also delves into the history of sex changes and provides archival footage on Hitler's persecution of transsexuals.

Paris Is Burning
*(1990, 78 min, US,
Jennie Livingston)*

Welcome to the world of the Ball, where everyone is Cinderella. The balls in question are the voguing and drag balls of Harlem, the subject of lesbian director Jennie Livingston's award-winning and sensationally entertaining documentary. Voguing, an underground dance invented

Paris Is Burning

by black and Latino queers, burst upon the pop scene when Madonna "took" voguing for herself and popularized it. But it's the originators of the form who are the film's subject. Voguers, or "ball walkers," affiliate themselves with "Houses," the equivalent of gay street gangs, and compete for trophies at the late-nite balls. For some, these balls are the only escape they have from their otherwise poverty-stricken lives. Livingston uses sensitivity and compassion in documenting her stars. From legendary drag queen Dorian Corey, to multi-grand prize winner Pepper Labeija, to hot-voguer Willi Ninja, all are fierce, friendly and for real. Snubbed at the Oscars, *Paris* is one of the liveliest and most touching movies in recent memory. Madonna's production company financed it out of limbo and onto video release. ⊛

Privates on Parade

Privates on Parade
(1984, 95 min, GB, Michael Blakemore)

Alternately hilarious and heartwarming, this gem covers the comic adventures of a theatrical troupe of British soldiers tap-dancing and cross-dressing their way through WWII. Monty Python-ite John Cleese stars as the commander of this motley crew and Denis Quilley is ferociously funny as the campy director whose productions would make a USO show look like Shakespeare-in-the-Park. Don't miss the uproarious closing credits sequence. ⊛

The Queen *(1968, 80 min, US, Frank Simon)*

This outlandish behind-the-scenes look at the drag Miss All American Beauty Pageant of 1967 has gotten better over the years, offering the viewer a fascinating and humorous peek into the world of drag, its memorable participants and a glimpse at one aspect of pre-Stonewall gay life. Staged in New York, the film captures the frantic days of preparation for the elaborately staged finals as the 40 regional contestants arrive, meet the exacting Edith Head-like coordinator, rehearse their stage entrance and dance numbers, and exchange makeup, fashion and beauty secrets. The pageant itself is a glamorous, sensational affair which gives center stage to these beauties, especially Philadelphia's Harlow, a willowy blonde waif with a mysterious and vulnerable air. After the crowning of the new queen, many of the attitude-throwing, jealous losers bare their sharp claws and venomous tongues, bitching about the winner and her oh-so-tacky dress! Meow! A camp delight and finger-snapping fun.

Second Serve
(1986, 100 min, US, Anthony Page)

The much publicized life of transsexual Renee Richards is given an above average made-for-television treatment in this drama starring Vanessa Redgrave. Being tall with mannish features (characteristics also used wonderfully in *Ballad of the Sad Cafe*), Redgrave not only physically fills the part, but her acting ability realistically brings to life both the characterizations of Richards as a man (successful eye surgeon Richard Radley) and as a woman (tennis pro, coach and cause célèbre Renee Richards). Based on Richards' autobiography.

Sex Change — Shock! Horror! Probe! *(1989, 50 min, GB, Jane Jackson)*

Written and produced by Chris Clarke, a transsexual herself, this inside look into the lives of transsexuals makes for a compelling and well-tempered documentary. Made for Britain's Channel 4, Jackson focuses on a group of opinionated transsexuals who recount their pre-operation lives as well as their much-changed (for the better) post-operational ones.

> "Groundbreaking video work — the stuff of change and revolution. It is well-made, entertaining, enlightening and provocative."
> — *Bay Area Reporter*

Le Sexe Des Étoiles

(1993, 100 min, Canada, Paule Baillargeon)
This Canadian melodrama details the difficult relationship between a young girl and her estranged father, who returns to her life a transsexual woman. I will leave it to the straight press (and this film is geared towards a straight, "sympathetic" audience) to bestow the accolades to this "daringly different and touching family drama." But taking a gay male (non transsexual) point of view, the politics of the film and its preachy attitudes toward atypical sexual preferences borders on the vicious. The story follows Camille, "12 and ¾-years-old," lost in a fantasy of her long-gone "perfect" father. He returns to Montreal after several years in New York City intent on rekindling, however awkwardly, his relationship with his daughter. Camille accepts the obvious, that is, that her father is now a woman, but refuses to alter any of the traditional father-daughter dynamics that she so desperately wants. How the two work out their personal needs and reconcile with each other is the crux of this drama. But to straight audiences the film is a "feel good" movie: It supports family life and reinforces the notion that deviant homosexuality is a sad, violent and unfulfilling world. The father, Marie-Pierre, is played by Denis Mercier in the John Lithgow-in-*The World According to Garp*-style of transsexual: a big, gangly, not at all feminine woman who is not fooling anyone. His life, when not with his daughter, consists of dreamily reading ladies' fashion magazines and sewing dresses, "For a girl loves new dresses." He is sexless in his new persona — his one attempt at sex with a man ends in disaster. Although he had decided to have the drastic operation to change his sex, Marie-Pierre is oddly naive towards her new being, deep down feeling a bit grotesque, and in the end, in "an act of courage and self-awareness," begins dressing as a man again. To the straight audience, his downfall is gentle, but necessary; to a

The Queen

gay/lesbian/transgender audience, she is a fool who doesn't know the first thing about herself. Another gay subplot also begins promisingly, only to end homophobically. Lucky, a handsome 13-year-old boy, befriends Camille and, during her ordeal, offers her advice in handling her newly feminized father, and takes her to a drag bar. He is sensitive, worldly (welcomed to a drag bar at the tender age of 13!), attractive and, as he reveals late in the film, gay. But he also prostitutes himself to a rich old geezer. He warns the girl at one point of the dangers of living like he and her father "in the mud, the shit" and is eventually beaten up by his sugar daddy. Possibly the worst kind of gay-themed film, it depicts images of the lifestyle as grotesquely sad, the characters must pay the price and the audience leaves feeling superior, pitying the poor homosexuals and happy that they and their children are "not that way." ⊛

Shadey *(1987, 90 min, GB, Philip Saville)*

This eminently strange, offbeat espionage spoof stars Anthony Sher as Shadey, a garage mechanic who has special powers — the ability to read minds and project those images on film — but whose only real concern is to find the money for a sex change operation. While the film acknowledges his desire to "move to a different part of the human race," Shadey's sexuality and deeper reasons for wanting the sex change are never explored, but hints are offered. Billie Whitelaw is featured as a crypto-lesbian govern-

The boys of *Summer Vacation 1999*

celebrity, is recounted in this fascinating documentary. Through interviews with Chrysis, her fellow drag queen friends and archival and home movie footage we learn of her inspiring rise to showgirl stardom only to succumb to cancer in 1990 at age 39, her death caused by the seepage of wax and silicone from her artificial breasts. Looking like a cross between Raquel Welsh and a young Joan Collins, we listen to her struggles as well as her witty, fanciful tales in this tender and entertaining portrait of an unforgettable "chick with a dick."

Storme: The Lady of the Jewel Box *(1987, 21 min, US, Michelle Parkerson)*

This captivating portrait of Storme DeLarverie, emcee and male impersonator of the legendary Jewel Box Review, offers an overview of America's first integrated female impersonation show. The show toured black theatres across America from 1939 to 1973.

Summer Vacation 1999
(1988, 90 min, Japan, Shusuke Kaneko)

A provocative and lushly photographed tale of budding sexuality and the loss of innocence that owes more to French cinema than that of Japanese filmmaking. Four teenage boys (all intriguingly played by young girls) are left behind in their boarding school during the summer. Their idyllic world is forever changed after another youth, who bears an uncanny resemblance to a dead friend, joins them. By using women to play the leads, the film takes on an interestingly androgynous angle while at the same time hauntingly explores the fragile period in time when youth is suspended between innocence and experience, uncomplicated friendships and the initial pangs of romantic love and sexual awareness. ✪

Switch *(1991, 103 min, US, Blake Edwards)*

Blake Edwards wrote and directed this occasionally amusing though ordinary body-switching comedy. Ellen Barkin single-handedly saves the picture from mediocrity with a vibrant portrayal of a sexist philanderer who is murdered and comes back as a beautiful blonde. Perry King is what she used to look like; Jimmy Smits is his partner who is now attracted to his associate. In view of Edwards' brilliant sex farce *Victor/Victoria*, *Switch* is all the more disappointing. ✪

Time Expired *(1992, 30 min, US, Donny Leiner)*

While only 30 minutes long, this delightfully wacky love story packs both a comedic and emotional wallop and suggests great promise for director Donny Leiner. The winner of the Grand Prize at the USA Film Festival in 1992 and the Grand Prize at the Aspen Short Film Festival, the film begins with the release from prison of a butch, "straight" thug from Brooklyn who is greeted by his understanding wife and mother. But this is no typical ex-con tale, as he also must contend with Ruby, his former cell-mate — a Puerto Rican spitfire transvestite lover who is now working as a manicurist at a beauty salon and longs to resume their affair. The character of the no-nonsense Ruby, played with compassion

ment official who hopes to reign Shadey's power for military gain. Before his operation, Shadey dons full feminine attire for a night out on the town, and concocts a plan to get rid of his dick in a most grisly fashion! Weird and downright ridiculous, but interesting. ✪

Something Special
(1986, 90 min, US, Paul Schneider)

Cleverly written and brilliantly cast, *Something Special* is a Hollywood teen transgender comedy about a girl who gets to be a boy. Milly Niceman gets her "deepest, darkest heart's desire" when she wishes on a magical Indian eclipse powder. She awakes in the middle of the night to discover she's grown "a guy's thing down there." When Mr. and Mrs. Niceman tell her she must choose between being a boy or a girl, she asks innocently, "can't I be both?" After Milly becomes a boy, her/his girlfriend develops a new kind of interest in him/her; so does another girl at Willy's new school; and so does Willy's new pal Alfie (a disabled boy who refers to his wheelchair as a lunar module). When Alfie confesses his "unnatural desires" to Willy, Willy shoots for the hetero option and decides he wants to be a girl again. Wishing upon a star does the trick, and Alfie and Milly go off together as happy hets. Although the film ultimately doesn't allow for homosexuality as an option, it plays extensively on homoerotic potentials, and problematizes gender construction in a very pleasurable manner. Patty Duke gives an outstanding performance as Mrs. Niceman, and Pamela Segall is uncannily butch and boyish as Willy (and as Milly). ✪

Split William to Chrysis, Portrait of a Drag Queen
(1992, 58 min, US, Andrew Weeks & Ellen Fisher Turk)

The fascinating yet tragic "rags-to-riches-and-fabulous frocks" story of International Chrysis, a glamorous beauty who ran away from the poverty of his Brooklyn boyhood to become a charismatic drag artist, friend of Salvador Dali and underground and verve by John Leguizamo (star of off-Broadway's "Mambo Mouth" and "Spic-O-Rama," and the film *To Wong Foo, Thanks for Everything, Julie Newmar*) is the real attraction in this hilarious human comedy as she demands both respect and affection from her befuddled, loutish beau who faces the dilemma of choosing between his "normal" family life and Ruby. ☮

Too Outrageous!
(1987, 110 min, Canada, Richard Benner)
Ten years after making the acclaimed, small-budget *Outrageous!*, director Richard Benner and actor Craig Russell re-teamed for this not all-together successful sequel. Plump, wise-cracking hairdresser Robin (Russell), now a big hit as a female impersonator in New York, must still contend with his lack of a love life, hampered primarily by his friend and room-mate Liza (Holly McLaren) who still suffers from debilitating bouts of schizophrenia. This is a disappointing backstage memoir that is a bit stilted, oddly dated and not possessing the offbeat charms of the first film. Craig Russell, who, like writer/director Benner, died of AIDS in 1990, provides the only real attraction with his biting and on-target impersonations of Eartha Kitt, Tina Turner and Mae West.

La Travestie
(1988, 108 min, France, Yves Boisset)
Thirty-year-old lawyer Nicole has spent most of her adult life living in the country and unsuccessfully seeking true love with a man. Aware of her dull, unfulfilling life, she finally discovers pleasure when she dresses up as a man. Her transvestism evolves from solitary dressing up to eventually venturing into the outside world in her new persona.

Vera

La Travestie

Triple Echo *(1972, 94 min, GB, Michael Apted)*
Although understated in both its acting and direction, this film, adapted from an H.E. Bates story, is nevertheless quite bizarre. With her husband a prisoner-of-war, Glenda Jackson is a woman living alone in a farmhouse in a windswept, almost desolate landscape. She meets up with a young soldier (Brian Deacon) who, swayed by his attraction for her, impulsively deserts his unit and hides out in Jackson's house. When investigators begin snooping around, Jackson proposes that he dress in her clothing and pass himself off as her sister. The ruse works too well as burly sergeant Oliver Reed takes a fancy to the fetching lass. Enjoying his new role as a woman a bit too much, he accepts an invitation when the lecherous Reed invites him to a party, much to Jackson's trepidation. Disaster strikes when Reed, rubbing his date as he tries to cop a kiss, discovers to his horror a below-the-belt growth on his coy beau! A strange little cross-dressing drama and reportedly one of Jackson's favorite starring roles. ☮

Turnabout *(1940, 83 min, US, Hal Roach)*
Husband and wife change bodies halfway through this screwball comedy. The comic talents of Carole Landis bring a measure of intelligence and hilarity to a fairly lightweight script. She dresses up in men's clothes, and mimics male body language, speech and gesture. Robert Montgomery is pretty funny too as he minces and flits around the office to the amusement of his male co-workers.

Vera *(1987, 87 min, Brazil, Sergio Toledo)*
A fine example of the denial of sexual orientation and confused identity, *Vera* is an intriguing account of a woman who wants to invent herself as a man. Upon her release from a boarding school for girls, where she developed a strong masculine persona and was both feared and respected by her fellow classmates, 18-year-old Vera (Ana Beatriz Nogueria) finds herself adrift in the outside world. She is attracted to women but refuses to see herself as a lesbian, but rather as a man trapped in a woman's body. In an effort to become more like a man, she adopts a full-time male persona which in turn strengthens her resolve to pursue Clara, a beautiful co-worker. But Vera's single-mindedness only isolates

her further and forces the woman to confront her conflicting feelings of sexuality.

> "A deeply rewarding film. *Vera* has a haunting resonance and a profound emotional impact...a fascinating debut."
> — Joel Weinberg, *New York Native*

Victor/Victoria

(1982, 133 min, US, Blake Edwards)

This stylish, gender-bending, sexual/musical comedy stars Julie Andrews as a female who poses as a gay man impersonating a woman. Although Andrews is quite appealing in the role(s), it is Robert Preston who steals the show as her best friend Toddy, an exuberant, liberated and witty older gay man. James Garner also stars as a Chicago gangster confusingly enchanted and attracted to Andrews, who he thinks is a man. While gay positive, the film disappoints a bit in this relationship, for although he is attracted to Count Victor (Andrews), Garner's attraction is based on his male intuition that there is something just not quite right with the guy and he does not kiss "him" until he secretly discovers that he is actually a she. Coming up from the rear is former footballer Alex Karras as Squash, Garner's gay bodyguard who eventually beds Preston. Based on the 1933 German cross-dressing comedy, *Viktor und Viktoria*, the film, which received seven Academy Award nominations, is full of snappy tunes and sophisticated, harmless hilarity. ⊛

> "An unqualified hit...as happens in farce, everyone falls in love with everyone else, and because this is a liberated farce, the possible combinations are more than doubled — they're squared."
> — Vincent Canby, *The New York Times*

Viktor und Viktoria

(1933, 101 min, Germany, Reinhold Schunzel)

The inspiration for Blake Edwards' 1982 *Victor/Victoria*, this cross-dressing musical comedy was a big hit when it was first released. Viktor (Hermann Thimig) is a professional drag queen who persuades singer Susanne (Renate Mueller, one of Germany's most popular stars at the time) to perform as a male female impersonator. Her success is immediate; he becomes her manager and they tour Europe prompting a series of comedy-of-sexuality escapades. Charming and fast-paced, the film spurred several remakes including a 1934 French film, *Georges et Georgette*.

What Sex Am I?

(1984, 58 min, US, Lee Grant)

The often misunderstood subject, even for gays and lesbians, of transvestism and transsexualism is sensitively explored in this documentary, narrated and directed by actress and director Lee Grant. Through interviews with several transsexuals, mostly male-to-female, but with one female-to-male, the film charts their case histories and elicits their feelings about why they believe that their sex was wrong for them, examines the psychological and medical procedures they underwent to make their sex change, and profiles their present, post-operation lives. While this part of the film is fascinating, Grant also takes a look into the better known world of transvestites, although much less successfully. Because of her serious, almost clinical approach, and the straight, older and tartish men interviewed, this segment lacks the conviction and insightfulness of the earlier part. Over all, a compassionate, non-exploitative look at these two alternative lifestyles. ⊛

Alex Karras (r.) expresses his gayness to James Garner in *Victor/Victoria*

8

CAMP

The films in this chapter focus on entertainingly cheesy films
that feature gay, lesbian or transgendered characters. And it is
obviously the most politically incorrect but most entertaining chapter
in the book.

"The wedding was gorgeous. The best man gave the groom
away. My father gave the bride away and the fact that I
wanted to be flower girl...gave me away!"
— Malcolm de John (Michael Greer)
in *The Gay Deceivers*

"It's such a shame you're so lovely. To think of you all cut
and bruised. But it has to be done. Turn Over!"
— Lesbian starship captain "Mother"
(with whip in hand) to her two-timing
lover Porche in *Space Thing*

Addams Family Values

(1993, 87 min, US, Barry Sonnenfeld)

Dripping with deliciously mordant one-liners and infused with an almost palpable gay sensitivity, this outlandish follow-up to *The Addams Family* was written by openly gay Paul Rudnick, and his deft touch is much in evidence as this sequel soars above its more pedestrian original. Morticia (the unearthly and serene Anjelica Huston) has a baby, Pupert, much to the joy of her husband Gomez (Raul Julia), grandma (Carol Kane) and Uncle Fester (Christopher Lloyd). The children, Pugsly (Jimmy Workman) and Wednesday (Christina Ricci), however, see the little nipper as nothing more than an usurper and respond to his arrival with murderous zeal. The kids are soon dragged off to summer camp due to the urging of the baby's new nanny (Joan Cusack), a gold-digging black widow with her homicidal eyes on the transfixed Fester. This broad plot outline is all Rudnick needs as he furnishes it with hilariously morbid jokes and a sly fable on the revenge of the outcasts. All (except an under-used Pugsly) are great in their roles, especially the pale-faced, death-obsessed Wednesday who supplies the film with its best retorts. Look for Charles Busch's cameo as Countess Aphasia du Barry-Addams at Fester's wedding ceremony. ⊛

Focus on: *Paul Rudnick*

A New Jersey native born in 1957, Paul Rudnick has had a remarkable couple of years as a writer. Rudnick attended Yale (he picked that college because Cole Porter attended there), and he moved to New York after graduation. Since the late 1980s, Rudnick has had an enviable string of plays and novels. The books "I'll Take It" and "Social Disease" were both well reviewed; his first Broadway production, "I Hate Hamlet," was nominated for a Tony and "Jeffrey," thought to be the first comedy about AIDS, was an off-Broadway success. Rudnick, who possesses the subversive wit of an Oscar Wilde or Joe Orton, once commented when asked about "gay" writing, "The whole question of whether there is a gay sensibility can be debated endlessly...you're not born, you know, with an epigram on your tongue and a pair of tickets to 'Sunset Boulevard.'" Rudnick is also known, to faithful Premiere Magazine readers, as the alter-ego of that housewife/critic, Libby Gelman-Waxner. Although Addams Family Values is Rudnick's first screenwriting credit, he has previously worked on several other films. He did a substantial re-write on the screenplay for The Addams Family in 1991, although he wasn't given screen credit. His other film was Sister Act in 1992. Rudnick wrote the screenplay for this highly successful comedy with Bette Midler, the original star, in mind. But when Midler left the project he disassociated himself with the film, and had his name removed from the credits, substituting the pseudonym "Joseph Howard." Rudnick's latest work is the screen version of his comedy "Jeffrey," which stars Steven Weber, Sigourney Weaver, Patrick Stewart and Nathan Lane.

Aliens Cut My Hair

(1992, 58 min, US, Michael McIntosh)

This transvestite science fiction "spectacular" demonstrates what can happen when a group of tacky, cross-dressing queens get their hands on a video camera. Trying hard to be both camp and post-modern, this queer *Star Trek* space opera features a scissor-clipping drag queen alien (Stephen Maxxine) from the planet Hairdo who is determined to undermine the stability of the

Barbarella

Spaceship Penetrator and get to the hair of its square-jawed commader, Captain Dick Priapus. Self-indulgent, talky and delightfully cheesy, the film, based on the comic strip "Fabulous Space Stories," can be a lot of fun if viewed with the right crowd, in the proper attire and with lots of accessories. ⊛

Auntie Mame

(1958, 143 min, US, Morton DaCosta)

Rosalind Russell shines in a career-topping performance as everybody's favorite relative: Auntie Mame. Based on the hit play by Patrick Dennis, this gloriously funny adaptation follows the comic antics of an orphaned nephew who moves in with his eccentric aunt. A classic instance in which role and performer were destined for each other. Auntie Mame's best lesson: "Life is a banquet and most poor suckers are starving to death." ⊛

Barbarella

(1968, 98 min, France/Italy, Roger Vadim)

There's something for everyone in this imaginative, sexually charged sci-fi camp classic. Featuring a young Jane Fonda who, before Vietnam, exercise videos and rich Southern media moguls, was a fetching, pre-liberated sex goddess, this wacky film shows off all of her best bodily talents. There are plenty of strange characters in her 40th-century space travels. There's the gay computer control voice in Barbarella's fur-lined space ship; the beautiful, blond blue-eyed angel, John Philip Law ("Angels don't make love, angels are love"); and finally Anita Pallenberg as the Great Tyrant of planet Sorgo, a sexy lesbian who, from her opening lines of "Hello pretty, pretty" through the destruction of her empire, cannot keep her hands off our luscious heroine. Fonda, as the sexy siren and adventurer, has never been better (remember, this is the camp section!), for when she is not fighting off demonic, razor-teethed dolls or killer canaries, she displays a wonderful assortment of the latest in revealing intergalactic fashion. ⊛

Beyond the Valley of the Dolls
(1970, 109 min, US, Russ Meyer)

Russ Meyer's only major studio production, this purposefully over-the-top melodrama follows a group of four young women and their male manager as they make it big in the music world, only to be seduced by the tempting lure of ogasmatic sex and drugs. The loud and tacky side of the mod Sixties are wonderfully captured and hilariously lampooned as Meyer tells his own special kind of morality tale. Sexy, innocent and big-haired Kelly is the lead singer of The Carrie Nations, an all-female rock group. Trouble rears its head when the group goes to an L.A. party hosted by Ronnie (John LaZar), aka the Z-Man, a psychotic sexual misfit and fashion nightmare. Among his more memorable lines is this tasty tidbit, "This is my happening and it freaks me out!" Viewers will watch in horror as the bisexual Z-Man is transformed into Superwoman and stalks his/her chiseled *objet d'amour*, Lance Rock. Another sexually deviant character is the naive Casey (Cynthia Meyers), a Carrie Nation member who falls prey to the alluring charms of Roxanne (Erica Gavin). Their love blossoms, but Sapphic love has its price as the unseen narrator warns that "Theirs was not an evil relationship, but evil did come because of it." There are several additional peripheral finger-snapping gay characters (Rob Bach, Tim Louie, Chris Riordian, George Stratton) who add some queer spice to this wonderfully hallucinogenic hippie-era potboiler. ⊗

Can't Stop the Music
(1980, 124 min, US, Nancy Walker)

Let's boogie! Although its production date is listed as 1980, this campy musical comedy's disco-pulsating heart lies squarely in the tacky '70s. Featuring the "acting" and singing talents of the Village People along with a slumming Valerie Perrine and an atrocious Steve Guttenberg (although my opinion would change if his Barry ("The Brady Bunch") Williams imitation was intentional). The story's "Let's Put on a Show" plot is the very definition of inanity, with the attraction being a bevy of terrible lines, awful acting (Bruce Jenner!?), ridiculous musical numbers and the Village People's six members acting curiously straight (maybe they *can* act). Enjoyable cheese with the highlight being a tantalizing rendition of "YMCA" set in a hunk-filled locker room and shower. Yes, that is actress Nancy Walker ("Rhoda," "McMillan and Wife") listed as director. ⊗

Chained Heat
(1983, 95 min, US/Germany, Paul Nicolas)

One of the great treats (meaning sleaziest) in the women-in-prison genre, this violent and sexually explicit exploitation film stars the genre's reigning queens: Linda Blair and Sybil Danning. When naive Carol (Blair) is sent to prison for involuntary vehicular homicide, she's in for a quick and brutal education, for the prison is headed by a drug-dealing wretch of a warden, controlled by a sadistic chief guard and populated with hard-as-nails, knife-wielding peroxide babes (probably culled from many a casting couch afternoon — remember, this is a straight man's fantasy film). Plenty of full frontal nudity and lingering, voyeuristic shower scenes are peppered through-

out, and at one point, a lonely and agressive Danning puts the make on poor Blair. Lesbianism is, of course, rampant, especially at night when a bevy of tanned, buxom prisoners in tight-fitting T-shirts go bed-hopping, looking for love and relief from the daily horrors of this hell-on-earth prison. If Blair thought being possessed by the devil was tough, she's never spent time in a women's prison! The plot revolves around drug dealing and white slavery, but the director's interest is really in scantily clad beauties showering, having sex, fighting, taking drugs, having sex, having their clothes torn off, killing, having sex, being raped and finally revolting. And if director Nicolas was next, who could blame them? ⊗

Chained Heat 2
(1993, 98 min, US, Lloyd Simanl)

An exploitative lesbian *Midnight Express*, this women-in-prison actioner is great, politically incorrect fun. All hope seems lost for pretty strawberry blonde Alex when she is falsely imprisoned in a hellish all-female Czechoslovakian prison for drug smuggling. The hell-hole is headed by Magda Kassar — a suit-and-tie attired warden (played by Brigette Nielsen) who, aided by her knife-wielding, cigar-chomping Lotte Lenya-wannabe henchwoman Rosa, rules her roost, which is really a front for heroin manufacturing (forcing the inmates to work in the nude and using the prettiest ones as personal sex slaves!). Will our heroine ever escape? Will any of the actresses ever attend acting classes? Filmed in an actual Prague prison, the film is laughably bad, featuring the requisite bevy of beauties, plenty of gratuitous flesh and several lesbian lovemaking scenes. Nielsen is memorable as the stiletto-wearing warden with a weakness for "pretty young things" and hip-hugging outfits. *Chained Heat 2* is filled with poor acting, a terrible (but fun) script, kinky lesbian S&M sex and lines like, "Dance for me bitch!" How would you like your exploitation? With cheese, please! ⊗

Chopper Chicks in Zombietown
(1990, 86 min, US, Dan Hoskins)

The surprise hit of the Montreal Lesbian and Gay Film Festival, *Chopper Chicks in Zombietown* contrasts the rampant heterosexuality of the "Cycle Sluts" with the outspoken lesbianism of their

Chopper Chicks in Zombietown

gangleader. Although the lesbian content of he film is limited, this is first-rate trash filmmaking with campy gender politics, a wacko plot and six female s/heroes. For fans of camp this one is not to be missed. Produced by Maria Snyder. ☮

The Curse of Her Flesh

(1968, 75 min, US, Michael and Roberta Findlay)
Take a little New York avant-garde theatre, blend in some psychedelic '60s sexual revolutionism and some purely gratuitous "T&A" action and the result is this entertainingly weird low-budgeter that, at times, seems to be a straight man's wet dream of lesbian S&M. This is a guilty pleasure for those who appreciate lines like, "I was once told by a girlfriend that my big toe was better than any man's." Oh, and the plot? Something about a nightclub owner on a killing spree. ☮

Curse of the Queerwolf

(1987, 90 min, US, Mark Pirro)
One of the funnier low-budget horror/sexploitation flicks to come around in some time, this wacky variation on the werewolf legend is, at times, a genuinely hilarious spoof that is marred only by an insidious streak of homophobia. The story follows Larry, a typical straight-as-an-arrow guy who, much to his horror, is bitten on the ass by a pretty "girl," turning him into a queerwolf — male by day and tarty, heavily rouged "lady" by full moon. The target of the film's antic humor is primarily gay men (watch out ACT-UP and Queer Nation members) and innocent little dogs. But while offensive to some, it is more harmless camp than incendiary hatred. ☮

The Day the Fish Came Out

(1967, 109 min, Greece/GB, Michael Cacoyannis)
Disastrously aiming to satire *Dr. Strangelove*, this comedy of a lost A-bomb, mutated fish and lustful homosexuals is set in the future (1972) on an idyllic Greek island where an American warplane loaded with nuclear weapons crashes. The search for the weapons turns the island into a frenzied tourist attraction. The befuddled cast includes Tom Courtenay, Colin Blakely, Sam Wanamaker and Candice Bergen as a whip and leather dominatrix/architect.

Desperate Remedies

(1993, 92 min, New Zealand, Stewart Main & Peter Wells)
Campy to an outrageously shameless fault, this deliriously enjoyable and visually explosive costume romp is infused with more than its fair share of hyperventilating passions, luscious bosom-popping women and seductively thick-lipped men yearning for fulfillment. All this is presented in blinding colors and with a convoluted plot that seems to have combined (and "queerized") a dozen Harlequin romance novels. Set in Hope, a rugged 19th-century New Zealand pioneer

seaport (strongly reminiscent of the setting to Fassbinder's *Querelle*), the story revolves around the efforts of Doretha (Jennifer Ward-Lealand), a strong-willed rich girl, and a sneering fop, Fraser (Cliff Curtis), to set up her pregnant opium-and-love-addicted sister Anna with newly arrived but befuddled hunk Lawrence (Kevin Smith). The operatic plot soon falls to the background as the heaving breasts, lust-filled eyes and seething passions of all concerned envelop the audience. A delightful romp that should have both gay men and lesbians howling with laughter.

Focus on: *Peter Wells and Stewart Main*

Formerly lovers, now collaborators, Stewart Main and Peter Wells have been working together since 1982 in their native New Zealand and have produced such films as Jewel's Diary *(1987), a candid "day-in-the-life" of a transsexual;* A Death in the Family *(1989), a family drama on AIDS;* The Nighty Civic *(1990), a docu-drama on an opulent movie palace and winner of the Special Jury Prize at the San Francisco International Film Festival; and* A Taste of Kiwi *(1991), a banned short which juxtaposed a beer ad in which rugby players were dressing and a hard-core porn film.*

Faster, Pussycat! Kill! Kill!

(1966, 83 min, US, Russ Meyer)
Tura Satana stars as Varla, the tough-talking ringleader of a wild gang of out-of-control go-go girls in this thoroughly outrageous cult classic. Varla, a proto-lesbian killer with a taste for fast cars and helpless girls, rules with a leather-gloved fist over blonde beauty Billie (aka Boom Boom) (Lori Williams) and dark toughie Josie (Haji), two hot-rodding chicks in skin-tight clothes (calling them buxom would be redundant when talking about a Russ Meyer babe). Set in the California desert, these violent femmes kill a male and kidnap his bikini-wearing cutie pie girlfriend and go on a reckless, violent road to inevitable ruin. Filled with hilarious dialogue and hellacious catfights, this potboiler is one of Meyer's best. ☮

Desperate Remedies

Fertile La Toyah Jackson Video
Magazine/ Kinky *(1993, 58 min, US)*

Imagine combining Divine with Elizabeth Taylor's Martha from *Who's Afraid of Virginia Woolf?* and one might get an idea of Fertile La Toyah Jackson who, with her much more visible (and hilariously funny) partner Vaginal Creme Davis, takes the viewer on a bizarre video tour featuring the more unconventional nocturnal denizens of sunny California. Super low-budget and patchy (both in humor and producton values), this wacky cross-dressing travelogue visits a star-packed Jean-Paul Gaultier fashion show; interviews Kembra Pfahler (lead "singer" of the rock group Voluptuous Horror of Karen Black); takes a trek to the San Francisco Folsom Street Fair (sort of a leather, S&M and piercing Halloween extravaganza); records an astonishing live human mummification; and even tries to get some sense out of crazed and now-dead rocker gg allin. A fabulously entertaining party tape that promises to show, among other things, "How voluptuousness can carry you into a state of being that never existed before." ⊛

The Gang's All Here
(1943, 103 min, US, Busby Berkeley)

Musical comedies won't come any campier than this outrageously entertaining peek into the mindset of 1940s Americana. Alice Faye stars as a nightclub singer who is pursued by G.I. James Ellison. Their repartee — while amusing — is really imitation Astaire-Rogers. The real star of the film is the gloriously overblown dance numbers choreographed by director Busby Berkeley and performed by the legendary Carmen Miranda. The film's biggest production number, "The Lady in the Tutti-Frutti Hat," makes "Springtime for Hitler" look like a highlight from *Singin' in the Rain*. In it, Miranda is adorned with baskets of fruit upon her head, and in a surreal sequence, giant bananas come from all directions engulfing chorus girls and Miranda, alike. Reissued in the early 1980s to enthusiastic response, this is an absolute don't-miss entry in the chapter of American movie camp. In support, the wonderfully comic Charlotte Greenwood sizzles as a wise-cracking society matron with the longest legs on screen, and Edward Everett Horton, Benny Goodman and Eugene Pallette also star.

The Girl with the Hungry Eyes
(1967, 85 min, US, William Rotsler)

From the Russ Meyer school of exploitation filmmaking comes this sultry tale of a hot-rodding lesbian bent on keeping her gal. Restless, man-hating Tigercat (Cathy Crowfoot) and her bisexual lover Kitty (Vicky Dee) are first seen cruising the California roads in their souped-up Corvette on a collision course with trouble! We soon find out that the honeymoon's over for the two as pony-tailed Kitty starts with the roving eye, despite Tiger's protestations that men "all want the same thing...to use you; you're better off with me." But after one tryst (and a bludgeoned male corpse), Kitty knows that getting out of the clutches of her jealous lover will be no easy task and she turns to dreaming of heterosexual bliss, telling Tiger that being with a man is "happier, it's different being with a real man, somehow not so desperate" (remember this was made by straight men). Kitty eventually finds her escape when, at a lesbian birthday party thrown for her, a vicious cat fight erupts

between Tiger and another butch who took a fancy to Kitty, and she runs out of of the house and right into the arms of her understanding former boyfriend. Most of the film is a scream, but it ends with an anti-lesbian diatribe, calling love between two women a "dead end...destructive...it's like death...a woman was made for man and vice versa." But it's best to ignore the ranting at the end and enjoy the wild, lesbian abandon. ⊛

Guilty as Charged
(1991, 95 min, US, Sam Irvin)

A black comedy and cult film candidate, this is openly gay director Sam Irvin's first film. Rod Steiger, with a nod to Mr. Joyboy from *The Loved One*, appears to be having a good time chewing the scenery even while underplaying in this spoofy thriller. Steiger plays the owner of a meat packing company who moonlights as a vigilante judge and executioner. Kidnapping paroled or escaped convicted murderers, Steiger imprisons and then zaps the convicts in a homemade electric chair. Heather Graham plays a pretty social worker who begins to notice and investigate the disappearances. The film also sets its sights on political tomfoolery, with Lyman Ward as a seedy congressman running for Governor who secretly endorses Steiger's sideline. Lauren Hutton vamps it up as Ward's disdainful wife, and Isaac Hayes has fun as Steiger's bible-quoting sidekick. ⊛

How to Impersonate a Woman
(1993, 60 min, US, Janus Rainer)

Finally, a QVC for cross-dressers and "big girls!" This shamelessly self-promotional video, where transvestite secrets are revealed, is a hilariously tacky instructional guide on makeup, prosthetic aids and clothing tips for men who like to dress up as women. While there is nothing inherently funny in transvestism, this video unintentionally goes out of its way to be pure camp. The first part of the film takes a serious, if awkward approach in offering different options for the female impersonator — with director/narrator Janus Rainer providing a valid defense for its adherents and then, with the aid of several models, demonstrates — for those who "adore the feminine mystique" — the proper application of makeup, selection of clothing, padding and wigs. The second half is where the film takes off, when Michael Salem, the corpulent self-styled "Lingerie King of Park Avenue," demonstrates, in a bizarre, hilarious, Tupperware party fashion, the various items he has for sale to a chunky, seemingly bewildered transvestite. Shrill and priceless. ⊛

Johnny Guitar
(1954, 110 min, US, Nicholas Ray)

A true original from Nicholas Ray (*Rebel without a Cause*), this is the story of a cowboy who carries a guitar instead of a pistol and believes that, "...when you boil it all down, all a man needs is a good smoke and a cup of coffee." Joan Crawford plays Vienna, a saloon keeper who enlists Johnny's aid, and Mercedes McCambridge is incomparable as Emma Small, the local crusader who simply can not rest until she sees them all hang. As played by McCambridge, Emma is a sneering zealot who wears black and can't accept her attraction to Vienna. Insightful and intoxicating, the film has been cited as a source of inspiration by such contemporaries as Wim Wenders and Jim Jarmusch. ⊛

The King *(1968, 60 min, US, Looney Bear)*

Little more than a simple '60s soft-core "nudie," *The King* is notable for its near-complete emphasis on lesbian sex and relationships. Filmed in non-sync sound with a voice-over narration that reads like a cheap but torrid lesbian potboiler, the film focuses on Carol, a dark-haired beauty who, after being seduced by her female boss two minutes on the job ("She was stimulating me as only a woman knows how"), returns home to strange relationships with her two roommates. At the center of her homelife is Mickie (The King), a dark-haired butch who emotionally and sexually dominates both Carol and the third roommate, Lisa. This being a nudie, all three are soon naked making love set to generic, upbeat elevator music. After the fun, the three go off to the beach, where Carol cruises other women and pines for a relationship that is not so abusive (Mickie not only denies her emotional stability, but beats her with a belt when so moved). But depsite these problems, Carol does not crave men, instead enjoying both the company of and sex with women, saying at one point that she is "Free from the constant harassment of men, men trying to talk to me, men trying to date me, men following me. They are devious, insincere and cruel — I know all about them, I know they want to abuse my body without giving me any affection." ☻

The Lonely Lady

(1983, 92 min, US, Peter Sasdy)

Tacky, tasteless and completely satisfying in a campy way, this Hollywood exposé, adapted from the Harold Robbins novel, was made to showcase the talent and body of the spunky Pia Zadora. The story begins with young Pia, a talented high school virgin (now that's great acting), who after being raped by a garden hose wielded by a Hollywood brat, quickly learns that being good is not all that it's cracked up to be. On recovery, she is determined to become a successful writer in the shark-infested swamp that is Hollywood. Sleeping her way to the top, our chipmunk-faced Pia achieves the success she sought, only to find emptiness and remorse, proving that it is indeed a lonely road up the ladder of fame and fortune. Her eagerness for success is so intense that she has sex not with one but two different women; one an Italian beauty who croons to her, "Your eyes are beautiful, your script is beautiful, everything is beautiful," before devouring her. Pia also drops her drawers when, ever the trouper, she climbs into a hot tub with a lesbian producer. Anthony Jackson puts in a great performance as Guy, a gay film director and the only character that cares for Pia...but in a sexless, best-friend way. Also, gay Kenneth Nelson (Michael from *The Boys in the Band*) puts in a cameo as a catty hairdresser. ☻

Love Bites *(1988, 60 min, US, Marvin Jones)*

The bat-flying, blood-sucking vampire legend takes a decidedly gay twist in this lighthearted romp which features porn stars Kevin Glover and Christopher Ladd. Love and sex come to the 437-year-old West Hollywood Count when his dangerously seductive charms entrap a novice vampire stalker. This unlikely love story between the sucker and the suckee is the main course in this delightfully erotic romance. ☻

"Best soft-core film of 1989." — *Advocate Men*

The Magic Christian

(1969, 95 min, GB, Joseph McGrath)

Although this wackily funny comedy (adapted by Terry Southern from his novel) is essentially straight, there are some points of interest for gays. Peter Sellers is Guy Grand, the world's richest man, who enjoys testing people's greed and proving that everyone has their price. Guy picks up street vagabond Ringo Starr and proceeds to adopt him as his son. Together, this unusually close "father-son" team proceed to play practical jokes on the unsuspecting. One of the best of these episodes features a seductive diva played by Yul Brynner (looking sluttishly ravishing in full drag regalia) singing a torch song ("Mad About the Boy") to a boyish, confused and sexually intrigued Roman Polanski; it culminates in a juicy kiss! Gay actor Leonard Frey (*The Boys in the Band, Fiddler on the Roof*), who died of AIDS at age 49 in 1988, is featured as a fussy, alarmist doctor-cum-vampire "administering" to the sick on a sinking luxury cruiser and Laurence Harvey does a striptease in the middle of playing "Hamlet." A hilarious camp comedy with cameos by Raquel Welch, Richard Attenborough, John Cleese and Graham Chapman, and with music by Badfinger. ☻

The Magic Christian

Manuel and Clemente

(1985, 100 min, Spain, Javier Palermo Romero)

A deliriously sacrilegious comedy, based on the history of the Carmelites of the Holy Shroud sect. Two gay lovers cash in on the religious prophesy racket in a scam that culminates with Clemente's coronation as Pope.

Medusa: Dare to Be Truthful

(1992, 90 min, US)

Julie Brown, spooftress extraordinaire, first made herself known to the world via her "Just Say Julie" show on MTV, and later in the camp/farce musical *Earth Girls Are Easy*. And now, her masterpiece. Yes, too strong a word; but her send-up of pop icon Madonna's documentary *Truth or Dare* is dead-on and absolutely brilliant. From the oh-so pretentious black-and-white photography, to the letter-perfect costumes and production, right down to the "I'm queen bitch of the world" tantrums and diatribes for which Ms. M. is famous, Brown has it *down*. Highlights include a hilarious (and unbelievably rude) take on Madonna's infamous visit to her mother's gravesite — including a side-splitting sight gag (watch for the shovel) — and a takeoff on "Vogue" entitled, smartly enough, "Vague," that is a jaw-dropper. Familiarity with *Truth or Dare* is a near-requirement, so get comfy, watch them back to back, and go into pop culture overdrive. ⊛

Mommie Dearest

(1981, 129 min, US, Frank Perry)

The campy, spirited version of Christina Crawford's novel detailing her abused childhood as the adopted daughter of actress Joan Crawford. Faye Dunaway pulls out all the stops in a no-holds-barred portrayal of the movie queen. (Ironically, Crawford herself remarked that if her life story were ever filmed, she wanted Dunaway to play her.) The film which immortalized the line, "No wire hangers!" ⊛

Monaco Forever

(1984, 43 min, US, William A. Levey)

This cheesy short film, from the director of *Skatetown USA,* has been recently released on video with Jean-Claude Van Damme's face and muscles prominently displayed on the cover. Tricky promotion, because Van Damme is actually in the film for only a little over two minutes — but what a two minutes! With the credits naming him the "Gay Karate Man," our hunky star-to-be plays a driver of an XK150 Jaguar who picks up a hitchhiker, makes some "advances" by placing his hand on his crotch, and when he is rebuked and threatened (the passenger was obviously deranged!), tears off his shirt and teaches the unresponsive tease a lesson. What makes this film interesting is not only Van Damme's choice of roles, but the unusual image of a sexually aggressive gay man, young rich and handsome, who instead of becoming a victim of queer-bashing, more than defends himself. ⊛

Monster in the Closet

(1986, 87 min, US, Bob Dahlin)

"Destroy All Closets!" No, this isn't the rallying cry of ACT-UP, but the battle hymn for the gallant cast of characters belonging to

Faye Dunaway is Joan Crawford. A star...a legend...and a mother... The illusion of perfection.

To my darling Christina with love

Mommie Dearest

this low-keyed, low-budget horror parody. Spoofing *Superman*, *King Kong* and *The Exorcist*, among many others, *Monster in the Closet* is probably the first film to feature a monster with a decidedly alternative sexual preference. A Clark Kent-type reporter investigates a series of killings in a small town, aided by a teacher and her young son. There are a few laughs, most of them in-jokes; and for a Troma release, the film is surprisingly non-offensive. ⊛

99 Women

(1968, 90 min, Spain/Ger/GB/It, Jess Franco)

The women-in-prison genre gets the European "art" treatment in this lurid drama set in a bizarre, fortress-like castle on a Mediterranean island. Sexy, scantily clad women are hauled to prison and are greeted by Thelma (Mercedes McCambridge), a hellish superintendent with looks suggesting a Prussian Sister George (with a bit of Lotte Lenya's Rosa Klebb thrown in). The usual elements of the genre are present: beautiful women, cat fights, lots of skin and sex; but the most interesting aspect of the film is its treatment of lesbianism. For when the lights go out, a veritable hotbed of Sapphic love percolates, though most of it is presented as perverse (and oddly only butch Thelma seems to be straight!). A rape of one woman by several others goes from being

CAMP

Ren & Stimpy

antics that often involve expulsions of bodily fluids (farts, spittle, "nose goblins"), not to mention hair balls, toe cheese and other such forbidden roughage. The pair — Ren being an effete Peter Lorre-voiced Chihuahua and Stimpy the dim-witted feline — get into the usual cartoon shenanigans but their "friendship" suggests more than simple pals. The two sleep together and are especially close. In the episode "Stimpy's Inventions" (which was banned by the television network and is available only on home video), the twosome's sexual antics are exposed for all to see. Stimpy's beloved fart, "Stinky," escapes his master's bottom and ventures into the big city leaving the chunky cat sobbing and distraught. Ren, hoping to change his mood, looks up and sees mistletoe above them. He becomes all coquettish and excited, fluttering mischievous bedroom eyes and wiggling his hairless ass at Stimpy. The distracted cat, realizing that all Ren has on his mind is sex, dismisses his horny hound-lover with "Is that all you can think of?" Not surprisingly, creator Kricfalusi was replaced after the first year. Openly gay producer Jim Ballantine stayed on with the new, less adventurous regime. ⊛

The Ritz
(1976, 91 min, US, Richard Lester)
Adapted from openly gay playwright Terrence McNally's hilarious Broadway hit, this riotous farce stars Jack Weston as a straight Cleveland garbage collector on the lam from his Mafioso brother-in-law who hides out in a New York gay bathhouse. There, he encounters the spitfire Googie Gomez (Rita Moreno reprising her Tony Award-winning role); a hunky, high-pitch-voiced Treat Williams; F. Murray Abraham; an active steam room; and a bevy of half-naked studs. At one point, the frazzled and corpulent Weston almost loses his virginity to a smitten "chubby chaser." Although quite funny, many in and out of the gay community view the film as a one-joke fag comedy that borders on the homophobic. But politics aside, the film is an innocent frenetic comedy that gently pokes fun at gays. ⊛

The Rocky Horror Picture Show
(1975, 95 min, GB, Jim Sharman)
"Come up to the lab, and see what's on the slab." In *the* cult-midnight show attraction, scientist, alien and bisexual transvestite Dr. Frank N. Furter is visited by average Americans Brad and Janet; the latter two giving themselves over to "absolute pleasure." A wacked-out, spoofy, goofy, hip and campy one-of-a-kind musical. Tim Curry is the Doc, with Susan Sarandon as Janet, Barry Bostwick as Brad, Richard O'Brien as the hunchback valet Riff-Raff, Meatloaf (again!) as rock 'n' roller Eddie, Little Nell as Columbia, and Patricia Quinn as Magenta. Based on the British stage musical, with lyrics and music by O'Brien. "Let's do the Time Warp again!" ⊛

Scarecrow in a Garden of Cucumbers
(1972, 95 min, US, Robert Kaplan)
Warholite Holly Woodlawn (*Trash, Women in Revolt*) is Eve Harrington, the effervescent ingenue who ventures to New York City and overcomes slimeballs, creeps and heartbreaking men to win fame and fortune. A hilarious spoof of Hollywood's star-is-born sagas with music by Bette Midler.

violent to a scene of tender, sensual caressing while the victim's lover helplessly watches, slightly aroused. Also shown is an exclusively lesbian house of prostitution catering to "a special kind of customer with very special tastes." As the female prisoner enters the room and performs an erotic striptease and masturbation performance, the camera pans over a menagerie of lesbian "types." The star of the film and her lover eventually break out only to be hunted down both by the guards and a group of sexually ravenous male prisoners. Ridiculous, but nonetheless thoroughly enjoyable. ⊛

Our Miss Fred *(1975, 96 min, GB, Bob Kellett)*
A guilty, campy pleasure if there ever was one, starring female impersonator Danny LaRue as a soldier who, during WWII, is caught in drag just when the Germans invade France. The admittedly ridiculous story follows his inventive attempts to get through Nazi-infested lands (under the nom de guerre of Frederika) without the Germans catching on to his identity — sort of a slapstick/drag version of *Europa, Europa*! Determinedly heterosexual, although there are plenty of double entendres to the contrary, our wonderfully fashion-accessorized heroine, who "has every little thing a woman should have and more," traipses through the countryside dazzling the enemy (and even a few horny Frenchmen) with her fabulously outrageous frocks, wigs and sharp-tongued wit. ⊛

Reform School Girls
(1986, 94 min, US, Tom DeSimone)
It's women behind bars, complete with young innocent (Linda Carol), sadistic disciplinarian (Pat Ast), witchy warden (Sybil Danning) and kinky con (Wendy O. Williams). Wendy O. also sings the title song ("So Young, So Bad, So What!"). ⊛

Ren and Stimpy
Other than Bugs Bunny's penchant for cross-dressing and his ongoing sadomasochistic relationship with the gun-toting Elmer Fudd, no other stars of cartoonland have come out, that is until the arrival of television's most unusual cat and dog team, Ren and Stimpy (no last names, please!). These creations by John Kricfalusi and first seen on cable TV's Nickelodeon shook up the standards of acceptable behavior by their wacky, no-holds-barred

The Seducers
(1970, 86 min, Italy, Ottavio Alessi)

A sexually kinky *L'Avventura*, this weird tale of love, power and violence is set in the Mediterranean on a yacht where a rich lesbian holds court over a group of sexually ravenous and/or psychotic characters. Mudy (Maude de Bellerouche) is a scowling lesbian with the looks of Buster Keaton and attired in Mary Quant dresses and Louise Brooks hair. She's a rich, butch power queen who is accompanied by two female prostitutes; one for her and the other for her near-catatonic teenage son who is still a virgin. In addition to loads of lesbian sex (all of the women get involved at some point), there is also some ordinary heterosexual sex and an amazing scene of a goat giving oral sex to an enraptured woman (a woman's answer to gerbils?). Although an exploitation film with despicable characters, lesbianism is shown as normal, sensuous and epidemic! (Also known as: *Sensation*; *Top Sensation*) ⊛

Sextette *(1978, 91 min, US, Ken Hughes)*

Four on the floor is standard equipment with this classic beauty, as Mae West returned to the showroom after an absence of almost 40 years loaded with options and ready for action. Her turbo-charged headers make it clear that this is one body that was built to go the distance. This camp classic about international superstar Margo Manners, whose honeymoon keeps getting interrupted by her many ex-husbands, co-stars a pre-James Bond Timothy Dalton, who faces his most dangerous challenge as Mae requires more servicing than a Buick Skylark. Ringo Starr, Tony Curtis, George Hamilton and Alice Cooper are just a few of the others who take her out for a spin after a quick look under the hood. Her farewell performance, this adaptation of her own play finds the octogenarian West offering an embarrassing litany of her most famous lines. ⊛

She-Male by Choice
(1993, 60 min, US, Marc Antonio)

On the (high)heels of her first entertaining video, *How to Be a Female Impersonator*, producer Janus Rainer delves deeper into man's eternal fascination with female beauty, attire and allure. This amateurish but eye-opening video promises to teach one and all "how to transform yourself into the beautiful female creature of your fantasies." Two "she-males" (Bill Fenway, aka Virginia, and "underground TV starlet" Ava Hollywood) offer contrasting tips on makeup, clothing, hip swiveling, latex breast simulators and, in the

The Rocky Horror Picture Show

Shock Treatment

advanced steps, how to attain the actual "look and style of total femininity." Virginia's transformation from a nerdy male to beauty queen (actually the final look will remind one more of Milton Berle in drag!) is done in ten easy steps, a must for cross-dressers whose moms were "too busy or unwilling to offer her beauty secrets." The more feminine and attitude-dripping instructor Ava, "a model and socialite in her Manhattan penthouse" (actually a windowless, painted brick-walled room), offers her own makeup tips. For Halloween dragsters, listen to Virginia; for those a bit more serious in dressing as a woman, follow Ava's advice (and seek an instructive girlfriend as well!).

She Mob
(1968, 79 min, US, Alfred Sack)
Start by making a cheap "nudie," throw in some Russ Meyer touches (see *Faster, Pussycat! Kill! Kill!*), and top off with "Big Shin" (a tough-talkin' power-hungry dyke with a penchant for conical shaped bras and leather undies), and you've got yourself 79 minutes of cheesy, guilty-pleasure excitement. Ringleader Big Shin (Marni Castle) and four of her girls break out from a women's prison and hole up in a farmhouse. The women, all sexually starved, silicone-breasted beauties, are tired of masturbating (with Big Shin watching and slobbering) and want a man (read: dick). So to keep her girls in line, Shin kidnaps a rich businesswoman's paid stud, and while waiting for the ransom, lets her ravenous underwear-clad women at him. Things get out of hand when Baby, Shin's favorite, joins in the hetero fun. The businesswoman (also played by Castle) has balls herself and hires "girl detective" Sweetie (Monique Duvall) (read: bimbo with a gun) to rescue her invaluable gigolo. Truly a '60s camp wonder with outrageous outfits and an unbelievably vicious lesbian villain who dies in a blaze of gunfire in a grand "Is this the end of Rico?" finale. ☻

Shock Treatment
(1981, 90 min, US, Jim Sharman)
The dynamic musical-comedy sequel to *The Rocky Horror Picture Show* finds Brad and Janet prisoners in demented Denton, home of

happiness and TV game shows. Richard O'Brien leads the fun as a mentally suspect medic in this twisted satire on The American Way (greed, lust, media-manipulation and skimpy attire). ☻

Sin in the Suburbs
(1964, 88 min, US, Joseph W. Sarno)
This early "nudie" that entertainingly exposes the teeming sexual corruption lurking behind the well-tended lawns of suburbia is a film ahead of its time with its depiction of extramarital group sex, a mysterious cloak-and-mask sex club and jailbait lesbianism! After their husbands take the 7:21 to the city, a group of sexually frustrated wives go about their daily activities: paying their bills (by fucking the bill collector), boozing it up with their equally horny neighbors, dancing the twist with their children's teenage boyfriends and generally acting like the Romans before the fall. The lesbian action finds pretty high school student Cathy coming home unexpectedly early only to witness mom naked on top of a stranger. She runs out of the house and into the understanding arms of Yvette (Lahna Monroe), a thirtyish neighbor who quickly takes a liking to the distraught girl, and they soon end up in bed. But when her sex club operations get in the way of their tryst, Yvette callously gives her the brush-off, explaining that, "I'm not good for you," prompting Cathy to run back into the loving embrace of her mommy. Absurdly funny and scandalous — in a clean-cut American way. ☻

Slumber Party Massacre
(1982, 78 min, US, Amy Jones)
Lesbian and feminist novelist Rita Mae Brown ("Rubyfruit Jungle," "Venus Envy") penned this horrific lampoon of mad-slasher films which, with the exception of the male driller killer and an "at the wrong place, at the wrong time" pizza delivery boy, has an all-female cast and crew. You've seen it all before: Pretty young teenage girls are terrorized when a psycho escapes from the hospital and goes on a bloody rampage. Brown has persistently defended her "I've gotta pay the rent" screenplay as a feminist parody of the genre, in which the women, initially the victims, react to repel their attacker. Nice try Rita! Interestingly, the relative success of this film spawned two sequels, both directed by women as well. ☻

Sometimes Aunt Martha Does Dreadful
Things *(1971, 95 min, US, Thomas Casey)*
Gay relationships don't come any sicker than in this enjoyably bizarre drive-in slasher-cum-camp pic. On the lam after murdering a rich old lady in Baltimore, Paul and Stanley, partners in bed and crime, end up in Miami, where Paul assumes the new drag identity of the demented Aunt Martha. Martha, a dominating bitch who would intimidate Joan Crawford, becomes alternately possessive and protective when his hippie boyfriend starts playing around with "loose" women. These seduction scenes are possibly the most interesting, with Stanley being passively receptive to the aggressive women only to become psychotic when it gets down to actually fucking. A truly kinky relationship in the tradition of Beryl Reid and Susannah York in *The Killing of Sister George*, which features a queasy "birthing" scene that would make John Waters proud. ☻

Transvestite Secrets Revealed

Ten Violent Women

(1979, 95 min, US, Ted V. Mikels)
The always fun women-in-prison genre is expanded by one with this poorly acted, incredibly insipid film. In the beginning there were ten good girls all working as coal miners (?!) in Southern California. But soon they leave their law-abiding ways behind and evolve into ten swinging, boozing, water gun-toting Farrah Fawcett-hair-wearing violent femmes bent on attaining quick, easy money. A jewel heist succeeds, but a drug deal goes bust, sending seven of our joy-riding chicks off to prison, headed by the nortorious Miss Terry, a sadistic butch lesbian warden with a penchant for wearing nautical-themed suits and, in the evenings, sexy lingerie. Keeping to the theme's rules, the slammer is filled with beautiful but dangerous she-cats and there are plenty of shower scenes, sex between prisoners and hellacious cat-fights. A terrible, but enjoyable exploitation flick that is notable for its depiction of lesbianism. Yes, the warden is a crazed dyke and female rape is shown, but two of the heroines are also lesbians before, during and after their stay in the big house and the depiction of ten women who band together without the company of men is certain to please many women while instilling fear in the hearts of many an insecure man! ✪

That Tender Touch

(1969, 88 min, US, Russell Vincent)
One from the vaults of American independent soft-core exploitation films that titillated the audience with the forbidden theme of lesbianism. This very "'60s" drama stars Sue Bernard (*Playboy*'s Miss December 1966 and star of Russ Meyer's *Faster, Pussycat! Kill! Kill!*) as Terri, a young woman whose brief lesbian interlude one idyllic summer is quickly forgotten when she breaks up with her lesbian lover to take the "respectable" heterosexual route. Recently married to a young man (who knows nothing of her sexual wanderings), she is eager to enjoy the rewards and privileges of suburban life. But those Orange County dreams of normalcy are threatened when her relentless ex, Marsha (Bee Thompson), arrives at her doorstep determined to rekindle that old Sapphic feeling. While Marsha tries to convince her that they should be together, several of Terri's female friends take an interest in Marsha — the British maid, the next-door neighbor and the neighbor's daughter all flirt with her. But Marsha only has eyes for Terri. She ends up face down in the swimming pool in the end, but not before jumping Terri one more time and getting her to admit that she is still in love with her. "I want you Marsha, but it's wrong," Terri pleads as Marsha tries to pull off her bikini on the bedroom floor. With lots of flesh and tantalizing lesbian sex, this entertaining camp potboiler is great cheesy fun and a fine example of the 1960s exploitation films that depicted lesbianism as enticing, but oh so wrong! ✪

A Thousand Pleasures

(1968, 68 min, US, Michael Findley)
The term "baby love" takes on a new dimension when wife-slayer Richard Davis, on his way to dispose of the body, picks up a pair of hitchhiking lesbians. Upon his arrival at their compound, he meets the colorful group of residents that include a full grown, full-figured diaper-wearing thumb sucker, and a pair of ill-tempered male-loathing dykes. After a lecture on the joys of woman-love, Davis is drugged and his "seed" is used to provide a child for one of the group. Catapulted into their demented world of sick pleasures, Davis is driven once again to violence in order to escape his well-earned woman-hell; he fails, however, and is suffocated at the hands (make that breasts) of a well-endowed member of the brood.

Transvestite Secrets Revealed

(1992, 60 min, US)
Super low-budget and entertainingly sleazy, this unusual how-to video is part of the tacky camp trilogy of cross-dressing how-to tapes (which include *How to Impersonate a Woman* and *She-Male by Choice*). Our corpulent host Michael Salem reveals the secrets to achieving a successful transformation from male to female. Bill Fenway, an amazingly geeky man, is miraculously transformed, with the assistance of fellow TVers Karen Dior, Krissie Orchide and Francis, into an equally geeky woman. As Salem explains, "One out of eight males are involved in some way with TV," one can understand why the avalanche of drag instruction is flooding the market. So for those who seek the "most intimate secrets of female attire" and how to achieve that lovely curvacious body

Vegas in Space

Gordon meets *Forbidden Planet*. Prohibited from landing on the "babes only" planet Clitoris, four men (actually two men and two women — the cross-dressing begins early) from a 23rd-century Earth patrol ship take a gender-bending pill that changes them into fabulously attired women enabling them to go undercover as 20th-century showgirls. Doris Fish is the enchanting ringleader who, along with Ginger Quest and "Tippi," attempt to uncover the bad guy/gal on the fun-filled, spiked-heeled pleasure planet where Miss X reigns as the planet's regal queen (and possible villain). The plot sputters a bit and there is tons of static filler, but despite its less-than-stellar production values (nothing was spared when it came to the frocks, however) the film is entertaining and harmless fun.

> "I see it as a sophisticated art film cleverly disguised as trash."
>
> — director Philip R. Ford

> "See it and surrender yourself to fabulousness."
> — *San Francisco Examiner*

nature denied you, this is the video for you. If drugs were not used during the production of this video, they should have been. ⊛

The Ultimate Degenerate
(1969, 70 min, US, Michael Findley)
Sleazy does not begin to describe this exploitation shocker that features lesbian nymphomaniacs, deadly hallucinations, whipped cream, a mad sexual ringmaster and a bushel of corn. Sex-loving Maria, a beautiful blonde, tires of her more traditional roommate/lover Tonya and answers a classified ad that promises wild sex. She goes to a run-down house ruled over by a handicapped sex fiend (director Michael Findley) and his strange assistant Bruno. Lesbian promiscuity goes into high gear as horny Maria beds several complying women. But the fun ends when the drugs get out of hand and the sex is a bit excessive — one of the more disturbing scenes shows a woman shoving several ears of corn into a woman's orifice in which one would have been enough. Death and violence ensue with the only happy survivor being a cackling gay man — the ultimate degenerate! Ludicrous fun for camp entertainment-starved queers. ⊛

Valley of the Dolls
(1967, 123 min, US, Mark Robson)
Trashy, melodramatic piece of camp heaven based on Jacqueline Susann's best-selling novel that takes us on a hell-bound highway of drugs, sex, drinks and infidelity. The story focuses on the rise and fall of starlets in the entertainment biz. Starring Patty Duke, Sharon Tate, Susan Hayward, Lee Grant and Martin Milner, the film at times drifts into cliché-riddled waters, but is nevertheless chock full of those absolutely absurd soap opera-ish elements which make this genre so much fun! A must see. ⊛

Vegas in Space
(1992, 90 min, US, Philip R. Ford)
Low-budget filmmaking is given a new definition in this outrageous sci-fi musical spoof: a cross-dressing version of *Flesh*

Zorro, the Gay Blade
(1981, 93 min, US, Peter Medak)
After successfully spoofing the vampire movie (in *Love at First Bite*), George Hamilton set his sights on the Zorro legend, with uneven results. Hamilton plays the twin sons of Zorro, one a swashbuckler, the other a gay bon vivant. Some laughs, and to its credit, not offensive. ⊛

Zorro, the Gay Blade

9

HONORABLE AND DISHONORABLE MENTIONS

The films in this chapter feature lesbian, gay, bisexual or transgendered characters in secondary or bit roles and/or make references to homosexuality.

"I've been with a man...which is a sin against nature, a sin against God!"
—Billy Joe McAllister's reason for jumping off the Tallahatchie Bridge in *Ode to Billy Joe*

"I happen to be a proud homo sex child. That makes me a woman by desire and a man by nature. Now which do you want to deal with, mother fucker!"
—The cross-dressing Mistress C.'s (Vaughn Cromwell) response after being called a "faggot" in *Street Wars*

The Adjuster

(1991, 102 min, Canada, Atom Egoyan)

Atom Egoyan's twisted tale follows Noah (Elias Koteas), an methodically opportunistic but strangely sympathetic insurance claim adjuster who sleeps with many of his female customers. At one point while taking down information on a gay couple's fire insurance claim, one of the men, Matthew (Raoul Trujillo), a leather-clad, long-haired beauty, cruises the increasingly uncomfortable Noah. In ensuing scenes, the erotically charged seduction continues until they eventually sleep together. This effectively handled depiction of a hitherto straight man's physical attraction to and seduction by another man is quite rare in mainstream films. ⊛

The Adventurers

(1970, 171 min, US, Lewis Gilbert)

Following up on her role as a lesbian in *The Group*, Candice Bergen reprises as a wealthy American heiress who, after losing her baby in an accident, prefers the sexual company of women. This big-budget fiasco was based on Harold Robbins' sex-filled best-seller and while eminently awful, this cheesy soap opera has developed a camp cult following. ⊛

The Adventures of Picasso

(1978, 88 min, Sweden, Tage Danielsson)

The wacky life of Pablo Picasso is imaginatively played out in this mad farce which, despite its biographical structure, has nothing to do with the actual life of the famous painter. Narrating the proceedings is Gertrude Stein who, when introduced, is a cigar-chomping drag queen; as is her "friend and constant companion" Alice B. Toklas. Labored but occasionally funny, the comedy is told in pantomime, simple words from many languages, and grunts. Gertrude is seen as the first to recognize Picasso's greatness and at one point expresses her jealousy when she sees Alice dancing with a man. ⊛

After Dark, My Sweet

(1990, 114 min, US, James Foley)

Jason Patric stars as Collie, a literally punch-drunk ex-boxer who meets his downfall in the person of an alcoholic widow (Rachel Ward) who, along with her "uncle" Bud (Bruce Dern), involves him in a complicated kidnapping scheme that goes sour. Before the kidnapping, Collie is befriended by a helpful older man, Doc Goldman (George Dickerson), who takes more than a medical interest in the strapping young man when he invites him to stay at his house for awhile. But Collie distrusts the Doc's motives, moves out and later, when he needs medicine for the kidnapped diabetic boy, steals it from the doc's office. The doctor, determined to confront (and reform?) Collie, is accidentally killed when a struggle turns deadly. Remarking on charges that the killing smacked of homophobia and gay-bashing, director James Foley stated, "If someone senses any homoerotic yearnings on the part of the doctor for Collie, they should attribute it to (original author Jim) Thompson." ⊛

After Hours

(1985, 97 min, US, Martin Scorsese)

Robert Plunkett plays a closeted gay man cruising the streets of New York for his first pick-up. He meets and takes back to his place yuppie Griffin Dunne, who is on an "Alice in Wonderland" tour of Greenwich Village. There's also an extremely affectionate leather duo at the bar tended by John Heard, and various gay characters are featured in extra roles. ⊛

Airplane! *(1980, 86 min, US, Jim Abrahams, David Zucker & Jerry Zucker)*

As a gay air traffic controller, Stephen Stucker brings inspired, campy lunacy to an already delightfully wacky romp; Peter Graves shows an interest in a young boy and likes gladiator movies. ⊛

All Men Are Apes!

(1965, 85 min, US, Joseph Narwa)

A delightfully cheesy, tongue-in-cheek T&A flick that follows the rise, fall and rise again of blonde bombshell Diane, who thrives (just like good old mom) in the bars of New York. She's thrown out of the house by mom after a tryst with mom's sailor trick, and tries to make a living with her looks — a mix of Mae West (*Sextette* era) and a beguiling Debbie Harry. Queer characters include Marcel (Tom O'Horgan), the campy gay host of a party full of "kinky sophisticates," a sexy transvestite belly dancer (Ceylon) and Barbara, Diane's lesbian friend who is interested in her and comes to her when she is date raped. Barbara complains that love is unfair saying, "If I could once find a broad who could give me a fair shake." ⊛

Amor Bandido

(1979, 98 min, Brazil, Bruno Barreto)

Told with melodramatic gusto, this torrid, sexy and brutal story of doomed (heterosexual) love follows

Airplane!: "Do you like gladiator movies?"

the relationship of Sandra, a 17-year-old exotic dancer/prostitute, and Tony, a baby-faced killer. The two meet after Sandra's transvestite roommate commits suicide and Tony, a former lover of the transvestite, comes to the apartment looking for photos of the two of them. An intensely violent love blossoms. Handsome bisexual Tony is an interesting depiction of a street thug, unapologetic of his lifestyle.

And Now My Love
(1974, 121 min, France, Claude Lelouch)
This charming love story of super rich girl Sara (Marthe Keller) and enterprising crook/filmmaker Simon (André Dussollier) features the cute hook that the two do not actually meet until the final scene. Keller is shown to be a bored jet-setter longing for true love. While visiting Italy she meets a bisexual woman (Carla Gravina) who is attracted to her. In one scene, Sara asks her why she is attracted to women and she replies, "Blacks prefer blacks, Arabs prefer Arabs, the blind prefer the blind. We all belong to our own group, we have the same tastes. What counts is getting along with someone else, that's all." Sara rejects her advances and the two become close friends, much to the discomfort of Sara's marriage-minded father. ⊛

The Anderson Tapes
(1971, 98 min, US, Sidney Lumet)
Martin Balsam gives a prissy characterization as Tommy, a limp-wristed and ultimately cowardly antique dealer who's part of Sean Connery's burglary ring. When federal officials are in court to get permission to bug his shop, they refer to him as "the fag who owns the joint." New legal jargon, no doubt. One of the tenants of the building the gang hits is as stereotypical as Tommy. ⊛

Angel *(1984, 93 min, US, Robert Vincent O'Neil)*
A hilarious exploitation film definitely a cut above the rest. With an ad campaign that featured a pony-tailed innocent on one side and the same 15-year-old as a stiletto-heeled streetwalker on the other, the tag line read: "Honor student by day, hooker by night." The sleazy streets of Hollywood provide the backdrop to this tale of one girl's descent into hell and back. Helping throughout is Dick Shawn as Mae, a hulking six-foot transvestite who acts as Angel's surrogate mother and, when Angel is threatened with violence, father, as well. Susan Tyrrell is her raspy-voiced, hard-as-nails lesbian landlady. Cliff Gorman (*The Boys in the Band*) is also featured as a cop. The film was a big hit and spawned two sequels, *Avenging Angel* and *Angel III: The Final Chapter*, both of which featured down-and-out gays and drag queens trying to make a life on the streets. The first sequel featured the return of Solly, Angel's alcoholic lesbian friend and former landlady.

Are You Being Served?
(1977, 95 min, GB, Bob Kellett)
This tepid film version of the British television series features the familiar employees of Grace Brothers Department Store who embark on a cruise to Costa Plonka. The humor, much of which centers on sexual innuendos, takes special inoffensive aim at the flamboyantly stereotypical and gay Mr. Humphries (John Inman).

Around the World in 80 Ways
(1986, 90 min, Australia, Stephen MacLean)
Philip Quast is Wally, a resourceful and cash-poor tour guide who comes up with the wackiest of schemes: Take dear old, senile dad on an improvised and very fake tour around the world and pocket the money that would have gone for the trip. This is one of only a handful of films in which the main character is gay, but his sexual orientation has nothing to do with the film's plot. Quast gives a fast, funny performance — impersonating everyone from Hawaiian hula dancers to Elvis to the Pope. ⊛

Backbeat *(1994, 100 min, GB, Iain Softley)*
This fictionalized account of the early years of The Beatles and of Stu Sutcliffe, the "fifth Beatle," centers on the interesting premise that John Lennon and he were the closest of friends broken apart by Lennon's repressed physical attraction for Sutcliffe. When the group travels to Hamburg to perform in basement dives, Stu (Stephen Dorff) meets Astrid (Sheryl Lee) and her sexually ambiguous boyfriend. The entranced Stu (sort of a pre-Jim Morrison Jim Morrison) soon falls in with the city's art crowd, a group that includes gays and lesbians (but who are kept at a distance from the camera's interest). This affair with Astrid quickly strains his relationship with Lennon (Ian Hart), a primarily heterosexual who can't accept his love for his boyhood mate. Being straight, working-class Liverpudians at heart, the two never initiate a physical relationship — much to the frustration of a gay audience who wish they would just jump on each other and get it over with. While some see only a "spiritual" bond between the two attractive young men, it is obvious in a queer interpretation that the dynamics of their friendship (and, ultimately, The Beatles) was fueled by their mutual, although unequal homo-feelings. ⊛

Bank Robber *(1993, 94 min, US, Nick Ward)*
Writer-director Nick Ward has combined the outline of a typical heist film with a story line inspired by Eugene Ionesco's Theatre of the Absurd, and the result is an entertainingly bizarre and challenging film. A pumped-up Patrick Dempsey is Billy, a nice enough guy who decides to rob a bank. But when he's caught on camera, he is forced to hide out in a creepy L.A. hotel till the heat blows over. His nightmare soon begins as he is visited by a succession of characters who know he's the bank robber and are out to scam him for a bit of his fortune. While in love with a girl (Olivia D'Abo) and infatuated by a hooker (Lisa Bonet), Billy is visited one evening in a gay dream (or was it?). He opens his eyes and finds towering over his bed Officer Ted (Mark Pellegrino), a cute leather-freak motorcycle cop. Officer Ted begins to play an erotic S&M game with the dazed Billy, placing a gun next to his head and his crotch in front of Billy's face. He wakes up in the morning in his underwear and with a bottle of oil on the floor. Following that episode, a dirty-talking blonde transvestite (Scott Kaske) appears at his door requiring "a good hard fuck." Billy's not interested, but after the transvestite begs him to "shoot me in the stomach and fuck my heart out," he eventually has sex with him. When the prostitute is counting his take, he observes, "It's amazing how reality falls back in place after all the passion is spent." Strange, absorbing and oddly queer-friendly. ⊛

Barefoot in the Park

(1967, 105 min, US, Gene Saks)

Neil Simon's marital comedy has newlywed Robert Redford saying of his Greenwich Village neighbors: "We have some of the greatest weirdos in the country living in this building." That includes "a lovely young couple who happen to be of the same sex." The lovely young couple is never seen. ⊛

Barry Lyndon

(1975, 183 min, GB, Stanley Kubrick)

Two gay soldiers, Jonathan and Frederick, bid farewell as they bathe in a stream together. Ryan O'Neal happens along and steals Frederick's clothes and horse. ⊛

Batman — The Movie

(1966, 105 min, US, Leslie Martinson)

Crash! Pow! Bang! Sexual Hijinks with a Minor!? Just what was this "ward" relationship between Bruce Wayne (Adam West) and his teenage cutie Dick Grayson (Burt Ward)? Chaste to a fault, this camp classic still has inquiring minds aflutter and entranced eyes affixed on the Dynamic Duo's form-fitting and crotch-teasing crime-fighting tights. Conspicuously absent from the two Tim Burton *Batman* films is The Boy Wonder — Robin. No wonder Michael Keaton looks so forlorn! ⊛

Bedazzled *(1967, 107 min, GB, Stanley Donen)*

This hysterical adaptation of the Faust legend stars Peter Cook as a mischievous Mephistopheles who grants the nebbish Dudley Moore seven wishes in exchange for his soul. All of the wishes end in disaster for Moore who only wants his Whimpy Burger co-worker Margaret (Eleanor Bron) to love him. The final wish finds Moore transformed into Sister Luna, a lesbian nun in love with Sister Margaret. The Seven Deadly Sins are the Devil's incompetent collection of employees and include Raquel Welch as Lust and Barry Humphries (Dame Edna Everage) as the queeny, bitchy and quite gay Envy. ⊛

Beetlejuice

(1988, 92 min, US, Tim Burton)

Glenn Shadix is Otho, the interior designer who dabbles in the paranormal ("Is that what they're calling your kind, now?"), and makes a fabulous bass for "Day-O." Written by openly gay Michael McDowell, who also adapted Tim Burton's original idea in Burton's *The Nightmare Before Christmas*. ⊛

The Bell Jar

(1979, 107 min, US, Larry Peerce)

Based on the autobiographical novel by Sylvia Plath, the movie fails to capture the frustration and conflict experienced by the main character, Esther Greenwood. Of interest: In the book, the lesbian character Joan is a minor one; but in the film, she becomes Esther's best friend as well as a freak and a foil. The two end up in the same "Ivy League loony bin" where Joan professes her sexual attraction for Esther, saying that they should make a suicide pact and die like lovers. Esther rejects her advances and Joan promptly hangs herself. Ironically, the rejection is life-affirming for Esther, as she chooses life over suicide and begins her road to recovery. And though Esther had made homophobic remarks prior to Joan's death, her choice is probably attributed more to a desire to live rather than homophobia. ⊛

Belle de Jour

(1967, 100 min, France/Italy, Luis Buñuel)

Dreams and reality merge with surrealism in this, Buñuel's sex comedy that wittily skewers the pretensions of the bourgeoisie. A luminous Catherine Deneuve stars as a rich but bored housewife who unaccountably takes up prostitution during the afternoons in a high-class brothel where she complacently acquiesces to the strange sexual requests of her kinky clients. Genevieve Page was featured as the whorehouse's elegant madam, a lesbian who fancies the icy beauty of her newest employee.

Belle Epoque

(1993, 108 min, Spain, Fernando Trueba)

The winner of the 1993 Academy Award for Best Foreign-Language Film, *Belle Epoque* is a disarmingly gentle and comic tale of female seduction set in the Civil War-plagued Spain of 1931. AWOL soldier Fernando (Jorge Sanz), a handsome, rogue-wannabe finds brief solace, love, sex and emotional turmoil in the home of an elderly gentleman who has four beautiful and flirtatious daughters. Each woman, with a different reason for doing so, seduces the confused but eagerly accommodating young man although it is the first seduction, by Violeta (Ariadna Gil), which is of interest here. Violeta was brought up by her mother as a boy resulting in a boyish-

Belle de Jour

ly attractive (almost manly) and willfully independent young lady. She takes Fernando to a costume party with him dressed as a demure girl (complete with full-length dress and makeup) and she as a mustached soldier. Turned on by his femininity, she has her way with him in a hayloft, playing the part of the man to Fernando's astonished enjoyment. Come morning, Violeta couldn't care less for the male Fernando, despite his pleas for marriage. When he brings this up with her father, he replies, "How can you marry a man?" Later, Violeta's liberal mother encourages her to find a nice girl who loves her. An amazingly positive approach to a lesbian character, especially in a Spanish film.

Ben-Hur
(1959, 212 min, US, William Wyler)
In this epic's beginning scenes, Stephen Boyd's warrior Messala is in love with his childhood friend, Ben-Hur (Charlton Heston). In interviews, Boyd admitted playing the role as a former lover who wanted to rekindle the relationship, but had to settle for friendship. Later, they become enemies, and vent their sexual frustrations in the famous chariot race. ⊗

Stephen Boyd (l.) and Charlton Heston exchange affection in *Ben-Hur*

Best of the Fests *(1990, 60 min)*
This video compilation of various award-winning shorts feature two that are gay themed. *Song of a Angel* (1988, 5 min, US, David Weissman) stars Rodney Price, a founding member of San Francisco's theatrical troupe Angels of Light, who is gaunt, wheelchair-bound and obviously suffering from AIDS. Yet despite the look and his pain, his sings Kurt Weill's "Less Time Than You," a defiantly upbeat and satiric musical number. *Triangle* (1989, 6 min, US, Robert Anthony Doucette) is a short that uses animation, live action and paintings to tell its expressionistic history of the destruction and repression of Berlin's bustling pre-war gay life by Nazi forces. ⊗

The Betsy
(1978, 120 min, US, Daniel Petrie)
An all-star cast, headed by a slumming Laurence Olivier, gives varying degrees of over-the-top performances in this overwrought potboiler adapted from Harold Robbins' best-seller. Olivier is Loren Hardeman, Sr., an aging patriarch and retired Detroit car tycoon whose company is now headed by his grandson, Loren III (Robert Duvall). In addition to the usual cacophony of lurid melodramatic loves and familial treachery, it is revealed that Olivier's son, Loren II (Paul Rudd), though married and a father, was a homosexual who eventually killed himself — after discovering his wife and father in bed together! Also featured is Loren II's lover, Joe Warren (Clifford David), who is killed off by the father after a bungled blackmail attempt. ⊗

Beverly Hills Cop
(1984, 105 min, US, Martin Brest)
As Serge, a gay Beverly Hills art gallery employee, Bronson Pinchot upstages Eddie Murphy. Damon Wayans does his Blaine schtick long before "In Living Color" as — and he's billed as this — Banana Man, a gay waiter. And let's not forget Murphy's fag routine at an exclusive Beverly Hills club. Serge, incidentally, returned in the second sequel released in 1994, *Beverly Hills Cop 3*. ⊗

Beyond Passion (Além da Paixão)
(1984, 90 min, Brazil, Bruno Barreto)
This offbeat tale follows Regina, a seemingly contented middle-class housewife, who leaves her husband and stable life when she falls in love with a young hustler and "budding transvestite." Barreto has used gay themes in the past with films such as *Amor Bandido* and *The Kiss*.

The Big Bird Cage
(1972, 88 min, US, Jack Hill)
Blaxploitation superstar Pam Grier stars in this women-in-prison drama, a hilariously bad actioner filmed in The Philippines and featuring a bevy of often naked beauties. But while films of this type often feature lesbianism at its cheesy core, this oddity mentions but never explores it. Rather, male homosexuality is present, and the gay men are seen as buffoonish and stereotypical fairies and sadistic bullies who deserve their eventual punishment. For the jungle enclave, home to the women prisoners, is ruled by a number of gay prison guards. Rocco, the head guard, is portrayed as an obese, bottom-pinching, giggling thug and is, during the film's requisite prison break, repeatedly raped (!) by the sexually starved women. The revolutionary who assists in the breakout infiltrates the prison by posing as a purse-carrying, limp-wristed, lisping queen who entrances the smitten prison guards with his promise of sex. A pre-liberated example of how gays were used as comic relief fodder. ⊗

The Big Combo
(1955, 89 min, US, Joseph Lewis)
A shadowy noirish thriller, *The Big Combo* revolves around a police detective's (Cornel Wilde) determined efforts to imprison

Mr. Brown (Richard Conte), the boss of a crime syndicate. In what is quite a daring depiction, Mr. Brown's two henchmen, Fante (a pre-spaghetti western Lee Van Cleef) and Mingo (Earl Holliman), are a covertly gay couple. Although they are ruthless killers, the men, who share a bedroom, are seen in some scenes touching; and when Fante is killed by his double-crossing boss, Mingo cries and exacts revenge for his lover by spilling his guts to the cops. ⊗

The Big Doll House
(1971, 93 min, US, Jack Hill)
Valley girls and Hollywood starlets trapped in a hellhole Filipino prison! One of the earliest and most commercially successful of the women-in-prison films which were popular in the '70s, this is almost chaste compared to its more cheesier successors. Filmed in a breezy, comedic fashion, the film features the requisite S&M beatings, a shower sequence and "claws out girls" fighting; though lesbianism is strangely underdeveloped. The one relationship shown is between Collier (Judy Brown), a red-headed vixen in jail for killing her bisexual boyfriend, and Grear, played by exploitation queen Pam Grier. Although there is no kissing or other signs of affection, the two get involved in a close, protector-protectee relationship. Wardress Dietrich, despite the promising name, is frustratingly heterosexual. ⊗

The Big Sky
(1952, 122 min, US, Howard Hawks)
As fur-trappers roughing it up in the great outdoors, Kirk Douglas and Dewey Martin make goo-goo eyes at each other through the whole movie. ⊗

Billy Bathgate
(1991, 106 min, US, Robert Benton)
In this flavorful adaptation of E.L. Doctorow's gangster story, Nicole Kidman plays a flirtatious free-spirit who becomes involved with Dutch Schultz (Dustin Hoffman). When he tires of her, he puts a hit on her, and her gay husband Harvey, played by Xander Berkeley, comes to her rescue in the nick of time. Christopher Rubin plays Harvey's boyfriend. ⊗

Biloxi Blues *(1988, 106 min, US, Mike Nichols)*
Michael Dolan nicely plays Pvt. Hennesey, a gay soldier stationed in Mississippi during WWII whose sexuality is discovered, prompting his discharge. It's interesting that Hennesey is the only one in the barracks to stand up to anti-Semitics and racial bigots. As Neil Simon's alter ego Eugene Jerome, Matthew Broderick writes of his heterosexual though fussy friend Arnold Epstein (Corey Parker): "I have the instinctive feeling that Arnold is a homosexual...and it bothers me." Private Lindstrom (Ben Hynum) is the soldier caught having sex with Hennesey. ⊗

Bird on a Wire
(1990, 110 min, US, John Badham)
On-the-run witness protectee Mel Gibson visits the faggy hairdressers he used to work with. Mel's lisp routine is offensive, and these hairdressers bring new definition to the word "stereotype." One of the hairdressers insinuates that there was a relationship between him and Mel, but Gibson just smirks and nothing more is made of it. ⊗

The Boys Next Door

Bitter Moon
(1993, 135 min, France/GB, Roman Polanski)
Polanski fans who have not seen this trashy but fun psychosexual drama (comedy?) should read no further: for the queer angle of the film is in the final scene. Humorously uptight Britisher Nigel (Hugh Grant) and Fiona (Kristen Scott-Thomas) meet up with the wheelchair-bound American expatriate Oscar (Peter Coyote) and his voluptuously sexy wife Mimi (Emmanuelle Seigner) on a Mediterranean cruise. Much to his frustration, Nigel becomes transfixed on Oscar's near pornographic accounts of their tumultuous relationship — one that includes obsessive love, excessive sex, playful sadomasochism, water sports, betrayal, bitter hatred and sick revenge (it's a long cruise). The end result is that Mimi, hurt terribly by Oscar before his "accident," abusively takes care of him and mercilessly teases him with her wanton sexuality. Oscar manipulates both events and people so that the nerdish Nigel beds his wife; but, in a surprise move, it is Nigel's wife Fiona who seduces Mimi in plain view of the startled men. This lesbian twist is sensuously executed in this bizarrely entertaining drama described by Janet Maslin of *The New York Times* as "a world-class, defiantly bad film that has a life of its own." ⊗

Black Eye *(1974, 98 min, US, Jack Arnold)*
Blaxploitation mystery-thriller that adopts Sam Spade-like conventions to tell its tale of Southern Californian corruption. Fred Williamson stars as a former police lieutenant turned P.I., and the film also features Teresa Graves as his bisexual girlfriend Cynthia who is getting it on with white girl "Miss Francis" (Rosemary Forsyth).

Black Shampoo

(1976, 83 min, US, Greydon Clark)
This little seen and cheaply made blaxploitation gem has little in common with the Warren Beatty vehicle *Shampoo* other than featuring an indefatigable ladies' man who wields his scissors, hair blower and cock with equal abandon. John Daniels is the black superstud and owner of Jonathan's, where two stereotypical nelly queens — white Artie (Skip E. Lowe) and black Richard (Gary Allen) — work. Essentially there to make the lead look that much more masculine and for comic relief, the two caricatures are soon surprisingly fleshed out. They defend women threatened by thugs and prove to be supportive and loyal friends to Jonathan. But while the straight gets the girl, the two gays, called "fucking little faggots" by the bad guys, are eventually tortured (they stick a hot curler up Artie's ass), beaten and presumably killed. A troubling but interesting image of gays. ⊛

Blacula

(1972, 92 min, US, William Crain)
Antique dealers Ted Harris and Rick Metzler buy Blacula's coffin in Transylvania and transport it to L.A.; they become vampire William Marshall's first victims. Kindly doctor Thalmus Rasulala calls them "two faggot interior decorators." ⊛

Blazing Saddles

(1973, 93 min, US, Mel Brooks)
Choreographer Dom DeLuise pleads to his basher, "Not the face," as a western brawl interrupts his musical dance sequence. An all-out fight ensues between the film's cowpokes and an all-gay male chorus line ("let's get them, girls!"). One of the rowdy cowboys is parked by the Commissary and walks off with one of the dancers. ⊛

Blood and Concrete

(1991, 97 min, US, Jeffrey Reiner)
An offbeat, almost hallucinatory comedy/thriller/love story that features a lumbering, opera-loving gangster (Nicolas Worth) and his muscular bodyguard/companion (Mark Pellegrino). The sex-obsessed twosome make life miserable for straight hero Billy Zane. Pellegrino even tries to rape Zane in one scene, though it's done for laughs. ⊛

Blood In, Blood Out

(1993, 180 min, US, Taylor Hackford)
An epic (at least in the realm of time) drama about the lives of three friends born and raised on the mean *calles* of East L.A. One gets beaten up badly as a teen, becomes a successful artist only to succumb to drugs; another, a teen thug, becomes a respected cop; the third, Miklo (Damian Chapa) — a blond, blue-eyed Anglo-Chicano — becomes a macho-posturing gang member who enters into a life of crime. The gay angle does not begin at home (despite his young mother looking suspiciously like a drag queen) but at San Quentin Prison. From the moment he gets off the bus, the pretty boy becomes the object of sexual taunts from whites, Chicanos and even a tough gathering of black drag queens. After fighting off one attempted rape from a muscle-bound thug, Miklo realizes that he is going to have to use his good (white) looks if he's going to survive. At one point, Miklo, as part of an initiation rite, must kill a particularly obnoxious white prisoner. He insinuates himself in the man's favor, promising him hot sex. He gives a blow job to the bewitched man's finger, and right before killing him he goes down on him promising the horny thug, "I'm gonna lick you clean." The doomed prisoner responds, "Do it bitch." Those are his last words — no blow job and no heart beat. Although homo-sex soaks the air in the prison scenes, there is no additional overt action, just lots of ass-pinching and talk. (Also known as: *Bound by Honor*) ⊛

Bloody Mama

(1970, 90 min, US, Roger Corman)
Roger Corman's exploitative answer to *Bonnie and Clyde* is notable for Shelley Winters' over-the-top performance as "Ma" Kate Barker, sleazy, white trash mother, protector and ringleader to her four hooligan sons. When the "sensitive" son Freddie (Robert Walden) is thrown in jail, he begins a sadomasochistic relationship with fellow con Bruce Dern. Their affair begins with Dern purring, "I'm not going to hurt you, I really like you." Upon their release, the two stay together, with Dern sharing Freddie's bed and becoming one of mom's "boys." When Ma kills Dern, Freddie has matricide on his mind. Their obvious sexual pairing goes unnoticed or is taken in a matter-of-fact fashion by the other brothers. Look for a young and surprisingly attractive Robert De Niro as one of Ma's crazed, drug addicted sons. ⊛

Body Puzzle

(1993, 90 min, US/Italy, Lamberto Bava)
A grisly but mediocre thriller that postulates the following theme of a gay relationship: homosexual attraction leads to sexual obsession which in turn leads to a psychologically deranged murder spree. When his bisexual married lover Abe is killed in a motorcycle accident, Tim goes berserk with grief, leading him to become a crazed serial killer who collects body parts of his victims (those victims were all recipients of organ transplants from the body of Abe). The plot gets even more convoluted, but the basic premise is that it doesn't take much for an emotionally disturbed gay man to become a tormented psycho-killer. ⊛

Borderline

(1930, 60 min, GB/Switzerland, Kenneth McPherson)
This silent, independently made avant-garde film features lesbian poet H.D. (Hilda Doolittle) and her real-life lover Bryher as Swiss innkeepers who become immersed in sexual and psychological game-playing with an interracial American couple (Paul Robeson and his wife Eslanda). The film's subject of racial prejudice and sexual ambiguity was remarkable for its time.

Born Innocent

(1974, 100 min, US, Donald Wrye)
Linda Blair is a runaway who is sent to a juvenile detention center where she is at one point raped by a lesbian, Moco (Nora Heflin), and a fellow gang of ravenous friends in the shower. (This isn't the first time our Miss Blair has had trouble in the showers — see the attempted lesbian rape scene in *Chained Heat*.) Made for TV, the film's rape scene was eventually cut from all future showings. ⊛

The Boston Strangler

(1968, 116 min, US, Richard Fleischer)

Hurd Hatfield is Terence Huntley, a gay antique dealer who is a suspect in the Boston strangulation cases ("Whenever there are sex crimes, the police crack down on us"). Investigator Henry Fonda visits him in a gay bar; Fonda was tipped off by Huntley's two lesbian neighbors, Ellen Ridgeway (Eve Collier) and Alice Oakville (Gwyla Domhome). This film may have the dubious distinction to be the first film to have a male character called "she" by a gay man; and one of the first films to use the word "gay" to describe a homosexual. ☉

The Boys Next Door

(1984, 90 min, US, Penelope Spheeris)

Charlie Sheen and Maxwell Caulfield are high school teens who go on a killing rampage. They stop off in West Hollywood, pick up Paul C. Dancer in a gay bar, and brutally murder him. It's a disturbing scene, as are all the killings in the film, but illustrates both the twisted minds of these two psychos and the ultimate consequences of homophobia. Kenneth Cortland is Dancer's boyfriend, who is left behind to mourn. Later when Bo (Sheen) makes love to a pickup (Patti D'Arbanville), Roy (Caulfield) goes into a jealous rage and kills her. Caulfield's closeted, sexually repressed high school grad is a terrifying, but unfortunately, all-too-real characterization. ☉

The Broadway Melody

(1929, 104 min, US, Harry Beaumont)

The costume designer for a Ziegfeld-type show is a "sweet little cutie." When he tells the dresser "I design the costumes for the show, not the doors for the theatre," she responds, "I know that, if you had, they'd been done in lavender." The film is based on an original story by gay director Edmund Goulding. ☉

Buffy the Vampire Slayer

(1992, 86 min, US, Fran Rubel Kuzui)

As a villainous vampire, Paul Reubens' seductive pose atop a carousel, all to grab the attention of the handsome jock who's about to be his next victim, could give a clue as to why Reubens' bloodsucker only attacks guys. ☉

Bump in the Night

(1991, 100 min, US, Karen Arthur)

A made-for-TV movie that stars Christopher Reeve as a convicted gay pedophile who abducts the eight-year-old son of alcoholic writer Meredith Baxter-Birney. Before Reeve can sexually abuse the boy or turn him over to a child pornography ring, mom and the police rescue him. Reeve is done in by his sexual urges, and is punished with a swift death.

The Butcher's Wife

(1991, 125 min, US, Terry Hughes)

Demi Moore stars in this whimsical romantic comedy as a Southern clairvoyant who impulsively marries a doughy butcher (George Dzunda) from Greenwich Village. In her new surroundings, she sets off a farcical chain reaction of sexual trysts through

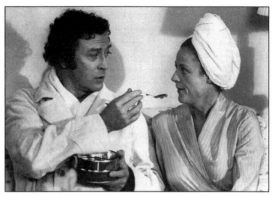

California Suite

her predictions of love to a neighborhood starving for it. Frances McDormand is featured as an owner of a clothing store to whom Moore promises that she'll meet a "kind lover" and the woman of her dreams. It is a wonderful portrayal of a lesbian — she is completely at ease with her sexual orientation and her friends as well. When asked by a "straight" woman why women waste their time on men, she replies, "Not all of us do." Unlike most films, this charming dyke finds love and sexual happiness at the end. As good as her character is, however, it is counterbalanced with a stupid cameo appearance by a dripping-with-attitude, unsympathetic drag queen (minus a wig) played by Thomas Mikal Ford. ☉

Caged   *(1950, 96 min, US, John Cromwell)*

This harrowing and trendsetting women-in-prison drama features Eleanor Parker as a waifish 19-year-old who is sent to the slammer for her involvement in a robbery and slowly becomes hardened after her encounters with brutalizing prison officials and fellow inmates. Hope Emerson is the sadistic matron who rules with an iron hand. She is subtly depicted as a lesbian — mannish in appearance, tough, mean and more than mildly interested in "her gals." Elvira Powell is featured as another thinly veiled lesbian and fellow inmate. Agnes Moorehead co-stars as the warden in this starkly grim account which received Academy Award nominations for Best Actress (Parker), Best Supporting Actress (Emerson) and Best Original Story. ☉

Caged Heat

(1974, 84 min, US, Jonathan Demme)

Jonathan Demme's directorial debut is an above average women-in-prison potboiler and semi-skin flick/morality play. Barbara Steele is featured as the sadistic (is this a requirement for the job?) warden who lords over her subjects. Lesbianism is hinted at, all as part of the corrupting and degenerate atmosphere. ☉

California Suite

(1978, 103 min, US, Herbert Ross)

This funny film version of Neil Simon's Broadway comedy focuses on the misadventures of a disparate group of travelers staying at the Beverly Hills Hotel. Two of those include an actress (Maggie Smith), who's an Academy Award nominee attending the Oscar ceremonies, and her bisexual antique dealer husband, played with great depth and conviction by Michael Caine. Theirs is a strained relationship but a loving friendship prevails. Ironically, Smith won an Oscar for her portrayal of an Oscar nominated actress. ✪

Car Wash *(1976, 97 min, US, Michael Schultz)*

Antonio Fargas is Lindy, the spunky gay car wash employee who is "more man than you'll ever be and more woman that you'll ever get." In one scene, car wash owner Sully Boyar worries that his son may be gay (he's not, "not yet"). Vincent Canby of *The New York Times* called Fargas' character, "The homosexual whose wrist is limp and whose mouth is loud." ✪

Chantilly Lace
(1993, 102 min, US, Linda Yellen)

Half a female *Big Chill* and half a primarily straight *Boys in the Band*, this improvisational drama centers around several "girls only" getaways set at a rural Colorado house. Filled with yuppie angst and the requisite laughter, tears, regrets, hugs and "secret" revelations, the story seems to yearn to be an all-star dyke drama but slips back to heterosexuality every time the dreaded "L" word is mentioned. Essentially a gushy talk fest starring Lindsay Crouse, Jill Eikenberry, Talia Shire, JoBeth Williams, Martha Plimpton, Ally Sheedy and Helen Slater, the film's queer moments are few but sensitively handled. Ann (Plimpton) asks the group one evening if any of them has slept with another woman. Tensions rise as Hannah (Slater) admits to a lesbian affair a few years back. She calls it a positive experience that has had an effect on the rest of her life. There is also the big coming out scene in which Liz (Sheedy) admits her love for Ann. In what is supposed to be a surprise (to all but the viewer), she calls her lover a "dream person" and reveals to the group and her startled sister (Williams) that she has been a lesbian all of her life. ✪

The Color Purple

Chastity
(1969, 85 min, US, Alessio de Paola)

Cher stars in this Sonny Bono-produced drama about the wanderings of an aimless, child-abused young woman who has renamed herself Chastity. At one point, after an unsuccessful try at being a prostitute, she is seduced by the whorehouse's owner, Diana (Barbara London). She quickly flees the scene.

A Chorus Line
(1985, 113 min, US, Richard Attenborough)

Having British director Richard Attenborough (*Gandhi, Cry Freedom*) adapt Michael Bennett's groundbreaking, long-running Broadway musical to the screen seemed from the beginning an inappropriate choice. The result is an uninspired, sanitized, heteroized musical that arrived DOA at the cinemas. One of the play's leading gay characters has been eliminated, and the two remaining, Gregory and Paul, have been greatly reduced in importance. Gregory (Justin Ross) has been made both gay and Jewish, and in his small amount of screen time projects a palpable obnoxiousness; Paul (Cameron English), the young Puerto Rican and former drag queen, has one of the few moving scenes in the film. Attenborough defended his cutting away of the gay themes by saying that homosexuality was no longer "shocking" to film audiences. ✪

Cleopatra Jones
(1973, 89 min, US, Jack Starrett)

Shelley Winters is "Mommy," the lesbian crime boss — she's butch, sadistic, wears a leather coat and fright wig — who runs afoul with special agent Cleopatra Jones (Tamara Dobson). ✪

Cleopatra Jones and the Casino of Gold *(1975, 94 min, US, Chuck Bail)*

Stella Stevens is the Dragon Lady, yet another lesbian crime boss who goes up against agent Cleopatra Jones (Tamara Dobson). The Dragon Lady is less cartoonish than Winters' "Mommy" from the first film, and there's a discreet love scene between Stevens and her female staffers. ✪

The Color Purple
(1985, 152 min, US, Steven Spielberg)

Spielberg's screen adaptation of Alice Walker's epistolary novel is a poignant movie but is ultimately disappointing in that it downplays much of what the book emphasizes, mainly the power of love between women. Whoopi Goldberg plays Celie, who after having two children by her dad, is married off to Mister (Danny Glover) with the warning, "She's not fresh." Nettie, Celie's sister, comes to live with them in order to keep away from her father, but Mister subjects her to the same sexual harassment. When she refuses him with a kick to the groin, he sends her away in a classic Spielberg five-hanky scene (you hate to cry because you know you're supposed to, but what the hell!). When Mister is doing "his business" on top of Celie, she sees the image of Shug (Margaret Avery), Mister's real love and soon to be Celie's. Tune your gaydar. Celie bathes Shug, combs her hair, spits in the drink of Mister's father who slanders her, and, in turn, Shug sings a song to her, "Sista, You've Been on My Mind," and gets to smile without covering her mouth. After Celie confides that she hates having sex with Mister and has never had an orgasm, Shug exclaims, "Then you're still a virgin!" They exchange a series of innocuous kisses and the camera pans away. Unfortunately, as with *Fried Green Tomatoes*, the lesbianism that was prominent in the novel is de-emphasized in the film adaptation for fear of losing mainstream appeal. See the movie, but read the book, too. ⊗

Come Back to the 5 & Dime, Jimmy Dean, Jimmy Dean

(1982, 110 min, US, Robert Altman)
Karen Black is featured as a transsexual who returns to her dust-bowl Texas town for a 20-year reunion of a James Dean fan club. Her transformation from gay Joe to slinky Josephine produces shock, disgust and admiration from her old girlfriends (Cher, Sandy Dennis, Kathy Bates, Sudie Bond). Josephine, embittered by many of the townspeople's mistreatment of her when she was a man, seeks psychological self-healing in her return to her pain-filled past. Black is especially good as Josephine, projecting a subtly masculine femininity. ⊗

Confessions of a Serial Killer

(1992, 80 min, US, Mark Blair)
This "exposé" on Texas serial killer Daniel Ray Hawkins (based on real-life killer Henry Lee Lucas) is, in fact, a sleazy low-budget exploitation flick that revels in the many depictions of Hawkins terrorizing, raping and brutally killing women. What makes the film a bit strange is his relationship with his overweight, goonish buddy Moon Lewton. Moon is "queer," which don't bother Hawkins none; and he later admits that not only did they have "homosexual relations" several times with each other (Hawkins is supposedly bi, with a preference towards heterosexuality), but they also lived together and killed together. Disturbing in its gratuitous violence, but also disturbing in depicting homosexuality as another facet of a killer's deranged behavior. ⊗

Conjugal Warfare

(1981, 116 min, Brazil, Joaquim Pedro de Andrade)
From one of the founding filmmakers of the "Cinema Novo" movement comes this deliciously black, surrealist-tinged comedy with a theme described by de Andrade himself as "redemption through excessive sex." The film features three interconnecting stories on sex — Brazilian style. And while the second and third tales are purely heterosexual, the first is far from it. A cocksure, middle-aged lawyer pursues his sexual obsession by having sex with as many women as he can — be they young, old, beautiful or homely. But the tables are turned when an old male classmate succeeds in seducing the seducer, unleashing his pent-up homosexual desires.

Coonskin

(1975, 82 min, US, Ralph Bakshi)
An offensively "funny" look at 1970s ghetto life, this part-live-action part-animation satire comes from a straight white man's point of view with the butt of the jokes coming from the director's grotesque caricatures of women, blacks and gays. The story revolves around a trip to an animated Harlem where the denizens of this crime, drug and violence-infested neighborhood include black hustlers, pimps and prostitutes as well as several stereotypical gays. They include black drag queen Snowflake, a freak who enjoys S&M sex behind trucks on the waterfront; a swishy bartender named Queenie who puts the make on a burly white thug only to receive a hairy knuckle sandwich in return; and two gays who enjoy sex in a trash can. (Also known as: *Streetfight*) ⊗

Cover Me Babe

(1970, 89 min, US, Noel Black)
Described by *Variety* as "tasteless, ludicrous and artistically offensive," this low-budget disaster follows a fledgling filmmaker's increasingly desperate efforts to secure a studio deal. Working on a documentary on "human depravity," the filmmaker (Robert Forster) gets his former girlfriend to seduce a gay student (Floyd Mutrux).

"Crocodile" Dundee

(1986, 98 min, Australia, Peter Faiman)
In a New York bar, a transvestite (actress Anne Carlisle, in a nod to *Victor/Victoria*, playing a man dressed as a woman) is almost picked up, and then ridiculed, by Australian "Everyman" "Crocodile" Dundee (Paul Hogan), who doesn't know "he's a fag." It's a stupid, unnecessary fag joke. ⊗

"Crocodile" Dundee II

(1988, 110 min, US/Australia, John Cornell)
In this witless sequel, "Crocodile" Dundee (Paul Hogan) tries to convince a potential jumper (Vincent Jerosa) to come off an office building ledge. Offering sympathy to him, Hogan falls off the ledge himself when he discovers Jerosa is distraught over a "him." With Hogan barely holding on, Jerosa walks away without offering assistance. Not as offensive as it could have been, but a fag joke nonetheless. ⊗

Cross My Heart

(France, 1990, 105 min, Jacques Fansten)
This endearing comedy about a group of classmates who protect a friend from placement in an orphanage features a young teacher who is seemingly the only "cool" adult around. At one point, some of the boy's friends ask the teacher to adopt the parentless 12-year-old Martin. He confesses to them that he can't adopt because he is a homosexual. This revelation brings a sharp reaction from one boy who thinks it is disgusting — not that he is gay, but that authorities give such a hard time to homosexuals. ⊗

Danzòn *(1991, 103 min, Mexico, Maria Novaro)*

Julia (Maria Rojo), a thirtyish Mexico City telephone operator, finds herself emotionally adrift when her ballroom dancing partner suddenly disappears. Her search for him leads to the coastal city of

Veracruz, where she is soon befriended by Susy (Tito Vasconcelos), a raven-haired transvestite who performs Carmen Miranda-like drag shows. They soon become best friends, and Susy, accompanied by her gay friends and fellow drag queens, lift Julia's spirits and give her a renewed love of life. The freshness and openness of the Susy character is especially surprising due to the political climate in Mexico, where police raids on gay clubs continue today. ⊛

Day for Night
(1973, 120 min, France/Italy, François Truffaut)
In this loving ode to the intricacies of filmmaking, François Truffaut plays the compassionate director of a beleaguered production. Jean-Pierre Aumont plays Alexandre, an aging international film star, once known as "The Continental Lover." Twice married and divorced, the bisexual actor brings his young male lover with him on the set. However, death comes to the gay man when, before filming is completed, Alexandre is killed and his lover injured in an auto accident. ⊛

The Day of the Jackal
(1973, 141 min, GB/France, Fred Zinnemann)
As a hired assassin eluding a police dragnet, Edward Fox visits a Turkish bath in Paris and picks up and moves in with Anton Rodgers, only to kill him when the gay man discovers his real identity. ⊛

Dazed and Confused
(1993, 113 min, US, Richard Linklater)
Although this *American Graffiti* for the stoned-out '70s is completely heterosexual, the comedy, set in Texas on the final day of high school, features among its ensemble young gay actor Anthony Rapp as Tony. His funniest lines recount a dream he had of making love to a woman's body who has the face of Abraham Lincoln. Rapp can also be seen in *Six Degrees of Separation*, in which he plays Ben, the son of one of the wealthy parents duped by Will Smith. ⊛

The Decline of the American Empire
(1986, 101 min, Canada, Denys Arcand)
Yves Jacques plays Claude, a gay teacher who, after the death of his lover, says he "only feels alive" when he's cruising. This Canadian comedy, whose pretense of honesty and character is an exchange of ideas you wouldn't tell your psychiatrist, has the teacher, among other things, talking about the beauty of 12-year-old boys. ⊛

Def by Temptation
(1990, 95 min, US, James Bond III)
Michael Rivera plays a gay man who gets picked up by vampiress Cynthia Bond. She tells him "it's much better with a woman," and then, to his surprise ("girlfriend, where did *that* come from?"), literally fucks him to death. ⊛

Deliverance *(1972, 109 min, US, John Boorman)*
A rousing adventure thriller about four men who go on a rugged Appalachian canoeing trip only to meet up with some toothless,

buggery-minded hillbillies. The greasy low-lifes bypass hunky Burt Reynolds and pretty boy Jon Voight for the ample ass of chubby Ned Beatty. For most American audiences, this was their first view of homosexual anal sex — a violent, repugnant act that called for murderous revenge. Although "Sowee!" was soon heard all across the land. ⊛

Designing Woman
(1957, 118 min, US, Vincente Minnelli)
As an effeminate choreographer, Jack Cole proves his masculinity to Gregory Peck by taking care of a couple of thugs — in a choreographed kick-boxing routine! Then, he proves his heterosexuality by showing pictures of his kids. ⊛

Diamonds Are Forever
(1971, 119 min, GB, Guy Hamilton)
Gay lovers and ruthless killers Mr. Wint (Bruce Glover) and Mr. Kidd (Putter Smith) prove to be formidable foes to James Bond — almost. ⊛

Diary of a Mad Housewife
(1970, 103 min, US, Frank Perry)
Frank Langella is George, a possibly bisexual writer who becomes involved with Carrie Snodgress (the housewife of the title). She discovers another man's tie in his bathrobe, and accuses him of being "a fag." ⊛

Doctors' Wives
(1971, 100 min, US, George Schaefer)
A glossy but sleazily melodramatic soap opera about the sexual philanderings of a group of middle-aged doctors and their bored but horny wives. In one scene, Rachel Roberts tells her psychiatrist husband Gene Hackman of a college-era lesbian affair with a woman he, too, had bedded. After initial disbelief and a slap to her face, he calms down and "forgives" her indiscretion. Also starring Carroll O'Connor, Janice Rule and Dyan Cannon. ⊛

La Dolce Vita
(1960, 175 min, Italy, Federico Fellini)
Marcello Mastroianni stars as a cynical gossip columnist who weaves in and out of the hollow lives of Rome's decadent, amoral upper crust. In the famous orgy scene, several gay men and one lesbian are featured — although not in the best light. Towards the end, one exuberant transvestite claims that "by the year 2000, the whole world will be homosexual!" ⊛

Drum
(1976, 102 min, US, Steve Carver)
A limp sequel to the guilty pleasure *Mandingo*, *Drum* stars Ken Norton as Drum, a muscular slave who refuses to be broken. The gay images include a lesbian whorehouse madam (Isela Vega), her lover/black maid (Paula Kelly), and a whip-wielding white slaver (John Colicos), who has a lover (Alain Patrick) but gets his kicks raping and disfiguring male slaves. An exploitative yawn that also stars Warren Oates, Pam Grier and Yaphet Kotto. ⊛

Europa, Europa

Dune

(1984, 137 min, US, David Lynch)

Frank Herbert's 1965 sci-fi classic comes to cinematic semi-life in this uneven but visually impressive adaptation. Set in the year 10,991, the film follows the battle between the universe's superpowers over Melange, a mind-expanding spice found only on the desert planet of Arrakis. Kyle MacLachlan plays the heterosexual hero/warrior while a bloated, puss-spewing Kenneth McMillan is the evil megalomaniac Baron Vladimir Harkonnen, who opposes him. Sting also stars as Harkonnen's grinning nephew Feyd-Rautha. Suggested, in the kinkiest and sleaziest fashion, is a sexual relationship between the beauty and the beast — at one point, Sting struts about clothed only in a loincloth for his leering uncle. Yet another example of equating homosexuality with the dark forces of man. ⊛

The Eiger Sanction

(1975, 128 min, US, Clint Eastwood)

Jack Cassidy is Miles, an effeminate and cowardly government agent who tangles with hired assassin Clint Eastwood. Miles is so gay he even has a dog named "Faggot." With this level of stereotyping, it's no surprise that it's the gay man who turns out to be the villain. ⊛

El Topo

(1971, 124 min, Mexico, Alexandro Jodorowsky)

A "hippie western" that gained cult status during the 1970s, *El Topo* is a religious allegory imbued with cryptic symbolism and graphically detailed violence set amidst a strange anti-hero's (director Jodorowsky) bloody odyssey through the 1800s Western frontier seeking revenge and spiritual enlightenment. There are several gay and lesbian images sprinkled throughout. The first involves a band of grungy desperadoes who capture four virginal monks and, attracted to their boyish good looks, fair beardless skin and flowing robes, proceed to dance with, forcibly kiss and eventually rape (implied) and humiliate them. El Topo comes on the scene and exacts bloody justice, much to the demure monks'

delight. Later in his wanderings, he begins to travel with two women — one a dark-haired gunslinger (Paula Romo) and the other a fair maiden (Mara Lorenzio). Initially attached to El Topo, the two women soon find bloodied pleasure and loving S&M fulfillment in each other's arms.

Entangled

(1993, 98 min, Canada, Max Fischer)

Sorry, but in order to explain the gay angle in this terrible mystery-thriller, I must reveal its "secret" ending. Set in Paris and starring a wooden Judd Nelson as an aspiring novelist jealously in love with vacuous model Annabelle (Laurence Triel), the story has Nelson accidentally killing a man whom he thinks is sleeping with his girlfriend. But when another suspected boyfriend of Annabelle (sexy Pierce Brosnan) becomes obsessed with tracking down the man's killer, his motives only become clear at the end when it is revealed that he is, in fact, gay and the man killed was not sleeping with the woman but was his lover! A twist that any self-respecting queer sees early on. A good gay subplot that is wasted in this otherwise wretched film. ⊛

Escalier C

(1985, 102 min, France, Jean-Charles Tacchella)

Set primarily in the stairway of a 14th arrondissement apartment building, this lightweight drama centers on Forster, a cynical, misogynistic young man and art critic who learns about the possibilities of life through the course of his interactions with his neighbors. One of whom includes Claude (Jacques Bonnafé), an openly gay and intelligent young man, wounded by love affairs gone sour but nonetheless caring and, as the promotional material describes, "the neighbor of your dreams." Although Forster is attracted to the man, he begins a relationship with a female neighbor.

Europa, Europa

(1991, 110 min, France/Germany, Agnieszka Holland)

A powerful WWII and Holocaust drama, this sweeping statement about the resilience of the human spirit stars Marco Hofschneider as Solomon Perel, a Jewish youth who alternately pretends to be a Nazi and a Russian during the war. With bee-stung lips, clear pale skin and a sexy innocence, the teenager's beauty becomes his protector — disarming both women and men. While masquerading as a German soldier, Perel is befriended by Robert (Andre Wilms), who discovers his Jewish identity (by seeing his circumcised penis) after an awkward seduction attempt. Instead of turning him in, Robert, an "other kind of German" and clearly in love with him, treats him like a brother and protects him. With the exception of a farewell kiss, nothing more develops between the two. ⊛

Evil Under the Sun

(1982, 102 min, GB, Guy Hamilton)

Roddy McDowall plays Rex Brewster, a prissy gossip columnist and possible murder suspect in this Agatha Christie mystery. Brewster — like the film — has no class nor wit. Clifton Webb's

Waldo Lydecker (*Laura*), George Sanders' Addison DeWitt (*All About Eve*) and Monty Woolley's Sheridan Whiteside (*The Man Who Came to Dinner*) are the real McCoys. ☻

Eyes of Laura Mars
(1978, 103 min, US, Irvin Kershner)
Faye Dunaway is Laura Mars, a fashion photographer whose portraits of murder and mayhem become all-too real. As her gay manager, Rene Auberjonois fleshes out a sympathetic portrait of the flamboyant Donald. He, as well as lovers and models Lulu (Darlanne Fluegel) and Michelle (Lisa Taylor), become victims to a vicious murderer. ☻

Falling Down
(1993, 115 min, US, Joel Schumacher)
As Michael Douglas wanders throughout Los Angeles experiencing '90s urban angst, he stops by the Army-Navy shop owned by fascist Frederic Forrest. Also there are two gay men, played by Peter Radon and Spencer Rochfort. When Forrest taunts them with verbal assaults of "faggot," instead of cowering, these masculine, in-shape men are ready to stand their ground. ☻

Fame   *(1980, 134 min, US, Alan Parker)*
Paul McCrane plays Montgomery, the gay son of a popular movie actress. He attends New York's High School of the Performing Arts (evidently he's the only gay there), and his sexuality is rather incidental. Though he is the only lead character not romantically paired. (In the TV version, the character's gayness was dropped completely.) ☻

The Fan   *(1981, 95 min, US, Edward Bianchi)*
Michael Biehn plays Douglas Breen, an all-American boy psychotic killer in this creepy thriller about a fan's obsessive attraction to a famous actress (Lauren Bacall). As the young man begins to become increasingly crazed, he stalks and slashes his way to the object of his "desires." With the police on his trail, Douglas con-cocts a plan to fake his own suicide — he visits the Haymarket, a gay bar in midtown Manhattan, silently picks up look-alike Terence Marinan and while receiving a blow job, knifes him and then sets the gay man afire. Whether the killer was a bisexual or a repressed homosexual is left vague, although in keeping with such films as *Cruising, Windows* and *The Detective*, the latter is inferred. ☻

Farewell My Lovely
(1975, 97 min, US, Dick Richards)
This modern film noir update of Raymond Chandler's classic murder mystery stars Robert Mitchum as an older, more tired and increasingly cynical Philip Marlowe, private eye. While searching for a mobster's sultry girlfriend, Velma, his investigation leads him into a brothel where he comes face to face with L.A.'s most notorious dyke madam, Frances Anthor (Kate Murtagh). The woman is huge and mean and a fervent non-smoker. She puts out her cigarette and slaps the smugness off his face; he punches her; she drugs him. She is eventually shot while beating up Doris (Rainbeaux Smith), "her favorite girl" who was caught sleeping with thug Johnnie (a pre-stardom Sylvester Stallone). The steely Murtagh coolly out-evils Barbara Stanwyck's madam in *Walk on the Wild Side.* ☻

Father of the Bride
(1991, 105 min, US, Charles Shyer)
In this remake of the Spencer Tracy 1950 classic, Steve Martin and Diane Keaton prepare for daughter Kimberly Williams' wedding. As a mincing caterer, Martin Short does a variation of his agent in *The Big Picture*, but here it's nothing more than a rehash of the decades-old and very tired queeny decorator. Why would someone of Short's cleverness resort to such a cheap, offensive laugh? ☻

Fear City
(1984, 95 min, US, Abel Ferrara)
Contentious independent filmmaker Abel Ferrara (*King of New York, Ms. 45*) delivers a violent crime melodrama set in the sleazy sex world of New York's 42nd Street. Melanie Griffith stars as a stripper who, after breaking up with pimp Tom Berenger, becomes the lover of Rae Dawn Chong. Keeping the Hollywood tradition (as first noted by Vito Russo) that the lesbian/gay man more often than not dies, the sensuous Chong is brutally slashed by a serial killer, suffering terribly before dying. Griffith freaks out at the news and refuses to strip (her form of wearing black); but she is eventually persuaded that "the show must go on." A tender relationship while it lasted. ☻

The Fearless Vampire Killers
(1967, 111 min, US/GB, Roman Polanski)
In Roman Polanski's witty vampire comedy/satire, Professor Abronsius (Jack MacGowran) and his bumbling assistant Alfred (Polanski) hunt the dreaded vampire Count Von Krolock. Iain Quarrier is Herbert, the Count's gay vampire son who takes a liking to the nerdy Alfred. Original title: *The Fearless Vampire Killers, or Pardon Me, But Your Teeth Are in My Neck.* (Also known as: *Dance of the Vampires*) ☻

Paul McCrane as a gay teen in *Fame*

52 Pick-Up
(1986, 114 min, US, John Frankenheimer)
Roy Scheider stars as a businessman being blackmailed by John Glover and his gang. Robert Trebor plays Leo, a "wimpering" gay crook, one of Glover's flunkies who also runs an adult bookstore. William J. Murphy is Leo's boyfriend. ⊛

The Fisher King
(1991, 137 min, US, Terry Gilliam)
In this extraordinary comic fable, Jeff Bridges plays a disc jockey searching for redemption. He crosses paths with homeless Robin Williams, who's searching for the Holy Grail. On their travels, they befriend gay, homeless, ex-cabaret performer Michael Jeter. He touchingly recalls the death of all his friends to AIDS, and does Ethel Merman proud in a knockout version of "Everything's Coming Up Roses." Jeter — who should have been nominated for an Academy Award — gives a bravura performance. ⊛

Five Easy Pieces
(1970, 96 min, US, Bob Rafelson)
As lovers hitchhiking to Alaska, Helena Kallianiotes and Toni Basil are given a ride by Jack Nicholson and Karen Black. In a brief sequence, Kallianiotes steals the show with her passionate diatribes on the world's ills, which drives Nicholson to the point of ejecting his newly acquainted passengers. ⊛

Flesh Gordon
(1973, 78 min, US, Michael Benveniste & Howard Ziehm)
This no-budget but often hilarious X-rated sci-fi spoof features John Hoyt as the gay Prince Precious, the "rightful heir to the throne of Porno." After one of their many adventures, the Prince saves the life of Flesh Gordon (Jason Williams); our appreciative hero allows the Prince to go down on him, eliciting groans of ecstasy from the essentially straight Gordon. ⊛

Flesh Mirror (Espelho de Carne)
(1983, 90 min, Brazil, Antonio Carlos Fontoura)
One of the many soft-core sex films made in Brazil, this fantasy centers on a mirror that brings out the lust in the uptight bourgeois men and women who gaze on it. While mostly heterosexual, the sex scenes include one explicit homosexual act.

Fly by Night
(1992, 93 min, US, Steve Gomer)
This ambitious drama, set in the black ghettos of New York, follows a young man's quest to become a rap star. Rich (Jeffrey Sams) is a college student, husband, father and city worker who gives it all up in his ambitious goal for fame in the tough inner-city world of Gansta Rap music. The film is harmless entertainment until the introduction of Rich's white girlfriend's gay roommate Sam. When we get our first real look at Sam (Yul Vazquez), he is exercising — while looking at himself in the mirror and wearing high heels, fishnet stockings and a black leather miniskirt (typical attire for athletically minded queers!). Straight black man Rich is disgusted by the sight and begins giving him shit on the way he looks and talks, calling him "fag," "freak," "ass-bucket"

From Russia with Love: Lotte Lenya as the deadly Rosa Klebb

and "clone." Sam shows some queer spunk by verbally fighting back, but Rich's hate-filled tirade lingers in one's mind. While the introduction of gay/lesbian characters in straight films is usually laudable, this depiction is confusing and troubling.

Freebie and the Bean
(1974, 112 min, US, Richard Rush)
A pedestrian police comedy-drama which features Christopher Morley as a blackmailer and killer transvestite who tangles with cop James Caan in the ladies' room during the Super Bowl. Caan refers to Morley, who he has just killed, as a "faggot." ⊛

From Russia with Love
(1963, 118 min, GB, Terence Young)
Super spy James Bond (Sean Connery) must retrieve a top secret Russian decoder machine and return it to England. In his way stands lethal lesbian Russian agent Rosa Klebb, menacingly played by Lotte Lenya. When she kicks up her heels, watch out! ⊛

The Front Page
(1974, 105 min, US, Billy Wilder)
Third screen version of the Hecht-MacArthur classic, with Jack Lemmon and Walter Matthau as the feuding newspapermen Hildy Johnson and Walter Burns. David Wayne is Bensinger, prissy reporter extraordinaire. Jon Korkes is the youthful journalist who, as the end titles tell, moves to Cape Cod with Bensinger and together they open an antique shop. Director-writer Billy Wilder is in a particularly and surprisingly insensitive mood. ⊛

Funeral in Berlin
(1966, 102 min, US, Guy Hamilton)
In a brief scene, agent Michael Caine visits a transvestite bar in Berlin, the Chez Nous, which is very tasteful and also a hotbed of spies and political intrigue. ⊛

Gas Food Lodging

(1992, 102 min, US, Allison Anders)

Former Wim Wenders assistant Allison Anders made her directorial debut with this heartfelt tale of familial discord. The story tells of a single, lonely mother (Brooke Adams) and her two daughters (Ione Skye and Fairuza Balk.) All three are seeking a man — a theme that has drawn some fire from feminists. In the early parts of the film, Shade's (Balk) only male friend is Darius (Donovan Leitch), an androgynous teen obsessed with Olivia Newton-John. Although to the viewer he is obviously gay, Shade, in a desperate attempt to find a lover, misinterprets his kindness and affection for heterosexual shyness and eventually pounces on the shocked (and made-up) youth. When nothing happens, she feels like a fool, and he apologizes ("It's not you, it's me"). She eventually finds what she needs in a handsome (and straight) Mexican-American. ⊛

Georgia, Georgia

(1972, 91 min, US, Stig Bjorkman)

Adapted by Maya Angelou from one of her own stories, this independent drama dealing with racial prejudice features Diana Sands as an American singer who, while on tour in Sweden, meets and falls in love with white photographer and Vietnam deserter Dirk Benedict. Roger Furman is featured as Herbert, Sands' gay road manager.

The Getting of Wisdom

(1977, 100 min, Australia, Bruce Beresford)

Two school girls' crushes at a repressive and snobbish Melbourne ladies academy are featured in this pleasant if unimaginative coming-of-age drama. Set before the turn-of-the-century, intelligent but impetuous Laura (Susannah Fowle) leaves her rural home for higher education in the big city. There, she overcomes the school's petty regulations, schoolgirl rivalries and the authority's herd mentality. Chinky (Alix Longman) is a new student who develops an unrequited love for the energetic Laura. She talks about how she would marry her if she were a man, admires her body and steals money from the other girls in order to buy Laura a ring. She is caught, however, and expelled, leaving unrepentant. Laura soon falls for a woman herself in the person of a pretty young teacher, Evelyn (Hilary Ryan). Her jealousy and possessiveness soon breaks up the affair but not before Beresford hints that the two women were physically involved. Funnywoman Dame Edna Everidge's alter ego, Barry Humphries, appears as the school's principal in a wasted performance. ⊛

Gilda *(1946, 110 min, US, Charles Vidor)*

Businessman Ballin Mundson (George MacReady) "picks up" drifter Johnny Farrell (Glenn Ford), makes him #2 man at his Buenos Aries casino. You have to read between the lines, but you only have to look at the way they gaze at each other to grasp the situation. Then Rita Hayworth arrives on the scene. Ford once commented that he and MacReady played their parts as gay lovers. ⊛

Girls in Prison

(1994, 85 min, US, John Naughton)

Made by cable's Showtime as part of a series dedicated to cheesy 1950s teen flicks, this hilariously bad (bad story line, bad acting, bad hair) women-in-prison yarn is a howling delight. While the film does not have sadistic guards and a lecherous warden who lusts over the girls, it does have catfights, gratuitous shower scenes, knife-wielding hit girls and plenty of lesbianism. When innocent Aggie (Missy Crider) asks fellow prisoner Melba if she is a lesbian, she replies that on the outside she isn't, but inside she is (her prison lover Carol, played by Ione Skye, always has liked girls). When asked to describe the sex, she stumbles, "It's like the same, it's uh, the same except it's different." A highlight is a striptease show in which cross-dressing prisoners shed their shirts and pants to the excited delight of a roomful of horny women.

The Glitter Dome

(1984, 95 min, US, Stuart Margolin)

James Garner is a jaded detective working the Hollywood beat in this well-made but standard made-for-TV police yarn based on Joseph Wambaugh's 1981 novel. His investigation into the murder of a Hollywood honcho takes him through the dark side of filmdom — a world of gay and kiddie porn, drugs, murder, sexual aberrations and exploitation. One of the suspects in the murder is script supervisor Lorna Dilman (Colleen Dewhurst), the middle-aged lover to 15-year-old Jill (Christine Hirt), a sometime prostitute and porn actress. She is not cowed by the accusing cops and is portrayed as both loving and protective to the much younger girl. Interestingly, the girl's father has no problems with the relationship. Also featured is Cooley (Real Andrews), a handsome Marine who poses nude for gay porn magazines but insists that he isn't gay. A pity. ⊛

The Goddess

(1958, 105 min, US, John Cromwell)

Subtle but distinct lesbianism can be found near the end of this ambitious melodrama centering around the doomed life and film career of a Marilyn Monroe-like actress. After her rise to stardom, Emily Ann (Kim Stanley) finds herself alone at the top, suffering from alcoholism and psychiatric problems. Her companion/nurse is Miss Haywood (Elizabeth Wilson), a protective even mothering woman with a stern demeanor. When Emily Ann's (now Rita) ex-husband visits and upsets her, it is Miss Haywood who calms and comforts her — calling her "my girl" and "baby." Miss Haywood assures the ex-husband that she will take good care of her, explaining, "I kind of love her." ⊛

Going Places (Les Valseuses)

(1974, 117 min, France, Bertrand Blier)

Gérard Depardieu and Patrick Dewaere star as two thoroughly degenerate thugs who nonchalantly steal from, molest and terrorize the general population while staying one step ahead of the police and angry mobs. At one point, Depardieu is turned on while washing his injured bosom buddy (who was shot in the balls by an armed victim); with no women in sight, he takes a fancy to Dewaere's ass, and, after being fought off, rapes him. The next day, Dewaere complains about the assault, but Depardieu dismisses it by saying "between friends it's normal." They then continue their reign of terror whose victims include Jeanne Moreau and a masochistic Miou-Miou. ⊛

MENTIONS

Goldfinger *(1964, 108 min, GB, Guy Hamilton)*

"You can turn off the charm," Pussy Galore purrs to James Bond, "I'm immune," and for the first three-quarters of this 007 actioner, she is. Pussy (Honor Blackman) is the right-hand woman to the evil Goldfinger and she manages a group of all-female pilots called Pussy's Flying Circus. But as Sean Connery's Bond works at keeping Goldfinger from poisoning the country's gold supply, he also works at lowering Pussy's resistance. When Goldfinger tells Pussy to entertain Mr. Bond, she replies "Business before pleasure." But after a rousing judo match, the two fall rather randily in the hay. Pussy then helps James by calling the police and when they ask James why she helped him, he replies, "I must have appealed to her maternal instincts." ⊗

The Goodbye Girl

(1977, 92 min, US, Herbert Ross)

Exaggerated gay stereotypes done strictly for comedy relief and a mother-fixated homosexual theatre director mar this Neil Simon-written, homophobe Herbert Ross-directed comedy about divorcée Marsha Mason falling in love with egocentric actor Richard Dreyfuss. Off-Broadway director and obnoxious homophile Mark (Paul Benedict) pontificates that both William Shakespeare and Richard III were "flaming homosexuals" and that his play on the hunchback king should have been called "The Queen Who Would Be King." So in presenting his version of "Richard III," he forces actor Dreyfuss to play the lead clothed in lavender robes, to speak with a pronounced lisp, and to swish about on stage. The play closes after one performance; although the damage done to gays lingers. ⊗

The Grasshopper

(1970, 96 min, US, Jerry Paris)

A beautiful Jacqueline Bisset stars in this "small-town girl tries to make it in the big city" melodrama. Bisset is Christine, an ambitious young woman who seeks success as a chorus girl in a Las Vegas revue. Many men romantically enter and exit her tumultuous life, but Buck Brown (Roger Garrett), fellow dancer and a non-stereotypical gay man, is her best friend and constant emotional support. They even double date two different blond members of a rock band called The Ice Pack. There is also a quick scene with an ass-slapping lesbian chorus girl. ⊗

The Great Escape

(1963, 168 min, US, John Sturges)

Though there is really nothing overtly gay in this classic WWII adventure film, one question does remain: Just what was going on between the daddyish Danny (Charles Bronson) and the fairish Willy (John Leyton)? ⊗

The Group *(1966, 150 min, US, Sidney Lumet)*

Based on Mary McCarthy's best-seller, Sidney Lumet's adaptation follows the lives of eight Vassar women in the 1930s. In her film debut, Candice Bergen plays Lakey, one of the college grads of the title, who returns from Europe with a mannish female lover called the Baroness (Lidia Prochnicka). As Larry Hagman observes to Lakey, "I never pegged you for a Sapphic. To put it crudely, a lesbo." ⊗

Hair *(1979, 121 min, US, Milos Forman)*

As Wolf, Don Dacus says: "I wouldn't kick Mick Jagger out of bed, but I'm not homosexual." His part was considerably toned down from the original Broadway production. One of the film's musical highlights is the production number "Black Boys/White Boys," with its male and female singers/admirers. That's Michael Jeter as the inductee wearing nail polish on his toes. ⊗

Hanging Out (Tagediebe)

(1985, 90 min, Germany, Marcel Gisler)

This drama of misplaced youth eking out an existence in Berlin treads similar ground covered in *Christiane F.*, but without the drugs; and is also reminiscent of the hard-hitting gay drama of life-on-Berlin-streets, *Prince in Hell*. The story revolves around Max, Lola and Laurids, three young people who are roommates without a flat of their own. Told in an episodic fashion, we find that Max loves Lola but Lola wants her freedom while Laurids is a fun-loving gay. An interesting story of several souls lost in the inhumanity of a harsh city.

The Haunting *(1963, 112 min, US, Robert Wise)*

Julie Harris plays Eleanor Lance, a high-strung spinster who joins a group of "professionals" in spending and documenting their stay in Hill House, a notorious haunted mansion. She is soon befriended by Theodora (Claire Bloom), a pretty, stylish lesbian who strangely takes a fancy to Eleanor. Their friendship is stormy and in one argument Eleanor calls her "nature's mistake," just in case somebody didn't pick up on her sexual orientation. The covert lesbian context is handled in a non-offensive, even positive manner. And the film is darn scary, too. ⊗

Headhunter

(1989, 92 min, US, Francis Schaeffer)

A low-budget horror film that involves voodoo, a mysterious beast and Nigerian immigrants. The police investigate a series of bizarre decapitations in Miami (though shot in South Africa). In a subplot, one of the detectives (Wayne Crawford) leaves his wife after he discovers that she is sleeping with another woman.

He's My Girl

(1987, 104 min, US, Gabrielle Beaumont)

This "straight" cross-dressing comedy features black comedian T.K. Carter as Reggie, an always-on-the-make music manager who is transformed into Regina, a six-foot conical-breasted "woman" in order to accompany his friend (cute blond David Hallyday) on a prize-winning trip to Hollywood. Regina sashays and finger-snaps with the best of them and she has her hands full when a sleazy record executive gets the hots for her curvacious bod. While the only gay shown is a typically swishy, limp-wristed photographer (who exclaims upon seeing Regina, "Well, aren't we just a little petite thing!"), there is enough drag queen humor and interpretive gay jokes to make this film enjoyable. ⊗

Heathers *(1989, 102 min, US, Michael Lehmann)*

Among the many classmates murdered in this wickedly funny black comedy, the deaths of jocks Lance Fenton and Patrick Labyorteaux are made by Christian Slater and Winona Ryder to look like a sui-

Julie Harris (l.) and Claire Bloom in *The Haunting*

cide love-pact. At the funeral, one father says "I love my dead gay son." To which Slater responds sarcastically, "How do you think he'd react to a son that had a limp wrist with a pulse." ☮

The Heavenly Kid
(1985, 89 min, US, Cary Medoway)
In this awfully acted and terribly unfunny comedy, Lewis Smith plays a teenaged '50s greaser, killed in a chicken race, whose spirit returns in the '80s to look after nerdy Jason Gedrick — who turns out to be his son. In one scene, Smith visits an old hangout which is now home to a heavy-duty gay leather bar. Smith observes it's now "the wrong turf." ☮

Hiding Out
(1987, 98 min, US, Bob Giraldi)
The 1987 "Homosexual Panic Award" goes to Keith Coogan for the tizzy he goes into when incognito cousin Jon Cryer makes eyes at him in the classroom trying to get his attention. C'mon, running down the school hallway, arms flailing, and hiding in a toilet? ☮

History of the World, Pt. 1
(1981, 92 min, US, Mel Brooks)
Mel Brooks presents an episodic view of, well, the history of the world. In a segment called "The Roman Empire," Howard Morris camps it up as Brooks lets loose with a barrage of fag jokes (again). ☮

The Hitcher *(1986, 97 min, US, Robert Harmon)*
Crazed killer Rutger Hauer chases boyish C. Thomas Howell through the desert in this eerie thriller awash in homoeroticism. The simple premise: Howell picks up the murderously psychotic Hauer who, instead of killing him like all of his other victims, plays a psychological cat-and-mouse game with the confused youth. Soon after getting into the car, the bug-eyed Hauer threatens him and, when help possibly comes Howell's way, Hauer diverts suspicion when he grabs the teen's crotch and acts like the two are lovers. Later, Hauer ominously caresses Howell's face with a knife, putting the phallic symbol into his terrified victim's mouth. When the teen asks why is he doing this to him, Hauer replies, "You're a smart kid. Figure it out." Even outsiders catch on to the game, with a sheriff remarking at one point, "There's something strange going on between the two of you." Other startling images involve the sultry Jennifer Jason Leigh who befriends Howell, only to fall victim to a horribly violent, jealous rage by Hauer. The final gay hint is near the end when Howell spits in the face of an appreciative Hauer who spreads the cum-like liquid over his face accompanied by a dreamy smile. Ah! Love! ☮

House of Angels
(1992, 119 min, Sweden, Colin Nutley)
An endearing comedy-drama that is a plea for tolerance as well as a celebration of being different. When an eccentric old man dies in a bizarre accident, his greedy neighbor expects to snatch up his

property for a song. But the old man's will gives it all to his hitherto unknown granddaughter Fanny who is living in Germany. Her arrival to claim her land startles the townsfolk for not only is she an outlandish, sexy blonde with a suggestive swagger, but she arrives on a motorcycle driven by Zak, a menacing, leather-jacketed Alice Cooper-looking man. We soon discover that Zak is not her lover but is instead gay as well as her best friend and performance partner. Zak's specialty is cross-dressing musical numbers. The townspeople's initial horror of the two and their skinny-dipping, partying friends soon turns to acceptance in this amiable satire. One of the most successful Swedish films ever made, Colin Nutley, an Englishman living in Sweden, has an adroit hand when it comes to creating interesting characters. Of note: Miramax Films announced that it is producing an American remake of the film to be directed by Nutley. It will be interesting to see if they retain the gay subplot or whether Zak will turn into a booze-guzzling, woman-loving hetero stud! ⊛

The House of the Spirits

(1994, 109 min, Portugal/US, Billie August)
While overall this adaptation of Isabel Allende's novel reads more like a dispassionate Cliff Notes version of the turbulent tale of family turmoil and political upheaval, the book's subtle lesbian subplot not only remains intact, but has been enlarged. Jeremy Irons stars as Esteban, an ambitious landowner whose heartless drive for success destroys his family and nearly crushes his humanity. Glenn Close stars a Ferula, Esteban's sexually repressed virgin spinster sister who develops a love for his beautiful wife Clara (Meryl Streep). Ferula, who had led a life lacking in love and tenderness, becomes extremely attached to gentle, caring Clara and moves in with her and Esteban when they marry. The two women never develop a sexual relationship, although the lonely Ferula harbors lustful thoughts. At one point, she goes to a priest and confesses "sins" involving Clara. She whispers excitedly, "She looks like the angel of light, I want to climb into her bed, to feel the warmth of her skin, her gentle breathing." Later, she is dicovered by Esteban

sleeping (fully clothed) in the same bed with Clara, and he promptly throws her out of the house despite her protestations that "it's never been the way you imagine between us, never." Allende commented that the two loved each other, but the sexual angles were left ambiguous. "And if there was a sexual attraction on the part of Ferula in Latin culture at the time, it would have never been acknowledged. She wouldn't even have known what it was about. Of course, things have changed." ⊛

In a Lonely Place

(1950, 91 min, US, Nicholas Ray)
Humphrey Bogart plays a hot-tempered, down-on-his-luck screenwriter in this film noir murder mystery set in Hollywood. Gloria Grahame co-stars as an actress who becomes involved with Bogart after being his sole alibi when he is accused of murder. As the police investigation continues, she becomes increasingly worried that he may be the killer. In a role that must have been edited to some degree before final release, Hadda Brooks is Martha, Grahame's stern, masculine and stocky masseuse who doesn't trust Bogey. There are hints that there is something between the two, especially when Martha, the prototypical lesbian, is obviously comfortable in calling her employer "angel" and being quite open about their life together. But Grahame chooses the man and fires her, only to frantically call her butch protector when she gets into trouble. What was going on with the two of them? ⊛

In a Shallow Grave

(1987, 92 min, US, Kenneth Bowser)
Eminently strange, slow moving and oddly interesting, this film version of James Purdy's novel of redemption through homosexual love centers around Garnet (Michael Biehn), a WWII vet who was horribly disfigured in the war and who has returned to his Virginia farm to seek solitude, wallow in self-pity and pine for love. Drifter Daventry (Patrick Dempsey) arrives and soon becomes his helper. But the story takes an unusual shift when Daventry claims Garnet to be his "other self" and professes his love for him. There is one memorable scene in which the two men longingly embrace. Charles Silver of *The Village Voice* wrote, "Bowser handles the homoeroticism central to the novel with such obliquity and discretion, one can almost feel the fetid breath of Jesse Helms overseeing the 'morality' of this destined-for-PBS production." ⊛

The Incident

(1967, 99 min, US, Larry Peerce)
This edgy, violent drama, reminiscent of the raw intensity of the works of The Living Theatre, is an early precursor to the urban terrors of today. Two young thugs, Artie (Martin Sheen) and Joe (Tony Musante), terrorize the trapped passengers of a New York City subway car one late summer night. Included in

Kevin Bacon (c.) as a gay hustler in *JFK*

the collection of hapless stereotypical urbanites is Kenneth (Robert Fields), a nervous, lonely and pitiful homosexual. Seen first in a bar where he almost comes on to the older but straight Gary Merrill, Kenneth becomes the bullies' first victim. Artie immediately spots him as a fag and while he is tormented and humiliated by both men, the other passengers simply look on, with one remarking, "So what, so they found a queer." There is a subtle eroticism to the bashing as the gay man takes the beating and punishment he feels he deserves. ⊛

Inside Daisy Clover

(1965, 128 min, US, Robert Mulligan)
In one of his earliest screen roles, Robert Redford is Wade Lewis, a gay 1930s screen idol who "never could resist a charming boy." He marries unsuspecting 15-year-old Venice vagabond Daisy (played by 27-year-old Natalie Wood), who is discovered by film executive Christopher Plummer, and the marriage lasts for one day. Redford's homosexuality was blurred by worried studio executives resulting in an ill-defined character who is presented as a bisexual. ⊛

Inspector Lavardin

(1986, 103 min, France, Claude Chabrol)
A cast of kinky and suspicious characters meet Inspector Lavardin as he tries to solve the murder of a prominent Catholic found naked on the Brittainy beach. In this effective thriller, the normally taciturn inspector discovers that the bourgeoisie can very well be "different" as he tries to unravel the mystery. People involved in his investigation include the man's surprisingly calm wife (who coincidentally was a former lover of Lavardin) and the victim's eccentric gay brother (played by Jean-Claude Brialy) who hints that he knows something as he shows off his collection of glass eyes.

Irreconcilable Differences

(1984, 117 min, US, Charles Shyer)
Young Drew Barrymore goes to court to "divorce" her parents — director Ryan O'Neal and writer Shelley Long. As one of Long's employees, Richard Minchenberg is Howard, a stereotypical, "screaming" nellie secretary. ⊛

Jacqueline Susann's Once Is Not
Enough *(1975, 121 min, US, Guy Green)*

This film version of Jacqueline Susann's final novel is a wonderfully campy and trashy melodrama examining the lives and sexuality of a group of unhappy jet-setters. The plot centers on January (Deborah Raffin), an innocent but father-fixated daughter of a has-been movie producer (Kirk Douglas) who grows up awfully fast in this laughably tawdry tale. In a small subplot, Alexis Smith appears as the super-rich Deidre who is secretly involved in a lesbian affair with Karla (Melina Mercouri), a Greta Garbo-esque actress. The two kiss and are affectionate towards one another. ⊛

JFK *(1991, 188 min, US, Oliver Stone)*

Oliver Stone's controversial investigation into the murder of President John F. Kennedy suggests that businessman Clay Shaw (Tommy Lee Jones), petty criminal David Ferrie (Joe Pesci) and

Inside Daisy Clover

male hustler Willie O'Keefe (Kevin Bacon), all of them gay, were government dupes and possible lower-level CIA operatives involved to some degree in the assassination. As heterosexual family man and do-gooder New Orleans D.A. Jim Garrison (Kevin Costner) digs deeper into the possible conspiracy, he finds most local roads lead to the gay underworld — a link that suggests an association between wholesome American life and the moral and criminal degeneracy of homosexuals. Bacon comes off best (in comparison to the others) as a Marine-like racist/fascist party boy, Pesci is a lying ex-priest defrocked for his "one fucking weakness" and Jones felt it necessary to feminize himself in his offensive (but Oscar nominated) portrayal of Shaw. ⊛

Justice de Flic (Deadly Aim)

(1986, 85 min, France, Michel Gérard)
This typical French police thriller features an atypical gay angle in its plot. After a bloody bank heist, one of the crooks, Alan Jefferson, flees to the United States with all of the money, leaving his partners-in-crime, the Satori brothers, holding the bag. In order to get their money and lure Jefferson back to France, they force his younger brother, Hervé, into male prostitution on the streets of Paris. At the same time, the police inspector, whose bungling of the investigation allowed Jefferson to flee, also uses dirty tricks — by sending him a photo of his brother soliciting male customers and writes on the back, "The Satoris have turned your brother into a faggot whore." With his former crime partners and the police waiting, Jefferson returns to France to save his brother.

The Krays

Killer Nun *(1978, 87 min, Italy, Giulio Berruti)*

This shock-schlock flick is not as violent nor as promisingly funny as the title suggests, yet any film that features crazed, sexually starved nuns, ensuing carnal indulgences, sadomasochism and violence can't be all bad. Alida Valli stars as Sister Gertrude, a nun tormented by evil demons and who is beginning to crack up in the most violent fashion. Featured is a man-hating lesbian nun who has the hots for our statuesque sister, but she is violently and humiliatingly rebuffed. Joe Dallesandro has a small role as an investigator. Good exploitative fun.

King Rat *(1965, 133 min, US, Bryan Forbes)*

Based on the novel by James Clavell, this powerful adaptation focuses on the lives of a group of American and British soldiers confined to a Japanese POW camp during WWII. George Segal stars as the title character, an American black market scavenger who rules his barracks. James Fox is the fairish British soldier he takes under his wing, and they are very likely lovers, although this relationship is only hinted at. ☻

Knightriders
(1981, 146 min, US, George Romero)

An interminably long and insufferably trite tale of modern day "knights" who put on traveling stunt jousting matches on motorcycles for Renaissance Fair-type tournaments. The bikers include a constipated and self-important Ed Harris as their King Arthur-like leader. While the bikers are macho and hetero, their announcer Pippin (Warner Shook) is quite different — a sensitive and closeted young man who is eventually teased by the group for being gay. He doesn't deny it, claiming that he doesn't know what orientation he is. But later he comes out to a female friend and amazingly finds happiness when one of the strapping knights asks to be his boyfriend. They are seen together, and while their only sign of affection is a manly hug, their gay lovey-dovey inclusion into the action-oriented story is nothing less than amazing. ☻

The Krays
(1990, 119 min, GB, Peter Medak)

Chillingly effective, although perhaps too maudlin for American shoot-'em-up audiences, this film works both as a psychological gangster flick and as a violent, dysfunctional family drama. The coldly handsome twin brothers Gary and Martin Kemp (of Spandau Ballet) star as the Krays — two of England's most notorious criminals. Formed under the smothering, obsessive love of their mother (Billie Whitelaw), the two young men begin a reign of terror through 1960s London as they ruthlessly grasp power. The interesting and well-handled aspect of the story is that Ron is gay and his brother Reg is straight. Ron is seen kissing and in bed with one of the blond members of their gang but as soon as tenderness and affection rises to the top, Ron destroys it through mistreatment and intimidation towards his long-suffering lover. Much to Ron's jealousy, Reg falls in love with a woman, a situation that threatens their nearly incestuous closeness. Initially, Reg's love story suggests that heterosexuals are capable of a more normal relationship than a gay one, but as soon as this point is made, Reg's coldness resurfaces, prompting the girl's suicide and his re-commitment to crime, his mom and brother. It is also interesting that Ron's gayness, ridiculed by his enemies, is taken much more nonchalantly by all the others. ☻

The Kremlin Letter
(1970, 113 min, US, John Huston)

This convoluted but involving Cold War espionage thriller centers on an incendiary letter sent by an American official to the Soviet Union regarding the destruction of China's nuclear weapons capability. Providing some enjoyable moments is George Sanders in perhaps his strangest role — playing, in full regalia, a gay San Francisco drag queen with a penchant for knitting. Another queer scene is when a kidnapped Russian official is forced to watch his daughter being seduced by a black lesbian. ☻

The L-Shaped Room
(1962, 142 min, GB, Bryan Forbes)

Sort of a "kitchen sink *Tales of the City*," this touching drama stars Leslie Caron as a pregnant French woman who moves to a seedy boarding house in London to have her baby. The group of offbeat lodgers include Tom Bell as a struggling writer who falls in love with her; Brock Peters as a gay West Indian jazz musician who is in turn secretly in love with Bell; and Cicely Courtneidge as a lesbian vaudeville performer, now retired.

Lady Beware
(1987, 108 min, US, Karen Arthur)

Diane Lane stars in this erotic thriller as a department store window dresser who becomes the victim of a psychopath's obsession.

Other than the unusually hunky and often shirtless villain (Michael Woods), a supporting gay stereotype is also featured. Peter Nevargic plays Lionel, the comic relief assistant window dresser (what, Meshach Taylor wasn't available?) who introduces himself as the employee "nobody wants to work with." He's saddled with such tired lines as "I love the hair. It's luscious!" ☻

The Lady Vanishes
(1938, 97 min, GB, Alfred Hitchcock)
This quintessential train murder mystery stars Michael Redgrave and Margaret Lockwood as a pair of travelers who undertake a search for a missing passenger: a diminutive old woman who may possibly hold secrets of international espionage. Among the many characters are Caldicott (Naughton Wayne) and Charters (Basil Radford), two men traveling together. Forced to share a bedroom (and a single bed) together in a hotel, Caldicott is seen topless and Charters is seen without his pajama bottoms — what could Hitchcock have been trying to tell us about them? Unlike typically negative or stereotypical images of gays, these two are seen as cool, collective Englishmen who pitch in when needed. ☻

Lakki: The Boy Who Grew Wings
(1993, 104 min, Norway, Svend Wam)
Nominally a straight drama about a teenage boy's emotional problems, *Lakki* features plenty of male nudity (both the calf and beefcake variety), a closeted bisexual gym instructor and a pitiful child molester. Lakki (Andres Borchgrevink), an attractive 14-year-old youth, is in the throngs of a nervous breakdown — his alcoholic, nympho mother is mercurial at best when it comes to care and support and his yuppie father proves to be a complete, unreliable jerk. His search for understanding outside of his home leads Lakki into the apartment of a mousy, middle-aged man who, when he makes the moves on the troubled boy, is beaten senseless. ☻

Landscape in the Mist

Landscape in the Mist
(1988, 126 min, Greece, Theo Angelopoulos)
Two children — a 13-year-old girl and her seven-year-old brother — leave the squalor of their home in Athens and journey north to Germany in hopes of finding their long-lost father in this moving allegorical drama. The rough odyssey, which includes a rape of the girl by a trucker and other hardships, is lessened when they meet and are befriended by Orestes (Stratos Tzortzoglou), a handsome young man cruising the countryside on his motorcycle before his induction into the armed forces. He seems too good to be true and for gay audiences he proves to be — for near the end of the film, he is seen picking up another young man in a bar. The subtle revelation that he is gay is skillfully handled in this haunting tale of hope and survival. ☻

The Last Emperor
(1987, 164 min, Italy/China, Bernardo Bertolucci)
A much-lauded (winner of nine Academy Awards) historical epic that chronicles the turbulent life and times of China's last emperor, Pu Yi. John Lone stars as the weak-willed man who began his life as the all-powerful emperor of the Dragon Throne and ended as a simple gardener. After he is dethroned and expelled from the Forbidden City in the late 1920s, he enjoys a Western-style playboy life while the Japanese, needing a puppet head in their invasion and take-over of Manchuria, cunningly recruit him to their cause. They use as their bait Eastern Jewel (Maggie Han) — Pu Yi's sexy, modern-looking cousin sent under the guise to "protect the emperor and his wife." Jewel, first seen in a fetching leather aviation outfit (and later in suits and ties), is a bewitching bisexual who soon realizes she must get rid of his wife Wam Jung (Joan Chen), a vocal opponent to her husband's planned collaboration. Eastern Jewel soon addicts her to opium, sexually seduces her and, after arranging for a soldier to impregnate her, sends her away in disgrace. Much like the evil Nazi lesbian in *Rome — Open City*, the film presents a disturbing image of a villainous, calculating and predatory lesbian — a woman who uses her (lesbian) sexuality to destroy. ☻

The Last Metro
(1980, 133 min, France, François Truffaut)
Catherine Deneuve stars as the owner of a Parisian theatre trying to keep her house open in the face of Nazi oppression in Occupied France. Among the cast members and staffers, gay and lesbian personnel include a substitute director (Jean Poiret), a costume designer (Andrea Ferreal), and an actress (Sabine Haudepin). ☻

The Last of Sheila
(1973, 120 min, US, Herbert Ross)
In this perplexing and complex mystery written by Anthony Perkins and Stephen Sondheim, movie producer James Coburn gathers six Hollywood types for a week of sailing and games. Each of the guests have a "dark secret." As a screenwriter, Richard Benjamin's is that he had an affair with his host. ☻

The Laughing Policeman

(1973, 111 min, US, Stuart Rosenberg)

Walter Matthau and a hot-headed Bruce Dern star as two moralistic San Francisco cops who, while working on cracking the mass killing on a city bus, are led through the underbelly of the city — its porno district, prostitutes, crazed Vietnam veterans, drug addicts and gay scene. They scan several gay bars, including the Frolic Room and the Ramrod, a leather/western bar. One of their leads takes them to a hospital where they meet a lesbian nurse (Joanna Cassidy) who is unresponsive to their strong-arm tactics. In the end, they uncover the killer: Henry Camerero, a closeted gay man (Albert Paulsen). ⊛

Lawrence of Arabia

(1962, 216 min, GB, David Lean)

As a Turkish bey, Jose Ferrer is attracted to the fair-complexioned T.E. Lawrence, played by Peter O'Toole. Thinking he may have found a fellow spirit, Ferrer thinks "that would be too lucky." Lawrence's homosexuality is not mentioned in the film; he's sexually ambiguous more than anything else, although the film does show Lawrence demonstrating a deep affection for an Arab boy (who in real life may have been his lover). It's also suggested that Lawrence is raped by Ferrer's military leader. ⊛

League of Gentlemen

(1960, 114 min, GB, Basil Dearden)

This exciting and exceedingly witty bank heist caper is very queer indeed. The story revolves around an unlikely group of retired military men who are brought together for a big bank robbery. The sharp dialogue and fast-moving story line includes several gay references. Fran Stevens is a gay man and is one of the ex-Army officers involved in the plan. We find out that he caused a scandal and was thrown out of the service for a sexual indiscretion; the ringleader dryly notes, "Nothing the British public likes better than catching the odd man out." He is now a trainer at a gym (seen giving a massage to an athlete) but is being blackmailed for his sexuality (being gay at the time was illegal in Britain). The seen-it-all Cockney blackmailer remarks, "They say girls are expensive enough...but it takes all sorts." There are several jokes (none mean-spirited) referring to him being gay. In another queer reference, a member of the gang always refers to people as "old darling." When asked to stop, he apologizes and explains, "One gets such terrible bad habits at the YMCA." And adding to the festivities is a cameo by tough guy Oliver Reed who plays an outrageously queeny acting student who would make Emory in *The Boys in the Band* look thuggish by comparison. ⊛

The Legend of Lylah Clare

(1968, 127 min, US, Robert Aldrich)

A critical disaster and box-office bomb, this now-campy melodrama stars Kim Novak in a dual role: as Lylah Clare, a Hollywood star who mysteriously died on the night of her wedding night, and Elsa, Lylah's spitting image. Twenty years after her death, Lylah's husband, director Lewis Zarkan (Peter Finch), hires Elsa to portray his former wife in a biopic he hopes will mark his comeback. Rossella Falk is featured as Rossella, an on-the-prowl, drug-addicted lesbian who, while her dialogue coach, was having an affair with Lylah.

Lenny *(1974, 112 min, US, Bob Fosse)*

A documentary-style film on the life and death of controversial comic Lenny Bruce, who is memorably played by Dustin Hoffman. After falling in with a swinging drug crowd, Bruce convinces his wife and professional stripper Honey (Valerie Perrine) to have sex with another woman, and then reproaches her for liking it too much. During his stand-up nightclub routine, Bruce tells a "joke" about two gay schoolteachers who were fired after authorities discovered they were having sex together. He says that it's not like any of the children went home and told their parents, "We had five minutes of geography and ten minutes of cocksucking." This precipitated the first of Bruce's many arrests for obscenity, which eventually bankrupted him. ⊛

Leon Morin, Priest

(1961, 118 min, France, Jean-Pierre Melville)

Emmanuelle Riva stars as an unhappy atheist and communist widow who decides to convert to Catholicism after being befriended by a young priest (Jean-Paul Belmondo playing against type). During their nightly discussions, she reveals to him that she has fallen in love with her equally interested female supervisor, observing, "When I saw her, time stood still...only the beautiful should give orders." The women's relationship, however, is never consummated. ⊛

Less Than Zero

(1987, 96 min, US, Marek Kanievska)

Slimy drug dealer Rip (James Spader) pimps boyish, troubled and straight teen Julian (Robert Downey, Jr.) to his male clients. It seems Julian gives good head, or at least that's what the graffiti says. Downey's touching performance is wasted in this otherwise awful film. ⊛

Light Sleeper

(1992, 103 min, US, Paul Schrader)

David Clennon is Robert, a drug dealer who works for small-time operator Susan Sarandon. His character is neither sleazy nor offensive, and his sexuality is incidental. ⊛

Little Big Man

(1970, 150 min, US, Arthur Penn)

Robert Little Star plays Little Horse, a gay Cheyenne Indian who doesn't have "the temperament" to be a warrior. The tribe calls him a "humanie," and he is thought highly of. ⊛

Little Darlings

(1980, 92 min, US, Ronald F. Maxwell)

No direct lesbian characters here, but there is a palpable dyke undercurrent running between fellow virgins Ferris (Tatum O'Neal) and Angel (Kristy McNichol) in this mildly amusing comedy-drama set at summer camp. McNichol smokes Marlboros in a hard pack and thinks "guys are a pain in the ass" while Tatum is the rich and pampered femme. The other girls write Angel off as lezzie and conclude that Ferris is not, she's simply immature. They are cajoled into a $100 bet on who can lose their virginity first. Neither are particularly interested in boys, and they accept the bet only due to peer pressure. *Little Dykes*? If only they had lost their virginity to each other (do lesbians ever lose their virginity!?). Dream on. Angel goes to the boys' camp to seduce Matt Dillon (they both have the same hair-do) and Ferris tries for coach Armand Assanti. One does, the other doesn't. ⊕

The Long Good Friday

(1980, 114 min, GB, John Mackenzie)
In this outstanding crime drama, Paul Freeman plays a gay underworld figure who double-crosses the wrong organization (the IRA). Pierce Brosnan is the pretty boy who lures him to his death. ⊕

Love Child *(1982, 97 min, US, Larry Peerce)*

The legal nightmares of an angry young woman caught up in the Florida penal system is the theme to this based-on-fact drama. Amy Madigan stars as 19-year-old Terry Jean, who is sent to prison for 15 years after she naively became involved in an armed robbery. The prison, bright, clean and safe in comparison to the many other women-in-prison tales, still has its tense and threatening moments for the young woman. Her first encounters are with several leering lesbians headed by J.J. (Mackenzie Phillips), a butched-up, slicked-back-haired beauty who, though "married" to a blonde femme inmate, still has time to appreciate the new kid on the cell block. Terry Jean rejects all comers but eventually becomes platonic best friends with J.J. Overly balanced in its depiction of prison life to be campy fun (despite a prison full of beautiful women, a fleeting shower scene, a cat fight and one "Keep your hands off my lady!" outburst by J.J.), the story drops the lesbian angle when Terry Jean becomes pregnant by a prison guard (Beau Bridges) and begins an impassioned battle to keep her child. ⊕

Love in a Women's Prison

(1972, 100 min, Italy, Rino Di Silvestro)
The title tells it all in this amusingly terrible exploitation "sizzler." All of the ingredients of the women-in-prison genre are evident: lesbianism, skin, catfights, bondage, drug smuggling and not-terribly-helpful guards. Ridiculous and tiring.

Love Potion #9

(1992, 97 min, US, Dale Launer)
This lightweight fluff — a failed screwball comedy wannabe — is taken from the hit pop tune of the same name and follows the hormonal hijinks of Paul and Diane, two nerdy scientists (Tate Donovan and Sandra Bullock) who accidentally take a powerfully heterosexual love potion. The few fleeting gay references come early. In the first scene, a Gypsy (Anne Bancroft) reads Paul's palm and sees no women in his life, prompting her to ask, "Are you a boy-kissy-boy? A homosexual?" He says "no," but takes the potion just in case. Can this potion be seen as a drug to change gays into straights? Nah...although there is a scene in which Diane goes to an office where in a cubicle is a (gay) male secretary

The Maltese Falcon

(Scott Higgs) — we know he's gay because he is listening to the Village People's "YMCA" on the radio and graces his walls with pictures of half-naked men and Marilyn Monroe! Try as he may against his "nature," he eventually succumbs to her womanly charms. A disturbing idea but not to worry, it's only an insipid comedy. ⊕

Made in America

(1993, 110 min, US, Richard Benjamin)
Whoopi Goldberg stars as Sarah, owner of an African-American bookstore called African Queen. She has one employee, James (Jeffrey Joseph). When James is first introduced, he is miming the words to Judy Garland's "Over the Rainbow," and later in conversation with her boss, he says that it would be bad luck not to have "a real African queen working on the premises." Will Smith also stars as Tea Cake, lifelong friend to Sarah's daughter, Zora (Nia Long). Though the script requires him to be straight and in love with Zora, Smith plays the role so campy that several reviewers thought Smith's character to be gay. ⊕

The Maltese Falcon

(1941, 101 min, US, John Huston)
John Huston made his directorial debut with this classic mystery and second screen version of Dashiell Hammett's novel. Humphrey Bogart stars as Sam Spade, tough-guy private eye whose investigation into the death of his partner leads him to tangle with underworld art collector Kasper Gutman and his associates. Sydney Greenstreet also made his debut (and received an Oscar nomination for it) as Gutman, the eloquent "fat man" who is partners with the primpering Joel Cairo (Peter Lorre) and lovers with his bodyguard Wilmer (Elisha Cook, Jr.) — though the relationship must be read between the lines. In one scene, Wilmer is referred to as a "gunsel," which is period slang for homosexual. ⊕

Man of Flowers

(1984, 110 min, Australia, Paul Cox)

An unusual, understated drama about a rich, sexually repressed lover of art and flowers (Norman Kaye) who pays a model, Lisa (Alyson Best), to strip for him weekly as he sets the erotic encounter to classical music. His lonely life, caused by childhood sexual traumas, is enlivened and upset as he reluctantly becomes involved with her tumultuous personal life. One such encounter is when Lisa leaves her no-talent artist boyfriend and enters into a relationship with her friend, Jane (Sarah Walker), an attractive lesbian. The scenes of the two women together are handled so matter-of-factly that it makes bisexuality seem to be the norm. Wonderfully captured is a bedroom scene before their first sexual encounter. As they lie about naked and drinking, Lisa anticipates the inevitable and says, "Am I gonna like this? I don't know how I feel...I reserve the right to be disgusted." Jane responds, "You won't be, it grows on you." They kiss...fade out. Later, the man tells them that he knows they have a loving relationship and would like to add their lovemaking to his voyeuristic arrangement. ✪

The Man without a Face

(1993, 125 min, US, Mel Gibson)

Homophobe and heartthrob Mel Gibson's directorial debut is this by-the-numbers adaptation of Isabelle Holland's touching coming-of-age story. Gibson stars as Justin McLeod, a horribly disfigured loner whose life and appearance are a mystery to his New England neighbors. A former teacher, he is approached for tutoring sessions by a troubled teenaged boy, Chuck (Nick Stahl). A friendship develops between them, and McLeod serves as mentor to the youth until news of child molestation charges in McLeod's past begin to surface. (In the original novel, McLeod is gay, but almost all references to that have been dropped for the screen version.) The boy's mother questions Chuck on his relationship with McLeod, asking if he had been abused by the older man. And, the

Manhattan

town's sheriff also investigates their friendship, actually coming to McLeod's house at one point to take the boy away from him. ✪

Manhattan

(1979, 96 min, US, Woody Allen)

Woody Allen's ex-wife Meryl Streep and her lover Karen Ludwig are raising Allen and Streep's son ("How's Willie...does he play baseball? Does he wear dresses?"). As Michael Murphy observes: Streep under Allen's "personal vibrations...went from bisexuality to homosexuality." ✪

Manhunter   *(1986, 119 min, US, Michael Mann)*

This stylish, tough police thriller stars William L. Petersen as an intensely troubled ex-FBI agent who comes out of retirement to track down the Tooth Fairy, a serial killer who murders entire families but only sexually molests his male victims. The FBI and police deduce that he is a homosexual who "is impotent to members of the opposite sex and may have had sexual relations with his mother." He instructs his officers to immediately check out the "KY cowboys and the leather bars" of Atlanta. When the deranged queer is introduced, we meet Frances Dollarhyde (Tom Noonan), a geeky, ugly, polyesterized outcast. The gay angle is inexplicably dropped as he falls in love with a sensitive blind woman; although he eventually feels betrayed by her and turns on her. It is interesting that this film and its sequel, *The Silence of the Lambs* (Brian Cox plays Dr. Hannibal Lecter in this first film), both feature a sexually confused, presumably gay and certainly sicko killer. ✪

Mannequin

(1987, 90 min, US, Michael Gottlieb)

Set at a major Philadelphia department store, this lifeless comedy stars Andrew McCarthy as a store employee who discovers that a mannequin has come to life in the form of Kim Cattrall — but only he can see her. As the store's queeny and flamboyant window dresser, Meshach Taylor minces, prances and swishes as Hollywood. He drives a pink convertable with a licence plate that reads "Bad Girl" and is continually bawling over his ex-lover Alfred. ✪

Mannequin Two: On the Move

(1991, 95 min, US, Stewart Raffil)

Cartoonish and embarrassingly amateurish, this sequel to the equally appalling *Mannequin* sees the return of Meshach Taylor as Hollywood, the elaborately costumed walking caricature who is the film's comic foil. Elevated to a co-starring role (pretty easy when competing against leads William Ragsdale and Kristy Swanson), Hollywood is a window dresser *artiste* with a flair for stereotypical outrageousness and a penchant for pink Cadillacs, garish jewelry and flailing of the arms when excited. Some of his admittedly humorous lines include him quoting from *Mahogany* with "Give me cheekbones or give me death!"; doing a fag version of DeNiro's "You lookin' at me?" from *Taxi Driver*; and when it is revealed that he was in the Marines

Le Marginal

he explains that "They were looking for a few good men and so was I." A ridiculous, potentially insulting role that Taylor imbues with a certain amount of panache and humor. ⊛

Le Marginal

(1983, 101 min, France, Jacques Deray)
A veteran of French crime thrillers (*Borsalino, He Died with His Eyes Opened*), Jacques Deray has fashioned a Gallic *French Connection* meets *Cruising*. Jean-Paul Belmondo stars as a cop assigned to the narcotics squad of Marseilles who is determined to get his man — in this case Mecacci, an illusive drug warlord. But Mecacci pulls some strings and Belmondo finds himself instead reassigned to a neighborhood police station in Paris. Undeterred, his private investigation leads him to a gay leather bar in search of an informant. But the crime boss kills the gay man, which in turn gets Belmondo to play dirty — by concocting a crime and getting rid of his enemy illegally.

Mass Appeal

(1984, 100 min, US, Glenn Jordan)
Knowing the Monsignor has vowed to "stop the flow of neurotic priests into the church" — meaning gays — newly appointed deacon Mark Dolson (Zeljko Ivanek) defends two suspected gay seminarians; and to thine own self stays true by declaring his bisexuality. Deacon Dolson also suggests there may have been something between Jesus and St. John. ⊛

May Fools

(1990, 108 min, France/Italy, Louis Malle)
This mildly entertaining comedy-of-manners centers around the return of the disparate but equally selfish members of a wealthy family to their ancestral country mansion to pick through the possessions of their recently deceased matriarch. Claire (Dominque Blanc), a sophisticated but impassioned lesbian, brings Marie-Laure, her young, wannabe-ballerina/lover (Rozenn Le Tallec) home for the family squabbling. But much to Claire's dismay, Marie-Laure soon falls for Claire's radically minded male cousin. Threatened, Claire suggests a parlor game where the men and women draw lots to see who will have sex in front of the others (purely heterosexual); the outcome (and the corrupt bourgeois

morality) is interrupted when news of the 1968 student riots in Paris is heard on the radio. Another scene that suggests that all is not right/normal with the two women's relationship is when a young niece walks into the bedroom where Claire and her lover are sleeping (in separate beds). Later, when the girl asks why Marie-Laure was handcuffed to the bedpost, Claire's grandfather responds, so "that she will stay there." (GB title: *Milou en mai*) ⊛

Me, Myself & I

(1993, 97 min, US, Pablo Ferro)
George Segal stars in this comedy about mental illness as a writer separated from his L.A.-based wife who meets up with a paranoid, nymphomaniac wacko in the personage of JoBeth Williams. We discover that his wife (Shelly Hack), an award-winning actress is now living with another woman (Cheryl Paris). Calling herself Segal's "future ex-wife," she is depicted as a coke-sniffing, bitchy woman who in the end, drops her female lover when she tries to get her husband back, claiming that she and her shrink had worked all of the lesbianism out! ⊛

Mean Dog Blues

(1978, 108 min, US, Mel Stuart)
Homosexuality is a fact of life inside a Southern penitentiary in this gritty but strictly by-the-numbers prison drama. Musician Paul Ramsey (Greg Henry) is falsely accused of a deadly hit-and-run accident while hitchhiking and is summarily sent to a hellish (is there any other kind?) lockup where homosexuality among prisoners and guards, alike, is the norm. Hopelessly heterosexual, despite advice that "it helps to be a little queer," Paul battles his fellow inmates, sadistic guards as well as the demented warden (the always enjoyable George Kennedy) and his trusty band of blood-thirsty Dobermans. ⊛

Mediterraneo

(1991, 92 min, Italy, Gabriele Salvatores)
This charming but lightweight Oscar winner for Best Foreign Film is set on an idyllic Greek island during WWII. After spending three years together, Italian soldier Ugo Conti tells his sergeant Diego Abatantuono he loves him. Nothing before that moment suggests Conti's character is gay, and he only expresses his affection upon learning they are going home. ⊛

Meet the Feebles

(1992, 92 min, Australia, Peter Jackson)
If you've ever wondered what becomes of Muppets when they go bad, then this determinedly disgusting (but unfunny) comedy reveals all. Marketed as "one of the sickest movies ever made," this drug, sex and bodily fluid-immersed backstage tale includes such characters as lovelorn Heidi Hippo (a big-titted serial-killing Miss Piggy), a drug-addicted, knife-throwing frog, and many other animal grotesques. Though almost entirely straight, the gay angle to this ultimately numbing spectacle includes Harry, a sexually promiscuous bunny, who possibly contracts AIDS (with the illness depicted as horribly disfiguring and puss-excreting), and Sebastian, a gay fey fox who ends the show with a musical number called "Sodomy." Life will go on quite well if you never get to see this one.

Meeting Venus

(1991, 124 min, GB, Istvan Szabo)

A world-famous conductor (Niels Arestrup) mounts an international production of Wagner's "Tannhauser" while maintaining an affair with his tempestuous diva (Glenn Close). Among the supporting players, tenor Jay O. Sanders bickers a lot with boyfriend and house manager Dieter Laser during the rehearsals. There are other peripheral gay characters, also. ⊗

Mercedes

(1993, 100 min, Egypt/France, Yousry Nasrallah)

Gay filmmaker Yousry Nasrallah's turbulent political drama and family soap opera features an unusually sensitive handling of a gay character and his relationship with his lover. The central story concerns Noubi, a young man from a rich Egyptian family who is released from prison (on political charges) only to become embroiled in a tawdry family mess. His gay brother Gamal is seen as a strong, moralistic man who would rather become disinherited and estranged from his father rather than leave his beloved Achraf, a dark-skinned Egyptian. But at his death bed, Gamal's father has a change of heart for his youngest son and leaves him millions. Family infighting over the money begins immediately as Noubi sets off on a search through Cairo for his long-lost brother. The depiction of a positive gay character in an Arabic film is amazing and the sight of a loving gay relationship, depicted so matter-of-factly, is even more startling.

Miracle Mile

(1989, 87 min, US, Steve DeJarnatt)

In this off-the-wall, strangely upbeat and thoroughly entertaining nuclear annihilation yarn, musician Anthony Edwards learns that L.A. has a little over an hour until a nuclear strike. In an attempt for him and girlfriend Mare Winningham to leave the city, he hires rugged helicopter pilot Brian Thompson, whom he meets working out at a gym. When Thompson says he's bringing someone with

him, his youthful lover Herbert Fair accompanies him. This is "not a problem" to Edwards as they all try to escape the Apocalypse. In a near-ending scene, a bloodied Thompson heroically returns to rescue the two leads. ⊗

Mirror Images

(1991, 92 min, US, Gregory Hippolyte)

An entertainingly bad T&A (men and women) political mystery thriller that stars *Penthouse* pet Delia Sheppard in the dual roles of twin sisters: one a stripper and full-time slut and the other a bored housewife and part-time slut. When the housewife becomes frustrated by the lack of attention she receives from her boorish husband, she is easily enticed into a steamy lesbian lovemaking encounter with a secretary, Gina (Julie Strain). Although Gina is positively portrayed, she is immediately killed. The wife then embarks on a ludicrous amateur sleuthing determined to uncover her lesbian lover's killer. ⊗

Mistress *(1992, 109 min, US, Barry Primus)*

Jerome Dempsey is Mitch, a gay voice teacher for whom a would-be-movie producer (Eli Wallach) throws a birthday batch. As a Donald Trump-like businessman, Robert DeNiro observes: "Who cares about this fag's birthday?" ⊗

Mo' Money *(1992, 91 min, US, Peter MacDonald)*

Damon Wayans rehashes his once-scathingly funny "Men on Film" characterization (from TV's "In Living Color") to poor effect. In one scene, Wayans and brother Marlon impersonate a pair of queens trying to scam a jewelry store employee. ⊗

Mona Lisa *(1986, 104 min, GB, Neil Jordan)*

Bob Hoskins is riveting as George, a dim-witted Cockney thug who falls hopelessly in love with Simone (Cathy Tyson), a beautiful, high-priced prostitute. Initially hired as her chauffeur/bodyguard, George plays detective to track down Simone's missing lover, Cathy (Kate Hardie). ⊗

Mondo Balordo

(1964, 86 min, Italy, Roberto Montero)

The "freak show" that is life is humorously explored in this harmless *Mondo Cane* rip-off. Narrated by an amused Boris Karloff, the film features all kinds of oddities from around the world including singing midgets, opium-taking Asians, African tribes, female wrestlers and...drag queens and lesbians! The film ventures first to a party where German transvestites are seen dancing the night away with Karloff somberly intoning that transvestism has "spread like a spot of oil to every corner of the world until it spread to its present frightening proportions!" Undaunted, the film visits a German lesbian bar

Mountains of the Moon

where women are seen innocently talking or dancing, but the narration explains that "this small world of unsatisfied women who founded a club for those with "special tastes" are apart from and above every moral rule." Boys, hang on tight to your girlfriends!

A Month in the Country
(1987, 96 min, GB, Pat O'Connor)
A beautifully filmed, sensitive adaptation of J.L. Carr's novel about two emotionally scarred WWI veterans who come to terms with their past during an idyllic summer in the English countryside. Colin Firth plays Birkin, an artist restoring a church's medieval wall painting. He finds a soulmate in the form of the brooding Moon (Kenneth Branagh), who is excavating the church's graveyard. It is revealed later on in the film that the gay Moon was sent to "a glass house for buggery." Moon's sexuality throughout the film is incidental. ⊛

Mountains of the Moon
(1990, 135 min, US, Bob Rafleson)
Iain Glen is 19th-century British explorer John Hanning Speke who, while traveling with fellow explorer Sir Richard Burton (played by Patrick Bergen), discovered the source of the Nile. Richard H. Grant is Speke's close friend (and possible lover?), a publisher who is instrumental in Speke terminating his association with Burton. This version of the story contradicts (or ignores) the many reports of Burton's bisexuality; though a sexual tension exists between both characters. ⊛

The Music Teacher
(1988, 100 min, Belgium, Gerard Corbiau)
Set in turn-of-the-century France, this opulent yet winsome drama centers on a world renowned opera singer (Jose Van Dam) who retires from the stage and becomes a teacher to two exceptional students. His pupils eventually compete in an international singing competition. Another teacher whose students are entering the contest is the gay Prince Scotti (Patrick Bauchau), the maestro's longtime adversary who, with pursed lips and slinty eyes, almost oozes evil. Though Scotti's homosexuality is not overtly related to him being the villain, the film is yet another example of equating a gay man with decadence and sleaze. While the heterosexuals all seem to fall in love at one point in the film, Scotti is simply icy cold and manipulative. His relationship with his young (and probable boy-toy) protégé Arcas (Marc Schreiber, a Nigel Kennedy look-alike) is far from romantic and, at one point, while Scotti plots Machiavellian revenge against the young singers, he remarks, "If I had a heart, I'd pity him." Overall, another troubling depiction of a gay man in a role that needn't have included his sexuality. ⊛

Naked in New York
(1994, 91 min, US, Dan Algrant)
Twentysomething kvetching couched in the form of a whimsical Woody Allen-style comedy, *Naked in New York* stars Eric Stoltz as Jake, a talented New York Jew (with red hair, freckles and glasses — remind you of anyone?) who, despite the love of a beautiful woman and praise for his writing ability, remains vaguely unfulfilled and unhappy. Tough luck! Of interest here, though, is Chris (Ralph Macchio), his best friend in college and the one who helps him get his big break off-Broadway. Macchio is sur-

Next Stop, Greenwich Village

prisingly effective as a closeted gay man who carries a quiet torch for his straight friend. In the film's most affecting scene, Chris takes the plunge and plants a loving kiss on the lips of the startled Jake — an act that immediately distances them. In quick order, Jake betrays him professionally and Chris is soon dropped from the plot. While many viewers will identify with the handsome Jake and his situation, for many gays Chris will be seen as the real tragic hero: unloved, rejected and dumped by the man he loves, an egocentric and uncaring straight man. Blink during the Cape Cod party scene and you'll miss Quentin Crisp. ⊛

The Name of the Rose *(1986, 128 min, Italy/France/Germany, Jean-Jacques Annaud)*
Sean Connery and Christian Slater star as a visiting monk and his apprentice who are sent to a troubled monastery in 13th-century Italy to investigate a series of bizarre deaths. Homosexual lust figures prominently in this visually rich medieval murder mystery. The ominous gay subtext is introduced by the leering William Hickey who warns the two new arrivals that "The devil is throwing beautiful boys out of windows." Proving that abbey life can be a dangerously lonely place for young men, Connery, a Dark Ages Sherlock Holmes, eventually unravels the bloody mystery. Brother Berringer (Michael Habeck), an obscenely corpulent monk, made "unnatural advances" on the innocent Adelmo (Lars Bobin-Jorgensen), causing him to commit suicide by throwing himself down a deep embankment. Several more deaths ensue as a cover-up is made to hush up the scandal (Church policy which still exists today). ⊛

Next Stop, Greenwich Village
(1976, 109 min, US, Paul Mazursky)
Paul Mazursky's affectionate and winning semiautobiographical tale is an account of his early adulthood in 1950s Greenwich Village. Lenny Baker plays the director's alter ego, an aspiring actor who befriends a group of Village eccentrics. One of the bohemian members of his clique is played by Antonio Fargas, who gives a touching performance as Bernstein, a gay bon vivant who has a penchant for sailors. Though marvelously performed by the entire cast, the acting honors go to Shelley Winters for her quintessential turn as Baker's over-protective Jewish mother. ⊛

Night Angel

(1990, 90 min, US, Dominique Othenin-Girard)
The ill-fated owner of a modeling agency (Karen Black) falls under the spell of a seductive, soul-stealing succubus (Isa Andersen) who'll stop at nothing — not even lesbianism — to achieve her goal of world domination. Intelligent handling makes this better than it sounds. ⊗

Night Shift *(1982, 105 min, US, Ron Howard)*

Henry Winkler, jailed for pimping, says "I've sunk as low as I can go." Then the queer next to him cuts out paper hearts and blows him a kiss. Winkler responds: "I was wrong." ⊗

A Nightmare on Elm Street Part 2 — Freddy's Revenge

(1985, 87 min, US, Jack Sholder)
Thought to be the weakest in the *Nightmare* series, this time around Freddy takes over the cute (often shirtless) body of a teen, Jesse (Mark Patton), in his ongoing killing dream quest. At one point, Jesse leaves his suburban home and enters a wild, bisexual S&M bar where one of its patrons is his coach (Marshall Bell). The two wind up naked in the high school showers where ropes and Freddy's razor-like claws make for awfully short foreplay. ⊗

Nineteen Nineteen

(1984, 99 min, GB, Hugh Brody)
This ambitious, mesmerizing drama alternates between the Viennas of 1970 and 1919 as it weaves its story of self-discovery, memory, regret and possible reconciliation as two of the last surviving patients of Sigmund Freud come together after 50 years to answer whether his analysis helped or emotionally crippled them. The 1919 segments are set in Freud's consulting room, where Jewish would-be radical Sophie (Claire Higgens) is sent after attempting suicide when her relationship with another woman ends. She tells Freud that she is there because of the suicide, not because she was in love with another woman. She soon describes both her hatred/obsessive love for her father and her great passion for Anna (Diana Quick), a beautiful bourgeois woman. Soon after, she is summarily sent to

No Exit (1955)

No Exit (1962)

America by her family to avoid scandal. Years later, now an old woman (played by Maria Schell), she returns to Vienna to meet Alexander (Paul Scofield), the other surviving patient who could never desire the woman he loved and only found passion with women he despised. Reflecting on the only person she really loved, Sophie reminisces about a night she and Anna spent together, calling it "the happiest night of my life." Trivia note: Fiona Cunningham Reid, lesbian director of the documentary *Feed Them to the Cannibals*, was the "clapper loader" on this production. ⊗

1969 *(1988, 93 min, US, Ernest Thompson)*

Kiefer Sutherland, Robert Downey, Jr. and Winona Ryder star in this sincere though dramatically impotent teen drama set against the backdrop of the 1960s social upheaval and anti-war protests. Sutherland and Downey are the best of buddies who hitchhike from college back to their home town. On one trip, they are picked up by a nerdish, Neru jacket-wearing hippie named Marshall who quickly makes the moves on the blond Sutherland. When the boys jump out of the car screaming "Fuckin' homo," the would-be molester explains, "I didn't know you two were married!" Chalk up an other negative, albeit witty depiction of a gay man. ⊗

No Exit (Huis Clos)

(1955, 99 min, France, Jacqueline Audry)
Jean-Paul Sartre's existential short play about three people trapped in a hotel room after their death stars Frank Villard, Arletty, and Gaby Sylvia as an embittered lesbian. The people, all with dark secrets, find that their personal hell is to be condemned for an eternity surrounded by people they despise. From the director of the lesbian classic *Olivia*.

No Exit

(1962, 85 min, US/Argentina, Tad Danielewski)
This second film adaptation of Sartre's play about an unusual hell — three people doomed to spend an eternity in a single room — was a sensation at the 1962 Berlin Film Festival. Actresses Viveca Lindfors and Rita Gam shared the Best Actress award. Lindfors is Inez, the lesbian of the trio.

No Small Affair

(1984, 102 min, US, Jerry Schatzberg)
Jock Tim Robbins and friends taunt straight, shy-guy Jon Cryer about being gay. ⊛

No Way Out

(1987, 116 min, US, Roger Donaldson)
Kevin Costner stars as a CIA liaison agent who investigates the murder of his girlfriend — and he's the top suspect. Costner's boss, the Secretary of Defense (Gene Hackman), is the actual killer. Will Patton is the gay, blindly devoted assistant to Hackman. In a poorly conceived part, Patton's desperate portrayal of a man who would ultimately kill to protect his boss could only fuel the argument for those against lifting the ban on gays and lesbians in the military. Patton's character eventually blows his brains out when he realizes that Hackman doesn't love him. ⊛

No Way to Treat a Lady

(1968, 108 min, US, Jack Smight)
As a serial killer with a penchant for disguises, Rod Steiger minces as a gay hairdresser ("it doesn't make you all bad"); and dresses in drag to befriend an intended victim. ⊛

Norma *(1970, 77 min, US, Ted Roter)*

This enjoyable 42nd Street special stars Mady Maguire as an intelligent, seemingly normal farm girl who is unaccountably transformed into an "insatiable nymphomaniac." There's plenty of T&A as the young woman explores her sexual appetite. It's pretty straight stuff, but at a groovy sex party, Robert Redding becomes the life of the joint as a flailing-of-the-arms drag queen. The film's "shocking" ending features gratuitous display of transvestism.

The Nun (La Religieuse)

(1965, 130 min, France, Jacques Rivette)
Anna Karina stars as Suzanne, a young woman who suffers physical and emotional anguish at the hands of her family, a religious order and society at large in this intensely somber drama set in 18th-century France. Suzanne is sent by her family to a convent against her will. There, rebellious and unmoved by the religious life, she is beaten and semi-starved. Sent to another convent, she is initially befriended by its Mother Superior, who then attempts to entrap her in a lesbian relationship; Suzanne resists the sexual demands. Although the lesbian nun is seen as calculating and abusive, she is no different than the other people who contribute to destroy the young woman's life. ⊛

Ode to Billy Joe

(1976, 106 min, US, Max Baer)
What *did* cause Billy Joe McAllister to jump off the Tallahatchie Bridge? Bobbie Gentry's 1967 hit song was the inspiration for this initially touching drama of first love starring Robby Benson as Billy Joe and Glynnis O'Connor as his girlfriend Bobbie Lee. But while the story is pleasant enough, the reason for Billy Joe's suicide is unconsciously homophobic, for after much sweating and wringing of the hands, Billy Joe (cute in a goofy sort of way), on the night before his leap, blurts out "I ain't all right! I have been with a man...which is a sin against nature, a sin against God!" And even though his girlfriend takes the revelation calmly, a devastated Billy Joe, convinced that he's a hopeless faggot, jumps off the Tallahatchie Bridge — surfacing years later on AM radios all across the nation. James Best is the 50-ish Dewey Barksdale, who eventually comes forward and admits that it was he who deflowered her boyfriend (and he got there first!); strangely enough, the chicken hawk lives. ⊛

Once Bitten

(1985, 97 min, US, Howard Storm)
This broad comedy about modern-day neck-biters more often misses than not. There are several gay references of note. After innocent shenanigans in the showers, two teen boys are called fags by the rest of the school (and it's "the suckiest thing ever to have happened" to one of the boys); and look for a bewitching drag queen who almost gets his/her man. There is also Cleavon Little, camping it up (but none too effectively) as swishy Sebastian, limp-wristed valet to chief vampire Lauren Hutton. ⊛

Once Upon a Time in the East

(1975, 100 min, Canada, Andre Brassard)
Based on Brassard's successful stage play, this drama about the down-and-out denizens of a dumpy East Montreal tenement is amateurish, stage-bound and, with exception of several gay film festivals, never received commercial distribution outside Canada. The characters include Hosanna, a past-her-prime drag queen who lives with an abusive gay roommate.

One Flew Over the Cuckoo's Nest

(1975, 133 min, US, Milos Forman)
As the intellectual Harding, William Redfield has "allusions, not illusions" made that his marital problems stem from homosexuality. ⊛

The Onion Field

(1979, 126 min, US, Howard Becker)
This hard-hitting version of Joseph Wambaugh's best-seller does not contain the vitriolic homophobia much in evidence in *The Choirboys*, but still has several anti-queer moments. "Based on a true story," the crime actioner stars Ted Danson and John Savage as two undercover cops assigned as partners. In an early throwaway scene at the police

The Nun

station, the two watch as a poorly dressed, flailing-of-the-arms black drag queen (Rene La Vant) is brought in, followed by a respectable looking white man who suddenly goes berserk, needing several cops to subdue him. When Savage asks what set him off, a nonchalant Danson explains, "Homosexual panic, I've seen it before. The boy suddenly realized who he is, he's confused and he's scared." With the homophobia out of the way, the story begins. James Woods, in his screen debut, is memorable as a sleaze-ball psychotic thug who kidnaps the two cops and cold-bloodily kills one of them (Danson). Woods and his Latino partner-in-crime (Franklyn Seales) are soon caught as the story follows their legal maneuvering to avoid the gas chamber. In prison, Seales begs Woods to tell the authorities that he is innocent and gives a smirking Woods a blow job to convince him. Watch as Woods becomes a brainy jailhouse lawyer and predatory fag. Nothing like a Wambaugh film to get an activist's heart racing. ☮

The Other Woman
(1992, 99 min, US, Jag Mundhra)
Produced by Gregory Hippolyte, director of such steamy lesbian-tinged thrillers as *Night Rhythms* and *Mirror Images*, this soft-core porn drama concerns a woman's initiation and eventual rejection of lesbian sex. Jess (Lee Anne Beaman) is a beautiful but sexually uptight blonde married to a handsome best-selling author. After she finds photos of another woman in a suit of his, she begins to stalk the woman and eventually meets her. The "other woman," Traci (Jenna Persaud), is a sultry Latina prostitute who seems to enjoy the bedding of both men and women. Jess is slowly drawn to her, allowing her pent-up lesbian desires to rise to the surface. They eventually make it with each other. But her foray into Sapphic love was just a "phase" as she runs back into the arms of her husband. ☮

Papillon *(1973, 150 min, US, Franklin J. Schaffner)*
Adapting a Jean Genet-like setting — that is, the brutalized existence of male prisoners in a French penal colony — this rousing adventure tale stars Steve McQueen and Dustin Hoffman as two dissimilar men banded together during their incarceration at the dreaded Devil's Island. Despite glimpses of the tough tenderness of the inmates and two gay characters, the subject of homosexuality is assiduously avoided. McQueen, falsely charged with murder, is obsessed with escape and enlists fellow prisoner Maturette (Robert Deman) in a plan. When first seen, handsome young Maturette is being caressed and groped by a lecherous trustee. In the film's one overt homage to Genet, the sleazy older man places a red flower into Maturette's mouth. McQueen tells the young prisoner to have sex with the guard; he also tells him he's going to escape. Maturette wants to escape with him and proves that he is capable by telling McQueen that yes he's "a fag, queer, fairy, poof" but that he's already killed a man and is up to the challenge. The three (Hoffman as well) do escape but are soon re-arrested with both McQueen and Maturette sentenced to five years solitary confinement. Overall a positive portrayal of a gay man who is seen as tougher and more dependable than the other presumably straight prisoners. ☮

Pardon Mon Affaire
(1977, 110 min, France, Yves Robert)
This frantic, wry French boudoir comedy follows four buddies who, all in their own way, cheat on their loved ones. Jean

Rochefort is their ringleader and chief erotic provocateur and when the film begins to seem hopelessly heterosexual in scope, a gay mini-subplot develops. Daniel (Guy Bedos), the most normal and even-headed of the bunch, seen previously mostly as a friend in need, has his own little affair that involves a much younger, doe-eyed blond beauty he meets at a wedding. In the next scene, his longtime lover calls him a bitch and throws him out of their house. Daniel's character and his homosexuality is much more developed in the sequel, *Pardon Mon Affaire, Too*. ☮

Pardon Mon Affaire, Too
(1977, 110 min, France, Yves Robert)
While Hollywood continues to have a difficult time incorporating well-drawn gay characters into their major releases, this Gallic comedy is a pleasant example of how to successfully accomplish it. This gentle satiric farce centers on the extramarital affairs of four middle-aged but still boyish friends. Extramarital is actually too hetero-centric, for one of the men cheats on his overly domineering mother and another, Daniel (Guy Bedos), cheats on his homosexuality. Daniel is a car mechanic who is open about his sexuality with his three friends, who in turn accept it readily, except for a few name-calling incidents when they fight. He does not have a lover, but is seen cruising men and is once seen with a cute blond Polish youth in his bed. When the demands for conformity and wanting children overwhelm him, he suffers a sexual midlife crisis and quickly begins dating an older woman and soon plans to marry her. But the woman, told by Daniel of his sexual bent early on, backs out at the last moment. Daniel is relieved and resumes his gay life and friendship with the boys. A surprisingly complex, sympathetic and knowing portrait of a gay man in sexual confusion. ☮

Pas Très Catholique
(1993, 100 min, France, Tonie Marshall)
An unusual film in its refreshingly casual depiction of the lead character's bisexuality, this drama focuses on the frantic life of a still youthful (she insists on being addressed as "mademoiselle" rather than "madame") 40-year-old woman, Maxime (Anémone). Working all hours as a private detective, chain-smoking cigarettes and generally mistreating all those who love her, Maxime's free-spirited but selfish and self-destructive life is saved when she comes upon her 18-year-old son (Gregoire Colin from *Olivier, Olivier*), a boy she has not seen since his birth. One of the people who puts up with her antics is her part-time lover Florence (Christine Boisson), a beautiful woman a few years younger who, while the two are in bed together, is successful in softening the usually hard-as-nails Maxime. Their relationship is only touched on, but the film, by making the lead character a lesbian (with hetero leanings) without affecting the story is hopefully a sign of cinematic things to come.

The Pawnbroker
(1965, 116 min, US, Sidney Lumet)
Brock Peters plays Rodriguez, a shady gay businessman with interests in everything from a whorehouse to a laundramat to a pawn shop (the latter is run by Rod Steiger). Not a flattering portrait but daring for its time as his sexuality really has nothing to do with the plot (although one could interpret his gayness as just another example of his decadence). ☮

A Perfect Couple

(1979, 110 min, US, Robert Altman)
This quirky romantic comedy centers around the unlikely love affair between uptight Alex (Paul Dooley) and rocker Sheila (Marta Heflin), a pair who find each other through an L.A. video dating service. Among the many characters that continuously weave in and out of the tale are Mary (Heather McCrea) and Sydney-Ray (Tommi-Lee Bradley) — members of a musical group as well as a happy lesbian couple. In a rare instance in movies, the two women are introduced without the typical stereotypes or lurid sexual innuendo.

Pete 'n' Tillie

(1972, 100 min, US, Martin Ritt)
Rene Auberjonois is a standout in a supporting role as the witty, bitchy but understanding gay friend to Carol Burnett in this engaging marital comedy-drama co-starring Walter Matthau. Auberjonois plays Jimmy Twitchel, an Oscar Wilde-type described as "a cultural Robin Hood who steals from the witty and gives to the dull." He is alternately a catty gossiper and supportive to both friends and charitable events. When Burnett signs herself into a "hospital" after a nervous breakdown caused by her marital breakup, Jimmy arrives and — in a sympathetic, friendly gesture designed to get her out of there — offers to marry her; he promises her better wardrobe and hair, and a good time. Sex would presumably not enter the picture. She appreciates the offer but reunites with Matthau. ⊛

Peter's Friends

(1992, 102 min, GB, Kenneth Branagh)
With its heart lying squarely on the side of heterosexuality, this slight comedy and British equivalent to *The Big Chill* is set in a large English manor house where six old university friends meet for a ten-year reunion. This cast of stock characters include Kenneth Branagh as a talented writer who sells himself off for money in Hollywood; his vulgar, loud-mouthed wife Rita Rudner (the film's co-writer); Stephen Fry as the lumbering host harboring a "secret"; and Emma Thompson, who outshines them all, as a gawky, eccentric woman trying desperately to change. What makes the film of interest to gay audiences is the fact that Peter reveals to his friends that he is bisexual (although to queers watching the film, it is obvious that he is gay and just not ready to admit it). Their matter-of-fact acceptance of this "revelation" is well presented, but when he also tells them that he is HIV-positive, it triggers an onslaught of sappy liberal sympathies and ignorant thinking that people with HIV should not have sex and should be pitied for their "imminent" death. Straight liberal thinking has never looked more callous and insipid. ⊛

Focus on: *Stephen Fry*

With his droopy eyes, ever-present sarcastic smirk and droll deadpan delivery, openly gay British actor Stephen Fry has a body made for comedy. In addition to Peter's Friends, *Fry has enjoyed success in several British stage and television productions including his slyly underplayed role as the imperturbable super-manservant Jeeves in the BBC television series "Jeeves and Wooster," based on the novels of P.G. Woodehouse. The series has been shown in the U.S. on PBS and several episodes are available on video. His longtime comedy partner Hugh Laurie also stars in that series playing the bungling poor little rich boy Wooster. Fry's comedy series with Laurie, "A Bit of Fry & Laurie" was a hit that spawned two best-selling books of their sketches. Fry also played Lord Melchett in "Blackadder II" (1986) and was the dramatic lead in the 1989 production "This Is David Lander." Fry has also written two hilarious novels: "The Liar," his 1991 autobiography that opens with the disclaimer, "Not one word of the following is true"; and "Paperweight," written in 1992. He was also one of the many signers of a public letter to Ian McKellen urging him to accept the Queen's knighting, a controversy which had split England's gay community.*

Pigs *(1984, 79 min, Ireland, Cathal Black)*

The inner-city squalor of Dublin provides the derelict backdrop to this tough drama about a group of divergent outcasts who squat in an abandoned mansion. The far from traditional household drawn together by mutual need includes a prostitute, a black pimp, a drug dealer and a sweetly hopeless homosexual. Jimmy Brennan (who also wrote the screenplay) is the gay man who is the main organizer in making the dump a "home."

La Pirate *(1984, 88 min, France, Jacques Doillon)*

Made a year before the similarly themed *Thelma and Louise* and *Bound and Gagged: A Love Story*, this French drama begins as Carol arrives in Paris to seek her ex-lover Alma, who is now married to Andrew. With the aid of another woman, they cart Alma away from Andrew, prompting his frantic search for her through the French countryside. Tragedy befalls all when he finally meets up with them in Dunkirk.

Pleasure Principal

(1991, 100 min, GB, David Cohen)
Peter Firth is Dick, a freelance journalist and unlikely womanizer in this low-budget sex comedy. Despite his philandering, he still longs for his lesbian ex-wife Ann (Sara Mair-Thomas).

Police Academy

(1984, 97 min, US, Hugh Wilson)
The first in the series of what would incredibly be seven films, this comedy follows the insipidly funny slapstick misadventures of a group of bungling misfit police cadets. Scott Thomson and Brant Van Hoffman plays two of the neo-Nazi cadets (read: bad guys) who are tricked into visiting The Blue Oyster, a seriously all-leather gay bar whose patrons welcome the unsuspecting cadets with open arms. The homophobes-to-be get swept to the dance floor for a spirited tango as well as a soulful slow dance. Fade out. Another gay aside is when the dim-witted commandant thinks that Steve Guttenberg gave him a quite satisfying blow job. He didn't. ⊛

Police Squad!

(1982, 25 min each episode, US, Jim Abrahams, David Zucker, Jerry Zucker & Joe Dante)
Years before the hilarious *Naked Gun* trilogy, bungling Lt. Frank Drebin (Leslie Nielsen) roamed the city streets in this inspired but short-lived (six episodes) television series. And while the feature films feature Priscilla Presley as his sexy love interest, we discover that silver-maned Frank harbors a sexual secret that is never men-

tioned, except in the very first episode of the TV show when he recounts a youthful gay love affair! During a routine interrogation of a woman whose husband has been murdered, Frank's memory of his gay past is rekindled after the women says, "Do you know what it's like to be married to a wonderful man for 14 years?" Out of nowhere, Frank reminisces about a guy he lived with for a couple of years, "a man who had a brain, not just a body and sinuous muscles." Their relationship was strained by "the usual slurs, rumors and innuendos. People just didn't understand. They ran him out of town." His old flame eventually married and had three kids, but Frank "never cared for her, sent her a nice gift, never got back a note." Knowing what he likes, Frank tells the widow that he also lived with the man's son for a year, but "it wasn't the same, you can't go back." ☮

Pornography-Prostitution USA
(1970, 88 min, US, Alvin Tokunow)

Structured as an exposé documentary on prostitution, this sexually explicit (towards the women only — the men are mainly clothed) film is rather entertaining and an informative celebration of sex. Where else could you hear "real-life" prostitutes saying lines such as, "Your vagina really gets a lot of wear" or "I avoid sadists...they take too long and it's always risky." Filmed primarily behind two-way mirrors (but not really), the final segment features a hooker whose specialty is lesbians ("It takes a real professional to take care of a woman"). It shows her having enthusiastic sex with a female customer. And joining in (presumably at a surcharge) is the prostitute's friend — a dildo-wearing male-to-female transsexual.

Prisoner: Cell Block H
(1979-87, 692 episodes, Australia)

This very popular Australian television soap opera set in a women's prison has all of the needed ingredients of the genre: a tough-talking warden, tougher guards, a desperate cast of inmates, catfights and lesbianism. Because the entertaining series was made for TV and targeted to a mass market, the lesbian undertones are muted, with the women sleeping with women for convenience and never any overt displays of Sapphic attraction and, of course, no lovemaking. The most prominent lesbian at the Wentworth Detention Centre is Frieda "Franky" Doyle (Carol Burns), a tough, bib overall-wearing inmate with a nasty sneer. This bad-tempered blonde is featured in the early episodes as she attempts to stake her claim as the inmate's top dog as well as make sexual moves on husband killer and pretty femme Karen Travers (Peta Toppano). Their first encounter and attempted seduction scene is as follows:

Franky: "It's up to you, love, you can really enjoy yourself if   you put your mind to it."

Karen: "I'm not like that, Franky."

Franky: "You're gonna have to be, and anything you don't know,

     I'll teach you."

Franky then playfully pounces on her. Karen runs away and as punishment, Franky has her lover and friend Doreen (Colette Mann) moved from her cell. Franky is eventually killed off, but other lesbians, though not as deliciously camp, take her place.

Private Benjamin
(1980, 110 min, US, Howard Zieff)

In one of her most popular comedies, Goldie Hawn stars as an initially ditsy "Jewish American Princess" who enlists in the Army and becomes a new woman. Eileen Brennan co-stars as the tough Captain Lewis who becomes adversaries with Hawn. Seen in training camp as a heterosexual, later scenes find the captain switching jobs (to a desk job in France) and sexual orientations (with a hulking blonde named Helga). Initially drawn in a sympathetic comic light, Brennan's character gets increasingly mean-spirited and unlikable, with her lesbian conversion being the filmmaker's not-so-subtle and certainly homophobic indication of her "problems." ☮

The Private Life of Sherlock Holmes
(1970, 125 min, GB, Billy Wilder)

A hugely enjoyable and superbly melancholy whodunit which shows the famous sleuth as a cocaine fancier, an unrepentant misogynist and a possible homosexual. When a famous Russian ballerina asks Holmes (Robert Stephens) to father her child, Holmes begs off the invitation by suggesting that he and Dr. Watson (Colin Blakely) —two bachelors living together for "five very happy years" — are more than just roommates. The ballerina's manager commiserates on his situation calling it a "cruel caprice of Mother Nature." But while Dr. Watson is revealed to be a heterosexual and upset at the "dastardly lies," the sexual orientation of Holmes remains suggestively vague. ☮

Private Resort
(1985, 82 min, US, George Bowers)

A young Johnny Depp, sporting all-American good looks, stars in this tepid teen sex comedy, an unbridled celebration of harmless heterosexual lust. But if so hetero, why do Depp and attractive co-star Rob Morrow ("Northern Exposure") drop their clothes so often with the camera leeringly transfixed on their exposed flesh (taking exceptional delight in their butts). The only real scene to warrant inclusion in this section is when Morrow, hiding from a jealous husband and an obsessive hotel detective, dons drag and while in an elevator with his two pursuers, finds his ass caressed by both appreciative men. ☮

The Producers: "Where do you keep your wallet?"

The Producers

(1968, 88 min, US, Mel Brooks)
The worst director on Broadway is Roger DeBris, engagingly played by Christopher Hewett. His lover is Carmen Gia (Andreas Voustinas). Hewett brings such high spirits to the flamboyant showman that you want to overlook the fag caricatures. After all, Mel Brooks' broad farce satirizes everything and everyone. ⊛

Proof

(1992, 91 min, Australia, Jocelyn Moorhouse)
At the local drive-in, blind, straight photographer Hugo Weaving is mistaken by the jerks in the next car as making a pass at them. His friend Russell Crowe comes back from the concession stand and fights them off. They write "Fag" all over Crowe's car. ⊛

Protocol   *(1984, 96 min, US, Herbert Ross)*
In this agreeable if slight comedy, Goldie Hawn plays a down-to-earth waitress who saves the life of a foreign dignitary. The press examines every detail of her life — including her two gay and supportive roommates, Ben (Joel Brooks) and Jerry (Grainger Hines). When asked about the living arrangements, she responds that she lives "in a small part of the house that belongs to two men who live together," rather than living with two men. ⊛

Pump Up the Volume

(1990, 100 min, US, Allan Moyle)
Chris Jacobs plays Matt, a troubled gay teen who talks hard with pirate D.J. Christian Slater (aka Happy Harry Hard-On), and he gets some good advice. For once, it's not the gay kid who commits suicide. ⊛

Pumping Iron II — The Women

(1985, 107 min, US, George Butler & Robert Rider)
Several years after *Pumping Iron*, his acclaimed documentary on men's bodybuilding which introduced American audiences to the physique and charms of a playful Arnold Schwarzenegger, George Butler returned to the gyms in this engaging look at female bodybuilding. Despite the presence of muscle-building, macho women, the film assiduously avoids the issue of lesbianism. And when the subject *is* brought up, denials — though non-homophobic — flow. Champion bodybuilder Bev Francis remarks, "I don't object to anyone else being lesbian. Muscles don't make a woman a lesbian." Her fiancé (at the time), weightlifter Steve Weinberger, also says, "Male bodybuilders are accused of being faggots, too. I'm sure that there are lesbians who lift weights, but there are lesbians who do everything — so what?" The camera oogles at the bronzed women pumping up, but in order to keep it all-American, the femininity and heterosexuality of the women is constantly brought up, with one female bodybuilder even receiving a man's proposal of marriage in front of the camera. ⊛

Q & A   *(1990, 132 min, US, Sidney Lumet)*
As Lt. Mike Brennan, a bigoted, sexually repressed New York City cop, Nick Nolte goes on an anti-gay rampage. Paul Calderon and International Chrysis are two transvestites he harasses and eventually kills. The caricatures of the drag queens are of cowardly, untrustworthy wantons; and "faggot" seems to be about every other word. Of all the primary cast members, only Timothy Hutton's Assistant D.A. — who is battling his own prejudicial demons — refrains from using homophobic epithets. For a supposedly intelligent examination of bigotry, the film is shockingly callous in its depiction of gays. ⊛

Queens Logic

(1991, 112 min, US, Steve Rash)
A group of friends gather in New York's Queens borough for a wedding. John Malkovich is Elliott ("I'm a homosexual who cannot relate to gay men"), and he attacks his role with his usual intensity. Elliott's sexuality isn't revealed until halfway through the film, and he's supported and loved by his macho pals. Terry Kinney is Jeremy, whom Elliott meets in a bar and doesn't like; Michael Zelniker is Marty, a sensitive pianist with whom Elliott connects. ⊛

Rachel, Rachel

(1968, 101 min, US, Paul Newman)
An intensely somber but affecting drama of a woman who, after years of self-imposed fear, decides to experience life. Joanne Woodward is Rachel, a 35-year-old schoolteacher and walking tinderbox of repressed emotions and sexual frustrations. One of the people who attempts to get her out of her shell is Calla (Estelle Parsons), a fellow "spinster" teacher, Pentecostal Christian and frustrated lesbian who develops a crush on her heterosexual friend. After encouraging Rachel to accompany her to a revival service, a visit that upsets Rachel, Calla tenderly holds the crying woman, eventually planting kisses on her face and lips. Both are immediately stunned and embarrassed by the act, with Calla ineffectually explaining, "I didn't mean *that*." But Rachel is so shocked that she cuts off her friendship although they are reconciled when Rachel fears she is pregnant and needs comforting and advice. Rachel eventually comes to accept Calla's feelings for her and when Rachel decides to leave her small town, she says to the upset Calla, "I wish I could have been different for you." Parsons' Calla is not exactly a glowing portrayal of lesbianism, but it is tender, understanding and, for its time, an advancement in Hollywood. Both actresses received Oscar nominations. ⊛

Radio Days   *(1987, 85 min, US, Woody Allen)*
Woody Allen wrote and directed this affectionate look at his youth set in 1940s New York. His aunt, played by the wonderful Dianne Wiest, goes on a date with a sensitive young man (Robert Joy), but he still can't get over the breakup with his male lover. ⊛

A Rage in Harlem

(1991, 115 min, US, Bill Duke)
Distinguished South African actor Zakes Mokae, in one of his few film appearances, plays Big Kathy, the transvestite madam of a 1950s Harlem bordello. In helping brothers Forest Whitaker and Gregory Hines fight the bad guys, he gets killed for his troubles. ⊛

Raiders of the Lost Ark

(1981, 115 min, US, Steven Spielberg)
Don't blink, or you'll miss this cute bit that has a male student, amongst a class of adoring female classmates, leaving an apple on the desk of Harrison Ford's Professor Indiana Jones. ⊛

MENTIONS

Reality Bites *(1994, 99 min, US, Ben Stiller)*

The inclusion of a gay character in this engaging comedy on twentysomething kvetching has been one of debate. Is the presence of gay Sammy (Steven Zahn) in this otherwise heterosexual coming-of-life tale a great sign of Hollywood including gays and lesbians into the fabric of their movies, or has the homosexual replaced the black as the token minority presence? The latter argument seems to be the feeling among opinioned queers: for Sammy is an underused and ultimately unneeded character — cut out his character and dialogue, and the film would be unaffected. Although a close friend to the four main characters — aspiring videomaker Lelaina (Winona Ryder), her hip grunger friend/love interest Troy (Ethan Hawke), her roommate and Gap manager Vickie (Janeana Garofalo) and outsider Michael (Ben Stiller), a post-yuppie square — he doesn't have much of a reason to be in the film. He doesn't live with them (he's always hanging around), doesn't share in any of the many witty lines bandied about, has no subplot to call his own, doesn't have sex (he's celibate because of AIDS) or a relationship (other than an unseen "friend" at the end), doesn't "seem" gay at all (my own gaydar did not register a beep) and doesn't even get to suffer through an AIDS scare (that falls on the promiscuous heterosexual Vickie.) So why include him? Is the film jumping on the "year of the queer" bandwagon? Does his inclusion make the others seem hip because they're friends with an actual gay person? And what are they saying when the only gay character is a sexless semi-nerd hanger-on? Sexual politics aside, *Reality Bites* is a bright romantic comedy that takes acerbic aim on aimless, middle-class, white, straight, TV-obsessed American youth. ☻

Reform School Girl

(1957, 71 min, US, Edward Bernds)

Sally Kellerman, in her feature film debut, is featured as a tool case-carrying, black leather-wearing lesbian in this low-budget women-in-prison potboiler. A naive teenage girl, Gloria (Donna Price — Linda Blair was unavailable for the part, she wasn't born yet) is wrongly sent to a women's penitentiary, taking the rap for a hit-and-run automobile death caused by her boyfriend. But prison life soon proves to be nearly as fatal as she soon gets involved in run-ins with several of the hardened dames in the joint. Kellerman has said that this role was a big mistake, as it took over three years for her to get another acting role. ☻

Republic of Assassins

(1985, 199 min, Brazil, Miquel Faria)

Political corruption during a military dictatorship, the "death squads" who roam the streets and the press who plays along with the rulers are the indicted in this ambitious melodrama. After his petty thief boyfriend is taken away and presumedly killed, his plucky transvestite boyfriend braves the odds and demands justice.

Revenge of the Nerds

(1984, 90 min, US, Jeff Kanew)

The Nerds go to college! Robert Carradine and Anthony Edwards (much too cute for the role) are the heads of a nerd fraternity called Lambda Lambda Lambda; one of the members is the black Lamar (Larry B. Scott), a swishy stereotype always flitting about attired in fabulous frocks and easily identified with his high-pitched squeal.

Reality Bites

Despite the stereotype (the Japanese are handled just as insensitively), however, Lamar's sexual orientation is never questioned, and when they are deciding on the rules for admittance to their fraternity, he chimes in that sexual preference should not be a barrier. When they throw a party, he's only one of two frat members with a date (albeit another disco-loving fag) and when they need to win one more event to beat the homophobic jocks in a sporting tournament, Lamar develops a special pole vault that takes into account "his limp-wristed throwing style" and saves the day. ☻

Ricochet *(1991, 97 min, US, Russell Mulcahy)*

An impressively violent action film that stars John Lithgow as a crazed serial killer who plots the downfall of a politically ambitious cop (Denzel Washington) who had previously sent him to prison. Throughout the film, Lithgow keeps a much younger (and very West Hollywood cute) partner (Josh Evans) around. This unlikely coupling suggests a sexual like between the two, although that link would be strictly master-slave. Their relationship is not unlike a psychotic and sexually tinged one between Gilligan and the Skipper — Evans is the puppy dog Gilligan to Lithgow's seriously evil Skipper. ☻

The Road Warrior

(1982, 94 min, Australia, George Miller)

Mel Gibson writes the book on existential cool as the light-lipped, leather-clad loner who roams the arid plains of a post-apocalyptic wasteland. Two groups of survivors share the barren wasteland with Mel: one a petrol-rich, peace-loving but fortressed community, and the other, a roving gang of murderous thugs. Among the hooligans is a Mohawked, motorcycle-driving wild man, also leather-clad (but with exposed ass cheeks), whose constant companion is his cute, bleached-blond boyfriend. But the youth is soon cut down by a steel boomerang, sending his macho lover in a hot-headed rage. ☻

S.O.B. *(1981, 121 min, US, Blake Edwards)*

Robert Preston is both hilarious and positively portrayed as a quick-witted doctor who — though it is never mentioned — is certainly gay. ☻

St. Elmo's Fire

(1985, 108 min, US, Joel Schumacher)

Possibly the quintessential Brat Pack ensemble film, the entire gang is here in this awful "We're-out-of-college/doesn't-life-suck" young adult drama. Demi Moore, Andrew McCarthy, Emilio Estevez, Rob Lowe, Ally Sheedy and Judd Nelson are some of the cast members. As Moore's gay neighbor Ron, Matthew Laurance is unable to flesh out an unflattering, poorly written character; who, among other things, has suspected closet case McCarthy's heterosexuality flaunted in his face. Given a line like "I just had my nose done" as a response to a barroom brawl, it's little wonder why Ron is simply another stereotype. ⊗

Saint Jack
(1979, 112 min, US, Peter Bogdanovich)
Ben Gazzara stars as a pimp who runs a hotel in the sleazier side of Singapore. George Lazenby plays an American senator who becomes a target for blackmail when he picks up a male prostitute (Edward Tan) while on a visit there. ⊗

Saturday Night Fever
(1977, 119 min, US, John Badham)
John Travolta's Tony Manero is conspicuously not interested in taunting the two "fairies" being harassed by his friends. ⊗

The Sentinel
(1977, 92 min, US, Michael Winner)
The Exorcist meets *Rosemary's Baby* in this hilariously hyperventilating horror film about a young model who rents an apartment in an old Brooklyn townhouse only to discover that it is the gateway to Hell! Among the many ghosts who haunt the place are Sylvia

Miles and Beverly D'Angelo as two stealthy lesbians, who in their earthly lives were both murderesses. Miles is a hoot as the butch Gerda (she plays the part as a Prussian Bette Davis), and D'Angelo is Sandra, a bug-eyed china doll femme prone to public displays of masturbation. When asked what the two do for a living, Gerda slinkingly replies, "We fondle each other." Later in the film, the two are seen naked, ravenously eating the flesh of a recently deceased male. Enjoyably bizarre trash.

Scarecrow
(1973, 115 min, US, Jerry Schatzberg)
A subtle gay male camaraderie in the tradition of *Midnight Cowboy* develops between two beautiful losers on the road in this buddy drama. Gene Hackman is the taciturn hothead who is befriended by the boyishly clownish Al Pacino. After a bar skirmish throws the two back in jail, Pacino develops a puppy dog devotion to Jack Riley (Richard Lynch), a fellow inmate. Riley takes him under his wing, tries to rape him ("How 'bout it? Be a pal"), and when that fails, beats him to a pulp. Hackman is the protective "Daddy" who avenges the unwanted advances. Riley is another example of a nearly devilish homosexual who preys on the unsuspecting but who gets his punishment in the end. ⊗

Serial *(1980, 92 min, US, Bill Persky)*
Dated, heavy-handed but funny at times, this satire takes the "us (the sane) vs. them (the weirdos)" approach in its lampoon of "eccentrics" living in wealthy Marin County during that fertile period when

The Road Warrior

flower-power philosophy met '80s greed. Martin Mull and Tuesday Weld star as a confused couple trying to remain sane through the social madness. And this being the San Francisco area, gays play a big part of the weirdos. There's a touchy-feely aerobic instructor, a catty and violent gay hairdresser, a bitchy society gal who comes out, and a bisexual dog-groomer. There is also the Gay Bruce doll, described by Sally Kellerman in that "Gay Bruce comes in a box shaped like a little closet." The doll becomes a victim to a queer-bashing by a nasty 10-year-old boy who "killed him because he was a fag." There is also a dignified Christopher Lee who is featured as the leader of the Road Reamers, a tough motorcycle gang described by Mull as "during the week, they are completely normal; but on weekends, they dress up like Hell's Angels and listen to Judy Garland a lot." But unlike most gay relationships, Lee happily gets the boy in the end! ☺

Le Sex Shop

(1973, 92 min, France, Claude Berri)
This congenial satire wittily explores the sexual revolution and society's rapidly changing sexual mores. Claude, the nebbish owner of a failing bookstore, enjoys financial success when he transforms his store into a sex paraphernalia shop. But he and his wife soon become involved with the "fast crowd" when a night on the town comes to include wife-swapping, group sex and an "anything goes" mentality. There are a few queer images in the bevy of horny Parisians, including Claude's pretty, young shop assistant who is involved with a butch, suit-and-tie wearing beauty but who also takes a fancy to Claude's wife. The wife, anxious to make Claude jealous, plays around with her for a night. The character is quite positive; an attractive, uninhibited, untroubled young woman

Single White Female

who goes after what she likes. Other characters include some additional lesbian coupling and one memorable customer — a middle-aged vibrator-loving size queen, who prefers the pink models! They give and they take. ☺

Sexuality in Chains (Geschlecht in Fesseln)

(1928, Germany, 78 min, William Dieterle)
Before becoming a top Hollywood director (*The Devil and Daniel Webster, Hunchback of Notre Dame*), William Dieterle directed this melodramatic prison film that, despite its determinedly heterosexual outlook, features some early glimpses of homosexuality in prison. Franz is an impetuous young man who accidentally kills a man who was harassing his girlfriend Helen. He is sent to prison and shares a cell with several others, including a flamboyant homosexual. Without the accompaniment of women, Franz discreetly enters into a sexual relationship with a handsome cell mate. Upon his release, Franz walks out, saying nothing to his prison lover (he doesn't even look back — just like a man!) as he runs back into the arms of his woman. Strange, interestingly suggestive and quite provocative for its time.

She Done Him Wrong

(1933, 66 min, US, Lowell Sherman)
Mae West appears as Diamond Lil in this classic screen comedy. In one scene, she visits a prison and is greeted enthusiastically by the prisoners. Upon passing the cell of two smiling cons, she refers to them (in a pre-Code remark) as "The Cherry Sisters." ☺

She's Gotta Have It

(1986, 84 min, US, Spike Lee)
Tracy Camila Johns is the "She" of the title, who besides driving three boyfriends mad with desire, also turns the head of Raye Dowell, who doesn't understand "No" for an answer. Spike Lee's otherwise pleasant comedy is surprisingly insensitive in its portrayal of Dowell's lesbian character. ☺

Showdown in Little Tokyo

(1991, 76 min, US, Mark L. Lester)
Though his character isn't gay, Brandon Lee can't help saying to partner Dolph Lundgren before a deadly stand-off: "Just in case we get killed, I wanted to tell you: You have the biggest dick I've ever seen on a man." He also ponders on being on the receiving end of his well-endowed co-hort. ☺

Single White Female

(1992, 107 min, US, Barbet Schroeder)
Bridget Fonda plays Allie, a benevolent woman looking for a roommate after breaking up with her fiancé, thinking "it will be nice to have a girlfriend, again." She chooses frumpy and idiosyncratic Hedra (Jennifer Jason Leigh), who gradually assumes Allie's identity in an effort to either coexist as twins (Hedra's twin was stillborn) or to

destroy her. Is this an anti-lesbian movie, or just another story about a sociopath who happens to have those "inclinations?" Hedra shows her affection for Allie twice in the movie. The first time she is holding a butcher knife to Allie's neck; the second time Allie is unconscious. Of course, one must die. One of them does, and no more girlfriends. ☻

Soapdish *(1991, 95 min, US, Michael Hoffman)*
A terrific cast headlines this very funny spoof on soap operas. Sally Field is the reigning Queen of the Soaps, Whoopi Goldberg is a scriptwriter and her longtime friend, and Kevin Kline is Field's down-on-his-luck ex who reenters her life when he is cast on the show. Providing the comic villain roles are Robert Downey, Jr. as the program's ass-kissing producer and Cathy Moriarty as Montana Moorehead, a scheming actress bent on replacing Field. The queer twist is at the end (read no further if you haven't seen the film!) as it's revealed that the luscious blonde Montana used to be a boy — Milton Moorehead! ☻

Son-in-Law *(1993, 95 min, US, Steve Rash)*
A very positive lesbian scene and the promise of a great lesbian relationship are buried within the mediocrity of this tepid comedy starring the curly haired Pauly Shore, a kinetic but unfunny product of MTV and a harmless '90s version of Cheech and Chong. The story centers on the unlikely love between farm girl Rebecca (Carla Gugino) and beach bum Shore. In an early scene, innocent Rebecca enrolls in a free-spirited L.A. university. On moving-in day, she meets her roommate, Carol (Ria Pavia), a friendly and attractive redhead of whom Rebecca's mother remarks, "What a nice girl." Later, Carol arrives with her friend, Lisa (Lisa Lawrence), and upon Lisa's departure, the two women exchange a long, passionate kiss in front of a startled Rebecca and her family. Although their relationship is never explored (the two remain peripheral figures in the story of the romance between Rebecca and Shore), their nonchalant but ardent kiss remains the only memorable moment of the film. ☻

Sonny Boy *(1990, 96 min, US, Martin Carroll)*
This extremely weird film features a family that would feel right at home in John Waters' Mortville. A dark tale of family love gone berserk, the film features Paul L. Smith as a 300-pound psychotic crook who with his wife, Pearl, raise an orphan boy to become an animal-like killing machine to advance their criminal enterprise. The role of the sweet, loving mother Pearl is played oddly enough by David Carradine, who plays the part entirely as a woman — wearing polka dot dresses, makeup and jewelry and sensible hair, although she does like her occasional cigar. As they go about their murderous ways, all involved ignore the fact that Pearl is a transvestite, which only adds to the pleasure of this mean-spirited oddity. ☻

Space Thing *(1968, 69 min, US, B. Ron Elliot)*
Picture a live-action "Josie and the Pussy Cats" where everyone is on ecstasy and you'll have a pretty good idea of what *Space Thing* is like. The crew of a small and extremely cheesy space craft is

headed by a militant lesbian, who after watching on closed circuit TV two of her crew members having heterosexual sex, proceeds to whip the female and then reprimand her, "Maybe that'll teach you that men are off-limits." Adding spice to the galactic tale are a few well-placed lesbian lovemaking scenes. ☻

Starstruck *(1982, 95 min, Australia, Gillian Armstrong)*
Jo Kennedy stars in this high-spirited musical romp as a Sydney teenager working in her mother's near-bankrupt pub who dreams of fame and fortune as a singer. When the local MTV-like show stages a contest, she can achieve her goal and save her mother's bar. The host of the TV show is played by John O'May, who befriends Kennedy and invites her to an intimate swimming party. She thinks it's romantic, but when she's greeted by an all-male chorus line, she realizes he's not the man for her. The party guests perform what is probably the first "coming out" musical production number. ☻

Steel Magnolias *(1989, 118 min, US, Herbert Ross)*
An alternately charming, funny and sentimental comedy-drama with Sally Field, Dolly Parton, Shirley MacLaine, Olympia Dukakis, Julia Roberts and Daryl Hannah as a group of Southern ladies who meet regularly at Parton's beauty shop. During one of their conversations, the ladies figure out how to tell if someone is gay: track lighting. ☻

Stephen King's Sleepwalkers *(1992, 91 min, US, Mick Garris)*
Predatory schoolteacher Mr. Fallows (Glenn Shadix) bites off more than he can chew (and gets even more bitten off) when he makes sexual advances to the new kid in school (Brian Krause), who is in reality a shape-shifting catboy from beyond antiquity. As stupid as it sounds. ☻

Stir Crazy *(1980, 111 min, US, Sidney Poitier)*
A lame comedy (but box-office smash) about two misfits (Gene Wilder and Richard Pryor) who are innocently sent to the slammer, *Stir Crazy* features some standard homosexuality-in-prison situations as well as one prominent gay character. When the two men are convicted of bank robbery, they're sent to a California penitentiary and are quickly faced with the prospect of rape, "kissing the baby" and of being suspected of being "sweet pants." Adding to the situation is Georg Stanford Brown as Rory, an effeminate black inmate who has the hots for Pryor. First seen as simply a leering but harmless caricature of a fag, Rory soon develops into a well-defined character who joins Pryor and Wilder in their prison breakout. Although he's the one who must sport drag in their plot (being the gay man, drag must come more naturally) and he does not get his man (Pryor), he does get to plant a big wet one on his *objet d'amour*'s startled lips. ☻

Storyville *(1992, 112 min, US, Mark Frost)*
This thriller, steeped in dirty politics, sex and murder features James Spader as a blindly ambitious New Orleans political novice who becomes involved in a murder scenario in the midst of his

campaign for Congress. The person who witnesses the murder and testifies in Spader's defense is transvestite and "model" Tom Plunkett (Bernard Zette). Initially seen in enticing leather regalia, he meets Spader in a gay bar (dressed as a man) and at court appears in a fetching Camelot-era Jackie Kennedy outfit (minus the pillbox). The film does not make fun of him, he does not get killed and he is the hero/heroine. ⊛

Strangers in Good Company

(1990 110 min, Canada, Cynthia Scott)
A gentle, quietly moving drama of seven elder women who become stranded in the Canadian countryside and are forced to fend for themselves for a few days after their bus breaks down. The non-professional cast includes Mary Meigs as Mary, a 70-ish lesbian painter who, in one of the best scenes of the film, tells wide-eyed Cissy that she is a lesbian, with Cissy replying, "Oh, that's good." ⊛

Strangers on a Train

(1951, 101 min, US, Alfred Hitchcock)
A slick psychological thriller that tackles blackmail, murder and latent homosexuality. Farley Granger is a handsome tennis player who meets the flamboyant Robert Walker on a train and soon becomes his unwilling partner in crime. Walker plays it thick as Bruno, the spoiled, middle-aged rich kid whose hatred of and devotion to his mother turns him into a subtly gay would-be seducer and psychopath. ⊛

Street Wars

(1994, 90 min, US, Jamaa Fanaka)
Disguised as simply another direct-to-video action film set in the black subculture of drugs and violence is this entertaining and spoofy adaptation of *The Godfather*. What is startling in this independently made film from the director of *Penitentiary* is its handling of one of the supporting characters, Mistress C. (aka Christy, played by Vaughn Cromwell), a cross-dressing henchman (henchperson?) of Sugar Pop (Alan Joseph), a 17-year-old who aspires to be the unrivaled honcho of an urban drug empire. Christy's thuggish beauty (lace stockings, never smudged makeup and some fetching outerwear) coupled with his ballsy gun-toting love of violence makes him an unforgettable black Rambo in drag. The story centers around Sugar Pop, a brainy, green-eyed calfcake and West Point aspirant whose military career gets sidetracked when his drug lord brother is gunned down. With a few of his trusted pals behind him (including Mistress C.), he makes a bloody drive for power and control. This film is a great example of incorporating queers into mainstream films. Mistress C., while an unconventional portrait of a drag queen, is nonetheless seen as a respected and feared member of the gang who takes shit from no one. He's trusted, brave, a good shot and, unlike so many films of the past, is not dropped from the plot nor killed off. He struts his stuff, brings his boyfriend to a gangster party and the only time someone mentions his looks (or calls him a "faggot"), his response is unforgettable and militant (see the first page of this chapter for his quote). ⊛

Strangers in Good Company

Sudden Impact

(1983, 117 min, US, Clint Eastwood)
Audrie J. Neenan is Ray, a foul-mouthed, lip-curling lowlife, referred to as "the dyke," who participates in the rape of Sondra Locke and her sister, an act which sends Locke over the edge. It would be difficult to imagine a more conspicuous stereotype. ⊛

Summer Wishes, Winter Dreams

(1973, 93 min, US, Gilbert Cates)
Ron Richards is Bobby, Joanne Woodward and Martin Balsam's estranged gay son whose move to Amsterdam upsets his mother. Joffrey Ballet dancer Dennis Wayne appears briefly in a flashback as Bobby's stateside boyfriend. ⊛

Supergirls in 3-D

(1983, 90 min, Germany, Horst Alexander)
This otherwise forgettable exploitation flick from Germany has a few queer images of note. The girls' photographer, Jon, is the typical nelly homo who, against his wishes, is forced to give a half-hearted hand in the staged orgy scene. Also featured is a bisexual named Angie who is used only as the star's helping friend. And as all great works of (3-D) cinema must, the film ends in a food fight, including the requisite flying custard pies.

The Supergrass

(1987, 105 min, GB, Peter Richardson)
This outrageous hit-or-miss farce features many of the biggest names in British comedy today including Adrian Edmonson and Nigel Planner ("The Young Ones"), Dawn French and Jennifer Saunders, Alexie Sayle and Robbie Coltrane. The story revolves around a brainless but strangely sympathetic idiot who claims he is involved in a drug smuggling ring to impress a girl and ends up unwittingly embroiled in a real drug scheme. The real criminals are two men who, while waiting for the drug ship to arrive, masquerade as a married couple with Planner as the stylishly dressed wife. His partner in crime (Keith Allen) soon takes a fancy to him,

turned on by his partner's silk stockings and more than respectable legs. The drag is strictly for laughs but the two do fight like a couple with the two hurling sexual remarks ("You broken down old drag queen" and "Admit you're gay and get out of the closet") with vicious abandon. ⊛

Swashbuckler
(1976, 101 min, US, James Goldstone)
Peter Boyle is a gay villain with a penchant for S&M in this forgettable big-budget pirate satire. As the corrupt governor of early 18th-century Jamaica, Boyle camps it up, enjoying the attentions of a galley of black male slaves as well as a submissive young lute player (Mark Baker). The story centers around a sword-wielding pirate (Robert Shaw) who comes to the rescue of a beautiful damsel-in-distress (Genevieve Bujold) but the fun is undermined (for politically sensitive queers) by the mean-spirited depiction of the film's bad guy as a homosexual, a role that even had *The New York Times* critic Vincent Canby remark at the time that the film made an uneasy association between Boyle's homosexuality and political and moral corruption. ⊛

Switch *(1991, 103 min, US, Black Edwards)*
An occasionally amusing though ultimately frustrating body-switching comedy which stars the sensuous Ellen Barkin as the female incarnation of a murdered homophobic and sexist philanderer. The lesbian possibilities of a transgendered horny man trapped in a woman's body is almost ignored as Edwards trods the safer terrain of pratfall comedy. The only lesbian subplot involves Lorraine Brocco as Sheila Faxton, the beautiful young president of a cosmetics firm and out lesbian, who is on the prowl after the breakup of a ten-year relationship. Barkin makes the move and Brocco responds, but the awkward seduction scene ends when the edgy Barkin faints, preserving her lesbian virginity. Straight man Edwards' vision of a lesbian bar is also shown — an elegant club filled with glam femmes and fist-flying butches (Faith Minton steals the scene as Nancy the bouncer). A mainstream film that offered the possibility of dealing with lesbianism in a progressive fashion but fails miserably to do so. ⊛

Sylvia
(1965, 115 min, US, Gordon Douglas)
Private investigator George Maharis delves into the life of a prostitute (Carroll Baker) who turned her life around in this episodic and flashback-laden drama. On his rounds, he meets a librarian (Viveca Lindfors) who confesses her love for the beautiful Sylvia.

Sylvia *(1985, 99 min, New Zealand, Michael Firth)*
Eleanor David stars as an unorthodox teacher of Aborigine children in a small New Zealand village. Married to an understanding man, she still feels pangs of dissatisfaction with her life. She meets a kindred spirit in Opal Saunders (Mary Regan), a pretty district nurse whose favorite attire is a suit and tie (a hackneyed directorial hint on her sexuality). The two become close friends, and although there are signs of sexual tension between them (Opal writes poetry about Sylvia; Sylvia lovingly sculpts her muse, and the two hug and touch), nothing more develops. ⊛

The Tamarind Seed
(1974, 123 min, GB, Blake Edwards)
Blake Edwards directed this romantic espionage thriller that can best be summed up as a Cold War "Romeo and Juliet." Julie Andrews stars as a British Home Office secretary who falls in love with KBG operative Omar Sharif. Dan O'Herlihy co-stars as a British double agent who is also a closet homosexual. Sylvia Syms plays his long-suffering but loyal wife. Can't trust those gay spies! ⊛

Tango and Cash
(1989, 98 min, US, Andrei Konchalovsky)
One of the most homoerotic of the countless "buddy movies" to come from Hollywood, this over-the-top police actioner stars a foppish Sylvester Stallone and a pumped-up Kurt Russell as two rivaling supercops who team to bust the drug empire of an evil Jack Palance. Stallone stretches his acting ability as Tango, an bespectacled, Armani-wearing aesthete who always gets his man. Cutesy dialogue filled with sexual innuendo adds spice to the overladened violence and sadism. On their first encounter, Tango thrusts his gun into the crotch of a stoic Cash. From then on, the machismo posturing of the two gives way to constant sexual references including a naked shower scene (with Russell dropping his soap!) and a memorable cameo of Russell in knockout drag —leather mini-skirt, good legs, big hair and a fetching come-hither look. At the end, even Tango's sister gets frustrated about all this verbal foreplay when she says, "Why don't you admit that you two work well together?" The final shot has them gazing into one another's eyes. Sadly, there was no sequel keeping us in the dark as to who was the top man. ⊛

A Taste of Flesh
(1967, 73 min, US, Lou Silverman)
Sexy exploitation queen Doris Wishman directed under one of her several pseudonyms in this claptrap about a political assassination and an apartment full of lesbians. Filled with several dreamy episodes of slinky women making it with each other, the film features Carol and Bobbi, two lesbian roommates and lovers, one of whom invites another young woman to stay with them while she visits the city. But before any shenanigans can commence, two men break into the apartment and hold the three captive while they plot to kill a European government official from their apartment window. Not withstanding its cheesy '60s erotica intentions, the lesbian sex is portrayed as enticing and loving while the men are seen as violent brutes. The non-sync post-dubbing, turgid pacing and terrible acting only enhances the film's tackiness. ⊛

10 *(1979, 122 min, US, Blake Edwards)*
As a gay composer, Robert Webber sobs in his beer through the whole movie about: a) no relationship; b) his new lover; c) their breakup. ⊛

Theatre of Blood
(1973, 105 min, GB, Douglas Hickcox)
An unsettling film to watch for any critic, this entertaining horror film stars Vincent Price as an over-the-top Shakespearean

MENTIONS

actor who exacts bloody revenge on eight critics who gave him thumbs down. The gay references are two-fold. Robert Morley is featured as Meredith Merridew, an effeminate critic replete with poofed-up pinkish hair, outrageous "faggot" wardrobe and two pink-ribboned French poodles. He's made as the cheap joke whose death mirrors that of the queen in Shakespeare's "Titus Andronicus" — that is, he's served his "children" baked in a pie and then force-fed to death. Grisly, funny and completely politically incorrect! The other gay reference is Price himself — in his scheme to kill Coral Browne, he plays Butch, a killer hairdresser who still has time to make goo-goo eyes with a police constable. ⊛

There Was a Crooked Man
(1970, 126 min, US, Joseph L. Mankiewicz)
A fast-paced, likable western take on the men-in-prison genre, this actioner stars Kirk Douglas as Paris Pitman, Jr., a wise-guy rogue (looking a lot like a dimple-cheeked John Lennon) who is sent to a territorial prison. His cell mates include Burgess Meredith, Warren Oates and, for comic relief, Hume Cronyn and John Randolph as a pair of bickering, often whimpering homosexuals. The two are obvious longtime partners, though no love nor affection for each other is demonstrated. During one of their arguments, Dudley (Cronyn) blames Cyrus (Randolph) for their predicament, nagging, "We could have had a nice little house — you could have had a decent job and I could have cooked and cleaned." Although they are seen as selfish and outwardly uncaring (except for a tender scene of Dudley washing Cyrus' back), they aren't killed when Kirk spearheads a bloody prison outbreak and, as a matter of fact, are seen planning their domestic life after their sentence. Another depiction of homosexuality is not so complex. Prison guard Skinner (Bert Freed), looking like a 19th-century version of a Nazi, takes a fancy to Coy Cavendish (Michael Blodgett), a bronzed, blond youth and cell mate of Kirk. When Cavendish rejects the older man's lascivious advances, the guard begins to whip him, prompting a riot and the death of the evil homosexual. ⊛

They Only Kill Their Masters
(1972, 98 min, US, James Goldstone)
James Garner is a self-described "normal heterosexual" and small-town police chief who becomes embroiled in a case involving the murder of a bisexual woman. The film begins with the mutilated and pregnant body of a woman (Jennie Campbell) washing up on the northern California shore. In the ensuing investigation, Garner finds that she left her husband (Peter Crawford) for another woman. In the end, the murderer confesses and who should it be but none other than her jealous lover, June Allyson! So the film has it both: the lesbian murder victim and the murderous lesbian. ⊛

This Boy's Life
(1993, 115 min, US, Michael Caton-Jones)
Based on the autobiography of writer Tobias Wolff, this intensely moving and powerful coming-of-age drama is a courageous tale examining the hopes and desperation of an unsettled youth. The

remarkable Leonardo DiCaprio plays a troubled teen who relocates to a small town when his mother (Ellen Barkin) remarries. In a volatile performance, Robert DeNiro plays his abusive stepfather. As one of DiCaprio's only friends, Jonah Blechman gives an astonishing performance as Arthur, a gay teen — a rustic Oscar Wilde trapped in a world of uncivility and ignorance who is both flamboyant and quietly determined. Handled particularly well is a scene in which Arthur — who has a crush on his heterosexual friend — plants a kiss on Tobias, whose only reaction seems to be one of flattery. Afterwards, nothing is made of it and they remain the best of friends. It is one of the finest portraits of gay youth ever put on screen. ⊛

Three Lives
(1970, 75 min, US, Kate Millett & Susan Kleckner)
This early women's liberation documentary captures the opinionated thoughts of three disparate women. One of the women, Robin Mide, discusses her lesbian feelings.

Tightrope *(1984, 114 min, US, Richard Tuddle)*
A sex-obsessed serial killer is stalking the streets of New Orleans and it is up to detective Clint Eastwood to track him down in this gritty crime thriller. During his investigation in the seedy French

Jason Priestley in *Tombstone*

Quarter's sex-for-hire underworld, his own sexually aberrant desires are exposed and acted upon. Instead of being disgusted by the flesh market, Clint displays his usual cool. A male street hustler asks him, "You want some honey?" Clint succinctly replies, "I don't eat sweets." One of the women he interrogates is a high-price bisexual call girl whose pretty working partner and former lover is killed — she shows little remorse as she quickly gives a wide-eyed Clint a blow job. The best queer scene occurs later when Clint is sent to Praline's, a smokey gay bar, to meet a possible informant. A leatherized patron (Robert Harvey) gives Clint the once over and ominously (and humorously) asks, "Looking for something, Alice?" Before Clint can respond, he meets his informant, who is actually a male hustler (Jonathan Sacher) sent to service Clint. Clint declines the offer, and the man asks, "How do you know if you haven't tried it?" Clint says in a deadpan voice, "Maybe I have." ☻

To Be or Not to Be

(1983, 108 min, US, Mel Brooks)
Mel Brooks and Anne Bancroft reprise the roles created by Jack Benny and Carole Lombard in Ernest Lubitsch's 1942 comedy classic. The story has to do with a group of Polish actors outwitting the Nazis. Taking over Maude Eburne's role in the original, James Haake plays the flamboyant Sasha, dresser to stage star Bancroft. Brooks' film may be the first Hollywood feature film — albeit a comedy — to address the rounding up and internment of gays at the hands of the Nazis (the play "Bent" has yet to be filmed). In one scene, Sasha's quick thinking saves the lives of several Jewish refugees. ☻

The Todd Killings

(1970, 93 min, US, Barry Shear)
Robert F. Lyons stars as Skipper Todd, a kill-for-thrills psycho in this tense and atmospheric drama. Based on real-life accounts, and predating the similarly themed *River's Edge*, the film offers a look into the twisted mind of a killer who provides drugs and parties to a group of bored, alienated teens who in turn protect him from the law. Although a ladies' man, Skipper admits to an officer at his draft hearing that he's had affairs with men: "I tried not to, but sometimes there's a guy who's really sweet," and also reveals that he "screws chicks once because it makes them dirty." This charming but fucked-up rogue and possibly repressed homosexual befriends delinquent Richard Thomas but otherwise is shown as straight. Look for singer Holly Near as one of his murderous accomplices. ☻

Tombstone

(1993, 132 min, US, George P. Cosmatos)
This '90s version of Wyatt Earp and his famous shoot-'em-up at the O.K. Corral stars Kurt Russell as the slinty-eyed lawman and a seductively droll Val Kilmer, who steals the show as the acerbic but sickly Doc Holliday. Being a revisionist western, the film allows some mention of gays. Playing against type, heartthrob Jason Priestley plays Billy Breckenridge, the town's lovable fag (or as one character calls him, "sister boy"), a bespectacled, goateed cowpoke who is laughed at but accepted by the other cow-

boys. Billy Zane is a traveling actor who catches Priestley's eye. Although nothing more of their possible tryst is shown, it is broadly hinted that the two began something that ended when Zane gets caught in the crossfire of the good and the bad guys. Priestley, who reluctantly joined the posse, is seen visibly upset by his love's limp body. Before his corpse is taken away, he affectionately places has hand on Zane's, much to the shocked tittering of teenage girls throughout America's multiplexes. ☻

Tony Rome

(1967, 110 min, US, Gordon Douglas)
As private eye Tony Rome, Frank Sinatra investigates the goings-on of a society girl. In his travels, he talks to Georgia, a lesbian stripper, and her whining "roommate" Irene. Neither actress is given screen credit, so we don't know who gave life to these insulting portrayals. Disapproving Sinatra grimaces at their sight and proclaims they're in "the wrong ballpark." Lloyd Bochner does get screen credit as Vic, a homosexual drug dealer whose apartment is laid out in the gayest '60s interior décor. ☻

Tough Guys   *(1986, 104 min, US, Jeff Kanew)*

Kirk Douglas returns to his favorite saloon after a 30-year prison stint to discover it's now a gay bar. His first time there, he gets asked to dance — beginner's luck. You'd think all those years behind bars he wouldn't get so freaked. ☻

The Turning Point

(1977, 119 min, US, Herbert Ross)
Shirley MacLaine and Anne Bancroft star in this drama about the reunion of two friends who were aspiring ballet dancers. Didi (MacLaine) is now a housewife and dance teacher while Emma (Bancroft) became a star ballerina. They meet again in New York City when Didi's daughter moves there to study dance. Didi is plagued with wondering if she could have made it, while Emma is envious of Didi's family. There is a definite repudiation of gay involvement in the dance world and exaltation of heterosexuality that is especially disturbing for a movie about the artistic community; although this is not surprising coming from director Ross. Wayne (James Mitchell) is a choreographer whose gayness is referred to as his "ambivalence" and Didi admits that she got married (to Tom Skerritt) and got pregnant to prove that her dancer/husband was not gay. ☻

Two for the Seesaw

(1962, 120 min, US, Robert Wise)
Bohemian Shirley MacLaine tells businessman Robert Mitchum about her dance partner (who is not seen). Mitchum asks: "Do you sleep with him?" She responds: "He's a dancer...you think I'm peculiar?" She then asks him, "Hey, are you queer?" ☻

Two Moon Junction

(1988, 104 Min, US, Zalman King)
A bored, blonde Sherilyn Fenn (looking like an overly officious nurse) dumps her privileged life and vapid beau (Martin Hewitt) and takes up with a brutish, muscle-bound carnival worker (Richard Tyson). Kristy McNichol adds some real interest and life

to this cheesy T&A tale as Patti Jean, a fast-talking, truck-driving, fist-throwing bisexual cowgirl who takes a strong interest with Fenn's ice princess. There's a lot of teasing between the two of them, highlighted by a lustful dance together — sadly, the two go no further. ⊛

The Uninvited *(1944, 98 min, US, Lewis Allen)*

With more than one similarity to *Rebecca*, this atmospheric ghost story is both chilling and eerie, with more than its fair share of good humor. Londoner Ray Milland and his sister Ruth Hussey buy an abandoned mansion located off the rocky cliffs of the English coastline. When they move in, they discover their new home is haunted by the spirit of the possibly murdered daughter of the ex-owner. Cornelia Otis Skinner plays a former nurse to the dead woman, and Skinner's devoted companion — who may hold the secret of the tragedy — seems to be cousin to Judith Anderson's Mrs. Danvers in the Hitchcock classic. Gazing at the portrait of her former employer, she calls her "My darling" and talks lovingly of their close association. ⊛

A Very Curious Girl
(Dirty Mary, La Fiancée Du Pirate)
(1969, 105 min, France, Nelly Kaplan)

Bernadette Lafont plays Mary, a poor peasant girl, alternately reviled as a daughter of a Gypsy and a tramp and lusted after by every man in the farming village. Claire Maurier plays Irene, Mary's lecherous boss who, like the loutish men, lusts after the comely girl. She is seen as "one of the boys"; a leather-jacketed, tough-as-nails butch who, when not lunging for our heroine's breasts, takes a whip to a stealing worker. This sexy, satiric fable has Mary turning the tables on them all, first by charging them for her services and then eventually exposing them for their hypocrisies and cruelty. ⊛

A View from the Bridge
(1962, 110 min, US, Sidney Lumet)

Like the previous year's *The Children's Hour*, this family drama deals, in part, with rumors and accusations of homosexuality and features a startling (for its time) man-to-man kiss. From Arthur Miller's acclaimed play, the story focuses on a Brooklyn dock worker (Raf Vallone) and his tempestuous relationship with his wife (Jean Stapleton) and her niece (Carol Lawrence), whom he secretly lusts after. His repressed desire for her erupts when she begins to date a sensitive Italian longshoreman, Rodolpho (Jean Sorel). When his disapproval of the man falls on deaf ears, he resorts to accusing him of being a homosexual and to "prove" it, plants a kiss smack on the man's lips. The ploy does not work.

Vixen
(1968, 70 min, US, Russ Meyer)

Exploitation-cum-social satirist and buxom bosom-loving fetishist Russ Meyer brings his usual frenetic style of sex, camp, humor and politics with this outrageous tale of a sexually charged young woman and the men (and a woman) she seduces and sets it in the tranquil Canadian wilderness. Erica Gavin stars as Vixen, a sultry temptress who, when not having sex with her pilot hus-band, is making it with visitors, neighbors and even her brother. When the kittenish redhead Janet arrives on the scene with her husband, it doesn't take long for Vixen to seduce both. As she is slowly aroused by the teasing of Vixen, the "innocent" Janet comments, "Is something wrong with us?...Ahh, your hands sure feel good!" ⊛

WR: Mysteries of the Organism
(1971, 86 min, Serbia/US, Dusan Makavejev)

This strikingly original film from the director of *Montenegro* and *The Coca-Cola Kid* is a clever, amusing and, at times, exasperating political satire which quite seriously proposes sex as the ideological imperative for liberation — a plea for Erotic Socialism. Interwoven into his complicated tale is an examination/celebration of sexologist and Communist Wilhelm Reich; a story of a Yugoslavian woman's quest for political and sexual liberation; and some segments featuring Warholite Candy Darling. The Darling footage begins with her walking down 42nd Street with a pretty blond boy, both of them innocently eating ice cream cones. Further "interviews" involve Candy's love for a man named Eric (the boy?) and her plans to marry him. Don't expect to easily link this transsexual love affair with the rest of the heterosexually themed film — just keep your eyes wide open and take it like a man/woman! ⊛

Wagons East
(1994, 100 min, US, Peter Markle)

In his last role, John Candy plays a drunken, incompetent wagon-master who leads a group of dissatisfied settlers of the Old West on a journey back to a more civilized East. Unfunny to the point of embarrassment, the film features as one of its main characters a gay bookseller. As Julian, John C. McGinley — who on-screen usually has the intensity of a James Woods — is an effeminate, googly-eyed "sissy boy" who, when not washing the back of a hunkish young straight guy (causing Julian to get an underwater hard-on), is flittering around the camp with a perpetual grin. As if to try to make amends for the stereotypical mannerisms of Julian, the story at one point has him saving the day when he engages in a Clint Eastwood-inspired showdown with a hired gunslinger — proving to have the fastest, and limpest, gun in the West. At the film's end, and with a handsome Indian brave in tow, Julian decides to head back West — his destination provides one of the only real laughs in this otherwise amiable bomb.

Warm Nights on a Slow Moving Train
(1987, 91 min, Australia, Bob Ellis)

Wendy Hughes plays a Catholic schoolteacher who, while on the Melbourne to Sydney overnight train she takes every weekend to visit her ailing brother, transforms into a classy hooker and nonchalantly turns tricks with the passengers. A funny and erotic drama, the film features Peter Whitford as the train's steward, a middle-aged gay man who is Hughes' confidant and sometime protector. After Whitford leaves his lover for bringing home "rough trade" and is single and alone, Hughes suggests she and him marry. This prompts Whitford to remark (and in keeping with the train analogy), "Yes, switch tracks and go on down the line...and think of him." He also predicts, "We'll never agree on the lampshades." Ⓐ

Wayne's World 2
(1993, 96 min, US, Stephen Sujik)
Alternately witty and insipid, this pleasant comedy, which spoofs 1960s and early '70s movies and music, stars the two effervescent innocents, Wayne (Mike Myers) and Garth (Dana Carvey). Thoroughly heterosexual, there is a brief but hilarious episode in which Wayne and his friends don disguises (a telephone man, a policeman, a sailor) to spy on his possibly cheating girlfriend. But they are spotted and chased by the incensed Christopher Walken into the backdoor entrance of a gay bar where, accompanied by a mysterious, half-naked Indian, they lip-sync to the Village People's hit "YMCA" to an enthusiastic response from the crowded bar. Quite gay-friendly. Ⓐ

When the Party's Over
(1991, 114 min, US, Matthew Irmas)
The fun-loving L.A. twentysomething crowd is the focus of this "serious" look at youthful love, sex, deception and "growing up." Rae Dawn Chong plays a power and sex hungry bitch who shares a house with four others. Included in the yuppie-wannabe heterosexual coupling is Banks (Kris Kamm), an aspiring gay actor. His gayness is accepted without thought by the other members of the household, although the brother of one of his roommates does question him, and another wonders if he "just hasn't met the right woman." While this inclusion of a secondary character who just happens to be gay is great, there are some troubling thoughts — although there is no overt homophobia, words like "fag", "butt pirate" and "tinkerbell" are thrown at the young man by his "friends." And like the gay character in *Reality Bites*, Banks remains curiously non-sexual. He doesn't have a boyfriend (he does remark at one point that a guy is cute), isn't romantically involved, doesn't have sex; and when others recall how they lost their virginity, he remembers not a male but a female! While giving with one hand (by including a gay character), the picture takes with the other (by making him a sexless, non-threatening extra). Ⓐ

Where the Day Takes You
(1992, 92 min, US, Marc Rocco)
It's *Young Guns Go Homeless* in this seedy, moralistic drama about teens eking out a living on the not-so-mean streets of Los Angeles. Dermot Mulroney returns from jail to reclaim his leadership over a motley gang of runaways, drug addicts and losers. One of the runaways,

Little J. (Balthazar Getty), a cute and curiously well-groomed teen, is encouraged to help out a male prostitute who has too much on his plate. Despite saying that he's "not down on that shit," J. does agree to meet the gentle and sensitive Charles (Stephen Tobolowsky) in his West Hollywood apartment. Their first tentative session — a little face touching and mutual J.O. — develops into a semi-Pygmalian situation as the boy (despite initial anger and spitting out "faggot" several times) moves in and begins to enjoy the advantages of being the boy-toy of the generous older gay man. But too many show tunes and Charles' discovery of a gun in J.'s pocket causes the boy to snap, beat up his benefactor and split. The boy eventually takes out his "rage" (is it anger over being a short-lived prostitute or unsettled questions of his sexuality?) by killing a homeless thug. Jail and his friends put him back on the straight track. Ⓐ

Where Sleeping Dogs Lie
(1991, 92 min, US, Charles Finch)
Though neither character is gay, there's a sexual tension between handsome writer Dylan McDermott and his weird tenant Tom Sizemore. In a scene which firmly establishes their relationship, the muscular McDermott, wearing only a towel and aware of his physical appeal, is gazed upon by the almost-aroused Sizemore. The encounter underscores the sexual repression between them. Ⓐ

Where's Poppa?
(1970, 82 min, US, Carl Reiner)
One of the seminal comedies of the 1970s, this scathingly irreverent cult film stars George Segal as an Upper West Side mama's boy who has had enough of his scheming, senile mother (the hilarious Ruth Gordon). Ron Liebman is featured as Sidney, Segal's beleaguered married brother who, during his nightly runs through Central Park on his way to Mom's apartment, is repeatedly mugged by a group of black thugs. On one of these dashes through

Wings

the park, he is encouraged by the mischievous thieves to rape a woman. He does, but the woman turns out to be a male undercover cop. Instead of pressing charges, the thankful cop sends him flowers (long stem roses!) with the note, "Thanks for a wonderful evening." Sidney's touched by the gesture and seriously considers responding. Ⓐ

Who's the Man?
(1993, 85 min, US, Ted Demme)
In the tradition of *House Party*, this harmless and often times funny urban comedy stars MTV VJs (and a black 1990s version of Abbott and Costello) Ed Lover and his corpulent partner Dr. Dré. The plot centers on the bungling pair going from spastic barbers to New York City policemen battling corrupt, white, real estate speculators. A recurring minor character in the film is Lamar, a gay barber played by Andre B. Blake. First seen preening over a cute male customer's hair, the flamboyant Lamar responds to his costumer's complaint of his excessive touchiness by responding, "You know you like it. You'll be my way soon...I'll ride you like one of those go-go dancers on *Soul Train*." Later, this lisping stereotype sees the two stars for the first time dressed as cops and says the tired line, "I love a man in uniform." Although he is slightly offensive and appears for cheap comic relief, he isn't killed off or beaten up and is an interesting example of acceptance of a fellow black gay. Ⓐ

Wild in the Streets
(1968, 97 min, US, Barry Shear)
Christopher Jones stars in this '60s camp/exploitation classic as Max, a millionaire rock star who becomes President of the United States on the platform of lowering the voting age to 14. Once in office, he spikes Congress' water with LSD and sets up "Paradise Camps" for senior citizens (including his hellish mother, Shelley Winters). Max's right-hand boy is openly gay 15-year-old Billy (Kevin Coughlin), guitarist, manager and genius who has his eyes on Daddy figure Hal Holbrook. Groovy. Ⓐ

Wings
(1927, 139 min, US, William Wellman)
The first film to win an Academy Award for Best Picture, this silent WWI drama and 1920s gay wet dream focuses on the friendship between two men and the woman they both

love. While superficially heterosexual, there is no denying a subtle but persistent homosexual inference between the two handsome young men. Jack (Charles Rogers) and David (Richard Arlen) both enlist in the early Air Force at the outbreak of war. Being rivals for the heart of Mary (Clara Bow), the two initially dislike each other, despite their constant gazing into each others eyes. At boot camp their animosity turns to affection during an out-of-control boxing match. David is knocked to the ground and with a puppy dog look of hurt and blood (semen?) dripping out of the sides of this mouth, he gazes lovingly at his opponent...they leave the scene arm in arm and become the best of pals. Their closeness is tested after Mary enlists as a nurse and threatens their relationship; oh, and then there is the war. For nudity fans, early on in the film, when the men enlist, there is a scene at the recruiting office that quickly shows the shapely rears of several aspiring soldiers-to-be. Ⓐ

Withnail and I
(1987, 105 min, GB, Bruce Robinson)
This sardonic comedy features Richard E. Grant and Paul McGann as two unemployed actors living on the edge in a seedy flat in the before-it-was-fashionable Camden Town in 1969. They have an opportunity to go on holiday when Grant's rich gay uncle offers them his "country cottage" (actually a dilapidated dump). While the two young men seem like gay lovers and are even accused of being so in a pub, they are indeed heterosexuals. The eccentric uncle Monty (Richard Griffiths) is the true homo, sort of an obese, slightly deranged Oscar Wilde gone to lecherous seed. From his first conversation with them when he lectures almost orgasmicly on the pleasures of vegetables, to his humorous attempts of seduction

Young Man with a Horn

on the handsome but ridiculously jumpy McGann, he is seen as a funny, sexually harmless character. ⊛

Without a Trace
(1983, 120 min, US, Stanley R. Jaffe)
Keith McDermott plays Philippe, Kate Nelligan's gay houseboy. When her six-year-old son becomes missing, Philippe is arrested; after all, he's a "convicted sex offender and avowed homosexual." The film goes to great lengths not to offend nor equate gayness with perversity. Nelligan even remarks: "Practically all child molesters are heterosexual...a gay man (is) the least likely candidate." ⊛

The Woman Next Door
(1981, 106 min, France, François Truffaut)
Roger Van Hool plays Roland, a gay publisher whose sexuality is incidental. His youthful lover accompanies him on a resort holiday. ⊛

The Year of Living Dangerously

The World According to Garp
(1982, 136 min, US, George Roy Hill)
John Irvin's quirky best-seller makes for a most entertaining and first-rate comedy-drama. In her dynamic film debut, Glenn Close plays Jenny Fields, a nurse who impregnates herself with the semen of a comatose soldier. She gives birth to Garp (Robin Williams). Later in life, Jenny becomes a leader in the feminist movement with her autobiographical novel, "A Sexual Suspect." One of the many people to surround Jenny is Roberta Muldoon (John Lithgow), a transsexual who used to be a former tight end for the Philadelphia Eagles. Lithgow received an Oscar nomination for his splendid portrayal; the actor never condescends, and paints a vivid, touching characterization. After Jenny is assassinated, Roberta helps Garp dress in drag so he can attend his mother's funeral — the first feminist funeral which is women only! ⊛

The Year of Living Dangerously
(1982, 114 min, Australia, Peter Weir)
Mel Gibson stars as a naive foreign correspondent who becomes involved with British attache Sigourney Weaver during the midst of the turbulent 1965 Indonesian military coup. Linda Hunt, in a role that won her an Academy Award, stars as Billy Kwan, a Chinese-Australian photographer who not only is the only character with a political and moral understanding of the soon-to-explode revolution, but who also takes the cute Mel under his wing and, quite possibly, falls in love with him. This positive, cross-dressing image is offset by a negative one of gay, drunken and obnoxious English newspaperman Wally O'Sullivan (Noel Ferrer), who, when his sexuality is discovered says, "I'll pack my bags tonight." ⊛

Young Man with a Horn
(1950, 112 min, US, Michael Curtiz)
Lauren Bacall marries Kirk Douglas, not out of love. There are several references to hint at Bacall's lesbianism, including describ-

ing her party guests as "colorful characters" and her leaving her husband to tour Europe with a young female art student. (GB title: *Young Man of Music*) ⊛

Young Törless
(1966, 85 min, Germany/France, Volker Schlöndorff)
This trenchant drama on the cruelty of man is set in a boys' boarding school in rural Germany before World War I. There, in a grey, lifeless environment, the intelligent Törless (Mathhieu Carriere) witnesses the sadistic hazing of a pudgy, disliked boy (Marian Seidowsky) by two of his friends. When Törless becomes sensitive to the boy's plight, he confronts the sadistic bullies, who in turn accuse him of being the boy's lover.

Z
(1969, 127 min, France, Costa-Gavras)
This Oscar-winning Best Foreign Film is a swiftly moving political thriller examining corruption in the Greek government. Marcel Bozzufi plays the gay fascist killer Vago, whose first concern is politics; sexuality is secondary. ⊛

Zazie Dans Le Metro
(1960, 88 min, France, Louis Malle)
A colorful, frenetic slapstick comedy which revolves around the anarchic fun enjoyed by the precocious 10-year-old Zazie as she spends a mischievous weekend in Paris with her uncle (Philippe Noiret). Evoking an effervescent zaniness copied with similar effect in The Beatles' 1967 film *Magical Mystery Tour*, the film's gay angle is that her uncle is a professional female impersonator (although we never get to see chubby Noiret in drag). At one point, the girl repeatedly and bluntly asks him if he is a homosexual; he evades her and never does respond to the question — although the answer is obvious. ⊛

INDEX:
TITLES

Index: Titles (cont.)

Index: Titles (cont.)

Index: Titles (cont.)

Index: Titles (cont.)

Index: Titles (cont.)

Index: Titles (cont.)

Index: Titles (cont.)

INDEX: DIRECTORS

Index: Directors (cont.)

Index:
Personalities

INDEX:
THEMES

Index: Themes (cont.)

Index: Themes (cont.)

Index: Theme (cont.)

IMAGES IN THE DARK

Selective Bibliography

THE ALYSON ALMANAC
 Alyson Publications
 Boston, MA
 1990

THE CELLULOID CLOSET
 by Vito Russo
 Harper & Row, Publishers
 New York, NY
 1981, 1987

CONVERSATIONS WITH MY ELDERS
 by Boze Hadleigh
 St. Martin's Press - Stonewall Inn Editions
 New York, NY
 1986

THE GAY BOOK OF DAYS
 by Martin Greif
 Carol Publishing Group
 New York, NY
 1989

THE GAY BOOK OF LISTS
 by Leigh W. Rutledge
 Alyson Publications,
 Boston, MA
 1987

THE GAY FIRESIDE COMPANION
 by Leigh W. Rutledge
 Alyson Publications
 Boston, MA
 1989

GAYS & FILM
 edited by Richard Dyer
 BFI Publishing
 London, England
 1980

GAYS AND LESBIANS IN MAINSTREAM CINEMA
 by James Robert Parrish
 McFarland & Company, Inc.
 Jefferson, NC
 1993

HALLIWELL'S FILMGOER'S COMPANION
 by Leslie Halliwell
 Harper & Row
 New York, NY
 1985

JONATHAN TO GIDE —
THE HOMOSEXUAL IN HISTORY
 by Noel I. Garde
 Vantage Press
 New York, NY
 1964

LAVENDER LISTS
 by Lynne Yamaguchi Fletcher & Adrien Saks
 Alyson Publications
 Boston, MA
 1990

MORE FROM HOLLYWOOD
 by DeWitt Bodeen
 A.S. Barnes and Co., Inc
 Cranbury, NJ
 1977

MOVIE JOURNAL — THE RISE OF A NEW
AMERICAN CINEMA, 1959-1971
 by Jonas Mekas
 Collier Books
 New York, NY
 1972

NOW YOU SEE IT — STUDIES ON
LESBIAN AND GAY FILM
 by Richard Dyer
 Routledge
 London and New York
 1990

VAMPIRES & VIOLETS — Lesbians in Cinema
 by Andrea Weiss
 Jonathan Cape
 London, England
 1992

WOMEN IN FILM - AN INTERNATIONAL GUIDE
 (originally published in Great Britain as
 The Women's Companion to International Film)
 Edited by: Annette Kuhn with Susannah Radstone
 Fawcett Columbine Books
 New York, NY
 1990

ABOUT THE AUTHOR

Born in 1954, Raymond Murray has been involved with film for over twenty years. Having started as a projectionist at Philadelphia's most popular repertory cinema, he eventually became the movie house's programmer and co-owner before transforming the theater into a chain of successful alternative video stores specializing in foreign, cult and gay/lesbian cinema. *Images in the Dark* benefits from Mr. Murray's frequent travels which, for the past fifteen years, have landed him at gay/lesbian film festivals in London, New York, Los Angeles and San Francisco.

VIDEOS FOR SALE

A Selection of Lesbian and Gay Themed Films and Films of Queer Interest Available on Home Video in the United States

The following videos are available at these suggested retail prices. Please note that the prices and availablity are subject to change (many times coming down in price).

* Titles marked with an asterisk are on sale through TLA Video at 10% off the price shown.

Accattone (subtitled)..$29.95	Becoming Colette (EP) $9.95
Aclà (subtitled)..$69.95	Beethoven's Nephew $14.95
Acting on Impulse $89.95	*Before Stonewall $29.95
An Actor's Revenge (subtitled)...................................$79.95	Being at Home with Claude (subtitled) $89.95
Addams Family Values...$94.95	Benjamin Britten's Death in Venice $39.95
Advise and Consent $19.98	The Best Man $19.98
AIDS — What You Need to Know $14.95	The Best of Kids in the Hall..$59.95
Akermania, Vol. 1 (subtitled) $19.95	Best of Soap Vol. 1 & 2 (sold separately)..................$14.98
Aliens Cut My Hair...$39.95	The Best Way (subtitled)..$69.95
All Out Comedy $29.95	Betty Dobson: Self Loving $39.98
Amazing Grace..$79.95	Beyond the Valley of the Dolls $19.98
American Fabulous $29.95	Beyond Therapy $14.95
AMG — The Fantasy Factory.......................................$39.95	Les Biches (subtitled) $79.95
AMG — The Fantasy Factory Revisited........................$49.95	Billy Budd $59.98
AMG — The Third Visit $39.95	Billy Liar (EP)..$9.95
And the Band Played On..$49.99	The Bitter Tears of Petra von Kant (subtitled)...................$79.95
The Angelic Conversation $29.95	Bittersweet...$29.95
Anita: Dances of Vice $39.95	Black Lizard $79.95
Another Way (subtitled) $59.95	Black Widow...$19.98
Antonia and Jane $19.95	Blonde Venus $14.98
Apartment Zero $14.95	Blood and Roses (EP) $9.95
Arabian Nights (subtitled) $79.95	Blood for Dracula $29.95
Aria...$14.95	Blood of a Poet (subtitled) $29.95
*Armistead Maupin's Tales of the City $59.95	The Blue Angel (subtitled) $24.95
The Art of Touch...$24.95	*The Blue Hour (subtitled)..$39.95
The Art of the Touch II $24.95	Blue Jeans (subtitled)...$59.95
As Is $19.98	Blunt — The Fourth Man $19.98
Auntie Mame $19.98	Body & Soul: The Complete Workout............................$29.98
The Balcony $29.95	Boots, Biceps and Bulges $59.95
The Ballad of Little Jo $94.95	The Bostonians $19.95
The Ballad of the Sad Cafe $89.95	Bound and Gagged: A Love Story................................$89.95
Barbarella..$14.95	The Boyfriend $19.98
Basic Instinct $19.98	The Boys in the Band...$59.98
Bathroom Sluts $39.95	*The Boys of Cell Block Q..$39.95
Beautiful Dreamers..$14.95	The Boys of St. Vincent (Canada Only) $94.95
*Beauty and the Beast (Cocteau) (subtitled)..................$24.95	Boys' Shorts $39.95

ORDER THESE VIDEOS THROUGH TLA VIDEO • 1-800-333-8521

Brideshead Revisited (Vol. 1-6 Sold Separately)	$19.95
Brittania Hospital	$9.95
Broken Noses	$29.95
BurLEZk	$29.95
BurLEZk II Live!	$29.95
Busting	$14.95
Cabaret	$19.98
The Cage	$39.95
La Cage aux Folles (subtitled)	$19.98
La Cage aux Folles — 2 (subtitled)	$19.98
La Cage aux Folles — 3 (subtitled)	$19.98
Calamity Jane	$19.98
Camille	$19.98
*Can't Stop the Music	$14.95
Canterbury Tales (subtitled)	$79.95
Car Wash	$19.95
Caravaggio	$79.95
Cat on a Hot Tin Roof (1958)	$19.98
*Caught Looking/North of Vortex	$39.95
Chain of Desire	$92.95
Chained Heat 2	$89.95
*Changing Face	$19.95
Cheers: The Boys in the Bar	$14.98
Chi Chi Larue's Hardbody Video Mag Vol.1 or 2	$49.95
The Children's Hour (GB: The Loudest Whisper)	$19.98
The Chippendales — A Musical with Muscle	$59.95
The Chippendales — Tahitian Adventure/Stranded	$19.95
The Chippendales — Tall, Dark & Handsome	$19.95
The Choirboys	$14.98
Chopper Chicks in Zombietown	$19.95
Christopher Strong	$19.95
Ciao! Manhattan	$19.95
Citizen Cohn	$89.95
Claire of the Moon	$89.98
Clay Farmers/My First Suit	$69.95
Clips	$39.95
Club de Femmes (subtitled)	$39.95
Colegas (subtitled)	$69.95
The Color Purple	$19.98
The Comfort of Strangers	$89.98
Coming Out is a Many Splendored Thing	$24.98
Common Threads	$19.98
Confessions of a Serial Killer	$89.95
The Conformist (dubbed)	$49.95
Coup de Grace (subtitled)	$59.95
Craig's Wife	$19.95
Cruising	$19.98
Crush (1994)	$89.95

Cry-Baby	$19.98
*The Crying Game	$19.98
Curse of Her Flesh	$24.95
*Da Vinci Body Series	$29.95
*Da Vinci Body Series II — Lower Body Workout	$29.95
*Da Vinci Body Series III — Aerobic Workout	$39.95
Daddy and the Muscle Academy	$49.95
The Damned	$59.95
Dance, Girl, Dance	$19.98
Dancing to the Promised Land: Bill T. Jones	$24.95
Danzón (subtitled)	$94.95
Dark Habits (subtitled)	$79.95
The David Burrill Nude Aerobic Workout	$34.95
David Hockney: Portrait of an Artist	$39.95
A Day on the Grand Canal with the Emperor of China	$39.95
Dear Boys	$69.95
Death in Venice	$59.95
Deathtrap	$19.98
The Decameron (subtitled)	$79.95
Desert Hearts	$29.98
Desire	$39.9
*Desperate Living	$19.95
Devil in the Flesh (1947)	$34.95
Devil in the Flesh (1987) (subtitled)	$19.98
The Devils	$19.98
Bette Midler — Divine Madness	$19.95
Diabolique (subtitled)	$39.95
Diary of a Lost Girl (subtitled)	$29.95
A Different Story	$19.95
El Diputado (subtitled)	$69.95
Distant Voices, Still Lives	$89.95
Dog Day Afternoon	$19.95
La Dolce Vita (subtitled)	$24.95
Doña Herlinda and Her Son (subtitled)	$79.95
Donna E: Learn to Country Western Dance	$19.95
Dr. Jekyll & Sister Hyde	$14.95
Dracula's Daughter	$14.95
Drag Shorts	$19.95
Drawing the Line: Keith Haring	$19.95
Dreaded Experimental Comedies	$49.95
Dream Boys Revue	$9.95
Dream Man	$19.95
Dreamers of the Day	$39.95
Dress Grey	$89.95
Dress Up for Daddy	$39.95
Drifting (subtitled)	$69.95
Eat the Rich	$89.95
Eating Raoul	$19.95

These titles are on sale through TLA Video at 10% off price shown.

ORDER THESE VIDEOS THROUGH TLA VIDEO • 1-800-333-8521

Ed Wood: Look Back in Angora	$19.95
*Edward II	$19.95
8 1/2 (subtitled)	$59.95
The Eighties (subtitled)	$79.95
The Elegant Criminal (subtitled)	$89.95
The Elegant Spanking	$14.97
Elton John: Live in Australia	$14.95
An Empty Bed	$29.95
An Englishman Abroad	$49.95
Entre Nous (subtitled)	$19.98
Ernesto	$69.95
Erotic Choices	$39.95
Erotic in Nature	$39.95
*Erotikus: History of the Blue Movie	$19.95
Et L'Amour	$24.95
The Eternal Return (subtitled)	$29.95
Even Cowgirls Get the Blues	$96.89
The Everlasting Secret Family	$79.95
Every Night in Thailand	$69.95
Exquisite Corpses	$79.95
Extramuros (subtitled)	$39.95
Fantasy Dancer	$39.95
*Fantasy Men Volumes I & II (2-tape set)	$39.95
Farewell My Concubine (subtitled)	$96.89
Faster, Pussycat!...Kill! Kill!	$69.95
Fellini Roma (subtitled)	$19.98
*Fellini Satyricon (subtitled)	$19.98
*Female Misbehavior	$29.95
Fertile LaToyah Jackson	$49.95
Films of Barbara Hammer (4 vol. ea. sold separately)	$59.95
Films of James Broughton: 6-tape collection	$149.80
Films of James Broughton: My Autobiographical	$29.95
Films of James Broughton: Dreamwood	$29.95
Films of James Broughton: Erotic Celebrations	$29.95
Films of James Broughton: Parables of Wonder	$29.95
Films of James Broughton: Rituals of Play	$29.95
Films of James Broughton: The Pleasure Garden	$29.95
The Flavor of Corn	$69.95
Flesh	$29.95
Flesh for Frankenstein	$29.95
A Florida Enchantment	$39.95
For a Lost Soldier (subtitled)	$89.95
Forbidden Love: Stories of Lesbian Lives	$69.95
Forbidden Passion: Oscar Wilde	$79.95
Forever Mary	$79.95
*Fortune and Men's Eyes	$19.98
Four Weddings and a Funeral	$94.95
The 4th Man (subtitled)	$24.95
Fox and His Friends (subtitled)	$79.95
Framing Lesbian Fashion	$39.98
Francis Bacon: Portrait of a Painter	$39.95
Frankie and Johnny	$19.98
*Fried Green Tomatoes	$19.95
Friends Forever (subtitled)	$69.95
Fun Down There	$39.95
Fun with a Sausage	$39.95
The Garden	$19.98
The Gay Deceivers	$14.95
Gay Erotic Video Awards, The First Annual	$19.95
*Gay Erotic Video Awards, The Second Annual	$29.95
Gay Erotica From the Past Vol. 1	$44.95
Gay Erotica from the Past Vol. 2	$44.95
Gay Games III & Cultural Festival	$34.98
Gay Games IV From A to Q	$24.95
The Gay Man's Guide to Safer Sex	$39.98
*Gay, Gay Hollywood	$39.95
The Genesis Children	$69.95
*Getting It Right: Safer Sex for Younger Men	$39.95
The Girl with the Hungry Eyes	$24.95
Girlfriends (1993)	$59.95
Glen or Glenda? (aka "I Changed My Sex")	$24.95
The Glitter Goddess of the Sunset Strip	$69.98
Gore Vidal's Billy the Kid (EP)	$9.95
Gore Vidal: Profile of a Writer	$39.95
The Gospel According to Matthew (subtitled)	$29.95
Grief	$92.95
Guilty as Charged	$89.95
*Gymnastikos	$39.95
Gypsy (1993)	$14.95
Hairspray	$14.95
The Handmaid's Tale	$19.98
Happy Birthday, Gemini	$14.95
Hay Fever	$39.95
He and She and Him	$24.95
Hearing Voices	$79.95
Heat	$29.95
Heavy Petting	$14.95
*Henry & June	$19.95
High Heels (subtitled)	$89.95
Highlights — Pet Shop Boys	$16.98
*Hin Yin for Men	$29.95
The Hitcher	$14.98
Hockney at the Tate	$39.95
L'Homme Blesse (subtitled)	$79.95
Homo Promo	$39.95
The Hours and Times	$19.95

These titles are on sale through TLA Video at 10% off price shown.

IMAGES IN THE DARK

How to Female Ejaculate	$39.95
How to Find Your Goddess Spot	$29.95
How to Have a Sex Party	$29.95
How to Impersonate a Woman	$59.95
*The Hunger	$19.98
Hungry Hearts	$39.95
I Am My Own Woman	$79.95
I Wanna Be a Beauty Queen	$19.95
*I've Heard the Mermaids Singing	$14.95
If...	$29.95
Images: A Lesbian Love Story	$59.95
Improper Conduct (subtitled)	$79.95
In a Glass Cage (subtitled)	$79.95
In the Life: The Funny Tape	$39.98
The Incredible Shrinking Woman	$14.98
Inside Monkey Zetterland	$92.95
Internal Affairs	$19.98
International Sweethearts of Rhythm	$29.95
je tu il elle	$29.98
Jean Cocteau: Autobiography of an Unknown	$19.95
Jeffrey Dahmer — The Secret Life	$89.95
Jerker	$19.95
The Jim Bailey Experience	$39.95
Joey Breaker	$92.95
Jubilee	$29.95
Judgment	$89.95
Julia	$19.95
Just a Gigolo	$59.95
k.d. lang — Harvest of the Seven Years	$19.98
Kamikaze Hearts	$39.95
Kenneth Anger's Magick Lantern Cycle (3 vol. each sold separately)	$29.95
The Krays	$19.95
Labyrinth of Passion (subtitled)	$79.95
The Lair of the White Worm	$14.98
Lakki: The Boy Who Grew Wings (subtitled)	$69.95
Last Call at Maud's	$39.95
Last Exit to Brooklyn	$89.95
The Last of England	$29.95
Law of Desire (subtitled)	$79.95
The Left Handed Gun	$14.95
Lesbian Avengers Eat Fire, Too!	$21.00
Lesbian Tongues	$29.95
Lesbionage	$59.95
Let Me Die a Woman!	$24.95
The Life and Times of Allen Ginsberg	$79.95
Lifetime Commitment: A Portrait of Karen Thompson	$39.98
Lily Tomlin — Appearing Nitely	$19.98
Linda, Les and Annie	$39.95
The Living End	$89.95
London Kills Me	$89.98
The Lonely Lady	$59.95
Long Awaited Pleasure	$59.95
The Long Day Closes	$94.95
Longtime Companion	$19.95
Looking for Langston	$39.95
Los Placeros Ocultos (subtitled)	$79.95
*The Lost Language of Cranes	$19.98
Lot in Sodom (American Avant — Garde Films)	$49.95
Love Bites	$19.95
Love Game	$39.95
Lust in the Dust	$14.95
M. Butterfly	$19.95
Macho Dancer	$79.95
Madonna: Truth of Dare (In Bed with Madonna))	$19.98
Mädchen in Uniform (1931) (subtitled)	$24.95
The Magic Christian	$14.98
Magic of Female Ejaculation	$19.95
Making Love	$69.98
Male Escorts of San Francisco	$29.95
Malerotic	$24.95
*Mambo Mouth	$19.95
A Man Like Eva (subtitled)	$79.95
The Man Who Fell to Earth	$19.95
Marcel Proust: A Portrait of a Writer	$24.95
*Mardi Gras 1991 (r-rated)	$39.95
*Mardi Gras 1991 (x-rated)	$39.95
*Mardi Gras 1992 (x-rated)	$39.95
*Mardi Gras 1993 (x-rated)	$39.95
*Mardi Gras 1994 (x-rated)	$39.95
Marquis (subtitled)	$29.95
*Mascara	$19.98
Matador (subtitled)	$79.95
*Maurice	$19.98
Medusa: Dare to Be Truthful	$14.95
Men in Love	$39.95
Ménage (subtitled)	$29.98
Midnight Cowboy	$19.95
Miller's Crossing	$14.98
Mishima (subtitled)	$79.95
Moments — The Making of Claire of the Moon	$39.98
Mommie Dearest	$14.95
Monaco Forever	$29.95
Monster in the Closet	$19.95
Morocco	$14.95

These titles are on sale through TLA Video at 10% off price shown.

ORDER THESE VIDEOS THROUGH TLA VIDEO • 1-800-333-8521

Movie Buff — The Video	$49.95
Movie Buff — The Sequel	$49.95
Movie Buff — The Threesome	$49.95
Movie Buff — The Four Play	$49.95
Mr. Nude Universe: The Video (Playgirl))	$24.95
Mrs. Doubtfire	$19.98
*Multiple Maniacs	$29.95
*The Music Lovers	$19.98
My Beautiful Laundrette	$19.98
*My Father Is Coming	$29.95
*My Own Private Idaho	$19.95
The Mystery of Alexina	$19.95
The Naked Civil Servant	$19.98
Naked Lunch	$94.98
Naturally Naked	$24.95
Navajeros (subtitled)	$89.95
Network Q Series (each monthly vol. sold separately)	$19.95
Never Give Up, Imogen Cunningham	$29.98
News from Home	$79.95
Nice Girls...Films By & About Women	$19.95
The Night of the Iguana	$19.98
Night Rhythms	$89.95
Night Visions	$89.95
Night Zoo (subtitled)	$14.95
Nighthawks	$14.95
Nijinsky	$14.95
Nitrate Kisses	$39.95
No Alternative	$14.95
No Skin Off My Ass	$39.95
Nocturne (1993)	$34.95
*Norman, Is That You?	$19.98
*North of Vortex/Caught Looking	$39.95
*Northern Exposure: Cicely	$14.95
Nothing to Lose	$29.98
Nude Dudes	$39.95
The Nun (subtitled)	$59.95
Ode to Billy Joe	$19.95
Oedipus Rex (subtitled)	$59.95
Okoge (subtitled)	$79.95
Olivia (subtitled)	$29.98
Olivier, Olivier (subtitled)	$94.95
On Being Gay	$39.95
On Common Ground	$19.95
*One Nation Under God	$29.95
Only When I Laugh	$19.95
Orlando	$94.95
Orpheus (subtitled)	$19.95
Out for Laughs	$29.98
Outcasts (subtitled)	$69.95
Pandora's Box	$24.95
*Paris Is Burning	$19.98
Parting Glances	$29.95
Partners	$79.95
Pat Rocco: Bi-Centennial Gala	$19.95
Pat Rocco: Mondo Rocco	$39.95
Pat Rocco: One Adventure	$19.95
Paul Bowles in Morocco	$29.95
Paul Cadmus: Portrait of a Painter	$39.95
Pepi, Luci & Bom (subtitled)	$79.95
Performance	$19.98
Persona (subtitled)	$19.98
Personal Best	$19.98
Peter's Friends	$19.98
Philadelphia	$99.95
Poetry in Motion	$59.95
Poison	$19.95
Poison Ivy	$19.95
Polyester	$19.95
Positive	$29.95
Positive Image	$29.95
Prelude to a Kiss	$19.98
Prelude to Victory	$19.95
Pretty Boy (subtitled)	$69.95
Pride Time Travels — Key West	$19.95
Pride Time Travels — London & Brighton	$19.95
Pride Time Travels — Montreal	$19.95
Pride Time Travels — Palm Springs	$19.95
Pride Time Travels — Provincetown I	$19.95
Pride Time Travels — Provincetown II	$19.95
Pride Time Travels — Rehobeth	$19.95
Pride Time Travels — San Francisco	$19.95
The Private Life of Sherlock Holmes	$9.98
Private Parts	$19.98
Private Pleasures	$34.95
Privates on Parade	$19.95
Profile of Benjamin Britten: A Time There Was	$39.95
Que Viva Mexico	$59.95
Queen Christina	$19.98
*Querelle	$14.95
Question of Attribution/ An Englishman Abroad	$89.95
A Question of Silence (subtitled)	$29.95
Rachel, Rachel	$19.95
The Rainbow	$89.95
Rebel without a Cause	$19.95
Red, Hot & Blue	$19.98
Red, Hot & Dance	$19.98

These titles are on sale through TLA Video at 10% off price shown.

ORDER THESE VIDEOS THROUGH TLA VIDEO • 1-800-333-8521

VIDEOS FOR SALE

Reflections — A Moment in Time $39.95
Reflections in a Golden Eye $19.98
Reform School Girls $14.95
Ren & Stimpy: Stinky Christmas $14.95
Les Rendez-vous D'Anna..$29.95
Rich Boy, Poor Boy (subtitled) $69.95
Riot $14.95
*The Ritz $19.98
Robby $69.95
Rocco and His Brothers (subtitled)................................$79.95
Rock Hudson's Home Movies $39.95
The Rocky Horror Picture Show $19.98
Sacred Passions $39.95
Safe Is Desire $39.95
*Salmonberries...$29.95
*Saló, or the 120 Days of Sodom (subtitled) $69.95
Salome (silent) $19.95
Salome's Last Dance $89.98
Salut Victor! $39.95
Sammy and Rosie Get Laid $19.98
Sand and Blood (subtitled) $79.95
Savage Nights (subtitled) $94.99
Search for Signs of Intelligent Life in the Universe...........$89.95
Secret Passions $39.95
The Seducers $24.95
*Seduction: The Cruel Woman (subtitled)......................$29.95
Seize the Day: A Guide to Living with HIV $29.95
Sensual Men $19.95
A Separate Peace $49.95
Serial Mom $94.95
*Sex Is...$39.95
Shadows...$39.95
She Must Be Seeing Things...$29.95
She's Safe! $39.95
She-Male By Choice..$59.95
She-Mob $24.95
The Sheltering Sky $19.95
Shock Treatment $14.98
Siegfried (aka "Zygfryd") (subtitled) $39.95
Silence = Death $29.95
The Silence of the Lambs..$19.95
The Silence $24.95
Silverlake Life: The View from Here $39.95
Sin in the Suburbs $24.98
Since Stonewall $19.95
Six Degrees of Separation $96.89
The Sluts and Goddesses Workshop $39.95
Smoke $39.95

Some Like It Hot...$19.98
Something for Everyone...$59.98
Something Special $29.98
Song of the Loon $49.95
Sonia Speaks: Going Farther Out of Our Minds..............$39.98
Space Thing $24.95
Spetters (dubbed)...$19.98
Der Sprinter (subtitled) $79.95
The Spy Who Came $24.95
Stonewall 25: Voices of Pride & Protest.........................$24.95
Stop the Church $39.95
Straight for the Heart $39.95
Street Kid (subtitled) $69.95
Suburban Dykes $39.95
Suddenly, Last Summer $19.98
The Summer of Miss Forbes (subtitled) $19.95
Summer Vacation 1999 (subtitled) $69.95
Sun Chi..$19.95
Sunset Boulevard $14.98
The Supergrass $19.95
Superstar: Life and Times of Andy Warhol.....................$14.98
Switch $19.98
*Swoon...$19.95
Taboo $49.95
Tao Yin: Chinese Art of Self -Massage $39.95
The Taste of Her Flesh..$24.95
Taxi Zum Klo (subtitled) $79.95
Tea and Sympathy $19.98
Teorema (subtitled) $79.95
Terrorist Bridesmaids $29.95
The Testament of Orpheus (subtitled)............................$29.95
Thank You and Goodnight $29.95
That Tender Touch $24.95
Thelma and Louise $19.98
These Three $19.98
The Third Sex $24.98
This Special Friendship (subtitled) $69.95
A Thousand Pleasures $24.95
Three of Hearts $19.95
Threesome $99.95
Tidy Endings...$79.95
Tie Me Up! Tie Me Down! (subtitled) $19.95
Time Expired $14.95
Time Out: The Truth About HIV and You $9.95
Tiny and Ruby: Hell Divin' Women $29.95
To Catch a Killer...$89.95
To Play or Die (subtitled) $39.95
Together Alone $39.95

*These titles are on sale through TLA Video at 10% off price shown.

ORDER THESE VIDEOS THROUGH TLA VIDEO • 1-800-333-8521

Tom's Men	$39.95
Tommy	$14.95
Tongues Untied	$39.95
Too Much Sun	$89.95
Torch Song Trilogy	$89.95
Toute Une Nuit (subtitled)	$29.95
Towers Open Fire	$29.95
Transvestite Secrets Revealed	$59.95
Trash	$29.95
Trouble in Mind	$14.95
Truman Capote's A Christmas Memory	$19.95
Two in Twenty (3 tape set)	$99.98
The Ultimate Degenerate	$24.95
Urinal	$39.95
Valentino	$19.98
Valley of the Dolls	$19.98
Via Appia (subtitled)	$39.95
Victor/Victoria	$19.98
*The Virgin Machine (subtitled)	$29.95
Virginia Woolf	$24.95
A Virus Knows No Morals	$39.95
Vito and the Others (subtitled)	$69.95
Voices from the Front	$39.95
Waiting for the Moon	$79.98
Waking Up	$29.95
Walk on the Wild Side	$59.95
War Requiem	$29.95
Warhol: Portrait of an Artist	$39.95
We Think the World of You	$19.95
We Were One Man (subtitled)	$69.95
The Wedding Banquet	$94.95

Well Sexy Women	$24.95
West Coast Crones	$39.95
Westler: East of the Wall (subtitled)	$39.95
What Have I Done to Deserve This? (subtitled)	$79.95
What Sex Am I?	$59.95
Who Killed Cock Robin?	$59.95
Who's Afraid of Virginia Woolf?	$19.95
Whoever Says the Truth Shall Die	$59.95
Wild Blade	$29.95
Wild Life	$49.95
William Burroughs: Commissioner of Sewers	$29.95
Window Shopping (subtitled)	$29.95
Without You, I'm Nothing	$19.98
The Wizard of Oz	$19.95
Women in Love	$19.98
Women on the Verge of a Nervous Breakdown (subtitled)	$19.98
Wonderland (The Fruit Machine)	$29.95
Word Is Out	$79.95
Working Girls	$14.95
The World According to Garp	$19.98
Wrecked for Life: The Trip & Magic of Trocadero	$39.95
Xanadu	$14.98
Yentl	$19.95
Yes (To Ingrid, Love Lisa)	$24.95
You Are Not Alone (subtitled)	$69.95
Young Hearts, Broken Dreams	$39.95
Young Man with a Horn	$19.98
Zero Patience	$79.95
Zorro, the Gay Blade	$59.98

Please call for information and availability of films not listed

1·800·333·8521

Also, see our order form on the back page

VIDEOS FOR SALE · GREAT BRITAIN

A Selection of Lesbian and Gay Themed Films Available on Home Video in Great Britain

The following videos are available at these suggested retail prices. Please note that the prices and availablity are subject to change (many times coming down in price).

Accattone (subtitled)	£15.99
An Actor's Revenge (subtitled)	£15.99
And the Band Played On	£64.99
The Angelic Conversation	£14.99
Another Country	£14.99
The Art of Touch	£14.99
The Ballad of the Sad Cafe	£15.99
Beauty and the Beast (Cocteau) (subtitled)	£15.99
Before Stonewall	£14.99
Being at Home with Claude (subtitled)	£14.99
Best of "Out" and "Out on Tuesday"	£15.99
Beyond the Valley of the Dolls	£10.99
Les Biches (subtitled)	£15.99
Blood of a Poet	£15.99
The Boys in the Band	£10.99
Boys of Cellblock Q	£14.99
Boys on Film 1	£14.99
Boys on Film 2	£14.99
Boys on Film 3	£14.99
Boys on Film 4	£14.99
La Cage aux Folles (subtitled)	£12.99
Caligula	£12.97
Caravaggio	£15.99
Cat on a Hot Tin Roof (1958)	£ 9.99
Caught Looking/The Attendant	£14.99
Claire of the Moon	£14.99
Color Me Lurid	£12.99
Coming Out	£14.99
Crush (1994)	£15.99
Daddy and Muscle Academy	£14.99
Danzón	£15.99
Death in Venice	£12.99
Desperate Living	£10.99
Desperate Remedies	£15.99
Diary of a Lost Girl	£15.99
A Different Story	£14.99
Dog Day Afternoon	£ 9.99
Doña Herlinda and Her Son (subtitled)	£14.99
Dr. M (US — Club Extinction)	£15.99
Dream Man	£14.99
The Dresser	£ 6.99
8 1/2 (subtitled)	£15.99
Entertaining Mr. Sloane	£10.99
Farewell My Concubine (subtitled)	£15.99
Feed Them to the Cannibals!	£12.99
Female Trouble	£10.99
For a Lost Soldier (subtitled)	£14.99
Forbidden Love: Stories of Lesbian Lives	£14.99
The Fruit Machine (Wonderland)	£10.99
Gay Classics	£15.99
The Gay Man's Guide to Safer Sex	£17.99
Getting It Right: Safer Sex for Younger Men	£14.99
Glitterbug	£14.99
Gospel According to Matthew (subtitled)	£15.99
Hairspray	£ 6.99
Hamlet (Quentin Crisp)	£10.99
Henry & June	£10.99
The Hitcher	£11.99
Homework (subtitled)	£15.99
The Hours and the Times	£10.99
In Bed with Madonna	£ 6.99
Je T'Aime Moi Non Plus (subtitled)	£14.99
Jerker	£14.99
Jubilee	£14.99
k.d. lang — Harvest of the Seven Years	£10.99
Kenneth Anger's Magick Lantern Cycle (4 vol. each sold separately)	£10.99
Labyrinth of Passion (subtitled)	£15.99
Last Exit to Brooklyn	£ 5.99
Law of Desire	£15.99
Lesbian Leather Shorts	£14.99
Lesbian Lykra Shorts	£12.99
The Lie (subtitled)	£15.99
Liquid Sky	£15.99
The Living End	£14.99
The Long Day Closes	£15.99
Man for Man — Vols 1, 2 & 3 (sold separately)	£14.99
Marquis (subtitled)	£12.99

Matador (subtitled)	£15.99	Prick Up Your Ears	£10.99
Medea (subtitled)	£15.99	Queen Christina	£10.99
Midnight Express	£10.99	The Rainbow	£10.99
A Midsummer Night's Dream	£14.99	Red, Hot & Dance	£12.99
Mishima (subtitled)	£ 9.99	Reflections in a Golden Eye	£15.99
Mona Lisa	£14.99	Rocco and His Brothers (subtitled)	£15.99
Mr. Gay UK	£14.99	The Rocky Horror Picture Show	£12.99
Multiple Maniacs	£10.99	Salmonberries	£15.99
My Own Private Idaho	£12.99	Salon Kitty	£12.99
Myra Breckenridge	£10.99	Savage Nights (subtitled)	£15.99
Naked Lunch	£12.99	Sebastiane (subtitled)	£12.99
Nighthawks	£15.99	Seduction: The Cruel Woman (subtitled)	£14.99
No Skin Off My Ass	£14.99	Strip Jack Naked (Nighthawks 2)	£15.99
Noir Et Blanc (subtitled)	£15.99	Swoon	£15.99
North of Vortex	£14.99	Taxi Zum Klo (subtitled)	£14.99
Oedipus Rex (subtitled)	£15.99	The Terence Davies Trilogy	£15.99
Olivier, Olivier (subtitled)	£15.99	Testament of Orpheus	£15.99
Oranges Are Not the Only Fruit	£19.99	Three of Hearts	£65.99
Orlando (box set)	£22.99	Tie Me Up! Tie Me Down! (subtitled)	£ 6.99
Orlando (widescreen)	£15.99	Torch Song Trilogy	£ 6.99
Orpheé (subtitled)	£15.99	Two of Us	£12.99
Ossessione (subtitled)	£15.99	The Virgin Machine	£14.99
Pandora's Box (subtitled)	£15.99	Well Sexy Women	£14.99
Parting Glances	£14.99	What Have I Done to Deserve This? (subtitled)	£15.99
Pepi, Luci & Bom (subtitled)	£15.99	Without You, I'm Nothing	£15.99
Pink Flamingos	£10.99	Wittgenstein	£15.99
Pink Narcissus	£14.99	Young Soul Rebels	£10.99
Poison	£12.99		

For orders or additional information

call **CHANNEL** VIDEO FILMS

Phone or Fax • **071-372-2025**